AF782010

Econometrics and the Philosophy of Economics

Econometrics and the Philosophy of Economics

Theory-Data Confrontations in Economics

Bernt P. Stigum

PRINCETON UNIVERSITY PRESS
PRINCETON AND OXFORD

Copyright © 2003 by Princeton University Press

Published by Princeton University Press, 41 William Street, Princeton, New Jersey 08540
In the United Kingdom: Princeton University Press, 3 Market Place, Woodstock, Oxfordshire OX20 1SY

All Rights Reserved

Library of Congress Control Number: 2003106662

ISBN: 0-691-11300-9

British Library Cataloging-in-Publication Data is available

This book has been composed in Times Roman and Abadi Extra Light by Princeton Editorial Associates, Inc., Scottsdale, Arizona

Printed on acid-free paper. ∞

www.pupress.princeton.edu

Printed in the United States of America
10 9 8 7 6 5 4 3 2 1

To Clive, Christophe and Grayham, Dale, David and Hans-Martin, Erik, Geir, Harald, Heather, Herman, Jeffrey and Dan, and Tore and Nils
— for collaborating

To Herman Ruge Jervell
— for an unforeseen appendix

To Douglas V. DeJong, Cathrine Hagem, Per Richard Johansen, and Henry, Richard, and Yngvild
— for most wanted examples

To Anna, Helena, Magnus Walker, and Mary Sofie
— my grandchildren

To Erik and Carol, Tove and Jonathan, and Anne Olaug, Fia and Earl Spencer
— for making me feel a very privileged person

Contents

summary

Figures

Tables

Preface

In this book I point out and unravel an intriguing philosophical puzzle: How is a science of economics possible? Economic science is systematized knowledge about the nature of social reality that pertains to economic matters. Economists derive such knowledge from theories about toys in toy economies and sophisticated statistical analyses of data whose references belong in a socially constructed world of ideas. The toy economies and economists' world of ideas have little in common with social reality—a fact that renders successful searches for knowledge about economic aspects of social reality questionable. Yet the science of economics is not fictional. The book demonstrates that a proper understanding of the purport of an economic theory and meaningful bridge principles that link up theoretical variables and relevant data enable economists to learn about characteristic features of social reality. In doing so, it unravels the riddle and shows how economists can ensure their science an interesting future.

This book is meant to be a companion to my book *Toward a Formal Science of Economics*, which was published by MIT Press in 1990, and provides the philosophical foundations that are missing in the earlier volume. It also presents a clear and understandable picture of my methodology at a mathematically comfortable level for an applied econometrician and, by way of many examples, shows how to apply the methodology in relevant economic situations. Finally, it includes chapters by a group of my colleagues that exemplify contemporary applied econometrics at its best.

Although written independently of mine, the chapters of my collaborators play important roles in the structure of the ideas that I am trying to convey. The four chapters in Part IV develop sophisticated means to construct the framework within which an applied econometrician's theory-data confrontation is taking place. The four chapters in Part VII and Chapters 19 and 21 illustrate some of the questions today's applied econometricians dare ask and how they go about answering them. In that way the authors give readers an idea of the kind of future they envision for the science of economics.

MY DISTINGUISHED COLLABORATORS

Tore Schweder (Chapter 13) is a professor of statistics in the Department of Economics at the University of Oslo. His Ph.D., from the University of California at Berkeley (1974), dealt with stochastic point processes with application to abundance estimation of whales. He has continued his interest in marine biology with emphasis on stock assessment and fisheries management, and is a member of the Scientific Committee of the International Whaling Commission. He is also interested in the foundations of statistics, the history of statistics, event history analysis, and simulation-based estimation. He is an elected fellow of the Norwegian Academy of Science and Letters.

Nils Lid Hjort, Tore's co-author, is professor of statistics in the Department of Mathematics at the University of Oslo. He has contributed to the theory and practice of statistics in matters concerning the foundations of statistics, nonparametric function estimation, spatial statistics, nonparametric Bayesian statistics, statistical model selection, and modeling and inference for event history analysis. He is an elected fellow of the Norwegian Academy of Science and Letters.

Harald E. Goldstein (Chapter 14) is an associate professor of statistics in the Department of Economics at the University of Oslo. The Academic Kollegium of the University of Oslo awarded him a Ph.D. in 1981 for a thesis entitled "Robust Inference in Contingency Tables." His research interests focus on inference in contingency tables, frontier production models, and statistical problems that arise in the study of labor markets. He has served for a number of years as a scientific advisor at the Frisch Centre, an institute for applied economic research in Oslo, and has been heavily involved in a joint project between the Departments of Economics at the University of Zimbabwe and the University of Oslo.

Christophe Bontemps (Chapter 15) is an econometrician in the Department of Economics and Rural Sociology of the French National Institute for Agronomic Research (INRA) in Toulouse. He has an engineering degree in computer science, optimization, and parallelism from the Toulouse Ecole Nationale Supérieure d'Electrotechnique, d'Informatique, d'Hydraulique, et des Télécommunications and a Ph.D. in mathematics from the Université des Sciences Sociales in Toulouse. His research interests concern specification tests and nonparametric methods as well as irrigation water demand and market relations in the agrofood industry.

Grayham E. Mizon, Christophe's co-author, is Leverhulme Professor of Econometrics at the University of Southampton and is joint editor with Clive Granger of the series Advanced Texts in Econometrics (Oxford University Press). He has held positions at the European University Institute, the London School of Economics, and Oxford University, and visiting posts at the Australian National University and University of California at San Diego. He has edited the *Review of Economic Studies,* has been an associate editor of *Econometric Reviews,* and has published widely on econometric theory, methods, and modeling, as well as applied econometric studies of macroeconomic time series. He is a foreign member of the Polish Academy of Science.

David F. Hendry (Chapter 16) is professor of economics and a fellow of Nuffield College, Oxford. He is one of the world's leading experts on econometric methodology, economic forecasting, and the history of econometrics and has published extensively in these areas, including such works as *Dynamic Econometrics* (Oxford University Press, 1995), *Forecasting Non-Stationary Economic Time Series* (with M. P. Clements; MIT Press, 1999), and *Foundations of Econometric Analysis* (with M. S. Morgan; Cambridge University Press, 1995). He has been an editor of *Review of Economic Studies, Economic Journal,* and the *Oxford Bulletin of Economics and Statistics* and an associate editor of *Econometrica* and the *International Journal of Forecasting.* He has served as president of both the Royal Economic Society and Section F of the British Association for the Advancement of Science. A fellow of both the Econometric Society and the British Academy, he is also a foreign honorary member of the American Economic Association and the American Academy of Arts and Sciences.

Hans-Martin Krolzig, David's co-author, has been a research fellow of Nuffield College and the Department of Economics, Oxford, since 1995. He received a diploma in economics from the University of Bielefeld in 1992 and a doctorate in rer. pol. from the Humboldt University in Berlin in 1996. Hans-Martin's research focuses on regime-switching models, analyses of the business cycle, and computer-automated econometric modeling. His previous publications include articles in international scientific journals and the books *Markov Switching Vector Autoregressions: Modeling Statistical Inference and Application to Business Cycle Analysis* (Springer, 1997) and *Automatic Econometric Model Selection with PcGets* (with David Hendry; Timberlake Consultants Press, 2001). He is the original developer of the Ox package MSVAR.

Clive W. J. Granger (Chapter 19) was awarded a Ph.D. in mathematics from the University of Nottingham in 1959. From 1956 to 1974 he served as an assistant lecturer, lecturer, reader, and professor in the Departments of Economics and Mathematics at Nottingham, and since 1974 he has been a professor of economics at the University of California at San Diego. His research concerns time-series analysis, forecasting, applied econometrics, and finance, and he has published numerous articles and ten books in these areas. He is a fellow of the American Academy of Arts and Sciences, the Econometric Society, and the International Institute of Forecasters.

Herman Ruge Jervell, who contributed the appendix to Chapter 20, studied mathematics at the University of Oslo and Stanford University and received his Dr. philos. from the University of Tromsø in 1974. From 1974 to 1985 he was assistant, then associate, professor of mathematics at the University of Tromsø, and from 1985 he was professor of computer science at the University of Oslo. Since 1988 he has been professor in language, logic, and information at the University of Oslo. His main interests lie in logic, with special emphasis on proof theory. His research activities also cover such varied fields as artificial intelligence and computational logic.

Heather Anderson (Chapter 21 and co-author of Chapter 23) was awarded a Ph.D. in economics from the University of California at San Diego in 1992. She taught at the University of Texas at Austin and Texas A&M University and is currently an associate professor in the Department of Econometrics and Business Statistics at Monash University in Australia. Her research interests include nonlinear time-series analysis, empirical finance, and empirical macroeconomics, and she has published in the *Review of Economics and Statistics*, the *Journal of Applied Econometrics*, and the *Journal of Econometrics*. She is currently on the editorial board of the *Journal of Applied Econometrics*.

Geir Storvik (co-author of Chapter 23) is an associate professor of statistics in the Department of Mathematics at the University of Oslo. He received his Ph.D. from the University of Oslo in 1993 for a thesis entitled "Automatic Object Recognition in Images and Markov Chain Monte Carlo Methods." Since then he has continued his work on image analysis, stochastic computation, Monte Carlo methods, spatial and spatiotemporal modeling, and dynamic state space models. He spends part of his time as a researcher at the Norwegian Computing Center.

Erik Biørn (Chapter 24) has been professor of economics at the University of Oslo and scientific advisor at the research department of Statistics Norway since 1986. He teaches econometrics and his research interests include panel data econometrics, econometrics of latent variables, time-series econometrics, and the aggregation problem in econometrics. He is the author of *Taxation, Technology and the User Cost of Capital* (Elsevier, 1989), several Norwegian textbooks in econometrics, as well as many articles in international scientific journals.

Herman K. van Dijk (Chapter 25) is a professor of econometrics and director of the Econometric Institute at Erasmus University in Rotterdam. Formerly chairman of the Tinbergen Institute, his research interests are in Bayesian inference and decision analysis, computational economics, time-series econometrics, and income distribution analysis. He serves on the editorial boards of several scientific journals.

Jeffrey A. Dubin (Chapter 26) was awarded a Ph.D. in economics by the Massachusetts Institute of Technology in 1982. He is currently an associate professor of economics at the California Institute of Technology. His research focuses on microeconomic modeling with particular emphasis on discrete-choice econometrics, energy economics, sampling and survey methods, valuation of intangible assets, and studies of ballot proposition voting. He is the author of *Empirical Studies in Applied Economics* (2001) and *Studies in Consumer Demand-Econometric Methods Applied to Market Data* (1998), both published by Kluwer Academic Publishers. In 1986 he received the Econometric Society's Frisch Medal, together with Daniel McFadden, for the article that is reprinted as Chapter 26 in this book.

Daniel McFadden, Jeffrey's co-author, has published many studies in applied econometrics and has developed a variety of tools that draw upon economic theory and statistics to integrate the analysis and interpretation of economic data. He is recognized particularly for his work on the theory and empirical analysis of demand for discrete alternatives and cost and profit functions. He earned a Ph.D. in behavioral science from the University of Minnesota in 1962, and has been a faculty member at MIT and the University of California at Berkeley. He is a Nobel Prize laureate in economics and the recipient of the John Bates Clark Medal, the Frisch Medal (with Jeffrey A. Dubin), and the Nemmers Prize.

Dale W. Jorgenson (Chapter 27) is the Samuel W. Morris University Professor at Harvard University. He earned his Ph.D. in economics from Harvard in 1959, has been a professor in Harvard's Department of Economics since 1969, and has served as director of the Program on Technology and Economic Policy at the Kennedy School of Government since 1984. His work covers almost all areas of economic theory and theoretical econometrics, and he has shown an incredible ability to find data and to combine these data with theory in studying a wide range of important economic phenomena. The results that he and his collaborators have obtained have been collected in eleven volumes published by MIT Press. He has served as president of both the American Economic Association and the Econometric Society and has received several prestigious honors for his work, including the John Bates Clark Medal of the American Economic Association and honorary doctorates from Uppsala University and the University of Oslo. He is an elected member of the American Philosophical Society, the Royal Swedish Academy of Sciences, and the American Academy of Arts and Sciences, and a fellow of the American Association for the Advancement of Science, the American Statistical Association, and the Econometric Society.

ACKNOWLEDGMENTS

It has taken me more than 10 years to put together this long essay in the philosophy of science, and I owe many friends and colleagues hearty thanks for their help and moral support.

First of all, I thank Heather Anderson, Erik Biørn, Christophe Bontemps and Grayham E. Mizon, Harald E. Goldstein, Clive W. J. Granger, David F. Hendry and Hans-Martin Krolzig, Tore Schweder and Nils Lid Hjort, Geir Storvik, and Herman van Dijk for all the time they spent writing their respective chapters for me. I am also grateful to Dale W. Jorgenson and Jeffrey A. Dubin and Daniel L. McFadden for letting me reprint seminal articles of theirs as chapters. Finally I thank Herman Ruge Jervell for the appendix to Chapter 20 and Douglas V. DeJong, Cathrine Hagem, Per Richard Johansen, Richard Keesey, Henry McKean, and Yngvild Wasteson for their generosity in providing some of the examples that appear scattered throughout the book.

During these 10 years of hard work I have spent extended periods of time at several universities far from Oslo. Thanks are due to Rob Engle at the University of California at San Diego and to Marjorie McElroy at Duke University for inviting me to spend my sabbatical years in 1990–1991 and 1998–1999 at their respective institutions. Thanks are also due to Salvador Barbera at the Universidad Autonoma for arranging for free office space and a friendly ambience during my sojourns in Barcelona, and to Anthony D. Hall at the University of Technology Sydney for inviting me to spend a glorious month in his School of Finance and Economics. Finally, I thank Heather Anderson, Grayham E. Mizon, Hans-Werner Sinn, Rajiv Sarin, Professor Wilhelm Keilhaus Minnefond, and the Norwegian Research Council for Science and the Humanities for the weeks I spent at Texas A&M University, the European University Institute in Florence, the University of Munich, and the Maison des Sciences de l'Homme in Paris.

During the years that I worked on this book I had occasion to lecture on various related topics at the World Congresses in Tokyo and Seattle, at the European Econometric Society Meetings in Uppsala, at the Australasian Meetings of the Econometric Society in Sydney, and at faculty seminars at many distinguished universities. In the United States I gave talks at the University of California at San Diego and Davis, the University of Southern California at Los Angeles, the University of Arizona at Tucson, and Stanford, Northwestern, Harvard, Yale, Columbia, Princeton, and Duke Universities. In England I gave talks at Oxford and Cambridge Universities and at the London School of Economics. In Europe I spoke at the Universidad Autonoma in Barcelona, the Universidad Carlos III in Madrid, the Université de Paris at Dauphine, the CREA/Ecole Polytechnique in Paris, GREQE at the Université d'Aix-Marseille, the European University Institute in Florence, the University of Munich, the University of Aarhus, and the University of Oslo. In Australia I lectured at the University of Technology

Sydney and at Monash University in Melbourne. In Canada I gave a talk at the Université de Québec at Montréal. The talks, and the discussions during the seminars and afterward, helped me clarify the ideas that I have developed in this book. Thanks are due both to those who invited me and to the participants in these seminars.

I have also benefited from comments from those who have taken time to read parts of the manuscript: Chapter 1: Heather Anderson, Guttorm Fløistad, and Grayham E. Mizon; Part II: Fredrik Engelstad, Kathinka Frøystad, and Nils Roll-Hansen; Chapter 1 and Parts I and II: Martin Eide; Chapters 6 and 7: Kjell Arne Brekke; Chapter 9: Jon Wetlesen; Part III: Michael Massmann; Chapter 20: Roger Antonsen, Jens Erik Fenstad, and Herman Ruge Jervell; Chapter 23: Clive W. J. Granger and Ragnar Nymoen. I thank John Driffill, Alberto Holy, Svend Hylleberg, Dale W. Jorgenson, Alan Kirman, Tor Jakob Klette, Maurice Lagueux, Neil De Marchi, Robert Nadeau, Mats Persson, Steinar Strøm, and Michel de Vroey, who read and commented on papers of mine that became chapters in the book, and Kåre Bævre and Dag Fjeld Edwardsen, who helped me with calculations that provided insights for Chapter 5, 10, and 23. Thanks are also due to Carsten Smith for providing a hard-to-find published report of the Norwegian Supreme Court that I needed for Chapter 9, and to Paul Schreyer at the OECD and Torbjørn Hægeland, Per Richard Johansen, Tom Kornstad, Baard Lian, Lasse Røgeberg, and Karin Snesrud at Statistics Norway (SN) for furnishing data that I needed for Chapter 17. Finally, thanks for their friendly support are due to Liv Simpson, head of SN's National Accounts section, and to three successive heads of SN's research division: Olav Bjerkholt, Øystein Olsen, and Ådne Cappeln.

Three of the chapters in the book—Chapters 21, 26, and 27—have been published previously. The sources are as follows: Chapter 21 is based on "Explanations of an Empirical Puzzle: What Can Be Learnt from a Test of the Rational Expectations Hypothesis?" by Heather Anderson, *Journal of Economic Methodology* 6(1), 31–59, 1999 [http://www.tandf.co.uk/journals]; Chapter 26 comes from "An Econometric Analysis of Residential Electric Appliance Holdings and Consumption," by Jeffrey A. Dubin and Daniel L. McFadden, *Econometrica* 52(2), 74–100, 1984; Chapter 27 is from "Econometric Methods for Applied General Equilibrium Analysis," in: *Growth*, Vol. 2: *Energy, the Environment, and Economic Growth*, by Dale W. Jorgenson, MIT Press, pp. 89–155, 1998. Thanks are due to the *Journal of Economic Methodology*, *Econometrica*, and MIT Press for permission to republish this material. In Chapter 22 I used the equivalent of roughly three pages of material from my article "Scientific Explanation in Econometrics," in: *Econometrics and Economic Theory in the 20th Century*: *The Ragnar Frisch Centennial Symposium*, Cambridge University Press, 1998, and I thank Cambridge University Press for letting me use this previously published material. Finally, I am grateful to MIT Press for allowing me to use the equivalent of six pages of excerpts from my earlier book, *Toward a Formal Science of Economics*, MIT Press, 1990, in Chapters 5 and 6.

Last but not least, I thank Professor Wilhelm Keilhaus Minnefond, the Norwegian Research Council for Science, and the Humanities and the Economics Department at the University of Oslo for financial support, and Vidar Christiansen, chair of the Department of Economics, for friendly support and help. I also express my appreciation to Merethe Aase, Grethe Stensbøl, and the other members of the staff of the Economics Department at the University of Oslo for all the assistance they have given me over the years. Their cheerful demeanor and positive attitude help make the department a good place to work. Finally, I thank two anonymous referees for constructive criticism; Peter Strupp, Cyd Westmoreland, and Evelyn Grossberg at Princeton Editorial Associates for helpful advice and super service in the copyediting and typesetting of the book; and Terry Vaughn and Tim Vaughan at Princeton University Press for their cordial support.

Bernt P. Stigum
Oslo

Econometrics and the Philosophy of Economics

Chapter One

Introduction

This is a book about econometrics and the philosophy of economics, two topics that seem worlds apart. Econometrics is a study of good and bad ways to measure economic relations. Philosophy is a study of the nature of things and the principles governing human behavior. And the philosophy of economics is a study that searches for truth and knowledge about the part of reality that pertains to economic matters. This book will show that in economic theory-data confrontations the two topics are inextricably conjoined. Meaningful applied econometrics requires proper understanding of the purport of economic theory, and empirically relevant economic theorizing requires knowledge of the power of applied econometrics.

1.1 THEORY-DATA CONFRONTATIONS IN ECONOMICS

A *theory-data confrontation* is an empirical analysis in which theoretical arguments play an essential role. Economic theory-data confrontations occur in many different situations. In some of these confrontations economists try to establish the empirical relevance of a theory. In others econometricians search for theoretical explanations for observed regularities in their data. In still others economic researchers produce evaluations of performance and forecasts for business executives and government policy-makers.

1.1.1 A Unifying Framework

There is a unifying framework within which we can view the different activities in economic theory-data confrontations. All have a core structure consisting of three parts: two disjoint universes, one for theory and one for data, and a bridge between them. The theory universe is populated by theoretical objects that have all the features that the theory ascribes to them. The elements in the data universe are observations from which we create data for the theory-data confrontation. The bridge is built of assertions that describe the way that elements in the two universes are related to one another.

I think of an economic theory T as one of two abstract ideas. In one case T is a pair (ST, M), where ST denotes a finite set of assertions concerning some economic situation and M is a family of models of these assertions that delineates the relevant characteristics of the situation in question. The other T is a formal theory AT that is developed by the axiomatic method. It consists of the axioms and all the theorems that can be derived from them with the help of logical rules of inference. The intended interpretation of AT delineates the characteristics that its originator considered sufficient to describe the kind of economic situation about which he or she was theorizing.[1]

In economic theory-data confrontations the "theory" (IT) is either the M of a pertinent ST or an interpretation of some AT. For example, let T denote the theory of consumer choice under certainty. In one theory-data confrontation of T, IT might present the way Franco Modigliani and Richard Brumberg's (1955) life-cycle hypothesis views consumer allocation of resources over time. In another confrontation, IT might delineate Kenneth Arrow's (1965) ideas of how consumers allocate their net worth to safe and risky assets. There are many possibilities. Note, therefore, that regardless of what IT supposedly describes, the elements in the corresponding theory universe remain theoretical objects.

The characteristics of theoretical objects are not interesting per se. Hence in a theory-data confrontation, econometricians do not question the validity of IT in its own universe. Instead they ask whether, when the objects in the theory universe have been interpreted by certain bridge principles, they can use IT to deduce true assertions about elements in the data universe. These principles constitute the bridge between the theory universe and the data universe.

In a given theory-data confrontation, the data universe consists of a collection of observations and data. The nature of the observations depends both on IT and on the original purposes for which those observations were collected. The purpose of an empirical analysis need not be the same as the purposes for which the observations were collected. The observations are used to create data for the theory-data confrontation. The makeup of the data depends on IT and the design of the particular empirical analysis.

The theory-data confrontation that I have described above is pictured in Fig. 1.1. On the right-hand side of the figure we see at the bottom the sample population on whose characteristics observations are based. Econometricians use their observations to create data that they feed into the data universe on top. On the left-hand side of the figure we find at the bottom the theory, that is, (ST, M) or AT as the case may be. Thereupon follows IT, the relevant parts of which are fed into the theory universe on top. The bridge between the two universes contains all the bridge principles and nothing else, and the arrows describe the flow of information in the system. Finally, the numbered ellipses are nodes in which researchers receive and send information and decide on what to feed into the pertinent boxes.

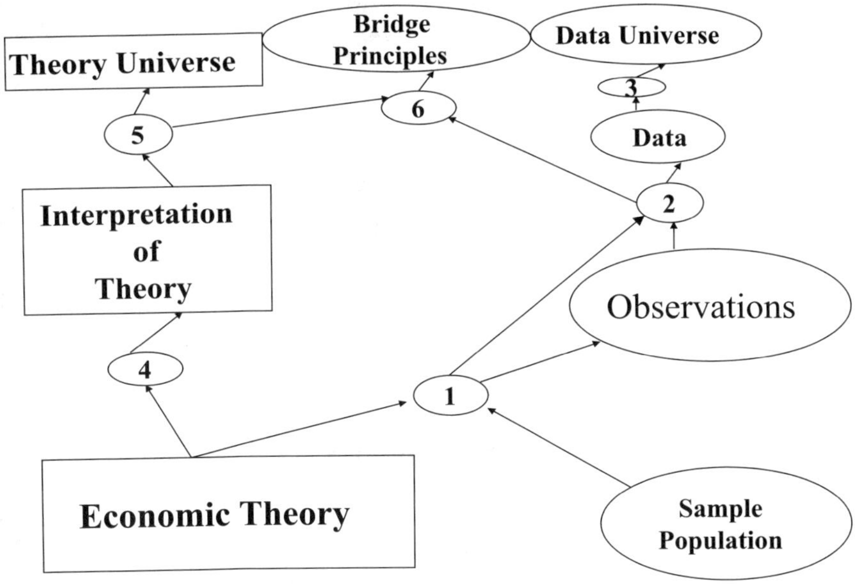

Fig. 1.1 A theory-data confrontation.

1.1.2 A Disturbing Riddle

Economic theory is developed and econometrics is used in the theory-data confrontation to obtain knowledge concerning relations that exist in the social reality. Generating such knowledge is problematic. We have seen that the references of the variables in the theory universe are theoretical objects, for example, toys in a toy economy.[2] It appears, therefore, that meaningful econometric work stands and falls with the references of observations and data in the data universe belonging to the social reality. In Chapter 3, I demonstrate that the references of most variables in contemporary econometric data universes live and function in a socially constructed world of ideas. This world of ideas has little in common with the true social reality. That fact raises a serious question concerning the relevance of contemporary econometrics: How is it possible to gain insight into the social reality with data concerning a socially constructed world of ideas?

Figure 1.2 illustrates the gravity of the situation in which econometricians find themselves. At the top of that figure we discover the top of Fig. 1.1, that is, the theory and data universes and the bridge between them. Below them on the left-hand side is the toy economy in which reside the references of all the variables in the theory universe. On the right-hand side we observe the socially constructed world of ideas that contains the references of all the variables in

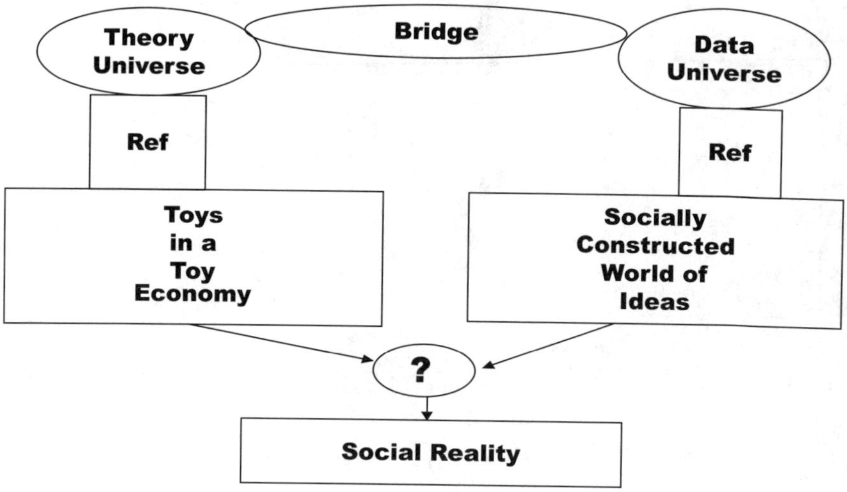

Fig. 1.2 A disturbing riddle.

the data universe. Finally, at the bottom we find the elements that constitute the social reality. The arrows and the question mark underscore the fact that it is uncertain how combining elements from a toy economy with elements from a socially constructed world of ideas enables econometricians to learn interesting things about the social reality.

1.1.3 The Resolution of the Riddle

The question I posed above amounts to asking, *how is a science of economics possible*? A long time ago, Immanuel Kant (1781, 1787) asked a similar question: "Wie ist reine Naturwissenschaft möglich?" ["How is pure natural science possible?"] The answer he gave to his question differs from the answer that I give to mine. Since both the differences and the similarities are interesting to us, I shall recount Kant's answer and the reasons he posited in support of that answer.[3]

Kant's (1787) book, *Kritik der reinen Vernunft*, which in F. Max Müller's translation (Kant, 1966) became *Critique of Pure Reason*, is an analysis of the powers of human reason in gaining knowledge about the world independently of all experience. He argued that knowledge begins with experience but insisted that all knowledge need not arise from experience. Experience suffices to establish that "snow is melting in the streets today." A priori reasoning is needed to ascertain that "every change has its cause." Knowledge gained from experience alone Kant called *empirical knowledge*. All other knowledge he referred to as *knowledge a priori*. Some knowledge a priori can be obtained independently of experience. For example, it can be known from a priori reasoning alone that, "all instances of seven added to five result in twelve." Such knowledge Kant referred to as *pure knowledge* (p. 3).

There are two sources of human knowledge in Kant's theory: sensibility and understanding. The first is the faculty by which objects are received as data. The other is the faculty of judging. Knowledge of objects requires the cooperation of both faculties. "Without sensibility objects would not be given to us; without understanding they would not be thought by us" (p. 45).

Kant distinguished between two kinds of judgments: the *analytic* and the *synthetic*. A judgment is an operation of thought that connects a subject and a predicate. In an *analytic judgment* the concept of the subject contains the idea of the predicate. Examples are "all bachelors are unmarried" and "all bodies are extended." In both cases the idea of the predicate is contained in the idea of the subject. The validity of an analytic judgment can be established by a priori arguments that appeal to the logical relation of subject and predicate.

A *synthetic judgment* is one in which the idea of the subject does not contain the idea of the predicate. Examples are "the object in my hands is heavy" and "seven plus five equals twelve." In either case the predicate adds something to the concept of the subject. Most synthetic judgments are judgments a posteriori in the sense that they arise after an experience. There are also synthetic judgments that are judgments a priori, and their validity can be established by a priori reasoning alone. Of the two examples above, the first is a synthetic judgment a posteriori and the second is a synthetic judgment a priori (pp. 7–10).

Kant believed that necessity and strict universality were characteristic features of synthetical judgments a priori (p. 3). He also insisted that such judgments permeated the sciences. For example, mathematical propositions, such as $5 + 7 = 12$, "are always synthetic judgments a priori, and not empirical, because they carry along with them necessity, which can never be deduced from experience" (p. 10). Similarly, in geometry a proposition such as "between any two points the straight line is the shortest line that connects them" is a synthetic judgment. It is also a priori because it carries with it the notion of universality (p. 11). Finally, natural science (Physica) contains synthetical judgments a priori as principles. Examples are "in all changes of the material world the quantity of matter always remains unchanged" and "in all communication of motion, action and reaction must always be the same." Both judgments are obviously synthetical. They are also a priori since they carry with them the idea of necessity (pp. 10–12).

To solve his original problem Kant had to figure out how synthetical judgments a priori were possible. The best way to do that was to study the functioning of the human mind, and he thought of that functioning as occurring in three stages. In the first, the mind places in *space* and *time* the manifold of experiences that humans receive through their senses. Space and time are not empirical concepts. They are pure forms of sensuous intuition (*Anschauung*) that are necessary representations a priori of all intuitions (pp. 23–35). In the second stage, the mind organizes the manifold matter of sensuous intuitions in forms of sensibility that constitute concepts of the understanding that humans use to judge the meaning of their experiences. Kant believed that the forms exist in the mind a priori, and he attributed the synthesizing act of arranging different representations in forms to twelve basic categories of thought (pp. 54–66). In the third stage, the mind combines categories of thought and established concepts to give a unifying account of the manifold world of sense impressions that humans face. He ascribed the mind's ability to accomplish that to what he deemed the highest principle of cognition: the existence of an a priori synthetical unity of apperception that is constitutive of the synthetical unity of consciousness and hence the *self* (pp. 76–82).

In this context there are two especially interesting aspects of Kant's view of the functioning of the human mind. First, he distinguished between two kinds of reality: the world of phenomena that human beings experience and the world of things as they are in themselves independently of human observation. One can have knowledge about phenomena but not about things-in-themselves (*Dinge-an-sich*). Secondly, knowledge of phenomena is limited by the way human faculties of perception and understanding synthesize experiences. In doing that, the two faculties with application of the ideas of space and time and the twelve categories of thought structure the world of phenomena in accordance with their own way of knowing.

It is remarkable that two abstract ideas, space and time, and just twelve a priori categories of thought should enable humans to relate meaningfully to the world of phenomena and to make synthetic judgments about its constituents that have the marks of necessity and universality. To understand how that is possible requires a closer look at the categories of thought. Kant arranged the categories in four groups with names, *quantity*, *quality*, *relation*, and *modality*. In the quantity group one finds three categories: *unity*, *plurality*, and *totality*. In the quality group reside three other categories: *reality*, *negation*, and *limitation*. In the relation group one finds the categories *inherence and subsistence*, *causality and dependence*, and *community*. Finally, in the modality group resides a fourth triple of categories: *possibility*, *existence*, and *necessity* (pp. 62–66). Kant believed that the categories enabled the mind to delineate characteristic features of objects in the world of phenomena. Examples of how the mind accomplishes that can be found in E 1.1. In reading the examples, note that even the simplest judgments make use of a combination of several categories.[4]

E 1.1 *Consider the collection of four balls on my desk. To say something about all of them, one must perceive what the balls have in common, for example, that "they are all billiard balls." To insist that "only one ball is red," one must be able to comprehend the totality of balls. In such judgments one uses the categories in the quantity group. To judge that "there is a black ball and no green ball" and that "the balls are not soft," one applies the categories in the* *quality group. To judge that "one ball is smaller than the others," that "if one ball is given a push, it will start rolling," and that "the balls are either black or red or blue," one employs the categories in the relation group. Finally, to judge that "it is possible that the balls, if pushed, will roll at uneven speeds," that "one ball has a hole in it," and that "the balls are billiard balls and billiard balls are round," one uses the categories in the modality group.*

Kant believed that the ideas of space and time and the twelve categories enable humans to gain a unified account of the world of phenomena. He also believed that humans are able to use their imagination to develop theories about relations that exist among elements in the world of phenomena. These beliefs and the a priori existence in the human mind of the notion of space and time and the twelve categories provided him with the ideas he needed to show how pure natural sciences such as Euclid's geometry and Newton's dynamics are possible.

The arguments that I shall advance to substantiate my claim that a science of economics is possible differ in many ways from those that Kant used in support of his claim. In my case social reality appears in place of Kant's world of phenomena and the "things-in-themselves" are not in sight. Further, the theories are about toys in a toy economy instead of phenomena and the a priori notion of space and time does not appear. Finally, I make no use of Kant's twelve categories. Even so there is one significant similarity. The unified account of the world of phenomena that Kant's humans gain with the help of categories and an a priori notion of space and time is an account of characteristic features of the objects in the world they experience. Consequently, if he is right in insisting that humans structure the world in accordance with their way of knowing phenomena, the theories that humans develop must also be about characteristic features of objects and relations in the world of phenomena. I believe that economic theories, be they about toys or abstract ideas, attempt to delineate characteristic features of behavior and events that the originators of the theories have observed in the social reality in which they live. I also believe that econometricians can assess the likelihood of the empirical relevance of the characteristic features about which economic theories talk. This book will show that my belief is right, and in doing that it will establish the possibility of a science of economics.

1.1.4 A Final Remark on the Riddle

Wassily W. Leontief (1982), Lawrence H. Summers (1991), Tony Lawson (1997), and many others worry about the dire straits of econometrics and economic theory, and all of them give weighty arguments for their concern. Be that as it may, I have tried to write a book that gives an econometrician the idea that he or she should "get on with the job" while keeping Fig. 1.2 clearly in mind. Cooperating economic theorists and econometricians, the references of their theory and data variables notwithstanding, can learn about characteristic features of the workings of the social reality. Such a happy ending, however, depends crucially in each case on the cooperating scientists delineating the purport of the particular economic theory and giving details of all the relevant bridge principles.

1.2 THE ORGANIZATION OF THIS BOOK

The book deals with social reality and the means economists use to learn about those of its characteristics that they find interesting. That involves saying what social reality means, discussing what the purport of an economic theory is, delineating formal aspects of economic theory-data confrontations, and exhibiting salient features of contemporary applied econometrics. To accomplish that my collaborators and I have written twenty-six chapters that are arranged in seven parts with meaningful titles. In this section I describe briefly the contents of the various parts.

1.2.1 Facts and Fiction in Econometrics

Part I concerns facts and fiction in econometrics. I begin by discussing the facts. To me that means describing how human beings create social reality. I then discuss the fiction, that is, the social construction of reality in economics and econometrics. Finally, I show how, in a fictional reality, cooperating economic theorists and econometricians can gain insights into essential characteristics of the social reality in which we live.

This part covers topics that have occupied the minds of philosophers of social science ever since the publication of Peter L. Berger and Thomas Luckmann's (1966) *The Social Construction of Reality*. The philosophers' discussions centered on two basic problems. How do human beings go about creating the social reality in which they live? What is the "reality" philosophers have in mind when they discuss the "social construction of reality?" Judging from Finn Collin's (1997) authoritative account of the subject matter, there does not seem to be a consensus as to the right answer to either of these two questions.

John R. Searle (1995) gives a philosopher's answer to the first question in his book on *The Construction of Social Reality*. I give an economist's answer in Chapter 2. Searle identifies social reality with the totality of social facts, and he insists that all social facts are facts involving collective intentionality.[5] There is no room in his social reality for things, personal facts, and personal and social possibilities. In my conception, social reality comprises all the things and facts there are, all the possibilities that one or more persons envisage, and nothing else. The missing elements in Searle's notion of social reality constitute fundamental parts of mine. Without them I would have no chance of analyzing the workings of an economic system.

There are several answers to the second question. To Berger and Luckmann the "reality" in the "social construction of reality" is an ordered world of institutions that through a process of socialization receives a certain stability over time. In her book *The Manufacture of Knowledge*, Karin D. Knorr-Cetina (1981) studies life in a laboratory. To her, the scientific products that such a laboratory engenders constitute the reality in the social construction of reality. My vision of the social construction of reality is not about the construction of institutions and not about the production of scientific artifacts. It is rather about the social construction of "objects of thought and representation" (Sismondo, 1993). Thus, the reality in my vision of the social construction of reality is the socially constructed world of ideas that I describe in Chapter 3.

There is one aspect of the production of artifacts in Knorr-Cetina's laboratory that is particularly interesting. The artifacts are produced in a preconstructed artificial reality with purified chemicals, and specially grown and selectively bred plant and assay rats that are equally preconstructed. Such products cannot be part of "nature" as I understand the term. Nevertheless scientists use such products to further their understanding of processes that are active in nature. For me, the interesting aspect is that it illustrates how knowledge of relations in one world, the laboratory, can be used to gain insight about relations that exist in another world, nature. Analogous problems arise each time an econometrician attempts to use relations in the data universe to establish properties of relations in social reality. I devote Chapter 4 to sorting out the latter problems as they relate to individual choice, market characteristics, and macroeconomic policies.

1.2.2 Theorizing in Economics

Economics is a branch of knowledge concerned with the production and consumption of goods and services and with the commercial activities of a society. In Part II, I discuss the art of theorizing in economics and the purport of an economic theory. My aim is to determine what attitude one ought to adopt toward such a theory.

I begin in Chapter 5 by detailing salient features of the axiomatic method. Greek scientists knew of and used this method more than 2,000 years ago. It was only introduced to economics in William N. Senior's (1836) treatise, *An Outline of the Science of Political Economy*. Today the axiomatic method constitutes the primary way of theorizing in economics. It features a finite number of assertions, the axioms, and a few rules of inference. The axioms delineate pertinent properties of certain undefined terms, and the rules of inference tell the user how to pass from axioms to theorems and from axioms and theorems to new theorems. The totality of theorems that can be derived from the axioms makes up the searched-for theory. For this book it is important to keep in mind that the theory is about undefined terms, not about anything specific in the world. In different words, it is a theory about symbols and nothing else.

The axiomatic method is powerful and provides intriguing possibilities for theorizing in science as well as in mathematics. Examples of its use in economics and econometrics can be found in Stigum (1990). However, the method is also treacherous. Beautiful theoretical structures have collapsed because the axioms harbored surprising contradictory statements. A well-known example of that is George Cantor's theory of sets (1895, 1897).

A theory is said to be consistent if no contradictory statements can be derived from its axioms. A consistent theory can be made to talk about objects of interest by giving the undefined terms an interpretation that renders all the axioms simultaneously true. Such an interpretation is called a *model* of the axioms and the theory derived from them. Different models of one and the same theory may describe very different matters. For example, one model of the standard theory of consumer choice under certainty may be about the allocation of an individual's income among various commodity groups. Another model may be about the allocation of an individual's net worth among safe and risky assets. In either case the individual may, for all I know, be a family, a rat, or a pigeon.

There are philosophers of science, for example, Wolfgang Balzer, C. Ulises Moulines, and Joseph Sneed (1987), who believe that the best way to think of a scientific theory is to picture it as a set-theoretic predicate that prescribes the conditions that the models of a theory must satisfy. Some of these conditions determine the conceptual framework within which all the models of the theory must lie. Others describe lawlike properties of the entities about which the theory speaks. If one adopts this view of scientific theories, one can think of the scientist as formulating his theory in two steps. He begins by writing down the assertions that characterize the conceptual framework of the theory. He then makes simplifying assumptions about the various elements that play essential roles in its development. The latter assumptions determine a family of models of the original assertions that I take to constitute the searched-for theory. I refer to this way of constructing a scientific theory as *model-theoretic* or *semantic* (cf. Balzer et al., 1987).

I consider that an economic theory of choice or development delineates the positive analogies that the originator of the theory considered sufficient to describe the kind of situation that he had in mind. For example, in an economic theory of choice, a decision-maker may choose among uncertain prospects according to their expected utility. This characterization describes succinctly a particular feature of behavior in the intended reference group of individuals in social reality. Similarly, in an economic theory concerning a given kind of financial market the theory may insist that the family of equilibrium yields on the pertinent instruments are cointegrated ARIMA processes. This characterization describes a characteristic feature of the probability distributions that govern the behavior over time of equilibrium yields in such a market. Whether the positive analogies in question have empirical relevance can only be determined by confronting the given theories with appropriate data.[6]

In reading the preceding observations on the purport of an economic theory it is important to keep the following points in mind: (1) To say that expected utility maximization is a positive analogy of individual choice among uncertain prospects is very different from saying that an individual chooses among such prospects as if he were maximizing expected utility. An individual in the theory's intended reference group, by hypothesis, does choose among uncertain prospects according to their expected utility. (2) Even though an accurate description of the behavior of a decision-maker in a given reference group would exhibit many negative analogies of individual behavior, the positive analogies that the theory identifies must not be taken to provide an approximate description of individual behavior. (3) One's understanding of the theory and the data one possesses determine what kind of questions about social reality one can answer in a theory-data confrontation. With the first and third point I want to rule out of court Milton Friedman's (1953) instrumentalistic view of economic theories. With the second and the third point I want to distance my view from the idea that economic theorems are tendency laws in the sense that John Stuart Mill (1836) gave to such laws.[7]

I confront my view of the purport of an economic theory with the views of leading economic theorists in Chapter 6. It differs both from Max Weber's (1949) and from the classical English economists' view of economic theories. However, I believe that it is very much like the way in which John Maynard Keynes (1936) and Robert M. Solow (1956) think of the import of their theories, and Chapter 6 gives ample evidence of that.

I believe that "rationality" is one of the most misused terms in economics. The concept is ill-defined, and it often gets in the way of sound reasoning. Moreover, we can do without the term and we would be better off if we did. In Chapter 7, I advance arguments to show that my opinion is well taken. Three of these arguments are as follows: (1) Theories of choice for consumers and firms can be formulated and discussed without ever mentioning rationality. (2) The positive analogies that two models of one and the same theory identify may be very different. (3) In a given situation, the optimal choice that two different theories prescribe need not be alike. These and other arguments suggest to me that we ought to substitute for "rational agent" and "rational choice and judgment" less loaded terms such as "rational animal" and "good choice and judgment," the meaning of which I explicate in Chapter 9.[8]

It is interesting to note that the adoption of my view of rationality has an important consequence for applied econometrics. Econometricians cannot use economic theories and data to test the rationality of members of a given population. This is true of human populations since their members are "rational animals" and hence rational by definition. It is also true of other kinds of populations, such as those of rats or pigeons. Their members are not rational. Whether a given population possesses the positive analogies on which an economic theory insists is a matter to be settled in a relevant theory-data confrontation.

Much of economic theorizing today is carried out by mathematical economists at a level of sophistication that is way beyond the comprehension of a large segment of contemporary economic theorists. This work has resulted in beautiful theorems, which have provided important insights in both economics and mathematics. The economic insights come with the interpretations that the mathematical economists give their theories. The importance of such insights, therefore, depends on the relevance of the associated interpretations. In Chapter 8, I discuss two of the most beautiful theorems in mathematical economics. One is by Gerard Debreu and Herbert Scarf (1963) and the other is by Robert J. Aumann (1964, 1966). Both theorems concern the relationship between core allocations and competitive equilibrium allocations in large economies. My results demonstrate that the insight that these theorems provide depends as much on the appropriateness of the topologies that the authors have adopted as on the number of agents in the economy. These results are not meant to detract from the unquestioned importance of the two theorems to mathematical economics. Instead, they provide evidence that it is not sufficient to assign names to the undefined terms and to check the mutual consistency of the axioms when interpreting an economic theory. The originator of a theory owes his readers a description of at least one situation in which the empirical relevance of the theory can be tested.[9]

1.2.3 Theory-Data Confrontations in Economics

The chapters in Part II concern subject matter that belongs in the economic-theory and the interpretation-of-theory boxes in Fig. 1.1. In Part III I discuss topics that concern the contents of the remaining boxes in the same figure.

I begin in Chapter 9 with a discussion of what characteristics an econometrician can, in good faith, expect rational members of a sample population to possess. The characteristics I end up with have no definite meaning. Rather, they are like undefined terms in mathematics that can be interpreted in ways that suit the purposes of the research and that seem appropriate for the population being studied. My main sources here are translations of and philosophical commentaries on Aristotle's treatises, *De Anima* and the *Nicomachean Ethics*. In their spirit I designate a "rational individual" by the term rational animal and identify "rational" choices and judgments with good choices and judgments.

In Chapters 10–12, I search for good ways to formalize the core of an economic theory-data confrontation. In such a formalization the theory universe is a pair (Ω_T, Γ_t), where Ω_T is a subset of a vector space and Γ_t is a family of assertions that the vectors in Ω_T must satisfy. The axioms of the theory universe, Γ_t, need not be the axioms of the pertinent IT in the interpreted-theory box in Fig. 1.1. In the intended interpretation of Γ_t, the members of Γ_t delineate just the characteristics of IT that are at stake in a given theory-data confrontation. Moreover, Γ_t need not constitute a complete axiomatic system. Chapter 10 contains examples of theory universes from consumer choice, the neoclassical theory of the firm, and international trade in which I describe the theory-data confrontation that I have in mind, delineate the salient characteristics of IT, and formulate the axioms in Γ_t.

In Chapter 11, I discuss the contents in the observations and data boxes of Fig. 1.1 and describe ways to construct a data universe to go with a given theory universe. In my formalization of a theory-data confrontation the data universe is a pair (Ω_P, Γ_p), where Ω_P is a subset of a vector space and Γ_p is a family of assertions that the vectors in Ω_P must satisfy. The assertions in Γ_p describe salient characteristics of the observations on which the theory-data confrontation is based and delineate the way the pertinent data are constructed from the observations. Like the axioms of the theory universe, the members of Γ_p need not constitute a complete axiomatic system. In economic theory-data confrontations the data universe is usually part of a triple $[(\Omega_P, \Gamma_p), \Im_p, P_p(\cdot)]$, where $\Im_p$ is a σ-field of subsets of Ω_P, and $P_p(\cdot) : \Im_p \to [0, 1]$ is a probability measure. The probability distribution of the data that $P_p(\cdot)$ generates plays the role of the true probability distribution of the vectors in Ω_P. I call this distribution FP.

The bridge in Fig. 1.1 is composed of assertions $\Gamma_{t,p}$ that, in a subset of $\Omega_T \times \Omega_P$ named the *sample space* and denoted Ω, relate variables in the theory universe to variables in the data universe. Bridges and their principles seem to be objects of thought that econometricians avoid at all costs. Hence, in order not to scare friendly readers I try in Chapter 12 to introduce the topic in a logical way. I begin by discussing theoretical terms and interpretative systems in the philosophy of science. I then give the reasons why bridge principles are needed in applied econometrics and describe ways to formulate such principles in empirical analyses of consumer and entrepreneurial choice. Finally, I present an example that exhibits the functioning of bridge principles in a formal theory-data confrontation.

Traditionally, in philosophy as well as in economics, researchers have learned that the bridge between the two universes in Fig. 1.1 is to be traversed from the theory universe to the data universe and that the empirical analysis is to be carried out in the latter. The last section of Chapter 12 shows that the bridge can be traversed equally well from the data universe to the theory universe and that an interesting part of the empirical analysis can be carried out in the theory universe. That sounds strange, but it is not. In the example E 12.5, I contrast the process of testing a theory in the data universe with testing the same theory in the theory universe. The example shows that the formulation of the bridge principles and the econometrician's inclinations determine in which universe he ought to try his theory. That insight throws new light on the import of exploratory data analysis and also suggests new ways for theorists and econometricians to cooperate in their pursuit of economic knowledge.

In theory-data confrontations in which the data-generating process is random, there are three probability distributions of the variables in the data universe for which the econometrician in charge must account. One is the true probability distribution *FP*. Another, the so-called *MPD*, is the probability distribution of the data variables that is induced by $\Gamma_{t,p}$ and the joint probability distribution of the variables in the theory universe. The third is the probability distribution that, in David Hendry's (1995) terminology, is a minimal congruent model of the data, a model that mimics the data-generation process and encompasses all rival models.[10] The *MPD* plays a pivotal role in the empirical analysis when the econometrician traverses the bridge from the theory universe to the data universe. The probability distribution of the vectors in Ω_T that one of the minimal congruent models of the data and the bridge principles induce play an equally pivotal role in theory-data confrontations in which the econometrician traverses the bridge from the data universe to the theory universe. Example E 12.5 demonstrates this idea.

When an econometrician traverses the bridge from the theory universe to the data universe, the bridge principles enter his empirical analysis in two ways. First, since the *MPD* depends on the pertinent bridge principles, those become essential parts of the econometrician's characterization of the empirical context in which his theory is being tried. Vide, for example, the errors-in-variables and qualitative-response models in econometrics. The errors in the former and the relationship between true and observed variables in the latter help determine the characteristics of the associated data-generating processes. Second, when confronting his theory with data, the econometrician uses the bridge principles to dress up his theory in terms that can be understood in the given empirical context. The empirical relevance of a theory depends on the extent to which the dressed-up version can make valid assertions about elements in the empirical context that it faces. Since the *MPD* is different from the *FP*, the double role of the bridge principles in theory-data confrontations raises interesting philosophical problems about the status of bridge principles in empirical analyses. Some of these problems are discussed in Chapters 11 and 17 and others in Chapter 22.

1.2.4 Data Analyses

As a graduate student at Harvard, I learned that it was a sin to "look at the data" before confronting a theory with data. Since then, I have come to believe that the alleged sin need not be a sin at all. In fact, such exploratory data analyses play an important role in my methodological scheme.

The axioms in the theory universe have many models. Thus, in a theory-data confrontation econometricians are usually confronting data with a family of models rather than a single model of the theory. From this it follows that a complete analysis of the empirical relevance of a theory should delineate the contours of a pair of families of models: one for the theory universe and one for the data universe and the *MPD*. The latter family is to characterize the empirical context within which the theory is tested or applied. If this context does not allow us to reject the theory's empirical relevance, the former family of models will delimit the models of the theory that might be empirically relevant in the given context.

In Chapter 13, the first chapter in Part IV, Tore Schweder and Nils Lid Hjort develop a statistical method by which outside information and a novel frequentist prior and posterior analysis can be used to delimit the family of models of the data universe. Briefly, they argue as follows.

In 1930 R. A. Fisher introduced fiducial probability as a means of presenting in distributional terms what has been learned from the data given the chosen parametric model. In clear-cut cases, J. Neyman (1941) found that the fiducial distribution corresponds to his confidence intervals in the sense that fiducial quantiles span confidence intervals with coverage probability equal to fiducial mass between the quantiles. B. Efron (1998) and others picked up the fiducial thread, but used the term confidence distribution because the confidence interpretation is less controversial than the fiducial probability interpretation.[11] Chapter 13 discusses the basic theory of confidence distributions, including a new version of the Neyman-Pearson lemma, which states that confidence distributions based on the optimal statistic have stochastically less dispersion than all other confidence distributions, regardless of how that dispersion is measured.[12] A version of Efron's (1982) abc-method of converting a bootstrap distribution to an approximate confidence distribution is also presented.

To allow data summarized in distributional terms as input to a frequentist statistical analysis, the authors identify the likelihood function related to the prior confidence distribution when the prior is based on a pivotal quantity.[13] This likelihood is termed the reduced likelihood, since it represents the appropriate data reduction, and nuisance parameters are reduced out of the likelihood. The reduced likelihood is a proper one and is often a marginal or a conditional one. It is argued that meta-analyses are facilitated when sufficient information is reported to recover the reduced likelihood from the confidence distribution of the parameter of primary interest. The theory is illustrated by many examples, among them one concerning the Fieller method of estimating the ratio of two regression parameters in a study of monetary condition indexes where no proper confidence distribution exists and one example concerning the assessment of the Alaskan stock of bowhead whales.

In Chapter 14 Harald Goldstein shows how the *corrected ordinary least squares* (COLS) method can be combined with sophisticated moment analyses to determine a statistically adequate characterization of the error-term distribution in stochastic frontier production models. In such models the structure of the error term constitutes an essential element in the description of the empirical context in which the pertinent theory is to be tried. Often the error-term distribution is specified in an ad hoc manner. The diagnostic that Harald develops can help an econometrician make better assumptions about the error term and, in that way, lend increased credibility to an efficient estimation procedure, such as maximum likelihood, at a later stage in his data analysis. In the univariate case he discusses the characteristics of several common specifications of the error-term distribution as well as a semiparametric generalization of the normal-gamma model.

To the best of my knowledge, there is no generally accepted statistical method for analyzing multivariate stochastic frontier models. Harald shows how to analyze one kind of multivariate case by combining the moment method on the residuals with the generalized method of moments (GMM) estimation of the system. He applies his method to studying the model of the transportation industry in Norway that I present in Chapter 12. His results are not quite what I wanted them to be, but such is the life of an applied econometrician. The exciting thing to note is the extraordinary diagnostic opportunities that his method affords econometricians when they search for an adequate characterization of the empirical context in which they are to try their multivariate stochastic frontier models.

In Chapter 15 Christophe Bontemps and Grayham E. Mizon discuss the importance of *congruence* and *encompassing* in empirical modeling and delineate the relationship between the two concepts. They give a formal definition of congruence and discuss its relationship with previous informal definitions. A model is congruent if it fully exploits all the information implicitly available once an investigator has chosen a set of variables to be used in modeling the phenomenon of interest. Though congruence is not testable directly, it can be tested indirectly via tests of misspecification, but as a result more than one model can appear to be congruent empirically. A model is encompassing if it can account for the results obtained from rival models and, in that sense, makes the rivals inferentially redundant. Thus a congruent and encompassing model has no sign of misspecification and is inferentially dominant. A feature of empirically congruent models is that they mimic the properties of the data-generation process: They can accurately predict the misspecifications of noncongruent models; they can encompass models nested within them; and they provide a valid statistical framework for testing alternative simplifications of themselves. These results are consistent with a general-to-simple modeling strategy that begins from a congruent general unrestricted model being successful in practice. An empirical example illustrates these points.

Finally, in Chapter 16 David Hendry and Hans-Martin Krolzig describe a general method that computes a congruent model of the data-generating process that does not nest a simpler encompassing model. Their results constitute a giant step toward the goal of automating the process of model selection in time-series analyses of nonstationary random processes. They argue as follows.

Scientific disciplines advance by an intricate interplay of theory and evidence, although precisely how these should be linked remains controversial. The counterpart in "observational" (as against experimental) subjects concerns empirical modeling, which raises the important methodological issue of how to select models from data evidence. The correct specification of any economic relationship is always unknown, so data evidence is essential to separate the relevant from the irrelevant variables. David and Hans-Martin show that simplification from a congruent general unrestricted model (GUM)—known as general-to-specific (*Gets*) modeling—provides the best approach to doing so.

Gets can be implemented in a computer program for automatic selection of models, commencing from a congruent GUM. A minimal representation is chosen consistent with the desired selection criteria and the data evidence. David and Hans-Martin explain the analytic foundation for their program (*PcGets*) and show, on the basis of simulation studies, that it performs almost as well as could be hoped. With false acceptances at any preset level the correct rejections are close to the attainable upper bound. Yet the study of automatic selection procedures has barely begun—early chess-playing programs were easily defeated by amateurs, but later ones could systematically beat grandmasters. David and Hans-Martin anticipate computer-automated model selection software developing well beyond the capabilities of the most expert modelers: "Deep Blue" may be just around the corner.

1.2.5 Empirical Relevance

The way in which the formal structure of a theory-data confrontation is applied depends on the purpose of the particular empirical analysis. Harald Goldstein and I used it in Chapters 10, 12, and 14 to evaluate the performance of firms in the Norwegian transportation sector. In Part V I use it to determine the empirical relevance of an economic theory. We can check the empirical relevance of one theory at a time. It is also possible to confront two theories with each other and check their empirical relevance in some given situation. I demonstrate that the formal structure is equally applicable in both cases.

In Chapter 17, I begin by discussing how my views of the purport of a theory-data confrontation differs from Karl Popper's (1972) ideas. Then I give a formal characterization of what it means to say that a conjecture or a theory has empirical relevance. Finally, I construct formal tests of the empirical relevance of expected utility theory, of Eli Heckscher (1919) and Bertil Ohlin's (1933) conjecture concerning factor endowments and trade flows, and of Milton Friedman's (1957) permanent-income hypothesis.

The tests in Chapter 17 differ in interesting ways. In the trial of expected utility theory there is only one model of the theory universe and many models of the data universe. The bridge principles come with many models, all of which are independent of the models of the two universes. In the trial of Heckscher and Ohlin's conjecture the data universe has only one model. The theory universe has many models with controversial import. Moreover, it is hard to delineate the subfamily that is relevant in the given empirical analysis. The bridge principles come with many models. Their formulation depends on the models that are chosen for the two universes. Finally, in the trial of the permanent-income hypothesis both universes and the bridge principles come with many models. Further, the bridge principles relate variables in one universe to variables and pertinent parameters in the other universe. In the trials of expected utility theory and of Heckscher and Ohlin's conjecture there is no sample population and no probability measure on the subsets of the sample space. In the trial of the permanent-income hypothesis there is a sample population, a probability measure on the subsets of the sample space, and a sampling scheme. The trial of Friedman's hypothesis has many interesting features, one of which concerns Duhem's trap. I believe that the trial describes a way in which judicious use of my methodology can help circumvent the difficulties about which Pierre Duhem (1954) warned.

In Chapter 18, I confront two theories with the same data. The theories in question concern choice in uncertain situations: the Bayesian theory and a formal version of Maurice Allais's (1988) (U, θ) theory in which uncertain options are ordered according to the values of a Choquet integral rather than their expected utility. I check whether neither, one, or both of them are empirically relevant in a given laboratory situation. In this case the formal structure of the theory-data confrontation contains two disjoint theory universes, one data universe, and two sets of bridge principles. Each theory has its own theory universe and its own set of bridge principles that relate the theory's variables to the variables in the data universe. One interesting aspect of the test is that the set of sentences about the data on which the empirical relevance of one theory hinges is different from the set of sentences that determine the empirical relevance of the other theory. Thus, econometricians may find that they reject the relevance of one theory on the basis of sentences that are irrelevant as far as the empirical relevance of the other theory is concerned. In the chapter I formulate the axioms for a test of the two theories, derive theorems for the test, and present results of a trial test that Rajiv Sarin and I carried out with undergraduate economics majors at Texas A&M University.

There are distinguished econometricians who believe that econometrics puts too much emphasis on testing hypotheses and gives too little weight to evaluating the performance of theories. Clive Granger is one of them. Part V contains a very interesting chapter, "Evaluation of Theories and Models," in which Clive elaborates on ideas that he presented in his 1998 Marshall Lecture at the University of Cambridge. He presents several examples that ought to give food for much afterthought on this matter.

1.2.6 Diagnostics and Scientific Explanation

Scientific explanation is a multifaceted topic of interest to scholars, government policy-makers, and men and women in charge of business operations. Whatever the call for an explanation might be, for example, a faulty economic forecast or a test of a hypothesis that failed, researchers in artificial intelligence (AI) have developed ideas for both the design and the computation of such explanations. The ideas for design delineate criteria that good explanations must satisfy. Those for computation describe efficient ways of calculating the explanation whenever such calculations make sense. I believe that economic and econometric methodology can benefit from adopting ideas that the researchers in AI have generated. Therefore, I begin Part VII by discussing some of these ideas as they appeared in Raymond Reiter's (1980, 1987) seminal articles on diagnostics and default logic.[14]

In Chapter 20, I present Reiter's interesting logic for diagnostic reasoning and discuss its salient characteristics. His diagnostic arguments delineate ways to search for cures of ailing systems, for example, a car that refuses to start, and they provide researchers with means to find reasons for faulty predictions. It is also the case that Reiter's logic can be used to rationalize reasoning that appears in economic journals and books. A good example is Maarten Janssen and Yao-Hua Tan's (1992) use of Reiter's logic to rationalize the arguments that Milton Friedman (1957) advances in support of the permanent-income hypothesis. In the context of this book it is particularly interesting to contrast Reiter's arguments with the kind of diagnostic reasoning that is exemplified in Heather Anderson's extraordinary econometric analysis of the rational expectations hypothesis in Chapter 21.

Most diagnostic reasoning in econometrics is carried out entirely in the realm of a data universe.[15] In the last half of Chapter 20, I use Reiter's default logic as a vehicle to see what happens to such analyses in the broader context of a theory-data confrontation in which bridge principles play an essential role. Formally, the bridge principles are similar to the axioms in the theory and data universes. However, there should be a difference in the attitude that an econometrician ought to adopt toward them. The axioms in the theory universe concern objects in a toy economy. Those in the data universe concern observations and data that the econometrician has created himself. Hence, there is no reason why he should doubt the validity of the axioms in the two universes. In contrast, he usually has no firm evidence as to whether the bridge principles are valid. In the vernacular of logicians, the most he can claim is that he is sure that there are worlds in which they are valid.

When abstracting from my formalism, the role I assign to bridge principles in theory-data confrontations is the one factor that sets my methodology apart from Trygve Haavelmo's (1944) methodology. For that reason it is important that I be able to explicate the logical status of bridge principles in economic theory-data confrontations. I do that in Section 20.3 with the help of a multi-sorted modal language for science that I developed in Stigum (1990). In this language I postulate that the logical representatives of Γ_t and Γ_p are valid in all possible worlds and that the logical representative of $\Gamma_{t,p}$ is valid in at least one world, but that that world need not be the Real World (RW). From this it follows, in the given language, that a logical consequence A of Γ_t, Γ_p, and $\Gamma_{t,p}$ in the proof of which a member of $\Gamma_{t,p}$ plays an essential role need not be valid in RW. If $\Gamma_{t,p}$ is valid in a world H, then A must be valid in H. A may be valid in many other worlds as well, but I cannot be sure that one of them is RW. Hence, I cannot have more confidence in the validity of A than I have in the validity of $\Gamma_{t,p}$. If I find that A is not valid in RW, I have not run across a contradiction in the ordinary sense of this term. The only thing of which I can be certain is that one of the members of $\Gamma_{t,p}$ that I used in the proof of A is not valid in RW. In the context of a theory-data confrontation, finding that A is not valid in RW calls for a diagnosis in Reiter's sense of the term. I give an example of such a diagnosis at the end of the chapter.

In Herman Ruge Jervell's appendix to Section 20.3, he establishes interesting properties of my language, which he describes in three theorems: a completeness theorem, a cut elimination theorem, and an interpolation theorem, the last of which provides a new grounding for the logical status of bridge principles in theory-data confrontations. Equally important for me, the appendix shows that my arguments have a firm basis.

In Chapter 21 Heather Anderson illustrates the interplay between theory development and data analysis by considering the ability of the rational expectations hypothesis to explain the empirical cointegration structure found in the term structure. She finds that although a standard no-arbitrage theory that incorporates rational expectations can explain some of the properties of Treasury bill yields, this theoretical explanation is incomplete. A broader-based explanation that accounts for government debt and time-varying risk premia can improve predictions of yield movements relative to those predictions based solely on a bill yield spread.

In Chapter 22, I give a formal characterization of the meaning of scientific explanations in economics and econometrics. An explanation is an answer to a why question. It makes something that is not known or understood by the person asking the question clear and intelligible. A scientific explanation is one in which the ideas of a scientific theory play an essential role. In economics this scientific theory is an economic theory, and its ideas are used to provide scientific explanations of regularities that applied economists and econometricians have observed in their data.

The form in which the causes of events and the reasons for observed phenomena are listed and used in scientific explanations differ among scientists, even within the same discipline. There is, therefore, a need for formal criteria by which one can distinguish the good from bad. These criteria must list the necessary elements of a scientific explanation and explicate the ideas of a logically and an empirically adequate scientific explanation. I provide such criteria for scientific explanations in economics and econometrics.

My formal account of scientific explanations in Chapter 22 differs in many ways from Carl G. Hempel's (1965, pp. 245–251) deductive-nomological scheme (DNS) for scientific explanations. According to Hempel, a scientific explanation of an event or a phenomenon must have four elements: (1) A sentence E that describes the event or phenomenon in question; (2) a list of sentences $C_1, \ldots, C_n$ that describes relevant antecedent conditions; (3) a list of general laws $L_1, \ldots, L_k$; and (4) arguments that demonstrate that E is a logical consequence of the C's and the L's. In my account, E describes salient features of a data universe, the C's are axioms of the data universe, the L's are axioms of a theory universe, and the logical arguments demonstrate that E is a logical consequence of the C's, the L's, and bridge principles that, in a pertinent sample space, relate variables in the two universes to one another. The explanation is logically adequate if E is not a logical consequence of the C's. It is empirically adequate if the L's are relevant in the empirical context in which the explanation takes place.

The important differences between the DNS and my account of scientific explanation are twofold: (1) The L's of the DNS concern matters of facts in a data universe. My L's concern life in a toy economy. (2) The L's of the DNS are laws that are valid irrespective of time and place. My L's are theoretical claims of limited empirical relevance. The differences notwithstanding, Hempel's fundamental symmetry thesis concerning explanation and prediction is valid for a logically and empirically adequate explanation in my account of scientific explanation as well as for an adequate explanation in the DNS.

Since the L's are about life in a toy economy and the E concerns matters of facts in a data universe, the relevant bridge principles play a pivotal role in my account of scientific explanations in economics. To make sure that the role of the bridge principles is understood I formulate two equivalent explications of such explanations, SE 1 and SEM 1, the first with the means of real analysis and the second with the help of the modal-logical language that I developed in Chapter 20. I exemplify the use of SE 1 and SEM 1 by giving a real-valued and a modal-logical scientific explanation of a characteristic of individual choice that Maurice Allais and his followers have observed in their tests of the expected utility hypothesis.

The situations that call for scientific explanations in econometrics differ from the situations already envisaged in one fundamental way. In SE 1, E is a family of sentences each one of which has a truth value in every model of (Ω_P, Γ_p). In econometrics E is often a family of statistical relations. For example, in econometrics an E may insist that "the prices of soybean oil and cottonseed oil vary over time as two cointegrated ARIMA processes." This E has no truth value in a model of (Ω_P, Γ_p). To provide scientific explanations of such E's statistical arguments are required.

At the end of Chapter 22, I list the elements and the requirements of a logically and empirically adequate scientific explanation in econometrics. In the situations that econometricians face, the E is a pair (H_1, H_2), where H_1 describes conditions that the vectors in (Ω_P, Γ_p) satisfy and H_2 delineates salient characteristics of the *FP*. As in economics, the antecedent conditions are members of Γ_p, the L's are axioms in a theory universe (Ω_T, Γ_t) and the bridge principles $\Gamma_{t,p}$ describe how variables in the theory universe are related to variables in the data universe. In addition, there is a probability measure $P(\cdot)$ on subsets of the sample space Ω, and logical arguments that show that H_1 is a consequence of Γ_t, Γ_p, and $\Gamma_{t,p}$ and that the *MPD* that Γ_t, Γ_p, and $\Gamma_{t,p}$ and the axioms of $P(\cdot)$ determine has the characteristics that H_2 imposes on *FP*. The explanation is logically adequate if (H_1, H_2) is not a logical consequence of Γ_p and the axioms of the probability measure on subsets of Ω_P that generates *FP*. It is empirically adequate if the theory is relevant in the empirical context in which the explanation is taking place. Chapter 23 contains an example of such an explanation.

In Chapter 23 Heather Anderson, Geir Storvik, and I give a logically and empirically adequate scientific explanation of a characteristic of the Treasury bill market that Anthony Hall, Heather Anderson, and Clive Granger observed in Hall et al. (1992). The economic-theoretic formalism and the statistical analysis of the data that our explanation comprises differ in interesting ways from the arguments that Hall et al. advanced in explaining their findings. Our arguments also differ from the diagnostic arguments that Heather uses in Chapter 21 to assess the ability of the rational expectations hypothesis to account for the stochastic properties of the Treasury bill market. In the context of the book the interplay between economic theory and statistical arguments that the chapter exhibits and the new insight that it offers concerning the relationship between the *MPD* and the *FP* are particularly exciting.

1.2.7 Contemporary Econometric Analyses

In theory-data confrontations econometricians test hypotheses and estimate parameters of interest. When testing hypotheses, they base their procedures on several fundamental ideas. One of them originated in Neyman and Pearson (1928, 1933) and concerns the relative importance of the chance of rejecting a hypothesis when it is true versus the chance of accepting it when it is false. Another is the notion of *optimum confidence sets* as set forth in Neyman (1937). A third, of more recent origin, is the idea of *an encompassing data-generating process* as formalized in Mizon (1984). When estimating parameters, econometricians also base their procedures on several fundamental ideas. One of them is *the principle of maximum likelihood*, which originated in Fisher (1922). Another is L. Hansen and K. Singleton's (1982) idea of a *generalized method of moments estimator*). A third is a cluster of ideas concerning the conditions that an equation's independent variables must satisfy, for example, exogeneity (Koopmans, 1950) and Granger causality (Granger, 1969).

Hypothesis testing and parameter estimation can be viewed as characteristic aspects of games that statisticians play against Nature. Abraham Wald (1947, 1950) used this idea to develop a formal unifying account of hypothesis testing and estimation in his theory of decision procedures. In Wald's theory a game is a quadruple consisting of a sample space S; a set of pure strategies for Nature, Φ; a space of randomized strategies for the econometrician, Ψ; and a risk function $\rho(\cdot)$. Each part of the quadruple varies with the statistical problem on hand. Here it suffices to identify a strategy of Nature in tests with the true hypothesis and in estimation problems with the true parameter values. Moreover, the sample space is a triple $[\mathrm{O}, \Phi, q(\cdot|\cdot)]$, where $\mathrm{O} \subset R^n$ is the space of observations, $q(\cdot|\cdot) : \mathrm{O} \times \Phi \to R_+$ is a function, and $q(\cdot|\theta)$ is the probability density of the econometrician's observations for each choice of strategy by nature, θ. The space of randomized strategies is a triple $[\mathrm{A}, \mathrm{O}, \psi(\cdot|\cdot)]$, where A is a set of acts, $\psi(\cdot|\cdot) : \{\text{subsets of A}\} \times \mathrm{O} \to [0, 1]$ is a function, and $\psi(B|r)$ measures the probability that the econometrician will choose an act in B for each $B \subset A$ and each observed r. In tests A may be a pair {accept, reject} and in estimation problems it may be a subset of R^k, where k is the number of relevant parameters. Finally, the risk function $\rho(\cdot)$ is defined by the equation

$$\rho(\theta, \psi) = \int_{\mathrm{O}} \int_A L(\theta, a) d\psi(a|r) q(r|\theta) dr,$$

where $L(\cdot) : \Phi \times A \to R$ is the econometrician's loss function. In tests of hypotheses the range of $L(\cdot)$ may be a triple $\{0, b, 1\}$, and in estimation problems $L(\theta, a)$ may simply equal $\|\theta - a)\|^2$, where $\|\cdot\|$ is a suitable norm.

The econometrician's optimal strategies depend on the assumptions that he makes about nature's choice of strategies. I consider three possibilities: (1) Nature has chosen a pure strategy and the econometrician must guess which one it is. (2) Nature has chosen a mixed strategy, which I take to be the econometrician's *prior* on Φ. (3) Nature is out to do the econometrician in and has chosen a strategy that maximizes the econometrician's expected risk.

Corresponding to Nature's choice of strategies, there are three classes of the econometrician's optimal strategies to consider: the admissible strategies, the Bayes strategies, and the minimax strategies. These are defined as follows.

1. A given $\psi \in \Psi$ is *inadmissible* if and only if there is a $\psi^* \in \Psi$ such that for all $\theta \in \Phi$, $\rho(\theta, \psi^*) \leq \rho(\theta, \psi)$ with inequality for some θ. Otherwise ψ is *admissible.*
2. For a given prior $\xi(\cdot)$ on the subsets of Φ, ψ^* is a *Bayes strategy* if

$$\int_\Phi \rho(\theta, \psi^*) d\xi(\theta) \leq \int_\Phi \rho(\theta, \psi) d\xi(\theta) \text{ for all } \psi \in \Psi.$$

The value of the left-hand integral is called the *Bayes risk* of $\xi(\cdot)$.

3. A pair (ξ^*, ψ^*) constitutes a pair of "good" strategies for Nature and the econometrician if, for all priors $\xi(\cdot)$ on the subsets of Φ and for all $\psi \in \Psi$,

$$\int_{\Phi} \rho(\theta, \psi^*) d\xi(\theta) \leq \int_{\Phi} \rho(\theta, \psi^*) d\xi^*(\theta) \leq \int_{\Phi} \rho(\theta, \psi) d\xi^*(\theta).$$

Here it is interesting to note that the econometrician's "good" strategy minimizes his maximum risk, and Nature's "good" strategy maximizes the econometrician's minimum risk. Hence, in the vernacular of game theorists, the econometrician's "good" strategy is a *minimax* strategy, and Nature's "good" strategy is a *maximin* strategy.

It seems beyond dispute that an econometrician's choice of strategy is justifiable only if it is admissible. When Φ is discrete and $\xi(\cdot)$ assigns positive probability to each and every strategy of nature, the econometrician's Bayes strategy against $\xi(\cdot)$ is admissible. Moreover, if there is one and only one minimax strategy ψ^*, then ψ^* is admissible. Finally, if ψ^* is admissible and $\rho(\cdot, \varphi^*)$ is constant on Φ, then ψ^* is a minimax strategy. However, Bayes's strategies and minimax strategies need not be admissible. In fact, in many multivariate estimation problems the standard minimax estimator is inadmissible, as was first noted by Stein (1956).[16]

Viewing statistical problems as games against Nature gave statisticians a new vista that engaged the best minds of statistics and led to a surge of interesting new theoretical results in mathematical statistics. It also brought to the fore philosophical issues, the discussion of which split econometrics into two nonoverlapping parts: *classical* and *Bayesian* econometrics. I believe that this split was fortuitous rather than detrimental. It added a second dimension to econometrics that gave econometricians a deeper understanding of the implications of their basic attitudes. Information concerning the development and achievements of statistical decision theory during the last half of the twentieth century can be found in James O. Berger's (1985) book *Statistical Decision Theory and Bayesian Analysis.*[17] Details of the philosophical issues that concern choice of priors and the characteristics of exchangeable processes on ordinary and conditional probability spaces can be found in Stigum (1990, chs. 17, 18).

Part VII includes four chapters—one "Bayesian" and three "classical"—that illustrate four different ways that econometricians analyze important economic problems today. These chapters are important in the context of this book as they provide an indication of the kind of questions that econometricians dare to ask and how they go about answering them. Moreover, they exemplify contemporary applied econometrics at its best.

In Chapter 24, Erik Biørn analyzes an 8-year panel of Norwegian manufacturing firms to determine how materials and capital inputs respond to output changes. Panel data from microunits are a valuable source of information for theory-data confrontation in econometrics. They give the researcher the opportunity of "controlling for" unobserved individual and/or time-specific heterogeneity, which may be correlated with the included explanatory variables. Moreover, when the distribution of latent regressors and measurement errors satisfy certain weak conditions, it is possible to handle the heterogeneity and the errors-in-variables problems jointly and estimate slope coefficients consistently and efficiently without extraneous information. Finally, they make the errors-in-variables identification problem more manageable than unidimensional data (i.e., pure cross-section or pure time-series data) partly because of the repeated measurement property of panel data and partly because of the larger set of linear data transformations available for estimation. Such transformations are needed to compensate for unidimensional "nuisance variables" such as unobserved heterogeneity. Erik illustrates this in Chapter 24. The estimators considered are standard panel-data estimators operating on period specific means and GMM's. The latter use either equations in differences with level values as instruments or equations in levels with differenced values as instruments. Both difference transformations serve to eliminate unobserved individual heterogeneity. Erik illustrates these approaches by examples relating the input response to output changes of materials and capital inputs from the panel of Norwegian manufacturing firms.

In Chapter 25, Herman van Dijk surveys econometric issues that are considered fundamental in the development of Bayesian structural inference within a simultaneous equation system (SEM).

The difficulty of specifying prior information that is of interest to economists and yields tractable posterior distributions constitutes a formidable problem in Bayesian studies of SEMs. A major issue is the nonstandard shape of the likelihood owing to reduced rank restrictions, which implies that the existence of structural posterior moments under vague prior information is a nontrivial issue. Herman illustrates the problem through simple examples using artificially generated data in a so-called limited information framework, where the connection with the problem of weak instruments in classical economics is also described.

A promising new development is Bayesian structural inference of implied characteristics, in particular dynamic features of an SEM. Herman illustrates the potential of such Bayesian structural inference, using a predictivist approach for prior specification and Monte Carlo simulation techniques for computational purposes, by means of a prior and posterior analysis of the U.S. business cycle in a period of depression. A structural prior is elicited through investigation of the implied predictive features.

Herman argues that Bayesian structural inference is like a phoenix. It was almost a dead topic in the late 1980s and early 1990s. Now, it has new importance in the study of models where reduced rank analysis occurs. These models include structural VARs, APT asset price theory models of finance, dynamic panel models, time-varying parameter models in the structural time-series approach, and consumer and factor demand systems in production theory.

In Chapter 26, Jeffrey Dubin and Daniel McFadden discuss and derive a unified model of the demand for consumer durables and the derived demand for electricity. They point out that within the context of their model it becomes important to test the statistical exogeneity of appliance dummy variables that are included in the demand for electricity equations. If the demand for durables and their use are related decisions by the consumer, specifications that ignore this fact will lead to biased and inconsistent estimates of price and income elasticities.

In their chapter Jeffrey and Dan set out to test the alleged bias using observations on a sample of households that the Washington Center for Metropolitan Studies gathered in 1975.

In Chapter 27, Dale Jorgenson develops new econometric methods for estimating the parameters that describe technology and preferences in economic general equilibrium models. These methods introduce a whole new line of research in which econometrics becomes an essential ingredient in applied general equilibrium analysis. Dale applies his methods to studying the behavior of samples of U.S. firms and consumers. The chapter, as it appears in this book, is an edited version of Chapter 2 in Volume 2 of a monograph on issues of economic growth that MIT Press published for Dale in 1998.

NOTES

1. Here the S in ST is short for "semantic" and (ST, M) is a theory that has been developed by model-theoretic means. In addition, the A in AT is short for "axiomatic" and AT is a formal axiomatic theory, that is, a theory that has been developed by the axiomatic method. Chapter 5 describes characteristic features of these two different ways of developing economic theories.

2. I owe the idea of a toy economy to a lecture that Robert Solow gave in Oslo on his way back from the 1987 Nobel festivities in Stockholm. However, I am not sure that Solow will accept the way I use his ideas here.

3. My main sources of reference are the 1966 Anchor edition of F. Max Müller's (1881) translation of Immanuel Kant's (1781, 1787) *Kritik der reinen Vernunft, Critique of Pure Reason*, and relevant chapters in Frederick Coplestone's (1994) *History of Philosophy, Filosofi og Vitenskap* by T. Berg Eriksen et al. (1987), and S. E. Stumpf's (1977) *Philosophy: History and Problems*. If nothing else is said, the page numbers in the text refer to pages in the Anchor edition of Müller's translation.

4. I owe the idea of this example to Guttorm Fløistad's marvelous account of Kant's theory of knowledge in Berg Eriksen et al. (1987, pp. 485–503)

5. I explicate the ideas of "intentionality" and "collective intentionality" in Chapter 2. Here it suffices to say that collective intentionality refers to the intentional mental state of a group of individuals who have a sense of doing something together.

6. I explicate the ideas of a positive analogy and a negative analogy in Chapter 6. Here it suffices to say that a positive analogy for a group of individuals (or a family of events)

is a characteristic that the members of the group (family) share. A negative analogy is a characteristic that only some of the members of the group (family) possess. When one searches for the empirical relevance of a given set of positive analogies, one is checking whether there are groups of individuals or families of events, as the case may be, whose members share the characteristics in question.

7. There are interesting observations on *ceteris paribus* clauses and tendency laws in Mark Blaug's (1990, pp. 59–69) discussion of Mill and in Daniel M. Hausmann's (1992, ch. 8) account of inexactness in economic theory. Also, Lawrence Summers' (1991, pp. 140–141) stories of successful pragmatic empirical work provide insight into the way economic theorists learn about the positive analogies that their theories identify.

8. Chapter 1 of Hausmann (1992) has a good account of the average economist's idea of rationality.

9. This view of mathematical economics I share with Trygve Haavelmo. In his treatise Haavelmo (1944, p. 6) observes that "[many] economists consider 'mathematical economics' as a separate branch of economics. The question suggests itself as to what the difference is between 'mathematical economics' and 'mathematics.' Does a system of equations, say, become less mathematical and more economic in character just by calling x 'consumption,' y 'price,' etc.? . . . [Any piece of mathematical economics remains] a formal mathematical scheme, until we add *a design of experiments* that [details] what real phenomena are to be identified with the theoretical [variables, and describes how they are to be measured]."

10. The ideas of congruence and encompassing are discussed in depth in Chapters 15 and 16. For a summary account of these ideas the reader can consult Section 1.2.4.

11. Fisher intended his fiducial probability to be an alternative to the Bayesian posterior distribution of a parameter with a noninformative prior. The corresponding fiducial distribution contains all the information about a parameter that one can obtain with a given statistical model from the data alone without use of an informative prior distribution.

12. A statistic is optimal if it leads to most powerful tests or most discriminating confidence intervals. In the Fisherian likelihood tradition, optimal statistics might also emerge from conditioning on ancillary statistics.

13. A pivotal quantity (a pivot) is a function of the parameter and the data that satisfies two requirements. First, it should be monotone in the parameter for all possible data. Second, it must have a fixed distribution, regardless of the value of the parameter. The t-statistic is the archtypical pivot. All confidence intervals are essentially built on pivots.

14. For more recent literature on diagnostics the interested reader can refer to W. Marek and M. Truszczynski's (1993) book *Nonmonotonic Logic*.

15. A good example is Anthony Hall and Adrian Pagan's (1983) marvelous account of "Diagnostic Tests as Residual Analysis."

16. The reader can find an interesting discussion and instructive examples of inadmissible Bayes and minimax strategies in Berger (1985, pp. 253–256, 359–361).

17. For a discussion of some of these matters as they concern tests of hypotheses, prediction, and sequential analysis in the econometrics of nonstationary time series the interested reader is referred to Stigum (1967).

REFERENCES

Allais, M., 1988, "The General Theory of Random Choices in Relation to the Invariant Cardinal Utility Function and the Specific Probability Function," in: *Risk, Decision and Rationality*, B. R. Munier (ed.), Dordrecht: Reidel.

Arrow, K. J., 1965, *Aspects of the Theory of Risk Bearing*, Helsinki: Academic Book Store.

Aumann, R., 1964, "Markets with a Continuum of Traders," *Econometrica* 32, 39–50.

Aumann, R., 1966, "Existence of Competitive Equilibria in Markets with a Continuum of Traders," *Econometrica* 34, 1–17.

Balzer, W., C. U. Moulines, and J. Sneed, 1987, *An Architectonic for Science: The Structuralist Program*, Dordrecht: Reidel

Berg Eriksen, T., K. E. Tranøy, and G. Fløistad, 1987, *Filosofi og Vitenskap*, Oslo: Universitetsforlaget AS.

Berger, J. O., 1985, *Statistical Decision Theory and Bayesian Analysis,* 2nd Ed., New York: Springer-Verlag.

Berger, P. L., and T. Luckmann, 1967, *The Social Construction of Reality*, New York: Anchor Books, Doubleday.

Blaug, M., 1990, *The Methodology of Economics*, Cambridge: Cambridge University Press.

Cantor, G., 1895, "Beitrage zur Begrundung der transfiniten Mengenlehre, Part I," *Mathematische Annalen* 46, 481–512.

Cantor, G., 1897, "Beitrage zur Begrundung der transfiniten Mengenlehre, Part II," *Mathematische Annalen* 47, 207–246.

Collin, F., 1997, *Social Reality*, New York: Routledge.

Coplestone, F., 1994, *A History of Philosophy, Vol. 6,* New York: Doubleday.

Debreu, G., and H. Scarf, 1963, "A Limit Theorem on the Core of an Economy," *International Economic Review* 4, 235–246.

Duhem, P., 1954, *The Aim and Structure of Physical Theory*, P. P. Wiener (trans.), Princeton: Princeton University Press.

Efron, B., 1982, *The Jackknife, the Bootstrap and Other Resampling Plans*, Philadelphia: Society for Industrial and Applied Mathematics.

Efron, B., 1998, "R.A. Fisher in the 21st Century (with Discussion)," *Statistical Science* 13, 95–122.

Fisher, R. A., 1922, "On the Mathematical Foundation of Theoretical Statistics," *Philosophical Transactions of the Royal Society of London*, Series A 222, 309–368.

Fisher, R. A., 1930, "Inverse Probability," *Proceedings of the Cambridge Philosophical Society* 26, 528–535.

Friedman, M., 1953, "The Methodology of Positive Economics," in: *Essays in Positive Economics*, Chicago: University of Chicago Press.

Friedman, M., 1957, *A Theory of the Consumption Function*, Princeton: Princeton University Press.

Granger, C. W. J., 1969, "Investigating Causal Relations by Econometric Models and Cross-spectral Methods," *Econometrica* 37, 424–438.

Granger, C. W. J., 1999, *Empirical Modeling in Economics*, Cambridge: Cambridge University Press.

Haavelmo, T., 1944, "The Probability Approach in Econometrics," *Econometrica* 12 (Suppl.), 1–118.

Hall, A. D., and A. R. Pagan, 1983, "Diagnostic Tests as Residual Analysis," *Econometric Reviews* 2, 159–218.

Hall, T., H. Anderson, and C. W. J. Granger, 1992, "A Cointegration Analysis of Treasury Bill Yields," *The Review of Economics and Statistics* 74, 116–126.

Hansen, L. P., and K. J. Singleton, 1982, "Generalized Instrumental Variables Estimators of Nonlinear Rational Expectations Models," *Econometrica* 50, 1269–1286.

Hausman, D. M., 1992, *The Inexact and Separate Science of Economics*, Cambridge: Cambridge University Press.

Heckscher, E., 1919, "The Effect of Foreign Trade on the Distribution of Income," *Ekonomisk Tidsskrift*, 21, 497–512.

Hempel, C. G., 1965, *Aspects of Scientific Explanation and Other Essays in the Philosophy of Science*, New York: The Free Press.

Hendry, D. F., 1995, *Dynamic Econometrics*, Oxford: Oxford University Press.

Janssen, M. C. W., and Yao-Hua Tan, 1992, "Friedman's Permanent Income Hypothesis as an Example of Diagnostic Reasoning," *Economics and Philosophy* 8, 23–49.

Kant, I., 1966, *Critique of Pure Reason*, F. M. Müller (trans.), New York: Doubleday.

Keynes, J. M., 1936, *General Theory of Employment, Interest and Money*, New York: Harcourt Brace.

Knorr-Cetina, K. D., 1981, *The Manufacture of Knowledge*, Oxford: Pergamon Press.

Koopmans, T. C. (ed.), 1950, *Statistical Inference in Dynamic Economic Models*, Cowles Commission Monograph 10, New York: Wiley.

Lawson, T., 1997, *Economics and Reality*, London: Routledge

Leontief, W., 1982, Letter in *Science* 217, 104–107.

Marek, W., and M. Truszczynski, 1993, *Nonmonotonic Logic*, Berlin: Springer-Verlag.

Mill, J. S., 1836, "On the Definition of Political Economy; and on the Method of Investigation Proper to It" reprinted in 1967, in: *Collected Works, Essays on Economy and Society, Vol. 4*, J. M. Robson (ed.), Toronto: University of Toronto Press.

Mizon, G. E., 1984, "The Encompassing Approach in Econometrics," in: *Econometrics and Quantitative Economics*, D. Hendry and K. F. Wallis (eds.), London: Blackwell.

Modigliani, F., and R. Brumberg, 1955, "Utility Analysis and the Consumption Function: An Interpretation of Cross-section Data," in *Post-Keynesian Economics*, K. K. Kurihara (ed.), London: Allen and Unwin.

Neyman, J., 1937, "Outline of a Theory of Statistical Estimation Based on the Classical Theory of Probability," *Philosophical Transactions of the Royal Society of London*, Series A 236, 333–380.

Neyman, J., 1941, "Fiducial Argument and the Theory of Confidence Intervals," *Biometrika* 32, 128–150.

Neyman, J., and E. S. Pearson, 1928, "On the Use and Interpretation of Certain Test Criteria for Purposes of Statistical Inference," *Biometrika* 20A, 175–240, 263–294.

Neyman, J., and E. S. Pearson, 1933, "On the Problem of the Most Efficient Test of Statistical Hypotheses," *Philosophical Transactions of the Royal Society of London*, Series A 231, 289–337.

Ohlin, B., 1933, *Interregional and International Trade*, Cambridge: Harvard University Press

Popper, K. R., 1972, *Conjectures and Refutations*, London: Routledge & Kegan Paul.
Reiter, R., 1980, "A Logic for Default Reasoning," *Artificial Intelligence* 13, 81–132.
Reiter, R., 1987, "A Theory of Diagnosis from First Principles," *Artificial Intelligence* 32, 57–95.
Searle, J. R, 1995, *The Construction of Social Reality*, New York: Penguin.
Senior, W. N., 1836, *An Outline of the Science of Political Economy*, reprinted in 1965, New York: A. M. Kelley.
Senior, W. N., 1850, *Political Economy*, London: Griffin.
Sismondo, S., 1993, "Some Social Constructions," *Social Studies of Science* 23, 515–553
Solow, R. M., 1956, "A Contribution to the Theory of Economic Growth," *Quarterly Journal of Economics* 70, 65–94.
Stein, C. M., 1956, "Inadmissibility of the Usual Estimator for the Mean of a Multivariate Normal Distribution," in: *Proceedings of the Third Berkeley Symposium on Mathematical Statistics and Probability, Vol. I*, Berkeley: University of California Press.
Stigum, B. P., 1967, " A Decision Theoretic Approach to Time Series Analysis," *The Annals of the Institute of Statistical Mathematics* 19, 207–243.
Stigum, B. P., 1990, *Toward a Formal Science of Economics*, Cambridge: MIT Press.
Stumpf, S. E., 1977, *Philosophy: History and Problems*, New York: McGraw-Hill.
Summers, L. H., 1991, "The Scientific Illusion in Empirical Macroeconomics," *Scandinavian Journal of Economics* 93, 128–148.
Wald, A., 1947, *Sequential Analysis*, New York: Wiley.
Wald, A., 1950, *Statistical Decision Functions*, New York: Wiley.
Weber, M., 1949, *The Methodology of the Social Sciences*, E. Shils and H. Finch (trans.). New York: Free Press.

PART I
Facts and Fiction in Econometrics

Chapter Two

The Construction of Social Reality

In this chapter I present my view of the way human beings construct their social reality. The meaning of "social reality" is controversial and demands explication. To provide such explication, I need the use of several basic terms: "Truth," "Facts," the "World of Things," the "World of Facts," and the "World of Possibilities." I define them in a way that suits the purposes of the chapter. In spirit, if not in detail, my definitions of the first three concepts accord, respectively, with the notions of truth, fact, and reality that John R. Searle (1995) expounds in his book *The Construction of Social Reality*.

2.1 TRUTH

Some of the English words that I need to explicate the idea of truth, "name" and "declarative sentence," require careful definition. I use the word name in the same way that A. Church (1956, p. 3) uses "proper name." Examples are Oslo, the capital of Denmark, eight, and three hundred and twenty-nine. A name names something. We say that a name *denotes* that which it names, and we call the thing denoted its *denotation.* Different names may denote the same thing; for instance, Copenhagen and the capital of Denmark denote the same city in Denmark. In natural language a single name may also have different denotations. Thus Bergen denotes a city in Norway and a town in New Hampshire.

Names of a particular kind are "declarative sentences." Such sentences are aggregations of words that express an assertion, and they denote one or the other of two abstract objects called truth values: *truth* and *falsehood.* A true declarative sentence denotes truth and a false one falsehood. Thus "Copenhagen is the capital of Denmark" is a name that denotes truth, whereas "de Gaule was a Nazi" is a name that denotes falsehood. I conclude:

Truth is the denotation of a true declarative sentence, and *falsehood* is the denotation of a false declarative sentence.

But what is the meaning of "true"? The simplest declarative sentences predicate an attribute of some object; for example, "Snow is white." Complicated declarative sentences are compounds of simpler sentences; for example, "All the cats I know are ichthyophagous" is a compound of the sentences "c_i is a fish-eating cat," $i = 1, \ldots, n$, and "$c_1, \ldots, c_n$ are all the cats I know." Consequently, with a little stretch of the imagination we can think of a declarative sentence either as a sentence that predicates one or more relations among various objects or as a compound of such sentences. For such declarative sentences we can say that *they are true if and only if the denotations of the names in the sentence satisfy the relations predicated of them by the sentence.*

Unfortunately, the structure of a declarative sentence need not be as simple as I have suggested above. Two troublesome examples are: (1) It is true that "Peter owes Smith a horse." Yet there is no particular horse that Peter owes Smith. (2) It is true that "Frank believes that Copenhagen is in Sweden." Yet it is false that "Frank believes that the capital of Denmark is in Sweden."

We can account for such declarative sentences (and the simpler ones as well) if we amend our characterization of true as follows:

A declarative sentence is *true* if and only if the conditions on which the sentence insists are satisfied.

In short, if p is a declarative sentence, the sentence "p" is *true* if and only if p. Thus, the sentence "Snow is white" is true if and only if snow is white. Similarly, the sentence "Peter owes Smith a horse" is true if and only if Peter owes Smith a horse.

2.2 FACTS

The notion of truth that I am trying to convey accords with the spirit, if not the details, of Alfred Tarski's (1964, pp. 52–65) semantic conception of truth. It also accords with Aristotle's definition: "Falsehood consists in saying of that which is that it is not, or of that which is not that it is. Truth consists in saying of that which is that it is, or of that which is not that it is not" (Warrington, 1978, p. 142). Finally, it accords in spirit with John Searle's version of the correspondence theory of truth. I next use Searle's (1995, pp. 199–221) own arguments to show why that is so.

Searle (p. 213) characterizes his notion of truth as follows:

Declarative sentences are true if and only if they correspond to the facts.

Here facts are neither complex objects nor linguistic entities. Instead:

A *fact* is that in virtue of which a true statement is true.

As such, facts are "conditions in the world that satisfy the truth conditions specified by statements" (p. 211). But if that is so, then identifying that which makes a declarative sentence true by repeating the sentence means that repeating a true declarative sentence is the same thing as stating a fact. Consequently, my explication of a true sentence can be rephrased as follows:

A declarative sentence "p" is true if and only if it is a fact that p.

Now, Searle designates the relation between declarative sentences and stated facts as "corresponds to." With his understanding of corresponds to and fact my idea of a true declarative sentence can be made to sound like his. To wit:

A declarative sentence "p" is true if and only if it corresponds to the fact that p.

For the rest of this chapter it is important to keep in mind that facts are neither complex objects nor linguistic entities. *Facts are simply that in virtue of which true statements are true.*

2.3 THE WORLD OF THINGS

PW: The *World* is a nonempty set of things that exist independently of all human representations.

In this definition "thing" is an undefined term that varies from one science to another. In geology the World is full of rocks. In botany the World abounds with flowers, and in economics it is full of goods and consumers. Scientists have many ways of having access to and representing features of the World, for example, perception and language. From a philosopher's point of view, it is a strong assumption that the things in the World exist independently of such representations.

In searching for knowledge about the World scientists use observations and inference by induction and analogy to develop useful hypotheses. Their quest has a good chance of being successful only if the World is not too complicated. For that reason I adopt two hypotheses about the World that philosophers have proposed. The first is John Stuart Mill's (1843) principle of *the uniformity of nature* (PUN). The second is John Maynard Keynes's (1921) principle of *the limited variability of nature* (PLVN).

In Mill's words (cf. Robson, 1973, p. 306), PUN asserts that, "there are such things in nature as parallel cases, that what happens once will, under sufficient degree of similarity of circumstances happen again, and not only again, but as often as the same circumstances recur." For our purposes the most useful formulation of the principle is due to Keynes (1921, p. 226):

PUN: Mere differences in time and space of our sense data are inductively irrelevant.

It is difficult to fathom what Mill had in mind when he talked of parallel cases. It is equally hard to delineate criteria for ascertaining whether we face situations that, from an inductive point of view, differ only in time and space. For instance, it is easy to judge that the maple tree I see outside my house today is the same as the one I saw yesterday. That is so even though it has grown a smidge and lost a branch in the storm that raged last night. However, it is hard to determine all those factors that would render time and space inductively irrelevant in inferences concerning the composition of consumer expenditures on goods and services. Even so, in one form or another PUN appears explicitly or implicitly in many contemporary econometric models.

Keynes believed that the characteristics of the objects in which we are interested adhere in groups of invariable connection, which are finite in number. He formulated this belief roughly as follows (see Keynes 1921, pp. 252, 256):

PLVN: The qualities of an object are bound together in a limited number of *groups*, a subclass of each group being an infallible symptom of the coexistence of certain other members of the group. Moreover, the objects in the field, over which our generalizations extend, have a finite number of independent qualities.

Keynes used PUN and PLVN in his theory of induction to ensure that *any* inductive hypothesis would have a positive initial probability of being valid. In the context of this chapter, PUN and PLVN can be used to establish the possibility of ostensive definitions of universals such as chair, cat, blackness, and justice. The two postulates can also be used to explain scientists' successful search for useful ways to classify both animate and inanimate matters. Hence they form a basis on which one can use sense data, induction, and analogy to assign truth values to sentences such as, "the object next to which I sit is an iron desk" and "the body I perceive in front is a man wearing a red tie."

Lord Russell (1948) rejected both PUN and PLVN on the grounds that they are prescientific.[1] However, most reasoning done outside of laboratories and the ivory towers of academia *is* prescientific. In adapting to life, people more or less consciously trust the validity of variants of these principles. This is implicit both in their belief in the existence of physical objects and other minds and in the confidence they place in their ability to recognize objects. Thus in preparing for a bicycle ride, we look for our bicycles where we think we left them. If we experience emotional problems, we may confide our woes to a friend and hope for comfort and advice. If we notice an object on the road that is the size of a football but looks like a stone, we do not kick it. The fact that most people manage to cope with life may be taken as testimony to the considerable extent to which PUN and PLVN provide a reasonable basis for inference by induction and analogy in everyday situations.

Since the *World*, as defined above, is a set of things, in the remainder of the chapter I refer to the *World* by the name, *World of Things*. Moreover, I take PWE for granted.

PWE: The World of Things evolves in indefinite ways with the passage of time.

I consider social reality to be a superstructure of things and facts that human beings construct on top of the World of Things. It has three basic constituents: the World of Things, the World of Facts, and the World of Possibilities. I discussed the World of Things above. Next I describe how one generates the World of Facts.

2.4 THE WORLD OF FACTS

I denote the World of Facts by Ω_F, and in Ω_F one finds facts concerning members of the World of Things, facts concerning members of Ω_F, and facts concerning collections of things and facts. As time passes, the World of Things and the content of Ω_F change in indefinite ways. Hence, Ω_F is a collection of elements in flux.

2.4.1 Personal and Social Facts

In the World of Facts I distinguish between personal and social facts:

A *personal fact* is a fact that pertains to the mental states of a given person.

A *social fact* is a fact that more than one person accepts as a fact.

There are intentional and nonintentional personal facts. Here, "intentionality is that property of the mind by which it is directed at objects and states of affairs in the world" (Searle, 1995, p. 18). Assertions that at some point in time might express intentional personal facts are "I want to rest" and "I believe that the interest rates in Norway will rise this year." Assertions that at some point in time might express nonintentional personal facts are "I feel good today" and "My back is aching." These facts pertain to the mental state of a single person—me. Moreover, they are not social facts since they concern mental states that belong to me alone. Only the fact that I can be in such mental states is a social fact.

There are also intentional and nonintentional social facts. Not all intentional mental states are *singular* in the way "I want to rest" is singular. Some of them are *plural* and concern the collective intentionality of two or more individuals. Here *collective intentionality* refers to the intentional mental state of a group of individuals seen as a whole.[2] We presume that the members of the group have a sense of doing something together. In carrying out their tasks each member has his own intentionality. This intentionality he (or she or it) derives from the collective intentionality that he shares with the other members. Assertions that at some point in time might express intentional social facts are "Gerd and Anne Olaug are skiing together at Tryvann" and "The Norwegian Symphony Orchestra is giving a concert performance." Assertions that at some point in time might express nonintentional social facts are "The earth is moving around the sun" and "Water freezes at a temperature of 0°C."

As I have identified a fact with that in virtue of which a true statement is true, it might be disconcerting that a fact that just two people accept as a fact is a social fact.. However, this aspect of my definition is not as bad as it sounds. Disagreements about what is a fact are common in all walks of life—even in the sciences. Fuzzy borders and overlaps in classifications account for scientific facts that not all scientists are willing to accept. Moreover, disagreements about the axioms of mathematical logic account for mathematical facts that not all mathematicians can accept. Finally, technological inventions and the progress of knowledge account for facts that scientists of an earlier time accepted and their contemporary colleagues reject.

Human beings create social facts in many ways. For example, they create social facts when they classify elements of the World of Things and when they devise blueprints for combining elements in the making of new elements. They also create social facts when they establish institutions that regulate their lives and when, with the guidance of blueprints, they produce goods that they use for all sorts of purposes. Finally, they create social facts when they accumulate records of how their social reality has evolved from the beginning of time to the present. Each of these activities creates social facts in its own characteristic way. I show how this occurs below.

2.4.2 The Social World

It is obvious that the World of Things plays a pivotal role in the way human beings create social facts. Since my goal here is to describe the construction of social reality, the World of Things in question is the *Social World* (W_S). It contains elements from the worlds of all the different sciences, from the world of mathematics, and from the world of music. Thus in W_S one finds all the rocks of geology, all the plants of botany, and all the living organisms of zoology. In W_S one also finds elements of the world of astronomy, basic elements in the world of music, and various elements in the world of mathematics, such as the empty set and a set-theoretic representation of the real numbers.

For the purposes of this book it is important that we be able to identify W_S with the world as the latter appears to a person at *the beginning of the current period of time*. Therefore, I insist that in W_S there are real mountains and valleys, real solar systems and galaxies, and billions of real human beings. In particular, there is a planet in W_S that truthfully can be designated by the expression "the earth." On the earth there is a mountain that truthfully can be referred to by the words "Mount Everest." There is even a landmass full of lakes and fjords and fair-headed, blue-eyed people that can truthfully be denoted by the word "Norway." Finally, on the earth, human beings live in houses, drive cars, and play all sorts of musical instruments.

2.4.3 Typology (CL)

Human beings assign names to those elements of W_S of which they are aware and provide descriptions of classes of individuals or objects in W_S that share certain attributes. In that way they learn to distinguish even from odd numbers in mathematics and how to identify members of the families of igneous, sedimentary, and metamorphic rocks in geology. They also learn to distinguish different kinds of moving vehicles and learn where to place living organisms in the five kingdoms of biology. Finally, they learn to distinguish people living in Norway from people living in the United States, and how to identify members of the "accepted" classes of mental disorders in humans. The classes in question often have fuzzy borders. Moreover, they may overlap with one another horizontally and form intricate hierarchical systems vertically.

E 2.1 *In biology an animal is a multicellular organism whose cells are bound by a plasma membrane and who obtains energy by acquiring and ingesting food. The basic unit in the classification of animals is the species, a group of organisms that resemble each other closely and are able to mate with one another and produce fertile offspring. Biologists arrange species with similar characteristics and origins into higher groupings that are progressively more inclusive. Thus they group related species into a genus, genera into a family, families into an order, orders into a class, classes into a phylum, and phyla into a kingdom, Animalia. For example, there are many kinds of house cats. They form a species,* Felix catus, *that belongs to* Felis, *one of four genera.* Felis, *in turn, is a member of the family Felidae, which belongs to the order Carnivora. Finally, Carnivora is a member of the class Mammalia, which belongs to the phylum Chordata.*[3]

There are several things to note about these classifications. In delineating the various classes of the given classifications one uses ordinary English augmented with names of the elements of W_S. The classifications are not absolutes, but vary over time with the progress of knowledge. They may even vary among scientists in the same field of research. Most importantly here, the given classifications come without reasons for their existence. They are to be viewed as useful information storage and retrieval systems that scientists or others have devised to further communication among people. In performing this function successfully the classifications determine facts that I consider to be social facts.

The following is an example that illustrates how classifications determine social facts. Consider the assertion "The object in my hand is an apple." If the assertion is true, then it is a fact that the object in my hand is an apple. Searle would call that fact a *brute fact* because it concerns a physical object in the world of things (cf. Searle 1995, p. 122). Now, the given assertion can be true only if it accords with a system of classifications of elements of W_S. That system of classifications belongs to the information-retrieval system of many people. Consequently, the fact in question would be accepted by many and is, therefore, a social fact.

2.4.4 Blueprints (BP) and Production (PR)

Apart from classifying the elements of W_S, human beings create blueprints that indicate how to combine things in W_S to form both existing and new things. Moreover, with the blueprints in hand they devise ways to produce all sorts of interesting products and figure out means by which people residing in different parts of the earth can communicate with each other. The blueprints may surface on the drawing boards of scientists, be recorded in articles and books, or be hidden in the brains of skilled workmen and farmers, and the associated production processes may be carried out on farms, in factories, or in laboratories as the relevant case may require. The following are a few examples to indicate what I have in mind.

E 2.2 *Apples are interesting. They grow on trees, and their process of production is relatively simple and well understood. Existing blueprints detail all the impersonal facets of the production of apples. They also describe how apples combine with other products to form cider and various tarts and pies. The blueprints for apple production and the recipes for cider and tarts and pies can be used to express social facts that belong to* Ω_{F}. *For example, it is a social fact that "apples are used in the production of cider."*

As far as the world of facts is concerned, farm-grown apples do not differ from other man-made products. Take an industrial product such as aluminum. It is a social fact that "most aluminum produced today is made from bauxite." Existing blueprints detail all the impersonal facets of the production of aluminum from bauxite. They also describe how aluminum combines with other products to form all sorts of aluminum alloys. One can use the blueprints for the production of aluminum and the "recipes" for aluminum alloys to express social facts that belong to Ω_F.

E 2.3 *Gene splicing is a procedure whereby segments of genetic material from one organism, the donor, are transferred to another, the recipient. In most experimental situations genetic engineers combine fragments of the donor's DNA with viruses or plasmids and transfer the resulting DNA molecule into cells of the recipient. Each time a recipient cell divides, the inserted DNA molecule is replicated along with the recipient's DNA. Such divisions produce clones of identical cells that have the potential to translate the donor DNA fragment into the protein that it encodes.*[4]

Development of the gene-splicing technique has had many useful results. Using bacteria as recipient cells, genetic engineers have helped increase the availability of several medically important substances, for example, insulin for diabetes and interferon for viral infections. They have also managed to produce bacteria that can break down oil slicks and decompose many forms of garbage. Finally, they have demonstrated that it is possible to use plant cells as hosts, which is a possibility that has far-reaching consequences for the world's food production.[5] The blueprints that the genetic engineers have discovered and the production process they have designed can be used to express social facts that belong to Ω_F.

In this context it is relevant that a blueprint may exist in the mind of a single person, in which case it will determine personal as well as social facts. Moreover, not all blueprints will result in viable production processes. There may be many reasons for that, for example, nonexistence of markets and prohibitive laws and regulations. Finally, the products that human beings produce can usually be used for many different purposes. Each of these uses determines families of social facts that belong to Ω_F. Many of these social facts are institutional facts. We attend to them next.

2.4.5 Institutions (IN) and Institutional Facts

On earth human beings observe the production of goods and services and confront markets in which these goods and services are sold. They encounter institutional factors such as property rights, corporate structures, political parties, and games that humans use to entertain themselves and observe the existence of different kinds of governments and all sorts of national and international organizations. Most of these aspects of human life determine institutional facts. I follow Searle in describing how they do that.

Social facts whose existence depends on human institutions are *institutional facts* in Searle's terminology (cf. Searle 1995, p. 2). According to Searle, specific instances of institutional facts, such as "Magnus and Anne Olaug won the mixed-doubles final in tennis," are applications of specific constitutive rules. The constitutive rules in question come in systems and have a remarkably simple form:

"X counts as Y in the context C."

For example, there is a well-defined and agreed-upon system of rules for playing tennis. These rules are constitutive of tennis in the sense that playing tennis is constituted in part by acting in accordance with these rules. Magnus and Anne Olaug's winning the mixed-doubles final was an application of the rule: In three-set doubles (C) winning six of ten games in the first set and seven of twelve in the second set (X) counts as victory in the match (Y).

It is hard to fathom that systems of simple constitutive rules can create the very possibility of all the institutional facts one meets in Ω_F. To understand why, we must take a closer look at the prototype of a constitutive rule that I described earlier. I begin with X. The range of "things" that can be substituted for X in this formula depends on the system of constitutive rules of which the given rule is a part. For example, money is anything that can function widely as a medium of exchange. Consequently, in a family of rules that constitutes a monetary system one may substitute for X such varied kinds of entities as a certain "valuable commodity," certain "coins that a monetary authority issues," certain "notes that a bank issues," and various "bank deposits." In each case the

X in question supposedly counts as money (*Y*) in a specified situation (*C*). For example, since $20 Federal Reserve notes count as money in the United States today, I can use the $20 note in my pocket to pay for lunch.

Both in the case of tennis and in the case of a monetary system the terms, I substituted for *X* in Searle's prototype of a constitutive rule had a simple structure. Constitutive rules need not be that simple. For example, in a system of rules that constitutes the marriage institution, the entities I substitute for *X* are sequences of speech acts that the bride and the groom and the presiding official are to perform. The speech acts and the official differ from one situation to the next. However, in a given context (*C*), accurate performances of an appropriately chosen sequence of speech acts (*X*) count as the bride and groom getting married (*Y*).

There are several interesting aspects of Searle's formula for constitutive rules. One is the intended relationship between the entities one substitutes for the *X* and the *Y* terms. In order that for the formula to determine an institutional fact, the *Y* term must assign a status to the basic elements of the *X* term that they do not possess themselves just by virtue of satisfying the conditions that *X* specifies. Further, there must be collective agreement both about assigning that particular status to the item to which the *X* term refers and about imposing on individuals or objects the functions that possibly go with such a status. Thus, it is a fact that, "In my dining room (*C*) a piece of furniture consisting of a flat top set horizontally on four legs (*X*) counts as a table (*Y*)." However, that fact is not institutional since I can use this furniture as a table regardless of what anyone else thinks. In contrast, the generally agreed-upon rules of tennis are needed when assigning the status of winning the mixed-doubles match to Magnus and Anne Olaug. Therefore, the fact that Magnus and Anne Olaug won the mixed-doubles match is an institutional fact. Similarly, there is collective agreement in the United States that Federal Reserve notes have the status of money and that they, as such, are to function as mediums of exchange. Moreover, these notes cannot function as money without such collective agreement. Therefore, it is an institutional fact that the $20 Federal Reserve note in my pocket is money in the United States. Finally, there is collective agreement on assigning the status "married" to a couple only if they have accurately performed the required speech acts of an official wedding ceremony, and there is collective agreement on the functions that the given status imposes on the couple. Those status-functions are usually marked by the terms "husband" and "wife."

Another interesting feature of Searle's constitutive formula is the way such formulas interlock. The *Y* term in one system of constitutive rules might be part of an *X* term and/or a *C* term in the same system or in other systems. For example, in the system of rules that constitute citizenship it is the case that, "In Norway (*C*) being born in Norway and having Norwegian parents (*X*) counts as having Norwegian citizenship (*Y*)." Further, in the system of constitutive rules for travel "For Norwegian citizens (C), having a Norwegian passport (X) counts as having a permit to travel anywhere in Europe (Y)." Finally, in the system of constitutive rules for elections it is a fact that, "In Norway (C) a Norwegian citizen being eighteen or more years old (X) counts as a potential voter in national elections (Y)."

2.4.6 The Historical Records (H-)

There is a last way in which human beings create social facts. They accumulate records of the development of the world and the factual aspects of social reality in the past. These records tell of times when ice and snow covered all of Scandinavia and the first modern human being, Cro-Magnon, appeared in Europe. The records also tell of Aristotle's method of classifying animals and plants by logical division and of the alchemists' attempts to convert mercury and lead into gold. Finally, the records relate the tragic end of the Incan and Mayan civilizations and trace the development of the loom from the ancient Egyptian hand-weaving looms to the modern steam-powered mechanical looms. These and the many other matters that the historical records contain appear in scholarly articles and books. One also hears of them in classroom lectures, and one listens to the marvelous music of old masters on CDs. In that way the historical records constitute bricks and yarn in the fabric of culture. They also make up important parts of the background abilities and the tacit knowledge with which one faces the problems of life. Finally they determine matters of facts that for the current period I consider to be social facts.

2.5 THE WORLD OF POSSIBILITIES

The view of social reality that I tried to describe above reveals the content of W_S and the factual aspects of social reality at the beginning of the current period of time. Since both W_S and the World of Facts are in flux at all times, many details of this part of social reality will change during the current period. The changes that occur cannot be foreseen with certainty. From the vantage point of the present, therefore, the development of things and facts, that is, of W_S and Ω_F, in the future belongs to the World of Possibilities, which consists of all the paths along which W_S and Ω_F might evolve.

2.5.1 Changes in the World of Things and the World of Facts

I next describe briefly changes that occur in W_S and Ω_F with the passage of time. Such changes often take many years to materialize. I give examples both of changes that happened in the past and of changes that might materialize before the current year ends.

ΔW_S: The world W_S at one instant of time is never quite the same as at another instant of time. Living organisms reproduce, age, and die. Erupting volcanoes and earthquakes cause changes in the earth's crust, leave houses in ruin, and kill animals and people. Seasons, el Niño, and changes in the atmosphere modify the conditions of life for plants and living organisms alike. The changes in W_S need not be permanent, and some of them can be controlled. The following is an interesting case in point.

E 2.4 *Moas are extinct flightless birds that once inhabited New Zealand. The Maoris hunted them for food and used their bones and eggshells for tools and ornaments. Now researchers at the Otago University in Dunedin, New Zealand, have succeeded in extracting a DNA molecule from a preserved Moa leg bone. By implanting the molecule in a chicken egg they hope to develop a bird that will share many of the characteristics of the Moa.*[6]

It is important to keep in mind here that the elements of W_S are things that are *known* to exist. Hence, W_S also changes with the development of knowledge of things. Examples are geologists mapping a new oil field, a successful search for a missing element in Mendeleyev's table, the discoveries of HIV and Ebola, and the establishment of nonstandard numbers in mathematics.

ΔCL: The classifications of the elements in W_S change over time in various ways. A given class may gain new members, lose some members, or simply cease to exist. The changes may occur for all sorts of reasons, for example, new and successful product developments. Last year's inclusion of snowboarding in the class of Olympic events came as the result of an amazing product development. There may also be reclassifications because of new discoveries.

E 2.5 *Some years ago, an evolutionary microbiologist, C. Woese, and his collaborator G. E. Fox (cf. Woese and Fox 1977) succeeded in using rRNA analysis to construct a tree of life that consists of three kingdoms, the Bacteria, the Archaea, and the Eukarya. Of these, the first two make up the former kingdom of prokaryotes and the third includes the kingdoms of higher plants and animals. According to Woese's tree, billions of years ago a common ancestor gave rise to the two bacterial kingdoms, and later the Archaea gave rise to the Eukarya.*

Current research seems to throw doubts on Woese's ideas. For one thing, newly sequenced microbial genomes suggest that the chances are high that the Bacteria rather than the Archaea gave rise to the Eukarya. For another, counterfactual analysis of RNA metabolism in modern organisms suggests that eukaryote-like cells might have existed earlier than the cells of the Bacteria and the Archaea.[7]

ΔBP: The blueprints BP that detail ways of combining elements of W_S to produce new things or to create synthetic equivalents of the elements of W_S also change over time. These changes are mainly due to technological innovations and to the general growth of knowledge. They come in various forms. Some describe new ways of producing a given product. Others delineate ways to produce entirely new products. Still others detail new ways to combat the harm that human activities inflict on the environment and describe possible means to solve pressing world problems.

E 2.6 *In 1997 the state-owned Norwegian Oil Company, Statoil, decided to build two gas-fired power plants on the west coast of Norway. The decision resulted in a storm of protest from environmental activists, who claimed that the CO_2 emissions from such plants are much too high. The activists managed to stall the project temporarily. They also saw to it that the project became a hot political issue.*

For us the interesting aspect of the story is that Statoil might never build the two plants. Last year Norsk Hydro, a competitor, succeeded in developing new technology for producing electric power that uses natural gas to generate hydrogen-fueled electric power and produces clean CO_2 gas as a by-product. The latter can be injected into North Sea oil reservoirs. Such injections not only enlarge the supply of extractable oil but also reduce the power plant's CO_2 emissions into the atmosphere by a factor of 0.9 as compared with the emissions of modern gas-fired plants.[8]

Norsk Hydro's technological innovation changed BP in 1998. Whether it will also change PR remains to be seen. Hydrogen-fueled electric power is more costly than gas-fired electric power. The commercial feasibility of the hydrogen-fueled option therefore depends on the extent to which injection of CO_2 gas into North Sea reservoirs will increase the extractable supplies of oil.

ΔPR: Changes in PR take various forms. Firms may produce more or less of a given product, change the combinations in which they use required factors of production, replace old machinery with new models, and relocate. They may also cease production of some commodities, change the design of others, and prepare for the supply of entirely new products. These changes in PR have many causes. Some occur as the result of prospective changes in market conditions. Others happen because of changes in BP. Still others may be the result of government intervention.

E 2.7 *The* virtual office *of an employee in a given firm is a workplace that is geographically separate from but linked to the firm's main office through the use of telecommunication technology. A teleworker is an employee who spends at least half his working time in his virtual office. The virtual offices of most teleworkers are in their homes. There are, however, two interesting alternatives. One is an office in a satellite work center that a firm has created within easy commuting distance for a number of employees and the other is the telecottage of several offices that a given community or a number of firms equip and support financially. A large number of business organizations* *support teleworking either explicitly or tacitly. In the United States in 1995, for example, 18 percent of American companies had technology-based work-at-home programs. In Norway, the largest state-owned company, Statoil, now has an ongoing experiment in which 500 of its employees work in virtual offices.*

The steady advances in telecommunications technology and the concomitant increase in the use of virtual offices will have important effects on the social reality that the world's population will face as the new century progresses. Technological advances are leading to an ever increasing globalization of production as well as to an extraordinary decrease in the employed part of the industrial labor force and the middle-management of large firms. The increasing use of virtual offices in the operations of firms and public and private organizations will affect the mobility of firms, the demographic structure of cities and their rural peripheries, and the family lives of employees.[9]

ΔIN: The changes in IN come in various forms. The lives of individuals and the structures of organizations change, individuals and institutions change their legal status and exchange ownership, and rules and regulations change over time. When these rules and regulations are parts of a general policy, they become in Searle's terminology constitutive of families of new institutional facts. The changes may concern local or national matters or may result from international agreements. I describe one example of the latter in E 2.8.

E 2.8 *In December 1997, delegates to the third conference of the Parties to the U.N. Framework Convention on Climate Change (UNFCCC) agreed upon the Kyoto Protocol, which sets binding targets for the emission of greenhouse gases (GHG) for each industrial country (IC) during the years from 2008 to 2012. The Protocol also suggests ways in which the ICs can meet their targets. Three such methods are of interest here. The ICs may establish a market for trade in quotas. In this case ICs with high abatement costs buy quotas from ICs with low abatement costs. The ICs may also collaborate and help pay for each other's abatement costs. In such cases one IC obtains additional quotas by helping to pay for the cost of reducing the GHG emissions of another IC. Finally, an IC may obtain additional quotas by investing in projects in developing countries that contribute to the ultimate objectives of the Clean Development Mechanism.*

All the ICs, including the United States, signed the agreement. However, it will not enter into force until it has been ratified by at least fifty-five countries, and these ratifying countries must have accounted for at least 55 percent of the industrialized world's CO_2 emissions in 1990.[10] *The United States subsequently announced that it does not intend to ratify the Protocol.*

In November 2001, at the seventh conference of the Parties in Marrakech, negotiators reached agreement on rules for implementing the Kyoto Protocol. The Marrakech Accords include operating rules for international emission trading, the Clean Development Mechanism, and joint implementation.

By now, many countries have expressed their intention to ratify the agreement. When adopted, these rules and regulations will be constitutive of families of new institutional facts for all the Parties to the UNFCCC.[11]

ΔH*-:* The changes in H- are changes in our knowledge concerning the periods that preceded the current period. These changes occur partly as the results of fieldwork, partly as the results of studying old documents, and partly as the results of laboratory experiments.

E 2.9 *Spanish archaeologists insist that all artifacts and skeletal remains that have been found on the Canary Islands and date prior to the fifteenth century belong to the islands' aborigines. Members of the Society for Atlantic History Research are not so sure. They have recently found intriguing remains of a ship in a burial mound in Galdar on Grand Canary. The remains date back to the ninth century and contain strakes with cleats for lashing ribs to planks that are similar to the characteristic strakes of a Viking ship. Now the researchers are hoping that DNA tests of skeletal remains from the same burial mound will provide further evidence for the possibility that Vikings used the Canary Islands as a base during their raids in the Mediterranean.*[12]

2.5.2 Personal Possibilities and Social Possibilities

So much for changes in the Worlds of Things and Facts. In the resulting World of Possibilities I distinguish between personal possibilities and social possibilities:

A *personal possibility* is a future state of the Worlds of Things and Facts that is of importance to a given person and that he or she, as the case may be, believes is possible.

A *social possibility* is a future state of the Worlds of Things and Facts that is of importance to more than one person and that at least two of the individuals concerned believe is possible.

In reading these definitions one must keep in mind that the World of Possibilities does not vary over individuals or over groups of individuals. Only the probabilities that individuals assign to various future events differ among persons. It must also be noted that a personal possibility is an event in the World of Possibilities and not a single path. The same goes for social possibilities. For example, it is a personal possibility that I will spend the next academic year in the United States. To do that I have to receive an invitation from a suitable university and find someone to rent my apartment. It is irrelevant whether the current Norwegian government remains in power or the price of oil falls to an unprecedented low level. Similarly, today January 12, 2003, it is a social possibility that George W. Bush will declare war against Iraq before the end of

February 2003 and that Norway will join the war effort before the end of May 2003 even if Bush does not have the backing of the UN Security Council. The possibility of my going to the US will remain a personal possibility as long as I do not share it with others. The moment I mention the possibility to my wife and she thinks that it might be possible, it becomes a social possibility that we may work together to make happen. My wife's view of the given possibility and its good and bad consequences is likely to be very different from mine.

2.6 SOCIAL REALITY

We have now come so far that I can give a succinct definition of "social reality." My idea of social reality is an economist's vision of the reality in which he lives. It differs from that of others. Therefore, to give the reader a better idea of the meaningfulness of my definition, I first present brief characterizations of Ludwig Witgenstein's "reality" and John Searle's "social reality."

In his *Tractatus Logico-Philosophicus* Witgenstein (1974, pp. 5, 8) insists that, "[the] world is all that is the case. The world is the totality of facts, not things. The world is determined by the facts, and by their being *all* the facts. For the totality of facts determines what is the case. And also whatever is not the case. What is the case—a fact—is the existence of states of affairs. A state of affairs (a state of things) is a combination of objects (things). The existence and non-existence of states of affairs is reality."

On the surface of things it looks as though Witgenstein's reality is identical to my World of Facts. There are, however, two important differences. Witgenstein's facts are given and not to be disputed. In contrast, my facts need not be absolutes. People may disagree about some of them. Moreover, we create the facts there are in Ω_F.

In his account of the construction of social reality Searle (1995, p. 26) insists that all social facts are facts involving collective intentionality. He also claims that his "investigation into the nature of social reality has proceeded by investigating the status of the facts by virtue of which our statements about social reality are true" (p. 199). From the last assertion I conclude that Searle identifies social reality with the totality of all social facts. This totality and Searle's definition of social facts provide a succinct characterization of his concept of social reality.

Searle's concept of social reality differs from mine in two ways. It is based on ideas of social facts that differ from mine. His social facts are intentional social facts. My nonintentional social facts are not facts in his social reality. Further, he leaves no room in his social reality for things, personal facts, and possibilities. The missing elements constitute fundamental parts of my concept of social reality. Without them I would have no chance of analyzing the workings of an economic system.

So much for Witgenstein's reality and Searle's social reality. My discussion of the World of Things, the World of Facts, and the World of Possibilities provides me with all the elements I need to propose a succinct definition of my own concept of social reality:

At a given point in time *social reality* comprises all the things and facts there are, all the personal and social possibilities that one or more persons envisage, and nothing else.

As such, social reality does not vary over individuals, and it does not vary over groups of individuals. Still, the part of social reality that one person or one group experiences differs from the part that another person or group experiences. An individual's views of personal relationships and his or her choice of activities vary with sex, age, and physical and psychological characteristics. Similarly, an individual's ability to cope with life in the society in which he or she lives varies with family background, work experience, and education. A group may be a family, a political party, or an international conglomerate. Such groups differ in size and in the activities in which they engage. The ability of a group to perform well in the environment in which it functions determines the group's experience with its part of social reality. The degree of success that a group's performance achieves will vary with the cohesiveness of the group, the structure of its organization, and the attitudes of its members.

2.7 CONCLUDING REMARKS

In this chapter I have explicated the idea of social reality and described how human beings go about creating the social reality in which they live. I think of this social reality as a superstructure of personal and social facts and personal and social possibilities on top of the World of Things, and the chapter shows how it is put together. My vision differs from the ideas of others, and there need not be anybody else whose mental picture of social reality is like mine. Be that as it may, I believe that this chapter gives a good description of the social reality about which economists theorize. If I am right, the social reality that I have described can play the same role in my quest to establish the possibility of a science of economics that Kant's world of phenomena played in his search for the possibility of a pure natural science.

NOTES

1. A prescientific assumption is a "transitional assumption on the road toward fundamental laws of a different kind" (Russell, 1948, p. 444).

2. The idea of collective intentionality that I am describing here I learned from Searle (cf. Searle, 1995, pp. 23–26).

3. I owe this example to Yngvild Wasteson.

4. I learned about gene splicing from an article on genetic engineering by Louis Levine in the 1995 *Grolier Multimedia Encyclopedia.*

5. The development of biotech food, vaccines, and by-products is increasing at a rapid rate. Concerned people fear that this development will eventually sow an ecological catastrophe.

6. I learned about the Moa experiment from an NTB news dispatch in *Aftenposten*, March 10, 1998. It is interesting here that the experiment might not take place because of a dispute about ownership of DNA molecules. The inhabitants of Ngai-Thaus on the South Island of New Zealand claim that they as aborigines have the ownership rights of the Moa DNA molecules. If they do, they may choose to stop the experiment.

7. I learned of Woese's ideas from an article in *Science* (cf. Pennisi, 1998).

8. I obtained the information concerning Norsk Hydro's discovery from a Norsk Hydro press release dated April 23, 1998.

9. I learned of the virtual office from Nasjonale informasjonsnettverk reports on Norwegian experiences with such offices (e.g., Bakke et al., 1998) and from a paper by Laurence Habib and Tony Cornford (cf. Habib and Cornford, 1997). The remainder of my comments are based on pertinent chapters in Rifkin (1989). The establishment of virtual offices is interesting in this context because it can be viewed as the beginning of a reversal of the development that England and other countries experienced during the industrial revolution (cf. Plumb, 1970; Smelser, 1959).

10. Ratification of the agreement by a country means that the country's legislative body has approved agreement.

11. I owe this example to Cathrine Hagem. It is based on an article by Hagem (1997), a 1998 CICERO Report by Ringius et al. (1998), and an article by Hagem and Holtsmark (2001).

12. This example is based on an article by Helge Sandvig in *Aftenposten*, July 5, 1998.

REFERENCES

Bakke, J. W., E. Bergersen, E. Fossum, T. E. Julsrud, H. Opheim, and U. Sakshang, 1998, "Erfaringer med fjernarbeid i norske bedrifter," Unpublished Memorandum, NIN, Oslo.

Church, A., 1956, *Introduction to Mathematical Logic*, Princeton: Princeton University Press.

Habib, L., and T. Cornford, 1997, "The Virtual Office and Family Life," Unpublished Paper, London School of Economics.

Hagem, C., 1997, "Klimaforhandlinger og kostnadseffektivitet," *Sosialoekonomen* 51(8), 26–32.

Hagem, C., and B. Holtsmark, 2001, "From Small to Insignificant: Climate Impact of the Kyoto Protocol with and without the US," CICERO Policy Note 2001:1.

Keynes, J. M., 1921, *A Treatise on Probability*, London: Macmillan.

Mill, J. S, 1843, "On the Ground of Induction," reprinted in 1973, in: *A System of Logic Ratiocinative and Inductive*, Collected Works of John Stuart Mill, Vol. 7, J. M. Robson (ed.), Toronto: University of Toronto Press/London: Routledge & Kegan Paul.

Pennisi, E., 1998, "Genome Data Shake Tree of Life," *Science* 280, 672–674.

Plumb, J. H., 1970, *England in the Eighteenth Century*, New York: Penguin.

Ringius, L., L. O. Næss, and A. Torvanger, 1998, "Muligheter og betingelser for felles gjennomfoering etter Kyoto," A CICERO Report, April 29, 1998.

Rifkin, J., 1989, *The End of Work*, New York: G. P. Putnam's Sons.

Russell, B., 1948, *Human Knowledge*, New York: Simon and Schuster.

Sandvig. H., 1998, "Kanariøyene kan ha hatt vikingkoloni," *Aftenposten*, July 5, 1998.

Searle, J. R, 1995, *The Construction of Social Reality*, New York: Penguin.

Smelser, N. J., 1959. *In the Industrial Revolution*, London: Routledge & Kegan Paul.

Tarski, A., 1964, "The Semantic Conception of Truth and the Foundations of Semantics," in: *Readings in Philosophical Analysis*, H. Feigl and W. Sellars (eds.), New York: Appleton-Century-Crofts.

Warrington, J. (ed., trans.), 1978, Aristotle's *Metaphysics*, London: Dent.

Witgenstein, L., 1974, *Tractatus Logico-Philosophicus*, London: Macmillan.

Woese, C. R., and G. E. Fox, 1977, "Phylogenetic Structure of the Prokaryotic Domain: The Primary Kingdoms," *Proceedings of the National Academy of Sciences USA* 74, 5088–5090.

Chapter Three

The Social Construction of Reality

Scientists study the Worlds of Things and Facts and make predictions about the World of Possibilities. They search for an understanding of the relationships that exist among things and facts and hope to be able to predict future events and prepare for them. In this chapter and the next we see how scientists in general and social scientists in particular go about solving the related problems. But first, a remark concerning the notion of a social construction of reality and some of its meanings.

The concept, "social construction of reality," is composed of two parts, "social construction" and "reality." The first part signifies the process by which the second is formed. The description of the process of construction varies from one author to the next. So does also the idea of reality. For our discussion in this chapter I have chosen three interesting notions of reality. In one of them, reality is a world of institutions. In another, it is a world of scientific artifacts. In the third, it is a world of ideas. To go with these three concepts I have chosen three views of the processes that engender the social construction of such realities. The first is Berger and Luckmann's (1967) wonderful account of the processes by which human beings construct the world of institutions. The second is Knorr-Cetina's (1981) vision of the social construction of artifacts in scientific laboratories. The third is my own mental image of the way economists go about constructing their own world of ideas.[1]

3.1 BERGER AND LUCKMANN

"The social construction of reality" comes in many guises. One of them is described in Berger and Luckmann (1967).[2] To Peter Berger and Thomas Luckmann *reality* is a quality appertaining to phenomena that have a being independent of human volition. This reality varies over individuals and societies, and it might vary over situations as well. What is real to a Tibetan monk need not be real to an American businessman. Moreover, the objects that a person perceives in his dreams might be very different from the objects that present themselves to his consciousness in everyday life. The only reality that Berger and Luckmann consider seriously is the reality of everyday life. I believe that their idea of that is like my notion of social reality as I described it in Chapter 2 (to wit: Berger and Luckmann, 1967, pp. 19–28).

According to Berger and Luckmann, *knowledge* is the certainty that phenomena are real and possess specific characteristics. Such knowledge obviously varies over individuals. For example, what passes as knowledge by a criminal differs from what passes as knowledge by a criminologist. Such knowledge also varies over societies. The observable differences between societies in what is taken for granted as knowledge bear witness to that. They insist that the sociology of knowledge must concern itself with whatever passes for knowledge in a society regardless of its ultimate validity. Inasmuch as all human knowledge is developed, transmitted, and maintained in social situations, the sociology of knowledge must also seek to understand the processes by which the social construction of reality occurs (Berger and Luckmann, 1967, p. 3). The latter problem is of special interest here.

In Berger and Luckmann's book the processes that engender the social construction of reality are threefold: *institutionalization*, *legitimation*, and *socialization*. The first creates institutions and the other two ensure that institutions hang together and possess a certain degree of stability. The institutions in question range from the regulatory patterns that recurrent face-to-face interaction among individuals establish to the various institutions of a country's government. All of them are real and cannot be wished away. They have coercive power and moral authority. And they have historicity in the sense that they have been created in the course of a shared history (Berger and Luckmann, 1967, 54–55, 60–61).

Institutionalization supposedly happens "whenever there is a reciprocal *typification* of *habitualized* actions by types of actors" (Berger and Luckmann, 1967, p. 54). An action is habitualized when it is repeated often enough to be cast into a pattern that allows reproduction with an economy of effort. A typification of an action is an assignment of distinctive characteristics to the relevant action. Typifications of habitualized actions that constitute institutions are always shared, and the actors in an institution as well as the actions concerned are typified.

Institutionalization happens in many areas of collectively relevant conduct, and at all times sets of institutionalization processes take place concurrently. There is no a priori reason why these processes must hang together functionally, let alone as a logically consistent system. They hang together only as a result of a process of *legitimation*, which involves all sorts of explanations and justifications as well as promises and threats. With the help of language, legitimation superimposes a quality of logic on the institutional order. The resulting logic of the system of institutions becomes part of the socially available stock of knowledge and is taken for granted as such (Berger and Luckmann, 1967, pp. 63–64).

Each generation transmits an ordered world of institutions to the next generation. The members of the new generation learn to understand the order of the institutional system by a process of *socialization*. Here socialization refers to "the comprehensive and consistent induction of an individual into the objective world of a society" (Berger and Luckmann, 1967, p. 130). In this process, the individual learns to understand his fellowmen and to apprehend the world as a meaningful social reality. To the extent that individuals accept the institutions as they are, the order of the institutional system achieves a certain stability over time.

The reality that Berger and Luckmann's process of institutionalization generates is a world of institutions. This world is like Searle's social reality. Thus it is possible to view Berger and Luckmann's account of the social construction of reality as a description of the social processes that generate Searle's social reality. As we shall see, this reality is very different from that in my own social construction of reality.

3.2 KNORR-CETINA

In her treatise *The Manufacture of Knowledge*, Karin Knorr-Cetina (1981) insists that scientific inquiry is a process of production that constructs scientific products out of objects that exist in the World of Things. The products are contextually specific constructions that bear the mark of the situational contingency and interest structure of the process by which they are generated. Put differently, scientific products are highly internally structured, and the process of their fabrication involves decisions and social negotiations that determine chains of selections from which the final outcomes are derived. In that way the products of science are socially constructed (Knorr-Cetina, 1981, pp. 3–5).

Knorr-Cetina bases her claims on the insight she gained from studying work in a scientific laboratory. The "laboratory" was a government-financed research center in Berkeley, California, that employed 330 scientists and engineers and housed 86 students and visiting scientists. The work at the center comprised basic and applied research in chemical, physical, microbiological, and toxicological engineering and economic areas and was conducted under the auspices of seventeen separate research units. Almost every scientist at the center had a small laboratory connected with his or her office, as well as access to several large facilities that the members of a research unit shared. Various lines of research were conducted concurrently, and each scientist seemed to be engaged in many different projects.

Knorr-Cetina's observations focused on plant protein research, which included, among other subjects, protein generation and recovery with applications in the area of human nutrition. She recounts that the language of truth and hypothesis testing was ill equipped to describe work in the laboratory. Most of the reality with which the scientists dealt was highly preconstructed, being a local accumulation of materializations from previous selections in the fabrication process. Moreover, in the manufacture of knowledge success in making things work seemed more important than the pursuit of truth. Finally, the theories that one usually associates with science adopted in the laboratory a peculiarly atheoretical character. They assumed the appearance of discursively crystallized experimental operations that were woven into the process of performing experimentation (Knorr-Cetina, 1981, p. 4).

In Knorr-Cetina's laboratory the social aspects of the construction of scientific products permeated all parts of the fabrication process. Thus, the choice of projects as well as the design of the published research reports appeared to be determined by a social process of negotiation situated in time and space rather than by a logic of individual decision making. Further, the social negotiations that determined the chains of selections from which the scientific products emerged seemed to be governed by an opportunistic logic in which both incorporation of earlier results and transscientific resource relationships played important roles. Finally, the process of validation, like that of discovery, was seen to be a process of selective incorporation of previous results with due attention to the expected response of likely "validators" (Knorr-Cetina, 1981, pp. 68–93).

The scientific products that the laboratory engenders constitute the reality in Knorr-Cetina's social construction of reality. Some of these products are new objects in the World of Things, for example, a new medicament to combat breast cancer. Others are new facts in the World of Facts, for example, that the chemical composition of TRF (thyrotropin releasing factor) is Pyro-Glu-His-Pro-NH_2. Still others belong to the World of Possibilities, for example, Norsk Hydro's promise that in a year it will deliver a profitable technology that uses natural gas to generate hydrogen-fueled electric power with clean CO_2 gas as a by-product. Knorr-Cetina's social construction of reality can, therefore, be viewed as an unfolding of an important part of my World of Possibilities.

The realities in Berger and Luckmann's and Knorr-Cetina's social constructions of reality are very different. Berger and Luckmann theorize about the social construction of institutions. Knorr-Cetina deliberates about the social construction of artifacts in the laboratory. In the next three sections of this chapter I present my own vision of the social construction of reality. Mine is the vision of an economist and it differs fundamentally from the other two conceptions. It is not about institutions nor is it about scientific artifacts. In the words of Sergio Sismondo (1993, p. 516), my vision of the social construction of reality is about the social construction of "objects of thought and representation." In my words, my vision is about the social construction of a world of ideas.

3.3 A SOCIALLY CONSTRUCTED WORLD OF IDEAS

Universals such as table and justice live and function in Plato's world of ideas.[3] The same must be true of economic universals such as money and income. Now, the words table and justice have different meanings depending on the contexts in which they appear. In the present context, "table" is a name given to the collection of all pieces of furniture that consist of a flat top set horizontally on legs. Similarly, "justice" is a name given to the collection of all acts that have the quality of being righteous. Thus both universals have reference in the social reality I described above. The words money and income also have different meanings depending on the contexts in which they appear. In the present context "money" is a name given to the collection of all things that function as media of exchange, and "income" is a name given to all those things that some economist might consider to be income. Then money has reference in the social reality we experience, whereas income has reference in a socially constructed world of ideas. Figure 3.1 illustrates what I have in mind.

My insistence that the reference of income belongs to a socially constructed world of ideas requires an explanation of the way in which economic theorists and econometricians conceive of income. In mathematics a *universal term* is a term that needs no definition. Most economic theorists treat income as a universal term. However, the definitions of the term that leading economists have given cast doubt on its universality. The following three examples attest to that. *Income* is "a series of events," and *real income* consists "of those final physical events in the outer world which give us our inner enjoyments" (Fisher, 1961, pp. 3, 6). An individual's *income* equals his incomings in money and the payments in kind that he receives for his services (Marshall, 1953, p. 71). An

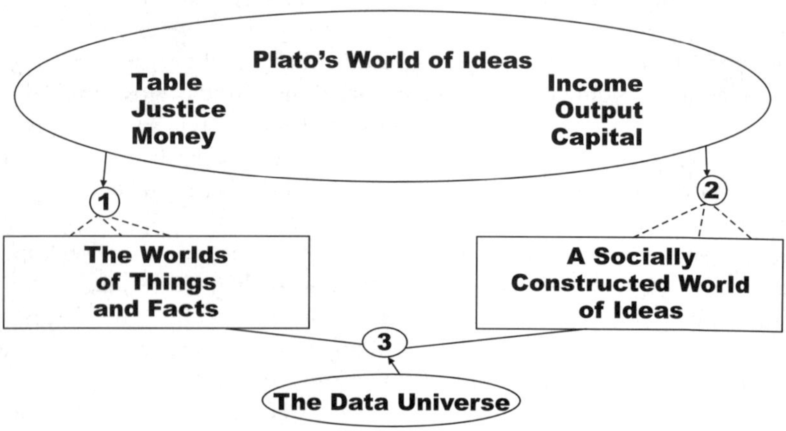

Fig. 3.1 Universals and the reference of variables in the data universe.

individual's *yearly income* equals the maximum value that he could consume during the year and still expect to be as well off at the end of the year as he was at the beginning (Hicks, 1953, p. 172).

Econometricians who study consumer choice cannot treat income as a universal term. They must use the data they have to define an aggregate that they can use to measure it. If an econometrician's data originate in budget studies of consumer expenditures, he might identify a family's income with its total outlays for goods and services (cf., e.g., Houthakker and Taylor, 1966, p. 33). If the econometrician's data stem from Norwegian tax statements, he might insist that a consumer's yearly income equals a sum that comprises her salary, the dividends and interests that she earns on her financial investments, and an imputed income on her residence and summer house. If the econometrician's data originate in a field survey of consumer finances, he might add to the latter sum realized and nonrealized appreciation of financial assets and pension plans. He might also include earnings on lotteries and the money value of gifts. Finally, he might add an estimate of the money value of the services that an unemployed family member provides.

The upshot of these observations is as follows: In economic theory the term income has no well-defined reference in the social reality I described in Chapter 2. The reference varies with the ideas of individual theorists. Similarly, in econometrics the term income has no well-defined reference in social reality. Instead, the reference varies both with the econometrician's data and with his understanding of the term. From this I conclude that the reference of the universal, income, belongs to a world of ideas that I consider to be socially constructed.

Income is not exceptional in that its reference belongs to a socially constructed world of ideas. Here is a second example to establish that fact. Most economic theorists treat the universal output as a universal term. In fact, the term output seems to be so universal that it deserves no place in the subject indexes of books concerning economic theory. Ragnar Frisch's book, on *Produksjonsteori* (*The Theory of Production*) is an exception. There he takes output to be the outcome of a process that changes the form and arrangement of matter (Frisch, 1971, p. 15). Now, a producer of output may be a nurse or a professor, a farm or a bank, an industry or a whole macro economy. That describing the output of such producers is not easy is attested to by the following observations.

In the spirit of Frisch's idea of output, we may take education to be "a service that transforms fixed quantities of inputs (i.e., individuals) into individuals with different qualities" (Hanushek, 1986, p. 1150). Here the quality differences that count as outputs of the education process concern individuals' health status, their performance in the labor market, and their ability to cope with life in a democracy. Economists have succeeded in measuring the differential impact of education on the earning power and cognitive skills of individuals. They have also succeeded in ascertaining the differential impact of education on such varied parameters as an individual's job satisfaction, his ability to maintain personal health, his voting behavior, and his criminal record. However, they have not managed to construct a generally agreed-upon index whose value can be used by researchers to measure the output of an education system. Therefore, for now I may insist that the reference "output of an education system" belongs to a socially constructed world of ideas.

Even when economic concepts have reference in social reality, the values econometricians use to measure the pertinent variables usually have reference only in a socially constructed world of ideas. Money and commodity prices are good examples. Money as a medium of exchange has reference in social reality. Yet the measures of national stocks of money that statistical offices publish and econometricians use in their analyses of monetary policy have no such reference. They are aggregates whose values refer to a world of ideas that economic theorists have created. Similarly, prices of commodities have reference in social reality. However, the variables that econometricians use in their analyses of price formation have no such reference. They are price indexes the details of which vary with the ideas of individual theorists. Thus their values have reference in a socially constructed world of ideas.

We think of income as the income of an individual and output as the output of a firm. In the socially constructed world of ideas to which economists' notions of income and output refer, individuals and firms exist only as "representative individuals." Representative individuals appear in all sorts of contexts in econometrics. They surface in the construction of vital statistics, for example, in estimates of the mortality rates of 40-year olds and the school-enrollment rate of 14-year olds. They appear in the equations of applied economists who study characteristics of individual behavior, for example, the behavior of consumers or firms. Further, they permeate the ideas on which econometricians base their models of the functioning of macro economies. The following example illustrates the way in which the latter is the case.

E 3.1 *Dale Jorgenson and Barbara Fraumeni agree that education is a service industry. Still, they insist that the best way to think of the output of education is as an investment in human capital (cf. Jorgenson and Fraumeni, 1992, p. 333). Thus a good measure of the output of education is the effect of an increase in an individual's educational attainment on his or her lifetime income. Moreover, a good measure of the output of an economy's educational system is the differential impact of the system on the lifetime incomes of all of the individuals that are enrolled in schools. Following up this idea, Jorgenson and Fraumeni have constructed estimates of the output of the U.S. educational system in every year during the period 1948–1986. The system of equations below gives a shorthand description of the structure of their estimates:*

For each year t *in the period 1948–1986 Jorgenson and Fraumeni (1992) collected information on the values of a huge family of variables and constants.*

Specifically, they gathered observations on the average number of hours worked whrs *and the average hourly compensation* com *for a total of 2,196 groups that they indexed by sex* s, *age* a, *and years of education,* e. *For the same groups they also obtained information on the employment rate* empr, *the school enrollment rate* senr, *the probability of survival* sr, *the average tax rate* tax, *and the average marginal tax rate* taxam. *They used the given constants and some others together with the preceding variables to construct, for each group and year, estimates of several functional constants. Four of them are the average annual market and nonmarket income,* ymi *and* ynmi, *and the average lifetime market and nonmarket income,* mi *and* nmi. *Two others are the average lifetime income* life *and the average investment in human capital* ih.

It is easy to write down the definition of ymi *for any group and the definition of* mi *for those who are above 35 years of age:*

$$ymi_{t,s,a,e} = (whrs_{t,s,a,e} \cdot empr_{t,s,a,e}) \cdot com_{t,s,a,e}$$

and

$$mi_{t,s,a,e} = ymi_{t,s,a,e} + sr_{t,s,a+1} \cdot mi_{t,s,a+1,e} \cdot (1.0132/1.0458),$$

where 1.0132 and 1.0458, respectively, equal a presumed average rate of growth of real income and a representative rate of time preference. From the present point of view, the interesting feature of the last equation is that it allows the authors to calculate the value of $\mathrm{mi}_{\mathrm{t,s,a,e}}$ *recursively from the observed values of* $\mathrm{sr}_{\mathrm{t,s,a+j}}$ *and* $\mathrm{ymi}_{\mathrm{t,s,a+j,e}}$ *for* $\mathrm{j} = 1, 2, \ldots, 75 - \mathrm{a}$.

The corresponding equations for ynmi *and* nmi *are as follows:*

$$ynmi_{t,s,a,e} = nmhrs_{t,s,a,e} \cdot com_{t,s,a,e} \cdot (1 + tax_t) \cdot (1 - taxam_t)$$

and

$$nmi_{t,s,a,e} = ynmi_{t,s,a,e} + sr_{t,s,a+1} \cdot nmi_{t,s,a+1,e} \cdot (1.0132/1.0458).$$

In the first equation the value of nmhrs *equals the average nonmarket labor time. It takes too much space to write down the equations that determine the value of* nmhrs. *Here it suffices to note that in defining the latter variable the authors make use of several basic assumptions: (1) Individuals have just 14 hours per day for work, education, and leisure. (2) The value of leisure time equals* com. *(3) A student spends 1,300 hours in school during the year. Further, the value of each hour spent in school is set equal to 0. As in the case of* mi, *the last equation allows the authors to calculate the value of* nmi *by recursion from the values of* $\mathrm{sr}_{\mathrm{t,s,a+j}}$ *and* $\mathrm{ynmi}_{\mathrm{t,s,a+j,e}}$ *for* $\mathrm{j} = 1, 2, \ldots, 75 - \mathrm{a}$.

The authors define the values of life *and* ih *by the equations*

$$life_{t,s,a,e} = mi_{t,s,a,e} + nmi_{t,s,a,e}$$

and

$$ih_{t,s,a,e} = senr_{t,s,a,e} \cdot (life_{t,s,a,e+1} - life_{t,s,a,e}).$$

One interesting aspect of these equations is that both life *and* ih *depend on the value of* nmi *as well as* mi. *That provides us with one more example of the elusiveness of the universal income.*

It is difficult to pinpoint the reference of Jorgenson and Fraumeni's (1992) interesting estimates. In a given period the lifetime income of an individual is an event in the World of Possibilities that has no obvious numerical name. Similarly, the lifetime income of a group of people, for example, a family or all those enrolled in an economy's schools, is an event in the World of Possibilities that has no obvious numerical name. The reason for this lack of names is that there is no generally accepted theory of choice for such uncertain situations as those envisaged here. Moreover, even if one of the available theories were to be adopted, the task of assigning weights to the elements of the various events in question would be more than staggering. To me the natural way to describe the references of Jorgenson and Fraumeni's estimates is as measures of the differential impact of education on the lifetime income of representative individuals in the subgroups that the authors consider.

3.4 THEORY-LADEN DATA

To establish relationships between elements in the Worlds of Things and Facts, scientists develop formal theories about factual aspects of social reality and confront their theories with data. Theory-data confrontations seem to happen in different ways in different sciences. Even so, I believe that they can all be pictured as having the same structure: two disjoint universes, one for theory and one for data, and a bridge between them. The bridge consists of principles that relate variables in the theory universe to variables in the data universe. One of the characteristics of this structure is of relevance here. It concerns the extent to which scientists' observations are theory laden. *Theory-laden data have reference in a socially constructed world of ideas that is essentially disjoint from the Worlds of Things and Facts.*

Theory-data confrontations in economics happen in many different situations. In each situation the pertinent data universe contains information on the values of a finite set of variables $X_1, \ldots, X_n$; a finite set of constants $C_1, \ldots, C_m$; a finite set of functional constants $F_1, \ldots, F_k$; and a finite set of predicate constants $Q_1, \ldots, Q_l$. Researchers observe the values of the X's in field surveys, in publications of central bureaus of statistics, and in the records of governmental agencies. They receive information about the C's from various external sources, and they use the X's and the C's to construct their observations on the F's and the Q's. We shall infer from relevant examples the extent to which such X's, C's, F's, and Q's are theory laden and contain information on a socially constructed world.

Observations can be theory laden in two ways. For one thing, the theory in a theory-data confrontation may impose restrictions on the way scientists sample information on pertinent X's and on the way they use X's and C's to construct F's and Q's. I think of such observations as being theory laden *by hypothesis.* For another, scientists may have preconceived ideas about the meaning of a variable, say an X or an F, and about the theoretically correct way to construct an estimate of the value of the given variable. I think of such observations as being theory laden *by prescription.* Examples E 3.1 and E 3.2 illustrate what I have in mind.

Economists test the descriptive validity of all sorts of economic theories in their laboratories, for example, von Neumann and Morgenstern's (1953) expected utility theory and Nash's (1950) bargaining theory. In each test the experimenter obtains his data in accordance with the prescriptions of the relevant theory. Similarly, when evaluating the benefits of possible public projects, economists use economic theory and estimates of hedonic price indexes and/or estimates of individuals' willingness to pay. In each case the researcher obtains his or her observations in more-or-less strict accordance with the prescriptions of the theory.[4]

E 3.2 *I believe that my students rank uncertain prospects according to their expected utility. I also believe that their utility functions of gains are linear. To test these hypotheses I confront one of the students with a sequence of prospects* $P(\pi_j; 1{,}000, 0), j = 1, \ldots, r$, *of the form kr 1.000 with probability* π_j *and kr 0 with probability* $(1 - \pi_j)$. *For each* j, *I ask the student to tell me his certainty equivalent,* $X(\pi_j)$, *of the given prospect.*[5] *Then I construct a sequence of values of the student's utility function in accordance with the formula*

$$F[X(\pi_j)] = \pi_j, \; j = 1, \ldots, r.$$

The resulting data universe contains r *observations on a pair of* X*'s and a partial observation on one* F. *I have constructed these observations in accordance with a known theorem of von Neumann and Morgenstern's expected utility theory. They are, therefore, theory laden* by hypothesis.

Indexes permeate economic statistics. For example, when studying the demand for commodities such as apples or automobiles, economists use observations on the values of quantity indexes for the relevant commodities and price indexes for the same commodities' prices. Similarly, when evaluating the benefits of medical treatments and public health projects economists use observations on an index that measures the quality of individuals' adjusted life years (QALY). Many of these indexes have an underpinning in economic theory.[6]

E 3.3 *I have developed a dynamic general equilibrium model to study the characteristics of economic growth and the effects on the environment of various* *economic policies. For the purpose of estimating the parameters of the model, I collect information on the values of many variables and constants. Four sets of the variables pertain to yearly consumption in Norway of electric power,* E, *and oil,* G, *and to the prices of* E *and* G: P_E *and* P_G. *The units of measurement of* E *and* G *are, respectively, Gwh and tons. The years in question are those since World War II. In addition to the mentioned variables I need information on the consumption of energy,* U, *and the price of energy,* P_U, *in Norway during the same period. I construct yearly values of U with the following formula:*

$$U = \left(C_E^{-1/\rho} E^{(1+\rho)/\rho} + C_G^{-1/\rho} G^{(1+\rho)/\rho}\right)^{\rho/(1+\rho)}$$

The corresponding values of the price of energy, P_U, *I obtain from the formula*

$$P_U = \left(C_E P_E^{(\rho+1)} + C_G P_G^{(\rho+1)}\right)^{1/(\rho+1)}$$

In these formulas the constants C_E *and* C_G *record the base period unit demand for electricity and oil raised to the power* $(\rho + 1)$; ρ *denotes an estimate of the elasticity of substitution in energy consumption between electricity and oil. I discovered that estimate in an earlier Central Bureau of Statistics paper.*

In the present context my construction of the values of U *and* P_U *is interesting for several reasons. First, the energy aggregate that I chose is just one of many such aggregates. Moreover, my choice was entirely independent of the dynamic general equilibrium model whose parameters I am out to estimate. Second, I chose a formula for* P_U *such that* P_U *equals the minimum cost of one unit of energy. From these two observations it follows that my data on the pair* (U, P_U) *are theory laden by prescription.*[7]

Knorr-Cetina insists that in her laboratory scientific theories assumed the appearance of discursively crystallized experimental operations. She also claims the process of fabrication of scientific products there was anything but deterministic. Still, I believe that theory-laden observations are facts of life in all sciences. E 3.4, which presents relevant features of a case study by Trevor Pinch (cf. 1985, pp. 4–16), shows that it must be the case in physics.

E 3.4 *According to theory, stars derive their energy from nuclear fusion. If that is so, the nuclear fusion that occurs in the interior of the sun will produce solar neutrinos as a by-product. The latter are massless and chargeless particles that interact only weakly with matter. They pass through the outer layers of the sun and reach the earth within 8 minutes of the time that they are produced.*

Scientists can observe solar neutrinos only indirectly with the help of sophisticated measuring instruments. In the present case the apparatus is a 100,000-gallon tank of dry-cleaning fluid, C_2Cl_4, *that they have placed in a shaft a mile below the surface of the earth. The fluid contains an isotope of chlorine,* Cl^{37}, *with which the neutrinos can interact. Such interaction results in a radioactive isotope of argon,* Ar^{37}*, whose atoms will be swept off the tank and placed in a tiny Geiger counter. The counter will respond to the* Ar^{37} *atoms by clicking. As some of the observed clicks might arise from background radiation in the counter rather than from* Ar^{37} *atoms, the scientists involved will have to use sophisticated electronics and data analysis to determine the extent to which the clicks of the Geiger counter are due to the* Ar^{37} *atoms.*

Interpreting the results of the experiment involves theory at several stages. The scientists use physical theory to describe the characteristics of solar neutrinos and the way the latter interact with Cl^{37} *isotopes. They also use chemical theory to describe the properties of argon and to explain why argon ions readily become free atoms. Finally, the same scientists must appeal to statistical theory to describe the statistical properties of their observations. In my terminology the production of argon isotopes is theory laden* by hypothesis, *whereas the process of placing* Ar^{37} *atoms in a Geiger counter is theory laden* by prescription.

3.5 THE SOCIAL CONSTRUCTION OF VALIDITY

Relations among variables whose references belong to a socially constructed world of ideas need not have any relevance for the study of social reality. In order for attention to focus on such relations one of two cases must obtain. Either the relations can be interpreted in light of an interesting theory or some authority dictates how one should relate to them in any given situation. The first case requires a detailed specification of both the theory and the construction of pertinent data. It also demands a clear description of the bridge principles that relate variables of the theory to variables in the data universe. In the other case an official of the government or an acknowledged committee of experts offers a convincing argument that there is one and only one way to construct measures of the concepts in question and that a certain theory enables interpretation of the relevant relations. I deal with the first case in the next chapter on "Facts and Fiction in Econometrics." Here I discuss briefly the characteristics and the prevalence of situations that the second case envisages. They are all situations in which various aspects of *the social construction of validity* are confronted.

The social construction of validity is met in all walks of life, for example, in education, in economic affairs, and in politics. The following are a few examples from Norway: In Norway the social construction of validity comes in many forms. Published opinion polls indicate that about 54 percent of the Norwegian population is against Norway joining the EEC, and farmers are hoping that such estimates will keep the Norwegian government from applying anew for membership. More than a decade ago U.S. experts decided that smoking might be a cause of lung cancer. As a consequence one now reads on the front of every pack of cigarettes that smoking is dangerous and may lead to lung cancer, and smoking is forbidden inside the buildings of all Norwegian universities and hospitals. In a recent publication of the Norwegian Department of Justice an interdepartmental panel of experts insists that punishment is not always the ideal deterrent of crime. For example, the best way to deal with violent gangs of immigrant youths in Oslo might be to send their members to a counselor rather than to lock them behind bars. This sounds like a hopeless suggestion. However, if "a counselor" is taken to be a common denominator for concerted efforts to give gang members a reason to leave the gangs and join the rest of society, the suggestion reflects an attitude that Norwegians, through laws and regulations, will learn to accept.

The social construction of validity also surfaces in the relations that Norway has with other nations. Four years ago the KGB decided that it had good reason to believe that there were Norwegian spies in Russia. As a consequence Russia expelled three unsuspecting Norwegian diplomats for espionage. The International Whaling Commission is refusing to accept the official Norwegian estimate of the stock of minke whales in the North Atlantic and keeps maintaining its moratorium on all commercial whaling. The Norwegians have ignored the moratorium and engaged in commercial whaling of minke whales in the northeastern Atlantic since 1992. According to Schweder (2001): "This whaling is legal under international law since Norway objected to the moratorium on commercial whaling [when it was imposed] in 1982." Currently a UN panel of experts is working hard to figure out the best way to measure CO_2 emissions from land use, land-use change, and forestry. The panel's results will have fundamental consequences for the abatement costs that Norway will incur in abiding with the Kyoto Protocol.

What one society considers valid need not be valid in another. Moreover, what is accepted as valid once need not be taken to be valid later. For example: Blood revenge was a way of life in early Viking communities, but today such a form of revenge has no place in Norway or any other Scandinavian country. Similarly, circumcision of young girls is a way of life in Sudan and some other African countries, but it is considered a crime of violence in most Western societies. Less dramatically but equally telling, in a referendum a few years ago Californians decided to abolish the State's commitment to teach children of Spanish-speaking immigrants Spanish. The reason given was that such education tends to hamper the children in their attempt to learn English and thus ensure themselves a good life in the United States. In contrast, the authorities in Norway still insist that immigrant children will have a better chance of eventually mastering Norwegian and adjusting to life in Norway if the government provides them with lessons in their mother tongue.

Within the science of economics the social construction of validity is ubiquitous. Through readings and lectures at university economists learn to distinguish good reasoning from bad. They also learn to avoid pitfalls in collecting data for applied economic research and to appreciate good statistical arguments in econometrics. The knowledge economists acquire in this way is common knowledge. As such it determines for the science of economics what counts as a valid argument and what the characteristics are of a valid result. In doing that, this common knowledge structures both the way economists go about solving their research problems and the way they choose to present their results.

There are many interesting sides to the social construction of validity in economics. Some supposedly valid measures of economic variables are senseless. Others make sense theoretically but are false in the light of the purposes for which economists and government policy-makers use them. Still others made sense in theory once but are now false because of changes in the relevant theories. From our point of view, the interesting aspects of these possibilities are the ways in which theorists and statisticians interact to determine what counts as a valid measure of an economic variable. The following three examples will show what I have in mind.

First an example of a measure that, given what it is supposed to measure, seems perfectly senseless.

E 3.5 *Roughly speaking,* national income *(NY) designates the total income earned and received by a nation during a given year. Economists have adopted two measures of this concept. One is the nation's net final output (NNP) evaluated at current market prices, and the other is the sum of all factor incomes (including profits) generated through the production of the nation's final output (NI). Economists may disagree on the actual computations of NNP and NI. However, in theory the two measures are almost equivalent. Specifically,* $\text{NNP} = \text{NI} + \text{IBT}$, *where IBT is short for indirect business taxes. Moreover, by* social construction *the two measures share an important characteristic: They assign zero value to all housework. A housewife receives no income, and the output of her labor is not included in NNP. From a theorist's point of view, this last feature of NNP and NI is illogical and renders the two measures of national income senseless.*

The NI and the NNP measures of national income have been used for many purposes, for example, as economic indicators, as measures of a nation's ability to meet heavy demands on its resources, and as measures of economic welfare. The present measures are not ideal for any of these purposes and have been severely criticized. For instance, those who would like to use national income as a measure of economic welfare lament the measures' failure to allow for externalities such as pollution and congestion. They also question the evaluation of public expenditures in a cost-input manner rather than in a welfare-oriented manner. Finally, they complain about the measures' failure to account for home-produced goods, which may constitute a large fraction of the total output in poorer countries. Whatever the criticisms are, the critics are searching for a meaningful concept in our socially constructed world of ideas and for a valid way to measure its value. The concept that a critic eventually chooses will vary with the purpose for which the relevant measure of national income is to be used.

Next an example of a theoretically sensible measure of one variable that economic policy-makers often use inappropriately as a measure of a different variable.

E 3.6 *A country's* Consumer Price Index *(CPI) equals the ratio of the current-period cost to the base-period cost of a "market basket" of goods and services that consumers in the country acquired during a given base period. Here market basket refers to a representative sample of the expenditures on goods and services that "consumers" buy for day-to-day living. Further, the term consumers designates either all consumers or a specific part of the population of consumers in a given country. For example, in the United States the term refers to all urban consumers, and the market basket comprises items that the Bureau of Labor Statistics (BLS) has chosen by a scientifically profound multistage sampling process. Finally, the current-period (base-period) cost of a market basket of goods and services denotes the value of this market basket when its components are evaluated by their current-period (base-period) prices.*

A country's Cost-of-Living Index *(CLI) equals the ratio of the minimum current-period cost of a market basket of goods and services that would leave consumers in the country as well off in the current period as they were in a given base period to the base-period cost of the market basket that the consumers acquired then. For a one-person economy the idea of a CLI is meaningful. The index for such an economy is even computable when the consumer's preferences belong to the "right" class of preference orderings. For a large economy the meaning of such an index is elusive for many reasons, one being that the required current-period market basket might not be available at current prices. Still, we can make the idea of a CLI meaningful for a large economy by thinking of the CLI as an index of the cost of living of a representative consumer.*

Economic policy-makers use estimates of the CLI for all sorts of purposes, for example, for adjusting pensions and for fixing wage agreements. The measure of the CLI that most policy-makers use is the CPI. Since the CPI concerns a fixed market basket of goods and services, it cannot provide an accurate estimate of the CLI. The values of the CPI fail to account for consumers' opportunities to substitute cheaper for more expensive goods. It also fails to account for consumers' ability to substitute new and better products for old ones. As a result of these and other failures, changes in the values of the CPI tend to overvalue changes in the CLI.

In the United States a committee of experts has suggested that the U.S. CPI overvalues the true CLI by as much as 1 percent. This inaccuracy has awesome consequences for the U.S. economy as witnessed by a 1995 report of the Congressional Budget Office (CBO). According to the CBO, if the changes in the CPI were to overstate the changes in the CLI "by an average of 1.1

percentage points per year over the next decade, this bias would contribute about $148 billion to the deficit in 2006 and $691 billion to the national debt by then. This bias alone would be the fourth largest federal program, after social security, health care and defense" (Boskin et al., 1996, p. i).

The last example is of a measure of an economic variable, depreciation, that made sense in the 1950s but fails to satisfy the demands of economic theorists today.

E 3.7 Depreciation *designates the decline in value of a physical asset that results from wear and tear, obsolescence, and aging. In a 1957 paper E. F. Denison argued for measures of capital stocks that presumed the relative efficiencies of equipment and structures to be constant over their lifetimes. He also insisted that depreciation be viewed as the cost of using a physical asset in the production of goods and that it be distributed evenly over the lifetime of the asset. In the United States the Bureau of Economic Analysis (BEA) adopted Dennison's ideas in its estimates of both U.S. stocks of depreciable assets and of depreciation for the National Income and Product Accounts (NIPA).*

At the end of the 1960s and the beginning of the 1970s Dennison's ideas came under heavy attack. Critics pointed out that the BEA's measurements of capital stocks and depreciation were internally inconsistent. If the efficiencies of physical assets were constant over their lifetimes, their depreciation must decline geometrically and not linearly. The critics also introduced a system of capital-vintage accounts that could be used to produce internally consistent measures of capital stocks and depreciation for the U.S. NIPA. In the 1980s econometricians picked up on the latter ideas and proceeded to estimate systems of vintage price functions and depreciation profiles for such varied assets as tractors, construction machinery, metal-working machinery, general industrial equipment, trucks, autos, industrial buildings, and commercial buildings. The estimated profiles suggested that a geometric pattern of depreciation for these assets was a much more interesting hypothesis than Denison's linear pattern.

Now, 45 years after the publication of Denison's paper life has taken a turn for the better in the U.S. NIPA. Econometricians have produced all the ingredients that were needed to construct the internally consistent system of measurements of physical assets and their depreciation that the theorists requested in the 1970s. Moreover, the BEA has adopted the new ideas and has revised its estimates of depreciation and net capital stocks for the U.S. NIPA accordingly.

Barbara Fraumeni (1997, pp. 7–23) and Dale Jorgenson (1996, pp. 24–42) give details of the preceding development of a socially constructed valid estimate of depreciation in the U.S. NIPA. The process lasted for almost half a century and involved many individuals situated in scattered locations all around the United States. They interacted via working papers and the exchange of ideas at specially scheduled workshops and conferences. They published papers in learned journals along the way so that the respective authors would receive due credit for their original ideas and results. Even though it is hard to envision this process of constructing a valid estimate of depreciation as work in a laboratory, it shares many of the characteristics of laboratory work that Knorr-Cetina (1981, pp. 5–6) describes in her book . There was a *primus motor*, Dale Jorgenson, and a core group of scientists who were either his former students or his co-authors on significant papers. The process was a cumulative effort in which each participant contributed building blocks to a formidable structure that made it possible for the BES to mend its ways and to produce better estimates of depreciation for the U.S. NIPA.

3.6 CONCLUDING REMARKS

In this chapter we have seen how two sociologists, a philosopher of science, and an economist view the social construction of reality. The sociologists depict it as a construction of a world of institutions. The philosopher of science insists that it is a process by which researchers in scientific laboratories produce artifacts. The economist looks at it as a cumulative process in which economists and econometricians create a world of ideas. The interesting aspects of Berger and Luckmann's and Knorr-Cetina's views of the social construction of reality notwithstanding, in the context of this book it is my view that counts. There are two reasons for this. The "reality" in my view of the social construction of reality is a world of ideas that is essentially disjoint from the social reality about which economists theorize, and this world of ideas comprises most of the references of the data variables in economic theory-data confrontations. These two aspects of the reality that economists and econometricians create make the possibility of a science of economics a tricky problem. In the next chapter I show how economists and econometricians go about solving that problem.

NOTES

1. There are many ways to envision the construction of social reality and the social construction of reality. One good way to learn about them is to read Finn Collin's (1997) book *Social Reality.*

2. In writing my account of Berger and Luckmann's understanding of the social construction of reality I benefited from reading Ragnvald Kalleberg's article, "Kombinering av forsknings-tradisjoner I sosiologien" (Dale et al., 1985, ch.7) and William Lafferty's article, "Externalization and Dialectics: Taking the Brackets Off Berger and Luckmann's Sociology of Knowledge" (Lafferty, 1977).

3. I follow in Bertrand Russell's footsteps (cf. Russell, 1976, p. 53) when I refer to the members of Plato's "World of Ideas" as universals. A universal is a relation that has both an extension and an intension. In a given world the extension of a universal is the set of objects in the world that satisfy the relation that it prescribes, for example, the

set of all just acts in the case of justice. The intension of the universal is the graph of a set-valued function on the set of all possible worlds whose values are the respective extensions of the universal (cf. Stigum, 1990, pp. 52–53). Two universals have the same meaning if and only if they have the same intension. The meaning of a universal is that which is grasped when one understands its name; that is, the common nature of which the members of its extension partake. For example, the meaning of "justice" is the common nature in virtue of which all just acts are just (Russell, 1976, p. 52).

4. Good references are Raymond B. Palmquist's "Hedonic Methods" and Richard T. Carson's "Constructed Markets," in Braden and Kolstad (1991, chs. 4 and 5).

5. The certainty equivalent of a prospect $P(\pi; 1{,}000, 0)$ in E 3.2 equals the minimum number of kroners that the student would be willing to accept in exchange for his opportunity to participate in the prospect.

6. The reader can find an interesting discussion of QALY in Erik Nord's (1996) critical review of health status index models.

7. The aggregates that I describe in this example have been used both by Haakon Vennemo and Hans Terje Mysen in studying various aspects of the Norwegian economy (cf. Vennemo, 1994; Mysen, 1991).

REFERENCES

Berger, P. L., and T. Luckmann, 1967, *The Social Construction of Reality*, New York: Anchor Books–Doubleday.

Boskin, M. J., E. R. Dulberger, R. J. Gordon, Z. Griliches, and D. Jorgenson, 1996, "Toward a More Accurate Measure of the Cost of Living," Final Report to the Senate Finance Committee, December 4, 1996.

Braden, J. B., and C. D. Kolstad (eds.), 1991, *Measuring the Demand for Environmental Quality*, Amsterdam: North-Holland.

Carson, R. T., 1991, "Constructed Markets," in: *Measuring the Demand for Environmental Quality*, J. B. Braden and C. D. Kolstad (eds.), Amsterdam: North-Holland.

Collin, F., 1997, *Social Reality*, New York: Routledge.

Denison, E. F., 1957, "Theoretical Aspects of Quality Change, Capital Consumption, and Net Capital Formation," in: *Problems of Capital Formation, Studies in Income and Wealth, Vol. 19*, Princeton: Princeton University Press, pp. 215–284.

Fisher, I., 1961, *The Theory of Interest*, New York: Kelley.

Fraumeni, B., 1997, "The Measurement of Depreciation in the U.S. National Income and Product Accounts," *Survey of Current Business* 77 (July), 7–23.

Frisch, R., 1971, *Produksjonsteori*, Oslo: Universitetsforlaget.

Hanushek, E. A., 1986, "The Economics of Schooling: Production and Efficiency in the Public Schools," *The Journal of Economic Literature* 24(3), 1144–1177.

Hicks, J. R., 1953, *Value and Capital*, 2nd. Ed., London: Oxford University Press.

Houthakker, H. S., and L. D. Taylor, 1966, *Consumer Demand in the United States, 1929–1970: Analyses and Projections*, Cambridge: Harvard University Press.

Jorgenson, D. W., 1996, "Empirical Studies of Depreciation," *Economic Inquiry* 34 (Jan.), 24–42.

Jorgenson, D. W., and B. M., Fraumeni, 1992, "The Output of the Education Sector," in: *Output Measurement in the Services Sector*, Z. Griliches (ed.), Studies in Income and Wealth, Vol. 55, Chicago: University of Chicago Press.

Kalleberg, R., 1985, "Kombinering av forsknings-tradisjoner I sosiologien." in *Metode på Tvers*, Dale, B., M. Jones, and W. Martinussen (eds.), Oslo: Tapir.

Knorr-Cetina, K. D., 1981, *The Manufacture of Knowledge*, Oxford: Pergamon.

Lafferty, W., 1977, "Externalization and Dialectics: Taking the Brackets Off Berger and Luckmann's Sociology of Knowledge," *Cultural Hermeneutics* 4, 139–161.

Marshall, A., 1953, *Principles of Economics*, 8th Ed., London: Macmillan.

Mysen, H. T., 1991, "Substitusjon mellom Olje og Elektrisitet I Produksjonssektorene I en Makromodell," Unpublished Paper, Central Bureau of Statistics Norway, Oslo.

Nash, J. F., 1950, "The Bargaining Problem," *Econometrica* 18, 155–162.

Nord, E., 1996, "Health Status Index Models for Use in Resource Allocation Decisions," *International Journal of Technology Assessment in Health Care*, Cambridge: Cambridge University Press.

Palmquist, R. B., 1991, "Hedonic Methods," in: *Measuring the Demand for Environmental Quality*, J. B. Braden and C. D. Kolstad (eds.), Amsterdam: North-Holland.

Pinch, T. J., 1985, "Towards an Analysis of Scientific Observation: The Externality and Evidential Significance of Observational Reports in Physics," *Social Studies in Science* 15(1), 3–35.

Russell, B., 1976, *The Problems of Philosophy*, Oxford: Oxford University Press.

Schweder, T., 2001, "Protecting Whales by Distorting Uncertainty: Non-precautionary Mismanagement?" *Fisheries Research* 52, 217–225.

Sismondo, S., 1993, "Some Social Constructions," *Social Studies of Science* 23(3), 515–553.

Stigum, B. P.,1990, *Toward a Formal Science of Economics*, Cambridge: MIT Press.

Vennemo, H., 1994, "A Growth Model of Norway with a Two-Way Link to the Environment." Unpublished Paper, Central Bureau of Statistics Norway, Oslo.

von Neumann, J., and O. Morgenstern, 1953, *Theory of Games and Economic Behavior*, Princeton: Princeton University Press.

Chapter Four

Facts and Fiction in Econometrics

In her book *The Manufacture of Knowledge*, Knorr-Cetina (1981) is mostly concerned with scientific laboratory products that end up in the World of Things. Some of their characteristics are of special interest to us. They are produced in a preconstructed artificial reality, the laboratory, with purified chemicals and specially grown and selectively bred plant and assay rats that are equally preconstructed. Such products cannot be part of the "nature" or "reality" that is so crucial to a descriptivist interpretation of scientific inquiry. Still, scientists use such products in concerted efforts to further their understanding of processes that are active in nature. "Through comparative studies and experimental investigations, [scientists] create general concepts and ideas about causal mechanisms which make it possible to explain or predict natural events. Experiments, in this interpretation, become an instrument for the broad description and explanation of the development of natural phenomena over time" (Roll-Hansen, 1998, p. 167). Here is a pertinent example that I owe to a generous friend, Richard Keesey. The results on which the example is based were published in Schwid et al. (1992).

E 4.1 *In controlled experiments with rats, it has been observed that subcutaneous injection of nicotine, in amounts capable of producing circulating blood levels of nicotine comparable to those seen in heavy smokers, has the following effects. Initially, the rat's food intake is reduced and its level of resting metabolism increases. With its caloric intake reduced and its expenditure increased, the body weight of the nicotine-treated rat declines. However, over time its food intake gradually increases while its energy expenditure decreases until a balance of intake and expenditure is restored and a stable, but reduced, level of body weight is then maintained for as long as the nicotine is administered.*

Upon cessation of nicotine treatment, the preceding syndrome is reversed. First food intake is elevated and resting energy expenditure is reduced, leading to an increase in body weight. However, as weight is gained, both food intake and resting metabolism gradually return to normal levels. A balance of energy intake and expenditure is restored when the rat's body weight reaches the level that it had maintained prior to the start of nicotine treatment.

These observations suggest that a primary physiological effect of nicotine is to lower the level at which body weight is regulated. Thus, the initial decline in food intake and the associated increase in metabolic rate are adaptive responses that lower the rat's body weight to the reduced level set by the nicotine. When nicotine treatment is terminated, the adjustments in energy intake and expenditure act to elevate body weight to the level normal for the untreated rat.

The relevance of these findings in rats to the human condition can be appreciated from the following observations: (1) Smokers on average weigh less than nonsmokers. (2) Smokers are often reported to eat less and to expend energy at higher rates than nonsmokers. (3) When individuals stop smoking, they typically eat more and gain weight. (Physicians at the smoking clinic in Madison, Wisconsin, tell me that concern about weight gain is the biggest obstacle to getting individuals, particularly women, to stop smoking.) (4) Individuals using a nicotine patch after they stop smoking display not only reduced craving but reduced weight gain as well.

For us the interesting aspect of Keesey's example is that it illustrates how knowledge of relations in one world, the laboratory, can be used to gain insight about relations that exist in another world, in this case social reality. Analogous problems arise each time an econometrician attempts to use relations in the data universe to establish properties of relations in social reality. I devote this chapter to sorting out the latter problems.

We have seen that economic theory-data confrontations abound with data that are theory laden by hypothesis or by prescription. We have also understood that most of the same data have reference in a socially constructed world of ideas that is essentially disjoint from the social reality I described in Chapter 2. The question arises: How can econometricians with such data hope to learn anything of value about the social reality in which they live? The answer hinges on the way they view the purport of pertinent economic theories. To demonstrate this, I consider three different cases: theories of choice, theories of markets, and macroeconomic theories.

4.1 THEORIES OF CHOICE AND REPRESENTATIVE INDIVIDUALS

A long time ago, A. Quetelet—the creator of the abominable *l'homme moyen*—claimed that what related to the human species, considered en masse, was of the order of physical facts. "The greater the number of individuals," he said, "the more the individual will is effaced and leaves predominating the series of general facts which depend on the general causes, in accordance with which society exists and maintains itself. These are the causes we seek to ascertain, and when we shall know them, we shall determine effects for society as we determine effects by causes in the physical sciences" (Stigler, 1965, p. 202).

Quetelet's dictum contains a postulate and a prescription. The postulate asserts that in the human race there are positive analogies, that is, characteristic features, of human behavior worth knowing. The prescription tells us how to look for these analogies. The following is a simple example to fix the ideas.

E 4.2 *Caroll Wright (1875) of the Massachusetts Bureau of Labor Statistics conducted a survey of incomes and expenditures of the State's workers' families. Table 4.1 is taken from p. 380 of that report. It gives a summary statement of the workers' incomes and savings. The relationship between savings and incomes seen in the table and Quetelet's dictum gave Wright the idea for the following law: The higher the income of a family, the greater is the amount it will save, actually and proportionately.*

The econometricians of today do not believe in Quetelet's statistical methods, as exemplified in Wright's use of the data in Table 4.1. However, they do share Quetelet's belief that there are in the human race positive analogies of human behavior worth knowing. In their search for such analogies they make use of a distinguished *alias* of Quetelet's *l'homme moyen*, the representative individual. Economic theories of choice delineate positive analogies of individual behavior. The representative individuals are ideal persons whose behavior is stripped of all characteristics other than such positive analogies. By studying the behavior of representative individuals, econometricians can establish the empirical relevance of the positive analogies of individual behavior about which economists theorize.

As an illustration of the usefulness of representative individuals in applied economics, I consider their role in the theory of choice under uncertainty. This theory comes in many guises. One of them, owing to John von Neumann and Oscar Morgenstern (1953), appears in the form of a family of models of eight axioms concerning six *undefined* terms, a *universe*, an *operation*, a *preference*

TABLE 4.1
Gradations of Income and Relative Surplus in Dollars

Gradations	Number of families	Their earnings	Their expenses	Average yearly surplus
300–500	10	4,308	4,466	−15.80
500–700	140	86,684	86,023	4.72
700–900	181	143,281	138,747	25.05
900–1100	54	52,708	49,720	55.33
1100–1300	8	9,729	8,788	117.63
> 1300	4	6,090	5,241	212.25
Total	397	302,800	292,987	24.72

relation, an *option,* a *decision-maker,* and a *choice function.* In reading the axioms, note that αu is short for $\alpha \cdot u$. Note, also, that I treat $\cdot$, $+$, $=$, the $\times$ in $U \times U$, and $[0, 1]$ and $(0, 1)$ as *universal* terms. Finally, $\prec$ denotes the strict preference relation determined by $\preceq$.

NM 1 *The* universe *is a system of utilities,* U.

NM 2 *An* operation *is a function* $f(\cdot) : U \times U \to U$ *for which there is an* $\alpha \in [0, 1]$ *such that* $f(u, v) = \alpha u + (1 - \alpha)v$ *for all* $(u, v) \in U \times U$. *There is an operation for every* $\alpha \in [0, 1]$.

NM 3 *A* preference relation $\preceq$ *is a complete, reflexive, and transitive ordering of* U.

NM 4 *If* $u, v, w \in U$ *and* $\alpha \in (0, 1)$, *then* $u \preceq v$ *if and only if* $\alpha u + (1-\alpha)w \preceq \alpha v + (1-\alpha)w$, *and* $u \prec v$ *implies that* $u \prec \alpha u + (1-\alpha)v \prec v$. *Also,* $u \prec w \prec v$, *implies that there is an* α *and a* $\beta \in (0, 1)$ *such that* $\alpha u + (1 - \alpha)v \prec w$ *and* $w \prec \beta u + (1 - \beta)v$.

NM 5 *If* $u, v \in U$ *and* $\alpha, \beta \in [0, 1]$, *then* $\alpha u + (1 - \alpha)v = (1 - \alpha)v + \alpha u$, *and* $\alpha[\beta u + (1 - \beta)v] + (1 - \alpha)v = \alpha\beta u + (1 - \alpha\beta)v$.

NM 6 *An* option *is a member of* $\wp_F(U)$, *the family of finite subsets of* U.

NM 7 *A* decision-maker *is a pair* $(\preceq, A)$, *where* $\preceq$ *is a preference relation and* A *is an option.*

NM 8 *A* choice function *is a function* $C(\cdot) : \wp_F(U) \to U$ *such that if* $A \in \wp_F(U)$, $C(A) \in A$, *and if* $v = C(A)$, $v \succeq u$ *for all* $u \in A$.

Known as axioms of expected utility for the reasons listed in theorem T 1, NM 1–NM 5 are due to John von Neumann and Oscar Morgenstern, who give a proof of T 1 in von Neumann and Morgenstern (1953, pp. 617–628).

T 1 *Suppose that NM 1–NM 5 are valid, and let* R *denote the set of real numbers. Then there exists a real valued function* $V(\cdot) : U \to R$ *that satisfies the conditions: If* $u, v \in U$ *and* $\alpha \in [0, 1]$, $u \prec v$ *if and only if* $V(u) < V(v)$, *and* $V[\alpha u + (1 - \alpha)v] = \alpha V(u) + (1 - \alpha)V(v)$. *The function* $V(\cdot)$ *is uniquely determined up to a positive linear transformation.*

I have formulated the axioms NM 1–NM 5 so that they both accord with their original formulation (cf. von Neumann and Morgenstern, 1953, p. 16) and can serve the purposes that I have in mind for them.[1] In current mathematical jargon, axioms NM 1, NM 2, and NM 5 insist that the universe of utilities with its operations is a mixture space. Further, axioms NM 3 and NM 4 claim that the universe is endowed with a complete weak-order preference relation that is vNM-independent and Jensen-continuous.

A system of axioms that has a model is consistent. The axioms NM 1–NM 8 have many models. A description of a family of them follows.

E 4.3 *To describe a family of models of NM 1–NM 8, I begin with the models of NM 1–NM 5: Let* $X = \{x_1, \ldots, x_n\}$, *and let* U *denote the set of all probability distributions on* X. *Then* $u \in U$ *only if* u *is a function* $u(\cdot) : X \to [0, 1]$ *that satisfies the condition* $u(x_1) + \ldots + u(x_n) = 1$. *Next, let* $R_+ = [0, \infty)$*; and let* $W(\cdot) : X \to R_+$ *and* $V(\cdot) : U \to R_+$ *be functions that satisfy the condition: For all* $u \in U$, $V(u) = W(x_1)u(x_1) + \ldots + W(x_n)u(x_n)$. *Finally, let* $\preceq$ *be a complete, reflexive, and transitive ordering of* U *that satisfies the condition: For all* $u, v \in U$, $u \preceq v$ *if and only if* $V(u) \leq V(v)$. *The given* U *and* $\preceq$ *and the operations on* $U \times U$ *satisfy NM 1–NM 5. By varying* X *and* $W(\cdot)$ *I obtain a family of models of NM 1–NM 5.*

I can use the family of models of NM 1–NM 5 to obtain a family of models of NM 1–NM 8 as follows: For each pair $[X, W(\cdot)]$, *I let a decision-maker be an individual who orders probability distributions on* X *in accordance with the* $\preceq$ *determined by* X *and* $W(\cdot)$. *Moreover, I insist that this decision-maker, when faced with an option* A, *always chooses a probability distribution in* A *that is maximal in* A *with respect to* $\preceq$. *Finally, I let the choice function be a function that records the probability distributions that the individual would choose in the various options in* $\wp_F(U)$. *By varying* X *and* $W(\cdot)$, *I obtain the sought for family of models of NM 1–NM 8.*

I do not know the intended interpretation of NM 1–NM 8. However, for the purposes of this chapter, the family of models delineated earlier can be thought of as the intended interpretation of the axioms. In that interpretation the preference order is that of some individual, for example, a consumer or a bank director. Further, the probability distributions on *X* are taken to be gambles of various sorts that the same individual might face. Finally, the probabilities of the outcomes of these gambles are the probabilities that the given individual assigns to these outcomes. I presume that if the individual were to choose one gamble from a finite subset of possible gambles, he would always choose a gamble that his preferences ranked the highest. To me, that is an *accurate* description of individual behavior in the intended universe of NM 1–NM 8. It also provides a succinct description of a *characteristic feature* of choice under uncertainty in the social reality I described in Chapter 2.

Now, take a second look at E 3.2 in Chapter 3. My student is a handsome young man who is too fond of chocolates and madly in love with a fellow student. He is also an average student in math, very good at languages, and hopelessly lost in philosophy. Finally, he has an older sister, an unhappy, single mother, and much too little money to live the kind of life for which he believes himself best suited. All this information is of no avail in my test of the empirical relevance of the expected utility hypothesis. As far as my experiment goes, the student appears stripped of all characteristics other than his way of ordering uncertain prospects and his willingness to choose among such prospects in accordance with this ordering, So I may treat him in the experiment as a representative individual.

Suppose next that I were to use several of my students in a test of the expected utility hypothesis. Not all of them are equally clever in calculating certainty equivalents, and some may have a tendency to overvalue low probabilities and undervalue high probabilities. In order that observations that pertain to different students be observations on the same variables, I must account for such errors. I can do that in various ways. One possibility is as follows: I let x and z, respectively, denote the true and the reported certainty equivalent of a given prospect, and I insist that $z = x + \eta$, where η is an error term. Also, I let p and q, respectively, denote perceived and quoted probability in the given prospect, and I insist that $p = \alpha + \alpha^{-2}(q - \alpha)^3$ if $0 \leq q \leq \alpha$, and $p = \alpha + (1-\alpha)^{-2}(q-\alpha)^3$ if $\alpha < q \leq 1$, where $\alpha \in [0, 1]$. The values of η and α vary over my students, and I may choose $(\eta, \alpha) = (0, 0.5)$ as the value of the pair that pertains to the representative individual. The latter value and an appropriate probabilistic specification of the extent to which a student's answers to my queries may differ from those of the representative individual will provide the ingredients I need for a test of the expected utility hypothesis.

In a given theory-data confrontation several representative individuals may be in action simultaneously. For example, in Chapter 18 Rajiv Sarin and I give a different interpretation of NM 1–NM 8 that allows us to test several different hypotheses concerning positive analogies of individual choice under uncertainty.[2] We associate a representative individual with each hypothesis. One of them is an optimist, one is a pessimist, and one is a Bayesian. The representative individuals are identified by a sequence of answers to our queries, and the rules of the experiment that we adopt specify the calculating errors that we are willing to allow each subject. I believe that our test of the relative empirical relevance of the three hypotheses concerning choice under uncertainty that we considered was successful.

Strictly speaking, Quetelet's *l'homme moyen* is not a representative individual in the sense I have given to the term. The *l'homme moyen* surfaces in the construction of vital statistics as well as in the conception of estimates such as Jorgenson and Fraumeni's (1992) "average life-time income" and "average investment in human capital." In such cases the statistics that researchers produce do not pertain to individual members of the pertinent sample populations. Instead *they are parameters that describe properties of a given sample population seen as a whole.* Such characteristics need not be the characteristic features of the behavior of any individual in the pertinent population. For example, the mortality tables for Norway insist that 3/1,000 of all Norwegian 40-year-olds will not live to become 41. From such tables one cannot deduce that it is a characteristic feature of a Norwegian 40-year-old that he with probability 0.003 will die before becoming 41.

Quetelet considered individual behavior en masse and claimed that with a large enough number of subjects the search for positive analogies of such behavior would be successful. The number of individuals on which we have observations matters as much to us today as it did to Quetelet more than a century and a half ago. Statistical measures of the goodness-of-fit and the significance of test statistics attest to that. So does the way in which econometricians use consistency and limiting probability distributions to justify their parameter estimates. In fact, econometricians still believe that with enough observations and with an appropriate statistical analysis they will be able to test the empirical relevance of the set of positive analogies on which any theory of individual choice may insist.

4.2 THEORIES OF MARKETS AND STATISTICAL AGGREGATES

Economists do not theorize about particular markets, such as the market for Golden Delicious apples or the market for Ascentia-J-Series of laptop computers. Instead they theorize about *characteristic features* of different kinds of markets. Markets are typified according to the number of participants. Thus, a commodity market is perfectly competitive if it contains many buyers and sellers no one of which alone can affect the equilibrium price of the commodity. A commodity market is monopolistic if it contains one seller and many buyers no one of which alone can affect the price at which the seller chooses to sell his product. The characteristic features of such markets that interest economists concern, among many other matters, the stability of a market and the efficiency of the allocation of resources that it affects. I discuss some of these characteristics in more detail in the pages that follow.

4.2.1 Perfectly Competitive Markets

No one knows how numerous sellers and buyers must be in order that a commodity market or a financial market be perfectly competitive. So the essential characteristic of such a market is that no one of the participants tries to influence the price that equates supply and demand within it. All of them behave as price-takers. It is hard to determine whether or not perfectly competitive markets exist. However, it seems a good guess that on days when the Federal Reserve and the Treasury are not active, the U.S. money market functions in a perfectly competitive fashion, and that on days when large central banks are inactive, the foreign exchange market acts like a perfectly competitive one

In economic theory one learns of sufficient conditions that an exchange economy (a production economy) with m consumers (m consumers and n producers) and a finite number of goods possesses a competitive equilibrium, that is, an equilibrium in which supply and demand are equal in all markets. One also learns that if the same conditions are satisfied, in a competitive equilibrium the allocation of resources is Pareto optimal and any Pareto-optimal allocation can be realized as the allocation of a suitable perfectly competitive equilibrium. Finally, one learns that if the aggregate excess demand functions of the economy satisfy a version of Samuelson's (1955, p. 111) weak axiom of revealed preference, there are dynamic price-adjustment processes in which such an economy in disequilibrium will converge to a perfectly competitive equilibrium. Of these characteristics, the existence of a competitive equilibrium ensures that the economists' vision of exchange and production in a perfectly competitive economy is objectively possible. The other two characteristics ensure that the same vision is nomologically adequate. Details of all this can be found in Stigum (1990, ch. 14) and Debreu (1959, ch. 6).

There are several ways in which an econometrician can study the workings of a perfectly competitive economy. He may assume that the economy he is looking at contains a finite number of participants all of whom differ in characteristic ways and formulate the family of models that he will confront with data accordingly. He may also assume that there is a representative consumer and a representative producer that he can use to rationalize his observations. In this case, the theory in the theory-data confrontation will consist of a family of models of an economy with m identical consumers and n identical firms. Differences in the families of models that the data confront may influence both the way the econometrician questions his data and the kind of answers he gives to the questions he asks. I now take a closer look at some of the pertinent questions.

A perfectly competitive economy may be in equilibrium or in disequilibrium. A disequilibrium situation is marked by nonclearing of markets and inefficiencies in the allocation of the economy's resources. When econometricians analyze the behavior of a perfectly competitive economy in equilibrium, the models of the economy that they confront with data will make sure that in the theory universe all the relevant markets are cleared and the allocation of resources is efficient. The other characteristics of the economy that the models may reflect depend on the questions they ask. An example of such an analysis can be found in Chapter 23. There Heather Anderson, Geir Storvik, and I delineate a family of models of a system of financial markets in equilibrium and confront the models with data from the U.S. money market. The questions we ask and answer concern the extent to which yields on U.S. Treasury bills are cointegrated random processes. When econometricians analyze the behavior of a perfectly competitive economy in disequilibrium, they often seek to determine the extent to which the allocation of resources is inefficient. Examples of such an analysis can be found in Chapters 10, 12, and 14. There Harald Goldstein and I search for possible inefficiencies in the Norwegian bus transportation sector. Bus transportation in Norway is regulated both as to quantity and price of outputs. However, the bus companies are free to choose their inputs as they see fit. They behave as price-takers in all input markets. Hence, for the purposes of the empirical analysis, we can treat the Norwegian transportation sector as a perfectly competitive economy. In Chapter 10 I delineate the family of models that Harald and I are to confront with data, and in Chapter 12 I describe how the theoretical variables are related to the data we have. Finally, in Chapter 14 Harald carries out a GMM analysis of the data that allows us to quantify the technical and allocative inefficiencies for which we were searching.

In the two examples that I referred to above, the theory-data confrontation did not appeal to the existence of a representative consumer. If we were to invoke the assumption that our data can be rationalized as choices of a representative consumer and a representative producer, we could answer new questions about a perfectly competitive economy. For one thing, we could infer from the existence of a representative consumer that Samuelson's fundamental theorem of consumer choice must be true of perfectly competitive markets. Thus we may assert and test the empirical relevance of the following proposition: Any commodity that is known always to increase in demand when the income of users alone rises must definitely shrink in demand when its price alone rises (Samuelson, 1953, p, 107). Further, when a representative consumer exists, it must be the case that the market demand functions satisfy Samuelson's weak axiom of revealed preference, which is an assertion whose empirical validity can be tested on financial instruments in the U.S. money market.[3]

4.2.2 Imperfectly Competitive Markets

There are all sorts of imperfectly competitive markets. I mentioned monopolistic markets earlier. Apart from these, there are monopolistically competitive markets, oligopolistic markets of various sorts, and many others. According to economic theory, they all have one characteristic in common: Their production processes are inefficient in economically interesting ways. For example, in imperfectly competitive markets prices are usually higher than marginal cost, and the value of a factor of production's marginal product is usually higher than the cost of an extra unit of the factor in question. These conditions imply that the level of output in such markets is too low to be efficient. Econometricians can use quantity and price indexes in a meaningful search for the empirical relevance of such claims.

In addition to numbers of participants, economists typify imperfectly competitive markets by product differentiation, concentration ratios, and kinds of entry barriers. A product is said to be differentiated if buyers can in any way distinguish it from other products designed to serve the same function. Such distinctions may be made on differences in physical characteristics, identifying characteristics, and packaging. They may also be made on differences in the conditions under which they are sold. A market is characterized by seller (buyer) fewness when a small number of sellers (buyers) dominate it. A concentration ratio indicates what percentage of total market sales is dominated by the k largest sellers (buyers), where k is some small integer such as four or six. A barrier to entry in a market comprises the advantages that established participants have over potential entrants into the market. Barriers to entry fall into three broad categories: economies of scale in production, product differentiation, and absolute cost advantages. The importance of scale economies in discouraging entry into a market depends on the size of the market and the range of output in which such economies occur. Product differentiation in a brand-conscious market creates a barrier of entry when a successful entry requires formidable initial outlays on product design, advertisement, and retail-dealer systems. Finally, established participants in a market are said to have absolute cost advantages vis-à-vis potential entrants if there is a barrier to entry that will cause the costs of new entrants to exceed those of the established participants at every level of output. Examples of such barriers are control of the supply of raw materials and patents.

Under the assumption that firms are profit maximizers, economists have theorized extensively about the characteristics of different kinds of imperfectly competitive markets. For example, they have considered the extent to which products in differentiated product markets can differ without causing the market failure of one of the products. Good examples of such failures in the car market are the demise of the Studebaker company and Ford's terrible experience with its Edsel model. They have also theorized about characteristic features of the degree of concentration in various markets. Two examples of the latter are relevant here: (1) In a homogeneous-good market in which outlays for advertisement and research and development are small, and in which the entry barrier is determined by the cost of a minimal efficient plant, the concentration ratio has no positive lower bound as the size of the market increases. (2) In a differentiated-product market in which sales are responsive to advertisement, the concentration ratio has a strictly positive lower bound that is independent of the size of the market (cf. Sutton, 1991, chs. 2 and 3).

In his interesting 1991 book, *Sunk Costs and Market Structure*, John Sutton set out to test the empirical relevance of the two above assertions concerning concentration ratios in oligopolistic markets. A market in Sutton's study is one of twenty industries in the food and drink sector that resides in one of the six largest Western economies, the United States, Japan, the Federal Republic of Germany, France, Italy, and the United Kingdom. Sutton divided the industries into two groups, a homogeneous-good group and a high-advertisement group. The first comprised six industries that, respectively, produced salt, sugar, flour, bread, processed meat, and canned vegetables. The other comprised fourteen industries that, respectively, produced frozen food, soup, margarine, soft drinks, RTE cereals, mineral water, sugar confections, chocolate confections, roast and ground coffee, instant coffee, biscuits, pet foods, baby foods, and beer. He obtained estimates of the concentration ratio, the setup cost, and the level of advertisement in each industry in each of the six countries for the year 1986. As a measure of the concentration ratio he used the sum of the market shares of the top four firms. He represented the setup cost by the cost of constructing a single plant of minimum efficient scale, and he designated the level of advertisement by the ratio of advertising expenditure to the total value of industry sales. With the two sets of data—one for the homogeneous-goods group and one for the high-advertisement group—he managed to estimate a function for each of the two groups that depicts the way the lower bound of the concentration ratio varies with total industry sales. He concluded from his results that his data did not give him reason to reject the empirical relevance of the two propositions.[4]

There are several aspects of Sutton's analysis that are relevant here. Finding propositions concerning oligopolistic markets that may constitute positive analogies in a suitable sample population is difficult. The available class of models of such markets admits of a wide range of detailed specifications, and the market characteristics that the models portray have a sensitive dependence on such details. Sutton formulates several propositions that he believes are valid in poorly delimited large families of theoretical models. Two of them are the ones I quoted above. He chose the food and drink sector for testing the empirical relevance of his propositions. His reason for the choice was that this sector, among all broadly defined industry groups (two-digit SIC level), has one of the lowest levels of R&D intensity together with the highest level of advertising intensity. Moreover, the intensity of advertising in the sector is not only high on average but varies very widely from one product market to another, providing an unusually good context in which to examine its effects (Sutton, 1991, p. 84). Now, an industry is an aggregate of firms that are active in many different markets. Similarly, the measures that Sutton uses to assess the concentration ratio and the size of an industry are aggregates that have no obvious referents in his theoretical models. Still, his study shows how statistical aggregates can be used to study characteristic features of oligopolistic markets.

4.3 STATISTICAL AGGREGATES AND MACROECONOMIC THEORIES

There is no doubt that the measures of aggregates such as the "money supply," the "level of employment," and "national income" that we find in government publications have no reference in the social reality I described in Chapter 2. It is equally obvious that the theoretical counterparts of these measures have no reference in social reality either. Both the latter and their measures have reference in the socially constructed world of ideas that I described in Chapter 3. So a question comes to mind. Why do economists and econometricians spend so much time and energy studying the dynamic characteristics of such variables? In different words, what is the raison d'être of macroeconomics?

Economists theorize about the behavior of individual consumers and firms, about the dynamics of various kinds of markets, and about the functioning of a nation's economy. The various facets of the last problem constitute the subject matter of macroeconomics. As such, macroeconomics is a study of the economic aspects of choices that millions of individuals and a large number of institutions make. Studying such aspects efficiently requires that the economic theorists find sound and relatively simple ways to account for the choices of all of these individuals and institutions seen as a whole. In different words, the theorists must find sound and simple ways of arguing about a nation's economy in terms of pertinent aggregates. Examples of aggregates about whose behavior macroeconomists theorize are the theoretical counterparts of the three aggregates that I mentioned earlier. Roughly speaking, the first of these refers to the total quantity of liquid funds that consumers, firms, and institutions hold as cash and/or as demand and savings deposits in banks. The second refers to the sum total of persons who, at the going level of wages, are willing to work and are able to find suitable jobs. The third refers to the total income earned by all the individuals in the economy.

Economists are not the only scientists who face situations in which it is useful to argue in terms of aggregates. The following is a simple example that shows that physicists also often find themselves in such situations.[5]

E 4.4 *Consider a closed cube* A *that contains one kind of gas, for example, neon or just air. The gas has neither a fixed shape nor a fixed volume, and it fills its container. Also, if physics is right, the gas is made out of a great many atoms, or elementary parts, that obey the laws of mechanics and may interact electrically.*

Physicists study the characteristics of gases both from a macroscopic and a microscopic point of view. In thermodynamics scientists search for relationships among the various properties of gases that can be ascertained without knowledge of their internal structure. In kinetic theory and statistical mechanics researchers seek characteristic features of the behavior of interacting particles that can be used to explain known macroscopic properties of gases. The behavior of interacting particles may satisfy the laws of classical mechanics or the laws of quantum mechanics, and in either case there are all sorts of special cases to consider.

The gas in A *is one special case. It satisfies the* ideal gas law, $\mathrm{PV} = \mathrm{NkT}$, *where* k *is a universal constant and* P, V, T, *and* N *are measures of various aggregates. Specifically,* P *is a measure of the pressure that the gas exerts on* A*'s walls,* V *is the volume of* A, T *is a measure of the temperature of the gas, and* N *is the number of molecules in* A. *According to kinetic theory, the gas in* A *also satisfies the law* $\mathrm{PV} = \frac{3}{2}\mathrm{N}(\frac{1}{2}\mathrm{mv}^2)$, *where* m *is a measure of the mass of a molecule and* v *equals the mean velocity of the molecules in* A. *From the two laws together one can infer a second interesting relationship between a macro-variable,* T, *and a micro-variable,* v, $\frac{1}{2}\mathrm{mv}^2 = \frac{3}{2}\mathrm{kT}$. *Finally, the second law of thermodynamics insists that heat flows naturally from a hot object to a cold* *one, and will not flow spontaneously from a cold object to a hot one. Thus if* A *is placed in a closed room with a lower temperature than the temperature of the gas in* A, *heat will flow from* A *into the room until* A *and the room arrive at a state of thermal equilibrium in which they have the same value of* T. *During this heat flow process the probability distributions of the velocities of the particles in* A *and the room change in such a way that the distribution of velocities in the system as a whole becomes more disorderly. The physicists' measure of such disorder,* entropy, *is a measure of a microscopic characteristic of the molecules in* A *and the given room.*

I believe that the physicists' macroscopic and microscopic views of the characteristics of gases are reflected in contemporary macroeconomic theories. Some of the latter concern relationships among economic aggregates that can be determined without due attention to individual behavior. Others describe ways in which properties of individual behavior can be used to explain relationships among economic aggregates.[6]

Finding variables and interesting relations among them that can help us understand the functioning of a nation's economy is difficult. The number of possible variables is large, and the number of possible relations among them is gargantuan. To get a feeling for how large these numbers are, we can envision ourselves submerged in the data bank of the National Bureau of Economic Research (NBER). We are surrounded by time-series observations on more than 2,000 macroeconomic variables. With them we can estimate more than 2.65×10^{14} different linear functions in five variables (Leamer, 1983). If 1 second is spent on each such equation, it would take more than 31 million years to estimate all of them. Being in the NBER data bank gives one a good idea of the extraordinary feat that John Maynard Keynes accomplished more than half a century ago. In his *General Theory of Employment, Interest and Money* (Keynes, 1936), he showed that seven variables, the three that I mentioned earlier together with "total outlays on consumer goods," "net additions to the 'nation's stock of capital,' " the "going interest rate," and the "price level," suffice to develop an interesting theory about the functioning of a nation's economy.

There are all sorts of macroeconomic theories. They differ in the choice of variables and in the selection of the characteristic features of a nation's economy that they are designed to explain. Two examples will suffice to illustrate the kind of differences I have in mind. Keynes's macroeconomic theory appeared in 1936 in the midst of a period of severe unemployment. He used his seven variables to explain how the equilibrium level of national income and employment was determined. In doing that he established possible reasons for the employment crisis, namely, insufficient aggregate demand for goods and sticky nominal wage rates. That set the stage for using increased government expenditures to reduce the level of unemployment.[7]

Robert Solow's macroeconomic theory of growth appeared in 1956 in the midst of a period in which the Western economies were rapidly emerging from the ravages of war and the threat of a new war with the countries behind the Iron Curtain was a constant fear. It was also a period in which economists believed that there existed appropriate economic measures by which a mixed capitalist society could keep unemployment at low levels and promote a precarious growth. Solow (1956) used three variables, "national income," the "nation's stock of capital," and the "nation's labor force," to show that growth was not precarious. Economists' knife-edge vision of a capitalistic economy's growth path was based on false assumptions about the characteristics of the aggregate production function. With the "right kind" of aggregate production function, growth in a capitalistic economy was stable. He also demonstrated that in this kind of economy there were no limits to growth.[8]

Macroeconomic theories also differ because the originators of the theories have fundamentally different views of the way an economy ticks. Two examples illustrate what I have in mind. First a case where the differences seem trivial but, judging from the voluminous literature that they have engendered, are not. Consider modeling of the monetary sector in traditional Keynesian macroeconomics. Many economists insist that the demand for money M is determined by the liquidity preference schedule $L(\cdot) : R_{++} \times R_{+} \to R_{++}$, so that $M = L(r, Y)$, where r denotes the interest rate and Y the national income. Others claim that the demand for money satisfies the equation $M = kY$, where k is a positive constant. The difference looks trivial because the second case seems to be a special case of the first. However, looks can be deceiving. The development of monetarist economics at the hands of Milton Friedman (1991) shows that the given difference in Keynesian macroeconomic theories reflects a fundamental disagreement about the way an economy ticks.

The second example concerns economic growth. In Solow's theory both the rate of growth of the labor force and technological progress are exogenously determined. This and the other assumptions on which the theory is based have interesting implications for equilibrium growth. Along a growth path in which flows are in equilibrium and flows and stocks are in equilibrium vis-à-vis each other, capital per capita grows at the same rate as national income per capita. Moreover, national income per capita grows at a rate that is entirely determined by the rate of technological progress. Many economists have doubts about the empirical relevance of Solow's assumption that labor growth and technological progress are exogenously determined. They observe that new technology can be shared and that Solow's theory, therefore, implies that the rate of growth of per capita national income in different countries ought to tend to a common value. Yet empirical studies of postwar economic growth by Summers and Heston (1984, 1991) indicate that there is no such tendency in sight. This has led doubters to develop alternative theories that economists label theories of endogenous economic growth. Early contributions to the new kind of theory were Gary S. Becker, Kevin M. Murphy, and Robert Tamura's "Human Capital, Fertility, and Economic Growth" (Becker et al., 1990) and Paul M. Romer's (1990) "Endogenous Technological Change." The first looked for ways to endogenize population growth and the growth of human capital, and the second proposed a way to endogenize technological progress. So far, the theory of endogenous growth has been a theory in flux with an ever growing list of contributors all of whose articles have had one common theme: The engine of economic growth is the result of choices that numerous interacting utility and profit-maximizing individual agents make in national and international markets. A good reference on this subject is Philippe Aghion and Peter Howitt's (1998) *Endogenous Growth Theory*.

The variables that appear in macroeconomic theories and the aggregates used to measure their values mean different things to different people depending on the roles they play in these individuals' decision-making processes. For example, to a government policy-maker statistics concerning last year's level of national income, end-of-year level of unemployment, and end-of-year value of the price index carry shorthand information about his fellow citizens' standard of living and his country's ability to provide adequately for the sick and the aged. To a central banker the same statistics may carry information about a possible onslaught of inflationary pressures and warn him of difficulties that he will face in keeping the country's exchange rate at an adequate level. To an employed person such statistics may provide clues as to the chances of his losing his job and indicate the dire consequences for him of being unemployed. How meaningful the given shorthand information is to the three decision-makers depends, of course, on their ability to supplement it with information on the values of other relevant macro-variables. Here the thing to note is that macro-variables and the aggregates that are used to measure them carry information that is of use to economic decision-makers.

The values of many of the macro-variables about which economists theorize can be affected by the actions of the decision-makers involved. For example, a government policy-maker may increase government expenditures and raise tax rates on personal incomes to pay for the additional outlays. Similarly, a central banker may sell government bonds to increase the level of interest rates in financial markets. He may also enter the foreign exchange market to support the exchange value of his country's currency. Macroeconomic theory and a decision-maker's goals single out the macro-variables whose values he should try to affect. For example, suppose that the decision-maker's goal is to bring the rate of unemployment down to an acceptable level. Elementary macroeconomic theory will tell a government policy-maker that higher government expenditures might lead to a higher net national product (NNP) and help lower the unemployment rate. The same theory will tell a central banker that an increase in the money supply might lower interest rates, increase business investment, raise NNP and, hopefully, help reduce the unemployment rate.

The two decision-makers may, of course, encounter difficulties. Increases in the money supply need not have any effect on the level of interest rates. Moreover, additional government expenditures must be financed by loans or by an increase in taxes. Borrowing might raise interest rates and hikes in tax rates might reduce aggregate consumption, two prospects that are not likely to help reduce the rate of unemployment. Such difficulties are not important here since I only want to establish that macro-variables and their measures play an important role in the decision-making processes of all sorts of individuals in an economy.

In the vernacular of economists, an acceptable level of unemployment and an acceptable rate of increase in the price level are policy targets. The means that policy-makers use to affect government expenditures and the money supply are policy instruments. Policy-makers must choose appropriate values for the instruments and determine reasonable levels for the targets. Instruments such as the central bank's discount rate, changes in given tax rates, and sales and purchases of foreign exchange belong to the social reality that I described in Chapter 2. The targets, however, are usually values that the economic policy-makers assign to variables in our socially constructed world of ideas. I say "usually" to account for the following possibility. According to a given country's published statistics, 124,000 persons are unemployed. One policy target for the coming year is "to create 6,200 new jobs." Another target is "to reduce unemployment by 5 percent." If two or more persons are aware of the first target, the first target belongs in our World of Possibilities. The other target assigns a number to a variable in our socially constructed world of ideas.

4.4 CONCLUDING REMARKS

In this first part of the book I have discussed a problem that ought to be a matter of concern to serious students of economics and econometrics: How is a science of economics possible? I have delineated the characteristic features of the social reality in which we all live and figured out how human beings go about constructing it. The parts of this social reality that pertain to economic phenomena constitute the intended subject matter of economic theory. We have studied the ways in which economists construct a world of ideas that comprises the references of most of the data they employ when they confront their theories with data. This world of ideas has little in common with their social reality, a fact that seems to render the idea of a science of economics a hopeless thought. In this chapter I have tried to show that economists, the references of their data notwithstanding, can learn interesting things about economic phenomena, be they phenomena that belong to their social reality or characteristic features of the way they think about social reality. The validity of my arguments depends upon my contention that economic theory is about characteristic features of social reality and nothing else. If my contention is right, my arguments show that a science of economics is possible.

Learning about characteristic features of phenomena in social reality is not easy. It is also not easy to find good ways to think about the behavior of aggregates of elements that belong to social reality.[9] In Sections 4.1 and 4.2, I gave examples of how cooperating economists and econometricians go about solving the first learning problem. I now conclude the chapter with an example that shows how the same researchers with good solutions to the second problem can help economic policy-makers resolve serious economic dilemmas. I owe this example to a generous colleague, Per Richard Johansen. In the example, Johansen uses a large econometric model, called MODAG, to study the effect on the Norwegian economy of changes in two policy instruments. A more detailed description of MODAG and an analysis of the effects of changes in many other policy instruments is to be found in P. R Johansen and Inger Holm's article on "Macroeconomic Effects of Different Ways of Using the Real Return on the Government Petroleum Fund" (cf. http://www.ssb.no/english/subjects/08/05/10/es/ or Johansen and Holm (2002).[10]

E 4.5 *A Norwegian policy package for using oil money to rehabilitate schools and hospitals without causing increased inflationary pressures*

Norway is at the moment one of the world's major exporters of crude oil and natural gas. It is also a country with a growing population of retired people. The steady depletion of the country's oil and gas resources and the expected increase in demand for pensions have been matters of great concern. To prepare for expected lower incomes and much higher expenditures on public pensions the government has put its income from oil and gas production into a government-owned petroleum fund and is using as little as possible from the fund to cover current needs in the economy.

Last year an interesting economic problem arose. Owing to high oil prices during the years 1999–2001 the petroleum fund grew faster than anticipated. At the same time public expenditures to meet needs in the health and education sectors of the economy proved to be inadequate. Finally, the rate of unemployment was low, the Central Bank kept raising interest rates to fight inflationary pressures, and political pressure to use more of the oil and gas income for current needs instead of saving it all for the future mounted. As a result, the government decided that it would be all right to spend as much as 4 percent of the value of the fund to meet pressing needs in the economy. The problem was how to spend that much money without adding to the already existing inflationary pressures in the economy. We shall use a large macroeconometric model—MODAG, belonging to Statistics Norway and used by the Norwegian Ministry of Finance—to solve this problem as it relates to the rehabilitation of schools and hospitals.

MODAG contains almost 230 econometric equations that include both the variables that one expects to find in a disaggregated macro-model and a detailed set of policy instruments. One uses MODAG to study how changes in one or more of these instruments affect the growth of the economy as compared with a baseline growth scenario. The baseline scenario is designed in such a way that it reflects reasonable trends in the Norwegian economy, with a stable unemployment rate of 3.5 percent and a 2.5 percent rate of inflation, both of which are close to the levels recorded in Norway over the last 5 years. All the policy actions and macroeconomic effects reported herein are expressed as deviations from the baseline scenario.

Our problem is to find a way of using oil money to rehabilitate schools and hospitals without causing increased inflationary pressure. To solve the problem we must make assumptions about the extra number of Norwegian kroners (NOK) that will be needed over the next 10 years to provide for the pressing need to rehabilitate hospitals and schools. For what it is worth, we assume that an extra NOK15 billion will be required each year for gross fixed capital formation in the health and education sector. Such a boost in government expenditures, about 1 percent of the GDP, is likely to reduce unemployment and put pressure on both wages and prices. To counteract the pressures on prices it was decided to instigate a gradual reduction in the 24 percent VAT rate—nothing in 2002, −0.3 percent in 2003, −0.6 percent in 2004, −0.8 percent in 2005, −0.9 percent in 2006, and −1 percent in 2007 and −1 percent thereafter—so that from 2007 on the VAT would be 23 percent.

The NOK15 billion of extra expenditures and the specified changes in the VAT resulted in interesting changes in the growth path of the economy. Table 4.2 shows the changes in relevant economic variables from their values in the baseline scenario. Calculations show that both the price level and inflation rates will be the same as in the baseline scenario—not just for the 10 years accounted for in the table, but for a period of at least 20 years. Since inflation rates remain unaltered over such a long period, interest rates and the exchange rate are not likely to be affected by the instigated changes.

Table 4.2 also shows interesting changes in other variables. In the medium and long term the level of GDP is increased by a good 1 percent, unemployment is reduced by some 0.1 of a percentage point, and real wages are increased by about 1.5 percent, compared to the baseline scenario. The negative budget balance impact of the policy package is calculated to increase from approximately NOK10 billion in 2002 to NOK20 billion in 2010, in current prices. This is well below the expected extra amounts of money that the new policy rule allows. In fact this extra amount is estimated to be about NOK50 billion in 2010. The costs for Norway as a nation are even smaller, just some NOK10 billion every year. The difference is made up by increased net financial investments in the private sector that partly compensate for the reduced financial investments in the government sector.

TABLE 4.2
A Fine-Tuned Policy Package

Deviations from the baseline scenario	2002	2003	2004	2005	2006	2007	2008	2009	2010
GDP (percent)	0.9	1.0	1.1	1.1	1.2	1.2	1.3	1.3	1.3
Unemployment rate (percentage points)	−0.3	−0.3	−0.3	−0.1	−0.1	−0.1	−0.1	−0.1	−0.2
Wage per hour (percent)	0.3	0.7	1.0	1.2	1.4	1.5	1.6	1.6	1.7
Consumer price index (percent)	0.0	0.0	0.0	0.0	0.0	0.0	0.0	0.0	0.0
Current account (NOK bn in current prices)	−7.2	−8.5	−10.0	−10.7	−11.2	−11.7	−12.2	−12.8	−13.5
Budget balance (NOK bn in current prices)	−9.1	−10.8	−12.7	−14.6	−16.4	−18.1	−19.3	−20.6	−21.6

NOTES

1. I have stated the axioms in terms of $\preceq$ rather than $\prec$. I have also added Paul Samuelson's independence axiom $u \preceq v$ if and only if $\alpha + (1-\alpha)w \preceq \alpha v + (1-\alpha)w$ and $w \in U$ to the original axioms (cf. Samuelson, 1952).

2. The interpretation that I have in mind is due to Jean-Yves Jaffray and presented in (Jaffray, 1989).

3. In the last paragraph the assumption that there exists a representative consumer (and a representative producer) insists that the consumers (the producers) in the market are all alike. For a different use of representative consumers the interested reader can take a look at Section 10.3.2. There I discuss trade in a two-country input-output economy with two representative consumers—one for each country.

4. Identifying a market with an industry does not sound like a good idea. Whether it is a good idea depends on the choice of industries and the kind of queries the researcher in question seeks to answer. In Chapter 4 of his book Sutton argues that treating the two-digit SIC level industries of the food and drink sector as markets makes good sense in his case study.

5. I owe the original idea of this example to Henry P. McKean.

6. In James E. Hartley's (1997, ch. 13) account, *The Myth of Microfoundations*, the interested reader can learn about many of the ideas that economists have generated in their search for a microeconomic foundation for macroeconomics. Cf. in this respect also Kirman (1992, 1999).

7. In Chapter 6, Section 6.3, I present the salient characteristics of Keynes's macroeconomic theory and discuss Keynes's view of the purport of an economic theory.

8. I present a discrete-time version of Solow's theory and discuss some of its salient characteristics in Section 6.4.1.

9. Here I have in mind, for example, characteristics of the behavior of aggregates of elements that belong to social reality and properties of probability distributions of variables that have reference in social reality.

10. P. R. Johansen and Inger Holm's analyses provide ample evidence for how economic policy-makers can make good use of disaggregated large-scale econometric models. Such models vary in interesting ways over countries. For comparative analyses of English and Scandinavian models the interested reader may consult Wallis and Whitley (1991) and Andersen et al. (1991).

REFERENCES

Aghion, P., and P. Howitt, 1998, *Endogenous Growth Theory*, Cambridge: MIT Press.

Andersen, E., Å. Cappelen, K.-G. Löfgren, P. S. Andersen, and W. Fricz, 1991, "The Nordic and International Experience with Large-Scale Econometric Models," *The Scandinavian Journal of Economics* 93, 315–348.

Becker, G. S., K. M. Murphy, and R Taumura, 1990, "Human Capital, Fertility, and Economic Growth," *Journal of Political Economy* 98, 12–37.

Debreu, G., 1959, *Theory of Value,* New York: Wiley.

Friedman, M., 1991, *Monetarist Economics*, Oxford: Blackwell.

Hartley, J. E., 1997, *The Representative Agent in Macroeconomics*, New York: Routledge.

Jaffray, J.-Y., 1989, "Linear Utility Theory and Belief Functions," *Operations Research Letters* 8, 107–112.

Johansen, P. R., and I. Holm, 2002, "Macroeconomic Effects of Different Ways of Using the Real Return on the Norwegian Government Petroleum Fund," *Economic Survey*, Statistics Norway, 12, 36–48.

Jorgenson, D. W., and B. M., Fraumeni, 1992, "The Output of the Education Sector," in: *Output Measurement in the Services Sector*, Z. Griliches (ed.), Studies in Income and Wealth, Vol. 55, Chicago: University of Chicago Press.

Keynes, J. M., 1964, *The General Theory of Employment, Interest and Money*, London: Harcourt Brace.

Kirman, A., 1989, "The Intrinsic Limits of Modern Economic Theory: The Emperor Has No Clothes," *The Economic Journal* 99, 126–139.

Kirman, A., 1992, "Whom or What Does the Representative Individual Represent?" *Journal of Economic Perspectives* 6, 117–136.

Knorr-Cetina, K. D., 1981, *The Manufacture of Knowledge*. Oxford: Pergamon.

Leamer, E. E., 1983, "Model Choice and Specification Analysis," in: D. Belsley, Z. Griliches, M. Intriligator, and P. Schmidt (eds.), *Handbook of Econometrics, Vol. I*, Amsterdam: North-Holland.

Romer, P. M., 1990, "Endogenous Technological Change," *Journal of Political Economy* 98, 71–102.

Roll-Hansen, N., 1998, "Studying Natural Science without Nature? Reflections on the Realism of So-called Laboratory Studies," *Studies in the History and Philosophy of Biology and the Biomedical Sciences* 29, 165–187.

Samuelson, P. A., 1952, "Probability, Utility, and the Independence Axiom," *Econometrica* 20, 670–678.

Samuelson, P. A., 1953, "Consumption Theorems in Terms of Overcompensation Rather that Indifference Comparisons," *Economica* 20, 1–9.

Samuelson, P. A., 1955, *Foundations of Economic Analysis*, Cambridge: Harvard University Press.

Schwid, S. R., M. D. Hirvonen, and R. E. Keesey, 1992, "Nicotine Effects on Body Weight: A Regulatory Perspective," *American Journal of Clinical Nutrition*, 55, 878–874.

Solow, R. M., 1956, "A Contribution to the Theory of Economic Growth," *Quarterly Journal of Economics* 70, 65–94.

Stigler, G. J., 1965, *Essays in the History of Economics*, Chicago: University of Chicago Press.

Stigum, B. P., 1990, *Toward a Formal Science of Economics*, Cambridge: MIT Press.

Summers, R., and Heston, A., 1984, "Improved International Comparisons of Real Product and Its Composition: 1950–1980," *Review of Income and Wealth* 30, 207–262.

Summers, R., and A. Heston, 1991, "The Penn World Table (Mark 5): An Expanded Set of International Comparisons, 1950–88," *Quarterly Journal of Economics* 106, 327–368.

Sutton, J., 1991, *Sunk Costs and Market Structure*, Cambridge: MIT Press.

von Neumann, J., and O. Morgenstern, 1953, *Theory of Games and Economic Behavior*, Princeton: Princeton University Press.

Wallis, K. F., and J. D. Whitley, 1991, "Large-Scale Econometric Models of National Economies," *The Scandinavian Journal of Economics* 93, 283–314.

Wright, C., 1875, Sixth Annual Report of the U.S. Bureau of Labor Statistics, Boston.

PART II
Theorizing in Economics

Chapter Five

Theories and Models

This book is about theory-data confrontations in economics. The theory in such confrontations is a family of models of a finite number of assertions that has been formulated according to formal-axiomatic or model-theoretic principles. In this chapter we study the axiomatic method and see how it is related to the model-theoretic way of theorizing that W. Balzer, C. Moulines, and J. Sneed have advocated (cf. Balzer et al., 1987). The purpose is to become familiar with useful concepts and to gain insight into the treacherous business of developing economic theories. In a later chapter we see that for the data confrontation it matters little whether the theory is formulated in an axiomatic or model-theoretic way.

5.1 AXIOMS AND UNDEFINED TERMS

Consider a scientist who is developing a theory about some subject such as probability or consumer choice. He cannot offer a rigorous proof of each assertion of his theory. In fact, to avoid vicious-circle arguments, he must postulate some assertions and from them deduce the validity of others. Aristotle was aware of this over 2,000 years ago (see Warrington, 1964, pp. 165, 168, 183; Wilder, 1965, pp. 3–4): Every demonstrative science must proceed from primary, indemonstrable principles; otherwise the steps of demonstration would be endless. Of these indemonstrable principles some are (a) common to all sciences and others are (b) special to each science.

Originally, the principles under (a) were called axioms. They were, supposedly, self-evident truths such as, "the whole always exceeds each of its parts." The principles under (b) were called postulates. They pertained to facts considered so obvious that their validity could be assumed: for example, "through a point P not on a given line L there is one and only one line parallel to L." Today all the basic assertions of a theory are called *axioms*.

A scientist is in the same situation vis-à-vis concepts as he is vis-à-vis assertions. He can define some concepts in terms of others, but he cannot define all his concepts that way. Instead he must start from certain undefined concepts, usually referred to as *undefined terms*, and use them to develop other concepts referred to as *defined terms*.

In choosing basic concepts (i.e., undefined terms), the scientist looks for concepts so simple that they can be understood without precise definition. Examples are "point" and "line" in geometry and "commodity" and "money" in economic theory. The number of concepts a researcher leaves undefined and the number of axioms that he postulates is arbitrary, their number depending on how he wants to use his theory and how others may use it.

5.2 RULES OF INFERENCE AND DEFINITION

To go beyond axioms and basic concepts, a theorist needs certain *rules of inference* that tell him how to pass from axioms to theorems and from axioms and theorems to other theorems. He also needs some *rules of definition* that tell him how he may introduce new concepts based on existing ones.

5.2.1 Valid Rules of Inference

There are all sorts of rules of inference. Two of them are the *modus ponens* and the *dictum de omni et nullo.* The first concerns two assertions, A and B, and insists that, "if A implies B and A is true, then B is also true." The other claims that, "what is true of all individuals is also true of any one individual." In E 3.1, I illustrate the use of these rules.

E 5.1 *Each and every human being is mortal.*
Per is a human being.
Therefore, Per is mortal.

In this example, lines 1 and 2 state the premises, line 3 states the conclusion. We use the *dictum de omni et nullo* to infer from "each and every human is mortal" that "if Per is a human being, Per is mortal." We also use *modus ponens* to infer from the last assertion and from "Per is a human being" that "Per is mortal."

A rule of inference is *valid* if it leads from true premises to true conclusions. Only valid rules of inference interest our scientist. Whether a rule of inference is valid depends on the class of sentences to which it is applied. E 5.2 below bears witness to that.

E 5.2 *Let us call a set* regular *if it is not an element of itself. The set of all barbers in Paris is a regular set; the set of all abstract ideas is not. Sets that are not regular must be treated with care:*
Each and every regular set and nothing else belongs to F.
F *is a regular set.*
Therefore, F *belongs to* F.

In E 5.2 I use two premises and the same rules of inference as in E 5.1 to deduce a conclusion that contradicts one of the premises. Thus, unless two contradictory statements can both be true, E 5.2 depicts a situation in which the given rules of inference cannot be applied.

5.2.2 Valid Definitions

Most theories would be unreadable if scientists did not simplify the statements of some assertions by the use of defined terms. The defined terms are of various kinds depending on the circumstances in which they are introduced. In one case a scientist may introduce a symbol and insist that it be understood as shorthand for a longer expression. For example, an economist may insist that NIPA be short for "national income and product accounts." In another case a scientist may introduce a word and insist that anything that has a certain property be referred to by this word. For example, an economist may insist that "money" is to denote anything that serves as a unit of account and is used as medium of exchange. In a third case, a scientist may substitute a functional constant for a long expression of mathematical symbols to simplify the arguments of a proof. For example, an economist may substitute a functional constant for a sum of excess demand functions in his proof of the existence of competitive equilibria in an economy.

Introducing defined terms seems to be a way of life in economics and econometrics. It is, therefore, important to observe that not all ways of defining terms are valid. Moreover, seemingly valid ways of defining terms may have unwanted consequences. Some of them may even lead to anomalous situations. As we shall see, such possibilities are not to be dismissed as innocuous. They have plagued the theories of philosophers of science and led to interesting work in mathematical logic.

A definition is *valid* only if it meets two conditions: (1) it must be *dispensable*; that is, the scientist must be able to do without it; and (2) it must be *noncreative*; that is, the scientist cannot use the definition to establish assertions that do not contain the defined terms, unless these assertions can be proved without using the definition.

It is easy to see that the three terms that the economists introduced above are dispensable. Whenever one observes NIPA in a sentence, one can substitute for it the longer expression "national income and product accounts" without changing the meaning of the sentence. Similarly, when an economist asserts that "x is money," one can equally well substitute for his expression "x is serving as a unit of account and used as a medium of exchange." The definitions are also noncreative. That is obviously true of NIPA and money. It is also true of the functional constant in the third example if the individual excess demand functions share certain required properties, which is illustrated in E 5.3.

E 5.3 *Consider an exchange economy with* m *consumers, and let* $p \in R^n_{++}$ *and* $\omega_i \in R^n_{++}$ *denote, respectively, a price vector and a vector of initial quantities of commodities owned by the* i*th consumer. Also, let* $z_i(p, \omega_i)$, $i = 1, \dots, m$, *be the individual excess demand functions of the* m *consumers in the economy, and define the aggregate excess demand function by the equation*

$$z(p, \omega_1, \dots, \omega_m) = \sum_{1 \le i \le m} z_i(p, \omega_i),\ p \in R^n_{++},\ \omega_i \in R^n_{++},\ i = 1, \dots, m.$$

Finally, suppose that the $z_i(\cdot, \omega_i)$ *are continuous on* R^n_{++} *and share the following three properties: (1)* $pz_i(p, \omega_i) = 0$*; (2)* $z_i(\lambda p, \omega_i) = z_i(p, \omega_i)$ *for any* $\lambda \in R_{++}$*; and (3)* $z_{ij}(p, \omega_i) > \sum_{1 \le i \le m} \omega_{ij}$ *if* $p_j = 0, j = 1, \dots, n$*. Then* $z(\cdot, \omega_1, \dots, \omega_m)$ *will have the same properties, and when I set out to establish the existence of a competitive equilibrium in the economy, I can substitute* $z(\cdot, \omega_1, \dots, \omega_m)$ *for the sum of the individual excess demand functions in those parts of the proof in which only the given four characteristics play a role.*

Even valid definitions may have unwanted implications. Often such undesirable implications are due to characteristics of the language in which the scientist formulates his theory. In Chapter 12, I discuss some that arise in the philosophy of science because of the properties of the first-order logic's material implication sign. Here I am content to exhibit a well-known semantic analogue of the anomaly discovered in E 5.2.

E 5.4 *Let us agree to say that an adjective is* autological *if the property denoted by the adjective holds for the adjective itself. Otherwise the adjective is* heterological. *An example of an autological adjective is "abstract." The adjective "good" is heterological. Now, "heterological" is an adjective. If "heterological" is heterological, it is not heterological. If "heterological" is not heterological, it is heterological.*

5.3 UNIVERSAL TERMS AND THEOREMS

There are all sorts of ways a scientist can develop a theory. For example, an idealistic scientist may begin with first-order logic and develop set theory and the theory of natural numbers the way I did (see Stigum, 1990, ch. 9). With the sets and natural numbers on hand an economist can develop the theory of real numbers and all the elements of real analysis that he might need for his economic theorizing. In the same way a statistician can develop the theory of real numbers and all the elements of probability theory that he might need for his statistical theorizing. In fact, on top of the set theory of Chapter 9 in my earlier book it is possible to construct a set-theoretic superstructure in which all of mathematics resides. Chapters 20–22 in the same book bear witness to that.

Now, few scientists are as idealistic as the one I envisioned above. Most will assume the validity of certain parts of mathematics and develop their theories within the framework that these parts of mathematics provide. For example, an economist will take basic characteristics of sets and real numbers as givens and develop his theories with their help. Similarly, a statistician will take basic characteristics of sets, probability distributions, and random processes as givens and use them to develop his theories. The same is true of most mathematicians as well. The axioms and theorems of elementary probability theory in E 5.5 illustrate what I have in mind.

E 5.5 *Elementary probability theory has two undefined terms: an* experiment *and a* probability. *These terms satisfy the following axioms:*

A 1 *An* experiment *is a pair* $(\Omega, \aleph)$, *where* Ω *is a nonempty set of objects and* $\aleph$ *is a family of subsets of* Ω.

A 2 $\Omega \in \aleph$.

A 3 *If* A *and* B *are members of* $\aleph$, *then* $A \cup B \in \aleph$ *and* $A - B \in \aleph$.

A 4 *A* probability *is a function* $\wp(\cdot) : \aleph \to [0, 1]$, *with* $\wp(\Omega) = 1$.

A 5 *If* $A, B \in \aleph$ *and* $A \cap B = \emptyset$, *then* $\wp(A) + \wp(B) = \wp(A \cup B)$.

There are two defined terms, an outcome *and an* event.

D 1 *An* outcome ω *is any one of the objects in* Ω.

D 2 *An* event *is a member of* $\aleph$.

In deducing theorems from these axioms I use standard rules of inference and the properties of sets and real numbers. For example, from $\Omega - \Omega = \emptyset$ *and A 2 and A 3, I deduce that* $\emptyset \in \aleph$. *From this, from* $\Omega \cup \emptyset = \Omega$ *and* $\Omega \cap \emptyset = \emptyset$, *and from A 4, A 5, and a property of real numbers I deduce that* $\wp(\emptyset) = 0$. *Similarly, if* $A_I \in \aleph$, $i = 1, \ldots, n$, *and* $A_i \cap A_j = \emptyset$ *for all* i, j *with* $i \neq j$, *then I can use A 3, A 5, and mathematical induction to show that* $(\cup_{i=1}^{n} A_i) \in \aleph$ *and that* $\sum_{1 \le i \le n} \wp(A_i) = \wp(\cup_{i=1}^{n} A_i)$.

Theorems are assertions concerning the undefined and defined terms that can be proved from accepted premises with the help of valid rules of inference. As can be seen from E 5.5, the accepted premises are either axioms, already proved theorems, or so-called *universal theorems.* The last are theorems that have been established in other areas of mathematical inquiry, for example, in set theory and real analysis as in E 5.5. Good examples of universal theorems in economic theory are the implicit function theorem and Kakutani's fixed-point theorem. Economists use the former in their search for salient properties of demand functions. They use the latter in their proofs of the existence of competitive equilibria.

When formulating theorems a scientist often makes use not only of undefined and defined terms but also of a collection of so-called *universal terms*. The latter denote supposedly commonly understood logical and mathematical terms. In E 5.5, for example, the collection of universal terms comprised mathematical concepts, such as pair, nonempty set, family of subsets, member, and function, and mathematical symbols, such as $\in$, $\cup$, $\cap$, $\emptyset$, $\rightarrow$, and $\sum$. The use of universal terms and theorems is not prescribed by logic. It depends on both the scientist's interests and his audience.

5.4 FORMAL THEORIES AND THEIR MODELS

The undefined and defined terms, the axioms, and all the theorems that can be derived from them constitute a *formal theory*. The method of constructing such a theory from basic concepts and principles is called the *axiomatic method*. I summarize my description of this method schematically in Fig. 5.1. All the collecting and processing of information takes place in nodes I and II. Node I operations use the rules of definition; node II operations use the rules of inference. The arrows indicate information flows within the system.

The scientist can make his theory "talk about" objects of interest by giving the undefined terms an interpretation that renders all the axioms simultaneously true. Such an interpretation is called a *model* of the axioms and the theory derived from them. For illustration, I present in E 5.6 a model of E 5.5's elementary probability theory.

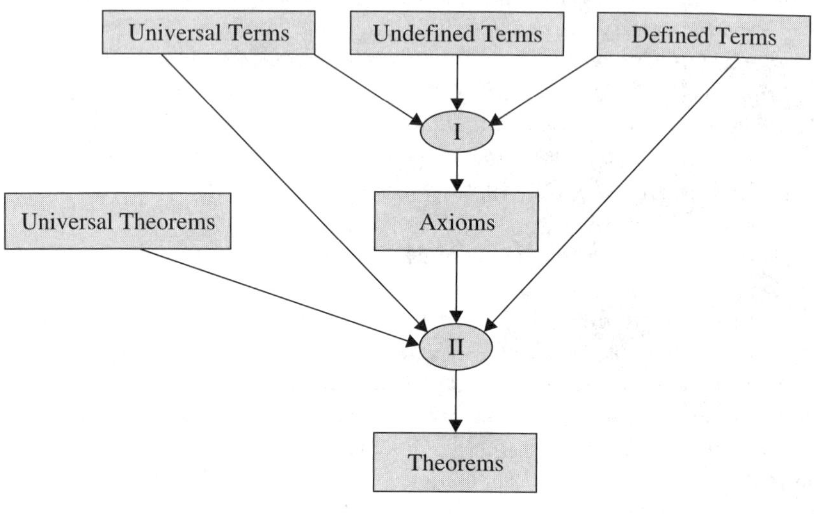

Fig. 5.1 The axiomatic method.

E 5.6 *It is soccer season. Each week any Norwegian can bet on the results of twelve soccer games that are being played at different locations in England. For each match there are three possible results: the home team wins,* H*; the visiting team wins,* V*; or there is a tie,* U*. The games are numbered from 1 to 12. In this case I choose* $(\Omega, \aleph)$ *so that* Ω *denotes the set of all sequences of twelve letters taken from the triple* (H, V, U) *and* $\aleph$ *denotes the family of all subsets of* Ω*. Also, for each* $\omega \in \Omega$*, I let* $\wp(\{\omega\}) = 3^{-12}$*, and for each* $B \in \aleph$*, I let* $\wp(B) = \sum_{\omega \in B} \wp(\{\omega\})$*. Then the pair* $(\Omega, \aleph)$ *satisfies A 1–A 3, and the function* $\wp(\cdot) : \aleph \to [0, 1]$ *satisfies A 4 and A 5.*

Not all axiom systems have models. We learn from mathematical logic that an axiom system that harbors contradictory assertions has no models. The converse is also true. Hence, it is a fact that an axiom system has a model if and only if one cannot derive contradictory assertions from its axioms (cf. Stigum, 1990, pp. 97–105). In the vernacular of mathematical logicians, an axiom system that does not harbor contradictory assertions is *consistent.*

An axiom system that has one model usually has many. The model or, as the case may be, the family of models for which the theory was developed I call the *intended interpretation* of the theory. For instance, the intended interpretation of the standard theory of consumer choice describes a consumer's choice of commodity bundles in various price-income situations. The theory can also be interpreted as describing a consumer's optimal investment in safe and risky assets in various price—net worth situations. In naming his undefined terms, the scientist indicates the intended interpretation of his theory.

5.5 MODELS AND HIERARCHIES OF THEORIES

If we look back at E 5.5 and E 5.6, it ought to be obvious that the triple $[\Omega, \aleph, \wp(\cdot)]$ can represent many different things. For example, Ω may be an urn with 100 red and white balls, the set of grown-up citizens of Zambia with and without AIDS, or the collection of all possible outcomes of a game of Lotto in Norway. Further, $\aleph$ may contain two sets $\emptyset$ and Ω; four sets $\emptyset$, Ω, R, and W, where R denotes the set of red balls (people with AIDS) and W denotes the set of white balls (people without AIDS), or some other interesting collection of subsets of Ω. The possible assignment of values to $\wp(\cdot)$ is equally numerous.

One thing that is not so obvious is that theories come in hierarchies in which all theories but one are families of models of another theory. That may sound strange. So to bring the point home, I next describe the beginnings of a hierarchy of theories of consumer choice. This hierarchy may be thought of as a tree of nodes like the one in Fig. 5.2. The initial node is a pair (T_0, M_0), where T_0 denotes the basic theory and M_0 is a family of models of T_0. The terminal nodes are theories of various kinds that can be derived from T_0 by specialization. In

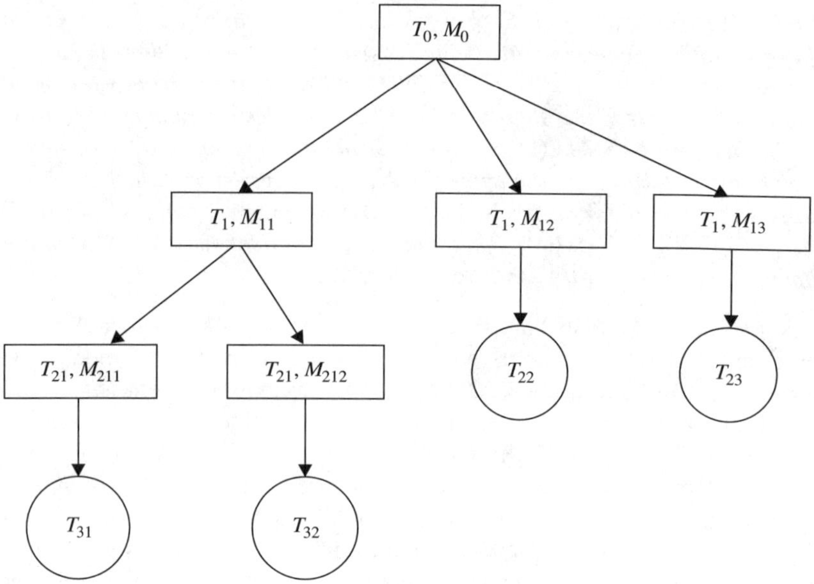

Fig. 5.2 A hierarchy of consumer choice theories.

between there are nodes of pairs whose first components denote theories and whose second components denote families of models of the respective theories. The distinguishing characteristic of the tree is that the family of models of a theory at one level is the largest family of models of the pertinent next-level theory.

In my hierarchy of theories of consumer choice the basic theory T_0 has four undefined terms, *commodity bundle*, *price*, *consumer*, and *consumption bundle*, and six axioms, H 1–H 6 , which may be phrased as follows:

H 1 *Let* X *be a nonempty, closed, convex subset of* R^n_+. *A* commodity bundle *is an* $x \in X$.

H 2 *Let* P *be a nonempty subset of* R^n_{++}. *A* price *is a vector* $p \in P$.

H 3 *A* consumer *is a pair* $(\preceq, A)$, *where* $A \in \mathrm{R}_+$ *and* $\preceq$ *is a complete, reflexive, and transitive ordering of* X.

H 4 $\forall y \in X, \exists x \in X$ *such that* $y \preceq x$ *and* $\sim x \preceq y$.

H 5 *A* consumption bundle *is a vector* $c \in X$ *that in some* (p, A) *situation satisfies two conditions:* $pc \leq A$ *and, for all* $x \in X$ *such that* $px \leq A, x \preceq c$.

H 6 *For all* $y \in X$, *the set* $\{x \in X : y \preceq x\}$ *is closed and convex, and the set* $\{x \in X : x \preceq y\}$ *is closed. Also, for all* $y, x \in X$ *and all* $\lambda \in (0, 1)$, *if* $x \neq y$ *and* $x \preceq y$, *then* $x \preceq \lambda x + (1 - \lambda)y$ *and* $\sim \lambda x + (1 - \lambda)y \preceq x$.

The preceding axioms are variants of the axioms of consumer choice under certainty that are encountered in most intermediate economic theory texts. A family M_0 of models of these axioms is obtained by letting X, P, and A be unspecified and by insisting that $\preceq$ satisfy the following condition: There is a continuous, strictly increasing, strictly quasi-concave function, $U(\cdot) : X \to R_+$, such that for all $x, y \in X$, $x \preceq y$ if and only if $U(x) \leq U(y)$.

The pair (T_0, M_0) that I described above constitutes the initial node of the tree in Fig. 5.2. The nodes at the next level of the tree contain one theory, T_1, and three models, M_{11}, M_{12}, and M_{13}. Here T_1 is short for T(H 1, H 2, H 31, H 41, H 51), where H 31, H 41, and H 51 are, respectively, analogues of H 3, H 5, and (H 4, H 6) with $U(\cdot)$ in place of $\preceq$:

H 31 A consumer *is a pair* $[\mathrm{U}(\cdot), \mathrm{A}]$, *where* $\mathrm{U}(\cdot) : \mathrm{X} \to \mathrm{R}_+$ *and* $\mathrm{A} \in \mathrm{R}_+$.

H 41 A consumption bundle *is a vector* $\mathrm{c} \in \mathrm{X}$ *that, in some* (p, A) *situation, satisfies two conditions:* $\mathrm{pc} \leq \mathrm{A}$ *and, for all* $\mathrm{x} \in \mathrm{X}$ *such that* $\mathrm{px} \leq \mathrm{A}$, $\mathrm{U(c)} \geq \mathrm{U(x)}$.

H 51 $\mathrm{U}(\cdot)$ *is continuous, strictly increasing, and strictly quasi-concave.*

It ought to be evident that M_0 is the largest family of models of T_1. Note, therefore, that the three families of models that appear at the second level of the tree in Fig. 5.2 are also families of models of T_1. Their descriptions are as follows:

***M*₁₁** *Let* X *and* A *be unspecified and let* P *be such that the first component of a price vector equals 1. Also, let* $\mathrm{F}(\cdot) : \mathrm{P} \to [0, 1]$ *be a nondegenerate probability distribution with compact support, let* $\mathrm{V}(\cdot) : \mathrm{R}_+ \to \mathrm{R}_+$, *be a twice differentiable function with* $\mathrm{V}'(\cdot) > 0$ *and* $\mathrm{V}''(\cdot) < 0$, *and insist that* $\mathrm{U(x)} = \int_{\mathrm{P}} \mathrm{V(rx)dF(r)}$.

***M*₁₂** *Let* $\mathrm{X} = \mathrm{R}^{\mathrm{n}}_+$, *and let* $\mathrm{p} \in \mathrm{P}$ *and* A *be as follows: There exist variables,* $\beta \in (0, 1)$ *and* $\mathrm{A}_{-1} \in \mathrm{R}$, *and a sequence of numbers,* $\mathrm{y_i} \in \mathrm{R}_+$, $\mathrm{i} = 0, \ldots, \mathrm{n}-1$, *such that* $\mathrm{A} = \mathrm{A}_{-1} + \sum_{0 \leq \mathrm{i} \leq \mathrm{n}-1} \beta^{\mathrm{i}} \mathrm{y_i}$, *and* $\mathrm{p} = (1, \beta^1, \ldots, \beta^{\mathrm{n}-1})$. *Also,* $\mathrm{U}(\cdot)$ *is a homothetic function.*

***M*₁₃** *Let* δ, α_{i}, *and* γ_{i}, $\mathrm{i} = 1, \ldots, \mathrm{n}$, *be positive constants such that* $\sum_{1 \leq \mathrm{i} \leq \mathrm{n}} \alpha_{\mathrm{i}} = 1$ *and assume that, for all* $\mathrm{x} \in \mathrm{X}$, $\mathrm{x_i} \geq \delta + \gamma_{\mathrm{i}}$, $\mathrm{i} = 1, \ldots, \mathrm{n}$. *Also, insist that* $\mathrm{A} > \delta + \sum_{1 \leq \mathrm{i} \leq \mathrm{n}} \gamma_{\mathrm{i}}$, *and that, for all* $\mathrm{p} \in \mathrm{P}$, $\sum_{1 \leq \mathrm{i} \leq \mathrm{n}} \mathrm{p_i} = 1$. *Finally, suppose that* $\log \mathrm{U(x)} = \sum_{1 \leq \mathrm{i} \leq \mathrm{n}} \alpha_{\mathrm{i}} \log(\mathrm{x_i} - \gamma_{\mathrm{i}})$, $\mathrm{x} \in \mathrm{X}$.

Together with T_1, M_{11}, M_{12}, and M_{13}, form three different nodes of the tree (T_1, M_{11}), (T_1, M_{12}), and (T_1, M_{13}).

At the third level of the tree in Fig. 5.2 there are three different theories, T_{21}, T_{22}, and T_{23}; two different families of models, M_{211}, M_{212}; two ordinary nodes, (T_{21}, M_{211}) and (T_{21}, M_{212}); and two terminal nodes, T_{22}, and T_{23}. In the same way that M_0 was the largest family of models of T_1, M_{1j} is the largest family of models of T_{2j}, $j = 1, 2, 3$. Also, M_{211} is M_{11} with the additional assumption that $n = 2$. Finally, M_{212} is M_{11} with the additional assumption that $V(\cdot)$ has one or the other of the following two properties:

1. For appropriate values of the constants, D, ϕ, η, and φ, $V'(t) = D(\phi + \eta t)^{\varphi}, t \in R_+$.
2. For appropriate values of the constants b and d, $V'(t) = be^{dt}, t \in R_+$.

At the fourth level we find two theories, the one determined by M_{211}, T_{31} and the one determined by M_{212}, T_{32}. There are also two terminal nodes, T_{31} and T_{32}.

In subsequent chapters I discuss the theories that appear as terminal nodes in Fig. 5.2 in more detail. Here it suffices to point out that T_{31} constitutes Kenneth Arrow (1965) and John Pratt's (1964) theory of consumer choice among one safe and one risky asset,[1] while T_{32} extends the same theory to choice among one safe and many risky assets (cf. Stigum, 1990, pp. 223–236).[2] Further, T_{22} constitutes the theory of consumer choice from which Milton Friedman (1957, ch. 2) developed his theory of the consumption function. Finally, T_{23} is the theory of consumer choice that underlies the so-called linear expenditure system in econometrics (cf. Stone, 1954).

5.6 PITFALLS IN THE AXIOMATIC METHOD

The axiomatic method is used to develop theories in such varied areas as mathematical logic, economics, and astronomy. Although it appears to be simple, the method has caused much controversy as self-evident postulates have turned out not to be obvious and carefully constructed theories have proved to be contradictory.

Many of the "self-evident truths" common to all sciences are not *generally* valid. The *law of contradiction* insists that nothing can both be and not be. Yet an Australian and a Norwegian will disagree on whether today is Sunday. Similarly, the *law of the excluded middle* insists that something must be or not be, but how can one be sure? Consider sentences such as: "All angels have wings." and "There are natural numbers of which no one has ever thought." Finally, "The whole is always larger than any of its parts."; whether the whole is larger, depends on the meaning of "larger" as witnessed by the one-to-one correspondence between positive and even integers.

The postulates that pertain to particular branches of science also often turn out to be neither simple nor obviously valid. For instance, non-Euclidean geometries shattered the idea that through a point P not on a line L, one and only one line can be drawn that is parallel to L. In the geometry of Lobachevski

(1829) there exist infinitely many lines through P that are parallel to L; in Riemann's (1854) geometry there are no such lines.

Of the various theories whose axioms imply contradictory assertions, one of fundamental importance to modern mathematics is Cantor's (1895, 1897) set theory. As originally conceived, Cantor's theory contained contradictions such as E 5.3 and paradoxes such as, "The power set of the set of all sets, U, has a greater cardinal than U itself." Russell (1903) discovered the contradiction and Cantor (1895, 1897) found the paradox. Logicians refer to the contradiction and the paradox, respectively, as Russell's and Cantor's *antinomies*.

The preceding examples indicate not that the axiomatic method should never be used, but rather that it must be applied with care. Specifically, since most "obvious truths" are not generally valid, a scientist employing the axiomatic method must delineate the logic he is using to justify his rules of inference and rules of definition. He must also specify the mathematical theory that supplies the theorems in the universal-theorems box of Fig. 5.1, and he must check the axioms as a possible source of contradictory statements.

5.7 THE ART OF THEORIZING

It is clear that the axiomatic method has pitfalls, some of which have caused the collapse of beautiful theoretical structures. The method has its limitations as well, and I confront them later. Here I take a look at examples that illustrate the interesting possibilities for theorizing that the method offers.

It is a fact that a theory that has been developed from one set of axioms can be developed from other axioms as well. In different words, if $T(\Gamma)$ is a theory with basic axioms Γ one can find a family of assertions Δ that belongs to $T(\Gamma)$, differs from Γ, and is such that $T(\Delta)$ and $T(\Gamma)$ have the same theorems. I use elementary probability theory to illustrate this. For that purpose I need the following theorem:

T 1 *If A 1–A 5 in E 5.5 are valid, then there exists a family of events* $\Re$ *and a function* $\wp(\cdot|\cdot) : \aleph \times \Re \rightarrow [0, 1]$, *with the following properties:*

- ***R 1*** $\Omega \in \Re$.
- ***R 2*** *If* $\mathrm{B}_1 \in \Re$ *and* $\mathrm{B}_2 \in \Re$, *then* $(\mathrm{B}_1 \cup \mathrm{B}_2) \in \Re$.
- ***R 3*** $\emptyset \notin \Re$.
- ***R 4*** *If* $\mathrm{B} \in \Re$, *then* $\wp(\cdot|\mathrm{B}) : \aleph \rightarrow [0, 1]$ *with* $\wp(\mathrm{B}|\mathrm{B}) = 1$.
- ***R 5*** *If* $\mathrm{B} \in \Re$, *then* $\wp(\cdot|\mathrm{B})$ *satisfies A 5.*
- ***R 6*** *If* $\mathrm{B}, \mathrm{C} \in \Re$ *and* $\mathrm{C} \subset \mathrm{B}$ *then* $\wp(\mathrm{C}|\mathrm{B}) > 0$ *and, for all* $\mathrm{A} \in \aleph$,

$$\wp(A|C) = \wp(A \cap C|B)/\wp(C|B).$$

To prove the theorem I define $\Re$ and $\wp(\cdot|\cdot)$ by D 3 and D 4.

D 3 *If* $\mathrm{B} \in \aleph$, *then* $\mathrm{B} \in \Re$ *if and only if* $\wp(\mathrm{B}) > 0$.

D 4 *For every* $\mathrm{B} \in \Re$ *with* $\wp(\mathrm{B}) > 0$ *and for every* $\mathrm{A} \in \aleph$,

$$\wp(A|B) = \wp(A \cap B)/\wp(B).$$

Then it is easy to verify that $\Re$ and $\wp(\cdot|\cdot)$ satisfy the conditions of T 1.

Suppose next that $(\Omega, \aleph)$ satisfies A 1–A 3 and that $\Re$ and $\wp(\cdot|\cdot)$ satisfy the conditions of T 1. Then, for all $A \in \aleph$, we can define $\wp(A)$ by D 5 and show that $\wp(\cdot)$ satisfies A 4 and A 5.

D 5 *For all* $\mathrm{A} \in \aleph$, $\wp(\mathrm{A}) = \wp(\mathrm{A}|\Omega)$.

From the preceding observations it follows that T(A 1–A 5) with D 1–D 4 has the same theorems as T(A 1–A 3, R 1–R 6) with D 1, D 2, and D 5.

Next I look at the consequences of seemingly innocuous additional axioms. Suppose that two axioms concerning the properties of $\aleph$ and $\wp(\cdot)$ are added to A 1–A 5 in E 5.5.

A 6 *If* $\mathrm{A} \in \aleph, \mathrm{i} = 1, 2, \ldots,$ *then* $\left(\cup_{\mathrm{i}=1}^{\infty} \mathrm{A_i}\right) \in \aleph$.

A 7 *If* $\mathrm{A} \in \aleph, \mathrm{i} = 1, 2, \ldots,$ *and* $\mathrm{A_i} \cap \mathrm{A_j} = \emptyset$ *for all* $\mathrm{i} \neq \mathrm{j}, \mathrm{i}, \mathrm{j} = 1, 2, \ldots,$ *then* $\wp(\cup_{\mathrm{i}=1}^{\infty} \mathrm{A_i}) = \sum_{\mathrm{i}=1}^{\infty} \wp(\mathrm{A_i})$.

These axioms have interesting implications. Here is the first.

E 5.7 *Let* Ω *denote the set of real numbers and suppose that* $\aleph$ *contains all subsets of* Ω *that are either bounded left closed, right open intervals or are finite unions of such sets. If* $\aleph$ *satisfies A 1–A 3 and A 6 it must also contain all open intervals, all closed intervals, and all denumerable subsets of* Ω.

Here is a second implication.

E 5.8 *Let* $\Omega = [0, 1)$ *and let* $\Im$ *be the family of all subsets of* Ω *that are either left closed, right open intervals or finite unions of such sets. Further, suppose that* $\aleph$ *is the smallest family of sets that contains* $\Im$ *and satisfies A 1–A 3 and A 6. Finally, suppose that* $\mathrm{P}(\cdot) : \Im \to [0, 1]$ *satisfies A 4, A 5, and A 7 and is such that, for any pair* (a, b) *with* $\mathrm{a} < \mathrm{b}, \mathrm{P}([\mathrm{a}, \mathrm{b})) = \mathrm{b} - \mathrm{a}$. *Then there exists a unique probability* $\wp(\cdot) : \aleph \to [0, 1]$ *that agrees with* $\mathrm{P}(\cdot)$ *on* $\Im$ *and satisfies A 7. This probability is called the* Lebesgue measure *and has the interesting property that, for all* $\omega \in \Omega$, $\wp(\{\omega\}) = 0$.

There is a third implication of far-reaching importance. To describe this consequence of adding A 6 and A 7 to A 1–A 5, several preliminary remarks are required. First two definitions:

D 6 *A family of events* $\Re$ *is a* bunch of events *if it satisfies R 2 and R 3 and if there exists a sequence* $\mathrm{B_n} \in \Re, \mathrm{n} = 1, 2, \ldots,$ *such that* $\left(\cup_{\mathrm{n}=1}^{\infty} \mathrm{B_n}\right) = \Omega$.

D 7 *A function,* $\mathrm{v}(\cdot) : \aleph \rightarrow \mathrm{R}_{+}$, *is* σ-finite *if* $\mathrm{v}(\cdot)$ *satisfies A 5 and A 7, and if there exists a sequence of events* $\mathrm{A_n}$, $\mathrm{n} = 1, 2, \ldots$, *such that* $\mathrm{v}(\mathrm{A_n}) < \infty$ *and* $\left(\cup_{\mathrm{n}=1}^{\infty} \mathrm{A_n}\right) = \Omega$.

It is interesting to observe here that if $(\Omega, \aleph)$ is an experiment that satisfies A 6, and if $\Re$ is defined by D 3, then $\Re$ is a bunch of events that contains Ω. Note also that if $\wp(\cdot)$ satisfies A 7, and if $\wp(\cdot|\cdot) : \aleph \times \Re \rightarrow [0, 1]$ is defined by D 4, then for all $B \in \Re$, $\wp(\cdot|B)$ satisfies A 7 as well as R 4 and R 6. Hence, it is easy to see that the elementary probability theory with A 6 and A 7, that is, T(A 1–A 7) with D 1–D 4, has the same theorems as T(A 1–A 3, R 1–R 6) with D 1, D 2, and D 5 when $\Re$ is a bunch of events that contains Ω and when the function $\wp(\cdot|\cdot) : \aleph \times \Re \rightarrow [0, 1]$ satisfies R 5 with A 7 instead of A 5.

It is exciting now to observe what happens to this probability theory when I refrain from insisting that a bunch of events must include Ω. Alfred Renyi's fundamental theorem, T 2, bears witness to that (Renyi, 1970, Theorem 2.2.1, p. 40).

T 2 *Let* $(\Omega, \aleph)$ *be an experiment that satisfies A 1–A 3 and A 6; let* $\Re$ *be bunch of events; and let* $\wp(\cdot|\cdot)$ *be a function* $\wp(\cdot|\cdot) : \aleph \times \Re \rightarrow [0, 1]$ *that satisfies R 4, R 6, and R 5 with A 7 instead of A 5. Then there exists a function* $\mathrm{v}(\cdot) : \aleph \rightarrow \mathrm{R}_{+}$ *that is σ-finite and that, for all* $\mathrm{B} \in \Re$ *and all* $(\mathrm{A}, \mathrm{B}) \in \aleph \times \Re$, *satisfies the conditions* $0 < \mathrm{v}(\mathrm{B}) < \infty$ *and* $\wp(\mathrm{A}|\mathrm{B}) = \mathrm{v}(\mathrm{A} \cap \mathrm{B})/\mathrm{v}(\mathrm{B})$. *The function* $\mathrm{v}(\cdot)$ *is determined uniquely up to a positive constant factor.*

From T 2 it follows that, by taking conditional probability as an undefined term and probability as a defined term, and by postulating A 1–A 3, A 6 and R 2–R 6 with $\Re$ a bunch of events and with A 7 replacing A 5 in R 5, one can enlarge the scope of probability theory significantly. The enlargement allows the defined probability term to assume any nonnegative values on R_{+}. In doing that, it provides justification for the use of improper priors in Bayesian econometrics.

5.8 LIMITS TO THE AXIOMATIC METHOD

The simplicity of the axiomatic method and the realization of its power that followed in the wake of the non-Euclidean geometries engendered the idea that every branch of mathematics could be developed in its totality from a finite set of axioms. Boole (1847) and Schröder (1890) carried out this idea for the algebra of classes. Peano (1889) did it for natural numbers, and Cantor (1895, 1897) tried to do it for set theory. At about the same time Frege (1879, 1884, 1893) axiomatized the propositional calculus, created a formal system of logic that incorporated both his propositional calculus and a first- and second-order quantification theory, and used the latter to formulate an axiomatic theory of sets. Finally, following in the footsteps of Frege and Cantor, Bertrand Russell (1903) and later Russell and Alfred North Whitehead (1910–1913) set out to demonstrate that there are axioms of formal logic from which all of mathematics can be derived.

Mathematicians' search for knowledge was beset with difficulties. There were all sorts of stumbling blocks to overcome. There were treacherous fata morganas to dispel. And there were absolute limits to their endeavors that they, eventually, had to accept. Russell's and Cantor's antinomies demonstrated that the set theories of Cantor and Frege were inconsistent. In doing that, they engendered successful searches for axioms of set theory that outlaw troublesome objects such as the F in E 5.2 and the set of all sets. One interesting example of such axioms is Jon Barwise's (1975, pp. 9–11) axioms for admissible sets with urelements. Similarly, semantic paradoxes, such as the one encountered in E 5.4, caused mathematical logicians to search for characterizations of formal languages in which they could explicate interesting semantical concepts. The first successful characterization of a language in which one can explicate the idea of "truth" appeared in Tarski's (1964) article on "The Semantic Conception of Truth and the Foundations of Semantics." Finally, a rapid development of mathematical logic led to the discovery of new and exciting methods of proof and to the establishment of magical theorems. Some of these theorems set definite limits to the power of the axiomatic method and demonstrated that the vision of Russell and Whitehead was in fact a fata morgana that could not be dispelled.

Three of the theorems that set limits to the power of the axiomatic method were due to Gödel and Skolem.

Gödel (1931): There is no finite set of axioms (formulated in a first-order logic) from which all the true propositions about natural numbers can be derived.

Skolem (1922): There is a theory of real numbers (formulated in a first-order language) that has a model with a countable universe.

Skolem (1934): In a first-order language in which the theory of natural numbers can be formulated, there is no collection of well-formed formulas that can provide a complete characterization of natural numbers.

In the statement of Gödel's theorem, a first-order language is a symbolic language with individual variables, function and predicate symbols (one of which is equality), the logical connectives "not" and "imply," and the quantifier "for all." A development of such a symbolic language and an outline of a proof of Gödel's theorem can be found in Stigum (1990, chs. 5, 8). The import of the theorem is that Russell and Whitehead's dream of creating a basis for all of mathematics in mathematical logic cannot be realized.

In Skolem's first theorem a model of a theory is an interpretation of the theory's undefined terms that renders its axioms (simultaneously) true statements.

The theorem insists that if our comprehension of the continuum is as described in a first-order theory, then there is no loss in generality in assuming that the "continuum" is countable. I give a proof of a generalization of this theorem in Stigum (1990, ch. 6). The general version of Skolem's theorem has important implications for applied econometrics.

Skolem's second theorem can be paraphrased to say that any finitely axiomatized first-order theory of natural numbers has nonisomorphic models. Specifically, any such theory has a model whose universe is uncountable. In proving the theorem, Skolem established the existence of a universe of nonstandard natural numbers. This result and the generalizations that were to come at the hands of Abraham Robinson (1966) opened up a new branch of mathematical inquiry: nonstandard analysis. I give a proof of Skolem's theorem, present nonstandard analysis from a modern point of view, and discuss interesting economic applications in Stigum (1990, chs. 20–22) and in Chapter 8 of this book.

The implications for formal economic theory of the preceding theorems are easy to divine. Any first-order language in which we can embed an economic theory must be rich enough to develop a theory of both the natural and the real numbers. By Gödel's theorem it follows that any model of a given axiomatized economic theory will necessarily contain true sentences that are not logical consequences of the axioms. Similarly, by Skolem's second theorem one can infer that any axiomatic characterization of an economic concept will have nonisomorphic models. Finally, by Skolem's first theorem it follows that, for most purposes in econometrics, discrete-time dynamic models are as good as continuous-time models.

5.9 THE RISE OF FORMAL ECONOMICS

The axiomatic method is a systematic way of developing a concept such as natural number or consumer choice from a few basic propositions using only generally accepted logical rules of inference. When and where this method originated is uncertain. However, Euclid's *Elements of Geometry* (ca. 300 B.C.) and the Archimedes treatises in theoretical mechanics (ca. 240 B.C.) demonstrate that the method was well known to Greek mathematicians several hundred years before the Christian era. Senior introduced it into economics in A.D. 1836 in his *Outline of the Science of Political Economy* and it is today more or less consciously adopted by most economic theorists as the way of theorizing in economics.

The advent of Senior's treatise came during a period in which the non-Euclidean geometries of Lobachevski (1829) and Riemann (1854) appeared. These geometries shattered the pedestal on which Euclid's geometry resided. They demonstrated that scientists' notions of straight lines, planes, and distances were vague and subject to a large number of tacit assumptions. They also showed that observations on physical space as it appears to the senses of a given individual would not enable that individual to decide whether Euclid's geometry or the new geometries provide the more accurate description of his world. In doing that, the non-Euclidean geometries set the stage for acceptance of formal geometries whose theorems lay down laws for imaginary matters only.

Senior's treatise indicates that he was unaware of the development of formal geometries. He set out to formulate a theory that could describe the actual workings of the economy he had in mind. In that respect his ideas as to the purport of economic theory were similar to the ideas of his fellow scientists who conceived of Euclid's geometry as a description of physical space as it appears to the senses.

Senior defined economics to be, "the Science which treats of the Nature, the Production, and the Distribution of Wealth" (1850, p. 1). To develop this science, he adopted as axioms four general propositions that he considered to be "the result of observation, or consciousness, and scarcely requiring proof" (p. 3), and that he formulated as follows (see p. 26):

S 1 *Every "man desires to obtain additional Wealth with as little sacrifice as possible."*

S 2 *The "Population of the World . . . is limited only by moral or physical evil, or by fear of a deficiency of those articles of wealth which the habits of the individuals of each class of its inhabitants lead them to require."*

S 3 *The "powers of Labour, and of the other instruments which produce wealth, may be indefinitely increased by using their Products as the means of further Production."*

S 4 *Agricultural "skill remaining the same, additional Labour employed on the land within a given district produces in general a less proportionate return."*

From looking at Senior's four axioms, one cannot divine what kind of economics he intended to develop. To find out one must add definitional axioms that explicate his idea of the terms "Wealth," "Labour," "Production," and "the other instruments of production" (see Senior 1850, pp. 6–22, 50–81). One must also add axioms that delineate Senior's conception of the laws of production and the behavior of man. When one does, one finds that Senior's theory was developed to explicate the workings of an economy in which there are both consumers and producers, some of whom are laborers, others capitalists, and still others owners of natural agents of production, and in which services, farm products, and manufactured goods are produced and exchanged (for the most part) in perfectly competitive markets.

For the purposes of this chapter it is not necessary to know the exact contours of Senior's economy. For later use, I need only reiterate that he intended his theory to be about the actual workings of an economy and that he believed that his axioms were so certain that they scarcely required proof.

In the 100 years that followed publication of Senior's treatise, leading English economists modified his theory in various ways. John Stuart Mill (1836) introduced "the economic man," Alfred Marshall (1890) introduced 'the representative firm,' and Lionel Robbins (1935, p.16) insisted that economics was, "a science which studies human behavior as a relationship between ends and scarce means which have alternative uses." All of them agreed with Senior that the basic principles of economics are based on indubitable facts of human nature and the world However, they seemed to be at odds about the extent to which the propositions of economics are about the actual workings of the economy. Marshall as well as Mill insisted that the laws of economics are tendency laws that describe what will occur in the world if there are no disturbing causes. John Neville Keynes (1897, p. 221), on the other hand, claimed that an economic law, "notwithstanding the hypothetical element that it contains, still has reference to the actual course of events; it is an assertion respecting the actual relations of economic phenomena one to another." Finally, Robbins (1935, p. 116) asserted that the *validity* of an economic theory is "a matter of its logical derivation from the general assumptions which it makes." In contrast, its *applicability* in a given situation "depends upon the extent to which its concepts actually reflect the forces operating in that situation."

For the development of formal economics, the upshot of the preceding observations is that the economic theories of the English economists in question were axiomatic but not formal in the current understanding of "formal." I believe that the theories that economists such as Trygve Haavelmo (1954), J. R. Hicks (1939), and Paul Samuelson (1948, 1949) developed in the years that followed Robbins's essay were also not formal in the current sense of the term. Their way of theorizing seems to me to be a reflection of John Maynard Keynes's (1973, p. 297) view that economics is "a science of thinking in terms of models joined to the art of choosing models which are relevant to the contemporary world." If I am right in this, it is also true that a general acceptance of formal economic theory first came with the publication of Gerard Debreu's *Theory of Value* in 1959.

5.10 MODEL-THEORETIC CHARACTERIZATIONS OF THEORIES

Judging from Wofgang Balzer, C. Ulises Moulines, and Joseph Sneed's book *An Architectonic for Science: The Structuralist Program* (Balzer et al., 1987), Keynes's view of economics as a science of thinking about models may be a valid view of all sciences. Balzer et al. view a scientific theory as a set-theoretic predicate. For example, the theory of consumer choice under certainty is a predicate, *consumer,* where a "consumer" is any quadruple $(X, \Im, H, h)$ that satisfies the following conditions:

K 1 X *is a nonempty, closed, convex subset of* $\mathrm{R}^{\mathrm{n}}_{+}$.

K 2 $\Im$ *is a family of compact, convex subsets of* X.

K 3 H *is a reflexive, transitive, and complete binary relation on* X.

K 4 h *is a function* $\mathrm{h}(\cdot) : \Im \rightarrow \mathrm{X}$, *such that for all* $\mathrm{B} \in \Im, \mathrm{h}(\mathrm{B}) = \{\mathrm{x} \in \mathrm{B} : \forall \mathrm{y} \in \mathrm{B}, \mathrm{x}\,\mathrm{H}\,\mathrm{y}\}$.

K 5 $\forall \mathrm{y} \in \mathrm{X}, \exists \mathrm{x} \in \mathrm{X}$ *such that* $\mathrm{x}\,\mathrm{H}\,\mathrm{y}$ *and* $\sim \mathrm{y}\,\mathrm{H}\,\mathrm{x}$.

K 6 $\forall \mathrm{y} \in \mathrm{X}$, *the sets* $\{\mathrm{x} \in \mathrm{X} : \mathrm{x}\,\mathrm{H}\,\mathrm{y}\}$ *and* $\{\mathrm{x} \in \mathrm{X} : \mathrm{y}\,\mathrm{H}\,\mathrm{x}\}$ *are closed in* X.

K 7 $\forall \mathrm{x}, \mathrm{y} \in \mathrm{X}$ *and* $\lambda \in (0, 1)$, *if* $\mathrm{x} \neq \mathrm{y}$ *and* $\mathrm{x}\,\mathrm{H}\,\mathrm{y}$, *then* $[\lambda\mathrm{x} + (1 - \lambda)\mathrm{y}]\,\mathrm{H}\,\mathrm{y}$ *and* $\sim \mathrm{y}\,\mathrm{H}[\lambda\mathrm{x} + (1 - \lambda)\mathrm{y}]$.

In different words, a quadruple $\{X, \Im, H, h\}$ satisfies the predicate, consumer, if and only if it is a model of K 1–K 7.

There are many interesting families of models that satisfy the predicate, consumer. One of them is the family of all models of H 1–H 6. To show why, insist first that $B \in \Im$ if and only if $\exists p \in R^n_{++}$ and $A \in R_{++}$ such that $B = \{x \in X : px \leq A\}$. Then, demand that $\forall x, y \in X, x\ H\ y$ if and only if $y \preceq x$. Finally, identify a consumption bundle with the pertinent value of $h(\cdot)$.

According to Balzer et al. (1987), the assertions that delineate the characteristic features of a scientific-theory predicate are of two kinds. Some of them determine the conceptual framework to which all the models of the pertinent theory must belong. Others describe lawlike properties of the entities about which the given theory speaks. Balzer et al. suggest that the models of the first kind of assertions be labeled the *potential models* of the theory. The subfamily of the potential models whose members satisfy all the axioms of the theory they label the family of *actual models* of the theory. In the case of the consumer one may identify the family of potential models with the family of models of K 1–K 3. The family of actual models consists of all models that satisfy the predicate, consumer.

5.10.1 Set-Theoretic Predicates in Economics

I believe that many economic theorists formulate their theories in two steps. First they write down assertions that characterize the conceptual framework of the theory. Then they make simplifying assumptions about the various elements that play essential roles in the development of the theory. It is probably good to think of the conceptual framework as a family of potential models of the theory. It is also good to think of the simplifying assumptions as determining the family of actual models of the theory. In the remainder of the book I refer to this way of constructing a theory as *model-theoretic* or *semantic*. Moreover, I consider a model-theoretic formulation of a theory not as a set theoretic predicate, but as a theory about certain undefined terms that economists in theory-data confrontations seek to relate to variables in the pertinent data universes.

Judging from the characterization of scientific theories by Balzer et al. and from the examples that Erwin Klein (1998) gives in his book *Economic Theories and their Relational Structures*, the choice of axioms that form the basis of the pertinent family of potential models is rarely well defined and is sometimes arbitrary. I believe that it is wrong to view the choice of basic axioms in economics as arbitrary. Economic theorists who adopt the model-theoretic way of formulating theories make a conscious choice when they write down the assertions that form the basis of their families of potential models. Vide, for example, John M. Keynes's (1936) presentation of his theory of the determination of an equilibrium level of national income and employment and Paul A. Samuelson's (1948, 1949) seminal articles on the factor price equalization theorem

To illustrate the model-theoretic way of formulating an economic theory, I conclude the chapter by discussing an interesting family of models of Senior's (1850) four basic postulates for the science of economics.

5.10.1.1 An Example

The model of Senior's postulates that I have in mind is a discrete-time variant of Robert Solow's (1956) growth model that Richard Day invented 30 years ago. It concerns four macro-variables, consumption C, net national product Y, aggregate stock of capital K, and the labor force L. For each $t = 1, 2, \ldots$ the behavior of these variables is determined by the following equations:

$$C_t = \sigma L_t + (1 - \mu)(Y_t - \sigma L_t), \tag{1}$$

$$Y_t = f(K_t, L_t), \tag{2}$$

$$K_{t+1} = K_t + (Y_t - C_t), \tag{3}$$

$$L_{t+1} = \min[(1 + \lambda)L_t, C_t/\sigma]. \tag{4}$$

I assume that the constants, σ, μ, and λ, satisfy the inequalities

$$\lambda > 0, \sigma > 0, \text{ and } \mu \in (0, 1). \tag{5}$$

Also, $f(\cdot)$ is a real-valued function on R^2_{++} that is homogeneous of degree one, strictly increasing, strictly quasi-concave, twice differentiable, and satisfies the condition

$$\lim_{x \to 0} \partial f(x, 1)/\partial K = \infty. \tag{6}$$

Finally, there exist positive constants, k^s, k^w, k_0, and k_1 that satisfy the equations

$$f(k^s, 1) = \sigma;\ f(k^w, 1) = [(1 + \lambda - \mu)/(1 - \mu)]\sigma; \quad \text{and } f(k_j, 1) = \sigma + (\lambda/\mu)k_j,\ j = 0, 1, \tag{7}$$

where $k^s < k^w < k_0 < k_1$, from which I deduce that

$$k^w > \sigma\mu/(1-\mu). \tag{8}$$

Since Senior's treatise appeared 100 years before Keynes's (1936) *General Theory of Employment, Interest and Money*, it is unlikely that Senior had any vision of the advent of contemporary macroeconomics. For that reason I cannot claim that there are models of Eqs. (1)–(8) that belong to the *intended* family of potential models of Senior's economic theory. Still, I may claim that among the macroeconomic models of his postulates, there is an interesting subfamily that satisfies the conditions that I delineate in Eqs. (1)–(8). Certainly, models of (1), (2), and (5) that satisfy the conditions I impose on $f(\cdot)$ capture the ideas of his first and fourth postulates, and models of (2)–(4) satisfy the conditions on which his second and third postulates insist. Moreover, as we shall see, (6)–(8) impose conditions on a nation's economic development that accord with the ideas underlying his second and fourth postulates.

To tell a simple story about the economics of Eqs. (1)–(8) I fix t and see what happens to C, L, K, and K/L when (K_t/L_t) resides in one of various intervals of the real line.

When $(K_t/L_t) \in (0, k^s)$, $C_{t+1} < C_t$, $L_{t+1} < L_t$, and $K_{t+1} < K_t$; and when $(K_t/L_t) \in (k^s, \infty)$, $C_{t+1} > C_t$, $L_{t+1} > L_t$, and $K_{t+1} > K_t$. Hence, for C, L, and K, the region $(0, k^s)$ appears to be a true "Malthusian trap."

The behavior of (K/L) in the given regions depends on the value of the ratio, $\sigma\mu/(1-\mu)$.

1. When $\sigma\mu/(1-\mu) < k^s$, then $K_{t+1}/L_{t+1} < K_t/L_t$ if $(K_t/L_t) \in (0, \sigma\mu/(1-\mu)) \cup (k^s, k_0) \cup (k_1, \infty)$ and $K_{t+1}/L_{t+1} > K_t/L_t$ if $(K_t/L_t) \in (\sigma\mu/(1-\mu, k^s) \cup (k_0, k_1)$.
2. When $k^s < \sigma\mu/(1-\mu)$, then $K_{t+1}/L_{t+1} < K_t/L_t$ if $(K_t/L_t) \in (0, k^s) \cup (\sigma\mu/(1-\mu), k_0) \cup (k_1, \infty)$ and $K_{t+1}/L_{t+1} > K_t/L_t$ if $(K_t/L_t) \in (k^s, \sigma\mu/(1-\mu)) \cup (k_0, k_1)$.

There are several stationary points:

3. When $\sigma\mu/(1-\mu) < k^s$, then $\sigma\mu/(1-\mu)$, k^s, k_0, and k_1 are stationary points. Of these the first and the third are unstable and the second and fourth are stable.
4. When $k^s < \sigma\mu/(1-\mu)$, then k^s, $\sigma\mu/(1-\mu)$, k_0 and k_1 are stationary points. Of these the first and third are unstable and the second and fourth point are stable.

From all of this it follows that, in the region (k_0, ∞) the Senior model behaves like the original Solow model, which I discuss in the next chapter.

NOTES

1. In Stigum (1990, Ch. 12) I demonstrated that Arrow and Pratt's theory can be viewed as a family of models of H 1–H 6.

2. I learned of the candidate families of utility functions in M_{212} from Cass and Stiglitz (1970). They enabled me to extend Arrow and Pratt's theory to a theory of choice among one safe and several risky assets.

REFERENCES

Arrow, K., 1965, *Aspects of the Theory of Risk Bearing*, Helsinki: Academic Book Store.

Balzer, W. , C. U. Moulines, and J. Sneed, 1987, *An Architectonic for Science: The Structuralist Program*, Dordrecht: Reidel.

Barwise, J., 1975, *Admissible Sets and Structures*, New York: Springer-Verlag.

Boole, G., 1847, *The Mathematical Analysis of Logic*, Cambridge: Macmillan, Barclay and Macmillan.

Cantor, G.,1895, "Beiträge zur Begründung der transfiniten Mengenlehre, Part I," *Mathematische Annalen* 46, 481–512.

Cantor, G., 1897, "Beiträge zur Begründung der transfiniten Mengenlehre, Part II," *Mathematische Annalen* 47, 207–246.

Cass, D., and J. E. Stiglitz, 1970, "The Structure of Investor Preferences and Asset Returns, and Separability in Portfolio Allocation: A Contribution to the Pure Theory of Mutual Funds," *Journal of Economic Theory* 2, 102–160.

Debreu, G., 1959, *Theory of Value*, New York: Wiley.

Frege, G., 1879, *Begriffsschrift eine der arithmetischen nachgebildeten Formelsprachen des reinen Denkens*, Halle: Nebert.

Frege, G., 1884, *Die Grundlagen der Arithmetik*, Breslau: Verlag Wilhelm Koebner.

Frege, G., 1893, *Grundgesetze der Arithmetik begriffsschriftlich abgeleitet, Band I*, Jena: Verlag Hermann Pohle.

Friedman, M., 1957, *A Theory of the Consumption Function*, Princeton: Princeton University Press.

Gödel, K., 1931, "Über formal unentscheidbare Sätze der Principia Mathematica und verwandter Systeme I," *Monatshefte für Mathematik und Physik* 38, 173–198.

Haavelmo, T., 1954, *A Study in the Theory of Economic Evolution*, Amsterdam: North-Holland.

Hicks, J. R., 1939, *Value and Capital*, Oxford: Oxford University Press.

Keynes, J. M., 1936, *General Theory of Employment, Interest and Money*, New York: Harcourt Brace.

Keynes, J. M., 1938, "Letter to Roy Harrod, July 4," reprinted in 1973, in: *Collected Writings of John Maynard Keynes, Vol. 14*, D. Moggridge (ed.), London: Macmillan.

Keynes, J. N., 1897, *The Scope and Method of Political Economy*, 2nd Ed., London: Macmillan.

Klein, E., 1998, *Economic Theories and their Relational Structures*, New York: Harcourt Brace.

Lobachevski, N. I., 1829, "Über die Anfangsgründe der Geometrie," *Kasaner Bote, Theil* 25; translated by F. Engel and published in 1898, in: *Urkunden zur Geschichte der Nichteuklidischen Geometrie, Vol. 1*, Leipzig: Druck und Verlag von B.G. Teubner.

Marshall, A., 1890, *Principles of Economics*, 1st Ed., London: Macmillan.

Mill, J. S., 1836, "On the Definition of Political Economy," reprinted in 1967, in: *Collected Works, Essays on Economy and Society, Vol. 4*, J. M. Robson (ed.), Toronto: University of Toronto Press.

Peano, G., 1889, *Arithmetices Principia Nova Methodo Exposita*, Turin: Bocca.

Pratt, J., 1964, "Risk Aversion in the Small and the Large," *Econometrica*. 32, 122–136.

Renyi, A., 1970, *Foundations of Probability*, San Francisco: Holden Day.

Riemann, B., 1854, *Über die Hypothesen welche der Geometrie zu Grunde liegen*, Berlin: Verlag von Julius Springer.

Robbins, L., 1935, *An Essay on the Nature an Significance of Economic Science*, 2nd Ed., London: Macmillan.

Robinson, A., 1966, *Non-Standard Analysis*, Amsterdam: North Holland.

Russell, B., 1903, *Principles of Mathematics*, New York: Norton.

Russell, B., and A. N. Whitehead, 1910–1913, *Principia Mathematica*, Cambridge: Cambridge University Press.

Samuelson, P. A. 1948, "International Trade and the Equalization of Factor Prices," *Economic Journal* 58, 163–184.

Samuelson, P. A., 1949, "International Factor Price Equalization Once Again," *Economic Journal* 59, 181–197.

Schröder, E., 1890, *Vorlesungen über die Algebra der Logik*, Leipzig: Druck und Verlag von B.G. Teubner.

Senior, N. W., 1836, *Outline of the Science of Political Economy*, reprinted in 1965, New York: A. M. Kelley.

Senior, N. W., 1850, *Political Economy*, London: Griffin.

Skolem, T., 1922, "Einige Bemerkungen zur axiomatischen Begründung der Mengenlehre," in: *Proceedings of the 5th Scandinavian Mathematics Congress in Helsinki*, Helsingfors: Akademiska Bokhandelen.

Skolem, T., 1934, "Über die Nicht-characterisierbarkeit der Zahlenreihe mittels endlich oder abzählbar unendlich vieler Aussagen mit ausschliesslichen Zahlenvariabeln," *Fundamenta Mathematicae* 23, 150–161.

Solow, R. M., 1956, "A Contribution to the Theory of Economic Growth," *Quarterly Journal of Economics* 70, 65–94.

Stigum, B. P., 1990, *Toward a Formal Science of Economics*, Cambridge: MIT Press.

Stone, J. R. N., 1954, "Linear Expenditure Systems and Demand Analysis: An Application to the Pattern of British Demand," *Economic Journal* 64, 511–527.

Tarski, A., 1964, "The Semantic Conception of Truth and the Foundations of Semantics," in: *Readings in Philosophical Analysis*, H. Feigel and W. Sellars (eds.), New York: Appleton-Century-Crofts.

Warrington, J. (ed., trans.), 1964, Aristotle's *Prior and Posterior Analytics*, London: Dent.

Wilder, R. L., 1965, *Introduction to the Foundations of Mathematics*, 2nd Ed., New York: Wiley.

Chapter Six

The Purport of an Economic Theory

There are many economists in the world and probably equally many views of the purport of an economic theory. There are also quite a few "right" ways of developing an economic theory, each of which has many true believers. In this chapter I present my own view of the purport of an economic theory and demonstrate its ability to explicate the meaning of theories that have been developed in accordance with the ideas of Max Weber, John Maynard Keynes, Robert Solow, and Gerard Debreu.

6.1 A VIEW OF THE PURPORT OF AN ECONOMIC THEORY

We learned in the preceding chapter that an economic theory—whether developed by the axiomatic method or in accordance with the semantic view of theories—is a theory about undefined terms. In the intended interpretation of the theory the undefined terms carry names that indicate the economic situation to which the theory pertains. It is, therefore, important to observe that, many of these names have no reference in the social reality I described in Chapter 2. Instead, their references belong to a socially constructed world of ideas. Since this might not be obvious, a few clarifying remarks will prove useful.

Universals, such as table and justice, live and function in Plato's world of ideas. The same is true of economic universals, such as money and income. In Chapter 3, I observed that money as well as table and justice have reference in the social reality that I described in Chapter 2 while income has no such reference. Instead income has reference in a socially constructed world of ideas. Income is not exceptional in this respect. The same is true of output, capital, and many other economic concepts. Even when economic concepts have reference in the social reality, the references of the variables that carry their names in an economic theory have no such reference. Money is a good example. Money as a medium of exchange has reference in the social reality. Yet the variables in macroeconomic theories that carry the name "money" have no such reference. Their references are aggregates whose values belong to a world of ideas that economists have created.

If most of the variables in economic theories have references in a socially constructed world of ideas, it becomes important for the purposes of this book that I state clearly what I consider to be the purport of an economic theory. To do that, I must first explain what I mean by a positive analogy. *Analogy* is a process of reasoning in which objects or events that are similar in one respect are judged to resemble each other in certain other respects as well. A *positive analogy* for a group of individuals, $\Im$, is a propositional function satisfied by all the individuals in $\Im$. A *negative analogy* for $\Im$ is a propositional function satisfied by some but not all individuals in $\Im$.

My way of looking at an economic theory of some economic situation (e.g., an act or a historical development) is that the intended interpretation of the theory delineates the positive analogies that the originator of the theory considered sufficient to describe the kind of situation that he had in mind. For example, in the intended interpretation of an axiomatized version of the theory of the firm, such as an augmented version of N 1–N 7 in Chapter 10, the firm chooses its input-output strategy so as to maximize its profits. I consider this an accurate description of firm behavior in the theory universe of N 1–N 7. Supposedly, it also describes succinctly a characteristic of behavior in the intended reference group of firms in social reality. Whether the latter supposition has empirical relevance is a question that can be answered only in a pertinent theory-data confrontation.

In reading my characterization of the meaning of economic theories, it is important to keep in mind the following observations: (1) To say that profit maximization is a positive analogy of firm behavior is very different from saying that the firm behaves *as if* it were maximizing profits. Firms in the theory's intended reference group do, by hypothesis, maximize profits. (2) Even though an accurate description of the behavior of a firm in a given reference group would exhibit many negative analogies of firm behavior, the positive analogies that the theory identifies must not be taken to provide an *approximate* description of firm behavior. (3) The hypotheses that are comprised of a theory's basic postulates and the theorems that can be deduced from them are valid in the theory's intended universe. Understanding of the theory and the data that one possesses determine what kind of questions about social reality one can answer in a theory-data confrontation. With the first and third point I rule out of court the instrumentalistic view of economic theories expounded by Friedman (1953). With the second and third point I distance my view from the idea that the theorems of an economic theory are tendency laws in the sense Mill (1836) gave to this term.

6.2 MAX WEBER AND HIS IDEAL TYPES

For all I know, Max Weber probably endorsed many parts of John Stuart Mill's political economy and Alfred Marshall's (1890) economics. However, his ideas as to the purport of an economic theory differed markedly from theirs. So did his vision of the role theory should play in a social science search for knowledge about concrete reality.

Weber (1949) insisted that the only social science in which he was interested was an empirical science of concrete reality. Such a science should help him understand the relationships and cultural significance of individual events in their contemporary manifestations and should also help him trace the causes of their being historically so and not otherwise (p. 72).

Establishing a science with such powers was problematic for many reasons. Life seemed to evolve in an infinite multiplicity of successively and coexistently emerging and disappearing events. Moreover, social scientists were at odds about the proper aims of their science. Finally, the available data were mostly historical and qualitative, and the extraordinary development of econometrics during the last half of the twentieth century was not in sight.

The existence of an infinite multiplicity of events in concrete reality led Weber to believe that a presuppositionless social science made no sense. To cope with the infinity of events and to provide a reasonable foundation for his science he proposed several "suppositions" with which he hoped social scientists would agree.

One of Weber's suppositions concerned the makeup of a social science empirical reality. His social science was to be a science that analyzed the phenomena of life in terms of their *cultural significance.* As culture is a value concept, the significance of a configuration of cultural events presupposes a value orientation toward these events. Therefore, in Weber's social science, empirical reality included only those segments of concrete reality that had become significant because of their value relevance (p. 76).

A second supposition concerned the possibility of obtaining knowledge about the essential characteristics of empirical reality. Specifically, Weber supposed that, at any given point in time, only a finite portion of concrete reality is important in the sense of being worthy of being known. Thus, empirical reality is a finite structure that evolves in indefinite ways over time (p. 78).

Weber also tried to refocus his fellow scientists' views of the aims of social science. Many of them believed that the best way to gain knowledge about reality was to search for pertinent "laws." Some of them thought that they could find such laws by generalized induction over recurrent sequences of historical events and by studying the characteristics and interrelationships of psychic factors that underlie complicated social phenomena. Others were convinced that they could find such laws by combining knowledge of recurrent historical events with the laws of economics. Weber insisted that they were all wrong.

In Weber's view, his fellow scientists were wrong because the cultural significance of an event cannot be deduced from empirical laws. He also insisted that their way of searching for such laws was misguided. Concrete reality cannot be deduced from knowledge of psychic factors. Such hypothetical factors might, at best, create cultural phenomena that are historically significant.

Moreover, economic "laws" are not laws in the precise natural science sense. They are rules that, with the application of the logical category "objective possibility," might, at best, express adequate causal relationships among culturally significant phenomena. Finally, the social laws that recurrent historical events determine do not constitute knowledge of concrete reality. "Knowledge of *cultural* events is inconceivable except on a basis of the *significance* which the concrete constellations of reality have for us in certain *individual* concrete situations" (p. 80).

In spite of the preceding contention, Weber considered the search for empirical laws to be a useful endeavor for social scientists on the grounds that such laws constitute an invaluable aid in finding causes that can be imputed to essential features of culturally significant events. Here the emphasis is on "imputation." "Where the individuality of a phenomenon is concerned, the question of causality is not a question of laws but of concrete causal relationships; it is not a question of the subsumption of the event under some general rubric as a representative case but of its imputation as a consequence of some constellation" (pp. 78–79).

Given the state of the art in econometrics and the kind of data that were available, Weber's vision of an empirical social science was of a science in which most empirical studies would consist of qualitative historical analyses. In such analyses the scientists were to search for significant cultural relationships that they thought were objectively possible and adequate from a nomological point of view. In each case the success of their endeavor would depend on their knowledge of historical regularities and well- established theoretical "laws" and on their ability to develop relevant ideal-typical concepts.

Ideal-typical concepts play an important role in the search for significant cultural relationships. Here an "ideal-type concept" is one that "is formed by the one-sided *accentuation* of one or more points of view and by the synthesis of a great many diffuse, discrete, more-or-less present and occasionally absent *concrete individual* phenomena, which are arranged according to those one-sidedly emphasized viewpoints into a unified *analytical* construct." As such, an ideal type is not to be viewed as a hypothesis. It only offers guidance to the construction of hypotheses. Moreover, an ideal type is not to be viewed as a description of reality. It is only designed to give unambiguous means of expression to such a description. In its purity, an ideal type cannot be found empirically anywhere in reality. It is *utopia* (pp. 43, 90).

It is far from obvious why ideal-typical concepts are required for the development of social science, so a few comments in that regard are in order.

Historical studies are replete with concepts such as "individualism," "feudalism," "mercantilism," and "Christianity." For the kind of studies Weber had in mind, it made no sense to define these concepts in accordance with the scheme of *genus proximum* and *differentia specifica.*[1] A descriptive analysis of such concepts into their components either did not exist or was illusory because it left unanswered which of these elements were essential in the historically unique configuration under study. In Weber's kind of historical studies such concepts required a genetic definition, and genetic definitions give ideal-type explications of the concepts in question.

E 6.1 *According to the 1982 Second College Edition of* The American Heritage Dictionary, *"Christianity" can be one of three things: the Christian religion that is founded on the teachings of Jesus, Christians as a group, or the state or fact of being a Christian. In Weber's historical studies of the Christianity of the Middle Ages, Christianity is a fusion of the Christianity of the people living in the Middle Ages and the Christian elements that one finds in the institutions of the Middle Ages. From that point of view, the genetic definition of "Christianity" delineates a fusion of a combination of articles of faith, norms from church law and custom, maxims of conduct, and countless concrete interrelationships (p. 96).*

Ideal types do not just appear as abstract concepts of stable relationships in historically individual complexes in which developments occur. Developmental sequences can also be conceived as ideal types to be used in counterfactual analyses of the cultural significance of historical events. Such ideal types abstract from concrete reality essential characteristics of a historical development that historians, from a certain point of view, can use to impute causes to a past or present event as the case may be.

E 6.2 *Consider the year 490 B.C. and the Battle of Marathon between Persia and Athens. According to a distinguished historian, Eduard Meyer (1900), the outcome of the battle was to decide among two objectively possible and causally adequate consequences. One represented a theocratic-religious culture under the aegis of a Persian protectorate. The other envisioned the triumph of a free Hellenic circle of ideas that were to provide those cultural values from which Western civilization still draws sustenance. The objective possibility and adequacy of the first consequence stemmed from Meyer's knowledge of how in other cases victorious Persians had used the religion of conquered nations as an instrument of domination. The objective possibility and causal adequacy of the second consequence stemmed both from his belief that an Athenian victory was essential for the subsequent construction of the Attic fleet and the happy end of the war of liberation and from his knowledge of the actual subsequent course of history (pp. 171–175).*

In commenting on Meyer's view of the Battle of Marathon, Weber insists that the two outcomes of the battle with their objectively possible and causally adequate consequences are the only reasons for any interest in the battle. Without such an appraisal of the possible outcomes a statement regarding the battle's significance would be impossible. In fact, without Meyer's appraisal, "there would . . . be no reason why we should not rate that decisive contest equally with a scuffle between two tribes of Kaffirs or Indians . . . (p. 172).

The main function of ideal types is to help analyze historically unique configurations by means of genetic concepts. Whether they can do that successfully cannot be determined by a priori means alone. In each case, it depends on whether the concepts exhibit the essence of the interdependencies, causal conditions, and significance of existing concrete cultural phenomena. Weber believed that if his presuppositions were valid, judicious constructions of ideal types would serve their purpose successfully. If he is right, it is very interesting for empirical work in the social sciences because the success of ideal-type concepts that he envisioned for them does not make them less abstract. We see next how these concepts fare in economics.

Weber insisted that it is an essential characteristic of social-economic phenomena that physical existence and the satisfaction of human needs everywhere confront quantitative limits and qualitative inadequacies of external means. Solving the associated social-economic problems requires planful provision and work, struggle with nature, and the association of human beings (p. 64).

Many of the social-economic phenomena that Weber had in mind pertain to economics proper, for example, commodity markets, commercial banks, and the state. They are economically significant either because of their constitutive role in the material struggle for existence or because of their existence having consequences that are interesting from an economic point of view. It is the task of economic theory to throw light on the ramifications of problems that are associated with economic phenomena.

According to Weber, economic theory is an axiomatic discipline that utilizes exclusively "ideal types" such as Mill's "economic man" and Marshall's "representative firm." It assumes the dominance of economic interests and leaves out of account political and other noneconomic considerations. It also, supposedly, bases its arguments on assumptions concerning the environment that are never quite right and tries to determine what rational actors would do under such conditions (pp. 42–43).

E 6.3 *Consider the exchange economy in economic theory. It offers an ideal picture of a society's commodity market organized according to the principles of free competition and rigorously rational conduct. This construct is like a utopia that has been arrived at by the analytical accentuation of certain elements of reality. Its relationship to the empirical data consists solely in the following fact: "Where market-conditioned relationships of the type referred to by the abstract construct are discovered or suspected to exist in reality to some extent, we can make the characteristic* features of this relationship pragmatically clear and *understandable* by reference to an *ideal type*" (p. 90).

Many of the ideas on which Weber bases his economic methodology have counterparts among those that I try to convey in the first few chapters of this book. Both the differences and the similarities are relevant here, and I comment on those that concern the domain and promise of economics, the formal characteristics of economic theories, and the purport of such theories.

According to Weber, economics is a science of "concrete reality" that studies the interrelationships, "causal conditions," and significance of "cultural" phenomena. Moreover, the success of such a science hinges on the presupposition that only a finite segment of infinite concrete reality is culturally significant in the sense of being worth knowing. My economists study, for the most part, interesting economic phenomena in the social reality I described in Chapter 2. Their success hinges on the validity in the social world W_S of Mill's axiom of the uniformity of nature, PUN, and Keynes's principle of the limited variability of nature, PLVN. Since Weber does not say what he means by "concrete reality," "culture," and "causal conditions," his ideas of the domain of economics and of economists' chances of success in their endeavors do not seem to differ much from mine.

Weber's notion of an economic theory does not seem to differ much from my notion of such a theory either. We agree that economics is an "axiomatic discipline." However, since Weber does not explain what he means by an axiomatic discipline, we might disagree on the meaning of that term. Weber insists that pure economic theory in its analysis of past and present phenomena uses ideal-type utopian concepts exclusively. I agree that an economic theory—be it an axiomatized theory or a family of models of a few assertions concerning an economic event—is utopian in Weber's sense of the term. I also agree that it is likely that most economists in the process of developing a theory have ideal-type concepts in mind. However, once a theorist has formulated his theory, that theory takes on a life of its own that is independent of the ideal-type with which he might have started out.

There is an important difference in Weber's and my ideas of the purport of an economic theory. An ideal-type concept is formed by the synthesis of many diffuse, discrete, more-or-less present, and occasionally absent concrete individual phenomena. Thus Weber's ideal types comprise both positive and negative analogies of the kind of events or phenomena to which they apply. In contrast, I consider that an economic theory delineates only positive analogies of the kind of events or phenomena that the originator of the theory had in mind. The negative analogies will only enter upon my stage when I search for the theory's empirical relevance.[2]

6.3 KEYNES AND THE SEMANTIC VIEW OF THEORIES

In a letter to Roy Harrod, Keynes insisted that economics was a branch of logic, a way of thinking. More specifically, he thought that economics was a science of thinking in terms of models joined to the art of choosing models that are relevant to the contemporary world. One could make worthwhile progress merely by using axioms and maxims. However, one could not get very far except by devising new and improved models (Keynes, 1938).

It is not easy from a short letter alone to determine Keynes's views about the purport of economic theories. However, his letter to Harrod and the way he argued in his *General Theory* suggest that Keynes's prescription for theorizing in economics was semantic: Formulate, explicitly or implicitly, a few assertions about the pertinent subject matter and proceed to develop models of these assertions that are relevant to the purpose at hand.

6.3.1 Macroeconomics à la Keynes

John Maynard Keynes's *General Theory of Employment, Interest and Money* introduced macroeconomics to economic theory. As such the work marks a singular event in the history of economic science. It also stands as an extraordinary example of an economic theory that the author has developed in accordance with the semantic view of theories. I subsequently show why this is so.[3]

Keynes's theory is about how a closed economy without taxes and government expenditures determines its equilibrium levels of "national income" Y and "aggregate employment" L. Here Y equals the sum total of income that accrues to the factors of production plus the sum of all profits that the firms in the economy earn and L denotes the total number of units of labor employed in the economy. Keynes suggested that Y be measured in "wage-units" and L in "labor-units." A wage-unit was to equal the money-wage of a labor-unit and a labor-unit was synonymous with an hour's employment of ordinary labor. An hour of special labor that was remunerated at twice the ordinary rate would count as two labor-units (Keynes, 1936, p. 41).

Keynes began by insisting on the validity of several assertions concerning the values that pertinent variables assume during a given period of unspecified length:

1. The aggregate net "final output" of the economy consists of consumer goods C and net additions to the nation's stock of capital I. This final output is measured in the same units as Y, for example, wage-units, and $C + I = Y$ (pp. 29, 61–65).
2. For each value of $C + I$ there is a minimum number of labor units that can produce it with the existing stock of capital. The relation between this minimal value of L and the value of $C + I$ can be represented by a function $f(\cdot) : R_+ \to R_+$ that is an increasing function of L (p. 25).
3. For each value of Y and for each value of the price level P, there is a maximum number of labor-units that the economy's entrepreneurs find it worth their while to employ. The relationship between this maximal value

of L, P, and Y can be represented by a function $\phi(\cdot) : R_+ \times R_{++} \to R_+$ that is an increasing function of L and P (pp. 24–25).[4]

4. For given values of P, the equilibrium values of Y and L are solutions to the equations (i) $Y = f(L)$ and (ii) $Y = \phi(L, P)$.

Keynes referred to $f(\cdot)$ as the *aggregate demand function* for L and called $\phi(\cdot)$ *the aggregate supply function.* As he did not include P as an argument of $\phi(\cdot)$, a remark in that regard is called for. In Keynes's theory, as I understand it, unions and firms bargained to determine the wage-unit at the beginning of the period in which he sought equilibrium values for Y and L (pp. 13, 247). Hence, decisions concerning the wage-unit were made long before anybody knew the value of L at which the aggregate demand function would intersect the aggregate supply function. The process of finding equilibrium values of Y and L might involve adjustments in both prices and nominal wage rates (p. 25). To account for such changes, I have included P as an argument of $\phi(\cdot)$.

Most of the *General Theory* is about the way consumers and firms determine the values of C and I. Keynes thought that the value of C depended on the consumers' propensity to consume out of current income. Further, the value of I depended on the interest rate and the marginal efficiency of capital, and the interest rate depended on the economy's stock of money and consumers' and firms' liquidity preference. Here the meanings of the propensity to consume, the marginal efficiency of capital, and the liquidity preference are as I describe them in what follows.

Keynes believed that "men [were] disposed, as a rule and on the average, to increase their consumption as their income increases, but not by as much as the increase in their income" (p. 96). From this belief he inferred the validity of assertion 5.

5. Consumers' propensity to consume is a function, $\chi(\cdot) : R_+ \to R_+$ that delineates the relationship between national income and aggregate consumption (p. 90). The term $\chi(\cdot)$ is an increasing function of Y, and changes in Y always result in less than proportionate changes in the value of $\chi(\cdot)$; that is, for all values of Y, $\Delta\chi(Y)/\Delta Y < 1$ (p. 96).

The marginal efficiency of capital equals the rate of discount that will make the present value of the future yields on an additional dollar of investment equal to \$1. Keynes was convinced that firms were disposed to push their investments to the point where the marginal efficiency of capital equaled the interest rate (p. 136). From this conviction he inferred the validity of assertion 6.

6. The aggregate amount of investments is a function $I(\cdot) : R^2_{++} \to R_+$ that is a decreasing function of the interest rate and an increasing function of the price level (pp. 136–137).

I have included P in the investment function to emphasize that in Keynes's theory it is mainly through the marginal efficiency of capital that "the expectation of the future influences the present" (p. 145). The current value of P carries information about future prices, and expectations of future price movements will influence the marginal efficiency of a given stock of capital (pp. 142–143).

Keynes believed that the amount of loanable funds that firms and consumers want to keep in liquid assets depended on their liquidity preference, their income, and the going rate of interest. On that basis he insisted on the validity of assertion 7.

7. The aggregate demand for liquid assets is a function $M(\cdot) : R_{++} \times R_{+} \rightarrow R_{+}$ that is a decreasing function of the interest rate and an increasing function of national income (pp. 166–172).

Keynes's macroeconomic theory is a family of models of the seven assertions that I have just listed. When understood in this way, his theory becomes a family of models of equations that determine an economy's equilibrium levels of national income and aggregate employment. With r denoting the interest rate and M^s the economy's stock of money, the pertinent equations can be formulated as follows:

$$Y = C + I \tag{1}$$

$$C = \chi(Y) \tag{2}$$

$$I = I(r, P) \tag{3}$$

$$M = M(r, Y) \tag{4}$$

$$M = M^s \tag{5}$$

$$Y = f(L) \tag{6}$$

$$Y = \phi(L, P), \tag{7}$$

where $(Y, C, I, M, L) \in R^5_{+}$, $(r, P) \in R^2_{++}$, and $\chi(\cdot)$, $\phi(\cdot)$, $I(\cdot)$, $M(\cdot)$, and $f(\cdot)$, respectively, have the properties ascribed to them in assertions 5, 3, 6, 7, and 2.

Equations (1)–(7) are consistent. To show why, I delineate a simple family of models of these equations and demonstrate that a member of this family has an equilibrium:

$$\chi(Y) = a + bY, \text{ with } 0 < b < 1,$$

$$I(r, P) = dP - er,$$

$$M(r, Y) = g - hr + kY, \text{ with } 0 < k < 1,$$

$$M^s > 0,$$

$$f(L) = L^{1/2},$$

and

$$\phi(L, P) = [\max\{0, P(L - t)\}]^2,$$

where a, d, e, g, h, and t are appropriately chosen positive constants. When $a = 10, b = 0.8, d = 20, e = 1{,}000, g = 100, h = 2{,}000, k = 0.2, M^s = 100$, and $t = 9{,}990$, the equilibrium values of Y and L are, respectively, 100 and 10,000. The corresponding value of the vector (P, r, C, I) is (1, 0.01, 90, 10).

Keynes did not specify an intended family of models of his basic assertions in mathematical terms. However, he spent much time discussing properties that the functions $\chi(\cdot)$, $I(\cdot)$, $M(\cdot)$, $f(\cdot)$, and $\phi(\cdot)$ must possess. I listed some of these properties in assertions 2–7 and detail a few others later.

Keynes believed that it was "an outstanding characteristic of the economic system in which we live that, whilst it is subject to severe fluctuations in respect of output and employment, it is not violently unstable" (p. 249). In order that his model economy be stable, he imposed conditions on $\chi(\cdot)$, $I(\cdot)$, and $M(\cdot)$ that are of interest here.

First $\chi(\cdot)$: To ensure stability of his model economy, Keynes thought it necessary that the multiplier that related changes in investment to changes in national income be "greater than unity but not very large." What he meant by "not very large" is uncertain. Most estimates of the marginal propensity to consume of which I am aware have been larger than 0.8. If a multiplier greater than five is "large," it is possible that Keynes would have objected to a linear version of $\chi(\cdot)$.

Next $I(\cdot)$: Keynes also thought that his model system would be stable only if "moderate changes in the prospective yield of capital or in the interest rate [would] not be associated with very great changes in the rate of investment" (p. 250). In different words, he suggested that the relevant values of the interest elasticity of the demand for investment, $(r/I)dI/dr$, must be low. This suggests that he would have objected to a linear investment demand function.

Finally $M(\cdot)$: Keynes envisioned three motives for holding liquid funds: the transactions motive, the precautionary motive, and the speculative motive. He worried that there might be a value of r for each value of Y at which the speculative and precautionary motives would lead most firms and consumers to keep their loanable funds liquid rather than invest them in bonds or other money market instruments. He thought that for an economic system to be stable it is essential that there always "exists a variety of opinion about what is uncertain" (p.172). The variety of opinions, supposedly, would reduce the system's sensitivity to changes in the rate of interest. I believe that Keynes would have objected to a linear version of $M(\cdot)$ for the United States since there "everyone tends to hold the same opinion at the same time" (p. 172).

Keynes reiterated time and again that the wage bargains between entrepreneurs and workers did not determine the real wage. There simply was no way "by which labour as a whole [could] reduce its *real* wage to a given figure by making revised *money* bargains with the entrepreneurs" (p. 15). The equilibrium level of the real wage was determined by the value of L at which $f(L)$ and $\phi(L, P)$ were equal with the proviso that this level of L could not be larger than the full-employment value of L. In different words, the real wage at the equilibrium value of L had to be at least as large as the marginal disutility of labor.

Keynes did not elaborate on how the marginal disutility of labor was to be determined. Still, one thing is certain. Any model of Eqs. (1)–(7) that he would have found acceptable would have to have an equilibrium value of L at which the real wage was above or equal to the marginal disutility of labor. That alone might rule out $\surd(\cdot)$ as a functional form for $f(\cdot)$.

My comments concerning the equilibrium level of L and the properties of $\chi(\cdot)$, $I(\cdot)$, and $M(\cdot)$ suggest that the family of models of Eqs. (1)–(7) that I described earlier would not have been acceptable to Keynes. However, it serves no purpose in this chapter to try to formulate a more acceptable family of models. The only thing that is important here is to see clearly the intent and purport of his theorizing about a macro economy.

6.3.2 The Purport of the General Theory

In his *General Theory* Keynes did not formulate a theory that was to describe the actual workings of a given economy. Instead, he searched for an understanding of one particular aspect of the functioning of an economy on the national level: What determines the equilibrium values of the economy's national income and aggregate employment? (p. 247) For that purpose he singled out five characteristic features of an economic system: the aggregate demand function, the aggregate supply function, consumers' propensity to consume, the marginal efficiency of capital, and the liquidity preference schedule. He ascribed properties to them that, presumably, were positive analogies for the group of economies about which he was theorizing. Moreover, the five of them sufficed to determine the sought for equilibrium values of Y and L.

Keynes suggested that one think of Y, C, I, and M as so many wage-units and measure L in labor-units. He also gave meaningful names to his variables and argued in interesting ways about the possible comparative-statics properties of his economic system. All of this notwithstanding, careful reading of the *General Theory* reveals that Keynes's theory is a theory about symbols and nothing else. Its empirical relevance cannot be established by a priori means. It must be tested in a well-designed theory-data confrontation.

6.4 TWO AXIOMATIZED ECONOMIC THEORIES

There is one feature that sets axiomatized theories apart from theories that have been developed in accordance with the semantic view of theories. Their basic assertions constitute complete systems of axioms from which the theorems of the pertinent theories can be derived. Except for that, the purport of axiomatized theories is similar to that of theories that have been developed by model-theoretic arguments.

In this section of the chapter I discuss the purports of two very different axiomatized economic theories. One of the theories concerns economic growth. It is simple and elegant, caught the imagination of young theoreticians early on, and resulted in two decades of search for interesting extensions and imaginative theorems in mathematical economics.[5] For us it raises intriguing questions about the nature of the positive analogies of economic growth that it exhibits.

The other theory concerns choice under uncertainty. It is mathematically involved and contains interesting theorems that imply that in a world in which current prices carry information about future prices, long heralded truths such as Houthakker's strong axiom of revealed preference, Samuelson's fundamental theorem of consumer choice, and the noncomparability of competitive equilibria are not valid. The theory was launched in Stigum (1969). It did not catch the imagination of young economists, and it has not led to a search for interesting extensions and imaginative new theorems. In fact, its contrary theorems notwithstanding, those engaged in developing the positive heuristics of the scientific research program on consumer choice and competitive equilibria have ignored it.

The disregard of the second theory must stand as a startling example of an attitude that Lakatos (1978, pp. 50, 52) thought permeated scientific research programs: scientists ignoring counterexamples in the hope that they will turn in due course into corroboration of the program.

6.4.1 Robert Solow's Theory of Economic Growth

Robert Solow (1956) suggested that the growth of an economy can be characterized by a simple axiomatic system, and in the following I formalize the discrete-time version of that system.

Solow's theory concerns five undefined terms, *net national product, consumption, investment, capital,* and *labor*, which satisfy eight axioms with $T = \{0, 1, \ldots\}$.

S 1 Net national product *is a function* $Y(\cdot) : T \to R_+$.

S 2 Consumption *is a function* $c(\cdot) : T \to R_+$.

S 3 Investment *is a function* $I(\cdot) : T \to R_+$.

S 4 Capital *is a function* $K(\cdot) : T \to R_+$.

S 5 Labor *is a function* $L(\cdot) : T \to R_+$.

S 6 *For each* $t \in T$, $y(t) = c(t) + I(t)$. *Also, there is an* $s \in (0, 1)$ *such that* $c(t) = (1 - s)y(t)$.

S 7 *For each* $t \in T$, $K(t+1) - K(t) = I(t)$. *There also exists a constant* $\lambda \in (1, \infty)$ *such that* $L(t+1) = \lambda L(t)$.

S 8 *There is a function* $F(\cdot) : R^2_+ \to R_+$ *such that, for all* $t \in T$, $y(t) = F[L(t), K(t)]$. $F(\cdot)$ *is differentiable, nondecreasing, strictly quasi-concave, linearly homogeneous, and strictly increasing on* R^2_{++}. *Also,* $\lambda - 1 > sF(0, 1)$.

The axioms S 1–S 8 are consistent. I obtain a model of them by letting $F(L, K) = L^{1/2}K^{1/2}$, by choosing s and λ such that that $s \in (0, 1)$ and $\lambda \in (1, \infty)$, and by assigning arbitrary positive values to $L(0)$ and $K(0)$.

A consistent theory can be used to discuss many different matters. In the intended interpretation of Solow's axioms, the members of T represent time periods and the properties of the vector-valued function $(y, c, I, K, L)(\cdot) : T \to R^5_+$ portray characteristic features of the growth of an economy at the national level. In this scenario, $y(t)$, $c(t)$, and $I(t)$, respectively, represent the economy's net national product, aggregate consumption, and aggregate net investment in period t; $K(t)$ and $L(t)$, respectively, represent the economy's aggregate stock of capital and labor force at the beginning of period t; and finally, $F(\cdot)$ stands for the economy's aggregate production function, $(\lambda - 1)$ is the rate of growth of the labor force, and $(1 - s)y(t)$ equals, in Keynes's terminology, the consumers' propensity to consume in period t.

In comparing the theories of Solow and Keynes it is important to note the different perspectives from which the two theorists viewed their economic systems. Keynes set out to characterize, *for a given period*, the way an economy's equilibrium levels of national income and aggregate employment are determined. Solow was trying to characterize *the behavior over time* of Keynes's two variables. For that purpose, Solow insisted on Keynes's accounting relationship among y, c, and I, that is, $y = c + I$. He also adopted a simple form of Keynes's consumption function $\chi(y) = (1 - s)y$ and postulated a deterministic growth rate for the nation's labor force. Solow found the justification for his choice of consumption function and labor growth rate in published time-series data on (c/y) and L.

There is one particularly interesting aspect of the two theories that should not go unnoticed. Keynes's theory is about the determination of equilibrium flows of aggregate output and labor, whereas Solow's is about equilibrium flows of output, equilibrium stocks of capital and labor, and the relationship between stocks and flows. In each period in Solow's model the demand and supply for output (flows) are equal. Hence, there is a flow equilibrium. Moreover, in each period the demand for stocks of capital and labor is equal to the supply of capital and labor. Hence there is a stock equilibrium. However, the relationship between stocks and flows need not be one of equilibrium. In fact, stocks and flows cannot be in equilibrium vis-à-vis each other unless the economy travels along a balanced growth path.

In theorem T 1 I show for Solow's economy that if flows and stocks are not in equilibrium vis-à-vis each other, there is an inexorable force that moves them closer to an equilibrium configuration in each period.

T 1 *Suppose that* L(0) > 0 *and* K(0) > 0. *Then there exist a vector* $V \in R^2_{++}$ *and a continuous increasing function* $\gamma(\cdot) : R_+ \rightarrow R_+$ *such that*

$$(\lambda - 1)V_2 = sF(V),$$

$$\lim_{t\to\infty} [(L(t), K(t))/\lambda^t] = \gamma[L(0)]V,$$

and

$$\lim_{t\to\infty} y(t)/\lambda^t = \gamma[L(0)]F(V).$$

It might not be obvious that the asymptotic state to which T 1 refers is a state in which the flows and stocks are in equilibrium vis-à-vis each other. To make sure that they are, let us see what happens if $[L(0), K(0)] = aV$ for some positive constant a and the vector $V = (V_1, V_2)$ on whose existence T 1 insists. Then it is easy to verify that for all $t > 0$,

$$c(t)/y(t) = (1 - s), I(t)/y(t) = s,$$

$$L(t)/K(t) = V_1/V_2,$$

$$y(t)/L(t) = F(1, V_2/V_1),$$

and

$$y(t)/K(t) = F(V_1/V_2, 1).$$

Hence, along the given path there is a flow equilibrium, a stock equilibrium, and an equilibrium configuration of stocks and flows.

Solow did not say whether his theory applied to an uncertainty economy as well as to a certainty economy. I have my doubts about the empirical relevance of two of his equations for an economy that functions in an uncertain environment. One determines the growth of the labor force, and the other determines the growth of the stock of capital:

$$L(t + 1) = \lambda L(t), t \in T,$$

and

$$K(t + 1) = K(t) + sF[L(t), K(t)], t \in T.$$

I find the first suspect because the size of the labor force in period $t + 1$ depends on both the size and the composition of the labor force in period t. The composition of the labor force in period t will depend on many past random events. Hence, the best for which one can hope is that the labor equation holds on the average in the sense that

$$E\{L(t+1)|L(t), \ldots, L(0)\} = \lambda L(t) \text{ w. pr. 1.}$$

where $E\{A|B\}$ designates the conditional expectation of A for a given value of B, and w. pr. 1 is short for "with probability one."

I consider the second equation suspect because the propensity to consume is probably misspecified for an uncertainty economy. Solow's propensity to consume might be valid in the long run in the sense that over time consumers tend to spend a constant proportion of their disposable income on consumer goods. However, it is likely to be a poor assumption in the short run for an uncertainty economy. If that is so, the best one can hope for is that the second equation holds on the average in the sense that

$$E\{K(t+1)|[L(t), K(t)], \ldots, [L(0), K(0)]\} = K(t) + sF[L(t), K(t)] \text{ w. pr. 1.}$$

If my reasons for having qualms about the two equations that determine the growth of capital and the labor force are legitimate, it becomes interesting to check whether Solow's main result, theorem T 1, is valid even if the relations that the two equations depict hold only on the average. In a paper on growth under uncertainty, Harry Kesten and I established conditions on the probability distributions of the $[L(t), K(t)]$ that will ensure the possibility of balanced growth in an uncertainty version of Solow's economy theory in which the two equations hold only on the average. Specifically, we established the existence of a random variable g that conditional upon the value of $[L(0), K(0)] \in R^2_{++}$ has a positive, finite mean and satisfies the relation,

$$\lim_{t\to\infty} [(L(t), K(t))/\lambda^t] = gV \text{ w. pr. 1,}$$

where V is as described in T 1. The proof is involved, so I refer the interested reader to Kesten and Stigum (1974) for the details.

The preceding observations leave us with an interesting question. What is the correct interpretation of the positive analogies of economic growth that Solow's theory identifies? As I understand him, Solow takes for granted that the right way to view economic growth is to think of it as a deterministic process. If he is right, the positive analogies that his theory identifies are characteristic features of the behavior over time of the kind of economic system Keynes was considering. I believe that economic growth is essentially stochastic. If that is so, and if the probability distributions of Solow's variables satisfy the strictures that Kesten and I imposed on them, then the positive analogies that Solow's theory identifies become characteristic features of the probability distributions of stochastic processes that govern the behavior over time of the kind of economies Solow was considering.

It is relevant here that most macroeconomists today view the behavior over time of an economy as the realization of a stochastic process. In their theories they search for characteristics of the pertinent probability distributions that are positive analogies for the kind of economic systems they are considering. It is also relevant that economists today tend to view the behavior over time of markets as realizations of random processes. In their theories they search for characteristics of the pertinent probability distributions that are positive analogies for the kind of markets they are considering. Chapters 21 and 23 provide ample evidence of the usefulness of such studies.

6.4.2 Consumer Choice under Uncertainty

The theory of consumer choice under uncertainty in what follows is a streamlined version of the theory that I developed in *Toward a Formal Science of Economics* (Stigum, 1990, pp. 795–804).[6] Its axioms are involved. Hence, for brevity's sake, I deal here only with the basic ones.

6.4.2.1 The Basic Axioms and Their Potential Models

My theory of consumer choice under uncertainty concerns seven undefined terms: *the world*, a *commodity bundle*, a *security*, a *price system*, a *consumer*, an *expenditure sequence*, and a *consumption-investment strategy*. There are seven basic axioms.

CBS 1 *The* world *is a pair* $(\Omega, \aleph)$, *where* Ω *is a set that contains all states of the world and nothing else, and* $\aleph$ *is a* σ*-field of subsets of* Ω.

CBS 2 *A* commodity bundle *is a vector* $x \in \cup_{i=1}^{M}(R_+^n \times R_+)^i$. *When* $x \in (R_+^n \times R_+)^i$, *I often write* x *as an* i*-tuple of pairs* $[(q, L)(1), \ldots, (q, L)(i)]$, *where* $q \in R_+^n$ *is a commodity vector,* $L \in R_+$ *denotes units of labor, and* $(q, L)(j)$ *is a commodity-service vector for period* $j, j = 1, \ldots, i$.

CBS 3 *A* security *is a* $\mu \in R$.

CBS 4 *Let* $T = \{1, 2, \ldots\}$. *Then a* price system *is a vector-valued function* $(p, w, \alpha)(\cdot) : T \times \Omega \to R_{++}^n \times R_{++} \times R_{++}$. *Also, for all* $t \in T$, $\aleph[(p, w, \alpha)(t)] \subset \aleph$, *where* $\aleph[(p, w, \alpha)(t)]$ *is the* σ*-field generated by* $(p, w, \alpha)(t, \cdot)$.

CBS 5 *A* consumer *is a six-tuple* $[Z, V, A, Q, \xi, (N_L, N_\mu)]$, *where:*

- *(i)* $Z = \cup_{i=1}^{M}[(R_+^n \times R_+)^i \times R])$.
- *(ii)* $V(\cdot) : Z \to R$.
- *(iii)* $A(\cdot) : \Omega \to R_{++}$ *and* $\aleph(A) \subset \aleph$.
- *(iv)* $Q(\cdot) : \aleph \to [0, 1]$ *is a* σ*-additive probability measure.*
- *(v)* $\xi(\cdot) : \Omega \to \{1, 2, \ldots, M\}$, *and* $\aleph(\xi) \subset \aleph$.
- *(vi)* $(N_L, N_\mu)(\cdot) : T \times \Omega \to R_{++}^2$, *and for all* $t \in T$, $\aleph[(N_L, N_\mu)(t)] \subset \aleph$.

CBS 6 *An* expenditure sequence *is a vector-valued function* $(q, L, \mu)(\cdot) : \{1, 2, \ldots, M\} \times \Omega \to R_+^n \times R_+ \times R$ *that for all* $t \in \{1, 2, \ldots, M\}$ *satisfies the following conditions:*

(i) $\aleph[(q, L, \mu)(t)] \subset \aleph[A, (p, w, \alpha, N_L, N_\mu)(s), 1 \le s \le t, I_{\ge t}(\xi)]$,

where $I_{\ge t}(\xi)$ is a random variable that assumes the values 1 or 0 according as $\xi \ge t$ or $\xi < t$.

(ii) *On the set* $\{\omega \in \Omega : \xi(\omega) \le t\}$, $(q, L, \mu)(s, \omega) = 0$ *for* $s = t + 1, \ldots, M$.

(iii) *On the set* $\{\omega \in \Omega : \xi(\omega) = t\}$, *the following conditions hold:*

(a) $p(1, \omega)q(1, \omega) + \alpha(1, \omega)\mu(1, \omega) \le A(\omega) + w(1, \omega)L(1, \omega)$.

(b) $p(s, \omega)q(s, \omega) + \alpha(s, \omega)\mu(s, \omega) \le w(s, \omega)L(s, \omega) + \mu(s - 1, \omega)$ *for* $1 < s \le t$.

(c) $0 \le L(s, \omega) \le N_L(s, \omega)$ *and* $-N_\mu(s, \omega) \le \mu(s, \omega)$ *for* $1 \le s \le t$.

CBS 7 *For all* $i = 1, \ldots, M$, *let* $U_i(\cdot) : (R_+^n \times R_+)^i \times R \to R$ *be defined by* $U_i(x, y) = V(x, y)$, *for* $x \in (R_+^n \times R_+)^i$ *and* $y \in R$. *A* consumption-investment strategy *is an expenditure sequence* $(q, L, \mu)(\cdot)$, *such that if* $(q^*, L^*, \mu^*)(\cdot)$ *is any other expenditure sequence, then*

$$\begin{aligned}
&\sum_{\xi=1}^{M} E\left\{U_\xi\Big[(q, L)(1, \omega), \ldots, (q, L)(\xi, \omega), \mu(\xi, \omega)\Big]\Big|A, (p, w, \alpha, N_L, N_\mu)(1), \xi(\omega) = \xi\right\} \\
&\qquad \times Q\Big[\{\omega \in \Omega : \xi(\omega) = \xi\}\Big|A, (p, w, \alpha, N_L, N_\mu)(1)\Big] \\
&\ge \sum_{\xi=1}^{M} E\left\{U_\xi\left[(q^*, L^*)(1, \omega), \ldots, (q^*, L^*)(\xi, \omega), \mu^*(\xi, \omega)\right]\Big|A, (p, w, \alpha, N_L, N_\mu)(1), \xi(\omega) = \xi\right\} \\
&\qquad \times Q\Big[\{\omega \in \Omega : \xi(\omega) = \xi\}\Big|A, (p, w, \alpha, N_L, N_\mu)(1)\Big]
\end{aligned}$$

The preceding axioms call for several comments concerning the intended interpretation of the undefined terms. In the intended interpretation of the axioms a commodity-service vector (q, L) is a vector in which the first n components denote so many units of various commodities and the last denotes so many units of labor. A security μ is a security each unit of which pays one unit of the next-period unit of account. Further, to each component of (q, L, μ) corresponds a component of the (price) vector (p, w, α) that records its price. Finally, a consumer is an individual living alone or a family with a common budget. The consumer orders sequences of commodity-service vectors and securities in accordance with the values of a utility function $V(\cdot)$, and he chooses a consumption-investment strategy from among all available expenditure sequences for each value of A and the price system.

In the intended interpretation of the axioms the consumer has well-defined price expectations; expectations concerning the institutional constraints (N_L, N_μ) that he will face; and ideas about when he will die, that is, the value of ξ. These expectations call for remarks concerning the state of nature, the state of the world, price expectations, and the nature of expenditure sequences.

First, the state of nature: A *state of nature* is a description of the environment as it was in the past, as it is in the present, and as it will be in the future. In the preceding axioms, the environment is represented by the triple

$[A, \xi, \{(N_L, N_\mu)(t, \omega); t \in T\}]$. Hence, in the intended interpretation of the axioms, a state of nature is a description of: (1) the consumer's initial claim on first-period units of account, $A(\omega)$; (2) the period in which the consumer will die, $\xi(\omega)$; and (3) the values of the institutional constraints $(N_L, N_\mu)(t, \omega)$ that the consumer will face in the labor and loan markets in period $t, t = 1, 2, \ldots$.

Next the world: A *state of the world* is an $\omega \in \Omega$. In the intended interpretation of the axioms, a state of the world is a complete description (i.e., one that leaves no relevant detail undescribed) of the world as it was in the past, as it is in the present, and as it will be in the future. It is assumed that the description of the world describes the state of nature and the values of prices in all relevant periods. However, the state of the world does not describe the actions of individual consumers in the economy.

Then *price expectations*: I presume that the consumer has expectations concerning what the price of any given commodity, service, or security might be in each period under every possible set of circumstances. Specifically, I assume that, for each t, there exists a vector-valued function $(p, w, \alpha)(t, \cdot) : \Omega \to R_{++}^{n+2}$, whose value at ω, $(p, w, \alpha)(t, \omega)$, represents the price that the consumer believes a commodity-service-and-security vector would assume in period t if the true state of the world were ω. Since I intend that the description of the world associated with ω is to specify the value of all prices in each and every period, the value of $(p, w, \alpha)(t, \cdot)$ at ω must necessarily coincide with the value of this price vector specified in the description of the world.

As suggested by the preceding remarks, in the intended interpretation of the axioms, the consumer's price expectations are point expectations with respect to the state of the world and multivalued with respect to the state of nature. Price expectations do not appear explicitly in my description of a "consumer." They appear by implication in the role of $Q(\cdot)$. In the intended interpretation of the axioms, $Q(\cdot)$ represents the consumer's subjective probability measure on $(\Omega, \aleph)$, and $Q(\cdot), A(\cdot), (p, w, \alpha, N_L, N_\mu)(t, \cdot), t = 1, 2, \ldots, M$, and $\xi(\cdot)$ determine the consumer's subjective probability distributions of the price system, the institutional constraints, and ξ.[7]

Finally, *expenditure sequences:* These sequences describe possible sequences of acquisitions of commodities and securities and supplies of labor that satisfy the consumer's budget constraint and are compatible with the consumer's information structure.

6.4.2.2 *An Example*

The following is an example to help the reader's intuition about the meaning of the axioms. Let $M = 3, Z = \cup_{i=1}^{3}(R_+^i \times R), \Omega = \{\omega_1, \ldots, \omega_8\}$, and $\aleph = \wp(\Omega)$, the family of all subsets of Ω. Then suppose that the consumer

TABLE 6.1
Prices and Constraints during a Life Cycle

ω	$(p, \alpha, N_\mu)(1, \cdot)$	$(p, \alpha, N_\mu)(2, \cdot)$	$(p, \alpha, N_\mu)(3, \cdot)$	$\xi(\cdot)$
ω_1	(1, 0.9, 10)	(1.1, 0.8, 12.5)	(1.2, 0.85, 15)	1
ω_2	(1, 0.9, 10)	(1.1, 0.8, 12.5)	(1, 0.9, 15)	1
ω_3	(1, 0.9, 10)	(1.1, 0.8, 12.5)	(1, 0.95, 15)	1
ω_4	(1, 0.9, 10)	(1.1, 0.9, 11.5)	(1.2, 0.9, 16)	2
ω_5	(1, 0.9, 10)	(1.1, 0.9, 11.5)	(1.2, 0.75, 16)	2
ω_6	(1, 0.9, 10)	(1.1, 0.9, 11.5)	(1.2, 0.75, 16)	3
ω_7	(1, 0.9, 10)	(0.905, 1, 12)	(0.85, 1.1, 14)	3
ω_8	(1, 0.9, 10)	(0.905, 1, 12)	(1, 0.95, 14)	3

does not work, that $A(\omega) = 50$ for all $\omega \in \Omega$, and that the ranges of $\xi(\cdot)$ and $(p, \alpha, N_\mu)(t, \cdot), t = 1, 2, 3$, are as specified in Table 6.1. Moreover, suppose that the $U_i(\cdot)$ in CBS 7 are given by

$$U_1(x, y) = (1 + x)^{1/8}(2.855 + y)^{3/8}, x \in R_+, y \geq -2.855,$$

$$U_2(x, y) = (1 + x_1)^{1/8}(1 + x_2)^{1/8}(1.95 + y)^{1/4}, x \in R_+^2, y \geq -1.95,$$

and

$$U_3(x, y) = (1 + x_1)^{1/8}(1 + x_2)^{1/8}(1 + x_3)^{1/8}(1 + y)^{1/8}, x \in R_+^3, y \geq -1.$$

There are four states of nature, $s_1 = \{\omega_1, \omega_2, \omega_3\}$, $s_2 = \{\omega_4, \omega_5\}$, $s_3 = \{\omega_6\}$, and $s_4 = \{\omega_7, \omega_8\}$. Moreover, the consumer faces the information structure shown in Fig. 6.1, where e_{ij} is an event that might occur in period $i, i = 1, 2, 3$. The probabilities that $Q(\cdot)$, the probability measure on $(\Omega, \aleph)$, assigns to the various states of the world are as listed in Table 6.2. Finally, the main characteristics of expenditure sequences are shown in the equations below, where I record the consumer's consumption-investment strategy:

$$(q, \mu)(1, \omega) = (12.392375, 41.78625) \text{ for all } \omega \in \Omega,$$

$$(q, \mu)(2, \omega) = \begin{cases} (15.442449, 27.810833) & \text{if } \omega \in e_{21}, \\ (12.527652, 31.117593) & \text{if } \omega \in e_{22}, \\ (0, 0) & \text{if } \omega \in e_{23}, \end{cases}$$

$$(q, \mu)(3, \omega) = \begin{cases} (13.880417, 14.663596) & \text{if } \omega \in e_{31}, \\ (16.506372, 12.527651) & \text{if } \omega \in e_{32}; \\ (12.778164, 21.045062) & \text{if } \omega \in e_{33}, \\ (0, 0) & \text{if } \omega \in e_{23} \cup e_{34}. \end{cases}$$

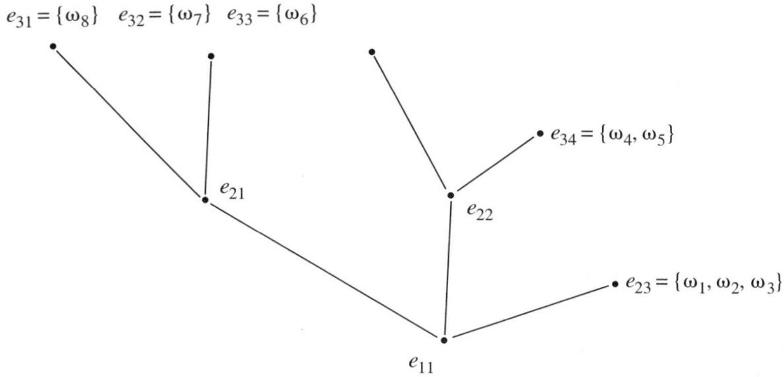

Fig. 6.1 A life-cycle information structure.

6.4.2.3 *The Fundamental Theorems*

Faced with a vector $[A, (p, w, \alpha, N_L, N_\mu)(1)]$ and knowing that $\xi \geq 1$, the consumer determines his consumption-investment strategy and goes to the market to acquire the corresponding vector $(q, L, \mu)(1)$. In order to be sure that the consumer has a consumption-investment strategy, I must introduce additional axioms concerning $V(\cdot)$ and $Q(\cdot)$. The ones I require are analogues of axioms CBS 9–CBS 12 in Stigum (1990, pp. 800–801). They ensure that the consumer's utility function in CBS 1–CBS 7 has properties analogous to the properties of the utility function in (T_0, M_0) in Fig. 5.2 and that the consumer's expectations vary continuously with the information he possesses. Moreover, they insist that the consumer is convinced that he might die during any one of the periods $t = 1, \ldots, M$, and that he believes that his creditors will never force him into bankruptcy.

For brevity's sake I omit the details of the additional conditions on $V(\cdot)$ and $Q(\cdot)$ and note that their analogues can be found in Stigum (1990). These conditions and CBS 1–CBS 7 enable me to establish theorems T 2 and T 3 below, which are the *fundamental theorems* of my theory of consumer choice under uncertainty.[8]

T 2 *If CBS 1–CBS 7 and the additional conditions on* $V(\cdot)$ *and* $Q(\cdot)$ *are valid, then for each value of* A *and* $(p, w, \alpha, N_L, N_\mu)(1)$, *there is a consumption-investment strategy.*

TABLE 6.2
States of the World and Their Respective Probabilities

$\{\omega\}$	$\{\omega_1\}$	$\{\omega_2\}$	$\{\omega_3\}$	$\{\omega_4\}$	$\{\omega_5\}$	$\{\omega_6\}$	$\{\omega_7\}$	$\{\omega_8\}$
$Q(\{\omega\})$	1/18	1/18	1/18	1/9	1/9	4/9	1/12	1/12

T 3 *Let* $\gamma(t, \omega) = [(p, w, a, N_L, N_\mu)(1, \omega), \ldots, (p, w, \alpha, N_L, N_\mu)(t, \omega)]$, $t = 1, 2, \ldots, \omega \in \Omega$, *and suppose that CBS 1–CBS 7 and the additional conditions on* $V(\cdot)$ *and* $Q(\cdot)$ *are valid. Then there exists a continuous real-valued function* $W(\cdot)$ *on the set* $\{[A, \gamma(1), q, L, \mu] \in \text{range}[A, \gamma(1)] \times R_+^n \times R_+ \times \{\mu \in R : \mu \geq -N_\mu\}\}$ *that, for each value of* $[A, \gamma(1)]$, *satisfies the conditions: (i)* $W[A, \gamma(1), \cdot]$ *is a strictly increasing, strictly concave function on* $R_+^n \times R_+ \times \{\mu \in R : \mu \geq -N_\mu\}$. *(ii) The consumer can determine the* $(q, L, \mu)(1)$ *component of his consumption-investment strategy by setting it equal to the* (q, L, μ) *vector that maximizes the value of* $W[A, \gamma(1), q, L, \mu]$ *subject to the conditions:* $p(1)q + \alpha(1)\mu \leq A + w(1)L$; *and* $(q, L, \mu) \in R_+^n \times R_+ \times \{\mu \in R : \mu \geq -N_\mu\}$. *(iii) Let* $(q, L, \mu)(\cdot) : \text{range}[A, \gamma(1)] \rightarrow R_+^n \times R_+ \times R$ *be the solution to the maximum problem in (ii). Then,* $(q, L, \mu)(\cdot)$ *is continuous on range*$[A, \gamma(1)]$, *homogeneous of degree zero in* $[A, (p, w, \alpha)(1)]$, *and satisfies a version of Walras's law* $(p, w, \alpha)(1)(q, L, \mu)[A, \gamma(1)] = A$.

The preceding theorems indicate in shorthand the positive analogies of consumer behavior that the theory identifies. The theory insists that the consumer can order current-period budget vectors and that his ordering depends on the prices that he observes in the present and on those that he has observed in the past. Moreover, the consumer always chooses a budget vector that has the highest rank among all such vectors. Finally, the consumer's choice of budget vectors varies with his net worth and with the prices and institutional constraints that he faces in accordance with the strictures of T 3(ii) and (iii). These are the only positive analogies of a consumer's current-period behavior that the theory identifies.

6.5 CONCLUDING REMARKS

I believe that the intended interpretation of an economic theory delineates the positive analogies that the originator of the theory considered sufficient to describe the situation about which he was theorizing. In this chapter we have studied different kinds of economic theories to see if the intended interpretation of these theories is in accord with my idea of the purport of an economic theory.

I began by discussing Max Weber's vision of a social science of concrete reality in which he could use ideal-type constructs to understand the relationships and cultural significance of the individual events that he faced. Since an ideal-type construct might comprise negative as well as positive analogies of the kind of situations about which Weber was theorizing, his idea of the purport of an axiomatized economic theory is not quite like mine. However, we seem to agree that an economic theory is not meant to describe all the varied and sundry details of a situation. Rather, it delineates characteristic features of the kind of situations that its originator had in mind.

I then discussed Keynes's model-theoretic account of the determination of an economy's equilibrium level of "national income" and "aggregate employment" and Solow's axiomatized theory of economic growth. Even though I had difficulties pinpointing the positive analogies about which Solow was theorizing, I am convinced that my idea of the purport of an economic theory is similar to the ideas of Keynes and Solow.

At the end of the chapter I discussed a theory of choice under uncertainty that I developed in Stigum (1969) in the spirit of Gerard Debreu's (1959) remarkable book *Theory of Value*. Debreu theorized about general equilibria in economies with complete sets of securities markets. I theorized about temporary equilibria in economies with incomplete sets of securities markets. The reference to Debreu here is interesting because the positive analogies that T 2 and T 3 identify are so different from the positive analogies of consumer behavior that Debreu's book recognizes. I note three essential differences in the following[9]:

1. In the intended interpretation of the axioms, $(q, L, \mu)(\cdot)$ is a function of parameters whose values are observable. Hence, the demand function of my consumer can be used as a basis for an econometric analysis of consumer choice under uncertainty.

This property of my consumer's demand function is not shared by the demand function of Debreu's consumer. His consumer's demand function is a function of future prices and incomes as well as of current prices and income. Future prices and incomes are not observable in social reality.

2. In contradistinction to the demand function of Debreu's consumer, $(q, L, \mu)(\cdot)$ satisfies neither the strong nor the weak axiom of revealed preference. Therefore, in the intended interpretation of the axioms, the consistency of my consumer's market behavior cannot be tested by the strong (or weak) axiom of revealed preference.

The reason for the failure of $(q, L, \mu)(\cdot)$ is simple: The first-period prices (i.e., current prices) of q, L, and μ are components of $\gamma(1)$. As current prices change, $\gamma(1)$ changes, and as $\gamma(1)$ changes, the consumer's ordering of first-period budget vectors also changes.

3. Again, in contradistinction to Debreu's consumer, $(q, L, \mu)(\cdot)$ does not satisfy Samuelson's (1953) fundamental theorem of consumer choice [theorem T 10.16 in Stigum (1990)]. In the intended interpretation of my axioms, it is not sufficient to consult my consumer's Engel curves to determine whether he will respond to a fall in the price of a commodity by buying more of that commodity.

The reason for the nonapplicability of Samuelson's theorem is that three and not just two "effects" determine my consumer's response to a price change. First, there is the *substitution effect*, which determines how the consumer would react to a price change if: (1) his expectations, that is, if the $[A, \gamma(1)]$ argument of $W(\cdot)$, were not allowed to change, and if (2) his initial net worth were adjusted so that he could maintain the same level of expected utility after the price change as before. Then there is the *income effect*, which determines the reaction of the consumer when I undo the net-worth compensation but keep expectations constant. Finally, there is the *expectation effect*, which determines the consumer's response when I at last remove the lid on his expectations. Since $W[A, \gamma(1), \cdot]$ is increasing and strictly concave, the substitution effect is always negative. The signs of the other two effects, however, are indeterminate. Only if both signs are positive can we be sure that our consumer would respond to a fall in the price of a commodity by buying more of that commodity.

There may be economists who think that the failure of my consumer's behavior to satisfy the strictures on which Debreu's theory of consumer choice insists detracts from the import of my theory. Even so, I believe it worthwhile to end this chapter with one more example of a failure of my theory to identify positive analogies that another well-known theory recognizes.

Arrow's theory (1965) of choice among safe and risky assets is a wonderful example of the import of models in economic theorizing. In Chapter 12 of *Toward a Formal Science of Economics* (Stigum, 1990) I demonstrated that Arrow's theory can be viewed as a family of models of the certainty theory of consumer choice. While the latter theory has few interesting theorems, Arrow's theory is full of thought-provoking theorems relating a consumer's demand for safe and risky assets to the properties of his or her absolute and relative risk-aversion functions. It is, therefore, relevant here that it is impossible within my theory of consumer choice under uncertainty to give a meaningful definition of the consumer's absolute and relative risk aversion.[10] A careful perusal of the proof of T 3 in my earlier book attests to that.

Finally, I must reiterate that the positive analogies of individual behavior that a theory identifies are accurate descriptions of behavior in its own theory universe. Whether these positive analogies depict characteristic features of behavior in the Real World is a question that can be answered only in a theory-data confrontation.

NOTES

1. The requirement that a definition be stated in terms of *genus proximum* and *differentia specifica* is a doctrine of classical logic. Such a definition characterizes a class or a property as the logical product of two other classes or properties and cannot be applied when the definiendum is a relation or a function (Hempel, 1952, p. 5). Hence, Weber is not the only one who has reasons to complain about the given requirement of classical logic.

2. The difference in Weber's and my views of the purport of an economic theory is significant. To see how important it is, consider the idea of a medieval city economy. I

would characterize such an economy by listing characteristics that I believe medieval city economies have in common and check whether these characteristics constitute positive analogies of a given family of medieval cities. In contrast, Weber would construct the concept of a medieval city economy as an ideal type and check "the extent to which this ideal-construct approximates to or diverges from reality, to what extent, for example, the economic structure of [one of the cities in the given family of medieval cities can] be classified as a 'city economy' " (cf. Weber, 1949, p. 90).

3. My assessment of the import of Keynes's *General Theory* is very different from the value J. R. Hicks (1937) confers on Keynes's book in his famous review, "Mr. Keynes and the 'Classics': A Suggested Interpretation." Hicks's analysis of the book differs from my analysis as well. However, here the similarities are more important than the differences inasmuch as Hicks seems to view Keynes's theory as a theory that has been developed by model-theoretic means.

4. I have designated P by the name "price level." Chances are that Keynes would have objected strenuously to the name. He thought that the idea of a general price level was vague and that the vagueness made the term unsatisfactory for the purposes of a causal analysis. In fact, for his own analysis he deemed the concept not only vague but also unnecessary (Keynes, 1936, p. 39).

5. The reader can get an idea of how fast the topic of economic growth developed after Solow's pathbreaking article by looking at Edwin Burmeister and A. Rodney Dobell's (1970) textbook *Mathematical Theories of Economic Growth*. The book is also interesting in this context because it contains a foreword by Solow in which he details his 1970 views on the economic theory of growth.

6. This version has only one security and no shares. The other details have not changed.

7. The past does not figure explicitly in the axioms. Note, therefore, that the past values of prices and institutional constraints are important determinants of both $Q(\cdot)$ and $\aleph$. I left them out of the axioms to simplify my notation.

8. In the statement of T 3, range$[A, \gamma(1)] = \{x \in R_{++}^{(n+5)} : x = [A(\omega), \gamma(1, \omega)]$ for some $\omega \in \Omega\}$. Proofs of the theorems can be found in Stigum (1990, pp. 827–833).

9. Debreu's consumer's demand function is, strictly speaking, a demand correspondence. Be that as it may, to simplify my arguments I choose as the intended interpretation of Debreu's axioms a family of models in which the consumer's preferences can be represented by a continuous, strictly increasing, and strictly quasi-concave utility function.

10. In Arrow's theory, a decision maker is an expected utility maximizer with a utility function, $U(\cdot) : R_+ \to R$, that satisfies the condition $U'(\cdot) > 0$. The decision maker is risk averse if $U''(\cdot) < 0$. Moreover, his absolute and relative risk aversion at a given level of net worth, A, is given, respectively, by the value of $-U''(A)/U'(A)$ and $-AU''(A)/U'(A)$.

REFERENCES

Arrow, K. J., 1965, *Aspects of the Theory of Risk Bearing*, Helsinki: Academic Book Store.

Burmeister, E., and A. R. Dobell, 1970, *Mathematical Theories of Economic Growth*, New York: Macmillan.

Debreu, G., 1959, *Theory of Value*, New York: Wiley.

Friedman, M., 1953, "The Methodology of Positive Economics," in: *Essays in Positive Economics*, Chicago: University of Chicago Press.

Hempel, C. G., 1952, *Fundamentals of Concept Formation in Empirical Science*, Chicago: University of Chicago Press.

Hicks, J. R. 1937, "Mr. Keynes and the 'Classics': A Suggested Interpretation," *Econometrica* 5, 147–159.

Kesten, H., and B. Stigum, 1974, "Balanced Growth under Uncertainty in Decomposable Economies," in: *Essays on Economic Behavior under Uncertainty*, M. S. Balch, D. L. McFadden, and S. Y. Wui, (eds.), New York: North-Holland/American Elsevier.

Keynes, J. M., 1936, *General Theory of Employment, Interest and Money*, New York: Harcourt Brace.

Keynes, J. M., 1938, "Letter to Roy Harrod, July 4," reprinted in 1973, in: *Collected Writings of John Maynard Keynes, Vol. 14*, D. Moggridge (ed.), London: Macmillan.

Lakatos, I., 1978, *The Methodology of Scientific Research Programmes*, Cambridge: Cambridge University Press.

Marshall, A., 1890, *Principles of Economics*, London: Macmillan.

Meyer, E., 1900, *Zur Theorie und Methodik der Geschichte*, Halle: Niemeyer.

Mill, J. S., 1836, "On the Definition of Political Economy," reprinted in 1967, in: *Collected Works, Essays on Economy and Society, Vol. 4*, J. M. Robson (ed.), Toronto: University of Toronto Press.

Samuelson, P. A., 1953, "Consumption Theorems in Terms of Overcompensation Rather than Indifference Comparisons," *Economica* 20, 1–9.

Solow, R. M., 1956, "A Contribution to the Theory of Economic Growth," *Quarterly Journal of Economics* 70, 65–94.

Stigum, B. P., 1969, "Competitive Equilibria under Uncertainty," *Quarterly Journal of Economics* 83, 533–561.

Stigum, B. P., 1990, *Toward a Formal Science of Economics*, Cambridge: MIT Press.

Weber, M., 1949, *The Methodology of the Social Sciences*, E. Shils and H. Finch (trans.), New York: Free Press.

Chapter Seven

Rationality in Economics

Although I dealt with the purport of economic theories at length in Chapter 6, the concept of rationality played no role in the discussion. In fact, rational agents and rational choice were hardly mentioned at all. This aspect of that chapter reflects a deeply felt belief of mine that rationality is one of the most abused terms in economics. Certainly, the concept of rationality is ill defined and it often gets in the way of sound reasoning. At times it even makes economists talk at cross purposes with each other. Much abuse and agitated counterarguments have taught me that such opinions are not welcome in economic circles. Still, I consider the matter is important enough to make another try at explaining to friend and foe alike why my opinions are sound. In the process of doing that, I hope to convince economists that for "rational agent" and "rational choice and judgment," they should substitute less loaded terms such as "rational animal" and "good choice and judgment." I explicate the meaning of the latter terms in Chapter 9.

7.1 A MISCONCEPTION

According to Robert Aumann, an economic theory is a theory "concerned with the interactive behavior of *Homo rationalis*—rational man. *Homo rationalis* is the species that always acts both purposefully and logically, has well-defined goals, is motivated solely by the desire to approach these goals as closely as possible, and has the calculating ability to do so." Such species are as mythical as the unicorn and the mermaid (Aumann, 1985, p. 35).

There is a sense of Aumann's *dictum* with which most economists will agree. An economic theory, whether developed by the axiomatic method or formulated as a family of models of a finite number of assertions, is a theory about undefined terms. These undefined terms with their intended interpretations comprise all sorts of abstract ideas, and in theories of choice and games some of them may be members of Aumann's family of *Homo rationalis.* All of them have one characteristic in common: They live and function in a socially constructed world of ideas frequented by Hans Christian Andersen's mermaid and the unicorn.

Seen in the context of this book, Aumann's view of economic theory is misconceived. I detail three reasons why. One reason is as follows: Take a look at the axioms of the theory of consumer choice in Chapter 5, H 1–H 6, and the basic assertions of the neoclassical theory of the firm in Chapter 10, N 1–N 7. Within the theory that economists derive from H 1–H 6 they can delineate the characteristics of a rational-choice function for the consumer to show that, in each (p, A) situation, the consumer's consumption bundle is a rational choice of a commodity bundle. Similarly, within the theory that they derive from N 1–N 7 and an additional eighth axiom they can delineate the characteristics of a rational-choice function for the producer to show that, in each (a, w) situation, the firm's input-output strategy is a rational choice of inputs and output. Note that the word "rational" does not appear in H 1–H 6, and that the concept of rationality played no role in the intended interpretation of the axioms. Consequently, one can develop the theory of consumer choice and test the empirical relevance of its intended interpretation without ever introducing the idea of a rational consumer. For the same reasons one can use N 1–N 7 to develop the neoclassical theory of the firm and try the empirical relevance of its intended interpretation without ever introducing the idea of a rational producer.

There is another reason why Aumann's idea of economic theory is misconceived when viewed in the context of this book. An economic theory of choice characterizes a choice situation and exhibits a set of choices that it insists are optimal in the given choice situation. The optimal choice may be a commodity vector that maximizes a consumer's utility subject to his budget constraint. It may also be an input-output vector that maximizes a firm's profit subject to a production constraint. Whatever the theory and the pertinent choice situation, the theory comes with many families of models. The characteristic features of optimal choice in one family of models need not be the characteristic features of optimal choice in another such family. It seems unreasonable to single out one family of models and insist that the characteristic features of optimal choice in that family of models are the characteristic features of rational choice in the given choice situation. For example, in Milton Friedman's theory (1957) of the consumption function, a consumer's optimal outlay on consumer goods in the current period, c, satisfies an equation of the form $c = k(r)y_p + c_t$, where y_p denotes the consumer's permanent income, r is the interest rate, and c_t designates the consumer's transitory consumption. In Franco Modigliani and Richard Brumberg's (1955) life-cycle theory of consumer choice, a consumer's optimal outlay on consumer goods in the current period t satisfies an equation of the form $c = H(r)[A_{t-1} + y_t + (M - \alpha)y_t^e]$, where A_{t-1} denotes the consumer's net worth at the end of year $t - 1$, y_t is his labor income in year t, M is his expected life span in years, α denotes his age in year t, and $y_t^e = (M - \alpha)^{-1} \sum_{1 \leq i \leq (M-\alpha)} [1/(1 + r)]^i y_{t+i}$. The theories of Friedman and Modigliani and Brumberg constitute different families of models of one and the same formal theory. Note that the characteristic features, that is, the positive analogies, of optimal choice that the two theories identify are very different. I doubt that Friedman would insist that his consumer is rational and that Modigliani and Brumberg's consumer is not.

There is a third important reason why Aumann's view of economic theory in the context of this book is misconceived. Often economists develop several theories of choice for one and the same situation. The optimal choices that these theories identify are usually very different. Just think of choice with priors and expected utility versus choice with superadditive probabilities and Choquet integrals in uncertain situations. In such cases it seems meaningless to argue that the optimal choices in one theory are more rational than the optimal choices in the others. At most one can attribute to rational individuals the common elements of the theories and try the empirical relevance of the other elements in various relevant situations. Even that may be too much to hope for since these common elements might have no empirical relevance.

There are all sorts of economic theories of choice. Some pertain to choice under certainty. Others concern choice under uncertainty. Still others delineate strategies in various game-theoretic situations. I believe that the proper attitude to adopt toward these theories is as follows: The intended interpretations of the theories concern the behavior of *rational animals* in situations that are interesting to economists. The theories delineate positive analogies of behavior in the populations of rational animals that the originators of the theories might have considered relevant. In Chapter 9, I give a characterization of rational animals that I believe is suitable for econometrics. These rational animals are not mythical characters. They are ordinary human beings experiencing the social reality that I described in Chapter 2. Whether the positive analogies that the various economic theories attribute to populations of such animals have empirical relevance is a question for applied econometricians.

In the remainder of this chapter I discuss some of the characteristic features of rational choice on which economic theories insist and the circumstances under which and the populations for which these characteristics may depict positive analogies of individual behavior.

7.2 CHOICE UNDER CERTAINTY

Adoption of the attitude toward economic theory that I advocated earlier is conditioned on a tacit agreement that econometricians cannot use economic theories and data to test the rationality of members of a given population. This is obviously true of human populations. Their members are rational animals and, hence, rational by definition. It is also true of other kinds of populations, for example, rats or pigeons; their members are not rational. Whether a given population possesses the positive analogies on which an economic theory insists is a matter to be settled in a pertinent theory-data confrontation.

7.2.1 Consumer Choice with Rational Animals

Consider the standard theory of consumer choice under certainty that is derived from axioms H 1–H 6 in Chapter 5. In the intended interpretation of the theory, a consumer is a human being, that is, a rational animal, who possesses "good judgment." A commodity bundle is an ordinary commodity vector. It may also be a vector of safe and risky assets or a life-cycle plan of consumer expenditures. The consumer's choices are always "good choices." Here, "good judgment" is taken to mean that the consumer can order the commodity bundles he faces. Moreover, "good choice" means the consumer choosing the one that ranks the highest from among the available bundles. Finally, an available commodity bundle is a commodity bundle that satisfies the consumer's budget constraint. The main purport of the theory is to delineate two characteristic features of consumer choice, "good judgment" and "good choice," and to show how they are reflected in consumer behavior.

The given interpretation of the theory of consumer choice is often ridiculed for outlandish assumptions by students of economics as well as by learned people in noneconomic academic disciplines. This scorn is the result of a fundamental misunderstanding of the purport of the theory. These critics do not understand that the theory does not describe individual behavior. It only delineates characteristic features of consumer behavior that may or may not constitute positive analogies of behavior in a population of interest. Moreover, they seem to think, in error, that the empirical relevance of the theory can be determined by a priori reasoning alone. The following is a simple example to illustrate what I have in mind.

E 7.1 *Consider my daily shopping for food in the neighborhood grocery store and the standard theory of consumer choice under certainty. I usually buy a loaf of bread and I might buy coffee if the price is right. Sometimes the store is out of my family's favorite brand of bread. Then I buy another brand that I believe my little daughter will like. I will do that even if the other brand costs twice as much and even if there is another grocery store, 10 minutes away, that might have the brand I want. As to coffee, I will buy coffee only if I judge the price to be low. Then I buy many more bags of coffee than I need, and I store them for later use. The theory insists that a consumer chooses among available commodity bundles the one he prefers. Since I am a rational animal, the theory cannot be used to question the rationality of my shopping in the neighborhood grocery store. Whether the theory has empirical relevance in my situation is another matter. The theory does not account for the costs of search. It provides no opportunity for storing goods. And it denies current prices the ability to convey information about future prices. Of these failures I may ignore the first and circumvent the second by choosing the length of a time period appropriately. The third failure, however, cannot be dismissed. It renders the empirical relevance of the theory in the situation under consideration problematic.*[1]

In theory-data confrontations of the given interpretation of H 1–H 6, the consumer is usually identified with an individual living alone or a family living together and having a common budget. Econometricians have used the theory successfully to study how consumers' expenditures on various categories of commodities vary with their incomes (Engel, 1857; Aasnes et al., 1985). They have also used it successfully to determine how a consumer's choice of safe and risky assets varies with his net worth (Arrow, 1965; Stigum, 1990) and how his consumption-savings decision varies with his expected life-cycle income stream (Modigliani and Brumberg, 1955; Friedman, 1957; Stigum, 1990).

7.2.2 Consumer Choice with Rats

In the intended interpretation of the theory of consumer choice, the consumers are rational animals. According to my characterization of such animals in Chapter 9, rational animals are human beings. It is, therefore, interesting that there are valid interpretations of the theory of consumer choice in which a consumer may be a rat or a pigeon. Rats and pigeons are not rational animals.

In the early 1970s, John H. Kagel, Raymond C. Battalio, and Leonard Green began a series of experimental studies of rats and pigeons to see if economic choice theory can account for animal behavior. Their work culminated in a monograph entitled *Economic Choice Theory: An Experimental Analysis of Animal Behavior* (Kagel et al., 1995). I recount some of their results in what follows.

Consider a male albino rat that lives in an experimental chamber fitted with two levers. By pressing a lever a certain number of times the rat can obtain delivery of a premeasured amount of food or liquid, as the case may be. The food comes in buckets with a certain number of food pellets. The liquid comes in buckets with a certain number of milliliters of liquid such as water, root beer, and Tom Collins mix without alcohol. Pressing on one of the levers is effective in delivering a commodity only when two lights located above the lever are on. Each day the rat has on hand a limited number of effective lever presses that it can distribute in any combination between the two levers. When the rat has used up its allotment of lever presses, the lights are automatically extinguished. The number of lever presses that are required for delivery of a commodity, the magnitude of the commodity delivered, and the effective number of lever presses at the rat's disposal are subject to experimental control.

The life of an albino rat in an experimental chamber may not be especially good. Still, I can use it to describe an interesting interpretation of the axioms for consumer choice in Chapter 5, H 1–H 6. In this interpretation a commodity is a pair (x_1, x_2), where x_1 denotes so many buckets of food and x_2 designates so many buckets of root beer. In each bucket there is a given number of food pellets and a given number of milliliters of root beer as the case may be. A price is a pair (p_1, p_2), where $p_1(p_2)$ denotes the number of lever presses that are required to obtain delivery of one bucket of food (root beer). A consumer is a pair $(\preceq, A)$, where $\preceq$ is a complete reflexive and transitive ordering of the commodity space, and A denotes so many units of lever presses that the consumer has on hand each day. Finally, the consumption bundle in a given (p, A) situation is the most preferred commodity bundle among all the commodity bundles that satisfy the budget constraint determined by (p, A).

In a theory-data confrontation of the preceding interpretation of H 1–H 6, Kagel and his colleagues identified a consumer with an albino rat in an experimental chamber such as the one I described. They also assumed that they had accurate observations on p_1, p_2, and A. Finally, they associated a consumption bundle with a "stable choice" of commodity bundles in the pertinent (p, A) situation. By a stable choice in a (p, A) situation they meant the following: The rat faced the same (p, A) pair during an experimental session that lasted for at least 14 days and was as long as it took for the rat's choices of (x_1, x_2) pairs to be relatively stable over at least 10 consecutive days. The "stable choice" was taken to be the mean value of the chosen commodity bundles during the final 10 days of the experimental session.

With the help of thirteen albino rats, Kagel et al. were able to try the empirical relevance of two of $T(\text{H } 1, \ldots, \text{H } 6)$'s main theorems. Both of them concern characteristic features of the way a consumer's consumption bundle varies with the price-income situation he faces. I can state them roughly as follows: Let (c_1^0, c_2^0) be the consumer's consumption bundle in the price-income situation (p^0, A^0). Also, let $(p^1, A^1) = (p_1^0 + \Delta p_1, p_2^0, A^0 + \Delta A)$, where ΔA is chosen such that $p_1^1 c_1^0 + p_2^1 c_2^0 = A^1$. Finally, let (c_1^1, c_2^1) and (c_1^2, c_2^2) be, respectively, the consumption bundle in the price-income situation (p^1, A^0) and the price-income situation (p^1, A^1). Then

1. Slutsky (1915): $c_1^2 > (<) c_1^0$ according as $\Delta p_1 < 0 (> 0)$.
2. Samuelson (1953): If the first component of the consumption bundle in the price-income situation (p^1, A) is an increasing function of A, $c_1^1 > (<) c_1^0$ according as $\Delta p_1 < 0 (> 0)$.

Here the first theorem insists that the sign of the Slutsky income-compensated substitution effect is negative. The other gives a symbolic rendition of Samuelson's fundamental theorem of consumer choice.

The empirical results of Kagel et al. were interesting. Thirty-five out of forty of the income-compensated price changes resulted in increased (reduced) consumption of the commodity whose price decreased (increased). Thus, in 87 percent of all cases the Slutsky income-compensated substitution effect was negative. With the assumption that the rats' responses to the price changes were random, the probability of observing so many consistent responses is less than 0.01 (Kagel et al., 1995, p. 20).

As to the trial of Samuelson's theorem, the researchers viewed the price change as a change that has two component parts: (1) an income-compensated price change, and (2) a parallel shift in the budget line that undoes the original compensation of income. They observed that whenever a subject responded to an increase in A by consuming more of x_1, it would also respond to an uncompensated decrease in p_1 by increasing its consumption of x_1 (Kagel et al., 1995, pp. 24–25). Thus, their subjects responded to price changes in accordance with Samuelson's theorem.

7.3 CHOICE UNDER UNCERTAINTY

Most economic theories of choice under uncertainty agree that "good judgment" is synonymous with "ability to rank available options." The characteristics of the rankings in question, however, vary over theories as well as over the situations the decision-maker faces.

An uncertain option can be many things, for example, a gamble, an insurance policy, or an investment in the stock market. I distinguish between two kinds of uncertain options—those that pertain to risky situations and those that pertain to uncertain situations. Here a *risky situation* is taken to be one in which the likelihoods of all possible events are known or can be calculated by reason alone. An *uncertain situation* is one in which the likelihoods of all possible events are not known and cannot be calculated with reason alone. I begin by discussing choice in risky situations.

7.3.1 Risky Situations

To make my discussion of choice in risky situations as simple as possible I consider an uncertain option in such situations as a prospect. A *prospect* is an n-tuple of pairs $\{(x_1, p_1), \ldots, (x_n, p_n)\}$, where $x_i \in R$ is an outcome, $p_i \in R_+$ is a measure of the likelihood of x_i happening, and $p_1 + \ldots + p_n = 1$.

7.3.1.1 Assigning Probabilities to Events

Showing "good judgment" in risky situations involves carrying out two successive tasks. The first task consists of assigning numbers to the p_i in the prospects that the decision-maker is facing, which is sometimes easy and other times not. Moreover, a given task may be easy for some and much too difficult for others. Examples E 7.2 and E 7.3 illustrate what I have in mind.

According to Laplace (1820, pp. 6–7, 11), the probability of an event is the ratio between the number of cases favorable to it and the number of possible cases, when there is nothing to make one believe that one case should occur rather than another, so that in that particular instance the cases are equally likely. With this definition in mind and, if need be, with a little bit of coaching I believe that most people would agree with the probability I assign in E 7.2.

E 7.2 *A blindfolded man,* A, *is to pull a ball from an urn with* k *red balls and 100-*k *white balls. The urn is shaken well, so the probability of* A *pulling a red ball from the urn is* k/*100.*

With coaching most people might be able to determine the probability of more complicated events, for example, the probability of E_1, four red balls in four draws with replacement from an urn with $k = 84$, or the probability of E_2, at least four red balls in ten draws with replacement from an urn with $k = 50$. However, without coaching it is unlikely that most people would manage to figure such probabilities.

D. Kahnemann and A. Tversky (1972) believe that most people in assessing likelihoods rely on a limited number of heuristics that help them reduce complex computational tasks to manageable proportions. One such heuristic, *anchoring*, leads people to overestimate the probability of conjunctive events and to underestimate the probability of disjunctive events. Thus chances are that most people would overestimate the probability of E_1 and underestimate the probability of E_2. Experimental evidence bears out this prediction (cf., e.g., Bar-Hillel, 1973).

What untutored people might do in the case I describe in E 7.3 is anybody's guess.

E 7.3 *Consider a mechanical system of* r *indistinguishable particles. The phase space has been subdivided into a large number* n *of cells and each particle is assigned to a cell. There are* $\mathrm{n^r}$ *different ways in which* r *particles can be arranged in* n *cells. I have no reason to believe that one way is more likely than another, so I take all ways to be equally likely. Since there are* $\mathrm{r!/r_1!r_2!\ldots r_n!}$ *indistinguishable ways in which I can arrange* r *particles so that* $\mathrm{r_i}$ *particles are in cell* i, $\mathrm{i = 1, \ldots, n}$, *I conclude that the probability that cells* $1, \ldots, \mathrm{n}$ *contain* $\mathrm{r_1, \ldots, r_n}$ *particles with* $\mathrm{r_1 + \ldots + r_n = r}$ *is* $\mathrm{(r!/r_1!r_2!\ldots r_n!)n^{-r}}$.

The interesting aspect of E 7.3 is that I have used Laplace's definition of probability correctly and come up with a wrong probability assignment. According to Feller (1957, pp. 38–39), numerous experiments have shown beyond doubt that the probabilities I calculated in E 7.3 are not the true probabilities of any known mechanical system of particles. For example, photons, nuclei, and atoms containing an even number of elementary particles behave as if they considered only distinguishable arrangements of the relevant system's particles. Since there are just $(n + r - 1)!/(n - 1)!r!$ distinguishable arrangements of r particles in n cells, and since all of them seem to be equally likely, the true probability of the given event for photons, nuclei, and atoms containing an even number of elementary particles is $[(n + r - 1)!/(n - 1)!r!]^{-1}$.

Few if any would question Feller's authority in E 7.3. So from E 7.2 and E 7.3 I conclude that I can know which prospects a given decision-maker chooses from only in trivial cases. This is true even if I help him determine the values of the pertinent probabilities because the values I assess may be very different from those that the decision-maker perceives. For example, the high probabilities may be higher and the low probabilities may be lower than the corresponding perceived probabilities. Many experimental studies bear witness to such a possibility (cf., e.g., Mosteller and Nogee, 1951; Preston and Baratta, 1948).

7.3.1.2 *Ordering Prospects*

To show "good judgment" in risky situations the decision-maker must carry out a second difficult task: determining his ordering of the prospects he faces. For that purpose, consider a decision-maker B, whose perceived probabilities often differ from the true probabilities in the prospects he faces. I think of a prospect to B as a measurable function on a probability space $(\aleph, \Re, \wp)$, where $\aleph$ is a finite set of states of nature, $\Re$ is the field of all subsets of $\aleph$, and $\wp$ is a probability measure on $\Re$. In a given situation the functions take only a finite number of values, all of which belong to a set of real numbers X, and the value of $\wp$ at any $A \in \Re$ equals the likelihood of A happening that B perceives. I assume that B's ordering of prospects induces an ordering of functions in which the indicator functions of subsets of $\aleph$ are ranked in accordance with the $\wp$-values of the respective sets. Further, I assume that, with a slight modification of one of the axioms, SSA 4, B's ordering of prospects satisfies the axioms concerning $\aleph$ and the ordering of measurable functions that I listed in Stigum (1990, pp. 434–439).[2] That ensures the existence of a function $U(\cdot) : X \to R$ that is determined up to a positive linear transformation and is such that if x and y are any two of the prospects B faces, B will prefer x to y if and only if

$$\sum_{\eta \in \aleph} U[x(\eta)]\wp(\{\eta\}) > \sum_{\eta \in \aleph} U[y(\eta)]\wp(\{\eta\}).$$

Thus, if $\aleph$ and B's ordering of measurable functions satisfy my axioms, B will order the pertinent prospects according to their perceived expected utilities.

The axioms to which I referred earlier represent a modification of L. J. Savage's (1954) axioms for choice under uncertainty that pertain to risky situations in which $\aleph$ contains a finite number of states of nature. My theory differs from Savage's in two respects. In Savage's theory the utility function and the decision-maker's subjective probability measure are determined simultaneously by his or her risk preferences. Further, he seems to believe that the utility function and the subjective probability measure are determined once and for all for all the risky situations that the decision-maker might face. I believe that $U(\cdot)$, $\aleph$, and $\wp(\cdot)$ may vary from one choice situation to the next.

Moreover, in the situations I envisioned earlier "good judgment" is obtained sequentially in two steps. One first determines B's perceived probabilities and then his or her ordering of the prospects in question. That allows me to rephrase my SSA 4 axiom in the obvious way such that the a_i in Stigum (1990, p. 435, eq. 19.22) can be interpreted as B's perceived probability of the ith state of nature.

The empirical relevance of my theory is uncertain. To see why, consider the following example.

E 7.4 *Consider an urn with 100 balls that differ only in color and assume that there are 89 red balls, 10 black balls, and 1 white ball. The urn is shaken well and a blindfolded man is to pull one ball out of it. We ask a decision-maker* B *to rank the components of the following two pairs of prospects in which he will receive:*

- α_1: *\$1,000 regardless of which ball is drawn.*
- α_2: *Nothing, \$1,000, or \$5,000 according as the ball drawn is white, red, or black.*
- β_1: *Nothing if the ball is red and \$1,000 otherwise.*
- β_2: *Nothing if the ball is either red or white and \$5,000 if the ball is black.*

If B*'s preferences satisfy my axioms,* B *will prefer* α_1 *to* α_2 *if and only if he prefers* β_1 *to* β_2. *Also,* B *will prefer* α_2 *to* α_1 *if and only if he prefers* β_2 *to* β_1.

Ever since 1952 when Maurice Allais started dreaming up examples such as E 7.4 (cf. Allais, 1979), numerous individuals have been asked to rank similar pairs of prospects. Judging from the experiments of which I am aware, at most 60 percent of the subjects answer in accordance with the prescriptions of my theory. Those who "fail" the test usually prefer α_1 to α_2 and β_2 to β_1. Their preferences seem to reveal an aversion to uncertainty that is characteristic of individuals who shade their probabilities in uncertain situations. More on that in what follows.

7.3.2 Uncertain Situations

In discussing the choice of options in uncertain situations I shall again, for simplicity, think of an option as a prospect, $\{(x_1, p_1), \ldots, (x_n, p_n)\}$. In this case the x_i are known, but the p_i are not. In addition, the true values of the p_i cannot be calculated by reason alone. I consider two prominent ways of dealing with such prospects. In one of them the decision-maker assigns values to the p_i in accordance with Bayesian principles and chooses among options according to their expected utility. In the other the decision-maker assigns values to the p_i in accordance with ideas developed by A. P. Dempster (1967) and G. Shafer (1976). Moreover, he chooses among options according to the values of a Choquet integral that he associates with them. I begin with the Bayesians.

7.3.2.1 *Bayesian Choice of Prospects*

Consider the following example and take special note of the forty-five subjects who were indifferent in their choice of urns.

E 7.5 *Two urns,* A *and* B, *contain 100 balls that are either red or white. There are 50 red balls in* A, *but nobody knows how many there are in* B. *A blindfolded man is to pull a ball from one of the urns, and you are to choose the urn for him. If he pulls a red ball, you will receive $100, otherwise nothing. Of 140 colleagues, students, and friends in Evanston and Oslo who were faced with the given choice, 82 chose* A, *45 could not make up their minds, and 13 chose* B.

Each one of the 45 indifferent persons may have argued like true Bayesians. The probability of pulling a red ball from A is 1/2. Also, there is one of 101 possible combinations of red and white balls in B, and there is no reason why one combination is more likely than another. So, in accordance with Laplace, one should assign prior probability $(101)^{-1}$ to each of them and insist that the probability of picking a red ball in B equals $\sum_{i=0}^{100}(i/100) \cdot (101)^{-1} = (101)^{-1} \cdot [100 \cdot 101/2 \cdot 100] = 1/2$. If the Bayesian arguments are right, there is no reason to prefer one urn to the other.

A Bayesian prior is supposed to reflect the decision-maker's knowledge about the p_i in a given prospect. Assigning such priors can be problematic. A case in point follows.

E 7.6 *Consider two diseases,* X *and* Y, *which require different treatments and are equally fatal if untreated. A person* A *is taking a test to determine whether he is suffering from* X *or* Y. *He knows that the probability that the test result will be accurate is 4/5. He also knows that* X *for a variety of demographic reasons is nineteen times as common as* Y. *The test reports that* A *suffers from* Y. *From this* A *deduces that the probability is 4/23 that he is suffering from* Y *and 19/23 that he is suffering from* X. *So he asks his doctor to treat him for* X.

I became aware of this example from reading an article by L. J. Cohen (1981, p. 329). Cohen insists that A has used a prior concerning the relative prevalence of the two diseases and computed the probability that an instance of a long run of patients that take the test will suffer from disease X. He should have used, instead, a prior that assesses A's own predisposition to the two diseases. If A has no known predisposition to either disease, he should have concluded from the test results that the probability is 4/5 that he is suffering from Y and ask his doctor to treat him for Y rather than X. Among probabilists and statisticians Cohen's arguments are controversial. However, results of experimental tests in comparable situations indicate that subjects tend to judge the values of analogous probabilities in accordance with Cohen's analysis (cf., e.g., Hammerton, 1973).[3]

We saw earlier that learned people may disagree on the appropriate prior to use in evaluating a given option. It is also the case that Bayesians argue among themselves as to the best way to model ignorance. They worry when their way of modeling ignorance of a parameter p suggests that they are not that ignorant about the value of $1/p$. They are also concerned when use of a diffuse prior to model ignorance of a parameter θ may swamp the information that a researcher can obtain from sample information about θ (cf. Lindley, 1977). The important thing to observe here is that not everybody is a Bayesian—at most 45 of the 140 subjects in E 7.5. Moreover, even one who tends to think like a Bayesian will have difficulties calculating the posteriors that are required for proper use of Bayesian ideas. Finally, in whatever way a Bayesian chooses his priors and calculates his posteriors, both the priors and the posteriors are honest probabilities, they are nonnegative, and their sums or their integrals, as the case may be, equal 1.

To a Bayesian decision-maker D, a prospect x is like a probability distribution $F_x(\cdot) : R \to [0, 1]$. D orders probability distributions in accordance with NM 1–NM5 in Chapter 4.[4] Consequently, if $x = \{(x_1, p_1), \ldots, (x_n, p_n)\}$ and $y = \{(y_1, q_1), \ldots, (y_m, q_m)\}$ are two prospects with probabilities that D has calculated, then D will prefer x to y if and only if the expected utility of x is larger than the expected utility of y.

Allais and his followers are as critical of von Neumann and Morgenstern's (1953) theory, that is, of NM 1–NM 5, as they are of Savage's theory. Moreover, many of the tests that they have conceived have been good tests of both theories (cf. MacCrimmon and Larsson, 1979). The dismal results of these tests have motivated researchers to look for alternative theories. I discuss the most promising of them next.

7.3.2.2 *Choice of Prospects with Capacities and Choquet Integrals*

Many knowledgeable persons will insist that the 82 subjects in E 7.5, by choosing A over B, have revealed an aversion to uncertainty. Specifically, so the argument goes. For any one of these subjects, one can find a number $k < 50$ and an urn $C(k)$ with k red balls and 100-k white balls such that the given person would be indifferent between having the blindfolded man pull a ball from B or $C(k)$. This indifference indicates that the person is assigning probability $k/100$ to the event that the blindfolded man might pull a red ball from B. By a similar argument, he would assign probability $k/100$ to the event that the blindfolded man might pull a white ball from B. But if that is true, the given subject is a person who reacts to uncertainty by shading his probabilities. Chances are good that the other members of the group of 82 in E 7.5 react to uncertainty in the same way.

When people shade their probabilities, they assign superadditive probabilities to the possible events in an uncertain situation. In the vernacular of probabilists, such a probability measure is designated by the name *capacity.* Capacities have interesting properties. To study them I assume, for simplicity, that there are only a finite number of states of nature, that is, that $\aleph = \{\eta_1, \ldots, \eta_n\}$ for some n. Also, I take $\Re$ to be the set of all subsets of $\aleph$ and let $\text{Bel}(\cdot) : \Re \to [0, 1]$ be a function that records the values that a given decision-maker D assigns to the subsets of $\aleph$. D shades his probabilities in the face of uncertainty. Hence, for any two disjoint events, A and C, I find that $\text{Bel}(A) + \text{Bel}(C) \leq \text{Bel}(A \cup C)$. Finally, I assume that there exists a function $m(\cdot) : \Re \to [0, 1]$, with $m(\emptyset) = 0$, $\sum_{A \subset \aleph} m(A) = 1$, and $\text{Bel}(A) = \sum_{C \subset A} m(C)$ for all $A \in \Re$. Then $\text{Bel}(\cdot)$ is a capacity and $m(\cdot)$ is, in Shafer's (1976) terminology, the associated *basic probability assignment.*

Shafer (1976) develops interesting ways for D to combine belief functions so as to update his beliefs. However, he has little to say about how D should order the options he faces. There are several alternatives (cf. Chateauneuf, 1986; Gilboa, 1987; Jaffray, 1989). I use a method I learned from Kjell Arne Brekke in 1986 (cf. Stigum,1990, pp. 445–455). Let $\aleph$, $\Re$, $\text{Bel}(\cdot)$, and $m(\cdot)$ be as above, and think of a prospect as a function $x(\cdot) : \aleph \to X$, where $X = \{x_1, \ldots, x_n\}$ is the set of all consequences of the prospects that decision-maker D faces. I assume that D orders consequences according to the values of a function $U(\cdot) : X \to R$. Also, for each prospect $x(\cdot)$ and every $A \in \Re$, I let $W_x(A) = \min_{\eta \in A} U[x(\eta)]$, and I insist that the utility that D receives from prospect $x(\cdot)$ equals $V(x)$, where

$$V(x) = \sum_{A \subset \Re} W_x(A) m(A).$$

The ordering of prospects that $V(\cdot)$ induces has many interesting characteristics. The ordering cannot be rationalized by an expected utility index. Instead,

$$V(x) = \int_0^\infty \text{Bel}(\{\eta \in \aleph : U[x(\eta)] \geq t\})\, \text{dt},$$

where the integral is a *Choquet integral* that reduces to an expected utility index only when $\text{Bel}(\cdot)$ is additive. Also, the ordering exhibits a remarkable aversion to uncertainty that I can document in the following way: Let $P = \{p(\cdot) : \aleph \to [0, 1] : \sum_{i=1}^n p(\eta_i) = 1\}$ and, for each $p \in P$, let $Pp(\cdot) : \Re \to [0, 1]$ be such that $Pp(A) = \sum_{\eta \in A} p(\eta)$ for each $A \in \Re$. Also, let

$$C = \{p \in P : \text{for all } A \in \Re,\ Pp(A) \geq \text{Bel}(A)].$$

Then

$$V(x) = \min_{p \in C} \sum_{i=1}^{n} U[x(\eta_i)] p(\eta_i).$$

Finally, the ordering satisfies neither Savage's axioms nor mine. I have much to say about that in Chapter 18.

The way $V(\cdot)$ orders prospects is fundamentally different from the way Bayesians order prospects in uncertain situations. It makes no sense to insist that one of these orderings is rational and the other is not. However, it does make sense to question the empirical relevance of the positive analogies of choice that the two theories are depicting. In Chapter 18 I describe a formal test that is designed to answer that question.[5]

7.3.3 Game-Theoretic Situations

In consumer choice under certainty the consumer knows the values of all relevant current and future prices. In consumer choice under uncertainty the consumer knows all relevant current and past prices and uses the information they convey to form his ideas about the probability distributions of future prices (cf. Chapter 6, Section 6.4.2). In both theories the consumer forms his judgments and makes his choices independently of the judgments and choices of other consumers. In particular, he does not take into account that his ability to implement his choices depends on the choices of other consumers. There are various sufficient conditions on preferences and expectations that ensure the existence of prices at which all consumers can implement their choices. Examples of such conditions for the certainty case can be found in Debreu (1959). Analogous conditions for the uncertainty case are given in Stigum (1969, 1972).

In game-theoretic situations each participant has on hand a set of pure strategies and faces a set of consequences, each one of which results from the particular combinations of pure strategies chosen by the participants. Moreover, each participant orders consequences according to the values of a utility function and may use mixed as well as pure strategies. Finally, each participant knows the rules of the game, his own and his opponents' sets of pure strategies, the consequences for him and the others of his and their choice of strategies, his own utility function, and the families of functions to which his opponents' utility functions belong. Game theorists usually add to this that it is common knowledge among participants that each of them possesses such knowledge.

There are all sorts of games. Some are noncooperative; others are cooperative. Some are static; others are dynamic. Whatever the game, the novel aspect of a game-theoretic situation is that each participant in his search for good choices must take into account the possible choices of his opponents. Game theorists agree that a good choice of strategy for a given player must be a best response to the strategies of his opponents. However, it is often hard to determine what constitutes a best response in situations in which an opponent's choice of strategy is not well defined. Moreover, even in situations where all the participants' best responses are common knowledge, it may be impossible for a participant to single out a good choice of strategy before he knows what his opponents will do. The following example of a noncooperative static game illustrates what I have in mind.

E 7.7 *Consider a game with two players,* A *and* B*, in which* A *has three pure strategies,* b, c, *and* d*;* B *has two pure strategies,* α *and* β*, and the payoff matrix is:*

		B's strategies	
		α	β
	b	200, 75	40, 300
A's strategies	*c*	50, 300	200, 65
	d	100, 50	100, 45

Thus if A *chooses* b *and* B *chooses* β, A *will receive utility 40 and* B *will receive utility 300. We take for granted that* A *and* B *are rational animals and that that fact is part of the players' common knowledge.*

In this game *B*'s best responses to *A*'s pure strategies, *b*, *c*, and *d* are β, α, and β, respectively. Similarly, *A*'s best responses to *B*'s pure strategies, α and β, are *b* and *c*, respectively. Moreover, the utility that *A* can gain from playing *d* is smaller than the expected utility that he would obtain by playing *b* with probability 1/2 and *c* with probability 1/2. Thus most game theorists would insist that a rational animal in *A*'s situation would never play *d*. However, this need not be so. Unless it is common knowledge that players in a game rank uncertain prospects according to their expected utility, one cannot take for granted that *A* will never employ *d*.[6] More on that later.

A Nash equilibrium in a game is a combination of strategies in which each participant has played his best response against the chosen strategies of the other players. In the given game there is no Nash equilibrium in pure strategies. If it is common knowledge that *A* and *B* rank uncertain options according to their expected utility, there is, instead, a Nash equilibrium in mixed strategies. In this equilibrium *A* plays *b* with probability 47/92 and *c* with probability 45/92 and *B* plays α with probability 16/31 and β with probability 15/31. There is no other Nash equilibrium.

There are many interesting aspects of the preceding example. For instance, a Nash equilibrium in pure strategies is an equilibrium in which each participant in the game, after learning his opponents' chosen strategies is satisfied with the strategy he chose for himself. A Nash equilibrium in mixed strategies is nothing of the sort, since in such an equilibrium the game participants never know what strategies their opponents have adopted. Consider, for example, the Nash equilibrium in E 7.7, where *A* is to play *b* and *c* with respective probabilities 47/92 and 45/92 and *B* is to play α and β with respective probabilities 16/31 and 15/31. In this equilibrium *A* receives expected utility 122.58. As long as *B* sticks to his equilibrium mixed strategy, *A* can obtain the same expected utility from playing *b* or *c* or any possible probabilistic combination of the two. Which one of the infinitude of equivalent strategies that *A* ends up adopting *B* never knows. He only observes the pure strategy, b or c, that results from A's decision-making deliberations.[7]

Game theorists seek to ameliorate the given deficiency of mixed-strategy Nash equilibria by adding two conditions to this characterization of games. They insist that it must be common knowledge that each participant is "rational" and that "rational" individuals limit their choice of good strategies to Nash equilibrium strategies. In a game with a unique Nash equilibrium, therefore, the players need not observe the strategies of their opponents. They can calculate their own and their opponents' equilibrium strategies, choose their own equilibrium strategies, and be sure that their opponents will do the same. What the participants are supposed to do in games with multiple Nash equilibria, however, is problematic to say the least.

It is one thing to argue that it is "rational" for the players of a game to adopt mutually consistent Nash equilibrium strategies. It is another thing to insist that in game-theoretic situations rational animals tend to choose mutually consistent Nash equilibrium strategies. The former is an assertion about what rational animals *ought* to do when they participate in games. The latter is an assertion about what rational animals *actually* do. Most economists seem to agree that game theorists' arguments in support of Nash equilibrium strategies make wonderful sense for a *normative* theory of games. However, these arguments are of little help in the search for ways to develop a *positive* theory of games. To describe actual behavior in games I must introduce other ideas.

Players in the kind of games I consider are rational animals. To describe the behavior of rational animals in game-theoretic situations, I must introduce ideas about the players' expectations and about their risk preferences. Take another look at the game in E 7.7. From the point of view of A, his three pure strategies are three prospects with known consequences and unspecified probabilities. The probabilities specify A's ideas as to how B goes about choosing his two strategies. Similarly, to B his two strategies are prospects with known consequences and unspecified probabilities. The probabilities describe B's ideas as to how A goes about choosing his three strategies. A and B must use the information they possess about each other to evaluate the relevant probabilities, rank the resulting prospects, and determine their respective good choices. In the social reality that I described in Chapter 2, A's and B's probability assignments and risk preferences are not common knowledge. The next example elaborates on these ideas.

E 7.8 *Consider the game in E 7.7, and assume that both* A *and* B *assign probabilities to the strategies of their opponent in accordance with the principles of Dempster (1967) and Shafer (1976).* A *argues that* B *has no good reason for preferring* α *to* β. *So he assigns the following basic probabilities to* B*'s choice of strategies:*

$$m_A(\{\alpha\}) = 1/4 = m_A(\{\beta\}) \text{ and } m_A(\{\alpha, \beta\}) = 1/2.$$

B for his part argues that A has no good reason for preferring b to c and that there is a chance that A is averse to uncertainty. So he assigns the following basic probabilities to A's choice of strategies:

$$m_B(\{b\}) = 1/4 = m_B(\{c\}), m_B(\{b, c\}) = 1/4, m_B(\{d\}) = 1/6, \text{ and } m_B(\{b, c, d\}) = 1/12.$$

Also, both A and B in uncertain situations rank their prospects according to the prescriptions of Kjell Arne Brekke that I noted above. Thus, for A we find that

$$W_A(\{\alpha\}|b) = 200, W_A(\{\beta\}|b) = 40, W_A(\{\alpha, \beta\}|b) = 40,$$

with

$$V_A(b) = (1/4)(200 + 40) + (1/2)40 = 80;$$

$$W_A(\{\alpha\}|c) = 50, W_A(\{\beta\}|c) = 200, W_A(\{\alpha, \beta\}|c) = 50,$$

with

$$V_A(c) = (1/4)(50 + 200) + (1/2)50 = 87.5;$$

and

$$W_A(\{\alpha\}|d) = 100, W_A(\{\beta\}|d) = 100, W_A(\{\alpha, \beta\}|d) = 100,$$

with

$$V_A(d) = 100.$$

For B we find that

$$W_B(\{b\}|\alpha) = 75, W_B(\{c\}|\alpha) = 300, W_B(\{d\}|\alpha) = 50, W_B(\{b, c\}|\alpha) = 75, W_B(\{b, c, d\}|\alpha) = 50;$$

and

$$W_B(\{b\}|\beta) = 300, W_B(\{c\}|\beta) = 65, W_B(\{d\}|\beta) = 45, W_B(\{b, c\}|\beta) = 65, W_B(\{b, c, d\}|\beta) = 45,$$

with

$$V_B(\alpha) = (1/4)(75 + 300 + 75) + (1/6)50 + (1/12)50 = 1500/12 = 125$$

and

$$V_B(\beta) = (1/4)(300 + 65 + 65) + (1/6)45 + (1/12)45 = 1425/12 = 118.75.$$

From this we conclude that A will choose strategy d and that B will choose strategy α. Neither one of them has reason to regret his choice. This solution shows why A's d strategy in the E 7.8 game cannot be eliminated unless it is common knowledge that A is an expected utility maximizer.

Several remarks and disclaimers are called for in regard to E 7.8: (1) *A* and *B* order their prospects with capacities and Choquet integrals. They could, as well, have ordered them the way Bayesians order prospects in uncertain situations. (2) A player's assignment of probabilities to his opponent's pure strategies is not to be identified with the opponent's mixed strategy. Each player's choice of strategy is independent of the other player's ordering of prospects. (3) *A* and *B* end up with a unique pair of optimal pure strategies. That is not always the case. A player with several optimal pure strategies may choose among them according to the outcome of a random device. (4) The ideas that E 7.8 exemplifies are shared by others. Vide, for instance, Jürgen Eichberger and David Kelsey's (1993) paper on nonadditive beliefs and equilibria in game theory.[8] However, most game theorists seem to find them unacceptable solely on theoretical grounds. A good reference for that opinion is Harsanyi (1982).

The game-theoretic situations that I considered above are prototypes of a small percentage of the game situations researchers face in economics. In other cases they must consider the possibility of preplay communication, the strategic aspects of threats, and the advantages of cooperation. Economists have devised all sorts of theoretical models to go with such possibilities. Some are easy to grasp and others are quite complex. Here the important thing to note is that the rationality that these theoretical models prescribe need not have much in common with the rationality of rational animals. The empirical relevance of the characteristics of rational choice in these models must be confronted with data before they can be accepted. The following are two examples to illustrate what I have in mind.

More than a half-century ago John Nash (1950) insisted that any solution of a two-person bargaining problem must satisfy four, supposedly reasonable conditions: Pareto optimality, symmetry, independence of irrelevant alternatives, and invariance to linear transformations of utility. Ingenious experiments in economics laboratories have demonstrated that most experimental bargaining outcomes satisfy the first three conditions and fail to satisfy the fourth (cf. Davis and Holt, 1993, pp. 242–275). The failure in regard to the fourth condition is problematic for game theorists who insist that it is common knowledge in games that players rank mixed strategies according to their expected utility. The utility function of an expected-utility maximizer is determined up to a positive linear transformation.

Multistage games usually have many Nash equilibria. Multiple equilibria are problematic for a positive theory of games and have led game theorists to look for refinements of Nash equilibria. One such refinement is Reinhard Selten's idea of a subgame perfect Nash equilibrium (SPNE) in which the players' strategies establish Nash equilibria in each and every subgame (cf. Selten, 1965). The SPNEs have interesting characteristics. For example, they limit the number of relevant Nash equilibria by ruling noncredible threats off the equilibrium path out of order. They also, unfortunately, carry with them problematic questions for rational choice in multistage games. The following illustrates one of them. In any given case we find Selten's SPNEs by so-called backward induction, and backward induction arguments are questionable. A number of laboratory experiments have demonstrated that subjects are not good at backward induction (cf. Davis and Holt, 1993, pp. 102–109). Moreover, as evidenced by Selten's (1978) own "chain-store paradox," they can lead to unreasonable equilibria. Finally, one aspect of rational choice in a SPNE, on which Selten insists, is dubious: If your opponent makes a draw that seems foolish to you, do not question his rationality! Just treat the draw as the result of an inconsequential lapse of concentration. To me that is dubious advice.[9]

My concern about rationality and backward induction is shared by many others. Thoughtful discussions of rationality and backward induction can be found in Aumann (1995), Binmore (1997), and Dekel and Gul (1997, sec. 5).

7.4 RATIONAL EXPECTATIONS

John Muth (1961) suggested that individual decision-makers' expectations be considered as informed predictions of future events that coincide with the predictions of the relevant economic theory. Doing that could ensure that the theories' descriptions of individual behavior would be consistent with the decision-makers' beliefs about the behavior of the economic system. Muth's idea of expectations formation constitutes the essential ingredient of the *rational expectations hypothesis* (REH) in economics.

Largely due to the seminal works of Robert E. Lucas (Lucas, 1972a,b, 1975), the REH surfaced in macroeconomic studies of inflation and the natural rate of unemployment in the 1970s. In these studies economists hypothesized that it served the best interests of utility-maximizing consumers and profit-maximizing firms to predict the rate of inflation as accurately as possible. To do that successfully the individuals in question needed to take all available information into account, including forecasts of changes in monetary and fiscal policies. With such information they might make inaccurate assessments of probable changes in the price level, and different individuals were likely to make different forecasts. Still, so economists hypothesized, on the average the predictions would be right. Moreover, the mistakes that the given individuals as a group made in forecasting the rate of inflation would be random and uncorrelated with the information they possessed. These ideas find expressions in the macroeconomic model I describe in E 7.9, which I have got from Hashem Pesaran, who ascribes it to Lucas (cf. Pesaran, 1987, pp. 26–29).

E 7.9 *Suppose that the behavior over time of an economy can be described by the following system of equations:*

$$y_t^d + p_t = m_t + v, t = 1, 2, \ldots \qquad (1)$$

$$y_t^s - \ddot{y}_t = \alpha\left(p_t - p_t^*\right) + \varepsilon_t, t = 1, 2, \ldots \quad (2)$$

$$y_t^s = y_t^d, t = 1, 2, \ldots \quad (3)$$

Here y^d, y^s, *and* $\ddot{y}$ *are the logarithms, respectively, of the demand (for), supply, and natural level of aggregate output;* p *and* p^* *are the logarithms, respectively, of the actual price level and the price level that the members of the economy in one period expected to prevail in the next period;* m *and* v *are the logarithms, respectively, of the money supply and the velocity of money;* t *records relevant periods, and* $\{\varepsilon_t, t = 1, 2, \ldots\}$ *constitutes a purely random process with mean zero and finite variance whose members, for each* t, *are uncorrelated with* $\ddot{y}_s$, m_s, *and* v, $s \leq t$.

Suppose next that m *is an exogenous policy variable and adopt the rational expectations hypothesis that for each* t, p_t^* *equals the economic system's best prediction of the value of* p_t *in period* $t-1$. *By solving Eqs. (1)–(3) for* p_t, *one finds that*

$$p_t = [\alpha/(1+\alpha)]p_t^* + [1/(1+\alpha)](m_t + v - \ddot{y}_t - \varepsilon_t). \quad (4)$$

Also, by taking expectations of both sides of (4) conditional on the information set in period $t-1$, Ω_{t-1}, *one finds that the best predictor of* p_t, Þ_t *is given by the equation*

$$\text{Þ}_t = [\alpha/(1+\alpha)]p_t^* + [1/(1+\alpha)]E\left\{m_t + v - \ddot{y}_t - \varepsilon_t | \Omega_{t-1}\right\}. \quad (5)$$

It follows from (5) and the REH that

$$p_t^* = E\left\{m_t + v - \ddot{y}_t - \varepsilon_t | \Omega_{t-1}\right\}. \quad (6)$$

If one now combines (6) and (4) and takes expectation of both sides in (4) with respect to Ω_{t-1}, *one can conclude that*

$$E\{p_t | \Omega_{t-1}\} = E\left\{m_t + v - \ddot{y}_t - \varepsilon_t | \Omega_{t-1}\right\} \quad (7)$$

and hence that

$$p_t^* = E\{p_t | \Omega_{t-1}\}. \quad (8)$$

The last equation shows that the price expectations of the members of the economy are valid on the average. Further, since $E\left\{p_t - p_t^* | \Omega_{t-1}\right\} = E\{p_t | \Omega_{t-1}\} - p_t^* = 0$, *the equation implies that the prediction error in one period is uncorrelated with the variables in the preceding period's information set.*

In E 7.9 I did not characterize the DGP of the exogenous variables. One way to accomplish that is to assume that the m_t and the ε_t in Eqs. (1) and (2) satisfy the following set of equations:

$$m_t = \rho m_{t-1} + \xi_t, t = 1, 2, \ldots, \quad (9)$$

where $\rho \in (0, 1)$, and $\{\xi_t, t = 1, 2, \ldots\}$ is a purely random process with mean zero and finite variance that is distributed independently of the ε_t.

$$E\{\varepsilon_t|\Omega_{t-1}\} = E\{\xi_t|\Omega_{t-1}\} = 0, t = 1, 2, \ldots \quad (10)$$

When one adds Eqs. (9) and (10) to (1)–(3), one can show that

$$y_t = \ddot{y}_t + [1/(1+\alpha)](\alpha\xi_t - \varepsilon_t), t = 1, 2, \ldots, \quad (11)$$

and

$$p_t = \rho m_{t-1} + v - \ddot{y}_t + [1/(1+\alpha)](\xi_t - \varepsilon_t), t = 1, 2, \ldots. \quad (12)$$

Thus, if the postulates (1)–(3) and (9)–(10) are valid, it follows from (11) that only unforeseen changes in the money supply affect the equilibrium level of y. Equation (12) also provides an explicit form for the linear best predictor of the price level.

Its simplicity notwithstanding, E 7.9 and Eqs. (9)–(12) give a good idea of the role the REH plays in macroeconomic models. Note how involved the conditional expectation of the policy variable m_t and the two exogenous variables $\ddot{y}_t$ and v is in forming the expectation of the endogenous variable p_t. This involvement exemplifies a general characteristic of REH macroeconomic models (Pesaran, 1989, p. 28). Note also that (9) is meant to convey the idea that in the given economy, there is a fixed rule underlying the government's monetary policy. Deviations from the rule are unforeseen and happen only at random. This, again, is a general characteristic of monetary policy in REH macroeconomic models. Finally, note the severe knowledge requirements that the REH places on the members of the economy. They are supposed to know both the true structural model of the economy and the data-generating process of endogenous and exogenous variables alike. For an ordinary rational animal, that is a very tall order whose empirical relevance data alone can determine.[10]

I have considered the import of REH in macroeconomics. The REH plays an important role in other areas of economics as well, for example, in general equilibrium theory and in the theory of financial markets. For an interesting study of the import of REH in real-life financial markets one reader can consult Chapter 21, where Heather Anderson tries the empirical relevance of the REH with data from the U.S. money market.

7.5 CONCLUDING REMARKS

In this chapter I have discussed consumer choice under certainty, choice in risky and uncertain situations, choice in various game-theoretic situations, and the rational expectations hypothesis. The purpose of the discussion was to describe the attitude that I think we ought to adopt toward these theories. I believe that they delineate positive analogies of behavior in the populations of rational animals that their originators had in mind. Whether these positive analogies have empirical relevance is a question for applied econometricians to answer. In that regard one last remark is in order.

I have tried to convey the idea that in the tests of theories of choice that econometricians carry out, the rationality of the members of the sample populations is not at stake. The only point in question is the empirical relevance of the positive analogies of behavior that the theories identify, and this ought to be evident from the tests of the theory of consumer choice that I describe in the book. In one of the tests the sample population comprises families and single individuals living in the United States in 1962. In another test the sample population consists of albino rats in a laboratory at the Texas A&M University. In a third test the sample population consists of psychotics at Central Islip State Hospital in New York. The theory tested out in the second and third test and failed in the first. The failure occurred not because the 1962 U.S. consumers were irrational, but because the characteristics that Milton Friedman's (1957) theory attributed to them were not positive analogies for that population. Similarly, the rationality of members of the sample populations was never at stake in the tests of the expected utility theory that Maurice Allais (1979), Daniel Ellsberg (1961), and many others have carried out. Those who failed these tests did not fail them because they were irrational. They failed because the positive analogies that the theory identifies were not characteristic features of their way of ordering uncertain prospects.

NOTES

1. Here it is interesting to recall theorem T 3 of Section 6.4.2. If the prices of bread and coffee were arguments of my utility function, as they are in T 3, it is not far fetched to claim that I, in the neighborhood grocery store and within the budget that my wife has allotted to me, always choose the pair of commodities that I most prefer.

2. The idea is to rephrase my SSA 4 axiom so that the α_i in Eq. (19.22) of Stigum (1990, p. 435) can be identified with B's perceived probabilities of the respective events.

3. In an experimental situation, knowledge of the percentage of the pertinent population that suffers from a given disease is likely to influence a subject's prior probability that he himself might suffer from the disease. For that reason it is not obvious that Hammerton's results can be interpreted so as to support the view that subjects tend to act in accordance with Cohen's ideas.

4. Von Neumann and Morgenstern's axioms and a precise statement of their theorem can be found in Section 4.1.

5. The ordering of prospects that $V(\cdot)$ induces satisfies neither Savage's axioms nor mine. For a discussion of how the ordering differs from Savage's axioms one may consult Stigum (1990, pp. 445–455).

6. Even then there may be difficulties. For evidence of that, compare, for example, the interesting article by Van Huyck et al. (1999), "What Does It Take to Eliminate the Use of a Strategy Strictly Dominated by a Mixture?"

7. In this context the interested reader will find Marco Mariotti's (1997, pp. 47–50) analysis of the principle of "equal treatment of payoff-equivalent strategies" relevant.

Mariotti claims that it is inconsistent with Bayesian ideas of rationality to discriminate between two strategies that have the same expected payoff. If he is right, the mixed-strategy Nash equilibrium in E 7.7 cannot be considered an equilibrium in a game between two Bayesian decision-makers.

8. J. Eichberger and D. Kelsey consider game-theoretic equilibria in which each player's optimal strategy is required to be a best response to his own superadditive beliefs over the possible optimal strategies of his opponents. Their kind of equilibria is related in interesting ways to Nash equilibria and maximum equilibria.

9. Dow and Werlang (1994) show that Nash equilibrium exists for any degree of uncertainty aversion and that backward induction breaks down in the twice-repeated prisoners dilemma.

10. For a discussion of the empirical relevance of the REH and the intricacies of estimating REH econometric models one should consult Sheffrin (1996) and Pesaran (1987).

REFERENCES

Aasnes, J., E. Bjoern, and T. Skjerpen, 1993, "Engel Functions, Panel Data, and Latent Variables," *Econometrica* 61, 1395–1422.

Allais, M., 1979, "The So-Called Allais Paradox and Rational Decisions under Uncertainty," in: *Expected Utility Hypothesis and the Allais Paradox*, M. Allais and O. Hagen (eds.), Dordrecht: Reidel.

Arrow, K. J., 1965, *Aspects of the Theory of Risk Bearing*, Helsinki: Academic Book Store.

Aumann, R., 1985, "What is Game Theory Trying to Accomplish?" in: *Frontiers of Economics*, K. J. Arrow and S. Honkapohja (eds), Oxford: Blackwell.

Aumann, R., 1995, "Backward Induction and Common Knowledge of Rationality," *Games and Economic Behavior* 8, 6–19.

Bar-Hillel, M., 1973, "On the Subjective Probability of Compound Events," *Organizational Behavior and Human Performance* 9, 396–406.

Binmore, K., 1997, "Rationality and Backward Induction," *Journal of Economic Methodology* 4, 23–1.

Chateauneuf, A., 1986, "Uncertainty Aversion and Risk Aversion in Models with Non-additive Probabilities," Mimeographed Paper, Université de Paris.

Cohen, L. J., 1981, "Can Human Irrationality be Experimentally Demonstrated?" *Behavioral and Brain Sciences* 4, 317–370.

Davis, D. D., and C. A. Holt,1993, *Experimental Economics*, Princeton: Princeton University Press.

Debreu, G., 1959, *Theory of Value*, New York: Wiley.

Dekel, E., and F. Gul, 1997, "Rationality and Knowledge in Game Theory," in: *Advances in Economics and Econometrics: Theory and Applications, Seventh World Congress, Vol. I*, D. M. Kreps and K. Wallis (eds.), Cambridge: Cambridge University Press.

Dempster, A. P., 1967, "Upper and Lower Probabilities Induced by a Multivalued Mapping," *Annals of Mathematical Statistics* 38, 325–339.

Dow, J., and S. R. da C. Werlang, 1994, "Nash Equilibrium under Knightian Uncertainty: Breaking down Backward Induction," *Journal of Economic Theory* 64, 305–324.

Eichberger, J., and D. Kelsey, 1993, "Non-additive Beliefs and Game Theory," Unpublished Paper, University of Melbourne, Australia.

Ellsberg, D., 1961, "Risk, Ambiguity, and the Savage Axioms," *Quarterly Journal of Economics* 75, 643–669.

Engel, E., 1857, "Die Produktions- und Consumptionsverhältnisse des Königsreichs Sachsen," *Zeitschrift des Statistischen Büreaus des Königlich*, Sächsischen Ministeriums des Innern, Dresden, November.

Feller, W., 1957, *An Introduction to Probability Theory and Its Applications. Vol. 1*, 2nd Ed. New York: Wiley.

Friedman, M., 1957, *A Theory of the Consumption Function*, Princeton: Princeton University Press.

Gilboa, I., 1987, "Expected Utility with Purely Subjective Non-additive Probabilities," *Journal of Mathematical Economics* 16, 65–88.

Hammerton, M., 1973, "A Case of Radical Probability Estimation," *Journal of Experimental Psychology* 101, 252–254.

Harsanyi, J. C., 1982, "Subjective Probability and the Theory of Games: Comments on Kadane and Larkey's Paper, and Rejoinder to Kadane and Larkey," *Management Science* 28, 120–124.

Jaffray, J.-Y., 1989, "Linear Utility Theory and Belief Functions," *Operations Research Letters* 8, 107–112.

Kahnemann, D. and A. Tversky, 1972. "Subjective Probability: A Judgement of Representativeness," *Cognitive Psychology* 3, 430–454.

Kagel, J. H., R. C. Battalio, and L. Green, 1995, *Economic Choice Theory: An Experimental Analysis of Animal Behavior*, Cambridge: Cambridge University Press.

Laplace, P. S.,1820, *A Philosophical Essay on Probabilities*, F. W. Truscott and F. L. Emory (trans.), New York: Dover, 1951.

Lindley, D. V., 1977, "A Problem in Forensic Science," *Biometrica* 64, 207–213.

Lucas, R. E., 1972a, "Expectations and the Neutrality of Money," *Journal of Economic Theory* 4, 103–124.

Lucas, R. E., 1972b, "Econometric Testing of the Natural Rate Hypothesis," in O. Eckstein (ed.), *The Econometrics of Price Determination Conference*, Washington, D.C.: Board of Governors of the Federal Reserve System.

Lucas, R. E., 1975, "An Equilibrium Model of the Business Cycle," *Journal of Political Economy* 83, 1113–1144.

MacCrimmon, K. R., and S. Larsson, 1979, "Utility Theory: Axioms Versus Paradoxes," in: *The Expected Utility Hypothesis and the Allais Paradox*, M. Allais and O. Hagen (eds.), Dordrecht: Riedel.

Mariotti, M., 1997, "Decisions in Games: Why There Should be a Special Exemption from Bayesian Rationality," *Journal of Economic Methodology* 4, 43–60.

Modigliani, F., and R. Brumberg, 1955, "Utility Analysis and the Consumption Function. An Interpretation of Cross-Section Data," in: *Post-Keynesian Economics*, K. K. Kurihara (ed.), London: Allen and Unwin.

Mosteller, F. C., and P. Nogee, 1951, "An Experimental Measurement of Utility," *Journal of Political Economy* 59, 371–404.

Muth, J. F., 1961, "Rational Expectations and the Theory of Price Movements," *Econometrica* 29, 315–335.

Nash, J. F., 1950, "The Bargaining Problem," *Econometrica* 18, 155–162.

Pesaran, M. H., 1987, *The Limits to Rational Expectations*, London: Blackwell.

Preston, M. G., and P. Baratta, 1948, "An Experimental Study of the Auction Value of an Uncertain Income," *American Journal of Psychology* 61, 183–193.

Samuelson, P. A., 1953, "Consumption Theorems in Terms of Overcompensation Rather than Indifference Comparisons," *Economica* 20, 1–9.

Savage, L. J., 1954, *The Foundations of Statistics*, New York: Wiley.

Selten, R., 1965, "Spieltheoretische Behandlung eines Oligopolmodells mit Nachfragetragheit," *Zeitschrift für die gesamte Staatswissenschaft* 121, 301–324, 667–689

Selten, R., 1978, "The Chain Store Paradox," *Theory and Decision* 9, 127–159.

Shafer, G., 1976, *A Mathematical Theory of Evidence*, Princeton: Princeton University Press.

Sheffrin, S. M., 1996, *Rational Expectations*, 2nd ed., Cambridge: Cambridge University Press.

Slutsky, E., 1915, "Sulla Teoria del Bilancio del Consumatore," *Giornale degli Economisti* 51, 1–26.

Stigum, B. P., 1969, "Competitive Equilibria under Uncertainty," *Quarterly Journal of Economics* 83, 533–561.

Stigum, B. P., 1972, "Resource Allocation under Uncertainty," *International Economic Review*. 13, 431–459.

Stigum, B. P., 1990, *Toward a Formal Science of Economics*, Cambridge: MIT Press.

Van Huyck, J., F. Rankin, and R. Battalio, 1999, "What Does It Take to Eliminate the Use of a Strategy Strictly Dominated by a Mixture?" *Experimental Economics* 2, 129–150.

von Neumann, J., and O. Morgenstern, 1953, *Theory of Games and Economic Behavior*, Princeton: Princeton University Press.

Chapter Eight

Topological Artifacts and Life in Large Economies

This chapter is about competitive equilibria and core allocations in large economies. According to standard theory, in a competitive equilibrium the allocation of an economy's resources is a core allocation. Moreover, if the economy is large, every core allocation is close to some competitive equilibrium allocation. In fact, if the economy is large enough, so the theory says, the set of core allocations coincides with the set of competitive equilibrium allocations. I show here that the last two observations are topological artifacts that have little to do with the size of the economy. I also demonstrate a characteristic of resource allocation in large economies that renders the purport of the second assertion dubious.

8.1 TWO BEAUTIFUL THEOREMS IN MATHEMATICAL ECONOMICS

The strategy behind my demonstration that two supposedly fundamental properties of large economies are topological artifacts is simple: Pick two central theorems in mathematical economics—one that concerns the possibility of approximating core allocations by competitive equilibrium allocations and one that establishes the equality of the set of core allocations and the set of competitive equilibrium allocations. Then show that in each case there are large nonstandard economies that satisfy all the conditions of the theorem and yet satisfy the conclusions only if the topology is right.

To make my case as strong as possible I have singled out two of the most beautiful theorems in mathematical economics. One of them is due to Gerard Debreu and Herbert Scarf (1963) and paraphrased in theorem T 1. The other is due to Robert Aumann (1964, 1966) and paraphrased in T 2.

8.1.1 Debreu and Scarf's Theorem

Debreu and Scarf's theorem T 1 depicts the relation of core allocations and competitive equilibrium allocations in m-fold replications E_m of an exchange economy E with k consumers of different types. In E_m an *allocation* is a function

$$X^m(\cdot) : \{1, \ldots, k\} \times \{1, \ldots, m\} \to R^n_+ \tag{1}$$

that satisfies the condition

$$\sum_{i=1}^{k} \sum_{j=1}^{m} X^m(i, j) = \sum_{i=1}^{k} \sum_{j=1}^{m} \omega(i, j), \tag{2}$$

where the pair (i, j) designates the jth consumer of the ith type, $\omega(i, j) \in R^n_{++}$ denotes his initial endowment of commodities, and $X^m(i, j)$ is the commodity bundle that $X^m(\cdot)$ allocates to him. Moreover, a *competitive equilibrium* is a pair $[p, X^m(\cdot)]$, where $p \in R^n_{++}$ and $X^m(\cdot)$ is an allocation that, for each pair $(i, j) \in \{1, \ldots, k\} \times \{1, \ldots, m\}$, satisfies

$$pX^m(i, j) \leq p\omega(i, j) \tag{3}$$

and

$$V^i[X^m(i, j)] = \max_{y \in R^n_+, py \leq p\omega(i,j)} V^i(y) \tag{4}$$

with $V^i(\cdot) : R^n_+ \to R_+$ as the type i consumer's utility indicator, $i = 1, \ldots, k$. Finally, the *core* of E_m consists of all allocations that cannot be blocked by some coalition. Here a *coalition* is a nonempty subset of $\{1, \ldots, k\} \times \{1, \ldots, m\}$, and a coalition H is said to *block* an allocation $X^m(\cdot)$ if there is an allocation $Z^m(\cdot)$ in E_m such that $\sum_{(i,j)\in H} Z^m(i, j) = \sum_{(i,j)\in H} \omega(i, j)$ and such that for all $(i, j) \in H$, $V^i[Z^m(i, j)] \geq V^i[X^m(i, j)]$ with inequality for at least one pair $(i, j) \in H$. Under the conditions that T 1 imposes on the $V^i(\cdot)$ and the $\omega(i, \cdot)$ it is well known that a competitive equilibrium in E_m exists and that the associated allocation is a core allocation. Hence the core in E_m is nonempty and contains E_m's set of competitive equilibrium allocations. Theorem T 1 describes in what way the set of core allocations in E_m approaches E_m's set of competitive equilibrium allocations as m tends to infinity.

T 1 *Let* E *be a standard exchange economy with* k *consumers; that is, let*

$$E = \left[\left(V^1(\cdot), R^n_+, \omega^1\right), \ldots, \left(V^k(\cdot), R^n_+, \omega^k\right)\right],$$

where for each $\mathrm{i} = 1, \ldots, \mathrm{k}$*: (a)* $\omega^{\mathrm{i}} \in \mathrm{R}^{\mathrm{n}}_{++}$*, (b)* $\mathrm{V}^{\mathrm{i}}(\cdot) : \mathrm{R}^{\mathrm{n}}_+ \to \mathrm{R}_+$ *is strictly increasing, strictly quasi-concave, and continuous; and (c)* $[\mathrm{V}^{\mathrm{j}}(\cdot), \omega^{\mathrm{j}}] \neq [\mathrm{V}^{\mathrm{i}}(\cdot), \omega^{\mathrm{i}}]$ *for* $\mathrm{j} \neq \mathrm{i}, \mathrm{j} \in \{1, \ldots, \mathrm{k}\}$. *Next, let* $\mathrm{E_m}$ *be an* m*-fold replication of* E*, name the consumers in* $\mathrm{E_m}$ *by pairs* $(\mathrm{i}, \mathrm{j}) \in \{1, \ldots \mathrm{k}\} \times \{1, \ldots, \mathrm{m}\}$*, and identify consumer* $(\mathrm{i}, 1)$ *with the* i*th consumer in* E, $\mathrm{i} = 1, \ldots, \mathrm{k}$. *Moreover, designate the endowments of the consumers in* $\mathrm{E_m}$ *by a function* $\omega(\cdot) : \{1, \ldots, \mathrm{k}\} \times \{1, \ldots, \mathrm{m}\} \to \mathrm{R}^{\mathrm{n}}_{++}$*, whose values satisfy* $\omega(\mathrm{i}, \mathrm{j}) = \omega^{\mathrm{i}}$*, for all* $\mathrm{j} \in \{1, \ldots, \mathrm{m}\}, \mathrm{i} = 1, \ldots, \mathrm{k}$*, and let* $\mathrm{X^m}(\cdot) : \{1, \ldots, \mathrm{k}\} \times \{1, \ldots, \mathrm{m}\} \to \mathrm{R}^{\mathrm{n}}_{++}$ *be an allocation in* $\mathrm{E_m}$*. The following two assertions about* $\mathrm{E_m}$ *are valid:*

(I) If $\mathrm{X^m}(\cdot)$ *is a core allocation, then* $\mathrm{X^m}(\mathrm{i}, \mathrm{j}) = \mathrm{X^m}(\mathrm{i}, 1)$ *for all* $\mathrm{j} = 2, \ldots, \mathrm{m}$*, and* $\mathrm{i} = 1, \ldots, \mathrm{k}$.

(II) *Let* $C_m = \{x \in R_+^{kn} : x = [X^m(1,1), \ldots, X^m(k,1)]$ *for some core allocation* $X^m(\cdot)\}$. *Then* $C_{(m+1)} \subset C_m$, *and if* $x \in C_m$ *for all* $m = 1, 2, \ldots,$ *then there exists a* $p \in R_{++}^n$ *such that* (p, x) *is a competitive equilibrium in* E.

In the intended interpretation of T 1, the components of a w denote units of ordinary commodities such as apples, oranges, and potatoes, and R_+^n is taken to denote the set of all available commodity vectors. For each component of w, there is a component of the p in (3) that denotes the number of units of account that are needed in a given competitive equilibrium to purchase one unit of the commodity in question. Further, a consumer is an individual living alone or a family living together with a common household budget and an initial endowment of commodities, w, and orders commodity vectors in accordance with the values of their utility indicator $V(\cdot)$. Finally, an economy is a finite set of consumers with resources equal to the sum $\sum_{i=1}^k w^i$ or $\sum_{i=1}^k \sum_{j=1}^m w(i, j)$ as the case may be, and an allocation is a distribution of these resources among the consumers in the economy.

8.1.2 Aumann's Theorem

In the intended interpretation of E_m, the existence of a competitive equilibrium is taken to establish the objective possibility of a perfectly competitive exchange economy arriving at an equilibrium in which all markets are cleared. There is, however, an important proviso to the possibility: In a perfectly competitive economy a single trader alone, even if he should care to, cannot influence the equilibrium level of prices in the economy. The proviso does not hold for E_m no matter how large m is. That led Robert Aumann to believe that the appropriate model for a perfectly competitive exchange economy is one with a continuum of traders. I consider Aumann's (1964, 1966) core equivalence theorem for such an economy next.

In the statement of Aumann's theorem, T 2, the closed unit interval [0,1] designates the set of consumers and R_+^n denotes the set of available commodity vectors; $w(\cdot) : [0,1] \to R_+^n$ depicts the initial commodity vectors of the respective consumers, and for each $r \in [0,1]$, $V(r, \cdot)$ denotes the utility indicator of the rth consumer. Finally, an exchange economy is a triple, $\{V(\cdot), [0,1] \times R_+^n, w(\cdot)\}$, where $V(\cdot) : [0,1] \times R_+^n \to R_+$ and [0,1], R_+^n, and $w(\cdot)$ have the interpretation already given to them.

In the Aumann economy, EA, an *allocation* is a Lebesgue measurable function $x(\cdot) : [0,1] \to R_+^n$ that satisfies

$$x(r) \leq c \qquad (5)$$

for some constant c and *a.a.* $r \in [0,1]$ (μ measure), and

$$\int_0^1 x(r)\, d\mu(r) = \int_0^1 w(r)\, d\mu(r), \qquad (6)$$

where $\mu(\cdot)$ denotes the Lebesgue measure.[1] Also, a *competitive equilibrium* is a triple $[p, x(\cdot), K]$, where $p \in R^n_{++}$, $x(\cdot)$ is an allocation, $K \subset [0, 1]$, and K and $x(\cdot)$ satisfy

$$\mu(K) = 1, \tag{7}$$

$$px(r) \leq pw(r), \qquad r \in K, \tag{8}$$

and

$$V[r, x(r)] = \max_{y \in R^n_+, py \leq pw(r)} V(r, y), \qquad r \in K. \tag{9}$$

Finally, the *core* consists of all allocations that cannot be blocked by some coalition. Here a *coalition* is a nonnull Lebesgue measurable subset of [0, 1], and a coalition H is said to *block* an allocation $x(\cdot)$ if there exists a Lebesgue measurable function $z(\cdot) : [0, 1] \to R^n_+$ that satisfies (5) and

$$V[r, z(r)] > V[r, x(r)] \tag{10}$$

for a.a. $r \in H$ (μ measure), and

$$\int_H z(r)\, d\mu(r) = \int_H w(r)\, d\mu(r). \tag{11}$$

T 2 *Let* $\text{EA} = \{\text{V}(\cdot), [0, 1] \times \text{R}^n_+, \text{w}(\cdot)\}$ *be an exchange economy with a nonatomic measure space of consumers* $[[0, 1], \mathcal{L}, \mu(\cdot)]$, *where* $\mathcal{L}$ *denotes the family of Lebesgue measurable subsets of [0, 1] and* $\mu(\cdot) : \mathcal{L} \to [0, 1]$ *denotes the Lebesgue measure. Assume that (i)* $\text{w}(\cdot) : [0, 1] \to \text{R}_{++}$ *is a.e. uniformly bounded and Lebesgue measurable, and (ii)* $\text{V}(\cdot) : [0, 1] \times \text{R}^n_+ \to \text{R}_+$*; for a.a.* $\text{r} \in [0, 1]$ *(μ measure),* $\text{V}(\text{r}, \cdot)$ *is strictly increasing and continuous; and for all* $\text{x}, \text{y} \in \text{R}^n_+$, $\{\text{r} \in [0, 1] : \text{V}(\text{r}, \text{x}) > \text{V}(\text{r}, \text{y})\} \in \mathcal{L}$. *In* EA *the core equals the set of competitive equilibrium allocations.*[2]

With the exception that Aumann's economy consists of a nonatomic measure space of consumers, the intended interpretation of T 2 is similar to the interpretation I gave of T 1. I discuss the differences that matter, that is, the role of K in (7)–(9) and the interpretation of (6), in Section 8.4.

8.1.3 A Preview

I demonstrate that there are economies that have many more consumers than Aumann's economy and for which theorems T 1 and T 2 are not true. For that purpose I have to make use of nonstandard analysis. Section 8.2 contains the information concerning nonstandard numbers and sets that the reader needs to understand the import of my results. In writing the section I have borrowed ideas freely from Tom Lindstrøm's (1988) marvelous article, "An Invitation to Nonstandard Analysis." For both insight and missing details the reader is referred to Section 1 in Lindstrøm's article.

In Section 8.3 I first delineate salient characteristics of a topology for the nonstandard real numbers $^*R$, and the corresponding n-dimensional hyperspace $^*R^n$ that has most of the characteristics one associates with the standard topology for R and R^n, for example, the intervals $[a, b]$ are closed in $^*R$ and $\{x \in {}^*R^n : px \leq a \text{ and } x \geq 0\}$ is closed in $^*R^n$. Then I demonstrate that in this topology neither T 1 nor T 2 is true of exchange in hyperspace.

In Section 8.4 I begin by describing the topology for $^*R$ and $^*R^n$ in which most economic analyses in hyperspace are carried out. In this topology the intervals $[a, b]$ in $^*R$ and the sets $\{x \in {}^*R^n : px \leq a \text{ and } x \geq 0\}$ are neither closed nor open, yet the neighborhoods of the topology are standard ε-neighborhoods filled with nonstandard numbers or vectors as the case may be. Then I demonstrate that when hyperspace is given the second topology, a nonstandard analogue of T 2, T 28, is valid.

There is one interesting aspect of the last core equivalence theorem that should be noted. Theorem T 28 concerns a hyperfinite alias of Aumann's economy. The discreteness of this nonstandard economy allows me in Section 8.4.2.2 to show the import of two disturbing features of theorem T 2:

1. $[0, 1] - K$ may contain infinitely many consumers.
2. One competitive equilibrium allocation in *EA* may let large quantities of resources go to waste; another may insist on distributing much larger quantities of resources than are available in the economy.

These disturbing features cannot be shrugged off simply by insisting that in large economies single consumers have a negligible influence on prices and by pointing out that in Aumann's economy allocations are only determined up to a set of Lebesgue measure zero. They affect the very possibility of giving a reasonable interpretation to exchange in *EA*.

In Section 8.5 I use the two disturbing characteristics of *EA*'s competitive equilibrium to show that the equilibrium prices in *EA* cannot be used to decentralize the distribution of core allocations in large finite economies.

Many of the ideas and results that I present in Sections 8.3 and 8.4 are developed at greater length in my book *Toward a Formal Science of Economics* (Stigum, 1990). For both insight and missing details the reader is referred to Chapters 20–22 therein.

8.2 CONSTRUCTION OF THE NONSTANDARD UNIVERSE

In this section I use the set of real numbers R to construct the set of nonstandard real numbers $^*R$ and classify the subsets of $^*R$. Since my construction of $^*R$ is similar to the standard construction of R from the set of rational numbers Q, for the sake of intuition, I begin by recalling the construction of R from Q.

8.2.1 Construction of the Reals from the Rationals

To construct R from Q I let C denote the set of Cauchy sequences in Q, and define the relation $\equiv$ on C by[3]

$$\{a_n\} \equiv \{b_n\} \text{ iff } \lim_n (a_n - b_n) = 0. \tag{12}$$

It is easy to see that $\equiv$ is reflexive, symmetric, and transitive. Hence, $\equiv$ is an equivalence relation on C. Next I let $R = C/\equiv$, that is, R equals the set of equivalence classes of C under $\equiv$. Then R is well defined since the limits of Cauchy sequences are uniquely determined. Moreover, if I let $\langle a_n \rangle$ denote the equivalence class of $\{a_n\}$, Q can be identified with a subset of R through the embedding

$$q \to \langle q \rangle, \tag{13}$$

where $\langle q \rangle$ denotes the equivalence class of the sequence $q, q, \ldots$ in C. In particular,

$$0 \to \langle 0 \rangle \quad \text{and} \quad 1 \to \langle 1 \rangle. \tag{14}$$

I can also add and multiply numbers in R by the schemes

$$\langle a_n \rangle + \langle b_n \rangle = \langle a_n + b_n \rangle \quad \text{and} \quad \langle a_n \rangle \cdot \langle b_n \rangle = \langle a_n b_n \rangle; \tag{15}$$

and can introduce order in R by the scheme $\langle a_n \rangle < \langle b_n \rangle$ iff there exists an $\varepsilon > 0$ such that

$$a_n + \varepsilon < b_n \qquad \text{for all large } n. \tag{16}$$

If all this is done, R with 0, 1, $+$, $\cdot$, and $<$ as defined in (14)–(16) becomes a complete ordered field.

8.2.2 Construction of the Hyperreals from the Reals

Before I begin my construction of $^*R$ from R it is instructive to observe that $\langle a_n \rangle$ is identified with the set of Cauchy sequences in C with the same limit point as $\{a_n\}$. For example,

$$\langle n^{-1/2} \rangle = \langle n^{-1} \rangle = \langle n^{-2} \rangle = \langle 0 \rangle. \tag{17}$$

When $^*R$ is constructed, I shall be much more choosy about the sequences I agree to identify. This is necessary because $^*R$ is to have both infinitesimally small numbers and infinitely large numbers.

In order to choose between sequences of real numbers I must introduce the idea of a free ultrafilter over the set of natural numbers N. A *free ultrafilter* over N is a family of subsets of N, denoted by $\mathcal{U}$, with the following properties:

1. $A \in \mathcal{U}$, $B \subset N$ and $A \subset B$ imply $B \in \mathcal{U}$.
2. $A, B \in \mathcal{U}$ imply $(A \cap B) \in \mathcal{U}$.

3. $N \in \mathcal{U}$ and $\sim [\phi \in \mathcal{U}]$.
4. $A \subset N$ implies that either $A \in \mathcal{U}$ or $(N - A) \in \mathcal{U}$.
5. If $A \subset N$ and A is finite, then $\sim [A \in \mathcal{U}]$.

In this definition conditions 1–3 assert that $\mathcal{U}$ is a *filter*, condition 4 adds that $\mathcal{U}$ is an *ultrafilter*, and condition 5 insists that $\mathcal{U}$ is *free*. An example of a filter that is not an ultrafilter is the family of all subsets of N containing all but a finite number of elements of N. For $\mathcal{U}$ to be an ultrafilter, either the set of all odd numbers or the set of all even numbers and zero, but not both, must belong to $\mathcal{U}$. An example of an ultrafilter that is not free is the family of all subsets of N that has $\{x_0\}$ as a subset, where $x_0 \in N$ is an arbitrarily chosen number.

There exist infinitely many free ultrafilters over N.[4] I use one of them, $\mathcal{U}$, to construct $^*R$ from R. For that purpose let

$$R^N = \{\{a_n\} : a_n \in R,\ n = 0, 1, \ldots\},$$

and let the relation $\sim_{\mathcal{U}}$ on R^N be defined by

$$\{a_n\} \sim_{\mathcal{U}} \{b_n\} \quad \text{iff} \quad \{n \in N : a_n = b_n\} \in \mathcal{U}. \tag{18}$$

Since $N \in \mathcal{U}$, $\{a_n\} \sim_{\mathcal{U}} \{a_n\}$. In addition, $\{a_n\} \sim_{\mathcal{U}} \{b_n\}$ if and only if $\{b_n\} \sim_{\mathcal{U}} \{a_n\}$. Finally, properties 1 and 2 of $\mathcal{U}$ ensure that if $\{a_n\} \sim_{\mathcal{U}} \{b_n\}$ and $\{b_n\} \sim_{\mathcal{U}} \{c_n\}$, then $\{a_n\} \sim_{\mathcal{U}} \{c_n\}$ as well. Hence, $\mathcal{U}$ is an equivalence relation on R^N. Next, for each $a \in R^N$, let $a_u = \left\{b \in R^N : a \sim_{\mathcal{U}} b\right\}$ and define $^*R$ by

$$^*R = R^N / \sim_{\mathcal{U}} = \left\{a_{\mathcal{U}} : a \in R^N\right\}. \tag{19}$$

Then $^*R$ is well defined since if $\{a_n\} \in a_{\mathcal{U}}$ and $\{b_n\} \in b_{\mathcal{U}}$, then

$$a_{\mathcal{U}} = b_{\mathcal{U}} \quad \text{iff} \quad \{n \in N : a_n = b_n\} \in \mathcal{U}. \tag{20}$$

Moreover, R can be identified with a subset of $^*R$ through the embedding

$$r \rightarrow r_{\mathcal{U}}, \tag{21}$$

where $r_{\mathcal{U}}$ denotes the equivalence class of the sequence $r, r, \ldots$ in R^N. In particular

$$0 \rightarrow 0_{\mathcal{U}} \quad \text{and} \quad 1 \rightarrow 1_{\mathcal{U}}, \tag{22}$$

I can also introduce addition and multiplication in $^*R$ with the schemes

$$a_{\mathcal{U}} + b_{\mathcal{U}} = c_{\mathcal{U}} \quad \text{iff} \quad \{n \in N : a_n + b_n = c_n\} \in \mathcal{U} \tag{23}$$

and

$$a_{\mathcal{U}} \cdot b_{\mathcal{U}} = c_{\mathcal{U}} \quad \text{iff} \quad \{n \in N : a_n \cdot b_n = c_n\} \in \mathcal{U}, \tag{24}$$

and can order the elements in $^*R$ by the scheme

$$a_{\mathcal{U}} < b_{\mathcal{U}} \quad \text{iff} \quad \{n \in N : a_n < b_n\} \in \mathcal{U} \tag{25}$$

If all that is done, then $^*R$ with 0, 1, +, ·, and < as defined in (22)–(25) becomes an ordered field with a complete ordered field as a proper subset.

The set of hyperreals $^*R$ that has been constructed contains *infinitesimals*, that is, numbers that are smaller in absolute value than any arbitrarily chosen positive real number. One example is $\{n^{-1}\}_{\mathcal{U}}$. $^*R$ also contains *infinitely large numbers*, that is, numbers that are larger in absolute value than any arbitrarily chosen real number. One example is $\{n\}_{\mathcal{U}}$. Finally, note that the infinitesimals in $^*R$ are ordered, for example,

$$\{n^{-1}\}_{\mathcal{U}} < \{n^{-1/2}\}_{\mathcal{U}}, \tag{26}$$

which contrasts sharply with (17). The infinite numbers in $^*R$ are also ordered, for example,

$$\{n\}_{u} < \{n^2\}_{\mathcal{U}}.$$

8.2.3 Internal Sets and Functions

The subsets of $^*R$ and the functions from $^*R$ to $^*R$ can be classified in various ways. I identify internal sets and functions, standard sets and functions, and external sets, and also delineate the hyperfinite subsets of $^*R$. I begin with the internal sets and functions.

A sequence $\{A_n\}$of subsets of R determines a subset $\{A_n\}_{\mathcal{U}}$ of $^*R$ in accordance with the scheme

$$\{x_n\}_{\mathcal{U}} \in \{A_n\}_{\mathcal{U}} \quad \text{iff} \quad \{n \in N : x_n \in A_n\} \in \mathcal{U} \tag{27}$$

Similarly, a sequence $\{f_n(\cdot)\}$ of functions $f_n(\cdot) : A_n \rightarrow R$ determines a function $f(\cdot) : \{A_n\}_{\mathcal{U}} \rightarrow {}^*R$ in accordance with the scheme

$$f(\{x_n\}_{\mathcal{U}}) = \{f_n(x_n)\}_{\mathcal{U}}, \quad \{x_n\}_{\mathcal{U}} \in \{A_n\}_{\mathcal{U}} \tag{28}$$

Sets and functions obtained in this way are called, respectively, *internal sets* and *internal functions*. Subsets of $^*R$ that are not internal are *external*.

Examples of internal sets are the intervals (a, b) and $[a, b]$. When $a = \{a_n\}_{\mathcal{U}}$ and $b = \{b_n\}_{\mathcal{U}}$ and $a < b$, then

$$[a, b] = \{[a_n, b_n]\}_{\mathcal{U}}$$

and

$$\{x_n\}_{\mathcal{U}} \in [a, b] \text{ iff } \{n \in N : x_n \in [a_n, b_n]\} \in \mathcal{U}.$$

An example of an internal function is $\sin cx$. When $c = \{c_n\}_{\mathcal{U}}$,

$$\sin cx = \{\sin c_n x_n\}_{\mathcal{U}}, x = \{x_n\}_{\mathcal{U}}.$$

Examples of external sets are N and R.

A subset A of R can be embedded in $\mathcal{P}({}^*R)$, the family of subsets of ${}^*R$, by the scheme

$$A \to A_{\mathcal{U}}, \tag{29}$$

where $A_{\mathcal{U}}$ denotes the subset of ${}^*R$ determined by the sequence $A, A, \ldots$. The resulting subset is internal and called *standard*, henceforth denoted by ${}^*A$, in accordance with denoting $R_{\mathcal{U}}$ by ${}^*R$. One other important example is $N_{\mathcal{U}}$, which is denoted by ${}^*N$.

A function $f(\cdot) : A \to R$ has a nonstandard alias, denoted ${}^*f(\cdot)$ and defined by

$${}^*f(x) = \{f(x_n)\}_{\mathcal{U}}, \qquad x = \{x_n\}_{\mathcal{U}} \tag{30}$$

This function is internal, called *standard*, and has domain ${}^*A$, that is,

$${}^*f(\cdot) : {}^*A \to {}^*R.$$

Note that if $a = \{a\}_{\mathcal{U}}$ and $a \in {}^*A$, then ${}^*f(a) = \{f(a)\}_{\mathcal{U}} = f(a)$. Hence, ${}^*f(\cdot)$ can be viewed as an extension of $f(\cdot)$ to ${}^*A$.

A certain class of internal sets is particularly important for my purposes: the class of hyperfinite subsets of ${}^*R$. If $B \subset {}^*R$, B is *hyperfinite* if and only if (1) B is internal and (2) there is an internal bijection from an initial segment of ${}^*N$ onto B.

If B is hyperfinite and mapped onto $\{n \in {}^*N : n \leq m\}$ by an internal bijection, then m is called the *internal cardinality* of B and denoted by $|B|$.

Two theorems for the reader's intuition about hyperfinite sets are in order here.

T 3 *Let* $\mathrm{E} \subset \mathrm{R}$ *and let* $\mathcal{P}_{\mathrm{F}}(\mathrm{E})$ *denote the family of finite subsets of* E. *Suppose that* A *is a hyperfinite subset of* ${}^*\mathrm{E}$. *Then* $\mathrm{A} \in {}^*\mathcal{P}_{\mathrm{F}}(\mathrm{E})$.[5]

T 4 *If* $\mathrm{B} \subset {}^*\mathrm{R}$ *is internal and countable from the outside, then* B *is finite.*

Proofs of these theorems are given in Stigum (1990, pp. 480, 485).

8.2.4 Hyperspace ${}^*R^n$ and the Internal Subsets of and Functions on ${}^*R^n$

By letting ${}^*R^n = {}^*R \times {}^*R \times \cdots \times {}^*R$ I obtain a representation of n-dimensional hyperspace. The internal subsets of ${}^*R^n$ are obtained from the subsets of R^n in the same way the internal subsets of ${}^*R$ were obtained from the subsets of R. Similarly, the internal functions on ${}^*R^n$ to ${}^*R^m$ are obtained from functions on R^n to R^m in the same way the internal functions on ${}^*R$ to ${}^*R$ were obtained from functions on R to R. Finally, the characterization of hyperfinite sets in ${}^*R^n$ is identical to the characterization of hyperfinite sets in ${}^*R$. There is no need to elaborate on any of these constructions here.

Internal subsets of $^*R^n$ have many interesting properties. For ease of reference I record two of them here.

T 5 *Suppose that* A_i, $i \in N$, *are nonempty internal subsets of* $^*R^n$ *that satisfy the condition* $A_0 \supset A_1 \supset \cdots$. *Then* $\sim [\cap_{i \in N} A_i = \phi]$, *that is, there is an internal object that belongs to all the* A_i.

T 6 *Let* Ω *be an internal subset of* $^*R^n$ *and let* B *and* A_i, $i \in N$, *be internal subsets of* Ω *such that* $B = \cup_{i \in N} A_i$. *Then there exists an* $m \in N$ *such that* $B = \cup_{i=0}^{m} A_i$.

Proofs of these theorems for the case $n = 1$ are given in Lindstrøm (1988, pp. 12–13). Lindstrøm's arguments are valid for the case $n > 1$ as well.

8.2.5 A Note of Warning

I have described one way in which the nonstandard reals can be constructed from the reals and used the same method to delineate the class of internal subsets of $^*R$ and the class of internal functions from $^*R$ to $^*R$. In the same way internal families of subsets of $^*R$ can be constructed from families of subsets of R (see note 3 for an example) and internal measures on internal families of subsets of $^*R$. Hence the content of this section ought to give the reader the intuition about nonstandard concepts that he or she will need to read and understand the next two sections of the chapter. However, my description of nonstandard numbers and internal sets and functions does not provide the tools needed to construct proofs of all the theorems I record in Sections 8.3 and 8.4. The missing details for that purpose are given in Stigum (1990, pp. 470–480).

8.3 EXCHANGE IN HYPERSPACE I

In this section we first study the salient characteristics of a topology for $^*R$ and $^*R^n$ in which the standard intervals $^*[a, b]$ and their n-dimensional analogues are closed. Then I show that in such a topology neither Aumann's theorem nor Debreu and Scarfs' theorem holds true for exchange in hyperspace.

8.3.1 The *Topology of $^*R^n$

Let X be a nonempty set and let τ be a family of subsets of X. Then (X, τ) is a topological space and τ is a topology for X if τ satisfies the following conditions:

1. $\phi \in \tau$ and $X \in \tau$.
2. If $G_i \in \tau, i, \ldots, m$, then $\cap_{i=1}^{m} G_i \in \tau$.
3. If I is an index set and $G_i \in \tau$, $i \in I$, then $\cup_{i \in I} G_i \in \tau$.

In this topology, the members of τ are the open subsets of X, and a set A is *closed* if and only if its complement A^c is open. Note that any finite union of closed sets is closed, and any intersection of closed sets is closed. Finally, the closure of a set A, denoted $clo(A)$, is the intersection of all closed subsets of X that contain A; and the interior of A, denoted $int(A)$, is the union of all the open subsets of A. For all $A \subset X$, $int(A)$ is open, $clo(A)$ is closed, and $int(A) \subset A \subset clo(A)$.

The standard topology for R^n is obtained in the following way: Let $\|\cdot\|$ denote the norm in R^n, that is, let $\|x\| = \left(\sum_{i=1}^{n} x_i^2\right)^{1/2}$, and for each $x \in R^n$ and $q \in Q \cap R_{++}$, let

$$S(x, q) = \{y \in R^n : \|y - x\| < q\}.$$

Then define the family S of subsets of R^n by

$B \in S$ iff there is an $x \in Q^n$ and a $q \in Q \cap R_{++}$ such that $B = S(x, q)$.

Finally, let τ_{R^n} consist of ϕ and all $A \subset R^n$ with the property that if $x \in A$, there is a $B \in S$ such that $x \in B$ and $B \subset A$. Then (R^n, τ_{R^n}) is a topological space. In fact, τ_{R^n} is the *standard topology* for R^n.

The alias of S in ${}^*R^n$ can be used to construct the required topology for ${}^*R^n$. For each $A \subset {}^*R^n$ let A be **-open* if and only if A is internal and, for each $x \in A$, there is a $B \in {}^*S$ such that $x \in B$ and $B \subset A$. Also let $\tau_{{}^*R^n}$ consist of ϕ and all the *-open subsets of ${}^*R^n$. Then $\tau_{{}^*R^n}$ satisfies the following conditions:

1. $\phi \in \tau_{{}^*R^n}$ and ${}^*R^n \in \tau_{{}^*R^n}$.
2. If $m \in {}^*N$ and if G_i is internal and $G_i \in \tau_{{}^*R^n}$, $i = 0, \ldots, m$, then $\cap_{i=0}^{m} G_i \in \tau_{{}^*R^n}$.
3. If I is an internal index set and $G_i \in \tau_{{}^*R^n}$ for all $i \in I$, then $\cup_{i=I} G_i \in \tau_{{}^*R^n}$.

A family of internal sets satisfying these three conditions is an *internal topology* for ${}^*R^n$ and $\tau_{{}^*R^n}$ is called the **topology* for ${}^*R^n$.

Since the union of a set of open sets need not be internal, $\tau_{{}^*R^n}$ is not a topology in the ordinary sense. It is, therefore, interesting to observe that $\tau_{{}^*R^n}$ constitutes a base for a topology in ${}^*R^n$. A. Robinson called the topology generated by $\tau_{{}^*R^n}$ the Q topology for ${}^*R^n$ and showed that an internal set B is open in the Q topology if and only if B belongs to $\tau_{{}^*R^n}$ (see Robinson 1966, p. 99, th. 4.2.9).

The relationship between the *topology of ${}^*R^n$ and the standard topology of R^n is described in the following theorem:

T 7 $\quad \tau_{{}^*\mathrm{R}^n} = {}^*\tau_{\mathrm{R}^n}$.

The *topology has many interesting characteristics—some familiar and some not. To discuss these characteristics I must introduce the idea of a monad. For each $x \in {}^*R^n$, let

$${}^*S\left(x, l^{-1}\right) = \{y \in {}^*R^n : \|x - y\| < l^{-1}\}.$$

Then the *monad* of x is defined as

$$m(x) = \bigcap_{l \in N} {}^*S\left(x, l^{-1}\right).$$

It follows from T 5 that $m(x) \neq \phi$. If $y \in m(x)$, one writes $y \approx x$ and reads aloud, "y is infinitesimally close to x." For all $x \in {}^*R^n$, $x \approx x$. Also, $y \approx x$ if and only if $x \approx y$. Finally, if $x \approx y$ and $y \approx z$, then $x \approx z$. Hence, $\approx$ is an equivalence relation. From this one can infer T 8.

T 8 *If* $x, y \in {}^*R^n$, *either* $m(x) = m(y)$ *or* $m(x) \cap m(y) = \phi$.

The monad of an $x \in {}^*R^n$ need not be an internal subset of ${}^*R^n$. However, for each $x \in {}^*R^n$, there is an internal open set $B \subset m(x)$. To wit: T 9.

T 9 *If* $x \in {}^*R^n$, *there is a* $B \in \tau_{{}^*R^n}$ *such that* $x \in B$ *and* $B \subset m(x)$.

Here is an example to aid intuition.

E 8.1 *Let* $n = 1$ *and consider the set* ${}^*(0, 1)$. *This set is open in the* **topology. Note, therefore, that*

$$m(0) \cap {}^*(0, 1) \neq \phi. \tag{31}$$

Also, if $x \in R \cap {}^*(0, 1)$, *then* $m(x) \subset {}^*(0, 1)$, *and there is a* $B \in \tau_{{}^*R^n}$ *such that* $x \in B$ *and* $B \subset m(x)$.

An internal set B *is* *-compact *if and only if* B *is closed in the* **topology and there is an* $m \in {}^*N$ *such that* $B \subset \{x \in {}^*R^n : \|x\| \leq m\}$. *The* **-compact internal subsets of* ${}^*R^n$ *share a familiar property—see T 10.*

T 10 *Suppose that* $A \subset {}^*R^n$ *is internal and* **-compact and let* $\mathcal{G}$ *be an internal family of open sets that cover* A. *There is an* $m \in {}^*N$ *and a sequence of sets* $G_i, i = 0, 1, \ldots, m$, *such that* $G_i \in \mathcal{G}$ *and* $A \subset \cup_{i=0}^m G_i$.

An internal $A \subset {}^*R^n$ is **-convex* if and only if, for all $x, y \in A$ and all $\lambda \in {}^*(0, 1)$, $\lambda x + (1 - \lambda) y \in A$. Also, an internal function $f(\cdot) : A \rightarrow B$ is **-continuous* if it is continuous in the *topology. The *-convex internal sets and *-continuous internal functions have familiar properties—see T 11 and T 12.

T 11 *Let* B *be a* **-convex internal subset of* ${}^*R^n$ *and suppose that* $x \in {}^*R^n - B$. *Then there is a* $p \in {}^*R^n - \{0\}$ *such that*

$$B \subset \left\{y \in {}^*R^n : px \leq py\right\}.$$

T 12 *Let* A *be an internal* **-compact,* **-convex subset of* ${}^*R^n$ *and suppose that* $f(\cdot) : A \rightarrow A$ *is internal and* **-continuous. Then there is an* $x \in A$ *such that* $x = f(x)$.

Proofs of theorems T 11 and T 12 as well as of theorems T 7–T 10 are given in Stigum (1990, pp. 488–490).

8.3.2 Exchange in Hyperspace When *R^n Is Given the *Topology

A hyperfinite exchange economy is a triple,

$$HE = \left\{U(\cdot), T \times {}^*R^n_+, A(\cdot)\right\},$$

that satisfies the conditions

1. $T = \{1, \ldots, \gamma\}$ for some $\gamma = {}^*N - N$.
2. $U(\cdot) : T \times {}^*R^n \to {}^*R_+$ is internal and, for each $t \in T$, $U(t, \cdot)$ is strictly increasing, strictly quasi-concave, and continuous in the *topology.
3. $A(\cdot) : T \to {}^*R^n_{++}$ is internal, and there is an $r \in R_{++}$ such that $A(t) \leq r$ for all $t \in T$.

In reading this definition note that T denotes the set of consumers in the economy and that it may contain many more elements than there are real numbers in [0, 1]. Note also that, for each $t \in T$, $U(t, \cdot)$ and $A(t)$, respectively, denote the utility indicator and the initial endowment of consumer t. It will be seen that this economy has all the properties associated with ordinary finite exchange economies.

First a few definitions: A **-allocation* is an internal function $X(\cdot) : T \to {}^*R^n_+$ such that $\sum_{t \in T} X(t) = \sum_{t \in T} A(t)$. A **-competitive equilibrium* is a pair $[p, X(\cdot)]$, where $p \in {}^*R^n_{++}$, $X(\cdot)$ is a *-allocation, and for all $t \in T$,

$$pX(t) \leq pA(t), \tag{32}$$

and

$$U[t, X(t)] = \max_{y \in {}^*R^n_+, py \leq pA(t)} U(t, y) \tag{33}$$

Finally, the **-core* of *HE* consists of all allocations that cannot be blocked by some coalition. Here a *coalition* is an internal subset of T, and a *-allocation $X(\cdot)$ is blocked by a coalition S if and only if there is a *allocation $Y(\cdot)$ such that

$$U[t, X(t)] \leq U(t, Y(t)) \tag{34}$$

for all $t \in S$ with strict inequality for some $t \in S$; and

$$\sum_{t \in S} Y(t) = \sum_{t \in S} A(t). \tag{35}$$

With these definitions two interesting theorems can be noted, the proofs of which are given in Stigum (1990, pp. 496–498).

T 13 *There exists a *-competitive equilibrium in* HE.

T 14 *Let* $\left[\mathrm{p}, \mathrm{X}(\cdot)\right]$ *be a *-competitive equilibrium in* HE. *Then* X(·) *belongs to the *-core of* HE.

T 13 and T 14 are interesting for several reasons. First, they demonstrate that theorems that hold true for ordinary exchange economies are true of hyperfinite economies as well if $^*R^n$ is given the *topology. Second, since the converse of T 14 is false (that is, since it is not true of *HE* that the *-core is contained in the set of *-competitive equilibrium allocations) and since γ may be so large that T contains more members than there are real numbers in [0, 1], the existence of *HE* demonstrates that the conclusion of Aumann's theorem T 2 has little to do with the size of Aumann's economy.

Next I demonstrate that Debreu and Scarf's (1963) theorem T 1 is also not true in the setting of the present hyperfinite exchange economy. For that purpose I denote *HE* by E_η and hypothesize that *HE* has k different types of consumers and η consumers of each type so that $\gamma = \eta \cdot k$ with $k > 1$. Also I denote by $X^\eta(\cdot)$ a *-allocation in E_η and let

$$X^\eta = \left[X_1^\eta(1), \ldots, X_k^\eta(1)\right]$$

be the vector of commodities allocated by $X^\eta(\cdot)$ to the first consumer of each type. Finally, I let

$$C_\eta = \left\{x \in {}^*R_+^{kn} : x = X^\eta \text{ for some } X^\eta(\cdot) \text{ in the *-core of } E_\eta\right\}.$$

Then I can state the following analogue of T 1, the proof of which is given in Stigum (1990, pp. 498–500).[6]

T 15 *Let* $X^\eta(\cdot)$ *be an allocation in the *-core of* E_η *and let* $X_i^\eta(j)$ *be the commodities allocated by* $X^\eta(\cdot)$ *to the* j*th consumer of the* i*th kind. Then for* $j = 2, \ldots, \eta$,

$$X_i^\eta(j) = X_i^\eta(1), \qquad i = 1, \ldots, k.$$

Moreover, if $X \in {}^*R_+^{kn}$ *and* $X \in C_\eta$ *for all* $\eta \in {}^*N$, *then there exists a* $p \in {}^*R_{++}^n$ *such that* (p, X) *is a competitive equilibrium in* E_1.

I claim that the Debreu-Scarf theorem T 1 is not valid in the setting of the present hyperfinite exchange economy because one cannot replace the $^*N$ in T 15 by N.

8.4 EXCHANGE IN HYPERSPACE II

In this section I first characterize a new topology for $^*R^n$ and then describe a hyperfinite exchange economy for which the conclusion of Aumann's theorem holds true.

8.4.1 The *S*-Topology in $^*R^n$

If $A \subset {}^*R^n$, one says that A is *S-open* if and only if, for all $x \in A$, there is a $q \in Q \cap R_{++}$, such that $^*S(x, q) \subset A$. The S-open sets in $^*R^n$ form a topology for $^*R^n$ called the *S-topology* and denoted by τ_S.

The *topology and the S-topology for $^*R^n$ are very different, as witnessed by the following theorems:

T 16 *ϕ and $^*R^n$ are the only* S-open *internal subsets of* $^*R^n$.

T 17 *For $A \subset {}^*R^n$, let* S-int(A) *be the union of all the* S-open *subsets of* A. *If* $x \in {}^*R^n$ *and* $x \notin$ S-int(A), *then* $m(x) \cap$ S-int$(A) = \phi$.

T 18 *If $A \subset {}^*R^n$ is internal, then* $x \in$ S-int(A) *iff* $m(x) \subset$ S-int(A).

T 19 *For $A \subset {}^*R^n$, let* S-clo(A) *denote the intersection of all the* S-closed *sets in $^*R^n$ that contain* A. *If $A \subset {}^*R^n$ is internal, then* $x \in$ S-clo(A) *iff* $m(x) \cap A \neq \phi$. *Moreover,* $x \in$ *boundary of* A *iff both* $m(x) \cap A \neq \phi$ *and* $m(x) \cap A^c \neq \phi$, *where the boundary of* A *equals* S-clo(A) $\cap$ S-clo(A^c).

Of these theorems T 16 is due to Robinson and proved in Robinson (1966, p. 121). The other three are due to Brown and Robinson (1975), and proofs can be found in Stigum (1990, pp. 491–492).

The following examples should aid intuition concerning the differences between the *topology and the S-topology.

E 8.2 *Let* $n = 1$. *Then the set* $^*(0, 1)$ *is open in the *topology but not in the* S*-topology. The* S-clo$[^*(0, 1)] = m(1) \cup {}^*(0, 1) \cup m(0)$ *and the boundary of* $^*(0, 1)$ *equals* $\{0, 1\}$ *in the *topology and* $m(0) \cup m(1)$ *in the* S*-topology.*

E 8.3 *Let* $A = \{x \in {}^*R^n : a \leq px\}$, *where* $a \in {}^*R$, $p \in {}^*R^n_{++} - m(0)$, *and both* $m(a) \cap R$ *and* $m(p) \cap R^n$ *are nonempty. Then*

$$S\text{-}clo\,(A) = \left\{x \in {}^*R^n : a \lesssim px\right\},$$

and

$$S\text{-boundary of } A = \left\{x \in {}^*R^n : a \approx px\right\},$$

where $a \lesssim px$ *iff* $a \leq px$ *or* $a \approx px$.

If $A \subset {}^*R^n$, the S-*convex* hull of A consists of all $x \in {}^*R^n$ for which there is an $m \in N$ and pairs $(x_i, \lambda_i) \in A \times {}^*[0, 1]$, $i = 1, \ldots, m$, such that $\sum_{i=1}^m \lambda_i = 1$ and $x = \sum_{i=1}^m \lambda_i x_i$. A set $A \subset {}^*R^n$ that contains its S-convex hull is said to be S-*convex*. S-convex sets have several interesting properties, which are detailed next.

T 20 *If $A \subset {}^*R^n$ is* S*-convex,* S-int(A) *is* S*-convex.*

T 21 *Let* $N_S({}^*R^n) = \{x \in {}^*R^n : m(x) \cap R^n \neq \phi\}$. *If* $A \subset N_S({}^*R^n)$ *is* S*-convex, and if* $x \in R^n$ *and* $x \notin$ S-int(A), *then there is a* $p \in R^n - \{0\}$ *such that*

$$S\text{-}int(A) \subset \left\{y \in {}^*R^n : px \lesssim py\right\}$$

Both theorems are due to Brown and Robinson (1975), and proofs can be found in Stigum (1990, p. 494).

8.4.2 Exchange in Hyperspace When $^*R^n$ Is Given the S-Topology

In order to describe the hyperfinite exchange economy I have in mind for this section, I must introduce several new concepts. Suppose that $x \in N_S(^*R^n)$ and let $\{^\circ x\} = m(x) \cap R^n$. Suppose next that $B \subset {}^*R^n$ and let $^\circ B = \{x \in R^n : x \in m(y) \text{ for some } y \in B\}$. Finally, let $T = \{1/\gamma \ldots, 1\}$ for some $\gamma \in {}^*N - N$ and assume that there is an $\eta \in {}^*N - N$ such that $\gamma = \eta!$. Then all the rationals in (0, 1) belong to T. Also, if r is an irrational number in (0, 1), there is a unique $k \in {}^*N$ such that $k/\gamma < r < (k+1)/\gamma$ (Keisler, 1984, p. 13). Moreover $^\circ T = [0, 1]$.

Next I construct a useful probability space on T. For that purpose, let $\mathcal{A}$ be the set of all internal subsets of T and define $v(\cdot) : \mathcal{A} \to {}^*[0, 1]$ by

$$v(A) = |A|/\gamma, \quad A \in \mathcal{A} \tag{36}$$

Then $v(\cdot)$ is an internal, finitely additive probability measure on $\mathcal{A}$; and $[T, \mathcal{A}, v(\cdot)]$ is *an internal probability space*. Next, let $\sigma(A)$ denote the σ-algebra generated by $\mathcal{A}$, and let

$$^\circ v(A) = {}^\circ[v(A)] \quad \text{for } A \in \mathcal{A}. \tag{37}$$

Then by T 6 for $n = 1$, $^\circ v(\cdot)$ is σ-additive on $\mathcal{A}$. Hence, $^\circ v(\cdot)$ can be extended in one and only one way to a σ-additive probability measure on $\sigma(\mathcal{A})$, which is denoted by $\tilde{P}_v(\cdot)$. Finally, let $[T, \mathcal{F}_\mathcal{A}, P_v(\cdot)]$ denote the completion of $[T, \sigma(\mathcal{A}), \tilde{P}_v(\cdot)]$, Then $[T, \mathcal{F}_\mathcal{A}, P_v(\cdot)]$ is the Loeb probability space associated with $[T, \mathcal{A}, v(\cdot)]$.

8.4.2.1 *Description of the Economy*

Suppose that $^*R$ and $^*R^n_+$ have been endowed with the S-topology. In this environment a hyperfinite exchange economy is a triple:

$$HEA = \{U(\cdot), T \times {}^*R^n_+, A(\cdot)\},$$

where $U(\cdot) : T \times {}^*R^n_+ \to [{}^*R_+ \cap N_S({}^*R)]$, $T = \{1/\gamma, \ldots, 1\}$ for some $\gamma \in {}^*N - N$, and $A(\cdot) : T \to {}^*R^n_{++}$. One assumes that

1. $A(\cdot)$ is internal and there is an $r \in R^n_{++}$ such that, for a.a $t \in T(P_v$ measure), $A(t) \leq r$.
2. $U(\cdot)$ is internal and, for a.a. $t \in T$ (P_v measure), $U(t, \cdot)$ is *S-continuous* and strictly increasing in the *S-topology*; that is, if $x, y \in {}^*R^n_+$, $x \leq y$, and $x \neq y$, then $U(t, x) < U(t, y)$, and if in addition $x \not\approx y$, then $U(t, x) \not\approx U(t, y)$.

3. $\gamma = \eta!$ for some $\eta \in {}^*N - N$ and there are functions $V(\cdot) : [0,1] \times R^n_+ \rightarrow R_+$ and $w(\cdot) : [0,1] \rightarrow R^n_{++}$, such that[7]

$$w(°t) = °A(t) \text{ a.e. } (P_v \text{ measure}) \tag{38}$$

and such that, for some P_v null set $\mathcal{N}$,

$$V(°t, °x) = °U(t,x), (t,x) \in (T - \mathcal{N}) \times N_S({}^*R^n) \tag{39}$$

In *HEA* an allocation is an S-allocation; and an S-*allocation* is an internal function $X(\cdot) : T \rightarrow {}^*R^n_+$ that is a.e. (P_v measure) uniformly bounded by some $r \in R_{++}$ and satisfies

$$\gamma^{-1} \sum_{t \in T} X(t) \approx \gamma^{-1} \sum_{t \in T} A(t) \tag{40}$$

Also, a competitive equilibrium in *HEA* is an S-competitive equilibrium; and an S-*competitive* equilibrium is a pair $[p, X(\cdot)]$, that satisfies the conditions

1. $p \in {}^*R^n_{++} - m(0)$ and $X(\cdot)$ is an S-allocation.
2. There is an internal $K \subset T$ such that $|K|/\gamma \approx 1$ and, for all $t \in K$, $pX(t) \lesssim pA(t)$, and

$$U[t, X(t)] = \max_{y \in {}^*R^n_+, py \lesssim pA(t)} U(t,y).$$

Finally, the S-core of *HEA* consists of all S-allocations that cannot be blocked by some coalition. Here a *coalition* G is an internal subset of T such that $\gamma^{-1}|G| \not\approx 0$. Moreover, a coalition G is said to block an allocation $X(\cdot)$ if there is an S-allocation $Y(\cdot)$ such that

$$\gamma^{-1} \sum_{t \in G} Y(t) \approx \gamma^{-1} \sum_{t \in G} A(t) \tag{41}$$

and such that, for all $t \in G$,

$$U[t, Y(t)] > U[t, X(t)] \quad \text{and} \quad U[t, Y(t)] \not\approx U[t, X(t)]. \tag{42}$$

In Section 8.4.2.3 I demonstrate that the set of core allocations in *HEA* equals the set of competitive equilibrium allocations, but first a few remarks concerning the relationship between *HEA* and Aumann's economy, *EA*.

8.4.2.2 *The Relationship between* HEA *and* EA

For the purposes of this chapter the relationship between *HEA* and *EA* is of paramount importance, so a few remarks in that regard are in order. I begin by relating the measure space of consumers in *EA* $[[0,1], \mathcal{L}, \mu(\cdot)]$ to the internal probability space of consumers in *HEA* $[T, \mathcal{A}, v(\cdot)]$.

T 22 *Suppose that* $B \subset [0,1]$. *Then* $B \in \mathcal{L}$ *iff* $\{t \in T : °t \in B\} \in \mathcal{F}_{\mathcal{A}}$. *Moreover, if* $B \in \mathcal{L}$, *then*

$$\mu(B) = P_v(\{t \in T : {}^\circ t \in B\}). \tag{43}$$

Thus $\mu(\cdot)$ can be viewed as the natural extension of Laplace's counting measure. Also, in *EA*, $\mu(B)$ can be taken to record the mean number of consumers in B. To wit: If $B \in \mathcal{L}$ and $\{t \in T : {}^\circ t \in B\} \in \mathcal{A}$, then by (36), (37), and (43),

$$\mu(B) = {}^\circ v(\{t \in T : {}^\circ t \in B\}) = {}^\circ\left(|\{t \in T : {}^\circ t \in B\}| / \gamma\right) \tag{44}$$

In particular, if $B = [0, 1] - K$ with K as described in (7)–(9) and if $\{t \in T : {}^\circ t \in [0, 1] - K\} \in \mathcal{A}$, then

$$0 = \mu([0, 1] - K) = {}^\circ\left(|\{t \in T : {}^\circ t \in [0, 1] - K\}| / \gamma\right),$$

and

$$|\{t \in T : {}^\circ t \in [0, 1] - K\}| / \gamma \approx 0.$$

So even though $[0, 1] - K$ may contain infinitely many consumers, as asserted in Section 8.1.2 the mean number of consumers in $[0, 1] - K$ is negligible.

Next the allocations in *EA* and *HEA*: To compare them we need the following theorems concerning random variables on $[[0, 1], \mathcal{L}, \mu(\cdot)]$ and $[T, \mathcal{A}, v(\cdot)]$:

T 23 *Suppose that* $\mathrm{x}(\cdot) : [0, 1] \to \mathrm{R}^{\mathrm{n}}_{++}$. *Then* $\mathrm{x}(\cdot)$ *is Lebesgue measurable iff there exists an internal function* $\mathrm{F_x}(\cdot) : \mathrm{T} \to {}^*\mathrm{R}^{\mathrm{n}}_{++}$ *such that*

$$x({}^\circ t) = {}^\circ F_x(t) \text{ a.e. } (P_v \text{ measure}). \tag{45}$$

T 24 *Suppose that* $\mathrm{x}(\cdot) : [0, 1] \to \mathrm{R}^{\mathrm{n}}_{+}$ *is bounded and Lebesgue measurable, and let* $\mathrm{F_x}(\cdot) : \mathrm{T} \to {}^*\mathrm{R}^{\mathrm{n}}_{+}$ *be an internal function that satisfies (45). Then,*

$$\int_0^1 x(r)\, d\mu(r) = {}^\circ\left[\int_T F_x(t)\, dv(t)\right] = {}^\circ\left[\gamma^{-1} \sum_{t \in T} F_x(t)\right]. \tag{46}$$

From these two theorems it follows that if $x(\cdot) : [0, 1] \to R^n_+$ is an allocation in *EA* and $F_x(\cdot) : T \to {}^*R^n_+$ is an internal function that satisfies (45), then $F_x(\cdot)$ is an S-allocation in *HEA*. Further, if $F_x(\cdot)$ is an S-allocation in *HEA* and $x(\cdot) : [0, 1] \to R^n_+$ is a Lebesgue measurable function that satisfies (45), then $x(\cdot)$ is an allocation in *EA*. Proofs of T 22–T 24 are given in Stigum (1990, pp. 512–514, 519–520).

The last two theorems also allow us to compare the meaning of (2) and (6). Equation (2) insists that $X^m(\cdot)$ is an allocation only if the total quantity of commodities to be allocated to the various consumers in E_m equals the sum total of initial quantities that the consumers in E_m possess. In contrast, according to (6), $x(\cdot) : [0, 1] \to R^n_+$ is an allocation only if the mean commodity bundle allocated by $x(\cdot)$ to consumers in *EA* equals the mean initial commodity bundle possessed by the consumers in *EA*. That allows the possibility that $x(\cdot)$ might insist on distributing a larger quantity of commodities than the consumers in *EA* possess or that $x(\cdot)$ might leave large quantities of resources go to waste as asserted in Section 8.1.2.

Finally, to compare the consumers in *EA* and *HEA* I need the following interesting theorem, the proof of which can be found in Albeverio et al. (1986, pp. 136–137).

T 25 *Let* $\mathrm{V}(\cdot) : [0, 1] \times \mathrm{R}^n_+ \to \mathrm{R}_+$, *and suppose that* $\mathrm{V}(\cdot, \mathrm{x})$ *is Lebesgue measurable for all* $\mathrm{x} \in \mathrm{R}^n_+$. *Then, for a.a.* $\mathrm{r} \in [0, 1]$ *(Lebesgue measure),* $\mathrm{V}(\mathrm{r}, \cdot)$ *is continuous if and only if there exists a* $\mathrm{P_v}$ *null set* $\mathcal{N} \subset \mathrm{T}$ *and an internal function* $\mathrm{U}(\cdot) : \mathrm{T} \times {}^*\mathrm{R}^n_+ \to \left[{}^*\mathrm{R}_+ \cap \mathrm{N_S}({}^*\mathrm{R}_+)\right]$ *such that*

$$V({}^\circ t, {}^\circ x) = {}^\circ U(t, x) \text{ for } (t, x) \in (T - \mathcal{N}) \times N_S\left({}^*R^n_+\right).$$

With the help of this theorem, T 23–T 24, and arguments that are spelled out in Stigum (1990, pp. 520–523) it can be shown that *EA* and *HEA* are aliases of one another—see T 26 and T 27.

T 26 *Let* $\mathrm{V}(\cdot)$ *and* $\mathrm{w}(\cdot)$ *be as in the description of* HEA. *Every hyperfinite economy* HEA *has an alias* $\left\{(\mathrm{V}(\cdot), [0, 1] \times \mathrm{R}^n_+, \mathrm{w}(\cdot)\right\}$ *that is an Aumann economy; that is,* $\mathrm{w}(\cdot) : [0, 1] \to \mathrm{R}^n_{++}$ *is Lebesgue measurable and a.e. (Lebesgue measure) bounded above; for a.a* $\mathrm{r} \in [0, 1]$ *(Lebesgue measure),* $\mathrm{V}(\mathrm{r}, \cdot)$ *is continuous and increasing, and for all* $\mathrm{x}, \mathrm{y} \in \mathrm{R}^n_{++}$,

$$\{r \in [0, 1] : V(r, x) < V(r, y)\} \in \mathcal{L}.$$

T 27 *Every Aumann economy* $\mathrm{EA} = \left\{\mathrm{V}(\cdot), [0, 1] \times \mathrm{R}^n_+, \mathrm{w}(\cdot)\right\}$ *has a hyperfinite alias* $\left\{\mathrm{U}(\cdot), \mathrm{T} \times {}^*\mathrm{R}^n_+, \mathrm{A}(\cdot)\right\}$, *that satisfies the conditions of* HEA *with* $\mathrm{V}(\cdot)$ *and* $\mathrm{w}(\cdot)$ *as specified in the description of the Aumann economy.*

8.4.2.3 A Core Equivalence Theorem

So much for the relationship between *HEA* and *EA*. Now on to the sought for core equivalence theorem for *HEA*:

T 28 *There exists an* S*-competitive equilibrium in* HEA. *Moreover. if* $[\mathrm{p}, \mathrm{X}(\cdot)]$ *is an* S*-competitive equilibrium in* HEA, *then* $\mathrm{X}(\cdot)$ *belongs to the* S*-core of* HEA. *Finally, if* $\mathrm{X}(\cdot)$ *is in the* S*-core of* HEA, *then there exists a* $\mathrm{p} \in {}^*\mathrm{R}^n_{++} - \mathrm{m}(0)$ *such that* $[\mathrm{p}, \mathrm{X}(\cdot)]$ *is an* S*-competitive equilibrium in* HEA.

The arguments needed to establish the existence of an *S*-competitive equilibrium in *HEA* are detailed in Stigum (1990, pp. 520–523). Moreover, the arguments needed to establish the last half of T 28 are spelled out in Stigum (1990, pp. 503–506). Here I need only add that the role played by δ in the arguments just referred to must be taken over by $w(\cdot)$.

As suggested by results of Donald Brown and M. Ali Kahn (1976, 1980), T 28 may not constitute the most general core equivalence theorem for hyperfinite exchange economies. However, both the theorem and my proof of it serve the purposes for which they were designed: to exhibit the topological aspects of T 1 and T 2 and to draw attention to the import of two disturbing features of T 2.

8.5 PRACTICAL IMPLICATIONS

I consider that the results of this essay have two practical implications—one for economic theory and one for the science of economics.

First *economic theory*: In spite of all the interesting core equivalence and core convergence theorems that they have produced in the last two decades, mathematical economists are far from having a good idea of the workings of large economies. For example, in large economies consumers are supposed to have a negligible influence on price. When price changes are measured in terms of nonstandard ε-neighborhoods, the actions of a single consumer have as much effect on prices in a hyperfinite economy as they have in an ordinary finite economy. When price changes are measured in terms of standard ε-neighborhoods, even coalitions with uncountably many consumers might have a negligible influence on the prices at which trading occurs. Yet economic theory provides no hint as to how one can determine which topology is the right one for the study of exchange in hyperfinite economies.

Next *the science of economics*: Ideally, a scientist interprets his theory to see if his axioms are consistent. If they are, he proceeds to search for consequences of the axioms that seem interesting from a scientist's point of view. Finally he uses his results to describe an experiment by which the empirical relevance of the intended interpretation of his theory can be tested. Mathematical economists are usually content when they, to their own satisfaction, have carried out the first two steps of this theory development. The necessity of describing ways in which their theories can be confronted with data occurs to only a few. This is unfortunate since, as my results suggest, the empirical relevance of an interpretation of a theory cannot be determined by a priori reasoning alone.

Since the preceding point concerns the import of this chapter, a striking example is in order here. In the example, the idea of which I have taken from Werner Hildenbrand's (1974) extraordinary account, *Core and Equilibria of a Large Economy*, J_{sco} denotes the set of all strictly increasing and strictly convex preference relations on $R^n_+ \times R^n_+$, and $J_{sco} \times R^n_+$ is the space of agents' characteristics. Further, an exchange economy is a measurable mapping, $\varepsilon : [[0, 1], \mathcal{L}, \mu(\cdot)] \to J_{sco} \times R^n_+$, e is the projection of $J_{sco} \times R^n_{++}$ onto R^n_{++}, and $\gamma(\cdot) : \mathcal{P}\left(J_{sco} \times R^n_{++}\right) \to [0, 1]$ is the preference-endowment distribution of ε, which is defined by $\gamma(B) = \mu\varepsilon^{-1}(B)$, $B \in \mathcal{P}(J_{sco} \times R^n_{++})$. Finally, a simple economy is a mapping $\varepsilon_n(\cdot) : \left[A_n, \varphi_n, \mu_n(\cdot)\right] \to J_{sco} \times R^n_{++}$, where $A_n \subset [0, 1]$ is finite, φ_n is the family of all subsets of A_n, and $\mu_n(B) = (\#B/\#A_n)$, $B \in \varphi_n$.

E 8.4 *In Chapter 3 of his 1974 treatise Hildenbrand sets out to show that* "in a simple exchange economy *with* sufficiently many *participants, every allocation in the core can be* approximately *decentralized by a suitably chosen price system. The more agents that participate in the economy, the better the approximation will be" (cf. Hildenbrand, 1974, p. 177). One part of the evidence that he cites for such a claim is paraphrased in the following theorem:*[8]

T 29 *Consider an Aumann economy with preference-endowment distribution* $\gamma(\cdot)$, *and let* ε_n *be a sequence of simple exchange economies with preference endowment distribution,*

$$\gamma_n(\cdot) : \mathcal{P}\left(J_{sco} \times R^n_{++}\right) \to [0, 1].$$

Suppose also that the ε_n *satisfy the following conditions: (1)* $\lim_n \#A_n = \infty$; *(2) the sequence* $\gamma_n(\cdot)$ *converges weakly on* $J_{sco} \times R^n_{++}$ *to* $\gamma(\cdot)$; *(3)* $\lim_n \int e d\gamma_n = \int e d\gamma$; *and (4)* $\int e d\gamma > 0$. *Finally, let* $\tau(\gamma)$ *denote the set of competitive equilibrium prices in the Aumann economy, and let* $\psi[\varepsilon_n(a), \cdot] : R^n_{++} \to R^n_+$, *denote the demand function of* $a \in A_n$. *Then, for every* $\delta > 0$ *and* $\eta > 0$, *there exists an integer* $\tilde{n}$ *such that for every* $n > \tilde{n}$ *and for every core allocation* $f(\cdot)$ *in* ε_n *there is a* $p \in \tau(\gamma)$ *such that*

$$(1/\#A_n)\#\{a \in A_n : |f(a) - \psi[\varepsilon_n(a), p]| > \eta\} < \delta$$

Since, as my results demonstrate, the allocation achieved by $\psi[\varepsilon(\cdot), p]$ might leave vast quantities of some commodities going to waste and allocate vast nonexisting quantities of other commodities to frustrated consumers, the preceding theorem does not provide any evidence in support of Hildenbrand's dictum.

NOTES

1. In equation (5) a.a. is short for "almost all."
2. In the statements of his two theorems, Aumann (1964, 1966) did not insist that his consumers' endowments were bounded.
3. In equation (12) iff is short for "if and only if."
4. For a proof of the existence of a free ultrafilter over N see Stigum (1990, pp. 464–465). In this context it is interesting to observe that if $M(\cdot) : \mathcal{P}(N) \to \{0, 1\}$ is an additive measure on the set of all subsets of N, $\mathcal{P}(N)$, such that $M(N) = 1$, then the family of sets $\mathcal{F}_M$ that satisfy the conditions, $A \subset N$ and $M(A) = 1$, constitutes an ultrafilter over N. If one adds to the conditions on $M(\cdot)$ that $M(A) = 0$ if A is finite, then $\mathcal{F}_M$ becomes a free ultrafilter over N.
5. In reading T 3, note that $\mathcal{P}_F(E)$ is not a subset of $^*R$. Still $^*\mathcal{P}_F(E)$ is to be thought of as the equivalence class $\mathcal{P}_F(E)_{\mathcal{U}}$. Thus, if $A \subset {^*R}$, then $A \in {^*\mathcal{P}_F(E)}$ if and only if there is a sequence of subsets of R, $\{A_n\}$, such that $A = \{A_n\}_u$ and $\{n \in N : A_n \in \mathcal{P}_F(E)\} \in \mathcal{U}$.

6. There is a misprint on p. 499, line 18, in the proof of T 21.28 in Stigum (1990). There Σ should be replaced by $\cup$ so that $G = \cup_{i=1} G_i$.

7. In equation (38) a.e. is short for "almost everywhere."

8. Note that in T 2 the initial commodity bundles are positive and uniformly bounded. Here I have added the assumption that consumer preferences are strictly convex.

REFERENCES

Albeverio, S., J. E. Fenstad, R. Hoegh-Krohn, and T. Lindstrøm, 1986, *Nonstandard Methods in Stochastic Analysis and Mathematical Physics*, New York: Academic Press.

Aumann, R., 1964, "Markets with a Continuum of Traders," *Econometrica*, 32, 39–50.

Aumann, R., 1966, "Existence of Competitive Equilibria Ill Markets with a Continuum of Traders," *Econometrica* 34, 1–17.

Brown, D. J., 1976, "Existence of a competitive Equilibrium in a Nonstandard Exchange Economy," *Econometrica* 44, 537–546.

Brown, D. J., and M. A. Kahn, 1980, "An Extension of the Brown-Robinson Equivalence Theorem," *Applied Mathematics and Computation* 6, 167–175.

Brown, D. J., and A. Robinson, 1975, "Nonstandard Exchange Economies," *Econometrica*, 43, 355–369.

Debreu, G., and H. Scarf, 1963, "A Limit Theorem on the Core of an Economy," *International Economic Review* 4, 235–246.

Hildenbrand, W., 1974, *Core and Equilibria of a Large Economy*, Princeton: Princeton University Press.

Keisler, H. J., 1984, "An Infinitesimal Approach to Stochastic Analysis," *Memoirs of the American Mathematical Society*, 297.

Lindstrøm, T., 1988, "An Invitation to Nonstandard Analysis," in *Nonstandard Analysis and its Applications*, N. Cutland (ed.), Cambridge: Cambridge University Press.

Robinson, A., 1966, *Non-Standard Analysis*, Amsterdam: North-Holland.

Stigum, B. P., 1990, *Toward a Formal Science of Economics*, Cambridge: MIT Press.

PART III
Theory-Data Confrontations in Economics

Chapter Nine

Rational Animals and Sample Populations

The idea of rationality enters an econometrician's work in many ways, for example, in his presuppositions about sample populations, in his model selections and data analyses, and in his choice of projects. In this chapter I establish the characteristics that an econometrician can, in good faith, expect rational members of a sample population to possess. The characteristics I end up with have no definite meaning. Rather, they are like undefined terms in mathematics that the econometrician can interpret in ways that suit the purposes of his research and seem appropriate for the population he is studying. When interpreted, the pertinent characteristics of the rational members of a given population become hypotheses whose empirical relevance must be tested.

To emphasize the undefined aspect of the characteristics that constitute my idea of rationality, I designate a rational individual by the term "rational animal." As such, my rational animal shares many of the characteristics of Thomas Paine's "common man" and John Stuart Mill's "economic man." My rational animal also looks like Donald Davidson's rational animal, whose rationality is made up of all sorts of propositional attitudes (cf. Davidson, 1982). Whether my rational animal, like Davidson's, does have the use of language is a question that I do not raise. However, all the populations that I have in mind have the use of some kind of language. Finally, the fact that the empirical relevance of a given interpreted version of my rational animal cannot be taken for granted accords with Hempel's insistence that the assumption that man is rational is an empirical hypothesis (cf. Hempel, 1962, p. 5).

9.1 A PHILOSOPHER'S CONCEPT OF RATIONALITY

One of the many socially constructed facts that I have learned to accept is that *a human being is a rational animal.* Philosophers, usually without proper reference, attribute this assertion to Aristotle. I begin my search for a suitable concept of rationality for econometrics by delineating Aristotle's idea of a rational animal. My primary sources are translations of Aristotle's treatises *De Anima* and *Nicomachean Ethics* and relevant philosophical commentaries.[1]

9.1.1 Rational Animals

Aristotle had a simple scheme for classifying elements in the physical world. There were two realms: the inorganic world and the organic world. All living things and nothing else belonged to the organic world, and he arranged the living things in turn into three life classes according to their possession of various basic faculties. Vegetable life consisted of all living things that had only the powers of nutrition and reproduction. Animal life consisted of all living things that had the powers of nutrition and reproduction and the sensation of touch. Finally, human life consisted of all living things that had the powers of nutrition and reproduction, the sensation of touch, and the faculty of deliberative imagination.

For my purposes here it is important to keep in mind the role of touch and deliberative imagination in Aristotle's characterizations of animal and human life. He allowed that animals may have many sensations in addition to touch. However, touch was to him "the only sense, the deprivation of which necessitates the death of animals. For neither [was] it possible for anything that is not an animal to have this sense, nor [was] it necessary for anything that is an animal to have any sense beyond it" (*De Anima*, p. 143). Consequently, an animal was a living thing that had the sensation of touch as well as the faculties of a member of vegetable life.

The case of deliberative imagination is a bit more involved. According to Aristotle, imagination was the faculty of mind by which an animal forms images of things that are not present to the senses or within the actual experience of the organism involved. As such imagination was not sensation, although an animal could not have imagination without having the faculty of sensation. Aristotle conceived of two kinds of imagination: imagination derived from sensation and deliberative imagination. The former, he claimed, "[was] found in the lower animals but deliberative imagination [was] found only in those animals which [were] endowed with reason" (*De Anima* Book III, Chapter XI). Moreover, an animal could not have the power of reason without having deliberative imagination. Since none of the lower animals had reason, it follows that the higher animals, that is, human beings, had to be animals with the power of deliberative imagination.

A rational animal is more than an animal with deliberative imagination because an animal with deliberative imagination has the faculty of reason, and an animal with reason has the faculty of deliberative imagination. To deliberate means to weigh alternatives and that is an act of reason. Therefore, an animal with the faculty of deliberative imagination and the power of reason would also have the ability to form opinions. Finally, an animal could not have the ability to form opinions without having the faculty of deliberative imagination (*De Anima*, Book III, Chapter III). But if that is so, one may claim that a human being is an animal with the faculties of deliberative imagination, opinion, and reason. Consequently, if a human being is a rational animal, one may adopt the following characterization of rational animals: *An animal is rational if and only if it has the faculty of deliberative imagination and is able to form opinions and reason.*

9.1.2 Deliberative Imagination, Opinion, and Reason

I believe that the preceding assertion provides an adequate rendition of Aristotle's idea of *rational* animals. However, to get a good idea of what it means for an animal to be rational, one must take a closer look at the meanings of deliberative imagination, opinion, and reason.

I consider the three terms, deliberative imagination, opinion, and reason, to be like undefined terms in mathematics. They have no definite agreed-upon meaning. Rather, their meanings are culturally determined and vary over individuals as well as over groups of individuals.

The wealth of images that an individual can create with his deliberative imagination is a function of many things. It depends on the physical and mental sensations that he has experienced, for example, the places he has visited and the people he has met. It also depends on his schooling and his abilities and inclinations. Finally, it depends on the cultural traditions with which he grew up. A Californian might dream of UFOs traversing the sky, and a Norwegian youngster might fantasize about trolls and seductive maidens with long tails roaming a nearby forest at night.

Individuals have all sorts of opinions. Some pertain to their personal lives and determine their likes and dislikes of things and ideas and their proper attitudes toward their fellowmen. Others pertain to the society in which they live and may concern the appropriateness of customs, for example, the circumcision of women, and the usefulness of various structural aspects, for example, the political independence of a central bank. Still others pertain to the validity of theories and socially constructed facts and may concern the power of ghosts and the right of biologists to clone human beings. Opinions may vary in surprising ways over individuals, as witnessed in the next example.

E 9.1 *In her book* In a Different Voice *Carol Gilligan theorizes about differences in character development between men and women. One of the experiments she describes is relevant here.*

A psychiatrist tells two eleven-year-old children, a boy and a girl, a sad story. Al and Liz are happily married. Liz is sick and will die unless she gets a medicament C. Al has no money to buy C and the nearest druggist refuses to give it to him. That presents Al with two options—steal C to save his wife's life or watch his wife die. What should he do? The boy argues that Al ought to steal C since the druggist's loss of C would be minor relative to Al's gain from C saving Liz's life. He also suggests that if Al were caught, he would receive a light sentence, since the judge would agree that Al did the right thing. The girl insists that it is not right that a person should die if her life could be saved. Still Al ought not to steal C. Instead he should try to persuade the druggist to give him C and promise to pay him later.

Gilligan recounts that the boy in the experiment actually preferred English to math and that the girl aspired to become a scientist. Still, the boy relied on conventions of logic to resolve the dilemma, assuming that most people would agree to these conventions. The girl relied on a process of communication to find a solution to the dilemma, assuming that most people will respond to a reasonable plea for help (cf. Gilligan, 1982, pp. 24–32).

It is interesting to note here that Aristotle insisted that a person could not have an opinion without believing in what he opined. Hence, opinion was followed by belief. In fact, "every opinion [was] followed by belief, as belief [was] followed by persuasion, and persuasion by reason" (*De Anima*, p. 108). Persuasion concerns all matters on which an individual might have an opinion. It occurs in familiar places, for example, at home, in classrooms and lecture halls, and in day-to-day interactions with friends and acquaintances. It is experienced in different forms, for example, as gentle parental coaxing, as socially constructed facts in books and newspapers, and as results of heated discussions. The beliefs acquired in this way may be well founded or just fixed ideas as evidenced in E 9.2, where I paraphrase an observation of E. E. Evans-Pritchard.[2]

E 9.2 *I have no particular knowledge of meteorology. Still I insist that rain is due to natural causes. This belief is not based on observation and inference but is part of my cultural heritage. A savage might believe that, under suitable natural and ritual conditions, the appropriate magic can induce rain. His belief is not based on observation and inference either, but. is part of his cultural heritage, and he adopts it simply by being born into it. Both he and I are thinking in patterns of thought that the societies in which we live provided for us.*

For Aristotle, reason was the instrument by which a person thinks and forms conceptions and it could be passive or active. The passive reason in an infant was pure potentiality. In a learned person the passive reason became the capacity of thinking itself (*De Anima*, Book III, Chapter IV). The active reason was reason activated by desire (*De Anima*, Book III, Chapters IX and X). Depending on the particular object of desire the active reason would result in choice of action, judgment concerning truth and falsehood, or judgment of what is right or wrong. The reasoning involved was *true* if it was logical and based on premises that were either true by necessity or accepted as true by the wise. Moreover, the desire was right if it reflected an appetition for a good end. The choices and judgments concerning right or wrong were good if they resulted from true reasoning and a right desire. The judgments concerning truth and falsehood were good if they were logical consequences of premises that were true by necessity (*Nicomachean Ethics*, Book VI, see Ross, 1925, pp. 138–139).

The validity of necessary truths and the well-foundedness of premises that the wise have accepted are often questionable. Moreover, some of the premises of the wise may reflect attitudes that one cannot condone. The following are a few illustrations to demonstrate my point.

Consider the law of the excluded middle. Aristotle believed that the law was true by necessity, and most mathematicians today agree with him. The Dutch intuitionists, however, think differently. They insist that a declarative sentence denotes truth or falsehood according as it, or its negation, can be verified. If neither the sentence nor its negation is verifiable, the sentence is neither true nor false. Here are two cases in point: (1) *There are three consecutive 7's in the decimal expansion of* π. (2) *There are integers of which nobody ever will have thought.* At present the truth value of the first sentence is unknown, and it is conceivable that no human being will ever determine it. Satisfying the predicated relation in the second sentence involves a contradiction, and determination of its falsehood is inconceivable. According to the Dutch intuitionists these sentences are at present neither true nor false.

Similarly, the well-foundedness of premises that the wise have accepted is often uncertain. This can be seen in the way scientific knowledge changes over time. For example, Aristotle believed that water was one of five basic substances that could combine with other substances to form compounds but could not be broken down to simpler substances. His idea was dispelled in 1775 when Cavendish succeeded in showing that hydrogen and oxygen combined to form water. It can also be seen in historical records describing dire consequences of government policies that were based on irrelevant economic theories. One recent example is from Peru, where the changes in land ownership that the military junta carried out between 1968 and 1980 had a disastrous effect on farm output. The military and their economic advisers based their policies on the theory of labor-managed firms, an interesting economic theory that had next to no empirical relevance under Peruvian conditions. The Peruvian farm laborers did not have the knowledge or the ability to acquire the knowledge of how to manage large farms.[3]

Finally, some of the premises that the wise accept may reflect attitudes that one cannot condone, for instance, the maxim that *the end always justifies the means.* When other arguments fail, governments use this notion to justify all sorts of interventions. One example is from the 1990s "Bank Crisis" in Norway. To solve the crisis the Labor government assumed ownership of the three largest Norwegian banks. As far as I can tell, there was no good economic reason for the takeovers. Moreover, the government's handling of the case displayed a shocking disregard for the individual citizen in its refusal to compensate the stockholders. The Russian massacres of innocent people in Hungary in 1956 and in Czechoslovakia in 1968 provide a different example. In private conversations, an internationally known scientist, that is, a very wise man, told me that the Russians' vision of Eastern Europeans living in bliss under communism justified the atrocities.

Now the conclusion concerning Aristotle's active reason: If necessary truths might be invalid and if the judgments of the wise may be questioned, then true reason and right desire cannot be well determined. They must vary with the culture in which an individual has been raised and are likely to vary among individuals even in the same community. If that is so, then Aristotle's active reason is like an undefined term with no definite meaning. This indefiniteness faces us everywhere and always. We become acutely aware of it when we meet people and experience events in real life or in books and newspapers that we cannot understand. The associated problems may concern family relations or the increasing violence in the streets. They may concern aspects of human rights or just the senseless wars in the Balkans. Finally, they may concern the disparate premises of the religions that provide people with standards of right and wrong. The next example describes an important case in point.

E 9.3 *The question is:* Should a doctor be allowed to help a mortally ill patient die prematurely? *In Norway the Church and the law say no. However, many influential people say yes and argue strongly for changing the law accordingly.*

In 1996 a forty-five-year old woman mortally ill with multiple sclerosis asked her doctor to help her die. The doctor agreed and gave her an overdose of morphine. Later, the doctor asked the courts to try him for murder. He was hoping that the trial would start the process of changing the law so that active death help under strict provisions would be allowed.

As the first of its kind, the case went through the court system in Norway. The lower court found the doctor guilty of premeditated manslaughter, but refused to punish him. Both the doctor and the prosecutor appealed the verdict to a higher court. In the higher court the jury found him not guilty of manslaughter. The judges, however, insisted that the doctor was guilty and overruled the jury. That meant that the same court had to convene once more with different judges and try the case anew. In the new trial the court found the doctor guilty of premeditated manslaughter and postponed the determination of the sentence with a probation period of 2 years. Again the doctor and the prosecutor appealed the verdict—this time to the Supreme Court of Norway. On April 14, 2000, the Supreme Court denied the appeals.

9.1.3 Good Choices and Judgments

The preceding discussion leaves one with the idea that a rational animal is one with deliberative imagination, beliefs, opinions, and reason and that these four characteristic features have no definite meaning. The same vagueness must be a quality of Aristotle's idea of rational animals. Hence, if one accepts Aristotle's ideas, one should expect to meet all sorts of rational animals, which is not disconcerting as the people one meets in life are all so different.

Aristotle's idea of rationality had two interesting characteristics. First, his notion of a rational animal was universal in the sense that it characterized all human beings, be they atheists or priests, ignoramuses or scholars, or just infants or grown-ups. Second, the choices and judgments that a rational animal made were rational only if they were good choices and judgments that, in accordance with the rules of logic, followed from proper premises and right desires. Here the logic in question was the syllogistic logic that Aristotle developed in his treatise *Prior Analytics* (see Barnes, 1984). Moreover, depending on the subject matter, the premises were the results either of intuitive reasoning and arguments by induction and analogy or of ratiocinative deliberations. Finally, the desires were right only if they reflected an appetition for a good end.

Since rational choices and judgments were to be good choices and judgments, a few remarks concerning Aristotle's idea of the "good" are called for. To Aristotle the good was that toward which every art and inquiry and every action and pursuit aim. It was also something that people searched for for its own sake. Finally, it was an activity of the soul in accordance with moral and intellectual virtue. This extraordinary good Aristotle identified with *happiness* (*Nicomachean Ethics*, see Ross, 1925, pp. 1–24).

Most people associate living well and faring well with being happy. Yet, different individuals are likely to differ considerably in their ideas as to what actually constitutes happiness. A sick person might identify happiness with health and a poor one might associate it with wealth. Similarly, a youngster might associate happiness with pleasure and a politician might identify it with honor. According to Aristotelian thinking, they are all wrong. In Aristotle's vocabulary health, wealth, pleasure, and honor were not different aspects of the good. Rather, they were means in the pursuit of the good, which he designated as happiness.

According to Aristotle, happiness was an activity of the soul in accordance with perfect virtue, and a virtue was a state of character. Virtues came in two forms: moral and intellectual. Individuals acquired moral virtues by habit; for example, they became just by carrying out just acts and brave by performing brave acts. Similarly, people developed intellectual virtues in schools and through individual studies; for example, they acquired philosophical wisdom from intuition of basic premises, scientific research, and deductive reasoning and practical wisdom by developing a true and reasoned capacity to act with regard to the things that are good or bad for man. Thus a person acquired virtues by habit and practice and in the process learned to appreciate the virtuousness and to enjoy the happiness it brought him.

What is virtuous in one society need not be virtuous in another. Moreover, what one wise person considers virtuous another may dispute. In the *Nicomachean Ethics* Aristotle insisted that in all situations that involve choice and moral judgments truly virtuous persons would adhere to the so-called *right rule* (*Nicomachean Ethics*, see Ross, 1925, p. 30). In such situations, "excess [was] a form of failure, and so [was] defect, while the intermediate [was] praised and [was] a form of success; and being praised and being successful [were] both characteristics of virtue." Thus virtue was kind of a mean. For example, courage was a mean between fear and confidence and pride was a mean between dishonor and honor (pp. 38–41). Interesting aspects of this doctrine have a good hold on the minds of many of my fellow citizens in Norway. There children grow up with the idea that it is not virtuous to show off. The school system is designed so that poor students can survive, average students can do well, and bright students have little or no opportunity to perform according to their abilities. And the solidarity principle, which underlies the income-distribution policy of the government, ensures that disposable income does not vary too much over a large majority of the population.

In my search for a concept of rationality for econometrics, I am looking for a concept that shares the two characteristics of Aristotle's idea of rationality. Thus, I insist that *a rational person is an animal with deliberative imagination, beliefs, opinions, and reason.* Moreover, *rational choices and judgments are good choices and judgments that, in accordance with the pertinent rules of logic, follow from appropriate premises and right desires.* However, I do not limit the rules of logic to Aristotle's syllogistic logic, but allow the logic to vary with situation as well as subject matter. For example, I might use rules of the first-order predicate calculus in mathematics and the sciences, rules of deontic logic in juridical matters, and the language that I developed in Stigum (1990, pp. 583–611) in matters that pertain to the theory of knowledge. Furthermore, I do not insist that a rational animal's appetition for a good end be in accord with Aristotle's idea of the right rule. However, as the examples from Norway indicate, I cannot ignore the fact that rules and regulations that are engendered by lawmakers and other authorities have a determining influence on what the average citizen considers virtuous. To the extent that these rules and regulations reflect aspects of Aristotle's doctrine, that doctrine forms a part of my concept of what constitutes rational conduct and judgment.

9.2 RULES OF LOGIC, PROPER PREMISES, AND RIGHT DESIRES

Rational animals live and function in the social reality I described in Chapter 2. They are all alike in having deliberative imagination, beliefs, opinions, and reason. In this section I try to determine whether they are alike in other respects as well. To do this, I look for answers to three questions: Is it true that two different rational animals in a given choice situation will necessarily make the same choice? If they happen to make different choices, what are the chances that one might be persuaded to change his or her choice? Finally, is it likely that two individuals from one and the same society will act and make judgments on the basis of premises that all the members of their society accept? The answers to these questions provide a good understanding of the roles "rules of logic," "proper premises," and "right desire" play in my idea of a rational animal's rational choice and judgment.

9.2.1 Rational Animals in Choice Situations

People go through life experiencing all sorts of situations in which they are called upon to make a choice. Sometimes the number of alternatives is small: for example, the choices open to Norwegian parents when their children come of age and *must* attend primary school. There are many public schools and just a few private schools. Most parents send their children to a public school in their neighborhood. Other times the number of alternatives is considerable: for example, the options for the unfortunate person who must acquire a new car. There are many different car makes, each comes in many different models, and every model has any number of styles to choose from. Finally, there are times when the number of alternatives is hard to fathom: for example, the situation of the young man who must choose an education for access to a life-long stream of income that will enable him to meet his future needs. He can decide to start his education now or wait a year. If he waits a year, he can take a part-time job and devote lots of time to his favorite hobbies and leisure activities. He can also take a full-time job and save money to pay for his education.

It is improbable that two rational animals in one and the same choice situation are alike in all pertinent matters. A second look at the choice situations I described earlier bears witness to that. In the choice of school for a child the abilities and character of the child are pertinent matters, as are the parents' upbringing, their visions for the child's future, and the roles they play in the neighborhood in which they live. In the choice of a new car the buyer's budget constraint, his knowledge of cars, and the purposes for which he needs the car are pertinent matters as are the time he has allotted to searching for a new car, the supply of cars in his neighborhood, and his ideas as to the kind of car he ought to be driving. In the choice of career the number of pertinent matters are as numerous as the alternatives the young man faces, among them are his character and upbringing, his abilities and the state of his health, his financial constraints, the availability and costs of schooling, the current employment situation, and his visions of opportunities and the kind of life he wants to live.

I am looking for a concept of rationality according to which rational choices, in accordance with the rules of logic, follow from appropriate premises. The preceding observations suggest that there are only two reasonable ways to test whether the choices of rational animals have this property: One can either observe the actions of a given individual in similar choice situations or construct simple choice experiments in which a subject's impertinent attributes are stripped of influence. I describe two such tests in what follows.

If a given rational animal's choices follow from proper premises following the rules of logic, one should expect that he will always make the same choice in similar choice situations. In the following example I question such consistency of a single rational animal's choices. Specifically, the example describes a way of testing the consistency of consumer choice of commodity vectors. The test is one that Paul Samuelson suggested many years ago (cf. Samuelson, 1938, pp. 61–71).

E 9.4 *Consider a consumer* A *and suppose that in the price-income situation* (p^0, I^0), A *chooses the commodity vector* x^0. *Suppose also that* x^1 *is another commodity vector, which satisfies the inequality,* $p^0x^1 \leq p^0x^0$. *Then* A *has revealed that he prefers* x^0 *to* x^1. *Consequently, if* A *in some price-income situation* (p^1, I^1) *buys* x^1, *it must be the case that* $p^1x^1 < p^1x^0$.

In this case the premises are threefold: A *has a consistent ordering of commodity vectors; in a given price-income situation,* A *always chooses the vector in his budget set that he ranks the highest; and.* A*'s ordering of commodity vectors is such that there always is just one vector in a budget set that he will rank the highest.*

If A *is rational in accordance with the concept of rationality that I am seeking, the conclusion, that is, the claim that the inequality* $p^1x^1 < p^1x^0$ *must hold, is valid with one very strong proviso:* A*'s ordering of commodity vectors when he chooses* x^1 *is the same as when he chose* x^0.

The proviso in E 9.4 is hard to accept. A consumer's ordering of commodity vectors is likely to change over time for many reasons. It may change with the ages of family members or because some family member develops a liking for a special component of the commodity vector. The ordering may also change with the price-income expectations of the consumer. If the expectations at (p^1, I^1) differ from those at (p^0, I^0), Samuelson's test would be invalid.[4]

Two-person noncooperative game theory is full of possibilities for laboratory experiments in which one can check whether two persons in one and the same choice situation will make the same choices. I describe one of them in E 9.5.

E 9.5 *Consider two individuals* A *and* B *who dislike each other enough so that they are not willing to communicate under any circumstances. A third person* C *has persuaded them to participate in a game of the following sort:* A *and* B *are to choose one of two letters* α *and* β. *If they both choose* $\alpha(\beta)$, C *will pay them each \$100 (\$10). If* A *chooses* $\alpha(\beta)$ *and* B *chooses* $\beta(\alpha)$, C *will charge* A *\$200 for the game and pay* B *\$300 (pay* A *\$300 and charge* B *\$200 for the game).* A(B) *must make his choice without knowing which letter* B(A) *is choosing.* A *and* B *both know all the consequences of the game and have agreed to the rules*

A *and* B *will be playing a model of the game called "Prisoner's Dilemma" with a payoff matrix as shown below. All the entries in the matrix denote so many dollars.*

		B's strategies	
		α	β
A's strategies	α	100, 100	−200, 300
	β	300, −200	10, 10

An equilibrium in game theory is a Nash equilibrium. It has the property that each player, once his opponent's strategy has been revealed, is satisfied with his own choice of strategy. In the present game there is one and only one equilibrium, and it prescribes that both A *and* B *choose the letter* β.

In E 9.5, *A* and *B* start out with the same premises and the same information, and the payoff matrix is symmetric in the sense that neither *A* nor *B* would have anything against exchanging names. It seems, therefore, that if *A* and *B* are rational, according to any concept of rationality that one might seek, they must end up choosing the same letter. Game theorists insist that the rational thing for *A* and *B* to do is to choose β because β is the only choice that they will not regret having made afterward. So far the idea of regret has played no part in this discussion of rationality. Hence, a philosopher is still free to reject the game theorists' claim by arguing as follows: *A* and *B* are both rational. Therefore, in the given choice situation they will choose the same letter. Being rational, they will figure out that they will choose the same letter, and as the best one for them both is α, the rational thing for them to do is to choose α (cf. Brown, 1990, pp. 3–6).

It is one thing to argue about what rational people ought to do when facing a prisoner's dilemma but another to find out what people actually do in such a choice situation. The evidence from experimental economics is mixed. In some cases the pair chooses an α. In other cases the pair chooses a β. In still other cases one member of the pair chooses an α while the other chooses a β. On the whole, there seem to be more β's among the chosen letters than α's. That is not strange since choosing β is not just a Nash equilibrium strategy for the two players, but a dominant strategy for both players. Further, if that is not enough, it is also a *maximin* strategy for them. To wit: If *A* (or *B*) chooses α he might *lose* \$200 (\$200). If he chooses β, he might *receive* \$10 rather than \$100.

The experiment in E 9.6, which was conceived and carried out by Russell W. Cooper, Douglas V. DeJong, Robert Forsythe, and Thomas W. Ross (cf. Cooper et al., 1996), bears out the import of the preceding remarks. Douglas DeJong provided the numbers I have recorded in Table 9.1.

TABLE 9.1
Prisoner's Dilemma Matchings

Matchings	1–5	6–10	11–15	16–20
Percentage of (α, α) pairs	17	10	7	6
Percentage of (β, β) pairs	32	45	57	67
Percentage of (α, β) and (β, α) pairs	51	45	36	27

E 9.6 *Consider a prisoner's dilemma experiment in which forty-two subjects are paired with each other in a sequence of* matchings. *By letting each subject encounter every other subject only once, a sequence of forty different matchings can be generated in which each matching contains twenty single-stage games. In 1991 Cooper et al. carried out such an experiment, with the results shown here in Table 9.1.*

9.2.2 Regrets and Rational Choice

We have seen that it is next to impossible to divine circumstances in real life in which one can check whether rational animals in one and the same choice situation make the same choice. We have also seen that in experimental settings in which one would expect rational animals to make the same choice, they need not do so. The last example suggests that when two individuals in a prisoner's dilemma situation make different choices, one of them will have regrets and choose differently the next time he is called upon to choose. That fact raises an interesting question: Suppose that one has observed that a supposedly rational person makes a choice that the observer thinks is not rational. Is it be possible for the observer to persuade him to change his choice? I try to answer that question next.

Philosophers believe that it is an essential characteristic of a rational person that he be willing to mend his ways if he discovers that he has erred in choice or conduct (cf., e.g., Foellesdal, 1982, p. 316). I am not so sure. If two rational animals in the same choice situation make different choices, one of three things must obtain. Both individuals consider the consequences of their choices equivalent; one of them has made a logical error; or each has made use of a different logic. In the first case it makes no sense to ask one of the two individuals to mend his ways. In the other two the success of persuasion may depend on many factors, some of which I indicate in what follows.

First logical errors: Logical errors in reasoning crop up in many situations. Since a logical error is like a false arithmetical calculation, one would expect that an erring person who discovers his error will recalculate and change his choice. Whether he actually does recalculate, however, may depend on the situation. For example, at home a given individual may miscalculate the remaining balance in his checking account and write a check too many. Then the bank makes sure that he mends his ways. At work his search for solutions to a given problem may be based in part on unfounded beliefs and flimsy evidence. What is worse, the arguments he employs may suffer from poorly specified a priori assumptions that are either inapplicable in the circumstances he envisages or lead to circular reasoning. If he is a reasonable person, he probably would rethink his reasoning if he became aware of such fallacies. Finally, as a consultant on the side, he may base his forecasts of future business conditions on assumptions that others might consider utterly unrealistic. Even if these others manage to convince him of that, he might not change his ways as long as his forecasts are good.

There is an interesting example from experimental economics that is relevant here.

E 9.7 *In a given laboratory a subject is asked to rank pairs of prospects of the following form:*

P: \$4 w. pr. 0.99 and −\$1 w. pr. 0.01

and

Q: \$16 w. pr. 0.33 and −\$2 w. pr. 0.67,

where w. pr. is short for with probability. After a break the subject is confronted with the same prospects in different order and asked to indicate the minimum prices at which he would be willing to sell the respective prospects if he owned them.

In their seminal 1971 article, "Reversals of Preference between Bids and Choices in Gambling Decisions," Sarah Lichtenstein and Paul Slovic found that a large percentage of their subjects often ranked a P *prospect above a* Q *prospect and yet insisted on a higher sales price for the* Q *prospect than for the pertinent* P *prospect. This kind of preference reversal has been observed by others, and some of them have tried hard to discredit its relevance for economic theorizing (cf., e.g., Grether and Plott, 1979). Here the interesting part of Lichtenstein and Slovic's paper is that the authors faced eleven of the sinners with their inconsistent behavior and asked them if they saw any reason to mend their ways. Two refused, and of the nine others only six were willing to mend their ways without much ado (Lichtenstein and Slovic, 1971, pp. 53–54).*

Next different logics: It might at first sound impossible that in a given situation two people might choose differently because they make use of different logics. However, E 9.5 provides us with a good illustration of such a possibility. There A might argue as a game theorist and choose β, while B argues as a philosopher and chooses α. One might convince B that his logic is fallacious. However, it would be to no avail since the rules of the game do not allow him to change his strategy.

There are many reasons why two supposedly rational individuals in a given choice situation might make use of different logics. For example, their attitudes toward relevant logical and nonlogical premises may differ, as may their conceptions of the choice alternatives they face. The possibility that decision-makers utilize different logics is important to econometrics, so I give several examples later that illustrate how that can happen.

When I compare the choice of two rational animals in a given choice situation, I presume that the two start out with the same premises and face the same consequences of their actions. The premises may insist that the two obey the laws of their society and adhere to a certain moral code. For example, you shall not steal or cheat on taxes, and you shall not inflict wounds on other persons willfully. The consequences may include a record of possible monetary gain as well as a list of various penalties for breaking the law. If two individuals' premises and consequences are the same, only different logics cause them to make different choices. Different logics may reflect different attitudes toward the strictures of the law as well as different assignments of probabilities to possible gains and losses. E 9.8 bears witness to that.

E 9.8 *In Norway many people find it to their advantage to sneak out of paying fares on trolleys and buses. The fares are high, the chance of being caught sneaking is small, and the penalty when caught is light. Since there are no public records of who has been caught sneaking, the punishment for sneaking amounts to only a smidgen more than the fine and a day of bad mood.*

The sneaking on trolleys and buses is extensive enough to cause the transportation companies some concern. A few years back these companies launched a campaign in which they appealed to the moral attitudes of their customers and asked them to mend their ways. The campaign had no appreciable effect. It seemed that the only way to induce a sneaking person to stop sneaking was to make the penalty more severe and increase the frequency of controls. The companies ended up doubling the penalty for being caught while leaving the frequency of controls more or less as it had always been.

In the next example I describe a choice situation in which a very wise person and an ordinary citizen apply different logics because of their radically different attitudes toward uncertainty.

E 9.9 *In a classic article on exchangeable events and processes Bruno de Finetti insisted that subjective probabilities had to be additive. If a person's assignments of probabilities to mutually exclusive uncertain events were not additive, he could make a fool of that person by inducing him to take an unfavorable bet (cf. de Finetti 1964, pp. 102–104). I long considered this an incontestable fact, but I now show that it is no fact at all.*

Consider an ordinary grown-up rational animal A *who faces two events,* E_1 *and its complement* E_2*. One may think of* E_1 *as the event that* bin Laden was killed during one of the American air raids last year. *Further, suppose that* A *is a person who deals with uncertainty by shading his subjective probabilities. He assigns probability one-third to the occurrence of* E_1 *and probability one-third to the occurrence of* E_2*. Finally, suppose that* A*'s utility function on the set of consequences is linear in all situations in which gains and losses can be measured in dollars. Let us see how de Finetti would make a Dutch Book against* A.

To present de Finetti's arguments I let $S = (S_1, S_2)$ *designate a security that will pay the owner* $\$S_1$ *if* E_1 *occurs and* $\$S_2$ *if* E_2 *occurs. De Finetti takes for granted that* S *is worth* $(1/3)\$S_1 + (1/3)\$S_2$ *to* A *and that* A *should be willing to issue* S *and sell it for a smidgen more than what it is worth to him. With that assumption in hand, he shows that, for any positive pair of numbers* (g, h)*, he can find a pair* (S_1, S_2) *that satisfies the equations*

$$g = S_1 - (1/3)S_1 - (1/3)S_2$$

and

$$h = S_2 - (1/3)S_1 - (1/3)S_2.$$

From these equations it follows that by buying the solution $S = (S_1, S_2)$ *from* A*, de Finetti can ensure himself a gain of about* \$g *if* E_1 *were to occur and* \$h *if* E_2 *were to occur.*

In the present case de Finetti is wrong about the value of S *to* A*. In choice under uncertainty* A *orders uncertain options in accordance with the axioms that I discussed in Section 7.3.2.2. If* $S = (S_1, S_2)$ *is the solution to the two equations, then to him* $(S_1, 0)$ *is worth* $(1/3)\$S_1$*,* $(0, S_2)$ *is worth* $(1/3)\$S_2$*, and* S *is worth* $(1/3)\$S_1 + (2/3)\$S_2$ *if* $S_2 \leq S_1$ *and* $(2/3)\$S_1 + (1/3)\$S_2$ *if* $S_1 \leq S_2$*. There is no way in which de Finetti can make a Dutch Book against* A.

In E 9.9 I followed de Finetti in assuming that *A*'s utility function is linear in money. Also, for simplicity, I considered a case with just two events. Neither of these assumptions is critical for the conclusion: It need not be irrational to shade one's probabilities in the face of uncertainty. If it is not, it makes no sense to ask *A* in E 9.9 to mend his ways.

There are many situations in which it makes no sense to ask somebody to mend his ways if his ways appear irrational. In some such cases the attempt would be futile. For example, persuasion is of no avail in the case of an alcoholic. He must find out by himself that life would improve if he were to stop drinking. In other cases sound arguments will have next to no effect. Certainly, a lecture on the characteristics of purely random processes is unlikely to find an open mind in somebody who is suffering from an acute case of the gambler's fallacy. In still other cases any arguments that one might dream up might be incomprehensible to the supposedly irrational person and hence come to naught. The following is an example that illustrates what I have in mind.

E 9.10 *The African Azande entertain beliefs that appear strange to us. For example, they believe that certain fellow members are witches who exercise* *malignant occult influence on the lives of others. They also engage in practices that are incomprehensible to us, such as performing rituals to counteract witchcraft and consulting oracles to protect themselves from harm.*

Since oracles often contradict themselves and come up with fallacious prophecies, it seems that an Azande's life must be filled with disturbing contradictions. Although contradictions once brought down George Cantor's (1895, 1897) beautiful "house" of sets, they do not seem to have much effect on the lives of the Azande. According to E. E. Evans-Pritchard (1934), using contradictions in which oracles are involved to demolish the oracles' claim to power would be to no avail. If such arguments were translated into Zande modes of thought, they would serve to support the Azande's entire structure of belief. The Azande's mystical notions are eminently coherent . They are interrelated by a network of logical ties and are so ordered that they never too crudely contradict sensory experience. Instead, experience seems to justify them (cf. Winch 1964, p. 89).

It is interesting to me that the Azande's mystical notions are ordered so that they *never too crudely* contradict sensory experience. In that way the Azande are able to function in a world filled with contradictions. I believe that they may not be too different from other rational animals in this respect. A rational animal has all sorts of beliefs. Moreover, if he believes in the propositions p, q, r, s, and t, logic demands that he must believe in all the logical consequences of these propositions as well. Satisfying the latter requirement is beyond the intellectual capacity of most individuals. Hence, rational animals are likely to entertain systems of beliefs that harbor a myriad of contradictory propositions. Most individuals probably cope with such contradictions in two ways. They do not push their search for logical consequences too far, that is, they go only as far as it is in their interest to search (Jones, 1983, p. 52). Moreover, when they run across contradictions, they are content to make minimal changes in their belief systems, for example, changes that are in rough accord with the prescriptions of the AGM paradigm (Alchourónet al., 1985).

9.3 PROPER PREMISES FOR CHOICE AND JUDGMENTS

We have seen that two rational animals in the same choice situation need not make the same choice and that there are all sorts of reasons for that, for instance, differences in attitudes toward premises and the use of different logics. We have also seen that it is only when a person's logical arguments are fallacious that one has a good chance of persuading him to mend his ways. In this section I explore the question of whether it is reasonable to believe that individuals in the same society make choices and pass judgments on the basis of the same scientific and ethical principles.

Aristotle insisted that a rational animal's reasoning was *true* if it was logical and based on premises that either were true by necessity or accepted as true by the wise. Moreover, true reasoning would result in *good* choices and judgments if it was activated by an appetition for the *good.* In Aristotle's day, a person's reasoning was logical only if it adhered to the rules of Aristotle's own syllogistic logic. Today most people would insist that to be logical a person's arguments would have to satisfy the strictures of the first-order predicate calculus (FPC). However, there are many dissenters. For example: In FPC the law of the excluded middle (LEM) is a tautology. In the formal logic of the Dutch intuitionists LEM is true in some cases and not in others. Furthermore, in FPC reasoning is monotonic in the sense that if C follows from A necessarily, then C follows by necessity from A and B as well. In the formal logic that artificial-intelligence people have developed for choice with incomplete information, nonmonotonic reasoning abounds.[5]

It is here useful to distinguish between logical and nonlogical premises. Different logics make use of different axioms and different rules of inference. The mixture of axioms and rules of inference in a given formal logic may vary from one presentation to another. Therefore, I think of the rules of inference of a formal logic as premises on a par with the axioms of the same logic. Logical premises are premises that belong to some formal logic. Two individuals who make use of different formal logics base their arguments on different families of logical premises. It is possible that one and the same person might make use of one formal logic in one situation and another in a different situation. In that case the family of logical premises that the person employs varies over the situations he faces. As long as he keeps the different families of logical premises apart, this variation need not involve him in contradictions.

I distinguish between two families of nonlogical premises: one concerning scientific matters and the other matters of ethics. The scientific principles are of two kinds: those that are true by necessity and those that wise men have surmised from theory and from observations by inductive and appropriate analogical reasoning. The ethical premises are also of two kinds: those that concern moral virtues and those that pertain to political science proper.

The scientific premises that are true by necessity comprise a varied lot of assertions. Some of them are true by definition: for example, "all widows have had husbands." Others can be established by analysis: for example, "for all integers n, $1 + 2 + \ldots + n = n(n + 1)/2$." Still others are intuitively obvious: for example, "agricultural skill remaining the same, additional labor employed on the land within a given district produces in general a less-than-proportionate return." Finally, there are some assertions for the truth of which wise men provide both inductive and theoretical reasons: for example, "any living organism has or has had a parent."

The second class of scientific premises includes propositions that the wise, without good theoretical reasons, believe to be true. Some are laws that scientists have established by induction: for example, "all ruminants have cloven hooves." Others are laws that can be inferred by analogy from introspection or other pertinent observations: for example, "any man is either in selfless pursuit of some spiritual goal or desires to obtain additional wealth with as little sacrifice as possible." Still others are laws of nature that knowledgeable wise men, on rather flimsy evidence, take to be valid: for example, John M. Keynes's (1921) principle of the limited variability of nature that I adopted in Chapter 2.

It is possible that in a given society there is a family of scientific premises that all the members, if prodded, would accept as valid. Still, *the scientific premises on which one person in the society bases his reasoning varies over the situations he faces. Moreover, the scientific premises that different individuals employ in similar situations are likely to differ for various reasons. Their educational background and their stock of tacit knowledge may differ, and their access to information retrieval systems may be very different.* These facts of life have interesting analogues in mathematics. In developing one and the same theory different mathematicians may make use of different axioms and rules of inference. Moreover, what are axioms in one theory may appear as theorems in another. For example, the axioms of the theory of real numbers are derived theorems in set theory and universal theorems in Euclidean geometry.

The ethical premises that concern moral virtues are prescriptions for good behavior. Some describe what it is morally right to do: for example, "you shall honor your mother and father." Others list actions that are morally wrong: for example, "you shall not kill." Still others formulate general principles for right behavior: for example, "do to others only what you would have them do to you." Prescriptions for good behavior as well as sanctions for bad behavior vary with both the codes of honor of secular societies and with the commandments of religious societies. For instance, a woman's bare ankle is hardly noticed in the United States, but in Taliban Afghanistan it was cause for a public beating. Moreover, the interpretation that different wise give to one and the same ethical premise may differ. For instance, act-Utilitarians disagree with rule-Utilitarians about whether one can ever justify punishing an innocent person. Similarly, proponents of Natural-Law ethics disagree with Utilitarians about justifiable reasons for killing a fetus to save the mother's life.[6]

The ethical premises that concern matters of political philosophy prescribe basic rights of human beings and the essential characteristics of a just society. Examples of fundamental human rights are "freedom of thought and worship" and "freedom of speech and assembly." Examples of the elements of a just society are "equality before the law" and "equality of opportunity." Philosophers agree that there are such things as fundamental human rights. However, they disagree as to whether to look for the origin of such rights in natural law or in social-contract theory. They are equally at odds about how to characterize a just society. For example, Aristotle accepted the subjugation of women to men, slaves to citizens, and barbarians to hellenes. He reserved justice for those who were "free and either proportionately or arithmetically equal" (*Nicomachean Ethics*, see Ross, 1925, pp. 106–125). In contrast, Rawls (1971, pp. 54–83) insists that a just society is one in which equality of opportunity reigns and each person has an equal claim to the basic rights and liberties. In a just society social and economic inequalities arise only if they contribute to the welfare of the least advantaged members of that society.

The ethical premises determine what is right or wrong in a person's relation to other human beings. They also structure a rational animal's appetition for the good. *It is quite clear that different secular as well as religious societies adopt different families of basic ethical premises. Still there may be a core of ethical premises that reasonable secular and religious societies accept so that their respective nations can survive as free democratic societies.* If such principles exist, we may find them among the principles of justice that reasonable and rational persons in a Rawlsian Original Position would adopt for a democratic society of free and equal citizens. These reasonable and rational persons have a sense of justice, a conception of the good, and the required intellectual powers of judgment, thought, and inference. Moreover, in the Original Position they search for principles of justice that specify fair terms of social cooperation between free and equal citizens and ensure the emergence of just institutions in a democratic society. Rawls (1996, pp. 47–88) believes that the resulting principles would enable even a society of individuals who are profoundly divided by reasonable religious, philosophical, and moral doctrines to exist over time as a just and stable society of free and equal citizens. There are in the social reality examples of just and stable democratic societies with free and equal citizens. Norway is one of them. I believe that Rawls's reasonable and rational persons would accept the principles that the Norwegian constitution incorporates. I also believe that it is fair to say that Norwegians today are "profoundly divided by reasonable religious, philosophical, and moral doctrines." It will be interesting to see how the tolerance of the doctrines fares as the population of African and Asian immigrants in Norway grows.

9.4 RIGHT DESIRES AND RATIONAL CHOICE IN THE SOCIAL REALITY

We have seen that it is possible for a given society to have a set of basic scientific principles that all its members, if prodded, would consider valid. Still, it is not certain that two of the same society's members in a given choice situation would reason with the same basic principles. We have also seen that in a society in which members are at odds about fundamental religious, philosophical, and moral issues, only the principles that concern political justice have a good chance of being accepted by all. But if that is so, there are better ways to think of a rational animal's proper premises than to identify them with the basic principles I discussed above. One such way follows.

Scientific and ethical premises influence a rational animal's acts and judgments in interesting ways. Note, therefore, that whatever are the scientific premises on which a given person bases his acts and judgments, they express facts. Some of these premises originate in scientific classifications and blueprints and others are determined by institutional constraints, but they all express factual aspects of the social reality the person is experiencing. Similarly, whatever the ethical premises on which a given person bases his acts and judgments, they and the sanctions that the person associates with them determine institutional facts. These institutional facts also express factual aspects of the social reality the person is experiencing. Both the scientific and the ethical premises vary with individuals and with the situations that different individuals face. For a U.S. farmer, some of the premises may describe ways to produce his products. Others may tell him how to rank those products according to their profitability and insist that he not employ illegal immigrants. For a given physicist at CERN, some of the premises may instruct him as to how to read tracks in a cloud chamber. Others may tell him how to report his results and insist that he do it truthfully.

In the remainder of this chapter I consider a person's basic principles facts in the social reality that he is experiencing. He carries some of these facts with him as easily accessible explicit or tacit knowledge. Others he can, if need be, acquire by reading books and journals or by simply picking the brains of friends and foes. The sentences that, by virtue of these facts, he believes to be true may harbor contradictions. They may also express facts that are not accepted as such by others. In each choice situation the person makes his decisions on the basis of pertinent facts only. If the latter harbor contradictions, and if he becomes aware of it, one expects that he will make changes in his basic principles locally and, if possible, adjust his choice or judgment accordingly. *The facts that determine a person's choice and judgments in a given situation depend on his desires and vary with the situation he faces.*

A person's desires are right if they reflect an appetition for the good. In the history of moral philosophy the good has been interpreted as many different things. For Plato the good was a form in a world of ideas whose reference in his social reality consisted of all those things that one truthfully could describe as good.[7] For medieval Christian philosophers the good was God, and eternal life with God was the goal of all right desires. To nineteenth-century Utilitarians the good was the sum total of happiness that the members of a given population experienced, and happiness was pleasure and freedom from pain. Here I give good the interpretation that Aristotle gave to the term: *The good is that at which every art and inquiry and every action and pursuit aim. The good is also something people search for for its own sake.* Aristotle identified this good with happiness, and I insist that the happiness in question is the good that any given individual experiences. As such, happiness is an undefined term that economists usually designate by "utility."

Aristotle insisted that the good was an activity of the soul in accordance with moral and intellectual virtues. This connection between the good and all the virtues that he listed in his *Nicomachean Ethics* was an essential characteristic of his idea of the good. I obtain an analogous connection by insisting that: *happiness, that is, the good, is a function of variables some of which I associate with Aristotle's virtues and some of which I associate with members of Rawls's list of primary goods.* Examples are knowledge, esteem, friendship, justice, basic rights and liberties, and income and wealth. The function may but need not be additively separable, and the arguments as well as the function itself may vary from one individual to the next. Here it is important to observe that an appetition for the good may lead to increased values of some factors affecting happiness and to decreased values of others. Thus it is perfectly possible that the act of a Norwegian who fails to pay a bus ticket and the act of a North Carolina business man who sees fit to employ an illegal immigrant may reflect an appetite for the good.

With the preceding observations in mind I can conclude this section with the following characterization of rational choice and judgments: *Rational choices and judgments are good choices and judgments that, in accordance with the rules of logic, follow from pertinent facts and right desires.*

NOTES

1. The translations with commentaries I have relied on are: Foster and Humphries (1951), Hammond (1902), Lawsen-Tancred (1986), Ross (1980), and parts of Jon Wetlesen's unpublished lecture notes on Aristotle at the University of Oslo. The page references in *De Anima* refer to pages in Hammond's book.

2. The idea of this example is taken from an article by Evans-Pritchard (1934) on "Lévy-Bruhl's Theory of Primitive Mentality." I learned of it from reading Peter Winch's article on "Understanding a Primitive Society" (cf. Wilson, 1970, pp. 79–80).

3. Jaroslav Vanek's (1970) book *The General Theory of Labor-Managed Market Economies* and Norman J. Ireland and Peter J. Law's (1982) book *The Economics of Labour-Managed Enterprises* contain interesting discussions of the economics of labor-managed firms. Vanek (1977, ch. 2) also gives an authoritative account of the economics of the Peruvian law defining the self-managed sector of social property.

4. All of this goes to show how difficult it is to dream up situations that are similar enough for a good test of the consistency of a decision-maker's choices. The results of Section 6.4 substantiate my claim that changes in expectations may invalidate Samuelson's test.

5. The reader can find examples of nonmonotonic reasoning in my discussion of Raymond Reiter's default logic in Chapter 20.

6. *Utilitarianism* is a doctrine of moral philosophy that is based on a *principle of utility* according to which an action is right if it is conducive to furthering the greatest happiness of the greatest number of people. The origin of the doctrine is usually attributed to Jeremy Bentham (1780) and John Stuart Mill (1861), who identified happiness with

pleasure and absence of pain. In recent times the doctrine has appeared in several different guises, two of which are *act-utilitarianism* and *rule utilitarianism*. According to the former, an action is right if, among all available actions, it produces a state of conscious beings of maximal intrinsic worth. According to the latter, an action is right if it is not prohibited by the relevant ideal rules of the society in which it is performed. The ideal rules in question are rules that ensure maximum welfare in the given society if its members make a conscientious effort to abide by them (Brandt, 1959, pp. 253–254, 380–381). Natural law ethics is a doctrine of moral philosophy that dates back to Thomas Aquinas. According to Aquinas, Natural Law consists of the portion of God's Eternal Law that pertains to human beings. In this doctrine an action is right if it promotes the preservation of life, the propagation of offspring, and the pursuit of truth and a peaceful society (Stumpf, 1977, pp. 197–201).

7. It is not clear from Plato's writings what was his idea of the good. In the *Republic* he lets Socrates claim that the good is the supreme form of all the forms and the source of being and reality of forms (Plato, 1974, p. 309). There Socrates also claims that God is the creator of the forms (425). From this it might appear that Plato identifies the good with God. However, scholars are at odds about that (cf., for example, Coplestone, 1994, pp. 190–193).

REFERENCES

Alchourón, C., P. Gärdenfors, and D. Makinson, 1985, "On the Logic of Theory Change: Partial Meet Functions for Contraction and Revision," *Journal of Symbolic Logic* 50, 510–530.

Barnes, J., 1984, *The Complete Works of Aristotle*, Princeton: Princeton University Press.

Bentham, J., 1780, *An Introduction to the Principles of Morals and Legislation*, reprinted in: *A Bentham Reader*, M. P. Mack (ed.), New York: Hafner.

Brandt, R. B., 1959, *Ethical Theory*, Englewood Cliffs: Prentice-Hall.

Brown, H. I., 1990, *Rationality*, New York: Routledge.

Cantor, G., 1895, "Beitrage zur Begrundung der transfiniten Mengenlehre,"Part I, *Mathematische Annalen* 46, 481–512.

Cantor, G., 1897, "Beitrage zur Begrundung der transfiniten Mengenlehre," Part II, *Mathematische Annalen* 47, 207–246.

Cooper, R. W., D. V. DeJong, R. Forsythe, and T. W. Ross, 1996, "Cooperation without Reputation: Experimental Evidence from Prisoner's Dilemma Games," *Games and Economic Behavior* 12, 187–218.

Coplestone, F., 1994, *A History of Philosophy, Vol. 1*, NewYork: Doubleday.

Davidson, D., 1982, "Rational Animals," *Dialectica* 36, 317–327.

de Finetti, B., 1964, "La Prévision: ses Lois Logiques, ses Sources Subjectives," in: *Studies in Subjective Probability*, H. E. Kyburg, Jr., and H. E. Smokler (eds.), New York: Wiley.

Evans-Pritchard, E. E., 1934, "Levy-Bruhl's Theory of Primitive Mentality," *Bulletin of the Faculty of Arts*, University of Egypt.

Foellesdal, D., 1982, "The Status of Rationality Assumptions in Interpretation and in the Explanation of Action," *Dialectica* 36, 301–316.

Foster, K., and S. Humphries (transl.), 1951. *Aristotle's De Anima in the Version of William of Moerbeke and the Commentary of St. Thomas Aquinas*, New Haven: Yale University Press/Dresden: Ministeriums des Innern.
Gilligan, C., 1982, *In a Different Voice*, Cambridge: Harvard University Press.
Grether, D., and C. Plott, 1979, "Economic Theory of Choice and the Preference Reversal Phenomenon," *American Economic Review* 69, 623–638.
Hammond, W. A., 1902, *Aristotle's Psychology: A Treatise on the Principle of Life*, London: Swan Sonnenschein.
Hempel, C. G., 1962, "Rational Action," *Proceedings and Addresses of the American Philosophical Association, 1961–1962*, 35, 5–23.
Ireland, N. J., and P. J. Law, 1982, *The Economics of Labour-Managed Enterprises*, London: Croom Helm
Jones, A. J. I., 1983, *Communication and Meaning*, Boston: Reidel.
Keynes, J. M., 1921, *A Treatise on Probability*, London: Macmillan.
Lawson-Tancred, H., 1986, *Aristotle: De Anima*, London: Penguin.
Lichtenstein, S., and P. Slovic, 1971, "Reversal of Preference Between Bids and Choices in Gambling Decisions," *Journal of Experimental Psychology* 89, 46–55.
Plato, 1974, *The Republic*, D. Lee (trans.), Baltimore: Penguin Books.
Rawls, J., 1971, *A Theory of Justice*, Cambridge: Harvard University Press.
Rawls, J., 1996, *Political Liberalism*, New York: Columbia University Press.
Ross, D. (trans), 1980, *Aristotle: The Nicomachean Ethics*. Revised by J. L. Ackrill and J. O. Urmson. Oxford: Oxford University Press.
Samuelson, P. A., 1938, "A Note on the Pure Theory of Consumer Behavior," *Economica* 5, 61–71.
Stigum, B. P., 1990, *Toward a Formal Science of Economics*, Cambridge: MIT Press.
Stumpf, S. E., 1977, *Philosophy: History and Problems*, New York: McGraw-Hill.
Vanek, J., 1970, *The General Theory of Labor-Managed Market Economies*, Ithaca: Cornell University Press.
Vanek, J., 1977, *The Labor-Managed Economy*, Ithaca: Cornell University Press.
Wetlesen, J., 2000, *Aristotle*, Unpublished lecture notes, Oslo: Department of Philosophy, University of Oslo.
Wilson, B. R. (ed.), 1970, *Rationality*, New York: Blackwell.
Winch, P., 1964, "Understanding a Primitive Society," reprinted in 1970, in: *Rationality*, B. R. Wilson (ed.), New York: Blackwell.

Chapter Ten

The Theory Universe

In Chapter 5, I discussed two different ways of developing scientific theories: the semantic way and the axiomatic way. A semantically developed theory consists of a finite set of more-or-less coherent assertions concerning certain undefined terms and a family of models of these assertions. The models interpret the undefined terms, delineate their characteristics, and indicate the kind of situation with which the theory is concerned. An axiomatized theory is a formal theory about certain undefined terms whose characteristics are delineated in a finite set of axioms and in the theorems that can be derived from them with logical rules of inference. The theory is meaningful only if its axioms are consistent, that is, if no pair of contradictory assertions can be derived from them. One can make a meaningful theory talk about many different matters by interpreting the undefined terms appropriately. Here the important thing to note is that it makes no sense to search for a test of the validity of a consistent formal theory. One can only ask whether a given family of models of the theory's axioms has empirical relevance.[1] Therefore, in a theory-data confrontation it matters not whether the particular theory is semantically developed or a family of models of an axiomatized theory. In either case, the theory in the theory-data confrontation is a family of models of a finite set of assertions.

In Chapter 6, I searched for the purport of economic theories. There I tried to convey the idea that an economic theory, whether developed in the axiomatic or the semantic way, depicts positive analogies of the kind of situations about which the theory talks.[2] Thus the theory of consumer choice delineates characteristic features of consumer behavior. Similarly, the economic theories of markets delineate positive analogies of various kinds of markets, for example, of perfectly competitive or monopolistically competitive markets. Today's macroeconomic theories describe characteristic features of the dynamics of specific classes of economies, for example, of industrially advanced or underdeveloped economies. The relevance of this here is that in a theory-data confrontation the theory depicts the positive analogies and nothing else is at stake.

A theory universe is a pair (Ω_T, Γ_t), where Ω_T is a subset of a vector space and Γ_t is a finite set of axioms that the elements of Ω_T must satisfy. The theory universe is always part of a six-tuple $\{(\Omega_T, \Gamma_t), (\Omega_P, \Gamma_p), \Omega, \Gamma_{t,p}, S, \Psi(\cdot)\}$ that describes the formal structure of a theory-data confrontation. Here (Ω_P, Γ_P) denotes the data universe, $\Omega \subset \Omega_T \times \Omega_P$ is the sample space, and $\Gamma_{t,p}$ designates the family of bridge principles that in the sample space relates variables in the theory universe to variables in the data universe. Also S denotes the sample population from which the pertinent observations are collected, and $\Psi(\cdot) : S \to \Omega$ is a function that associates a pair of vectors, $(\omega_{Ts}, \omega_{Ps}) \in \Omega$ with each $s \in S$. I discuss the data universe and the bridge principles in subsequent chapters. Here, by way of examples, I show the construction of the theory universe of various theories and demonstrate how the positive analogies on which the theories insist are reflected in the members of the respective Γ_t.

The theory universe in a theory-data confrontation depends on many things —the relevant family of models of the theory and the positive analogies whose empirical relevance the data confrontation is to determine. Usually, only a few of the positive analogies that the theory identifies are under scrutiny. For example, in one data confrontation of the theory (T_0, M_0) illustrated in Fig. 5.2, the positive analogies at stake might claim that a consumer's good choices vary with p and A in accordance with Samuelson's (1953, p. 107) fundamental theorem of consumer choice, and Walras's law.[3] In another confrontation of the same theory, the positive analogies at stake might insist that a consumer's good choices vary with p and A in accordance with Houthakker's (1950) strong axiom of revealed preference and Walras's law.

The theory universe also depends on the sample population and on the kind of data that the particular scientist possesses, as well as on his ideas and the empirical analysis that he intends to carry out. For example, the dimensions of the universe depend on the kind and the number of observations that the scientist has on each member of his sample population. Moreover, the positive analogies at stake and, hence, the members of Γ_t vary with the ideas of the scientist and the data he possesses. I try to demonstrate some of these dependencies in the examples that I recount later.

A disclaimer is in order here. In an economic theory-data confrontation one sets out to confront a family of models of a finite set of assertions with data, and the empirical relevance of the whole family is at stake. Ideally, therefore, one ought to delineate the relevant family of models of (Ω_T, Γ_t) before one tries the theory out against data. I assume a less idealistic attitude and let the data determine the contours of a family of models of (Ω_T, Γ_t) whose empirical relevance the given data would not reject. Accordingly, in this chapter I present examples of theory universes in which I describe the members of Γ_t without saying much about the interpretation of (Ω_T, Γ_t), and discuss the relevant family of models of (Ω_T, Γ_t) later.

10.1 CONSUMER CHOICE AND SOME OF ITS THEORY UNIVERSES

From my discussion of rational animals and rationality in economics it follows that one cannot impose stringent requirements on the characteristics of rational animals' good choices. One can insist that in a given choice situation a rational animal ranks available alternatives and chooses the one that he ranks the highest. One can probably also insist that a rational animal in similar choice situations makes the same choices. If one insists on more than that, one is likely to find that there are sample populations in which these requirements have little empirical relevance.

The preceding facts do not deter economists from imposing severe requirements on rational choice in the situations that they consider. Consumer choice under certainty is a good example. In this theory the consumer ranks commodity bundles according to the values of a utility function. The available bundles are the ones that satisfy the consumer's budget constraint. Moreover, the consumer's good choice is the commodity bundle among all available bundles that maximizes his utility. The theory's demands on rational behavior come as a consequence of the conditions it imposes on the domain and functional characteristics of the utility function. For example, consider the family of models of the theory that the pair (T_0, M_0) in Fig 5.2 delineates. In these models a commodity bundle is identified with a vector in R^n_+ and the utility function $U(\cdot)$ is assumed to be real valued, continuous, strictly increasing, and strictly quasi-concave with domain R^n_+. With these assumptions in hand it can be shown that the consumer's choice of commodity bundle x varies with his income A and with the commodity prices he faces, p, in accordance with the values of a well-defined vector-valued function $f(\cdot) : R^n_{++} \times R_+ \rightarrow R^n_+$. The function $f(\cdot)$ is the consumer's demand function. It is continuous, homogeneous of degree zero (cf. Stigum, 1990, pp.184–189), and satisfies Samuelson's fundamental theorem, Houthakker's strong axiom, and Walras's law.

A starting point for econometric studies of consumer demand is often a system of equations that relate the quantities demanded of each commodity to the prices of all commodities and total expenditures. Early examples are the studies by H. Schultz (1938), and Herman Wold and Lars Jurêen (1953). The functional form of the equations varies from one study to another. In some cases the econometrician assumes that his sample consumers' utility functions have a specific structure and formulates a system of equations whose estimated version may be a demand function for such a utility function. A good example is J. R. N. Stone's (1954) study of demand in England during the years 1920–1938. Stone derived his linear expenditure system from the M_{13} class of utility functions in Fig. 5.2. In other cases the econometrician makes assumptions about his sample consumers' cost functions or indirect utility functions and uses them to formulate a system of equations whose estimated version he believes will approximate the demand function of a representative consumer in his sample. One example of such a system is the almost ideal demand system (AIDS) of Angus Deaton and John Muellbauer (1980). Another example is the family of systems that Russell Cooper and Keith McLaren (1996) invented. Neither Deaton and Muellbauer nor Cooper and McLaren claim that the estimated version of their respective systems has the properties of a (T_0, M_0) demand function at all values of (p, A) in $R^n_{++} \times R$. Deaton and Muellbauer insist that the form of their AIDS is flexible enough to provide a good linear approximation to a demand function $f(\cdot)$ at any given point $(p, A) \in R^n_{++} \times R$. Cooper and McLaren claim that the estimated version of their kind of equation system has the properties of a demand function at any observed pair of prices and expenditures.[4]

In Sections 10.1.1 and 10.1.2.2, I formulate theory universes for studies that seem less trying than those I described earlier. In the first example, the CISH experiment, I have observations on triples (x, p, A) that I insist belong to the graph of a vector-valued demand function, and ask if they satisfy Houthakker's strong axiom of revealed preference. In the other, the permanent-income hypothesis, I deal with characteristic properties of the first component of a vector-valued demand function that I insist has been generated by a member of the class of homothetic utility functions in M_{12} of Fig. 5.2.

10.1.1 The CISH Experiment

More than 30 years ago researchers at Texas A&M University set out to test the empirical relevance of the theory of consumer choice in a token economy on a ward for chronic psychotics at Central Islip State Hospital in New York (CISH). A token economy is an organized system in which individuals live for extended periods of time. The individuals in the economy receive tokens for work performed and use them to buy consumer goods. At the time of the CISH experiment the given token economy had been in operation on the ward for 1 year, and about half the patients had been in it for more than 6 months (Battalio et al., 1973, p. 416).

10.1.1.1 The Design of a Test

The researchers thought that the CISH token economy would provide an ideal setting for a test of the empirical relevance of Houthakker's revealed-preference axiom. In their test they identified a commodity with an item that the patients could buy with tokens and measured it by the number of units of the respective items that the patients purchased in a week. For convenience in administering price changes and studying demand behavior, they also divided the pertinent commodities into three groups and constructed three aggregates, X_1, X_2, and X_3, whose units they measured in terms of the preexperiment token values of the aggregates. Finally, they arranged for appropriate changes in the prices of the given aggregates and carried out a test of Houthakker's axiom with the records of thirty-eight patients' purchases over a period of 7 consecutive weeks.

10.1.1.2 A Theory Universe for the CISH Experiment

With this much said about the test one can formulate the theory universe of the CISH experiment (Ω_T, Γ_t) as follows:

C 1 $\omega_T \in \Omega_T$ *only if* $\omega_T = [(x_1, p_1), \ldots, (x_7, p_7), U(\cdot), \alpha]$, *where* $x_i \in R^3_+, p_i \in R^3_{++}, i = 1, \ldots, 7, U(\cdot) : R^3_+ \times \Im \rightarrow R_+$, *and* $\alpha \in \Im$, *where* $\Im$ *is an index set.*

C 2 *For each and every* $\omega_T \in \Omega_T$, *the components of* ω_T *must satisfy the following two families of conditions: (i)* $U(x_i, \alpha) = \max_{y \in \Psi(p_i, x_i)} U(y, \alpha), i = 1, \ldots, 7$, *where* $\Psi(p, x) = \{y \in R^3_+ : py \leq px\}$. *(ii) If, for some sequence* $i_j, j = 1, \ldots, m$, *with* $2 \leq m \leq 7, p_{i_j} x_{i_j} \geq p_{i_j} x_{i_{(j+1)}}, j = 1, \ldots, m-1$, *and if, for some pair* (j, k) *with* $1 \leq j, k \leq m, j \neq k$ *and* $x_{i_j} \neq x_{i_k}$, *then* $p_{i_m} x_{i_m} < p_{i_m} x_{i_1}$.

For the CISH experiment, C 1 and C 2 constitute Γ_t, the axioms of the theory universe. One obtains a family of models of the universe by describing characteristics of $U(\cdot)$ and by assigning ranges to the components of $[(x_1, p_1), \ldots, (x_7, p_7), \alpha]$.

In the intended interpretation of the axioms in Γ_t, condition (i) in C 2 insists that an individual in the relevant sample population orders available commodity bundles in accord with the values of a utility function and chooses the bundle that he or she ranks the highest. Condition (ii) in the same axiom insists that the choices that an individual makes in various price-income situations satisfy Houthakker's strong axiom of revealed preference. The utility function and Houthakker's axiom are features of consumer choice that I have not insisted on in my description of rational animals. It is, therefore, important to note here that it is innocuous to assume that the ordering in condition (i) is in accord with the values of a utility function. The only characteristic of consumer choice that is at stake in the CISH experiment is Houthakker's axiom.

10.1.1.3 Rationalizable Observations and GARP

To bring the assertion concerning the innocuous utility function in C 2 home, I next describe a nonparametric test of the utility hypothesis, an idea that originated with Sidney Afriat ((1976). For that purpose I have to clarify the meaning of two new concepts: *rationalizable observations* and Hal Varian's (1982) *GARP*.

First, rationalizable observations: Suppose that one has observed m pairs $(x^i, p^i) \in R^n_+ \times R^n_{++}, i = 1, \ldots, m$, where x^i and p^i, respectively, denote the commodity bundle that a given consumer acquired in period i and the price he paid for it. Further, let $u(\cdot) : R^n_+ \rightarrow R$ be a function that, for all $x \in R^n_+$, satisfies the conditions $u(x^i) \geq u(x)$ if $p^i x^i \geq p^i x, i = 1, \ldots, m$. Then $u(\cdot)$ *rationalizes* the observations on p and x.

Next, GARP: GARP is short for *generalized axiom of revealed preference.* To express GARP succinctly, I let $x^i Qx$ mean that there exists a sequence i_j, $j = 1, \ldots, k$, such that $p^i x^i \geq p^i x^{i_1}, p^{i_1} x^{i_1} \geq p^{i_1} x^{i_2}, \ldots, p^{i_k} x^{i_k} \geq p^{i_k} x$. Then GARP insists that for any pair $1 \leq i, j \leq m$, $x^i Qx^j$ implies that $p^j x^j \leq p^j x^i$. GARP is weaker than Houthakker's axiom inasmuch as it allows the possibility that $x^i Qx^j$, $x^i \neq x^j$, $p^i x^i = p^i x^j$, and $p^j x^j = p^j x^i$ may all hold.

With rationalizable observations and GARP, I can formulate a theorem, T 1, that justifies using GARP to test the validity of the utility hypothesis.

T 1 *Suppose that the data consist of pairs* $(\mathrm{x}^{\mathrm{i}}, \mathrm{p}^{\mathrm{i}}) \in \mathrm{R}^{\mathrm{n}}_{+} \times \mathrm{R}^{\mathrm{n}}_{++}$, $\mathrm{i} = 1, \ldots, \mathrm{m}$. *Then the following conditions are equivalent: (i) The data satisfy GARP. (ii) There exists a nonsatiated, continuous, concave monotonic function* $\mathrm{u}(\cdot) : \mathrm{R}^{\mathrm{n}}_{+} \rightarrow \mathrm{R}$ *that rationalizes the data.*

I prove this theorem in Stigum (1990, pp. 764–765). Here it suffices to observe that GARP alone allows me to claim that the pertinent data belong to the graph of a demand correspondence but not that they belong to the graph of a demand function.

10.1.2 The Permanent-Income Hypothesis

I constructed a theory universe earlier for the pair (T_0, M_0) in Fig. 5.2. In this section I construct a theory universe for the pair (T_1, M_{12}) in the same figure. The latter pair represents the theory from which Milton Friedman (1957) derived his permanent-income hypothesis. My intent is to construct a theory universe for a theory-data confrontation in which I test Friedman's hypothesis with data that researchers at the Federal Reserve Board in Washington, D.C., have collected (cf. Projector and Weiss, 1966). The data pertain to economic choices made by a group of U.S. consumers during 1962 and 1963. For each consumer in the sample, the data provide information on 1962 end-of-year net worth, on 1963 disposable income, on the change in net worth during 1963, and on the age of the head of the household in 1963.

10.1.2.1 Milton Friedman's Theory

To show how Friedman derived the permanent-income hypothesis from (T_1, M_{12}), I begin by renaming the components of x and p in M_{12} so that $x = (C_0, \ldots, C_{n-1})$ and $p = (1, [1/(1+r)], \ldots, [1/(1+r)]^{n-1})$ for some $r \in R_{++}$. Here, r and C_i, respectively, denote the rate of interest and the number of units of account that the consumer spends on consumer goods in period i, $i = 0, \ldots, n-1$. Next, I interpret A so that

$$A = A_{-1} + \sum_{0 \leq i \leq n-1} [1/(1+r)]^i y_i,$$

where A_{-1} and y_i, respectively, designate the consumer's net worth at the beginning of period 0 and his income from physical work in period $i, i = 0, \ldots, n-1$. Finally, I recall that the utility functions in M_{12} are continuous, strictly increasing, strictly quasi-concave, and homothetic.

The homotheticity of the utility functions in M_{12} plays an important role in Friedman's theory. From this property it follows that for each pair of a utility function $U(\cdot)$ and a demand function $f(\cdot)$, there exists a function $g(\cdot) : R^n_{++} \to R^n_+$ so that for all relevant (p, A), $f(p, A) = g(p)A$. Thus, if we let

$$C(r) = g_1(1, [1/(1+r)], \ldots, [1/(1+r)]^{n-1}), r \in R_+,$$

and write $C = C(r)A, r \in R_+$, then C denotes the consumer's optimal expenditure on consumer goods in period 0 when the interest rate is r.

The function $C(\cdot)(\cdot) : R^2_+ \to R_+$ ought to be called the consumption function of the consumer, but in Friedman's theory it is not because it is a function of the wrong variables. To derive the consumer's consumption function, Friedman observes that the designation of current receipts as "income" in statistical studies is an expedient enforced by the limitation of the data. On a theoretical level, income is generally defined as the amount a consumer unit could consume (or believes it could) while maintaining its wealth intact (Friedman 1957, p. 10). Consequently, the consumer's true first-period income should be defined, not as y_0, but as

$$y_p = [r/(1+r)]A.$$

Friedman called such income *permanent income* and used it to define his consumption function as follows:

$$C = k(r)y_p, (r, y_p) \in R_{++} \times R_+,$$

where $k(r) = [(1+r)/r]C(r), r > 0$.

In a given period a consumer's measured income is ordinarily taken to equal his salary plus any rent, interest, and/or dividends he earns. Friedman called the difference between measured and permanent income *transitory income.* Thus if y denotes measured income and y_t is transitory income, then $y = y_p + y_t$.

Friedman also hypothesized that a consumer's expenditures on goods and services, c, can be decomposed into a permanent component c_p and a transitory one c_t, so that $c = c_p + c_t$. The permanent component, supposedly, was the variable about which the theory of consumer choice was concerned. Hence, Friedman insisted that $c_p = k(r)y_p, r > 0$ and $y_p \geq 0$.

10.1.2.2 A Theory Universe for the Permanent-Income Hypothesis

With that much said about data and Friedman's theory, I can describe the sought for theory universe as follows:

PIH 1 $\omega_T \in \Omega_T$ *only if* $\omega_T = (r, y_p, y_t, c_p, c_t, A, a, u)$, *where* $(r, y_p, c_p, A) \in R^4_{++}$, $(y_t, c_t, u) \in R^3$, *and* $\alpha \in \{15, 16, \ldots, 100\}$.

PIH 2 *For all* $\omega_T \in \Omega_T$, $y_p = [r/(1+r)]A$.

PIH 3 *Let* $\Omega_T(a) = \{\omega_T \in \Omega_T : \alpha = a\}$, *with* $a \in \{15, 16, \ldots, 100\}$. *There exists a function* $k(\cdot) : R_{++} \times \{15, 16, \ldots, 100\} \to R_{++}$, *such that for all* $\omega_T \in \Omega_T(\alpha)$, $c_p = k(r, \alpha)y_p$.

PIH 4 *Let* $h(\cdot)$ *be defined by*

$$h(\alpha) = \begin{cases} 25 & \text{if } \alpha < 35, \\ 5(i+6)+5 & \text{if } (i+6)5 \leq \alpha \leq (i+8)5, i = 1, 3, 5, \\ 70 & \text{if } 65 \leq \alpha. \end{cases}$$

Then, for all $\alpha \in \{15, 16, \ldots, 100\}$, $k[r, h(\alpha)] = k(r, \alpha)$, $r > 0$.

PIH 1–PIH 4 constitute Γ_t, the axioms of a theory universe for the permanent-income hypothesis. In the intended interpretation of the axioms, the meaning of r, y_p, y_t, c_p, c_t, and A accords with the meaning I gave to these variables in my description of Friedman's theory. Thus, the relation $y_p = [r/(1+r)]A$ is a definition of y_p that is not at stake in the test I have in mind for the permanent-income hypothesis. Moreover, α designates the age of the consumer, and $h(\cdot)$ is used to partition the consumers into five age groups within which the consumption function does not vary over individuals. Finally, u is an error term. In reading the axioms, note that y_t, c_t, and u, do not appear in PIH 2–PIH 4. They enter the theory-data confrontation in the bridge principles, and I discuss them in Chapters 11 and 17.

10.2 A THEORY UNIVERSE FOR THE NEOCLASSICAL THEORY OF THE FIRM

In this section I construct a theory universe for a theory-data confrontation in which I determine the operative efficiency of an industry. The theory in question is a family of models of the neoclassical theory of the firm, and the industry is the Norwegian bus transportation sector. The operative efficiency that I have in mind is of two kinds: technical and allocative. *Technical efficiency* is a measure of the industry's ability to obtain maximal levels of output from given quantities of inputs. *Allocative efficiency* is a measure of the industry's ability to use optimal combinations of inputs to produce given levels of outputs.[5]

Determining the technical and allocative efficiency of a firm's operations is difficult without knowledge of the firm's production function. When such information is missing, there are two very different ways by which economists and econometricians study the efficiency characteristics of interesting production processes: "data envelopment analysis" and "stochastic frontier analysis." The former uses data on inputs and outputs of a sample of firms and linear programming methods to construct a piecewise linear production frontier relative to which the technical and allocative efficiency of each firm in the sample can be assessed. The latter assumes that the firms in a given sample have the same production function and that this function belongs to a well-defined family of such functions, for example, the family of Cobb-Douglas production functions. Then it uses data on inputs and outputs of the firms in the sample and econometric methods to estimate a linear function of the form $\log y = x\beta - U + V$, where y and x, respectively, designate a firm's output and inputs and $U \in R_+$ and $V \in R$ are random variables. The value of e^{-U} is taken to measure a firm's technical efficiency, and V accounts for errors in measurement and for unspecified input variables in the production function.

Interesting applications of data envelopment analysis and stochastic frontier analysis can be found, respectively, in Førsund and Hjalmarsson (1987) and Kittelsen (1998) and in Aigner et al. (1977) and Coelli et al. (1998, chs. 8, 9), and Førsund et al. (1980) and Green (1993) contain comprehensive surveys of these methods. My analysis of the operative efficiency of the Norwegian bus transportation sector builds on the ideas of stochastic frontier analysis.

10.2.1 The Neoclassical Theory of the Firm

The neoclassical theory of the firm concerns six undefined terms: *input*, *output*, *revenue*, *wage*, *firm*, and *input-output strategy*. The properties of these terms are delineated in the seven axioms listed below.

N 1 *An* input *is a vector* $x \in R^n_+$.

N 2 *An* output *is a number* $y \in R_+$.

N 3 wage *is a vector* $w \in R^n_{++}$.

N 4 *A* revenue *is a pair* $[H(\cdot), A]$, *where* $H(\cdot) : R_+ \times A \to R$ *and* $A \subset R_{++}$.

N 5 *A* firm *is a triple* $[f(\cdot), X, Y]$, *where* $f(\cdot) : X \to Y, X \subset R^n_+$, *and* $Y \subset R_+$.

N 6 *An* input-output strategy *is a pair* $(x^0, y^0) \in X \times Y$ *that, for some pair* $(a, w) \in A \times R^n_{++}$, *satisfies* $y^0 = f(x^0)$ *and* $H(y^0, a) - wx^0 \geq H(y, a) - wx$ *for all* $(x, y) \in X \times Y$ *for which* $y = f(x)$.

N 7 X *is a convex subset of* R^n_+ *and* $Y = R_+$. *Also,* $f(\cdot)$ *is twice differentiable, strictly increasing, and strictly quasi-concave; and for all* $a \in A, H(\cdot, a)$ *is twice differentiable and concave. Finally, there is a* $k \in R_+$ *such that* $f(\cdot)$ *is concave in the set* $\{x \in X : f(x) \geq k\}$.

To ensure existence and uniqueness of the firm's input-output strategy in arbitrarily given (a, w) situations, one must add restrictions on the structures of $H(\cdot)$, $f(\cdot)$, and X. I impose such conditions in the models of N 1–N 7 that I discuss below rather than in a formal eighth axiom.

Collections of axioms that have a model are consistent. I obtain a model of N 1–N 7 by letting $n = 2$, $Y = R_+$, $A = R_{++}$, $H(y, a) = ay$, $f(x_1, x_2) = x_1^{1/4}x_2^{1/4}$, $X = R_{++}^2$, $k = 0$, $x^0 = \left[(1/16)a^2 w_1^{-3/2} w_2^{-1/2}, (1/16)a^2 w_1^{-1/2} w_2^{-3/2}\right]$, and $y^0 = (1/4)aw_1^{-1/2}w_2^{-1/2}$. Hence N 1–N 7 are consistent. The theory derived from them (i.e., the neoclassical theory of the firm) is also meaningful, and the theory can be used to talk about many different economic matters.

In the intended interpretation of N 1–N 7, the components of x in N 1 denote units of ordinary inputs such as labor, fuel, and capital. For each component of x, there is a component of w in N 3 that denotes the number of units of account that are needed to purchase one unit of the input in question. Further, a firm is a producer with a production function $f(\cdot)$ that transforms an input x into an output y in accordance with the equation $y = f(x)$. The output is taken to be an agricultural or an industrial commodity that the producer sells in the market for such commodities. For a given $a \in A$, $H(\cdot, a)$ is taken to be the firm's total revenue function; and in a given (a, w) situation, $H(y, a) - wx$ equals the number of units of account of the firm's profit on the sale of y if it had used x to produce y. Finally, an input-output strategy is an input-output vector that the producer chooses in some (a, w) situation.

The firm, in the intended interpretation of N 1–N 7, is a profit-maximizing producer. It purchases its inputs in perfectly competitive markets and sells its product in a market that may or may not be perfectly competitive. For example, when $A \subset (0, 1)$ and $H(y, a) = y^{1-a}$, the firm's input-output strategy would be the (x, y) choice of a producer who is a monopolist in the market for y. When $A = R_{++}$, and $H(y, a) = ay$, a is taken to be the price of y, and the firm's input-output strategy will be the (x, y) choice of a producer who is a price-taker in the market for y. No matter what the characteristics of the firm's output market are, a profit-maximizing firm becomes a cost-minimizing firm when the value of its output is prescribed by some regulatory agency; that is, for a given y, the firm will choose an x that minimizes the value of wx over all x that satisfy $y = f(x)$ and $x \in R_+^n$.

10.2.2 A Theory Universe for Confronting N 1–N 7 with Data

The Norwegian Department of Commerce worries about the efficiency of its bus transportation industry and regulates its operation by fixing "production" and fares. The bus companies, in turn, provide their transportation services at minimum cost with generous subsidies, always making certain that they can cover eventual losses. However, Department officials are now questioning the reported costs of the services provided as they seem to be too high.

To ascertain the efficiency the industry, with the help of Harald Dale-Olsen, I obtained information on various economic choices that a group of bus companies made in 1991.[6] These choices concerned the number of kilometers of transportation (y) that a bus company provided and the number of liters of gasoline (x_1), the hours of labor (x_2), and the kroners of capital (x_3) that it used to produce y. I also obtained information on the total cost of gasoline (c_1), labor (c_2), and capital (c_3) that each company incurred in 1991. This information and the equations $w_i = (c_i/x_i), i = 1, 2, 3$, provided information about each company's cost per unit of gasoline (w_1) labor (w_2), and capital (w_3).

For the planned theory-data confrontation, I must delineate a family of models of N 1–N 7. In the present case, $n = 3, X \subset R^3_{++}, Y = R_+, A = \{\bar{a}\}, H(y, a) = ay$, and there exist functions $F(\cdot) : R^3_{++} \to R_+$ and $G(\cdot) : R_+ \to R_+$ such that for all $x \in X, f(x) = G[F(x)]$. The $\bar{a}$ is a positive real number. Also, $G(\cdot)$ and $F(\cdot)$ are strictly increasing and differentiable, and $F(\cdot)$ is homogeneous of degree one and strictly quasi-concave. In fact, the relation $y = G[F(x)]$ can be written in the form: $y^b e^{dy} = \Lambda x_1^{\alpha} x_2^{\beta} x_3^{\gamma}$, where $b, d, \Lambda, \alpha, \beta, \gamma$ are positive constants and $\alpha + \beta + \gamma = 1$. Then, when $b \geq 1$, the k in N 7 can be taken to equal zero.

The data I have and the preceding family of models of N 1–N 7 suggest that I adopt the following axioms for the theory universe:

NB 1 $\omega_T \in \Omega_T$ *only if* $\omega_T = (\mathrm{y, x, w, U, V})$, *where* $\mathrm{y} \in \mathrm{R}_{++}, \mathrm{x} \in \mathrm{R}^3_{++}, \mathrm{w} \in \mathrm{R}^3_{++}, \mathrm{U} \in \mathrm{R}_+$, *and* $\mathrm{V} \in \mathrm{R}$.

Here the intended meanings of y, x, and w are, respectively, the output of a firm, the inputs it uses, and the costs of these inputs, and U and V are error terms that I use to measure the technical and allocative efficiency of the firm's production of y, respectively.

NB 2 *There exist positive constants* $\mathrm{b, d}, \Lambda, \alpha, \beta, \gamma$, *such that* $\alpha + \beta + \gamma = 1$, *and for all* $\omega_T \in \Omega_T$, $\mathrm{y^b e^{dy}} = \Lambda \mathrm{x}_1^{\alpha} \mathrm{x}_2^{\beta} \mathrm{x}_3^{\gamma}$.

NB 3 *For all* $\omega_T \in \Omega_T$, $\alpha \mathrm{x}_2/\beta \mathrm{x}_1 = \mathrm{w}_1/\mathrm{w}_2$, *and* $\gamma \mathrm{x}_2/\beta \mathrm{x}_3 = \mathrm{w}_3/\mathrm{w}_2$.

In reading these axioms, note that I take for granted that a firm has no choice as to the proper value of y. The authorities fix the value of each firm's output. The fixity of y for a given firm is reflected in the conditions spelled out in NB 2 and NB 3, which are necessary and sufficient for x to be the cost-minimizing input vector for y. Note also that the production technology, $F(\cdot)$ and $G(\cdot)$, is taken to be the same for all firms in the industry being studied. The input-output strategy of a firm varies from one firm to another because y and w vary over firms. Finally, note that U and V do not appear in NB 2 and NB 3. I explicate their role in the theory-data confrontation when I discuss bridge principles in Chapter 12.

10.3 A THEORY UNIVERSE FOR A TEST OF THE HECKSCHER-OHLIN CONJECTURE

A country A is said to have a comparative advantage in producing a given good if the opportunity cost of producing x in terms of other goods is lower in A than elsewhere. There are many reasons why A might have a comparative advantage in the production of x, for example, climate and the supply of natural resources. Whatever the reasons, international trade allows A to specialize in producing goods in which it has a comparative advantage vis-à-vis its trading partners.

A long time ago, Eli Heckscher (1919) and Bertil Ohlin (1933) conjectured that a country exports (imports) goods in the production of which its relatively abundant (scarce) factors play a dominant role, their reasoning being that a country has a comparative advantage in producing goods whose production processes are abundant-factor intensive.

10.3.1 The Leontief Test

Wassily Leontief (1953) published a study in which he used input-output analysis to investigate the possible empirical relevance of the Heckscher and Ohlin (H&O) conjecture for U.S. trade. His principal findings are summarized in Table 10.1, which suggests that "America's participation in the international division of labor [in 1947 was] based on its specialization on labor-intensive, rather than capital-intensive, lines of production. In other words [the United States resorted] to foreign trade in order to economize its capital and dispose of its surplus labor, rather than vice versa" (Leontief, 1953, p. 343). Since the United States in 1947 possessed more productive capital per worker than any other country, Leontief's findings contradict the H&O conjecture.

Leontief's study was criticized for theoretical as well as statistical inadequacies. S. Valavanis-Vail (1954) insisted that Leontief's input-output approach could not be used to analyze international trade problems, and B. C. Swerling (1954) observed that as the production and trade conditions prevailing in 1947 were abnormal, Leontief's results were biased, and M. A. Diab (1956) complained that Leontief had not paid sufficient attention to the capital-intensive

TABLE 10.1
Domestic Capital and Labor Requirements per Million Dollars of U.S. Exports and of Competitive Import Replacements (of average 1947 composition)

	Exports	Import replacements
Capital (U.S. $, in 1947 prices)	2,550,780	3,091,339
Labor (man-years)	183.313	170.004

natural-resource component of U.S. imports. Be that as it may, Leontief's study is intriguing and makes me want to see whether the H&O conjecture is valid in an input-output model of world trade in which natural resources play a significant role.

10.3.2 Trade in a Two-Country Input-Output Economy

I scrutinize the Heckscher-Ohlin conjecture in a simple thought experiment. The world I imagine is like the world Paul Samuelson envisioned in his seminal articles on the factor-price equalization theorem (cf. Samuelson, 1948 and 1949). It features two countries, A and B, two commodities, x and y, two primary factors of production, K and L, and two natural resources, z and u. For these countries I assume that conditions 1–4 below are valid.

1. The initial endowments of primary factors in A, L_A, and K_A, and in B, L_B, and K_B, satisfy the conditions $0 < L_A < K_A$ and $L_B > K_B > 0$.
2. The production of x and y requires the use of both primary factors, and the production of both commodities occurs under conditions of constant returns to scale.
3. In A and B there are two natural resources, z and u, the extraction of which requires the use of both primary factors of production; z and u are essential factors of production of x and y; and neither z nor u is part of final demand; that is, they are not consumables.
4. The commodities, x and y, can flow freely without transport cost both within and between countries; the primary factors and natural resources move freely within countries but not between them; and the markets for goods and factors are perfectly competitive.

To simplify the discussion, I denote x, y, z, and u, respectively, by x_1, x_2, x_3, and x_4. Similarly, I denote the prices of the four commodities by P_1, P_2, P_3, and P_4. Finally, I denote the prices of L and K by w and q, the supply of and demand for commodities by superscripts s and d, and the commodities and primary factors that belong to A and B by subscripts A and B.

In my family of models of (1)–(4), I assume that the demand functions for x_1 and x_2 in the two countries can be rationalized by two utility functions, $U_A(\cdot) : R_+^2 \to R_+$ for A and $U_B(\cdot) : R_+^2 \to R_+$ for B, where

$$U_A(x_1, x_2) = x_1^\alpha x_2^\beta \text{ and } U_B(x_1, x_2) = x_1^\delta x_2^\mu, \text{ with } \alpha, \beta, \delta, \text{ and } \mu \in R_{++}.$$

I also assume that the production functions of the four commodities are constant-returns-to-scale Leontief-type functions that satisfy the following conditions:

$$x_1 = \min\{L/a_{L1}, K/a_{K1}, x_3/a_{31}, x_4/a_{41}\},$$

$$x_2 = \min\{L/a_{L2}, K/a_{K2}, x_3/a_{32}, x_4/a_{42}\},$$

$$x_3 = \min\{L/a_{L3}, K/a_{K3}\},$$
$$x_4 = \min\{L/a_{L4}, K/a_{K4}\},$$

where $(L, K) \in R_+^2$ and $a_{ij} \in R_{++}, i = L, K, 3, 4$ and $j = 1, 2, 3$, and 4. Thus, to produce one unit of x_1 one needs a_{L1} units of L, a_{K1} units of K, a_{31} units of x_3, and a_{41} units of x_4. Similarly for x_2, x_3, and x_4.

If the preceding conditions hold, a trade equilibrium in the world of A and B is a vector of prices and commodities $(P, w, q, x_A^d, x_A^s, x_B^d, x_B^s)$ that satisfies the following equations:

$$P \in R_{++}^4, w \in R_{++}, q \in R_{++}, \text{ and } (x_A^d, x_A^s, x_B^d, x_B^s) \in R_+^{16}, \quad (1)$$

$$x_{1A}^d = (\alpha/\alpha + \beta)[(wL_A + qK_A)/P_1]$$
$$\text{and } x_{2A}^d = (\beta/\alpha + \beta)[(wL_A + qK_A)/P_2], \quad (2)$$

$$x_{3A}^d = 0 = x_{4A}^d, \quad (3)$$

$$x_{1B}^d = (\delta/\mu + \delta)[(wL_B + qK_B)/P_1]$$
$$\text{and } x_{2B}^d = (\mu/\mu + \delta)[(wL_B + qK_B)/P_2], \quad (4)$$

$$x_{3B}^d = 0 = x_{4B}^d, \quad (5)$$

$$P_1 = a_{31}P_3 + a_{41}P_4 + a_{L1}w + a_{K1}q, \quad (6)$$

$$P_2 = a_{32}P_3 + a_{42}P_4 + a_{L2}w + a_{K2}q, \quad (7)$$

$$P_3 = a_{L3}w + a_{K3}q, \quad (8)$$

$$P_4 = a_{L4}w + a_{K4}q, \quad (9)$$

$$a_{L1}x_{1A}^s + a_{L2}x_{2A}^s + a_{L3}x_{3A}^s + a_{L4}x_{4A}^s \leq L_A, \quad (10)$$

$$a_{K1}x_{1A}^s + a_{K2}x_{2A}^s + a_{K3}x_{3A}^s + a_{K4}x_{4A}^s \leq K_A, \quad (11)$$

$$x_{3A}^s - a_{31}x_{1A}^s - a_{32}x_{2A}^s = 0, \quad (12)$$

$$x_{4A}s - a_{41}x_{1A}^s - a_{42}x_{2A}^s = 0, \quad (13)$$

$$a_{L1}x_{1B}^s + a_{L2}x_{2B}^s + a_{L3}x_{3B}^s + a_{L4}x_{4B}^s \leq L_B, \quad (14)$$

$$a_{K1}x_{1B}^s + a_{K2}x_{2B}^s + a_{K3}x_{3B}^s + a_{K4}x_{4B}^s \leq K_B, \quad (15)$$

$$x_{3B}^s - a_{31}x_{1B}^s - a_{32}x_{2B}^s = 0, \quad (16)$$

$$x_{4B}^s - a_{41}x_{1B}^s - a_{42}x_{2B}^s = 0, \quad (17)$$

$$x_{1A}^s + x_{1B}^s = x_{1A}^d + x_{1B}^d, \quad (18)$$

$$x_{2A}^s + x_{2B}^s = x_{2A}^d + x_{2B}^d. \quad (19)$$

In this system of equations, (2)–(5) show the four demand functions in A and B; (6)–(9) insist that in trade equilibrium the prices of the four commodities equal the unit costs of producing them; (10) and (11) and (14) and (15), respectively, demand that the indirect and direct use of primary factors in the production of x_1 and x_2 in A and B equal or be less than the supply of primary factors in the two countries; (12) and (13) and (16) and (17), respectively, require that the production of x_3 and x_4 in A and B equal the use in each country of these commodities in the production of x_1 and x_2; and (18) and (19) insist that in trade equilibrium the aggregate supply of x_1 and x_2 must equal the aggregate demand for the two commodities. There are twenty-two equations to determine the values of twenty-two variables. However, only twenty-one of the equations are independent, so they allow us to determine the values of five price ratios and not the values of six prices.

One interesting aspect of Leontief's analysis is the way he determines whether the production of a commodity is labor or capital intensive. The factor intensity of a production function is determined in his analysis by both the direct and the indirect uses that it makes of the primary factors of production. In my simple example the direct factor requirements in the production of x_1 and x_2 are determined by the respective outputs and by the values of the components of the D matrix below. The indirect factor requirements are determined by the outputs of x_1 and x_2 and by the C and F matrices below. Finally, the factor intensities of the production of x_1 and x_2 are determined by the entries in the G matrix below. The production of x_1 is relatively labor intensive if $g_{L1}/g_{K1} > g_{L2}/g_{K2}$, and the production of x_2 is relatively capital intensive if $g_{K2}/g_{L2} > g_{K1}/g_{L1}$:

$$D = \begin{pmatrix} a_{L1} & a_{L2} \\ a_{K1} & a_{K2} \end{pmatrix} \quad C = \begin{pmatrix} a_{L3} & a_{L4} \\ a_{K3} & a_{K4} \end{pmatrix} \quad F = \begin{pmatrix} a_{31} & a_{32} \\ a_{41} & a_{42} \end{pmatrix}$$

$$G = \{D + CF\} = \begin{pmatrix} g_{L1} & g_{L2} \\ g_{K1} & g_{K2} \end{pmatrix}$$

To get a good idea of the workings of an international economy such as the one I just described, I look at several contrasting cases. In all of them I assume that

$$a_{31} = 0.2, a_{32} = 0.1, a_{41} = 0.1, a_{42} = 0.3, a_{L1} = 2.04, a_{L2} = 0.67, a_{K1} = 1.06,$$
$$a_{K2} = 1.38, a_{L3} = 1.5, a_{L4} = 1.6, a_{K3} = 1.8, a_{K4} = 1.8.$$
$$L_A = 100,\ K_A = 150,\ L_B = 130, \text{ and } K_B = 100.$$

These numbers mean nothing by themselves. The only thing that matters is that they ensure that capital and labor, respectively, are the abundant primary factors in A and B. They also imply that:

$$D = \begin{pmatrix} 2.04 & 0.67 \\ 1.06 & 1.38 \end{pmatrix} C = \begin{pmatrix} 1.5 & 1.6 \\ 1.8 & 1.8 \end{pmatrix} F = \begin{pmatrix} 0.2 & 0.1 \\ 0.1 & 0.3 \end{pmatrix} G = \begin{pmatrix} 2.5 & 1.3 \\ 1.6 & 2.1 \end{pmatrix}$$

Hence, they ensure that the production of x_1 is labor intensive and the production of x_2 is capital intensive. The production of both natural resources, x_3 and x_4, is capital intensive.

Case 1 In this case we assume that $(\alpha/\beta + \alpha) = (\delta/\delta + \mu) = 1/2$. Then, with $P_2 = 1$, there is a unique trade equilibrium in the A and B world economy in which

$$\left(P_1, P_2, w, q, x_{1A}^d, x_{2A}^d, x_{1A}^s, x_{2A}^s, x_{1B}^d, x_{2B}^d, x_{1B}^s, x_{2B}^s\right) = (1.63, 1, 0.57, 0.12, 23.21, 37.76, 4.74, 67.82, 26.63, 43.31, 45.11, 13.25).^{7}$$

In this equilibrium, A imports 18.47 units of x_1 and exports 30.06 units of x_2, and the H&O conjecture is valid. Moreover, both factors are fully employed in A and B.

Case 2 In this case we assume that $(\alpha/\alpha + \beta) = 0.04$ and $(\delta/\mu + \delta) = 0.87$. Then, in autarky, there is a unique equilibrium in A in which

$$\left(P_1, P_2, w, q, x_{1A}^d, x_{2A}^d, x_{1A}^s, x_{2A}^s\right) = (1.6, 2.1, 0, 1, 3.75, 68.57, 3.75, 68.57),^{8}$$

and in which capital is fully employed and only 98.52 units of labor are used in the production of x_1 and x_2. Similarly, there is a unique autarkic equilibrium in B in which

$$\left(P_1, P_2, w, q, x_{1B}^d, x_{2B}^d, x_{1B}^s, x_{2B}^s\right) = (2.5, 1.3, 1, 0, 45.24, 13, 45.24, 13),^{9}$$

and in which labor is fully employed and only 99.68 units of capital are used in the production of x_1 and x_2. When A and B are allowed to trade in x_1 and x_2, one finds that there is a unique trade equilibrium in which

$$\left(P_1, P_2, w, q, x_{1A}^d, x_{2A}^d, x_{1A}^s, x_{2A}^s, x_{1B}^d, x_{2B}^d, x_{1B}^s, x_{2B}^s\right) = (1.37, 1, 0.40, 0.23, 2.17, 71.33, 4.73, 67.82, 47.67, 9.75, 45.11, 13.25).^{10}$$

In this equilibrium both primary factors are fully employed. Also, A exports 2.56 units of x_1 and imports 3.51 units of x_2 in contradiction to the H&O conjecture.

The preceding examples demonstrate that in an input-output model of international trade differences in demand among the two countries may lead to situations in which the H&O conjecture is not valid. If α and β are not too different from δ and μ, can one be sure that trade flows in the world economy of A and B accord with the H&O conjecture? The answer to this question plays a role in my empirical analysis of the H&O conjecture in Chapter 17.

10.3.3 A Theory Universe for a Test of the Heckscher-Ohlin Conjecture

Next I formulate a theory universe for a test of the Heckscher-Ohlin conjecture based on Norwegian data and a version of the input-output model that I discussed earlier. In reading the details of the theory universe, note that it can serve as a basis for a theory-data confrontation with cross-section data on one or more countries. If I had intended analyzing n yearly observations on Norwegian industries, each of the components of ω_T would have had to be n-dimensional instead of one-dimensional.

HO 1 $\omega_T \in \Omega_T$ *only if* $\omega_T = (x^s, x^d, x_3^f, x_4^f, L, K, p, w, q, L_A, K_A, EL_A, EK_A, EL_{TC}, EK_{TC})$, *where* $x^s \in R_+^4, x^d \in R_+^2 \times \{(0,0)\}, x_3^f \in R_+^2, x_4^f \in R_+^2, (L, K) \in R_+^8, p \in R_{++}^4, (w, q) \in R_{++}^2, (L_A, K_A) \in R_{++}^2$, *and* $(EL_A, EK_A, EL_{TC}, EK_{TC}) \in R_{++}^4$.

In the intended interpretation of this axiom, the country concerned, A, is a country in trade equilibrium with its trading community TC. It produces four commodities, $x_1, \ldots, x_4$, with two primary factors of production: labor and capital. I denote the pair of primary factors used in the production of x_i by $(L_i, K_i), i = 1, \ldots, 4$, and take L to stand for labor and K for capital. The first two commodities, x_1 and x_2, are consumables. The last two, x_3 and x_4, are natural resources that are not consumable. The country trades in x_1 and x_2 and uses x_3 and x_4 as factors in the production of x_1 and x_2, and x_{3i}^f and x_{4i}^f denote the amount of x_3 and x_4 used as factors in the production of $x_i, i = 1, 2$. The symbol p denotes the price of x; w and q are the wage of labor and the rental price of capital, respectively; and L_A and K_A designate country A's current stock of the respective primary factors. It is an interesting question in the theory-data confrontation of the H&O conjecture whether the two countries' endowments of labor and capital, EL_J and EK_J, $J = A, TC$, ought to be taken to equal their stocks of labor and capital. I come back to that question in Chapter 17.

Next the axiom concerning the demand for x_1 and x_2, HO 2, and those concerning the production of the components of x, HO 3 and HO 4.

HO 2 *There is a constant* $a \in (0, 1)$ *such that for all* $\omega_T \in \Omega_T, p_1 x_1^d = a(wL_A + qK_A)$ *and* $p_2 x_2^d = (1 - a)(wL_A + qK_A)$.

HO 3 *There are positive constants* a_{ki}, $k = 3, 4, L, K$, *and* $i = 1, \ldots, 4$, *such that, for all* $\omega_T \in \Omega_T$, $x_i^s = \min\left\{(L_i/a_{Li}), (K_i/a_{Ki}), \left(x_{3i}^f/a_{3i}\right), \left(x_{4i}^f/a_{4i}\right)\right\}$, $i = 1, 2$, *and* $x_i^s = \min\{(L_i/a_{Li}), (K_i/a_{Ki})\}, i = 3, 4$.

HO 4 *For all* $\omega_T \in \Omega_T$,

$$p_1 - p_3 a_{31} - p_4 a_{41} = w a_{L1} + q a_{K1},$$

$$p_2 - p_3 a_{32} - p_4 a_{42} = w a_{L2} + q a_{K2},$$

$$p_3 = w a_{L3} + q a_{K3},$$

and

$$p_4 = w a_{L4} + q a_{K4}.$$

In axiom HO 2, I assume that domestic demand for x_1 and x_2 in A can be rationalized by a utility function such as the ones I used to rationalize demand in A and B earlier. Here $a = [\alpha/(\alpha + \beta)]$ for some values of α and β. In HO 3, I also assume that the production of $x_1, \ldots, x_4$ in A satisfies the conditions that I imposed on the respective production functions in my trade model. Finally, the equations in HO 4 insist that the prices of the components of x equal the cost of producing them.

Axiom HO 5 below insists that the supply of x_3 and x_4 equals the demand for x_3 and x_4. Similarly, axiom HO 6 makes sure that the production of the respective components of x does not employ more of L and K than is available. Since A trades in x_1 and x_2, there are no analogous conditions on the supply and demand for x_1 and x_2. However, HO 7 is a partial substitute. In the intended interpretation of these axioms, HO 7 insists that in trade equilibrium the value of A's supply of x_1 and x_2 must equal the value of its demand for the same commodities.

HO 5 *For all* $\omega_T \in \Omega_T$, $x_3^s - x_{31}^f - x_{32}^f = 0$ *and* $x_4^s - x_{41}^f - x_{42}^f = 0$.

HO 6 *For all* $\omega_T \in \Omega_T$, $L_1+L_2+L_3+L_4 \le L_A$ *and* $K_1+K_2+K_3+K_4 \le K_A$.

HO 7 *For all* $\omega_T \in \Omega_T$, $p_1x_1^s + p_2x_2^s = p_1x_1^d + p_2x_2^d$.

In HO 8 below I formulate the version of the H&O conjecture that I intend to confront with data. In reading the axiom, note that the validity of the H&O conjecture depends on EL_J and EK_J, and not on the stocks of labor and capital in A and TC.

HO 8 *For all* $\omega_T \in \Omega_T$, *if* $EL_A/EK_A < (>)\ EL_{TC}/EK_{TC}$ *and*

$$[(a_{L1} + a_{L3}a_{31} + a_{L4}a_{41})/(a_{K1} + a_{K3}a_{31} + a_{K4}a_{41})] < [(a_{L2} + a_{L3}a_{32} + a_{L4}a_{42})/(a_{K2} + a_{K3}a_{32} + a_{K4}a_{42})]$$

then $x_1^s > (<)x_1^d$ *and* $x_2^s < (>)x_2^d$. *Also, if* $EL_A/EK_A < (>)EL_{TC}/EK_{TC}$, *then the preceding condition on the* a_{ki} *coefficients with* $<$ *replaced by* $>$ *implies that* $x_1^s < (>)x_1^d$ *and* $x_2^s > (<)x_2^d$.

There are several interesting aspects of the theory universe that I just delineated. First of all, HO 1–HO 8 do not constitute a complete set of axioms from which one can deduce a theory of a country's trade flows. Rather, I selected relevant elements of the family of models of the world economy that I discussed in Section 10.3.2. The models of the given world economy ensure that the axioms of my theory universe have meaningful models. Second, I have not insisted on possible values of a, L_A, and K_A that, with the appropriate choice of values for EL and EK, will ensure the validity of the H&O conjecture in a trade model such as the one I described in Section 10.3.2. Even so, in my test of the empirical relevance of the H&O conjecture the estimated values of a, L_A, and K_A play a significant role. Third, the incompleteness of HO 1–HO 8 raises a serious question. How am I to determine which factor, L or K, is the relatively abundant factor in A? That remains to be seen.

10.4 CONCLUDING REMARKS

In this chapter I discussed theory universes for four different theories. In looking back at them, one should note that the axioms express just a few of the positive analogies that the pertinent theories identify. Moreover, the axioms are in each case meant to constitute the first step in a model-theoretic development of a theory. I omitted the second step in which the intended family of models of the axioms is to be delineated. Later, in the empirical analyses of the respective theories, I search for contours of a family of models of the axioms whose empirical relevance cannot be rejected. Finally, it is important to note that I conclude the chapter with a theory universe whose adequacy hinges on a satisfactory answer to a serious question. Does there exist a reasonable family of models of the axioms that allows one to determine the relative abundance of the two primary factors of production? I return to this in Chapter 17.

NOTES

1. In Chapter 17, I give a formal definition of *empirical relevance.* Here it suffices to say that a theory is empirically relevant in a given empirical context if its assertions are valid in that context.

2. A positive analogy is a characteristic that all the members of a given population share.

3. The version of Walras's law that I have in mind here insists that in all price-income situations (p, A), the market value of the goods demanded $pf(p, A)$ equals the value of the funds supplied A.

4. According to the characterization of rational animals in Chapter 9, one expects a rational animal to be able to order available commodity bundles and to choose from among them the one he most prefers. It is, therefore, an attractive feature of Cooper and McLaren's theory that it puts restrictions on $f(\cdot)$ only at the observed values of prices and expenditures.

5. The idea of analyzing the operative efficiency of a firm in terms of technical and allocative efficiency dates back to M. J. Farrell's (1957) seminal article, "The Measurement of Productive Efficiency."

6. The data were based on observations that Harald Dale-Olsen (1994) used in writing his hovedoppgave (thesis), "Produksjon i Busstransportsektoren," for an embedseksamen (degree) in economics at the University of Oslo.

7. If I had been a numerical analyst, I would have been ashamed of presenting the equilibria in cases 1 and 2 without providing accuracy measures for the values of the respective components. However, for the purposes of this chapter the accuracy measures are not important. Hence, I leave it to the reader to get an indication of the inaccuracies by computing, as I have done, the values of the missing variables. The values of the missing variables in the case 1 trade equilibrium are as follows: $(P_3, P_4, x^s_{3A}, x^s_{4A}, x^s_{3B}, x^s_{4B}) = (1.07, 1.13, 7.73, 20.82, 10.35, 8.49)$.

8. In the case 2 autarky equilibrium in A the missing values are as follows: $(P_3, P_4, x^s_{3A}, x^s_{4A}) = (1.8, 1.8, 7.61, 20.95)$.

9. In the case 2 autarky equilibrium in B the missing values are as follows: $(P_3, P_4, x^s_{3B}, x^s_{4B}) = (1.5, 1.6, 10.35, 8.42)$.

10. In the case 2 trade equilibrium the missing values are as follows: $(P_3, P_4, x^s_{3A}, x^s_{4A}, x^s_{3B}, x^s_{4B}) = (1.01, 1.05, 7.73, 20.82, 10.35, 8.49)$.

REFERENCES

Afriat, S., 1976, *The Combinatorial Theory of Demand*, London: Input-Output.

Aigner, D., C. A. K. Lovell, and P. Schmidt, 1977, "Formulation and Estimation of Stochastic Frontier Production Function Models," *Journal of Econometrics* 86, 21–37.

Battalio, R. C., E. B. Fisher, J. H. Kagel, R. L. Basmann, R. C. Winkler, and L. Krasner, 1973, "A Test of Consumer Demand Theory Using Observations on Individual Consumer Purchases," *Western Economic Journal* 11, 411–428.

Coelli, T., D. S. Prasada Rao, and G. E. Battese, 1998, *An Introduction to Efficiency and Productivity Analysis*, Boston: Kluwer.

Cooper, R. J., and K. McLaren, 1996, "A System of Demand Equations Satisfying Effectively Global Regularity Conditions," *Review of Economics and Statistics* 78, 359–364.

Dale-Olsen, H., 1994, Produksjon i Busstransportsektoren, Unpublished Hovedoppgave, Department of Economics, University of Oslo.

Deaton, A. S., and J. Muellbauer, 1980, "An Almost Ideal Demand System," *American Economic Review* 70, 312–326.

Diab, M. A., 1956, *The United States Capital Position and the Structure of its Foreign Trade*, Amsterdam: North-Holland.

Farrell, M. J., 1957, "The Measurement of Productive Efficiency," *Journal of the Royal Statistical Society Series A* 120, 253–281.

Førsund, F. R., and L. Hjalmarsson, 1987, *Analyses of Industrial Structure: A Putty-Clay Approach*, Stockholm: Almquist & Wiksell International.

Førsund, F. R., C. A. K. Lovell, and P. Schmidt, 1980, "A Survey of Frontier Production Functions and of their Relationship to Efficiency Measurement," *Journal of Econometrics* 13, 5–25.

Friedman, M., 1957, *A Theory of the Consumption Function*, Princeton: Princeton University Press.

Green, W. H., 1993, "The Econometric Approach to Efficiency Analysis," in: *The Measurement of Productive Efficiency, Techniques and Applications*, H. O. Fried, C. A. K. Lovell, and S. S. Schmidt (eds.), New York: Oxford University Press.

Heckscher, E., 1919, "The Effect of Foreign Trade on the Distribution of Income," *Ekonomkisk Tidsskrift* 21, 497–512.

Houthakker, H. S., 1950, "Revealed Preference and the Utility Function," *Economica* 17, 159–174.

Kittelsen, S. A. C., 1998, "Using Data Envelopment Analysis to Measure Production Efficiency in the Public Sector," *Økonomiske Doktorgradsavhandlinger*, University of Oslo.

Leontief, W. W., 1953, "Domestic Production and Foreign Trade: The American Capital Position Re-examined," *Proceedings of the American Philosophical Society* 107, 332–349.

Ohlin, B., 1933, *Interregional and International Trade*, Cambridge: Harvard University Press.

Projector, D. S, and G. S. Weiss, 1966, Survey of Financial Characteristics of Consumers, Board of Governors of the Federal Reserve System, Washington, D.C.

Samuelson, P. A. 1948, "International Trade and the Equalization of Factor Prices," *Economic Journal* 58, 163–184.

Samuelson, P. A., 1949, "International Factor Price Equalization Once Again," *Economic Journal* 59, 181–197.

Samuelson, P. A., 1953, "Consumption Theorems in Terms of Overcompensation Rather than Indifference Comparisons," *Economica* 20, 1–9.

Schultz, H., 1938, *The Theory and Measurement of Demand*, Chicago: University of Chicago Press.

Stigum, B. P., 1990, *Toward a Formal Science of Economics*, Cambridge: MIT Press.

Stone, J. R. N., 1954, "Linear Expenditure Systems and Demand Analysis: An Application to the Pattern of British Demand," *Economic Journal* 64, 511–527.

Swerling, B. C., 1954, "Capital Shortage and Labour Surplus in the United States," *Review of Economics and Statistics* 36, 286–289.

Valavanis-Vail S., 1954, "Leontief's Scarce Factor Paradox," *Journal of Political Economy* 52, 523–528.

Varian, H. R., 1982, "The Non-parametric Approach to Demand Analysis," *Econometrica* 50, 945–973.

Wold, H., and L. Jurêen, 1953, *Demand Analysis*, New York: Wiley.

Chapter Eleven

The Data Universe

In this chapter I discuss properties of economic data, construct data universes, and derive salient characteristics of two kinds of data-generating processes. My goal is to impart a good understanding of various formal features of the empirical contexts in which economists try the relevance of their theories. Two of these features are the role of theory in data creation and the function bridge principles play in the characterization of data-generating processes.

11.1 OBSERVATIONS AND DATA

In economics an empirical analysis is usually carried out with two kinds of data: observed values of pertinent economic variables (e.g., appropriate entries on a financial statement and relevant parts of a country's vital statistics) and values of variables that have been created for analysis (e.g., values of suitable price indexes and chosen input-output combinations in an industry).

The variables for which there are observations pertain to individuals or to groups of individuals, and we index them by time and location. Cases in point are the expenditures on recreation of individual consumers in 1962 in the United States and the level of unemployment in postwar Western Europe. The values of these variables are observed in laboratory experiments, in specially designed field surveys, and in the publications of central bureaus of statistics. In each case, the process that generates the observations may be deterministic. However, the data-generating process (DGP) is usually considered to be random, and one imagines that the observations have been obtained by one of several possible sampling schemes.

There are many reasons why special variables are created for an empirical analysis in economics. One reason might be that the economist has observations on the values of certain variables and needs observations on the values of a combination of these variables. For example, he might have observed the income and savings of a 1962 U.S. consumer and needs to know that consumer's expenditures on goods and services. Another reason might be that the economist has information on the values of more variables than his data analysis can handle. For example, he might have observed the prices and the total sales of each of many services of a given kind. He has to construct an aggregate of these services and determine the appropriate price for the aggregate. A third reason might be that the theory in the pertinent theory-data confrontation involves variables on which he has no information, for example, permanent income or entrepreneurship. In his empirical analysis he may treat such variables as *latent* variables,[1] or he may construct variables that he can use to represent them.

In creating auxiliary variables for an empirical analysis one uses variables for which there are observations, previously created auxiliary variables, and various forms of indirect information. The last comprises physical constants, estimates of relevant economic constants, and various functional forms. In this book, for example, I use observed bids and a physical constant, the number of days in a year, to compute yields on U.S. Treasury bills. I also use an estimate of the elasticity of substitution between electricity and oil, a CES functional form, and both observed and created variables to construct the price of energy.

One's observations may be deficient in obvious ways. For one thing, one's information on pertinent constants might be incomplete, for example, the customs duties of a foreign country. One might also find that some of the observed values of the economic variables are faulty; for example, because they do not satisfy relevant accounting identities. Finally, one usually observes the arguments and the values of functions such as, for example, production functions, only in limited subsets of their graphs. There are many ways of treating such inadequacies, and different researchers handle them differently. Here it is important to observe that the deficiencies in question are characteristics of observations that arise independently of the theory to be confronted with data.

There are also less obvious ways in which observations might be deficient. Economists use observations on the choices of many different individuals to establish positive analogies of individual choice. Similarly they use observations on the state of an economy in many different periods to establish characteristic features of economic growth. When they do, it is important that their observations be complete and that they record *accurate* values of the *same* variables. That is a tall order that their observations rarely satisfy. For example, in field surveys of consumer finances the sample families often fail to answer all the questions. Moreover, chances are that they do not share the same understanding of terms such as "disposable income," "liquid and fixed assets," and "debt." In the latter case the observed values of the respective variables will not be comparable across the sample families.[2]

The fact that the observed values of an economic variable need not be comparable is a problem that comes up in all sorts of contexts. For example, in family tax statements the recorded earnings and the assessed taxable value of fixed assets need not be comparable across families. Similarly, the values of a firm's stock of capital or the prices of an industrial product at two different dates need not be comparable. Even the values of the same economic variable that an individual gives to two different researchers need not be the same. There may be many good reasons for these anomalies, but whatever they are, one must account for them when designing bridge principles for a theory-data confrontation.

An economist's description of the DGP is also often deficient. There are two obvious reasons for that. He might not, in a given sample population, know the probability distribution of the values of pertinent economic variables and assign an erroneous joint distribution to them. Just think of maintaining that 1/2 is the probability of drawing a red ball from an urn with unknown composition of red and white balls. He might also insist on a faulty sampling scheme for the sake of simplifying the statistical analysis. For example, in this book I make the seemingly doubtful claim that I have sampled inputs and output of Norwegian bus companies at random and with replacement. I require that the sampling be random to justify analyzing the sample by means of statistics and insist that I have sampled with replacement to simplify my analysis.

11.2 THE DATA UNIVERSE

The preceding observations provide all the ideas I need for a formal characterization of the data universe in an economic theory-data confrontation. The data universe is a pair (Ω_P, Γ_P), where Ω_P is a subset of a vector space. The components of a vector ω_P in Ω_P denote observed values of pertinent economic variables, indirect information as constants, and variables that have been created for the empirical analysis. Also Γ_P consists of axioms that describe characteristics of the components of ω_P and delineate the way these components relate to one another. Most economic theory-data confrontations take for granted that the DGP is random. The data universe, then, constitutes one part of a triple $[(\Omega_P, \Gamma_P), \Im_P, P_P(\cdot)]$, where $\Im_P$ denotes a family of subsets of Ω_P and $P_P(\cdot)$ designates a probability measure on $\Im_P$. The $P_P(\cdot)$ and the Γ_P induce a joint probability distribution of the components of ω_P. This distribution and the sampling scheme determine the representation of the *true* DGP in the particular theory-data confrontation.

There are different ways of formalizing an empirical analysis. Hence, different researchers may describe the data universe of a given theory-data confrontation differently. To fix these ideas, I next give examples of data universes that can be used to exemplify the import of the general remarks I made earlier. I begin with two examples of the pair (Ω_P, Γ_P).

11.2.1 A Data Universe for a Test of the Permanent-Income Hypothesis

Suppose that I possess information from a field survey on the disposable incomes and the balance sheets of a sample of U.S. families in 1962 and 1963 and that I intend to use this material to confront the permanent-income hypothesis with data.[3] For that purpose I must delineate a suitable data universe (Ω_P, Γ_P). Let e and y, respectively, denote the age of the head of a family and the dollar value of a family's yearly disposable income. Also, let b, h, and d, respectively, denote the dollar value of a family's liquid assets, fixed assets, and debt at the end of a year. Finally, let the subscripts 2 and 3 refer, respectively, to 1962 and 1963. I can then represent my observations by nine-dimensional vectors $(e_2, y_2, b_2, h_2, d_2, y_3, b_3, h_3, d_3)$, all of which satisfy the condition:

$$(y_2, b_2, h_2, d_2, y_3, b_3, h_3, d_3) \in R_+^8 \text{ and } e_2 \in \{15, \ldots, 100\} \quad (1)$$

To carry out the present theory-data confrontation, I also need information on each family's net worth w at the end of 1962 and 1963 and on its outlays on consumer goods and services, c, in 1963. I create these variables with

$$w_2 = b_2 + h_2 - d_2 \text{ and } w_3 = b_3 + h_3 - d_3 \quad (2)$$

and

$$c_3 = y_3 - (w_3 - w_2). \quad (3)$$

Evidently,

$$(c_3, w_2, w_3) \in R^3. \quad (4)$$

The variables on which I have observations and those I have created are all the variables I need to confront the permanent-income hypothesis with data. So I may insist that $\Omega_P \subset R^{12}$. Also, $\omega_P \in \Omega_P$ only if

$$\omega_P = (e_2, y_2, b_2, h_2, d_2, y_3, b_3, h_3, d_3, w_2, w_3, c_3),$$

and ω_P satisfies (1)–(4).

As to Γ_P, I insist that Γ_P comprises (1)–(4) above and (5)–(7) below. The latter equations concern the y, c, and d components of ω_P; the k_i, $i = y, c$, are nonnegative constants; and the m_i, $i = y, c, d$, are positive constants:

$$k_y < y_j < m_y,\ j = 2, 3, \quad (5)$$

$$k_c < c_5 < m_c, \quad (6)$$

and

$$b_j + h_j + m_d y_j > d_j,\ j = 2, 3. \quad (7)$$

With that much said about my observations and data, I can describe the data universe to go with the theory universe that I constructed for the permanent-income hypothesis in Chapter 10.[4]

PIH 8 $\omega_P \in \Omega_P$ *only if* $\omega_P = (e_2, y_2, b_2, h_2, d_2, y_3, b_3, h_3, d_3, w_2, w_3, c_3)$, *where* $(y_2, b_2, h_2, d_2, y_3, b_3, h_3, d_3, c_3) \in R_+^9$, $(w_2, w_3) \in R^2$, *and* $e_2 \in \{15, \ldots, 100\}$.

PIH 9 *For all* $\omega_P \in \Omega_P$, *it is the case that* $w_2 = b_2 + h_2 - d_2$, $w_3 = b_3 + h_3 - d_3$, *and* $c_3 = y_3 - (w_3 - w_2)$.

PIH 10 *There exist nonnegative constants* $\mathrm{k_i}$, $\mathrm{i = y, c}$, *and positive constants* $\mathrm{m_j, j = y, c, d}$, *such that for all* $\omega_P \in \Omega_P$, *the following inequalities hold:* $\mathrm{k_y < y_j < m_y, j = 2, 3, k_c < c_3 < m_c}$, *and* $\mathrm{b_j + h_j + m_d y_j > d_j, j = 2, 3}$.

The data universe I delineated above has many models. One obtains models of (Ω_P, Γ_P) by assigning specific values to the k_i and the m_i that satisfy the conditions $k_i \in R_+, i = y, c, k_I < m_i, i = y, c$, and $m_d \in R_{++}$. The values assigned to the k_i and the m_i depend on the particular theory-data confrontation on hand. If one were studying the behavior of the poor, one would assign a low value to m_y and ignore all observations that fail to satisfy (5) with that value of m_y. If one were studying the behavior of the rich, one would assign high values to k_y and the three m_i's and ignore all observations that fail to satisfy (5), (6), and (7) with those values of k_y, m_y, m_c, and m_d. The values one chooses for the k_i and the m_i also depend on the preliminary analysis carried out to determine the quality of the observations. For example, one might choose values for the m_i and k_c that help rule out outliers.

11.2.2 A Data Universe for a Test of the Heckscher and Ohlin Conjecture

In this section I describe a data universe for a test of the H&O conjecture. Looking at the data without harming the import of the theory-data confrontation is a serious problem in many situations. My search for an appropriate data universe in which to try the empirical relevance of the H&O conjecture provides a good illustration of how uncomfortable the problem can be. The data I possess comprise a 1997 input-output table for Norway with twenty-three industries and endogenous imports, the 1997 costs of production owing to wages and salaries for eighty-two Norwegian industries, and the 1997 kroner value of the stock of capital in thirty-eight Norwegian industries.[5] I have to create data to measure the inputs and outputs of four industries that I can relate to the four x_i's in my theory universe and find a way to measure final demand for the products of the two nonnatural-resource industries and the 1997 stocks of labor and capital in Norway. Finally, I have to construct estimates of the production coefficients on whose existence I insist in axiom HO 3 of the theory universe and find a good way of measuring the endowments of labor and capital in 1997 Norway and its trading community. That is a tall order when one considers the fact that the resolution of my problem must not affect the outcome of the test of the H&O conjecture.

Leaving out the details, I solve my problem in the following way. Let $Z_i, i = 1, \ldots, 23$, designate the twenty-three industries in the 1997 Norwegian Input-Output Table (Statistics Norway, 2000). The industries Z_{20} to Z_{22} concern various operations of public administration, and I lump them together in a "public sector" Z^5. Industry Z_3 comprises mining and oil production. With the help of Statistics Norway (SN), I split that industry in two and obtain an industry for mining Z^3 and an industry for oil production Z^4. Also with the help of SN, I combine all industries in $\{Z_1, Z_2, Z_4, \ldots, Z_{19}\}$ with more exports than imports and all industries with more imports than exports into two industries, Z^1 and Z^2, and construct an input-output table with endogenous imports for Z^1, Z^2, Z^3, Z^4, and Z^5. Finally, I asked SN to provide me with data on the total costs of salaries and wages and on the values of the stocks of capital in the five industries $Z^1, \ldots, Z^5$. With the constructed input-output table and the latter data in hand, I can divine a suitable data universe for a test of the H&O conjecture.[6]

HO 13 $\omega_P \in \Omega_P$ *only if* $\omega_P = (X^s, X^d, A, M, W, Q, AI, MI, AE, ME, AC, MC, AG, MG, A\sum, M\sum, W\sum, Q\sum, SL, SL\sum, SK, SK\sum, w^*, q^*, B, c, SL\sum_{TC}, SK\sum_{TC}, L^c, K^c, U)$, *where* $X^s \in R^5_+, X^d \in R^5_+, A = (A_{ij})$ *and* $M = (M_{ij})$ *are, respectively,* 5×5 *and* 4×5 *real-valued matrices with nonnegative components* $W \in R^5_{++}, Q \in R^5_{++}, AI \in R^5_+, MI \in R^4_+, AE \in R^5_+, ME \in R^4_+, AC \in R^5_+, MC \in R^4_+, AG \in R^5_+, MG \in R^4_+, A\sum \in R^5_+, M\sum \in R^4_+, W\sum \in R_{++}, Q\sum \in R_{++}, (SL, SK) \in R^{10}_{++}, (SL\sum, SK\sum) \in R^2_{++}, w^* \in R_{++}, q^* \in R_{++}$; B *is a* 2×9 *real-valued matrix with nonnegative components,* $c \in R^4_{++}, (SL\sum_{TC}, SK\sum_{TC}, L^c, K^c) \in R^4_{++}$, *and* $U \in R^4$.

In the interpretation of the axiom, the components of X^s and X^d denote the supply of and the final demand for the products of the respective industries in Z, where $Z = (Z^1, Z^2, Z^3, Z^4, Z^5)$. The components of Q and SL and SK designate, respectively, the gross surplus and the stocks of labor and capital in the respective industries in Z, and $SL\sum_{TC}$, $SK\sum_{TC}$, and L^c and K^c, respectively, denote stock of labor and capital in TC, and the amount of labor and capital used in the production of X^d_1 and X^d_2. Finally, w^*, q^*, and U indicate, respectively, the average wage rate, the average rental price of capital, and factors that are not accounted for; B is a matrix of coefficients that are to play the role of the HO 8 a_{ij}'s in my test of the empirical relevance of the H&O conjecture; and c is a vector of appropriately chosen constants. The remaining components of ω_P are entries in the input-output matrix that I show below. In this matrix, $Z = (Z^1, Z^2, Z^3, Z^4, Z^5)$ as above, and $MZ = (MZ^1, MZ^2, MZ^3, MZ^4)$. Also, respectively, MZ^j stands for imports of products pertaining to industry Z^j, $j = 1, \ldots, 4$, I and E for investment and export, C and G for household consumption and government, and $\sum$ for sum:

	Z	I	E	C	G	$\sum$
Z	A	AI	AE	AC	AG	$A\sum$
MZ	M	MI	ME	MC	MG	$M\sum$
Wages	W					$W\sum$
Gross surplus	Q					$Q\sum$

So much for HO 13. Axiom HO 14 guarantees that it makes sense to interpret $\sum$ as a sum and also provides a way to compute w^* and q^*.

HO 14 *For all* $\omega_P \in \Omega_P$, $\mathrm{A}_{j1} + \mathrm{A}_{j2} + \mathrm{A}_{j3} + \mathrm{A}_{j4} + \mathrm{A}_{j5} + \mathrm{AI}_j + \mathrm{AE}_j + \mathrm{AC}_j + \mathrm{AG}_j = \mathrm{A}\sum_j, \mathrm{j} = 1, \ldots, 5$; $\mathrm{M}_{j1} + \mathrm{M}_{j2} + \mathrm{M}_{j3} + \mathrm{M}_{j4} + \mathrm{M}_{j5} + \mathrm{MI}_j + \mathrm{ME}_j + \mathrm{MC}_j + \mathrm{MG}_j = \mathrm{M}\sum_j, \mathrm{j} = 1, \ldots, 4$; $\mathrm{W}_1 + \mathrm{W}_2 + \mathrm{W}_3 + \mathrm{W}_4 + \mathrm{W}_5 = \mathrm{W}\sum$; $\mathrm{Q}_1 + \mathrm{Q}_2 + \mathrm{Q}_3 + \mathrm{Q}_4 + \mathrm{Q}_5 = \mathrm{Q}\sum$; $\mathrm{SL}_1 + \mathrm{SL}_2 + \mathrm{SL}_3 + \mathrm{SL}_4 + \mathrm{SL}_5 = \mathrm{SL}\sum$; $\mathrm{SK}_1 + \mathrm{SK}_2 + \mathrm{SK}_3 + \mathrm{SK}_4 + \mathrm{SK}_5 = \mathrm{SK}\sum$; $\mathrm{w}^* = \mathrm{W}\sum/\mathrm{SL}\sum$, *and* $\mathrm{q}^* = \mathrm{Q}\sum/\mathrm{SK}\sum$.

The entries in the B matrix play the role of the HO 8 a_{ij}'s in my test of the H&O conjecture. In HO 15, I propose a possible way of measuring the respective components of B. The bridge principles that I formulate in HO 9–HO 12 in Chapter 17 will ensure that they actually can play the role that I have assigned to them.

HO 15 *For all* $\omega_P \in \Omega_P$, *the components of* c *and* B *satisfy the relations:*

$$c_i b_{Li} = W_i/A\sum_i \text{ and } c_i b_{Ki} = Q_i/A\sum_i, i = 1, \ldots, 4,$$

$$c_i b_{3i} = A_{3i}/A\sum_i \text{ and } c_i b_{4i} = A_{4i}/A\sum_i, i = 1, 2,$$

$$b_{L5} = W_5/A\sum_5, b_{K5} = Q_5/A\sum_5 \text{ and } c_i b_{5i} = A_{5i}/A\sum_5, i = 1, \ldots, 4.$$

Also, the $\mathrm{c_i}$ *are chosen such that*

$$(b_{Li} + b_{L5}b_{5i}) + (b_{Ki} + b_{K5}b_{5i}) + b_{3i} + b_{4i} = 1, i = 1, 2,$$

and

$$(b_{Li} + b_{L5}b_{5i}) + (b_{Ki} + b_{K5}b_{5i}) = 1, i = 3, 4.$$

Finally,

$$B = \begin{pmatrix} b_{L1} & b_{L2} & b_{L3} & b_{L4} & b_{L5} & b_{31} & b_{41} & b_{51} & b_{53} \\ b_{K1} & b_{K2} & b_{K3} & b_{K4} & b_{K5} & b_{32} & b_{42} & b_{52} & b_{54} \end{pmatrix}$$

The variables that play the roles in the data universe that the components of x^s and x^d play in the theory universe are X_i^s and X_i^d, $I = 1, \ldots, 4$. Precise definitions of the latter variables follow:

HO 16 *For all* $\omega_P \in \Omega_P$:

$$X_1^s = A\sum_1 - \sum_{1 \le j \le 5} A_{1j} + (AI_4 + AE_4 + AC_4 + AG_4) - M\sum_1 - M\sum_4$$

$$X_1^d = AI_1 + AC_1 + AG_1 + (AI_4 + AC_4 + AG_4),$$

$$X_2^s = A\sum_2 - \sum_{1 \le j \le 5} A_{2j} + (AI_3 + AE_3 + AC_3 + AG_3) - M\sum_2 - M\sum_3,$$

$$X_2^d = AI_2 + AC_2 + AG_2 + (AI_3 + AC_3 + AG_3),$$

$$X_3^s = A\sum_3 - \sum_{1\le j\le 5} A_{3j} - (AI_3 + AE_3 + AC_3 + AG_3) + M\sum_3,$$

$$X_3^d = 0,$$

$$X_4^s = A\sum_4 - \sum_{1\le j\le 5} A_{4j} - (AI_4 + AE_4 + AC_4 + AG_4) + M\sum_4,$$

$$X_4^d = 0.$$

11.3 THE DATA-GENERATING PROCESS AND THE DATA UNIVERSE

So much for data universes in empirical analyses with deterministic DGPs. Next I examine characteristics of the triples $[(\Omega_P, \Gamma_P), \Im, P_P(\cdot)]$ and the associated random DGPs. The triples differ from the pairs (Ω_P, Γ_P) I discussed earlier in that the vectors in Ω_P are random. I distinguish between two probability distributions of the components of ω_P. One is the joint probability distribution of the components of ω_P that, subject to the conditions on which Γ_P insists, is generated by $P_p(\cdot)$. I consider this as the *true* probability distribution of the components of ω_P and denote it by *FP*. The other is a probability distribution of the components of ω_P whose salient characteristics I deduce from a joint distribution of the components of (ω_T, ω_P) and from axioms that relate the components of ω_T to the components of ω_P. I denote the second probability distribution of the components of ω_P by *MPD*.

In most theory-data confrontations the econometrician in charge knows neither the characteristics of *FP* nor the joint probability distribution of the components of (ω_T, ω_P). He obtains ideas of the structure of *FP* from the kind of data analysis that my collaborators develop in Part IV of this volume. Moreover, he makes specific assumptions about the probability distribution of the components of ω_T and derives characteristics of the *MPD* from them and from the bridge principles. I discuss the construction of the *MPD* in this section and discuss data analysis and properties of the *FP* in Section 11.4. The relationship between *FP* and *MPD* is considered in Section 11.5 and in Chapter 17.

I denote the second joint probability distribution of the components of ω_P as *MPD* to emphasize the fact that the distribution in question is a marginal one. I now explain why this is so. I make use of two concepts, the *sample space* Ω and the *bridge principles* of the particular theory-data confrontation $\Gamma_{t,p}$. I explicate the meaning of these concepts in a subsequent chapter. Here it suffices to observe that $\Omega \subset \Omega_T \times \Omega_P$ and that for each $\omega \in \Omega$, the members of $\Gamma_{t,p}$ describe how the theory components and data components of ω are related.

In economic theory-data confrontations the data record information about individuals in a certain sample population S. The individuals in S may be consumers or firms, or industries or countries, or commodities or financial assets. They may even be historical data whose characteristics are of interest. I identify the individuals in S by name and event and think of the event as describing the circumstances under which an individual operates. The *current event* is the event that actually occurred when my sample observations were obtained. I refer to the individuals that I have identified by the current event as *actual* individuals. The others I call *hypothetical* individuals.

With each individual $s \in S$ I associate a pair of vectors $(\omega_{Ts}, \omega_{Ps})$ in the sample space Ω. I denote this pair by $\Psi(s)$ and insist that $\Psi(s)$ is the value at s of a function $\Psi(\cdot) : S \rightarrow \Omega$. The sample space is a subset of $\Omega_T \times \Omega_P$ and $\omega_{Ts} \in \Omega_T$. Hence, the Ts components of $\Psi(s)$ are unobservable, whereas the Ps components are in principle observable. However, I only observe the components of an ω_{Ps} vector that pertain to an actual s. I imagine that there is a probability measure $Q(\cdot)$ on a σ-field of subsets of S, $\Im_S$, that determines the probability of observing an s in the various members of $\Im_S$. The properties of $Q(\cdot)$ are determined by $\Psi(\cdot)$ and a probability measure $P(\cdot)$ that assigns probabilities to subsets of Ω. Specifically, there is a σ-field of subsets of Ω, $\aleph$ and a probability measure $P(\cdot) : \aleph \rightarrow [0, 1]$ such that $\Im_S$ is the inverse image of $\aleph$ under $\Psi(\cdot)$ and that for all $B \in \aleph$,

$$Q\left[\Psi^{-1}(B)\right] = P[B \cap \text{range}(\Psi)]/P[\text{range}(\Psi)],$$

where $\text{range}(\Psi) = \{\omega \in \Omega : \omega = \Psi(s) \text{ for some } s \in S\}$.

There is no definite relationship between the probability measure $P(\cdot)$ on subsets of Ω and the probability measure $P_P(\cdot)$ on subsets of Ω_P. The marginal distribution of the components of ω_P that $P(\cdot)$ and $\Gamma_{t,p}$ induce equals the probability distribution that I labeled *MPD*. The *MPD* may be very different from *FP*, the probability distribution of the components of ω_P that $P_P(\cdot)$, subject to the conditions on which Γ_P insists, generates. However, if the relations that the axioms of $P(\cdot)$ and the members of $\Gamma_{t,p}$ impose on functionals of *MPD* are not contradicted by my data, I can advance arguments as to why the corresponding functionals of *FP* satisfy the same relations. These arguments are good in moderately sized samples, but may be controversial in very large samples. I discuss them in Section 11.5. If I obtain a sample of N observations from S in accordance with some sampling scheme ξ, I call the marginal distribution of the sequence of ω_{Ps} that $P(\cdot)$, $\Gamma_{t,p}$, $\Psi(\cdot)$, and ξ determine the PDGP and refer to it as the pseudo-data-generating process. The distribution of the same sequence of ω_{Ps} that *FP*, $\Psi(\cdot)$, and ξ determine is the DGP, that is, the *true* DGP.[7]

It may seem strange that I associate a pair of vectors with each $s \in S$, the first component of which is unobservable and seems to play no role at all in the data analysis. Note, therefore, that the components of ω_{Ts} relate to one another by hypothesis the way the theory in the theory-data confrontation prescribes, that is, they satisfy the pertinent Γ_T. Also by hypothesis, the components of ω_{Ps} satisfy the pertinent Γ_p, and relate to the components of ω_{Ts} in the way the relevant bridge principles prescribe; that is, the components of the pair $(\omega_{Ts}, \omega_{Ps})$ satisfy the particular $\Gamma_{t,p}$. In a given theory-data confrontation I question the empirical relevance of the theory by checking whether the conditions that Γ_T, the axioms of $P(\cdot)$, and $\Gamma_{t,p}$ impose on (Ω_P, Γ_p) and the probability distribution of the components of ω_{Ps} are valid. Associating a pair of vectors $(\omega_{Ts}, \omega_{Ps})$ with an $s \in S$ allows me to use the theory systematically when I analyze the data.

It is not easy to fathom how $P(\cdot)$ and $\Gamma_{t,p}$ determine the characteristics of *MPD*. It is also hard to envision all the different kinds of *MPD*s that an econometrician might meet in his empirical analysis. Some of the components of ω_P may be independently distributed. Others may have a well-defined covariance structure. Still others may be cointegrated, generalized random walks. There seems to be no end to the possibilities. So, to fix my ideas, I give two examples in which I concentrate my discussion on the relationship among $P(\cdot)$, $\Gamma_{t,p}$, and characteristics of the *MPD*. I consider the relationship between the *MPD* and *FP* in Section 11.5.

11.3.1 Qualitative Response Models

I begin by discussing qualitative response models. Basically, *a qualitative response model* is an econometric model in which the range of the dependent variable is discrete or half-discrete and half-continuous. Such models surface in analyses of situations in which individuals are asked to choose from among a finite set of alternatives. One example might be a situation in which addicts are offered the opportunity to participate in a rehabilitation program, and a second might be a family setting in which a member must choose whether to search for part-time employment. In some situations the econometrician ends up analyzing a qualitative response model because his observations on the dependent variable of interest only indicate in which subset of alternatives the dependent variable must have appeared. This is the kind of model that I discuss in Section 11.3.1.1.

Qualitative response models come in many disguises. They may be univariate, multivariate, and multinomial. They may also be aliases of sample selection models. I show later how prototypes of these models can be analyzed within the methodological framework that I develop in this book. In this context the interesting aspect of my discussion is that each prototype has its own characteristic set of bridge principles. Moreover, these bridge principles differ from those that I discuss in subsequent chapters.

I do not develop an empirical analysis to exemplify my discussion of qualitative response models. Excellent introductions into the intricacies of estimating parameters in qualitative response models can be found in Greene (1997, chs. 20, 21) and Davidson and MacKinnon (1993, ch. 15). In addition, for applied work with such models one can consult some of the seminal articles of Daniel McFadden and James Heckmann, Nobel Prize laureates in Economics in 2001 (e.g., McFadden, 1974; Heckmann, 1976). Finally, the Nobel lecture of Heckmann and McFadden's survey article in the *Handbook of Econometrics* contains excellent surveys of the last 30 years of theoretical and applied work with qualitative response models (cf. Heckmann, 2001; McFadden, 1984).

11.3.1.1 An MPD *for a Qualitative Response Model*

Suppose that $\omega_T \in \Omega_T$ only if $\omega_T = (y, x, u)$, where $(y, x, u) \in R^{k+2}$. Also, suppose that there is a vector of constants $\beta \in R^k$ such that for all $\omega_T \in \Omega_T$, $y = \beta' x + u$. Finally, suppose that $\omega_P \in \Omega_P$ only if $\omega_P = (y^*, x^*)$, where $(y^*, x^*) \in \{0, 1\} \times R^k$. For all $(\omega_T, \omega_P) \in \Omega$, the components of ω_T and ω_P are related as follows:

$$y^* = 1 \text{ if } y > 0 \text{ and } y^* = 0 \text{ if } y \leq 0, \tag{8}$$

$$x = x^*. \tag{9}$$

In these bridge principles I insist that I have accurate observations on the components of x and am able to determine whether the value of y is or is not greater than zero.

For the statistical analysis, I assume that, relative to $P(\cdot)$, the components of (y, x, u) are jointly distributed with finite means μ_y, μ_x, and μ_u and finite variances σ_y^2, σ_x^2, and σ_u^2. Also, $\mu_u = 0$, $E[(x - \mu_x)u] = 0$, and $E\{u|x\}$ may or may not equal zero. From these assumptions and the bridge principles I deduce that relative to $P(\cdot)$: $P\{y^* = 1|x^*\} = P\{u > -\beta' x^* | x = x^*\}$, $P\{y^* = 0|x^*\} = P\{u \leq -\beta' x^* | x = x^*\}$, and $E\{y^*|x^*\} = P\{y^* = 1|x^*\}$.

To describe additional details of the *MPD* of (y^*, x^*) in my example, I must invoke further assumptions about the distribution of x and u, and in so doing, I consider a simple model of the axioms that I sketched above. The arguments that I need to derive the *MPD* in a simple model are much less involved than the ones that I would need to derive the *MPD* in a more elaborate model. Even so, the arguments are equally informative.

In the simple model, $x \in \{1, 3\}$, $u \in \{-1, 1\}$, u and x are independently distributed, and $y = -1 + 2x + u$. Also, relative to $P(\cdot)$, u assumes the values, 1 and -1, each with probability 1/2, and x assumes the values 1 and 3, with respective probabilities 1/3 and 2/3. From this and from the equation $y = -1 + 2x + u$, I deduce that y can assume the values 0, 2, 4, and 6, with respective probabilities 1/6, 1/6, 2/6, and 2/6. Now, there are sixteen possible values of the triple (y, x, u). However, only four of them belong to Ω_T, $(0, 1, -1)$, $(2, 1, 1)$, $(4, 3, -1)$, and $(6, 3, 1)$, and they occur with respective probabilities 1/6, 1/6, 2/6, and 2/6. I do not know how many possible values the pair (y^*, x^*) can assume in Ω_P. However, among the possibilities must be the pairs (0, 1), (1, 1), and (1, 3). Finally, in Ω there are four five-tuples, (0, 1, -1, 0, 1), (2, 1, 1, 1, 1), (4, 3, -1, 1, 3), (6, 3, 1, 1, 3), that relative to $P(\cdot)$ occur with respective probabilities 1/6, 1/6, 2/6, and 2/6. With the latter probabilities in hand, I find that the *MPD* of (y^*, x^*) in my model assigns probabilities, 1/6, 1/6, and 4/6, respectively, to the pairs (0, 1), (1, 1), and (1, 3). If there are pairs other than these in Ω_P, I let the *MPD* assign probability zero to them.

11.3.1.2 Variations on a Theme

The univariate qualitative response model in Section 11.3.1.1 generalizes in the obvious way to multivariate models. For example, in the bivariate case (8) and (9) become

$$y_j = \beta_j' x_j + u_j,\ y_j^* = 1 \text{ if } y_j > 0 \text{ and } 0 \text{ otherwise},\ j = 1, 2, \tag{10}$$

and

$$x_j^* = x_j,\ j = 1, 2. \tag{11}$$

By changing (10) a bit, one sees that the original model also generalizes to so-called multinomial qualitative response models. To wit: for the binomial case:

$$y_j = \beta' x_j + u_j,\ j = 1, 2, \tag{12}$$

$$y_1^* = 1 \text{ if } y_1 > y_2 \text{ and } 0 \text{ otherwise},\ y_2^* = 1 \text{ if } y_2 > y_1 \text{ and } 0 \text{ otherwise}, \tag{13}$$

$$x_j^* = x_j,\ j = 1, 2. \tag{14}$$

Finally the model generalizes to sample selection models. I obtain one example of a bivariate sample selection model by changing (8) and (9) as follows:

$$y = \beta' x + u \text{ and } Z = \gamma' w + v \tag{15}$$

$$y^* = y \text{ if } Z > 0 \text{ and } 0 \text{ otherwise},\ Z^* = 1 \text{ if } Z > 0 \text{ and } 0 \text{ otherwise}, \tag{16}$$

and

$$x^* = x \text{ and } w^* = w. \tag{17}$$

The models in this section are prototypes of models that have been applied in all sorts of situations. For example, in (10) and (11) one can imagine a situation in which a family has to decide whether to send at least one child to a public school and whether to vote for the school's budget. In (12)–(14) one can imagine that the subjects are facing a situation in which they have to choose between two different modes of transportation. In such situations the y_i typically measure the utilities that the subjects receive from each choice. Finally, in (15)–(17) one can imagine a situation in which a housewife has to decide whether to look for part-time employment. In that case y is a measure of the number of hours that she is willing to work and Z is a measure of the difference between the market wage she is offered and her reservation wage.

11.3.2 An *MPD* for the Permanent-Income Hypothesis

Next I look for an *MPD* in the data universe of the permanent-income hypothesis that I discussed in Section 11.2.1. I obtained the data for the given theory-data confrontation from a field survey of U.S. consumers. Econometricians regard such field surveys as random DGPs. Consequently, the data universe for the given empirical analysis is part of a triple $[(\Omega_P, \Gamma_P), \Im_P, P_P(\cdot)]$, where the pair (Ω_P, Γ_P) is as I described it in Section 11.2.1. To concretize my arguments I assume that in PIH 10 the k_y and k_c equal zero, the m_y and m_c equal infinity, and the m_d equals one. Also, since my arguments only involve e_2, y_3, c_3, and w_2, I can summarize the axioms of the data universe as follows:

PIH 8–PIH 10 $\omega_P \in \Omega_P$ *only if* $\omega_P = (e_2, y_3, c_3, w_2)$, *where* $e_2 \in \{15, \ldots, 100\}$, $(y_3, c_3) \in R_+^2$, *and* $w_2 \in R$.

I do not have a firm idea about the *FP* for the present case. Therefore, I would like to make my description of the *MPD* as general as possible. Since the relevant *MPD* is induced by a probability measure $P(\cdot)$ on subsets of the sample space Ω, I look for axioms concerning $P(\cdot)$ that I believe most econometricians will accept.

To state the axioms for $P(\cdot)$, I must refer to the theory universe of the permanent-income hypothesis and to the bridge principles that in the sample space of the theory-data confrontation relate variables in the given theory universe to variables in the present data universe. For ease of reference, therefore, I list the members of the particular Γ_t and $\Gamma_{t,p}$. First the members of Γ_t:

PIH 1 $\omega_T \in \Omega_T$ *only if* $\omega_T = (r, y_p, y_t, c_p, c_t, A, \alpha, u)$, *where* $(r, y_p, c_p, A) \in R_{++}^4$, $(y_t, c_t, u) \in R^3$, *and* $\alpha \in \{15, 16, \ldots, 100\}$.

PIH 2 *For all* $\omega_T \in \Omega_T$, $y_p = [r/(1+r)]A$.

PIH 3 *Let* $\Omega_T(a) = \{\omega_T \in \Omega_T : \alpha = a\}$, *with* $a \in \{15, 16, \ldots, 100\}$. *There exists a function,* $k(\cdot) : R_{++} \times \{15, 16, \ldots, 100\} \rightarrow R_{++}$ *such that for all* $\omega_T \in \Omega_T(\alpha)$, $c_p = k(r, \alpha)y_p$.

PIH 4 *Let* $h(\cdot)$ *be defined by*

$$h(\alpha) = \begin{cases} 25 & \text{if } \alpha < 35, \\ 5(i+6)+5 & \text{if } (i+6)5 \leq \alpha < (i+8)5,\ i = 1, 3, 5, \\ 70 & \text{if } 65 \leq \alpha. \end{cases}$$

Then, for all $\alpha \in \{15, 16, \ldots, 100\}$, $k[r, h(\alpha)] = k(r, \alpha)$, $r > 0$.

In reading these axioms again, recall that the relation $y_p = [r/(1+r)]A$, is intended to provide a definition of y_p that is not at stake in the test of Friedman's permanent-income hypothesis. Next, the members of $\Gamma_{t,p}$:

PIH 5 *For all* $\omega \in \Omega$, $\alpha = e_2$. *Also, there exists a function* $q(\cdot) : \{25, 40, \ldots, 70\} \rightarrow R$ *such that for all* $\omega \in \Omega$, $w_2 = q[h(\alpha)] + A + u$.

PIH 6 *For all* $\omega \in \Omega$, $c_3 = c_p + c_t$ *and* $y_3 = y_p + y_t$.

PIH 7 *Let* $G = \{25, 40, 50, 60, 70\}$ *and let* $\Omega[g] = \{\omega \in \Omega : h(\alpha) = g\}$, $g \in G$. *There exists a positive constant* r_g *such that for all* $\omega \in \Omega[g]$, $r = r_g$, *and* $[(1+r_g)/r_g] = b_3$, *where* b_3 *is a parameter of the joint distribution of* c_3, y_2, w_2, *and* y_p *that I specify later in T 1(ii).*

Here PIH 5 claims that I have accurate observations on the age of the consumer and that the value of his net worth at the end of 1962 is related in an interesting way to the A and u components of ω_T. The way w_2 is related to A and u is of no consequence for Friedman's hypothesis. However, as will be seen, it establishes the intriguing possibility of using w_2 as an instrumental variable in a factor-analytic test of the permanent-income hypothesis. In doing that it also illustrates how "outside" information can be introduced and used in the testing of a theory. PIH 6 formulates relations among c_3, c_p, c_t, y_3, y_p, and y_t that accord with the ideas that Friedman (1957) expounded in his treatise. Finally, PIH 7 claims that r is a constant r_g whose value is related to the value of a statistical parameter that is specified later in T 1(ii). In that way r_g becomes an important element in the search for a family of data universes in which a meaningful test of the empirical relevance of the permanent-income hypothesis can be constructed.

With the members of Γ_T and $\Gamma_{t,p}$ in sight, I can begin listing the axioms of the probability measure on subsets of Ω, $P(\cdot) : \aleph \rightarrow [0, 1]$.

PIH 11 *For each* $g \in G$, $\Omega(g) \in \aleph$ *and* $P[\Omega(g)] > 0$. *Moreover, relative to* $P[\cdot|\Omega(g)]$, *the variances of* y_p, y_t, c_p, *and* c_t *are positive and finite, and the covariances of the pairs* $(y_t, y_p), (y_p, c_t), (c_p, y_t)$, *and* (c_t, y_t) *are zero,* $g \in G$.

PIH 12 *Relative to* $P[\cdot|\Omega(g)]$, *the variance of* u *is positive and finite, and the covariances of the pairs* $(u, A), (u, y_t), (u, c_p)$, *and* (u, c_t) *are zero,* $g \in G$.

PIH 13 *Relative to* $P[\cdot|\Omega(g)]$, *the means of* y_t, c_t, *and* u *are zero, and the means of* y, c, *and* w_2 *are positive,* $g \in G$.

Except for the reference to u and w_2, these axioms express ideas Friedman insisted on in his treatise. Specifically, PIH 11 and the assertion concerning y_t and c_t in PIH 13 formalize for the present axiom system Friedman's assumptions 3.3 and 3.4 (Friedman, 1957, pp. 26, 30). However, the restrictions insisted upon in PIH 3 and PIH 4 are not heeded in either PIH 11 or PIH 13.

The axioms of $P(\cdot)$ together with the bridge principles imply that the mean and covariance structure of *MPD* has interesting characteristics. First the obvious: For all $g \in G$, that is, in all age groups, the variances of c_3, y_3, and w_2 are positive and finite. Also, the means of c_3, y_3, and w_2 are positive. Finally, the covariances of the pairs (c_3, y_3), (c_3, w_2), and (y_3, w_2) are finite.

To obtain more information about the mean and covariance structure of *MPD*, I need an auxiliary theorem, T 1, that gives the relation between the means and variances of c_3, y_3, and w_2 and y_p and c_p.

T 1 *Suppose that PIH 1, PIH 2, and PIH 5–PIH 13 are valid. Also, for each* $\mathrm{g} \in \mathrm{G}$, *let* $\mathrm{E}\{\cdot|\mathrm{g}\}$ *and* $\sigma^2(\cdot|\mathrm{g})$, *respectively, denote the expectation and variance of* $(\cdot)$ *with respect to* $\mathrm{P}[\cdot|\Omega(\mathrm{g})]$. *Then for each* $\mathrm{g} \in \mathrm{G}$:

(*i*) $\mathrm{E}\{c_3|g\} = \mathrm{E}\{c_p|g\}$ *and* $\mathrm{E}\{y_3|g\} = \mathrm{E}\{y_p|g\}$. *Also,* $\sigma^2(c_3|g) = \sigma^2(c_p|g) + \sigma^2(c_t|g)$ *and* $\sigma^2(y_3|g) = \sigma^2(y_p|g) + \sigma^2(y_t|g)$.

(*ii*) *There exist pairs of constants* (a_i, b_i), $i = 1, 2, 3$, *and a triple of random variables,* ξ_1, ξ_2, *and* ξ_3, *that have mean zero and finite variance, are orthogonal to* y_p, *and satisfy the equations* $c_3 = a_1 + b_1 y_p + \xi_1$, $y_3 = a_2 + b_2 y_p + \xi_2$, $w_2 = a_3 + b_3 y_p + \xi_3$, *with* $a_2 = 0$, $b_2 = 1$, $\xi_2 = y_t$, $\mathrm{E}\{\xi_1\xi_2|g\} = \mathrm{E}\{\xi_2\xi_3|g\} = \mathrm{E}\{\xi_3\xi_1|g\} = 0$, *and* $\xi_3 = u$.

Simple algebra, the relation, $y_p = [r/(1 + r)]A$, PIH 5–PIH 13, and an appeal to a standard theorem in mathematical statistics suffice to establish the theorem, so there is no need to give a detailed proof here. I consider that the most interesting aspect of the theorem is the role r_g plays in T 1(ii). The relation $b_3 = [(1+r_g)/r_g]$ that I postulated in the bridge principles relates a constant in the theory universe to a statistical parameter whose value can be estimated with observations on variables in the data universe. This bridge principle enables me to establish the relations, $E\{\xi_3\xi_1|g\} = 0$, and $\xi_3 = u$ in T 1(ii). As a consequence it becomes an essential element in my description of the family of models of the data universe within which I am to try the empirical relevance of the permanent-income hypothesis.

With T 1 in hand I can give a complete characterization of *MPD*s mean and covariance structure in T 2. In reading the theorem it is worth noting that its validity depends on the validity of the axioms of $P(\cdot)$ and the given bridge principles. I derived the conditions of T 4 without making use of PIH 3 and PIH 4, so the empirical relevance of the theorem is independent of the validity of the permanent-income hypothesis.

T 2 *Let* $\mathrm{a} = (a_1, a_2, a_3)'$, $\mathrm{b} = (b_1, b_2, b_3)'$, *and* $\xi = (\xi_1, \xi_2, \xi_3)'$ *be as in T 3. Also, let* $\mathrm{x} = (c_3, y_3, w_2)'$, $M_x^g = \mathrm{E}\{xx'|g\}$, $\sum^g = \mathrm{E}\{(x - \mathrm{E}\{x|g\})(x' - \mathrm{E}\{x'|g\})|g\}$, *and* $\Psi^g = \mathrm{E}\{\xi\xi'|g\}$. *Finally, recall that* a, b, *and* ξ *vary with* g, *and suppose that PIH 1, PIH 2, and PIH 5–PIH 13 are valid. Then, for each* $\mathrm{g} \in \mathrm{G}$, *(i)* $a = (a_1, 0, a_3)'$, $b = (b_1, 1, b_3)'$, *and* Ψ^g *is diagonal.*

(ii) $E\{x|g\} = a + bE\{y_p|g\}$.

(iii) $M_x^g = aa' + (ba' + ab')E\{y_p|g\} + bb'E\{y_p^2|g\} + \Psi^g$.

(iv) $\sum^g = bb'\sigma^2(y_p|g) + \Psi^g$.

It ought not go unnoticed that here as well as in the actual data confrontation of Friedman's hypothesis in Chapter 17, I choose to characterize the pertinent *MPD* entirely in terms of its mean and covariance structure. The *MPD* may have many other characteristics, but they are entirely irrelevant for the purposes of this chapter.

The values of the components of the mean and covariance structure of *MPD* are not known. For the purpose of estimating their values with my data I have to postulate two more axioms, which concern properties of $P(\cdot)$ and the sampling distribution. The researchers at the Board of Governors of the Federal Reserve System, who are responsible for these data, sampled U.S. consumers according to a stratified random sampling scheme in which consumers were stratified by income. I formalize some of the characteristics of the Federal Reserve researchers' sampling scheme in Chapter 17.

11.4 MODEL SELECTION AND THE DATA UNIVERSE

So far I have given several examples of data universes and sketched their roles in theory-data confrontations. However, I have had little to say about all the choices involved in deciding on the elements of an appropriate data universe. Moreover, I have only discussed data universes for theory-data confrontations in which there is a definite theory to be confronted with data. In doing that I have failed to account for all the exploratory analyses of data from which econometricians seek to acquire ideas for new theories, for better economic forecasts, and for explanations of the inefficiencies that they have discovered in production processes.

In most exploratory data analysis as well as in the choice of elements for a data universe the econometrician is engaged in what is called model selection. *Model selection* in econometrics is about how best to choose variables for an empirical analysis and how to search for the linear or nonlinear relations among them that will best serve the purposes of the analysis. I end this chapter by discussing one of the problems that arise in model selection and refer the reader to interesting discussions of related problems in Part IV of this volume, where the main concerns are various aspects of the data analysis that are required to construct a meaningful data universe when its variables are treated as random variables.

11.4.1 Confounding Causal Relations

Choosing variables for the data universe in a prospective theory-data confrontation is difficult. It is, therefore, important to be aware that the choice might have fundamental consequences for the relevance of the empirical results. Left-out variables can confound causal relationships and lead to misrepresentations of dynamic characteristics. To see how, just envision yourself studying the effect of a retraining program for unemployed workers on their employment possibilities. You have observations from two disjoint groups of individuals, one of which has been exposed to the retraining program. To avoid confounding causal effects, you must find a way of rendering the groups observationally equivalent, which requires having observations on a number of the salient characteristics of each group.

The idea of confounding causal relationships is related to the notion of noncollapsibility in regression analysis. Suppose that the theory in the theory-data confrontation insists on a causal relation between two variables, x and z, in which x is the dependent variable and z is the independent one. Suppose also that there are independently distributed observations in the data universe on x and z, and on the variable v. Finally, suppose that the three data variables have finite means and variances and that there exists a function $G(\cdot) : R \to R$ such that $G(E\{x|z\}) = \alpha + \beta z$, and $G(E\{x|z, v\}) = a + bz + cv$. Then the regression of x on z, v is *collapsible* for b over v if $b = \beta$ (cf. Greenland et al., 1999, p. 38). If it is, we may ignore v in our search for the causal relationship between x and z.

11.4.2 Second-Order Properties and Heteroskedasticity

It is not the place here to discuss sufficient conditions for collapsibility. However, there is a relationship between collapsibility and choice of variables for the data universe that is relevant here. For that purpose observe that in the case considered above, there exist vectors of constants (a_1, b_1) and (a_2, b_2, c_2) and variables u_1 and u_2 with finite means and variances that satisfy the conditions:

$$x = a_1 + b_1 z + u_1,\ E\{u_1\} = 0 \text{ and } E\{zu_1\} = 0,$$

$$x = a_2 + b_2 z + c_2 v + u_2,\ E\{u_2\} = 0 \text{ and } E\{zu_2\} = E\{vu_2\} = 0.$$

Certainly, b_1 need not equal β, and $b_1 = b_2$ only if $c_2 = 0$. Also, the a_i, b_i, and c_2 are statistical parameters and need not have an obvious relation to the behavioral parameters that might be of interest here. With my data I can obtain least squares estimates of the constants in these equations. The estimates are consistent, but might be biased. They are biased in the first (second) equation if $u_1(u_2)$ is heteroskedastic, that is, if $E\{u_1|z\}(E\{u_2|z, v\})$ varies with $z(z, v)$. A heteroskedastic $u_1(u_2)$ indicates that $E\{x|z\}(E\{x|z, v\}$ is nonlinear and suggests that one look for nonlinear relationships among the variables in which the error terms are homoskedastic. E 11.1 gives an example of a successful search for such a relation. The example is a freely recounted case study based on the research of Heather Anderson and Farshid Vahid (1997, pp. 480–481). In reading the example, note that nonlinear relations such as the ones arrived at by Anderson and Vahid need not be interesting in themselves. Even so, they may be very interesting in the context of a given theory-data confrontation because providing useful ideas for what variables to include in the particular data universe and what assumptions to make about the structure of their *FP*.

E 11.1 *Anderson and Vahid have James Tobin's (1950) data on food consumption and household income and size in the United States in 1941. To determine the causal relationship among these variables they begin by estimating a linear equation. The result, with the standard deviations of the parameter estimates in parenthesis below, is as follows:*

$$\log FOODCON_i = \underset{(0.1)}{0.82} + \underset{(0.03)}{0.56} \log HINC_i + \underset{(0.04)}{0.25} \log AHSIZE_i + u_i,\ i \in N.$$

Diagnostic specification tests show strong evidence of heteroskedasticity and nonnormality in the residuals. Moreover, a Lagrange multiplier (LM) test suggests that the variance of the residuals varies with the size of the sample's (income/household size) groups. This indicates that a weighted regression might be appropriate. Running the weighted regression, they obtain

$$\log FOODCON_i = \underset{(0.07)}{0.73} + \underset{(0.02)}{0.59} \log HINC_i + \underset{(0.03)}{0.23} \log AHSIZE_i + u_i,\ i \in N.$$

Tests for heteroskedasticity and nonnormality in the residuals fail to find evidence of misspecification. However, an LM test for omitted nonlinearity indicates that the log-linear specification they are using is inappropriate. They end up choosing the following (weighted) regression as a model of the causal relation among the three variables:

$$\log FOODCON_i = \underset{(0.11)}{0.91} + \underset{(0.04)}{0.54} \log HINC_i - \underset{(0.22)}{0.43} \log AHSIZE_i$$

$$+ \underset{(0.08)}{0.17} (\log AHSIZE_i)(\log HINC_i) + \underset{(0.09)}{0.14} (\log AHSIZE_i)^2 + u_i,\ i \in N.$$

Diagnostic tests based on this specification have failed to find any evidence of misspecification.

11.5 CONCLUDING REMARKS

I conclude this chapter with brief remarks on several of its interesting aspects that ought not go unnoticed: (1) The way in which hermeneutical arguments have been ruled out of court; (2) theory-laden data; (3) the incompleteness of the axioms of $P(\cdot)$ and the *FP*; (4) the two roles of bridge principles in theory-data confrontations; (5) the existence of data-admissible models of the *MPD*; and (6) why the *MPD* is not to be an approximation to the *FP*.

11.5.1 Hermeneutical Matters

It is quite clear that two researchers can have different opinions about the meaning of a given set of observations. It is equally clear that the same two researchers may differ in the ways they relate the given observations to variables in a particular theory universe. Be that as it may, for the purposes of this book, it is important that there be agreement that in any given theory-data confrontation, it is the opinion of the researcher in charge that counts. I always assume that he has definite opinions about the purport of his observations and that he makes conscious choices when he creates new data for his empirical analysis. I also assume that he always formulates bridge principles that he has good reasons to believe are valid in some world. Whether they are valid in the Real World is a question that he leaves up to the empirical analysis to answer.

11.5.2 Theory-Laden Data

I constructed data universes for two theory-data confrontations. The constructions exemplify many of the details that are characteristic features of econometric data universes. In looking back at them, note, in particular, the way ideas of the pertinent theory enter the creation of data. For example, the theory in the test of Heckscher and Ohlin's conjecture pertains to a two-country, four-commodity world in which two of the commodities, x_1 and x_2, are traded. Both countries are producers of x_1 and x_2. In trade equilibrium one of them exports x_1 and the other exports x_2. These exports are net exports. I have observations on the activities of twenty-three industries in a country in trade equilibrium with the rest of the world, and I construct two industries, Z^1 and Z^2, that I can associate with x_1 and x_2 : Z^1 comprises all the industries with positive net exports and Z^2 includes all industries with positive net imports.

11.5.3 The Incompleteness of the Axioms of $P(\cdot)$ and the *FP*

It is interesting to observe how the probability measure on the sample space $P(\cdot)$, the variables of the theory universe, and the bridge principles combine to determine the form of the pertinent *MPD*. The example I gave of a simple qualitative response model gave all the details of the construction of an *MPD*. With those details in mind, the construction of an *MPD* for the permanent-income hypothesis that followed ought to have been understandable as well. However, the latter construction comes with an important twist. The axioms for $P(\cdot)$ delineate only a few characteristics of $P(\cdot)$. From them and $\Gamma_{t,p}$, I am able to provide a characterization of the mean and covariance structure of the *MPD* and nothing else.

I believe that it is a general feature of formalized economic theory-data confrontations that the axioms for $P(\cdot)$ are incomplete. Sometimes, for example, when the empirical relevance of a theory is being tried, the incompleteness of the axioms of $P(\cdot)$ serves a purpose. Then the econometrician formulates axioms for $P(\cdot)$ that do not incorporate the strictures on which the theory insists, ascertains that the characteristics of the *MPD* that follow from these axioms and the bridge-principles are data admissible, and concludes the empirical analysis by checking whether the additional restrictions on the structure of the *MPD* that the theory imposes are data admissible.[8] As my analysis of the PIH in Chapters 10, 11, and 17 indicates, such a two-stage procedure may enable the econometrician to circumvent the Duhem trap.

When the axioms for $P(\cdot)$ are incomplete, econometricians are not able to identify their *MPD* with the pertinent *FP*. This inexact relationship between the *MPD* and the *FP* calls for a clarifying remark. In the theory-data confrontations that I consider in this book I do not ever present axioms that give a complete characterization of the *FP*. In most situations I envision that the ideas that the researcher in charge (RiC) has about the structure of *FP* are ideas that he has gathered from external sources, that is, from facts that do not constitute parts of the axioms of the theory-data confrontation itself. This is so even in the case of scientific explanation that Heather Anderson, Geir Storvik, and I consider in Chapter 23. We stipulate axioms concerning the *FP* that delineate just a single structural characteristic of the family of probability distributions that govern the behavior over time of yields in the money market.

The ideas about the *FP* that the RiC has gathered from external sources are implicitly accounted for in the axioms in the following way: Any functional of the *MPD* whose existence is derivable from the axioms of $P(\cdot)$ and the members of $\Gamma_{t,p}$ is taken to be a functional that may belong to the *FP* as well. For example, if the *MPD* has a finite mean and covariance structure, it is possible that the *FP* has a finite mean and covariance structure as well. Further, if the *MPD* insists that some components of the particular ω_P are normally distributed, the same components may also be normally distributed in *FP*. Whether the *FP* actually has the properties that the formal theory-data confrontation suggests is determined by the RiCs empirical analysis.

11.5.4 The Two Roles of the Bridge Principles

In Chapter 12 it will be seen that the bridge between a theory universe and a data universe can be traversed in both directions. However, in this chapter I assume that the relevant crossings take place from the theory to the data universe. When the crossings happen in that way, it is important to be aware of the roles that bridge principles play in the empirical analysis. Hence a remark in that regard is called for.

Strictly speaking, in a formalized economic theory-data confrontation the *empirical context* in which the confrontation takes place is a triple: an accurate description of a sampling scheme, an interpretation of the data universe (Ω_P, Γ_p), and the *true* probability distribution of the components of ω_P, FP. I refer to this empirical context by the name Real World. The empirical context in which the theory-data confrontation *actually* takes place is a different triple: a not-necessarily accurate description of a sampling scheme, an interpretation of (Ω_P, Γ_p), and an interpretation of the *MPD* of the components of ω_P. In the framework of this book it is useful to think of this empirical context as one of the worlds in which all the bridge principles are valid.

In a theory-data confrontation in which the empirical relevance of an economic theory is at stake, the bridge principles have two roles to play in the empirical analysis. First, as the preceding paragraph indicates, the bridge principles constitute essential elements in the characterization of the empirical context in which the confrontation takes place. Second, when the RiC tries the empirical relevance of the particular theory, he first uses the bridge principles to dress it up in terms that the empirical context can understand. Then he checks whether the dressed-up theory makes valid assertions about the data universe and the *MPD*.

11.5.5 The Existence of Data Admissible Models of the *MPD*

It is important for the theory-data confrontation that the econometrician be able to determine whether one of the worlds in which the bridge principles are valid is the Real World. For that purpose he has to ascertain that the sampling scheme that generated his data was adequate and that his interpretation of the *MPD* is data admissible. A sampling scheme is *adequate* if the data it generates enable the econometrician to obtain consistent estimates of the functionals of FP that he needs for his empirical analysis. *A model of the MPD is data admissible if its interpretation of the logical consequences of the axioms of $P(\cdot)$ and $\Gamma_{t,p}$ is not contradicted by the data.* For example, a model of the *MPD* in the PIH example is data admissible only if: (1) the estimated mean and covariance structure of the *MPD* satisfies the strictures of T 2, and (2) the model values of the means and covariances of the *MPD* satisfy the strictures of T 2 and lie within a 95 percent confidence band of the values of the estimated parameters.[9] *An interpretation of the MPD; that is, a family of models of the MPD is data admissible only if it with high probability contains a model whose functionals equal the corresponding functionals of the FP*. If the econometrician's sampling scheme is adequate and his interpretation of the *MPD* is data admissible, I insist that the Real World is one of the worlds in which his bridge principles are valid. In that case, the differences between the *FP* and the *MPD* notwithstanding, I consider the Real World the empirical context in which the theory-data confrontation is taking place.

The idea of a data-admissible model of the *MPD* plays a pivotal role in my view of a theory-data confrontation. It is, therefore, important that the concept not be misunderstood. A model of the *MPD* in a given theory-data confrontation is not an approximation of the *FP* in the ordinary sense. It is an approximation just to the extent that it does not have all the characteristics that the *FP* has. Checking for the data admissibility of a model of the particular *MPD* involves testing whether the model is a model of the logical consequences of the axioms of $P(\cdot)$ and $\Gamma_{t,p}$ and nothing else. The tests involved are misspecification tests, the results of which depend both on the validity of the logical consequences of $P(\cdot)$ and $\Gamma_{t,p}$ and on the chosen significance level.[10] The following is an example of what I have in mind.

E 11.2 *Consider an experiment in which I throw a die* N *times. The die has six sides. It is marked on each side with a different number of spots from one to six. The probability of observing* i *spots is* $\mathrm{p_i}, \mathrm{i} = 1, \ldots, 6$. *The* $\mathrm{p_i}$ *are nonnegative and* $\mathrm{p_1} + \mathrm{p_2} + \ldots + \mathrm{p_6} = 1$. *I believe that my die is perfect and that I have accurate records of the observed spots in each toss. Consequently, my* MPD *insists that* $\mathrm{p_i} = 1/6, \mathrm{i} = 1, \ldots, 6$. *I do not know whether or not the* FP *agrees with my* MPD. *I suppose that the true value of* $\mathrm{p_i}$ *is* $\mathrm{q_i}, \mathrm{i} = 1, \ldots, 6$. *I also assume that my tosses are identical and independent of each other. Then, if* $\mathrm{n_i}$ *equals the number of observed* i*'s and* $\mathrm{p_i^*(N)} = \mathrm{n_i/N}, \mathrm{i} = 1, \ldots, 6$, *as* $\mathrm{N} \to \infty$, $\mathrm{p_i^*(N)}$ *converges with probability one to* $\mathrm{q_i}$ *for all* i. *My* MPD *is data admissible only if my data do not reject the null hypothesis that all the* $\mathrm{q_i}$ *equal 1/6, that is, say, only if a 95 percent confidence region around* $[\mathrm{p_1^*(N)}, \ldots, \mathrm{p_6^*(N)}]$ *contains* $(1/6, \ldots, 1/6)$.

When the logical consequences of the axioms of $P(\cdot)$ and $\Gamma_{t,p}$ in a given theory-data confrontation do not pass all the misspecification tests to which the econometrician subjects them, the conclusion must be that the family of data-admissible models of the *MPD* is empty. If so, the econometrician has two options. He may treat the *MPD* as an approximation to *FP* and estimate the parameters of the *MPD* in a way that, in some sense, makes the estimated *MPD* a best possible approximation to the *FP*,[11] or he may insist that the emptiness of the family of data-admissible models of the *MPD* calls for a diagnosis in Raymond Reiter's (1987) sense of the term. Some of the axioms of $P(\cdot)$ and/or some of the members of $\Gamma_{t,p}$ must be invalid in the Real World, and the diagnosis is to determine which ones. In my opinion the econometrician ought to choose the second option. The part of Reiter's interesting logic that I present in Chapter 20 tells him how to proceed.

11.5.6 Why the *MPD* Is Not to Be an Ordinary Approximation to the *FP*

In looking back at E 11.2 three sobering thoughts come to mind: (1) It is hard to hit a point in Euclidean space. (2) If some of the q_i differ from 1/6 by an insignificant amount, it would make no difference to my comprehension of the die's characteristics. (3) If some of the q_i actually do differ from 1/6, I can be certain that my tosses eventually will produce a sample that will reject the data admissibility of my *MPD*. These thoughts suggest that it might be a good idea to relax my demands on data-admissible models of the *MPD*. For example, in E 11.2, I could pick a small value of ε and agree that a model of the *MPD* is data admissible if $\|p^*(N) - (1/6, \ldots, 1/6)\| < \varepsilon$, where $p^*(N) = [p_1^*(N), \ldots, p_6^*(N)]$. Also, in a more general setting, I could choose a suitable measure for the distance between two families of probability distributions and agree that a model of the *MPD* is data admissible if it differs from the *FP* by less than a preassigned value of ε. Examples of the kind of measures of distance that I have in mind can be found in Goldstein (1985) and Gourieroux and Montfort (1995, vol. 1, ch. 8).

I owe the idea underlying the preceding observations to Harald Goldstein, who made good use of the idea in his study of robust inference in contingency tables. I have not adopted his idea in this book because of the fundamental consequences that it would have for the roles that bridge principles play in theory-data confrontations. Adoption of Harald's idea would make it natural to think of the *MPD* as an approximation to the *FP* or as a misspecified version of the *FP*. And thinking of the *MPD* in that way would make it difficult to identify the World in which the theory-data confrontation is taking place with the World in which the bridge principles are valid. That is a consequence that I am not willing to accept here.

NOTES

1. A *latent* variable is a variable on whose values the pertinent researcher has no observations.

2. The reader can find interesting discussions of the reliability of consumer surveys of financial holdings, such as, time deposits, demand deposits and debts in (Lansing et al., 1961) and (Ferber, 1965, 1966).

3. The reference here is to a reinterview survey of consumer finances in the United States that researchers at the Board of Governors of the Federal Reserve System carried

out in 1962 and 1963. The survey is described and the data are analyzed in Projector and Weiss (1966) and Projector (1968).

4. Axioms PIH 5–PIH 7 concern the bridge principles that I have adopted for my test of the permanent-income hypothesis. They are stated and discussed in Section 11.3.2

5. The 1997 twenty-three-industry input-output table for Norway is published on pp. 128–129 in *Nationalregnskapsstatistikk 1992–1999, Statistisk Sentralbyraa, 2000*. The 1997 industrial data on the stock of capital and the labor force I obtained from Statistics Norway's National Accounts statistics.

6. Axioms HO 9–HO 12 concern the bridge principles that I have adopted for a test of Heckscher and Ohlin's conjecture. They are stated and discussed in Section 17.3.2.

7. To make my description of the PDGP and the DGP as simple as possible I have assumed implicitly that the sampling scheme is such that the ω_{ps} are identically and independently distributed.

8. I give a formal definition of a data-admissible *MPD* in Section 11.5.5. Here it suffices to say that a model of the *MPD* is data admissible if it is not contradicted by the data.

9. Here I have insisted on a 95 percent interval, which accords with my analysis of the empirical relevance of PIH in Chapter 17.

10. In order to understand the assertions that are being checked in the various misspecification tests, it is important to be aware that my concept of data admissibility differs from that of others. For example, in his book *Dynamic Econometrics*, David Hendry insists that an "[econometric] model is data admissible if its predictions automatically satisfy all known data constraints" (Hendry, 1995, p. 364). In Chapter 15 Christophe Bontemps and Grayham Mizon also insist that an econometric model is data admissible if it is "coherent with the properties of the measurement system."

11. The way to do that depends both on the chosen approximation measure and on the characteristics of the pertinent theory-data confrontation. The reader can find good examples in Goldstein (1985) and in Gourieroux and Montfort (1995, vol. 1, ch. 8). Harald Goldstein is concerned with statistical inference for contingency tables and the problem of how to choose simplified models that can be used as a basis for the final statistical interpretation of the tables without assuming that the submodels are true. Christian Gourieroux and Alain Montfort develop an interesting asymptotic theory for the behavior of pseudo-maximum-likelihood estimates of parameters in misspecified econometric models.

REFERENCES

Anderson, H. M., and F. Vahid, 1997, "On the Correspondence Between Individual and Aggregate Food Consumption Functions: Evidence from the USA and The Netherlands," *Journal of Applied Econometrics* 12, 477–507.

Davidson, R., and J. G. MacKinnon, 1993, *Estimation and Inference in Econometrics*, Oxford: Oxford University Press.

Ferber, R., 1965, "The Reliability of Consumer Surveys of Financial Holdings: Time Deposits," *Journal of the American Statistical Association* (March), 148–163.

Ferber, R., 1966, "The Reliability of Consumer Surveys of Financial Holdings: Demand Deposits," *Journal of the American Statistical Association* (March), 91–103.

Friedman, M., 1957, *A Theory of the Consumption Function*, Princeton: Princeton University Press.

Goldstein, H., 1985, "Robust Inference in Contingency Tables I, II, and III," *Scandinavian Actuarial Journal,* 157–178, 179–219, 220–247.

Gourieroux, C. and A. Monfort, 1995, *Statistics and Econometric Models, Vol. I and II,* Quang Vuong (trans.), Cambridge: Cambridge University Press.

Greene, W. H., 1997, *Econometric Analysis*, 3rd Ed., Englewood Cliffs, N.J.: Prentice-Hall.

Greenland, S., J. M. Robins, and J. Pearl, 1999, "Confounding and Collapsibility in Causal Inference," *Statistical Science* 14, 29–46.

Heckmann, J. J.,1976, "The Common Structure of Statistical Models of Truncation, Sample Selection, and Limited Dependent Variables and a Simple Estimator for Such Models," *Annals of Economic and Social Measurement* 5, 475–492.

Heckmann, J. J., 2001, "Micro Data, Heterogeneity, and the Evaluation of Public Policy: Nobel Lecture," *Journal of Political Economy* 109, 673–748.

Hendry, D. F., 1995, *Dynamic Econometrics*, Oxford: Oxford University Press.

Lansing, J. B., G. P. Ginsburg, and K. Braaten, 1961, "An Investigation of Response Error," University of Illinois, Bureau of Economic and Business Research, Studies in Consumer Savings, No. 2.

McFadden, D., 1974, "Conditional Logit Analysis of Qualitative Choice Behavior," in: *Frontiers in Econometrics*, P. Zarembka (ed.), New York: Academic.

McFadden, D., 1984, "Econometric Analysis of Qualitative Choice Models," in: *Handbook of Econometrics*, *Vol. 2*, Z. Griliches and M. D. Intriligator (eds.), Amsterdam: North-Holland.

Nationalregnskapsstatistikk 1991–1998, Statistisk Sentralbyrå, 1999.

Projector, D. S., 1968, "Survey of Changes in Family Finances," Board of Governors of the Federal Reserve System, Washington, D.C.

Projector, D. S., and G. S. Weiss, 1966, "Survey of Financial Characteristics of Consumers," Board of Governors of the Federal Reserve System, Washington, D.C.

Reiter R., 1987, "A Theory of Diagnosis from First Principles," *Artificial Intelligence* 32, 57–95.

Statistics Norway, 2000, "The 1997 Twenty-Three Industry Input-Output Table for Norway," in *Nasjonalregnskapsstatistikk 1992–1999*, pp. 128–129.

Tobin, J., 1950, "A Statistical Demand Function for Food in the U.S.A.," *Journal of the Royal Statistical Society, Series A* 113, 113–141.

Chapter Twelve

The Bridge Principles

In Chapters 10 and 11, I discussed two of the cornerstones in the structure that constitutes the formal part of a theory-data confrontation: the theory universe (Ω_T, Γ_t) and the data universe (Ω_P, Γ_p). It was seen that Ω_T is a vector space and that the vectors in Ω_T, ω_T, must satisfy the conditions on which Γ_t insists and, similarly, that Ω_P is a vector space and that the vectors in Ω_P, ω_P, must satisfy the conditions on which Γ_p insists.

In this chapter I deal with the intricacies of building bridges between theory universes and data universes in empirical economic analyses. The building blocks of these bridges are principles that indicate how the components of vectors in Ω_T are related to those in Ω_P. The bridge principles, which I denote by $\Gamma_{t,p}$, vary from simple identities to complicated dynamic stochastic relations and concern components of pairs of vectors (ω_T, ω_P) in a subset of $\Omega_T \times \Omega_P$, that I denote by Ω and call the *sample space*. The importance of the bridge principles in theory-data confrontations stems from the fact that they are the means by which the results of econometric studies become interpretable.

Judging from econometric literature, bridge principles seem to be principles that econometricians avoid at all costs. Hence, in order not to scare friendly readers, I must take care to develop the topic in a logical manner. I begin by discussing the role of correspondence rules in the so-called *Received View of scientific theories*. Then I detail reasons why bridge principles are needed in applied econometrics and present an example that demonstrates the functioning of bridge principles in a formal theory-data confrontation. Finally, I discuss how data analyses and bridge principles together determine the right universe for carrying out a given test of a hypothesis. The chapter concludes with a few words concerning the status of correspondence rules in the Received View and the status of bridge principles in an economic theory-data confrontation.

12.1 THEORETICAL TERMS AND INTERPRETATIVE SYSTEMS

We live in a marvelous world with all sorts of interesting people, with institutions and mechanical devices that humans have created, and with an extraordinary array of strange animals, beautiful plants, and useful minerals. To find our way in this world we observe and make inferences. A skier might watch the weather map on TV and look for signs of snow tomorrow. A fellow citizen might read of corruption in government and question a department secretary's willingness to lie to save his own skin irrespective of the dire consequences for others. An unemployed person might study series of statistics concerning emigration and wonder what the employment situation would have been today if the emigrants had stayed at home.

Scientists, too, observe facts and make inferences concerning relations among those facts. The facts become data, and the inferences provide the elements for predictions, scientific explanations, and counterfactual arguments. In carrying out their work scientists search for regularities in their data and formulate theories that can account for them. Establishing regularities is essential for meaningful predictions and counterfactual arguments. Moreover, their existence calls for explanations, and the theories make scientific explanations of the observed regularities possible.

The theories that scientists formulate are designed to explain matters of fact. Yet, they contain all sorts of *theoretical terms*, that is, terms that have no reference in the world that the scientists observe: For example, "utility" in economics, "id" in psychology, and "electron" in physics. The need for such theoretical terms is puzzling to some and disconcerting to others. Their prevalence in scientific theories, therefore, calls for some remarks concerning the way different philosophers of science think of them.

Some philosophers, the *conventionalists*, consider the use of theoretical terms in scientific theories to be an innocuous mathematical convention that helps scientists express their ideas in clear and concise ways. With the help of suitable definitions, scientists can replace all theoretical terms by expressions that relate to observation terms only. Theoretical terms that are mere abbreviations of expressions concerning observable objects have no meaning as such. The meaning of an expression containing such abbreviations is determined by its method of verification. Thus, understanding the meaning of assertions concerning definable theoretical terms amounts to understanding the circumstances under which there are good reasons to believe in them.[1]

The *logical positivists* of the Vienna Circle and their followers agree with the *conventionalists*' ideas and explicate the latter's *verification theory of meaning* as follows: Let T be a scientific theory and suppose that a scientist has formulated T in a first-order language L_T with nonlogical vocabulary V_T.[2] Suppose as well that he has formulated the observation statements of interest to him in a first-order language L_O with the same logical vocabulary as L_T and with a nonlogical vocabulary V_O that has no term in common with V_T. Finally, let L be a first-order language with the same logical vocabulary as L_T and L_O, and with nonlogical vocabulary $V_T \cup V_O$. The logical positivists insist that in such a case any term F and any predicate Q in L that are *theoretical terms* of T can be defined in terms of members of V_O alone. For example, if F is a one-place functional constant in L_T and a theoretical term of T, there exists a well-formed formula (wff) A in L_O with just two free variables, x and y, such that in L,

$$(\forall z)(\exists u)\left[[u = F(z)] \equiv A_{x,y}(z, u)\right]. \tag{1}$$

Similarly, if Q is a one-place predicate constant in L_T and a theoretical term of T, there exists a wff B in L_O with just one free variable x such that in L,

$$(\forall z)\,[Q(z) \equiv B_x(z)]. \tag{2}$$

If so, then any expression E in T that concerns F and Q can be rewritten with the help of A and B. Also, understanding the meaning of E amounts to understanding the method by which the translation of E can be verified.[3,4]

In this case the conventionalist philosophers and the logical positivists are wrong. Not all theoretical terms of a scientific theory can be defined by observational terms alone. Good examples of theoretical terms that cannot be so defined are disposition terms, such as "magnetic" and "fragile." The following is an example to fix these ideas.

E 12.1 *Let* L, L_T, *and* L_O *be as above. Also, let* M *be a one-place predicate in* L_T, *and* C *and* I *be one-place predicates in* L_O. *Finally, suppose that* M *in* L *can be defined in terms of* C *and* I *by*

$$(\forall x)[M(x) \equiv [C(x) \supset I(x)]]. \tag{3}$$

This assertion might insist that x *has the property* M *if and only if* x *under the test conditions described in* C *exhibits the response indicated in* I. *For example,* x *is magnetic if and only if whenever* x *is close to a small iron object, the iron object moves toward it.*

As a definitional scheme for science, (3) has a serious defect. It implies that any x that is not subjected to the test prescribed in C has the property M. To escape this unfortunate situation R. Carnap (1936, pp. 441–444) suggested that M be defined by a so-called *reduction sentence*,

$$(\forall x)\,[C(x) \supset [M(x) \equiv I(x)]]. \tag{4}$$

Then, if x is not tested, it need not satisfy M.

The reduction sentence in (4) provides only a partial definition of $M(\cdot)$. Also, any sequence of reduction sentences, one for each test condition in which an individual x might display the required characteristic M, would provide only a partial definition of $M(\cdot)$. Thus the content of relevant sequences of reduction sentences will not exhaust the meaning of a given disposition term.

There are many theoretical terms, for example, utility and electron, whose meanings cannot be described in terms of observables with sequences of reduction sentences. This fact and the way such terms function in scientific theories suggest that one might as well conceive of the interpretation of a scientific theory T as an interpretative system C whose interpretation of T by indirection explicates the meaning of T's theoretical terms. In first-order logic, systems of explicit definitions and sequences of reduction sentences may form parts of an interpretative system. There are, however, many other possible components of such a system. For ease of reference in D 12.1, I describe the most general interpretative system that has to be conceived of here.

D 12.1 Let T be a scientific theory that has been formulated in a first-order language L with equality and nonlogical vocabulary $V_T \cup V_O$. Assume that T has been expressed in terms of members of V_T alone and that $V_T \cap V_O = \emptyset$. Finally, assume that the members of V_O denote observational objects that concern the intended interpretation of T. Then *an interpretative system for T* is a finite set of wffs in L, C that satisfies the following conditions: (a) C and T must be logically compatible. (b) All the nonlogical terms of C belong to $V_T \cup V_O$. (c) Each sentence in C contains at least one term from V_O and one term from V_T essentially.

With the correspondence rules in D 12.1 the logical positivists' idea of a scientific theory becomes what I referred to earlier as the Received View of scientific theories. Specifically, let T, C, L, V_T, and V_O be as in D 12.1, and let *TC* denote the translation of T in L. Then *TC* comprises assertions about members of V_O. A scientist can use the members of *TC* and antecedently accepted assertions concerning V_O to infer the validity of other assertions concerning members of V_O. The Received View identifies a scientific theory with *TC* and insists that C specify the admissible experimental procedures for applying the theory to observational phenomena. Moreover, the terms in V_T receive no observational interpretation beyond what *TC* supplies.[5]

The import of the meaning that the terms of V_T in the Received View receives from *TC* faces serious problems, one of which is of particular interest here. When T is a formalization of a theory in physics, for example, the designations of the members of V_O and the antecedently accepted assertions about V_O pertain to experiments in which the relevance of T is at stake. The construction of such experiments depends both on T and on other theories of physics. The use of auxiliary theories in constructing experiments implies that the meaning of T becomes theory dependent. With time the auxiliary theories change and with them the designations of the members of V_O and the meaning of *TC* change as well.

To avoid facing up to the theory dependence of the meaning of scientific theories, the *scientific realists* insist that the theoretical terms that well-confirmed theories talk about are real. Such terms denote unobservable objects that exist independently of any theorizing about them and have a meaning that is independent of a scientist's observations. This view of scientific theories is controversial and very different from mine. I believe that in economics the terms of V_T pertain to matters of fact in a toy economy and nothing else.

I do not discuss the views of scientific realists here. In this chapter I focus on the role of bridge principles in economic theory-data confrontations and determine the extent to which the status of bridge principles in applied econometrics differs from that of correspondence rules in the Received View. An interesting discussion of scientific realism can be found in Van Frassen (1980, ch. 2), and Chapters 3 and 4 in this book deal in part with theory-dependent observations and include suggestions for how cooperating economists and econometricians can solve some of the problems about which scientific realists are concerned.

12.2 WHY BRIDGE PRINCIPLES IN ECONOMIC THEORY-DATA CONFRONTATIONS?

Economists theorize about many things, for example, consumer choice, oligopolistic markets, and economic growth. In these theories they discover variables that carry names such as "income," "output," and "capital." They read the names and believe that they understand what they mean. Moreover, in a first-order formalization of the theories in question one would expect the aliases in V_T of income, output, and capital to possess obvious definitions in terms of members of the pertinent V_O. But how can one be sure? The following sections give good reasons why economists should be aware.

12.2.1 Income

Most economic theorists treat "income" as a universal term that needs no definition. However, vide Section 3.4, the definitions of the term that leading economists have given and the measures of the term that econometricians have proposed throw doubt on its universality. Here it is important to note that in a theory-data confrontation in which a variable carries the name "income," the intended interpretation of the theory determines the meaning of income in the theory universe. Moreover, the intended interpretation of the aggregate that one uses to measure income in the data universe determines its meaning in that universe. Interpretations vary among researchers, and different interpretations determine different concepts. In order that the particular empirical analysis be meaningful, explicitly stated bridge principles must delineate the way income in the theory universe relates to income in the data universe.

E 12.2 *There are many ways in which income in a theory universe might be related to income in a data universe. I give three examples of such bridges. Let* y_t *and* $\acute{y}_t$*, respectively, denote income in period* t *in the theory and data universe. Then, for all relevant* t*, either*

$$y_t = \acute{y}_t \quad (5)$$

or

$$\acute{y}_t = y_t + \eta_t \tag{6}$$

or

$$y_t - \alpha y_{t-1} = (1-\alpha)\acute{y}_t + \zeta_t - \alpha\zeta_{t-1} \tag{7}$$

for some $\alpha \in (0, 1)$. *Here (5) indicates that one has accurate observations on* y_t *and (6) insists that these observations on* y_t *are marred by errors. One may think of the errors apparent from (6) as being due to inadequacies in the way income is being measured. One may also think of* η_t *as a measure of the value of the consumer's transitory income in period* t *(cf. Friedman, 1957, p. 21). As to (7), it postulates a dynamic relationship between* y_t *and* $\acute{y}_t$. *On the face of it, this relationship looks arbitrary. However, there is a reasonable way of justifying it: Insist that* y_t *can be approximated by the sum (cf. Friedman, 1957, p. 143),*

$$(1-\alpha)\sum_{0\le s<\infty} \alpha^s \acute{y}_{t-s},$$

and let

$$\zeta_t = y_t - (1-\alpha)\sum_{0\le s<\infty} \alpha^s \acute{y}_{t-s}$$

12.2.2 Output

Like "income," "output" is treated by most economists as a universal term. However, vide again Section 3.4, the definitions of the term that economists have given and the measures of the term that econometricians have proposed throw doubt on its universality. A producer of output may be a nurse or a professor, or a farm or a bank, or an industry or a whole macro economy. Describing the output of such a producer is not easy. In a given theory-data confrontation the axioms of the theory universe delineate the meaning of output in the theory universe. Similarly, the axioms of the data universe determine the meaning of output in the data universe. In order that the empirical analysis be meaningful, explicitly stated bridge principles must specify how the two concepts of output are related to each other.

E 12.3 *In the theory-data confrontation in this book in which Harald Goldstein and I study inefficiencies of production in the Norwegian bus transportation industry, the theory insists that output* y *is related to three inputs,* x_1, x_2, *and* x_3, *in accordance with*

$$y^a e^{by} = Ax_1^{\alpha}x_2^{\beta}x_3^{\gamma};\ (y, x_1, x_2, x_3) \in R^4_{++}, \tag{8}$$

where A, a, b, α, β, *and* γ *are positive constants and* $\alpha+\beta+\gamma = 1$. *The theory also claims that in the theory universe bus companies always choose to employ the combination of* x_1, x_2, *and* x_3 *that will minimize their cost of producing the prescribed value of* y. *We have observations on* y *and the* x_i *that pertain to many bus companies. Let* y^o, x_1^o, x_2^o, *and* x_3^o *be the observational counterpart of some quadruple,* y, x_1, x_2, *and* x_3. *The two sets of variables are related as follows:*

$$y = y^o. \tag{9}$$

Also, for some pair $(V_1, V_2) \in R^2$,

$$\left(x_1^o/x_2^o\right) = (x_1/x_2)e^{V_1}, \tag{10}$$

and

$$\left(x_3^o/x_2^o\right) = (x_3/x_2)e^{V_2}. \tag{11}$$

Finally, there is a $U \in R_+$ *such that*

$$y^a e^{by} = A\left(x_1^o\right)^\alpha \left(x_2^o\right)^\beta \left(x_3^o\right)^\gamma e^{-U}. \tag{12}$$

Here (9) expresses the idea that the bus company in question supplies whatever number of bus kilometers that the commerce department prescribes. Hence our observation on y is accurate. Equations (10) and (11) insist that the bus company's production is *allocatively* inefficient because it uses nonoptimal combinations of the factors of production. Equation (12) suggests that the bus company's production is also *technically* inefficient because it uses more of the factors of production than necessary.

12.2.3 Capital

Finally "capital": To those economic theorists who have managed to steer clear of the capital controversies of the past, capital is a universal term. Even less fortunate theorists treat capital as a term that needs no definition. J. R. Hicks (1953), for example, wrote a whole book, entitled *Value and Capital*, without ever caring to define capital. Similarly, J. M. Keynes (1936) in *The General Theory of Employment, Interest and Money* discusses the marginal efficiency of capital at length without providing a definition of capital. Whether one can justify such a cavalier attitude toward the term is doubtful. Two definitions that leading theorists have proposed attest to that. "A *person's capital* consists of the external goods that he uses in his trade, either holding them to be sold for money or applying them to produce things that are to be sold for money" (Marshall, 1953, p. 72). *Capital is* one of the three primary factors of production, the other two being labor and land, and as such is not a quantity in the ordinary sense of the term, but rather "an assemblage of physical goods—factories, machines, lubricants, raw materials and the like" (Schumpeter, 1976, pp. 899–900).

Econometricians cannot treat capital as a universal term. In a theory-data confrontation in which the term appears, the econometrician must use his data to define an aggregate that can play the role of capital. The aggregate he chooses depends on the theory as well as the data and on the purpose of the empirical analysis and the econometrician's comprehension of the theory and the data-generating process. For example, John Kendrick (1961) in his book *Productivity Trends in the United States* takes a macro economy's output to be a function of two factors of production: labor and capital. He identifies capital with a sum whose components are the real value of the economy's net foreign assets and monetary gold and silver and the real value of the economy's various physical assets. The latter comprise the real value of the economy's farm, forest, and park land, of its residential and nonresidential structures, and of its equipment and inventories. Here the real value of an asset is synonymous with the asset's dollar value in 1929 U.S. dollars (Kendrick, 1961, pp. 322–325).

Whatever they are, the designations of Hick's and Keynes's capital live and function in various theory universes. The aggregates that Kendrick and others use to measure capital in their studies live and function in various data universes. In order that the empirical analysis in a given theory-data confrontation make sense, the researcher in question must relate the capital in the data universe to the capital in the theory universe. The bridge principles that delineate this relation are not unique. For a given theory, they vary both with the data and the researcher in charge of the empirical analysis. The following is an example to fix these ideas.

E 12.4 *Consider a theory-data confrontation in which one studies the dynamics of production in U.S. manufacturing industries, and let* C *and* K *denote, respectively, capital in the theory and data universe. Also let* Y *denote output in the theory universe and assume that there is a constant* a *such that* $\mathrm{C} = \mathrm{aY}$. *Finally, assume that the demand for* Y *in the theory universe varies over time in accordance with a random process* $[\mathrm{y(t)} : \mathrm{t} \in \{0, 1, \ldots\}]$ *that satisfies the relation*

$$y(t) = \max\{0, z(t) - bz(t-1)\},$$

where b *is a positive constant and* $[\mathrm{z(t)} : \mathrm{t} \in \{0, 1, \ldots\}]$ *is a purely random process.*[6] *The value that* C *assumes in a given period* t *can be interpreted to represent an industry's optimal level of capital in that period. The value of the corresponding* K(t) *need not equal* C(t), *one of the reasons for that being that it is costly to adjust the level of* K. *I assume that it is expensive both to employ a nonoptimal level of capital and to adjust the level of capital. In period* t *these costs equal*

$$[K(t) - C(t)]^2 + c[K(t) - K(t-1)]^2.$$

I also assume that the particular U.S. industry's "producer" has an overly long planning horizon within which he chooses the values of the K(t) *so as to minimize the expected value of the sum,*

$$\sum_{t\leq s<\infty} (1+r)^{-(s-t)} \left\{[K(s)-C(s)]^2 + c[K(s)-K(s-1)]^2\right\},$$

where r *is an appropriate discount factor. Then we can use theorem T 32.12 and E 32.13 in Stigum (1990) to justify the following relation between* C *and* K*:*

$$dC(t) - eC(t-1) = K(t) - \alpha K(t-1) + \beta K(t-2),\ t \in \{2, 3, \ldots\}, \qquad (13)$$

where d, e, α, *and* β *are positive constants.*

12.2.4 Economic Aggregates and Theoretical Constructs

The preceding discussion shows that in economics universal terms need not have obvious definitions in terms of observables. As that is so, one should not expect variables in a theory universe to have obvious counterparts in the particular data universe. All the variables in the theory universe are theoretical terms. Some of them, however, are more theoretical than others. One is likely to find interesting bridge principles that relate income and capital to variables in the data universe and less likely to discover observable counterparts of utility and entrepreneurship. To distinguish the latter from the former I refer to the last two terms as *theoretical constructs.*

Utility functions in economic theory are theoretical constructs. Even so, there are situations in which econometricians may be able to construct these functions out of observables. Certainly, in properly structured laboratory tests of the expected utility hypothesis they might be able to construct a subject's utility function. Vide, for example, E 3.1 and the discussion of such tests in Chapter 17. Moreover, whenever the functions belong to well-defined parametric families of such functions, the data might allow an econometrician to estimate the values of the parameters and use the estimates to construct the relevant functions. To see how, let $x \in R^n_{++}$ be a commodity vector and assume that the utility function of a given sample population's representative consumer satisfies the equation

$$\log U(x) = \sum_{i=1}^{n} \beta_i \log(x_i - \gamma_i),$$

where $x_i > \gamma_i, \gamma_i \geq 0, \beta_i > 0$, and $\sum_{i=1}^{n} \beta_i = 1$. The demand function of this representative consumer is given by

$$f_i(p, A) = \left(\beta_i / \sum_{j=1}^{n} \beta_j\right)\left[\left(A - \sum_{j=1}^{n} p_j\gamma_j\right)/p_i\right]$$
$$+\gamma_i,\ p \in R^n_{++},\ A > \sum_{j=1}^{n} p_j\gamma_j,\ i = 1, \ldots, n \qquad (14)$$

With appropriate data an econometrician can estimate the parameters in (14) and construct the representative consumer's utility function out of observables.

In situations in which an econometrician cannot construct a utility function out of observables, there is still a chance that his data might enable him to determine interesting characteristics of the particular function. I next recount two successful searches for such characteristics. One interesting aspect of these stories is the role that economic theory plays in ensuring the successful results.

12.2.4.1 The CISH Experiment Revisited

Recall that the CISH experiment was conceived to test the theory of consumer choice in a token economy on a ward for chronic psychotics at Central Islip State Hospital in New York (CISH). A token economy, again, is an organized system in which individuals live for extended periods of time. The individuals receive tokens for work performed and use them to buy consumer goods.

Texas A&M University researchers thought that the CISH token economy would provide an ideal setting for a test of the empirical relevance of Houthakker's revealed-preference axiom. In their test they identified a commodity with an item that the patients could buy with tokens and measured such commodities by the number of units of the respective items that the patients purchased during a week. Also, for convenience in administering price changes and studying demand behavior, they divided the pertinent commodities into three groups and constructed three aggregates, X_1, X_2, and X_3, the units of which they measured in terms of the preexperiment token values of the aggregates. Finally, they arranged for appropriate changes in the prices of the given aggregates and carried out a test of Houthakker's axiom with the records of thirty-eight patients' purchases over a period of 7 consecutive weeks.

The validity of the test design the researchers derived from Hicks' (1953, pp. 312–313) and Leontief's (1936, pp. 53–59) aggregation theorem. In the framework of (T_0, M_0) illustrated earlier in Fig. 5.2, this theorem insists on the validity of the following assertion concerning a demand-function construct $F(\cdot)$:

T 1 *(Hicks-Leontief) Suppose that* $\mathrm{p}^0 \in \mathrm{R}^n_{++}$ *and that* $\mathrm{p}^0 = (\mathrm{p}^0_1, \ldots, \mathrm{p}^0_k)$, *where* $\mathrm{p}^0_i \in \mathrm{R}^{n_i}_{++}, \mathrm{i} = 1, \ldots, \mathrm{k}$, *and* $\sum_{1 \le i \le k} \mathrm{n_i} = \mathrm{n}$. *Also, let* $\mathrm{f}(\cdot) = [\mathrm{f}_1(\cdot), \ldots, \mathrm{f}_k(\cdot)]$, *with* $\mathrm{f_i}(\cdot) : \mathrm{R}^n_{++} \times \mathrm{R}_+ \to \mathrm{R}^{n_i}_+, \mathrm{i} = 1, \ldots, \mathrm{k}$, *be the demand function of a consumer in* $(\mathrm{T}_0, \mathrm{M}_0)$. *Finally, define the function* $\mathrm{F}(\cdot) : \mathrm{R}^k_{++} \times \mathrm{R}_+ \to \mathrm{R}^k_+$ *by*

$$F(\cdot) = [F_1(\cdot), \ldots, F_k(\cdot)]$$

$$\text{and } F_i(\lambda, A) = \sum_{1 \le j \le n_i} p^0_{ij} f_{ij}\left(\lambda_1 p^0_1, \ldots, \lambda_k p^0_k, A\right), i = 1, \ldots, k,$$

where p^0_{ij} *and* $\mathrm{f_{ij}}(\cdot)$, *respectively, are the* jth *component of* p^0_i *and* $\mathrm{f_i}(\cdot)$, $\lambda_i \in \mathrm{R}_{++}, \mathrm{i} = 1, \ldots, \mathrm{k}$, *and* $\mathrm{A} \in \mathrm{R}_+$. *Then* $\mathrm{F}(\cdot)$ *is the demand function of a consumer in* $(\mathrm{T}_0, \mathrm{M}_0)$ *with* $\mathrm{n} = \mathrm{k}$.

In the CISH test, p^0 was represented by the preexperiment token prices of the commodities, $k = 3, n_1 = 4, n_2 = 7, n_3 = 5$, and the λ_i assumed the values 1, 1/2, and 2. A statement and proof of the Hicks-Leontief aggregation theorem can be found in Stigum (1990, theorem T 10.17, pp. 191–193).

The researchers' analysis of their data proceeded in two steps. Initially, they assumed that they had accurate observations on the variables in the theory universe. With only identities as bridge principles, the results of the experiment showed that the purchases of nineteen of the thirty-eight subjects satisfied Houthakker's axiom. The researchers then made allowance for possible errors of observations on the choices of the remaining nineteen subjects and showed that the latter subjects' purchases, then, also satisfied Houthakker's axiom. From this and from theorem T 1 in Chapter 10 I may venture that, as functions of the three aggregates, the utility functions of the participants in the CISH experiment were nonsatiated and concave.

12.2.4.2 *Absolute and Proportional Risk Aversion in Risky Situations*

Next I consider a case in which I use theory, bridge principles, and observations to obtain information about the structural properties of a theoretical construct. The theory I have in mind is Kenneth Arrow (1965) and John Pratt's (1964) theory of choice among safe and risky assets. This is the kind of theory that econometricians dream of but rarely find. It gives conditions on consumer *behavior* that are necessary and sufficient to ensure that a consumer's *utility function* has specific and interesting characteristics. Moreover, on the surface of things, the conditions seem to be easy to test.

Arrow and Pratt's theory is about choice between one safe asset and one risky asset. Without specific assumptions about the structure of the decision-maker's utility function, the theory does not generalize to one about choice among one safe asset and several risky assets or between one safe asset and an aggregate of risky assets. In E 12.5 the axioms pertain to a decision-maker whose utility function possesses David Cass and Joseph Stiglitz's (1970) separation property.[7] Arrow and Pratt's theory can be used to depict characteristic features of the choices that such consumers make between an aggregate of safe assets and an aggregate of risky assets.

E 12.5 *In this example I sketch the deterministic part of a system of axioms for a test of Arrow and Pratt's theory of choice among safe and risky assets. I begin with the theory universe:*

AP 1 $\omega_T \in \Omega_T$ *only if* $\omega_T = (a, \mu, m, A, \xi, \delta)$, *where* $a \in R_{++}$, $(\mu, m) \in R_+^2$, $A \in R_+$, $\xi \in R$, *and* $\delta \in R$.

AP 2 *There exists a function* $h(\cdot) : R_{++} \times R_+ \to R_+$, *such that for all* $\omega_T \in \Omega_T$, $\mu + am = A$ *and* $m = h(a, A)$.

AP 3 *There exists a constant* $c \in (-\infty, 0)$, *two sets,* $D \subset R_{++}$ *and* $E \subset (-c, \infty)$, *and two functions,* $\varphi(\cdot) : D \to (-\infty, 0)$ *and* $\Psi(\cdot) : E \to R_{++}$ *such* *that for all* $\omega_T \in \Omega_T$, $a \in D$, $A \in E$, $c\psi(a) = \varphi(a)$, $h(a, A) = \varphi(a) + \psi(a)A$, *and* $0 < ah(a, A) < A$.

In the intended interpretation of the axioms, μ *and* m, *respectively, designate so many units of a safe asset and a risky asset. Also,* a *denotes the price of* m, A *stands for net worth, and* ξ *is an error term. Finally, the price of* μ *equals one, and the domain of* A *is taken to be* $[-c, \infty)$.

I have observations on an aggregate of safe assets μ^*, *on an aggregate of risky assets* m^*, *and on the net worth* A^* *of a sample of 1962 U.S. consumers. The data universe has two axioms:*

AP 4 $\omega_P \in \Omega_P$ *only if* $\omega_P = (\mu^*, m^*, A^*)$ *and* $(\mu^*, m^*, A^*) \in R^3_+$.

AP 5 *For all* $\omega_P \in \Omega_P$, $\mu^* + m^* = A^*$.

In the intended interpretation of the axioms μ^* *and* m^* *measure, respectively, the total value of a consumer's investments in safe and risky assets.*

The relation between the variables in the two universes can be formulated as follows:

AP 6 *For all* $(\omega_T, \omega_P) \in \Omega$, $m^* = am + \xi$, $A^* = A + \delta$, $a = a^*$, *where* a^* *is a member of* D *and* $\delta \in R$.

In reading this axiom, note that $m = h(a, A)$ *and that* $h(a, A) = h(a, A^* - \delta)$. *Hence, the axiom insists that* $m^* = a^*h(a^*, A^* - \delta) + \xi$.

From axioms AP 1–AP 6 I deduce that

$$m^* = a^*\varphi(a^*) + a^*\psi(a^*)A^* + (\xi - a^*\psi(a^*)\delta).$$

This equation, appropriate assumptions concerning $P(\cdot)$, *the probability measure of subsets of* Ω, *and the sampling scheme provide a way to test the empirical relevance of Arrow and Pratt's theory. In the version of the theory that is at stake here, both the absolute and the relative risk-aversion function are decreasing functions of net worth.*

It is interesting that the pertinent absolute and relative risk-aversion functions are also decreasing functions of c. *I used this property of the risk-aversion functions in Stigum (1990) to study how absolute and relative risk aversion varied over subgroups of the 1962 U.S. population. My results suggest, among other things, that both absolute and relative risk aversion increase with age and are higher among the self-employed than among those who work for others.*

Chapters 12 and 28 in Stigum (1990) include further details concerning Arrow and Pratt's theory and its empirical relevance.

12.3 THE TECHNICAL AND ALLOCATIVE EFFICIENCIES OF AN INDUSTRY

The time has come to give an example of how bridge principles function in a formal theory-data confrontation. The example I have in mind uses the ideas of E 12.3 to provide a set of bridge principles and a data universe for the theory universe that I formulated in Section 10.2. In this example of a formal theory-data confrontation the undefined terms are the *sample population* S; the *sample space* $(\Omega, \aleph)$, the *sampling distribution* $P(\cdot)$; and the *sample design* $(\omega_T, \omega_P, \Psi)$. These terms satisfy the following axioms:

GTU 1 *Let #S denote the number of elements in* S. *Then #S is finite or countably infinite.*

GTU 2 *There is a set* Ω_T *of ordered ten-tuples* ω_T *and a set* Ω_P *of ordered eleven-tuples* ω_P *such that* $\Omega \subset \Omega_T \times \Omega_P$. *Moreover,* $\aleph$ *is a σ-field of subsets of* Ω.

GTU 3 $P(\cdot)$ *is a probability measure on* $(\Omega, \aleph)$.

GTU 4 $\Psi(\cdot) : S \to \Omega$ *is a function.*

In my interpretation of the axioms, S is a population of actual and hypothetical bus transportation companies in Norway in 1991. The actual bus companies are those on which I have data and the other bus companies in Norway. The hypothetical bus companies are those that the actual companies could have been if the conditions under which they operated had been different.

The theory universe is a pair (Ω_T, Γ_t), where Ω_T is the Ω_T of GTU 2 and Γ_t is a family of axioms that consists of the axioms that I called NB 1–NB 3 in Section 10.2 and restate here as GTU 5–GTU 7.

GTU 5 $\omega_T \in \Omega_T$ *only if* $\omega_T = (y, x, w, U, V)$, *where* $y \in R_{++}$, $x \in R^3_{++}$, $w \in R^3_{++}$, $U \in R_+$, *and* $V \in R^2$.

GTU 6 *There exist positive constants* b, d, Λ, α, β, γ *such that* $\alpha+\beta+\gamma = 1$, *and that for all* $\omega_T \in \Omega_T$, $y^b e^{dy} = \Lambda x_1^\alpha x_2^\beta x_3^\gamma$.

GTU 7 *For all* $\omega_T \in \Omega_T$, $\alpha x_2/\beta x_1 = w_1/w_2$ *and* $\gamma x_2/\beta x_3 = w_3/w_2$.

In these axioms, y, x, and w are, respectively, the output of a firm, the inputs it uses, and the costs of these inputs. Also, U and the components of V are error terms. I presume that the firms in S have no choice as to the proper value of y. The fixity of y is reflected in the conditions in GTU 6 and GTU 7. These conditions are necessary and sufficient for x to be the cost-minimizing input for y.

The data universe is a pair, (Ω_P, Γ_p), that forms part of a triple $[(\Omega_P, \Gamma_p), \aleph_p, P_p(\cdot)]$, where Ω_P is the Ω_P of GTU 2, Γ_p is the pair of axioms GTU 11 and GTU 12, and $\aleph_p$ and $P_p(\cdot)$ satisfy GTU 13.

GTU 11 $\omega_P \in \Omega_P$ *only if* $\omega_P = (y^*, x^*, w^*, c^*, g^*)$, *where* $y^* \in R_{++}$, $x^* \in R^3_{++}$, $w^* \in R^3_{++}$, $c^* \in R^3_{++}$, *and* $g^* \in \{1, 2, \ldots, 19\}$.

GTU 12 *For all* $\omega_P \in \Omega_P$, $w_i^* = c_i^*/x_i^*$, $i = 1, 2, 3$.

GTU 13 $\aleph_p$ *is a σ-field of subsets of* Ω_P, *and* $P_p(\cdot) : \aleph_p \to [0, 1]$ *is a probability measure.*

In the intended interpretation of these axioms, y^*, x^*, and c^* are observations on y, x, and c, and w^* designates a datum on w that I have created. Also, g^* is an integer that I use to denote a *fylke* (county) in Norway. Finally, the *true* joint probability distribution of the components of ω_P in this example *FP* is the probability distribution of the components of ω_P that, subject to the conditions on which GTU 11 and GTU 12 insist, is generated by $P_p(\cdot)$.

The bridge principles for the present analysis are formalizations of the bridge principles that I delineated in E 12.3.

GTU 8 *For all* $(\omega_T, \omega_P) \in \Omega$, $y = y^*$ *and* $w = w^*$.

GTU 9 *For all* $(\omega_T, \omega_P) \in \Omega$, $y^a e^{by} = \Lambda x_1^{*\alpha} x_2^{*\beta} x_3^{*\gamma} e^{-U}$.

GTU 10 *For all* $(\omega_T, \omega_P) \in \Omega$, $(x_2^*/x_1^*) = (x_2/x_1)e^{V_1}$, *and* $(x_2^*/x_3^*) = (x_2/x_3)e^{V_2}$.

In the intended interpretation of the axioms, these bridge principles insist that I have accurate observations on w and that the firms in the data universe produce the y they are asked to produce. They also insist that the firms' production of output, for nonzero values of U and V is inefficient in two different ways. According to GTU 9 their production of y is technically inefficient because they use more inputs than necessary. According to GTU 10, their production of y is also allocatively inefficient because they use the wrong combination of inputs.

Finally, I formulate the $P(\cdot)$ axioms and the two axioms that characterize the sampling scheme by which my observations on the Norwegian bus companies were obtained:

GTU 14 *Let* $I_i = \{(\omega_T, \omega_P) \in \Omega : g^* = i\}$. *Then* $I_i \in \aleph$ *and* $P(I_i) > 0$ *for all* $i = 1, 2, \ldots, 19$.

GTU 15 *Let* $P(\cdot|I_i)$ *denote the conditional probability measure on* $(\Omega, \aleph)$ *given* I_i. *Then, relative to* $P(\cdot|I_i), i = 1, \ldots, 19$, V_1 *and* V_2 *have mean zero and finite variance,* U *has finite mean and variance, and* V_1, V_2, *and* U *are distributed independently of each other and orthogonal to* $\log y$ *and* $\log w$.

GTU 16 *Relative to* $P(\cdot|I_i), i = 1, \ldots, 19$, y *and the components of* x *and* w *have finite positive means and finite variances. The respective logarithms have finite means and variances.*

GTU 17 *There are* N *observations with* n_i *observations from* $I_i, i = 1, \ldots, 19$. *The probability distribution of the sample is given by* $\Pi_{1 \le i \le 19} P(\cdot|I_i)^{n_i}$.

GTU 18 *For each* N, *let* $n_i(N)$ *denote the number of observations in* $I_i, i = 1, \ldots, 19$. *The sampling scheme is designed in accordance with*

$$\lim_{N\to\infty} [n_i(N)/N] = P(I_i), i = 1, \ldots, 19. \tag{15}$$

The $P(\cdot)$ axioms speak for themselves. Here I need only observe that GTU 17 insists that the sampling scheme is stratified and random. In the intended interpretation of the axioms, I imagine that S has been divided into nineteen regions, $S_i = \Psi^{-1}(I_i)$, so that there is one region for each *fylke* in Norway. I also imagine that I have n_i observations from $S_i, i = 1, \ldots, 19$, and that each set of n_i observations has been obtained in accordance with a random-sampling scheme. With this interpretation of GTU 17, GTU 17 and GTU 18 insist that the sampling scheme is adequate.

There are two probability distributions of the components of ω_P that I must take account of in my empirical analysis: (1) the true distribution *FP*, and (2) the *MPD* whose properties I deduce from the axioms of $P(\cdot)$ and the bridge principles. The axioms of $P(\cdot)$ concern the means and covariances of the components of ω_T. From them, GTU 5–GTU 7, and GTU 8–GTU 10, I can derive two theorems, T 2 and T 3, that impose severe restrictions on the mean and covariance structure of the parameters of *MPD*.

T 2 *There exist a vector of constants* $\mathrm{K} \in \mathrm{R}^3$ *and a vector of error terms* $\mathrm{U}^* \in \mathrm{R}^3$ *such that for all* $(\omega_\mathrm{T}, \omega_\mathrm{P}) \in \Omega$ *and for* $\mathrm{i} = 1, 2, 3$,

$$\log c_i^* = K_i + a \log y^* + by^* + \alpha \log w_1^* + \beta \log w_2^* + \gamma \log w_3^* + U_i^*,$$

where $\mathrm{U}_1^* = \mathrm{U} - (\beta + \gamma)\mathrm{V}_1 + \gamma \mathrm{V}_2$, $\mathrm{U}_2^* = \mathrm{U} + \alpha \mathrm{V}_1 + \gamma \mathrm{V}_2$, *and* $\mathrm{U}_3^* = \mathrm{U} + \alpha \mathrm{V}_1 - (\alpha + \beta)\mathrm{V}_2$.

T 3 *For all* $(\omega_\mathrm{T}, \omega_\mathrm{P}) \in \Omega$, $\mathrm{V}_1 = \log(\alpha/\beta) + \log(\mathrm{c}_2^*/\mathrm{c}_1^*)$, *and* $\mathrm{V}_2 = \log(\gamma/\beta) + \log(\mathrm{c}_2^*/\mathrm{c}_1^*)$.

In the vernacular of modal logic, I am convinced that there are worlds in which my bridge principles are valid, but I cannot be sure that the Real World is one of them. Consequently, I cannot be sure that T 2 and T 3 are valid in the Real World. On the other hand, if my sampling scheme satisfies the conditions that I delineate in GTU 17 and GTU 18, I can obtain consistent estimates of the parameters in T 2 and T 3, perform appropriate diagnostic checks, and ascertain whether the estimated parameters are parameters of a data-admissible model of the *MPD*. If the estimates are such parameters, I can describe a family of models of the *MPD* that with high probability contains a model with values of $a, b, \alpha, \beta, \gamma$ and the means and variances of V_1, V_2, and U that it shares with *FP*. That is all I need to justify the two claims I make later. If my estimates of the parameters of the *MPD* are not data admissible, a diagnosis of my axioms is called for. One or more of them might not be valid in the Real World. For example, the bridge principles may fail to account for errors in the measurements of y and w. Moreover, the assumption that V_1 and V_2 are independently distributed may be false. There are many possibilities.

Suppose that the estimates of the parameters in T 2 are parameters in a data-admissible model of *MPD*. Then the meaning of T 2 and T 3 needs no further comment. However, there are two important observations: (1) The bridge principles allow me to decompose the error terms in T 2 and interpret estimates of the coefficients in the equations for $\log c_i^*$. In fact, estimates of the parameters in T 2 provide a consistent estimate of the relevant industry's production function. The production function of a firm, like the utility function of a consumer, is a theoretical construct in economic theory.[8] It is, therefore, interesting in this context that estimates of the parameters in T 2 and the bridge principles in GTU 8–GTU 10 allow me to write the production function as a function of observables. (2) With the help of the bridge principles and T 3 and T 2, I can estimate the allocative inefficiencies in each and every firm in the sample. Also, the bridge principles, T 2, T 3, and theorem T 4 below enable me to estimate the mean technical and allocative inefficiency in the sample. The latter I take to equal the mean value of the ratio $C(w, y^*, e^U)/w^*x^*$ as it varies over the firms in the sample.

T 4 *Let* $\mathrm{C(w, y, e^U)}$ *equal* $\mathrm{e^U}$ *times the minimum cost at* w *of producing* y. *Then, for all* $(\omega_T, \omega_P) \in \Omega$,

$$C\left(w, y, e^U\right) = wxe^U = e^{-\alpha V_1 - \gamma V_2}\left(w_1^* x_1^* e^{V_1} + w_2^* x_2^* + w_3^* x_3^* e^{V_2}\right).$$

Harald Dale-Olsen (1994) and Harald Goldstein (Chapter 14, this volume) have, with different methods, carried out analyses of the data admissibility of the intended family of models of *MPD*. In his analysis Dale-Olsen assumes that the V's are normally distributed and that there exists a normally distributed variable Z such that relative to $P(\cdot|I_i)$, $i = 1, \ldots, 19$, the distribution of U equals the conditional probability distribution of Z given that $Z \geq 0$. He ends up judging his estimate of a model of the *MPD* data admissible. Goldstein considers two possible distributions of U and makes no additional assumption about the probability distribution of the V's. He ends up being uncertain about the data admissibility of his estimate of a model of the *MPD*. For reference one can consult Dale-Olsen (1994), Stigum (1995), and Goldstein's extraordinary diagnostic analysis in Chapter 14.

12.4 BRIDGE PRINCIPLES AND DATA ANALYSES

In cases where the variables in the data universe are taken *to be random* I always assume that there is a probability measure, $P(\cdot) : \aleph \rightarrow [0, 1]$, on subsets of the sample space. Relative to $P(\cdot)$, the variables in the theory universe and those in the data universe are jointly distributed random variables. Hence, the econometrician can specify properties of the probability distribution of the theoretical variables and use them and his bridge principles to derive salient characteristics of the marginal probability distribution of his data—the *MPD*. If he proceeds in that way, he can test the empirical relevance of his theory by checking whether the theory, when translated by his bridge principles, makes statistically valid predictions about characteristics of the data.

An econometrician can also delineate properties of the DGP from scratch and then use them and his bridge principles to deduce salient characteristics of the probability distribution of the theoretical variables—the TGP.[9] If he proceeds in that way, he can test the empirical relevance of his theory by checking whether the properties of the TGP are in accord with the prescriptions of his theory.

It must not go unnoticed here that in the first case all tests concerning the empirical relevance of the theory are carried out in the data universe, whereas in the second they are carried out in the theory universe—the universe of the theoretical variables. Whether the econometrician has a choice of universe in which to carry out his tests depends on the way he chooses to formulate his bridge principles. Since this is an important point, I give several simple examples to illustrate what I have in mind.

E 12.6 *Consider the five-tuple of real-valued random variables* (y, u, c, x, z) *and assume that the first three components reside in the theory universe and that the last two roam around in the data universe. Suppose also that, according to theory, TH is valid.*

TH *There is a finite, positive constant* k *such that* $c = ky$.

Finally, assume that the variables in the two universes are related as follows:

B 1 $y + u = x$

and

B 2 $c = z$.

I consider three different cases for the analysis: I, II, and III. In each case I assume, without saying, that a demon has produced N *independent draws of the values of* y, u, c, x, *and* z, *and that he has only revealed the* N *values of the pair* (x, z).

Case I. In this case I impose conditions on the probability distribution of the theoretical variables and use these conditions and the bridge principles B 1 and B 2 to deduce restrictions on the marginal probability distribution of the pair (x, z)*; that is, the* MPD. *Specifically, I assume the validity of the following:*

A *The means and variances of* y, u, *and* c *are finite and satisfy the conditions* $Ey > 0, Eu = 0, Ec > 0, \rho_{yu} = 0, \sigma_y^2 > 0, \sigma_u^2 > 0,$ *and* $\sigma_c^2 > 0$.

From these conditions and the bridge principles I can deduce the validity of TI 1.

TI 1 *If A, B 1, and B 2 are valid, then the means and variances of* x *and* z *are finite and positive.*

Thus the only restrictions that A, B 1, and B 2 impose on a data-admissible model of MPD *are: (1) that the estimated mean and covariance structure of the distribution of x and z satisfies TI 1; and (2) that its own mean and covariance structure lies within a 95 percent confidence band of the estimates of the given parameters.*

The theory that I formulated in TH and the bridge principles impose further restrictions on the distribution of x *and* z *that a family of data-admissible models of the* MPD *might not satisfy. These are as follows:*

TI 2 *If TH, A, B 1, and B 2 are valid, then it must be the case that* $z/k = y$, $x - z/k = u$, $Ez/Ex = k$, $\sigma_z^2/k^2 = \sigma_y^2$ *and* $\sigma_x^2 - \sigma_z^2/k^2 = \sigma_u^2$.

The interesting part of TI 2 is that the conclusion holds only if the covariance of x *and* z *satisfies*

HI $\rho_{xz} = \sigma_z^2/k$.

Checking whether there is a data-admissible model of MPD *that satisfies HI with* $k = Ez/Ex$, *provides me with* a test of TH and A in the data universe.

Case II. In this case I start by deriving a distribution of x *and* z *that generates a particular congruent model of my data without making any assumptions about the distribution of* y, u, *and* c. *With this distribution and the bridge principles in hand I can establish the following theorems:*

TII 1 *Let* CGDII *be the distribution of* (x, z) *that in case II generates the particular congruent model of my data and assume that B 1 and B 2 are the bridge principles that relate the components of* (y, u, c) *to* (x, z). *Then the following equations must be valid:* $Ey + Eu = Ex$, $Ec = Ez$, $\sigma_y^2 + 2\rho_{yu} + \sigma_u^2 = \sigma_x^2$, *and* $\sigma_c^2 = \sigma_z^2$.

TII 2 *If TH, B1, and B2 are valid and if* (x, z) *is distributed in accordance with* CGDII, *then the following equations must hold:* $y = z/k$, $u = x - z/k$, $Ey = Ez/k$, $Eu = Ex - Ez/k$, $\sigma_y^2 = \sigma_z^2/k^2$, $\rho_{yu} = \rho_{xz}/k - \sigma_z^2/k^2$, *and* $\sigma_u^2 = \sigma_x^2 - 2\rho_{xz}/k + \sigma_z^2/k^2$.

TII.1 and TII.2 demonstrate that in this case, I cannot construct a test of TH in the theory universe *without making appropriate assumptions about the distribution of* (y, u, c).

Case III. Here I proceed the same way as in case II and let CGDII *be as described there. To obtain a test of TH in the theory universe I must add a condition on the distribution of* (y, u, c), *that is:*

TIII.1 *Suppose that TH, B 1, and B 2, are valid. Suppose also that* $Eu = 0$ *and that* $\rho_{yu} = 0$. *If* (x, z) *is distributed in accordance with* CGDII, *then the conclusion of TII 2 is valid. In addition, it must be the case that the following equation is valid as well:*

$$H^* : k\sigma_y^2 = \rho_{xz} \text{ with } k = Ez/Ex.$$

Then H* *provides a test of TH,* $Eu = 0$ *and* $\rho_{yu} = 0$ *in the theory universe.*

There is one aspect of the preceding example that is special. In discussing the three cases I implicitly assume that I am engaged in an analysis of *N* independently and identically distributed observations on the pair (x, z). That allows me to couch the discussion in terms of properties of the distribution of (y, u, c, x, z) instead of the distribution of the demon's N independent draws of the given five-tuple of random variables. Except for the simplicity in presentation, the ideas that the example illustrates also generalize to analyses of panel and time-series data.

I consider that this section on bridge principles and data analyses constitutes an exciting end to a long discussion of theory-data confrontations in economics. I have discussed characteristic features of two universes and the bridge that connects them. Traditionally, in philosophy as well as in economics, researchers have learned that the bridge is to be traversed from the theory universe to the data universe. This section makes the important point that the bridge can be traversed equally well from the data universe to the theory universe. In doing that it throws new light on the import of exploratory data analysis and suggests new ways for theorists and econometricians to cooperate in their pursuit of economic knowledge.

12.5 CONCLUDING REMARKS

This chapter is concerned with correspondence rules and bridge principles. In looking back at my deliberations, it is important to keep in mind that the sample space in a formalization of a theory-data confrontation is an undefined term whose properties are described in the pertinent bridge principles $\Gamma_{t,p}$. The members of $\Gamma_{t,p}$ rarely provide a complete characterization of Ω. Hence, if the axioms are consistent, there are all sorts of models of Ω. This is so even when $\Gamma_{t,p}$ contains identities only; that is, even if the researcher believes that he has accurate observations on the relevant theoretical variables. One can gain some idea of the range of possible models of Ω by looking at the examples I gave in Section 12.2. In E 12.2 the range of models of Ω varies with the probability distribution of η in Eq.(6) and with α and the probability distributions of the ζ process in Eq. (7). In E 12.3 the models of Ω vary with the constants in (8), with the value of y_0, and with the probability distributions of the V_i and U in (9)–(12). Finally, in E 12.4 the models of Ω vary with r and the constants in (13).

In looking back at the discussion of bridge principles it is also important to keep in mind that the status of the conditions on which the members of $\Gamma_{t,p}$ insist is very different from the status of the ones that Γ_T and Γ_P impose. Since the members of ω_T are theoretical objects, there is no need to question the validity of the members of Γ_t. One can treat them as if they were true by necessity. Similarly, provided a demon is not playing tricks, there is no need to question the validity of the components of Γ_P in the data universe. One can treat them as if they were true by necessity as well. It is quite a different story when one comes to the members of $\Gamma_{t,p}$. They reflect the ideas of the researcher and have no special claim to being valid. Consequently, if one deduces an assertion B concerning the vectors in the data universe from Γ_t and $\Gamma_{t,p}$, B has no more claim to being valid than the members of $\Gamma_{t,p}$. This aspect of theory-data confrontations is discussed at length in Chapter 20.

Finally, it is interesting to compare the status of correspondence rules in the Received View with the status of bridge principles in theory-data confrontations. In the Received View of a scientific theory, the theory is identified with TC. Hence, in the Received View, the correspondence rules C form an integral part of the theory in question. In contrast, the bridge principles in a theory-data confrontation vary with the researcher as well as with the data universe. They vary with the researcher because they reflect his, and not necessarily anybody else's, idea of how the variables in the theory universe are related to the variables in the data universe. Consequently, the bridge principles in a theory-data confrontation are anything but parts of the theory.

NOTES

1. For a discussion of conventionalism, logical positivism, and the origin of the Received View of scientific theories cfr. Suppe (1977, pp. 6–15).

2. In the first section of Chapter 20 there is a description of the essential characteristics of a first-order language with logical and nonlogical vocabulary. There one can find explanations of terms in the first section of this chapter that may be unfamiliar.

3. Here A is a wff with two free variables, x and y. Also, $A_{x,y}(z, u)$ is the wff that results when I substitute z for x and u for y at all free occurrences of x and y in A.

4. Here B is a wff with one free variable x. Also, $B_x(z)$ is the wff that results when I substitute z for x at all free occurrences of x in B.

5. For a discussion of the development of the Received View of scientific theories cfr. Suppe (1977, pp. 16–36).

6. Here, a random process $X = \{x(t); t = 0, 1, \ldots\}$ is purely random if and only if the $x(t)$ are identically and independently distributed with finite mean and variance.

7. Here the condition I have in mind concerns the derivative of the consumer's utility function $U'(\cdot)$. Specifically, for appropriate values of the pertinent parameters, the derivative of the consumer's utility function must assume one or the other of two forms: $U'(A) = D(\alpha + \beta A)^{\gamma}$, $A \in R_+$, where D, α, β, and γ are constants, or $U'(A) = be^{dA}$, $A \in R_+$, where b and d are constants. In E 12.4 I have assumed implicitly that the utility function belongs to the first family of functions with positive D and β, and negative α and γ. Also, the range of A is $(-(\alpha/\beta), \infty)$.

8. There probably are economists who do not agree that the production function in economic theory is a theoretical construct. Half a century ago two of them might have been Hollis B. Chenery and Vernon L. Smith. Evidence for that is an engineering production function for gas transmission that Chenery (1949) constructed and two production functions that Smith (1961, ch. 2) delineated, one for the production and transmission of electrical energy and one for a firm that employs capital equipment subject to wear and breakdown.

9. The TGP is a true alias of the PDGP for the theory universe. It constitutes the probability distribution of the theoretical variables that the marginal distribution of the theoretical variables and the sampling scheme determine.

REFERENCES

Arrow, K. J., 1965, *Aspects of the Theory of Risk Bearing*, Helsinki: Academic Book Store.

Carnap, R., 1936, "Testability and Meaning," *Philosophy of Science* 3.

Cass, D., and J. E. Stiglitz, 1970, "The Structure of Investor Preferences and Asset Returns, and Separability in Portfolio Allocation: A Contribution to the Pure Theory of Mutual Funds," *Journal of Economic Theory* 2, 102–160.

Chenery, H. B., 1949, "Engineering Production Functions," *Quarterly Journal of Economics* 63, 507–531.

Dale-Olsen, H., 1994, Produksjon i Busstransportsektoren, Unpublished Hovedoppgave, Department of Economics, University of Oslo.

Friedman, M., 1957, *A Theory of the Consumption Function*, Princeton: Princeton University Press.

Hicks, J. R., 1953, *Value and Capital*, Oxford: Oxford University Press.

Kendrick, J. W., 1961, *Productivity Trends in the United States*, Princeton: Princeton University Press.

Keynes, J. M., 1936, *The General Theory of Employment, Interest and Money*, New York: Harcourt Brace.

Leontief, W. W., 1936, "Composite Commodities and the Problem of Index Numbers," *Econometrica* 4, 39–59.

Marshall, A., 1953, *Principles of Economics*, 8th Ed., New York: Macmillan.

Pratt, J. W., 1964, "Risk Aversion in the Small and in the Large," *Econometrica* 32, 122–136.

Schumpeter, J. H., 1976, *History of Economic Analysis*, New York: Oxford University Press.

Smith, V. L., 1961, *Investment and Production*, Cambridge: Harvard University Press.

Stigum, B. P., 1990, *Toward a Formal Science of Economics*, Cambridge: MIT Press.

Stigum, B. P., 1995, "Theory-Data Confrontations in Economics," *Dialogue* 34, 581–604.

Suppe, F., 1977, *The Structure of Scientific Theories*, Urbana: University of Illinois Press.

Van Frassen, B. C.,1980, *The Scientific Image*, Oxford: Oxford University Press.

PART IV
Data Analyses

Chapter Thirteen

Frequentist Analogues of Priors and Posteriors

Tore Schweder and Nils Lid Hjort

In econometrics there is a tendency to focus on new data in isolation. Other sources of information about the parameters of the model might enter the analysis in, for example, the format of structural assumptions in the model, possibly as restrictions on certain parameters, or as hypotheses to be tested. Coherent learning in the Bayesian sense of updating distributional knowledge of a parameter in the light of new data has no parallel in the non-Bayesian likelihood or frequentist tradition. However, the likelihood function is the preeminent tool for integrating diverse data, and provided the distributional information concerning a parameter has a likelihood representation, it could simply be integrated with the likelihood of the new independent data by multiplication.

In the purist likelihood tradition of Edwards (1992) and Royall (1997), the likelihood function itself is the primitive. In this tradition, the likelihood function of the interest parameter is reported and interpreted without recourse to confidence intervals, p-values, or the like. The parallel to Bayesian updating is thus straightforward. This process of updating a likelihood we term *likelihood updating*. When the current knowledge of a parameter is represented by a likelihood function, this likelihood is updated when combined with the likelihood of new data. The ratio between the updated and the previous likelihood represents the new information.

Most statisticians and econometricians probably still belong to the frequentist camp. Their favorite formats for statistical reporting are the confidence interval, the p-values for certain hypotheses of interest, or point estimates accompanied by measures of uncertainty such as the standard error. The likelihood function is, of course, a central concept in the frequentist tradition, but is used mainly as a tool to obtain efficient statistics with (asymptotic) frequentist interpretations. Unfortunately, the statistics reported by frequentist statisticians are seldom sufficient as input to likelihood updating. To achieve this sufficiency, the reported statistics have to be converted to a likelihood function.

We are concerned mainly with the reporting of frequentist statistics related to a scalar parameter and their conversion to a likelihood component. Some thoughts on integrative likelihood analysis in multiparameter models are also provided. As in many Bayesian situations, prior information is assumed to come in independent packages, one for each one-dimensional parameter. As the Bayesians, we also assume that the prior information comes in the format of a distribution. Instead of regarding the prior distribution as a probability distribution, we assume that the distribution represents confidence intervals by its quantiles. Such distributions are called confidence distributions and are studied in some detail in Section 13.1.

Fiducial probability distributions were introduced by Fisher (1930). In clear-cut cases, fiducial distributions are identical to confidence distributions. We follow Efron (1998) and others in preferring the latter term, emphasizing the close connection between confidence distributions and confidence intervals. Following Neyman (1941), the quantiles of the confidence distribution do, in fact, span confidence intervals. Through the bootstrap and also other work of Efron (1987, 1993, 1998), Fraser (1996, 1998), and others, there is renewed interest in confidence distributions. Schweder and Hjort (2002) present theory for confidence distributions and the related reduced likelihoods and provide more depth and further examples to what is presented here.

The well-known duality between hypothesis testing and confidence intervals emerges as a relationship between the p-value for a test and the cumulative confidence distribution function. In Section 13.2 a version of the Neyman–Pearson lemma is provided, explaining the frequentist optimality of the confidence distribution in one-parameter models with monotone likelihood ratios. This also leads to optimal constructions of confidence distributions in parametric families of the exponential kind, via conditioning on appropriate statistics. These confidence distributions become uniformly most powerful in a sense made precise in Section 13.2.

We hold that for parameters of primary interest the complete confidence distribution should be reported rather than only a pair of quantiles such as the endpoints of the 95 percent confidence interval. We argue in particular that reporting the confidence density for interest parameters, the derivative of the cumulative confidence distribution, is an effective way of summarizing results from statistical analyses of data regarding both presentation and inference. This post-data parameter density curve shares some of the features and appealing aspects of the Bayesian posterior, but is purely frequentistic and should also be noncontroversial conceptually.

It is desirable to develop methods for obtaining approximate confidence distributions in situations where exact constructions either become too intricate or do not exist. In Section 13.3 we discuss various approximations, the simplest of which are based on the traditional delta method for asymptotic normality. Better versions emerge via corrections of various sorts. In particular we develop an acceleration and bias corrected bootstrap percentile interval method for constructing improved confidence densities. It has an appealing form and is seen to perform well in terms of accuracy.

For large samples, the asymptotic normality of regular statistics allows the confidence distribution to be turned into a likelihood function through its normal scores. This likelihood, called the normal-based likelihood, agrees with the so-called implied likelihood of Efron (1993). However, if the information content in the data is of small to moderate weight, the normal-based likelihood might be misleading. An example is provided in Section 13.4 to show that a given confidence distribution might relate to many different likelihood functions, depending on the sampling situation behind the confidence distribution. For this reason it is advisable to supplement the reported confidence distribution with sufficient information concerning its probability basis to enable future readers to recover an acceptable likelihood function related to the confidence distribution.

Section 13.5 develops theory for confidence and likelihoods in models with exact or approximate pivots. An illustration is given for the problem of assessing the stock of bowhead whales outside Alaska in Section 13.6. Finally supplemental remarks and discussion are found in Section 13.7.

There is considerable current interest in building principles for and evaluating applications of combining different information sources in nontrivial situations. Application areas range from economics to assessments of whale stocks. Schweder and Hjort (1997) introduced likelihood synthesis to deal with problems encountered with earlier attempts at Bayesian synthesis and reviewed part of the literature. Recent articles on this theme include Berger et al. (1999) on eliminating nuisance parameters via integrated likelihoods as well as Poole and Raftery (1998) on "Bayesian melding" (see also comments in Sections 13.6 and 13.7). Some discussion of bootstrap likelihoods and likelihoods based on confidence sets can be found in Davison and Hinkley (1997, ch. 10). Schweder and Hjort (2002) take the material of the present chapter further, and discuss the extent to which the methodology can be seen as an integrated Fisher–Neyman approach, with Fisher (1930) as an important starting point.

Fisher's fiducial distribution has been controversial, partly because he insisted that the fiducial distributions are probability distributions in line with all other probability distributions. Fisher is regarded as the most important statistician since Laplace and Gauss. Hald (1998) actually characterizes Fisher's work as a paradigmatic revolution on par with that of Laplace (inverse probability) and Gauss and Laplace (least squares). The controversy around the fiducial distribution has caused some authors to call it "Fisher's biggest blunder" (see Efron, 1998). This is not the view of Efron, who interprets the fiducial distributions as distributions of confidence and not of probability. Efron (1998) wrote, "I believe that objective Bayes methods will develop for such problems, and that something like fiducial inference will play an important role in this development. Maybe Fisher's biggest blunder will become a big hit in the 21st century!"

13.1 CONFIDENCE DISTRIBUTIONS

Before relating confidence distributions to likelihoods, a closer look at the concept as a format for reporting statistical inference is worthwhile.

13.1.1 Confidence and Statistical Inference

In a selected and validated econometric model, statistical inference is, to a large extent, carried out as follows. From optimality or structural considerations, an estimator of the parameter of interest, and possibly of the remaining (nuisance) parameters in the model, is determined. Then, the sampling distribution of the estimator is calculated, possibly by bootstrapping. Finally, statements of inference, for example, confidence intervals, are extracted from the sampling distribution and its dependence on the parameter.

Our context is a parametric model with an interest parameter ψ for which inference is sought. The interest parameter is assumed to be scalar and to belong to a finite or infinite interval on the real line. The space of the parameter is thus linearly ordered. With inference we understand statements of the type $\psi > \psi_0$, $\psi_1 \leq \psi \leq \psi_2$, and so on, where $\psi_0, \psi_1, \ldots$ are values usually computed from the data. We would like to associate how much confidence the data allow us to have for each statement.

As the name indicates, the confidence distribution is related to confidence intervals, which are interval statements with the confidence fixed ex ante, and with endpoints calculated from the data. A one-sided confidence interval with (degree of) confidence $1 - \alpha$ has as a right endpoint the corresponding quantile of the confidence distribution. If C is the cumulative confidence distribution calculated from the data, the left-sided confidence interval is $[-\infty, C^{-1}(1-\alpha)]$. A right-sided confidence interval $[C^{-1}(\alpha), \infty]$ has confidence $1-\alpha$, and a two-sided confidence interval $[C^{-1}(\alpha), C^{-1}(\beta)]$ has confidence $\beta - \alpha$. Two-sided confidence intervals are usually equitailed in the sense that $\alpha = 1 - \beta$.

Hypothesis testing and confidence intervals are closely related. We omit the instructive proof, and state this relation in the following lemma.

Lemma 1 *The confidence of the statement* $\psi \leq \psi_0$ *is the cumulative confidence distribution function value* $C(\psi_0)$, *and is equal to the* p-*value of a test of* $H_0 : \psi \leq \psi_0$ *versus the alternative* $H_1 : \psi > \psi_0$.

The opposite statement $\psi > \psi_0$ has confidence $1 - C(\psi_0)$. Usually, the confidence distributions are continuous, and $\psi \geq \psi_0$ has the same confidence as $\psi > \psi_0$.

When ψ_0 is fixed, the statement $\psi \neq \psi_0$ should, preferably, have confidence given by one minus the p-value when testing H_0: $\psi = \psi_0$. This can be calculated from the observed confidence distribution, and is $1 - 2\min\{C(\psi_0), 1 - C(\psi_0)\}$.

Confidence intervals are invariant with respect to monotone transformations. This is also the case for confidence distributions.

Lemma 2 *Confidence distributions based essentially on the same statistic are invariant with respect to monotone continuous transformations of the parameter: If* $\rho = \mathrm{r}(\psi)$, *say, with* r *increasing, and if* C^{ψ} *is based on* T *while* C^{ρ} *is based on* $\mathrm{S} = \mathrm{s}(\mathrm{T})$, *where* s *is monotone, then*

$$C^{\rho}(\rho) = C^{\psi}\left[r^{-1}(\rho)\right].$$

A sharp distinction should be drawn between the (estimated) sampling distribution and the confidence distribution. The sampling distribution of the estimator is the ex ante probability distribution of the statistic under repeated sampling, whereas the confidence distribution is calculated ex post and distributes the confidence the observed data allow to be associated with different statements concerning the parameter. Consider the estimated sampling distribution of the point estimator $\widehat{\psi}$, say, as obtained from the parametric bootstrap. If ψ^* is a random estimate of ψ obtained by the same method, the estimated sampling distribution is the familiar

$$S(\psi) = \Pr\left\{\psi^* \leq \psi \mid \widehat{\psi}\right\} = F_{\hat{\psi}}(\psi).$$

The confidence distribution is, in fact, an inversion of a sampling distribution. It is a distribution for the parameter and not for a stochastic variable. Ex ante, the confidence distribution is a stochastic element having a probability distribution. Ex post, however, it is a distribution for the parameter calculated from the observed data. Example 8.1 illustrates the inversion, which is also illustrated by several other examples.

Exact confidence distributions are equivalent to the infamous fiducial distributions in the sense of Fisher, at least in cases where Fisher would have considered the mechanism behind the confidence limits to be inferentially correct (see the discussion in Efron, 1998, sec. 8). In view of old and on-going controversies and confusion surrounding this theme of Fisher's, and the fact that such fiducial distributions have sometimes been put forward in ad hoc fashion and with vague interpretations, we emphasize that our confidence distributions are actually derived from particular principles in a rigorous framework and with a clear interpretation. Our work can perhaps be seen as being in the spirit of Neyman (1941). We share the view expressed in Lehmann (1993) that the division between the Fisherian and the Neyman–Pearson tradition is unfortunate. The unity of the two traditions is illustrated by our version of the Neyman–Pearson lemma as it applies to Fisher's fiducial distribution (confidence distribution). Note also that in Section 13.2, in particular, we work toward establishing confidence distributions that are inferentially correct. The following simple examples illustrate the approach.

E 13.1 *Consider the exponentially distributed variate* T *with probability density* $f(t; \psi) = (1/\psi)\exp(-t/\psi)$. *From the obvious* p*-value, the cumulative confidence distribution is* $C(\psi; t_{obs}) = \Pr_\psi\{T > t_{obs}\} = \exp(-t_{obs}/\psi)$. *Ex ante, the potentially observed value* $t_{obs} = T$ *is stochastic, whereas ex post it is simply an observed value. We often write* $C(\psi)$, *which is the stochastic quantity* $C(\psi; T)$ *or the realized confidence distribution* $C(\psi; t_{obs})$. *The interpretation will be clear from the context. The cumulative confidence distribution function for* ψ *is* $C(\psi; t) = \exp(-t/\psi)$. *The confidence density is thus* $c(\psi; t) = (d/d\psi)C(\psi; t) = t\psi^{-2}\exp(-t/\psi)$, *which not only has a completely different interpretation from the sampling density of the maximum likelihood estimator* T, *but also has a different shape.*

E 13.2 *Suppose the ratio* $\psi = \sigma_2/\sigma_1$ *between standard deviation parameters from two different data sets are of interest, where independent estimates of the familiar form* $\widehat{\sigma}_j^2 = \sigma_j^2 W_j/\nu_j$ *are available, and* W_j *is a* $\chi^2_{\nu_j}$. *The canonical intervals from inverting the optimal tests for single-point hypotheses* $\psi = \psi_0$ *take the form*

$$\left[\widehat{\psi}/K^{-1}(1-\alpha)^{1/2}, \widehat{\psi}/K^{-1}(\alpha)^{1/2}\right],$$

where $\widehat{\psi} = \widehat{\sigma}_2/\widehat{\sigma}_1$ *and* $K = K_{\nu_2,\nu_1}$ *is the distribution function for the* F *statistic* $(W_2/\nu_2)/(W_1/\nu_1)$. *Thus* $C^{-1}(\alpha) = \widehat{\psi}/K^{-1}(1-\alpha)^{1/2}$. *This corresponds to the confidence distribution function* $C(\psi \mid \text{data}) = 1 - K(\widehat{\psi}^2/\psi^2)$, *with confidence density*

$$c(\psi \mid \text{data}) = k(\widehat{\psi}^2/\psi^2)2\widehat{\psi}^2/\psi^3,$$

expressed in terms of the F *density* $k = k_{\nu_2,\nu_1}$. *See also Section 13.2 for an optimality result of the confidence density used here, and Section 13.3 for a very good approximation based on bootstrapping.*

The calculation of the confidence distribution is easy when a pivot statistic for ψ is available. The random variable $\text{piv}(X, \psi)$ is a pivot (Barndorff-Nielsen and Cox, 1994) in a model with nuisance parameter χ and data X if the probability distribution of $\text{piv}(X, \psi)$ is the same for all (ψ, χ), and if the function $\text{piv}(x, \psi)$ is monotone and increasing in ψ for almost all x.

When the confidence distribution is based on a pivot, and F is the cumulative distribution function of the pivot, the confidence distribution is

$$C(\psi) = F(\text{piv}(X, \psi)). \tag{1}$$

This can also be turned around. If, in fact, $C(\psi; X)$ is a cumulative confidence distribution based on data X, then it is a pivot since at ψ it is uniformly distributed. Thus, a confidence distribution based on a sufficient statistic exists if and only if there is a pivot based on the sufficient statistic. Moreover, the cumulative confidence distribution function is simply the probability transform of the pivot.

13.1.2 Linear Regression

In the linear normal model, the n-dimensional data Y of the response is assumed to be $N(X\beta, \sigma^2 I)$. With SSR being the residual sum of squares and $p =$ rank (X), $S^2 = \mathrm{SSR}/(n-p)$ is the traditional estimate of the residual variance. With S_j^2 being the mean-unbiased estimator of the variance of the regression coefficient estimator $\widehat{\beta}_j$,

$$V_j = (\widehat{\beta}_j - \beta_j)/S_j$$

is a pivot with a t-distribution of $\nu = n - p$ degrees of freedom. With $t_\nu(\alpha)$ the quantiles of this t-distribution, the confidence quantiles for β_j are the familiar $\widehat{\beta}_j + t_\nu(\alpha) S_j$. The cumulative confidence distribution function for β_j thus becomes

$$C(\beta_j;\ \text{data}) = 1 - G_\nu\left((\widehat{\beta}_j - \beta_j)/S_j\right) = G_\nu\left((\beta_j - \widehat{\beta}_j)/S_j\right),$$

where G_ν is the cumulative t-distribution with ν degrees of freedom. Note also that the confidence density $c(\beta_j;\ \text{data})$ is the t_ν-density centered at $\widehat{\beta}_j$, with the appropriate scale.

Now we turn our attention to the case where σ, the residual standard deviation, is the parameter of interest. Then the pivot $\mathrm{SSR}/\sigma^2 = \nu S^2/\sigma^2$ is a χ^2_ν, and the cumulative confidence distribution is found to be

$$C(\sigma \mid \text{data}) = \Pr\left\{\chi^2_\nu > \mathrm{SSR}/\sigma^2\right\} = 1 - \Gamma_\nu\left(\nu S^2/\sigma^2\right),$$

where Γ_ν is the cumulative distribution function of the χ^2_ν with density γ_ν. The confidence density becomes

$$c(\sigma \mid \text{data}) = \gamma_\nu\left(\frac{\nu S^2}{\sigma^2}\right)\frac{2\nu S^2}{\sigma^3} = \frac{2\left(\frac{1}{2}\nu\right)^\nu S^\nu}{\Gamma\left(\frac{1}{2}\nu\right)}\sigma^{-(\nu+1)}\exp\left(-\tfrac{1}{2}\nu S^2/\sigma^2\right),$$

which again is different from the likelihood. The likelihood for the SSR part of the data is the density of $\mathrm{SSR} = \sigma^2\chi^2_\nu$, which is proportional to

$$L(\sigma) = \sigma^{-\nu}\exp\left(-\tfrac{1}{2}\nu S^2/\sigma^2\right).$$

If we take logarithms, the pivot is brought on an additive scale, $\log S - \log\sigma$, and in the parameter $\tau = \log\sigma$ the confidence density is proportional to the likelihood. The log-likelihood also has a nicer shape in τ than in σ, where it is less neatly peaked.

13.1.3 Ratio Parameters and the Fieller Solution

Ericsson et al. (1998) discuss the empirical basis for the weights in monetary conditions indexes, MCI. With R being the interest rate and e the exchange rate, MCI $= \psi(R - R_0) + (e - e_0)$. The relative weight of the interest rate ψ is estimated as the ratio of two regression coefficients, $\widehat{\psi} = \widehat{\beta}_1/\widehat{\beta}_2$, in a linear regression. Both regression parameters are assumed to be nonnegative, and thus $0 \le \psi \le \infty$. For Norway, Ericsson et al. (1998) found $[0, \infty]$ as the 95 percent confidence interval for ψ. It is an embarrassing conceptual problem to have a 95 percent confidence interval covering the whole range of the parameter, which certainly should have had confidence 100 percent and not 95 percent. This is known as the Fieller problem (see, e.g., Koschat, 1987; Dufour, 1997).

Ratios of regression coefficients are often estimated in econometrics. The method of Fieller (1940, 1954), discussed later, should therefore be of interest. Staiger et al. (1997) used the Fieller method to estimate the nonacceleration rate of unemployment (NAIRU). They found in a simulation study that the Fieller method performs much better than the delta method. This is not surprising, since this method of constructing a confidence region for ψ is related to a t-test with the usual optimality properties [see Neyman's discussion of Fieller (1954)].

Assume $(\widehat{\beta}_1, \widehat{\beta}_2)^t$ to be $\mathrm{N}\left[(\beta_1, \beta_2)^t, \sum\right]$, with $\sum = \sigma^2 \sum_0$ estimated at df degrees of freedom. Confidence regions for the quotient $\psi = \beta_1/\beta_2$ are found from inverting the t-test of $H_0\colon \psi = \psi_0$ versus $H_1\colon \psi \ne \psi_0$. The hypothesis is first reformulated to $H_0\colon \beta_1 - \psi_0\beta_2 = 0$, and tested by $T(\psi_0)$, where

$$T(\psi) = \frac{\psi\widehat{\beta}_2 - \widehat{\beta}_1}{\widehat{\sigma}\sigma_0(\psi)} \qquad \text{and} \qquad \sigma_0^2(\psi) = (-1, \psi)\sum\nolimits_0(-1, \psi)^t.$$

This test statistic T is t-distributed with df degrees of freedom when $\psi = \psi_0$. It is, however, not a pivot since it is not monotone in ψ for all possible data. Over $[-\infty, \infty]$, T typically has two monotone branches. With $b = (\widehat{\beta}_2, -\widehat{\beta}_1)\sum_0$, the point of branching is $\psi_m = -b_1/b_2$, which is a minimum if $b_2 < 0$. The inversion of the two-sided test leads to the confidence regions of Fieller (1940, 1954). For a given level of confidence $1 - 2\alpha$, the region is determined by $\alpha \le G_{\mathrm{df}}[T(\psi)] \le 1 - \alpha$, where G_{df} is the distribution function of the t_{df} distribution. Depending on the confidence level and the estimates, we find that the confidence region can be either $[-\infty, \infty]$, $[-\infty, \widehat{\psi}_U]$, $[\widehat{\psi}_L, \infty]$, $[\widehat{\psi}_L, \widehat{\psi}_U]$, or even $[\widehat{\psi}_{L1}, \widehat{\psi}_{L2}] \cup [\widehat{\psi}_{U1}, \widehat{\psi}_{U2}]$ with $\widehat{\psi}_{L2} < \widehat{\psi}_{U1}$ and one or both interval pieces being infinite. Note that the coverage probability is exact.

The Fieller test statistic is $\widehat{\beta}_1 - \psi_0\widehat{\beta}_2$ and orders data differently from the more natural test statistic $|\widehat{\psi} - \psi_0|$. One might therefore suspect that something is lost by the Fieller solution. However, Koschat (1987) found that no reasonable method other than the Fieller solution provides confidence intervals with exact coverage probabilities when $\sum_0 = I$. This was shown for the angle related to the ratio. Consequently, if something is to be gained in power by another ordering of data sets, it must be at the price of obtaining only approximate null behavior.

Since $T(\psi)$ is not a pivot, standard confidence distributions for ψ are not available by the Fieller method, which has essentially three problems: (1) the confidence region can be infinite; (2) it can be a union of two intervals where at least one is infinite; and (3) it might, at some given degree of confidence less than 100 percent, lead to nonsense interval statements of the type $\psi \in [-\infty, \infty]$. That the confidence region might be infinite is due to the discontinuity of $\psi = \tan(\theta)$ at $\theta = \pi/2$. In polar coordinates, the Fieller method leads to either an interval for θ or to the whole half-circle $\widehat{\theta} \pm \pi/2$. If the region for θ is taken to be the fixed interval $(-\pi/2, \pi/2]$, the confidence region might consist of two intervals. The final, and for some, the most disturbing problem is the third: that the confidence region should have 100 percent confidence and not 95 percent when it includes the complete range of the parameter. However, following Neyman when discussing Fieller (1954), we do not see this as a disturbing phenomenon. Seen as as family of confidence intervals on the circle, the Fieller method determines a confidence distribution of mass less than 1. This is indeed possible. In such cases the total mass of the confidence distribution determines an upper limit on the confidence that can be associated with any informative statement. If this mass is less than 95 percent, it seems inappropriate to present the noninformative 95 percent region. One should rather reduce the ambition and report the confidence statements that the data allow.

E 13.3 *For Norway, Ericsson et al. (1998) found estimates* $\widehat{\beta}_1 = 0.34891$, $\widehat{\beta}_2 = 0.16264$, $\sigma_0^2(\psi) = 215.998 - 2 \cdot 7.992\psi + 57.935\psi^2$, *and* $\widehat{\sigma} = 0.01162$. *For these data,* T *is increasing over the positive axis. The transform* $C(\psi) = G_{df}(T(\psi))$ *can thus be taken as the cumulative confidence distribution. The cumulative confidence starts at* $C(0) = 0.025$ *and approaches* $C(\infty) = 0.962$. *Thus, no informative statements with confidence more than 0.937 are possible for these data. The confidence distribution represented as the family of equi-tailed confidence intervals is shown in Fig. 13.1.*

13.2 CONFIDENCE LEVEL AND CONFIDENCE POWER

Let $C(\psi)$ be the cumulative confidence distribution. The intended interpretation of C is that its quantiles are endpoints of confidence intervals.

For these intervals to have correct coverage probabilities, the cumulative confidence at the true value of the parameter must have a uniform probability distribution. This is an ex ante statement. Before the data have been gathered, the confidence distribution is a stochastic element and $C(\psi_{\text{true}})$ is a random variable. If

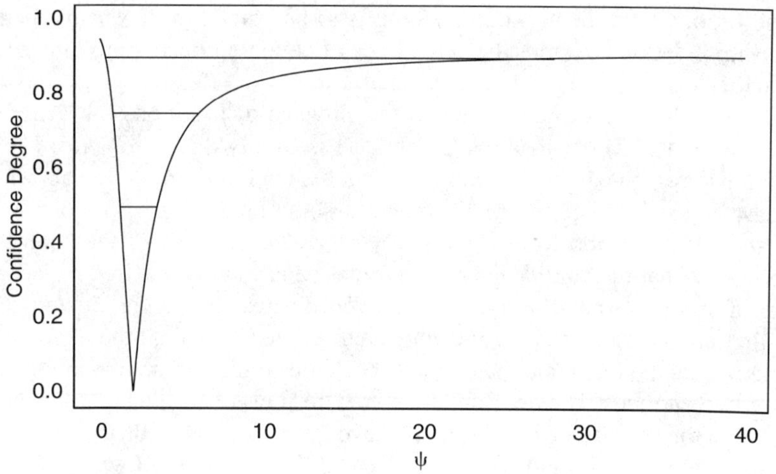

Fig. 13.1 Confidence distribution for the ratio ψ represented as confidence degree $2\left[C(\psi) - \frac{1}{2}\right]$, based on Norwegian data (Nymoen, personal communication). Equitailed confidence intervals at degree 0.50, 0.75, and 0.90 are shown as horizontal lines.

$$\Pr_{\psi}\{C(\psi) \leq c\} = c \quad \text{for } 0 \leq c \leq 1, \tag{2}$$

assuming the probability distribution to be continuous, the coverage probability of $\left[-\infty, C^{-1}(\alpha)\right]$ is

$$\Pr_{\psi}\left\{\psi \leq C^{-1}(\alpha)\right\} = \alpha,$$

which conventionally is called the confidence level of the interval. The confidence distribution is exact if (2) holds exactly, and thus the coverage probability of a confidence interval obtained from C equals the nominal confidence level.

Confidence distributions provide point estimates, the most natural being the confidence median, $\widehat{\psi} = C^{-1}\left(\frac{1}{2}\right)$. When the confidence distribution is exact, this point estimator is median unbiased. This property is kept under monotone transformations of the parameter.

The choice of statistic on which to base the confidence distribution is unambiguous only in simple cases. Barndorff-Nielsen and Cox (1994) are in agreement with Fisher when emphasizing the structure of the model and the data as a basis for choosing the statistic. They are primarily interested in the logic of statistical inference. In the tradition of Neyman and Wald, the emphasis has been on inductive behavior, and the goal has been to find methods with optimal frequentist properties. In nice models such as exponential families it turns out that methods favored on structural and logical grounds are also favored on grounds of optimality. This agreement between the Fisherian and Neyman–Wald schools is encouraging and helps to reduce the distinction between the two. This core of statistical theory needs to be reformulated in terms of confidence distributions.

13.2.1 Optimal Confidence Power

The Neyman–Pearson lemma is regarded as a cornerstone of frequentist theory (cf. Lehmann, 1959). It says that tests based on sufficient statistics with monotone likelihood ratio are uniformly most powerful. The power function of a test is an ex ante property. In the frequentist tradition, methods are judged by their ex ante properties, such as level and power for tests and inclusion-exclusion probabilities for confidence intervals. The null property of a confidence distribution is simply that $C(\psi)$ has a uniform probability distribution under ψ. The power properties of C are captured by the probability distributions of chosen functionals of C. These functionals will typically measure the spread of the confidence distribution.

The tighter the confidence intervals are, the better, provided they have the claimed confidence. Ex post, it is thus desirable to have as small a spread in the confidence distribution as possible. Standard deviation, interquantile difference, or other measures of spread could be used to rank methods with respect to their discriminatory power. The properties of a method must be assessed ex ante, and it is thus the probability distribution of a chosen measure of spread that would be relevant. The assessment of the information content in a given body of data is, however, another matter, and must clearly be discussed ex post.

When testing $H_0\colon \psi = \psi_0$ versus $H_1\colon \psi > \psi_0$, one rejects at level α if $C(\psi_0) < \alpha$. The power of the test is $\Pr\{C(\psi_0) < \alpha\}$ evaluated at a point $\psi_1 > \psi_0$. Cast in terms of p-values, the power distribution is the distribution at ψ_1 of the p-value $C(\psi_0)$. The basis for test optimality is monotonicity in the likelihood ratio based on a sufficient statistic S,

$$\mathrm{LR}(\psi_1, \psi_2; S) = L(\psi_2; S)/L(\psi_1; S) \tag{3}$$

is increasing in S for $\psi_2 > \psi_1$. When $\Pr\{X \leq x\} \leq \Pr\{Y \leq x\}$ for all values x, Y is stochastically smaller (no larger) than X, written $Y \leq_{\mathrm{st}} X$. From Schweder (1988) we have the following lemma.

Lemma 3 *Neyman–Pearson for* p-*values. Let* S *be a one-dimensional sufficient statistic with increasing likelihood ratio whenever $\psi_1 < \psi_2$. Let the cumulative confidence distribution based on* S *be* C^{S} *and that based on another statistic* T *be* C^{T}. *In this situation, the cumulative confidence distributions are stochastically ordered:*

$$C^S(\psi_0) \geq_{\mathrm{st}(\psi)} C^T(\psi_0) \qquad \text{at} \qquad \psi > \psi_0$$

and

$$C^S(\psi_0) \leq_{\mathrm{st}(\psi)} C^T(\psi_0) \qquad \text{at} \qquad \psi < \psi_0.$$

Now, every natural measure of spread in C around the true value of the parameter ψ_0 can be expressed as a functional $\gamma(C) = \int_{-\infty}^{\infty} \Gamma(\psi - \psi_0)\, C(d\psi)$, where $\Gamma(0) = 0$, Γ is nonincreasing to the left of zero, and nondecreasing to the right. Here $\Gamma(t) = \int_0^t \gamma(du)$ is the integral of a signed measure γ.

A confidence distribution C^S is said to be uniformly more powerful in the mean than C^T if

$$\mathrm{E}_{\psi_0}\gamma(C^S) \le \mathrm{E}_{\psi_0}\gamma(C^T)$$

holds for all spread functionals γ and at all parameter values ψ_0. With this definition, the Neyman–Pearson lemma for p-values yields the following.

Proposition 4 *[Neyman–Pearson for power in the mean.] If* S *is a sufficient one-dimensional statistic and the likelihood ratio* (3) *is increasing in* S *whenever* $\psi_1 < \psi_2$, *then the confidence distribution based on* S *is uniformly most powerful in expectation.*

Proof. By partial integration,

$$\gamma(C) = \int_{-\infty}^{0} C(\psi + \psi_0)\,(-\gamma)(\mathrm{d}\psi) + \int_{0}^{\infty} \left[1 - C(\psi + \psi_0)\right] \gamma(\mathrm{d}\psi). \quad (4)$$

By lemma 3, $\mathrm{E}C^S(\psi + \psi_0) \le \mathrm{E}C^T(\psi + \psi_0)$ for $\psi < 0$ while $\mathrm{E}(1 - C^S(\psi + \psi_0)) \le \mathrm{E}\left[1 - C^T(\psi + \psi_0)\right]$ for $\psi > 0$. Consequently, since both $(-\gamma)(\mathrm{d}\psi)$ and $\gamma(\mathrm{d}\psi) \ge 0$,

$$\mathrm{E}_{\psi_0}\gamma(C^S) \le \mathrm{E}_{\psi_0}\gamma(C^T).$$

This relation holds for all such spread measures that have a finite integral, and for all reference values ψ_0. Hence, C^S is uniformly more powerful in the mean than any other confidence distribution.

The Neyman–Pearson argument for confidence distributions can be strengthened. Say that a confidence distribution C^S is uniformly most powerful if, ex ante, $\gamma(C^S)$ is stochastically less than or equal to $\gamma(C^T)$ for all other statistics T, for all spread functionals γ, and with respect to the probability distribution at all values of the true parameter ψ_0. The following is proved in Schweder and Hjort (2002).

Proposition 5 *[Neyman–Pearson for confidence distributions.] If* S *is a sufficient one-dimensional statistic and the likelihood ratio* (3) *is increasing in* S *whenever* $\psi_1 < \psi_2$, *then the confidence distribution based on* S *is uniformly most powerful.*

13.2.2 Uniformly Most Powerful Confidence for Exponential Families

Conditional tests often have good power properties in situations with nuisance parameters. In the exponential family of models it turns out that valid confidence distributions should be based on the conditional distribution of the statistic that is sufficient for the interest parameter, given the remaining statistics informative for the nuisance parameters. That conditional tests are most powerful among power-unbiased tests is well known (see, e.g., Lehmann,

1959). There are also other broad lines of arguments leading to constructions of conditional tests (see, e.g., Barndorff-Nielsen and Cox, 1994). Presently we indicate how and why the most powerful confidence distributions are also of such a conditional nature.

Proposition 6 *Let ψ be the scalar parameter and χ the nuisance parameter vector in an exponential model, with density of the form*

$$p(x) = \exp\left\{\psi S(x) + \chi_1 A_1(x) + \cdots + \chi_p A_p(x) - k(\psi, \chi_1, \ldots, \chi_p)\right\}$$

with respect to a fixed measure, for data vector x *in a sample space region not dependent upon the parameters. Assume* (ψ, χ) *is contained in an open* $(p+1)$*-dimensional parameter set. Then, for* ψ *and hence for all monotone transforms of* ψ*, there exist exactly valid confidence distributions, and the uniformly most powerful of these takes the conditional form*

$$C_{S\,|\,A}(\psi) = \Pr_{\psi,\chi}\{S > S_{\text{obs}} \mid A = A_{\text{obs}}\}\,.$$

Here S_{obs} *and* A_{obs} *denote the observed values of* S *and* $A = (A_1, \ldots, A_p)$.

Strictly speaking this formula holds in the case of continuous distributions; a minor discontinuity correction amendment is called for in case of a discrete distribution.

The proof of this proposition and its extensions and applications are found in Schweder and Hjort (2002). One key ingredient here is that A is a sufficient and complete statistic for χ when $\psi = \psi_0$ is fixed. Note that the distribution of S given $A = A_{\text{obs}}$ depends on ψ but not on $\chi_1, \ldots, \chi_p$.

E 13.4 *Consider pairs* (X_j, Y_j) *of independent Poisson variables, where* X_j *and* Y_j *have parameters* λ_j *and* $\lambda_j\psi$*, for* $j = 1, \ldots, m$. *The likelihood is proportional to*

$$\exp\left\{\sum_{j=1}^{m} y_j \log\psi + \sum_{j=1}^{m}(x_j + y_j)\log\lambda_j\right\}.$$

Write $S = \sum_{j=1}^{m} Y_j$ *and* $A_j = X_j + Y_j$. *Then* $A_1, \ldots, A_m$ *become sufficient and complete for the nuisance parameters when* ψ *is fixed. Also,* $Y_j \mid A_j$ *is a binomial* $[A_j, \psi/(1+\psi)]$. *It follows from proposition 6 that the uniformly most powerful confidence distribution, used here with a half-correction for discreteness, takes the simple form*

$$\begin{aligned} C_{S|A}(\psi) &= \Pr_\psi\{S > S_{\text{obs}} \mid A_{\text{obs}}\} + \tfrac{1}{2}\Pr_\psi\{S = S_{\text{obs}} \mid A_{\text{obs}}\} \\ &= 1 - \text{Bin}\left(S_{\text{obs}}; \sum_{j=1}^{m} A_{j,\text{obs}}, \frac{\psi}{1+\psi}\right) + \tfrac{1}{2}\text{bin}\left(S_{\text{obs}}; \sum_{j=1}^{m} A_{j,\text{obs}}, \frac{\psi}{1+\psi}\right), \end{aligned}$$

where $\text{Bin}(\cdot; n, p)$ *and* $\text{bin}(\cdot; n, p)$ *are the cumulative and pointwise distribution functions for the binomial.*

13.3 APPROXIMATE CONFIDENCE DISTRIBUTIONS

Uniformly most powerful exact inference is only possible in a restricted class of models. In more complex models, the statistic upon which to base the confidence distribution might be chosen on various grounds: the structure of the likelihood function, perceived robustness, asymptotic properties, computational feasibility, and the perspective and tradition of the study. In a given model, with finite data, it might be difficult to obtain an exact confidence distribution based on the chosen statistic. There are, however, various techniques available to obtain approximate confidence.

Bootstrapping, simulation, and asymptotics are useful tools in calculating approximate confidence distributions and in characterizing their power properties. When an estimator, often the maximum likelihood estimator of the interest parameter, is used as the statistic on which the confidence distribution is based, bootstrapping provides an estimate of the sampling distribution of the statistic. This empirical sampling distribution can be turned into an approximate confidence distribution in several ways. The simplest and most widely used method of obtaining approximate confidence intervals is the delta method, which leads to first-order accuracy properties in smooth models. A more refined method to obtain confidence distributions is via acceleration and bias corrections on bootstrap distributions, as developed in Section 13.3.3. This method, along with several other venues for refinement, usually provides second-order accuracy properties.

13.3.1 The Delta Method

In a sample of size n, let the estimator $\widehat{\theta}_n$ have an approximate multinormal distribution centered at θ with a covariance matrix of the form S_n/n, so that $\sqrt{n}S_n^{-1/2}(\widehat{\theta}_n - \theta) \to_d \mathrm{N}(0, I)$. By the delta method, the confidence distribution for a parameter $\psi = p(\theta)$ is based on linearizing p at $\widehat{\theta}$ and yields

$$C_{\text{delta}}(\psi) = \Phi\left((\psi - \widehat{\psi})/\widehat{\sigma}_n\right) \qquad (5)$$

in terms of the cumulative standard normal Φ. The variance estimate is $\widehat{\sigma}_n^2 = \widehat{g}^{\,t} S_n \widehat{g}/n$, where $\widehat{g}$ is the gradient of p evaluated at $\widehat{\theta}$. Again, this estimate of the confidence distribution is to be displayed post-data with $\widehat{\psi}$ equal to its observed value $\widehat{\psi}_{\text{obs}}$.

This confidence distribution is known to be first-order unbiased under weak conditions. That $C_{\text{delta}}(\psi)$ is first-order unbiased means that the coverage probabilities converge at the rate $n^{-1/2}$ or that $C_{\text{delta}}(\psi_{\text{true}})$ converges in distribution to the uniform distribution at the $n^{1/2}$ rate. Note also that the confidence density as estimated via the delta method, say $c_{\text{delta}}(\psi)$, is simply the normal density $\mathrm{N}\left(\widehat{\psi}, \widehat{\sigma}_n^2\right)$.

13.3.2 The t-Bootstrap Method

For a suitable monotone transformation of ψ and $\widehat{\psi}$ to $\gamma = h(\psi)$ and $\widehat{\gamma} = h(\widehat{\psi})$, suppose

$$t = (\widehat{\gamma} - \gamma)/\widehat{\tau} \tag{6}$$

is an approximate pivot, where $\widehat{\tau}$ is proportional to an estimate of the standard deviation of $\widehat{\gamma}$. Let R be the distribution function of t, by assumption approximately independent of underlying parameters (ψ, χ). The canonical confidence intervals for γ then take the form $\widehat{\gamma} - R^{-1}(1-\alpha)\widehat{\tau} \leq \gamma \leq \widehat{\gamma} + R^{-1}(\alpha)\widehat{\tau}$, which backtransform to intervals for ψ, with

$$C^{-1}(\alpha) = h^{-1}\left(\widehat{\gamma} - R^{-1}(1-\alpha)\widehat{\tau}\right).$$

Solving for α leads to the confidence distribution $C(\psi) = 1 - R\big((h(\widehat{\psi}) - h(\psi))/\widehat{\tau}\big)$, with appropriate confidence density $c(\psi) = C'(\psi)$. Now R would often be unknown, but the situation is saved via bootstrapping. Let $\widehat{\gamma}^* = h(\widehat{\theta}^*)$ and $\widehat{\tau}^*$ be the result of parametric bootstrapping from the estimated model. Then the R distribution can be estimated arbitrarily well as $\widehat{R}$, say, obtained via bootstrapped values of $t^* = (\widehat{\gamma}^* - \widehat{\gamma})/\widehat{\tau}^*$. The confidence distribution reported is then as above but with $\widehat{R}$ replacing R:

$$C_{\text{tboot}}(\psi) = 1 - \widehat{R}\left((h(\widehat{\psi}) - h(\psi))/\widehat{\tau}\right). \tag{7}$$

This t-bootstrap method applies even when t is not a perfect pivot, but is especially successful when it is, since t^* then has exactly the same distribution R as t. Note that the method automatically takes care of bias and asymmetry in R and that it therefore aims at being more precise than the delta method above, which corresponds to zero bias and a normal R. The problem is that an educated guess is required for a successful pivotal transformation h and that the interval is not invariant under monotone transformations. The following method is not hampered by these shortcomings.

13.3.3 The Acceleration and Bias Corrected Bootstrap Method

Efron (1987) introduced acceleration and bias corrected bootstrap percentile intervals and showed that these have several desirable aspects regarding accuracy and parameter invariance. Here we exploit some of these ideas, but "turn them around" to construct accurate bootstrap-based approximations to confidence distributions.

Suppose that on some transformed scale, from ψ and $\widehat{\psi}$ to $\gamma = h(\psi)$ and $\widehat{\gamma} = h(\widehat{\psi})$, one has

$$(\widehat{\gamma} - \gamma)/(1 + a\gamma) \sim \mathrm{N}(-b, 1) \tag{8}$$

to a very good approximation for suitable constants a (for acceleration) and b (for bias). Both population parameters a and b tend to be small, as further commented upon later. Assumption (8) can be written $\widehat{\gamma}-\gamma = (1+a\gamma)(Z-b)$, where Z is standard normal. This leads to

$$1 + a\widehat{\gamma} = (1 + a\gamma)\,[1 + a(Z - b)]$$

and a canonically correct interval for γ and hence ψ, as explained shortly. The essentials of the following arguments are that (8) describes a pivotal model on a transformed scale and that the apparatus already established for deriving confidence distributions from pivots becomes applicable via the transformation lemma of Section 13.1 in conjunction with bootstrapping. We include a little more detail, however, to pinpoint the roles of the various elements.

Start with $z^{(\alpha)} \le Z \le z^{(1-\alpha)}$, the symmetric interval including Z with probability $1 - 2\alpha$, writing $z^{(\varepsilon)}$ for $\Phi^{-1}(\varepsilon)$. This leads after some algebra to

$$h^{-1}\left(\frac{\widehat{\gamma} - (z^{(1-\alpha)} - b)}{1 + a(z^{(1-\alpha)} - b)}\right) \le \psi \le h^{-1}\left(\frac{\widehat{\gamma} - (z^{(\alpha)} - b)}{1 + a(z^{(\alpha)} - b)}\right).$$

Writing this interval as $[C^{-1}(\alpha), C^{-1}(1 - \alpha)]$ and solving $C^{-1}(\alpha) = \psi$ for α gives the confidence distribution

$$C(\psi) = \Phi\left(\frac{h(\psi) - h(\widehat{\psi})}{1 + ah(\psi)} - b\right). \qquad (9)$$

This constitutes a good approximation to the real confidence distribution, say $C_{\text{exact}}(\psi)$, under assumption (8). But it requires h to be known, as well as values of a and b.

To get around this, look at bootstrapped versions $\widehat{\gamma}^* = h(\widehat{\psi}^*)$ from the estimated parametric model. If assumption (8) holds uniformly in a neighborhood of the true parameters, then also

$$(\widehat{\gamma}^* - \widehat{\gamma})/(1 + a\widehat{\gamma}) \mid \text{data} \sim N(-b, 1)$$

with good precision. Hence, the bootstrap distribution may be expressed as

$$\widehat{G}(t) = \Pr_*\{\widehat{\psi}^* \le t\} = \Pr_*\{\widehat{\gamma}^* \le h(t)\} = \Phi\left(\frac{h(t) - \widehat{\gamma}}{1 + a\widehat{\gamma}} + b\right).$$

It follows, again after some algebra, that the lower endpoint in the interval for ψ above satisfies

$$\widehat{G}(\widehat{\psi}^*) = \Phi\left(b - \frac{z^{(1-\alpha)} - b}{1 + a(z^{(1-\alpha)} - b)}\right).$$

This gives first the so-called BC_a intervals of Efron (1987), say $[\widehat{C}^{-1}(\alpha), \widehat{C}^{-1}(1 - \alpha)]$, where $\widehat{C}^{-1}(\alpha) = \widehat{\psi}^{(\alpha)}$.

Second, it gives us an acceleration and bias corrected approximation to the confidence distribution found in (9), through solving $\widehat{C}^{-1}(\alpha) = \psi$ for α. The result is the abc formula

$$\widehat{C}_{\mathrm{abc}}(\psi) = \Phi\left(\frac{\Phi^{-1}[\widehat{G}(\psi)] - b}{1 + a\left(\Phi^{-1}\left(\widehat{G}(\psi)\right) - b\right)} - b\right). \tag{10}$$

Note that an approximation $c_{\mathrm{abc}}(\psi)$ to the confidence density also emerges by evaluating the derivative of $\widehat{C}_{\mathrm{abc}}$. This can sometimes be done analytically, in cases where $\widehat{G}(\psi)$ can be found in a closed form, or can be carried out numerically.

It remains to specify a and b. The bias parameter b is found from $\widehat{G}(\widehat{\psi}) = \Phi(b)$. The acceleration parameter a is found as $a = \frac{1}{6}\mathrm{skew}$, where there are several ways in which to calculate or approximate the skewness parameter in question, at least in iid and regression situations. Extensive discussions can be found in Efron (1987), Efron and Tibshirani (1993, chs. 14, 22) and in Davison and Hinkley (1997, ch. 5). One option is via the jackknife method, which gives parameter estimates $\widehat{\psi}_{(i)}$ computed by leaving out data point i, and to use

$$a = \left(6\sqrt{n}\right)^{-1} \mathrm{skew}\left\{\widehat{\psi}_{(\cdot)} - \widehat{\psi}_{(1)}, \ldots, \widehat{\psi}_{(\cdot)} - \widehat{\psi}_{(n)}\right\}.$$

Here $\widehat{\psi}_{(\cdot)}$ is the mean of the n jackknife estimates. Another option for parametric families is to compute the skewness of the logarithmic derivative of the likelihood at the parameter point estimate inside the least favorable parametric subfamily (see again Efron, 1987, for more details).

Note that when a and b are zero, the abc confidence distribution becomes identical to the bootstrap distribution itself. In typical setups, both a and b will in fact go to zero with speed of order $1/\sqrt{n}$ in terms of sample size n. Thus (10) provides a second-order nonlinear correction of shift and scale to the immediate bootstrap distribution.

E 13.5 *Consider again the parameter* $\psi = \sigma_2/\sigma_1$ *of E 13.2. The exact confidence distribution was derived there and is equal to* $\mathrm{C}(\psi) = 1 - \mathrm{K}(\widehat{\psi}^2/\psi^2)$, *with* $\mathrm{K} = \mathrm{K}_{\nu_2,\nu_1}$. *We shall see how successful the abc apparatus is for approximating the* $\mathrm{C}(\psi)$ *and its confidence density* $\mathrm{c}(\psi)$.

In this situation, bootstrapping from the estimated parametric model leads to $\widehat{\psi}^* = \widehat{\sigma}_2^*/\widehat{\sigma}_1^*$ *of the form* $\widehat{\psi}\mathrm{F}^{1/2}$, *where* F *has degrees of freedom* ν_2 *and* ν_1. *Hence, the bootstrap distribution is* $\widehat{\mathrm{G}}(\mathrm{t}) = \mathrm{K}(\mathrm{t}^2/\widehat{\psi}^2)$, *and* $\widehat{\mathrm{G}}(\widehat{\psi}) = \mathrm{K}(1) = \Phi(\mathrm{b})$ *determines* b. *The acceleration constant can be computed exactly by looking at the log-derivative of the density* $\widehat{\psi}$, *which from* $\widehat{\psi} = \psi\mathrm{F}^{1/2}$ *is equal to* $\mathrm{p}(\mathrm{r}, \psi) = \mathrm{k}(\mathrm{r}^2/\psi^2)2\mathrm{r}/\psi^3$. *With a little work the log-derivative can be expressed as*

$$\frac{1}{\psi}\left\{-\nu_2 + (\nu_1+\nu_2)\frac{(\nu_2/\nu_1)\widehat{\psi}^2/\psi^2}{1 + (\nu_2/\nu_1)\widehat{\psi}^2/\psi^2}\right\}$$
$$=_d \frac{\nu_1+\nu_2}{\psi}\left\{\mathrm{Beta}\left(\tfrac{1}{2}\nu_2, \tfrac{1}{2}\nu_1\right) - \frac{\nu_2}{\nu_1+\nu_2}\right\}.$$

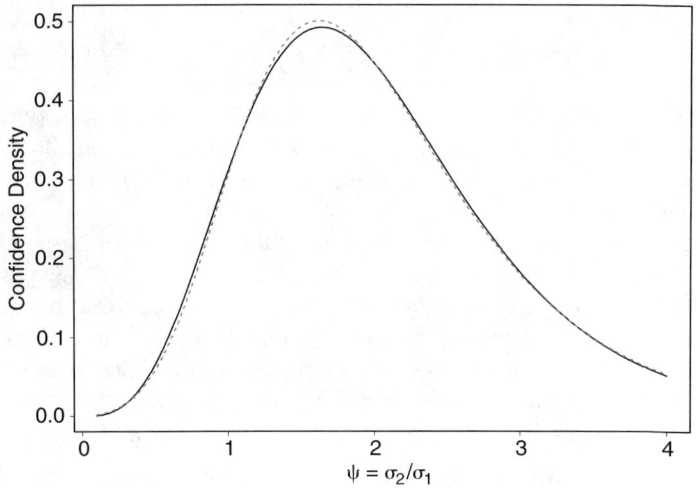

Fig. 13.2 True confidence density along with *abc*-estimated version of it, for parameter $\psi = \sigma_2/\sigma_1$ with four and nine degrees of freedom. The parameter estimate in this illustration is $\widehat{\psi} = 2.00$.

Calculating the three first moments of the Beta gives a formula for its skewness and hence for a. *(Using the jackknife formula or similar formulas based directly on simulated bootstrap estimates obviates the need for algebraic derivations, but give a good approximation only to the* a *parameter, for which we have now found the exact value.)*

Trying out the abc machinery shows that $\widehat{C}_{abc}(\psi)$ *is amazingly close to* $C(\psi)$*, even when the degrees-of-freedom numbers are low and unbalanced; the agreement is even better when* ν_1 *and* ν_2 *are more balanced or when they become larger. The same holds true for the densities* $\widehat{c}_{abc}(\psi)$ *and* $c(\psi)$ *(see Fig. 13.2).*

13.3.4 Comments

The delta and the abc methods remove bias by transforming the quantile function of the otherwise biased normal confidence distribution, $\Phi(\psi - \widehat{\psi})$. The delta method simply corrects the scale of the quantile function, whereas the abc method applies a shift and a nonlinear scale change to remove bias owing to both the nonlinearity in ψ as a function of the basic parameter θ and the effect on the asymptotic variance when the basic parameter is changed. The t-bootstrap method has good theoretical properties in cases where the $\widehat{\psi}$ estimator is a smooth function of sample averages, but has a couple of drawbacks compared to the abc method. It is, for example, not invariant under monotone transformations. Theorems delineating suitable second-order correctness aspects of both the abc and the t-bootstrap methods can be formulated and proved, with necessary assumptions having to do with the quality of approximations involved in (6) and (8). Methods of proof would involve, for example, Edgeworth or Cornish–Fisher expansion arguments (see, e.g., Hall, 1992), which could also be used to add corrections to the delta method [Eq. (5)].

Some asymptotic methods of debiasing an approximate confidence distribution involves a transformation of the confidence itself and not its quantile function. From a strict mathematical point of view there is of course no difference between acting on the quantiles or on the confidence. But methods such as the abc method are most naturally viewed as a transformation of the confidence for each given value of the parameter.

There are still other methods of theoretical and practical interest for computing approximate confidence distributions (cf. the extensive literature on constructing accurate confidence intervals). One approach would be via analytic approximations to the endpoints of the abc interval, under suitable assumptions; the arguments would be akin to those found in DiCiccio and Efron (1996) and Davison and Hinkley (1997, ch. 5) regarding "approximate bootstrap confidence intervals." Another approach would be via modified profile likelihoods, following work by Barndorff-Nielsen and others (see Barndorff-Nielsen and Cox, 1994, chs. 6, 7; Barndorff-Nielsen and Wood, 1998). Clearly more work and further illustrations are needed to better sort out which methods have the best potential for accuracy and transparency in different situations. At any rate the abc method [Eq. (10)] appears to be quite generally useful and precise.

13.4 LIKELIHOOD RELATED TO CONFIDENCE DISTRIBUTIONS

To combine past reported data with new data, as well as for other purposes, it is advantageous to recover a likelihood function or an approximation thereof from the available statistics summarizing the past data. The question we ask is whether an acceptable likelihood function can be recovered from a published confidence distribution, and if this is answered in the negative, how much additional information is needed to obtain a usable likelihood. When a confidence distribution relates to one of many parameters in the underlying model, the full multiparameter likelihood of the data cannot be obtained from the given one-dimensional confidence distribution. What might be recovered is a likelihood reduced of these other "nuisance" parameters, which will typically be a marginal or a conditional one. An example will show that a confidence distribution is in itself not sufficient to determine the likelihood of the reduced data, T, summarized by C. A given confidence distribution could, in fact, result from many different probability models, each with a specific likelihood.

Frequentist statisticians have discussed at length how to obtain confidence intervals for one-dimensional interest parameters from the likelihood of the data in view of its probability basis. Barndorff-Nielsen and Cox (1994) discuss adjusted likelihoods and other modified likelihoods based on saddle-point approximations, such as the r^*. Efron and Tibshirani (1993) and Davison and Hinkley (1997) present methods based on bootstrapping and quadratic approximations. These methods are very useful, and in our context they are needed when inference based on all the available data combined in the integrated likelihood is done. However, to obtain the integrative likelihood requires the likelihood components representing the (unavailable) data behind the confidence distributions. To recover a likelihood from a confidence distribution is a problem that, as far as we know, has not been addressed in the literature. In the Bayesian tradition, however, it is considered good practice to report separately the likelihood and the posterior distribution (Berger et al. 1999).

By definition, a likelihood is a probability density regarded as a function of the parameters, keeping the data at the observed value. A confidence distribution cannot be interpreted as a probability distribution. It distributes confidence and not probability. The confidence density is therefore not usually a candidate for the likelihood function we seek. It is the probability distribution of the confidence distribution, regarded as the data, that matters. We now demonstrate by means of a simple example that a given confidence distribution can relate to many different likelihoods, depending on its different probability bases.

E 13.6 *Consider the uniform confidence distribution over* [0.4, 0.8]. *The cumulative confidence distribution function is*

$$C(\psi) = (\psi - 0.4)/0.4 \quad \text{for } 0.4 \le \psi \le 0.8. \tag{11}$$

This confidence distribution could have come about in many different ways, and the likelihood associated with the confidence distribution depends on the underlying probability models.

Shift model. *In this model, the confidence distribution is based on a statistic with the sampling property*

$$T = \psi - 0.2 + 0.4\,U,$$

where U *is uniform (0, 1). The observed value is* $T_{obs} = 0.6$, *which indeed results in (11). The density of* T *is* $f(t; \psi) = 2.5$ *on* $-0.2 < t < \psi + 0.2$, *and the log-likelihood becomes 0 on* $(T_{obs} - 0.2, T_{obs} + 0.2)$ *and* $-\infty$ *outside this interval.*

Scale model. *The confidence distribution is now based on*

$$T = 0.4 + \left(\tfrac{1}{2}\psi - 0.2\right)/U.$$

The observed value $T_{obs} = 0.6$ *leads to the uniform confidence distribution over* [0.4, 0.8]. *In this scale model the density of* T *is*

$$f(t;\psi) = \frac{\frac{1}{2}\psi - 0.2}{(t-0.4)^2} \quad \text{for } t > 0.2 + \tfrac{1}{2}\psi,$$

and the log-likelihood is $\log(\psi - 0.4)$ *for* $0.4 < \psi < 2T_{obs} - 0.4$.

Transformed normal model. *Now let the confidence distribution be based on the statistic*

$$T = 0.4\left\{1 + \Phi\left(Z + \Phi^{-1}\left(\frac{\psi - 0.4}{0.4}\right)\right)\right\} \quad \text{for } 0.4 \le \psi \le 0.8,$$

where $Z \sim N(0,1)$. *Again, with* $T_{obs} = 0.6$, *the confidence distribution is uniform over the interval* $[0.4, 0.8]$. *The likelihood is invariant under a transformation of the data, say*

$$V = \Phi^{-1}(T/0.4 - 1) = Z + \Phi^{-1}\left[(\psi - 0.4)/0.4\right].$$

Since then $V_{obs} = 0$, *the log-likelihood is*

$$l(\psi) = -\tfrac{1}{2}\left\{\Phi^{-1}\left((\psi - 0.4)/0.4\right)\right\}^2 \quad \text{for } 0.4 \le \psi \le 0.8.$$

Three possible log-likelihoods consistent with the uniform confidence distribution are shown in Fig. 13.3. Other log-likelihoods are also possible.

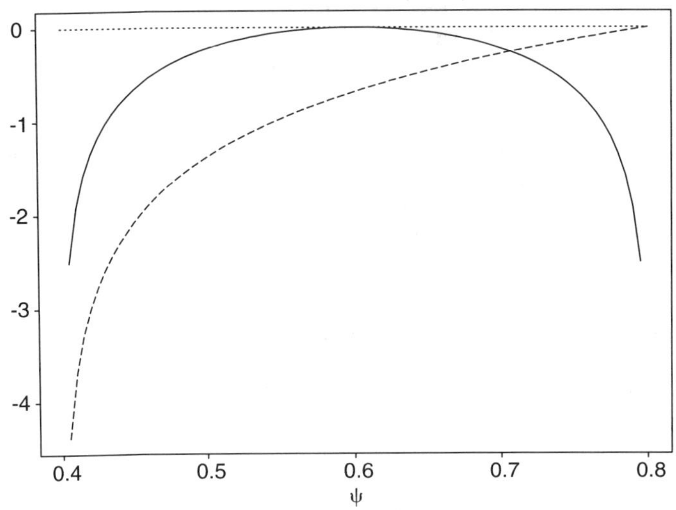

Fig. 13.3 Three log-likelihoods consistent with a uniform confidence distribution over [0.4, 0.8]. *"Many likelihoods informed me of this before, which hung so tottering in the balance that I could neither believe nor misdoubt."*—SHAKESPEARE.

13.4.1 Confidence and Likelihoods Based on Pivots

Assume that the confidence distribution $C(\psi)$ is based on a pivot piv with cumulative distribution function F and density f. Since ψ is one-dimensional, the pivot is typically a function of a one-dimensional statistic T in the data X. The probability density of T is (Fisher, 1930)

$$f^T(t;\psi) = f\,(\mathrm{piv}(t;\psi)) \left|\frac{d\mathrm{piv}(t;\psi)}{\mathrm{d}t}\right|. \tag{12}$$

Here $L(\psi; t) = f^T(t;\psi)$ is indeed a likelihood when regarded as a function of ψ for an observed value of t. If T is a sufficient statistic, L is typically the full likelihood. In other cases, when T is a one-dimensional function of a more complex sufficient statistic, T is the result of dimension reduction to obtain focused inference for ψ. Then the likelihood $L(\psi; t)$ is also the result of reducing the dimensionality of the full underlying likelihood, and we call it the reduced likelihood (Schweder and Hjort, 2002).

Since $\mathrm{piv}(T;\psi) = F^{-1}(C(\psi))$ we have the following.

Proposition 7 *When the probability basis for the confidence distribution is a pivot* piv (T; ψ) *in a one-dimensional statistic* T, *increasing in* ψ, *the reduced likelihood is*

$$L(\psi; T) = f\left(F^{-1}(C(\psi))\right) \left|\frac{d\mathrm{piv}(T;\psi)}{\mathrm{d}T}\right|.$$

The confidence density is also related to the distribution of the pivot. Since one has $C(\psi) = F(\mathrm{piv}(T;\psi))$,

$$c(\psi) = f(\mathrm{piv}(T;\psi)) \left|\frac{d\mathrm{piv}(T;\psi)}{d\psi}\right|. \tag{13}$$

Thus, the reduced likelihood is in this simple case related to the confidence density by

$$L(\psi; T) = c(\psi)\frac{d\mathrm{piv}(T;\psi)}{dT}\left(\left|\frac{d\mathrm{piv}(T;\psi)}{d\psi}\right|\right)^{-1}.$$

13.4.2 Normal-Based Reduced Likelihoods

There are important special cases. If the pivot is additive in T (at some measurement scale), say

$$\mathrm{piv}(T;\psi) = T - \mu(\psi), \tag{14}$$

for a smooth monotone function μ, the likelihood is $L(\psi; T) = f\left(F^{-1}(C(\psi))\right)$. Furthermore, when the pivot distribution is normal, we say that the confidence distribution has a normal probability basis.

Proposition 8 *[Normal-based likelihood.] When the probability basis for the confidence distribution is an additive and normally distributed pivot, the log-likelihood related to the confidence distribution is*

$$l(\psi) = -\tfrac{1}{2}\left[\Phi^{-1}\left(C(\psi)\right)\right]^2.$$

The normal-based likelihood might often provide a good approximate likelihood. Note that classical first-order asymptotics lead to normal-based likelihoods. The conventional method of constructing confidence intervals with confidence $1-\alpha$,

$$\left\{\psi\colon 2\left[l(\widehat{\psi}) - l(\psi)\right] < \Phi^{-1}\left(1-\tfrac{1}{2}\alpha\right)\right\},$$

where $\widehat{\psi}$ is the maximum likelihood estimate, is equivalent to assuming the likelihood to be normal based. The so-called ABC confidence distributions of Efron (1993), concerned partly with exponential families, have an asymptotic normal probability basis, as have confidence distributions obtained from the r^* (Barndorff-Nielsen and Wood, 1998).

In many applications, the confidence distribution is found by simulation. One might start with a statistic T which, together with an (approximate) ancillary statistic A, is simulated for a number of values of the interest parameter ψ and the nuisance parameter χ. The hope is that the conditional distribution of T given A is independent of the nuisance parameter. This question can be addressed by applying regression methods to the simulated data. The regression might have the format

$$T = \mu(\psi) + \tau(\psi)V, \tag{15}$$

where V is a scaled residual. Then $\mathrm{piv}(T;\psi) = [T - \mu(\psi)]/\tau(\psi)$, and the likelihood is

$$L(\psi) = f\left(F^{-1}\left(C(\psi)\right)\right)/\tau(\psi).$$

The scaling function τ and the regression function μ might depend on the ancillary statistic.

E 13.7 *Let* X *be Poisson with mean* ψ. *The half-corrected cumulative confidence distribution function is*

$$C(\psi) = 1 - \sum_{x=0}^{X} e^{-\psi}\frac{\psi^x}{x!} + \tfrac{1}{2}e^{-\psi}\frac{\psi^X}{X!}e^{-\psi}.$$

Here $\mathrm{Y} = 2(\sqrt{\psi} - \sqrt{\mathrm{X}})$ *is approximately* $\mathrm{N}(0,1)$ *and is accordingly approximately a pivot for moderate to large* ψ. *From a simulation experiment, one finds that the distribution of* Y *is slightly skewed, and has tails a bit longer than the normal. By a little trial and error, one finds that* $\exp(\mathrm{Y}/1000)$ *is closely Student distributed with* $\mathrm{df} = 30$. *With* Q_{30} *being the upper quantile function of this distribution and* t_{30} *the density, the log-likelihood is approximately*

$$l_s(\psi) = \log t_{30}\,(Q_{30}\,(C(\psi))) - \log t_{30}(0).$$

Examples are easily drawn to illustrate that the $l_s(\psi)$ *log-likelihood quite closely approximates the real Poisson log-likelihood* $l(\psi) = x - \psi + x \log(\psi/x)$.

Usually, the likelihood associated with a confidence distribution is different from the confidence density. The confidence density depends on the parameterization. By reparameterization, the likelihood can be brought to be proportional to the confidence density. This parameterization might have additional advantages.

Let $L(\psi)$ be the likelihood and $c(\psi)$ the confidence density for the chosen parameterization, both assumed to be positive over the support of the confidence distribution. The quotient

$$J(\psi) = L(\psi)/c(\psi)$$

has an increasing integral $\mu(\psi)$, with $(d/d\psi)\mu = J$, and the confidence density of $\mu = \mu(\psi)$ is $L[\mu(\psi)]$. There is thus always a parameterization that makes the likelihood proportional to the confidence density.

When the likelihood is based upon a pivot of the form $\mu(\psi) - T$, the likelihood in $\mu = \mu(\psi)$ is proportional to the confidence density of μ.

E 13.8 *Let* $\widehat{\psi}/\psi$ *be standard exponentially distributed. Taking the logarithm, one brings the pivot into translation form, and* $\mu(\psi) = \log\psi$. *The likelihood and the confidence density is thus* $c(\mu) \propto L(\mu) = \exp(\widehat{\mu} - \mu - \exp(\widehat{\mu} - \mu))$. *Bootstrapping this confidence distribution and likelihood is achieved by adding the bootstrap residuals* $\log V^*$ *to* $\widehat{\mu}$ *above, where* V^* *is standard exponentially distributed. The log-likelihood has a more normal-like shape in the* μ *parameterization than in the canonical parameter* ψ. *Also, as a translation family in* μ, *the likelihood and the confidence density are easily interpreted.*

Reduced likelihoods obtained from pivots (as in proposition 7) are reduced in more than one sense. Nuisance parameters are removed and the reduced likelihood is a likelihood only in the parameter of interest. The data are reduced to the scalar statistic in the pivot, and the model is in a sense reduced to the model for the pivot alone. Marginal and conditional likelihoods, when they exist, are often useful as reduced likelihoods. There is of course a substantial literature on likelihoods and their modifications (see, e.g., Barndorff-Nielsen and Cox, 1994).

Fisher (1930) introduced his fiducial distributions, here called confidence distributions, through pivots and (13). It is remarkable that en passant he also gave (12). He clearly understood (12) as a likelihood counterpart to (13). This insight seems not to have survived well in the literature.

13.5 ILLUSTRATION: A POPULATION DYNAMICS MODEL FOR BOWHEAD WHALES

The management of fisheries and whaling rests on the quality of stock assessments. Within the International Whaling Commission, the assessment of the stock of bowhead whales subject to exploitation by Native Americans in Alaska has been discussed repeatedly. The most recent assessment was done by Bayesian methodology (see International Whaling Commission, 1999; Poole and Raftery, 1998; Schweder, 2003).

Raftery and his co-workers have developed the Bayesian synthesis approach, and the most recent version of this approach is presented in Poole and Raftery (1998). They use "Bayesian melding" to harmonize conflicting prior distributions. In addition to using their method on the more complex age-specific population dynamics model used by the International Whaling Commission, they also illustrate their method on a simplified version of the model. We illustrate our method and compare it to the Bayesian synthesis approach by applying it to the simplified population dynamics model with the data used by Poole and Raftery (1998, sec. 3.6).

Poole and Raftery (1998) understand their prior distributions as prior probability distributions to be used in a Bayesian integration. We reinterpret these prior distributions as prior confidence distributions. Instead of a Bayesian integration, these confidence distributions are integrated with the likelihood of P_{1993} and yearly rate of increase ρ, after having been converted to likelihoods. To do this, we have to determine their probability basis. As Bayesians, Poole and Raftery are not concerned with this issue, and so no information is available. For simplicity, we chose to assume a normal probability basis for each of the three prior confidence distributions, which determines their likelihoods as follows.

At the beginning of year t, there are P_t bowhead whales. With C_t being the catch in year t, the deterministic dynamical model is

$$P_{t+1} = P_t - C_t + P_t\, 1.5\, \mu\{1 - (P_t/P_{1848})^2\},$$

where P_{1848} is taken as the carrying capacity of the stock, and μ (maximum sustainable yield rate) is the productivity parameter. Yankee whaling started in 1848. From that year on, the catch history $\{C_t\}$ is available and is assumed to be known exactly. There are two free parameters in this model. We choose these to be μ and P_{1848}. Stock sizes for other years are also parameters, but are determined by μ and P_{1848}. Poole and Raftery (1998) list the following independent priors:

$$P_{1848} \sim 6400 + \text{Gamma}(2.81, 0.000289),$$
$$\mu \sim \text{Gamma}(8.2, 372.7),$$

$$P_{1993} \sim N(7800, 1300^2),$$

where Gamma(a, b) denotes the gamma distribution with mean a/b and standard deviation $\sqrt{a}/b$.

In addition to prior information, there are two log-likelihood components based on recent survey data. One component concerns P_{1993}, and is the Gaussian

$$l_4(P_{1993}) = -\tfrac{1}{2}\{(P_{1993} - 8293)/626\}^2.$$

The source of this information is different from that for the prior distribution for P_{1993} above. The other component concerns the recent rate of increase in stock size ρ, which is defined through $P_{1993} = (1 + \rho)^{15} P_{1978}$. It has likelihood

$$l_5(\rho) = \frac{9}{2} \log \left\{ 1 + \frac{1}{8} \left(\frac{\log(1 + \rho) - 0.0302}{0.0069} \right)^2 \right\} - \log(\rho + 1)$$

obtained from the t-distribution with eight degrees of freedom, and an exponential transformation (Poole and Raftery, 1998).

The combined log-likelihood

$$l = l_1(P_{1848}) + l_2(\mu) + l_3(P_{1993}) + l_4(P_{1993}) + l_5(\rho)$$

is an extremely narrow curved ridge. (See the bootstrap sample of maximum likelihood estimate in Fig. 13.4.) The maximum likelihood estimate is presented in Table 13.1 together with quantiles of the confidence distributions for the various parameters obtained by the abc method, having employed 1,000 bootstrap replicates.

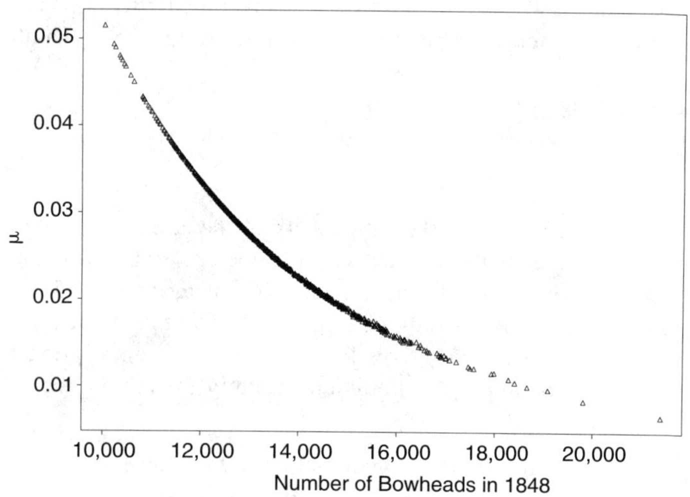

Fig. 13.4 One thousand bootstrap estimates of P_{1848} and μ.

TABLE 13.1
Maximum Likelihood Estimates and Quantiles for Prior and Posterior of Frequentist and Bayesian Distributions for Parameters of Interest

Parameter	Maximum likelihood estimate	Quantile	Prior	Posterior	Bayesian
		0.025	8,263	10,932	12,057
P_{1848}	13,152	0.5	14,997	13,017	14,346
		0.975	30,348	16,085	17,980
		0.025	0.0096	0.0157	0.0113
μ	0.0267	0.5	0.0211	0.0275	0.0213
		0.975	0.0394	0.0425	0.0333
		0.025		7,027	7,072
P_{1993}	8,117	0.5		8,117	8,196
		0.975		9,207	9,322
		0.025		0.0145	0.0105
ρ	0.0255	0.5		0.0261	0.0204
		0.975		0.0377	0.0318

The bootstrapping is determined by the probability bases of the likelihood components as follows:

$$l_1^*(P_{1848}) = -\tfrac{1}{2}\left[\Phi^{-1}(G_{2.81,0.000289}(P_{1848} - 6400)) + Z^*\right]^2,$$
$$l_2^*(\mu) = -\tfrac{1}{2}\left[\Phi^{-1}(G_{8.2,372.7}(\mu)) + Z^*\right]^2,$$
$$l_3^*(P_{1993}) = -\tfrac{1}{2}\{(P_{1993} - 7{,}800)/1300 + Z^*\}^2,$$
$$l_4^*(P_{1993}) = -\tfrac{1}{2}\{(P_{1993} - 8{,}200)/564 + Z^*\}^2,$$
$$l_5^*(\rho) = \frac{9}{2}\log\left\{1 + \frac{1}{8}\left(\frac{\log(1+\rho) - 0.0302}{0.0069} + T_8^*\right)^2\right\} - \log(\rho + 1).$$

Here the four Z^*s are independently drawn from the standard normal distribution and independently from T_8^*, which is drawn from the t_8-distribution. For each draw of these five "bootstrap residuals," the perturbed likelihood is maximized, leaving us with the bootstrap estimate $\theta^* = (P_{1848}^*, \mu^*)$.

Each bootstrap replicate θ^* induces bootstrap replicates of P_{1993} and ρ through the deterministic population dynamics model. The bootstrap distributions are nearly normal for the two induced parameters, $P_{1993}^* \sim N(8117, 556^2)$ and $\rho^* \sim N(0.0249, 0.0059^2)$. By simple bias correction relative to the maximum likelihood estimates, we obtain the quantiles in Table 13.1. For the primary parameters, transformation is necessary to obtain normality for the bootstrap sample. This is achieved by a Box–Cox transformation of exponent -1 : $10{,}000/P^*_{1848} \sim N(0.7525, 0.0748^2)$, whereas a square root transform normalizes the bootstrap distribution of μ:

$$(\mu^*)^{1/2} \sim N(0.1611, 0.0206^2). \tag{16}$$

Kolmogorov–Smirnov tests yielded p-values around 0.5 in both cases. A simple bias correction on these scales leaves us with the confidence quantiles in Table 13.1. For comparison, the corresponding quantiles obtained by the Bayesian analysis of Poole and Raftery (1998) are also included.

The probability basis of the input confidence distributions leading to the log-likelihoods l_1, l_2, and l_3 provides a basis for the bootstrap, as explained earlier. For ρ, we assume the likelihood given by Poole and Raftery (1998) to be based on the estimate of ρ, appropriately transformed, being a T_8 distance from the transformed parameter, where T_8 is drawn from a t-distribution with eight degrees of freedom.

The prior and posterior confidence densities of μ are shown in Fig. 13.5. The main reason for the posterior being shifted to the right of the prior confidence distribution is the influence of the data on ρ. The bootstrap density for μ is also shown. Note that the bias correction pushed the posterior confidence distribution toward higher values of μ. The bias correction is roughly +6 percent in this parameter.

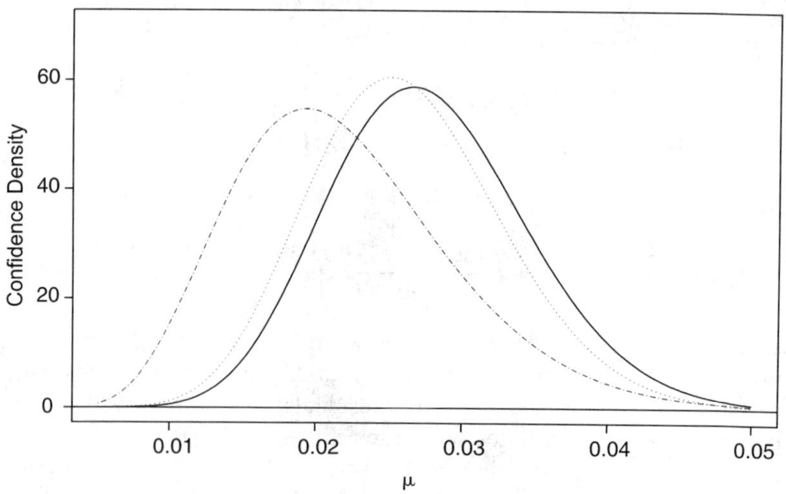

Fig. 13.5 Prior confidence density (broken line), bootstrap density (dotted), and posterior confidence densities for μ.

The probability basis for the posterior confidence distribution for μ is normal. It is, in fact, based on (16) and an assumption of the posterior confidence distribution on this scale only being shifted by a constant amount relative to the bootstrap distribution, $\mu^{1/2} \sim (\mu^*)^{1/2} + b$. The bias correction b is estimated as

$$2\left[(\widehat{\mu})^{1/2} - \text{mean}\left\{(\mu^*)^{1/2}\right\}\right] = 0.0046,$$

where $\widehat{\mu}$ is the maximum likelihood estimate of μ. With the probability basis being normal, the posterior log-likelihood of μ is

$$l_{\text{post}}(\mu) = -\tfrac{1}{2}\left(\mu^{1/2} - 0.166\right)^2/0.0206^2.$$

13.6 DISCUSSION

The confidence distribution is an attractive format for reporting statistical inference for parameters of primary interest. To allow good use of the results in the future it is desirable to allow a likelihood to be constructed from the confidence distribution. Alternatives are to make the original data available or to present the full likelihood. However, the work invested in reducing the original data to a confidence distribution for the parameter of interest would then be lost. To convert the posterior confidence distribution to a likelihood, the probability basis for the confidence distribution must be reported.

Our suggestion is to extend current frequentist reporting practice from reporting only a point estimate, a standard error and a (95%) confidence interval for the parameters of primary interest. To help future readers, one should report the confidence distribution fully and supplement it with information on its probability basis, for example, the pivot and its distribution. This latter information might be qualitative.

13.6.1 Frequentist Updating of Information

The advantages of representing the information contained in a confidence distribution in the format of (an approximate) likelihood function are many and substantial.

By adding the log-likelihoods of independent confidence distributions for the same parameter, an integrated likelihood, and thus a combined confidence distribution is obtained. The merging of independent confidence intervals, for example, has attracted considerable attention, and the use of reduced likelihoods offers a solution to the problem. One might, for instance, wish to merge independent confidence intervals for the same parameter to one interval based on all the data. When the probability basis and the confidence distribution are known for each data set, the related log-likelihoods can be added, and an integrative confidence distribution (accompanied with its probability basis) is obtained.

A related problem is that of so-called meta-analyses. If independent confidence distributions are obtained for the same parameter, the information is combined by adding the accompanying reduced log-likelihoods. A frequent problem in meta-analysis, however, is that the interest parameter might not have exactly the same value across the studies. This calls for a model that reflects this variation, possibly by including a random component. In any event, the availability of reduced likelihood functions from the various studies facilitates the meta-analysis, whether a random component is needed or not.

Studies in fields such as ecology, economics, and geophysics often utilize complex models with many parameters. To the extent that results are available for some of these parameters, it might be desirable to include this information in the study. If these previous results appear in the form of confidence distributions accompanied by explicit probability bases, their related likelihoods are perfectly suited to carry this information into the combined likelihood of the new and the previous data. If a confidence distribution is used that is not based on (previous) data, but on subjective judgment, its related likelihood can still be calculated and combined with other likelihood components, provided assumptions regarding its probability basis can be made. This subjective component of the likelihood should then, perhaps, be regarded as a penalizing rather than a likelihood term.

Finally, being able to obtain the related likelihood from confidence distributions and to calculate confidence distributions from data summarized by a likelihood within a statistical model leads to the emergence of a methodology that is parallel to and in competition with Bayesian methodology and is frequentist in its foundation. As the Bayesian methodology, it provides a framework for coherent learning and its inferential product is a distribution—a confidence distribution instead of a Bayesian posterior probability distribution. To highlight the parallel, the confidence distribution obtained in a study might be regarded as a frequentist posterior distribution. On the other hand, the reduced likelihood, related to an earlier confidence distribution, can be regarded as a frequentist prior when used in a likelihood synthesis.

13.6.2 Differences from the Bayesian Paradigm

It is pertinent to compare the Fisher–Neyman approach (Lehmann, 1993), as further developed in this chapter and in Schweder and Hjort (2002), with the Bayesian approach to coherent learning. Most importantly, the two approaches have the same aim: to update distributional knowledge in the view of new data within the frame of a statistical model. The updated distribution could then be subject to further updating at a later stage and so on. In this sense, our approach could be termed "frequentist Bayesian" (a term both frequentists and Bayesians would probably dislike). There are, however, substantial differences between the two approaches. Compared to the Bayesian approach, we emphasize the following.

Distributions for parameters are understood as confidence distributions and not probability distributions. The concept of probability is reserved for (hypothetically) repeated sampling and is interpreted frequentistically. To update a confidence distribution it must be related to its probability basis, as the likelihood related to the confidence distribution. To update a distribution the frequentist needs more information than the Bayesian, namely, its probability basis. On the other hand, the distinction between probability and confidence is basic in the frequentist tradition.

The frequentist can start from scratch, without any (unfounded) subjective probability distribution. In complex models, there might be distributional information available for some of the parameters, but not for all. The Bayesian is then stuck, or she has to construct priors. The frequentist, however, will not have principle problems in such situations. The concept of noninformativity is, in fact, simple for likelihoods. The noninformative likelihoods are simply flat. Noninformative Bayesian priors, on the other hand, are a thorny matter. In general, the frequentist approach is less dependent on subjective input to the analysis than the Bayesian. But if subjective input is needed, it can readily be incorporated (as a penalizing term in the likelihood).

In the bowhead example, there were three priors but only two free parameters. Without modifications of the Bayesian synthesis approach such as the melding of Poole and Raftery (1998), the Bayesian gets into trouble. Owing to the Borel paradox (Schweder and Hjort, 1997), the Bayesian synthesis will, in fact, be completely determined by the particular parameterization. With more prior distributions than there are free parameters, Poole and Raftery (1998) propose to meld the priors to a joint prior distribution of the same dimensionality as the free parameter. This melding is essentially a (geometric) averaging operation. If, however, there is independent prior distributional information on a parameter, it seems wasteful to average the priors. If, say, all the prior distributions happen to be identical, their Bayesian melding will give the same distribution. The Bayesian will thus not gain anything from k independent pieces of information, whereas the frequentist will end up with a less dispersed distribution; the standard deviation will, in fact, be the familiar $\sigma/\sqrt{k}$.

Nonlinearity, nonnormality, and nuisance parameters can produce bias in results, even when the model is correct. For example, the maximum likelihood estimator of variance in a standard regression model is biased. From a frequentist point of view, Bayesian posterior distributions can also be severely biased, and this has been emphasized repeatedly in the frequentist literature. Such bias should, as far as possible, be corrected in the reported results. The confidence distribution should be unbiased: When it is exact, the related confidence intervals have exactly the nominal coverage probabilities. Bias correction has traditionally not been a concern in the Bayesian tradition. There has, however, been some recent interest in the matter (see, e.g., Berger et al., 1999). To obtain frequentist unbiasedness, the Bayesian will have to choose her prior with unbiasedness in mind. Is she then a Bayesian? Her prior distribution will then not represent prior knowledge of the parameter in case, but an understanding of the model. Our "frequentist Bayesianism" solves this problem in principle. It takes as input (unbiased) prior confidence distributions and delivers (unbiased) posterior confidence distributions.

Efron (1998) regards Bayesians as the optimists among statisticians, while the frequentists are the pessimists. The Bayesian will always (in principle) obtain a proper posterior distribution when her prior is proper. (When it is improper, as is often the case, there might be unforeseen consequences (see, e.g., van Dijk, chapter 25, this volume). The frequentist, however, might end up with an improper confidence distribution, as was the case for Ericsson et al. (1998, see sec. 2.3). The frequentist might, in fact, find that the data only allow informative statements (finite confidence intervals) up to a certain level of confidence. "Life is easier" for the Bayesian in other respects as well. She has a clear concept of joint posterior distributions, and she obtains her one-dimensional posteriors by simple marginalization. Multivariate confidence distributions are difficult. Only in special cases are they available, and then marginalization leads to acceptable one-dimensional confidence distributions when further assumptions are satisfied. The difficulties stem from the insistence on the null property of confidence distributions—that any confidence interval shall have the nominal coverage probability. Unbiasedness in this sense has its price, which is usually disregarded by Bayesians.

REFERENCES

Barndorff-Nielsen, O. E., and D. R. Cox, 1994, *Inference and Asymptotics*, London: Chapman & Hall.

Barndorff-Nielsen, O. E., and T. A. Wood, 1998, "On Large Deviations and Choice of Ancillary for p^* and r^*," *Bernoulli* 4, 35–63.

Berger, J. O., B. Liseo, and R. L. Wolpert, 1999, "Integrated Likelihood Methods for Eliminating Nuisance Parameters (with Discussion)," *Statistical Science* 14, 1–28.

Davison, A. C., and D. V. Hinkley, 1997, *Bootstrap Methods and their Application*, Cambridge: Cambridge University Press.

DiCiccio, T. J., and B. Efron, 1996. "Bootstrap Confidence Intervals (with Discussion)," *Statistical Science* 11, 189–228.

Dufour, J. M., 1997, "Some Impossibility Theorems in Econometrics with Applications to Structural and Dynamic Models." *Econometrica* 65, 1365–1387.

Edwards, A. W. F., 1992, *Likelihood* (Expanded Ed.), Baltimore: John Hopkins University Press.

Efron, B., 1987, "Better Bootstrap Confidence Intervals (with Discussion), *Journal of the American Statistical Association* 82, 171–200.

Efron, B., 1993, "Bayes and Likelihood Calculations from Confidence Intervals," *Biometrika* 80, 3–26.

Efron, B., 1998, "R. A. Fisher in the 21st Century (with Discussion)," *Statistical Science* 13, 95–122.

Efron, B., and R. J. Tibshirani, 1993, *An Introduction to the Bootstrap*, London: Chapman & Hall.

Ericsson, N. R., E. S. Jansen, N. A. Kerbesian, and R. Nymoen, 1998, "Interpreting a Monetary Condition Index in Economic Policy," Technical Report, Department of Economics, University of Oslo.

Fieller, E. C., 1940, "The Biologial Standardization of Insuline," *Journal of the Royal Statistical Society Supplement* 7, 1–64.

Fieller, E. C., 1954, "Some Problems in Interval Estimation (with Discussion)." *Journal of the Royal Statistical Society Series B* 16, 175–185.

Fisher, R. A., 1930, "Inverse Probability," *Proceedings of the Cambridge Philosophical Society* 26, 528–535.

Fraser, D. A. S., 1996, "Some Remarks on Pivotal Models and the Fiducial Argument in Relation to Structural Models," *International Statistical Review* 64, 231–236.

Fraser, D. A. S., 1998, "Contribution to the Discussion of Efron's Paper," *Statistical Science* 13, 118–120.

Hald, A., 1998, *A History of Mathematical Statistics from 1750 to 1930*, New York: Wiley.

Hall, P., 1992, *The Bootstrap and Edgeworth Expansions*, Budapest: Springer-Verlag.

International Whaling Commission, 1999, Report of the Scientific Committee, Annex G. Report of the Sub-Committee on Aboriginal Subsistence Whaling. *Journal of Cetacean Research and Management* 1(Suppl.), 179–194.

Koschat, M. A., 1987, "A Characterisation of the Fieller Solution," *Annals of Statistics* 15, 462–468.

Lehmann, E. L., 1959, *Testing Statistical Hypotheses*, New York: Wiley.

Lehmann, E. L., 1993, "The Fisher, Neyman–Pearson Theories of Testing Hypotheses: One Theory or Two?" *Journal of the American Statistical Association* 88, 1242–1249.

Neyman, J., 1941, "Fiducial Argument and the Theory of Confidence Intervals," *Biometrika* 32, 128–150.

Poole, D., and A. E. Raftery, 1998, "Inference in Deterministic Simulation Models: The Bayesian Melding Approach," Technical Report No. 346, Department of Statistics, University of Washington.

Royall, R. M., 1997, *Statistical Evidence: A Likelihood Paradigm*, London: Chapman & Hall.

Schweder, T., 1988, "A Significance Version of the Basic Neyman–Pearson Theory for Scientific Hypothesis Testing (with Discussion)," *Scandinavian Journal of Statistics* 15, 225–242.

Schweder, T., 2003, "Integrative Fish Stock Assessment by Frequentist Methods: Confidence Distributions and Likelihoods for Bowhead Whales," *Scientia Marina* 67 (Suppl. 1), 89–97.

Schweder, T., and N. L. Hjort, 1996, "Bayesian Synthesis or Likelihood Synthesis: What Does the Borel Paradox Say?" *Reports of the International Whaling Commission* 46, 475–479.

Schweder, T., and N. L. Hjort, 1997, "Indirect and Direct Likelihoods and Their Synthesis," Statistical Research Report No. 12, University of Oslo.

Schweder, T., and N. L. Hjort, 2002, "Confidence and Likelihood," *Scandinavian Journal of Statistics* 29, 309–332.

Staiger, D., J. H. Stock, and M. W. Watson, 1997, "The NAIRU, Unemployment and Monetary Policy," *Journal of Economic Perspectives* 11, 33–49.

Chapter Fourteen

On the COLS and CGMM Moment Estimation Methods for Frontier Production Models

Harald E. Goldstein

This chapter is concerned with the estimation and specification problem of the error term distribution for stochastic frontier production models as introduced by Aigner et al. (1977) and Meeusen and van den Broeck (1977), in which the error term is decomposed in two parts, one representing efficiency differences between units and the other true random differences such as measurement errors (cf. Van den Broeck et al., 1980).

The models discussed are of Cobb-Douglas type:

$$\begin{aligned} y_i &= x_i'\beta + \varepsilon_i \\ \varepsilon_i &= V_i - U_i, \qquad i = 1, \cdots, n, \end{aligned} \tag{1}$$

where the observation units are firms; y_i is output measured on the logarithmic scale, ε_i is the error term, β is a vector of parameters, and x_i is a vector of inputs in addition to other relevant variables such as the constant 1, corresponding to the constant term. The model may also be written, $y_i = z_i - U_i$, where $z_i = x_i'\beta + V_i$ represents the stochastic frontier function. The (U_i, V_i) are considered to be iid as (U, V), where U, the inefficiency part, is distributed on the positive axis and V, the measurement error part, has a distribution usually assumed to be symmetric with expectation 0. If the assumption of symmetry for V is true, then evidence of nonsymmetry in the distribution of the residuals from (1) may be taken as evidence of the presence of inefficiencies in the class of firms studied.

One common motivation for this kind of model is the estimation of (technical) efficiency or inefficiency measures derived from the distribution of U for specified classes of firms (see, e.g., the survey paper by Schmidt, 1985–1986). I consider here two examples of such measures, "the average technical efficiency," (ATE) (Afriat, 1972), and "the average technical inefficiency" (ATI) (Schmidt and Lovell, 1979), defined by

$$\begin{aligned} \text{ATE} &= E(e^{-U}) \\ \text{ATI} &= E(U) \end{aligned} \tag{2}$$

If there are inefficiencies, that is, if $P(U_i > 0) > 0$, then the error term, ε_i has negative expectation $E(\varepsilon_i) = -E(U_i)$. Therefore, because of the constant term in the regression (1), it is clear that the location of the distribution of U is not identified, and thus neither is ATE nor ATI unless additional assumptions are imposed on the distribution of U. Such assumptions, combined with the symmetry assumption for V, are mostly ad hoc and hard to justify theoretically and empirically. They are usually imposed to allow identification and preferably efficient estimation of the model parameters by, for example, the maximum likelihood method (ML). However, owing to the ad hoc nature of the assumptions, both identification and efficiency are at best of uncertain value, unless such an analysis is accompanied by a diagnostic analysis with a focus on the identifying assumptions in particular. A complete diagnostic analysis may be too much to ask for, but whatever evidence can be found should be considered.

It is this accompanying diagnostic analysis that is the main theme of this chapter. In the univariate case described earlier I focus on the well-known "corrected least squares estimators" COLS as described, for example, in Olson et al. (1980), which is basically a moment method. In addition to that univariate case I also discuss a multivariate case in Section 14.5 utilizing the generalized moment method (GMM), called the corrected generalized moment method (CGMM) in the present context. It turns out that both methods offer diagnostic opportunities that are worth exploring. For illustration I use data from three Norwegian industrial sectors in the univariate case and data from the Norwegian bus sector in the multivariate case.

I start with the univariate case, where I first consider the "normal-truncated-normal" (NTN) specification for (U, V), introduced by Stevenson (1980). Then V is normally distributed,

$$V \sim N\left(0, \sigma_v^2\right) \tag{3}$$

and U is truncated normally distributed with $U \geq 0$, that is,

$$U = (A \mid A \geq 0) \tag{4}$$

where $A \sim N\left(\mu, \sigma_u^2\right)$. The parameter vector $\theta' = (\beta', \mu, \sigma_u, \sigma_v)$ may be efficiently estimated by the ML as indicated, for example, in Lee (1983). The COLS method involves OLS estimates of the regression model in (1) combined with the moment estimators of μ, σ_u, σ_v, based on the residuals, followed by an adjustment of the constant term in the regression. Although inefficient, COLS estimators are consistent and simpler to compute than the ML estimators. Thus, they may provide convenient starting values for ML or some efficient two-step estimator, as well as being of interest in their own right. For example, Monte Carlo evidence shows, at least in the restricted "half-normal case" (obtained by setting $\mu = 0$ in the distribution of U) that the COLS estimators sometimes behave quite well compared to ML (see Olson et al., 1980). When n is large, they may be of interest because of numerical reasons. The ML estimates may call for unwieldy computations as the likelihood function does not reduce to a simple form and requires separate calculations for each firm in each iteration.

For the purposes of this chapter it is interesting that the behavior of the COLS sometimes indicates defects in the model specification, in which case ML estimation on step two, without a respecification of the model, is less reasonable. In Section 14.1 a number of restrictions on the theoretical moments of ε are derived for the NTN model that may not be confirmed by empirical moments, as illustrated by the Norwegian data. The COLS procedure may therefore lead to various types of failures that suggest special corner solutions or a respecification of the error distribution. The specification tests presented in Section 14.1.3 may supplement other specification tests as given, for example, in Schmidt and Lin (1984) and Lee (1983).

In Sections 14.2, 14.5, I consider alternative specifications, of which the first is the normal-gamma model (see, e.g., Stevenson, 1980), where the distribution of U is specified as gamma. This intersects the NTN model in the sense that the exponential distribution can be regarded as a limiting case for the truncated-normal distribution. The normal-gamma model also has the advantage that it implies less strong restrictions on the moments of ε than the NTN model.

The normal assumption for V not only seems somewhat arbitrary but involves strong assumptions on the tail behavior of V that have consequences for the efficiency estimation. Recognizing this, I discuss two other specifications, "t-gamma," where V is t-distributed, and "s-gamma," where the distribution of V is specified as symmetric about zero with finite moments at least up to the tenth order. The last semiparametric case is of interest mainly when the sample size is large. The danger of concluding full efficiency when the error distribution is symmetrical is also pointed out.

Section 14.5 describes a multivariate case where the generalized method of moments is combined with the moment method for the residuals (CGMM). The multivariate situation offers additional opportunities to identify the shape of the distribution of U.

The final section contains some conclusions while theorems and proofs relevant for the previous discussion are collected in the appendix.

14.1 THE NTN MODEL AND ITS RESTRICTIONS

Assume that V is normal and U truncated normal as specified in (3) and (4). Let μ_j be the jth central moment about the mean of $\varepsilon = V - U$. The COLS moment method is based on the relationship

$$(\beta', \mu, \sigma_u, \sigma_v) \leftrightarrow (\beta', \mu_2, \mu_3, \mu_4), \tag{5}$$

which, as I prove, is one-to-one under a number of restrictions on μ_2, μ_3, μ_4. The relationship is somewhat complicated so I try to describe it in a form that is convenient for empirical analysis. It is also important to know the restrictions involved since, in a case in which the sample moments of the residuals from (1) do not satisfy the restrictions, one can conclude, first, that the moment estimates of μ, σ_u, σ_v do not exist as solutions of the moment equations and, second, that there is diagnostic evidence against the specification (3) and (4). An example of this is given in Section 14.1.3. I also discuss various corner solutions that are connected to the endpoints of the restrictions and also have a bearing on the measures of efficiency and inefficiency.

14.1.1 Characteristics of the Moments of $V - U$

For convenience I introduce the auxiliary parameter

$$t := \mu/\sigma_u \tag{6}$$

where ":=" means equality by definition. I also need the following version of Mills' ratio [$1/h(-t)$ is known as Mills' ratio (see, e.g., Ray and Pitman, 1963)].

$$h(x) := \phi(x)/\Phi(x), \tag{7}$$

where ϕ and Φ are the density and the distribution function, respectively, of the standard normal distribution. Some properties of h are given in lemma A.2 in the appendix.

The dependence of μ_j on μ, σ_u, σ_v is easily derived from the cumulant generating function for ε (see, e.g., Kendall and Stuart, 1969),

$$K(s) := \frac{s^2\sigma_v^2}{2} + \ln h(t) - \ln h(t - \sigma_u s), \tag{8}$$

which is defined as the log of the moment generating function and derived in (84)–(88). The jth cumulant κ_j is obtained from the jth derivative of K, that is, $\kappa_j = K^{(j)}(0)$.

Utilizing $h'(x)/h(x) = -(h(x) + x)$ (see lemma A.2) yields

$$K'(s) = \left(\sigma_u^2 + \sigma_v^2\right) s - \sigma_u t - \sigma_u h(t - \sigma_u s).$$

The relationship between the central moments and the cumulants is well known, giving:

$$\mathrm{E}(\varepsilon) = \kappa_1 = -\sigma_u[h(t) + t], \tag{9}$$

$$\mu_2 = \kappa_2 = \sigma_v^2 + \sigma_u^2[h'(t) + 1], \tag{10}$$

$$\mu_3 = \kappa_3 = -\sigma_u^3 h''(t), \tag{11}$$

$$\mu_4 = \kappa_4 + 3\kappa_2^2 = 3\mu_2^2 + \sigma_u^4 h'''(t). \tag{12}$$

The moment estimators are obtained by solving (10)–(12), with μ_j replaced by the sample moments of the residuals from (1), noting that the central moments for ε of order two and above are equal to the corresponding moments for $\varepsilon - E(\varepsilon)$.

By lemma A.2 we have that $h''(t) > 0$ for all t, which implies that

$$\mu_3 < 0 \tag{13}$$

and

$$\sigma_u = \left(\frac{|\mu_3|}{h''(t)} \right)^{1/3}. \tag{14}$$

Together with (10) this gives

$$\sigma_v^2 = \mu_2 - |\mu_3|^{2/3} R_1(t), \tag{15}$$

where

$$R_1(t) := \frac{1 + h'(t)}{h''(t)^{2/3}}. \tag{16}$$

Equations (12) and (14) yield

$$\mu_4 = 3\mu_2^2 + |\mu_3|^{4/3} R_2(t), \tag{17}$$

where

$$R_2(t) := \frac{h'''(t)}{h''(t)^{4/3}}. \tag{18}$$

According to lemma 1.1 $R_2(t)$ is monotone in t. Hence, by (17) we find t expressed by μ_2, μ_3, μ_4:

$$t = R_2^{-1} \left(\frac{\mu_4 - 3\mu_2^2}{|\mu_3|^{4/3}} \right). \tag{19}$$

This together with (14) and (15), shows how $(\mu = t\sigma_u, \sigma_u, \sigma_v)$ can be written as a function of (μ_2, μ_3, μ_4).

Some important properties of the auxiliary functions $R_1(t)$ and $R_2(t)$ are collected in the following lemma (see also Figs. 14.1 and 14.2):

Lemma 1.1 *(A)* $\mathrm{R}_1(\mathrm{t})$ *is an everywhere increasing function such that: (i)* $\mathrm{R}_1(\mathrm{t}) > 2^{-2/3}$ *for all* t, *and* $\mathrm{R}_1(\mathrm{t}) \to 2^{-2/3}$ *as* $\mathrm{t} \to -\infty$*; and (ii)* $\mathrm{R}_1(\mathrm{t}) \to \infty$ *as* $\mathrm{t} \to \infty$.

(B) $\mathrm{R}_2(\mathrm{t})$ *is an everywhere-decreasing function such that: (i)* $\mathrm{R}_2(\mathrm{t}) < 3 \cdot 2^{-1/3}$ *for all* t, *and* $\mathrm{R}_2(\mathrm{t}) \to 3 \cdot 2^{-1/3}$ *as* $\mathrm{t} \to -\infty$*; and (ii)* $\mathrm{R}_2(\mathrm{t}) \to -\infty$ *as* $t \to \infty$.

See the appendix for proof.

The plots of $R_1(t)$ and $R_2(t)$ given in Figs. 14.1 and 14.2 turn out to be useful in finding the moment estimates for (t, σ_u, σ_v), solving (14), (15), and (19) with μ_j replaced by the corresponding empirical moments of the residuals from the regression (1). Since $R_1(t)$ is bounded below and $R_2(t)$ is bounded above, they also show when the moment equations do not have solutions and when the estimate for t is unstable, that is, when $R_2(t)$ is nearly flat.

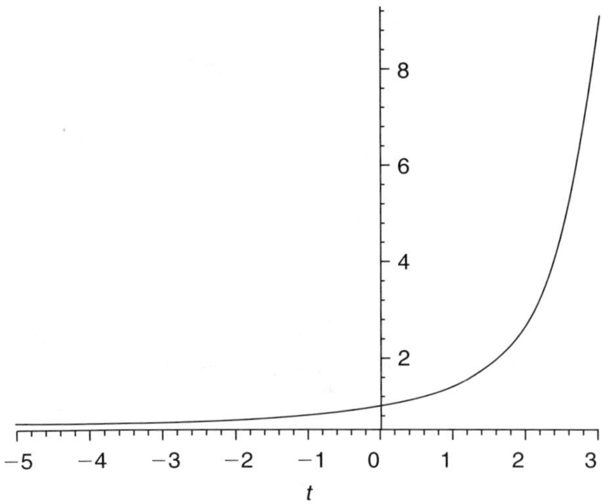

Fig. 14.1 Plot of $R_1(t)$.

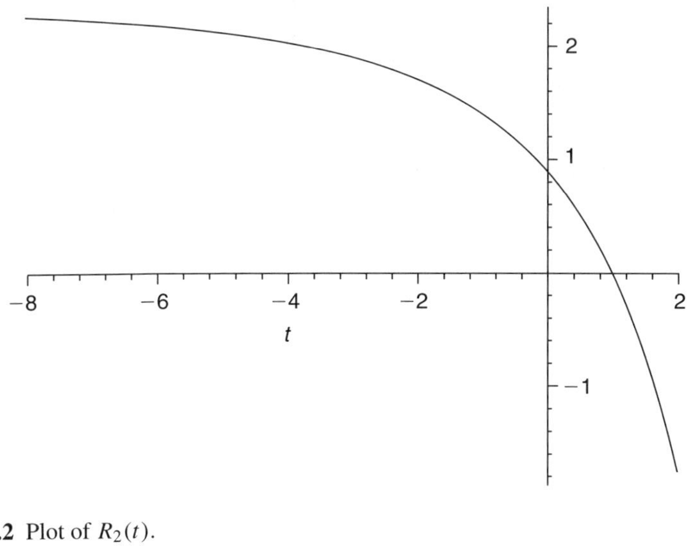

Fig. 14.2 Plot of $R_2(t)$.

The restrictions implied by the model now follow from lemma 1.1:

Theorem 1.1 *(A) Let* μ_j *be the* j*th central moment of* $\varepsilon = \mathrm{V} - \mathrm{U}$. *The parameters* $(\mu, \sigma_u, \sigma_v)$ *stand in a one-to-one relationship with* (μ_2, μ_3, μ_4) *satisfying*

$$-2\mu_2^{3/2} < \mu_3 < 0, \tag{20}$$

$$3\mu_2^2 + |\mu_3|^{4/3} R_2 \left[R_1^{-1}(c)\right] < \mu_4 < 3\mu_2^2 + |\mu_3|^{4/3} \cdot 3 \cdot 2^{-1/3}, \tag{21}$$

where

$$c := \mu_2/|\mu_3|^{2/3} \tag{22}$$

(B) The relation $(\mu, \sigma_u, \sigma_v) \longrightarrow (\mu_2, \mu_3, \mu_4)$ *is given by (10)–(12), where* $t := \mu/\sigma_u$. *The relation* $(\mu_2, \mu_3, \mu_4) \longrightarrow (\mu, \sigma_u, \sigma_v)$ *is given by (14), (15), (19), and* $\mu = t\sigma_u$.

(C) The auxiliary parameter t *satisfies the restriction* $t \leq t_0 := R_1^{-1}(c)$ *and* $t = t_0$ *is equivalent to* $\sigma_v = 0$.

See the appendix for proof.

The restrictions (20) and (21) can be expressed in a slightly simpler form by introducing the so-called "skewness" γ_1 and "kurtosis," sometimes called "excess kurtosis," γ_2 (see, e.g., Kendall and Stuart, 1969), defined by

$$\gamma_1 := \mu_3/\mu_2^{3/2},$$
$$\gamma_2 := \mu_4/\mu_2^2 - 3.$$

Then the restrictions (20) and (21) can be expressed as

$$-2 < \gamma_1 < 0, \tag{23}$$

$$|\gamma_1|^{4/3} R_2\left[R_1^{-1}(|\gamma_1|^{-2/3})\right] < \gamma_2 < |\gamma_1|^{4/3} \cdot 3 \cdot 2^{-1/3}. \tag{24}$$

Substituting the lower bound for γ_1 in (24) one obtains an upper bound for γ_2,

$$\gamma_2 < 6. \tag{25}$$

Empirical evidence (see, e.g., Section 14.1.3) suggests that these restrictions sometimes do not hold for real economic data, thus revealing potential deficiencies of the econometric model rather than expressing reasonable economic hypotheses.

14.1.2 Corner Solutions

I now show that all bounds in (23)–(25) represent meaningful corner solutions that are reasonable for inclusion in the model. The bounds -2 for γ_1 and 6 for γ_2 are both sharp in the sense that γ_1 and γ_2 can be arbitrarily close to their bounds within the model. In fact, keeping μ_3 fixed and letting $t \to -\infty$ and $\sigma_v \to 0$, we get from (15) and lemma 1.1 that $\gamma_1 \to -2$, which implies that both bounds in (24) approach 6 and hence $\gamma_2 \to 6$. Keeping μ_3 fixed and letting $t \to -\infty$, then, according to theorem A.1, the distribution of U converges with all its moments to an exponential distribution with density

$$f_u(x) = (1/a)e^{-x/a}, \qquad x \geq 0, \tag{26}$$

where

$$a = \mathrm{E}(U) = (\mid \mu_3 \mid /2)^{1/3}. \tag{27}$$

The skewness and kurtosis of an exponential distribution are 2 and 6, respectively, thus confirming the limits noted earlier. The similarity of the distribution of U with the exponential distribution for negative μ was also noted by Stevenson (1980).

Now look at the case, $\sigma_v = 0,\ t > -\infty$. Since by (17),

$$\gamma_2 = |\gamma_1|^{4/3} R_2(t), \tag{28}$$

from (15) one gets

$$\sigma_v = 0 \Leftrightarrow t = R_1^{-1}\left(|\gamma_1|^{-2/3}\right),$$

which, by (28), is equivalent to the lower bound of (24),

$$\gamma_2 = |\gamma_1|^{4/3} R_2\left[R_1^{-1}\left(|\gamma_1|^{-2/3}\right)\right]. \tag{29}$$

In this case, $\varepsilon = -U$, or, in other words, the nonstochastic frontier case with truncated-normal inefficiency. This corner solution may be tested by testing the condition (29) in terms of the sample moments of the residuals from the basic regression (1).

The case $\sigma_v = 0$ and $t = -\infty$ is characterized by $\varepsilon = -U$, that is, the nonstochastic frontier case, where U is exponentially distributed as (26), and occurs if and only if $\gamma_1 = -2$ (and $\gamma_2 = 6$). This is true because if $\sigma_v > 0$ and $t = -\infty$, then by (15) and $R_1(t) \geq R_1(-\infty) = 2^{-2/3}$, one gets

$$\gamma_1 = \frac{\mu_3}{\left[\sigma_v^2 + \left(|\ \mu_3\ |\ /2\right)^{2/3}\right]^{3/2}} > -2$$

Hence, this case can be tested by testing the condition $\gamma_1 = -2$ (or $\gamma_2 = 6$) in terms of the sample moments of the residuals.

The case $\sigma_v > 0$ and $t = -\infty$ is known as the stochastic frontier case, with $\varepsilon = V - U$, where U is exponentially distributed in accordance with (26). Then, by (28) and $R_2(-\infty) = 3 \cdot 2^{-1/3}$,

$$\gamma_2 = |\gamma_1|^{4/3} \cdot 3 \cdot 2^{-1/3}, \tag{30}$$

which is the upper bound in (24). Hence, this corner solution may be tested by testing the moment condition (30).

There is also a possible corner solution in connection with $t = \infty$. By letting $t \to \infty$ in the moment generating function (mgf) of U [see (87)], one finds

$$\lim_{\to\infty} Q_u(s) = \lim_{\to\infty} \frac{h(t)}{h(t + s\sigma_u)} = \lim_{\to\infty} \frac{\varphi(t)}{\varphi(t + s\sigma_u)} = \lim_{\to\infty} e^{s\sigma_u t + (s^2\sigma_u^2)/2} = e^{s\mu}$$

if $t \to \infty$ in such a way that $\mu > 0$ is fixed and $\sigma_u \to 0$. The mgf $e^{s\mu}$ represents a distribution with unit mass in μ. Thus, this corner solution is characterized by $\varepsilon = V - \mu$, where the inefficiency part is constant. The case of $\mu = \sigma_u = 0$ can clearly be included in the corner solution as well. Here $\mu_3 = \gamma_1 = 0$, that is, the upper bound of (23). Thus, the corner solution $\varepsilon = V - \mu$ for $\mu \geq 0$ is testable by means of the moment condition $\mu_3 = 0$.

14.1.3 Specification Tests for NTN, Illustrated by Norwegian Industry Data

Let m_j be the jth sample central moment of the residuals from a consistent estimation of (1). The residuals are estimates of $\varepsilon - E\varepsilon$ but, being translation invariant, the m_j are still consistent estimates of μ_j, $j \geq 2$. It is a consequence of the model that $\mu_3 < 0$. The case $\mu_3 = 0$ is also possible for $\mu \geq 0$, $\sigma_u = 0$. If $m_3 > 0$, then it is a question of whether it is significantly so. If it is significant, the model should probably be respecified. If it is not and the model is considered to be realistic, it may be interpreted as evidence for full efficiency, unless the inefficiency part U is a constant.

Assume that $m_3 < 0$. It is clear that specification tests can be constructed easily based on the restrictions (23) and (24). Consider, for example, the restriction based on the upper bound in (24), including the endpoint

$$\mu_4 \leq 3\mu_2^2 + |\mu_3|^{4/3} \cdot 3 \cdot 2^{-1/3}, \tag{31}$$

which may be rather important since μ_4 is sometimes large owing to large deviations in efficiency among some firms. If (31) is wrong, then neither the NTN model nor the normal-exponential border case is possible. It is therefore natural to test (31) based on the sample moments. That is, let

$$\delta = \mu_4 - 3\mu_2^2 - |\mu_3|^{4/3} \cdot 3 \cdot 2^{-1/3}.$$

Then, in order to test the hypothesis $\delta \leq 0$, which is implied by NTN, one may use

$$W = m_4 - 3m_2^2 - |m_3|^{4/3} \cdot 3 \cdot 2^{-1/3}. \tag{32}$$

The asymptotic distribution of W, obtained in "the usual way" by linearization, is normal with expectation δ and variance

$$\tau^2 = (1/n)c' \sum c,$$

where

$$c' = \left[-6\mu_2, 4(|\, \mu_3 \,|/2)^{1/3}, 1\right]$$

and the 3×3 matrix $\sum$ is the asymptotic covariance matrix of $\sqrt{n}(m_j - \mu_j)$, $j = 1, 2, 3$.

$$\begin{aligned}\sum = (\sigma_{ij}) = \big[&\mu_{i+j+2} - \mu_{i+1}\mu_{j+1} + (j+1)(k+1)\mu_2\mu_j\mu_k \\ &- (j+1)\mu_j\mu_{k+2} - (k+1)\mu_{j+2}\mu_k\big], \qquad i, j = 1, 2, 3.\end{aligned}$$

TABLE 14.1
Results of the Specification Test Eq. (32) for Three Sectors in 1982

Sector SIC-code	Number of firms	m_2	m_3	m_4	W	Standard Error	P-value
381** (tools, metal products)	1,426	0.2837	−0.1513	0.6258	0.1924	0.0909	0.017
382** (machinery)	1,138	0.3414	−0.00112	0.5923	0.2424	0.0894	0.003
341** (paper, pulp products)	125	0.5371	−0.6314	2.1234	−0.0317	—	> 0.5

As an example I report the results of applying this test to three sectors of Norwegian industry in 1982. The model used is a translog specification of the value added function

$$\ln(VA) = \beta_0 + \beta_1 \ln K + \beta_2 \ln L + \beta_3 (\ln K)^2 + \beta_4 (\ln L)^2 + \beta_5 (\ln K)(\ln L) + \varepsilon, \tag{33}$$

where VA, K, and L are measures of value added, capital, and labor, respectively, and the error term is specified as in (1). From Table 14.1 it can be seen that neither the normal-truncated-normal nor the normal-exponential error term distribution seems warranted for sectors 381 and 382. (381 is short for 381**, which means sector 38100–38199. Correspondingly for sector 382 and 341.)

For sector 341, (pulp products), the COLS moment estimate of t is found by solving [see (17)]

$$3m_2^2 + (| m_3 |)^{4/3} R_2(t) = m_4. \tag{34}$$

A plot of the left side gives $\hat{t} \approx -11$. The asymptotic standard error of $\hat{t}$ is obtained in the usual manner from the asymptotic distribution of (m_2, m_3, m_4) by differentiating [see (17)]

$$t = R_2^{-1}\left(\frac{\mu_4 - 3\mu_2^2}{| \mu_3 |^{4/3}}\right).$$

It may the be seen from lemma A.3 that the asymptotic standard error of $\hat{t}$, for which the estimated value is 54.9, is of order $O(| t^3 |)$ as $t \to -\infty$. This reveals an instability of $\hat{t}$ for large negative t. Note also that the left side of (34) is rather flat for large negative t.

14.1.4 Efficiency Estimation

In the NTN case the technical (in)efficiency measures (2) take the following form:

$$\text{ATE}(t) = Ee^{-U} = \frac{h(t)}{h(t-\sigma_u)}, \tag{35}$$

$$\text{ATI}(t) = EU = \sigma_u\,[t + h(t)] \tag{36}$$

[see, e.g., (96) and (90)]. For fixed μ_2, μ_3, it follows from theorem A.1 that, as $t \to -\infty$, ATE(t) and ATI(t) tend to the corresponding values for the limiting distribution of U:

$$\lim_{t\to-\infty} \text{ATI}(t) = a = \left(|\,\mu_3\,|\,/2\right)^{1/3}, \tag{37}$$

$$\lim_{t\to-\infty} \text{ATE}(t) = 1/(1+a). \tag{38}$$

Similar arguments as for $R_1(t)$ and $R_2(t)$ show that ATE(t) is a concave decreasing function with ATE($-\infty$) $= 1/(1+a)$ as an upper bound, whereas ATI(t) is convex increasing with ATI($-\infty$) $= a$ as a lower bound. As $t \to -\infty$ the derivatives are of order $O(1/t^3)$, and thus neither function varies much with t when t is large negative.

If, on the other hand, the main interest lies in estimating ATE or ATI, the instability of $\hat{t}$ is to a certain extent compensated by the fact that these functions vary only slightly for large negative values of t. For sectors 381 and 382 the estimation based on the NTN model is not meaningful since that model was rejected for both sectors. For sector 341, the (estimated) limiting values are ATE($-\infty$) $= 0.595$ and ATI($-\infty$) $= 0.681$, while the estimates are

$$\widehat{\text{ATE}} = \text{ATE}(-11) = 0.590,$$

$$\widehat{\text{ATI}} = \text{ATI}(-11) = 0.691.$$

The estimated standard errors, 0.29 and 0.14, respectively, are comparatively large here, which appears to be due mainly to the small sample size for this sector.

14.2 THE NORMAL-GAMMA MODEL

As the limit of the NTN model as $t \to -\infty$ entails an exponential distribution for U, it is natural to consider (as has been stressed in the literature) the gamma distribution family for U as an alternative specification (see, e.g., Stevenson, 1980). Thus, assume that V is normally distributed as before, while U is gamma distributed with density

$$f_u(x) = \frac{\lambda}{\Gamma(\psi)}(\lambda x)^{\psi-1}e^{-\lambda x}, \qquad x > 0,$$

with moment generating function

$$Q_u(s) = (1 - s/\lambda)^{-\psi}. \tag{39}$$

The distribution is defined for $\lambda > 0$, $\psi > 0$. Let the jth cumulant for a random variable X be denoted by $\kappa_j(X)$. The cumulants of V are 0 for $j \geq 3$ and for U

$$\kappa_1(U) = EU = \psi/\lambda, \tag{40}$$

$$\kappa_j(U) = (j-1)!\psi/\lambda^j, \quad j \geq 2. \tag{41}$$

Using $\kappa_j(\varepsilon) = \kappa_j(V) + (-1)^j \kappa_j(U)$, one derives the central moments of ε:

$$E\varepsilon = -\psi/\lambda, \tag{42}$$

$$\mu_2 = \kappa_2(\varepsilon) = \sigma_v^2 + \psi/\lambda^2, \tag{43}$$

$$\mu_3 = \kappa_3(\varepsilon) = -2\psi/\lambda^3, \tag{44}$$

$$\mu_4 = 3\kappa_2(\varepsilon)^2 + \kappa_4(\varepsilon) = 3\mu_2^2 + 6\psi/\lambda^4. \tag{45}$$

The skewness and kurtosis of ε are

$$\gamma_1 = -\frac{2\psi}{(\lambda^2\sigma_v^2 + \psi)^{3/2}},$$

$$\gamma_2 = \frac{6\psi}{(\lambda^2\sigma_v^2 + \psi)^2}.$$

It can be seen that the skewness is restricted to be negative and the kurtosis to be positive. Otherwise, unlike the NTN model, they can take on any value. These restrictions are equivalent to

$$\mu_3 < 0, \tag{46}$$

$$\mu_4 - 3\mu_2^2 > 0. \tag{47}$$

The parameters are easily expressed by the moments [putting $a = (| \mu_3 | /2)^{1/3}$ and $b = \mu_4 - 3\mu_2^2$]

$$\lambda = 6a^3/b \tag{48}$$

$$\psi = 216a^{12}/b^3 \tag{49}$$

$$\sigma_v^2 = \mu_2 - 6a^6/b \tag{50}$$

In addition, from (41) and (42),

$$\text{ATE} = Ee^{-U} = \lambda/(1+\lambda)^{\psi} \tag{51}$$

$$\text{ATI} = EU = 36a^9/b^2 \tag{52}$$

The full efficiency case, $U \equiv 0$, appears as a corner model when $\psi \to 0$, in which case the gamma distribution for U degenerates to the trivial distribution with unit mass in zero.

These expressions are well suited for the moment estimators. Formulas for asymptotic standard errors are obtained in the usual manner from the asymptotic distribution of the sample moments by linearization.

TABLE 14.2
Estimates for the Normal-Gamma and *t*-Gamma Model (standard errors in parentheses)

	Estimates					
	Normal-gamma			*t*-gamma		
Parameter	341**	381**	382**	341**	381**	382**
λ	1.5057	1.1810	0.0139	1.2838	1.3396	—
	(0.244)	(0.188)	(0.455)	(0.099)	(0.201)	
ψ	1.0776	0.1246	1.49×10^{-9}	0.6679	0.1819	—
	(0.627)	(0.053)	(1.96×10^{-7})	(0.225)	(0.061)	
σ_v^2	0.0618	0.1944	0.3414	0.1318	0.1824	—
	(0.123)	(0.019)	(0.020)	(0.080)	(0.017)	
ATE	0.5776	0.9264	1.0000	0.6806	0.9036	—
	(0.163)	(0.025)	(7.92×10^{-7})	(0.095)	(0.025)	
ATI	0.7157	0.1055	1.08×10^{-7}	0.5203	0.1358	—
	(0.357)	(0.035)	(1.06×10^{-5})	(0.194)	(0.036)	
ν				3.5206	8.3850	—
				(0.253)	(0.166)	

Table 14.2 shows the COLS estimation results for the example in Section 14.1.3 based on the normal-gamma model. It can be seen that the normal-gamma model in this case leads to a more satisfactory analysis than the NTN model. For sector 341 the efficiency measures are estimated with better precision and the efficiency estimates for sector 381 and 382 are meaningful. For section 382 the corner model of full efficiency seems to apply since $\widehat{\psi}$ is very close to zero. However, see the argument at the end of Section 14.4.

14.3 THE *t*-GAMMA MODEL

The only aspects of the normal distribution for V that have been used in the analysis so far are its skewness and kurtosis being zero. This makes it simple to calculate the effects of misspecification of the distribution of V, the normality assumption being somewhat arbitrary. Assume that the distribution of V is symmetric with the fourth cumulant, $q := \kappa_4(V) > 0$. This entails a larger kurtosis than the normal one, which is zero. Assume that the moments μ_j of ε are given. Then, for the normal-gamma case, the modified expressions for the parameters are obtained by replacing b in (48)–(52) by $b(q) = \mu_4 - 3\mu_2^2 - q = b - q$. It is now easy to see that ATE must decrease whereas ATI must increase as a result of the modification.

Thus, if the stochastic frontier function has a symmetric error distribution with larger kurtosis than the normal one, the COLS method based on the normal-gamma model will tend to overestimate the average efficiency. One should therefore be open to this possibility for the large efficiency estimates in Table 14.2.

One way to investigate this could be to postulate a symmetric distribution for V with more flexible tail behavior than normal. An example is the Student's t distribution, which is symmetric and allows a larger kurtosis. Thus, assume that U is gamma distributed as above and that V is given by

$$V = \sigma_v \sqrt{\frac{\nu - 2}{\nu}} T, \tag{53}$$

where the distribution of T is Student's t with ν degrees of freedom. Then $EV = 0$ and VAR $V = \sigma_v^2$. Here ν is considered a continuous parameter, for which the t distribution is still well defined, but it is required that $\nu > 5$ since the estimation of the parameters by the moment method is based on moments up to fifth order for this model. The central moments of $\varepsilon = V - U$ are easily derived:

$$\mu_2 = \sigma_v^2 + \psi/\lambda^2, \tag{54}$$

$$\mu_3 = -2\psi/\lambda^3, \tag{55}$$

$$\mu_4 = 3\mu_2^2 + 6\psi/\lambda^4 + 6\sigma_v^4/(\nu - 4), \tag{56}$$

$$\mu_5 = -\left(4\psi/\lambda^4\right)\left(5\sigma_v^2 + 6/\lambda^2\right). \tag{57}$$

For the moment estimators one must solve these equations with respect to the parameters. Elementary analysis leads to the following solutions.

Put $a = (\mid \mu_3 \mid /2)^{1/3}$ and $c = (2\mu_2 a^3 + \mu_5)/(60a^5)$. The form of the solution for ψ depends on the value of c. If $c^3 \geq -0.3$ then

$$\psi^{1/3} = c + d + c^2/d,$$

where

$$d = \left(\tfrac{3}{5} + c^3 + \tfrac{3}{5}\sqrt{1 + \tfrac{10}{3}c^3}\right)^{1/3}.$$

If $c^3 < -0.3$ then

$$\psi^{1/3} = -c\left[2\cos(\theta/3) - 1\right],$$

where

$$\theta = \text{arc cos}\left[-\left(3/5c^3\right) - 1\right] \in [0, \pi).$$

The other parameters are given by

$$\lambda = \psi^{1/3}/a,$$
$$\sigma_v^2 = \mu_2 - a^2\psi^{1/3},$$
$$\nu = 4 + 6\psi^{1/3}\frac{\mu_2 - a^2\psi^{1/3}}{\psi^{1/3}(\mu_4 - 3\mu_2^2) - 6a^2}.$$

Here ATI $= a\psi^{2/3}$ and ATE is as in (51).

The estimates obtained from these equations are given in Table 14.2. For sector 381, which has a sample of 1,426 firms, the degree-of-freedom parameter ν is estimated to be 8.4, which indicates that a normal V may be too restrictive for describing the tail behavior of the stochastic production function. On the other hand, the reduction observed in ATE compared to the normal-gamma analysis is not significant.

For sector 382, which contains 1,138 firms, there is little evidence for a non-symmetrical error distribution as both the third and the fifth moment are close to zero ($m_3 = -0.0011$, $m_5 = 0.0095$). (For example, the Wilcoxon test for symmetry about zero gave a p-value of 0.58.) The estimates have not been given since they are numerically difficult to determine and quite unreliable in this case. It is also questionable if the moment estimators exist at all since $m_5 > 0$, whereas the model implies that $\mu_5 < 0$. On the other hand, since m_3, m_5 are not significantly different from zero, there seems to be little evidence against the hypothesis of full efficiency for this sector, given that the model specification for U and V is true. If it is not true, the symmetry of the error distribution does not imply full efficiency in general, as argued at the end of Section 14.4.

For sector 341, there are only 125 firms and the information contained in higher moments is therefore more limited. For this reason the t-gamma analysis based on moments seems of less worth. Moreover, the estimated value of 3.5 for ν is outside the permitted region, reducing the credibility of the other estimates.

It should be pointed out that the standard errors in Table 14.2 for the t-gamma case are not strictly justified for $\nu \leq 10$ since the asymptotic distribution of the moment estimators depends on the moments up to the tenth order. For $\nu \leq 10$ the tenth moment does not exist in the t-distribution. On the other hand, other than its first ten moments no aspect of the t-distribution is used. Therefore, the assumptions of the argument can be modified by saying that the analysis is valid for any distribution of V having the same first five moments as (53) and for which the tenth moment exists. All things considered, the t-gamma model does not seem to be a good alternative to the normal-gamma model in this situation.

14.4 THE *s*-GAMMA MODEL

The last argument may be taken one important step further. Note that ν only occurs in the equation for μ_4 [see Eq. (56)], and that the other parameters are determined by μ_2, μ_3, and μ_5. Thus the t-gamma may be considered a special case of the following semiparametric specification, which is known as the symmetric-gamma (s-gamma) model: Let U be gamma as before and independent of V, which has an arbitrary symmetric distribution with expectation zero and for which the tenth moment exists. Actually only the third and the fifth moments of V have to be zero. Let VAR $V = \sigma_v^2$ and $\gamma := \mu_4(V)/\mu_2(V)^2 - 3$ be the kurtosis of V. Let μ_j denote, as before, the jth central moment of $\varepsilon = V - U$. Since $\mu_3(V) = \mu_5(V) = 0$, in the same way as for t-gamma, one obtains

$$
\begin{aligned}
E\varepsilon &= -\psi/\lambda, \\
\mu_2 &= \sigma_v^2 + \psi/\lambda^2, \\
\mu_3 &= -2\psi/\lambda^3, \\
\mu_4 &= 3\mu_2^2 + 6\psi/\lambda^4 + \gamma\sigma_v^4, \\
\mu_5 &= -\left(4\psi/\lambda^4\right)\left(5\sigma_v^2 + 6/\lambda^2\right).
\end{aligned}
$$

It is also clear that the s-gamma model implies that $\mu_3 < 0$ and $\mu_5 < 0$. Comparing with (54)–(57), one sees that the structure of the first five moments of this model is exactly the same as the t-gamma model except for a reparameterization of ν given by

$$\gamma = 6/(\nu - 4) \tag{58}$$

Thus, the solutions when solving for the parameters are the same as for the t-gamma model. One is rid of the t assumption for V, and ν is simply a reparameterization of γ with no restrictions attached to it (apart from $\nu \neq 4$).

The s-gamma model may seem more natural than the normal-gamma in the sense that it does not depend on the somewhat arbitrary assumption of a normal V. Its disadvantage is, of course, that it requires larger samples for a reliable estimation by the moment method. On the other hand, it is simple to compute, even for large samples.

I do not need to recalculate the estimates to see the effect of the respecification on my example because of the equivalence of the moment structure. The estimates and standard errors, which are justified by the standard asymptotic theory, are as in Table 14.2. The kurtosis can be calculated by (58) replacing ν by its estimate, and the asymptotic standard deviation is estimated by

$$\mathrm{sd}(\hat{\gamma}) \approx \frac{6}{(\hat{\nu} - 4)^2}\mathrm{sd}(\hat{\nu}).$$

Note that there are no restrictions on ν here. Thus, for sector 341, I estimate the kurtosis of V to be $\hat{\gamma} = -12.5$, with standard error 6.61. Hence, there is not strong evidence of a kurtosis for V different from the normal one, which may be due to the small sample size for this sector. On the other hand, Table 14.2 indicates that, for sector 341, the standard errors of the estimated parameters are substantially smaller for the s-gamma model compared to the normal-gamma ones. Considering the arbitrariness of the normality assumption for V, the s-gamma analysis seems to be preferable.

The analyses of sectors 381 and 382 are essentially the same as under the t-gamma model. The estimated kurtosis of V for sector 381 is 1.37 with standard error 0.052. For sector 382, assuming $U \equiv 0$, the kurtosis is 2.08 with standard error 0.61. Thus there is clear evidence against a normal V for both sectors.

The last conclusion, however, including the full efficiency of sector 382, must be taken with a grain of salt because it is based on the assumption that the proposed specification for U and V is true. For all the models studied here, symmetry of the distribution of $\tilde{\varepsilon} = \varepsilon - E(\varepsilon)$ about zero implies full efficiency, $U \equiv 0$ (unless, for the NTN case, U is a constant, which seems unrealistic). In general, however, this is not the case. Since the convolution of two distributions that are both symmetrical about zero is also symmetrical about zero, symmetry of $\tilde{\varepsilon}$ does not, in general, imply $U \equiv 0$. To illustrate this point, consider sector 382, for which the residual distribution is close to symmetrical about zero. Assume, for example, that $V \sim N(0, \sigma_v^2)$ and $U \geq 0$ is symmetrically distributed. This implies that the support of U is finite and included in an interval $(\eta - a, \eta + a)$, where $\eta = E(U)$. Assume further that U is uniformly distributed in $(\eta - a, \eta + a)$, where $\eta \geq a \geq 0$. Then $U - \eta$ is uniformly distributed in $(-a, a)$ and the moment equations for a and σ_v^2 are

$$\mu_2 = \sigma_v^2 + a^2/3,$$

$$\mu_4 = 3\sigma_v^4 + 6\sigma_v^2 (a^2/3) + a^4/5.$$

Applying the moments for sector 382 in Table 14.1 yields the estimates $\widehat{\sigma}_v^2 = 0.17$ and $\widehat{a} = 0.71$, giving the inefficiency estimate for sector 382, $\widehat{\text{ATI}} = \widehat{\eta} \geq 0.71$ and correspondingly for ATE. Thus, unless there are strong a priori reasons to believe in a particular specification of the type described above, the conclusion of full efficiency for sector 382 does not seem to be warranted.

14.5 A MULTIVARIATE CASE: CGMM ANALYSIS

In some cases the output can be considered as given and the efficiency formulated in terms of cost. Since there are usually several cost functions the problem is basically multivariate. In this section I look at one such example in which the data are based on a stratified cross-section sample of Norwegian bus transportation companies in 1991. The output is measured by the number of kilometers of transportation provided by a company, and the inputs are fuel, labor and capital. The data were originally analyzed by Dale-Olsen (1994), who kindly made it available to me for the present analysis, and later discussed by Stigum (1995). Dale-Olsen used a dummy variable technique to reduce the estimation problem to a univariate one. Here I present a multivariate analysis.

The econometric model is formulated by postulating links to the underlying theory, which is an interpreted version of the neoclassical theory of the firm. The link is briefly summarized in what follows (for details see Stigum, 1995).

Stigum operates with a theoretical universe and a data universe as separate entities. The theoretical universe consists of hypothetical firms characterized by the variables, (y, x, w, V, U) and a set of axioms. Here y represents output, kilometers of transportation provided; $x' = (x_1, x_2, x_3)$ denotes the input quantities, number of liters of gasoline, hours of labor, and kroners of capital, respectively; and $w' = (w_1, w_2, w_3)$ is interpreted as the corresponding vector of unit prices. In contrast to the univariate case I interpret $V' = (V_1, V_2)$ as measuring the allocative inefficiencies with U being the technical inefficiency as before.

The data universe representing the population from which the firms of the sample are actually drawn is characterized by the variables $(\widehat{y}, \widehat{x}, \widehat{w}, \widehat{c}, \widehat{g})$ observed in the sample; another set of axioms $\widehat{c}' = (\widehat{c}_1, \widehat{c}_2, \widehat{c}_3)$ represents the observed input costs; $\widehat{g}$ is an indicator identifying the strata (i.e., the nineteen Norwegian counties). The first three components have the corresponding meaning as the theoretical variables, with the exception that x represents the optimal, cost-minimizing inputs, given y, whereas the observed $\widehat{x}$ may include inefficiencies.

The production function is of the form $y = f(x) = G[F(x)]$, where G and F are strictly increasing and F is homogeneous of degree one and strictly quasi-concave. The specification of f is determined by

$$y^a e^{by} = \Lambda x_1^{\alpha} x_2^{\beta} x_3^{\gamma}, \tag{59}$$

where $\Lambda, a, b, \alpha, \beta, \gamma$ are positive constants such that $\alpha + \beta + \gamma = 1$. For this specification, minimum cost $(x'w)$, given y, is ensured by the postulate

$$\alpha x_2/\beta x_1 = w_1/w_2 \qquad \text{and} \qquad \gamma x_2/\beta x_3 = w_3/w_2. \tag{60}$$

The data universe contains only one axiom:

$$\widehat{c}_j = \widehat{x}_j \widehat{w}_j \qquad \text{for} \qquad j = 1, 2, 3. \tag{61}$$

The link between the theoretical universe and the data universe is expressed by the following three postulates. First the output and unit prices are observed without error:

$$y = \widehat{y} \qquad \text{and} \qquad w = \widehat{w}. \tag{62}$$

The technical inefficiency U satisfies

$$y^a e^{by} = \Lambda \widehat{x}_1^{\alpha} \widehat{x}_2^{\beta} \widehat{x}_3^{\gamma} e^{-U} \tag{63}$$

and V_1, V_2, determining the allocative inefficiencies, are expressed by

$$\widehat{x}_2/\widehat{x}_1 = (x_2/x_1)\, e^{V_1} \qquad \text{and} \qquad \widehat{x}_2/\widehat{x}_3 = (x_2/x_3)\, e^{V_2}. \tag{64}$$

For the sampling mechanism, it is assumed that the observed data vectors are drawn independently within each strata from the same distribution. There are no distributional differences among the strata. For each stratum, U, V_1, V_2 are independent random variables that are also assumed to be orthogonal to y, $\ln(y)$, and $\ln(w_j)$ for $j = 1, 2, 3$; thus there is the implicit assumption that the firms are price-takers. Furthermore, for the distribution of V_j one only postulates that it has expectation zero and variance σ_j^2 for $j = 1, 2$. The assumption of normality for V_j is tested later. As for the distribution of $U \geq 0$, I compare two different specifications: (1) truncated normal (NT) with parameters σ_u and $t = \mu/\sigma_u$, as in (4), and (2) generalized gamma (GGAM) with parameters p, k, λ [see (73) further on].

From the postulates it is straightforward to derive the following three theorems from Stigum (1995):

T 1 *Let* $\mathrm{C}(\mathrm{w}, \mathrm{y}, \mathrm{e}^{\mathrm{U}})$ *equal* e^{U} *times the minimum cost at* w *of producing* y. *Then*

$$C\left(w, y, e^{U}\right) = w'xe^{U} = e^{-\alpha V_1 - \gamma V_2}\left(\widehat{w}_1\widehat{x}_1 e^{V_1} + \widehat{w}_2\widehat{x}_2 + \widehat{w}_3\widehat{x}_3 e^{V_2}\right).$$

It follows readily from (59), (63), and (64) that $\widehat{x}_j = x_j e^U k_j(V_1, V_2)$ for $j = 1, 2, 3$, where k_j is a function such that $k_j = 1$ if $V_1 = V_2 = 0$. Therefore $C(w, y, e^U)$ can be interpreted as the cost for a firm with technical but no allocative inefficiency, and $C(\widehat{w}, \widehat{y}, e^U)/\widehat{w}'\widehat{x}$ is thus a measure of allocative efficiency for a firm with values $\widehat{x}$, $\widehat{y}$, and $\widehat{w}$.

T 2

$$V_1 = \ln(\alpha/\beta) + \ln\left(\widehat{c}_2/\widehat{c}_1\right)$$
$$V_2 = \ln(\gamma/\beta) + \ln\left(\widehat{c}_2/\widehat{c}_3\right).$$

T 3 *For* $\mathrm{j} = 1, 2, 3$,

$$\ln(\widehat{c}_j) = K_j + a\ln(\widehat{y}) + b\widehat{y} + \alpha\ln(\widehat{w}_1) + \beta\ln(\widehat{w}_2) + \gamma\ln(\widehat{w}_3) + \widetilde{V}_j + U,$$

where $\mathrm{K}_1 = -[\ln\Lambda + \beta\ln(\beta/\alpha) + \gamma\ln(\gamma/\alpha)]$, $\mathrm{K}_2 = -[\ln\Lambda + \alpha\ln(\alpha/\beta) + \gamma\ln(\gamma/\beta)]$, *and* $\mathrm{K}_3 = -[\ln\Lambda + \alpha\ln(\alpha/\gamma) + \beta\ln(\beta/\gamma)]$; *and where* $\widetilde{\mathrm{V}}_1 = -(\beta+\gamma)\mathrm{V}_1 - \gamma\mathrm{V}_2$, $\widetilde{\mathrm{V}}_2 = \alpha\mathrm{V}_1 + \gamma\mathrm{V}_2$, *and* $\widetilde{\mathrm{V}}_3 = \alpha\mathrm{V}_1 - (\alpha+\beta)\mathrm{V}_2$. *Note that the signs of* $\widetilde{\mathrm{V}}_{\mathrm{i}}$ *are different from those in Stigum (1995).*

In addition, the following is easily derived:

T 4

$$U = \ln\Lambda + \alpha\ln\widehat{c}_1 + \beta\ln\widehat{c}_2 + \gamma\ln\widehat{c}_3 - a\ln\widehat{y} - b\widehat{y} - \alpha\ln\widehat{w}_1 - \beta\ln\widehat{w}_2 - \gamma\ln\widehat{w}_3$$

It is somewhat complicated to estimate the reduced form derived in T 3 as there are restrictions, partly nonlinear, both in the expectation and the covariance matrix. Instead one reduces the system with respect to the error terms as in T 2 and T 4, which turns out to be more suitable for estimation. Defining the reparameterization: $\theta_1 = \ln(\beta/\alpha)$, and $\theta_2 = \ln(\beta/\gamma)$, or

$$\alpha = \frac{e^{\theta_2}}{e^{\theta_1} + e^{\theta_2} + e^{\theta_1+\theta_2}},$$
$$\beta = \frac{e^{\theta_1+\theta_2}}{e^{\theta_1} + e^{\theta_2} + e^{\theta_1+\theta_2}},$$
$$\gamma = \frac{e^{\theta_1}}{e^{\theta_1} + e^{\theta_2} + e^{\theta_1+\theta_2}},$$

it can be seen that there are no restrictions on θ_1, θ_2. Introducing the random variables, Z_1, Z_2, Z_3, I now write the system

$$Z_1 := \ln \widehat{c}_2 - \ln \widehat{c}_1 = \theta_1 + V_1, \tag{65}$$
$$Z_2 := \ln \widehat{c}_2 - \ln \widehat{c}_3 = \theta_2 + V_2, \tag{66}$$
$$\begin{aligned} Z_3 &:= \ln(\widehat{c}_2/\widehat{w}_2) - \alpha Z_1 - \gamma Z_2 - \alpha \ln(\widehat{w}_1/\widehat{w}_2) - \gamma \ln(\widehat{w}_3/\widehat{w}_2) \\ &= \theta_3 + a \ln \widehat{y} + b\widehat{y} + V_3, \end{aligned} \tag{67}$$

where $\eta = E(U)$, $\theta_3 = \eta - \ln \Lambda$, and $V_3 = U - \eta$. Conditional on the exogenous variables, the V_j's are independent with expectation zero and variances σ_j^2, $j = 1, 2, 3$. The exogenous variables are

$$d' := (d_0, d_1, d_2, d_3, d_4) := [1, \ln \widehat{y}, \widehat{y}, \ln(\widehat{w}_1/\widehat{w}_2), \ln(\widehat{w}_3/\widehat{w}_2)]. \tag{68}$$

The system written in this form appears well suited to the GMM estimation (see, e.g., Hansen, 1982). The GMM method provides consistent and asymptotically normally distributed estimates for $\theta' = (\theta_1, \theta_2, \theta_3, a, b)$, given a consistent estimate for $\sum_V = \text{Diag}(\sigma_j^2)$, that is, the covariance matrix of $V' = V(\theta)' = (V_1, V_2, V_3)$. The fifteen moment equations are given by

$$E[V(\theta) \otimes d] = 0, \tag{69}$$

and with empirical counterpart

$$m(\theta) := \frac{1}{n} \sum_{i=1}^{n} V_i \otimes d_i,$$

where n (=118) is the number of units observed, $V_i' = (V_{1i}, V_{2i}, V_{3i})$, and correspondingly for d_i.

Asymptotically optimal estimates of θ of the GMM type are obtained by minimizing

$$q = m(\theta)' \widehat{W}^{-1} m(\theta), \tag{70}$$

where $\widehat{W}$ is a consistent estimate of the asymptotic covariance matrix of $m(\theta)$:

$$W = \frac{1}{n^2} \sum_V \otimes D'D \tag{71}$$

and D is the $n \times 5$ matrix of rows d_i', $i = 1, 2, \ldots, n$.

Applying OLS on (65) and (66) yields consistent estimates of α, β, γ, and σ_j^2, $j = 1, 2$. Upon substituting the estimates for α, γ and applying OLS on

TABLE 14.3
GMM Estimates

Coefficient	Estimate	Standard deviation
θ_1	1.8544	0.0201
θ_2	1.3562	0.0362
θ_3	−1.4114	0.3405
a	0.9558	0.0262
b	6.2087×10^{-8}	1.5826×10^{-8}
α	0.1107	0.0021
β	0.7071	0.0049
γ	0.1822	0.0054
σ_1	0.2178	—
σ_2	0.3969	—
σ_3	0.1484	—

(67), one gets consistent estimates of θ_3, a, b, and σ_3^2, which provides starting values for the minimization of q. Gauss-Newton iterations were used. The GMM estimator $\widehat{\theta}$ obtained is asymptotically normal with expectation θ and covariance matrix $[GW^{-1}G']^{-1}$, where $G := \partial m/\partial\theta'$, consistently estimated by substituting $\widehat{\theta}$ for θ. For $\widehat{W}$ we use the updated estimates of σ_j, based on the residuals from the iterations. The results are given in Table 14.3.

The question of whether one should reiterate by substituting the updated estimate for $\sum_V$ until the estimates stabilize does not arise here since it turns out that in this case re-iteration only affects the estimates in the fourth decimal place.

The goodness-of-fit of the relationships in T 3 appears to be quite good, for example, measured by the squared correlation between $\ln(c_j)$ and its fitted value based on T 3, given by: Fuel (0.984), Labor (0.977), Capital (0.927). However, there is some evidence against the model. The GMM method provides a Wald test of the moment equations (69), as q [see (70)] is approximately χ^2-distributed with ten degrees of freedom (the number of moment equations minus the number of estimated parameters) if (69) is true. Since the observed value was $q = 104.8$ (p-value 0.000) there is evidence against (69), which may be interpreted as evidence against exogeneity of the explanatory variables in d. One possible explanation for this could be the presence of measurement errors in the exogenous variables, which I will not pursue here.

Since W is block diagonal [see (71)], q splits into $q = q_1 + q_2 + q_3$, where $q_j = m_j(\widehat{\theta})'\widehat{W}_j^{-1}m_j(\widehat{\theta})$ represents the five moment equations for V_j. The values are $q_1 = 42.9, q_2 = 53.7, q_3 = 8.2, q = 104.8$.

Thus it appears that it is V_1 and V_2 that are the main contributors to the high value of q. To improve on the situation one tries to omit some of the moment equations, for example, those corresponding to d_3, d_4 [see (68)], tentatively suspecting that these are nonexogenous. The exogenous variables are now $d' := (d_0, d_1, d_2) = (1, \ln\widehat{y}, \widehat{y})$, which gives nine moment equations as in (69), whereas the system is still (65)–(67). In this case one obtains $q = 22.57$ with $q_1 = 12.10$, $q_2 = 10.47$, and $q_3 = 0$. The null distribution for q is χ^2 with four degrees of freedom, which gives a p-value of 0.0002. Although q was substantially reduced by dropping the moment equations for d_3, d_4, it is still significant, and again it is V_1, V_2 that appear to be the cause.

On the other hand, owing to the special structure of the system (65)–(67), it can be seen that the question of the exogeneity of d can be addressed more directly by noting that d being uncorrelated with V_1 and V_2 is equivalent to d being uncorrelated with the observable Z_1 and Z_2. Thus, a test of exogeneity of d would be simply to determine whether the correlation $\rho(d_j, V_k) = \rho(d_j, Z_k)$ is zero for $j = 1, 2, 3, 4$ and $k = 1, 2$. This is done in Table 14.4, which is based on the well-known result that $\frac{1}{2}\ln(1 + r)/(1 - r)$ is approximately normally distributed with expectation $\frac{1}{2}\ln(1 + \rho)/(1 - \rho)$ and variance $1/(n - 3)$, where r and ρ denote sample and population product moment correlation coefficients, respectively, for two variables with iid data.

It can be seen that, except for $\widehat{\rho}(d_4, V_1)$, all the coefficients are significantly different from zero. Hence, all of d_1, d_2, d_3, d_4 fail this exogeneity test. However, because of the illustrative nature of the example I ignore this result in the subsequent discussion.

An advantage of the multivariate situation, in contrast to the univariate case, is that one can identify and estimate the error terms, V_1, V_2, and $V_3 = U - E(U)$, directly by means of the residuals from (65)–(67), $\widehat{V}_j$, $j = 1, 2, 3$. The decile histograms for $\widehat{V}_1$ and $\widehat{V}_2$, shown in Figs. 14.3 and 14.4, indicate that the normality assumption for V_1 and V_2 is not quite warranted (applying, e.g., the Anderson-Darling test for normality gives p-values of 0.032 and 0.002 for $\widehat{V}_1$ and $\widehat{V}_2$, respectively). In particular, the histogram for $\widehat{V}_2$ shows a clear tendency

TABLE 14.4
A Simple Exogeneity Test

Variables	Correlation (ρ)	p-value for $\rho = 0$
$\ln y,\ V_1$	0.307	0.0007
$\ln y,\ V_2$	0.282	0.0019
$y,\ V_1$	0.316	0.0005
$y,\ V_2$	0.200	0.0297
$\ln(w_1/w_2),\ V_1$	−0.580	0.0000
$\ln(w_1/w_2),\ V_2$	−0.446	0.0000
$\ln(w_3/w_2),\ V_1$	−0.151	0.1018
$\ln(w_3/w_2),\ V_2$	−0.641	0.0000

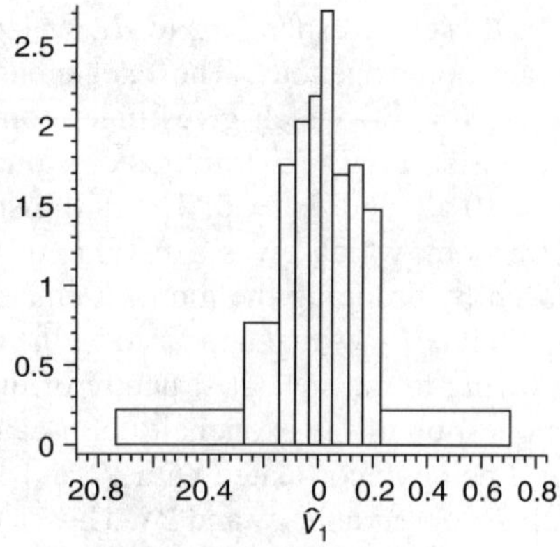

Fig. 14.3 Histogram of $\widehat{V}_1$.

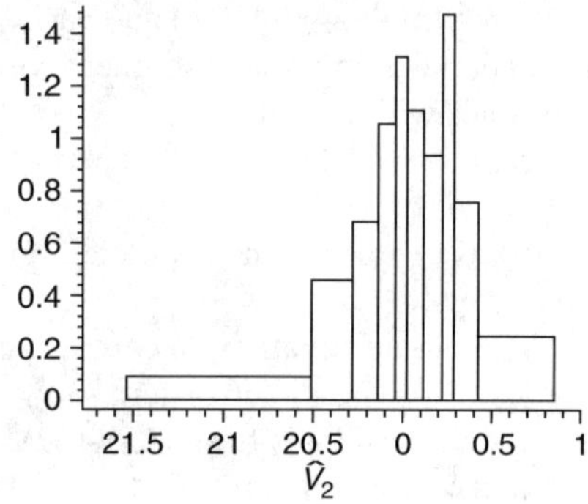

Fig. 14.4 Histogram of $\widehat{V}_2$.

toward left skewness. Thus, if one wishes to estimate the model by maximum likelihood based on normality for V_1 and V_2, it would be preferable to apply the pseudomaximum likelihood method to obtain proper asymptotic standard deviations. This is not pursued here since the focus of this discussion is more on the diagnostic possibilities of the moment methods.

The histogram of $\widehat{V}_3$ is given in Fig. 14.5. Let $\mu_r = \mu_r(U) = \mu_r(V_3)$ for $r \geq 2$ be the central moments, estimated by the sample moments of $\widehat{V}_3$, m_r. Then

	m_2	m_3	m_4
Value	0.021468	0.000167	0.001268
Standard error	0.002616	0.000434	0.000234

(72)

which values are needed to estimate the distribution of U by the moment method. One first assumes that U is truncated normal (TN) as in (4), with parameters, $t = \mu/\sigma_u$ and σ_u, so only two moment equations are needed to estimate this distribution. With notation from Section 14.1, one gets

$$\mu_2 = \sigma_u^2(h'(t) + 1),$$
$$\mu_3 = \sigma_u^3 h''(t).$$

The model implies that $\mu_3 > 0$ (see lemma A.2), which is not contradicted by the data (although m_3 is not significantly different from zero). Solved with respect to t, σ_u, from (16), one obtains

$$t = R_1^{-1}\left(\frac{\mu_2}{\mu_3^{2/3}}\right),$$
$$\sigma_u = \frac{1 + h'(t)}{h''(t)} \frac{\mu_3}{\mu_2},$$

which determine the moment estimators. The results are given in Table 14.5 with standard deviations calculated by the delta method. [For ATE and ATI see (35) and (36).]

Both the TN and the gamma specification imply a right-skewed distribution for U. Since there does not seem to be any a priori reasons why the distribution of U should not be symmetric or left-skewed, I now try the more flexible generalized gamma distribution, which includes the possibility of $\mu_3 \leq 0$. If X is distributed as Gamma$(k, 1)$, then $Y = X^{1/p}/\lambda$ is generalized gamma with parameters (p, k, λ), [in short, $Y \sim$ GGamma(p, k, λ)]. The density is given by

$$f(y) = \frac{p\lambda^{pk}}{\Gamma(k)} y^{pk-1} e^{-(\lambda y)^p}, \qquad \text{for } y > 0, \quad p > 0, \quad k > 0, \quad \lambda > 0. \tag{73}$$

If μ'_r is the rth moment about zero, then

$$\mu'_r = \frac{\Gamma[(r/p) + k]}{\Gamma(k)\lambda^r}, \qquad \text{for } r = 1, 2, \ldots. \tag{74}$$

Writing $B_r := B_r(p, k) := \Gamma(r/p + p)/\Gamma(k)$, one obtains the moment equations for (p, k, λ):

$$\mu_2 = \frac{1}{\lambda^2}\left[B_2 - B_1^2\right],$$
$$\mu_3 = \frac{1}{\lambda^3}\left[B_3 - 3B_2B_1 + 2B_1^3\right],$$
$$\mu_4 = \frac{1}{\lambda^4}\left[B_4 - 4B_3B_1 + 6B_2B_1^2 - 3B_1^4\right].$$

The solution of this system requires numerical iterations and can be found in Table 14.5. The efficiency measures are given by

TABLE 14.5
Estimates Related to the *U* Distribution

	TN		GGamma	
	Coefficient	Standard deviation	Coefficient	Standard deviation
t	2.8298	1.2175	—	—
σ_u	0.1481	0.0098	—	—
p	—	—	3.2863	0.8518
k	—	—	1.1708	1.1302
λ	—	—	1.9977	0.3323
ATI	0.4201	0.1676	0.4785	0.1660
ATE	0.6641	0.1110	0.6264	0.0858
Λ	6.2432	2.3691	6.6191	2.5070

$$\text{ATI} = E(U) = \frac{\Gamma[(1/p) + k]}{\Gamma(k)\lambda}$$

and

$$\text{ATE} = E(e^{-U}) = \frac{p\lambda^{pk}}{\Gamma(k)} \int_0^\infty x^{pk-1} e^{-x-(\lambda x)^p} dx,$$

which requires numerical integration. The calculation of standard deviations by the delta method also requires numerical evaluation of various integrals similar to ATE.

The allocative efficiency in the sample, measured by the mean value of $\left[C(\widehat{w}, \widehat{y}, e^U)/(\widehat{w}'\widehat{x})\right]_i$ is quite high—0.986.

Figure 14.5 shows the decile histogram of $\widehat{V}_3$, with the estimated densities [translated by E(U)]. Note that the two fits are almost identical. The choice between the TN or GGamma specification is, thus, not obvious in this case. GGamma appears to give slightly better precision for the estimation of ATI and ATE, but requires more extensive numerical calculations.

14.6 CONCLUSIONS

The NTN model has a number of disadvantages. It implies certain restrictions on the moments that seem hard to justify on economic grounds. In particular, the boundedness of the kurtosis appears doubtful. The normal-gamma model, on the other hand, contains no such restrictions.

The normal assumption for the symmetrical part of the error term implies strong assumptions on the tail behavior of the stochastic frontier function,

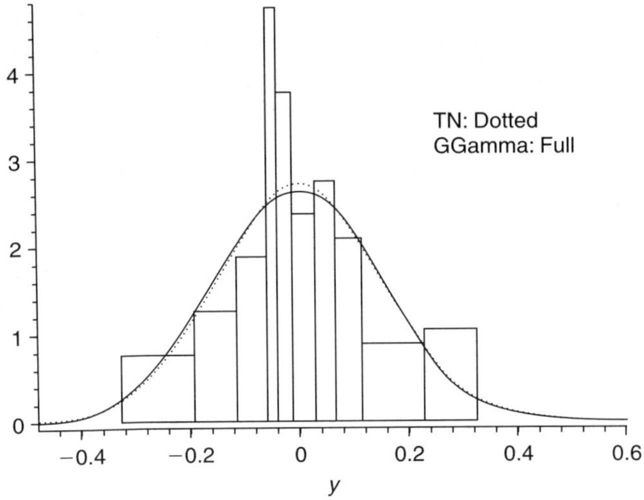

Fig. 14.5 Histogram of $\widehat{V}_3$.

which, considering the arbitrariness of the assumption, may lead to biased efficiency estimation.

The NTN model is somewhat complicated to estimate reliably from the numerical point of view since it involves the Mills' ratio both for ML and moment estimators, which needs careful handling to avoid misleading results.

The COLS estimators are inefficient with respect to the ML estimators for the NTN or the normal-gamma model. On the other hand, the efficiency of the ML estimators is only relevant to the extent that the error term is well founded. When the sample size is small, little information is contained in higher moments, and ad hoc distributional assumptions may lead to estimators that provide reasonable approximations. However, when the sample size is large it seems sensible to try to reduce the arbitrary parts of the model by exploiting the information contained in higher moments or other functionals of the empirical distribution. One possibility is to use the semiparametric model, s-gamma, which is simple to estimate by the COLS method. The gamma assumption for the efficiency part of the error distribution may itself be arbitrary, but the method of the chapter is clearly not limited to this specification. Other specifications for the efficiency part of the error may be treated similarly. For some specifications it is not true that symmetry of the distribution of $\varepsilon - E(\varepsilon)$ implies full efficiency.

The question of specification testing of the s-gamma model was not discussed. Neither did I consider individual efficiency estimation, which may be achieved in the s-gamma case by approximating $E(U \mid \varepsilon)$ in various ways.

The multivariate case has the important advantage that the distribution of $U - E(U)$ can be identified and estimated without ad hoc assumptions. This may lead to valuable information on the shape of U's distribution, which may be symmetrical or left-skewed, contrary to the right-skewed distributions most commonly suggested in the literature. The generalized gamma family of distributions offers such possibilities. The ad hoc assumptions on the distribution of U are still needed for identification of $E(U)$.

The multivariate situation studied also illustrates a case in which the reduced form with respect to the exogenous variables is complicated to estimate, whereas the reduced form with respect to the error terms is considerably simpler applying the GMM.

APPENDIX: PROOFS AND TECHNICAL COMMENTS

To help study asymptotic properties of $h(t)$ [see (7)], I approximate it from above and below by rational functions. A number of approximations have been developed in the literature (see, e.g., Ray and Pitman, 1963; Ruben, 1964). The following approximations, due to Laplace, are good mainly for large negative values of t, which is what they are needed for here.

Lemma A.1 *For* k *integer, define the rational function* g(t, k) *by*

$$g(t, 0) = -t \tag{75}$$

$$g(t, k) = \frac{t^{2k+1}}{-t^{2k} + \sum_{i=1}^{k}(-1)^{i+1} 1 \cdot 3 \cdots (2i-1)t^{2(k-i)}}. \tag{76}$$

Then, if k *is even,*

$$g(t, k) < h(t) < g(t, k+1).$$

The left inequality is valid for all $t < 0$ *and the right holds for all* $t < t_0$, *where* t_0 *is the smallest real root in the denominator of* $g(t, k+1)$; t_0 *exists and is negative.*

Proof. It follows readily from Feller (1964, p. 179) that, for every $t < 0$, $\Phi(t) < \phi(t)/g(t, k)$ when k is even or zero, and $\Phi(t) > \phi(t)/g(t, k)$ when k is odd. In particular, this shows that $g(t, k) > 0$ for every $t < 0$ when k is even. If k is odd, $g(t, k)$ may change sign for $t < 0$. By substituting 0 for t in the denominator of g, it is seen that the denominator must have at least one negative root. The lemma follows from these observations.

Some basic properties of h are collected in the following:

Lemma A.2 *(i)* h *is strictly decreasing.* $h(t) \downarrow 0$ *as* $t \to \infty$.
(ii) $h(t) > -t$, *and as* $t \to -\infty$, $h(t)/t \to -1$.

(iii) The first and second derivatives are

$$h'(t) = -h(t)[h(t) + t], \tag{77}$$

$$h''(t) = 2h^3(t) + 3th^2(t) - (1 - t^2)h(t). \tag{78}$$

(iv) $h''(t) > 0$ *for all* t, *that is,* h *is strictly convex.*
(v). $\lim_{t\to-\infty} t^3 h''(t) = -2$.

Proof. (iii) is straightforward, and (ii) follows from lemma A.1. by noting

$$0 < h(t) + t < \frac{-t^3}{t^2 - 1} + t = \frac{-t}{t^2 - 1}.$$

(i) that $\lim_{t\to\infty} h(t) = 0$ is immediate; (ii) and (iii) imply that h is strictly decreasing. From (78) it follows that the strict convexity of h is equivalent to

$$[2h(t) + t]\,[h(t) + t] - 1 > 0. \tag{79}$$

Equation (79) is clearly satisfied when $t \geq 1$. To prove that $h''(t) > 0$ for $0 \leq t \leq 1$ the inequality is transformed to

$$p(t) := 2\phi(t)^2 + 3t\phi(t)\Phi(t) - (1 - t^2)\Phi(t)^2 > 0$$

Now, since ϕ is concave in [0, 1], $l(t) \leq \phi(t) \leq \phi(0)$, where l is the secant $l(t) = \phi(0) - [\phi(0) - \phi(1)]t$. Thus, for $t \in (0, 1)$,

$$\Phi(t) < \tfrac{1}{2} + t\phi(0) =: c_u(t),$$

$$\Phi(t) > \tfrac{1}{2} + \tfrac{1}{2}\,[\phi(0) + l(t)]\,t =: c_l(t).$$

Hence,

$$\begin{aligned} p(t) &> 2l(t)^2 + 3tl(t)c_l(t) - (1 - t^2)c_u(t)^2 \\ &= 0.196115t^4 + 0.117141t^3 + 0.382133t^2 - 0.0510192t + 0.0683099, \end{aligned}$$

the roots of which are all complex. Therefore $p(t) > 0$.

To prove $h''(t) > 0$ for $t < 0$, I use Shenton's (1954) integral form, according to which

$$\int_0^\infty e^{-tx} e^{-x^2/2}\, dx = \frac{1 - \Phi(t)}{\phi(t)}.$$

Hence,

$$h(t) = 1/M(t),$$

where

$$M(t) := \int_0^\infty e^{tx} e^{-x^2/2}\, dx. \tag{80}$$

Now, $h''(t) > 0$ is equivalent to $T(t) := 2M'(t)^2 - M''(t)M(t) > 0$.

Since

$$M^{(j)}(t) = \int_0^\infty x^j e^{tx} e^{-x^2/2}\, dx = e^{t^2/2} \int_0^\infty x^j e^{-(x-t)^2/2}\, dx,$$

one can write

$$T(t) = e^{t^2} \int_0^\infty \int_0^\infty x(2y - x) e^{-\frac{1}{2}[(x-t)^2+(y-t)^2]}\, dx\, dy. \tag{81}$$

Assume $t < 0$. Introducing polar coordinates $x - t = r\cos\phi$ and $y - t = r\sin\phi$ yields

$$T(t) = e^{t^2/2} \int_{-t\sqrt{2}}^\infty r e^{-r^2/2} A(r)\, dr,$$

where

$$\begin{aligned} A(r) &= \int_{\alpha_r}^{(\pi/2)-\alpha_r} (t + r\cos\phi)(2r\sin\phi + t - r\cos\phi)\, d\phi \\ &= r^2 + 2t\sqrt{r^2 - t^2} + 2\left[t^2 - (r^2/2)\right]\left[(\pi/4) - \alpha_r\right] \end{aligned}$$

and

$$\alpha_r = \arcsin(-t/r)$$

I now prove that $A(r) > 0$ for all $r > -t\sqrt{2}$, which implies that $h''(t) > 0$. Put $s = \sqrt{r^2 - t^2} > -t$ and write $A_0(s) := A[r(s)]$ and $\alpha(s) := \alpha_{r(s)}$. Then $\alpha'(s) = t/(t^2 + s^2)$.

It is found that $A_0(-t) = A_0'(-t) = A_0''(-t) = A_0'''(-t) = 0$, and $A_0'''(s) = 8t^3(t^2 - s^2)/(s^2 + t^2)^3 > 0$ for all $s > -t$. Hence, $A(r) > 0$ for $r > -t\sqrt{2}$.

It remains to prove (v), that $t^3 h''(t) \to -2$ when $t \to -\infty$. Let h_l, h_u be approximations to h such that $h_l < h < h_u$. Then for $t < -1$

$$h'' > 2h_l^3 + 3th_u^2 + (t^2 - 1)h_l =: H_l, \tag{82}$$

$$h'' < 2h_u^3 + 3th_l^2 + (t^2 - 1)h_u =: H_u. \tag{83}$$

Choose $h_l(t) = g(t, 4)$ and $h_u(t) = g(t, 5)$ (see lemma A.1). It can be calculated that the smallest real root of the denominator of $g(t, 5)$ is $-1.953\cdots$. Therefore (82) and (83) hold for $t < -2$. For both $H_l(t)$ and $H_u(t)$ it turns out that when put on a common denominator, a number of the highest-order terms of the numerator cancel out, and they reduce to the following rational forms (checked by the computer program *Mathematica* (see, e.g., Wolfram (1991) or later):

$$H_l(t) = \frac{a_0 + a_1 t + a_2 t^3 + \cdots + a_{20} t^{39} - 2t^{41}}{b_0 + b_1 t^2 + b_3 t^4 + \cdots + b_{21} t^{42} + t^{44}},$$

$$H_u(t) = \frac{c_0 + c_1 t + c_2 t^3 + \cdots + c_{21} t^{41} - 2t^{43}}{d_0 + d_1 t^2 + d_3 t^4 + \cdots + d_{22} t^{44} + t^{46}},$$

where a_i, b_i, c_i, d_i are constants. Since, clearly,

$$\lim_{t \to -\infty} t^3 H_l(t) = \lim_{t \to -\infty} t^3 H_u(t) = -2,$$

(v) follows, which completes the proof of lemma A.2.

I now consider the distribution of $\varepsilon = V - U$, where V, U are independent, $V \sim N\left(0, \sigma_v^2\right)$, and $U = (A \mid A \geq 0)$, where $A \sim N\left(\mu, \sigma_u^2\right)$.

The moment generating function of ε is

$$Q(s) = Ee^{sV} \cdot Ee^{-sU} = e^{s^2\sigma_v^2/2} \int_0^\infty e^{-sx} f_u(x)\, dx, \tag{84}$$

where f_u is the density of U,

$$f_u(x) = \frac{\phi\left[(x - \mu)/\sigma_u\right]}{\sigma_u \Phi\left[(\mu/\sigma_u)\right]}, \qquad x \geq 0 \tag{85}$$

Utilizing (80), I get

$$Q(s) = e^{s^2\sigma_v^2/2} \frac{h(\mu/\sigma_u)}{h\left[(\mu/\sigma_u) - \sigma_u s\right]}. \tag{86}$$

In particular the moment generating function for U is:

$$Q_u(s) = Ee^{sU} = \frac{h(t)}{h(t + \sigma_u s)}, \tag{87}$$

where $t := \mu/\sigma_u$.

The cumulant generating function for ε becomes

$$K(s) := \ln Q(s) = s^2\sigma_v^2/2 + \ln h(t) - \ln h(t - \sigma_u s) \tag{88}$$

Using lemma A.2 (iii) gives

$$\begin{aligned} K'(s) &= \left(\sigma_u^2 + \sigma_v^2\right) s - \sigma_u t - \sigma_u h(t - \sigma_u s), \\ K''(s) &= \sigma_u^2 + \sigma_v^2 + \sigma_u^2 h'(t - \sigma_u s), \\ K^{(j)}(s) &= (-\sigma_u)^j h^{(j-1)}(t - \sigma_u s), \qquad \text{for } j \geq 3. \end{aligned} \tag{89}$$

Let μ_j, κ_j be the jth central moment and cumulant, respectively, for ε. Then $\kappa_j = K^{(j)}(0)$, and

$$E\varepsilon = \kappa_1 = -\sigma_u[t + h(t)], \tag{90}$$

$$\mu_2 = \kappa_2 = \sigma_v^2 + \sigma_u^2[1 + h'(t)], \tag{91}$$

$$\mu_3 = \kappa_3 = -\sigma_u^3 h''(t), \tag{92}$$

$$\mu_4 = \kappa_4 + 3\kappa_2^2 = 3\mu_2^2 + \sigma_u^4 h'''(t). \tag{93}$$

Theorem A.1 *Assume that* μ_3 *is fixed while* $t \to -\infty$. *Let* $Q_u(s) = Ee^{sU}$ *be the moment generating function for* U. *Then, for* $s < 1/a$, *where* $a = (|\mu_3|/2)^{1/3}$

$$\lim_{t\to-\infty} Q_u(s) = 1/(1-as) \tag{94}$$

Hence, U *converges in distribution and with all its moments and cumulants to an exponential distribution with density,* $(1/a)e^{-(u/a)}$.

Proof. Because of (92) and lemma A.2, one must have $\mu_3 < 0$ and, as $t \to -\infty$,

$$\frac{\sigma_u}{t} = -\left(\frac{|\mu_3|}{-t^3h''(t)}\right)^{\frac{1}{3}} \to -\left(\frac{|\mu_3|}{2}\right)^{\frac{1}{3}} = -a. \tag{95}$$

Then, for $s < 1/a$

$$t + \sigma_u s = t(1 + \frac{\sigma_u}{t}s) \to -\infty.$$

From (87) and lemma A.2 it now follows that

$$Q_u(s) = \frac{h(t)}{h(t+\sigma_u s)} = \frac{h(t)}{t} \cdot \frac{t+\sigma_u s}{h(t+\sigma_u s)} \cdot \frac{t}{t+\sigma_u s} \to \frac{1}{1-as}. \tag{96}$$

Since $Q_u(-s)$ and $1/(1+as)$ are the Laplace transforms for U and an exponential distribution, respectively, the convergence in distribution follows. The convergence of the moments and cumulants follows from the fact that Ee^{sU} is bounded in an interval around zero as $t \to -\infty$.

Lemma A.2 (v) can now be generalized:

Theorem A.2 *As* $t \to -\infty$,

$$t^2[1 + h'(t)] \to 1, \tag{97}$$

$$t^{j+1}h^{(j)}(t) \to j!(-1)^{j+1}, \qquad \text{for } j \geq 2. \tag{98}$$

Proof. It is well known that the jth cumulant of the exponential distribution in theorem A.1 is equal to $(j-1)!a^j$ for $j \geq 1$. Theorem A.1 then implies that $\kappa_{u,j} \to (j-1)!a^j$ for $j \geq 1$, where $\kappa_{u,j}$ is the jth cumulant of U. Since the cumulant generating function of U is $K_u(s) = \ln h(t) - \ln h(t - \sigma_u s)$, one gets from lemma A.2 that $K_u'(s) = \sigma_u[t + \sigma_u s + h(t+\sigma_u s)]$. Therefore $K_u''(s) = \sigma_u^2[1 + h'(t+\sigma_u s)]$ and $K_u^{(j)}(s) = (\sigma_u)^j h^{(j-1)}(t + \sigma_u s)$ for $j \geq 3$. Hence,

$$\kappa_{u,2} = (-\sigma_u/t)^2 t^2 \left[1 + h'(t)\right],$$

$$\kappa_{u,j} = (-\sigma_u/t)^j (-t)^j h^{(j-1)}(t), \qquad j \geq 3.$$

Since $\lim_{t\to-\infty}(-\sigma_u/t) = a$, [see (95)], the theorem follows.

From (90)–(93),

$$\sigma_v^2 = \mu_2 - |\mu_3|^{2/3} R_1(t), \tag{99}$$

$$\mu_4 = 3\mu_2^2 + |\mu_3|^{4/3} R_2(t), \tag{100}$$

where

$$R_1(t) := \frac{1 + h'(t)}{h''(t)^{2/3}}, \tag{101}$$

$$R_2(t) := \frac{h'''(t)}{h''(t)^{4/3}}. \tag{102}$$

Some properties of R_1 and R_2 are collected in the following.

Lemma A.3 *As* t $\to -\infty$, *the following limits hold*

(i)	$R_1(t) \to 2^{-2/3}$.
(ii)	$t^3 R_1'(t) \to -2^{4/3}$.
(iii)	$t^3 \frac{d}{dt}\left[t^3 R_1'(t)\right] \to -72 \cdot 2^{1/3}$.
(iv)	$R_2(t) \to 3 \cdot 2^{-1/3}$.
(v)	$t^3 R_2'(t) \to 12 \cdot 2^{2/3}$.
(vi)	$t^3 \frac{d}{dt}\left[t^3 R_2'(t)\right] \to 648 \cdot 2^{2/3}$.

If t $\to \infty$, *then* $\mathrm{R_1(t)} \to \infty$ *and* $\mathrm{R_2(t)} \to -\infty$.

Proof. (i) and (iv) follow from theorem A.2:

$$R_1(t) = \frac{t^2(1 + h')}{(t^3 h'')^{2/3}} \to 2^{-2/3},$$

$$R_2(t) = \frac{t^4 h'''}{(t^3 h'')^{4/3}} \to 6 \cdot (-2)^{-4/3} = 3 \cdot 2^{-1/3}.$$

For $R_j'(t)$ this method, unfortunately, only gives that $t R_j' \to 0$, so a stronger tool is needed. It turns out that the method used for proving (iv) in lemma A.2, works for (ii), (iii), (v) and (vi). I only sketch the proof for (ii):

$$R_1'(t) = \frac{3(h'')^2 - 2(1 + h')h'''}{3(h'')^{5/3}} = \frac{hT(t)}{3(h'')^{5/3}},$$

where

$$\begin{aligned} T(t) &:= h^3(t^2 + 8) + h^2(2t^3 + 20t) + h(t^4 + 14t^2 - 5) + (2t^3 - 6t) \\ &:= h^3 p_3 + h^2 p_2 + h p_1 + p_0. \end{aligned} \tag{103}$$

When t is large negative, the polynomials p_1, p_3 are positive while $p_2 < 0$. Let $h_l < h < h_u$ be rational approximations to h. Then

$$T > T_l := h_l^3 p_3 + h_u^2 p_2 + h_l p_1 + p_0,$$
$$T < T_u := h_u^3 p_3 + h_l^2 p_2 + h_u p_1 + p_0.$$

Choosing $h_l = g(t, 8)$ and $h_u = g(t, 9)$ in lemma A.1 (lower values for k in $g(t, k)$ do not lead to convergence) yields [checked by *Mathematica*, Wolfram, 1991]:

$$T_l = \frac{-24t^{75} + \cdots}{t^{84} + \cdots},$$
$$T_u = \frac{-24t^{77} + \cdots}{t^{86} + \cdots},$$

where I have written the highest-order terms only. This shows that $t^9 T(t) \to -24$ as $t \to -\infty$. Hence,

$$t^3 R_1'(t) = \frac{(h/t)t^9 T(t)}{3(t^3 h'')^{5/3}} \to \frac{(-1)(-24)}{3(-2)^{5/3}} = -2^{4/3}, \tag{104}$$

which proves (ii).

Now assume that $t \to \infty$. From lemma A.2 it follows that $h' \to 0$ and $h'' \to 0$. Hence, $R_1(t) \to \infty$. Since $h(t) \simeq \phi(t)$ for large t, from lemma A.2, one gets

$$h'' = h\left[t^2 - 1 + o(1)\right],$$
$$h''' = h\left[-t(t^2 - 3) - (7t^2 - 4)h - 12th^2 - 6h^3\right] = h\left[-t(t^2 - 3) + o(1)\right]. \tag{105}$$

Thus,

$$R_2(t) = \frac{h'''}{(h'')^{4/3}} = \frac{-t(t^2 - 3) + o(1)}{h^{1/3}\left[t^2 - 1 + o(1)\right]^{4/3}},$$

which shows that $R_2(t) \to -\infty$ as $t \to \infty$.

As a corollary of lemma A.3, one may put down the first three terms of an expansion around $-\infty$ of $R_j(t)$, for if a function with continuous second derivatives satisfies $R(t) \to c_0$, $t^3 R'(t) \to c_1$ and $t^3[t^3 R'(t)]' \to c_2$ when $t \to -\infty$, then

$$R(t) = c_0 - \frac{c_1}{2t^2} + \frac{c_2}{2 \cdot 4t^4} + o\left(\frac{1}{t^4}\right).$$

Thus, when $t \to -\infty$,

$$R_1(t) = 2^{1/3}\left(\frac{1}{2} + \frac{1}{t^2} - \frac{9}{t^4}\right) + o\left(\frac{1}{t^4}\right), \tag{106}$$

$$R_2(t) = 3 \cdot 2^{2/3}\left(\frac{1}{2} - \frac{2}{t^2} + \frac{27}{t^4}\right) + o\left(\frac{1}{t^4}\right). \tag{107}$$

Numerical calculations show that the approximations give three correct digits for $t \leq -7.5$ for R_1 and $t \leq -8$ for R_2. Both approximations give two correct digits for $t \leq -5.5$.

Proof of Lemma 1.1 (Partially Heuristic) From lemma A.3, $\lim_{t\to-\infty} R_1(t) = 2^{-2/3}$ and $\lim_{t\to\infty} R_1(t) = \infty$. For the derivative one has $\lim_{t\to-\infty} t^3 R_1'(t) = -2^{4/3}$. Therefore, at least one knows that there exists a number c_1 such that $R_1(t)$ is increasing for every $t < c_1$. The expression (103) shows that there is another constant c_2 such that $R_1(t)$ is increasing for every $t > c_2$.

Also from lemma A.3, $\lim_{t\to-\infty} R_2(t) = 3 \cdot 2^{-1/3}$, $\lim_{t\to\infty} R_2(t) = -\infty$, and $\lim_{t\to-\infty} t^3 R_2'(t) = 12 \cdot 2^{2/3}$. Therefore, R_2 is, indeed, bounded from above and decreasing for every $t < c_1$ for some $c_1 < 0$. Similarly to R_1 it is not hard to show that there is a c_2 such that R_2 is decreasing for every $t > c_2$.

Thus, what is lacking is a formal proof that R_1 and R_2 are monotone in the central region for t. However, from the plots in Figs. 14.1 and 14.2, and similar plots for the derivatives of R_1 and R_2 not presented, it seems fair to assume that this is true, which I do in this chapter.

Proof of Theorem 1.1 Suppose μ, σ_u, σ_v are given, where $\sigma_u > 0$, $\sigma_v > 0$, and $t = \mu/\sigma_u$. Then, by (13), $\mu_3 < 0$. From (15) and lemma 1.1,

$$\mu_2 > |\mu_3|^{2/3} R_1(t) > |\mu_3|^{2/3} 2^{-2/3}, \tag{108}$$

which, since $\mu_3 < 0$, gives $\mu_3 > -2\mu_2^{3/2}$, and, hence (20).

The right inequality in (21) follows directly from (17) and lemma 1.1. From the first inequality in (108) and the fact that R_1 is increasing, I obtain $t < R_1^{-1}(c)$, where $c := \mu_2/|\mu_3|^{2/3}$, and the endpoint is achieved if and only if $\sigma_v = 0$ by (15), which proves (C). Hence, since R_2 is decreasing, the left inequality in (21) follows directly from (17).

On the other hand, suppose that μ_2, μ_3, μ_4 are given such that (20) and (21) are fulfilled. Then, by lemma 1.1,

$$t = R_2^{-1}\left[\left(\mu_4 - 3\mu_2^2\right)/|\mu_3|^{4/3}\right]$$

has a (unique) solution if and only if $\left(\mu_4 - 3\mu_2^2\right)/|\mu_3|^{4/3} < 3 \cdot 2^{-1/3}$, which holds because of (21). Then,

$$\sigma_u = \left(|\mu_3|/h''(t)\right)^{1/3} > 0$$

is determined, and, by (15), it only remains to see that $\sigma_v^2 = \mu_2 - |\mu_3|^{2/3} R_1(t) > 0$. Write $d := \left(\mu_4 - 3\mu_2^2\right)/|\mu_3|^{4/3}$. Then, $t = R_2^{-1}(d)$ and, since R_1 is increasing and R_2 decreasing,

$$\sigma_v^2 = \mu_2 - |\mu_3|^{2/3} R_1\left[R_2^{-1}(d)\right] > 0$$

$$\Leftrightarrow c > R_1\left[R_2^{-1}(d)\right]$$
$$\Leftrightarrow R_2\left[R_1^{-1}(c)\right] < d.$$

The last inequality holds because of the left inequality in (21).

Lemma A.4 *Let* ATE(t) = h(t)/h(t − σ_u) *where* $\sigma_u = a(2/h'')^{1/3}$ *and* $a = (|\mu_3|/2)^{1/3}$. *Then, as* $t \to -\infty$

$$\mathrm{ATE}(t) \to 1/(1+a) \tag{109}$$

$$t^3(d/dt)\mathrm{ATE}(t) \to 2a(3a+2)/(1+a)^3 \tag{110}$$

Proof. Equation (109) follows from (94). I only sketch the proof for (110), which basically uses the same technique as for proving (104). It is, however, slightly more complicated since it involves irrational expressions.

First, introducing the function $w(t) = h(t) + t$, one gets, in the same way as (106),

$$w(t) = h + t = -1/t + 2/t^3 + o\big(1t^3\big). \tag{111}$$

One finds

$$\mathrm{ATE}'(t) = \mathrm{ATE}(t)W(t),$$

where

$$W(t) = w(s)s' - w(t), \tag{112}$$

$$s = s(t) = t - \sigma_u, \tag{113}$$

$$s' = 1 + aR_2(t)2^{1/3}/3. \tag{114}$$

It follows from (90), (107), and (111) that

$$W(t) = \left[-1/s + 2/s^3 + o\big(1/t^3\big)\right]\left[1 + a - 4a/t^2 + 54a/t^4 + o\big(1/t^4\big)\right] - \left[-1/t + 2/t^3 + o\big(1/t^3\big)\right] \tag{115}$$

Also $1/s$ has to be expanded. From (90),

$$t/s \to 1/(1+a).$$

By the same method as for (104), one obtains

$$t^3(t/s)' \to 8a/(1+a)^2.$$

Hence,

$$1/s = 1/t(1+a) - 4a/t^3(1+a)^2 + o\big(1/t^3\big).$$

Substituting this in (115) gives

$$W(t) = 2a(3a+2)/t^3(1+a)^2 + o\big(1/t^3\big),$$

which proves (110).

NOTE

I thank B. Stigum, whose comments led to substantial improvements of the present chapter.

REFERENCES

Afriat, S. N., 1972, "Efficiency Estimation of a Production Function," *International Economic Review* 13 (Oct.), 568–598.

Aigner, D., C. A. K. Lovell, and P. Schmidt, 1977, "Formulation and Estimation of Stochastic Frontier Production Function Models," *Journal of Econometrics* 6, 21–37.

Dale-Olsen, H., 1994, "Produksjon i Busstransportsektoren," Department of Economics, University of Oslo.

Feller, W., 1964, *An Introduction to Probability Theory and Its Applications,* Vol. 1, 2nd Ed. New York: Wiley.

Hansen, L., 1982, "Large Sample Properties of Generalized Method of Moments Estimators," *Econometrica* 50, 1029–1054.

Kendall, M. G., and A. Stuart, 1969, *Advanced Theory of Statistics*, Vol 1, 3rd Ed., High Wycombe: Griffin.

Lee, L. F., 1983, "A Test for Distributional Assumptions for the Stochastic Frontier Functions," *Journal of Econometrics* 22, 245–267.

Meeusen, W., and J. van den Broeck, 1977, "Efficiency Estimation from Cobb-Douglas Production Functions with Composed Error," *International Economic Review* 18, 435–444.

Olson, J. A., P. Schmidt, and D. M. Waldman, 1980, "A Monte Carlo Study of Estimators of Stochastic Frontier Production Functions," *Journal of Econometrics* 13, 67–82.

Ray, W. D., and A. E. N. T. Pitman, 1963, "Chebyshev Polynomial and Other New Approximations to Mills' Ratio," *Annals of Mathamatical Statistics* 34, 892–901.

Ruben, H., 1964, "Irrational Fraction Approximations to Mills' Ratio," *Biometrika* 51, 339–345.

Schmidt, P., 1985–86, "Frontier Production Functions," *Econometric Reviews* 4(2), 289–328.

Schmidt, P., and T. F. Lin, 1984, "Simple Tests of Alternative Specifications in Stochastic Frontier Models," *Journal of Econometrics* 24, 349–361.

Schmidt, P., and C. A. K. Lovell, 1979, "Estimating Technical and Allocative Inefficiency Relative to Stochastic Production and Cost Frontiers," *Journal of Econometrics* 9, 343–366.

Shenton, L. R., 1954, "Inequalities for the Normal Integral Including a New Continued Fraction," *Biometrika* 41, 177–189.

Stevenson, R. E., 1980, "Likelihood Functions for Generalized Stochastic Frontier Estimation," *Journal of Econometrics* 13, 57–66.

Stigum, B., 1995, Theory-Data Confrontations in Economics, *Dialogue XXXIV*, Canadian Philosophical Association, 581–604.

van den Broeck, J., F. R. Førsund, L. Hjalmarsson, and W. Meeusen, 1980, "On the Estimation of Deterministic and Stochastic Frontier Production Functions," *Journal of Econometrics* 13, 117–138.

Wolfram, S. 1991, *Mathematica: A System for Doing Mathematics by Computer,* 2nd Ed., New York: Addison-Wesley.

Chapter Fifteen

Congruence and Encompassing

Christophe Bontemps and Grayham E. Mizon

Economists and econometricians who undertake empirical modeling face many problems, not the least of which is how to deal with the fact that, with very rare exceptions, all the models analyzed are approximations of the actual processes that generate the observed data. The simplest approach to this problem is to ignore it, but potentially that is most likely to lead to invalid and misleading inferences. An alternative approach recognizes the problem explicitly by adopting misspecification-robust inference procedures, such as using heteroskedastic-autocorrelation-consistent standard errors (see inter alia Andrews, 1991; Gouriéroux and Monfort, 1995). However, this approach does not contribute anything specific toward tackling the problem; rather it is analogous to taking out an insurance policy while continuing to engage in hazardous activities—with the insurance eventually becoming more and more expensive, or redundant. Another approach, in addition to recognizing the problem explicitly, aims to alleviate it by establishing a statistically and economically well-specified framework within which to conduct modeling. This third approach is associated with the LSE methodology (see inter alia Hendry, 1995; Mizon, 1995a) in which the concepts of congruence and encompassing play important roles. Briefly, congruence is the property of a model that has fully exploited all the information implicitly available once an investigator has chosen a set of variables to be used in the modeling. Encompassing, on the other hand, is the property of a model that can account for the results obtained from rival models and, in that sense, makes the rivals inferentially redundant.

The present analysis emphasizes the importance of having a congruent model of the joint distribution of all relevant variables as a statistical framework for the evaluation of competing models nested within it. Such evaluation of models done using parsimonious encompassing has many advantages, including yielding transitive relations among the models and avoiding the anomaly of general models failing to encompass simplifications of themselves. By applying the concept of parsimonious encompassing to the relationship between a model and the corresponding data-generation process (DGP) a formal definition of congruence is obtained. It is further argued that nesting is more than one model being an algebraic simplification of another, that the congruence of a model is a sufficient condition for it to nest and encompass a simplification (parametric or nonparametric) of itself, and that consequently it plays a crucial role in the application of the encompassing principle.

The outline of this chapter is as follows. Section 15.1 presents notation and discusses the concepts of the data-generation process (DGP), the local data generating process (LDGP), an econometric model, and nesting, all of which play important roles in the rest of the chapter. Section 15.2 discusses the parametric relationship between the LDGP and an econometric model, prior to defining parametric and parsimonious encompassing. In Section 15.3 linear and nonlinear parametric and nonparametric examples of a general model failing to encompass a special case of itself are presented. Section 15.4 uses the concept of parsimonious encompassing to provide a formal definition of congruence, which is then shown to be a sufficient condition to preclude the anomaly of Section 15.3. Since the hypothesis defining congruence is not testable directly, alternative indirect methods for testing congruence are discussed in Section 15.5. This discussion highlights the distinction between misspecification and specification testing of models, and some of the limitations of misspecification hypotheses are analyzed. An illustration of an empirically congruent model that is not the DGP is presented in Section 15.6. Section 15.7 presents our conclusions.

15.1 PRELIMINARIES

It is assumed that a statistical representation can be given to the process by which observations are made on the phenomena of interest in the economy being studied. This is called the data-generation process.

15.1.1 The Data-Generation Process

Let the vector of N real random variables $\mathbf{w}_t$ characterize the economy under analysis. At each point in time $t \in \mathcal{T}$, the joint density $\mathsf{D}_{\mathbf{w}_t}(\mathbf{w}_t|\mathcal{F}_{t-1})$ of $\mathbf{w}_t$ has a sample space Ω and associated σ-field or event space $\mathcal{F}_{t-1}$ generated by $(\ldots \mathbf{w}_0, \mathbf{w}_{1t}, \ldots, \mathbf{w}_{t-1})$. This joint density is a statistical representation of the economy, and as such is the data-generation process (DGP) for $\mathbf{w}_t$. It is also assumed that this DGP can be represented as a vector stochastic process, with sufficient continuity to make it meaningful to postulate d parameters $\boldsymbol{\delta} \in \mathcal{D}^d \subseteq \mathbb{R}^d$ that do not depend on $\mathcal{F}_{t-1}$ at any t. It is not necessary to restrict the parameters to be constant over time or to exclude transient parameters. The history of the stochastic process $\{\mathbf{w}_t\}$ up to time $(t-1)$ is denoted by the notation $\mathbf{W}_{t-1} = (\mathbf{W}_0, \mathbf{w}_1, \ldots, \mathbf{w}_{t-1}) = (\mathbf{W}_0, \mathbf{W}^1_{t-1})$, where $\mathbf{W}_0$ is the set of initial conditions. Then, for a sample period $t = 1, \ldots, T$, the DGP is denoted by $\mathsf{D}_{\mathbf{W}}(\mathbf{W}^1_T|\mathbf{W}_0, \boldsymbol{\delta}_0)$ and is sequentially factorized as

$$\mathsf{D_W}\left(\mathbf{W}_T^1 \mid \mathbf{W}_0, \boldsymbol{\delta}_0\right) = \prod_{t=1}^{T} \mathsf{D_W}\left(\mathbf{w}_t \mid \mathbf{W}_{t-1}, \boldsymbol{\kappa}_t\right), \tag{1}$$

where $\boldsymbol{\delta}_0$ is a particular point in parameter space, and $\mathbf{g}(\boldsymbol{\delta}_0) = (\boldsymbol{\kappa}_1 \ldots \boldsymbol{\kappa}_T)$ for a $1-1$ function $\mathbf{g}(\cdot)$, so that the $\boldsymbol{\kappa}_t$ may be nonconstant over time owing to regime shifts and structural breaks. [See Hendry and Mizon (1998, 2000) for discussion of the distinction between these parameter changes.]

15.1.2 Econometric Models

Even when a sample of T time-series observations is available on all N variables in $\mathbf{w}_t$ it is not possible to analyze the interrelationships among all of them since N is usually large relative to T, and more importantly there may be particular interest in a transformed subset $\mathbf{x}_t$ of $\mathbf{w}_t$. Hence, econometric modeling typically employs knowledge from economic theory and the statistical properties of the observed $\mathbf{x}_t$ to guide model specification. An econometric model $\mathsf{f_X}(\cdot)$ for $n < N$ variables $\mathbf{x}_t$ implicitly derived from $\mathbf{w}_t$ by marginalization, aggregation, and transformation is denoted by

$$\mathsf{f_X}\left(\mathbf{X}_T^1 \mid \mathbf{X}_0, \boldsymbol{\xi}\right) = \prod_{t=1}^{T} \mathsf{f_X}\left(\mathbf{x}_t \mid \mathbf{X}_{t-1}, \boldsymbol{\xi}\right), \tag{2}$$

where $\boldsymbol{\xi} = \left(\xi_1, \ldots, \xi_k\right)' \in \Xi \subseteq \mathbb{R}^k$ when $\mathsf{f_X}(\mathbf{x}_t|\mathbf{X}_{t-1}, \boldsymbol{\xi})$ is the postulated sequential joint density at time t. It is assumed that $k < d$ and that $\boldsymbol{\xi}$ represents the constant parameters postulated by the modeler, so any time-dependent effects have been reparameterized accordingly [as in a "structural time-series model" re-represented as an ARIMA process (see Harvey, 1993)].

From the theory of reduction (see, inter alia, Hendry, 1995; Mizon, 1995a), there exists a local DGP (LDGP) for the chosen variables $\mathbf{x}_t$,

$$\mathsf{D_X}\left(\mathbf{x}_t|\mathbf{X}_{t-1}, \boldsymbol{\phi}\right), \tag{3}$$

where $\boldsymbol{\phi} = \left(\phi_1, \ldots, \phi_s\right)' \in \boldsymbol{\Phi} \subseteq \mathbb{R}^s$, which is derived from $\mathsf{D_W}\left(\mathbf{w}_t|\cdot\right)$ by reduction. In general, $\mathsf{f_X}(\cdot) \neq \mathsf{D_X}(\cdot)$, and this divergence has to be taken into account when making inferences about $\boldsymbol{\xi}$ (see inter alia Cox, 1961; White, 1982). Indeed, the modeler is free to specify any form of $\mathsf{f_X}(\cdot)$ independently of the process that has actually generated the data, which is almost always unknown. Precisely because the form of the econometric model is under the control of the investigator it is important that criteria be employed to assist in the specification of models. Designing a model to fully exploit the information available to the investigator is requiring the model to be congruent, and ensuring that it is at least as good as its rivals means that it is encompassing. Both of these concepts are analyzed in more detail in what follows.

15.1.3 Nesting

Not only is it usual for an econometric model to differ from the LDGP, but there is often more than one econometric model to be considered for the analysis of a particular economic phenomenon. For example, one parametric probability model for $\mathbf{x}_t$ might consist of the family of sequential densities indexed by the parameter vector $\boldsymbol{\beta}$:

$$\mathcal{M}_1 = \left\{\mathsf{G}_1\left(\mathbf{X}_T^1 \mid \mathbf{X}_0, \boldsymbol{\beta}_1\right), \boldsymbol{\beta}_1 \in \boldsymbol{\mathcal{B}}_1 \subseteq \mathbb{R}^{p_1}\right\} \quad (4)$$

when $\mathbf{X}_T^1 = (\mathbf{x}_1, \ldots, \mathbf{x}_T)$, with $\mathbf{X}_0$ being the initial conditions. Note that corresponding to the full sample density $\mathsf{G}_1\left(\mathbf{X}_T^1 \mid \mathbf{X}_0, \boldsymbol{\beta}_1\right)$, there are sequential densities $\mathsf{g}_1\left(\mathbf{x}_t \mid \mathbf{X}_{t-1}, \boldsymbol{\beta}_1\right)$ satisfying $\mathsf{G}_1\left(\mathbf{X}_T^1 \mid \mathbf{X}_0, \boldsymbol{\beta}_1\right) = \prod_{t=1}^T \mathsf{g}_1\left(\mathbf{x}_t \mid \mathbf{X}_{t-1}, \boldsymbol{\beta}_1\right)$ when $\mathbf{X}_{t-1} = (\mathbf{X}_0, \mathbf{x}_1, \ldots, \mathbf{x}_{t-1}) = (\mathbf{X}_0, \mathbf{X}_{t-1}^1)$. Denoting this probability model by $\mathcal{M}_1$ and considering the alternative probability model $\mathcal{M}_2$:

$$\mathcal{M}_2 = \{\mathsf{G}_2\left(\mathbf{X}_T^1 \mid \mathbf{X}_0, \boldsymbol{\beta}_2\right),\ \boldsymbol{\beta}_2 \in \boldsymbol{\mathcal{B}}_2 \subseteq \mathbb{R}^{p_2}\}, \quad (5)$$

allows nesting to be defined.

Definition 1 Nesting. $\mathcal{M}_1$ is nested within $\mathcal{M}_2$ if and only if $\mathcal{M}_1 \subseteq \mathcal{M}_2$.

Whenever $\mathcal{M}_1$ and $\mathcal{M}_2$ do not satisfy the conditions of this definition they are said to be nonnested. A particular form of nesting that yields a heuristic explanation of nesting arises when $\mathsf{G}_1(\cdot)$ and $\mathsf{G}_2(\cdot)$ are the same density function but $\boldsymbol{\mathcal{B}}_1 \subseteq \boldsymbol{\mathcal{B}}_2$ with $p_1 < p_2$, so that $\mathcal{M}_1$ is nested within $\mathcal{M}_2$ as a result of the restrictions on the parameter spaces defining the reduction from $\boldsymbol{\mathcal{B}}_2$ to $\boldsymbol{\mathcal{B}}_1$. In this case both models purport to represent the same probability distribution, but $\mathcal{M}_1$ is a parametric simplification of $\mathcal{M}_2$. Note, however, that one model being a parametric simplification of another does not by itself imply that it is nested in the more general model. [See Lu and Mizon (2000) and the discussion that follows for more details.] Throughout this chapter $\mathcal{M}_1$ and $\mathcal{M}_2$ are used as generic alternative parametric probability models of the same distribution, though the particular distribution varies from example to example. Also as a matter of notation in the sequel, models are denoted via their sequential densities rather than their full sample densities, for example, $\mathcal{M}_1 = \left\{\mathbf{g}_1\left(\mathbf{x}_t \mid \mathbf{X}_{t-1}, \boldsymbol{\beta}_1\right), \boldsymbol{\beta}_1 \in \boldsymbol{\mathcal{B}}_1 \subseteq \mathbb{R}^{p_1}\right\}$.

When the purpose of modeling is to use econometric models to learn more about the relationships among the elements of $\mathbf{x}_t$ in the DGP (as in theory testing and economic policy analysis), there is a premium to having an econometric model that provides a good approximation to the LDGP. Congruence, which is concerned with the relationship between a model f_x and the LDGP D_x, is discussed in detail in Section 15.4. When there is more than one econometric model available it is important to have criteria for assessing their merits, especially if they each appear to be congruent. Encompassing is concerned with the relationships between rival models and is discussed in detail in the next section.

15.2 ENCOMPASSING

Whether models are nested or nonnested it is important to be able to compare them and evaluate their relative merits: "The encompassing principle is concerned with the ability of a model to account for the behavior of others, or less ambitiously, to explain the behavior of relevant characteristics of other models" (Mizon, 1984). A model $\mathcal{M}_1$ encompasses another model $\mathcal{M}_2$ if $\mathcal{M}_1$ can account for results obtained from $\mathcal{M}_2$. In other words, anything that can be done using $\mathcal{M}_2$ can be done equally well using $\mathcal{M}_1$, and so once $\mathcal{M}_1$ is available $\mathcal{M}_2$ has nothing further to offer. These heuristic concepts are made more formal in the next two subsections.

15.2.1 Parametric Encompassing

The concept of encompassing considered in this chapter is that of population encompassing in a Neyman-Pearson hypothesis testing framework, which is in accord with the approach in Mizon (1984) and Mizon and Richard (1986) and as formally defined in Hendry and Richard (1989). Underlying all empirical econometric analyses is an information set (collection of variables or their σ-field), and a corresponding probability space. This information set has to be sufficiently general to include all the variables thought to be relevant for the empirical implementation of theoretical models in the form of statistical models. It is also important that this information set include the variables needed for all competing models that are to be compared; otherwise there can be noncomparabilities. Let these variables be $\mathbf{x}_t$ and the LDGP that generates them be the joint density $\mathsf{D}_{\mathsf{X}}(\mathbf{x}_t|\mathbf{X}_{t-1}, \boldsymbol{\phi})$ as defined in (3), at the particular parameter value $\boldsymbol{\phi} = \boldsymbol{\phi}_0$. Also let a parametric statistical model of the joint distribution be $\mathcal{M}_g = \{\mathsf{f}_g(\mathbf{x}_t|\mathbf{X}_{t-1}, \boldsymbol{\xi}), \boldsymbol{\xi} \in \Xi \subset \mathbb{R}^k\}$, as defined in (2). Let $\widehat{\boldsymbol{\xi}}$ be the maximum likelihood estimator of $\boldsymbol{\xi}$ so that $\widehat{\boldsymbol{\xi}} \underset{\mathcal{M}_g}{\overset{P}{\rightarrow}} \boldsymbol{\xi}$ and $\widehat{\boldsymbol{\xi}} \underset{LDGP}{\overset{P}{\rightarrow}} \boldsymbol{\xi}(\boldsymbol{\phi}_0) = \boldsymbol{\xi}_0$, which is the pseudotrue value of $\widehat{\boldsymbol{\xi}}$. Note that the parameters of a model are not arbitrary in that $\mathcal{M}_g$ and its parameterization $\boldsymbol{\xi}$ are chosen to correspond to phenomena of interest (such as elasticities and partial responses within the chosen probability space), although there may be observationally equivalent parameterizations. Moreover, estimation is an issue separate from that of model specification, in that an arbitrary estimation method does not define the parameters of a model.

Given a particular set of parameters there usually exist good and bad estimation methods for them, some of which are consistent and efficient, while others are inconsistent, and so on. The parameterization is an integral part of the specification of a model, and in many circumstances can be related to the moments of the variables $\mathbf{x}_t$. Given the specification of the model $\mathcal{M}_g$ the probability limit under $\mathcal{M}_g$ of the maximum likelihood estimator $\widehat{\boldsymbol{\xi}}$ (the optimal estimator under $\mathcal{M}_g$) defines the parameter $\boldsymbol{\xi}$. However, in general $\boldsymbol{\xi}$ will differ from its pseudotrue value $\boldsymbol{\xi}_0$ as a consequence of inadequate specification of $\mathcal{M}_g$.

With these definitions it is possible to give a more formal definition of encompassing in the present context.

Definition 2 Encompassing. $\mathcal{M}_1$ encompasses $\mathcal{M}_2$ (denoted $\mathcal{M}_1\mathcal{E}M_2$) with $\mathcal{M}_1 = \left\{g_1\left(\mathbf{x}_t|\mathbf{X}_{t-1}, \boldsymbol{\beta}_1\right), \boldsymbol{\beta}_1 \in \boldsymbol{\mathcal{B}}_1 \subset \mathbb{R}^{p_1}\right\}$ and $\mathcal{M}_2 = \left\{g_2\left(\mathbf{x}_t|\mathbf{X}_{t-1}, \boldsymbol{\beta}_2\right), \boldsymbol{\beta}_2 \in \boldsymbol{\mathcal{B}}_2 \subset \mathbb{R}^{p_2}\right\}$ if and only if $\boldsymbol{\beta}_{20} = \mathbf{b}_{21}(\boldsymbol{\beta}_{10})$ when $\boldsymbol{\beta}_{i0}$ is the pseudotrue value of the maximum likelihood estimator $\hat{\boldsymbol{\beta}}_i$ of $\boldsymbol{\beta}_i$, $i = 1, 2$, and $\mathbf{b}_{21}(\boldsymbol{\beta}_{10})$ is the binding function given by $\hat{\boldsymbol{\beta}}_2 \underset{\mathcal{M}_1}{\overset{P}{\rightarrow}} \mathbf{b}_{21}(\boldsymbol{\beta}_{10})$. (See Mizon and Richard, 1986; Hendry and Richard, 1989; Gouriéroux and Monfort, 1995.)

Note that this definition of encompassing applies when $\mathcal{M}_1$ and $\mathcal{M}_2$ are nonnested as well as nested. However, Hendry and Richard (1989) showed that when $\mathcal{M}_1$ and $\mathcal{M}_2$ are nonnested $\mathcal{M}_1\mathcal{E}M_2$ is equivalent to $\mathcal{M}_1$ being a valid reduction of the minimum completing model $\mathcal{M}_c = \mathcal{M}_1 \cup \mathcal{M}_2^{\perp}$ (so that $\mathcal{M}_1, \mathcal{M}_2 \subset \mathcal{M}_c$) when $\mathcal{M}_2^{\perp}$ is the model that represents all aspects of $\mathcal{M}_2$ that are not contained in $\mathcal{M}_1$. When this condition is satisfied $\mathcal{M}_1$ is said to parsimoniously encompass $\mathcal{M}_c$, a concept to which attention is turned in the next subsection.

15.2.2 Parsimonious Encompassing

Let $\mathcal{M}_s$ be a submodel of $\mathcal{M}_g$ (as defined in Section 15.2.1) that has the form $\mathcal{M}_s = \{\mathsf{f}_s(\mathbf{x}_t|\mathbf{X}_{t-1}, \boldsymbol{\alpha}), \boldsymbol{\alpha} \in \mathcal{A} \subset \mathbb{R}^n\}$, with $n = k - r, r > 0$, being the number of linearly independent restrictions on $\boldsymbol{\Xi}$ that define $\mathcal{A}$. Note that $\mathcal{M}_s \subseteq \mathcal{M}_g$ as a result of dimension-reducing constraints on the parameter space. Further, let the r constraint equations be $\boldsymbol{\psi}(\boldsymbol{\xi}) = \mathbf{0}$, which are such that rank $\left(\partial\psi/\partial\xi'\right)_{\xi_0} = r$, and consider the isomorphic reparameterization $\boldsymbol{\lambda}$ of $\boldsymbol{\xi}$: $\boldsymbol{\lambda} = \boldsymbol{\lambda}(\boldsymbol{\xi}) = \left[\boldsymbol{\lambda}_1(\boldsymbol{\xi})', \boldsymbol{\lambda}_2(\boldsymbol{\xi})'\right]' = \left[\boldsymbol{\alpha}', \boldsymbol{\psi}(\boldsymbol{\xi})'\right]'$, which is such that rank $\left(\partial\lambda/\partial\xi'\right)_{\xi_0} = k$ and $(\boldsymbol{\lambda}_1, \boldsymbol{\lambda}_2) \in \boldsymbol{\Lambda}_1 \times \boldsymbol{\Lambda}_2$. [See Sargan (1988) for discussion of such a reparameterization.) Hence $\mathcal{A} = \{\boldsymbol{\alpha} \mid \boldsymbol{\alpha} = \boldsymbol{\lambda}_1(\boldsymbol{\xi})$ such that $\boldsymbol{\psi}(\boldsymbol{\xi}) = \mathbf{0} \quad \forall\boldsymbol{\xi} \in \boldsymbol{\Xi}\}$. With this notation it is possible to define parsimonious encompassing in the following way.

Definition 3 Parsimonious Encompassing. $\mathcal{M}_s$ parsimoniously encompasses $\mathcal{M}_g$ with respect to $\boldsymbol{\xi}$ [denoted $\mathcal{M}_s\mathcal{E}_p(\boldsymbol{\xi})\mathcal{M}_g$] if and only if $\boldsymbol{\psi}(\boldsymbol{\xi}) = \mathbf{0}$ and $\mathcal{M}_s\mathcal{E}(\boldsymbol{\xi})\mathcal{M}_g$.

Hence, when $\mathcal{M}_s\mathcal{E}_p(\boldsymbol{\xi})\mathcal{M}_g$ the former model is a valid reduction of the latter, so efficient inference on $\boldsymbol{\alpha}$ can be obtained from $\mathcal{M}_s$. This interpretation of parsimonious encompassing is used in Section 15.4 to provide a formal definition of congruence.

Note that whenever $\mathcal{M}_1 \subset \mathcal{M}_2$ and $\mathcal{M}_1 \mathcal{E} M_2$, then $\mathcal{M}_1 \mathcal{E}_p \mathcal{M}_2$. Moreover, whenever $\mathcal{M}_1$ and $\mathcal{M}_2$ are nonnested, but $\mathcal{M}_1 \mathcal{E} M_2$, then $\mathcal{M}_1 \mathcal{E}_p \mathcal{M}_c$ with $\mathcal{M}_c = \mathcal{M}_1 \cup \mathcal{M}_2^{\perp}$. Hence, parsimonious encompassing plays an important role in the comparison of alternative models whether they are nested or nonnested. It is thus relevant to ask whether there is a separate role for encompassing as opposed to parsimonious encompassing: That there is can be seen from the following argument. Parsimonious encompassing means that a model is a valid reduction of a more general model. When a general-to-simple modeling strategy is adopted, the general model will embed the different econometric models implementing rival economic theories for the phenomenon of interest. Thus searching for the model that parsimoniously encompasses the general model is specification searching among models nested within a common general model. If after a modeling exercise is completed and the preferred model is determined, further information becomes available, a question arises as to whether the existing results are robust to the extension of the information set. The further information may take the form of new a priori theories that imply an extension of the information set to embrace the empirical models implementing them. Testing the preferred model's ability to encompass the newly available rival models (which can be done using nonnested test statistics) is a form of misspecification testing. Indeed it can be interpreted as testing the adequacy of the information set originally chosen for the modeling against extensions suggested by rival theories. However, given that one-degree-of-freedom nonnested test statistics, such as those of Cox (1961) and Davidson and MacKinnon (1981), have low power against a wide range of alternatives (see, e.g., Mizon and Richard, 1986) there will always be an argument for recommencing the modeling with a more general information set.

The above analysis has indicated that a general model that has rival models as simplifications of it underlies all encompassing comparisons. This general model might be one of the rival models that nests all its rivals, or it might be a completing model providing the statistical framework for model comparison. The next section discusses the relationship between encompassing and general models.

15.3 ENCOMPASSING AND GENERAL MODELS

The theory of reduction implies that for the variables in $\mathbf{x}_t$ there is a local DGP $\mathsf{D}_{\mathsf{X}}(\mathbf{x}_t|\mathbf{X}_{t-1}, \boldsymbol{\phi})$, which by definition encompasses all econometric models of the same distribution having the form $\mathsf{f}_{\mathsf{X}}(\mathbf{x}_t|\mathbf{X}_{t-1}, \boldsymbol{\xi})$. Therefore, it might be expected heuristically that general models encompass simplifications of themselves. Indeed Hendry 1995 states: "*A general model must encompass a special case thereof: indeed, misspecification analysis could not work without this result.*"

However, that this need not always be the case was pointed out by Gouriéroux and Monfort (1995) who state: *"A model $\mathcal{M}_2$ nesting a model $\mathcal{M}_1$ does not necessarily encompass $\mathcal{M}_1$."*

In the following subsections four examples are presented of general models that fail to encompass algebraic simplifications of themselves. Possible reasons for this phenomenon are then discussed.

15.3.1 A Linear Parametric Example

Consider the two linear models $\mathcal{M}_1$ and $\mathcal{M}_2$ of the conditional distribution $y_t \mid z_t, u_t$ defined by:

$$\mathcal{M}_1\colon\ y_t = \beta z_t + \zeta_{1t}, \qquad \zeta_{1t} \sim \mathcal{N}\left(0, \sigma^2_{\zeta_1}\right),$$

$$\mathcal{M}_2\colon\ y_t = \gamma z_t + \delta u_t + \varepsilon_{1t}, \qquad \varepsilon_{1t} \sim \mathcal{N}\left(0, \sigma^2_{\varepsilon_1}\right),$$

where (z_t, u_t) are independent and identically distributed variables, with ζ_{1t} and ε_{1t} asserted to be zero mean, constant variance Gaussian white noise processes, and the parameters β and $\boldsymbol{\pi}' = (\gamma, \delta)$ belong, respectively, to $\mathbb{R}^+$ and $\mathbb{R}^+ \times \mathbb{R}^+$. Clearly, $\mathcal{M}_1$ seems to be nested within $\mathcal{M}_2$ in the sense that $\mathcal{M}_1$ corresponds to the special case of $\mathcal{M}_2$ in which $\delta = 0$, and the parameter space for β is included in that of $\boldsymbol{\pi}$. Then, $\mathcal{M}_2$ should be able to explain the results of its own submodel, and so encompass $\mathcal{M}_1$. However, in general, this is not the case.

In the framework of Gouriéroux and Monfort (1995), who proposed this example, whether or not $\mathcal{M}_2$ encompasses $\mathcal{M}_1$ depends on the DGP. For example, if the DGP were nonlinear of the form

$$\mathcal{P}_0 : y_t = m_0(z_t, u_t) + v_t, \qquad v_t \sim \mathcal{N}\left(0, \sigma_0^2\right), \tag{6}$$

then $\mathcal{M}_1$ and $\mathcal{M}_2$ are misspecified, and the pseudotrue value β_0 of β under $\mathcal{P}_0$ is the L^2-projection of $m_0(z_t, u_t)$ onto the half line A_x defined by $\{\beta z_t, \beta \geq 0\}$, and $\boldsymbol{\pi}_0$, the pseudotrue value of $\boldsymbol{\pi}$ is the corresponding projection onto the cone C_{zu} defined by $\{\gamma z_t + \delta u_t, \gamma, \delta \geq 0\}$. [See Gouriéroux and Monfort (1995, fig. 1)]. The $\mathcal{M}_2$-pseudotrue value $\beta_2 = p\lim_{\mathcal{M}_2}(\widehat{\beta}) = \beta(\boldsymbol{\pi}_0)$ of β is in general different from β_0 (i.e., $\beta_2 = \beta(\boldsymbol{\pi}_0) \neq \beta_0$), so that $\mathcal{M}_2$ does not usually encompass $\mathcal{M}_1$. Gouriéroux and Monfort (1995) further argue that $\mathcal{M}_2 \mathcal{E} M_1$ occurs but only for those particular forms of the DGP in which $\beta_2 = \beta(\boldsymbol{\pi}_0) = \beta_0$.

One possible interpretation of this result is that whether or not a model encompasses a simplification of itself depends fortuitously on the nature of the unknown DGP. In this vein Gouriéroux and Monfort (1995) argue that whenever the unknown DGP is nonlinear, the law of iterated projections does not apply in general, and so a larger model may not encompass an algebraic simplification of itself, as in the above example. However, if in the above example the parameter spaces are unrestricted so that $\beta \in \mathbb{R}$ and $\pi \in \mathbb{R}^2$ and the assumption that z_t and u_t are identically independently distributed is dropped, but $\mathcal{M}_2$ now includes the false assertion that z_t and u_t are orthogonal, then even if the DGP were linear $\mathcal{M}_2$ would fail to encompass $\mathcal{M}_1$. This example was used by Govaerts et al. (1994) and Hendry (1995) to discuss the apparent anomaly of some models failing to encompass algebraic simplifications of themselves. The conclusion drawn by these authors was that as a result of the false assertion that z_t and u_t are orthogonal, $\mathcal{M}_1$ and $\mathcal{M}_2$ are nonnested—the orthogonality hypothesis having no role in $\mathcal{M}_1$ despite it being a part of the specification of $\mathcal{M}_2$. Hence, the problem is not simply associated with nonlinear DGPs. In particular, by reconsidering the models from the perspective of the joint density of (y_t, z_t, u_t), Hendry (1995) argues that the conditional model associated with $\mathcal{M}_1$ is not nested within the one associated with $\mathcal{M}_2$.

The anomaly for the linear example presented in this subsection has a nonlinear counterpart, as shown in the next subsection.

15.3.2 A Nonlinear Parametric Example

Let the two nonlinear conditional models $\mathcal{M}_1$ and $\mathcal{M}_2$ be defined as

$$\mathcal{M}_1\colon\ y_t = f_2(z_t, \beta) + \zeta_{2t},$$

$$\mathcal{M}_2\colon\ y_t = f_2(z_t, \gamma) + g_2(u_t, \delta) + \varepsilon_{2t},$$

where f_2 and g_2 are two regular functions defined on $\mathbb{R} \times \mathbb{R}$. Since $\mathcal{M}_1$ is a special case ($g_2 = 0$) of $\mathcal{M}_2$ it would appear to be nested in it, but it is not generally encompassed by $\mathcal{M}_2$. The restrictions on the form of $\mathcal{M}_2$, namely that the conditional mean of y_t is additively separable in z_t and u_t, will result in $\mathcal{M}_2$ failing to encompass $\mathcal{M}_1$ whenever the DGP does not have this property. For example, were the DGP to have the form of (6) then $\mathcal{M}_2 \mathcal{E} M_1$ would not hold, because the pseudotrue values of β under $\mathcal{P}_0$ and under $\mathcal{M}_2$ differ, and so $f_2\left(z_t, \beta_0\right) \neq f_2\left(z_t, \beta_2\right)$. Here again the situation in terms of pseudotrue values may be viewed as a sequence of projections that lead to different values of f_2. Hence, the failure of $\mathcal{M}_2 \mathcal{E} M_1$ to hold arises because of a false auxiliary hypothesis involved in $\mathcal{M}_2$, which can be interpreted as rendering $\mathcal{M}_2$ and $\mathcal{M}_1$ nonnested.

15.3.3 Comfac Example

In the process of illustrating the importance of modeling in a framework that has a congruent general model, Mizon (1993) produced the following illustration of a model failing to encompass an algebraic simplification of itself—the example is explored in more detail in Mizon (1995b):

$$\mathcal{M}_1\colon\ y_t = \delta z_t + \zeta_{3t},$$

$$\mathcal{M}_2\colon\ y_t = \rho y_{t-1} + \gamma z_t - \rho\gamma z_{t-1} + \varepsilon_{3t},$$

in which z_t is a white noise process with constant variance σ_z^2 distributed independently of ζ_{3t} and ε_{3t} . In this example it appears that $\mathcal{M}_1$ is nested within $\mathcal{M}_2$ with the restriction $\rho = 0$ rendering the models equivalent. However, when the DGP lies in the class of densities characterized by the stationary ($|\ \alpha\ | < 1$) linear partial adjustment model

$$\mathcal{P}_0\colon\ y_t = \alpha y_{t-1} + \beta z_t + v_t,$$

the pseudotrue value of $\widehat{\delta}$ is $\delta_0 = \beta$, whereas the pseudotrue values ρ_0 and γ_0 of $\widehat{\rho}$ and $\widehat{\gamma}$, respectively, are given as the solutions of the equations

$$\rho_0 - \alpha = -\,\alpha\gamma_0\left(\gamma_0 - \beta\right) / \left[\gamma_0^2 - 2\beta\gamma_0 + \sigma_0^2 / \left(1 - \alpha^2\right)\sigma_z^2\right],$$

$$\gamma_0 - \beta = -\,\alpha\beta\rho_0 / \left(1 + \rho_0^2\right).$$

The solution for γ_0 is

$$\gamma_0 = \beta\left[(1 + \rho_0^2) - \alpha\rho_0\right] / \left[1 + \rho_0^2\right]$$

when ρ_0 is a root of the fifth-order polynomial

$$aZ^5 + bZ^4 + cZ^3 + dZ^2 + eZ + f = 0,$$

with:

$$a = \sigma_0^2 + \beta^2\sigma_z^2\alpha^2 - \beta^2\sigma_z^2 \qquad b = \beta^2\sigma_z^2\alpha - \alpha\sigma_0^2 - \beta^2\sigma_z^2\alpha^3,$$

$$c = -2\beta^2\sigma_z^2 + 2\beta^2\sigma_z^2\alpha^2 + 2\sigma_0^2 \qquad d = -2\alpha\sigma_0^2 - 2\beta^2\sigma_z^2\alpha^3 + 2\beta^2\sigma_z^2\alpha,$$

$$e = -\beta^2\sigma_z^2 + \beta^2\sigma_z^2\alpha^4 + \sigma_0^2 \qquad f = \beta^2\sigma_z^2\alpha - \alpha\sigma_0^2 - \beta^2\sigma_z^2\alpha^3.$$

Further, the $\mathcal{M}_2-$pseudotrue value of $\widehat{\delta}$ is $\delta_2 = \gamma_0$, but $\gamma_0 = \beta$ if and only if $\alpha = 0$, in which case $\rho_0 = 0, \pm i$, and $\pm i$, implying that $\mathcal{M}_2\mathcal{E}M_1$ if and only if the DGP lies in the class of static densities—the four roots on the unit circle are ruled out by the stationarity condition. Hence, in general, $\delta_2 = \gamma_0 \neq \beta$ and so $\mathcal{M}_2$ does not encompass $\mathcal{M}_1$ despite the latter being an algebraic simplification of the former. Mizon (1995b) attributed this failure of $\mathcal{M}_2$ to encompass $\mathcal{M}_1$ to the false common factor auxiliary hypothesis implicit in $\mathcal{M}_2$ rendering it nonnested relative to $\mathcal{M}_1$, since the latter model does not involve the common factor hypothesis.

Similar anomalies can arise in a nonparametric context, as the next subsection shows for two nonparametric regression models.

15.3.4 A Nonparametric Example

Let $\mathcal{M}_1$ and $\mathcal{M}_2$ be two conditional models defined with respect to the conditional distribution $y_t|\ \sigma(z_t, u_t)$ but without any specified parametric form when

$\sigma(z_t, u_t)$ is the σ-field generated by z_t and u_t. $\mathcal{M}_1$ hypothesizes that the conditional mean only includes z_t, while $\mathcal{M}_2$ excludes the variable z_t:

$$\mathcal{M}_1\colon\ \mathsf{E}[y_t \mid \sigma(z_t, u_t)] = \mathsf{E}[y_t \mid \sigma(z_t)],$$
$$\mathcal{M}_2\colon\ \mathsf{E}[y_t \mid \sigma(z_t, u_t)] = \mathsf{E}[y_t \mid \sigma(u_t)].$$

Defining the functions f and g to be the following conditional expectations:

$$f(\cdot) = \mathsf{E}[y_t \mid z_t = \cdot]$$
$$g(\cdot) = \mathsf{E}[y_t \mid u_t = \cdot]$$

yields the nonparametric nonnested regression models:

$$\mathcal{M}_1\colon\ y_t = f(z_t) + \zeta_{4t},$$
$$\mathcal{M}_2\colon\ y_t = g(u_t) + \varepsilon_{4t}.$$

In this context a natural nesting model is

$$\mathcal{M}\colon\ y_t = m(z_t, u_t) + \eta_{4t},$$

where

$$m(z_t, u_t) = \mathsf{E}[y_t \mid \sigma(z_t, u_t)],$$

which as a result of unrestrictedly conditioning on both z_t and u_t nests both $\mathcal{M}_1$ and $\mathcal{M}_2$. Indeed, $\mathcal{M}$ is conditioned on the σ-field $\sigma(z_t, u_t)$, generated by the variables (z_t, u_t), and so will encompass all nonparametric submodels defined by hypotheses relating $\sigma(z_t, u_t)$ to σ-fields included within it. Consequently, $\mathcal{M}$ will encompass $\mathcal{M}_1$ and $\mathcal{M}_2$ whatever the DGP is, provided that the conditioning on $\sigma(z_t, u_t)$ is valid.

A situation similar to the previous parametric ones arises in considering the alternative "nesting" model $\mathcal{M}'$:

$$\mathcal{M}'\colon\ y_t = f(z_t) + g(u_t) + \nu_t.$$

In this case, $\mathcal{M}_1$ corresponds to the special case where $g \equiv 0$, and $\mathcal{M}_2$ corresponds to the special case where $f \equiv 0$; thus they appear to be nested in $\mathcal{M}'$. However, as a result of incorporating the restriction of additive separability in its specification $\mathcal{M}'$ does not nest either $\mathcal{M}_1$ or $\mathcal{M}_2$, both of which are defined with respect to the distribution $y_t \mid \sigma(z_t, u_t)$ with $\sigma(z_t, u_t)$ unrestricted. Thus $\mathcal{M}'$ will not encompass the submodels $\mathcal{M}_1$ and $\mathcal{M}_2$. This problem can be described alternatively as one in which $\mathcal{M}'$ is based on S', the union of the σ-fields $\sigma(z_t)$ and $\sigma(u_t)$, and as such is not a σ-field itself without the restriction of additive separability.

The next section provides a formal definition of congruence, which is then shown to be a sufficient condition to preclude the anomaly discussed in this section.

15.4 CONGRUENCE

Congruence has been discussed in numerous places, such as Hendry (1985, 1987), Hendry and Mizon (1990), and Mizon (1995a). From Hendry (1995) it can be defined in the following way.

Models are said to be congruent when they have:

1. Homoskedastic, innovation errors.
2. Weakly exogenous conditioning variables for the parameters of interest.
3. Constant, invariant parameters of interest.
4. Theory-consistent, identifiable structures.
5. Data-admissible formulations on accurate observations.

Thus, for example, if $\mathcal{M}_g = \{\mathsf{f}_g(\mathbf{x}_t|\mathbf{X}_{t-1}, \boldsymbol{\xi}), \boldsymbol{\xi} \in \Xi \subset \mathbb{R}^k\}$ is congruent it will be theory consistent (coherent with a priori theory), data coherent (coherent with observed sample information), and data admissible (coherent with the properties of the measurement system). Detailed explanations of each of these conditions, including discussion of how they might be tested, can be found in Hendry (1995) and Mizon (1995a). Theory consistency does not require that the model conform in all aspects to a very detailed statement of a theory, such as one associated with an intertemporal optimization problem. Rather it requires that $\mathbf{x}_t$ incorporate the relevant set of variables (transformed if necessary) to enable alternative densities to be specified that include the parameters of interest. Alternatively stated, a congruent model is coherent with low-level theory and provides a framework within which the hypotheses of high-level theory can be tested. The requirement that the model errors are innovations with respect to $\mathbf{X}_{t-1}$ ensures that all the information contained in linear functions of $\mathbf{X}_{t-1}$ has been fully exploited. If this is not the case, then there is unused information available that could improve the performance of the model. Note that this requirement does not rule out the possibility of specifying the model error to be generated by a moving average process, such as $\eta_t = \epsilon_t + \theta\epsilon_{t-1}$ for which η_t is not an innovation. What is required in such a case is that the white noise error ϵ_t be an innovation with respect to $\mathbf{X}_{t-1}$.

In each of the examples discussed in Section 15.3, $\mathcal{M}_2$ is not coherent with the "observed sample information" and so is not congruent. If the feature of each of these $\mathcal{M}_2$ models that leads to the lack of congruence were removed, the models would each encompass the corresponding $\mathcal{M}_1$ model. Accordingly, it would appear that a general model $\mathcal{M}_2$ that is congruent encompasses a simple model $\mathcal{M}_1$ that it nests. This surmise is proved later as a corollary to the following formal definition of congruence.

The interpretation of parsimonious encompassing presented in Section 15.2 immediately suggests the following definition of congruence.

Definition 4 Congruence. A theory-consistent, data-admissible model $\mathcal{M}_g = \{\mathsf{f}_g(\mathbf{x}_t|\mathbf{X}_{t-1}, \boldsymbol{\xi}), \boldsymbol{\xi} \in \boldsymbol{\Xi} \subset \mathbb{R}^k\}$ is congruent if and only if $\mathcal{M}_g \mathcal{E}_p(\boldsymbol{\phi})$LDGP at the point $\boldsymbol{\phi} = \boldsymbol{\phi}_0$ when LDGP $= \{\mathsf{D}_\mathsf{X}(\mathbf{x}_t|\mathbf{X}_{t-1}, \boldsymbol{\phi}), \boldsymbol{\phi} \in \boldsymbol{\Phi} \subset \mathbb{R}^s\}$, which means that $\mathcal{M}_g$ is a valid reduction of the local DGP. Equivalently, $\mathcal{M}_g$ is congruent if and only if $\boldsymbol{\mu}_2(\boldsymbol{\phi}_0) = \mathbf{0}$ when $\boldsymbol{\mu} = \boldsymbol{\mu}(\boldsymbol{\phi}) = \left[\boldsymbol{\mu}_1(\boldsymbol{\phi})', \boldsymbol{\mu}_2(\boldsymbol{\phi})'\right] = \left[\boldsymbol{\xi}', \boldsymbol{\mu}_2(\boldsymbol{\phi})'\right]$ is an isomorphic reparameterization of $\boldsymbol{\phi}$ with $\left(\partial\boldsymbol{\mu}/\partial\boldsymbol{\phi}'\right)_{\boldsymbol{\phi}_0}$ having full rank.

Congruence therefore requires a model $\mathcal{M}_g$, in addition to being data coherent $[\boldsymbol{\mu}_2(\boldsymbol{\phi}_0) = \mathbf{0}]$, to be defined with respect to a probability space that has a density function $\mathsf{f}_\mathsf{X}(\mathbf{x}_t|\mathbf{X}_{t-1}, \boldsymbol{\xi})$, a set of variables $\mathbf{x}_t$, and parameterization $\boldsymbol{\xi}$ that are capable of being (low-level) theory consistent and data admissible. Though many models that are commonly used in econometrics are linear in variables and parameters, it is conceivable that the unknown LDGPs are nonlinear. While finding a congruent nonlinear model would be invaluable, in its absence linear approximations may capture the main features of the data sufficiently well for there to be no evidence of noncongruence. Indeed, such linear econometric models can be highly effective vehicles for economic analysis using available information, despite not being observationally equivalent to the LDGP. Further positive consequences of a model being congruent are considered in the next two Sections.

15.4.1 General Models, Encompassing, and Nesting

From the example of Gouriéroux and Monfort (1995) discussed in Section 15.3 it might appear that whether a parametrically more general model encompasses a simplification of itself depends fortuitously on the nature of the unknown LDGP. However, this ignores the possibility that models can be designed to ensure that they encompass simple cases of themselves. Although Gouriéroux and Monfort argued that the LDGP can be such that $\mathcal{M}_2$ does not encompass its submodel $\mathcal{M}_1$, they also provided a zone that defines a class of LDGPs that enable $\mathcal{M}_2$ to encompass $\mathcal{M}_1$. Since the LDGP is unknown and cannot be designed (except in situations such as Monte Carlo simulation experiments), whereas models are artifacts that can be designed to have particular characteristics, it seems natural to consider what design features are required for models to encompass simplifications of themselves. Heuristically a congruent nesting model can be expected to encompass all submodels of itself. Hence, if a general model fails to encompass a simplification of itself it is possible that this has arisen as a result of the general model not being congruent or not nesting the simplification, or both. The examples in Section 15.3 suggest that a model encompasses an algebraic simplification of itself if and only if there are no false auxiliary hypotheses implicit in the nesting model that are not also an integral part of the "nested" model. When a general model $\mathcal{M}_g$ is data coherent [i.e., $\boldsymbol{\mu}_2(\boldsymbol{\phi}_0) = \mathbf{0}$], it is a valid reduction of the LDGP and so is be able to explain the properties of all models nested within it, as the following lemma records.

Lemma 1 *Since a data-coherent model is a valid reduction of the LDGP, and by definition the LDGP encompasses all models defined on the same probability space, a data-coherent model encompasses all models nested within it.*

A direct consequence of this lemma is the following corollary.

Corollary 2 *Since a congruent model is data coherent, it too encompasses all models nested within it [i.e., if* $\boldsymbol{\mu}_2(\boldsymbol{\phi}_0) = \mathbf{0}$ *then* $\mathcal{M}_g \mathcal{E} \mathrm{M}_i \; \forall \; \mathcal{M}_i \subseteq \mathcal{M}_g$*].*

Hence, congruence is a sufficient condition for a model to encompass models nested within it, and so provides a sufficient condition for the absence of the anomaly pointed out by Gouriéroux and Monfort (1995). The fact that it is not necessary is illustrated by the following example: Let the set of variables agreed on to be relevant for a particular problem be (y_t, x_t, z_t, u_t), and for the parameters of interest let (x_t, z_t, u_t) be weakly exogenous variables,[1] so that the LDGP lies in $\mathsf{D}(y_t \mid x_t, z_t, u_t)$. Consider the models

$$\mathcal{M}_1\colon\; y_t = \beta x_t + \zeta_{1t}, \qquad \zeta_{1t} \sim \mathcal{N}\left(0, \sigma^2_{\zeta_1}\right)$$

$$\mathcal{M}_2\colon\; y_t = \gamma x_t + \delta z_t + \varepsilon_{1t}, \qquad \varepsilon_{1t} \sim \mathcal{N}\left(0, \sigma^2_{\varepsilon_1}\right)$$

and note that, in general, $\mathcal{M}_2$ is not congruent since it wrongly excludes u_t and so is not a valid reduction of the LDGP. However, if it were the case that u_t were orthogonal to both x_t and z_t, then $\mathcal{M}_2$ would encompass $\mathcal{M}_1$ despite $\mathcal{M}_2$ not being congruent.

Further, note that since congruence is a sufficient condition for the absence of the anomaly it is possible for a noncongruent nesting model to encompass some, though not all, nested models. In fact, given that congruence cannot be directly established (see the subsequent discussion of testing congruence) it is fortunate that congruence is a sufficient, but not a necessary, condition for $\mathcal{M}_g \mathcal{E} M_s$ when $\mathcal{M}_s \subseteq \mathcal{M}_g$. Similarly, although congruence and nesting ensure that the nesting model encompasses the nested model, nesting alone does not ensure encompassing.

15.4.2 General-to-Specific Modeling

In addition to providing a sufficient condition for the anomaly noted by Gouriéroux and Monfort (1995) not to occur, congruence provides justification for the modeling strategy that seeks to evaluate alternative models of the phenomenon of interest in the framework of a congruent nesting model (see Hendry, 1995; Mizon, 1977a,b, 1995a). The above definitions, lemma, and corollary indicate that a good strategy to avoid misleading inferences is to test hypotheses such as $\mathcal{M}_s \mathcal{E}_p(\boldsymbol{\theta}) \mathcal{M}_g$ only when $\mathcal{M}_g$ is congruent. Similarly, they make it clear that the equivalence $\mathcal{M}_1 \mathcal{E} M_2 \Longleftrightarrow \mathcal{M}_1 \mathcal{E}_p \mathcal{M}_c$ requires that $\mathcal{M}_c$ be congruent, or at least data coherent (cf. Hendry and Richard, 1989; Hendry, 1995). Also note that since $\boldsymbol{\mu}(\boldsymbol{\phi})$ is an isomorphic reparameterization of $\boldsymbol{\phi}$ it follows that $\boldsymbol{\xi}$ and $\boldsymbol{\mu}_2$ are variation free, which is a convenient property for a model such as $\mathcal{M}_g$ to have given that the LDGP is in general unknown. However, despite $\boldsymbol{\xi}$ and $\boldsymbol{\mu}_2$ being variation free, fully efficient inference on $\boldsymbol{\xi}$ can only be obtained from $\mathcal{M}_g$ if it is congruent, that is, when $\boldsymbol{\mu}_2 = \mathbf{0}$. It is therefore important to test models for congruence.

15.5 TESTING CONGRUENCE

Unfortunately, the definition of congruence is nonoperational since the LDGP and, hence, its parameterization are unknown, so that a test of the hypothesis $\boldsymbol{\mu}_2(\boldsymbol{\phi}_0) = \mathbf{0}$ is not feasible. To the extent that part of $\boldsymbol{\mu}_2$ is known it would be possible to conduct a partial test of congruence, and this would be in the spirit of misspecification testing. Indeed, the fact that only a subset of $\boldsymbol{\mu}_2$ might be known, and thus only part of the condition for congruence testable, reflects the fact that at best it is only possible to test necessary conditions for congruence. A commonly adopted strategy for testing congruence is to test the adequacy of a model against misspecification in particular directions, such as having residuals that are serially correlated and heteroskedastic, there being invalid conditioning and parameter nonconstancies. Indeed, this is the basis of the definitions of congruence given in, for example, Hendry (1995) and Mizon (1995a). In the present context, misspecification testing applied to $\mathcal{M}_g$ in order to assess its congruence can be characterized as testing the m hypotheses $\rho_i = 0$ for $\mathcal{M}_g \mathcal{E}_p \mathcal{M}_g^i$ when the augmented models are given by $\mathcal{M}_g^i = \{\mathsf{f}_g^i(\mathbf{x}_t \mid \mathbf{X}_{t-1}; \boldsymbol{\xi}, \rho_i), \boldsymbol{\xi} \in \Xi, \rho_i \in \mathbb{R}\}$, with $\mathsf{f}_g^i(\mathbf{x}_t \mid \mathbf{X}_{t-1}; \boldsymbol{\xi}, 0) = \mathsf{f}_g(\mathbf{x}_t \mid \mathbf{X}_{t-1}; \boldsymbol{\xi}) \; \forall\, i$ and the ρ_i's might be residual serial correlation coefficients, parameter changes, or heteroskedasticity parameters. Note that in cases where $\boldsymbol{\mu}_2(\boldsymbol{\phi}_0) \neq \mathbf{0}$ the noncongruence of $\mathcal{M}_g$ can exhibit itself in many different ρ_i's being nonzero. For example, a shift in a long-run equilibrium of a system often results in serially correlated residuals. This illustrates the well-known fact that it is often (usually) inappropriate when a hypothesis $\rho_i = 0$ (such as zero residual serial correlation) is rejected to modify the tested model $\mathcal{M}_g$ in the direction of the alternative hypothesis for the misspecification test (e.g., by introducing a serially correlated error process). [See, inter alia, Mizon (1995b) for further discussion of this point.] In the present context note also that for a test of misspecification not to yield potentially misleading information it is necessary that the completing model $\mathcal{M}_g^i$ encompass $\mathcal{M}_g$. This accords with the quotation from Hendry (1995) given in Section 15.3, but note that $\mathcal{M}_g \subseteq \mathcal{M}_g^i$ does not ensure that $\mathcal{M}_g^i \mathcal{E} M_g$. To the extent that the misspecification hypotheses $\rho_i = 0$ for $i = 1, 2, \ldots, m$ are not orthogonal to each other this poses a problem. Were each $\mathcal{M}_g^i$ congruent the problem would disappear, but fortunately congruence of $\mathcal{M}_g^i$ is not essential for misspecification testing of $\mathcal{M}_g$ provided that the investigator does not adopt $\mathcal{M}_g^i$ as the preferred model if $\rho_i = 0$ is rejected.

Since the LDGP is not known, thus implying that $\boldsymbol{\mu}_2(\boldsymbol{\phi})$ is unknowable, whereas $\boldsymbol{\xi}$ can be estimated, the following restricted definition of parsimonious encompassing might be considered as the basis for an alternative way to test congruence.

Definition 5 Restricted Parsimonious Encompassing. Model $\mathcal{M}_s$ parsimoniously encompasses another model $\mathcal{M}_g$ with respect to $\boldsymbol{\alpha}$, $\left[\mathcal{M}_s\mathcal{E}_p(\boldsymbol{\alpha})\mathcal{M}_g\right]$ if and only if $\mathcal{M}_s \subseteq \mathcal{M}_g$ and $\mathcal{M}_s\mathcal{E}(\boldsymbol{\alpha})\mathcal{M}_g$.

Note that the encompassing comparison is made with respect to $\boldsymbol{\alpha}$, the parameter of the nested model $\mathcal{M}_s$, rather than $\boldsymbol{\xi}$ of the nesting model $\mathcal{M}_g$. However, the implicit null hypothesis (see Mizon and Richard 1986) associated with this definition has the same basic form as that of a Hausman (1978) specification test statistic, namely, the hypothesis that the contrast between the pseudotrue value of $\boldsymbol{\alpha}$ in $\mathcal{M}_s$ and that of $\boldsymbol{\alpha}$ in $\mathcal{M}_g$ [when $\boldsymbol{\xi}$ is reparameterized as $\boldsymbol{\xi}' = \left(\boldsymbol{\alpha}', \boldsymbol{\psi}'\right)$] is zero. Hence this hypothesis does not define a valid reduction from $\mathcal{M}_g$. Indeed, as shown by Holly (1982), the implicit null hypothesis holds if either (1) $\boldsymbol{\psi}(\boldsymbol{\xi}) = \mathbf{0}$ or (2) $\mathrm{p}\lim_{T\to\infty}\left[T^{-1}(\partial^2 L_g)/(\partial\alpha\partial\psi')\right] = 0$. The fact that (2) does not ensure that $\mathcal{M}_s$ contains all information relevant for inference on $\boldsymbol{\alpha}$ highlights the limitation of this approach. This is therefore not a promising route for testing for valid reductions from a fully specified alternative [e.g., $\mathcal{M}_s\mathcal{E}_p(\boldsymbol{\xi})\mathcal{M}_g$] and thus not for specification testing. On the other hand, when $\mathcal{M}_g$ is not a serious alternative to $\mathcal{M}_s$, but simply a vehicle for testing the adequacy of $\mathcal{M}_s$, then testing the hypothesis $\mathcal{M}_s\mathcal{E}_p(\boldsymbol{\alpha})\mathcal{M}_g$ can be useful as a misspecification test. Hence, the role of such restricted parsimonious encompassing hypotheses seems to lie in misspecification testing rather than specification testing. See Mizon (1977a) for discussion of this distinction. Thus there is a potential role for testing restricted parsimonious encompassing hypotheses of the type $\mathcal{M}_g\mathcal{E}_p(\boldsymbol{\xi})\mathcal{M}_g^i$ when $\mathcal{M}_g^i$ is not a serious alternative to $\mathcal{M}_g$ but simply a vehicle for indirectly testing the congruence of $\mathcal{M}_g$.

15.6 EMPIRICAL ILLUSTRATION

As a means of illustrating many of the concepts discussed in this chapter this section contains analysis of data generated from an artificial LDGP. Using artificial data rather than observed macroeconomic time-series data has the advantage of allowing the LDGP to be designed precisely to illustrate the chosen concepts. In particular, the LDGP is known as well, as the equivalence set of representations for it, and thus for this special circumstance they provide clear benchmarks against which empirical models can be compared. For the particular sample of data generated, the alternative representations of the LDGP that are known to be observationally equivalent can be estimated. In addition, there are other empirical models, which, despite not being observationally equivalent to the LDGP, display no evidence of misspecification and so cannot be rejected as congruent models.

Consider a situation in which the variable to be modeled y_t and an unrelated (and thus noncausal) variable z_t are generated by:

$$\begin{pmatrix} y_t \\ z_t \end{pmatrix} = \begin{pmatrix} \alpha & 0 \\ 0 & 0 \end{pmatrix} \begin{pmatrix} y_{t-1} \\ z_{t-1} \end{pmatrix} + \begin{pmatrix} \epsilon_{1,t} + \theta\epsilon_{1,t-1} \\ \epsilon_{2,t} \end{pmatrix} \tag{7}$$

when $(\epsilon_{1,t}, \epsilon_{2,t})' = \boldsymbol{\epsilon}_t \sim \mathsf{NI}(\mathbf{0}, \mathbf{I}_2)$. Hence y_t is generated from an $ARMA(1, 1)$, and z_t from an independent white noise process. An observationally equivalent representation of this LDGP is given with the first equation of (7) replaced by

$$y_t = \sum_{i=0}^{\infty} \phi_i y_{t-1-i} + \epsilon_{1,t}, \tag{8}$$

with $\phi_i = (-\theta)^i(\alpha + \theta)$. Note that $\phi_i \to 0$ as $i \to \infty$ for $|\ \alpha\ | < 1$ and $|\ \theta\ | < 1$, so that a finite-order autoregression gives a good approximation to (8) under these conditions. Further, although this particular LDGP has two observationally equivalent representations, the one involving the moving average error format in (7) might be preferred on grounds of parsimony *if the LDGP were known.* In fact, this $ARMA(1, 1)$ format was used to generate the sample of $T = 100$ observations on y_t and z_t (with $\alpha = 0.9$ and $\theta = 0.5$), rather than the less tractable $AR(\infty)$ representation in (8). However, in practice the LDGP is not known and the best that can be done is to compare the relative merits of alternative empirical models.

The following analysis illustrates how it is possible to find more than one empirical model for which there is no evidence in the sample of misspecification so that the hypothesis of congruence is not rejected, even though all but one of the models differ in the population from the LDGP. Hence, although in the population a congruent model is observationally equivalent to the LDGP, a model for which the hypothesis of congruence has not been rejected need not be equivalent to the LDGP. However, an important feature of models that are empirically congruent is that they are indistinguishable from the LDGP on the basis of sample information. Further, empirically congruent models have properties in the sample similar to those of the LDGP in the population, namely: (1) they will encompass models nested within them; (2) they provide a valid basis against which to test reduction or simplification hypotheses; and (3) they are able to successfully predict the properties of other models. [See Hendry (1995) for a discussion of misspecification encompassing.]

Consider the following classes of empirical model:

$$\begin{aligned}\mathcal{M}_1\colon\ y_t &= \delta_1 + \beta_1 y_{t-1} + u_{1,t} + \gamma_1 u_{1,t-1},\\ \mathcal{M}_2\colon\ y_t &= \delta_2 + \sum_{i=1}^{4} \beta_{2,i} y_{t-i} + \sum_{i=0}^{4} \lambda_{2,i} z_{t-i} + u_{2,t},\\ \mathcal{M}_3\colon\ y_t &= \delta_3 + \sum_{i=1}^{5} \beta_{3,i} y_{t-i} + u_{3,t}.\end{aligned} \tag{9}$$

$\mathcal{M}_1$ is an $ARMA(1,1)$ and includes the LDGP at $\delta_1 = 0, \beta_1 = 0.9$ and $\gamma_1 = 0.5$, plus $\mathsf{E}(u_{1,t}) = 0$, $\mathsf{Cov}(u_{1,t}, u_{1,s}) = 0$, $t \neq s$, and $\mathsf{V}(u_{1,t}) = 1$. $\mathcal{M}_2$ is an autoregressive-distributed lag model $AD(4,4)$, and although it does not include the LDGP and is thus not congruent in the population, the hypothesis of congruence is not rejected in sample. $\mathcal{M}_3$ is a fifth-order autoregression $AR(5)$, which neither includes nor is equivalent to the LDGP, but is a finite-order truncation of (8). As a preliminary to considering simplifications of them, these three models are now estimated and diagnostic statistics used to assess the evidence for their misspecification.

First, the LDGP, $\mathcal{M}_1$, was estimated and the particular sample evidence for misspecification assessed. The parameter point estimates and standard errors and the residuals $\widehat{u}_{1,t}$ were calculated using the exact maximum likelihood estimation option for linear regression models with moving average errors in *Microfit* (see Pesaran and Pesaran, 1997). The diagnostic statistics were calculated in *PcGive* (see Doornik and Hendry, 1996), which was used together with *PcGets* (see Krolzig and Hendry, 2001; Hendry and Krolzig, 2003) for the other results reported in this section. The diagnostic statistics reported are: single-equation residual standard deviations $\hat{\sigma}$; $F_{ar}(p, \cdot)$, a Lagrange multiplier test of pth-order residual serial correlation; F_{het} a test of residual heteroskedasticity; $F_{arch}(q, \cdot)$, a test of qth-order residual autoregressive heteroskedasticity; $\chi^2_{norm}(2)$, a test of residual normality; AIC, the Akaike information criterion; and SC, the Schwarz information criterion. [See Hendry and Doornik (1996) for more details.]

$$\left.\begin{aligned} y_t = -\underset{(0.164)}{0.1522} + \underset{(0.041)}{0.9188}\, y_{t-1} + \widehat{u}_{1,t} + \underset{(0.093)}{0.4483}\, \widehat{u}_{1,t-1},\\ R^2 = 0.919,\ s = 1.0357,\ T = 99,\ AIC = 0.100,\ SC = 0.179\\ F_{ar}(5,93) = 0.24[0.94],\ F_{arch}(4,90) = 0.70[0.59]\\ F_{het}(2,94) = 0.29[0.75],\ \chi^2_{norm}(2) = 0.21[0.90] \end{aligned}\right\}. \tag{10}$$

The point estimates of δ, α, and θ are close to, with none of them significantly different from, their population values, and there is no evidence of misspecification in the model. Hence this particular sample of data provides accurate estimates of the LDGP and does not give any indication of noncongruence via the reported diagnostic statistics.

The estimates for $\mathcal{M}_2$ are:

$$\left.\begin{aligned} \widehat{y}_t = & -\underset{(0.12)}{0.075} + \underset{(0.11)}{1.40}\, y_{t-1} - \underset{(0.19)}{0.59}\, y_{t-2} + \underset{(0.19)}{0.10}\, y_{t-3} + \underset{(0.11)}{0.03}\, y_{t-4} \\ & + \underset{(0.11)}{0.06}\, z_t - \underset{(0.11)}{0.16}\, z_{t-1} + \underset{(0.11)}{0.01}\, z_{t-2} + \underset{(0.11)}{0.002}\, z_{t-3} + \underset{(0.11)}{0.04}\, z_{t-4}, \\ R^2 = & \; 0.924,\ s = 1.0313,\ T = 96,\ AIC = 0.160,\ SC = 0.427 \\ & F_{ar}(5, 81) = 0.30\ [0.91],\ F_{arch}(4, 78) = 0.92\ [0.46] \\ & F_{het}(18, 67) = 0.88\ [0.61],\ \chi^2_{norm}(2) = 0.17\ [0.92] \end{aligned}\right\}. \quad (11)$$

Again there is no evidence of misspecification in this estimated model, so $\mathcal{M}_2$ also provides a valid basis from which to test the validity of reductions. Note, in particular, that $\mathcal{M}_2$ includes the irrelevant noncausal variables $z_t, z_{t-1}, \ldots, z_{t-4}$, none of whose estimated coefficients is significantly different from zero. In addition, the estimated coefficients of y_{t-1} and y_{t-2} are close to $\phi_1 = 1.4$ and $\phi_2 = -0.7$, while those of y_{t-3} and y_{t-4} corresponding to $\phi_3 = 0.35$ and $\phi_4 = -0.175$ are not significantly different from these values or zero. The fact that none of the diagnostic statistics indicates noncongruence implies that the fourth-order autoregression within $\mathcal{M}_2$ provides a good approximation to the LDGP.

The results from estimating $\mathcal{M}_3$ also yield a model with no evidence of misspecification and suggest that an *AR*(2) provides a good representation of these sample data:

$$\left.\begin{aligned} \widehat{y}_t = & -\underset{(0.12)}{0.08} + \underset{(0.11)}{1.39}\, y_{t-1} - \underset{(0.19)}{0.61}\, y_{t-2} + \underset{(0.20)}{0.14}\, y_{t-3} - \underset{(0.19)}{0.01}\, y_{t-4} + \underset{(0.11)}{0.02}\, y_{t-5}, \\ & R^2 = 0.920,\ s = 1.0278,\ T = 95,\ AIC = 0.116,\ SC = 0.277 \\ & F_{ar}(5, 84) = 1.53\ [0.19],\ F_{arch}(4, 81) = 1.102\ [0.36] \\ & F_{het}(10, 78) = 0.82\ [0.61],\ \chi^2_{norm}(2) = 0.29\ [0.86]. \end{aligned}\right\}. \quad (12)$$

On the basis of results so far it is concluded that:

1. Estimating "general" models involving the available data for y_t and z_t yields three models for which the hypothesis of congruence is not rejected, only one of which is equivalent to the LDGP.
2. The irrelevant noncausal variables $z_t, z_{t-1}, \ldots, z_{t-4}$ are not falsely indicated to be relevant.
3. The informal general-to-specific modeling within the autoregressive-distributed lag class of model reported above works well.
4. Estimating $\mathcal{M}_1$, which includes the LDGP, works best in terms of point estimates and goodness-of-fit adjusted for loss of degrees of freedom in higher dimensional parameterizations (see the *AIC* and *SC* values).

Although the use of information criteria to choose among congruent models as referred to in 4 leads to the choice of $\mathcal{M}_1$, it is clear that both $\mathcal{M}_2$ and $\mathcal{M}_3$ can be simplified and so further evaluation of their merits is in order. Note that $\mathcal{M}_1, \mathcal{M}_2$, and $\mathcal{M}_3$ are nonnested models and so strictly are only alternatives to each other in the context of an embedding model, such as the minimum completing model:

$$\mathcal{M}_4\colon\ y_t = \delta_4 + \sum_{i=1}^{5} \beta_{4,i} y_{t-i} + \sum_{i=0}^{4} \lambda_{4,i} z_{t-i} + u_{4,t} + \gamma_4 u_{4,t-1}, \tag{13}$$

which is an $AD(5,4)MA(1)$. When estimated using *Microfit*, this model also exhibited no evidence of misspecification as the following results show:

$$\left.\begin{array}{c} y_t = \underset{(0.19)}{-0.12} + \underset{(0.19)}{0.77}\, y_{t-1} + \underset{(0.23)}{0.31}\, y_{t-2} - \underset{(0.16)}{0.33}\, y_{t-3} + \underset{(0.13)}{0.13}\, y_{t-4} + \underset{(0.11)}{0.02}\, y_{t-5} \\ + \underset{(0.11)}{0.06}\, z_t - \underset{(0.13)}{0.13}\, z_{t-1} - \underset{(0.13)}{0.06}\, z_{t-2} + \underset{(0.13)}{0.03}\, z_{t-3} + \underset{(0.10)}{0.03}\, z_{t-4} + \widehat{u}_{4,t} + \underset{(0.17)}{0.65},\, \widehat{u}_{4,t-1} \\ R^2 = 0.924,\ s = 1.0362,\ T = 95,\ AIC = 0.188,\ SC = 0.511 \\ F_{ar}(5,78) = 0.99\ [0.43],\ F_{arch}(4,75) = 1.33\ [0.27] \\ F_{het}(20,62) = 0.73\ [0.78],\ \chi^2_{norm}(2) = 0.16\ [0.93] \end{array}\right\}. \tag{14}$$

It is important to note that typically models with moving average errors will only be considered if a general model with such an error is specified. In fact, regarding $\mathcal{M}_2$ and $\mathcal{M}_3$ as alternative general and unrestricted models (GUMs) makes it possible to get GUMs that exhibit no evidence of noncongruence without specifying moving average errors. However, for these sample data once the $MA(1)$ error specification is entertained the estimated moving average coefficient remains significant in all simplifications that have no evidence of misspecification. Indeed, applying a simplification strategy of sequentially deleting the least significant variable until all remaining variables are significant results in $\mathcal{M}_1$ being selected. If the $MA(1)$ error specification is not considered, then the minimum completing model for $\mathcal{M}_2$ and $\mathcal{M}_3$ is an $AD(5,4)$, which is (13) with $\gamma_4 = 0$. Denoting this model as $\mathcal{M}_5$ and estimating it yields the following results, which also reveal no evidence of misspecification:

$$\left.\begin{array}{c} \widehat{y}_t = \underset{(0.13)}{-0.08} + \underset{(0.11)}{1.40}\, y_{t-1} - \underset{(0.20)}{0.58}\, y_{t-2} + \underset{(0.21)}{0.07}\, y_{t-3} + \underset{(0.20)}{0.06}\, y_{t-4} - \underset{(0.11)}{0.01}\, y_{t-5} \\ + \underset{(0.11)}{0.06}\, z_t - \underset{(0.11)}{0.16}\, z_{t-1} + \underset{(0.11)}{0.02}\, z_{t-2} + \underset{(0.11)}{0.01}\, z_{t-3} + \underset{(0.11)}{0.03}\, z_{t-4}, \\ R^2 = 0.922,\ s = 1.0416,\ T = 95,\ AIC = 0.190,\ SC = 0.486 \\ F_{ar}(5,79) = 1.22\ [0.31],\ F_{arch}(4,76) = 0.91\ [0.47] \\ F_{het}(65,18) = 0.75\ [0.76],\ \chi^2_{norm}(2) = 0.21\ [0.90] \end{array}\right\}. \tag{15}$$

For models in the autoregressive-distributed-lag class a computer-automated general-to-specific modeling strategy has been implemented in *PcGets* (see Krolzig and Hendry, 2001), and this was applied to $\mathcal{M}_5$. The computer program *PcGets* first tests a GUM for congruence, then conducts variable elimination tests for "highly irrelevant" variables at a loose significance level (25 or 50%, say) in order to simplify the GUM. The program then explores the many paths that can be used to simplify the GUM by eliminating statistically insignificant variables on F- and t-tests, and applying diagnostic tests to ensure that only valid reductions are entertained. This ensures that the preferred model in each path is congruent. Encompassing procedures and information criteria are then used to select a model from this set of congruent models. As a final check of model adequacy, the constancy of the chosen model across subsamples is tested. Using $\mathcal{M}_5$ as a congruent GUM and applying *PcGets* finds the following $AR(2)$ (denoted by $\mathcal{M}_6$ below) as a unique valid reduction:

$$\left.\begin{array}{c} \widehat{y}_t = \underset{(0.12)}{-0.11} + \underset{(0.10)}{1.34}\, y_{t-1} - \underset{(0.10)}{0.41}\, y_{t-2}, \\ R^2 = 0.918,\ s = 1.0230,\ T = 95,\ AIC = 0.077,\ SC = 0.157 \\ F_{ar}(5,87) = 0.76\ [0.58],\ F_{arch}(4,84) = 1.31\ [0.27] \\ F_{het}(4,87) = 0.23\ [0.92],\ \chi^2_{norm}(2) = 0.67\ [0.72] \end{array}\right\}. \tag{16}$$

Hence the application of *PcGets* to these data selects $\mathcal{M}_6$ as a congruent reduction of $\mathcal{M}_5$. This is in conformity with the results in Hendry and Trivedi (1972) and Hendry (1977), who note that an $MA(p)$ is well approximated in terms of goodness-of-fit by an $AR(p)$, so that an $ARMA(p, q)$ is well approximated by an $AR(p+q)$. In the case of $\mathcal{M}_1$, $p = q = 1$ so that the $AR(2)$ in $\mathcal{M}_6$ is expected to provide a good approximation to $\mathcal{M}_1$.

Given that $\mathcal{M}_1, \mathcal{M}_2, \ldots, \mathcal{M}_6$ are all empirically congruent, it is interesting to compare their goodness-of-fit and the values of the *AIC* and *SC* information criteria. From inspection of Table 15.1 the best fit, as judged by the residual sum of squares (RSS), is obtained as to be expected by the most profligate

TABLE 15.1
A Comparison of Six Empirically Congruent Models

Model	*AIC*	*SC*	*RSS*	*Rank*
$\mathcal{M}_1$: *ARMA*(1, 1)	0.04266	0.09643	95.0531	1
$\mathcal{M}_2$: *AD*(4, 4)	0.15997	0.42709	91.4679	4
$\mathcal{M}_3$: *AR*(5)	0.11591	0.27721	94.0166	3
$\mathcal{M}_4$: *AD*(5, 4)*MA*(1)	0.18867	0.51127	89.1141	5/6/6
$\mathcal{M}_5$: *AD*(5, 4)	0.19012	0.48583	91.1416	6/5/5
$\mathcal{M}_6$: *AR*(2)	0.05630	0.10973	97.4153	2

TABLE 15.2
The Predictive Power of an Empirically Congruent Model

Model	$F_{ar}(5, \cdot)$	$F_{arch}(4, \cdot)$	$\chi^2_{norm}(2)$	$F_{het}(\cdot, \cdot)$	RSS	SC
$AD(1, 1)$	3.58 [0.01]**	0.24 [0.92]	0.05 [0.98]	0.89 [0.51]	119.717	0.376
$AD(1, 0)$	3.68 [0.00]**	0.44 [0.78]	0.09 [0.96]	0.80 [0.53]	120.514	0.336
$AR(1)$	3.55 [0.01]**	0.43 [0.78]	0.02 [0.99]	0.08 [0.92]	121.599	0.298
$AD(0, 0)$	198.0 [0.00]**	73.53 [0.00]**	4.80 [0.09]	1.54 [0.22]	1286.19	2.646

Note: The symbol ** denotes that the outcome is significant at the 1% level.

parameterization, namely $\mathcal{M}_4$. The other overparameterized models $\mathcal{M}_5$, $\mathcal{M}_2$, and $\mathcal{M}_3$ also perform well in goodness-of-fit. However, these four models are strongly dominated in terms of information criteria by $\mathcal{M}_1$ and $\mathcal{M}_6$, with $\mathcal{M}_1$ being preferred to $\mathcal{M}_6$ despite each model having three parameters plus the residual variance to be estimated.

The results for these estimated models can also be used to illustrate that a congruent model can predict the properties of other models, particularly those nested within it. For example, $\mathcal{M}_6$ [an $AR(2)$], which is empirically congruent and a valid reduction of $\mathcal{M}_5$, predicts that the errors of the parsimonious models $AR(1)$, $AD(1, 1)$, $AD(1, 0)$, and $AD(0, 0)$ will all be serially correlated. This is indeed the case as shown by the results in Table 15.2.

Finally, note that using the SC to select among the models in Table 15.2 would result in the $AR(1)$ model being selected, despite its noncongruence. Indeed, using the SC criterion results in the $AR(1)$ model being preferred to all models other than the $\mathcal{M}_1$, $\mathcal{M}_6$, and $\mathcal{M}_3$. Hence, selecting models solely on the basis of information criteria such as the SC and paying no attention to the congruence of the alternative models can result in a model being selected that is parsimoniously parameterized but misspecified. Noting that inferences based on misspecified models can be very misleading and that these models are not exploiting relevant information that is already available illustrates the value of seeking congruent and encompassing models and of adopting a general-to-specific modeling strategy.

15.7 CONCLUSIONS

In this chapter the relationship between alternative econometric models and the LDGP has been considered. In particular, an econometric model has been defined as congruent if and only if it parsimoniously encompasses the LDGP. In the population this implies that a congruent model is observationally equivalent to the LDGP and that they mutually encompass each other. Hence, by definition a congruent model contains the same information content as the LDGP. The fact that alternative parameterizations for a given density can exist means that the LDGP can be a member of an equivalence set of models. Ceteris paribus, the principle of preferring parsimonious to profligate parameterizations, can be applied to select the simplest representation of the LDGP (e.g., preferring the $ARMA(1, 1)$ representation over the $AR(\infty)$ in Section 15.6). However, congruence so defined is not directly testable in practice, and as a result is tested indirectly via tests for evidence of misspecification. Consequently, when the hypothesis of congruence is not rejected using sample data, it means that the present use that has been made of the available information has been unable to distinguish between the model and the LDGP. In Section 15.6 this was illustrated by the $AR(2)$ model providing an excellent approximation to the LDGP—an $ARMA(1, 1)$.

Another feature of empirically congruent models is that they mimic the properties of the LDGP: They can accurately predict the misspecifications of noncongruent models; they can encompass models nested within them; and they provide a valid statistical framework for testing alternative simplifications of them. The fact that there can be more than one empirically congruent model means that it is important to evaluate their relative merits, and this can be done via encompassing comparisons. A very powerful way to find congruent and encompassing models in practice is to use a general-to-specific modeling strategy, beginning from a congruent GUM. Hendry and Krolzig (2003) describe and illustrate the performance of a computer program that implements a general-to-specific modeling strategy. Finally, the arguments in this chapter apply equally to econometric systems and single-equation models. The empirical analysis in Section 15.6 only considers single-equation models to keep the illustration simple.

NOTES

The first version of this chapter was written while the first author was visiting the EUI between October and December 1995, and he wishes to thank the researchers and students of the Department of Economics there for their warm hospitality, and especially Massimiliano Marcellino for many discussions on encompassing. Valuable comments were received from John Aldrich, Clive Granger, Grant Hillier, Maozu Lu, Mark Salmon, Bernt Stigum, and Pravin Trivedi. Jean-Pierre Florens, David Hendry, Søren Johansen, and Jean-François Richard are also thanked for stimulating conversations on the topic. Financial support from the EUI Research Council and the UK ESRC under grant L138251009 is gratefully acknowledged.

1. This is not an essential feature of the example, but simplifies the presentation.

REFERENCES

Andrews, D., 1991, "Heteroskedasticity and Autocorrelation Consistent Covariance Matrix Estimation," *Econometrica* 59, 817–858.

Cox, D. R., 1961, "Tests of Separate Families of Hypotheses," in: *Proceedings of the Fourth Berkeley Symposium on Mathematical Statistics and Probability,* Vol. 1, Berkeley: University of California Press, pp. 105–123.

Davidson, R., and J. G. MacKinnon, 1981, "Several Tests for Model Specification in the Presence of Alternative Hypotheses," *Econometrica* 49, 781–793.

Doornik, J. A., and D. F. Hendry, 1996, *GiveWin: An Interactive Empirical Modelling Program,* London: Timberlake Consultants.

Gouriéroux, C., and A. Monfort, 1995, "Testing, Encompassing, and Simulating Dynamic Econometric Models," *Econometric Theory* 11, 195–228.

Govaerts, B., D. F. Hendry, and J.-F. Richard, 1994, "Encompassing in Stationary Linear Dynamic Models," *Journal of Econometrics* 63, 245–270.

Harvey, A. C., 1993, *Time Series Models,* 2nd Ed., Hemel Hempstead: Harvester Wheatsheaf.

Hausman, J. A., 1978, "Specification Tests in Econometrics," *Econometrica* 46, 1251–1271.

Hendry, D. F., 1977, "On the Time Series Approach to Econometric Model Building," in: *New Methods in Business Cycle Research,* C. A. Sims (ed.), Minneapolis: Federal Reserve Bank of Minneapolis, pp. 183–202. Reprinted in *Econometrics: Alchemy or Science?* D. F. Hendry, Oxford: Blackwell, 1993, and Oxford University Press, 2000.

Hendry, D. F., 1985, "Monetary Economic Myth and Econometric Reality," *Oxford Review of Economic Policy* 1, 72–84. Reprinted in *Econometrics: Alchemy or Science?* D. F. Hendry, Oxford: Blackwell, 1993, and Oxford University Press, 2000.

Hendry, D. F., 1987, "Econometric Methodology: A Personal Perspective," in: *Advances in Econometrics,* T. F. Bewley (ed.), Cambridge: Cambridge University Press, ch. 10.

Hendry, D. F., 1995, *Dynamic Econometrics,* Oxford: Oxford University Press.

Hendry, D. F., and J. A. Doornik, 1996, *Empirical Econometric Modeling Using PcGive for Windows,* London: Timberlake Consultants.

Hendry, D. F., and H.-M. Krolzig, 2003, "New Developments in Automatic General-to-Specific Modelling," in: *Econometrics and the Philosophy of Economics,* B. P. Stigum (ed.), Princeton: Princeton University Press, ch. 16.

Hendry, D. F., and G. E. Mizon, 1990, "Procrustean Econometrics: Or Stretching and Squeezing Data," in: *Modelling Economic Series,* C. W. J. Granger (ed.), Oxford: Clarendon Press, pp. 121–136.

Hendry, D. F., and G. E. Mizon, 1998, "Exogeneity, Causality, and Co-breaking in Economic Policy Analysis of a Small Econometric Model of Money in the UK," *Empirical Economics* 23, 267–294.

Hendry, D. F., and G. E. Mizon, 2000, "On Selecting Policy Analysis Models by Forecast Accuracy," in: *Putting Economics to Work: Volume in Honour of Michio Morishima,* A. B. Atkinson, H. Glennerster, and N. Stern (eds.), London School of Economics: STICERD, pp. 71–113.

Hendry, D. F., and J.-F. Richard, 1989, "Recent Developments in the Theory of Encompassing," in: *Contributions to Operations Research and Economics: The XXth*

Anniversary of CORE, B. Cornet and H. Tulkens (eds.), Cambridge: MIT Press, pp. 393–440.

Hendry, D. F., and P. K. Trivedi, 1972, "Maximum Likelihood Estimation of Difference Equations with Moving-average Errors: A Simulation Study," *Review of Economic Studies* 32, 117–145.

Holly, A., 1982, "A Remark on Hausman's Specification Test," *Econometrica* 50, 749–760.

Krolzig, H.-M., and D. F. Hendry, 2001, "Computer Automation of General-to-specific Model Selection Procedures," *Journal of Economic Dynamics and Control* 25, 831–866.

Lu, M., and G. E. Mizon, 2000, "Nested Models, Orthogonal Projection, and Encompassing," *Applications of Differential Geometry to Econometrics,* P. Marriott and M. Salmon (eds.), Cambridge: Cambridge University Press, pp. 64–84.

Mizon, G. E., 1977a, "Inferential Procedures in Nonlinear Models: An Application in a UK Industrial Cross Section Study of Factor Substitution and Returns to Scale," *Econometrica* 45, 1221–1242.

Mizon, G. E., 1977b, "Model Selection Procedures," in: *Studies in Modern Economic Analysis,* M. J. Artis and A. R. Nobay (eds.), Oxford: Blackwell, pp. 97–120.

Mizon, G. E., 1984, "The Encompassing Approach in Econometrics," in: *Econometrics and Quantitative Economics,* D. F. Hendry and K. F. Wallis (eds.), Oxford: Blackwell, pp. 135–172.

Mizon, G. E., 1993, "Empirical Analysis of Time Series: Illustrations with Simulated Data," in: *Advanced Lectures in Quantitative Economics,* Vol. II, A. de Zeeuw (ed.), New York: Academic Press, pp. 184–205.

Mizon, G. E., 1995a, "Progressive Modelling of Macroeconomic Time Series: The LSE Methodology," in: *Macroeconometrics: Developments, Tensions and Prospects,* K. D. Hoover (ed.), Dordrecht: Kluwer Academic Press, pp. 107–169.

Mizon, G. E., 1995b, "A Simple Message for Autocorrelation Correctors: Don't," *Journal of Econometrics* 69, 267–288.

Mizon, G. E., and J.-F. Richard, 1986, "The Encompassing Principle and Its Application to Non-nested Hypothesis Tests," *Econometrica* 54, 657–678.

Pesaran, M. H., and B. Pesaran, 1997, *Microfit for Windows, Version 4,* Oxford: Oxford University Press.

Sargan, J. D., 1988, *Lectures on Advanced Econometric Theory,* Oxford: Blackwell.

White, H., 1982, "Maximum Likelihood Estimation of Misspecified Models," *Econometrica* 50, 1–26.

Chapter Sixteen

New Developments in Automatic General-to-Specific Modeling

David F. Hendry and Hans-Martin Krolzig

Empirical econometric modeling is an integral aspect of the attempt to make economics a quantitative science, although it raises many important methodological issues. Not least among these is how to select models: by prior specification alone, by data evidence alone, or by some mixture of these, where the "weights" attached to the former could vary from unity to zero. Neither extreme seems tenable: Economies are so high dimensional, nonstationary, and complicated that pure theory can never precisely specify the underlying process, and there are simply too many variables to rely solely on data evidence. Thus, model-selection methods must be used, and the methodology thereof deserves careful attention.

When the prior specification of a possible relationship is not known for certain, data evidence is essential to delineate the relevant from the irrelevant variables. This is particularly true in nonstationary processes, as noted in Section 16.1, since retained irrelevant variables may be subject to deterministic shifts, inducing a structural break in the model under analysis. Thus, model selection is inevitable in practice, and while it may be accomplished in many possible ways, this chapter argues that simplification from a congruent general unrestricted model (GUM) embodies the best features of a number of alternatives. Some economists require the prior imposition of theory-based specifications, but such an approach assumes knowledge of the answer before the empirical investigation starts, thus virtually denying empirical modeling any useful role—and in practice, it has rarely contributed in that framework (see, e. g., Summers, 1991).

Unfortunately, there has been little agreement on which approaches should be adopted (see, inter alia, Leamer, 1983b; Pagan, 1987; Hendry et al., 1990; Granger, 1990; Magnus and Morgan, 1999). Hendry (2000b) discusses the rather pessimistic perceptions extant in the literature, including difficulties deriving from "data-based model selection" (see the attack by Keynes, 1939, 1940, on Tinbergen 1940a, b), "measurement without theory" (Koopmans, 1947), "data mining" (Lovell, 1983), pretest biases' (Judge and Bock, 1978), "ignoring selection effects" (Leamer, 1978), "repeated testing" (Leamer, 1983a), "arbitrary significance levels" (Hendry et al., 1990), "lack of identification" (see Faust and Whiteman, 1997, for a recent reiteration), and the potential "path dependence of any selection" (Pagan, 1987). Nevertheless, none of these problems is inherently insurmountable, most are based on theoretical arguments (rather than evidence), and most have countercriticisms. Instead, the sequence of developments in automatic model selection initiated by Hoover and Perez (1999) suggests the converse: The operational characteristics of some selection algorithms are excellent across a wide range of states of nature, as this chapter will demonstrate. Naturally, we focus on *PcGets* (see Hendry and Krolzig, 1999, 2001; Krolzig and Hendry, 2001).

PcGets is an Ox Package (see Doornik, 1999) implementing automatic general-to-specific (*Gets*) modeling for linear, dynamic, regression models based on the principles discussed in Hendry (1995). First, an initial general statistical model is tested for the absence of misspecification (denoted congruence), which is then maintained throughout the selection process by diagnostic checks, thereby ensuring a congruent final model. Next statistically insignificant variables are eliminated by selection tests, both in blocks and individually. Many reduction paths are searched to prevent the algorithm from becoming stuck in a sequence that inadvertently eliminates a variable that matters and thereby retains other variables as proxies. Path searches in *PcGets* terminate when no variable meets the preset criteria or any diagnostic test becomes significant. Nonrejected models are tested by encompassing. If several remain acceptable, so are congruent, undominated, mutually encompassing representations, the reduction process recommences from their union, providing that is a reduction of the GUM, till a unique outcome is obtained. Otherwise, or if all selected simplifications reappear, the search is terminated using the Schwarz (1978) information criterion. Lastly, subsample insignificance seeks to identify "spuriously significant" regressors.

In the Monte Carlo experiments in Hendry and Krolzig (1999) and Krolzig and Hendry (2001), *PcGets* recovers the data-generation process (DGP) with an accuracy close to what one would expect if the DGP specification were known, but nevertheless coefficient tests were conducted. Empirically, on the data sets analyzed by Davidson et al. (1978) and Hendry and Ericsson (1991b), *PcGets* selects (in seconds!) models at least as good as those developed over several years by their authors. Automatic model selection is in its infancy, yet exceptional progress has already been achieved, setting a high "lower bound" on future performance. Moreover, there is a burgeoning symbiosis between the implementation and the theory—developments in each stimulate advances in the other.

The structure of this chapter is as follows: Section 16.1 considers the main alternative modeling approaches presently available, which strongly suggest a focus on *Gets* modeling. Since the theory of reduction is the basis for *Gets* modeling, Section 16.2 notes the main ingredients of that theory. Section 16.3 then describes the embodiment of *Gets* in the computer program *PcGets* for automatic model selection. Section 16.4 distinguishes between the costs of inference and the costs of search to provide an explanation of why *PcGets* does so well in model selection: Sections 16.4.2 and 16.4.3 then discuss the probabilities of deleting irrelevant, and selecting relevant, variables, respectively. Section 16.5 presents a set of almost 2,000 new experiments that have been used to calibrate the behavior of the algorithm by varying the significance levels of its many selection procedures, then reports the outcomes of applying the released version of *PcGets* to both the Monte Carlo experiments in Lovell (1983) as reanalyzed by Hoover and Perez (1999), and in Krolzig and Hendry (2001), as well as noting the finite-sample behavior of the misspecification test statistics. Finally, Section 16.6 concludes the chapter.

16.1 WHAT ARE THE ALTERNATIVES?

Many investigators in econometrics have worried about the consequences of selecting models from data evidence, predating even the Cowles Commission, as noted earlier. Eight literature strands can be delineated, which comprise distinct research strategies, if somewhat overlapping at the margins:

1. Simple-to-general modeling [see, e.g., Anderson (1971), Hendry and Mizon (1978) and Hendry (1979) for critiques].
2. Retaining the general model [see, e.g., Yancey and Judge (1976) and Judge and Bock (1978)].
3. Testing theory-based models [see, e.g., Hall (1978) with Hendry and Mizon (2000), for a critical appraisal, and Stigum (1990) for a formal approach].
4. Other "rules" for model selection, such as step-wise regression [see, e.g., Leamer (1983a) for a critical appraisal], and "optimal" regression [see, e.g., Coen et al. (1969) and the following discussion].
5. Model comparisons, often based on nonnested hypothesis tests or encompassing [see, e.g., Cox (1961, 1962), Pesaran (1974), Deaton (1982), Kent (1986), and Vuong (1989), as well as Hendry and Richard (1982), Mizon (1984), Mizon and Richard (1986), and the survey in Hendry and Richard (1989)].
6. Model selection by information criteria [see, e.g., Schwarz (1978), Hannan and Quinn (1979), Amemiya (1980), Shibata (1980), Chow (1981), and Akaike (1985)].
7. Bayesian model comparisons [see, e.g., Leamer (1978) and Clayton et al. (1986)].
8. *Gets* [see, e.g., Anderson (1971), Sargan (1973, 1981), Mizon (1977a, 1977b), Hendry (1979), and White (1990)], with specific examples such

as COMFAC (see Sargan, 1980), as well as the related literature on multiple hypothesis testing (well reviewed by Savin, 1984).

We briefly consider these in turn.

16.1.1 The Problems of Simple-to-General Modeling

The paradigm of postulating a simple model and seeking to generalize it in the light of test rejections or anomalies is suspect for a number of reasons. First, there is no clear stopping point to an unordered search—the first nonrejection is obviously a bad strategy (see Anderson, 1971). Further, no control is offered over the significance level of testing, as it is not clear how many tests will be conducted.

Second, even if a general model is postulated at the outset as a definitive ending point, difficulties remain with simple-to-general. Often, simple models are noncongruent, inducing multiple test rejections. When two or more statistics reject, it is unclear which (if either) has caused the problem; should both, or only one, be "corrected"; or should other factors be sought? If several tests are computed *seriatim,* and a "later" one rejects, then that invalidates all the earlier inferences, inducing a very inefficient research strategy. Indeed, until a model adequately characterizes the data, conventional tests are invalid, and it is obviously not sensible to skip testing in the hope that a model is valid.

Third, alternative routes begin to multiply because simple-to-general is a divergent branching process—there are many possible generalizations, and the selected model evolves differently depending on which paths are selected, and in what order. Thus, genuine path dependence can be created by such a search strategy.

Fourth, once a problem is revealed by a test, it is unclear how to proceed. It is a potentially dangerous non sequitur to adopt the alternative hypothesis of the test that rejected, for example, assuming that residual autocorrelation is error autoregression, which imposes common factors on the dynamics (COMFAC: see Sargan, 1980; Hendry and Mizon, 1978).

Finally, if a model displays symptoms of misspecification, there is little point in imposing further restrictions on it. Thus, despite its obvious prevalence in empirical practice, there is little to commend a simple-to-general strategy.

16.1.2 Retaining the Initial General Model

Another alternative is to keep every variable in the GUM, but "shrink" the parameter estimates (see, e.g., Yancey and Judge, 1976; Judge and Bock, 1978). Shrinkage entails weighting coefficient estimates in relation to their significance, thus using a "smooth" discount factor rather than the zero-one weights inherent in retain-or-delete decisions. Technically, the latter are "inadmissible" (i.e., dominated on some criterion by other methods for a class of statistical problems). The shrinkage approach is also suggested as a solution to the "pretest" problem, whereby a biased estimator results when "insignificant" draws are set to zero. Naturally, shrinkage also delivers biased estimators, but is argued to have a lower "risk" than pretest estimators. However, such a claim has no theoretical underpinnings in processes subject to intermittent parameter shifts, since retaining irrelevant variables that are subject to deterministic shifts can be inimical to both forecasting and policy (see, e.g., Clements and Hendry, 2002). Moreover, progressivity entails explaining "more by less," which such an approach hardly facilitates. Finally, absent omniscience, misspecification testing is still essential to check the congruence of the GUM, which leads straight back to a testing—rather than a shrinkage—approach.

16.1.3 Testing Theory Models

Conventional econometric testing of economic theories is often conducted without first ascertaining the congruence of the models used: The dangers of doing so are discussed in Hendry and Mizon (2000). If, instead, misspecification testing is undertaken, then decisions on how to react to rejections must be made. One response is to assume that the observed rejection can be nullified by using a suitably "robust" inference procedure, such as heteroskedasticity-consistent standard errors as in White (1980), or also autocorrelation-consistent as in, say, Andrews (1991). Unfortunately, the symptoms of such problems may be due to other causes, such as unmodeled structural breaks, in which case the flaws in the inference are camouflaged rather than robustified. Another, earlier, response was to generalize the initial model by assuming a model for the problem encountered (e.g., an autoregressive error when autocorrelated errors were found), which brings us back to the problems of simple-to-general. By protecting against such serious problems, *PcGets* may yet help "data mining" to become a compliment.

16.1.4 Other Model-Simplification Approaches

There are probably an almost uncountable number of ways in which models can be selected from data evidence (or otherwise). The only other "rules" for model selection we consider here are "stepwise" regression (see, e.g., Leamer, 1983a, for a critical appraisal), and "optimal" regression (see, e.g., Coen et al., 1969, and the following discussion). There are three key problems with stepwise regression. First, it does not check the congruence of the starting model, so one cannot be sure that the inference rules adopted have the operational characteristics attributed to them (e.g., residual autocorrelation will distort estimated standard errors). Second, there are no checks on the congruence of reductions of the GUM, so again inference can become unreliable. Neither of these drawbacks is intrinsic to stepwise or optimal regression (the latter involves trying almost every combination of variables, so borders on an information criterion approach), and congruence testing could be added to those approaches. However, the key problem with stepwise regression is that only one simplification path is explored, usually based on successively eliminating the least-significant variable. Consequently, if a relevant variable is inadvertently eliminated early in the simplification, many others may be retained later to "proxy" its role, so the algorithm can get stuck and select far too large a model. Hoover and Perez (1999) found that to be a serious problem in early versions of their algorithm for *Gets* and, hence, implemented multiple-path searches.

16.1.5 Nonnested Hypothesis Tests and Encompassing

Model comparisons can be based on nonnested hypothesis tests or encompassing [see, e.g., Cox (1961, 1962), Pesaran (1974), Deaton (1982), Kent (1986), and Vuong (1989) for the former, and Hendry and Richard (1982), Mizon (1984), Mizon and Richard (1986), and the survey in Hendry and Richard (1989) for the latter]. In such an approach, empirical models are developed by "competing" investigators, and the "winner" selected by nonnested, or encompassing, tests. Encompassing essentially requires a simple model to explain a more general one within which it is nested (often the union of the simple model with its rivals); this notion is called parsimonious encompassing and is denoted by $\mathcal{E}_p$. An important property of parsimonious encompassing is that it defines a partial ordering over models, since $\mathcal{E}_p$ is transitive, reflexive, and antisymmetric. Since some aspects of inference must go wrong when a model is noncongruent, encompassing tests should only be conducted with respect to a 'baseline' congruent model, as pointed out by Gouriéroux and Monfort (1995), but is anyway unnecessary otherwise since noncongruence already demonstrates inadequacies (see Bontemps and Mizon, Chapter 15, this volume). Encompassing plays an important role in *PcGets* to select between congruent "terminal" models found by different search paths.

16.1.6 Selecting Models by Minimizing an Information Criterion

Another route is to select models by minimizing an information criterion, especially a criterion that can be shown to lead to consistent model selection (see e.g., Akaike, 1985; Schwarz, 1978; Hannan and Quinn, 1979). These three "selection" rules are denoted AIC (for the Akaike information criterion), SC (for the Schwarz criterion) and HQ (for Hannan–Quinn). The associated information criteria are defined as follows:

$$\begin{aligned}
\text{AIC} &= -2\log L/T + 2n/T,\\
\text{SC} &= -2\log L/T + n\log(T)/T,\\
\text{HQ} &= -2\log L/T + 2n\log[\log(T)]/T,
\end{aligned}$$

where L is the maximized likelihood, n is the number of estimated parameters, and T is the sample size. The last two criteria ensure a consistent model selection (see, e.g., Sawa, 1978; Judge et al., 1985; Chow, 1981). However, in "unstructured problems," where there is no natural order to the hypotheses to be tested (see, e.g., Mizon, 1977b), a huge number of potential combinations must be investigated, namely 2^m possible models for m candidate variables: For the Lovell (1983) database used below, that would be $2^{40} \simeq 10^{12}$ models, even restricting oneself to a maximum lag length of unity. To borrow an idea from Leamer (1983b), even at a 0.1 of a U.S. cent per model, it would cost U.S. \$1 billion. "Shortcuts" such as dropping all but the k "most significant" variables and exploring the remainder (as in Hansen, 1999), do not work well if more than k variables are needed. In practice, moreover, without checking that both the GUM and the selected model are congruent, the model that minimizes any information criterion has little to recommend it (see, e.g., Bontemps and Mizon, Chapter 15, this volume). Information criteria also play an important role in *PcGets* to select when congruent and mutually encompassing "terminal" models are found from different search paths.

16.1.7 Bayesian Model Comparisons

Again, there are important overlaps in approach: For example, the Schwarz (1978) criterion is also known as the Bayesian information criterion (BIC). Perhaps the most enthusiastic proponent of a Bayesian approach to model selection is Leamer (1978, 1983b), leading to his "practical" extreme-bounds analysis (see Leamer, 1983a, 1984, 1990), which in turn has been heavily criticized (see, *inter alia,* McAleer et al., 1985; Breusch, 1990; Hendry and Mizon, 1990). If there were a good empirical basis for nondistortionary "prior" information, it would seem sensible to use it; but since one of the claims implicit in Leamer's critiques is that previous (non-Bayesian) empirical research is seriously flawed, it is difficult to see where such priors might originate. All too often, there is no sound basis for the prior, and a metaphysical element is introduced into the analysis.

16.1.8 *Gets*

General-to-simple approaches have a long pedigree (see *inter alia,* Anderson, 1971; Sargan, 1973, 1981; Mizon, 1977a, b; Hendry, 1979; White, 1990). Important practical examples include COMFAC (see Sargan, 1980; Hendry and Mizon, 1978), where the GUM must be sufficiently general to allow dynamic common factors to be ascertained; and cointegration (see, e.g., Johansen, 1988), where the key feature is that all the inferences take place within the GUM (usually a vector autoregression). There is an extensive related literature on testing multiple hypotheses (see, e.g., Savin, 1984), where the consequences of alternative sequential tests are discussed.

16.1.9 Overview

PcGets blends aspects of all but the second-last of these many approaches, albeit usually with substantive modifications. For example, "top down" searches (which retain the most significant variables and block eliminate all others) partly resemble simple-to-general approaches in the order of testing, but with the fundamental difference that the whole inference procedure is conducted within a congruent GUM. If the GUM cannot be reduced by the criteria set by the user, then it will be retained, though not weighted as suggested in the "shrinkage" literature noted. The ability to fix some variables as always selected while evaluating the roles of others provides a viable alternative to simply including only the theoretically relevant variables. Next, the key problems noted with stepwise regression (that it only explores one path, so can get stuck, and does not check the congruence of either the starting model or reductions thereof) are avoided. Clearly, *PcGets* is a member of the *Gets* class, but also implements many presearch reduction tests, and emphasizes block tests over individual tests whenever that is feasible. Although minimizing a model-selection criterion by itself does not check the congruence of the selection (which could therefore be rather poor) between mutually encompassing congruent reductions, such criteria are applicable. Finally, parsimonious encompassing is used to select between congruent simplifications within a common GUM, once contending terminal models have been chosen. Thus, we conclude that *Gets* is the most useful of the available approaches and turn to a more formal analysis of its basis in the theory of reduction.

16.2 THE THEORY OF REDUCTION

Gets is the practical embodiment of the theory of reduction (see, e.g., Florens and Mouchart, 1980; Hendry and Richard, 1983; Florens et al., 1990; Hendry, 1987, 1995, ch. 9). That theory explains how the data-generation process (DGP) characterizing an economy is reduced to the "local" DGP (LDGP), which is the joint distribution of the subset of variables under analysis. By operations of aggregating, marginalizing, conditioning, sequentially factorizing, and transforming, a potentially vast initial information set is reduced to the small transformed subset that is relevant for the problem in question. These reduction operations affect the parameters of the process and thereby determine the properties of the LDGP.

The theory of reduction not only explains the origins of the LDGP, but the possible losses of information from any given reduction can be measured relative to its ability to deliver the parameters of interest in the analysis. For example, inappropriate reductions, such as marginalizing with respect to relevant variables, can induce nonconstant parameters, or autocorrelated residuals, or heteroskedasticity, and so on. The resulting taxonomy of possible information losses highlights six main null hypotheses against which model evaluation can be conducted, relating to the past, present, and future of the data, measurement and theory information, and results obtained by rival models.

A congruent model is one that matches the data evidence on all the measured attributes: The DGP can always be written as a congruent representation. Congruence is checked in practice by computing a set of misspecification statistics to ascertain that the residuals are approximately homoskedastic, normal, white noise, that any conditioning is valid, and that the parameters are constant. Empirical congruence is shown by satisfactory performance on all these checks. A model that can explain the findings of other models of the same dependent variables is said to encompass them, as discussed in Section 16.1.5 (see, e.g., Cox, 1961, 1962; Hendry and Richard, 1982, 1989; Mizon, 1984; Mizon and Richard, 1986). Since a model that explains the results of a more general model within which it is nested parsimoniously encompasses the latter (see Govaerts et al., 1994; Florens et al., 1996), when no reductions lose relevant information the LDGP parsimoniously encompasses the DGP with respect to the subset of variables under analysis.

To implement *Gets,* a general unrestricted model (GUM) is formulated to provide a congruent approximation to the LDGP, given the theoretical and empirical background knowledge. Bontemps and Mizon (Chapter 15, this volume) in an important finding show that an empirical model is congruent if it parsimoniously encompasses the LDGP. The empirical analysis commences from this GUM, after testing for misspecifications; if no problems are apparent, the GUM is simplified to a parsimonious, congruent model, each simplification step being checked by diagnostic testing. Simplification can be done in many ways, and although the goodness of a model is intrinsic to it, and not a property of the selection route, poor routes seem unlikely to deliver useful models. In the next section we investigate the impact of selection rules on the properties of the resulting models and consider the solution proposed in Hoover and Perez (1999) of exploring many simplification paths.

16.3 THE SELECTION STAGES OF *PcGets*

16.3.1 Formulating the GUM

Naturally, the specification of the initial general model must depend on the type of data (e.g., time series and cross section), the size of sample, the number of different potential variables, previous empirical and theoretical findings, likely functional-form transformations (e.g., logs) and appropriate parameterizations, known anomalies (such as, e.g., measurement changes and breaks), and data availability. The aim is to achieve a congruent starting point, so the specification should be sufficiently general that if a more general model is required, the investigator would be surprised, and therefore already have acquired useful information. Data may prove inadequate for the task, but even if a smaller GUM is enforced by presimplification, knowing at the outset what model ought to be postulated remains important. The larger the initial regressor set, the more likely adventitious effects are to be retained; but the smaller the GUM, the more likely key variables are to be omitted. Further, the less orthogonality between variables, the more "confusion" the algorithm faces, possibly leading to a proliferation of mutual-encompassing models, where final choices may only differ marginally (e.g., lag two versus one).

Davidson and Hendry (1981, p. 257) noted four possible problems facing *Gets*: (1) The chosen "general" model may be inadequate, by being too special a case of the LDGP. (2) Data limitations may preclude specifying the desired relationship. (3) The nonexistence of an optimal sequence for simplification leaves open the choice of reduction path. (4) Potentially large type-II error probabilities of the individual tests may be needed to avoid a high type-I error of the overall sequence. By adopting the "multiple path" development of Hoover and Perez (1999), and implementing a range of important improvements, *PcGets* overcomes the problems associated with points 3 and 4. However, the empirical success of *PcGets* depends crucially on the creativity of each researcher in specifying the general model, and the feasibility of estimating it from the available data—aspects beyond the capabilities of the program, other than the diagnostic tests serving their usual role of revealing model misspecification.

There is a central role for economic theory in the modeling process in "prior specification," "prior simplification," and suggesting admissible data transforms. The first of these relates to the inclusion of potentially relevant variables, the second to the exclusion of irrelevant effects, and the third to appropriate formulations in which the influences to be included are entered, such as log or ratio transforms, e.g., differences and cointegration vectors; and any likely linear transformations that might enhance orthogonality between regressors. The "LSE approach" argued for a close link of theory and model and explicitly opposed "running regressions on every variable on the database," as in Lovell (1983) (see, e.g., Hendry and Ericsson, 1991a). Unfortunately, economic theory rarely provides a basis for specifying the lag lengths in empirical macro-models: even when a theoretical model is dynamic, a "time period" is usually not well defined. In practice, lags are chosen either for analytical convenience (e.g., first-order differential equation systems) or to allow for some desirable features (as in the choice of a linear, second-order difference equation to replicate cycles). Therefore, it seems sensible to start from an unrestricted autoregressive-distributed lag model with a maximal lag length set according to available evidence (e.g., as four or five lags for quarterly time series, to allow for seasonal dynamics). Prior analysis also remains essential for appropriate parameterizations, functional forms, choice of variables, lag lengths, and indicator variables (including seasonals, special events, and so forth). Hopefully, automating the reduction process will enable researchers to concentrate their efforts on designing the GUM, which could significantly improve the empirical success of the algorithm.

PcGets conducts all inferences as if the data are I(0). Most selection tests will in fact be valid even when the data are I(1), given the results in Sims et al. (1990). Only t- or F-tests for an effect that corresponds to a unit root require nonstandard critical values. The empirical examples on I(1) data noted in Krolzig and Hendry (2001) did not reveal problems, but in principle it might be useful to implement cointegration tests and appropriate transformations prior to reduction. Care is then required not to "mix" variables with different degrees of integration, so our present recommendation is to specify the GUM in levels.

16.3.2 Misspecification Tests

Given the initial GUM, the next step is to conduct misspecification tests. There must be enough tests to check the main attributes of congruence, but, as discussed earlier, not so many as to induce a large type-I error. Thus, *PcGets* generally tests the following null hypotheses: (1) white-noise errors, (2) conditionally homoskedastic errors, (3) normally distributed errors, (4) unconditionally homoskedastic errors, and (5) constant parameters.

Approximate F-test formulations are used (see Harvey, 1981; Kiviet, 1985, 1986). Section 16.5.4 describes the finite-sample behavior of the various tests.

16.3.2.1 Significant Misspecification Tests

If the initial misspecification tests are significant at the prespecified level, the required significance level is lowered, and search paths terminated only when that lower level is violated. Empirical investigators would probably respecify the GUM on rejection, but as yet that relies on creativity beyond the capabilities of computer automation.

16.3.2.2 Integrated Variables

Wooldridge (1999) shows that diagnostic tests on the GUM (and presumably simplifications thereof) remain valid even for integrated time series.

16.3.2.3 Presearch Reductions

Once congruence of the GUM is established, groups of variables are tested in the order of their absolute t-values, commencing from the smallest and continuing up toward the preassigned selection criterion, when deletion must become inadmissible. A nonstringent significance level is used at this step, usually 90 percent, since the insignificant variables are deleted permanently. Such a high value might seem surprising given the claim noted above that selection leads to overparameterization, but confirms that such a claim is not sustainable. If no test is significant, the F-test on all variables in the GUM has been calculated, establishing that there is nothing to model.

Two rounds of cumulative simplification are offered, the second at a tighter level such as 25 percent. Optionally for time-series data, block tests of lag length are also offered.

16.3.3 Multiple Search Paths

All paths that commence with an insignificant t-deletion are explored. Blocks of variables constitute feasible search paths—such as the block F-tests in the preceding section, but along search paths—so these can be selected, in addition to individual-coefficient tests. Here we merely note that a nonnull set of "terminal" models is selected—namely all distinct minimal congruent reductions found along all the search paths—so when more than one such model is found, a choice between them is needed, which is accomplished as described in the next section.

16.3.4 Encompassing

Encompassing tests select between the candidate congruent models at the end of path searches. Each contender is tested against their union, and those that are dominated by, and do not dominate, another contender are dropped. If a unique model results, it is selected; otherwise, if some are rejected, *PcGets* forms the union of the remaining models and repeats this round till no encompassing reductions result. That union then constitutes a new starting point, and the complete path-search algorithm is repeated until the union is unchanged between successive rounds.

16.3.5 Information Criteria

When such a union coincides with the original GUM or with a previous union so no further feasible reductions can be found, *PcGets* selects a model by an information criterion. The current preferred "final-selection" rule is the Schwarz criterion, or BIC, defined earlier. For $T = 140$ and $m = 40$, minimum SC corresponds approximately to the marginal regressor satisfying $|t| \geq 1.9$.

16.3.6 Subsample Reliability

For the finally selected model, subsample reliability is evaluated by the Hoover–Perez overlapping split-sample criterion. *PcGets* then concludes that some variables are definitely excluded; some definitely included; and some have an uncertain role, varying from a reliability of, say, 0 percent (included in the final model, but insignificantly, and insignificant in both subsamples), through to 100 percent (significant overall and in both subsamples). Investigators are at liberty to interpret such evidence as they see fit, noting that further simplification of the selected congruent model may induce some violations of congruence or encompassing.

Recursive estimation is central to the *Gets* research program, but focused on parameter constancy, whereas Hoover and Perez use the split samples to help determine overall significance. A central t-test wanders around the origin, so the probability is low that an effect that is significant only by chance in the full sample will also be significant in two independent subsamples (see, e.g., the discussion in Campos and Ericsson, 1999). Conversely, a noncentral t-test diverges as the sample size increases, so it should be significant in subsamples, perhaps at a lower level of significance to reflect the smaller sample size. This strategy should be particularly powerful for model selection when breaks occur in some of the marginal relations over either of the subsamples.

16.3.7 Type-I and Type-II Errors

Whether or not *Gets* over- or underselects is not intrinsic to it, but depends on how it is used: Neither type-I nor type-II errors are emphasized by the methodology per se, nor by the *PcGets* algorithm, but reflect the choices of critical values in the search process. In the Hendry and Krolzig (1999) analysis of the Hoover and Perez (1999) rerun of the experiments in Lovell (1983), lowering the significance levels of the diagnostic tests from, say, 0.05 to 0.01 reduced the overall selection size noticeably (owing to the difference in powering up 0.95 and 0.99 repeatedly), without greatly affecting the power of the model-selection procedure. Smaller significance levels (1 versus 5%) for diagnostic tests probably have much to recommend them. Increasing the significance levels of the selection t-tests also reduced the empirical size, but lowered the power more noticeably for variables with population t-values smaller than 3. This trade-off can, therefore, be selected by an investigator. The next section addresses these issues.

16.4 ANALYZING THE ALGORITHM

We first distinguish between the costs of inference and the costs of search, then consider some aspects of the search process.

16.4.1 Costs of Inference and Costs of Search

Let $\mathsf{p}_{\alpha,i}^{dgp}$ denote the probability of retaining the ith variable in the DGP when commencing from the DGP using a selection test procedure with significance level α. Then,

$$\sum_{i=1}^{k}\left(1-\mathsf{p}_{\alpha,i}^{dgp}\right),$$

is a measure of the cost of inference when there are k variables in the DGP.

Let $\mathsf{p}_{\alpha,i}^{gum}$ denote the probability of retaining the ith variable when commencing from the GUM, also using significance level α. Let S_r denote the set of k relevant variables, and S_0 be the set of $(m-k)$ irrelevant variables. Then pure search costs are

$$\sum_{i\in S_r}\left(\mathsf{p}_{\alpha,i}^{dgp}-\mathsf{p}_{\alpha,i}^{gum}\right)+\sum_{i\in S_0}\mathsf{p}_{\alpha,i}^{gum}.$$

For irrelevant variables, $\mathsf{p}_{\alpha,i}^{dgp}\equiv 0$, so the whole cost of retaining adventitiously significant variables is attributed to search, plus any additional costs from failing to retain relevant variables. The former can be lowered by increasing the significance levels of selection tests, but at the cost of reducing the latter. However, it is feasible to lower size and raise power simultaneously by an improved search algorithm. When different selection strategies are used on the DGP and GUM (e.g., conventional t-testing on the former; preselection F-tests on the latter), then $\mathsf{p}_{\alpha,i}^{gum}$ could exceed $\mathsf{p}_{\alpha,i}^{dgp}$ (see, e.g., the critique of theory testing in Hendry and Mizon, 2000). We now consider the determinants of $\mathsf{p}_{\alpha,i}^{gum}$ for $i\in S_0$, namely the nondeletion probabilities of irrelevant variables, and then consider the probabilities $\mathsf{p}_{\alpha,i}^{dgp}$ of selecting the relevant variables assuming no irrelevant variables. The upshot of the analysis may be surprising: The former can be made relatively small for reasonable critical values of the tests *PcGets* uses, and it is retaining the relevant variables that poses the real problem—or the costs of search are small compared to the costs of inference.

16.4.2 Deletion Probabilities

One might expect low deletion probabilities to entail high search costs when many variables are included but none actually matters. That would be true in a pure t-testing strategy as we show now (see Hendry, 2000a). The probabilities p_j of $j=0,\ldots,m$ irrelevant variables being retained by t-testing are given by the jth-order coefficients in the expansion of $[\alpha+(1-\alpha)]^m$, namely,

$$\mathsf{p}_j=\frac{m!}{j!(m-j)!}\alpha^j(1-\alpha)^{m-j},\qquad j=0,\ldots,m. \tag{1}$$

Consequently, the expected number of variables retained in pure selection testing is

$$r=\sum_{j=0}^{m}j\mathsf{p}_j=m\alpha. \tag{2}$$

Per variable, this is a constant at $r/m=\alpha$. When $\alpha=0.05$ and $m=40$, r equals 2, falling to $r=0.4$ for $\alpha=0.01$: so even if only t-tests are used, few spurious variables would then be retained.

When there are no relevant variables, the probability of retaining none using only t-tests with critical value c_α is given by

$$\mathsf{P}(|\mathsf{t}_i| < c_\alpha, \forall i = 1, \ldots, m) = (1 - \alpha)^m. \tag{3}$$

When $m = 40$ and $\alpha = 0.05$, there is only a 13 percent chance of not retaining any spurious variables, but if $\alpha = 0.01$, this increases to a 67 percent chance of finding the null model. Even so, these constitute relatively low probabilities of locating the correct answer.

However, *PcGets* first calculates a one-off F-test, F_G, of the GUM against the null model using the critical value c_γ. Such a test has size $\mathsf{p}_G = \mathsf{P}(\mathsf{F}_G \geq c_\gamma) = \gamma$ under the null, so the null model is selected with probability γ, which will be dramatically smaller than (3) even if γ is set at quite a high value, such as 0.10 (so the null is incorrectly rejected 10 percent of the time). Thus, other searches only commence γ percent of the time, although (1) does not now describe the probabilities, as these are conditional on $\mathsf{F}_G \geq c_\gamma$, so there is a higher probability of locating significant variables, even when $\alpha < \gamma$.

In the Hendry and Krolzig (1999) rerun of the Hoover-Perez experiments with $m = 40$, using $\gamma = 0.01$ yielded $\widehat{\mathsf{p}_G} = 0.972$, as against a theory prediction from γ of 0.990. Let r variables be retained on t-testing using the critical value c_α after the event $\mathsf{F}_G \geq c_{0.01}$ occurs; then the probability $\bar{\mathsf{p}}_r$ that any given variable will be retained is $\bar{\mathsf{p}}_r \simeq (1 - \mathsf{p}_G)r/m$. The average "nondeletion" probability across all the null-DGP Monte Carlos was $\widehat{\bar{\mathsf{p}}}_r = 0.19$ percent, so $r \simeq 3$ when $\mathsf{F}_G \geq c_{0.01}$, and $r = 0$ otherwise. When a lower value of c_γ is set, using, say, $\gamma = 0.10$, the null model is retained 10 percent of the time, but providing the same c_α is used, fewer individually significant variables are retained in path searches, so the average size does not increase proportionally.

Overall, these are very small retention rates of spuriously significant variables from a larger number of irrelevant regressors, so it is easy to obtain a high probability of locating the null model even when forty irrelevant variables are included, providing that relatively tight significance levels are used—or a reasonably high probability using looser significance levels.

When only one, or a few, variables matter, the power of F_G becomes important, hence our suggestion of somewhat less stringent critical values. As described earlier, when F_G rejects, *PcGets* next checks increasing simplifications of the GUM using the ordered values $\mathsf{t}_1^2 \leq \mathsf{t}_2^2 \leq \ldots \leq \mathsf{t}_m^2$ in a cumulative F-test. Under orthogonality, after adding k variables we have the approximation:

$$\mathsf{F}(k, T - k) \simeq \frac{1}{k} \sum_{i=1}^{k} \mathsf{t}_i^2.$$

Once k variables are included, nonrejection requires that: (a) $k-1$ variables did not induce rejection; (b) $|\mathsf{t}_k| < c_\alpha$ for a critical value c_α; and (c) $\mathsf{F}(k, T-k) < c_\gamma$ for a critical value c_γ. Slightly more than half the coefficients will have $\mathsf{t}_1^2 < 0.5$ or smaller. Any $\mathsf{t}_i^2 \leq 1$ reduces the mean F-statistic, and since $\mathsf{P}(|\mathsf{t}_i| < 1) =$

0.68, when $m = 40$ then approximately twenty-eight variables fall into that group, leaving an F-statistic value of less than unity after their elimination. Also, $\mathsf{P}(|\mathsf{t}_i| \geq 2) = 0.05$ so only two out of forty variables should chance to have a larger $|\mathsf{t}_i|$ value on average. Thus, one can select surprisingly large values of γ, such as 0.75, for this step and yet have a high probability of eliminating most irrelevant variables. Since, e.g., $\mathsf{P}(\mathsf{F}(30, 100) < 1|\mathsf{H}_0) \simeq 0.48$, a first step with $\gamma = 0.5$ would on average eliminate twenty-eight variables with $\mathsf{t}_i^2 \leq 1$, when $m = 40$, and some larger t-values as well—hence the need to check that $|\mathsf{t}_k| < c_\alpha$.

Further, a "top down" search is also conducted, successively eliminating all but the largest t_m^2, and testing the remainder for zero, then all but the two largest and so on. This works well when only a couple of variables matter.

Thus, in contrast to the high costs of inference to be demonstrated in the next section, the costs of search arising from retaining irrelevant variables seem relatively small. For a reasonable GUM, with say twenty variables where fifteen are irrelevant, when using just t-tests at 5 percent, less than *one* spuriously significant variable will be retained by chance. Preselection tests lower those probabilities. Against such costs, the next section shows that there is at most a 50 percent chance of retaining variables with noncentralities less than two, and little chance of keeping several such regressors. Thus, the difficult problem is *retention of relevant, not elimination of irrelevant, variables.* Critical values should be selected with these findings in mind. Practical usage of *PcGets* suggests that its operational characteristics are quite well described by this analysis (see Section 16.5).

In applications, we often find that the multipath searches and preselection procedures produce similar outcomes, so although we cannot yet present a complete probability analysis of the former, it seems to behave almost as well in practice.

16.4.3 Selection Probabilities

When searching a large database for a DGP, an investigator might retain the relevant regressors less often than when the correct specification is known, as well as retaining irrelevant variables in the finally selected model. We now examine the difficulty of retaining relevant variables when commencing from the DGP, then turn to any additional power losses resulting from a search.

Consider a t-test, denoted $\mathsf{t}(n, \psi)$, of a null hypothesis H_0 (where $\psi = 0$ under the null), when for a critical value c_α, a two-sided test is used with $\mathsf{P}(|\mathsf{t}(n, 0)| \geq c_\alpha|\mathsf{H}_0) = \alpha$. When the null is false, such a test will reject with a probability that varies with its noncentrality parameter ψ, c_α, and the degrees of freedom n. To calculate its power to reject the null when $\mathsf{E}[\mathsf{t}] = \psi > 0$, we approximate by

$$\mathsf{P}(\mathsf{t} \geq c_\alpha \mid \mathsf{E}[\mathsf{t}] = \psi) \simeq \mathsf{P}(\mathsf{t} - \psi \geq c_\alpha - \psi \mid \mathsf{H}_0).$$

TABLE 16.1
t-Test Powers

ψ	α	$\mathsf{P}(\mathsf{t} > c_\alpha)$	$\mathsf{P}(\mathsf{t} > c_\alpha)^6$
1	0.05	0.165	0.000
2	0.05	0.508	0.017
2	0.01	0.267	0.000
3	0.05	0.845	0.364
3	0.01	0.646	0.073
4	0.01	0.914	0.583
5	0.01	0.990	0.941
6	0.001	0.995	0.968

Table 16.1 taken from Hendry and Krolzig (2001) records some approximate power calculations when a single null hypothesis is tested and when six are tested, in each case, precisely once for $n = 100$ and different values of ψ and α, for a two-sided test.

The third column of Table 16.1 reveals that there is little chance of retaining a variable with $\psi = 1$, and only a 50 percent chance of retaining a single variable with a population $|\mathsf{t}|$ of 2 when the critical value is also 2, falling to 25 percent for a critical value of 2.6. When $\psi = 3$, the power of detection is sharply higher for $\alpha = 0.05$, but still leads to more than 35 percent misclassifications at $\alpha = 0.01$. Finally, when $\psi \geq 4$, one such variable will almost always be retained, even at stringent significance levels. Note that no search is involved: These are the rejection probabilities of drawing from the correct univariate t-distribution and merely reflect the vagaries of sampling. Further, the noncentrality must have a unique sign (+ or −), so only one side of the distribution matters under the alternative, although two-sided nulls are assumed. These powers could be increased slightly by using a one-sided test when the sign is certain.

However, the final column shows that the probability of retaining all six relevant variables with the given noncentralities (i.e., the probability of locating the DGP) is essentially negligible when the tests are independent, except in the last three cases. Mixed cases (with different values of ψ) can be calculated by multiplying the probabilities in the third column (e.g., for $\psi = 2, 3, 3, 4, 5, 6$ the joint $\mathsf{P}(\cdot) \simeq 0.10$ at $\alpha = 0.01$). Such combined probabilities are highly nonlinear in ψ, since one is almost certain to retain six variables with $\psi = 6$, even at a 0.1 percent significance level. The important conclusion is that, despite "knowing" the DGP, low signal-noise variables will rarely be retained using t-tests when there is any need to test the null; and if there are many relevant variables, all of them are unlikely to be retained even when they have quite large noncentralities. The probabilities of retaining such variables when commencing from the GUM must be judged against this baseline, not against the requirement that the search procedure locate the "truth."

One alternative is to use an F-testing approach, after implementing, say, the first-stage preselection filters discussed earlier. A joint test will falsely reject a null model δ percent of the time when the implicit preselection critical value is c_δ, and the resulting model will then be the postselection GUM. However, the reliability statistics should help reveal any problems with spuriously significant variables. Conversely, this joint procedure has a dramatically higher probability of retaining a block of relevant variables. For example, if the six remaining variables all had expected t-values of two—an essentially impossible case above—then,

$$\mathsf{E}[\mathsf{F}(6,100)] \simeq \frac{1}{6}\left(\sum_{i=1}^{6} \mathsf{E}\left[\mathsf{t}_i^2\right]\right) \simeq 4. \tag{4}$$

When $\delta = 0.025$, $c_\delta \simeq 2.5$, so to reject we need

$$\mathsf{P}\left[\mathsf{F}(6,100) \geq 2.5 \mid \bar{\mathsf{F}} = 4\right],$$

which we solve by using a noncentral $\chi^2(6)$ approximation of $6\mathsf{F}(6,100)$ under the null, with critical value $c_{\alpha,k} = 14.5$, and the approximation under the alternative that

$$\chi^2(6,24) = h\chi^2(m,0),$$

where

$$h = \frac{6+48}{6+24} = 1.8 \qquad \text{and} \qquad m = \frac{(6+24)^2}{6+48} \simeq 17, \tag{5}$$

so using

$$\mathsf{P}\left[h\chi^2(m,0) > c_{\alpha,k}\right] = \mathsf{P}\left[\chi^2(m,0) > h^{-1}c_{\alpha,k}\right] \simeq \mathsf{P}\left[\chi^2(17,0) > 8\right] \simeq 0.97,$$

thereby almost always retaining all six relevant variables. This is in complete contrast with the near-zero probability of retaining all six variables using t-tests on the DGP as above. Thus, the power-size trade-off depends on the search algorithm and is not bounded above by the sequential t-test results.

The actual operating characteristics of *PcGets* are almost impossible to derive analytically given the complexity of the successive conditioning, so to investigate it in more detail, we consider some simulation studies.

16.5 MONTE CARLO EVIDENCE ON *PcGets*

Monte Carlo evidence on the behavior of earlier incarnations of *PcGets* is presented in Hendry and Krolzig (1999) for the Hoover and Perez (1999) experiments based on Lovell (1983), and in Krolzig and Hendry (2001), together comprising two very different types of experimental designs. Here we first consider a new set of almost 2,000 experiments that we used to calibrate the behavior of *PcGets*; then, based on the resulting settings, we reexamine its performance on both earlier designs, noting the simulation behavior of the misspecification tests en route.

16.5.1 Calibrating *PcGets* by Monte Carlo Experiments

We have also undertaken a huge range of Monte Carlo simulations across differing t-values in an artificial DGP, with different numbers of *relevant* regressors, different numbers of *irrelevant* regressors, and different critical values of most of the selection-test procedures. The outcomes of these experiments were used to calibrate the in-built search strategies, which we denote by liberal (minimize the nonselection probabilities) and conservative (minimize the nondeletion probabilities).

The DGP for $m = k + n + 1$ variables was:

$$y_t = \sum_{i=1}^{k} \beta_{i,0} x_{i,t} + u_t, \qquad u_t \sim \mathsf{IN}[0, 1],$$

$$\mathbf{x}_t = \mathbf{v}_t, \qquad \mathbf{v}_t \sim \mathsf{IN}_{m+n}\left[\mathbf{0}, \mathbf{I}_{m+n}\right]. \tag{6}$$

As shown, only k of these generated variables entered the DGP with potentially nonzero coefficients. However, the GUM was

$$y_t = \alpha y_{t-1} + \sum_{j=1}^{k+n} \beta_{j,i} x_{j,t} + \gamma + u_t. \tag{7}$$

We used a sample size of $T = 100$ and set the number of relevant variables k to eight. There were only $M = 100$ replications in each experiment, but 1,920 experiments in total. These comprised blocks of 320 experiments across different settings of every selection-test significance level from a wide range, designed to highlight problem areas as well as good choices. In the first two blocks of experiments, all $\beta_{i,0} = 0$ so the null model was the DGP; in the next two, the expected t-value of each $\beta_{i,0}$ was 2, and in the final two blocks, the expected t-value of each $\beta_{i,0}$ was 3. The two blocks corresponded to generating n equal to eight or twenty additional irrelevant variables for inclusion in the GUM.

The first figure has six plots, reporting the average null rejection frequency of each irrelevant variable included in the GUM, called the size for shorthand. As can be seen, the sizes in Figures 16.1a, b—when the DGP is the null model—are all quite small, around an average of 0.007–0.009. (The fluctuations in the graphs are probably due to sampling error from the small number of replications.) Thus, the algorithm embodies "automatic correction," in that although some significance levels are often set very loosely, other aspects compensate to

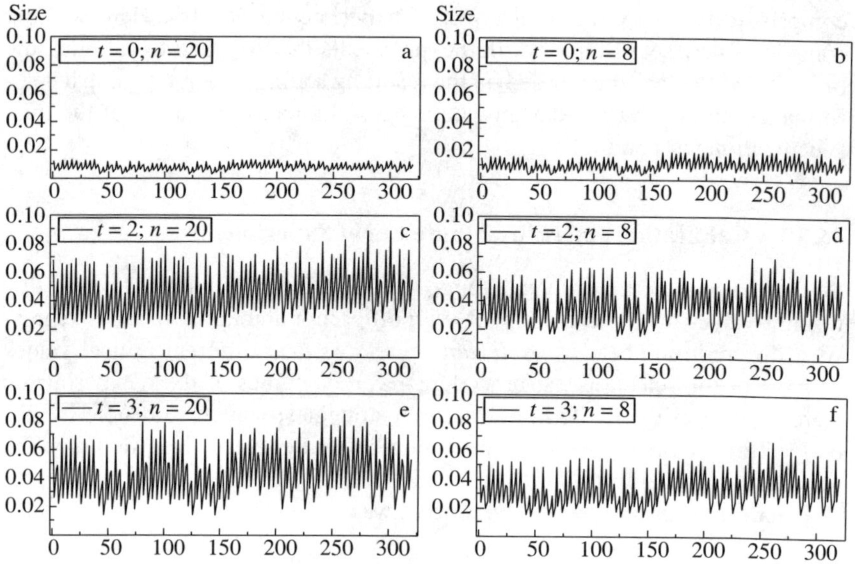

Fig. 16.1 Null rejection frequencies.

ensure a small overall size. For example, the F-test on the GUM against a null model has significance levels varying from 1 to 10 percent, with a negligible impact on the final sizes. More surprisingly, the average sizes per parameter in the GUM are higher for the smaller GUM. The increased null rejection frequency for $n = 8$ over $n = 20$ seems due to this property of the GUM and to preselection tests interacting with the number of variables retained when the null is rejected. Figures 16.1c–f show the corresponding sizes when there are relevant variables to be detected. The null rejection frequencies are higher in all states and for all critical value choices than for a null DGP, but range over 0. 015–0.075, thus remaining relatively small.

Of course, the choice of critical value also affects power, so we now consider the power-size trade-offs for the four blocks of experiments with nonnull DGPs. Figure 16.2 shows the outcome for the experiments where $\mathsf{E}[\mathsf{t}] = 2$ for the eight relevant variables, with both twenty and eight irrelevant regressors. The latter always attains a higher power than the former and comes close to the theoretical power of 0.5 applicable when drawing from a scalar t-distribution with a mean of two for $\alpha = 0.05$. Thus, the search induces only a small power loss at that size. The results for F_G at 10 and 5 percent illustrate the difficulties of deriving the characteristics of *PcGets* analytically: Lowering its critical value from $c_{0.05}$ to $c_{0.10}$ leads to noticeably higher power with little increase in size. The "upper envelope" (drawn by hand on the graphs) shows those combinations

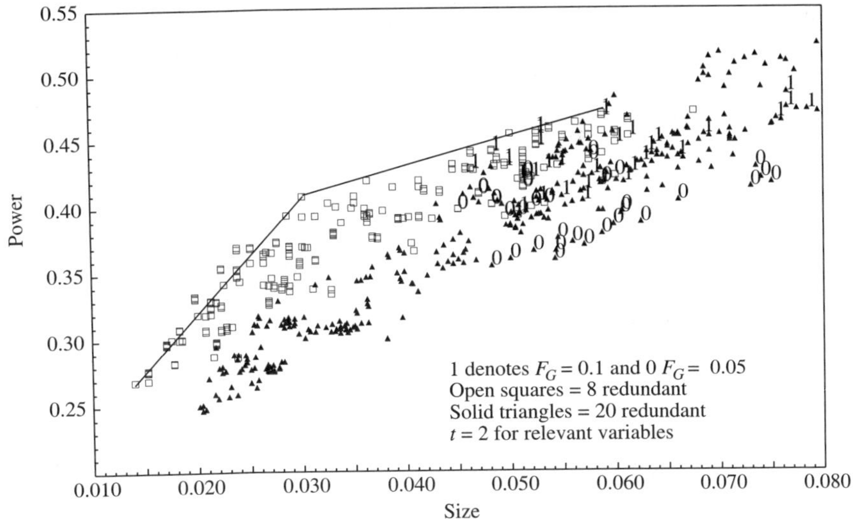

Fig. 16.2 Power-size trade-off: $\mathrm{t} = 2$.

of significance levels that do best in this category of experiments for eight irrelevant variables and guided our choice for the preset liberal and conservative strategies. Sizes smaller than 3 percent lead to relatively sharp falls in power, so are not recommended. Similarly, sizes much above 5 percent yield small gains in power, so again seem dominated.

Similar considerations apply to the remaining experiments shown in Figure 16.3. The experiments with F_G at 10 and 5 percent are not shown separately here as they were almost identical, supporting the selection of the former. Also, the theoretical power of 0.845 applicable when drawing from a scalar t-distribution with a mean of three for $\alpha = 0.05$ is nearly attained for eight irrelevant variables, and is only slightly smaller for twenty irrelevant variables. The range from the worst to the best selection of critical values is about 0.05 for a given number of variables, so the algorithm is remarkably stable, more so for these larger t-values than in Figure 16.2.

Table 16.2 reports more detailed statistical outcomes for the settings we finally selected. "T:" and "S:" respectively denote the "true" model [i.e., the DGP in (6)] and the specific model selected by *PcGets* in each replication. The evidence accords closely with the theory described above: When the population t-values are 2 or 3, it is almost impossible to retain the DGP specification even commencing from it when 1 percent critical values are used, and less than 25 percent likely for 5 percent critical values. Nevertheless, the actual sizes remain

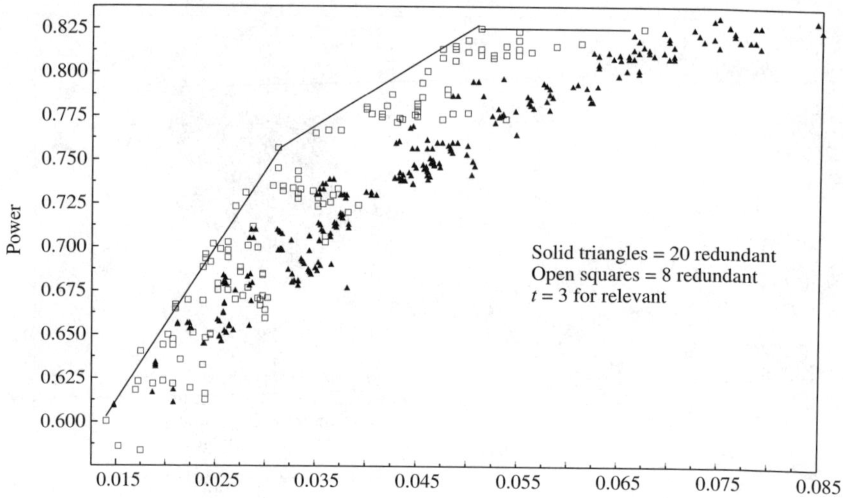

Fig. 16.3 Power-size trade-off: t = 3.

close to the nominal, and the powers for the specific model are close to the theoretical bound for the given choice of size.

At 1 percent, the sizes (per variable) are lower for the larger GUM, probably owing to the role of the block tests, which "throw out" more variables when they fail to reject. We also record how the use of the reliability measure of significance in subsamples to scale the outcomes would affect the size and power: that is, if the reliability is 0.2 for a given variable, we treat an investigator as eliminating it 80 percent of the time. The reliability measure reduces both size and power, but the former more than the latter (as Hoover and Perez also found). Finally, the conservative and liberal strategies seem to have the correct operational characteristics.

16.5.2 Reanalyzing the "Data Mining" Experiments

Lovell (1983) formed a databank of twenty macroeconomic variables; generated one (denoted y) as a function of zero to five others; regressed y on all others plus all lags thereof, four lags of y and an intercept; then examined how well some selection methods performed for the GUM:

$$y_t = \delta + \sum_{j=1}^{4} \alpha_j y_{t-j} + \sum_{i=1}^{18} \sum_{j=0}^{1} \gamma_{i,j} x_{i,t-j} + w_t. \qquad (8)$$

He found none did even reasonably, but we suggest that was mainly because of flaws in the search algorithms, not in the principle of selection.

TABLE 16.2
Liberal and Conservative Strategies

DGP design	A	B	C	D	E	F
t	0	0	2	2	2	3
k	8	8	8	8	8	8
n	8	20	8	20	8	20
Conservative						
T:DGP$_{\text{found}}$	1.0000	1.0000	0.0000	0.0000	0.0230	0.0280
S:DGP$_{\text{found}}$	0.8430	0.7870	0.0000	0.0000	0.0250	0.0230
S:Nondeletion	0.1570	0.2130	0.1780	0.2630	0.1800	0.2870
S:Nonselection	0.0000	0.0000	1.0000	1.0000	0.9690	0.9720
T:Dominated (0.025)	0.1560	0.2120	0.4730	0.4280	0.3530	0.3060
S:Dominated (0.025)	0.0010	0.0010	0.4270	0.4300	0.5160	0.4890
S:Size	0.0108	0.0093	0.0223	0.0166	0.0229	0.0178
S:Power	—	—	0.2800	0.2575	0.6091	0.5820
S:Selection error	—	—	0.3712	0.2240	0.2069	0.1321
Reliability based						
S:Size	0.0090	0.0084	0.0144	0.0131	0.0147	0.0141
S:Power	—	—	0.2398	0.2355	0.5539	0.5489
S:Selection error	—	—	0.3873	0.2278	0.2304	0.1390
Liberal						
T:DGP$_{\text{found}}$	1.0000	1.0000	0.0230	0.0050	0.1740	0.2000
S:DGP$_{\text{found}}$	0.4330	0.3590	0.0250	0.0010	0.1130	0.0680
S:Nondeletion	0.5670	0.6410	0.1800	0.6920	0.4570	0.6700
S:Nonselection	0.0000	0.0000	0.9690	0.9970	0.8220	0.8380
T:Dominated (0.075)	0.5670	0.6410	0.3530	0.7550	0.6270	0.6050
S:Dominated (0.075)	0.0000	0.0000	0.5160	0.0760	0.1470	0.1070
S:Size	0.0524	0.0479	0.0229	0.0627	0.0650	0.0595
S:Power	—	—	0.6091	0.4638	0.7900	0.7702
S:Selection error	—	—	0.2069	0.1980	0.1375	0.1082
Reliability based						
S:Size	0.0464	0.0429	0.0147	0.0556	0.0553	0.0530
S:Power	—	—	0.5539	0.4373	0.7559	0.7436
S:Selection error	—	—	0.2304	0.2005	0.1497	0.1111

In retrospect, despite using actual macroeconomic data, the Lovell experiments are not very representative of real situations likely to confront econometricians, for four reasons. First, the few variables that matter the most have (absolute) t-values of 5, 8, 10, and 12 in the population, so are almost always jointly detected, irrespective of the significance level set: even using $\alpha = 0.1$ percent only requires $|\mathsf{t}| > 3.4$. Second, the remaining relevant variables have population t-values of less than unity, so will almost never be detected:

$$\mathsf{P}(|\mathsf{t}| \geq 2 \mid \mathsf{E}[\mathsf{t}] = 1) \simeq \mathsf{P}(\mathsf{t} \geq 2 \mid \mathsf{E}[\mathsf{t}] = 1) = \mathsf{P}(\mathsf{t} \geq 1 \mid \mathsf{E}[\mathsf{t}] = 0),$$

which is less than 16 percent even at $\alpha = 5$ percent, and about 5 percent at $\alpha = 1$ percent. Thus, there is essentially a zero probability of retaining two such variables in those experiments (and hence no chance of locating the DGP), *even when no search is involved.* Third, including more than forty irrelevant variables when the sample size is $T = 100$ is hardly representative of empirical modeling. Finally, and true of most such Monte Carlo experiments, the DGP is a special case of the GUM, so misspecification tests play no useful role.

Combining these facets, any researcher running, or rerunning, such experiments knows this aspect, so is "biased" toward setting tough selection rules and ignoring diagnostic checks [see, e.g., the approach in Hansen (1999), commenting on Hoover and Perez (1999)]; *PcGets* would do best with very stringent significance levels. Unfortunately, in many practical applications, such settings will not perform well: t-values of 2 or 3 will rarely be retained, and badly misspecified models will not be detected. Consequently, we kept the critical value settings suggested by the calibration experiments described in Section 16.5.1 as well as all the diagnostic tests used therein.

Table 16.3 records the DGPs in those experiments that did not involve variables with population t-statistics less than unity in absolute value. In all cases, $\varepsilon_t \sim \mathsf{IN}[0, 1]$. The GUM nested the DGP, with the addition of between thirty-seven and forty irrelevant variables, depending on the experiment. The population t-values are shown in Table 16.4.

First, we record for convenience the original outcomes reported for our rerun of the Hoover-Perez experiments, shown in Table 16.5 (HP3 was not one of those we reran). While the performance was sometimes spectacular—as in

TABLE 16.3
Selected Hoover-Perez DGPs

HP1	$y_t = 130\varepsilon_t$
HP2	$y_t = 0.75y_{t-1} + 130\varepsilon_t$
HP2*	$y_t = 0.50y_{t-1} + 130\varepsilon_t$
HP7	$y_t = 0.75y_{t-1} + 1.33x_t - 0.975x_{t-1} + 9.73\varepsilon_t$

Note: The dependent variable choice differs across experiments.

TABLE 16.4
DGP t-Values in Hoover-Perez Experiments

	Experiment			
	HP1	HP2	HP2*	HP7
y_{t-1}	—	12.95	4.70	12.49
x_t	—	—	—	15.14
x_{t-1}	—	—	—	−8.16

HP1, where the DGP (which is the null model) is almost always found—it could also be less satisfactory, as in HP7 with $\alpha = 0.05$.

The basic *PcGets* setting used in Table 16.6 was the conservative strategy, with some variation in the two preselection tests, namely the F-test on the GUM being the null model (denoted F_G), and the F-test for the significance of the lag length F_P. The outcomes are based on $M = 1000$ replications of the DGP with a sample size of $T = 100$.

The probabilities of retaining the DGP when commencing from it, and from the GUM (denoted $\text{T:DGP}_{\text{found}}$ and $\text{S:DGP}_{\text{found}}$) are shown first: The former

TABLE 16.5
Original Outcomes for Hoover-Perez Experiments

	Experiment				
	HP1	HP2	HP2	HP7	HP7
Significance level	0.01	0.01	0.01*	0.01	0.05
Selection probabilities					
y_{t-1}		1.0000	1.0000	1.0000	1.0000
x_t				1.0000	1.0000
x_{t-1}				0.9970	0.9980
Power	—	1.0000	1.0000	0.9990	0.9990
Size	0.0019	0.0242	0.0088	0.0243	0.1017
Selected model					
DGP found	0.9720	0.6020	0.8520	0.5900	0.1050
Non-DGP var. included	0.0280	0.3980	0.1480	0.4100	0.8950
DGP var. not included	0.0000	0.0000	0.0000	0.0030	0.0020
DGP is dominated	0.0260	0.3830	0.1030	0.3900	0.8900
Specific is dominated	0.0020	0.0150	0.0450	0.0200	0.0050

* Using preselection tests.

TABLE 16.6
Simulation Results for Hoover-Perez Experiments

PcGets	Significance levels		
F-test of GUM	0.2500	0.5000	0.5000
Presearch (stage I)	0.5000	0.2500	0.5000
HP1	Probability	Probability	Probability
T:DGP$_{found}$	1.0000	1.0000	1.0000
S:DGP$_{found}$	0.8980	0.8800	0.8530
S:Nondeletion	0.1020	0.1200	0.1470
S:Nonselection	—	—	—
T:Dominated	0.1020	0.1200	0.1470
S:Dominated	0.0000	0.0000	0.0000
S:Size	0.0049	0.0049	0.0064
S:Power	—	—	—
S:Size (rel)	0.0041	0.0040	0.0054
S:Power (rel)	—	—	—
HP2			
T:DGP$_{found}$	1.0000	1.0000	1.0000
S:DGP$_{found}$	0.8090	0.8570	0.8100
S:Nondeletion	0.1910	0.1430	0.1900
S:Nonselection	0.0010	0.0000	0.0000
T:Dominated	0.1860	0.1430	0.1860
S:Dominated	0.0040	0.0000	0.0040
S:Size	0.0095	0.0073	0.0095
S:Power	0.9990	1.0000	1.0000
S:Size (rel)	0.0079	0.0058	0.0079
S:Power (rel)	0.9990	1.0000	1.0000
HP2*			
T:DGP$_{found}$	0.9940	0.9940	0.9940
S:DGP$_{found}$	0.6990	0.7710	0.7590
S:Nondeletion	0.2140	0.1780	0.2080
S:Nonselection	0.1100	0.0860	0.0490
T:Dominated	0.1960	0.1470	0.1970
S:Dominated	0.0850	0.0490	0.0310
S:Size	0.0104	0.0084	0.0102
S:Power	0.8900	0.9140	0.9510
S:Size (rel)	0.0088	0.0070	0.0086
S:Power (rel)	0.8894	0.9127	0.9501

TABLE 16.6
(Continued)

PcGets	Significance levels		
HP7	Probability	Probability	Probability
T:DGP_{found}	1.0000	1.0000	1.0000
S:DGP_{found}	0.8080	0.8460	0.8080
S:Nondeletion	0.1920	0.1540	0.1920
S:Nonselection	0.0060	0.0070	0.0060
T:Dominated	0.1850	0.1440	0.1850
S:Dominated	0.0010	0.0030	0.0010
S:Size	0.0096	0.0074	0.0096
S:Power	0.9980	0.9977	0.9980
S:Size (rel)	0.0081	0.0062	0.0081
S:Power (rel)	0.9979	0.9976	0.9979

is always close to unity and the latter almost always above 75 percent for the range of experiments shown. The power of *PcGets* (the probability of retaining the variables that matter) is close to that when commencing from the DGP, and the size is usually smaller than 0.75 percent: with more than thirty-seven irrelevant variables, the conservative strategy would almost certainly be the best choice.

Next the nondeletion and nonselection probabilities are shown: The latter are usually tiny, so the former are close to 1 – S:DGP_{found}. Finally, T:Dominated and S:Dominated record the probabilities that the DGP or the selected model dominates (i.e., encompasses) the other. As can be seen, the former occurs quite often, between 13–20 percent, whereas the latter is usually under 5 percent. Thus, the operating characteristics are stable between the experiments and everywhere well behaved.

Finally, we show how the latest version of *PcGets* (May 2001) would perform using both settings (see Table 16.7). The probabilities of locating the DGP are now constant across states of nature and remain high; this is due to both high power to retain relevant variables and a small size for irrelevant variables. The reliability measure again reduces the size, being everywhere less than 1 percent for the conservative, without much loss of power.

Overall, these findings cohere with those reported earlier (for a different version of the program, and very different settings for the significance levels), and suggest that *PcGets* performs well even in a demanding problem, where the GUM is hugely overparameterized. The outcomes suggest that relatively loose critical values should be chosen for preselection tests.

TABLE 16.7
Rerunning the Hoover-Perez Experiments

	Experiment			
	HP1	HP2	HP2*	HP7
Conservative				
T:DGP$_{\text{found}}$	1.0000	1.0000	0.9940	1.0000
S:DGP$_{\text{found}}$	0.8530	0.8100	0.7590	0.8080
S:Nondeletion	0.1470	0.1900	0.2080	0.1920
S:Nonselection	—	0.0000	0.0490	0.0060
T:Dominated (0.025)	0.1470	0.1860	0.1970	0.1850
S:Dominated (0.025)	0.0000	0.0040	0.0310	0.0010
S:Size	0.0064	0.0095	0.0102	0.0096
S:Power	—	1.0000	0.9510	0.9980
Reliability based				
S:Size	0.0054	0.0079	0.0086	0.0081
S:Power	—	1.0000	0.9501	0.9979
Liberal				
T:DGP$_{\text{found}}$	1.0000	1.0000	0.9990	1.0000
S:DGP$_{\text{found}}$	0.4700	0.3450	0.3440	0.3470
S:Nondeletion	0.5300	0.6550	0.6500	0.6530
S:Nonselection	—	0.0000	0.0220	0.0070
T:Dominated (0.075)	0.5290	0.6540	0.6380	0.6440
S:Dominated (0.075)	0.0010	0.0010	0.0050	0.0020
S:Size	0.0427	0.0549	0.0551	0.0541
S:Power	—	1.0000	0.9780	0.9977
Reliability based				
S:Size	0.0377	0.0476	0.0482	0.0470
S:Power	—	1.0000	0.9762	0.9976

16.5.3 Rerunning the JEDC Experiments

In this final set of experiments from Krolzig and Hendry (2001), the DGP is a Gaussian regression model, where the strongly exogenous variables are Gaussian white noise processes:

$$y_t = \sum_{k=1}^{5} \beta_{k,0} x_{k,t} + \varepsilon_t, \qquad \varepsilon_t \sim \mathsf{IN}[0, 1], \tag{9}$$

$$x_t = v_t, \qquad v_t \sim \mathsf{IN}_{10}[\mathbf{0}, \mathbf{I}_{10}] \quad \text{for } t = 1, \ldots, T,$$

where $\beta_{1,0} = 2/\sqrt{T}, \beta_{2,0} = 3/\sqrt{T}, \beta_{3,0} = 4/\sqrt{T}, \beta_{4,0} = 6/\sqrt{T}$, and $\beta_{5,0} = 8/\sqrt{T}$.

The GUM is an *ADL*(1, 1) model that includes as non-DGP variables the lagged endogenous variable y_{t-1}, the strongly exogenous variables $x_{6,t}, \ldots, x_{10,t}$ and the first lags of all regressors:

$$y_t = \pi_{0,1} y_{t-1} + \sum_{k=1}^{10} \sum_{i=0}^{1} \pi_{k,i} x_{k,t-i} + \pi_{0,0} + u_t, u_t \sim \mathsf{IN}\left[0, \sigma^2\right]. \quad (10)$$

The sample size used here is just $T = 100$, and the number of replications M is 1,000; the nonzero population t-values are therefore 2, 3, 4, 6, 8. In (10), seventeen of twenty-two regressors are "nuisance."

We record the performance of the original *PcGets* and that on the calibrated settings now embodied in the two formal strategies in Table 16.8 and 16.9. The progress is obvious: The sizes are generally similar with higher powers, again close to the upper bound of drawing from a scalar t-distribution. The search costs are generally negligible when compared to the costs of statistical inference. Under the default setting of *PcGets* (i.e., presearch and split-sample analysis are active), the costs of search are reduced to 0.0015 and 0.0054 per variable at nominal sizes of 0.01 and 0.05, respectively. Thus, they are just 2.12 percent (respectively, 8.49 percent) of the underlying costs of statistical inference.

Ensuring empirical congruence by checking the validity of the reductions is almost free: In the case of the liberal strategy, the diagnostic tests contributed only an estimated 0.0004 to the total costs of search, which are 0.0015. Partly, this is because the misspecification tests are well behaved, as we discuss next.

16.5.4 Small-Sample Properties of the Misspecification Tests

Krolzig and Hendry (2001) recorded quantile-quantile (QQ) plots of the empirical distributions of seven potential misspecification tests when estimating the correct specification, the general model, and the finally selected model in a Monte Carlo study with $T = 1{,}000$ and $T = 100$. In the larger sample, the tests were unaffected by the presence of (strongly exogenous) nuisance regressors (i.e., variables that entered the GUM but not the DGP). However, at the smaller sample size, some strong deviations were evident from the theoretical distributions for two tests: the portmanteau statistic (see Box and Pierce, 1970) rejected serial independence of the errors too often in the correct specification, never in the general, and too rarely in the final model; and the hetero-x test (see White, 1980) often had degrees-of-freedom problems for the GUM and performed badly for both the true and final models. Such incorrect finite-sample sizes of diagnostic tests would induce excess rejections of congruent GUMs, resulting in an increased overall size. Thus, the portmanteau diagnostic should

TABLE 16.8
JEDC Experiments: Conservative Strategy

	Theory	JEDC	JEDC (presearch)	*PcGets*	*PcGets* (presearch)	*PcGets* (presearch, split sample)
Size	0.0100	0.0185	0.0088	0.0162	0.0135	0.0102
vs. JEDC			−0.0097	−0.0023	−0.0050	−0.0084
vs. JEDC (%)			−52.43	−12.43	−27.19	−45.14
Power	0.7544	0.7598	0.6665	0.7582	0.7490	0.7312
vs. JEDC			−0.0933	−0.0016	−0.0108	−0.0286
vs. JEDC (%)			−12.28	−0.21	−1.42	−3.77
Selection error	0.0635	0.0689	0.0826	0.0675	0.0675	0.0689
vs. JEDC			0.0137	−0.0014	−0.0014	0.0001
vs. JEDC (%)			19.89	−2.05	−2.08	0.08
Costs of search		0.0053	0.0190	0.0039	0.0039	0.0054
Costs of search (%)		8.40	29.97	6.18	6.15	8.49
Expected number of						
NonDGP variables included	0.17	0.31	0.15	0.28	0.23	0.17
DGP variables deleted	1.23	1.20	1.67	1.21	1.26	1.34
Variables misplaced	1.40	1.52	1.82	1.48	1.48	1.52

Power function						
Power ($t = 2$)	0.2580	0.2820	0.1538	0.2850	0.2820	0.2559
Power ($t = 3$)	0.6130	0.6200	0.4278	0.6240	0.6190	0.5925
Power ($t = 4$)	0.9020	0.8980	0.7645	0.8820	0.8720	0.8577
Power ($t = 6$)	0.9990	0.9990	0.9865	1.0000	1.0000	0.9994
Power ($t = 8$)	1.0000	1.0000	1.0000	1.0000	1.0000	0.9997
Indicators						
T:DGP_{found}				0.1540	0.1540	0.1540
S:DGP_{found}				0.1290	0.1290	0.1290
S:Nondeletion				0.2130	0.1890	0.1890
S:Nonselection				0.8320	0.8390	0.8390
T:Dominated				0.6630	0.6490	0.6490
S:Dominated				0.1680	0.1850	0.1850

TABLE 16.9
JEDC Experiments: Liberal Strategy

	Theory	JEDC	JEDC (presearch)	*PcGets*	*PcGets* (presearch)	*PcGets* (presearch, split sample)
Size	0.0500	0.0677	0.0477	0.0666	0.0546	0.0447
vs. JEDC			−0.0200	−0.0011	−0.0131	−0.0230
vs. JEDC (%)			−29.54	−1.62	−19.36	−33.99
Power	0.8522	0.8532	0.8156	0.8556	0.8446	0.8274
vs. JEDC			−0.0376	0.0024	−0.0086	−0.0258
vs. JEDC (%)			−4.41	0.28	−1.01	−3.02
Selection error	0.0722	0.0857	0.0788	0.0843	0.0775	0.0738
vs. JEDC			−0.0069	−0.0014	−0.0082	−0.0119
vs. JEDC (%)			−8.06	−1.63	−9.54	−13.91
Costs of search		0.0135	0.0065	0.0121	0.0053	0.0015
Costs of search (%)		18.62	9.06	16.69	7.30	2.12
Expected number of						
NonDGP variables included	0.85	1.15	0.81	1.13	0.93	0.76
DGP variables deleted	0.74	0.73	0.92	0.72	0.78	0.86
Variables misplaced	1.59	1.88	1.73	1.85	1.71	1.62

Power function						
Power ($t = 2$)	0.4730	0.4930	0.4080	0.5000	0.4820	0.4494
Power ($t = 3$)	0.8120	0.8020	0.7330	0.8180	0.8080	0.7798
Power ($t = 4$)	0.9760	0.9720	0.9390	0.9600	0.9580	0.9455
Power ($t = 6$)	1.0000	0.9990	0.9980	1.0000	1.0000	1.0000
Power ($t = 8$)	1.0000	1.0000	1.0000	1.0000	1.0000	1.0000
Indicators						
T:DGP_{found}				0.3960	0.3960	0.3960
S:DGP_{found}				0.1410	0.1700	0.1700
S:Nondeletion				0.6290	0.5780	0.5780
S:Nonselection				0.5960	0.6150	0.6150
T:Dominated				0.7550	0.7000	0.7000
S:Dominated				0.0470	0.0520	0.0520

be excluded from any battery of test statistics and the hetero-x test from the GUM unless degrees of freedom are large. Overall, therefore, we recommend the five misspecification tests shown in Table 16.10.

We investigated the empirical distributions of these five remaining test statistics in the DGP, GUM, and selected model for the experiments in Section 16.6.3. The results are shown in Figure 16.4 at $T = 100$ for 1,000 replications, reporting midpoint and end-of-sample Chow tests. The graphs demonstrate that the test distributions in the selected model (bottom row) are both satisfactory and close to the distributions of those tests under the null of the DGP (first row). The properties of the misspecification tests were also satisfactory in the GUM (second row). In earlier versions of *PcGets*, the ARCH and hetero tests departed notably from their theoretical distributions in the GUM. A reviewer of Hendry and Krolzig (2001) (Dorian Owen) suggested that the degrees of freedom were inappropriate by using a correction like that in Lagrange-multiplier autocorrelation tests (see, e.g., Godfrey, 1978, and Breusch and Pagan, 1980). Instead, as argued in, for example, Davidson and MacKinnon (1993, ch. 11), since the covariance matrix is block diagonal between regression and skedastic function parameters, tests can take the former as given. Doing so changes the statistics from being regarded as $\mathsf{F}_{\mathsf{arch}}(p, T-k-2p)$ and $\mathsf{F}_{\mathsf{het}}(q, T-k-q)$ to $\mathsf{F}_{\mathsf{arch}}(p, T-2p)$ and $\mathsf{F}_{\mathsf{het}}(q, T-q)$, respectively, producing improved matches.

TABLE 16.10
Test Battery

Test	Alternative	Statistic	Sources
Chow (τT)	Predictive failure on $(1-\tau)T$ observed	$F[(1-\tau)T, \tau T - k]$	Chow (1960, pp. 594–595); Hendry (1979)
Normality	Skewness and excess kurtosis	$\chi^2(2)$	Jarque and Bera (1980); Doornik and Hansen (1994)
AR 1-p	pth Order residual autocorrelation	$F(p, T-k-p)$	Godfrey (1978); Harvey (1981, p. 173)
ARCH 1-p	pth Order ARCH	$F(p, T-2p)$	Engle (1982)
Hetero	Heteroskedasticity quadratic in regressors x_i^2	$F(q, T-q)$	White (1980); Nicholls and Pagan (1983)

Note: There are T observations and k regressors in the model under the null. The value of q may differ across statistics, as may those of k and T across models. By default, *PcGets* sets $p = 4$, $r = 12$, and computes two Chow tests at $\tau_1 = [0.5T]/T$ and $\tau_2 = [.09T]/T$.

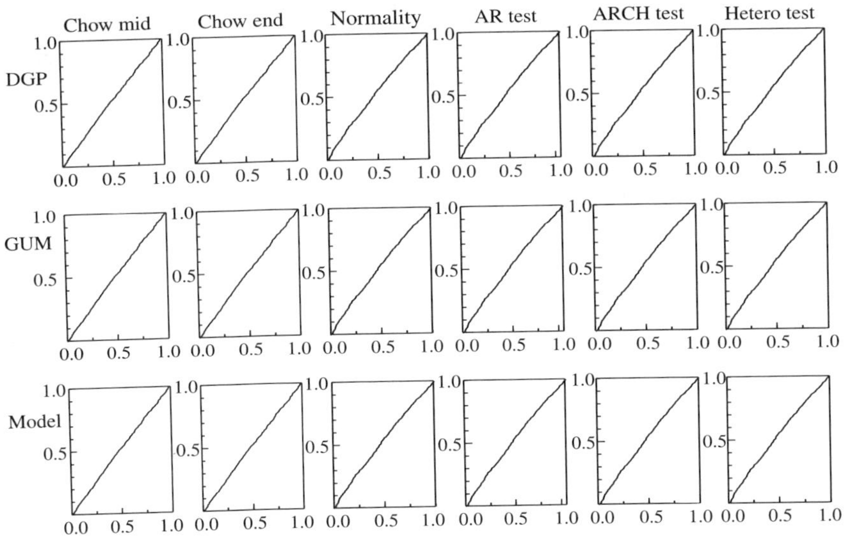

Fig. 16.4 Selecting misspecification tests: QQ plots for $T = 100$.

16.6 CONCLUSION

In his survey of model selection for the Handbook of Econometrics, Ed Leamer deems the need for model selection to be a serious drawback for economics research: *"On pessimistic days I doubt that economists have learned anything from the mountains of computer printouts that fill their offices. On especially pessimistic days, I doubt that they ever will."*

A lot has changed since he wrote in the early 1980s, not least the demise of "mountains of computer printouts." We have demonstrated that automatic model-selection procedures can perform almost as well as could be hoped, with size close to the desired level and power near that applicable when commencing from the DGP. Thus, the problem is not one of search costs owing to "the absence of completely defined models" (pace Leamer), but to the properties of statistical inference. However, here too we are more optimistic—at least in time-series applications, new data continually accrue, helping to weed out adventitiously significant variables and confirming the relevance of the remainder. Model selection is part of a progressive research strategy, not a one-off attempt to forge "economic laws" that hold forever.

Certainly, the context of regression with strongly exogenous variables is far too simple to characterize real-world econometrics. Empirical researchers confront nonstationary, mismeasured data, on evolving dynamic and high-dimensional economies, with at best weakly exogenous conditioning variables. At the practical level, *Gets* is applicable to systems, such as vector autoregressions (see Krolzig, 2000), and endogenous regressors where sufficient instruments exist, and it is just as powerful a tool on cross-section problems, as demonstrated by Hoover and Perez (2000).

Moreover, the study of automatic selection procedures has barely begun. As Hendry and Mizon (2000) remark, *"Early chess-playing programs were easily defeated, but later ones can systematically beat Grandmasters, so we anticipate computer-automated model selection software developing well beyond the capabilities of the most expert modellers."* Deep Blue may be just round the corner.

NOTE

Financial support from the U.K. Economic and Social Research Council under grant L11625015 is gratefully acknowledged. We are indebted to Mike Clements, Jurgen Doornik, David Firth, and Grayham Mizon for helpful comments. This chapter draws heavily on Hendry (2000b) and Hendry and Krolzig (2001).

REFERENCES

Akaike, H., 1985, "Prediction and Entropy," in: *A Celebration of Statistics,* A. C. Atkinson and S. E. Fienberg (eds.), New York: Springer-Verlag, pp. 1–24.

Amemiya, T., 1980, "Selection of Regressors," *International Economic Review* 21, 331–354.

Anderson, T. W., 1971, *The Statistical Analysis of Time Series,* New York: Wiley.

Andrews, D. W. K., 1991, "Heteroskedasticity and Autocorrelation Consistent Covariance Matrix Estimation," *Econometrica* 59, 817–858.

Box, G. E. P., and D. A. Pierce, 1970, "Distribution of Residual Autocorrelations in Autoregressive-integrated Moving Average Time Series Models," *Journal of the American Statistical Association* 65, 1509–1526.

Breusch, T. S., and A. R. Pagan, 1980, The Lagrange multiplier test and its applications to model specification in econometrics, *Review of Economic Studies* 47, 239–253.

Breusch, T. S., 1990, "Simplified Extreme Bounds," in: *Modelling Economic Series,* C. W. J. Granger (ed.), Oxford: Clarendon Press, p. 72–81.

Campos, J., and N. R. Ericsson, 1999, "Constructive Data Mining: Modeling Consumers' Expenditure in Venezuela," *Econometrics Journal* 2, 226–240.

Chow, G. C., 1960, "Tests of Equality Between Sets of Coefficients in Two Linear Regressions," *Econometrica* 28, 591–605.

Chow, G. C., 1981, "Selection of Econometric Models by the Information Criteria," in: *Proceedings of the Econometric Society European Meeting 1979,* E. G. Charatsis (ed.), Amsterdam: North-Holland, ch. 8.

Clayton, M. K., S. Geisser, and D. E. Jennings, 1986, "A Comparison of Several Model Selection Procedures," in: *Bayesian Inference and Decision Techniques,* P. Goel and A. Zellner (eds.), Amsterdam: Elsevier Science.

Clements, M. P., and D. F. Hendry, 2002, "Modelling Methodology and Forecast Failure," *Econometrics Journal* 5, 319–344.

Coen, P. G., E. D. Gomme, and M. G. Kendall, 1969, "Lagged Relationships in Economic Forecasting," *Journal of the Royal Statistical Society A* 132, 133–163.

Cox, D. R., 1961, "Tests of Separate Families of Hypotheses," in: *Proceedings of the Fourth Berkeley Symposium on Mathematical Statistics and Probability,* Vol. 1, Berkeley: University of California Press, pp. 105–123.

Cox, D. R., 1962, "Further Results on Tests of Separate Families of Hypotheses," *Journal of the Royal Statistical Society B* 24, 406–424.

Davidson, R., and J. G. MacKinnon, 1993, *Estimation and Inference in Econometrics,* Oxford: Oxford University Press.

Davidson, J. E. H., and D. F. Hendry, 1981, "Interpreting Econometric Evidence: The Behaviour of Consumers' Expenditure in the UK," *European Economic Review* 16, 177–192. Reprinted in *Econometrics: Alchemy or Science?,* D. F. Hendry, Oxford: Blackwell, 1993, and Oxford University Press, 2000.

Davidson, J. E. H., D. F. Hendry, F. Srba, and J. S. Yeo, 1978, "Econometric Modelling of the Aggregate Time-series Relationship between Consumers' Expenditure and Income in the United Kingdom," *Economic Journal* 88, 661–692. Reprinted in *Econometrics: Alchemy or Science?,* D. F. Hendry, Oxford: Blackwell, 1993, and Oxford University Press, 2000.

Deaton, A. S., 1982, "Model Selection Procedures or, Does the Consumption Function Exist?" in: *Evaluating the Reliability of Macro-Economic Models,* G. C. Chow and P. Corsi (eds.), New York: Wiley, ch. 5.

Doornik, J. A., 1999, *Object-Oriented Matrix Programming Using Ox,* 3rd Ed., London: Timberlake Consultants.

Doornik, J. A., and H. Hansen, 1994, "A Practical Test for Univariate and Multivariate Normality," Discussion Paper, Nuffield College.

Engle, R. F., 1982, "Autoregressive Conditional Heteroskedasticity with Estimates of the Variance of UK Inflation," *Econometrica* 50, 987–1008.

Engle, R. F., D. F. Hendry, and D. Trumbull, 1985, "Small Sample Properties of ARCH Estimators and Tests," *Canadian Journal of Economics* 43, 66–93.

Faust, J., and C. H. Whiteman, 1997, "General-to-specific Procedures for Fitting a Data-admissible, Theory-inspired, Congruent, Parsimonious, Encompassing, Weakly-exogenous, Identified, Structural Model of the DGP: A Translation and Critique," *Carnegie-Rochester Conference Series on Public Policy* 47, 121–161.

Florens, J.-P., and M. Mouchart, 1980, "Initial and Sequential Reduction of Bayesian Experiments, Discussion Paper 8015, CORE, Louvain-La-Neuve, Belgium.

Florens, J.-P., M. Mouchart, and J.-M. Rolin, 1990, *Elements of Bayesian Statistics,* New York: Dekker.

Florens, J.-P., D. F. Hendry, and J.-F. Richard, 1996, "Encompassing and Specificity," *Econometric Theory* 12, 620–656.

Godfrey, L. G., 1978, "Testing for Higher Order Serial Correlation in Regression Equations when the Regressors Include Lagged Dependent Variables," *Econometrica* 46, 1303–1313.

Gouriéroux, C., and A. Monfort, 1995, "Testing, Encompassing, and Simulating Dynamic Econometric Models," *Econometric Theory* 11, 195–228.

Govaerts, B., D. F. Hendry, and J.-F. Richard, 1994, "Encompassing in Stationary Linear Dynamic Models," *Journal of Econometrics* 63, 245–270.

Granger, C. W. J. (ed.), 1990, *Modelling Economic Series,* Oxford: Clarendon Press.

Hall, R. E., 1978, "Stochastic Implications of the Life Cycle-Permanent Income Hypothesis: Evidence," *Journal of Political Economy* 86, 971–987.

Hannan, E. J., and B. G. Quinn, 1979, "The Determination of the Order of an Autoregression," *Journal of the Royal Statistical Society* B 41, 190–195.

Hansen, B. E., 1999, "Discussion of 'Data Mining Reconsidered,' " *Econometrics Journal* 2, 26–40.

Harvey, A. C., 1981, *The Econometric Analysis of Time Series,* Deddington: Philip Allan.

Hendry, D. F., 1979, "Predictive Failure and Econometric Modelling in Macroeconomics: The Transactions Demand for Money," in: *Economic Modelling,* P. Ormerod (ed.), London: Heinemann, pp. 217–242. Reprinted in D. F. Hendry, *Econometrics: Alchemy or Science?,* Oxford: Blackwell, 1993, and Oxford University Press, 2000.

Hendry, D. F., 1987, "Econometric Methodology: A Personal Perspective," in: *Advances in Econometrics,* T. F. Bewley (ed.), Cambridge: Cambridge University Press, ch. 10.

Hendry, D. F., 1995, *Dynamic Econometrics,* Oxford: Oxford University Press.

Hendry, D. F., 2000a, *Econometrics: Alchemy or Science?* Oxford: Oxford University Press, New Edition.

Hendry, D. F., 2000b, "Epilogue: The Success of General-to-specific Model Selection," in: *Econometrics: Alchemy or Science?,* Oxford: Oxford University Press, New Edition, pp. 467–490.

Hendry, D. F., and N. R. Ericsson, 1991a, "An Econometric Analysis of UK Money Demand in 'Monetary Trends in the United States and the United Kingdom' by Milton Friedman and Anna J. Schwartz," *American Economic Review* 81, 8–38.

Hendry, D. F., and N. R. Ericsson, 1991b, "Modeling the Demand for Narrow Money in the United Kingdom and the United States," *European Economic Review* 35, 833–886.

Hendry, D. F., and H.-M. Krolzig, 1999, "Improving on 'Data Mining Reconsidered' by K. D. Hoover and S. J. Perez," *Econometrics Journal* 2, 202–219.

Hendry, D. F., and H.-M. Krolzig, 2001, *Automatic Econometric Model Selection,* London: Timberlake Consultants.

Hendry, D. F., and G. E. Mizon, 1978, "Serial Correlation as a Convenient Simplification, not a Nuisance: A Comment on a Study of the Demand for Money by the Bank of England," *Economic Journal* 88, 549–563. Reprinted in *Econometrics: Alchemy or Science?,* D. F. Hendry, Oxford: Blackwell, 1993, and Oxford University Press, 2000.

Hendry, D. F., and G. E. Mizon, 1990, "Procrustean Econometrics: Or Stretching and Squeezing Data," in: *Modelling Economic Series,* C. W. J. Granger (ed.), Oxford: Clarendon Press, pp. 121–136.

Hendry, D. F., and G. E. Mizon, 2000, "Reformulating Empirical Macroeconometric Modelling," *Oxford Review of Economic Policy* 16, 138–159.

Hendry, D. F., and J.-F. Richard, 1982, "On the Formulation of Empirical Models in Dynamic Econometrics," *Journal of Econometrics* 20, 3–33. Reprinted in *Modelling*

Economic Series, C. W. J. Granger (ed.), Oxford: Clarendon Press, 1990, and in *Econometrics: Alchemy or Science?,* D. F. Hendry, Oxford: Blackwell, 1993, and Oxford University Press, 2000.

Hendry, D. F., and J.-F. Richard, 1983, "The Econometric Analysis of Economic Time Series (with Discussion)," *International Statistical Review* 51, 111–163. Reprinted in *Econometrics: Alchemy or Science?,* D. F. Hendry, Oxford: Blackwell, 1993, and Oxford University Press, 2000.

Hendry, D. F., and J.-F. Richard, 1989, "Recent Developments in the Theory of Encompassing," in: *Contributions to Operations Research and Economics: The XXth Anniversary of CORE,* B. Cornet and H. Tulkens (eds.), Cambridge: MIT Press, pp. 393–440.

Hendry, D. F., E. E. Leamer, and D. J. Poirier, 1990, "A Conversation on Econometric Methodology," *Econometric Theory* 6, 171–261.

Hoover, K. D., and S. J. Perez, 1999, "Data Mining Reconsidered: Encompassing and the General-to-specific Approach to Specification Search," *Econometrics Journal* 2, 167–191.

Hoover, K. D., and S. J. Perez, 2000, "Truth and Robustness in Cross-country Growth Regressions," Unpublished Paper, Department of Economics, University of California, Davis.

Jarque, C. M., and A. K. Bera, 1980, "Efficient Tests for Normality, Homoscedasticity and Serial Independence of Regression Residuals," *Economics Letters* 6, 255–259.

Johansen, S., 1988, "Statistical Analysis of Cointegration Vectors," *Journal of Economic Dynamics and Control* 12, 231–254. Reprinted in *Long-Run Economic Relationships,* R. F. Engle and C. W. J. Granger (eds.), Oxford: Oxford University Press, 1991, pp. 131–152.

Judge, G. G., and M. E. Bock, 1978, *The Statistical Implications of Pre-Test and Stein-Rule Estimators in Econometrics,* Amsterdam: North-Holland.

Judge, G. G., W. E. Griffiths, R. C. Hill, H. Lütkepohl, and T.-C. Lee, 1985, *The Theory and Practice of Econometrics,* 2nd Ed., New York: Wiley.

Kent, J. T., 1986, "The Underlying Nature of Nonnested Hypothesis Tests," *Biometrika* 73, 333–343.

Keynes, J. M., 1939, "Professor Tinbergen's Method," *Economic Journal* 44, 558–568.

Keynes, J. M., 1940, "Comment," *Economic Journal* 50, 154–156.

Kiviet, J. F., 1985, "Model Selection Test Procedures in a Single Linear Equation of a Dynamic Simultaneous System and their Defects in Small Samples," *Journal of Econometrics* 28, 327–362.

Kiviet, J. F., 1986, "On the Rigor of Some Mis-specification Tests for Modelling Dynamic Relationships," *Review of Economic Studies* 53, 241–261.

Koopmans, T. C., 1947, "Measurement without Theory," *Review of Economics and Statistics* 29, 161–179.

Krolzig, H.-M., 2000, "General-to-specific Reductions in Vector Autoregressive Processes," Economics Discussion Paper, 2000-w34, Nuffield College, Oxford.

Krolzig, H.-M., and D. F. Hendry, 2001, "Computer Automation of General-to-specific Model Selection Procedures," *Journal of Economic Dynamics and Control* 25, 831–866.

Leamer, E. E., 1978, *Specification Searches: Ad-Hoc Inference with Non-Experimental Data,* New York: Wiley.

Leamer, E. E., 1983a, "Let's Take the Con out of Econometrics," *American Economic Review* 73, 31–43. Reprinted in *Modelling Economic Series,* C. W. J. Granger (ed.), Oxford: Clarendon Press, 1990.

Leamer, E. E., 1983b, "Model Choice and Specification Analysis," in: *Handbook of Econometrics,* Vol. 1, Z. Griliches and M. D. Intriligator (eds.), Amsterdam: North-Holland, ch. 5.

Leamer, E. E., 1984, "Global Sensitivity Results for Generalized Least Squares Estimates," *Journal of the American Statistical Association* 79, 867–870.

Leamer, E. E., 1990, "Sensitivity Analyses Would Help," in: *Modelling Economic Series,* C. W. J. Granger (ed.), Oxford: Clarendon Press, 1990, pp. 88–96.

Lovell, M. C., 1983, "Data Mining," *Review of Economics and Statistics* 65, 1–12.

Magnus, J. R., and M. S. Morgan, (eds.), 1999, *Methodology and Tacit Knowledge: Two Experiments in Econometrics,* Chichester: Wiley.

McAleer, M., A. R. Pagan, and P. A. Volker, 1985, "What Will Take the Con out of Econometrics?" *American Economic Review* 95, 293–301. Reprinted in *Modelling Economic Series,* C. W. J. Granger (ed.), Oxford: Clarendon Press, 1990.

Mizon, G. E., 1977a, "Inferential Procedures in Nonlinear Models: An Application in a UK Industrial Cross Section Study of Factor Substitution and Returns to Scale," *Econometrica* 45, 1221–1242.

Mizon, G. E., 1977b, "Model Selection Procedures," in: *Studies in Modern Economic Analysis,* M. J. Artis and A. R. Nobay (eds.), Oxford: Blackwell, pp. 97–120.

Mizon, G. E., 1984, "The Encompassing Approach in Econometrics," in: *Econometrics and Quantitative Economics,* D. F. Hendry and K. F. Wallis (eds.), Oxford: Blackwell, pp. 135–172.

Mizon, G. E., and J.-F. Richard, 1986, "The Encompassing Principle and Its Application to Non-nested Hypothesis Tests," *Econometrica* 54, 657–678.

Nicholls, D. F., and A. R. Pagan, 1983, "Heteroscedasticity in Models with Lagged Dependent Variables," *Econometrica* 51, 1233–1242.

Pagan, A. R., 1987, "Three Econometric Methodologies: A Critical Appraisal," *Journal of Economic Surveys* 1, 3–24. Reprinted in *Modelling Economic Series,* C. W. J. Granger (ed.), Oxford: Clarendon Press, 1990.

Pesaran, M. H., 1974, "On the General Problem of Model Selection," *Review of Economic Studies* 41, 153–171.

Sargan, J. D., 1973, "Model Building and Data Mining," presented to the Association of University Teachers of Economics Meeting, Manchester, April 1973. [*Econometric Reviews* (2001), 20, 159–170.]

Sargan, J. D., 1980, "Some Tests of Dynamic Specification for a Single Equation," *Econometrica* 48, 879–897. Reprinted *Contributions to Econometrics,* Vol. 1, J. D. Sargan, Cambridge: Cambridge University Press, 1988, pp. 191–212.

Sargan, J. D., 1981, "The Choice Between Sets of Regressors," Mimeo, Department of Economics, London School of Economics [*Econometric Reviews* (2001), 20, 171–186].

Savin, N. E., 1984, "Multiple Hypothesis Testing," in: *Handbook of Econometrics,* Vol. 2, Z. Griliches and M. D. Intriligator (eds.), Amsterdam: North-Holland, ch. 14.

Sawa, T., 1978, "Information Criteria for Discriminating Among Alternative Regression Models," *Econometrica* 46, 1273–1292.

Schwarz, G., 1978, "Estimating the Dimension of a Model," *Annals of Statistics* 6, 461–464.

Shibata, R., 1980, "Asymptotically Efficient Selection of the Order of the Model for Estimating Parameters of a Linear Process," *Annals of Statistics* 8, 147–164.

Sims, C. A., J. H. Stock, and M. W. Watson, 1990, "Inference in Linear Time Series Models with Some Unit Roots," *Econometrica* 58, 113–144.

Stigum, B. P., 1990, *Towards a Formal Science of Economics,* Cambridge: MIT Press.

Summers, L. H., 1991, "The Scientific Illusion in Empirical Macroeconomics," *Scandinavian Journal of Economics* 93, 129–148.

Tinbergen, J., 1940a, *Statistical Testing of Business-Cycle Theories, Vol. I: A Method and its Application to Investment Activity.* Geneva: League of Nations.

Tinbergen, J., 1940b, *Statistical Testing of Business-Cycle Theories, Vol. II: Business Cycles in the United States of America, 1919–1932,* Geneva: League of Nations.

Vuong, Q. H., 1989, "Likelihood Ratio Tests for Model Selection and Non-nested Hypotheses," *Econometrica* 57, 307–333.

White, H., 1980, "A Heteroskedastic-consistent Covariance Matrix Estimator and a Direct Test for Heteroskedasticity," *Econometrica* 48, 817–838.

White, H., 1990, "A Consistent Model Selection," in: *Modelling Economic Series,* C. W. J. Granger (ed.), Oxford: Clarendon Press, pp. 369–383.

Wooldridge, J. M., 1999, "Asymptotic Properties of Some Specification Tests in Linear Models with Integrated Processes," in: *Cointegration, Causality and Forecasting,* R. F. Engle and H. White (eds.), Oxford: Oxford University Press, pp. 366–384.

Yancey, T. A., and G. G. Judge, 1976, "A Monte Carlo Comparison of Traditional and Stein-rule Estimators under Squared Error Loss," *Journal of Econometrics* 4, 285–294.

PART V
Empirical Relevance

Chapter Seventeen

Conjectures, Theories, and Their Empirical Relevance

In this chapter I delineate formal characteristics of tests of economic conjectures and theories, and discuss the proper attitude to assume toward such tests. Throughout this chapter, I assume without saying so, that the bridge between the two universes is traversed from the theory universe to the data universe. This aspect of the formalism determines both the empirical context in which the relevance of a conjecture or a theory is tried and the sentences on whose validity the result of a test depends. Since many economists share Karl R. Popper's views on the import of tests of theories, a few remarks concerning how my views differ from his are called for.

17.1 POPPER ON CONJECTURES AND REFUTATIONS

Judging from a reading of his wonderful book *Conjectures and Refutations*, Popper (1972) identifies conjectures with theories. Such an understanding of the two concepts is at odds with their explication in leading English and American dictionaries. For example, both the *Oxford Reference Dictionary* (ORD) and *Webster's New World Dictionary* (WNWD) insist that "conjecture" is formation of an opinion on incomplete grounds, and they liken it to guesswork (cf. ORD, 1986, p. 182; WNWD, 1953, p. 310). In contrast, a "theory" is either an exposition of the principles on which a subject is based or a systematic statement of principles concerning certain observed phenomena (cf. ORD, 1986, p. 854, and WNWD, 1953, p. 1511).

In this book I adopt the meaning of "conjecture" given by the two dictionaries: A conjecture is guesswork based on incomplete evidence. Both implicitly and explicitly formulated conjectures permeate every person's conscious life. They surface in arguments by introspection and induction and help us determine the food we eat, the activities in which we engage, and the way we relate to other people. Some are well founded and prove valid most of the time, whereas others are based on flimsy evidence and often fail. However, the failure of a conjecture in one situation is not necessarily cause for its rejection, as it may be valid in other situations.

In econometrics conjectures enter both the choice of projects and the way one carries them out. Econometricians conjecture about positive analogies of the behavior of individuals and aggregates as well as about salient characteristics of data-generating processes. They deliberate about proper ways to measure significant variables and about where to find relevant data. And they argue about what constitutes a successful end to a project and the chances of being able to publish the results. Their conjectures are usually based on introspective and inductive arguments. E 17.1 presents a case in point.

E 17.1 *Researchers are studying the effect on employment of a retraining program for unemployed workers and are searching for data that pertain to two given disjoint groups of individuals, only one of which has been exposed to the retraining program. To avoid confounding causal effects, they must find a way of rendering the groups observationally equivalent, which requires having observations on a number of the salient characteristics of each group. Their conjectures concerning what these characteristics are depend on introspection, tacit knowledge, and the experience they have had in other related studies.*

In economics, as in econometrics, conjectures concern positive analogies of the behavior of individuals and aggregates and characteristics of relevant families of probability distributions. From a formal point of view a conjecture is like a hypothesis of an economic theory. However, economists' attitude toward a conjecture differs from the attitude they have toward a theoretical hypothesis. They are uncertain about the validity of a conjecture and believe that they have good reason to trust the validity of a theoretical hypothesis. This means that an assertion might be a conjecture at one point and a theoretical hypothesis later. Moreover, an assertion may be a theoretical hypothesis in one theory and a conjecture in another.

Conjectures in economics relate to theoretical hypotheses in many different ways. E 17.2 gives three examples.

E 17.2 *Heckscher (1919) and Ohlin's (1933) hypothesis concerning factor endowments and comparative advantage is a conjecture in Chapters 10 and 11. Yet, trade theorists treat it as a theorem, that is, as a theoretical hypothesis, and make extreme assumptions in their empirical work to justify such an attitude (cf. Leamer, 1984, p. 2, assumption 6).*

Richard Muth's (1961) rational expectations hypothesis is a consistency requirement in microeconomic models of individual behavior and a poorly substantiated conjecture about the predictive prowess of an aggregate of individuals in macroeconomics.

Paul Samuelson's (1955, p. 111) revealed-preference hypothesis was originally a conjecture concerning individual behavior from which followed "almost all the meaningful empirical implications of the whole pure theory of consumer's choice." It is now also a hypothesis concerning aggregate excess demand functions that will ensure the stability of perfectly competitive markets (Stigum, 1990, pp. 291–293).

Much of Popper's book deals with "refutation" of theories and the "demarcation" of scientific theories. He identifies "refutation" with "falsification" and insists that a theory is scientific only if it comprises statements that observations may refute. A test of a scientific theory is always an attempt to falsify the theory (Popper, 1963, pp. 36–37, 256). He also insists that a scientific theory "*tells us the more about observable facts the more facts it forbids*" and suggests that the empirical content of such a theory should be taken to equal the class of observational statements that contradict it (p. 385).

I consider Popper's attitude toward scientific theories unacceptable for several reasons. First, one confronts an economic theory with data not to seek its falsification, but to try its empirical relevance. An economic theory has empirical relevance in a given situation if the relations that the theory and the pertinent bridge principles prescribe among relevant variables in the data universe are valid. One cannot establish that a theory has empirical relevance in all pertinent situations. One can only ascertain that a given set of data does not contradict it.

Second, even if one sets out to falsify a theory, there are good reasons why one will not manage to do it. Pierre Duhem (1981, p. 187) pointed out one of these reasons a long time ago. A scientist can never subject an isolated hypothesis to an empirical test, as such a test always involves a set of auxiliary hypotheses. Consequently, if the predictions of his original hypothesis do not pan out, he is hard put to determine which one of the many hypotheses was the culprit in the failure. Whether there is a formal way of circumventing Duhem's problem is a matter that I deal with later in the chapter.

Third, it is awkward to measure the empirical content of a theory by the class of statements that contradict it. The family of statements that contradict the theory in a given theory-data confrontation depends on the bridge principles that the scientist has adopted. These principles are not an integral part of the theory. Rather, they comprise the scientist's conjectures about how variables in his theory are related to variables in the data universe. Such conjectures vary among scientists, which renders Popper's measure meaningless.

17.2 EMPIRICAL RELEVANCE: A FORMAL ACCOUNT

The positive analogies of an event or some phenomenon that a conjecture or an interpreted economic theory identifies need not have any empirical relevance. To ascertain that the given analogies are relevant, the conjecture or theory must be confronted with data. Such data confrontations happen in different contexts and for various reasons. However, formally speaking, all have the same core structure: two disjoint universes for theory and data, a bridge between the universes, and a sample population. I discuss this core structure at length in Part III of this book. For ease of reference I recount its salient features here.

17.2.1 The Core Structure of Theory-Data Confrontations

Let T be a conjecture or an economic theory, and let IT be an interpretation of T that an econometrician wants to confront with data. The theory universe for IT is a pair (Ω_T, Γ_t), where Ω_T denotes a set of vectors ω_T in a real vector space. The components of ω_T are variables and functional and predicate constants about which IT talks, and Γ_t comprises a family of axioms and/or theorems of IT. For example, let T be the neoclassical theory of the firm and suppose that IT presents the intended interpretation of T. Then some of the components of ω_T may carry names such as "labor" and "fuel"; others may be called "wage of labor" and "price of fuel"; and still others may have names such as "bus mileage" and "technical inefficiency." The members of Γ_t, in turn, may contain interpreted versions of N 1 to N 7 in Chapter 10 and delineate the classes to which the firm's revenue function $H(\cdot)$ and production function $f(\cdot)$ belong. They may insist that $H(y, a) = ay$ and that $f(\cdot)$ is a linearly homogeneous translog function.

It is important to keep in mind that regardless of the names they carry, the designations of the components of ω_T are units of theoretical objects, for example, toys in a toy economy that a demon has designed. All that is known of these objects is that they possess the characteristics on which the members of Γ_t insist.

Let T and IT be as above. The data universe for the empirical analysis of IT is a pair (Ω_P, Γ_p), where Ω_P is a set of vectors ω_P in a real vector space. The components of ω_P denote so many units of the individuals that the econometrician has observed and the data that he has created with them. Also, Γ_p comprises axioms that delineate the salient characteristics of the components of ω_P. When the data-generating process is taken to be random, the data universe forms part of a triple $[(\Omega_P, \Gamma_p), \Im_p, P_p(\cdot)]$, where $\Im_p$ is a family of subsets of Ω_P and $P_p(\cdot) : \Im_p \rightarrow [0, 1]$ is a probability measure. Subject to the conditions on which Γ_p insists, $P_p(\cdot)$ induces a joint probability distribution of the components of ω_P that I denote by FP. In a formalized theory-data confrontation with a random data-generating process, FP plays the role of the *true* probability distribution of the components of ω_p.

Again, let T and IT be as above. The bridge between the theory universe of IT and the corresponding data universe comprises a finite set of assertions. Formally speaking, these principles constitute a family of axioms, $\Gamma_{t,p}$, concerning pairs of vectors (ω_T, ω_P) in a subset Ω of $\Omega_T \times \Omega_P$. The members of $\Gamma_{t,p}$ delineate the way in which the components of ω_T are related to the components of ω_P. These relations reflect the econometrician's own views of the relationship between the variables of IT and his own observations. His views need not be correct. Hence, in any empirical analysis of the relevance of IT, the members of $\Gamma_{t,p}$ are as much under scrutiny as the members of Γ_t and Γ_p.

In reading this description of the three parts of the core structure, several facts should be kept in mind. The families of functions and predicates that constitute the intended interpretation of Γ_t belong to classes of functions and predicates on Ω_T that are described in IT. The families of functions and predicates that the intended interpretation of Γ_P comprises are unrestricted. Moreover, the bridge principles that relate components of ω_T to components of ω_P depend on IT and may depend on the various members of the intended interpretations of Γ_t and Γ_p.

The structure of a theory-data confrontation in which the data-generating process is stochastic has four parts. The first three are the two universes and the bridge between them. The fourth part comprises three elements: a sample population S, a function $\Psi(\cdot) : S \to \Omega$, and a probability measure $P(\cdot) : \aleph \to [0, 1]$ on subsets of Ω. I imagine that the econometrician is sampling individuals in S, for example, firms or historical data. S is usually a finite or a countably infinite set. I associate a pair of vectors $(\omega_{Ts}, \omega_{Ps}) \in \Omega$ with each point $s \in S$. I denote this pair by $\Psi(s)$ and insist that it is the value at s of the function $\Psi(\cdot)$. I also imagine that there is a probability measure $Q(\cdot)$ on a σ-field of subsets of S, $\aleph_S$, that determines the probability of observing an s in the various members of $\aleph_S$. The properties of $Q(\cdot)$ are determined by $\Psi(\cdot)$ and the probability measure $P(\cdot)$ that assigns probabilities to subsets of Ω in $\aleph$. Specifically, $\aleph_S$ is the inverse image of $\aleph$ under $\Psi(\cdot)$, and for all $B \in \aleph$,

$$Q\left[\Psi^{-1}(B)\right] = P\left[(B \cap \text{range}(\Psi)\right] / P\left[\text{range}(\Psi)\right],$$

where $\text{range}(\Psi) = \{\omega \in \Omega : \omega = \Psi(s) \text{ for some } s \in S\}$. Finally, I imagine that the econometrician has obtained a sample of N observations from S, $s_1, \ldots, s_N$, in accordance with a sampling scheme ξ. $P(\cdot)$ and ξ determine a probability distribution on subsets of Ω^N. I denote the marginal distribution of the components of ω_P determined by $P(\cdot)$ and $\Gamma_{t,p}$ by MPD. The marginal distribution of the sequence of ω_{Ps}'s determined by $P(\cdot)$, $\Gamma_{t,p}$, and ξ, I refer to as the pseudo-data-generating process and denote by PDGP.

For future purposes it is important to recall an important characteristic of the relationship between the MPD and the FP from Chapter 11. The intended interpretation of MPD need not contain a model that equals the FP. This is so even when the interpretation of MPD is data admissible in the sense that the interpretation it gives to the logical consequences of the axioms of $P(\cdot)$ and $\Gamma_{t,p}$ is not contradicted by the data. It goes without saying that an interpretation of the PDGP that is generated by ξ and a data-admissible interpretation of MPD need not contain a model that equals the *true* data-generating process either. The latter I identify with the joint distribution of the ω_{Ps}'s that is induced by FP and ξ, and I denote it by DGP.

17.2.2 The Empirical Relevance of Conjectures and Theories

With the preceding formal characterization of the core structure of a theory-data confrontation in hand I can now explain what is meant by saying that a theory is "relevant in a given empirical context." I begin with the empirical context. There are two cases to consider, depending on whether the DGP is taken to be deterministic or stochastic.

The deterministic case: When the DGP is deterministic, the empirical context in which the theory-data confrontation takes place is a pair: an accurate description of a sampling scheme and a family of data-admissible models of the data universe (Ω_P, Γ_p). A model of (Ω_P, Γ_p) is *data admissible* if the actual data in the particular theory-data confrontation satisfy the strictures on which the model insists.

The stochastic case: Strictly speaking, in a formalized economic theory-data confrontation in which the DGP is stochastic, the empirical context in which the theory-data confrontation takes place is a triple: an accurate description of a sampling scheme, the intended interpretation of the data universe (Ω_P, Γ_p), and the *true* probability distribution of the components of ω_P, FP. I refer to this empirical context by the name Real World. The empirical context in which the theory-data confrontation *actually* takes place is a different triple, a not-necessarily accurate description of a sampling scheme, the intended interpretation of (Ω_P, Γ_p), and an interpretation of the marginal probability distribution (MPD) of the components of ω_P. In Chapter 11, I insisted that this empirical context be thought of as one of the worlds in which all the bridge principles are valid. I also insisted that if the econometrician's sampling scheme was adequate and if his MPD is data admissible it makes good sense to assume that the bridge principles are valid in the Real World. In that case, the differences between the FP and the econometrician's MPD notwithstanding, I think of the Real World as the empirical context in which the theory-data confrontation is taking place.

Next, the relevance of an interpreted theory: Let T, IT, and the core structure of a data confrontation of IT be as described above, and let IM_p and IM_{MPD}, respectively, denote the intended family of data-admissible models of the data universe and the MPD. For simplicity I assume that the members of IM_{MPD} are parametric. Next, let $\Im_p$ denote the family of collections of sentences about individuals in the data universe that are logical consequences of Γ_t, Γ_p, and $\Gamma_{t,p}$. There is one collection of such sentences for each member of the intended interpretation of $(\Gamma_t, \Gamma_p, \Gamma_{t,p})$. Finally, let $\Im_{MPD}$ denote the family of collections of sentences about the parameters of the MPD that are logical consequences of Γ_t, Γ_p, $\Gamma_{t,p}$ and the axioms that determine the characteristics of $P(\cdot)$. Each member of $\Im_{MPD}$ is a collection of sentences about the parameters of the MPD that is determined by a member of the intended interpretation of Γ_t, Γ_p, $\Gamma_{t,p}$ and the axioms that determine the characteristics of $P(\cdot)$. Now, *IT is relevant* *in the empirical context that IM_p and IM_{MPD} delineate if and only if there is at least one member of the intended interpretation of Γ_t, Γ_p, $\Gamma_{t,p}$ and the axioms that determine the characteristics of $P(\cdot)$ such that: (1) the corresponding member of $\Im_p$ has a model that is a member of IM_p, and (2) the corresponding member of $\Im_{MPD}$ is valid in some member of IM_{MPD}*. In cases where there is no sample population and no probability measure $P(\cdot)$ on subsets of the sample space, only the first requirement matters.

The relevance criterion on which I insist is strong and as it is unfamiliar it may sound strange, four clarifying remarks are called for.

First, as I mentioned earlier, I do not adopt the idealistic attitude that an econometrician must specify the intended interpretation of (Ω_T, Γ_t) before he looks at the data. *I think it is better to adopt the attitude that an econometrician in a given theory-data confrontation is to search for an interpretation of (Ω_T, Γ_t) that might have empirical relevance*. An interpretation of the theory universe comprises a family of models of Γ_t. The requirement that there be a member of the intended interpretation of Γ_t, Γ_p, $\Gamma_{t,p}$ and the axioms that determine the characteristics of $P(\cdot)$ such that the corresponding members of $\Im_P$ *and $\Im_{MPD}$ are, respectively, valid in some member of IM_P and IM_{MPD}* singles out one model of (Ω_T, Γ_t) that is empirically relevant in the given theory-data confrontation. I believe that the econometrician ought to search for an as large as possible family of models of the theory universe that satisfies conditions (1) and (2) above. As my three examples show, that is easy in some cases and a daunting task in others.

Second, in theory-data confrontations in which $\Gamma_{t,p}$ has many models it is often the case that the econometrician ends up checking whether there is a model of $\Gamma_{t,p}$ that allows him to conclude that his theory has empirical relevance. This may sound strange, but is in accord with the two conditions of empirical relevance that I delineated earlier. The first example in Section 17.3 demonstrates what I have in mind.

Third, I have adopted my collaborators' idea that in each theory-data confrontation in which a sample population S and a probability measure $P(\cdot)$ on subsets of the sample space Ω figure, there is a true probability distribution of the components of ω_P, FP, and a true data-generating process. The econometrician does not know the details of FP. However, *ideally the family of models of the MPD in IM_{MPD} is meant to represent a set of possible data-admissible probability distributions of the components of ω_P that he believes has a high probability of containing a model of MPD whose parameters equal the corresponding parameters of the FP*. The third example in Section 17.3 shows the import of this remark, and the discussion in Section 11.5.4 about the existence of data admissible *MPD*s describes the difficulties that the idea faces in large samples.

Fourth, in a given situation the econometrician might not be able to check whether a member of IM_p is a model of all the sentences in the relevant member of $\Im_p$. Even when, in principle, he could check them all, he might not have the time and/or the resources to do it, and if he has the time and the resources, he might find that many of the checks are inconclusive. Certainly, they are likely to be inconclusive for most for-all sentences. Similarly, based on statistical estimates, attempts to make sure that a member of $\Im_{MPD}$ is valid in some member of IM_{MPD} are also likely to be inconclusive. Thus in most theory-data confrontations an econometrician is hard put to find an empirical context in which he can establish the relevance of a given IT. The best he can hope for are good statistical grounds for accepting or rejecting the relevance of an interpreted economic theory.

One aspect of my characterization of "relevance in an empirical context" in particular ought not go unnoticed. The family of sentences in $\Im_p$ and $\Im_{MPD}$ comprises all the sentences on whose validity the relevance of IT in the given empirical context depends. Note, therefore, that this family varies with $\Gamma_{t,p}$ and the axioms that determine the properties of $P(\cdot)$. Moreover, the collection of sentences in $\Im_p$ and $\Im_{MPD}$ to which conditions (1) and (2) refer need not contain all the sentences about the data universe and the parameters of MPD that are valid in the associated members of IM_p and IM_{MPD}. This is so because a finite set of axioms such as Γ_t, $\Gamma_{t,p}$, Γ_p and the axioms for $P(\cdot)$ might not suffice to give a complete characterization of a given empirical context.

When an econometrician, in accordance with my formal scheme, writes down axioms for testing the empirical relevance of an interpretation of an economic theory, only a few of them pertain to the theory itself. Consequently, on the surface of things it looks as though the prescriptions of my scheme always lead him to conduct tests on the basis of which he can never conclusively falsify the hypotheses being tested. But appearances can be deceiving. In the test of the permanent-income hypothesis that I describe in Section 17.5, I manage to isolate the theoretical hypothesis in such a way that, for any given sample population, the test has the power of statistics to reject the empirical relevance of the theoretical hypothesis. Hence, a judicious application of my formal scheme may help scientists circumvent the trap Duhem warns us about.

17.3 THREE EXAMPLES

It is easy to imagine tests of hypotheses in theory-data confrontations. However, as it is difficult to fathom all the details that make up a mathematical formalization of the corresponding empirical analysis, I discuss next three simple examples. In the first I present a theoretical hypothesis and formulate a test of its empirical relevance. In the second I complete the analysis that I began in Chapters 10 and 11 of Heckscher and Ohlin's conjecture and its empirical relevance for Norwegian trade flows. In the third I conclude the empirical analysis of Friedman's permanent-income hypothesis that I began in Chapters 10 and 11 and explore the possibility of finding ways to circumvent the Duhem trap.

Each of the three examples has distinguishing characteristics that one should be aware of. In the first, there is no sample population and no $P(\cdot)$. Moreover, Γ_t has only one model and Γ_p has an easily recognizable family of data-admissible models. In the second, there is also no sample population and no $P(\cdot)$. However, there is one model of Γ_P and many possible models of Γ_t, and the intended interpretation of Γ_t is hard to describe. In the third, there is a sample population and a $P(\cdot)$, and, further, the members of IM_p and IM_{MPD} determine what is to be the relevant family of models of Γ_t. Finally, the bridge principles in the first example are independent of the models of Γ_t and Γ_p; those in the second vary with the models of Γ_t; and the bridge principles in the third example vary with the parameters of MPD.

17.3.1 The Expected Utility Hypothesis

I believe that individuals rank random prospects according to their expected utility and that individual utility functions are linear. I also believe that people tend to overvalue low probabilities and undervalue high ones. To test these hypotheses I face a student with a large number N of simple prospects, ask for his certainty equivalents of these prospects, and construct his utility function.

The axioms of my test concern one undefined term, *the sample space* Ω, that must satisfy the following set of axioms. The definitional axiom is as follows:

U 1 *There are sets* Ω_T *and* Ω_P *of ordered* $(2N+1)$*-tuples,* ω_T *and* ω_P*, such that* $\Omega \subset \Omega_T \times \Omega_P$.

The Γ_t axioms are:

U 2 $\omega_T \in \Omega_T$ *only if* $\omega_T = (p, x, U)$*, where* $(p, x) \in ([0, 1] \times [0, 1{,}000])^N$ *and* $U(\cdot) : [0, 1{,}000] \rightarrow [0, 1]$.

U 3 *For all* $\omega_T \in \Omega_T, U(x_i) = p_i, i = 1, \ldots, N$*, where* (p_i, x_i) *is the* i*th component of* (p, x).

U 4 *For all* $\omega_T \in \Omega_T, x_i = 1{,}000p_i, i = 1, \ldots, N$.

The Γ_p axioms are:

U 5 $\omega_P \in \Omega_P$ *only if* $\omega_P = (q, z, W)$*, where* $(q, z) \in ([0, 1] \times [0, 1{,}000])^N$ *and* $W(\cdot) : [0, 1{,}000] \rightarrow [0, 1]$.

U 6 *For all* $\omega_P \in \Omega_P, W(z_i) = q_i, i = 1, \ldots, N$*, where* (q_i, z_i) *is the* i*th component of* (q, z).

The $\Gamma_{t,p}$ axioms are:

U 7 *For all* $(\omega_T, \omega_P) \in \Omega$, $x_i = z_i$, $i = 1, \dots, N$.

U 8 *There is an* $\alpha \in (0, 0.5]$ *such that for all* $(\omega_T, \omega_P) \in \Omega$ *and* $i = 1, \dots, N$,

$$p_i = \begin{cases} \alpha + \alpha^{-2}(q_i - \alpha)^3 & \text{if } 0 \leq q_i \leq \alpha. \\ \alpha + (1-\alpha)^{-2}(q_i - \alpha)^3 & \text{if } \alpha < q_i \leq 1. \end{cases}$$

In the interpretation of the Γ_t axioms that I intend, $U(\cdot)$ is the utility function of a student, p_i is the student's perceived probability, and x_i is his certainty equivalent of a random prospect that promises 1,000 with (perceived) probability p_i and 0 with (perceived) probability $(1 - p_i)$. With this interpretation of $U(\cdot)$, p, and x, it follows from U 3 and U 4 that for all $\omega_T \in \Omega_T$ and $i = 1, \dots, N$, $U(x_i) = x_i/1{,}000$.

In the intended interpretation of the Γ_P axioms, q_i is a probability with which I describe random prospects to my student, that is, 1,000 with probability q_i and 0 with probability $(1 - q_i)$. Also, for each q_i, z_i is the certainty equivalent of a random prospect that the student records. Finally, $W(\cdot)$ is the utility function that I construct on the basis of the student's responses to my q's.

In the interpretation of the $\Gamma_{t,p}$ axioms that I intend, U 8 describes how a student's perceived probabilities vary with quoted probabilities. The axiom delineates one way in which he might overvalue low probabilities and undervalue high ones. Finally U 7 insists that I obtain accurate observations on x.

From the preceding axioms I derive T 1 to test the empirical relevance of U 2–U 4. This theorem is a proposition concerning individuals in Ω_P.

T 1 *Let* $\alpha \in (0, 0.5]$ *be the* α *of U 8. Then, for all* $(\omega_T, \omega_P) \in \Omega$ *and* $i = 1, \dots, N$.

$$W(z_i) = \begin{cases} \alpha\left(1 + [(z_i - 1{,}000\alpha)/1{,}000\alpha]^{1/3}\right) & \text{if } 0 \leq z_i \leq 1{,}000\alpha \\ \alpha\left(1 + ((1-\alpha)/\alpha)\,[(z_i - 1{,}000\alpha)/1{,}000(1-\alpha)]^{1/3}\right) & \text{if } 1{,}000\alpha \leq z_i \leq 1{,}000. \end{cases}$$

This theorem is true in some model of U 5 and U 6 but not in all models of these axioms. Also T 1 is true in all models of U 1–U 8. Hence, I can use T 1 to test the empirical relevance of U 2–U 4 by checking whether T 1 is true in one of the data-admissible models of Γ_p that the intended interpretation of (Ω_P, Γ_p) contains. The intended interpretation of (Ω_P, Γ_p) in the present case is determined by my student's responses to my queries. A member of this interpretation is a model of Ω_P that contains the N values of q_i that I quoted, the corresponding certainty equivalents z_i that my student recorded, and a function $W(\cdot) : [0, 1{,}000] \to [0, 1]$ that satisfies the conditions $W(z_i) = q_i$, $i = 1, \dots, N$.

If there is no model of $\Gamma_{t,p}$, that is, if there is no $\alpha \in (0, 0.5]$ such that T 1 is valid in a member of the intended interpretation of (Ω_P, Γ_p), I must conclude that IT, $\Gamma_{t,p}$, or both lack relevance in the given empirical context.

The theory-data confrontation in the preceding example speaks for itself. Still a remark concerning the content of U 8 is called for. The phenomenon that individuals tend to overvalue low probabilities and undervalue high ones has been observed in many experimental studies and is discussed at some length in a survey article by R. D. Luce and P. Suppes (1965, pp. 321–327). By how much perceived and objective probabilities differ and how this difference varies with the characteristics of individuals are less well documented. It is, therefore, interesting that with $\alpha = 0.5$, the way in which perceived and quoted probabilities differ in U 8 accords with the way in which the psychological probabilities of F. Mosteller and P. Nogee's (1951, p. 397) guardsmen differed from the *true* probabilities. Also, with $\alpha = 0.2$, the functional relationship between perceived and quoted probabilities in U 8 is like the functional relationship between psychological and mathematical probabilities in Preston and Baratta (1948, p.188).

In the preceding theory-data confrontation I confronted my hypotheses with the responses of a single student. If I had confronted the same hypotheses with similar responses of n different students, I would have had to introduce a sample population, make assumptions about my sampling scheme, and formulate a statistical test of the hypotheses. For example, I might have agreed to reject the empirical relevance of my hypotheses if more than a suitable fraction of students failed the test.

17.3.2 The Heckscher and Ohlin Conjecture

In Chapters 10 and 11, I proposed axioms for a theory-data confrontation of the Heckscher and Ohlin (H&O) conjecture concerning factor endowments, comparative advantage, and trade flows. In this chapter I search for a way of measuring factor endowments that renders the conjecture empirically relevant for Norwegian trade flows (Heckscher, 1919; Ohlin, 1933).

17.3.2.1 A Recapitulation of Axioms

For ease of reference I begin by reviewing the axioms that I proposed in Chapters 10 and 11. First the axioms of the theory universe:

HO 1 $\omega_T \in \Omega_T$ *only if* $\omega_T = (x^s, x^d, x_3^f, x_4^f, L, K, p, w, q, L_A, K_A, EL_A, EK_A, EL_{TC}, EK_{TC})$, *where* $x^s \in R_+^4, x^d \in R_+^2 \times \{(0,0)\}, x_3^f \in R_+^2, x_4^f \in R_+^2, (L, K) \in R_+^8, p \in R_{++}^4, (w, q) \in R_{++}^2, (L_A, K_A) \in R_{++}^2$, *and* $(EL_A, EK_A, EL_{TC}, EK_{TC}) \in R_{++}^4$.

In the intended interpretation of this axiom, the country concerned, *A*, is a country in trade equilibrium with its trading community *TC*. It produces four commodities, $x_1, \ldots, x_4$, with two primary factors of production: labor and capital. I denote the pair of primary factors used in the production of $x_i, i = 1, \ldots, 4$, by (L_i, K_i) and take L to stand for labor and K for capital.

The first two commodities, x_1 and x_2, are consumables. The last two, x_3 and x_4, are natural resources that are not consumable. The country trades in x_1 and x_2 and uses x_3 and x_4 as factors in the production of x_1 and x_2. I denote by x_{3i}^f and x_{4i}^f the amount of x_3 and x_4 used as factors in the production of x_i, $i = 1, 2$. The symbol p denotes the price of x, the w and q are the wage of labor and the rental price of capital, and L_A and K_A designate country A's current stock of the respective primary factors. Finally, EL_J and EK_J denote country J's endowment of labor and capital, $J = A, TC$.

HO 2 *There is a constant* $\mathrm{a} \in (0, 1)$ *such that for all* $\omega_T \in \Omega_T$, $p_1 x_1^d = a[wL_A + qK_A]$ *and* $p_2 x_2^d = (1 - a)[wL_A + qK_A]$.

HO 3 *There are positive constants* a_{ki}, $k = 3, 4, L, K$, *and* $i = 1, \ldots, 4$, *such that for all* $\omega_T \in \Omega_T$, $x_i^s = \min\left\{(L_i/a_{Li}), (K_i/a_{Ki}), \left(x_{3i}^f/a_{3i}\right), \left(x_{4i}^f/a_{4i}\right)\right\}, i = 1, 2$, *and* $x_i^s = \min\{(L_i/a_{Li}), (K_i/a_{Ki})\}, i = 3, 4$.

HO 4 *For all* $\omega_T \in \Omega_T$, $p_1 - p_3 a_{31} - p_4 a_{41} = wa_{L1} + qa_{K1}$, $p_2 - p_3 a_{32} - p_4 a_{42} = wa_{L2} + qa_{K2}$, $p_3 = wa_{L3} + qa_{K3}$, *and* $p_4 = wa_{L4} + qa_{K4}$.

HO 5 *For all* $\omega_T \in \Omega_T$, $x_3^s - x_{31}^f - x_{32}^f = 0$, *and* $x_4^s - x_{41}^f - x_{42}^f = 0$.

HO 6 *For all* $\omega_T \in \Omega_T$, $L_1 + L_2 + L_3 + L_4 \leq L_A$ *and* $K_1 + K_2 + K_3 + K_4 \leq K_A$.

HO 7 *For all* $\omega_T \in \Omega_T$, $p_1 x_1^s + p_2 x_2^s = p_1 x_1^d + p_2 x_2^d$.

HO 8 *For all* $\omega_T \in \Omega_T$, *if* $EL_A/EK_A < (>) EL_{TC}/EK_{TC}$ *and* $[(a_{L1} + a_{L3}a_{31} + a_{L4}a_{41})/(a_{K1} + a_{K3}a_{31} + a_{K4}a_{41})] < [(a_{L2} + a_{L3}a_{32} + a_{L4}a_{42})/(a_{K2} + a_{K3}a_{32} + a_{K4}a_{42})]$, *then* $x_1^s > (<) x_1^d$ *and* $x_2^s < (>) x_2^d$. *Also, if* $EL_A/EK_A < (>) EL_{TC}/EK_{TC}$, *then the preceding condition on the* a_{ki} *coefficients with* $<$ *replaced by* $>$ *implies that* $x_1^s < (>) x_1^d$ *and* $x_2^s > (<) x_2^d$.

These axioms are easy to read, and supplementary commentary can be found in Chapters 10 and 11. Thus, here I need only recall that HO 8 delineates the version of the H&O conjecture that I intend to confront with data. In reading the axiom, note that it is *EL* and *EK*, and not L_A and K_A, on which the validity of the conjecture depends.

Next the five axioms of the data universe:

HO 13 $\omega_P \in \Omega_P$ *only if* $\omega_P = (X^s, X^d, A, M, W, Q, AI, MI, AE, ME, AC, MC, AG, MG, A\sum, M\sum, W\sum, Q\sum, SL, SL\sum, SK, SK\sum, w^*, q^*, B, c, SL\sum_{TC}, SK\sum_{TC}, L^c, K^c, U)$, *where* $X^s \in R_+^5$, $X^d \in R_+^5$, $A = (A_{ij})$ *and* $M = (M_{ij})$ *are, respectively,* 5×5 *and* 4×5 *real-valued matrices with nonnegative components* $W \in R_{++}^5$, $Q \in R_{++}^5$, $AI \in R_+^5$, $MI \in R_+^4$, $AE \in R_+^5$, $ME \in R_+^4$, $AC \in R_+^5$, $MC \in R_+^4$, $AG \in R_+^5$, $MG \in R_+^4$, $A\sum \in R_+^5$, $M\sum \in R_+^4$, $W\sum \in R_{++}$, $Q\sum \in R_{++}$, $(SL, SK) \in R_{++}^{10}$, $(SL\sum, SK\sum) \in R_{++}^2$, $w^* \in R_{++}$, $q^* \in R_{++}$, B *is a* 2×9 *real-valued matrix with nonnegative components,* $c \in R_{++}^4$, $(SL\sum_{TC}, SK\sum_{TC}, L^c, K^c) \in R_{++}^4$, *and* $U \in R^4$.

In the intended interpretation of the axiom, the components of X^s and X^d denote the supply of and the final demand for the products of the respective industries in Z, where $Z = (Z^1, Z^2, Z^3, Z^4, Z^5)$. The components of Q and SL and SK designate, respectively, the gross surplus and the stocks of labor and capital in the respective industries in Z, and $SL \sum_{TC}$ and $SK \sum_{TC}$ and L^c and K^c, respectively, denote the stock of labor and capital in TC and the amount of labor and capital used in the production of X_1^d and X_2^d. Finally, w^* and q^* and U record, respectively, the average wage rate and the average rental price of capital and factors that are not accounted for, B is a matrix of coefficients that are to play a_{ij}'s role in HO 7 in my test of the empirical relevance of the H&O conjecture, and c is a vector of appropriately chosen constants. The remaining components of ω_P are entries in the input-output matrix below. In this matrix, $Z = (Z^1, Z^2, Z^3, Z^4, Z^5)$ as above, and $MZ = (MZ^1, MZ^2, MZ^3, MZ^4)$. Also, MZ^j is short for "imports of products pertaining to industry Z^j," $j = 1, \ldots, 4$, I and E are short for "investment" and "export," C and G are short for "household consumption" and "government," and $\sum$ is short for "sum."

	Z	I	E	C	G	$\sum$
Z	A	AI	AE	AC	AG	$A\sum$
MZ	M	MI	ME	MC	MG	$M\sum$
Wages	W					$W\sum$
Gross surplus	Q					$Q\sum$

HO 14 *For all* $\omega_P \in \Omega_P$, $A_{j1} + A_{j2} + A_{j3} + A_{j4} + A_{j5} + AI_j + AE_j + AC_j + AG_j = A\sum_j, j = 1, \ldots, 5$; $M_{j1} + M_{j2} + M_{j3} + M_{j4} + M_{j5} + MI_j + ME_j + MC_j + MG_j = M\sum_j, j = 1, \ldots, 4$; $W_1 + W_2 + W_3 + W_4 + W_5 = W\sum$; $Q_1 + Q_2 + Q_3 + Q_4 + Q_5 = Q\sum$, $SL_1 + SL_2 + SL_3 + SL_4 + SL_5 = SL\sum$; $SK_1 + SK_2 + SK_3 + SK_4 + SK_5 = SK\sum$; $w^* = W\sum/SL\sum$; *and* $q^* = Q\sum/SK\sum$.

HO 15 *For all* $\omega_P \in \Omega_P$, *the components of* c *and* B *satisfy the relations* $c_i b_{Li} = W_i/A\sum_i$ *and* $c_i b_{Ki} = Q_i/A\sum_i, i = 1, \ldots, 4$, $c_i b_{3i} = A_{3i}/A\sum_i$ *and* $c_i b_{4i} = A_{4i}/A\sum_i, i = 1, 2$, $b_{L5} = W_5/A\sum_5$, $b_{K5} = Q_5/A\sum_5$, *and* $c_i b_{5i} = A_{5i}/A\sum_i, i = 1, \ldots, 4$. *Also, the* c_i *are chosen such that* $(b_{Li}+b_{L5}b_{5i})+(b_{Ki}+b_{K5}b_{5i})+b_{3i}+b_{4i} = 1, i = 1, 2$, *and* $(b_{Li}+b_{L5}b_{5i})+(b_{Ki}+b_{K5}b_{5i}) = 1, i = 3, 4$. *Finally,*

$$B = \begin{pmatrix} b_{L1} & b_{L2} & b_{L3} & b_{L4} & b_{L5} & b_{31} & b_{41} & b_{51} & b_{53} \\ b_{K1} & b_{K2} & b_{K3} & b_{K4} & b_{K5} & b_{32} & b_{42} & b_{52} & b_{54} \end{pmatrix}$$

HO 16 *For all* $\omega_P \in \Omega_P$,

$$X_1^s = A\sum\nolimits_1 - \sum_{1 \le j \le 5} A_{1j} + (AI_4 + AE_4 + AC_4 + AG_4) - M\sum\nolimits_1 - M\sum\nolimits_4$$

and

$$X_1^d = AI_1 + AC_1 + AG_1 + (AI_4 + AC_4 + AG_4),$$

$$X_2^s = A\sum\nolimits_2 - \sum_{1\leq j\leq 5} A_{2j} + (AI_3 + AE_3 + AC_3 + AG_3) - M\sum\nolimits_2 - M\sum\nolimits_3$$

and

$$X_2^d = AI_2 + AC_2 + AG_2 + (AI_3 + AC_3 + AG_3),$$

$$X_3^s = A\sum\nolimits_3 - \sum_{1\leq j\leq 5} A_{3j} - (AI_3 + AE_3 + AC_3 + AG_3) + M\sum\nolimits_3$$

and

$$X_3^d = 0,$$

$$X_4^s = A\sum\nolimits_4 - \sum_{1\leq j\leq 5} A_{4j} - (AI_4 + AE_4 + AC_4 + AG_4) + M\sum\nolimits_4,$$

and

$$X_4^d = 0.$$

I proposed the axioms for the data universe with the idea of testing the empirical relevance of the H&O conjecture for Norwegian trade flows. Hence, the axioms delineate the ways in which I constructed the variables that I needed for the test using data from Statistics Norway. Details concerning the measurement of my test variables can be found in Chapters 10 and 11. Here it is only important to note that a data-admissible model of Γ_p in this case is a set of vectors and matrices that satisfies the axioms and contains the vectors and matrices that constitute my data.

17.3.2.2 The Measurement of Factor Endowments

In HO 12 below I suggest two ways to measure a country's endowments of labor and capital: *EL* and *EK*. There are other ways to measure these variables, and they are all equally controversial. Therefore, I have to discuss the characteristics that measures of factor endowments must have in order to be appropriate for a test of the H&O conjecture.

Constructing appropriate measures for a test of the H&O conjecture is exceedingly difficult. So a thought comes to mind. I could admit that I do not know how to measure factor endowments in a meaningful way and infer the abundant factor in 1997 Norway from the results of my empirical analysis. It might be labor. If it is, the conclusion would not be quite as startling as Leontief's (1953) inference that labor was the abundant factor in 1947 United States. Still, an explanation would require sophisticated economic reasoning. Chances are good that my reasoning would fare no better than Leontief's insistence that labor was at least three times as productive in 1947 United States as it was in the rest of the world. Moreover, no matter how ingenious my arguments, proceeding in Leontief's way would be a bad approach to try the empirical relevance of the H&O conjecture. Therefore, I reject the thought and search for good measures of the endowments of labor and capital in 1997 Norway.

I can measure a country's endowments of labor and capital in many different ways. In the trade model in Section 10.3, the natural candidates for measures of A's factor endowments are L_A, K_A, and the equilibrium values of wL_A and qK_A. From them I obtain four possible measures of the relative abundance in A of the two factors (L_A/K_A), (wL_A/K_A) and (wL_A/qK_A), (L_A/qK_A). In case I (case II) the respective values were $(L_A/K_A) = 0.67(0.67)$, $(wL_A/K_A) = 0.38(0.267)$, $(wL_A/qK_A) = 3.17(1.159)$, and $(L_A/qK_A) = 5.56(2.899)$. The first two measures suggest that capital is the relatively abundant factor in A. The last two indicate that labor is the relatively abundant factor in A.

In international trade it is far from obvious that it is possible to determine the relative abundance of a country's factors of production simply by measuring the country's own stocks of such factors. Hence, the divergent views on the relative abundance of labor and capital in A that I obtained were to be expected. To determine the relative abundance of a factor in one country, I must compare its factor endowments with those of its major trading partners. Thus, in the trade model of Section 10.3 I must compare the measures of relative factor abundance in A with the corresponding measures for B. In case I (case II): $(L_B/K_B) = 1.3\ (1.3)$, $(wL_B/K_B) = 0.74\ (0.52)$, $(wL_B/qK_B) = 6.17\ (2.261)$, and $(L_B/qK_B) = 10.83\ (5.652)$. The first and the last two measures suggest that labor is the abundant factor in B, whereas the second measure insists that capital is the abundant factor in B. Note, therefore, that in all cases the value of the measure in B is larger than the equivalent measure in A. So, no matter how I decide to measure factor endowments in the given trade model, I conclude that labor is the abundant factor in B and capital the abundant factor in A.

When A has more than one trading partner, comparing its factor endowments with those of all of its trading partners need not lead to a meaningful assessment of the relative abundance of A's factors. There is, however, a better way to proceed. With reasonable measures of factor endowments in hand, I can estimate the total endowment of each factor in A's trading community and judge the factor in A that has the largest percentage of this total to be the abundant factor. Then, with TC denoting the trading community and with just two factors of production, L and K, I would judge capital to be the relatively abundant factor in A if the measure of EL_A/EL_{TC} is smaller than the measure of EK_A/EK_{TC}.[1] In HO 12 below I propose two different ways to measure factor endowments. Whether the chosen way of measuring EL and EK makes a difference as far the empirical assessment of the relative abundance of A's two primary factors is a question that I deal with in my empirical analysis of the H&O conjecture.

17.3.2.3 Bridge Principles for a Test of the H&O Conjecture

The bridge principles for the theory-data confrontation of the H&O conjecture are shown below. In reading them, recall that these principles concern vectors in the sample space Ω and that $\Omega \subset \Omega_T \times \Omega_P$. Remember also that the variables in the data universe are variables that I have constructed for the purpose of testing the empirical relevance of the H&O conjecture with Norwegian input-output data. Therefore, the formal appearance of the bridge principles notwithstanding, HO 9–HO 12 describe the way I perceive the relationship between my theory variables and those of the Norwegian data. In reading them, note that I conceive of two possible measures of the endowments of labor and capital.

HO 9 *For all* $(\omega_T, \omega_P) \in \Omega$, $p_j x_j^s = X_j^s - U_j, j = 1, \ldots, 4$, *and* $p_j x_j^d = X_j^d, j = 1, \ldots, 4$.

HO 10 *For all* $(\omega_T, \omega_P) \in \Omega$, $L_A = \sum_{1 \le i \le 5} SL_i$, $wL_A = W\sum$, $K_A = \sum_{1 \le i \le 5} SK_i$, $qK_A = Q\sum$.

HO 11 *For all* $(\omega_T, \omega_P) \in \Omega$, $wa_{Lj}/p_j = b_{Lj} + b_{L5}b_{5j}$, $qa_{Kj}/p_j = b_{Kj} + b_{K5}b_{5j}$, $j = 1, \ldots, 4$, $p_3 a_{3j}/p_j = b_{3j}$, *and* $p_4 a_{4j}/p_j = b_{4j}$, $j = 1, 2$.

HO 12 *Either, for all* $(\omega_T, \omega_P) \in \Omega$,

$$(EL_A, EK_A, EL_{TC}, EK_{TC}) = \left(SL\sum, SK\sum, SL\sum_{TC}, SK\sum_{TC}\right),$$

or for all $(\omega_T, \omega_P) \in \Omega$,

$$(EL_A, EK_A, EL_{TC}, EK_{TC}) = \left(W\sum, Q\sum, L^c, K^c\right).$$

In the intended interpretation of the axioms, the U_j account for matters that I have ignored in my analysis. Note that HO 11 provides an example of bridge principles that vary with models of Γ_t. Note also that it follows from HO 10 that for all $(\omega_T, \omega_P) \in \Omega$, $w = w^*$ and $q = q^*$. In different words, I assume that I have accurate observations on w and q. How L^c and K^c can be used to measure EL_{TC} and EK_{TC} is a question that I return to later.

The bridge principles allow me to establish several interesting properties of the variables in the data universe. I begin with a theorem, T 2, that shows how to use entries in the B matrix to determine the relative factor intensities of the production processes in Z^1 and Z^2. With T 2 and estimates of EL and EK, one can see if the 1997 Norwegian trade flows are in accord with the HO 8 version of the H&O conjecture.

T 2 *If HO 1–HO 7 and HO 9–HO 16 are valid, then for all* $(\omega_T, \omega_P) \in \Omega$ *and* j = 1, 2,

$$\begin{aligned}(w/q)(a_{Lj} + a_{L3}a_{3j} + a_{L4}a_{4j})/(a_{Kj} + a_{K3}a_{3j} + a_{K4}a_{4j}) \\ = \left[(b_{Lj} + b_{L5}b_{5j}) + (b_{L3} + b_{L5}b_{53})b_{3j} + (b_{L4} + b_{L5}b_{54})b_{4j}\right] / \\ \left[(b_{Kj} + b_{K5}b_{5j}) + (b_{K3} + b_{K5}b_{53})b_{3j} + (b_{K4} + b_{K5}b_{54})b_{4j}\right].\end{aligned}$$

Judging from the earlier discussion of factor endowments, it might seem impossible to use input-output tables and data on trade flows and factor endowments in only one country to test the validity of the H&O conjecture. It is, therefore, interesting to note that it is possible when the demand functions of the country in question, A, and its trading partners can be rationalized by one and the same homothetic utility function. In that case capital is the abundant factor in A if and only if $K_A/L_A > K^c/L^c$, where K^c and L^c, respectively, denote the stocks of capital and labor that are needed in A to produce the domestically consumed commodities. I state and prove this proposition in Section 17.3.2.6. I owe the idea of the proposition to Edward Leamer (cf. 1984, pp. 496–498).

In the universe of HO 1–HO 8 both primary factors are fully employed, and K^c and L^c are given by the following two equations:

$$L^c = (a_{L1} + a_{L3}a_{31} + a_{L4}a_{41})x_1^d + (a_{L2} + a_{L3}a_{32} + a_{L4}a_{42})x_2^d$$

and

$$K^c = (a_{K1} + a_{K3}a_{31} + a_{K4}a_{41})x_1^d + (a_{K2} + a_{K3}a_{32} + a_{K4}a_{42})x_2^d.$$

The next theorem shows how to measure qK^c/wL^c in the data universe.

T 3 *If HO 1–HO 7 and HO 9–HO 16 are valid, then for all* $(\omega_T, \omega_P) \in \Omega$,

$$\begin{aligned}(qK^c/wL^c) = \Big\{\big\{a\big[(b_{K1} + b_{K5}b_{51}) + b_{K3}b_{31} + b_{K4}b_{41}\big] \\ + (1-a)\big[(b_{K2} + b_{K5}b_{52}) + b_{K3}b_{32} + b_{K4}b_{42}\big]\big\}/ \\ \big\{a\big[(b_{L1} + b_{L5}b_{51}) + b_{L3}b_{31} + b_{L4}b_{41}\big] \\ + (1-a)\big[(b_{L2} + b_{L5}b_{52}) + b_{L3}b_{32} + b_{L4}b_{42}\big]\big\}\Big\}\end{aligned}$$

The validity of the theorem follows from HO 11 and the easily established equality,

$$\begin{aligned}(qK^c/wL^c) = \Big\{\big\{a\big[(qa_{K1}/p_1) + (qa_{K3}a_{31}/p_1) + (qa_{K4}a_{41}/p_1)\big]p_1x_1^d \\ + (1-a)\big[(qa_{K2}/p_2) + (qa_{K3}a_{32}/p_2) + (qa_{K4}a_{42}/p_2)\big]p_2x_2^d\big\}/ \\ \big\{a\big[(wa_{L1}/p_1) + (wa_{L3}a_{31}/p_1) + (wa_{L4}a_{41}/p_1)\big]p_1x_1^d \\ + (1-a)\big[(wa_{L2}/p_2) + (wa_{L3}a_{32}/p_2) + (wa_{L4}a_{42}/p_2)\big]p_2x_2^d\big\}\Big\}\end{aligned}$$

In this context, T 3 is particularly interesting since $K_A/L_A > K^c/L^c$ if and only if $qK_A/wL_A > qK^c/wL^c$. My observations on $W\sum$ and $Q\sum$, and HO 9 enable me to estimate the value of qK_A/wL_A, and T 3 tells me how to estimate qK^c/wL^c.

17.3.2.4 The Data and the 1997 Norwegian Trade Flows

To try the empirical relevance of the H&O conjecture for the 1997 Norwegian trade flows, I begin by listing the 1997 values of the entries in the input-output matrix in Section 17.3.2.1. The entries are in units of kr. 1.000 and the Z^d column records the sum of the relevant values of I, C, and G:

	Z^1	Z^2	Z^3	Z^4	Z^5	Z^d	Ex
Z^1	78.812.197	70.110.820	876.490	4.721.016	13.698.156	67.112.483	149.405.661
Z^2	82.322.282	196.287.679	1.279.485	15.171.473	38.915.025	303.373.923	88.131.933
Z^3	433.644	2.364.815	179.422	158.211	116.491	260.420	2.012.144
Z^4	1.578.874	16.946.653	120.679	3.439.795	773	15.093.513	167.733.943
Z^5	2.708.902	9.649.769	72.109	1.829.668	2.471.333	47.128.867	632.316
M^1	21.880.912	20.385.020	43.178	213.598	1.365.088	8.489.909	2.729.295
M^2	58.304.804	75.819.366	117.404	5.568.310	13.935.839	144.153.481	6.377.069
M^3	1.923.764	1.131.699	26.661	40.321	1.186	273.369	0
M^4	0	1.433.297	0	0	0	1.559.703	0
W	98.389.000	236.533.000	1.262.000	13.688.000	159.733.000		
Q	84.746.000	206.356.000	1.095.000	159.868.000	21.084.000		

	$A\sum_1$	$A\sum_2$	$A\sum_3$	$A\sum_4$	$A\sum_5$
$A\sum$	447.802.000	890.311.000	5.543.000	216.025.000	268.837.000

	$M\sum_1$	$M\sum_2$	$M\sum_3$	$M\sum_4$	$W\sum_5$
$M\sum$	55.107.000	304.652.000	3.397.000	2.993.000	470.566.000

	U_1	U_2	U_3	U_4	U_5
U	63.065.177	164.829.200	17.853	11.110.770	0

One can use these entries to calculate the values of X_j^s and X_j^d for $j = 1, \ldots, 4$.

	Z^1	Z^2	Z^3	Z^4
X^s	404.319.777	250.558.620	3.414.853	14.103.770
X^d	82.205.996	303.634.343	0	0

These values, the values of the respective U's, and the bridge principles in HO 8 show that

(I) Net exports are positive in Z^1 and negative in Z^2.

Then the B matrix: In computing the values of $b_{ki}, = 1, \ldots, 5$, I have used the following values of $c_i, i = 1, \ldots, 4$:

	Z^1	Z^2	Z^3	Z^4
$c.$	2.2624	1.8282	2.2763	1.2447

	Z^1	Z^2	Z^3	Z^4	Z^5
$b_{L\cdot}$	0.0971	0.1454	0.1000	0.0509	0.5942
$b_{K\cdot}$	0.0836	0.1268	0.0868	0.5945	0.0784
$b_{3\cdot}$	0.0009	0.0008			
$b_{4\cdot}$	0.0046	0.0102			
$b_{5\cdot}$	0.0135	0.0239	0.0092	0	

With the data shown above, the 1997 estimate of the values of the fraction,

$$\left[(b_{Lj} + b_{L5}b_{5j}) + (b_{L3} + b_{L5}b_{53})b_{3j} + (b_{L4} + b_{L5}b_{54})b_{4j}\right] / \left[(b_{Kj} + b_{K5}b_{5j}) + (b_{K3} + b_{K5}b_{53})b_{3j} + (b_{K4} + b_{K5}b_{54})b_{4j}\right],$$

in T 2 equals 1.2057 for $j = 1$ and 1.1884 for $j = 2$. From this and T 2 we infer that

(II) The production of X_1 is relatively labor intensive, and the production of X_2 is relatively capital intensive.

17.3.2.5 The H&O Conjecture and Norwegian Trade Flows

In the earlier discussion of relative factor endowments I considered several measures, for example, (K/L), (K^c/L^c), (qK/wL), and (qK^c/wL^c). Next I use HO 9–HO 12, the two ways of measuring EL and EK in HO 12, and the data I have to determine the empirical relevance of the H&O conjecture for Norwegian trade flows. I begin with $EL = SL\sum$ and $EK = SK\sum$.

CASE I: $EL = SL\sum$ AND $EK = SK\sum$

In 1997 Norway $SL\sum = 2{,}212{,}700$ (in millions of Norwegian kroners) and $SK\sum = 3{,}109{,}342$. So, if it makes sense to measure factor endowments of labor and capital, respectively, by the data-universe's version of L_A and K_A, then

(IIIa) 1997 Norway seems to have had a relative abundance of capital.

However, it makes little sense to try the H&O conjecture solely on the basis of the ratio L_A/K_A. One must compare this ratio with the corresponding one for Norway's trading community. Unfortunately, I do not have the required data for 1997, so I have to be content to recount pertinent details of the factor endowments in Norway and its trading partners in 1975 that Edward Leamer published in 1984.

In his 1984 study, *Sources of International Comparative Advantage,* Leamer carried out an analysis of the 1975 trade flows and endowments of various factors in forty-seven countries based on data that Harry Bowan constructed (cf. Leamer, 1984; Bowan, 1981). Table 17.1 presents the relevant results. In reading the table, note that Leamer's measure of a country's endowment of labor is a measure of the country's stock of labor, that is, of L_A. Also, his measure of a country's endowment of capital is a measure of the value of the country's net stock of capital, that is, of K_A.

TABLE 17.1
Endowment of Labor and Capital in OECD Countries, 1975

Country	Capital	Labor 1	Labor 2	Labor 3	L1 + L2 + L3
Australia	140,302	648.91	5,079.5	35	
Austria	64,792	299.42	2,932.1	20	
Benelux	93,700	464.43	3,385.7	43	
Canada	227,522	1,311.49	8,183.2	57	
Denmark	46,585	342.34	2,037.3	14	
Finland	53,987	329.71	1,902.8	13	
France	525,489	3,215.44	18,933.9	134	
Germany	641,369	3,376.34	24,428.8	168	
Greece	31,620	249.8	2,917.3	658	
Iceland	2,324	14.3	91.1	1	
Ireland	11,105	119.5	1,062.4	7	
Israel	21,006	220.5	873.9	126	
Italy	256,438	1,672.1	18,234.7	916	
Japan	930,860	4,438.5	52,025.7	513	
Korea	22,982	388.2	6,746.4	3552	
Netherlands	121,257	763.6	4,375.4	31	
Norway	53,475	227.5	1,284.3	9	1,520.8
Portugal	16,197	137.6	2,153.2	1,123.21	
Spain	153,243	775	10,572.7	973.36	
Sweden	102,201	694.8	2,911.5	21.77	
Switzerland	95,224	429.1	2,668.2	18.7	
United Kingdom	303,695	3,315.6	22,451.9	155.54	
United States	1,831,020	13,556.4	80,535.7	377.88	
Total	5,746,393	36,990.58	275,787.7	8,967.46	321,745.74

The data in Table 17.1 are from Leamer's Table B.1 (1984, pp. 221–227). According to his Table B.2 (pp. 228–229), capital is measured in millions of U.S. dollars and constitutes an estimate of the net stock of capital for a country. The estimate was obtained by summing gross domestic investment flows over the period 1948–1975 and applying depreciation factors based on the assumed average lifetimes of assets. Furthermore, labor is measured in thousands of economically active members of the relevant populations with labor 1 comprising the "professional technical and related workers," labor 3 comprising the illiterate workers, and labor 2 comprising all the rest. The capital data were derived from the World Bank's 1976 world tables, and the labor data were taken from ILO's 1965–1985 labor force projections.

The data in Table 17.1 suggest that in 1975 capital was the abundant factor in Norway. To wit: With N for Norway and TC for the totality of Norway's trading community,

$$K_N/K_{TC} = 0.009306 \text{ and } L_N/L_{TC} = 0.004727,$$

$$K_N/L_N = 35{,}162.41 \text{ and } K_{TC}/L_{TC} = 17{,}860.04.$$

If this relationship between K_N/L_N and K_{TC}/L_{TC} is not too different from that between the corresponding 1997 factor endowments, one must conclude that the H&O conjecture has little relevance for Norwegian trade flows.

Case II: $EL = L^c$ and $EK = K^c$

To overcome the problem caused by the lack of data on the factor endowments of Norway's trading partners, I adopt Leamer's (1984, p. 2) heroic assumption 6 that the demand functions of the relevant countries can be rationalized by one and the same homothetic utility function. In the case of A and its trading partners, in the intended interpretation of the theory universe the assumption implies that there is a constant $a \in (0, 1)$ and a positive constant s such that with the obvious notation,

$$p_1x_{1A}^d = a(wL_A + qK_A) \text{ and } p_2x_{2A}^d = (1-a)(wL_A + qK_A),$$

$$p_1x_{1TC}^d = a(wL_{TC} + qK_{TC}) \text{ and } p_2x_{2TC}^d = (1-a)(wL_{TC} + qK_{TC}),$$

and

$$\begin{aligned} s &= \left(p_1x_{1A}^d + p_2x_{2A}^d\right) / \left(p_1x_{1TC}^d + p_2x_{2TC}^d\right) \\ &= (wL_A + qK_A)/(wL_{TC} + qK_{TC}) \\ &= \left[\left(wL_{TC}^c\right)\left(L_A/L_{TC}^c\right) + \left(qK_{TC}^c\right)\left(K_A/K_{TC}^c\right)\right] / \left(wL_{TC}^c + qK_{TC}^c\right) \end{aligned}$$

The last equality follows from the fact that in trade equilibrium the Leontief world of the universe of HO 1–HO 8 must be such that $wL_{TC} + qK_{TC} = wL_{TC}^c + qK_{TC}^c$. From it one can deduce that

$$s \in \left[\min\left[\left(L_A/L^c_{TC}\right), \left(K_A/K^c_{TC}\right)\right], \max\left[\left(L_A/L^c_{TC}\right), \left(K_A/K^c_{TC}\right)\right]\right].$$

With similar arguments and the equality $wL_A + qK_A = wL^c_A + qK^c_A$, it follows that

$$s^{-1} \in \left[\min\left[\left(L_{TC}/L^c_A\right), \left(K_{TC}/K^c_A\right)\right], \max\left[\left(L_{TC}/L^c_A\right), \left(K_{TC}/K^c_A\right)\right]\right].$$

Now, in trade equilibrium the Leontief world of the universe of HO 1–HO 8 with Leamer's assumption must be such that

$$L^c_A = sL^c_{TC} \text{ and } K^c_A = sK^c_{TC}.$$

From these equalities, the preceding observations, and simple algebra follows the validity of theorem T 4

T 4 *If HO 1–HO 7 are valid and if demand in* A *and its trading community* TC *can be rationalized by the same utility function, then in the intended interpretation of the axioms it must be the case that either*

$$(L_A/K_A) = \left(L^c_A/K^c_A\right) = (L_{TC}/K_{TC})$$

or

$$(L_A/K_A) < (>) (L_{TC}/K_{TC}) \text{ if and only if } (L_A/K_A) < (>) \left(L^c_A/K^c_A\right).$$

For the country in question, A, in the theory universe of HO 1–HO 8,

$$(q/w)\left[(K_A/L_A) - (K^c/L^c)\right] = \left[(qK_A/wL_A) - (qK^c/wL^c)\right].$$

In the data universe, the value of the right-hand side equals

$$\left[q^* \sum_{\{1\le j\le 5\}} SK_j/w^* \sum_{\{1\le j\le 5\}} SL_j\right] - \Big\{\big\{a\left[(b_{K1} + b_{K5}b_{51}) + b_{K3}b_{31} + b_{K4}b_{41}\right]$$
$$+ (1-a)\left[(b_{K2} + b_{K5}b_{52}) + b_{K3}b_{32} + b_{K4}b_{42}\right]\big\}/$$
$$\big\{a\left[(b_{L1} + b_{L5}b_{51}) + b_{L3}b_{31} + b_{L4}b_{41}\right]$$
$$+ (1-a)\left[(b_{L2} + b_{L5}b_{52}) + b_{L3}b_{32} + b_{L4}b_{42}\right]\big\}\Big\}$$

Now, $[a/(1-a)] = X^d_1/X^d_2$ and $X^d_1/X^d_2 = 0.273$. Thus, $a = 0.21$. This value of a and the estimated values of the components of B imply that the value of the right-hand side of the last difference equals 0.8057. Since the value of this ratio is smaller than the value of the left-hand side of the same difference, 0.8696, one can conclude that

(IIIb) In 1997 Norway capital was the relatively abundant factor of production.

If Leamer's assumption is not too way off the mark, (IIIb) and (I) and (II) above throw doubt on the empirical relevance of the H&O conjecture.

SUMMING UP

It may look as though the conclusion to be drawn from the two case studies is that the H&O conjecture has little empirical relevance for 1997 Norwegian trade flows. However, looks can be deceiving. Testing the empirical relevance of a poorly specified conjecture is difficult. My empirical analysis of the H&O conjecture confronts a family of models of HO 1–HO 8 with data. When formulating these axioms I did not describe the contours of a two-country world economy that would have allowed me to delimit the family of models of the present theory universe. Consequently, I cannot be sure that the estimates of the relevant parameters that my data yield belong to a model of HO 1–HO 8 that pertains to a country in trade equilibrium with the rest of the world.

17.3.3 The Permanent-Income Hypothesis and Duhem's Trap

I conclude this chapter by presenting a statistical test of Friedman's (1957) permanent-income hypothesis. The test has several interesting features. It shows that sometimes seemingly irrelevant outside information can be of use in constructing interesting statistical tests of theoretical hypotheses. It also demonstrates that my scheme for theory-data confrontations might help scientists circumvent the Duhem trap.

17.3.3.1 A Recapitulation of the Axioms

I discussed the axioms of the test in Chapters 10 and 11. For ease of reference I repeat them here with a minimum of commentary. First the axioms for the theory universe:

PIH 1 $\omega_T \in \Omega_T$ *only if* $\omega_T = (r, y_p, y_t, c_p, c_t, A, \alpha, u)$, *where* $(r, y_p, c_p, A) \in R^4_{++}$, $(y_t, c_t, u) \in R^4$, *and* $\alpha \in \{15, 16, \ldots, 100\}$.

PIH 2 *For all* $\omega_T \in \Omega_T$, $y_p = [r/(1+r)]\,A$.

PIH 3 *Let* $\Omega_T(a) = \{\omega_T \in \Omega_T : \alpha = a\}$, *with* $a \in \{15, 16, \ldots, 100\}$. *There exists a function* $k(\cdot) : R_{++} \times \{15, 16, \ldots, 100\} \rightarrow R_{++}$ *such that for all* $\omega_T \in \Omega_T(\alpha)$, $c_p = k(r, \alpha) y_p$.

PIH 4 *Let* $h(\cdot)$ *be defined by*

$$h(\alpha) = \begin{cases} 25 & \text{if } \alpha < 35, \\ 5(i+6)+5 & \text{if } (i+6)5 \leq \alpha < (i+8)5, i = 1, 3, 5, \\ 70 & \text{if } 65 \leq \alpha. \end{cases}$$

Then, for all $\alpha \in \{15, 16, \ldots, 100\}$, $k[r, h(\alpha)] = k(r, \alpha)$, $r > 0$.

In reading these axioms again, recall that the relation $y_p = [r/(1+r)]\,A$ is intended to provide a definition of y_p that is not at stake in the test of Friedman's permanent-income hypothesis.

The axioms concerning the data universe, PIH 8–PIH 10, concern many variables only three of which, c_3, y_3, and w_2 are relevant for the present analysis. Since I can be certain that my data satisfy the axioms, I only paraphrase the relevant parts of PIH 8–PIH 10 here.

PIH 8–10 $\omega_P \in \Omega_P$ *only if* $\omega_p = (e_2, y_3, c_3, w_2)$, *where* $(y_3, c_3) \in R_+^2$, $w_2 \in R$, *and* $e_2 \in \{15, \ldots, 100\}$.

Next, the bridge principles:

PIH 5 *For all* $\omega \in \Omega$, $\alpha = e_2$. *There also exists a function* $q(\cdot) : \{25, 40, \ldots, 70\} \to R$ *such that for all* $\omega \in \Omega$, $w_2 = q\,[h(\alpha)] + A + u$.

PIH 6 *For all* $\omega \in \Omega$, $c_3 = c_p + c_t$, *and* $y_3 = y_p + y_t$.

PIH 7 *Let* $G = \{25, 40, 50, 60, 70\}$ *and let* $\Omega(g) = \{\omega \in \Omega : h(\alpha) = g\}$, $g \in G$. *There exists a positive constant* r_g *such that for all* $\omega \in \Omega(g)$, $r = r_g$ *and* $\left[(1 + r_g)/r_g\right] = b_3$, *where* b_3 *is a parameter of the joint distribution of* c_3, y_2, w_2, *and* y_p *that I specify in T 3(ii) below.*

In reading these bridge principles again, recall that the relation between w_2 and A that they specify is irrelevant for the permanent-income hypothesis. Still, with the observations on w_2, the relation enables one to formulate an interesting statistical test of Friedman's hypothesis.

Then the axioms for the probability measure $P(\cdot) : \aleph \to [0, 1]$ on subsets of Ω:

PIH 11 *For each* $g \in G$, $\Omega(g) \in \aleph$ *and* $P[\Omega(g)] > 0$. *Moreover, relative to* $P\left[\cdot \mid \Omega_g)\right]$, *the variances of* y_p, y_t, c_p, *and* c_t *are positive and finite and the covariances of the pairs* (y_t, y_p), (y_p, c_t), (c_p, y_t), *and* (c_t, y_t) *are zero,* $g \in G$.

PIH 12 *Relative to* $P\left[\cdot \mid \Omega(g)\right]$, *the variance of* u *is positive and finite and the covariances of the pairs* (u, A), (u, y_t), (u, c_p), *and* (u, c_t) *are zero,* $g \in G$.

PIH 13 *Relative to* $P\left[\cdot \mid \Omega(g)\right]$, *the means of* y_t, c_t, *and* u *are zero and the means of* y_p, c_p, *and* w_2 *are positive,* $g \in G$.

17.3.3.2 The Mean and Covariance Structure of MPD

The axioms for $P(\cdot)$ concern only the means and covariances of the components of ω_T. Hence, from the $P(\cdot)$ axioms and the bridge principles I can only determine the mean and covariance structure of the *MPD* in the empirical analysis of the PIH. The mean and covariance structure of *MPD* has interesting characteristics. For example, for all $g \in G$, that is, in all age groups, the variances of

c_3, y_3, and w_2 are positive and finite, the means of c_3, y_3, and w_2 are positive, and the covariances of the pairs (c_3, y_3), (c_3, w_2), and (y_3, w_2) are finite. With the added help of PIH 2, I can show that the mean and covariance structure of the *MPD* must also satisfy the conclusions of T 5 and T 6.

T 5 *Suppose that PIH 1, PIH 2, and PIH 5–PIH 13 are valid. Also, for each* $g \in G$, *let* $E\{\cdot \mid g\}$ *and* $\sigma^2(\cdot \mid g)$, *respectively, denote the expectation and variance of* $(\cdot)$ *with respect to* $P[\cdot \mid \Omega(g)]$. *Then, for each* $g \in G$,

(i) $E\{c_3 \mid g\} = E\{c_p \mid g\}$ *and* $E\{y_3 \mid g\} = E\{y_p \mid g\}$. *Also,* $\sigma^2(c_3 \mid g) = \sigma^2(c_p \mid g) + \sigma^2(c_t \mid g)$ *and* $\sigma^2(y_3 \mid g) = \sigma^2(y_p \mid g) + \sigma^2(y_t \mid g)$.

(ii) *There exist pairs of constants* (a_i, b_i), $i = 1, 2, 3$, *and a triple of random variables* ξ_1, ξ_2, *and* ξ_3 *that have mean zero and finite variance are orthogonal to* y_p *and satisfy the equations* $c_3 = a_1 + b_1 y_p + \xi_1$, $y_3 = a_2 + b_2 y_p + \xi_2$, $w_2 = a_3 + b_3 y_p + \xi_3$, *with* $a_2 = 0$, $b_2 = 1$, $\xi_2 = y_t$, $E\{\xi_1\xi_2 \mid g\} = E\{\xi_2\xi_3 \mid g\} = 0$, $E\{\xi_3\xi_1 \mid g\} = 0$, *and* $\xi_3 = u$.

T 6 *Let* $a = (a_1, a_2, a_3)'$, $b = (b_1, b_2, b_3)'$, *and* $\xi = (\xi_1, \xi_2, \xi_3)'$ *be as in T 5. Also, let* $x = (c_3, y_3, w_2)'$, $M_x^g = E\{xx' \mid g\}$, $\sum^g = E\{(x - E\{x \mid g\})(x' - E\{x' \mid g\}) \mid g\}$, *and* $\Psi^g = E\{\xi\xi' \mid g\}$. *Finally, recall that* a, b, *and* ξ *vary with* g, *and suppose that the conditions PIH 1, PIH 2, and PIH 5–PIH 13, are valid. Then, for each* $g \in G$,

(i) $a = (a_1, 0, a_3)'$, $b = (b_1, 1, b_3)'$, *and* Ψ^g *is diagonal.*

(ii) $E\{x \mid g\} = a + bE\{y_p \mid g\}$.

(iii) $M_x^g = aa' + (ba' + ab')E\{y_p \mid g\} + bb'E\{y_p^2 \mid g\} + \Psi^g$.

(iv) $\sum^g = bb'\sigma^2(y_p \mid g) + \Psi^g$.

In reading theorems T 5 and T 6, it is important to keep in mind that the validity of the theorems depends on the validity of PIH 1, PIH 2, PIH 8–PIH 10, the axioms for $P(\cdot)$, and the given bridge principles. I have derived the conditions of T 5 and T 6 without making use of PIH 3 and PIH 4. Hence, the empirical relevance of the theorems is independent of the validity of the permanent-income hypothesis.

To generate estimates of the T 6 parameters, I must add one more axiom for $P(\cdot)$.

PIH 14 *For each* g, $g = 25, 40, \ldots, 70$, *and relative to* $P[\cdot \mid \Omega(g)]$, *the probability distribution of* (c_3, y_3, w_2) *has finite fourth-order moments.*

This axiom differs from the other $P(\cdot)$ axioms in that it concerns components of ω_P rather than those of ω_T. There is a good reason for that. I believe that as long as I do not impose a structure on the fourth-order moments of *MPD*, the assumption that the *MPD* has finite fourth-order moments is innocuous. PIH 14 concerns the probability distribution of c_3, y_3, and w_2 rather than c_p, c_t, y_p, y_t, and u to avoid imposing a structure on the fourth-order moments of y_3, c_3, and w_2.

17.3.3.3 An Adequate Sampling Scheme

In addition to PIH 1–PIH 14, I must formalize axioms that characterize the Federal Reserve Board (FRB) sampling scheme:

PIH 15 *Let* τ_i *be one of the numbers, \$3,000, \$5,000, \$7,500, \$10,000, \$15,000, \$25,000, \$50,000, and \$100,000, with* $\tau_1 < \tau_2 < \ldots < \tau_8$. *Moreover, let* I_i *be defined by*

$$I_1 = \{(\omega_T, \omega_P) \in \Omega : y_3 < \tau_1\},$$

$$I_2 = \{(\omega_T, \omega_P) \in \Omega : \tau_{i-1} \leq y_3 < \tau_i\}, i = 2, \ldots, 8,$$

and

$$I_9 = \{(\omega_T, \omega_P) \in \Omega, y_3 \geq \tau_8\}.$$

Then $I_i \in \aleph$ and $P(I_i) > 0, i = 1, \ldots, 9$. Also, $P[I_i \cap \Omega(g)] > 0$ for all $(i, g) \in \{1, \ldots, 9\} \times G$.

PIH 16 *There are observations on* N *consumers with* n_i *observations from* $I_i, i = 1, \ldots, 9$. *The probability distribution of the sample is given, in short-hand* (!), *by* $\Pi_{1 \leq i \leq 9} [P(\cdot \mid I_i)]^{n_i}$, *where* $P(\cdot \mid I_i)$ *denotes the conditional probability measure on* Ω *given* I_i.

Axioms PIH 15 and PIH 16 describe characteristics of the FRB sampling scheme on which my test of Friedman's hypothesis is based. The researchers at the FRB intended the $n_i, i = 1, \ldots, 9$, in PIH 16 to equal 400. Instead they obtained sample sizes ranging from 385 for $i = 3$ to 453 for $i = 5$. I ignore this feature of the actual sampling scheme and assume that the FRB scheme was part of a larger one in which for all $g = 25, 40, \ldots, 70$, and $i = 1, \ldots, 9$,

$$\lim_{n \to \infty} n [I_i \cap \Omega(g)] / n = P [I_i \mid \Omega(g)]. \quad (1)$$

Here n and $n [I_i \cap \Omega(g)]$, respectively, designate the number of individuals in age group g and the number who belong to both age group g and income group i. This assumption ensures that the standard estimates of the means, variances, and covariances of *FP* are consistent. Since *MPD* is data admissible only if the estimates of these moments satisfy the strictures on which T 6 insists, Eq. (1) also ensures that my estimates of the T 6 parameters of a data-admissible *MPD* are consistent. To ensure that the same estimates in the limit are normally distributed, I assume in addition that for all $g = 25, 40, \ldots, 70$, and $i = 1, \ldots, 9$,

$$\lim_{n \to \infty} n^{1/2} \big\{ \{n [I_i \cap \Omega(g)] / n\} - P [I_i \mid \Omega(g)] \big\} = 0. \quad (2)$$

If PIH 15–PIH 16 provides an adequate description of the FRB sampling scheme, then Eqs. (1) and (2) ensure that the sampling scheme in my empirical analysis of PIH is adequate. The adequacy of PIH 15 and PIH 16 is not obvious. I have formulated PIH 15 in terms of the 1963 incomes of the sample consumers. The FRB researchers stratified their sample according to the 1960 incomes of their sample consumers. Moreover, PIH 16 describes characteristics of a stratified random sampling scheme. The FRB researchers sampled their population without replacement. As long as my data satisfy the two axioms as stated, *the noted inaccuracies make no difference as far as the data admissibility of my estimates is concerned.* My data satisfy PIH 15 and the first of the two strictures of PIH 16 by construction. Further, in the intended interpretation of PIH 1–PIH 16, my data satisfy the second stricture of PIH 16 to any degree of approximation. In the interpretation of the axioms that I intend, *S* is a population of actual and hypothetical consumers in 1962 United States. The actual consumers are those on whom I have data and the other U.S. consumers alive in 1962. The hypothetical consumers are the consumers that the actual consumers could have been if the conditions under which they lived had been different. But if that is so, the number of members of *S* is so large that the FRB sampling scheme can be likened to a stratified random sampling scheme in accord with PIH 16.

17.3.3.4 Estimates of the Mean and Covariance Structure of the MPD

In any data-admissible interpretation of the axioms PIH 1, PIH 2, and PIH 5–PIH 14, the mean and covariance structure of the *MDP*, as indicated in T 5 and T 6, can be estimated with standard factor-analytic methods. I used the LISEREL program to estimate the pertinent parameters. Table 17.2 presents

TABLE 17.2
Factor-Analytic Estimates with Bootstrap Standard Errors

Age group	b_1	$\sigma^2_{y_p} 10^{-8}$	$\sigma^2_{y_t} 10^{-8}$	a_1	$10^{-4}\mu_c$	$10^{-4}\mu_y$	χ^2	d.fr.
< 35	1.6994	0.0955	0.0782	−5402	0.5547	0.6443	0	362
	(0.568)	(0.046)	(0.044)	(260)				
35–44	7.1114	0.4640	1.2566	−69091	1.3735	1.1647	8.4069	408
	(4.286)	(0.242)	(0.452)	(4070)				
45–54	2.0647	2.2128	1.8128	−14046	1.6443	1.4767	0	426
	(1.066)	(1.598)	(0.457)	(1800)				
55–64	1.8760	3.1757	2.5346	−14307	1.7867	1.7150	0	403
	(0.835)	(1.573)	(1.364)	(1890)				
≥ 65	1.4664	5.5672	0.4727	−4883	1.6412	1.4523	0	313
	(0.282)	(1.408)	(0.402)	(1950)				
All	2.1221	2.0616	1.5526	−13464	1.4098	1.2988	0	1912
	(0.505)	(0.498)	(0.354)	(800)				

Source: Data from Tables 27.1, 27.2, and 27.5 in Stigum (1990).

a record of some of the results that concern c_3 and y_3. The standard errors in the table are bootstrap estimates that Petter Laake generated for me. Also, the χ^2, μ_c, and μ_y columns, respectively, show the estimated values of the χ^2 variable in LISEREL's factor-analysis program and the sample means of c_3 and y_3. Mathematical details concerning Laake's bootstrap estimates and the asymptotic distribution of the LISEREL parameter estimates in Tables 17.2 and 17.3 can be found in Stigum (1990, pp. 689–691, 709–719).

In a data-admissible model of PIH 1, PIH 2, PIH 5–PIH 14, the LISEREL estimates of the parameters that concern the distribution of w_2 carry interesting information. For example, from the estimate of b_3 and the equation $\left[(1+r_g)/r_g\right] = b_3$ I obtain an estimate of r_g for all age groups. These estimates of r_g can be interpreted so as to record the mean rate of time preference of the various age groups. Similarly, from the equations

$$q(g) = a_3$$

and

$$\begin{aligned} E\left[w_2 \mid \Omega(g)\right] &= q(g) + [(1+r_g)/r_g)E[y_p \mid \Omega(g)] \\ &= q(g) + E\left[A \mid \Omega(g)\right], \end{aligned}$$

I find that, for all age groups,

$$\begin{aligned} -a_3/E[w_2 \mid \Omega(g)] &= E(A - w_2 \mid \Omega(g)]/E[w_2 \mid \Omega(g)]. \\ &= E(\text{human wealth} \mid \Omega(g))/E[\text{nonhuman wealth} \mid \Omega(g)]. \end{aligned}$$

TABLE 17.3
Factor-Analytic Estimates of the Rate of Time Preference and the Human-Nonhuman Wealth Ratio

Age group	$10^{-4}\mu_w$	$10^{-4}a_3$	b_3	r_g	$[E(A-w_2\|g)/E(w_2\|g)]$	d.fr.
< 35	0.8970	−7.0076	12.2689	0.0887	7.8126	362
		(0.2264)	(0.7738)			
35–44	10.7684	−81.4855	79.2077	0.0128	7.5671	408
		(4.4029)	(6.4702)			
45–54	13.9745	−34.4984	32.8252	0.0314	2.4687	426
		(2.2643)	(1.9000)			
55–64	32.3511	−94.3699	73.8885	0.0137	2.9171	403
		(6.9248)	(4.8157)			
≥ 65	31.3004	−22.7029	37.1841	0.0276	0.7253	313
		(4.263)	(2.3107)			
All	17.5240	−52.4838	53.9038	0.0189	2.9950	1912
		(1.8635)	(1.8162)			

Source: Data from Table 27.2 in Stigum (1990).

I obtain an estimate of the right-hand side of the last equation by substituting the sample mean of w_2, μ_w, for $E\,[w_2 \mid \Omega(g)]$ in the respective age groups. This estimate and estimates of some of the other parameters in the distribution of w_2 are shown in Table 17.3. There the numbers in parentheses are LISEREL (not bootstrap) estimates of the standard errors of the respective parameter estimates.

There are interesting relationships among c_3, w_2, and y_3 that are not depicted either in Tables 17.2 and 17.3 or in T 6. Some of them play an important role in the test of Friedman's hypothesis. So, for ease of reference, I have shown their values in Table 17.4, where β is the regression coefficient in the regression of c_3 on y_3 in the gth age group. Thus, for all $\omega_P \in \Omega_P$, $c_3 = \alpha + \beta y_3 + \eta$, $E[\eta \mid \Omega(g)] = 0$, $E[\eta y_3 \mid \Omega(g)] = 0$, and $E[c_3 \mid \Omega(g)] = \alpha + \beta E[y_3 \mid \Omega(g)]$. Similarly, φ is the regression coefficient in the gth age group of w_2 on y_3. Thus, for all $\omega_P \in \Omega_P$, $w_2 = \gamma + \varphi y_3 + \zeta$, $E\,[\zeta \mid \Omega(g)] = 0$, $E\,[\zeta y_3 \mid \Omega(g)] = 0$, and $E\,[w_2 \mid \Omega(g)] = \gamma + \varphi E\,[y_3 \mid \Omega(g)]$.

If I let $\Phi = \left[\sigma^2(y_p \mid g)/(\sigma^2(y_p \mid g) + \sigma^2(y_t \mid g)\right]$, I can show that in any data-admissible interpretation of PIH 1, PIH 2, and PIH 5–PIH 14, $\beta = b_1\Phi$ and $\varphi = b_3\Phi$. Hence, in any data-admissible interpretation of PIH 1, PIH 2, and PIH 5–PIH 14, $\beta < b_1$ and $\varphi < b_3$ if and only if $\sigma^2(y_t \mid g) > 0$. For ease of reference, I show the estimated values of a_1, b_1, b_3, and the ratio of the sample means of c_3 and y_3, μ_c/μ_y, in Table 17.4.

TABLE 17.4
Factor-Analytic Estimates versus Least Squares Estimates of *MPD* Parameters

Age group	b_1	b_3	Φ	β	φ	μ_c/μ_y	a_1
< 35	1.6994	12.2689	0.5497	0.9342	6.7442	0.8609	−5,402
	(0.568)	(0.7738)					(260)
35–44	7.1114	79.2077	0.2697	1.6015	"21.3623"	1.1793	−69,091
	(4.286)	(6.4702)					(4,070)
45–54	2.0647	32.8252	0.5497	1.1351	18.0440	1.1135	−14,046
	(1.066)	(1.9000)					(1,800)
55–64	1.8760	73.8885	0.5561	1.0433	41.0893	1.0418	−14,307
	(0.835)	(4.8157)					(1,890)
≥ 65	1.4664	37.1841	0.9217	1.3516	34.2726	1.1301	−4,883
	(0.282)	(2.3107)					(1,950)
All	2.1221	53.9032	0.5704	1.2105	30.7464	1.0855	−13,464
	(0.505)	(1.8162)					(800)

Source: Data from Tables 27.1, 27.2, and 27.5 in Stigum (1990).

17.3.3.5 A Statistical Test of Friedman's Hypothesis

I am confronting a family of models of Friedman's hypothesis with data. It might be natural to delineate the contours of this family of models before I look at my data. Instead I allow the data to determine the extent of a family of models of (Ω_T, Γ_t) whose empirical relevance it does not reject. The models of Friedman's hypothesis depend on the range of values that two parameters r and $k(r, \alpha)$ may assume. I let a family of data-admissible interpretations of the *MPD* determine an empirically relevant range of values of these parameters.

With T 6 in hand I can describe the family of models of the *MPD*—one for each age group—with which I try the empirical relevance of the permanent-income hypothesis. Let MPD_g^0 be an *MPD* in a data-admissible interpretation of PIH 1, PIH 2, and PIH 5–PIH 14 for the gth age group, and denote the corresponding estimates of the parameters in T 6 by a_{gf}, b_{gf}, M_{gf}, $\sum_{gf}$, σ_{gf}, Ψ_{gf}, and μ_{gf}, where σ_{gf} and Ψ_{gf} are, respectively, estimates of $\sigma^2(y_p \mid g)$ and Ψ^g and μ_{gf} denotes the sample mean of x in age group g. Also, let $MPD_g \in PH$ have the meaning that MPD_g is an *MPD* in a data-admissible interpretation of PIH 1, PIH 2, and PIH 5–PIH 14 for the gth age group. Then the sought for family of *MPD*s can be defined as follows:

$\Re^{PIH}(g) = \{MPD_g \in PH$: for which the pertinent MPD_g's values of the components of $(a_g, b_g, M_g, \sum_g, \sigma_g, \Psi_g, \mu_g)$ differ from the corresponding values of $(a_{gf}, b_{gf}, M_{gf}, \sum_{gf}, \sigma_{gf}, \Psi_{gf}, \mu_{gf})$ by less than two standard deviations.

Then $MPD_g^0 \in \Re^{PIH}(g)$. If the MPD_g that my data determine, MPD_g^*, satisfies the condition $MPD_g^* \in PH$, I let MPD_g^* be the sought for MPD_g^0.

In reading this description of $\Re^{PIH}(g)$, note that the family of models of *MPD* that characterizes the empirical context in my test of Friedman's hypothesis consists of probability distributions of c_3, y_3, and w_2 that have finite fourth moments and a factor-analytic mean and covariance structure. Specifically, the respective means are finite and positive, the variances are finite and positive, and the first- and second-order moments satisfy the conditions listed in T 5 and T 6. The members of $\Re^{PIH}(g)$ may have other characteristics as well, but they are entirely irrelevant in this context.

I use Tables 17.2–17.4 to check whether the *MPD* that my data determine, say, MPD_g^*, constitutes a data-admissible interpretation of PIH 1, PIH 2, and PIH 5–PIH 14 for each of the g's in G. The means μ_c and μ_y in Table 17.2 and μ_w in Table 17.3 are finite and positive. Similarly, judging from the factor-analytic estimates of the parameters in T 6 that are shown in Tables 17.2 and 17.3, one sees that the variances of c_3, y_3, and w_2 are finite and positive. Finally, I may insist that $c_p = a_1 + b_1 y_p$ and $c_t = \xi_1$ and assume that the FRB sampling scheme was as described in PIH 15–PIH 16. If I do, I see from the estimates of T 6 parameters in Tables 17.2 and 17.3 that with the single possible

TABLE 17.5
Likely Range of Values of the Rate of Time Preference

Age group	< 35	35–44	45–54	55–64	≥ 65	All
min r_g	0.0830	0.0118	0.0297	0.0129	0.0260	0.0183
r_g estimate	0.0887	0.0128	0.0314	0.0137	0.0276	0.0189
max r_g	0.0953	0.0139	0.0334	0.0147	0.0295	0.0196

exception of the 35–44 age group, the MPD_g^* of the groups in Table 17.2, have the required factor-analytic mean and covariance structure on which PIH 1, PIH 2, and PIH 5–PIH 14 insist. The possibility that the 35–44 age group constitutes an exception is due to the large value of the χ^2-variable of this group in Table 17.2. From this I deduce that if it is the case that the probability distribution of c_3, y_3, and w_2 has finite fourth moments, it is also the case that the $MPDg$'s that my data determine constitute, for the nonexceptional groups, data-admissible interpretations of PIH 1, PIH 2, and PIH 5–PIH 14.

Suppose that PIH 15 and PIH 16 provide an adequate description of the FRB sampling scheme and that Eqs. (1) and (2) are valid. Then I may insist that in each nonexceptional group, the MPD that my data determine, MPD_g^*, satisfies the condition $MPD_g^* \in PH$. Consequently, I can identify MPD_g^* with the MPD_g^0 in the definition of $\Re^{PIH}(g)$ and use $\Re^{PIH}(g)$ with $MPDg^*$ as MPD_g^0 to delineate the contours of an empirically relevant family of models of PIH 1–PIH 4.

The contours of such a family of models of PIH 1–PIH 4 can be described by specifying the allowable values of the r_g and $k(r_g, \alpha)$. The estimates of b_3 and their standard errors that are found in Table 17.3 impose limits on the empirically relevant values of r_g that I show in Table 17.5. In reading the table, note that in each age group, $r_g = [1/(b_3 - 1)]$. Hence, the difference between max r_g and min r_g is not to be identified with two standard errors in the distribution of r_g.

Next I look at the sought for range of values of $k(r, \alpha)$. Now let k_g be the value of $k(r_g, \alpha)$ in age group g, $g = 25, 40, \ldots, 70$. According to PIH 1–PIH 4, PIH 6, and PIH 13,

$$c_3 = k_g y_p + c_t,\ E[c_3 \mid \Omega(g)] = k_g E[y_p \mid \Omega(g)],$$

$$k_g = E[c_3 \mid \Omega(g)]/E(y_p \mid \Omega(g)],$$

and

$$k_g = E\left\{\{c_3 - E\left[c_3 \mid \Omega(g)\right]\}\left\{y_p - E\left[y_p \mid \Omega(g)\right]\right\} \mid \Omega(g)\right\}/\sigma^2(y_p \mid g).$$

Similarly, from T 5 and T 6 it follows that

$$E[c_3 \mid \Omega(g)] = a_1 + b_1 E[y_p \mid \Omega(g)]$$

and that

$$b_1 = E\left\{\{c_3 - E\left[c_3 \mid \Omega(g)\right]\}\left\{y_p - E\left[y_p \mid \Omega(g)\right]\right\} \mid \Omega(g)\right\}/\sigma^2(y_p \mid g).$$

From these equations I deduce that in an empirically relevant interpretation of PIH 3 and PIH 4, it must be the case that

$$k_g \in (b_{1f} - 2\text{st.d.}, b_{1f} + 2\text{st.d.})$$

and that

$$0 \in (a_{1f} - 2\text{st.d.}, a_{1f} + 2\text{st.d.}).$$

Also, since $E\left[y_p \mid \Omega(g)\right] = E\left[y_3 \mid \Omega(g)\right]$, it must be the case that

$$k_g \in (\mu_{cf}/\mu_{yf} - 2\text{st.d.}, \mu_{cf}/\mu_{yf} + 2\text{st.d.}).$$

I do not have an estimate of the standard deviation of the distribution of μ_{cf}/μ_{yf}, so I rephrase the last relation as $(\mu_{cf}/\mu_{yf}) \in (b_{1f} - 2\text{std}, b_{1f} + 2\text{st.d})$, where the std refers to the st.d. of the distribution of b_{1f} in MPD_g^*. Tables 17.6–17.8 relate the three relations for each age group.

TABLE 17.6
Likely Range of Values of the Propensity to Consume

Age group	< 35	35–44	45–54	55–64	≥ 65	All
min k_g	0.5634	0	0	0.206	0.9024	1.1121
k_g estimates	1.6994	7.1114	2.0647	1.8760	1.4664	2.1221
max k_g	2.8354	15.6834	4.1967	3.546	2.0304	3.132

TABLE 17.7
Likely Values of a Critical Parameter

Age group	< 35	35–44	45–54	55–64	≥ 65	All
min a_1	−5,922	−77,231	−17,646	−18,087	−8,783	−15,064
a_1 estimates	−5,402	−69,091	−14,046	−14,307	−4,883	−13,464
max a_1	−4,882	−60,951	−10,446	−10,527	−983	−11,864

TABLE 17.8
Likely Values of a Second Critical Parameter

Age group	< 35	35–44	45–54	55–64	≥ 65	All
min b_{1f}	0.5634	0	0	0.206	0.9024	1.1121
(μ_{cf}/μ_{yf}) estimates	0.8609	1.1793	1.1135	1.0418	1.1301	1.0855
max b_{1f}	2.8354	15.6834	4.1967	3.546	2.0304	3.1321

The meaning of the relations illustrated in Tables 17.5–17.8 requires comment. In an economic theory-data confrontation an econometrician confronts a family of models of the theory with data. In the present case the relevant family of models can be described entirely in terms of regions in R^3 to which the triples $(r_g, 0, k_g)$ belong. Moreover, PIH 1–PIH 4 insist that for a given population, there is a value of $(r_g, 0, k_g)$ for each $g \in G$. I do not know what the values of these parameters are in the 1962 U.S. population. Tables 17.5–17.8 show estimates of the values of the parameters and describe the regions to which their values must belong in order that my data not reject the empirical relevance of Friedman's theory.

The intervals in Tables 17.5–17.8 to which the empirically relevant values of the pertinent parameters belong are wide. It is, therefore, of interest here that if the conditions on $n\,[I_i \cap \Omega(g)]\,/n$ that I listed in Eqs. (1) and (2) are satisfied, then the parameter estimates converge with probability one to their true values and the intervals will shrink so as to contain in the limit just the true values of the parameters of the *MPD*.

I consider that the fact that 0 does not belong to any of the intervals in which a_1 resides implies that PIH 3 and PIH 4 are not relevant in the empirical context of MPD_g^* in any of the nonexceptional groups, owing to the following: The empirical context of MPD_g^* varies with the bridge principles as well as with the axioms for $P(\cdot)$. When I try the empirical relevance of PIH 3 and PIH 4 in the empirical context of MPD_g^*, I use the bridge principles to translate PIH 3 and PIH 4 into terms that the empirical context of MPD_g^* can understand. Hence, since $MPD_g^* \in PH$, I cannot blame the failure of PIH 3 and PIH 4 on the bridge principles. *PIH 3 and PIH 4 are not empirically relevant in the empirical context of the* MPD_g^* *of the nonexceptional groups.* Whether the PIH 3 and PIH 4 are empirically relevant in the 35–44 age group, I cannot say since the MPD_g^* for that group does not satisfy the relation $MPD_g^* \in PH$.

In closing my empirical analysis of Friedman's permanent-income hypothesis I want to stick my neck out and claim that my results for the nonexceptional groups show that judicious use of my scheme for theory-data confrontations may help circumvent the Duhem trap.

17.4 CONCLUDING REMARKS

In looking back at Chapter 17 there are several important things to note. First, the empirical context in which an econometrician tries the relevance of an economic theory consists of two families of models, one for the data universe and one for the *MPD*. The available data determine the content of the intended family of data-admissible models of the data universe and the *MPD*. In considering these models there are two things to keep in mind: (1) The true probability distribution of the components of ω_P, *FP*, is not usually known. At least in ordinary-sized samples, the given family of models of the *MPD* is meant to be one of possible data-admissible models that with high probability contains a model whose parameters have the same values as their aliases in the *FP*. (2) The *MPD* depends on the bridge principles. Consequently, the empirical context in which an econometrician tries an economic theory depends on the bridge principles that he postulates.

Second, in an economic theory-data confrontation, the theory whose empirical relevance is on trial is not the theory that an econometrician may develop from Γ_t in his theory universe. It is rather the latter theory dressed in terms that can be understood in a given empirical context; that is, it is the composition of Γ_t with a pertinent $\Gamma_{t,p}$ that is at stake. Hence, the bridge principles in an economic theory-data confrontation constitute integral parts of both the theory on trial and the construction of the empirical context in which the trial takes place. Without this fact in mind, assertions such as "PIH is not relevant in the empirical context in which I tried PIH in Section 17.3.3," and "my arguments in the trial of PIH showed a way in which Duhem's trap can be circumvented," cannot be appreciated.

Third, it is important that econometricians who, like me, have grown up with Trygve Haavelmo's (1944) kind of applied econometrics not misunderstand my idea of a *true* probability distribution of the components of ω_P. In Haavelmo's econometrics there is one universe, the data universe, and conceptually three different measures of the values of the variables in that universe. The first measure assigns values to the components of ω_P in accordance with the values that the econometrician has observed. The second measure assigns values to the data variables that represent an ideal as to accurate measurements of reality "as it is in fact." The third measure assigns values to the data variables that are the "true measures that one would make if reality were actually in accordance with one's theoretical model" (Haavelmo, 1944, p. 5). The only measures of the data variables that I consider are the values of the variables that the particular econometrician has observed. Thus the *true* probability distribution of the components of ω_P is *FP*, and *FP* is the joint probability distribution of the econometrician's data. Moreover, a data-admissible model of the *MPD* is a joint probability distribution of the econometrician's data, that is, of the values of the components of ω_P that he has observed.[2]

Fourth, my analysis of the empirical relevance of an economic theory looks very different from the analysis that Haavelmo developed in his seminal treatise. It is, therefore, relevant here that in a one-universe world with accurate observations, my analysis would look very much like his.[3]

NOTES

1. This judgment is in accordance with Edward Leamer's (1980, p. 497) definition of a relatively abundant factor.

2. Being as involved as I am in my own views of econometric methodology, I might be misinterpreting the ideas that Trygve Haavelmo presented in his 1944 treatise, *The Probability Approach in Econometrics*. The reader can find two very different interpretations in Spanos (1989) and Juselius (1993).

3. Since 1944 econometric methodology has developed in several directions. For an authoritative account of the three leading methodologies see Pagan (1987). All three methodologies have important roles to play in the methodology developed in this book.

REFERENCES

Bowan, H. P., 1981, "A Multicountry Test of the Product Cycle Model," Paper presented to the Econometric Society Annual Meetings in Washington, D.C.

Duhem, P., 1981, *The Aim and Structure of Physical Theory*, P. P. Wiener (trans.), New York: Athenum.

Friedman, M., 1957, *A Theory of the Consumption Function*, Princeton: Princeton University Press.

Haavelmo, T., 1944, "The Probability Approach in Econometrics," *Econometrica* 12 (Suppl.), 1–118.

Heckscher, E., 1919, "The Effect of Foreign Trade on the Distribution of Income," *Ekonomkisk Tidsskrift* 21, 497–512.

Juselius, K., 1993, "VAR Modelling and Haavelmo's Probability Approach to Macroeconomic Modelling," *Empirical Economics* 18, 595–622.

Leamer, E. E., 1984, *Sources of International Comparative Advantage*, Cambridge: MIT Press.

Leontief, W. W., 1953, "Domestic Production and Foreign Trade: The American Capital Position Re-examined," *Proceedings of the American Philosophical Society* 107, 332–349.

Luce, R. D. and P. Suppes, 1965, "Preference, Utility, and Subjective Probability," in: *Handbook of Mathematical Psychology*, R. D. Luce, R. R. Bush, and E. Galanter (eds.), New York: Wiley.

Mosteller, F. C. and P. Nogee, 1951, "An Experimental Measurement of Utility," *The Journal of Political Economy* 59, 371–404.

Muth, J. F., 1961, "Rational Expectations and the Theory of Price Movements," *Econometrica* 29, 315–335.

Ohlin, B., 1933, *Interregional and International Trade*, Cambridge: Harvard University Press.

Pagan, A., 1987, "Three Econometric Methodologies: A Critical Appraisal," *Journal of Economic Surveys* 1, 3–24.

Popper, K. R., 1972, *Conjectures and Refutations*, London: Routledge & Kegan Paul.

Preston, M. G. and P. Baratta, 1948, "An Experimental Study of the Auction-Value of an Uncertain Income," *American Journal of Psychology* 61, 183–193.

Samuelson, P. A., 1955, *Foundations of Economic Analysis*, Cambridge: Harvard University Press

Spanos, A., 1989, "On Rereading Haavelmo: A Retrospective View of Econometric Modeling," *Econometric Theory* 5, 405–429.

Stigum, B. P., 1990, *Toward a Formal Science of Economics*, Cambridge: MIT Press.

Chapter Eighteen

Probability versus Capacity in Choice under Uncertainty

In Chapter 17, I used the framework of a theory-data confrontation that I developed in Part III of this book to delineate formal characteristics of tests of economic conjectures and theories. I also discussed the proper attitude to adopt toward such tests and explained what it means to say that a theory is relevant in a given empirical context. Finally I subjected three different economic theories to a test of their empirical relevance.

In this chapter I use the same framework for theory-data confrontations to delineate a scheme for testing one economic theory against another. I apply my scheme in the simple setting of an economic laboratory. The two theories at stake concern choice in uncertain situations. One is a formal version of Maurice Allais's (1988) (U, θ) theory with superadditive probabilities and the other is a version of the Bayesian theory of choice among random prospects.

18.1 INTRODUCTION

An economic theory is tested by confronting it with data and by checking whether it is relevant in the empirical context in which the data were generated. A theory may be relevant in one empirical context and not in another, and it is deemed potentially irrelevant if there is no known empirical context in which it has been proven relevant.

I noted in Chapter 5 that the meaning of the term "economic theory" varies among economists. To some an economic theory, such as the theory of consumer choice, is a formal theory that economists develop by the axiomatic method. To others an economic theory, such as the neoclassical theory of the firm, is a family of models of a finite set of assertions that pertain to various economic events. The two conceptions differ. However, from the point of view of testing an economic theory, it makes little difference which of the two conceptions of the term is adopted. In either case a test of its empirical relevance always amounts to checking whether a family of models of a finite set of assertions is relevant in a given empirical context.

Economists test one theory against another by confronting both with the same data and checking whether they are relevant in the empirical context in which the data were generated. In such situations they confront with data two families of models of two finite sets of assertions that may or may not be different. In such a test they may find that both are relevant (or irrelevant) or that one is relevant and the other is not.

The core structure of a theory-data confrontation of two rival theories comprises two disjoint theory universes, one data universe, bridges between each of the theory universes and the data universe, and a sample population. To see how, let T^1 and T^2 be the rival theories, and IT^1 and IT^2 be the interpretations whose empirical relevance is at stake. Associate two theory universes, (Ω_T^1, Γ_t^1) and (Ω_T^2, Γ_t^2), with IT^1 and IT^2 and let (Ω_p, Γ_p) denote the data universe that is to be used in the data confrontation of IT^1 and IT^2. Also, let Ω be a subset of $\Omega_T^1 \times \Omega_T^2 \times \Omega_p$ with vectors $(\omega_T^1, \omega_T^2, \omega_p)$ and $\Gamma_{t,p}^1$ and $\Gamma_{t,p}^2$ be the families of principles that, respectively, delineate the relationship between the components of ω_T^1 and ω_p and the components of ω_T^2 and ω_p. Finally, let S denote the relevant sample population, and $\Psi(\cdot)$, $P(\cdot)$, and $Q(\cdot)$ be as I described them in Chapter 17. These are all the components of the core structure of the theory-data confrontation of two rival theories. Except for two theory universes and two bridges, formally this core structure is like the core structure I described in Chapter 17.

18.2 PROBABILITIES AND CAPACITIES

In this chapter the rival theories whose empirical relevance is to be tested concern choice in uncertain situations. In the vernacular of economists a *risky* situation is an experiment in which the probabilities of all associated outcomes either are known or can be known by analysis. One example is a situation in which a blindfolded man is to draw a ball from a well-shaken urn with ninety balls of which thirty are red. The probability of the blindfolded man pulling a red ball from the urn is 1/3 and the probability of his pulling a ball that is not red is 2/3. In contrast, an *uncertain* situation is an experiment whose intrinsic probabilities neither are known nor can be known by reason alone. One obtains an example of such a situation by imagining that the sixty nonred balls in the urn are either yellow or black and insisting that one does not know how many of them are yellow. Then one cannot by reason alone determine the probability of the blindfolded man pulling a black ball or a ball that is either black or red.

The theories whose empirical relevance I test are variants of the theories of choice that I described in Sections 7.3.2.1 and 7.3.2.2 The distinguishing characteristic of the two theories is that the Bayesian decision-maker in Section 7.3.2.1 assigns additive probabilities to the events he faces, whereas the decision-maker in Section 7.3.2.2 assigns superadditive probabilities to the same events. Superadditive probability measures are *capacities* in the vernacular of probabilists. I discuss a subclass of these capacities that Glenn Shafer (1976) calls belief functions.[1]

18.2.1 Probabilities and the Bayes Theorem

For the purposes of this chapter it is important to have a clear idea of how a Bayesian's assignment of probabilities to events differs from Shafer's assignment of beliefs to the same events. The Bayesian bases his assignment on A. Kolmogorov's (1933, pp. 2, 13) axioms of probability theory and on various versions of Bayes's theorem. Here only the axioms that pertain to elementary probability theory and the simplest version of Bayes's theorem are significant.

As I noted in Chapter 5, elementary probability theory has two undefined terms, an *experiment* and a *probability*, which satisfy the following axioms:

K 1 *An* experiment *is a pair* $(\Omega, \aleph)$, *where* Ω *is a nonempty set of objects and* $\aleph$ *is a family of subsets of* Ω.

K 2 $\Omega \in \aleph$.

K 3 *If* A *and* B *are members of* $\aleph$, *then* $\mathrm{A} \cup \mathrm{B} \in \aleph$ *and* $\mathrm{A} - \mathrm{B} \in \aleph$.

K 4 *A* probability *is a function,* $\wp(\cdot) : \aleph \to [0, 1]$, *with* $\wp(\Omega) = 1$.

K 5 *If* $\mathrm{A}, \mathrm{B} \in \aleph$ *and* $\mathrm{A} \cap \mathrm{B} = \emptyset$, *then* $\wp(\mathrm{A}) + \wp(\mathrm{B}) = \wp(\mathrm{A} \cup \mathrm{B})$.

From these axioms it follows that $\wp(\emptyset) = 0$. Also, if $A_i \in \aleph$, $i = 1, \ldots, n$, and $A_i \cap A_j = \emptyset$ for all i, j with $i \neq j$, then $(\cup_{i=1}^n A_i) \in \aleph$ and $\sum_{1 \leq i \leq n} \wp(A_i) = \wp(\cup_{i=1}^n A_i)$. Finally, if C and D are members of $\aleph$ and $\wp(D) > 0$, one can define the conditional probability of C given D by $\wp(C \mid D) = \wp(C \cap D)/\wp(D)$ and show that $\wp(\cdot \mid D)$ is a probability on $\aleph$.

With the axioms of elementary probability and the definition of conditional probability in hand the simplest version of Bayes's theorem can be stated as follows: Suppose that $B_i \in \aleph$, $i = 1, \ldots, n$, and that $B_i \cap B_j = \emptyset$ when $i \neq j$. Suppose also that $E \in \aleph$, $E \subset \cup_{1 \leq i \leq n} B_i$, and $\wp(B_i) > 0$, $i = 1, \ldots, n$. Then,

$$\wp(E) = \sum_{1 \leq i \leq n} \wp(E \mid B_i)\wp(B_i),$$

and if $\wp(E) > 0$,

$$\wp(B_j \mid E) = \wp(E \mid B_j)\wp(B_j) / \sum_{1 \leq i \leq n} \wp(E \mid B_i)\wp(B_i), \; j = 1, \ldots, n. \quad (1)$$

In most applications of Bayes's theorem $\wp(B_i)$ is referred to as the *prior* measure of B_i, that is, the measure an individual would assign to B_i if he had no observations to guide him in assigning probabilities to the B_i, $i = 1, \ldots, n$.

In addition, $\wp(B_j \mid E)$ is referred to as the *posterior* measure of B_j, that is, the measure that an individual with prior probabilities $\wp(B_i)$, $i = 1, \ldots, n$, would assign to B_j after having observed E. Finally, the *conditional probabilities* $\wp(E \mid B_i)$, $i = 1, \ldots, n$, measure the likelihood of E as a function of B_i. In most applications the conditional probability measures $\wp(\cdot \mid B_i)$, $i = 1, \ldots, n$, are known.

E 18.1 *Consider the urn described above. It has thirty red balls and sixty balls that are either yellow or black. One does not know how many are yellow. The urn is shaken well, and a blindfolded man is about to pull a ball out of it. What is the probability that he will pick a red ball (yellow ball, black ball)?*

In this case a Bayesian would imagine that Ω *consists of 61 disjoint urns,* $\mathrm{B_i}$, $\mathrm{i} = 0, 1, \ldots, 60$, *with* $\mathrm{B_i}$ *containing 30 red balls,* i *yellow balls, and* $60 - \mathrm{i}$ *black balls. All the urns are shaken well. Hence, if the blindfolded man were to pick a ball in* $\mathrm{B_i}$, $\wp(\mathrm{A} \mid \mathrm{B_i}) = 1/3, (\mathrm{i}/90)$, *or* $[(60 - \mathrm{i})/90]$ *depending on whether* A *stands for picking a red ball, a yellow ball, or a black ball. The Bayesian believes that each combination of yellow and black balls is equally likely and figures that his prior measure over the* $\mathrm{B_i}$ *must satisfy the equation* $\wp(\mathrm{B_i}) = (1/61)$, $\mathrm{i} = 0, 1, \ldots, 60$. *Consequently, if* A *stands for picking a red ball (yellow ball, black ball),*

$$\wp(A) = (1/61) \sum_{0 \leq i \leq 60} \wp(A \mid B_i), \tag{2}$$

which equals 1/3 (1/3, 1/3).

Next, suppose that before the blindfolded man picks the ball, a demon tells us that he is sure that the ball will not be black. What is the probability that the ball will be red or that it will be yellow?

Well, the Bayesian recalls Eq. (2) and observes that

$$\wp(A \mid \text{not black ball}) = \wp[(A \cap \text{not black ball})]/\wp(\text{not black ball}),$$

and insists that the probability is 1/2 (1/2) depending on whether A stands for picking a red ball (yellow ball).

18.2.2 Capacities and Conditional Beliefs

Glenn Shafer's (1976) theory of belief functions has three undefined terms, an *experiment*, a *basic probability assignment*, and a *belief function*. These terms satisfy the following axioms:

G 1 *An* experiment *is a pair* $(\Omega, \aleph)$, *where* Ω *is a finite set of points* $\{\omega_1, \ldots, \omega_n)$ *and* $\aleph$ *denotes the family of all subsets of* Ω.

G 2 *A* basic probability assignment *is a function* $\mathrm{m}(\cdot) : \aleph \rightarrow [0, 1]$ *that satisfies the conditions* $\mathrm{m}(\emptyset) = 0$ *and* $\sum_{\mathrm{A} \subset \Omega} \mathrm{m}(\mathrm{A}) = 1$.

G 3 *A belief function is a function* $Bel(\cdot) : \aleph \rightarrow [0, 1]$ *that for each* $A \in \aleph$ *satisfies the condition* $Bel(A) = \sum_{B \subset A} m(B)$.

There are all sorts of belief functions. Interesting examples are the *vacuous belief function*, in which $m(\Omega) = 1$ and $m(A) = 0$ for all other members of $\aleph$, and the *simple support functions*, in which $m(\cdot)$ assigns an s in $(0, 1)$ to some given subset B of Ω, $1 - s$ to Ω, and 0 to all other members of $\aleph$. Whatever they look like, belief functions in contrast to probabilities are superadditive. Specifically, if A and B are members of $\aleph$ and if $A \cap B = \varnothing$, then $\text{Bel}(A) + \text{Bel}(B) \leq \text{Bel}(A \cup B)$:

A detailed analysis of Shafer's theory of belief functions can be found in Stigum (1990, pp. 317–326, 329–330). The only part of the analysis that need be noted here is Shafer's analogue of Bayes's theorem. For that purpose let A and E be members of $\aleph$, $\text{Bel}(\cdot)$ be a belief function with basic probability assignment $m(\cdot)$, and C be the union of all the members of $\aleph$ on which $m(\cdot)$ assumes a positive value. Suppose that $E \cap C \neq \varnothing$ and that $\text{Bel}(E^c) < 1$, where $E^c = \Omega - E$. Suppose also that E occurs. Then the *conditional belief in* A *given that* E *has occurred* is defined by

$$\text{Bel}(A \mid E) = \left[1 - \text{Bel}(E^c)\right]^{-1} \left[\text{Bel}(A \cup E^c) - \text{Bel}(E^c)\right] \qquad (3)$$

This relation does not look quite like an analogue of Bayes's theorem, but it is. Information of the kind the B's convey in Bayes's theorem is implicitly accounted for in $\text{Bel}(\cdot)$ and $m(\cdot)$. Moreover, when E occurs, new information is introduced in the form of a second basic probability assignment $m_2(\cdot)$ that satisfies the conditions $m_2(E) = 1$ and $m_2(A) = 0$ for all other members of $\aleph$. The two functions $m(\cdot)$ and $m_2(\cdot)$ combine to form a third basic probability assignment on $\aleph$ whose associated belief function is as described on the right-hand side of (3). Shafer insists that this belief function be adopted as the conditional belief in members of $\aleph$ that the occurrence of E causes.

E 18.2 *Consider again the urn in E 18.1: What answers might Shafer have given to the two questions I posed there.*

Shafer's Ω *would contain only three elements,* ω_R, ω_Y, *and* ω_B, *where* R, Y, *and* B *stand, respectively, for red, yellow, and black balls. He might have assigned the following basic probabilities to the subsets of* Ω : $m(\{\omega_R\}) = 1/3$, $m(\{\omega_Y\}) = m(\{\omega_B\}) = \varepsilon/6$, $m(\{\omega_R, \omega_B\}) = (2 - \varepsilon)/3$, *and* $m(A) = 0$ *for other* A*'s. Table 18.1 lists these values of* $m(\cdot)$ *and the resulting values of* $\text{Bel}(\cdot)$.

It can be seen from the table that Shafer's answer to the first question would have been $1/3(\varepsilon/6, \varepsilon/6)$, *and his answer to the second question would have been* $[1 - (\varepsilon/6)]^{-1}(1/3)$ *for the chance of picking a red ball and* $[1 - (\varepsilon/6)]^{-1}[(2/3) - (\varepsilon/6)]$ *for the chance of picking a yellow one. Note that for small values of* ε, *the latter is larger than the former.*

TABLE 18.1
A Basic Probability Assignment and Its Belief Function

A	$\varnothing$	$\{\omega_R\}$	$\{\omega_Y\}$	$\{\omega_B\}$	$\{\omega_R, \omega_Y\}$	$\{\omega_R, \omega_B\}$	$\{\omega_Y, \omega_B\}$	Ω
$M(\{A\})$	0	1/3	$\varepsilon/6$	$\varepsilon/6$	0	0	$(2-\varepsilon)/3$	0
$\text{Bel}(\{A\})$	0	1/3	$\varepsilon/6$	$\varepsilon/6$	$(2+\varepsilon)/6$	$(2+\varepsilon)/6$	2/3	1

18.3 CHOICE UNDER UNCERTAINTY

In Chapter 7, I noted that having good judgment in uncertain situations means being able to rank the available options and that the rankings in question vary over theories as well as over the uncertain options that the decision-maker faces. The options may be a gamble, an insurance policy, or an investment in the stock market. They may also be a job opportunity, a course of study, or a marriage partner. Whatever they are, in this chapter I consider such options *prospects*, that is, an n-tuple of pairs $\{(x_1, p_1), \ldots, (x_n, p_n)\}$, where $x_i \in R$ is an *outcome* and $p_i \in [0, 1]$ is a measure of the likelihood of x_i happening, $i = 1, \ldots, n$. The theories I consider are the Bayesian theory of choice, Maurice Allais's (U, θ) theory, and a formalized version of the latter.

In the Bayesian case, the p_i's in a prospect $\{(x_1, p_1), \ldots, (x_n, p_n)\}$ are probabilities that the Bayesian decision-maker has calculated. They are nonnegative and satisfy the condition, $p_1 + \ldots + p_n = 1$. The x_i belong to a compact subset of R, say X, and Bayesians assume that their decision-maker ranks outcomes according to the values of a utility function $U(\cdot) : X \to R$. They also assume that their decision-maker ranks prospects according to the expected value of $U(\cdot)$. Thus if $P = \{(x_1, p_1), \ldots, (x_n, p_n)\}$ and $Q = \{(y_1, q_1), \ldots, (y_n, q_n)\}$ are two prospects, the decision-maker ranks P higher than Q if and only if $\sum_{1\leq i\leq n} p_i U(x_i) > \sum_{1\leq i\leq n} q_i U(y_i)$.

The Bayesian theory of choice under uncertainty is well known, so I need not dwell on it here. Instead I focus on Allais's theory and on what I think of as a formalized version of that theory.

18.3.1 Allais's (U, θ) Theory of Choice under Uncertainty

Maurice Allais's (1988) theory of choice in uncertain situations is a good example of a theory that has been given a model-theoretic formulation. It consists of three basic assertions, A 1–A 3, and a family of models of these assertions that may vary with the intended application of the theory.

A 1 *A random prospect* P *is an* n*-tuple of pairs* $(\mathrm{x_i}, \mathrm{p_i})$, $\mathrm{i} = 1, \ldots, \mathrm{n}$, *where* $0 \leq \mathrm{x_1} \leq \mathrm{x_2} \leq \ldots \leq \mathrm{x_n}$, $\mathrm{p_i} \geq 0$, *and* $\sum_{1\leq i\leq n} \mathrm{p_i} = 1$. *The* n $\mathrm{x_i}$*'s are the returns* *that* P *will yield in* n *different states of the world. The probabilities that the associated states occur are given by the* p_i*'s.*

A 2 *The utility of a prospect* W(P) *is given by*

$$W(P) = u(x_1) + \theta(p_2 + \ldots + p_n)\,[u(x_2) - u(x_1)] + \ldots + \theta(p_n)\left[u(x_n) - u(x_{n-1})\right],$$

where $u(\cdot) : [1, \infty) \to [0, \infty)$ *and* $\theta(\cdot) : [0, 1] \to [0, 1]$ *are nondecreasing functions with* $\theta(1) = 1$. *Here* $u(\cdot)$ *measures the investor's utility of a sure monetary payoff and* $\theta(\cdot)$ *is his* specific probability function.

A 3 *The investor chooses the one prospect among those available that maximizes his utility.*

The preceding three assertions have many models. I obtain a family of models that serves my purposes by leaving the extensions of the x_i and the p_i unspecified and by insisting that $u(\cdot)$ and $\theta(\cdot)$ be continuous and strictly increasing. In doing that, I end up with a model-theoretic account of choice under uncertainty such as the one Allais presented in 1988.

Allais insists that $\theta(\cdot)$ reveals the investor's attitude toward risk and security. For example, an individual who is averse to uncertainty might have a specific probability function such as $\theta_1(\cdot)$ with a very small ε.

$$\theta_1(p) = \varepsilon p / [(1 + \varepsilon) - p], \; p \in [0, 1].$$

I believe that $\theta(\cdot)$ can also be taken to measure the investor's perception of the probabilities he faces. Thus an investor who overvalues low probabilities and undervalues high ones might have a specific probability function such as $\theta_2(\cdot)$:

$$\theta_2(p) = \begin{cases} p^{1/1.43} \text{ if } p \in [0, .1] \text{ and } p^5 & \text{if } p \in [.9, 1] \\ .01^{-1}\left[.1^{1/1.43} - .1^{1/1.5}\right](.11 - p) + p^{1/1.5} & \text{if } p \in [.1, .11] \\ .11^{1/1.5} + .79^{-1}\left[.9^5 - .11^{1/1.5}\right](p - .11) & \text{if } p \in [.11, .9] \end{cases}$$

The $U(\cdot)$ function in A 2 can have any shape. It may be concave or convex; it may also have an inflection point and be concave for small values of its argument and convex for large values. Since $W(P)$ is not equal to the expected utility of P, the shape of $U(\cdot)$ need not have any bearing on the decision-maker's attitude toward risk.

Allais insists that his theory can account for the experimental results that he and his followers have used during the last 50 years to reject the expected utility hypothesis. In E 18.3 I see if he is right by checking how an Allais decision-maker with a concave utility function and the specific probability function $\theta_2(\cdot)$ would have fared in one of Allais's experiments.

E 18.3 *Consider an urn with 100 balls that differ only in color and assume that there are 89 red balls, 10 black balls, and 1 white ball. The urn is shaken* *well and a blindfolded man is to pull a ball from it. An Allais decision-maker, Adam, is asked to rank the components of the following two pairs of prospects in which he will receive the following:*

α_1: *$1,000 regardless of which ball is drawn.*
α_2: *Nothing, $1,000, or $5,000 depending on whether the ball drawn is white, red, or black.*
β_1: *Nothing if the ball is red and $1,000 otherwise.*
β_2: *Nothing if the ball is either red or white and $5,000 if the ball is black.*

Adam's specific probability function is $\theta_2(\cdot)$, *and the utilities he obtains from the three gains are given by* $U(0) = 0$, $U(1{,}000) = .85$, *and* $U(5{,}000) = 1$.

It is now easy to figure out that, up to two decimals, the values of $W(\cdot)$ *at the four prospects are given by* $W(\alpha_1) = .85$, $W(\alpha_2) = .84$, $W(\beta_1) = .12$, *and* $W(\beta_2) = .2$. *According to these values Adam prefers* α_1 *to* α_2 *and* β_2 *to* β_1, *which is an ordering that contradicts the expected utility hypothesis.*

18.3.2 A Formalized Version of Allais's (U, θ) Theory

The axioms that I have in mind for a formalized version of Allais's (U, θ) Theory concern six undefined terms: *the world, a consequence, an act, an option, a decision-maker*, and a *choice function*. The eight axioms that follow delineate the properties of these terms. *R* denotes the set of real numbers, and A^N is shorthand for the set of all functions from N to A.[2]

B 1 *The* world *is a pair* $(\Omega, \Im)$, *where* $\Omega = \{\omega_1, \ldots, \omega_n\}$, *and* $\Im = \wp(\Omega)$, *the family of all subsets of* Ω.

B 2 *A* consequence *is a real number* $r \in R$.

B 3 *An* act *is a function* $x(\cdot) : \Omega \to R$.

B 4 *An* option *is a member of* $\wp_F(R^\Omega)$, *the family of all finite subsets of* R^Ω.

B 5 *A* decision-maker *is a quadruple* $(O, \Re, Bel(\cdot), V(\cdot))$, *where* $O \in \wp_F(\Re^\Omega)$, $\Re \subset R$, $Bel(\cdot) : \Im \to [0, 1]$, *and* $V(\cdot) : \Re^\Omega \to R$.

B 6 *There is a function,* $m(\cdot) : \Im \to [0, 1]$, *such that* $m(\emptyset) = 0$; $\sum_{A \subset \Omega} m(A) = 1$; *and* $Bel(B) = \sum_{A \subset B} m(A)$, $B \in \Im$.

B 7 *There are functions* $U(\cdot) : \Re \to R$ *and* $W_x(\cdot) : \Im \to R$ *such that for all* $B \in \Im$ *and all acts* $x \in \Re^\Omega$,

$$W_x(B) = \min_{\omega \in B} U(x(\omega))$$

and

$$V(x) = \sum_{A \subset \Omega} W_x(A) m(A).$$

B 8 *A choice function is a function* $C(\cdot) : \wp_F(\Re^\Omega) \to \Re^\Omega$ *such that if* $A \in \wp_F(\Re^\Omega)$, $C(A) \in A$, *and if* $v = C(A)$, *then* $V(v) \geq V(u)$ *for all* $u \in A$.

The axioms B 1–B 8 concern uncertain situations in which the decision-maker, for example, a consumer or the board of governors of an institution, is to choose among acts whose consequences depend on the occurrence of a finite number of states of the world Ω. One example is a choice among prospects whose outcomes depend on the color of the ball that the blindfolded man in E 18.3 is about to draw from an urn. I use the idea of such an experiment to construct a model of B 1–B 8.

18.3.2.1 The Intended Interpretation of B 1–B 8

To be certain that a system of axioms has a meaningful interpretation, I must construct a model of the axioms. The model that I have in mind for B 1–B 8 is as follows: First, let $n = 3$, let $\Omega = \{\omega_R, \omega_B, \omega_W\}$, and think of $\{\omega_i\}, i = R, B, W$, as being, respectively, a symbolic rendition of the event, "the blindfolded man pulls a red, a black, or a white ball from his urn." Also, let $\Re = \{0, 1{,}000, 5{,}000\}$; let O comprise just the following four acts:

$$\alpha_1(\{\omega_i\}) = 1{,}000 \text{ for } i = R, B, W,$$

$$\alpha_2(\{\omega_W\}) = 0,\ \alpha_2(\{\omega_R\}) = 1000, \text{ and } \alpha_2(\{\omega_B\}) = 5{,}000,$$

$$\beta_1(\{\omega_R\}) = 0 \text{ and } \beta_1(\{\omega_i\}) = 1{,}000 \text{ if } i = B \text{ or } W,$$

and

$$\beta_2(\{\omega_B\}) = 5{,}000 \text{ and } \beta_2(\{\omega_i\}) = 0 \text{ if } i = W \text{ or } R;$$

and let $U(O) = 0$, $U(1{,}000) = 0.85$, and $U(5{,}000) = 1$. These acts and the given utilities are analogues of Adam's prospects and utilities in E 18.3. Next let $m(\cdot) : \Im \to [0, 1]$ be defined by the following equations:

$$m(\{\omega_R\}) = 0.7, m(\{\omega_B\}) = 0.2, m(\{\omega_W\}) = 0.01, m(\{\omega_R, \omega_B\}) = 0.05,$$
$$m(\{\omega_R, \omega_W\}) = 0.03, m(\{\omega_B, \omega_W\}) = 0.01, \text{ and } m(A) = 0 \text{ for all other } A \in \Im.$$

These equations and B 6 determine the values of $\text{Bel}(\cdot) : \Im \to [0, 1]$. Finally, define $W_x(\cdot) : \Im \to R$ and $V(\cdot) : \Re^\Omega \to R$ as in B 7, and conclude the construction of the model by defining a choice function $C(\cdot)$ on $\wp_F(\Re^\Omega)$ that satisfies the prescriptions of B 8. In this model

$$V(\alpha_1) = 0.85,\ V(\alpha_2) = 0.84,\ V(\beta_1) = 0.12, \text{ and } V(\beta_2) = 0.2, \quad (4)$$

$$\alpha_1 = C(\{\alpha_1, \alpha_2\}),\ \beta_2 = C(\{\beta_1, \beta_2\}), \text{ and } \alpha_1 = C(O). \quad (5)$$

A system of axioms that has a model is consistent and can be used to talk about many different matters. In the intended interpretation of B 1–B 8 the $U(\cdot)$ and the $m(\cdot)$ in B 6 and B 7 are, respectively, the decision-maker's utility function of consequences and his basic probability assignment to the various subsets of Ω. Also, the Bel(·) in B 5 and B 6 is the decision-maker's belief function, that is, the function whose value at any $A \in \Im$ records the probability that the decision-maker assigns to the likelihood of observing A.

As to the $V(\cdot)$ and the $C(\cdot)$ in B 1–B 8: In the intended interpretation of the axioms the value of $V(\cdot)$ at an $x \in \Re^{\Omega}$ measures the utility that the decision-maker expects to obtain from x. Also, the value of $C(\cdot)$ on a subset A of $\Re^{\Omega}$ indicates the action that the decision-maker would take if faced with the option A. My interpretation of $V(\cdot)$ makes sense of using it to delineate the decision-maker's ordering of acts in $\Re^{\Omega}$. This ordering—arbitrary selections among equivalent maximal acts—and B 8 suffice to determine $C(\cdot)$. Except for the arbitrary choices among equivalent maximal acts, the interpretation of $C(\cdot)$ as the decision-maker's choice function is not problematic.

There are all sorts of utility functions. I conclude my description of the intended interpretation of B 1–B 8 by observing that $V(\cdot)$ is not an expected utility indicator. To wit: a theorem that I once learned from Kjell Arne Brekke (cf. Stigum, 1990, p. 449):

T 1 *Let* $\mathrm{x}(\cdot)$ *be an act. Then* $\mathrm{V}(\mathrm{x}) = \int_{(0,\infty)} \mathrm{Bel}(\{\omega \in \Omega : \mathrm{U}(\mathrm{x}(\omega)) \geq \mathrm{t}\})\mathrm{dt}$.

The theorem shows that $V(\cdot)$ is an expected utility indicator only if Bel(·) is additive.

18.3.2.2 B 1–B 8 and Allais's (U, θ) Theory

The axioms of Allais's (U, θ) theory, A 1–A 3, look very different from B 1–B 8. Hence, it is not obvious what I have in mind when I claim that the theory that I deduce from B 1–B 8 is a formalized version of Allais's theory. To show why, I begin by listing some of the most interesting similarities:

1. Both have models in which the respective utility functions, $W(\cdot)$ and $V(\cdot)$, rank prospects according to their expected utility. For example, let $\theta(\cdot) \equiv 1$ on (0, 1] and choose $m(\cdot)$ so that Bel(·) is additive.
2. Without special assumptions concerning the form of $\theta(\cdot)$ and Bel(·) the two theories do not satisfy Leonard Savage's sure-thing principle (STP). Allais's $W(\cdot)$ satisfies a modified version of the STP that heeds the inequalities in A 1, and $V(\cdot)$ satisfies a modified version of STP that I delineated in T 19.10 in Stigum (1990, pp. 446–447).
3. Allais's decision-maker and the decision-maker in B 1–B 8 "suffer" from an equivalent form of aversion to uncertainty. The uncertainty aversion of the B 1–B 8 decision-maker is displayed in theorem T 2, the proof of which can be found in Stigum (1990, pp. 451–452).

T 2 *Let* $\mathrm{P} = \left\{\mathrm{p}(\cdot) : \Omega \to [0, 1] : \sum_{1 \leq i \leq n} \mathrm{p}(\omega_i) = 1\right\}$ *and let* $\mathrm{x}(\cdot)$ *be an act.*

Also, for each $p \in P$, let $P_p(\cdot) : \Im \to [0, 1]$ be such that $P_p(A) = \sum_{\omega \in A} p(\omega)$, $A \in \Im$. Finally, let $G = \{p \in P : \text{for all } A \in \Im, P_p(A) \geq \text{Bel}(A)\}$. Then,

$$V(x) = \min_{p \in G} \sum_{1 \leq i \leq n} U(x(\omega_i))p(\omega_i).$$

I can obtain a similar expression for $W(P)$ by letting $p_{n+1} = 0$ and defining $p_i^*, i = 1, \ldots, n$, by

$$p_i^* = \theta(p_i + \ldots + p_n) - \theta(p_{i+1} + \ldots + p_n).$$

Then

$$\sum_{1 \leq i \leq n} p_i^* = 1$$

and

$$W(P) = \sum_{1 \leq i \leq n} U(x_i)p_i^*.$$

The last expression does not look quite like the conclusion of T 2. But looks can be deceiving.

Let $j_i, i = 0, 1, \ldots, n$, be such that if $U_{j_i} = U\left[x(\omega_{j_i})\right]$, then $U_{j_0} = 0$, and $0 \leq U_{j_i} \leq U_{j_{i+1}}, i = 1, \ldots, n-1$. Moreover, let

$$p(\omega_{j_i}) = \text{Bel}\left(\left\{\omega \in \Omega : U\left[x(\omega)\right] \geq U_{j_i}\right\}\right) \\ - \text{Bel}\left(\left\{\omega \in \Omega : U\left[x(\omega)\right] \geq U_{j_{i+1}}\right\}\right), i = 1, \ldots, n,$$

with U_{jn+1} being some number greater than U_{jn}. Then it is a fact that $\sum_{1 \leq i \leq n} p(\omega_{j_i}) = 1$ and that $p(\cdot) \in G$. Also, $V(x) = \sum_{1 \leq i \leq n} U\left[x(\omega_{j_i})\right] p(\omega_{j_i})$. Proof can be found in Stigum (1990, pp. 451–452).

4. If I define the U_{j_i} as I did in point 3, I can show that $V(\cdot)$ can be written in a functional form that is similar to the functional form of $W(\cdot)$. To wit: theorem T 3, the proof of which can be found in Stigum (1990, p. 450).

T 3 *Let* $\mathrm{x}(\cdot)$ *be an act and define* $\mathrm{j(i)}, \mathrm{i} = 0, 1, \ldots, \mathrm{n}$, *such that if* $\mathrm{U_{j(i)}} = \mathrm{U[x(\omega_{j(i)})]}$, *then* $\mathrm{U_{j(0)}} = 0$, *and* $\mathrm{U_{j(i)}} \leq \mathrm{U_{j(i+1)}}, \mathrm{i} = 1, \ldots, \mathrm{n} - 1$. *It is the case that*

$$V(x) = \sum_{1 \leq i \leq n} \left(U_{j(i)} - U_{j(i-1)}\right) \text{Bel}\left(\left\{\omega \in \Omega : U(x(\omega)) \geq U_{j(i)}\right\}\right).$$

The four points just delineated show some of the formal similarities of Allais's theory and the theory that I can derive from B 1–B 8. The last remark also suggests that for every Allais decision-maker, there is a B 1–B 8 decision-maker with the property that the choices that the two individuals make in identical uncertain situations cannot be distinguished. The converse is also true. E 18.3 and the model of B 1–B 8 that I sketched above provide good examples. The last equivalence is my justification for insisting that the test I formalize in what follows is a test of the empirical relevance of Allais's (U, θ) theory.

18.4 PROBABILITIES VERSUS CAPACITIES: AXIOMS AND THEOREMS FOR A TEST

A student M and a blindfolded man sit at two desks in my economics laboratory. The blindfolded man is to draw a ball from an urn. The urn is like the one in E 18.1 and E 18.2. It has ninety balls that differ only in color. Thirty of the balls are red and the remaining sixty are either yellow or black. They do not know how many of the balls are yellow. The urn is shaken well.

My intent is to use M, the blindfolded man, and the urn to test the empirical relevance of B 1–B 8 and the Bayesian theory of choice in uncertain situations. I begin the test by asking M to rank the acts $X_i, i = 1, \ldots, 14$, in Table 18.2. There C_R, C_Y, and C_B, respectively, denote the event that the blindfolded man pulls a red, a yellow, or a black ball from the urn. Also, the numbers in the table show the number of dollars of return to the respective acts when the three events occur, for example, the return to X_9 is \$100 in C_R, \$50 in C_Y and \$100 in C_B.

Thereafter, I suggest that M imagine an urn with ninety balls that are identical except for color. The urn contains thirty red balls, α yellow balls, and $60 - \alpha$ black balls, and it is shaken well. I ask M to write down the number of yellow balls, α_i, which in the case of $X_i, i = 2, \ldots, 5$, would have made him indifferent between having the blindfolded man draw a ball from the imagined urn and having him draw one from the original urn.

I conclude by asking M the following questions[3]:

Q 1. Suppose that you found out that the ball that the blindfolded man drew was not red. How would you then order the acts $X_2, X_3, X_6, X_7, X_{11}$?

Q 2. Suppose that you were told that the ball that the blindfolded man drew was not yellow. How would you then order the acts $X_1, X_3, X_5, X_8, X_{10}$?

Q 3. Suppose that you were told that the ball that the blindfolded man drew was not black. How would you then order the acts X_1, X_2, and X_{10}?

TABLE 18.2
A List of Prospects

	X_1	X_2	X_3	X_4	X_5	X_6	X_7	X_8	X_9	X_{10}	X_{11}	X_{12}	X_{13}	X_{14}
C_R	100	0	0	100	100	0	100	0	100	50	100	50	100	50
C_Y	0	100	0	100	0	100	0	100	50	100	50	100	50	100
C_B	0	0	100	0	100	100	200	200	100	100	200	200	25	25

18.4.1 The Data Universe

With M's answers in hand I can describe the data universe for my theory-data confrontation of the two rival theories of choice.

$\mathbf{\Gamma_{p1}}$ *Ω_p is a set of ordered eighteen-tuples ω_p.*

$\mathbf{\Gamma_{p2}}$ *Let* $\Re = (0, 25, 50, 100, 200)$ *and* $C = \{C_R, C_Y, C_B\}$. *Then,* $\omega_p \in \Omega_p$ *only if*

$$\omega_p = \left(\alpha_2, \ldots, \alpha_5, X_1, \ldots, X_{14}, \geq, \geq_{NR}, \geq_{NY}, \geq_{NB}, CH, CH_{NR}, CH_{NY}, CH_{NB}\right),$$

where $\alpha_i \in \{0, 1, \ldots, 60\}$, $i = 2, \ldots, 5$, $\geq$ *with or without subscripts is an ordering of the set of acts* $\Re^C$ *and the* CH *with and without subscripts are functions on* $\wp_F(\Re^C)$ *to* $\Re^C$.

$\mathbf{\Gamma_{p3}}$ *The four orderings of* $\Re^C$, $\geq$, $\geq_{NR}$, $\geq_{NY}$, *and* $\geq_{NB}$, *are complete, reflexive, and transitive.*

$\mathbf{\Gamma_{p4}}$ $CH(\cdot)$, $CH_{NR}(\cdot)$, $CH_{NY}(\cdot)$, $CH_{NB}(\cdot)$, *respectively, are choice functions on* $\wp_F(\Re^C)$ *determined by* $\geq$, $\geq_{NR}$, $\geq_{NY}$, *and* $\geq_{NB}$.

In reading these axioms, note that $X_i, i = 1, \ldots, 14$, the $\alpha_i, i = 2, \ldots, 5$, and M's rankings of acts constitute my observations. The same X_i and α_i, the four orderings $\geq$, $\geq_{NR}$, $\geq_{NY}$, and $\geq_{NB}$, and the corresponding four choice functions constitute my data. A model of the axioms is data-admissible only if the actual data satisfy the strictures on which the model insists. Consequently, in the present case, a model of the axioms is data-admissible only if: (1) its $\geq$-ordering of the $X_i, i = 1, \ldots, 14$ coincides with M's ordering of them; (2) its $\geq_{NR}$-ordering of the five X_i, for $i = 2, 3, 6, 7, 11$, accords with M's answer to Q 1; (3) its $\geq_{NY}$-ordering of the five X_i, for $i = 1, 3, 5, 8, 10$, accords with M's answer to Q 2; and (4) its $\geq_{NB}$-ordering of the three X_i, for $i = 1, 2$, and 10, accords with M's answer to Q 3. Since the orderings of acts are not uniquely determined, the intended interpretation of $(\Omega_p \Gamma_P)$ is either empty or comprises a whole family of models. The interpretation will be empty only if M's answers to all my queries are contradictory.

18.4.2 The First Theory Universe

So much for the data universe. Next I describe the theory universe of the intended interpretation of B 1–B 8.

$\mathbf{\Gamma^1_{t1}}$ *Ω^1_T is a set of twenty-one-tuples ω^1_T.*

$\mathbf{\Gamma^1_{t2}}$ *Let* $\Re = \{0, 25, 50, 100, 200\}$, $c = \left\{C_g, C_Y, C_B\right\}$, *and* $\Im_C$ *denote the set of all subsets of* c. *Then* $\omega^1_T \in \Omega^1_T$ *only if* $\omega^1_T = (x_1, \ldots, x_{14}, m(\cdot), Bel(\cdot), U(\cdot), V(\cdot), V(\cdot|\cdot), ch(\cdot), ch(\cdot|\cdot))$, *where* $x_i \in \Re^C, i = 1, \ldots, 14, m(\cdot) : \Im_c \rightarrow$

$[0, 1]$, $Bel(\cdot) : \Im_c \to [0, 1]$, $U(\cdot) : \Re \to [0, 1]$, $V(\cdot) : \Re^c \to R$, $V(\cdot|\cdot) : \Re^c \times \Im_c \to R$, $ch(\cdot) : \wp_F(\Re^c) \to \Re^c$, *and* $ch(\cdot|\cdot) : \wp_F(\Re^c) \times \Im_c \to \Re^c$.

$\mathbf{\Gamma^1_{t3}}$ $m(\emptyset) = 0$, $\sum_{A\subset c} m(A) = 1$, *and* $Bel(B) = \sum_{A\subset B} m(A)$ *for all* $B \in \Im_c$. *Also,* $Bel(\{C_R\}) = 1/3$ *and* $Bel(\{C_Y, C_B\}) = 2/3$.

$\mathbf{\Gamma^1_{t4}}$ $U(0) = 0, U(25) = 0.25, U(50) = 0.45, U(100) = 0.75, U(200) = 1.$

$\mathbf{\Gamma^1_{t5}}$ *For all* $A \in \Im_c$ *and* $x \in \Re^c$, *let* $W_x(A) = \min_{s\in A} U(x(s))$. *Then,* $V(x(\cdot)) = \sum_{A\subset c} W_x(A)m(A)$.

$\mathbf{\Gamma^1_{t6}}$ *Let* $E \in \Im_c$ *be such that* $Bel(c - E) < 1$, *and let*

$$\mathrm{Bel}(A \mid E) = [1 - \mathrm{Bel}(c - E)]^{-1}\{\mathrm{Bel}[A \cup (c - E)] - \mathrm{Bel}(c - E)\},\ A \in \Im_c.$$

Also, let

$$m(\{s\} \mid E) = \mathrm{Bel}(\{s\} \mid E) \text{ for } s = \{C_R\}, \{C_Y\}, \text{ and } \{C_B\},$$

$$m(\{C_R, C_Y\} \mid E) = \mathrm{Bel}(\{C_R, C_Y\} \mid E) - \mathrm{Bel}(\{C_R\} \mid E) - \mathrm{Bel}(\{C_Y\} \mid E),$$

$$m(\{C_R, C_B\} \mid E) = \mathrm{Bel}(\{C_R, C_B\} \mid E) - \mathrm{Bel}(\{C_R\} \mid E) - \mathrm{Bel}(\{C_B\} \mid E),$$

$$m(\{C_Y, C_B\} \mid E) = \mathrm{Bel}(\{C_Y, C_B\} \mid E) - \mathrm{Bel}(\{C_Y\} \mid E) - \mathrm{Bel}(\{C_B\} \mid E),$$

and

$$m(c \mid E) = 1 - \sum_{A\subset c, A\neq c} m(A \mid E).$$

Then for $x \in \Re^c$ *and the given* E, $V(x \mid E) = \sum_{A\subset c} W_x(A)m(A \mid E)$.

$\mathbf{\Gamma^1_{t7}}$ $ch(\cdot)$ *and* $ch(\cdot|\cdot)$, *respectively, are choice functions determined by* $V(\cdot)$ *and* $V(\cdot|\cdot)$.

In the intended interpretation of these axioms, (Ω^1_T, Γ^1_t) is the theory universe of an interpretation of B 1–B 8 concerning an uncertain situation such as the one I faced in my economics laboratory. In this interpretation $c = \{C_R, C_Y, C_B\}$ is the theory version of $\{C_R, C_Y, C_B\}$. Similarly, x_i is the theory clone of the X_i in Γ^1_{p2}, $i = 1, \ldots, 14$, and $V(x)$ measures the decision-maker's utility of choosing an act $x \in \Re^c$. I presume that the decision-maker orders acts in accordance with the values that $V(\cdot)$ assumes.

We have not encountered $V(\cdot \mid E)$ before. In the present interpretation of B 1–B 8, I follow Shafer in insisting that $\mathrm{Bel}(\cdot \mid E)$ indicates the probabilities that the decision-maker would assign to the subsets of c after having heard that E has occurred. Then the values of $V(\cdot \mid E)$ on $(0, 25, 50, 100, 200)^c$ determines the decision-maker's ordering of acts.

18.4.3 The Second Theory Universe

Next I describe the theory universe for the Bayesian theory of choice in uncertain situations. The situation I have in mind is identical to the one I considered in the discussion of (Ω^1_T, Γ^1_t).

Γ^2_{t1} Ω^2_Y *is a set of twenty-tuples* ω^2_T.

Γ^2_{t2} *Let* $\Re = (0, 25, 50, 100, 200)$, $b = \{b_R, b_Y, b_B\}$, *and* $\Im_b$ *be the set of all subsets of* b. *Then* $\omega^2_T \in \Omega^2_T$ *only if* $\omega^2_T = (y_1, \ldots, y_{14}, P(\cdot), U(\cdot), V^2(\cdot), V^2(\cdot|\cdot), ch^2(\cdot), ch^2(\cdot|\cdot)$, *where* $y_i \in \Re^b, i = 1, \ldots, 14, P(\cdot) : \Im_b \to [0, 1], U(\cdot) : \Re \to [0, 1], V^2(\cdot) : \Re^b \to [0, 1]$, *and* $V^2(\cdot|\cdot) : \Re^b \times \Im_b \to [0, 1], ch^2(\cdot) : \wp_F(\Re^b) \to \Re^b$, *and* $ch^2(\cdot|\cdot) : \wp_F(\Re^b) \times \Im_b \to \Re^b$.

Γ^2_{t3} $P(\cdot)$ *is an additive probability measure on* $\Im_b$. *Also,* $P(\{b_R\}) = 1/3$ *and* $P(\{b_Y, b_B\}) = 2/3$.

Γ^2_{t4} $U(0) = 0, U(25) = 0.25, U(50) = 0.45, U(100) = 0.75, U(200) = 1$.

Γ^2_{t5} *For all* $i = 1, \ldots, 14$, $V^2(y_i) = \sum_{s\in b} U(y(s))P(\{s\})$.

Γ^2_{t6} *If* $E \in \Im_b$ *and* $P(E) > 0$, *then for all* $A \in \Im_b$ *and all* $y \in \Re^b$,

$$P(A \mid E) = P(A \cap E)/P(E)$$

and

$$V^2(y \mid E) = \sum_{s\in b} U(y(s))P(\{s\} \mid E).$$

Γ^2_{t7} $ch^2(\cdot)$ *and* $ch^2(\cdot|\cdot)$, *respectively, are choice functions determined by* $V^2(\cdot)$ *and* $V^2(\cdot|\cdot)$.

The Γ^2_t axioms differ from the Γ^1_t axioms in that $P(\cdot)$ is additive and $\text{Bel}(\cdot)$ is superadditive. Furthermore, $V^2(\cdot)$ is an expected utility indicator and $V(\cdot)$ is not. I have not mentioned the decision-maker's prior probability distribution in the Γ^2_t axioms since the prior plays no role in the test I have designed.

18.4.4 The Bridge Principles

The bridge principles in the present theory-data confrontation are spelled out in the $\Gamma^1_{t,p}$ and $\Gamma^2_{t,p}$ axioms below. In reading them, note that the three acts $y(\cdot), x(\cdot)$, and $X(\cdot)$ are taken to be equal if the values of all three are the same, that is, if $y(\{b_R\}) = x(\{C_R\}) = X(\{C_R\})$, if $y(\{b_Y\}) = x(\{C_Y\}) = X(\{C_Y\})$, and if $y(\{b_B\}) = x(\{C_B\}) = X(\{C_B\})$. Similarly, the choice functions $ch^2(\cdot)$, $ch(\cdot)$, and $CH(\cdot)$ are taken to be equal if they assume the same values on corresponding subsets of $\wp_F(\Re^b)$, $\wp_F(\Re^c)$, and $\wp_F(\Re^C)$. Finally, the choice functions $ch^2(\cdot|\cdot)$, $ch(\cdot|\cdot)$, and $CH(\cdot|\cdot)$ are taken to be equal if they assume the same values in corresponding subsets of $\wp_F(\Re^b) \times \Im_b$, $\wp_F(\Re^c) \times \Im_c$, and $\wp_F(\Re^c) \times \Im_C$.

Γ^1_{tp} *Let* Ω *be a subset of* $\Omega^1_T \times \Omega^2_T \times \Omega_p$. *For all* $\omega \in \Omega$, *the components of* ω^1_T *are related to the components of* ω_p *in the following way:*

(*i*) $Bel(\{C_Y\}) = \alpha_2/90$, $Bel(\{C_B\}) = (60 - \alpha_3)/90$, $Bel(\{C_R, C_Y\}) = (30 + \alpha_4)/90$, *and* $Bel(\{C_R, C_B\}) = (90 - \alpha_5)/90$.

(*ii*) *Seen as vectors in* R^3, $x_i = X_i$, $i = 1, \ldots, 14$.

(*iii*) *With a suitable choice of equivalent acts, the choice functions* $\mathrm{ch}(\cdot)$ *and* $\mathrm{CH}(\cdot)$ *are equal.*

(*iv*) *With a suitable choice of equivalent acts, the choice functions* $\mathrm{ch}(\cdot|\cdot)$ *and* $\mathrm{CH}(\cdot|\cdot)$ *are equal.*

$\boldsymbol{\Gamma^2_{t,p}}$ *For all* $\omega \in \Omega$, *the components of* ω^2_T *are related to the components of* ω_p *in the following way:*

(*i*) $P(\{C_Y\}) = \alpha_2/90$, $P(\{C_B\}) = (60 - \alpha_3/90)$, $P(\{C_R, C_Y\}) = (30 + \alpha_4)/90$, *and* $P(\{C_R, C_B\}_= (90 - \alpha_5)/90$.

(*ii*) *Seen as vectors in* R^3, $y_i = X_i$, $i = 1, \ldots, 14$.

(*iii*) *With a suitable choice of equivalent acts, the choice functions* $\mathrm{ch}^2(\cdot)$ *and* $\mathrm{CH}(\cdot)$ *are equal.*

(*iv*) *With a suitable choice of equivalent acts the choice functions* $\mathrm{ch}^2(\cdot|\cdot)$ *and* $\mathrm{CH}(\cdot|\cdot)$ *are equal.*

18.4.5 Theorems for the Test

From the preceding system of axioms for a theory-data confrontation of B 1–B 8 and the Bayesian theory of choice in uncertain situations one can derive interesting theorems concerning characteristics of the data universe. I begin with two theorems, one of which imposes stringent conditions on the Bayesian theory:

T 4 *If* Γ^1_t, $\Gamma^1_{t,p}$, *and* Γ_p *are valid, then* $\alpha_2 \leq \alpha_4 \leq \alpha_5 \leq \alpha_3$.

T 5 *If* Γ^2_t, $\Gamma^2_{t,p}$, *and* Γ_p *are valid, then* $\alpha_2 = \alpha_3 = \alpha_4 = \alpha_5$.

If *M*'s answers do not satisfy T 4 and T 5, then neither B 1–B 8 nor the Bayesian theory is relevant in the given empirical context. If *M*'s answers satisfy both theorems, then the remainder of the test amounts to checking whether the Bayesian theory is empirically relevant in the given context. If *M*'s answers satisfy T 4 but not T 5, one must look to other theorems to check whether B 1–B 8 is relevant in the given empirical context.

Next I suppose that *M*'s answers satisfy T 4 but not T 5 and present several theorems for testing the empirical relevance of B 1–B 8.

T 6 *Suppose that* Γ^1_t, $\Gamma^1_{t,p}$, *and* Γ_p *are valid and that* $\alpha_2 < 30$ *and* $\alpha_5 > 30$. *Then,*

$$X_1 = CH(\{X_1, X_2\}),\ X_6 = CH(\{X_5, X_6\}),$$
$$X_{10} = CH(\{X_9, X_{10}\}),\ X_{12} = CH(\{X_{11}, X_{12}\}),$$

and

$$X_{13} = CH(\{X_{13}, X_{14}\}).$$

Here the choice of X_1 in the first option and the choice of X_6 in the second option violate Savage's (1954, p. 23) sure-thing principle. These choices reveal the B 1–B 8 decision-maker's preference for certainty over uncertainty.

There is an interesting modification of the sure-thing principle in which the preferences of a B 1–B 8 decision-maker satisfy T 19.10 in my earlier book. (cf. Stigum, 1990, p. 446). This fact is reflected in the choices of X_{10} in $\{X_9, X_{10}\}$, X_{12} in $\{X_{11}, X_{12}\}$, and X_{13} in $\{X_{13}, X_{14}\}$ and the (derived) choice of X_{15} in $\{X_{15}, X_{16}\}$, where X_{15} and X_{16} are described in Table 18.3. The characteristic of the acts $X_9, \ldots, X_{12}(X_{13}, \ldots, X_{16})$ that is relevant in this context is that the values they assume in $\{C_B\}$ are larger than or equal to (smaller than or equal to) the values they assume in $\{C_R, C_Y\}$.

Finally, for the import of the test it is significant that the choices that T 6 describes depend on $U(\cdot)$ being increasing but not on the form of $U(\cdot)$ as such.

T 7 *Suppose that* Γ_t^1, $\Gamma_{t,p}^1$, *and* Γ_{p2} *are valid and that* $\alpha_2 < 30$ *and* $\alpha_5 > 30$. *Then*

$$X_6 = CH(\{X_6, X_7\} \mid NR) \text{ and } X_6 = CH(\{X_6, X_{11}\} \mid NR),$$
$$X_3 = CH(\{X_1, X_3\} \mid NY) \text{ and } X_5 = CH(\{X_5, X_8\} \mid NY),$$
$$X_2 = CH(\{X_1, X_2\} \mid NB).$$

Here the choice of X_6 in $\{X_6, X_7\}$ and $\{X_6, X_{11}\}$ and the choice of X_5 in $\{X_5, X_8\}$ reflect the B 1–B 8 decision-maker's remarkable preference for certainty over uncertainty. Note also that the B 1–B 8 decision-maker upon knowledge of NY switches his choice in $\{X_1, X_3\}$ from X_1 to X_3. Similarly, upon knowledge of NB the decision-maker switches his choice in $\{X_1, X_2\}$ from X_1 to X_2. The reason is that knowledge of NY (NB) increases the decision-maker's belief in the possible occurrence of $\{C_B\}$ ($\{C_Y\}$).

The choice of X_6 in the first two options and the choice of X_5 in the fourth option depend on the form of $U(\cdot)$. The choice of X_3 in the third option and the choice of X_2 in the fifth option are independent of the form of $U(\cdot)$.

TABLE 18.3
An Interesting Pair of Prospects

	X_{15}	X_{16}
C_R	100	50
C_Y	50	100
C_B	50	50

Finally, suppose that M's answers satisfy both T 4 and T 5, and let α be the common value of the α_i, $i = 2, 3, 4, 5$, in T 5. Then the Bayesian theory and the B 1–B 8 theory are empirically relevant in the situation I consider only if the decision-maker's choices among acts accord with T 8 and T 9:

T 8 *Suppose that* Γ_t^2, $\Gamma_{t,p}^2$, *and* Γ_p *are valid, and let* α *be the common value of the* α_1 *in T 5. Suppose also that* $\alpha \leq 30$. *Then*

$$X_1 = CH(\{X_1, X_2\}),\ X_5 = CH(\{X_5, X_6\}),$$
$$X_9 = CH(\{X_9, X_{10}\}),\ X_{11} = CH(\{X_{11}, X_{12}\}),$$

and

$$X_{13} = CH(\{X_{13}, X_{14}\}).$$

Here the choice of X_5 in $\{X_5, X_6\}$ is in accord with the choice of X_1 in $\{X_1, X_2\}$ and the sure-thing principle. Similarly, the choice of X_{11} in $\{X_{11}, X_{12}\}$ is in accord with the choice of X_9 in $\{X_9, X_{10}\}$ and the sure-thing principle. Finally, X_{13} in $\{X_{13}, X_{14}\}$ is in accord with the choice of X_{11} in $\{X_{11}, X_{12}\}$ and the sure-thing principle. All the indicated choices are independent of $U(\cdot)$.

T 9 *Suppose that* Γ_t^2, $\Gamma_{t,p}^2$, *and* Γ_p *are valid, and let* α *be as in T 8. Suppose also that* $\alpha \leq 30$. *Then,*

$$CH(\{X_6, X_7\} \mid NR) = X_6 \text{ or } X_7 \text{ according as } \alpha \geq 15 \text{ or } \alpha \leq 15.$$
$$CH(\{X_6, X_{11}\} \mid NR) = X_6 \text{ or } X_{11} \text{ according as } \alpha \geq 27 \text{ or } \alpha \leq 27,$$
$$X_3 = CH(\{X_1, X_3\} \mid NY);\ X_5 = CH(\{X_5, X_8\} \mid NY),$$

and

$$X_1 = CH(\{X_1, X_2\} \mid NB).$$

When $\alpha = 30$, the decision-maker is indifferent between X_1 and X_3 in $\{X_1, X_3\}$ and between X_1 and X_2 in $\{X_1, X_2\}$. Note also that the numbers 15 and 27 vary with the $U(\cdot)$ function. The other choices are independent of $U(\cdot)$. Except for that, T 9 speaks for itself and needs no further comment.

18.5 AN EXPLORATORY CASE STUDY

I have not yet been able to conduct a full-fledged test of the two rival theories of choice under uncertainty. So I must be content to recount the results of an exploratory case study that Rajiv Sarin and I carried out at Texas A&M University.

The subjects in the test were thirty of Rajiv's undergraduate students majoring in economics. The laboratory was a classroom, and the blindfolded man was only present in the formulation of the questions we asked the subjects.

There were six different urns: A, $B20$, $B25$, $B30$, $B35$, and $B40$. All of them contained ninety M&M's, thirty of which were pink and sixty of which were yellow or green. The composition of yellow and green M&M's was uncertain in A and equaled i yellow and $60 - i$ green in Bi, $i = 20, 25, 30, 35, 40$.

The subjects were asked to choose between the components of nine pairs of lotteries the outcomes of which depended on the color of the M&M that the blindfolded outsider would pull from an urn. In nine of the lotteries the urn was A and in five of the lotteries the urn was one of the Bi. The lotteries are all shown in the top half of Table 18.4. There E is short for event, L is short for lottery, and R, Y, and G stand for a pink, yellow, and green M&M. Also, the numbers 4, 2, and 1 stand for so many U.S. dollars. In the analysis that follows I identify these numbers with the decision-maker's utility.

The pairs of lotteries among whose components the subjects were asked to choose were (LA_1, LA_2), (LA_3, LA_4), (LA_5, LA_6), (LA_7, LA_8), $(LA_9, LB20)$, $(LA_9, LB25)$, $(LA_9, LB30)$, $(LA_9, LB35)$, and $(LA_9, LB40)$. In the second half of Table 18.4, preference for a component of a pair of lotteries is indicated by a 1, indifference by 0.5, and not preferred by a 0. For example, PM prefers LA_1 to LA_2, OP prefers LA_5 to LA_6, and BA is indifferent between LA_7 and LA_8. Here PM is short for pessimist, OP for optimist, and BA for Bayesian. The sequences of 1's and 0's in the second half of the table describe the way I would expect a pessimist, an optimist, and a Bayesian to choose.

In Table 18.4 a pessimist is a decision-maker whose preferences satisfy axioms B 6 and B 7 and who chooses among options in accordance with B 8. Furthermore, a pessimist's basic probability assignment is taken to satisfy the conditions $m(\{R\}) = 1/3, m(\{Y\}) < 1/3, m(\{G\}) < 1/3, m(\{Y, G\}) = 2/3 - m(\{Y\}) - m(\{G\})$, and $m(\{R, Y\}) = m(\{R, G\}) = m(\{R, Y, G\}) = 0$. If these assumptions are correct and if we interpret the numbers in the top half of the table as utilities, it is straightforward to check that a pessimist's answers to our queries must be as I have indicated in Table 18.4.

An optimist in Table 18.4 is a decision-maker whose preferences satisfy B 6 and a modified version of B 7, and who chooses among options in accordance with B 8. In the modified version of B 7, $W_x^o(B) = \max_{\omega \in B} U[x(\omega)]$ and $V(x) = \sum_{A \subset \Omega} W_x^o(A)m(A)$. Also, an optimist's basic probability assignment is taken to satisfy the same conditions as the basic probability assignment of a pessimist. If that is correct and if the numbers in the top half of the table represent utilities, it is easy to check that an optimist's answers to our queries must be as I have indicated in Table 18.4.

A Bayesian in Table 18.4 is a decision-maker who assigns probabilities the way the Bayesian did in E 18.1 and who chooses among prospects according to their expected utility. If the numbers in the top half of the table represent utilities, then a Bayesian's answers to our queries must be as I have indicated in Table 18.4.

TABLE 18.4
Prospects for a Pessimist, an Optimist, and a Bayesian

$E\backslash L$	LA_1	LA_2	LA_3	LA_4	LA_5	LA_6	LA_7	LA_8	LA_9	$LB20$	$LB25$	$LB30$	$LB35$	$LB40$
$\{R\}$	4	0	4	0	4	2	4	2	0	0	0	0	0	0
$\{Y\}$	0	4	0	4	2	4	2	4	4	4	4	4	4	4
$\{G\}$	0	0	4	4	4	4	1	1	0	0	0	0	0	0
PM	1	0	0	1	0	1	1	0				1	1	1
OP	0	1	1	0	1	0	0	1	1	1	1	0		
BA	0.5	0.5	0.5	0.5	0.5	0.5	0.5	0.5	0.5	$<$	$<$	0.5	$>$	$>$

The results of our experiment can be summarized as follows:

1. Fifteen students answered in accordance with my prescriptions for a pessimist. Of these, four insisted that $\alpha < 20$, five that $20 < \alpha < 25$, and six that $25 < \alpha < 30$.
2. Eight answered the way a pessimist was expected to answer but with one "error." Of these, two insisted that $LA_1 \sim LA_2$ and that $25 < \alpha < 30$. Five insisted that $LA_8 > LA_7$. Of them one claimed that $\alpha = 20$, two claimed that $20 < \alpha < 25$, and two claimed that $25 < \alpha < 30$. Finally, one made an error in indicating the value of his α.
3. Two subjects answered the way a pessimist with $m(\{Y\}) > 1/3$, an optimist with $m(\{G\}) > 1/3$, or a Bayesian who assigns probability greater than 1/3 to $\{Y\}$ would have answered.
4. Five subjects answered in a way that I have not been able to understand.

In answering so many questions it must be all right to allow a student one mistake. If I do, I see that Allais's theory fared well in the test while the Bayesian theory of choice did poorly.[4]

NOTES

1. For an interesting article on the properties of capacities the reader is referred to (Chateauneuf and Jaffray, 1989).

2. The axioms B 1–B 8 are based on ideas that I have got from Glenn Shafer (1976), Kjell Arne Brekke, Alain Chateauneuf (1986), and Itzhak Gilboa (1987).

3. I owe the ideas for these questions to many interesting discussions with Michele Cohen and Jean-Yves Jaffray.

4. The Bayesians did not fare too well in the test. For that reason one might enjoy reading M. A. El-Gamal and D. M Grether's (1995) interesting article, "Are People Bayesian? Uncovering Behavioral Strategies."

REFERENCES

Allais, M., 1988, "The General Theory of Random Choices in Relation to the Invariant Cardinal Utility Function and the Specific Probability Function," in: B. R. Munier (ed.), *Risk, Decision and Rationality*, Dordrecht: Reidel.

Chateauneuf, A., 1986, "Uncertainty Aversion and Risk Aversion in Models with Non-additive Probabilities," Mimeographed Paper, Université de Paris.

Chateauneuf, A., and J.-Y. Jaffray, 1989, "Some Characterization of Lower Probabilities and Other Monotone Capacities Through the Use of Moebius Inversion," *Mathematical Social Sciences* 17, 263–283.

El-Gamal, M. A., and D. M. Grether, 1995, "Are People Bayesian?: Uncovering Behavioral Strategies," *Journal of the American Statistical Association* 90, 1137–1145.

Ellsberg, D., 1961, "Risk, Ambiguity and the Savage Axioms," *Quarterly Journal of Economics* 75, 643–669.

Gilboa, I., 1987, "Expected Utility with Purely Subjective Non-additive Probabilities," *Journal of Mathematical Economics* 16, 65–88.

Kolmogorov, A., 1933, *Grundbegriffe der Wahrscheinlichkeitsrechnung*, Berlin: Chelsea.

Savage, L. J., 1954, *The Foundations of Statistics*, New York: Wiley.

Shafer, G., 1976, *A Mathematical Theory of Evidence*, Princeton: Princeton University Press.

Stigum, B., 1990, *Toward a Formal Science of Economics*, Cambridge: MIT Press.

Chapter Nineteen

Evaluation of Theories and Models

Clive W. J. Granger

If one encounters or generates a new theory or model how does one know how good it is? To an econometrician, the immediate approach to this question is to ask how well the theory approximates or captures important features of the actual economy. However, there still remain many ways that the quality of this approximation can be measured. This chapter starts by surveying some of the statistical measures of quality considered by econometricians, then discusses the application concerning the U.S. Treasury bill market described by Heather Anderson in Chapter 21 of this volume, and after brief consideration of two other examples finally explores the use of economic criteria to evaluate economic theories.

19.1 BASIC STATISTICAL EVALUATION PROCEDURES

Within the process of building empirical models, economic theory can make a substantial contribution toward determining the specification of the model. The traditional contribution of econometrics was to provide estimates of any unknown parameters in the model. Under the assumption that the model is in some sense correct, or at least a good approximation to reality, the theory can be used to interpret the model so derived as well as to suggest any policy implications. However, this assumption is a substantial one and surely should be tested if possible. This introduces the question of how a model can be evaluated. In fact, the problem of how models, or economic theories, should be evaluated has received relatively little attention. In general it is quite difficult to answer the question whether a single model is satisfactory in quality; it is easier to determine if one model is better than another, which is largely a problem of choosing a relevant criterion.

When viewing a single model in sample, that is, using the same data that were used to estimate the parameters of the model, the classical measures of quality consider the goodness-of-fit of the model and the significance, or relevance, of individual or groups of parameters. Although the approaches to evaluation can be applied to wide classes of models, it is easiest to think of the linear regression model

$$Y_t = \boldsymbol{\beta}'\boldsymbol{X}_t + e_t,$$

where Y_t is the variable to be explained, usually called the dependent variable, and $\boldsymbol{\beta}'$ is the vector of explanatory variables with corresponding parameters stacked in the vector $\boldsymbol{\beta}$. It is called a linear model here because it is taken to be linear in the parameters. The two obvious measures of goodness-of-fit are: (1) R^2, which represents the proportion of the variance of Y_t that is explained by the X's; and (2) the likelihood value, which, if it is assumed that the e_t are independently and identically distributed with p.d.f. $P(e)$, is given by $L_t = \Pi_{t=1}^{T} P(e_t)$ for a sample $t = 1, \ldots, T$. If the e_t are not iid, L_t is obtained from the joint distribution.

Neither measure is actually very helpful in deciding if a model is good or not because there is no absolute value against which they can be compared. One might think of a rule such as an R^2 more than 0.7 is good but under 0.2 is unsatisfactory, but such rules are clearly arbitrary, as processes will vary in the extent to which they can be explained. A sequence of independent draws from a distribution can only have $R^2 = 0$, whereas a deterministic time series should have $R^2 = 1$ if the correct specification can be found. However, both measures can be useful for comparing alternative models for the same dependent variable, particularly if nested models are being compared by their likelihood values.

The difficulty with using R^2 with nonnested models can be simply illustrated by the two models

$$Y_t = \boldsymbol{\beta}'_1\boldsymbol{X}_t + e_{1t} \qquad R_1^2$$

and

$$Y_t = \boldsymbol{\beta}'_2\boldsymbol{Z}_t + e_{1t} \qquad R_2^2$$

with $R_1^2 < R_2^2$ but a theory says that the model involving X is interpretable and that Z should not be included in a model as it is not interpretable. At face value it appears that the theory using $\boldsymbol{X}_t$ does not fit the data as well as the alternative using $\boldsymbol{Z}_t$, and so the results do not support the theory. Of course, a cynic may say that another economic theory will be constructed to explain the new empirical fact that $\boldsymbol{Z}_t$ is a better explanatory set of variables than $\boldsymbol{X}_t$. Before taking this position it is necessary to carefully examine the contents of $\boldsymbol{Z}_t$ to make sure that a spuriously high fit is being achieved, as would occur if some components of Y_t are embedded within parts of $\boldsymbol{Z}_t$ or if the true causal relationship ran in the reverse direction, from Y_t to $\boldsymbol{Z}_t$. The problems are usually ameliorated if the model is carefully written as a reduced form. If, after such efforts, the "theoretically unacceptable model" continues to fit better than the "acceptable" form, the problem of interpretation is greater for the theorist than for the econometrician, although it might be better to attempt to nest the models when possible or to include the equation within a larger system of equations.

The significance or not of a parameter estimate can be judged from its associated estimated standard error and corresponding t-statistics. However, the interpretation of these quantities is not straightforward if the residuals of the model are autocorrelated. The earliest test proposed to investigate whether the residuals are serially correlated was based on the Durbin-Watson statistic, which is approximately $2(1 - \hat{\rho}_1)$, where $\hat{\rho}_1$ is an estimate of the correlation between a residual e_t and its lagged value e_{t-1}. Although still an important test statistic, its use can cause other important temporal structures in the residuals to be missed, such as a seasonal effect, represented by a high correlation between e_t and e_{t-12}, for monthly data.

Rather than just trying to evaluate a given form of a model, one common exercise is to compare, or nest, this model in one that is extended in a specific direction. These are considered to be *specification tests*, which enquire if the original model has an adequate specification in some direction or if an improved specification would provide a better model. The extensions usually take the form of missing components, such as particular lagged dependent variables, some specific missing X variables, a seasonality term, a trend (often approximated by a linear function of time), some specific nonlinear terms in the X's, such as powers X^P, autocorrelations in the residuals, or heteroskedasticity. As the original model is nested in the expanded one, the two likelihood values can be compared in the form of a likelihood ratio test (in practice, it is usual to express the test as the asymptotically equivalent Lagrange multiplier test). If the original model fails a specification test, an improved model is immediately suggested by the alternative model. However, interpretation is more difficult if the core model is tested simultaneously against a number of alternative specifications, as the test statistics are not independent and "fixing" one specification problem may also appear to solve several other such difficulties. A problem with this modeling strategy is that it clearly contains some elements of the process of "data mining," where one searches over many models to find the one that best fits the data, possibly ending up with a model that overfits. Some of the nonlinear model-fitting techniques, such as those based on neural networks, face this dilemma, which makes them difficult to evaluate in sample, that is, using the same data for evaluation as was used for the specification search and the model estimation.

For a careful analysis of the problems of fitting highly nonparsimonious nonlinear models in practice see Swanson and White (1995a,b), who consider the usefulness of artificial neural network models compared to linear models on various economic series. Their first paper considers the question of whether forward interest rates are useful in predicting future spot rates and the second investigates the forecastability of several major economic series. No one method appears to dominate the alternatives if one considers several criteria for evaluating forecasts, which probably suggests the need for a general theory of forecast evaluation.

There are various types of specification searching. The original specification tests compared a model, possibly derived from a theory of some level of sophistication, with a slightly extended model, adding just one or a few extra terms. All the models use the same information set, but if a missing variable is considered in the specification test, the information set is expanded by the extra variables, although these are traditionally only a few in number. More recently developed techniques, such as neural network models or semiparametric models use the same information set but much richer parametrifications, so that it is possible to move further away from the original specification. One protective strategy that has good statistical and intellectual credentials is modeling from general to simple, as discussed by Hendry (1995). Thus one starts with a prespecified model but in as general a form as considered plausible, and then goes through a process of simplification using the results of progressive tests, usually by dropping terms with insignificant parameters.

A different form of data mining involves expansion of the information set and asking if a new array of models using a wider set is better than models based on the smaller set. If the number of possible explanatory variables m becomes large enough and even if one decides to use a linear model involving just $p \ll m$ explanatory variables, then there are many possible specifications that can be considered, taking draws of size p from the m, and if one searches widely over the choices one has the specification search problem introduced by Leamer (1978). This says that if one searches enough, a model that fits spuriously well may be obtained. A related problem is that when reporting the research results, the discarded models may not be mentioned, so the quality of the model presented will be overemphasized, possibly even deliberately misrepresented.

In many of the physical sciences, including meteorology, there is a belief that if the information set is expanded sufficiently, the fit of the model becomes almost perfect, so that there is no, or essentially no, uncertainty in the system, except possibly for small amounts of measurement error. Fewer social scientists hold such a belief. Although a few econometricians consider chaotic processes and economic theorists often propose deterministic models, I think that most econometricians believe that asymptotically R^2 will not tend to one as the content of the information set is expanded. For any particular dependent variable there will be some upper bound in explainability, but given that any information set can be used, with any model, it is virtually impossible to determine this bound. Thus, measures of quality for a single model are difficult to interpret in any absolute sense. When applied to a pair of models they can be used to rank them but one still does not know how well the better of the two models (or some combination of them) compares to the best possible model.

The well-known model-selection criteria, such AIC, BIC, or Hannan-Quinn, are helpful when considering alternative model specification and emphasize parsimony in the number of parameters used, but they are not particularly helpful for overall model evaluation.

If one builds a model using k parameters, resulting in residuals with variance $\sigma^2(k)$, these criteria are defined as:

$$\text{AIC} = \log \sigma^2(k) + 2k/T,$$
$$\text{BIC} = \log \sigma^2(k) + k \log T/T,$$
$$\text{HIC} = \log \sigma^2(k) + \log \log T/T,$$

where T is the sample size (all logs are to base e). As k increases, the goodness-of-fit of the model will increase, and thus $\sigma^2(k)$ should decrease, so the final term is designed to be a penalty against lack of parsimony. One chooses k to minimize the criterion for fixed T. If the true model has a finite number of parameters, the BIC is generally considered to be the best criterion, but if this number is infinite then AIC is better. The criteria are rather arbitrary but nevertheless useful in preventing grossly overparameterized models. They are phrased in terms of $\log \sigma^2(k)$, but this can be written as $\log(1 - R^2(k))$ apart from the constant log VAR Y and so the criteria are related to the usual R^2. Although these quantities are certainly useful with the model specification process they are not relevant for model evaluation.

A technique that has been frequently used and often criticized is dynamic simulation of the model. As these simulations are not usually compared to the actual economy, one ends up learning something about the properties of the model but not its quality as an approximation to the economy. It might have theoretically desirable properties and also contain some stylized facts, but it may also miss many important features of reality.

A sophisticated approach to comparing models considered in a series of papers by Hendry, Mizen, and Richard, summarized in Hendry (1995, ch. 14), is called *encompassing*. Suppose that M_1 and M_2 are a pair of models, with M_1 the model of preference or of particular interest. In simple terms, M_1 will encompass M_2 if using M_1 one can deduce all of the properties, forecasts, and policy recommendations made by M_2. Thus essentially M_1 contains all the information that M_2 can provide. For example, "forecast encompassing" occurs if M_1, M_2 give forecasts $f_{1,f}$, $f_{2,t}$ for some variable and then no combination $\theta_1 f_{1,t} + \theta_2 f_{2,t}$ exists that is superior to $f_{1,t}$ according to a least-squares criterion. It will often be the case that for a pair of models, neither encompasses the other, so the approach does not always provide a ranking of models. Models may be nested but need not be for encompassing to occur. Clearly, testing is easier if the models are nested, with M_1 parsimonious compared to M_2, so that it has the same structural form, but some parameters in M_2 may be set to zero without loss of the usefulness of the model. This is known as *parsimonious encompassing*. If a model has a number of simplifying properties (such as homoskedasticity), has constant parameters, and agrees with the theory and the available data in various ways, it is called *congruent* (Hendry 1995, ch. 9). A model that is both congruent and encompasses alternative models is called *congruent encompassing* and is considered to be particularly desirable. In some realistic modeling situations, it may not be possible to achieve such a model.

Clearly encompassing is concerned with subtle, textual difference among empirical models and is thus unrelated to overall, summary measures, such as R^2.

Most comparisons of models use in-sample data. These data have already been used for estimation and for specification searches and thus have been somewhat bleached of their value. Many econometricians, but not all, feel that there is an advantage in evaluating and comparing models on a fresh, unused data set, such as a postsample in a time-series context or data held back for evaluation purposes in a panel or cross-section modeling exercise. There are a number of procedures available for evaluating and comparing forecasts, as discussed in Granger and Newbold (1987, ch. 7), Diebold and Mariano (1995), and Clements and Hendry (1993). For example, some simple procedures involve:

1. For a set of forecasts $f_{n,1}$ made at time n of X_{n+1}, regress

$$X_{n+1} = \alpha + \beta f_{n,1} + \varepsilon_{n+1}$$

then a necessary but not sufficient set of conditions that the forecasts are optimal for some information set that includes lagged X's is that $\alpha = 0, \beta = 1$, and the γ's should be zero mean white noise; that is the γ's should be temporarily uncorrelated.

2. If $f_{n,1}, g_{n,1}$ are a pair of one-step forecasts of X_{n+1} based on different models, then one can compare postsample mean-squared errors, but to perform a test, first form the series

$$s_n = ef_{n,1} + eg_{n,1},$$
$$d_n = ef_{n,1} - eg_{n,1},$$

where ef and eg are the errors arising from f and g and then test if $\text{corr}(s_n, d_n) = 0$. The null hypothesis is $E\left[ef^2\right] = E\left[eg^2\right]$ and it is assumed that each forecast is unbiased. Diebold and Mariano (1995) give a more sophisticated version of this test.

3. The estimated right-hand side, apart from the residual, of the regression

$$X_{n+1} = \alpha + \beta_1 f_{n,1} + \beta_2 g_{n,1} + \gamma X_n + \varepsilon_{n+1}$$

will provide a combined forecast that will often prove superior to each component. The weights represent some measure of the relative values of the two forecasts. This is clearly closely related to the idea of forecast encompassing. The means-squared error (MSE) of the best combined forecast can be compared to the MSE values of the individual forecasts, to get a simple numerical comparison.

All of the above techniques assume that the cost function being used to form the forecasts, and thus relevant to evaluating them, is the squared error. In most cases, equivalent results can be obtained for a general cost function if it is known, as discussed in Granger (1999).

A different type of "out-of-sample" evaluation technique, which is used mostly for cross-sectional and panel data, involves "cross-validation." Here part of the original sample is held back, the model specified and estimated on the rest of the data, and the model then used to predict the missing values, which can be compared to the actual values held out and squared errors recorded. This process can be repeated many times with parts of the original sample held back and the results averaged over all of the samples. Which part of the original sample is not used at any stage can either be decided from a random selection procedure or deterministically. The use of the procedure is illustrated in Granger and Huang (1997).

Many evaluation exercises consider a new model or technique and compare it with an older technology, usually with the objective of showing that it is better. A recently developed procedure, known as "data snooping," compares the new method with many alternative plausible methods and asks how well it performs within this larger group (White, 2000). For example, the well-known "January effect" (in which stocks do better in January than in other months) is compared to nearly 8,000 alternative plausible trading rules and is not found to be particularly spectacular (see Sullivan et al., 1999).

19.2 EVALUATION OF ANDERSON'S MODEL OF THE U.S. TREASURY BILL MARKET

Anderson (Chapter 21, this volume) discusses the specification, estimation, and evaluation of a time-series model for the U.S. Treasury bill market. The model uses rational-expectations theory in two forms: In the first an assumption is made that the term premium is constant over time and in the second this assumption is relaxed. The general specifications are thus theory based, within a linear framework, and a general-to-specific modeling strategy is used, starting with a parameter-rich form of the models, which is then pared down to a more parsimonious form by dropping insignificant parameters. Statistics that can be used to judge the relevance of the original, baseline model are given in Anderson's Table 3, and for the parsimonious model in her Table 7. The specification search includes examination of cointegration possibilities, and the search takes place within an error-correction model framework.

I would like to argue the position that when considering the value, or quality, of a model the method used to construct it, that is, how it was specified and estimated, is of no relevance. The final product is presented for evaluation and it is the properties of this model, particularly its output, that should be evaluated. Remember the famous aphorism, "judge a cigar by its flavor, not by who made it." (If that was not said by someone famous, then it should have been.)

When Jesus began to exposit His beliefs they were judged by their content not His background. Most people did not ask, "Who brought you up; what is your occupation; where have you been for the past 15 years?" They judged the beliefs in terms of their apparent strengths and quality. The only exceptions were those of His hometown of Nazareth, who knew of His early years and could not forget them when considering His speeches.

This being the case, it is interesting to see how an expert applied time-series economist, such as Anderson, looks at the results of her Table 1 and the LM diagnostic, or specification tests, and sees that the simple univariate model under the table heading is clearly misspecified, getting low p-values associated with the probability p that the null hypothesis of no misspecification is correct. If one is using a linear framework, cointegration and thus error-correction models become likely candidates and the results in Anderson's Tables 2 and 3 show that a plausible baseline model is achievable, which possesses the specification test properties. The next set of questions relates to whether one can apply constraints to the baseline model, reducing the number of parameters, and still have an apparently satisfactory model. This is discussed in Anderson's Tables 4 to 7.

In Tables 19.1 and 19.2 R^2 for the baseline and parsimonious models can be compared; the numbers are those provided by Heather Anderson.

If these are converted into corrected R^2 by the usual formula

$$R_c^2 = 1 - \frac{n-1}{n-k}\left(1 - R^2\right)$$

for sample size n and k parameter, Table 19.1 is modified into Table 19.2.

It can be seen from Tables 19.1 and 19.2 that one does not necessarily pay a penalty in terms of R_c^2 or in mean-squared error and likelihood by preferring a parsimonious model. The specification search, quite properly, was done just in sample, except for a postsample Chow test for change of structure using a very

TABLE 19.1
R^2 for Baseline and Parsimonious Models

	Endogenous variable			
R^2	$\Delta R(1,t)$	$\Delta R(2,t)$	$\Delta FF(t)$	$\Delta B(t)$
Baseline	0.8263	0.6969	0.6129	0.2986
(32 Parameters)				
Parsimonious	0.7687	0.6072	0.4997	0.1457
(Parameters)	(9)	(19)	(8)	(10)
Percent reduction	7	13	18	51

TABLE 19.2
Corrected R^2 for Models

R_c^2	Endogenous variable			
	$\Delta R(1,t)$	$\Delta R(2,t)$	$\Delta FF(t)$	$\Delta B(t)$
Baseline	0.7719	0.6020	0.4919	0.0799
Parsimonious	0.7687	0.6072	0.4997	0.1457
Percent reduction	0.4	−0.8	−1.6	−82

short interval, and all the measures of quality provided are also in sample. To compare models it is helpful to perform a postsample forecasting comparison exercise on data that were not involved with the fairly intense specification search and testing procedure that was used here. The results are shown in Anderson (Chapter 21, this volume, figs. 21.3, 21.4). It is shown that imposing rational expectations does not provide superior forecasts.

Overall, this is a good example of a modern piece of time-series econometrics, with evaluation based on statistical measures.

19.3 EVALUATION OF A THEORY OF UNCERTAIN UTILITY FOR LOW-PRICED GOODS

If, in a real world, a consumer is considering the purpose of a particular good or product with price P, then for each P there is a probability $B(P)$ that a member of the buying public, chosen at random, will find the article belonging within her acceptable price range. As P increases, one can expect that the probability will decrease, with more consumers finding the price unacceptably high. For goods that have not been purchased before, such as a new brand of shirt or wine, too low a price can lead to a belief that an unsatisfactory utility will be realized from the purchase. This is a component of the "price as an indicator of quality" argument. A specific functional form for $B(P)$ was given by Granger (1988) and Gabor (1988). Based on simple theory and experimental results, they suggested that $B(P)$ can be written as

$$B(P) = 1 - \Phi_1(p) - \Phi_2(p),$$

where $p = \log P$, Φ_1, Φ_2 are cumulative Gaussian distribution functions in $\log P$, $N(m_1, \sigma)$, $N(m_2, \sigma)$, and where there may be a linear relationship between $m_2 - m_1$ and σ. Knowing $B(P)$ is helpful in marketing strategies, particularly for new products.

To evaluate the theory one needs realistic data. An obvious source is asking consumers by a "doorstep" or telephone survey or when they enter or leave a store, "If a shirt that appears to be of satisfactory quality is priced P, would you buy it?" Different people would be offered different values of P. Although real potential consumers are used, they are placed in an artificial situation so that the collection of data will not provide a satisfactory evaluation of the theory. For that the consumer needs to be placed in a realistic situation. The researchers were initially allowed to offer prices of several items in a single supermarket over an 8- to 10-week period, and later the work was extended to several supermarkets within the same city. Prices were changed every 2 weeks, sales recorded, and a sample of consumers were given the "what would you do if the prices were . . . ?" questionnaire as they entered the shop. Another group was asked if they changed their minds in the store and, if so, why? The results obtained generally supported the theory within this realistic context; details can be found in Gabor (1988) and the papers discussed in that volume. As the experiments might have affected profits, the experimental design could not contain many lower prices as the stores were naturally reluctant to trade at a guaranteed loss. Nevertheless, a few low prices were included. It seems strange that more aspects of microeconomic theory are not evaluated by using in-store experiments as these experiments are frequently used to check marketing theories.

19.4 EVALUATION OF THE BLACK-SCHOLES OPTION-PRICING THEORY

In the area of finance the theory of option pricing owing to Black and Scholes (1973) is particularly well known. A description can be found in Campbell et al. (1997, ch. 9). Given certain assumptions, including a no-arbitrage condition, the options price will obey a second-order linear parabolic partial differential equation that, subject to two boundary conditions, has a unique solution, which is generally known as the Black-Scholes formula. This relates the option price and Φ the standard deviation, or volatility measure, of a variable that is assumed to have a normal distribution. In fact, if other observable parameters (some prices and an interest rate) are taken as given, there is a unique one-to-one relationship between the option prices and Φ. However, Φ is unobservable, at least directly, although it can be "implied" from the Black-Scholes formula.

How can one evaluate the Black-Scholes option-pricing theory? If the assumptions upon which it is based hold true then clearly the theory will be correct within that context. In practice, a couple of the assumptions are simplifications of the actual world and one assumption, that of normality, is generally acknowledged to be incorrect. Nevertheless, the theory may give an excellent approximation to reality, or it may not.

One obvious test is to see if the implied volatilities, which are estimates of forthcoming standard deviations, are better forecasts than alternatives using other standard techniques. There are, in fact, many empirical studies that consider forecasts of the variances of stock market returns, which have been summarized in Poon and Granger (2003). Different studies reach somewhat different conclusions: A few find that the "implied volatilities" from the Black-Scholes approach do rather well compared to alternatives, but the majority view seems to be that it is not necessarily the best method. Only a few studies consider combinations of volatility forecasts; those that do usually find that the combination forecast does better than the components and the combination will usually give positive weight to the implied volatility. The results suggest that the Black-Scholes theory does not completely agree with all aspects of the actual market, but it may contain useful aspects not captured by simple statistical models.

19.5 HOW SHOULD QUALITY BE JUDGED?

Suppose that I have to make an important decision about watermelons and that knowing the elasticity of demand for watermelons in my area would be helpful in making the decision. Using the same data set, three econometricians come up with three different estimates, so how do I choose the one I should use in my decision? If I ask other econometricians this question, I find that they want to base the choice on the perceived quality of the methods used to get the estimates: Is the procedure used known to produce consistent estimates, do the tests used have the correct sizes for the critical values, and so forth. What is interesting in this behavior is that their attention is directed toward technique and not toward the quality of the output of the procedures, in this case the estimates of elasticity. I suggest that it would be more appropriate to ask about the degree of success of previous decisions based on elasticity estimates using the particular techniques, assuming that there is some appropriate history. In a different context, when asked to evaluate forecasts, the response concentrates on how well a forecasting model has performed in the past, compared to alternatives, rather than on how the forecasts are formed. Of course, the comparison is easier with forecasts, as they can be directly compared to what actually happened and forecast errors used to quantify the costs of being wrong. In other areas of econometrics, such comparisons are less easy as the actual value is usually not observed, but the effectiveness of decisions based on models, theories, or specific estimates are sometimes observable, particularly in the area of finance, where the profitability of portfolios can be compared, or possibly in areas such as pollution control or the economics of the environment.

As seen in Section 19.1, the measures used by econometricians to evaluate and compare models are mostly purely statistical in nature. This is hardly surprising as most econometric textbooks appear to view the subject as a component of statistics. When economists consider the evaluation of their theories they generally do not do so in terms of economic quantities, such as improvement in utility, consumption, income, or profits; their measures are more likely to come from philosophy or history. For example, a theory may be required to be internally consistent, although consistency says little or nothing about relevance. It may be asked how well a theory explains the past but a model that is successful in looking backward is not necessarily good at looking forward; nonlinear dynamic stochastic models are not usually time reversible. Yet a popular and often cited book by Mark Blaug (1992), *The Methodology of Economics*, has the telling subtitle *Or How Economists Explain*. Surely economists have a greater ambition for their subject than merely to explain. How do you know if you have successfully explained something? Is there a unique explanation?

An alternative aim of economics might be thought to be prediction; in fact Hutchison (1977) says, "Perhaps a majority of economists—but not all—would agree that improved prediction of economic behavior or events is the main or primary task of the economist." However, Blaug (1992, ch. 4) suggests that if there is a majority, it is hardly more than 51 percent as there are plenty of groups that would not agree with the statement. Blaug (1992, ch. 1) also discusses the "notion that there is a perfect, logical symmetry between the nature of explanation and the nature of prediction," which is labeled the "symmetry thesis." Here a universal law, or theory, is used. The only difference is that explanations come after events and predictions come before them. Thus explanation is, in Blaug's words, simply "prediction written backwards." Prediction here means that an economy, or a data set, should have a previously unknown property according to analysis of the theory being considered. With this type of prediction there is not necessarily a clear time flow. A data set can be used to specify and estimate a model, a consequence of the model can be deduced in terms of some new property that should be found in the data, and a test can then be applied to the data to see if the new property is found. The difficulty is knowing how to evaluate the findings from the test, as it is possible that the "new" property was known by the builder of the model and the model was chosen to have this property. It is not difficult to build models to capture given features, as illustrated by those that include "stylized facts." A different example is the nonlinear deterministic model that has parameters chosen to produce chaos and thus share some properties with stochastic processes, as discussed in Benhabib (1992) and Granger (1994). The question of how one evaluates a claim of prediction is rarely discussed in the methodology literature.

I would like to put forward my personal beliefs about how an economic theory or model should be evaluated. I claim no originality for these proposals.

To concentrate the discussion I will consider economics to be a decision science, concerned with the decisions of many economic agents including investors, workers, employers, consumers, purchasing agents, sellers, government policy-makers, managers, and so forth. Every economic variable will be greatly affected by these decisions; in fact, they may be totally determined by them. The decisions will be determined by other decisions plus outside shocks, such as weather, earthquakes, "sunspots," and individual health hazards.

For a model to be successful I take the viewpoint that it has to lead to better decisions for some agents compared to the decisions that they would make using alternative available models. Thus, an evaluation experiment using agents in the actual economy is envisioned, including one group that uses the model in making its decisions and another group that does not, both groups containing enough agents, which are otherwise identical samples, to constitute a useful experiment. Some quantitative measure of the success of the decisions, such as average returns or profits, is required, and over a period of time statistical tests can determine which group performs better. I suggest that models be evaluated on their economic, market performance rather than on simply intellectual grounds. I realize that this is not a new idea. For example, it has been stated that there is little point in studying the history of economic thought because the efficiency of markets will ensure that good theories, that is, models, will push out the bad. Although I would not completely support such a viewpoint, as I am unsure that actual markets are so perfect, I do agree with its underlying tone. Rather than carrying out the evaluation experiment it may be possible to conduct a counterfactual analysis: That is, to determine two or more groups of agents with increasing economic success, such as profitability, and then to try to determine the differences in their past decision-making procedures that led to the success. Although one has less control than with an experiment, a counterfactual analysis may be more achievable.

Many real-economy experiments are conducted in the area of marketing and occasionally by economists; see, for example, the pricing experiments conducted in supermarkets described in Gabor (1988) and discussed earlier in Section 19.3.

In many cases it will not be easy to measure the benefits to decision-makers of some theory but thinking in such terms will often produce stronger, better-constructed theories or models. It will often be the case that no actual data will be available to compare the quality of decisions and so hypothetical, or thought, experiments will have to be discussed, which may not be satisfactory but will at least force consideration of the theory in a decision framework. It will also be important to have plausible alternative theories, or models, available for comparison. An example would be the efficient market hypothesis in its strong form, which says that there can be no consistently available profit-making strategies based on publicly available information, as otherwise arbitrage would remove their usefulness. (Here the problems of differing risk levels is assumed to be satisfactorily resolved.) An alternative model would attempt to make profits from some strategy, but if the market is efficient, not only will it fail but it will generate unnecessary transaction costs and thus create an extra loss.

Areas of economics where economic criteria are fairly well established are finance and forecasting. In finance, for example, McCulloch and Rossi (1990) consider both predictive and utility-based approaches to consider arbitrage pricing theory and Pesaran and Timmerman (1994) compare models by constructing portfolios from them and forming postsample average mean returns, allowing for transaction costs. There are many other examples. As an illustration, Pesaran and Timmerman (1994) build a model explaining monthly Standard & Poor's 500 index returns using lagged values of the dividend yield, the annual measure of inflation, the change in the 1-month T-bill rate, and the 12-month change in the industrial production index. All of these variables have significant coefficients if the model is estimated over the whole period 1954(1) to 1990(12) and an R^2 value of 0.09 is achieved. Starting in 1960(1) this model is estimated on the available data, a portfolio selected on the following criterion: Buy the index if the forecast predicts a positive excess return, otherwise buy Treasury bills, henceforth T-bills. This process is repeated monthly, with the model estimates being updated as new data become available, so that a switching portfolio is considered. With a 0.5 percent transactions cost, for the period 1960(1) to 1990(12), an initial investment of \$100 became \$2,289 using the switching portfolio compared with eventual values of \$1,756 from a buy-and-hold the market portfolio and \$608 from a hold T-bills investment. If the transactions costs are 1 percent per transaction the buy and hold has a higher final value (\$1,728) than the switching portfolio (\$1,542). These results are taken from Pesaran and Timmerman's Table IX. The work clearly illustrates the potential benefits of using alternative investment strategies, although the final outcome obviously depends on costs due to the number of transactions involved.

Forecasting methods are almost always compared by their actual postsample performance rather than by their in-sample properties. This is done by saying that a forecast $f_{n,h}$ made at time n of x_{n+h}, with horizon h, will produce an error of

$$e_{n,h} = x_{n+h} - f_{n,h}.$$

If decisions we based on the forecasts, then in a simple form of the theory, costs will arise because of the existence of error and will take the form $C(e)$ for some positive function C that is zero at $e = 0$ and monotonically increasing on each side of zero. A frequent assumption is that $C(e) = ae^2$ for some positive a, so that the cost function is symmetric and quadratic. Most of the procedures available for the evaluation of forecasts are based on this quadratic cost function. However, in reality, cost functions are probably usually nonsymmetric; for example, if you forecast when a bus will leave, the cost of being 3 minutes early is quite different from being 3 minutes late. Suppose, for the moment, that I decide to use a particular cost function $\widetilde{C}(e)$ to evaluate the point forecasts generated by a pair of particular models. I will prefer the model that generates the lowest average (or expected) cost. For a given cost function, one may require a complete model to form an optimum point forecast. Suppose that a model implies that the conditional distribution of x_{t+1} given an information set I_t is $f_t(x, \mu_t, \alpha_t)$, where μ_t is the conditional mean, α_t are other conditional parameters, both generally functions of the contents of I_t.

A complete model gives the whole of this one-step predictive distribution; a partial model gives only some of it, such as the conditional mean and/or the conditional variance. For certain cost functions, such as the quadratic, the optimum point forecast is just the conditional mean, and so the partial model can be sufficient. However, for all nonsymmetric cost functions, knowledge of more than just μ_t is required. In many circumstances it is clearly difficult to evaluate a partial model; one needs a complete model. It is rarely sufficient to casually complete a partial model by carefully specifying a conditional mean, and then just assuming that the distribution about this mean is Gaussian with a constant variance, for example. To put this another way, potential users of a model can be expected to have different cost functions, so that an incomplete model or a casually completed one will not be able to produce optimum point forecasts for all these customers, whereas a complete model will be able to do so. If the predictive distribution is, in fact, the true one for the relevant information set, then knowledge of which cost function is being used is irrelevant. It can be shown that for any cost function C_1,

$$\int_{-\infty}^{\infty} C(e)dF_0(e) \leq \int_{-\infty}^{\infty} C(e)d\widetilde{F}(e),$$

where $F_0(e)$ is the true distribution of the error, using the actual conditional distribution based on I_t, and $\widetilde{F}(e)$ is an approximation to the truth arising from a model using the same information set. This was proved independently by Granger and Pesaran (2000b) and by Diebold et al. (1996).

Note that the alternative model produces alternate forecasts, which then result in forecast errors generated by linking the optimum forecast errors with these alternative forecasts. One cannot assume that $\widetilde{F}(e)$ will take a particular shape, as that would imply that the errors from the alternative model could be controlled in some substantial way.

It follows that a complete model is potentially more useful to a wider group of consumers of its outputs and that its evaluation need not be tied to one or to a small group of specific cost functions. Instead, evaluation can be conducted in terms similar to those used when considering stochastic dominance, although the best way to do this has yet to be determined.

Further discussion of some of the topics in this section can be found in Granger and Pesaran (2000b).

19.6 CONCLUSION

When a researcher carefully states both the objective of the theory model that is being constructed and also considers how it can be evaluated, the research will achieve a clarity and a focus that is missing in many currently published papers. I think that an evaluation that is based on the usefulness of the research to economic agents who are decision-makers is likely to be particularly helpful, rather than just the statistical measures that are now available. Although new research on evaluation is required to determine how to do this, I believe that such research is worthwhile.

REFERENCES

Benhabib, J., 1992, *Cycles and Chaos in Economic Equilibrium*, Princeton: Princeton University Press.

Black, F., and M. Scholes, 1973, "The Pricing of Options and Corporate Liabilities," *Journal of Political Economy* 81, 637–654.

Blaug, M., 1992, *The Methodology of Economics*, 2nd Ed., Cambridge, Cambridge University Press.

Campbell, J. Y., A. W. Lo, and A. C. MacKinley, 1997, *The Econometrics of Financial Markets*, Princeton: Princeton University Press.

Clements, M. P., and D. F. Hendry, 1993, "The Limitations of Comparing Predictive Accuracy," *Journal of Forecasting* 12, 617–676.

Diebold, F. X., and R. S. Mariano, 1995, "Comparing Predictive Accuracy," *Journal of Business and Economic Statistics* 13, 253–263.

Diebold, F. X., T. A. Gunther, and A. S. Tay, 1996, "Evaluating Density Forecasts," Working Paper, Department of Economics, University of Pennsylvania.

Gabor, A., 1988, *Pricing,* 2nd Ed., Aldershot, U.K: Gower.

Granger, C. W. J., 1988, Appendix in: A. Gabor, *Pricing,* 2nd Ed., Aldershot, U.K: Gower.

Granger, C. W. J., 1994, "Is Chaotic Economic Theory Relevant for Economics?" (Review of Benhabib, 1992), *Journal of International and Comparative Economics* 3, 139–145.

Granger, C. W. J., 1999, "Outline of Forecast Theory Using Generalized Cost Functions," *Spanish Economic Review* 1, 161–173.

Granger, C. W. J., and L. Huang, 1997, "Notes on the Evaluation of Panel Models," Working Paper, University of California, San Diego.

Granger, C. W. J., and P. Newbold, 1987, *Forecasting Economic Time Series*, 2nd Ed., New York, Academic Press.

Granger, C. W. J., and H. Pesaran, 2000a, "A Decision Theoretic Approach to Forecast Evaluation," in: *Statistics and Finance: An Interface*, W.-S. Chan et al. (eds.), London: Imperial College Press, pp. 261–278.

Granger, C. W. J., and H. Pesaran, 2000b, "Economic and Statistical Measures of Forecast Accuracy," *Journal of Forecasting* 19, 537–560.

Hendry, D. F., 1995, *Dynamic Econometrics*, Oxford: Oxford University Press.

Hutchison, T. W., 1977, *Knowledge and Ignorance in Economics*, Oxford: Blackwell.

Leamer, F. E., 1978, *Specification Searches*, New York: Wiley.

McCulloch, R., and P. E. Rossi, 1990, "Posterior, Predictive, and Utility-Based Approaches to Testing the Arbitrage Pricing Theory," *Journal of Financial Economics* 28, 7–38.

Pesaran, H., and A. Timmerman, 1994, "Forecasting Stock Market Returns: An Examination of Stock Market Trading in the Presence of Transaction Costs," *Journal of Forecasting* 13, 335–367.

Poon, S.-H., and C. W. J. Granger, 2003, "Forecasting Financial Market Volatility: A Review," Forthcoming, *Journal of Economic Literature*.

Sullivan, R., A. Timmermann, and H. White, 1999, "Data Snooping, Technical Trading Rule Performance, and the Bootstrap," *Journal of Finance* 54, 1647–1692.

Swanson, N. R., and H. White, 1995a, "A Model-Selection Approach to Assessing the Information in the Term Structure Using Linear Models and Artificial Neural Networks," *Journal of Business and Economic Statistics* 13, 265–274.

Swanson, N. R., and H. White, 1995b, "Forecasting Economic Time Series Using Adaptive Versus Non-adaptive and Linear Versus Non-linear Economic Models," Working Paper, Department of Economics, University of California, San Diego, September 1995.

White, H., 2000, "A Reality-Check for Data Snooping," *Econometrica* 68, 1097–1127.

PART VI

Diagnostics and Scientific Explanation

Chapter Twenty

Diagnoses and Defaults in Artificial Intelligence and Economics

Scientific explanation is a multifaceted topic of interest to scholars, government policy-makers, and men and women in charge of business operations. When the call for an explanation concerns a faulty economic forecast or a test of a failed hypothesis, econometricians can take advantage of concepts from the field of artificial intelligence (AI), where researchers have developed ideas for the design and the computation of such explanations. The ideas for design delineate criteria that good explanations must satisfy and those for computation describe efficient ways of calculating the explanation whenever such calculations make sense.

In this chapter I discuss two AI subjects, *diagnoses* and *defaults*, and use the underlying ideas to: (1) determine the status of bridge principles in theory-data confrontations, and (2) find good ways to analyze the causes of a test failure of a given economic hypothesis. Since the ideas of diagnoses and defaults in AI are formulated within the context of various symbolic languages, I begin by reviewing the main characteristics of one of these languages.

20.1 FIRST-ORDER PREDICATE CALCULUS

The first-order predicate calculus (FPC) is a symbolic language that plays a fundamental role in economic theory and econometrics.[1] It provides rigorous justification for the rules of inference that economists and econometricians employ in their theoretical work and the means to ascertain the strength and weaknesses of research strategies. Moreover, it provides the domain within which they reason in many areas of economic theory and econometrics, for example, in the study of: (1) resource allocation in large economies, (2) common knowledge in game theory, (3) the logic of beliefs in choice under uncertainty, and (4) Bayesian methods in econometrics. Finally, it provides essential building blocks in the development of a formal theory of knowledge and the creation of a formal science. I use FPC as a point of reference in discussing the nonmonotonic logic of diagnoses and defaults in artificial intelligence and economics.

20.1.1 Symbols, Well-Formed Formulas, and Theorems

To describe a symbolic language means to list its symbols, delineate its well-formed formulas, formulate its rules of inference, and postulate its axioms.

The FPC is a symbolic language L with a logical and a nonlogical vocabulary. L's *logical vocabulary* comprises a denumerable infinity of *individual variables* $x, y, z, x_1, y_1, z_1, \ldots$, a *binary predicate* $=$, two *connectives* $\sim$ and $\supset$, a *universal quantifier* $\forall$, two kinds of *brackets* [,] and (,), and a *comma* ,.

The *nonlogical vocabulary* of L consists of indexed sets of function symbols, $\{f^i\}_{i \in I_n}$, and indexed sets of predicate symbols $\{P^j\}_{j \in J_n}, n = 0, 1, \ldots$. For each n and every $i \in I_n$, f^i is an *n-ary function symbol.* Similarly, for each n and every $j \in J_n$, P^j is an *n-ary predicate symbol.* A 0-ary function symbol is a *constant,* and a 0-ary predicate symbol is a *propositional variable.* The I_n and the J_n may be empty, finite, or countably infinite.

To explicate the notion of a *well-formed formula* (wff) in L one needs the concept of a *term* for which the inductive definition is as follows:

D 1 *An individual variable is a term.*

D 2 *If* $\mathrm{t}_1, \ldots, \mathrm{t}_\mathrm{n}$ *are terms and if* f *is an* n*-ary function symbol, then* $\mathrm{f}(\mathrm{t}_1, \ldots, \mathrm{t}_\mathrm{n})$ *is a term,* $\mathrm{n} = 0, 1, \ldots$.

There are no other terms. With these one can give an inductive definition of L's wffs:

FR 1 *If* $\mathrm{t}_1, \ldots, \mathrm{t}_\mathrm{n}$ *are terms, and if* P *is an* n*-ary logical or nonlogical predicate symbol, then* $\mathrm{P}(\mathrm{t}_1, \ldots, \mathrm{t}_\mathrm{n})$ *is a wff,* $\mathrm{n} = 0, 1, \ldots$.

FR 2 *If* A *is well formed (wf), then* $\sim$ A *is a wff.*

FR 3 *If* A *and* B *are wf, then* [A $\supset$ B] *is a wff.*

FR 4 *If* A *is wf and* a *is an individual variable, then* ($\forall$a)A *is a wff.*

The most important wffs of L are the *logical axioms* of L. In stating the axioms I use syntactical variables having wffs as values. The expressions that give the axioms are *axiom schemata.* They are not axioms themselves. Only their values are axioms.

The first three axiom schemata and the first rule of inference RI 1, noted later, determine the meaning of $\sim$ and $\supset$. They allow us to read $\sim A$ as "not A" and $[A \supset B]$ as "either not A or B" or simply as "A materially implies B":

LA 1 $[\mathrm{A} \supset [\mathrm{B} \supset \mathrm{A}]]$

LA 2 $[[\mathrm{A} \supset [\mathrm{B} \supset \mathrm{C}]] \supset [[\mathrm{A} \supset \mathrm{B}] \supset [\mathrm{A} \supset \mathrm{C}]]]$

LA 3 $[[\sim\mathrm{A} \supset \sim\mathrm{B}] \supset [\mathrm{B} \supset \mathrm{A}]]$

The next two axiom schemata concern the meaning of $\forall$. To state them one needs two new concepts: (i) a *free variable* and a *bound variable*, and (ii) a *syntactical symbol* $A_a(b)$. An occurrence of an individual variable a in a wff A is bound in A if it occurs in a wf subformula of A of the form $(\forall a)B$; otherwise it is free in A. One says that a is a free (or bound) variable of A if some occurrence of a is free (or bound) in A. The symbol $A_a(b)$ denotes the wff that results from substituting the term b for all free occurrences of a in A. Moreover, b is substitutable for a in A if for each individual variable x occurring in b, no part of A of the form $(\forall x)B$ contains an occurrence of a that is free in A.

LA 4 *Let* A *and* B *be wffs and let* a *be an individual variable that is not a free variable of* A. *Then* $[(\forall \mathrm{a})[\mathrm{A} \supset \mathrm{B}] \supset [\mathrm{A} \supset (\forall \mathrm{a})\mathrm{B}]]$.

LA 5 *Let* A *be a wff, let* a *be an individual variable, and let* b *be a term that is substitutable for* a *in* A. *Then* $[(\forall \mathrm{a})\mathrm{A} \supset \mathrm{A}_\mathrm{a}(\mathrm{b})]$.

These axioms and RI 2 below ensure that one can read $(\forall a)$ as "for all a." Then LA 5 becomes a symbolic rendition of the rule *de omni et nullo*.

The last two axiom schemata delineate the meaning of $=$. In stating the schemata I write $[x = y]$ rather than $= (x, y)$:

LA 6 *If* b *is a term* $[\mathrm{b} = \mathrm{b}]$.

LA 7 *Let* A *be a wff, let* a *be an individual variable, and let* b *and* c *be terms that are substitutable for* a *in* A. *Then* $[[\mathrm{b} = \mathrm{c}] \supset [\mathrm{A}_\mathrm{a}(\mathrm{b}) \supset \mathrm{A}_\mathrm{a}(\mathrm{c})]]$.

From these two axiom schemata and from LA 1–LA 3 and RI 1 one can deduce that $=$ is an equivalence relation. One can also show that $=$ has the following substitutive property: If f is an n-ary function symbol and s_i and t_i are terms, $i = 1, \ldots, n$, then either $\sim [t_i = s_i]$ for some i or $[f(t_1, \ldots, t_n) = f(s_1, \ldots, s_n)]$.

Finally, I adopt two *rules of inference* for L. The first is the *modus ponens*, and the second is the so-called *rule of generalization*:

RI 1 *Let* A *and* B *be wffs. From* $[\mathrm{A} \supset \mathrm{B}]$ *and* A, *one infers* B.

RI 2 *Let* A *be a wff. If* a *is an individual variable, from* A *one infers* $(\forall \mathrm{a})\mathrm{A}$.

In L a wff is a *theorem* if and only if it has a proof. A *proof* is a finite sequence of formulas, each of which is either an axiom or the conclusion of a rule of inference whose hypotheses precede that formula in the sequence. A proof is said to be a proof of the last formula in the sequence. A wff is a *logical theorem* if the axioms in its proof are logical axioms. Examples of proofs are values of the following sequence of assertions that establish the theorem schemata $[A \supset A]$:

$$[A \supset [[B \supset A] \supset A]].$$

$$[[A \supset [[B \supset A] \supset A]] \supset [[A \supset [B \supset A]] \supset [A \supset A]]]$$

$$[[A \supset [B \supset A]] \supset [A \supset A]]$$

$$[A \supset [B \supset A]]$$

$$[A \supset A]$$

Here we assert versions of LA 1 and LA 2, apply *modus ponens*, assert LA 1, and apply *modus ponens* again to conclude $[A \supset A]$. The values of the last theorem schemata are logical theorems since the axiom schemata that I used in its proof are logical axiom schemata.

The logical theorems of L provide symbolic renditions of rules for logical reasoning that economists and econometricians in their research activities apply without much thought. Good examples are the *law of contradiction* $\sim\sim[A \supset \sim\sim A]$, the *law of the excluded middle* $[A \supset A]$, the *converse law of contraposition,* LA 3, and the *law of reductio ad absurdum* $[[A \supset B] \supset [[A \supset \sim B] \supset \sim A]]$.[2] In the intended interpretation of L the values of these theorem schemata denote truth no matter what values A and B assume.

20.1.2 The Intended Interpretation of *L* and the Completeness Theorem

To interpret L, I must introduce the idea of a structure for L. A *structure* for L is a quadruple $(|\mathfrak{I}|, N^{\mathfrak{I}}, F^{\mathfrak{I}}, G^{\mathfrak{I}})$, where $|\mathfrak{I}|$ is a nonempty set of individuals; $N^{\mathfrak{I}}$ is a set of names of the individuals in $|\mathfrak{I}|$, with one name for each individual and different names for different individuals; $F^{\mathfrak{I}}$ is a family of functions from $|\mathfrak{I}|$ to $|\mathfrak{I}|$; and $G^{\mathfrak{I}}$ is a family of predicates in $|\mathfrak{I}|$. To each n-ary f in $\{f^i\}_{i \in I_n}$ corresponds an n-nary $f^{\mathfrak{I}}$ in $F^{\mathfrak{I}}$, and to each n-ary P in $\{P^j\}_{j \in J_n}$ corresponds an n-ary $P^{\mathfrak{I}}$ in $G^{\mathfrak{I}}$, $n = 0, 1, \ldots$.

The structure $\mathfrak{I}$ can be used to obtain an interpretation of L in the manner described below. I first add the names in $N^{\mathfrak{I}}$ to the 0-ary function symbols of L and denote the expanded first-order language by $L(\mathfrak{I})$. Then (by induction on the length of terms) I interpret :

(i) Each $a \in N^{\mathfrak{I}}$ as $\mathfrak{I}(a)$, the individual that a names.
(ii) Each variable-free term $a \in L(\mathfrak{I})$ of the form $f(a_1, \ldots, a_n)$ as $f^{\mathfrak{I}}[\mathfrak{I}(a_1), \ldots, \mathfrak{I}(a_n)]$, $n = 0, 1, \ldots$.

If a is a variable-free term in $L(\mathfrak{I})$, then a is a name or there exist an n, a unique n-ary function symbol f, and variable-free terms $a_1, \ldots, a_n$ such that a is $f(a_1, \ldots, a_n)$. Hence (i) and (ii) determine the interpretation of all variable-free terms in $L(\mathfrak{I})$.

Next let b be a term in L with n free variables $x_1, \ldots, x_n$; let $\phi_1, \ldots, \phi_n$ be names in $N^{\mathfrak{I}}$; and let $b_{x_1,\ldots,x_n}(\phi_1, \ldots, \phi_n)$ be the term one obtains by substituting ϕ_i for x_i at each occurrence of x_i in b, $i = 1, \ldots, n$. Then $b_{x_1,\ldots,x_n}(\phi_1, \ldots, \phi_n)$ is an $\mathfrak{I}$ *instance* of b. Conditions (i) and (ii) determine the interpretation of every $\mathfrak{I}$ instance of b and hence of b as well.

I interpret L by assigning truth values to its wffs. To do that, I must first assign truth values to the *closed* wffs of $L(\mathfrak{I})$, that is, to the wffs in $L(\mathfrak{I})$

in which no variable is free. I do this by induction on the length of wffs as follows:

(iii) Let A be the closed wff $[a = b]$, where a and b are terms. Since A is closed, a and b must be variable-free. I interpret A by letting $\Im(A) = t$ (for truth) or f (for falsehood) depending on whether $\Im(a) = \Im(b)$ holds or not.

(iv) Let A be the closed formula $P(a_1, \ldots, a_n)$, where P is not $=$. Since A is closed, the a_i must be variable-free terms. I interpret A by letting $\Im(A) = t$ or f depending on whether $P^{\Im}[\Im(a_1), \ldots, \Im(a_n)]$ holds or not.

(v) If A and B are closed wffs, then $\Im(\sim A) = t$ if $\Im(A) = f$ and $\Im(\sim A) = f$ if $\Im(A) = t$. Similarly, $\Im([A \supset B]) = t$ if $\Im(\sim A) = t$ or $\Im(B) = t$. Otherwise $\Im([A \supset B]) = f$.

(vi) If C is a wff that contains only one free individual variable x, then $\Im[(\forall x)C] = t$ if $\Im[C_x(a)] = t$ for all $a \in N^{\Im}$. Otherwise $\Im[(\forall x)C] = f$.

Conditions (iii)–(vi) determine the interpretation of all closed wffs of $L(\Im)$ and hence of L. To interpret the remaining wffs of L, consider a wff B of L with n free variables $x_1, \ldots, x_n$, and let $B_{x_1,\ldots,x_n}(\phi_1, \ldots, \phi_n)$ be the wff obtained by substituting the terms ϕ_i for each free occurrence of $x_i, i = 1, \ldots, n$. If the ϕ_i belong to $N^{\Im}$, $B_{x_1,\ldots,x_n}(\phi_1, \ldots, \phi_n)$ is a $\Im$ *instance* of B. Now (iii)–(vi) determine the interpretation of every $\Im$ instance of B and hence of B as well.

A wff B in L is valid in $\Im$ if and only if $\Im(B') = t$ for every $\Im$ instance B' of B. Then, in particular, a closed wff A in L is valid in $\Im$ if and only if $\Im(A) = t$. A wff B of L is valid if and only if B is valid in every structure for L. It is easy to verify that the values of LA 1–LA 7 are valid wffs. Consequently, all the logical theorems of L are valid wffs. It is also a fact, but much harder to prove, that a wff of L is valid only if it is a logical theorem of L. Consequently, one has TM 1, the *completeness theorem* of FPC.

TM 1 *A wff in* L *is a logical theorem if and only if it is valid.*

TM 1 is called a completeness theorem because it demonstrates that LA 1–LA 7 and RI 1–RI 2 account for all the valid wffs in L. In different words, TM 1 shows that one cannot add axioms and rules of inference to L and hope to derive new valid wffs.

20.1.3 First-Order Theories and Their Models

Almost all mathematical theories can be expressed in a first-order predicate calculus such as L. The same is true of most scientific theories that are developed by the axiomatic method. When one sets out to express a mathematical or scientific theory T in L, one begins by assigning symbols to the undefined terms of T and uses them and the logical vocabulary of L to formulate wffs that express the ideas of the axioms and the theorems of T. Then one adds to LA 1–LA 7 as new axioms the set Γ of wffs that express the axioms of T. In the expanded axiom system, a theorem is either a logical theorem or a symbolic rendition of a theorem of T. Moreover, a wff that expresses a theorem of T is a theorem in the expanded axiom system. I denote by $T(\Gamma)$ the collection of theorems that is derived from the expanded axiom system and refer to the wffs of L that express theorems of T as the *nonlogical theorems* of $T(\Gamma)$.

Let T denote a mathematical or scientific theory, and let $T(\Gamma)$ denote its *alias* in L, a first-order predicate calculus. The syntactical and semantic properties of T are reflected in the syntactical and semantic properties of Γ. Some of those properties are of interest here, so I note the salient ones of a given subset Γ of the wffs of my symbolic language L. I begin by generalizing upon TM 1. For that purpose let $\vdash A$ and $\models A$, respectively, be short for "A is a logical theorem of L" and "A is a valid wff." Also recall that TM 1 insists that $\vdash A$ if and only if $\models A$. Next let Γ be a collection of wffs in L; let $\Im$ be a structure for L; and observe that $\Im$ is a *model* of Γ if and only if every member of Γ is valid in $\Im$. Finally, let $\Gamma \vdash A$ and $\Gamma \models A$, respectively, be short for "A is derivable in L from Γ" and "A is valid in each and every model of Γ." Then one can state the sought for generalization of TM 1 as follows:

TM 2 *Let* Γ *be a collection of wffs in* L. *Also, let* A *be a wff in* L. *Then* $\Gamma \vdash$ A *if and only if* $\Gamma \models$ A.

TM 3 *Let* Γ *be a collection of wffs in* L. *Then* Γ *is consistent if and only if* Γ *has a model.*

20.2 DIAGNOSTIC REASONING IN ARTIFICIAL INTELLIGENCE AND ECONOMICS

Next, I discuss a logic for diagnostic reasoning (LDR) that researchers in AI have developed. The sentences of LDR are wffs in a suitable FPC, and the logical axioms and the rules of inference of LDR are LA 1–LA 7 and RI 1–RI 2 as I described them above. Still, LDR differs in a fundamental way from the logic of FPC: The logic of FPC is *monotonic*, whereas LDR is *nonmonotonic*.

20.2.1 Nonmonotonic versus Monotonic Reasoning

To show the way that reasoning with FPC is monotonic, it is convenient to add two new symbols to the pertinent version of L. Thus, here, for any wff B, $A =_{\mathrm{df}} B$ means that "A is an abbreviation for B" and implies that A may be substituted for B whether B stands alone or forms part of a longer wff. Then I can define $\vee$ (or) and $\wedge$ (and) by the expressions $[A \vee B] =_{\mathrm{df}} [\sim A \supset B]$ and

$[A \wedge B] =_{\text{df}} \sim [A \supset \sim B]$. Also, one can read $[A \vee B]$ and $[A \wedge B]$, respectively, as "either A or B" and "both A and B." The monotonic characteristic of the FPC is as indicated in TM 4.

TM 4 *Let* A, B, *and* Γ *be wffs of* L. *Then* $\Gamma \vdash A$ *only if* $[\Gamma \wedge B] \vdash A$.

In words TM 4 insists that if there is a proof of A from Γ in L, then there is also a proof of A from $[\Gamma \wedge B]$ in L. This follows from the easily established fact that $\vdash [[\Gamma \wedge B] \supset \Gamma]$.[3]

In social reality nonmonotonic reasoning surfaces in situations in which individuals must act or reason on the basis of incomplete information. E 20.1 is a simple example from the theory of choice under uncertainty.

E 20.1 *Consider an urn* U *with 90 colored balls. There are at least* a *red balls in* U *and no more than* (90 − a) *green and yellow balls. I have no idea of how many of the latter are green. The urn is shaken well, and a blindfolded man is in the process of picking a ball from the urn. I have a choice between two prospects,* PR *and* PG. PR *yields $100 if the ball is red and nothing otherwise.* PG *yields $100 if the ball is green and otherwise nothing. In making my choice I reason as follows:* C: *If* $a \geq 30$ *I choose* PR. D : $a = 30$. *Consequently,* A: *I choose* PR, *that is, from* $[C \wedge D]$ *I conclude* A. *But then* B: *A knowledgeable demon tells me that the ball is not yellow. So* E: *I choose* PG, *that is, from* $[[C \wedge D] \wedge B]$ *I conclude* E.

It may seem arbitrary to choose A in E 20.1 when faced with C and D and to switch to E when the demon reveals the truth of B. However, my risk preferences and my assignment of superadditive probabilities to the particular events are such that the reasoning underlying my choices accords with the strictures of FPC. Examples of this can be found in theorems T 6 and T 7 in Chapter 18.

20.2.2 Formal Diagnostic Reasoning in Artificial Intelligence and Economics

Raymond Reiter (1987) has developed an interesting logic for diagnostic reasoning that is nonmonotonic. Reiter's LDR is embedded in an FPC and comprises a quadruple of elements $\{T(S), Obs, C, Ab\}$. Here, $T(S)$ is a collection of closed wffs that describes the *system*, Obs is a collection of wffs that describes the available *observations*, C is an n-tuple of *system components* $\{c_1, \ldots, c_n\}$, and Ab is an n-tuple of unary *predicate symbols* $\{Ab_1, \ldots, Ab_n\}$. When interpreted, $T(S)$ describes a physical device, a real-world setting of interest, or an interpreted scientific theory, and Obs describes observed features of the way the system is functioning. Typically, $T(S)$ describes the way the system normally behaves. Description of abnormal behavior is left to the components of Ab. When interpreted, the unary predicates in Ab determine the extent to which the respective system components are functioning abnormally. If for some i, c_i malfunctions, $Ab_i(c_i)$ will denote truth. The system is functioning as it should only if the wffs in $\{T(S) \cup Obs \cup \{\sim Ab_1(c_1), \ldots, \sim Ab_n(c_n)\}\}$ are consistent.

When the system has malfunctioned, the wffs in $\{\{T(S) \cup Obs \cup \{\sim Ab_1(c_1), \ldots, \sim Ab_n(c_n)\}\}$ are inconsistent, in which case a diagnosis is called for. Here a *diagnosis* is a minimal family of system components Δ such that the wffs in $\{T(S) \cup Obs \cup \{Ab_i(c_i) : c_i \in \Delta\} \cup \{\sim Ab_j(c_j) : c_j \in (C - \Delta)\}$ are consistent. There may be just one or several diagnoses, as demonstrated by the next example.

E 20.2 *Consider a version* L *of FPC that is elaborate enough so that in its intended interpretation one can carry out elementary real analysis. In* L *there are seven special individual variables,* c, $\mathrm{c_p}$, $\mathrm{c_t}$, y, $\mathrm{y_p}$, $\mathrm{y_t}$, *and* η, *nine 0-ary function symbols,* k, a, b, α, β, 1, −1, $\mathrm{A_y}$, *and* μ_y, *two binary function symbols,* + *and* •, *and two tertiary predicate symbols,* P *and* Ab. *Also, in* L, T(S) *denotes the logical closure of the following wffs:*

1. $[\mathrm{c} = +(\mathrm{c_p}, \mathrm{c_t})]$
2. $[\mathrm{y} = +(\mathrm{y_p}, \mathrm{y_t})]$
3. $[\mathrm{c_p} = \bullet(\mathrm{k}, \mathrm{y_p})]$
4. $[\mathrm{c} = +(+(\mathrm{a}, \bullet(\mathrm{b}, \mathrm{y})), \eta)]$
5. $[\mathrm{b} = \bullet(\mathrm{k}, \mathrm{A_y})]$
6. $[\mathrm{a} = \bullet(\bullet(\mu_\mathrm{y}, +(1, \bullet(-1, \mathrm{A_y}))), \mathrm{k})]$
7. $\mathrm{P}(\mathrm{k}, \mathrm{A_y}, \mu_\mathrm{y})$.

Finally, in L,

8. $\mathrm{C} = \{\mathrm{A_y}, \mathrm{k}, \mu_\mathrm{y}\}$,

and Obs *is such that* Obs(α, β) *is a wff that insists that*

9. $[[\mathrm{a} = \alpha] \wedge [\mathrm{b} = \beta]]$

In the intended interpretation of L, T(S), *and* Obs*:*

$\mathrm{P}(\mathrm{k}, \mathrm{A_y}, \mu_\mathrm{y})$ *insists that* $[[[\mathrm{k} \in (0, 0.9]] \wedge [\mathrm{A_y} \in (0, 0.75]]] \wedge [\mu_\mathrm{y} \in [0, 1{,}000]]]$.

$\mathrm{Ab}(\mathrm{A_y}, \mathrm{k}, \mu_\mathrm{y})$ *asserts that* $[\mathrm{Ab_1}(\mathrm{A_y}) \vee [\mathrm{Ab_2}(\mathrm{k}) \vee \mathrm{Ab_3}(\mu_\mathrm{y})]]$, *where* $\mathrm{Ab_1}(\mathrm{A_y})$ *insists that* $[\mathrm{A_y} \neq 0.75]$, $\mathrm{Ab_2}(\mathrm{k})$ *claims that* $[\mathrm{k} \neq 0.9]$, *and* $\mathrm{Ab_3}(\mu_\mathrm{y})$ *insists that* $[\mu_\mathrm{y} \neq 500]]$.

The symbols +, •, 1, *and* −1 *stand for addition, multiplication, the number one, and the number minus one.*

With this interpretation in hand one can show that

$$T(S) \cup \sim Ab(A_y, k, \mu_y) \models [[a = 112.5] \wedge [b = 0.675]]$$

and that

$$T(S) \cup Obs(100, 0.6) \cup \sim Ab(A_y, k, \mu_y)$$

is inconsistent. The latter assertion requires a diagnosis. There are three explanations of the inconsistency $\mathrm{Ab}(\mathrm{A_y}, \mathrm{k}, \mu_\mathrm{y})$, $[[\mathrm{A_y} \neq 0.75] \wedge [\mu_\mathrm{y} \neq 500]]$, *and* $[\mathrm{k} \neq 0.9]$. *Of these, the last two provide two diagnoses of the inconsistency* $\Delta_1 = \{\mathrm{A_y}, \mu_\mathrm{y}\}$ *and* $\Delta_2 = \{\mathrm{k}\}$.

I got the idea for E 20.2 through reading Maarten Janssen and Yao-Hua Tan's (1992) analysis of Milton Friedman's (1957) theory of the consumption function. Janssen and Tan use Reiter's LDR to rationalize the arguments that Friedman advances in support of the permanent-income hypothesis (PIH). In their model for diagnostic reasoning the variables of $T(S)$ are random variables that satisfy the following additional conditions:

1. The expected values of c_t, y_t, and η equal 0, and the expected value of y_p is positive.
2. The variances of the respective variables are all finite.
3. The covariances of the components of (c_p, c_t), (y_p, y_t), (c_t, y_t), and (y, η) equal 0.

The additional axioms allow one to identify the system in E 20.2 with PIH, and to interpret μ_y as the mean of y and A_y as the ratio of the variance of y_p to the sum of the variances of y_p and y_t. With the symbol μ_c for the mean of c, one can also insist that $k = (\mu_c/\mu_y)$ and show that a and b are coefficients in the least squares regression of c on y.

Reiter's LDR has many interesting characteristics that he describes in several simple theorems, two of which I repeat here and exemplify with reference to the system in E 20.2.

TM 5 *A diagnosis exists for* {T(S), Obs, C} *if and only if the wffs in* T(S) ∪ Obs *are consistent.*

In the intended interpretation of the system in E 20.2, the wffs in $T(S) \cup Obs(100, 0.6)$ are consistent. The existence of two diagnoses are, therefore, in accord with TM 5.

TM 6 *If* Δ *is a diagnosis for* {T(S), *Obs*, C, Ab}, *then for each* $\mathrm{c_i} \in \Delta$,

$$T(S) \cup Obs \cup \{\sim Ab(c) : c \in C - \Delta\} \models Ab(c_i)$$

In E 20.2 with $\Delta = \{k\}$ one finds that

$$T(S) \cup Obs(100, 0.6) \cup \big\{[\mu_y = 500], [A_y = 0.75]\big\} \models [k \neq 0.9].$$

With $\Delta = \{\mu_y, A_y\}$ one finds that

$$T(S) \cup Obs(100, 0.6) \cup \{[k = 0.9]\} \models [[\mu_y \neq 500] \wedge [A_y \neq 0.75]],$$

in accord with TM 6.

The nonmonotonic feature of Reiter's LDR is apparent in cases where an additional observation annihilates a previously established diagnosis. The next definition and TM 7–TM 8 explains why.

Definition. A diagnosis Δ for $\{T(S), Obs, C\}$ predicts a closed wff Π in L if and only if $T(S) \cup Obs \cup \{Ab(c) : c \in \Delta\} \cup \{\sim Ab(c) : c \in C - \Delta\} \models \Pi$.

TM 7 *A diagnosis* Δ *for* {T(S), Obs, C} *predicts a closed wff* Π *if and only if* T(S) ∪ Obs ∪ {∼Ab(c) : c ∈ C − Δ} ⊨ Π.

TM 8 *Suppose that every diagnosis for* {T(S), Obs, C} *predicts one of* Π *or* $\sim\Pi$, *where* Π *is a closed wff. Then: (1) Every diagnosis for* {T(S), Obs, C} *that predicts* Π *is a diagnosis for* {T(S), Obs ∪ {Π}, C}. *(2) No diagnosis for* {T(S), Obs, C} *that predicts* $\sim\Pi$ *is a diagnosis for* {T(S), Obs ∪ {Π}, C}.

For example, in E 20.2 with $\Delta = \{k\}$ and Π asserting $[\mu_y = 500]$, one finds that $T(S) \cup Obs(100, 0.6) \cup \{Ab_2(k)\} \cup \{\sim Ab_1(A_y) \wedge \sim Ab_3(\mu_y)\} \models \Pi$, and that $\Delta = \{k\}$ is a diagnosis for $(T(S), [Obs(100, 0.6) \wedge \Pi], C)$. Also, with $\Delta = \{A_y, \mu_y\}$ and the same Π one finds that $T(S) \cup Obs(100, 0.6) \cup \{Ab_1(A_y) \wedge Ab_3(\mu_y)\} \cup \{\sim Ab_2(k) \models \sim\Pi$, and that Δ is not a diagnosis for $(T(S) \cup [Obs(100, 0.6) \wedge \Pi], C)$.

Reiter's diagnostic arguments delineate ways to search for cures for ailing systems, for example, a miserable stomachache and malfunctioning computer software. Moreover, as shown by TM 7–TM 8, they provide researchers with means to find reasons for faulty predictions. The latter aspect raises an intriguing question: Is it true that a diagnosis that, ex post, explains a faulty prediction would have been able, ex ante, to predict the relevant observation? Strange as it may seem, the answer is: Not necessarily. To see why, take another look at E 20.2 and $Obs(100, 0.6)$. The diagnosis $\Delta = \{k\}$ provides an explanation for $Obs(100, 0.6)$ by restoring consistency to the faulty system. Yet, it is false that $T(S) \cup \{Ab_2(k)\} \cup \{\sim Ab_1(A_y), \sim Ab_3(\mu_y)\} \models Obs(100, 0.6)$. As Janssen and Tan observed, this asymmetry between explanation and prediction in Reiter's logic is interesting because it contrasts with the symmetry thesis of Carl G. Hempel's deductive-nomological scheme for scientific explanation (cf. Hempel, 1965, pp. 335–375, and Section 22.1 in this volume).

20.3 DEFAULT LOGIC AND BRIDGE PRINCIPLES IN THEORY-DATA CONFRONTATIONS

Diagnostic reasoning also occurs in econometrics. Such reasoning surfaces in misspecification tests of the adequacy of an econometric model and in searches for the cause of faulty econometric forecasts, as well as in attempts to determine reasons for rejecting the empirical relevance of economic hypotheses. The sophisticated diagnostic analyses that Chapters 13–16 and 21 bring to the fore provide ample evidence of the import of diagnostic reasoning in econometrics.

20.3.1 Bridge Principles and Default Logic

Most diagnostic reasoning in econometrics is carried out entirely in the realm of a data universe. Next I describe what happens to such analyses in the broader context of a theory-data confrontation in which bridge principles play an essential role and I do it within the framework of a modified version of *default logic*.

In Reiter's seminal article on default logic, a closed *default theory* is a pair (D, W), where D is a set of closed defaults and W is a set of closed wffs. Further, a closed *default* is any expression of the form $[\alpha : M\beta_1, M\beta_2, \ldots, M\beta_m/\varphi]$, where α, φ, and the β_i, $i = 1, \ldots, m$, are closed wffs and $M\beta_i$ insists that it is consistent to believe that β_i. In shorthand, the expression claims that if α, and if it is consistent to believe that β_i, $i = 1, \ldots, m$, infer φ.

Default reasoning arises in situations in which conclusions must be drawn in spite of incomplete knowledge of relevant matters. For example, one knows that most birds can fly and that penguins and ostriches cannot. When one does not have a chance to check whether a given bird, Bob, is one of the exceptional birds, one concludes in the absence of information to the contrary that Bob can fly. In this section I describe characteristics of default reasoning when it is used in the context of an economic theory-data confrontation.

Like LDR, Reiter's default logic is embedded in a suitable FPC. I embed the required modified version of Reiter's default logic in a multisorted modal logic in which the modal operator $\sim\Box\sim$ takes the place of Reiter's M. When A is a closed wff, the intended interpretation of $\Box A$ is that "it is *necessarily* the case that A." Further, $\sim\Box\sim A$ reads as "it is possible that A is the case." Thus, in the standard vernacular of modal logic, $\Box A$ only if "in all possible worlds it is the case that A" and $\sim\Box\sim A$ only if "there are possible worlds in which it is the case that A." As such, the intended interpretation of $\sim\Box\sim A$ differs from Reiter's interpretation of MA. I chose $\sim\Box\sim$ in place of M because to my way of thinking, belief is a numerical relation between pairs of propositions p and h that measures the degree of belief in p that a person entertains upon knowledge of h (cf. Stigum, 1990, ch. 24). Reiter's M is not a numerical relation.

In my version of Reiter's default logic, a pair of hypotheses takes the place of Reiter's hypothesis $\{\alpha, M\beta_1, M\beta_2, \ldots, M\beta_m\}$. Furthermore, the inference is less certain than in Reiter's logic. Specifically, the hypotheses are

$$\left[\ldots\left[\left[\left[\alpha \wedge \sim\Box\sim\beta_1\right] \wedge \sim\Box\sim\beta_2\right] \wedge \ldots\right] \wedge \sim\Box\sim\beta_m\right]$$

$$\text{and } \left[\ldots\left[\left[\left[\alpha \wedge \beta_1\right] \wedge \beta_2\right] \wedge \ldots\right] \wedge \beta_m\right] \supset \varphi\right].$$

From them I infer that $\sim\Box\sim\varphi$. The reason for the weak inference is simple. If, at best, I can claim that there are possible worlds in which the β_i are valid, the most I can claim about φ is that there is a world in which φ is valid. Moreover, if I cannot be sure that all the β_i are valid in the Real World, I cannot be sure that φ is valid in the Real World either. The next example gives an idea of the import of such inferences in economic theory-data confrontations.

E 20.3 *Consider the test of the expected utility hypothesis that I described in Section 17.3.1. There* $\omega_T \in \Omega_T$ *only if* $\omega_T = (p, x, U)$, *where* $(p, x) \in ([0, 1] \times [0, 1{,}000])^N$ *and* $U(\cdot) : [0, 1{,}000] \to [0, 1]$. *Also,* $\omega_P \in \Omega_P$ *only if* $\omega_P = (q, z, W)$, *where* $(q, z) \in ([0, 1] \times [0, 1{,}000])^N$ *and* $W(\cdot) : [0, 1{,}000] \to [0, 1]$. *Finally,* $\omega \in \Omega$, $\omega = (\omega_T, \omega_P)$, *and* $\Omega \subset \Omega_T \times \Omega_P$.

In the given test one has no reason to doubt the validity of U 2–U 4 in the theory universe. Hence, for all $\omega_T \in \Omega_T$, *the respective components of* ω_T *must satisfy*

$$U(x_i) = p_i \tag{1}$$

and

$$x_i/1{,}000 = p_i, i = 1, \ldots, N. \tag{2}$$

One has also no reason to doubt the validity of U 5–U 6 in the data universe. Hence, for all $\omega_P \in \Omega_P$, *the respective components of* ω_P *must satisfy*

$$W(z_i) = q_i, i = 1, \ldots, N. \tag{3}$$

Suppose that one is less sure of the bridge principles in U 7–U 8. The most one can claim is

$$(\forall\omega \in \Omega) \sim\Box\sim\big[[x = z] \wedge [p = g(q)]\big], \tag{4}$$

where $g(q)$ *is short for* $[g(q_1), \ldots, g(q_N)]$ *and*

$$g(q_i) = \begin{cases} \alpha + \alpha^{-2}(q_i - \alpha)^3 \text{ if } 0 \le q_i \le \alpha \\ \\ \alpha + (1-\alpha)^{-2}(q_i - \alpha)^3 \text{ if } \alpha < q_i \le 1 \end{cases} \qquad i = 1, \ldots, N.$$

Now, it is the case that

$$\big[[[p = (x/1{,}000)] \wedge [[x = z] \wedge [p = g(q)]]] \supset [(z/1{,}000) = g(q)]\big]. \tag{5}$$

From (1)–(5) and standard arguments in S4 model logic (cf. the proof of TM 6 below), one can show that

$$[(\forall\omega \in \Omega)\sim\Box\sim[[x = z] \wedge [p = g(p)]] \supset (\forall\omega \in \Omega)\sim\Box\sim[z/1{,}000 = g(q)]]$$

and hence that

$$(\forall\omega \in \Omega)\sim\Box\sim[z/1{,}000 = g(q)]. \tag{6}$$

One can also show that

$$(\forall\omega \in \Omega)\sim\Box\sim\big[W(z_i) = g^{-1}(z_i/1{,}000), i = 1, \ldots, N\big]. \tag{7}$$

The analysis in E 20.3 is not quite like Reiter's default logic. In particular, it has one intriguing property that is not part of Reiter's analysis. It can be demonstrated that one may not be more sure that the components of ω_p satisfy the equations $z/1{,}000 = g(q)$ and $W(z) = g^{-1}(q)$ than that the components of ω satisfy U 7 and U 8. Moreover, the given equations need not be valid in the Real World.

In reading E 20.3, keep in mind that I intend to use the modified version of Reiter's default logic as a vehicle to study the status of bridge principles in economic theory-data confrontations. In so doing I may, for a good cause, run the risk of misrepresenting his theory in several ways, one of which is important. In the modal logic that underlies my arguments in E 20.3, the validity of a wff φ and the validity of $\Box\varphi$ are inextricably conjoined, and $\Box\varphi$ is taken to be valid if and only if φ is valid in all conceivable possible worlds. Other researchers think differently about the relationship between the truth values of φ and $M\varphi$. For example, in Grigoris Antoniou's (1997, p. 113) autoepistemic rendition of Reiter's theory, the validity of φ and $L\varphi$ (with L for M) "are totally unrelated because $L\varphi$ is treated as a new 0-ary predicate symbol. Intuitively, φ expresses truth of φ, whereas $L\varphi$ expresses belief in (or knowledge of) φ. One is allowed to believe in something false or not to believe in something that is true." No doubt, Antoniou takes his reading of Reiter's M to be correct.

20.3.2 A Multisorted Language for Theory-Data Confrontations

In Chapters 24 and 25 of Stigum (1990) I developed a multisorted first-order language for science and a formal theory of knowledge that can be of good use when analyzing relevant aspects of Reiter's default logic. Let $L_{tp} = (L_t, L_p, B_{tp})$ be a multisorted first-order language, where L_t and L_p are multisorted languages for discussing theory and data and B_{tp} comprises a finite number of predicates that relate individual variables of L_t to individual variables of L_p. The logical symbols of L_{tp} are the standard symbols $\sim$, $\supset$, [ ], (,), $\forall$, $=$; a modal operator $\Box$; k nonoverlapping lists of individual variables for L_t; and m nonoverlapping lists of individual variables for L_p. The nonlogical vocabulary of L_{tp} consists of the predicates in B_{tp}; a selection of constants, function symbols, and predicate symbols for L_t; and a selection of constants, function symbols, and predicate symbols for L_p. For ease of exposition, I assume that among the predicate symbols of L_{tp} there is a k-ary predicate symbol Ω_T, an m-ary predicate symbol Ω_P, and a $(k+m)$-ary predicate symbol Ω. The first two belong, respectively, to the vocabulary of L_t and L_p and the third is one of the predicate symbols in B_{tp}.

Space considerations preclude a detailed description of the formation rules and axioms of L_{tp}, so I provide only a sketchy outline here. Further details concerning L_{tp} and a discussion of the use of multisorted languages in science can be found in Stigum (1990, ch. 25).

A multisorted language with $(k+m)$ different kinds of individuals contains terms of $(k+m)$ kinds. One defines the terms of L_{tp} inductively in the obvious way. Thus constants and variables of the jth kind are terms of the jth kind, $j = 1, \ldots, (k+m)$. Also, if $f^{i,j}$ is an unary function symbol and t_j is a term of the jth kind, then $f^{i,j}(t_j)$ is a term of the ith kind, $1 \leq i, j \leq (k+m)$.

With the definition of terms in hand one can proceed to give an equally obvious inductive definition of the wffs of L_{tp}. Thus if t_i and t_j are terms of the ith and jth kind and R^{ij} is a binary predicate symbol, then $[t_i = t_j]$ and $R^{ij}(t_i, t_j)$ are wffs. Also, if A and B are wffs, then A and $[A \supset B]$ are wffs, and if A is closed, then $\Box A$ is wf as well. Finally, if a is an individual variable of the jth kind and A is a wff, then $(\forall a)A$ is wf.

The logical axiom schemata of L_{tp} are, with some modifications, similar to the axiom schemata of L that I delineated in Section 20.1. Specifically, the axiom schemata of L that determine the meaning of $\sim$ and $\supset$ are axiom schemata of L_{tp} as well.

LTPA 1 *Let* A, B, *and* C *be wffs. Then* $[\mathrm{A} \supset [\mathrm{B} \supset \mathrm{A}]]$, $[[\mathrm{A} \supset [\mathrm{B} \supset \mathrm{C}]] \supset [[\mathrm{A} \supset \mathrm{B}] \supset [\mathrm{B} \supset \mathrm{C}]]]$, *and* $[[\sim \mathrm{A} \supset \sim \mathrm{B}] \supset [\mathrm{B} \supset \mathrm{A}]]$.

In addition, there are the axiom schemata that determine the meaning of the universal quantifier $\forall$ and the $=$ predicate.

LTPA 2 *Let* A *be a wff, let* a *be an individual variable, and let* b *be a term of the same kind that is substitutable for* a *in* A. *Then,* $[(\forall \mathrm{a})\mathrm{A} \supset \mathrm{A_a(b)}]$.

LTPA 3 *Let* A *and* B *be wffs, and let* a *be an individual variable that is not a free variable in* A. *Then* $[(\forall \mathrm{a})[\mathrm{A} \supset \mathrm{B}] \supset [\mathrm{A} \supset (\forall \mathrm{a})\mathrm{B}]]$.

LTPA 4 *If* b *is a term and* t *and* s *are terms of different kinds, then* $[\mathrm{b} = \mathrm{b}]$ *and* $\sim [t = s]$.

LTPA 5 *Let* $\mathrm{t_1}, \ldots, \mathrm{t_n}$ *and* $\mathrm{s_1}, \ldots, \mathrm{s_n}$ *be terms, and let* P *be an* n*-ary predicate symbol. Then* $[[[\mathrm{t_1} = \mathrm{s_1}] \wedge [[\mathrm{t_2} = \mathrm{s_2}] \wedge \ldots \wedge [\mathrm{t_n} = \mathrm{s_n}] \ldots]]] \supset [\mathrm{P}(\mathrm{t_1}, \ldots, \mathrm{t_n}) \supset \mathrm{P}(\mathrm{s_1}, \ldots, \mathrm{s_n})]]$.

LTPA 6 *Let* A *be a wff; let* $\mathrm{a_j}$ *be an individual variable of the* 1_j*th kind,* $\mathrm{j} = 1, \ldots, \mathrm{n}$, *and let* $\mathrm{b_j}, \mathrm{c_j}$ *be terms that are substitutable for* $\mathrm{a_j}$ *in* A, $\mathrm{j} = 1, \ldots, \mathrm{n}$. *Then* $[[[\mathrm{b_1} = \mathrm{c_1}] \wedge [[\mathrm{b_2} = \mathrm{c_2}] \wedge \ldots \wedge [\mathrm{b_n} = \mathrm{c_n}] \ldots]]] \supset [\mathrm{A_{a_1,\ldots,a_n}}(\mathrm{b_1}, \ldots, \mathrm{b_n}) \supset \mathrm{A_{a_1,\ldots,a_n}}(\mathrm{c_1}, \ldots, \mathrm{c_n})]]$.

Finally, there are the standard S4 axiom schemata for $\Box$.

LTPA 7 *Let* A *and* B *be closed wffs. Then* $[\Box \mathrm{A} \supset \mathrm{A}]$, $[\Box[\mathrm{A} \supset \mathrm{B}] \supset [\Box \mathrm{A} \supset \Box \mathrm{B}]]$, *and* $[\Box \mathrm{A} \supset \Box\Box \mathrm{A}]$.

The nonlogical axioms of L_{tp} are threefold. First, there is the logical rendition of the axioms of the particular theory. I denote those axioms by Γ_t and note that the wffs in Γ_t are expressed exclusively with the vocabulary of L_t

and without the use of $\Box$. For ease of reference I summarize these axioms as follows:

LTPA 8 *Let* $\mathrm{a} = (\mathrm{a}_1, \ldots, \mathrm{a}_\mathrm{k})$, *where* a_j *is an individual variable of the* jth *kind,* $\mathrm{j} = 1, \ldots, \mathrm{k}$. *Then,* $(\forall \mathrm{a})[\Omega_\mathrm{T}(\mathrm{a}) \supset \Gamma_\mathrm{t}(\mathrm{a})]$.

Second, there is the logical rendition of the axioms that delineate characteristics of the data. I denote those axioms by Γ_p and note that the wffs in Γ_p are expressed exclusively with the vocabulary of L_p and without the use of $\Box$. For ease of reference, I summarize these axioms as follows:

LTPA 9 *Let* $\mathrm{a} = (\mathrm{a}_{\mathrm{k}+1}, \ldots, \mathrm{a}_{\mathrm{k}+\mathrm{m}})$, *where* $\mathrm{a}_{\mathrm{k}+\mathrm{j}}$ *is an individual variable of the* $(\mathrm{k}+\mathrm{j})$*th kind,* $\mathrm{j} = 1, \ldots, \mathrm{m}$. *Then,* $(\forall \mathrm{a})[\Omega_\mathrm{P}(\mathrm{a}) \supset \Gamma_\mathrm{p}(\mathrm{a})]$.

Third, there is the logical rendition of the bridge principles that in the particular theory-data confrontation relate theoretical variables to their counterparts in the data universe. I denote those axioms by $\Gamma_{t,p}$ and note that the wffs in $\Gamma_{t,p}$ are expressed with the help of the predicates in B_{tp} and the terms of L_t and L_p. To simplify my arguments I assume in the remainder of this chapter that $\Gamma_{t,p}$ can be written as a conjunction of the predicates in B_{tp}. Also, if $a = (a_t, a_p)$, where $a_t = (a_1, \ldots, a_k)$, $a_p = (a_{k+1}, \ldots, a_{k+m})$, and a_j, $j = 1, \ldots, (k+m)$, is an individual variable of the jth kind, I say that an assignment of values to a, σa, is *admissible* if it satisfies the predicate $[[\Omega_T \wedge \Omega_P] \wedge \Omega]$, that is, if $[[\Omega_T(\sigma a_t) \wedge \Omega_P(\sigma a_p)] \wedge \Omega(\sigma a)]$. That allows me to summarize the axioms in L_{tp} that concern bridge principles as follows:

LTPA 10 *Let* $\mathrm{a} = (\mathrm{a}_\mathrm{t}, \mathrm{a}_\mathrm{p})$, *where* $\mathrm{a}_\mathrm{t} = (\mathrm{a}_1, \ldots, \mathrm{a}_\mathrm{k})$, $\mathrm{a}_\mathrm{p} = (\mathrm{a}_{\mathrm{k}+1}, \ldots, \mathrm{a}_{\mathrm{k}+\mathrm{m}})$, *and* $\mathrm{a}_\mathrm{j}, \mathrm{j} = 1, \ldots, (\mathrm{k}+\mathrm{m})$, *is an individual variable of the* jth *kind. Also, let* $\sigma\mathrm{a} = (\sigma\mathrm{a}_\mathrm{t}, \sigma\mathrm{a}_\mathrm{p})$ *be an admissible assignment of values to* a *such that* $[[\Omega_\mathrm{T}(\sigma\mathrm{a}_\mathrm{t}) \wedge \Omega_\mathrm{P}(\sigma\mathrm{a}_\mathrm{p})] \wedge \Omega(\sigma\mathrm{a})]$. *Then* $\sim\Box\sim\Gamma_{\mathrm{t,p}}(\sigma\mathrm{a})$.

As rules of inference of L_{tp} I adopt those of L, that is, RI 1 and RI 2. In addition, I adopt a rule of inference that concerns the application of the modal operator $\Box$. In stating it, I take a nonmodal logical consequence to be an assertion in the proof of which the modal operator $\Box$ does not appear.

RI 3 *Let* $\mathrm{T}(\Gamma_\mathrm{t}, \Gamma_\mathrm{p})$ *denote the set of nonmodal logical consequences of LTPA 8, LTPA 9, and the axiom schemata LTPA 1–LTPA 6. If* A *is a closed wff that is a member of* $\mathrm{T}(\Gamma_\mathrm{t}, \Gamma_\mathrm{p})$, *infer* $\Box A$.

20.3.3 The Status of Bridge Principles

In E 20.3 I insisted that there was no reason not to believe in the axioms that delineated characteristics of individuals in the given theory and data universe. They must be valid. When I formulated RI 3, my intention was to go one step further. In economic theory-data confrontations the individuals who roam around in the theory universe are toys in a toy economy. The individuals in the data universe have been created by the economists themselves. Consequently, there are good reasons for claiming, as I do in RI 3, that the nonmodal logical closures in L_{tp} of the members of Γ_t and Γ_p are true in all possible worlds.

In E 20.3 I also insisted that I have inconclusive evidence for the validity of the given bridge principles. I believe that this uncertainty about the validity of bridge principles is a general feature of theory-data confrontations in economics. My belief finds expression in the axiom schemata of LTPA 10 when I insist that, for admissible assignments of values to a, $\sim\Box\sim\Gamma_{t,p}(\sigma a)$. The corresponding assertions in E 20.3 are conjunctions of $\sim\Box\sim P^{2,5}[\sigma(x,z)]$ and $\sim\Box\sim P^{1,4}[\sigma(p,q)]$, where $P^{2,5}(x,z)$ only if $[x = z]$, and $P^{1,4}(p,q)$ only if $[p = g(q)]$.

Uncertainty about the validity of the bridge principles necessarily carries with it uncertainty about the validity of assertions in the proof of which these principles play an essential role. The following theorem demonstrates what I have in mind:

TM 6 *Let* A *be a member of* Γ_t *with free variables* $a_{t_1}, \ldots, a_{t_r}$, *and let* $b_t = (a_{t_1}, \ldots, a_{t_r})$. *Also, let* C *be a wff in* L_p *that contains no appearance of* $\Box$ *and has free variables* $a_{p_1}, \ldots, a_{p_s}$, *and let* $b_p = (a_{p_1}, \ldots, a_{p_s})$. *Finally, let* $a = (a_t, a_p)$, *where* $a_t = (a_1, \ldots, a_k)$ *and* $a_p = (a_{k+1}, \ldots, a_{k+m})$*; let* B *be a member of* B_{tp} *with free variables* (b_t, b_p), *let* $(\sigma a_t, \sigma a_p)$ *be an admissible assignment of values to the respective components of* (a_t, a_p) *such that* $\sigma a_t \in \Omega_T$, $\sigma a_p \in \Omega p$, *and* $(\sigma a_t, \sigma a_p) \in \Omega$, *and suppose that*

$$[[A_{b_t}(\sigma a_t) \wedge B_{(b_t,b_p)}(\sigma a_t, \sigma a_p)] \supset C_{b_p}(\sigma a_p)]]$$

is a member of $T(\Gamma_t, \Gamma_p)$. *Then it is the case that* $\sim\Box\sim C_{b_p}(\sigma a_p)$.

The proof of TM 6 is as follows:

$$[[\Omega_T(\sigma a_t) \wedge \Omega_P(\sigma a_p)] \wedge \Omega(\sigma a_t, \sigma a_p)]$$

$$[[\Omega_T(\sigma a_t) \wedge \Omega_P(\sigma a_p)] \wedge \Omega(\sigma a_t, \sigma a_p)] \supset [[(\sigma a_t, \sigma a_p) \in \Omega]$$

$$[(\sigma a_t, \sigma a_p) \in \Omega]$$

$$[[(\sigma a_t, \sigma a_p) \in \Omega] \supset \sim\Box\sim B_{(b_t,b_p)}(\sigma a_t, \sigma a_p)]$$

$$\sim\Box\sim B_{(b_t,b_p)}(\sigma a_t, \sigma a_p)$$

$$A_{b_t}(\sigma a_t)$$

$$\Box A_{b_t}(\sigma a_t)$$

$$[[A_{b_t}(\sigma a_t) \wedge B_{(b_t,b_p)}(\sigma a_t, \sigma a_p)] \supset C_{b_p}(\sigma a_p)]$$

$$[[[A_{b_t}(\sigma a_t) \wedge B_{(b_t,b_p)}(\sigma a_t, \sigma a_p)] \supset C_{b_p}(\sigma a_p)] \supset$$
$$[\sim C_{b_p}(\sigma a_p) \supset \sim[A_{b_t}(\sigma a_t) \wedge B_{(b_t,b_p)}(\sigma a_t, \sigma a_p)]]]$$

$$[\sim C_{b_p}(\sigma a_p) \supset [A_{b_t}(\sigma a_t) \supset \sim B_{(b_t,b_p)}(\sigma a_t, \sigma a_p)]]$$

$$\square[\sim C_{b_p}(\sigma a_p) \supset [A_{b_t}(\sigma a_t) \supset \sim B_{(b_t,b_p)}(\sigma a_t, \sigma a_p)]]$$

$$\square[\sim C_{b_p}(\sigma a_p) \supset [A_{b_t}(\sigma a_t) \supset \sim B_{(b_t,b_p)}(\sigma a_t, \sigma a_p)]] \supset$$
$$[\square \sim C_{b_p}(\sigma a_p) \supset [\square A_{b_t}(\sigma a_t) \supset \square \sim B_{(b_t,b_p)}(\sigma a_t, \sigma a_p)]]$$

$$[\square \sim C_{b_p}(\sigma a_p) \supset [\square A_{b_t}(\sigma a_t) \supset \square \sim B_{(b_t,b_p)}(\sigma a_t, \sigma a_p)]]$$

$$[[\square \sim C_{b_p}(\sigma a_p) \supset [\square A_{b_t}(\sigma a_t) \supset \square \sim B_{(b_t,b_p)}(\sigma a_t, \sigma a_p)]] \supset$$
$$[[\square A_{b_t}(\sigma a_t) \wedge \sim\square\sim B_{(b_t,b_p)}(\sigma a_t, \sigma a_p)] \supset \sim\square\sim C_{b_p}(\sigma a_p)]]$$

$$[[\square A_{b_t}(\sigma a_t) \wedge \sim\square\sim B_{(b_t,b_p)}(\sigma a_t, \sigma a_p)] \supset \sim\square\sim C_{b_p}(\sigma a_p)]$$

$$[\square A_{b_t}(\sigma a_t) \wedge \sim\square\sim B_{(b_t,b_p)}(\sigma a_t, \sigma a_p)]$$

$$\sim\square\sim C_{b_p}(\sigma a_p)$$

My use of admissible assignments of values to variables in LTPA 10 may look disconcerting but is not. In economic theory-data confrontations, such as the one in E 20.3 and elsewhere in this book, Ω is an undefined term and the various terms that satisfy Ω_T are unobservable. Moreover, the number of observations that one has on individuals in the data universe is always finite. Hence, theorems in L_{tp} can be derived without concern about the exact assignment of values to members of Ω and correct required values on individuals in Ω_p provided once the observations have been collected.

20.3.4 The Intended Interpretation of L_{tp}

To provide the intended interpretation of L_{tp} I must sketch the contours of a structure for L_{tp}. In the required interpretation, $\square$ plays a special role, so I begin by describing a structure for L_{tp} without $\square$. Let M_{tp}, M_t, and M_p be, respectively, L_{tp}, L_t, and L_p without $\square$. A structure for M_{tp} is a triple $\mathfrak{I} = (\mathfrak{I}_t, \mathfrak{I}_p, G^{\mathfrak{I}})$, where $\mathfrak{I}_t = (|\mathfrak{I}_1|, \ldots, |\mathfrak{I}_k|, N^{\mathfrak{I}_1}, \ldots, N^{\mathfrak{I}_k}, F^{\mathfrak{I}_t}, G^{\mathfrak{I}_t})$ is a structure for M_t, $\mathfrak{I}_p = (|\mathfrak{I}_{k+1}|, \ldots, |\mathfrak{I}_{k+m}|, N^{\mathfrak{I}_{k+1}}, \ldots, N^{\mathfrak{I}_{k+m}}, F^{\mathfrak{I}_p}, G^{\mathfrak{I}_p})$ is a structure for M_p, and $G^{\mathfrak{I}}$ is an interpretation of the predicates in B_{tp}. Here, $|\mathfrak{I}_j|$ denotes the universe of the jth kind of individuals, and $N^{\mathfrak{I}_j}$ contains the names of the individuals in $|\mathfrak{I}_j|$, $j = 1, \ldots, (k+m)$. Also, $F^{\mathfrak{I}_t}$ and $G^{\mathfrak{I}_t}$ ($F^{\mathfrak{I}_p}$ and $G^{\mathfrak{I}_p}$), respectively, are collections of functions and predicates that provide the interpretation in $\mathfrak{I}_t(\mathfrak{I}_p)$ of the nonlogical vocabulary of $M_t(M_p)$. I assume throughout this discussion of default logic that for all $1 \leq i, j \leq (k+m)$ and $i \neq j$, $\mathfrak{I}_i \cap \mathfrak{I}_j = \emptyset$. Moreover, different individuals carry different names.

The structure for M_{tp} that I described above provides the means to interpret M_t, M_p, and M_{tp}. Since the procedure for carrying out this interpretation is analogous to the way I interpreted L in Section 20.1, I refer to Stigum (1990, pp. 626–627) for further details. The only thing needed for future reference here is an understanding that $M_{tp}(\Im)$, $M_t(\Im)$, and $M_p(\Im)$ denote, respectively, M_{tp}, M_t, and M_p with the names in the pertinent $N^{\Im_j}$ added to the constants of the nonlogical vocabulary of M_{tp}, M_t, and M_p as the case may be.

There are many different structures for M_{tp}. Some of the interpretations of M_{tp} that are obtained from them are models of LTPA 1–LTPA 6, LTPA 8, and LTPA 9. The structures in these models are the *possible worlds* of L_{tp}. A subset $\Re$ of these models has some interesting properties:

1. $\Re$ has a distinguishing member ξ_e that designates the *Real World.*
2. There is on $\Re$ a reflexive, transitive binary relation R.
3. The structures in $\Re$ are nonisomorphic and comprise all the possible worlds of relevance for the theory-data confrontation.
4. The structures in $\Re$ possess the same universe of discourse and name the individuals in the universe by the same names as ξ_e. Further, the given universe contains a denumerable infinity of individuals of each kind.
5. Let $a = (a_t, a_p)$, where $a_t = (a_1, \ldots, a_k)$, $a_p = (a_{k+1}, \ldots, a_{k+m})$, and a_j, $j = 1, \ldots, (k+m)$, is an individual variable of the jth kind. Also, let $\sigma a = (\sigma a_t, \sigma a_p)$, let H be an element in $\Re$, and suppose that

$$H\big([[\Omega_T(\sigma a_t) \wedge \Omega_P(\sigma a_p)] \wedge \Omega(\sigma a)]\big) = t.$$

   Then, there is an $H' \in \Re$ such that HRH' and $H'(\Gamma_{t,p}(\sigma a)) = t$.
6. Let a and σ be as in condition 5; let A be a wff in L_p with free variables, $ac = (ac_{(j1)}, \ldots, ac_{(jn)})$, where $ji \in \{k+1, \ldots, (k+m)\}$, $i = 1, \ldots, n$; and suppose that $A_{ac}(\sigma ac)$ is a logical consequence of Γ_t, Γ_p, $\Gamma_{t,p}$. Then, for all $H \in \Re$ in which $H([[\Omega_T(\sigma a_t) \wedge \Omega_P(\sigma a_p)] \wedge \Omega(\sigma a)]) = t$, there is an $H' \in \Re$ such that HRH' and $H'(A_{ac}(\sigma ac)) = t$.

The existence of such an $\Re$ is not obvious. So a few remarks in that regard are called for. Let T be a theory in M_{tp}, that is, let T be a deductively closed set in M_{tp}. Suppose that T has models whose universes contain infinitely many individuals of each kind. Then T has a model that contains just a denumerable infinity of individuals of each kind. In fact, every model of T whose universe contains infinitely many individuals of each kind has an elementary substructure whose universe contains only a denumerable infinity of individuals of each kind.[4] Suppose next that T is $T(\Gamma_t, \Gamma_p)$ and consider the structures in $\Re$. If all these structures have universes with a denumerable infinity of individuals of each kind, one can without loss of generality assume that they have the same universe and identify this universe with the universe of ξ_e. Justification for all these claims can be found in Stigum (1990, pp. 112–126, 640–644).

I can illustrate the preceding observations with the help of E 20.3, in which $T = T$(U 1–U 6). I obtain a structure $\Im$ for T by delineating the domains of $U(\cdot)$ and $W(\cdot)$, by assigning an appropriate value to α, and by noting the values of my observations on z, q, and $W(z)$. If a rational animal's comprehension of the continuum is as described in a first-order theory, I lose no generality in insisting that $|\Im_1| \times \ldots \times |\Im_6|$ contains only a denumerable infinity of individuals, that is, that the components of the vectors $[p, x, U(x), q, z, W(z)]$ can assume at most a denumerable infinity of values. In the ξ_e of E 20.3 these values are taken to belong to $[0, 1] \times [0, 1{,}000] \times [0, 1] \times [0, 1] \times [0, 1{,}000] \times [0, 1]$ and the pertinent α is an unspecified number in (0, 1). Finally, ξ_e and all the other structures of relevance for the theory-data confrontation have the same universe, different values of α, and the same or different sets of observations on $[q, z, W(z)]$.

Condition 6 looks innocent, but is not. To see why, one should take another look at E 20.3. There, with the domains of $U(\cdot)$ and $W(\cdot)$ given, one may think of the model H as being determined by the value of α and a student's answers to my queries. Conditions 5 and 6 insist that no matter who H is, if $H \in \Re$, one can find another student H' such that HRH' and such that $A_{ac}(\sigma ac)$ is consistent with H''s α and his answers to my questions. In different words, no matter what world H in $\Re$ is, if σac is an admissible assignment of values to ac in H, there is a world H' that is in the relation R to H and is such that the truth value of $A_{ac}(\sigma ac)$ in H' does not call for a diagnosis. I have insisted on condition 6 to simplify my arguments in the remainder of this chapter and in Chapter 22.

I can use the structures in $\Re$ to give an interpretation of $\Box$ and the remaining wffs of L_{tp}. For that purpose, let $M_{tp}(\xi_e)(L_{tp}(\xi_e))$ denote $M_{tp}(L_{tp})$ with the names in ξ_e added to the constants in the vocabulary of $M_{tp}(L_{tp})$. Also, let σ denote an assignment of values to the arguments of the predicates in B_{tp} that is admissible in ξ_e, and (with the given assignment of values to the arguments of the predicates in B_{tp}) let $C_{tp}^M(\xi_e, \sigma)(C_{tp}(\xi_e, \sigma))$ denote the collection of all closed wffs in $M_{tp}(\xi_e)(L_{tp}(\xi_e))$. Finally, for each $H \in \Re$, let $H(\cdot) : C_{tp}^M(\xi_e, \sigma) \rightarrow \{t, f\}$ be such that $H(A)$ denotes the truth value of A in H, let $\wp(\Re)$ denote the family of subsets of $\Re$, and let $\varphi(\cdot) : C_{tp}^M(\xi_e, \sigma) \times \Re \rightarrow \wp(\Re)$ be defined by

$$\varphi(A, H) = \{H' \in \Re : HRH' \text{ and } H'(A) = t\}.$$

Then $H(\cdot)$ and $\varphi(\cdot)$ are well defined. However, to use them in an interpretation of $\Box$ and $L_{tp}(\xi_e)$, I must extend their domain of definition to all of $C_{tp}(\xi_e, \sigma)$.

To extend the domain of $H(\cdot)$ and $\varphi(\cdot)$ to all of $C_{tp}(\xi_e, \sigma)$ I begin by letting $R_\Box \subset \Re \times \wp(\Re)$ be such that $(H, E) \in R_\Box$ if and only if $H \in \Re$ and $E = \{H' \in \Re : HRH'\}$. Thereafter I let C_i, $i = 0, 1, \ldots$ be an increasing sequence of collections of closed wffs that satisfy the conditions (i) $C_0 = C_{tp}^M(\xi_e, \sigma)$ and (ii) if $A \in C_i$ for some $i \geq 1$. Then there are wffs C and D in C_{i-1} such that A is C, $\sim C$, $[C \supset D]$, or $\Box C$. From my characterization of $C_{tp}(\xi_e, \sigma)$ it follows that $C_{tp}(\xi_e, \sigma) = \cup_{1 \leq i < \infty} C_i$. Hence, for each $H \in \Re$ and $\varphi(\cdot)$, I can obtain the required extensions by induction on the value of i. To wit: suppose that I have extended the required definitions to C_{n-1} and that A is a closed wff in C_n. Also, let H be an arbitrary member of $\Re$. If A is C and $C \in C_{n-1}$, I let $H(A) = H(C)$. If A is $\sim C$, I let $H(A) = f$ or t depending on whether $H(C) = t$ or f. If A is $[C \supset D]$, where $C, D \in C_{n-1}$, I let $H(A) = t$ if $H(C) = f$ or $H(D) = t$. Otherwise I let $H(A) = f$. If A is $\Box C$ for some $C \in C_{n-1}$, I let $H(A) = t$ if $(H, \varphi(C, H)) \in R_{\Box}$ and $H(A) = f$ otherwise. As soon as I have extended the definition of $H(\cdot)$ to C_n for all $H \in \mathfrak{R}$, I let $\varphi(A, H) = \{H' \in \mathfrak{R} : HRH' \text{ and } H'(A) = t\}$.

With the definition of $H(\cdot)$ and $\varphi(\cdot)$ extended to all of $C_{tp}(\xi_e, \sigma)$ for all $H \in \mathfrak{R}$ and for arbitrary assignments of values to the arguments of the predicates in B_{tp} that are admissible in ξ_e, I have delineated the sought for contour of the intended interpretation of $L_{tp}(\xi_e)$. In reading the interpretation, it is important to note that it constitutes one model of the axioms of L_{tp}. By varying $\mathfrak{R}$, ξ_e, and R, I can generate many different models.

20.4 DEFAULTS AND DIAGNOSES

The intended interpretation of L_{tp} has several interesting characteristics. I consider that the most interesting of them is a consequence of TM 6. According to the hypotheses of TM 6 and my interpretation of L_{tp}, for all $H \in \mathfrak{R}$,

$$H\left(\left[\left[A_{b_t}(\sigma a_t) \wedge B_{(b_t,b_p)}\left(\sigma a_t, \sigma a_p\right)\right] \supset C_{b_p}(\sigma a_p)\right]\right) = t.$$

But, if that is so, then—again according to TM 6 and the interpretation of L_{tp}—it must also be the case that for all $H \in \mathfrak{R}$ in which σa is an admissible assignment of values to a,

$$H\left(\sim\Box\sim C_{b_p}\left(\sigma a_p\right)\right) = t.$$

Consequently, for all admissible assignments of values to (a_t, a_p) in H, such as $(\sigma a_t, \sigma a_p)$, it must be the case that there is an $H' \in \mathfrak{R}$ such that HRH' and $H'[C_{b_p}(\sigma a_p)] = t$. The given H' may vary with H. More importantly, H' need not equal ξ_e for any H! Equally important, if $H'' \in \mathfrak{R}$ and $H''[B_{(b_t,b_p)}(\sigma a_t, \sigma a_p)] = t$, then $H''[C_{b_p}(\sigma a_p)] = t$! Thus, if $\xi_e[B_{(b_t,b_p)}(\sigma a_t, \sigma a_p)] = t$, then $\xi_e[C_{b_p}(\sigma a_p)] = t$ as well.

Suppose now that I have identified a structure as ξ_e and found that $\xi_e[C_{b_p}(\sigma a_p)] = f$. I conclude the chapter by discussing what the attitude toward this observation ought to be?

The observation that $\xi_e[C_{b_p}(\sigma a_p)] = f$ does not contradict any theorem in L_{tp}. However, as long as the validity of Γ_t is not at stake, the truth value of $C_{b_p}(\sigma a_p)$ in ξ_e implies that at least one of the components of Γ_{tp} is not true in the Real World. Moreover, as I noted above, if I can find a value of Γ_{tp} that is true in ξ_e, I can find a version of $C_{b_p}(\sigma a_p)$ that is valid in the Real World. Hence, the observed truth value of $C_{b_p}(\sigma a_p)$ demands a diagnosis. Carrying out such a diagnosis in the general case would take more space than is available here, so

I content myself with example E 20.5, in which I discuss a call for diagnosis in the context of E 20.3. E 20.4 provides the intuition needed to carry out a diagnosis in any relevant case.

E 20.4 *Consider the pairs* (Ω_T, Γ_t) *and* (Ω_P, Γ_p) *in E 20.3 and the bridge principles* $\Gamma_{t,p}$ *in the same example. Suppose that the* $W(\cdot)$ *that I constructed in E 20.3 does not satisfy the equation,* $W(z_i) = g^{-1}(z_i/1{,}000), i = 1, \ldots, N$, *for any* $\alpha \in (0, 1)$. *One must determine which of the axioms* Γ_t, $\Gamma_{t,p}$, *or* Γ_p *lack(s) relevance in the given empirical context*

In this case there is no reason to doubt the validity of Γ_p *and* Γ_t. *So the irrelevant axioms must be among the translations of* Γ_t *by* $\Gamma_{t,p}$. *One can insist on keeping* Γ_t *and adjust* $\Gamma_{t,p}$ *or one can modify* Γ_t *and leave* $\Gamma_{t,p}$ *as is. Suppose that I keep* Γ_t. *Then the present belief revision concerns the bridge principles alone. To streamline the argument let me restate the bridge principles as follows:*

$$x_i = H(z_i) \text{ and } p_i = G(q_i), i = 1, \ldots, N.$$

Then I can represent $T(S)$ *by the equations*

$$H(z_i) = 1{,}000G(q_i), i = 1, \ldots, N,$$

and

$$W(z_i) = q_i, i = 1, \ldots, N,$$

and let $C = \{H(\cdot), G(\cdot)\}$. *Also, I can represent* $Ab_1(\cdot)$ *and* $Ab_2(\cdot)$ *by the equations*

$$Ab_1(H) \text{ if and only if } H(\cdot) \neq 1(\cdot) \text{ on } [0, 1{,}000]$$

and

$$Ab_2(G) \text{ if and only if } G(\cdot) \neq g(\cdot) \text{ on } [0, 1].$$

Finally, I can postulate that Obs *is a wff* Obs(a, b) *that asserts*

$$[[q_i = a_i] \wedge [z_i = b_i]] \text{ for } i = 1, \ldots, N.$$

Now, if

$$T(S) \cup Obs(s, t) \cup \{\sim Ab_1(H)\} \cup \{\sim Ab_2(G)\}$$

is inconsistent, there are two possible diagnoses: $\Delta_1 = \{H(\cdot)\}$ *and* $\Delta_2 = \{G(\cdot)\}$. *Suppose that* $Ab_1(H)$ *is true. Then one can choose* $H(\cdot)$ *so that* $g^{-1}(H(t_i)/1{,}000) = s_i, i = 1, \ldots, N$. *If* $Ab_2(G)$ *is true, one can choose* $G(\cdot)$ *so that* $G^{-1}(t_i/1{,}000) = s_i, i = 1, \ldots, N$. *In that way the diagnoses provide two possible sets of bridge principles. I have no preference for either of the two.*

In reading the preceding example there is a significant point that ought not go unnoted here. If one had known of the culprit bridge principle in E 20.4, such knowledge would have carried no information about the truth value of $C_{b_p}(\sigma a_p)$

in the Real World! As is seen in Chapter 22, this fact has an important bearing on Hempel's (1965) symmetry thesis concerning prediction and explanation in science.

APPENDIX: SECTION 20.3 FROM A LOGICAL POINT OF VIEW

Herman Ruge Jervell

In Section 20.3 a number of logical matters are introduced:

1. Predicate logic
2. Default logic à la Reiter
3. Modal logic
4. Bridge principles

Let me look at this from a logical point of view. The predicate logic introduced is the standard one with quantifiers and connectives. It is a many sorted predicate calculus. Here the sorts are introduced by unary predicates $\Omega_a(x)$. The predicates are thought of as carving the universe into subuniverses. An alternative way might be to have a syntactical marking of the different sorts of variables and for an interpretation one gives a universe for each sort. The two ways of introducing sorts are equivalent—they can be easily translated into each other. In the formulation of the bridge principles—and in particular the proof of the interpolation theorem—there may be an advantage in the latter way of doing it.

In Section 20.3 a special modal logic is introduced as an alternative to Reiter's default logic, which I now explain. The modal logic is one with quantifiers introduced over an S4-type calculus. Then the problem is how to interpret quantification into a modal context. In particular, is there a way to understand formulas where one quantifies into a modal context such as

$$\forall x \Box \mathrm{P}x$$

In Section 20.3 the choice is: (1) Such formulas are syntactically meaningful. (2) The calculus prohibits essential use of them. The crucial rule is the rule of necessitation:

RI 3 *Let* $\mathrm{T}(\Gamma_{\mathrm{t}}, \Gamma_{\mathrm{p}})$ *denote the set of nonmodal logical consequences of LTPA 8, LTPA 9, and the axiom schemata LTPA 1–LTPA 6. If* A *is a closed wff that is a member of* $\mathrm{T}(\Gamma_{\mathrm{t}}, \Gamma_{\mathrm{p}})$, *infer* $\Box$A.

As usual it is assumed that *A* is a consequence derived from the axioms alone, that is, without extra assumptions. But here one also insists that *A* is a closed formula. This gives no way of deriving formulas where quantification into a modal context is used in an essential way.

The solid argument for the modal system is given by a completeness theorem. I have carried this out and give a rough sketch of the main elements below. But it seems worthwhile to reflect on why a completeness theorem is important. In this modal logic—as in all other logics—there is a tension between "logic as language" and "logic as calculus." One may be impressed by the expressive power of one's logic, but still think that there are unwanted interpretations of one's calculus. The completeness theorem demonstrates that there is an exact match between the valid propositions, that is, those that are true in all interpretations and the derivable propositions.

The argument for classical predicate calculus was first carried out by Thoralf Skolem in 1922, but is known mostly from the work of Kurt Gödel in 1930. Skolem and Gödel looked at systematic falsifications of propositions. If the falsifications did not succeed, then the propositions were derivable. The crucial point was that a nonsuccess—if it occurred—would occur after a finite time and this nonsuccess could be captured with the usual calculus for predicate logic. Now the systematic falsifications in the completeness proofs à la Skolem and Gödel give extra information. They show, for example, that the falsifications are controlled by the vocabularies of the propositions one tries to falsify. This is important in trying to understand the bridge principles in Section 20.3.

Now I turn to the completeness theorem. It is important here to carry out the completeness theorem in modal logic by using systematic falsifications. For propositional modal logic this is done, for example, by Grigori Mints (2000). I must extend this to the variant of modal predicate calculus used in Section 20.3. This requires more work but is helped by the extra restriction on the rule of necessitation RI 3. It can be shown that the modal logic is complete for formulas where one does not quantify into modal contexts. As usual my models are possible worlds where the possibility relation is reflexive and transitive since I have an S4 logic. But it is not necessary to insist that the universes in the possible worlds are the same. For the completeness theorem it does not matter. What about formulas where one has quantified into a modal context? The completeness result may be extended to such formulas by letting modal contexts with free variables play the role of atomic predicates.

I have carried out the proof by translating the system into a sequential calculus. As a bonus I find that the cut-free rules are complete. This gives cut elimination, which can be phrased here as:

If one has a derivation of a formula using auxiliary lemmas, then one also has a direct derivation of the formula without using the lemmas.

As another bonus I am led to a proof of the interpolation theorem:

If one has a proof of a formula A ⊃ B, *then there is a formula* C *in the language common to both* A *and* B *and proofs of both* A ⊃ C *and* C ⊃ B. *With common language one means, for example, that* C *uses only predicates and constants that are simultaneously in both* A *and* B.

The proof here requires some work. I have to be careful with the free variables common to both A and B. Here the assumption about quantification into modal contexts helps.

The interpolation theorem is of interest on its own. As a comment to Section 20.3 it gives a new grounding to the bridge principles. So let me recapitulate: For the bridge principles the following are essential:

1. There are two types of vocabularies: a theoretical vocabulary and a data vocabulary.
2. The theoretical axioms Γ_t are expressed as nonmodal propositions in the theoretical vocabulary.
3. The data axioms Γ_p are expressed as nonmodal propositions in the data vocabulary.
4. In addition there are bridge principles Γ_{tp} as axioms, which are expressed with predicates and propositions involving both vocabularies; they use the predicates in B_{tp}.
5. The bridge principles are satisfied in one of the possible worlds, say the Real World.

Here I have such a clean separation of vocabularies that I can use the interpolation theorem. Assume I have a derivation from the axioms of a proposition D in the data vocabulary:

$$(\Gamma_t \wedge \Gamma_{tp} \wedge \Gamma_p) \supset D.$$

This can be transformed into a derivation of

$$\Gamma_t \wedge \Gamma_{tp} \supset (\Gamma_p \supset D).$$

Now I am ready to use the interpolation theorem. The two sides of the conditionals have only the bridge predicates B_{tp} in common; hence there is an interpolant I built from the bridge predicates B_{tp} with

$$\Gamma_t \wedge \Gamma_{tp} \supset I$$

and

$$I \supset (\Gamma_p \supset D).$$

The last can be expressed as

$$\Gamma_p \supset (I \supset D) \text{ or } (\Gamma_p \wedge I) \supset D,$$

which may be easier to interpret. The proposition I may be said to be a bridge formula: It is a formula built up from bridge predicates and proved from the theoretical axioms and the bridge principles alone. Given the data axioms and the bridge formula one can derive proposition D.

I now look at what is really required to substantiate the considerations above. In the proof of the interpolation theorem there is always a hassle about the free variables. This is helped with the restriction in our modal logic: The rule of necessitation works only for closed propositions. On the other hand, one observes that this restriction paves the way for an interpolation theorem for modal as well as nonmodal formulas. The requirements that the axioms be nonmodal are not used yet. One may use modal axioms as well, but it is hard to imagine a situation where it is essential to use modal axioms in the theory, the data, or the bridge principles.

The bridge principles contain an extra element:

LTPA 10 *Let* $a = (a_t, a_p)$, *where* $a_t = (a_1, \ldots, a_k)$, $a_p = (a_{k+1}, \ldots, a_{k+m})$, *and* $a_j, j = 1, \ldots, (k+m)$, *is an individual variable of the* j*th kind. Also, let* $\sigma a = (\sigma a_t, \sigma a_p)$ *be an admissible assignment of values to* a *such that* $[[\Omega_T(\sigma a_t) \wedge \Omega_P(\sigma a_p)] \wedge \Omega(\sigma a)]$. *Then* $\sim\Box\sim\Gamma_{t,p}(\sigma a)$.

This goes beyond the separation of vocabularies mentioned—and used—above. LTPA 10 indicates that among the possible worlds there is one where all the bridge principles $\Gamma_{t,p}$ are satisfied. If I now have a nonmodal formula, then the consequences of the bridge principles $\Gamma_{t,p}$ are within this possible world: Satisfaction of a nonmodal formula in a world is a local property of that world. This gives rise to Bernt's TM 6.

TM 6 *Let* A *be a member of* Γ_t *with free variables* $a_{t_1}, \ldots, a_{t_r}$, *and let* $b_t = (a_{t_1}, \ldots, a_{t_r})$. *Also, let* C *be a wff in* L_p *that contains no appearance of* $\Box$ *and has free variables* $a_{p_1}, \ldots, a_{p_s}$, *and let* $b_p = (a_{p_1}, \ldots, a_{p_s})$. *Finally, let* $a = (a_t, a_p)$, *where* $a_t = (a_1, \ldots, a_k)$ *and* $a_p = (a_{k+1}, \ldots, a_{k+m})$. *Let* B *be a member of* B_{tp} *with free variables* (b_t, b_p); *let* $(\sigma a_t, \sigma a_p)$ *be an admissible assignment of values to the respective components of* (a_t, a_p) *such that* $\sigma a_t \in \Omega_T$, $\sigma a_p \in \Omega_p$, *and* $(\sigma a_t, \sigma a_p) \in \Omega$; *and assume that*

$$[[A_{b_t}(\sigma a_t) \wedge B_{(b_t,b_p)}(\sigma a_t, \sigma a_p)] \supset C_{b_p}(\sigma a_p)]]$$

is a member of $T(\Gamma_t, \Gamma_p)$. *Then it is the case that* $\sim\Box\sim C_{b_p}(\sigma a_p)$.

In the above I have not made a systematic distinction between proofs and derivations and formulas and propositions. I have used the one or the other part of the pair where it seemed suitable stylistically.

NOTES

1. In this book a *symbolic language* is a formalized language. Therefore, in Alonzo Church's (1956, pp. 47–58) terminology, a symbolic language is an uninterpreted calculus or a logistic system. In Joseph R Shoenfield's (1967, p. 4) terminology, my symbolic language is a *formal system,* and a formal system is the syntactical part of an axiom

system. A formal system has three parts: a language, a set of axioms, and a set of rules of inference. The language is completely specified when its symbols and formulas are specified.

2. My formulation of the law of the excluded middle and the law of contradiction is awkward. With $\wedge$ and $\vee$, as defined in Section 21.2.1, I can state the two laws in a more easily readable form. Then, the former becomes $[\sim A \vee A]$, and the latter becomes $\sim[A\wedge \sim A]$.

3. My notion of monotonicity is similar to the one that Yoav Shoham (1989, p. 76) formulated. He insists that L is monotonic if for all closed wffs A, B, and C in L, $A \models C$ only if $[A \wedge B] \models C$. My notion is also similar to Witold Lukaszewicz (1990, p. 77) formulation: L is monotonic if and only if for any sets of premises in L, S and S', $S \subset S'$ implies that {the wffs A in $L : S \vdash A$} $\subset$ {the wffs A in $L : S' \vdash A$}.

4. A formal definition of an elementary substructure can be found on in Stigum (1990, p. 117). Roughly speaking, if $\aleph_1$ and $\aleph_2$ are models of M_{tp}, then $\aleph_1$ is an elementary substructure of $\aleph_2$ if $\aleph_2$ is an extension of $\aleph_1$ and if a closed wff in $M_{tp}(\aleph_1)$ has the same truth value in $\aleph_2$ as in $\aleph_1$. The assertion itself is a consequence of Skolem's theorem, a proof of which is given in Stigum (1990, pp. 120–121).

REFERENCES

Antoniou, G., 1997, *Nonmonotonic Reasoning*, Cambridge: MIT Press.

Church, A., 1956, *Introduction to Mathematical Logic*, Princeton: Princeton University Press.

Friedman, M., 1957, *A Theory of the Consumption Function*, Princeton: Princeton University Press.

Gödel, K., 1930, "Die Vollständigkeit der Axiomen des logischen Funktionenkalküls," *Monatshefte für Mathematik und Physik* 37, 349–360.

Hempel, C. G., 1965, *Aspects of Scientific Explanation and Other Essays in the Philosophy of Science*, New York: The Free Press.

Janssen, M. C. W., and Y.-H. Tan,1992, "Friedman's Permanent Income Hypothesis as an Example of Diagnostic Reasoning," *Economics and Philosophy* 8, 23–49.

Lukaszewicz, W., 1990, *Non-Monotonic Reasoning*, New York: Ellis Horwood.

Mints, G., 2000, "A Short Introduction to Modal Logic," CSLI Lecture Notes, No. 30, Stanford University.

Reiter R., 1980, "A Logic for Default Reasoning," *Artificial Intelligence* 13, 81–132.

Reiter, R., 1987, "A Theory of Diagnosis from First Principles," *Artificial Intelligence* 32, 57–95.

Shoenfield, J. R., 1967, *Mathematical Logic*, Reading: Addison Wesley.

Shoham, Y., 1989, *Reasoning about Change, Time and Causation from the Standpoint of Artificial Intelligence*, Cambridge: MIT Press.

Skolem, T., 1922, "Einige Bemerkungen zur axiomatischen Begründung der Mengenlehre," in *Proceedings of the 5th Scandinavian Mathematics Congress in Helsinki*, Helsingfors: Akademiska Bokhandelen.

Stigum, B. P., 1990, *Toward a Formal Science of Economics*, Cambridge: MIT Press.

Chapter Twenty-One

Explanations of an Empirical Puzzle: What Can Be Learned from a Test of the Rational Expectations Hypothesis?

Heather M. Anderson

Economic theory, like theory in many disciplines, owes much of its development to observed phenomena. Economists frequently develop theories to explain observed patterns in economic data, and they often use data to verify or discredit various theories that they propose. Once researchers are satisfied that theory and data are mutually consistent, they can be confident that their understanding of the economy has developed. However, finding such consistency in this discipline is challenging. Sometimes appropriate data are not accessible to the researcher, and even when they are very plausible economic theories often appear to conflict with seemingly relevant data analysis.

The rational expectations hypothesis for the term structure of interest rates provides a well-known example. Based on a theoretically appealing "no-arbitrage" principle, this hypothesis (henceforth abbreviated by REH) asserts that the current yield on a long-term instrument equals a time-invariant premium plus the average level of current and expected future yields on shorter-term instruments. Researchers have tested this hypothesis extensively and have frequently been puzzled by their test results: REH implies that spreads should be able to predict future movements in interest rates, but regressions that study this implication often produce statistically insignificant spread coefficients.[1]

Some researchers have interpreted this failure to confirm REH as evidence against this hypothesis, but most term structure theorists have continued to believe in REH, despite this lack of empirical verification. Here, as with many tests of other economic theories, there has been a reluctance to see empirical work as a means of providing definitive answers, which is not unnatural given the many difficulties involved in testing economic hypotheses. The proponents of REH have, of course, been obliged to explain the observed regression results; their response has been to build up a particularly large literature that maintains REH and suggests that the data, the power of thc testing procedure, or factors such as time-varying premia or sluggish market adjustment might have unduly influenced the regression results.[2]

Sometimes a theory is said "to explain" the data if it implies a well-documented stylized fact. To continue with the REH example, researchers have sometimes used REH and an assumption that yields are integrated processes to explain cointegration between yields on Treasury bills.[3] Viewed from the prospective that this cointegration is found, the claim that REH explains the data is not without basis. However, it is reasonable to question whether REH explains this cointegration *adequately*; empirical studies have found that while some of the regressions that incorporate the cointegration implied by REH have statistically significant spread coefficients, REH predicts that these coefficients should be one, and the data typically reject this hypothesis .[4]

In these latter studies, the test of REH has been set up so that a statistical rejection of the theory's prediction falsifies the theory in Popper's (1968) sense. However, despite the fact that the researcher has now (empirically) rejected the theory, rather than failed to verify it, there is still a reluctance to take this finding at face value. One problem involved with the interpretation here is that tests of the "target" hypothesis (REH) cannot be made without incorporating several auxiliary assumptions. Thus, when one observes that the data reject the theory, it is not clear whether REH and/or the auxiliary assumptions are to blame.[5]

One has to question the value of testing REH, given the lack of faith in the test results. Indeed, one might even question whether it is appropriate to try testing this sort of theory. The problem here is that economic theories are not like theories found in the physical sciences, which can be tested in controlled and deterministic environments. Economic theories, by necessity, are tested via statistical rather than deterministic procedures, in environments where other potentially relevant factors are present and cannot be kept under control. Thus, regardless of how desirable it might be to use data to obtain a clear confirmation or rejection of REH, it is not obvious that this is possible in practice.

It is interesting to note, then, that while economists recognize the many difficulties inherent in the ceteris paribus testing of a single economic hypothesis, the vast majority of papers that purport to explain the REH theory-data discrepancy focus on one rather than many possible causes. Different researchers have noted that the problem might lie with the theory, the data, or how the data have been used to test the theory, but the various explanations that are put forward are typically considered in an ad hoc fashion rather than jointly. Standard research programs in economics are in themselves somewhat piecemeal because they are typically implemented in separate stages. As advocated by the hypothetico-deductive school of thought,[6] theory is usually developed first, and then its predictions are tested. This two-stage procedure, often viewed by economists as the "right way" to incorporate the data, generates rather than dispels the potential for situations in which theory and data disagree. Further fragmentation might then occur at the testing stage, since researchers often test just one rather than all of the implications of a theory. This allows situations to develop in which an empirical confirmation of the tested aspect of the theory does not necessarily mean that the theory and data are mutually consistent.

The problems that arise when one concentrates on just one of the many aspects of a theory-data relationship in economics have led econometricians such as Haavelmo (1944), Sims (1980), and Hendry (1995b), among others, to advocate broader research strategies. These strategies explicitly recognize that economic variables are simultaneously determined and that the econometric study of a single economic relationship may be invalid, unless an appropriate concept of exogeneity is applicable or one properly accounts for endogeneity. Within these more general approaches, data usage has gained a broader scope, providing information about interrelationships among variables, rather than just testing one aspect of an economic theory while assuming that other aspects of that theory are true. Sims (1980), Hendry (1995b), and others have explicitly avoided the use of economic theory to impose a priori restrictions on the data and have advocated working with general data representations that simply reflect the observed features of the data. These general representations can be consistent with many (potentially rival) economic theories. Pagan (1987) provides a discussion on different research strategies that attempt to allow for more than a single target hypothesis of interest.

A reluctance to impose a priori restrictions can be justified by the concern that such restrictions might be false, which would then invalidate all subsequent inference. Furthermore, true a priori restrictions implied by economic theory can be empirically invalid, if the observed data do not have a precise correspondence with the concept addressed by the theory. It is appropriate, also, to be concerned about the validity of the statistical assumptions that are made as a model is estimated and studied. Researchers such as Spanos (1995) have focused on this latter point and have advocated the development of "statistically adequate" models, in which the validity of a theory might be evaluated. The point emphasized by Spanos (1995) is that valid statistical inference can only be made on a model that is consistent with the empirical distribution properties of the data, so that the modeling process should address these properties first, before relating the inference based on the data back to the theory in question. Hendry's (1995b) related concept of a "congruent" model incorporates the requirement that models should empirically satisfy the statistical assumptions upon which valid inference relies, while Bontemps and Mizon's refinement of this concept in Chapter 15 of this volume emphasizes the need for a model to fully exploit all available information in the data.

In some recent work that addresses the issue of consistently relating economic theory and data, Stigum (1993, 1998) considers the question of whether REH explains cointegration in the U.S. Treasury bill market. He outlines theoretical issues associated with building a "scientific explanation" of this cointegration, and asks whether it is valid to consider just Treasury bill yields alone when factors such as debt and monetary policy potentially affect yields and therefore have the potential to influence relationships between yields. He suggests that an evaluation of the empirical adequacy of REH might be done using an empirical modeling framework such as Hendry's (1995b) general unrestricted model (GUM), but he does not undertake such an evaluation.

This chapter presents a study of the empirical adequacy of REH by analyzing the properties of various regression-based tests of REH. It first demonstrates that little is learned if the REH tests are conducted within the confines of a standard "textbook" regression framework. Such tests are shown to be invalid because they are based on models that fail a variety of misspecification tests. The chapter then develops a general empirical model of the term structure and related variables, which is carefully tested to show that it accords with the data. The statistical adequacy of this latter model ensures that when it is used for inference, such inference will be reliable. The broad nature of this more general model, and in particular the fact that it nests both REH and other, alternative, theories, allows inference to be made on both REH and other potentially interesting aspects of the theory.

While this chapter makes no formal attempt to replace REH with a better, rival, explanation of Treasury bill yield movements, it discusses various results of the general empirical analysis that are pertinent to such a development. The main result is that although yield spreads between Treasury bills *are* cointegrating, indicating a stable long-run relationship between the yields and that spreads can predict yield changes, the failure to include other variables in REH test regressions *does* influence the estimated spread coefficient. Both Government debt and monetary policy have important influences on Treasury bill yields and should therefore be part of any theory that explains yield movements. Moreover, once one allows for time-varying risk premia, which depend on the Federal Funds market and the market for longer-term instruments, then the explanation of Treasury bill movements is significantly improved.

The plan of the chapter is as follows. Section 21.1 briefly discusses REH and elaborates on some of its empirical implications. Then, in Section 21.2, two empirical analyses are undertaken. The first studies the regressions that are typically used to "test" REH and shows why inference based on these sorts of regressions can mask several potentially relevant aspects of the data. The second analysis then develops and presents a general and statistically adequate vector error-correction model of the Treasury bill market. The model versus data consistency in this second case ensures that all inference conducted within this framework will be reliable and that any inference that addresses any particular aspect of the theory will then lead to a valid assessment of whether that theory is consistent with the data. Section 21.3 compares the predictions of the general empirical Treasury bill model with the various implications of REH and discusses the empirical relevance of REH and other economic theory to the data at hand. Section 21.4 concludes the body of the chapter.

21.1 THE RATIONAL EXPECTATIONS HYPOTHESIS

21.1.1 Regression Implications of the Rational Expectations Hypothesis

Let $\boldsymbol{R(k,t)}$ be the continuously compounded yield to maturity of a k-period Treasury bill or bond ($k = 1, 2, \ldots$). Then, assuming that investors are risk-neutral and that they hold k-period bills until maturity, the principle of no arbitrage implies that

$$R(k,t) = \frac{1}{k}\left[\sum_{j=1}^{j=k} E_t[R(1, t+j-1)]\right] + L(k,t) \tag{1}$$

where E_t denotes expectations formed at time t of the distribution at time $t+j-1$ of the one-period bill, and the $L(k,t)$ are term premia. The simple expectations hypothesis is based on this "no-arbitrage" equilibrium condition (1), together with the assumption that the premia $L(k,t)$ do not vary over time. Other (more complicated) versions of the expectations hypothesis allow the premia to vary.

Expectations are usually assumed to be based on information available to agents at time t, and denoting the information set by I_t then the rational expectations hypothesis adds to Eq. (1), the assumption that $R(1,t+j) = E_t[R(1,t+j) \mid I_t] + \zeta_{t+j}$, where ζ_{t+j} is a forecast error such that $E_t(\zeta_{t+j} \mid I_t) = 0$. Linear forecasting rules are implicit in this statement of REH, and it is also assumed that agents can perfectly anticipate future changes in the density of $R(1,.)$. Agents' rational expectations of $R(1,t+j)$, that is, $E_t[R(1,t+j) \mid I_t]$, will depend on I_t, but the assumption that $E_t(\zeta_{t+j} \mid I_t) = 0$ ensures that these conditional expectations will be unbiased, regardless of what information might actually be contained in I_t.

If the term premia are assumed to be constant, standard versions of the REH for the term structure then assert that

$$R(k,t) = \frac{1}{k}\left[\sum_{j=1}^{j=k} [R(1, t+j-1)]\right] + L(k) + \upsilon_t, \tag{2}$$

where the error term

$$\upsilon_t = -\frac{1}{k}\sum_{j=1}^{j=k} \zeta_{t+j-1}$$

is orthogonal to the information set I_t, and $E_t[\upsilon_t | I_t] = 0$. It is then straightforward to rearrange this no-arbitrage equilibrium condition to obtain

$$S(k,1,t) = R(k,t) - R(1,t) = \frac{1}{k}\left(\sum_{r=1}^{k-1}\sum_{s=1}^{r} \Delta R(1, t+s)\right) + L(k) + \upsilon_t. \tag{3}$$

Equation (3) shows that when agents have rational expectations, these expectations about future yield movements and premia determine yield spreads. Since premia are assumed to be constant, any movement in the yield spread reflects changing expectations. Since the conditional expectations $E_t[R(1, t + s) \mid I_t]$ are assumed to be unbiased, it follows that the spread contains all the information that is relevant for forecasting changes in yields. Moreover, since $E_t[\upsilon_t \mid I_t] = 0$, it follows that all of the information in I_t has been incorporated into the spread.

For the special case when $k = 2$, lagging and rearranging (3) leads to

$$\tfrac{1}{2}[\Delta R(1, t)] = S(2, 1, t - 1) - L(2) + \upsilon_t, \tag{4}$$

and researchers frequently run regressions based on this, expecting a coefficient of one on the spread variable $S(2, 1, t - 1)$.[7] In this regression, a test of the null hypothesis that the spread coefficient is one is often interpreted as a test of REH. One might, however, question this interpretation for two reasons. The first is that although a rejection of the null provides evidence that something in the above derivations of Eq. (1), (2), or (3) might be wrong, it is not necessarily the case that REH is the culprit. Secondly, if one fails to reject the null, there is the problem that not all aspects of REH have been tested. Note that the implication of REH, that is, that the spread incorporates all of the information contained in I_t, has been imposed on (3) and (4), rather than tested. Specifically, tests that only examine the spread coefficient in (4) do not test the assumption that $E_t[\upsilon_t \mid I_t] = 0$ in (4).

An alternative approach to studying REH would be to include the variables in the information set I_t in the test regression, consider a test of the joint hypothesis that the spread coefficient is one and that the information coefficients are zero, and interpret this as a test of REH. In this joint testing setup, a failure to reject REH would then provide more information than a failure to reject REH in Eq. (4) (because a failure to reject in that equation does not tell us whether or not the information variables are orthogonal to υ_t). The joint test requires, of course, an explicit specification of the contents of I_t, and the test conclusion might change with the researcher's assumptions about what is contained in I_t.

The information set I_t presumably includes variables that are relevant for forecasting yields, and these might, in some cases, include current and lagged values of $R(k, t)$ (for $k = 1, 2, \ldots$), monetary policy variables, debt policy variables, and returns on alternative assets such as bonds, stocks, and foreign exchange. Some researchers discuss the contents of I_t,[8] pointing out that agents will know $S(k, 1, t-1) = R(k, t-1) - R(1, t-1)$. However, most studies based on (4) are not explicit about the agents' information because the assumptions already imposed on (4) imply that one can conduct the test on the spread without taking a stand on this matter.

Many rearrangements of (2) are possible, and for $k \geq 3$ the equation can be written as

$$\frac{1}{k}[\Delta R(1,t)] = S(k,1,t-1) + \frac{1}{k}\sum_{i=1}^{k-2}(k-1-i)\Delta R(1,t-i) - \sum_{i=1}^{k-2}\Delta R(k,t-i) - L(k) + \upsilon_t, \tag{5}$$

which shows that under REH, the spread $S(k, 1, t-1)$ is useful for predicting movements in $R(1, t)$. When $k \geq 3$, lags of $\Delta R(1, t)$ and $\Delta R(k, t)$ also have additional predictive content for $\Delta R(1, t)$.

Once one explicitly treats Treasury bill yields as integrated (unit root) processes,[9] the regressions (4) and (5) of $\Delta R(1, t)$ on a constant and the lagged spread (and the lags of the differenced yields) can be classified as error-correction models. Given the interpretation of Eq. (3) as an equilibrium condition and the additional interpretation of the mean spread as a measure of long-run equilibrium, the lagged spread then provides a measure of deviation of yields from the long-run equilibrium. One interpretation of these error-correction models is that yields move together over the long run and the coefficient on the lagged spread measures agents' short-run response to deviations from this long-run equilibrium. Error-correction models are often called "equilibrium-correction" models to reflect this interpretation. An alternative interpretation of the error-correction mechanism, owing to Campbell and Shiller (1988), is that the spread incorporates agents' rational expectations of future yield changes and that its predictive ability simply reflects these forecasts.

The error-correction Eqs. (4) and (5) impose the restriction that $R(1, t)$ and $R(k, t)$ are cointegrated with the cointegration vector of $(-1, 1)$,[10] and if the spread (error-correction term) is statistically significant in these regressions, then, via the Granger representation theorem, this implies that the restriction is valid. Thus, when researchers find that the spread has predictive power, they are implicitly confirming that the yields $R(1, t)$ and $R(k, t)$ are cointegrated with a cointegrating vector of $(-1, 1)$.

Viewed from a time-series perspective, the finding that $(-1, 1)$ is a cointegrating vector is consistent with REH, but does not confirm it. There are at least three reasons for this. First this type of cointegration between two yields implies that the spread is stochastically stationary, but this does not mean that risk premia are time invariant, as is usually assumed by REH. Second, cointegration with a vector $(-1, 1)$ does not imply a unit spread coefficient, or even that the spread can forecast $\Delta R(1, t)$,[11] but REH predicts these two properties. Third, cointegration with a vector $(-1, 1)$ is consistent with many different lag structures of $\Delta R(1, t)$ and $\Delta R(k, t)$ as explanatory variables in the error-correction regression, but REH imposes strong coefficient restrictions on these lags. Thus although cointegration is implied by REH, the sort of cointegration implied by REH can arise even if REH is not true.

21.1.2 Allowing for Departures from the Rational Expectations Hypothesis

Consider a very general reduced form statistical model of the Treasury bill market defined by

$$X_t = \mu + A(L)X_t + \varepsilon_t, \tag{6}$$

in which the data vector X_t includes observations on $R(1,t)$ and $R(k,t)$, as well as observations on other variables that might influence yields or expectations about yields (such as monetary or fiscal policy variables). $A(L)$ is a polynomial (of order $p \geq k-2$) in the lag operator L.[12] The variables in X_t need not be the same as those in the information set I_t discussed in Section 21.1.1, and in particular X_t might not contain all of the variables in I_t, possibly because the econometrician has limited access to the information available to market participants. The set X_t and the lag length in $A(L)$ are ideally chosen so that the residual term ε_t is a normally distributed homoskedastic innovation process with respect to X_t[13]; in practice this means that when Eq. (6) is estimated, the contents of X_t and the lag length of $A(L)$ should be sufficient to ensure that its empirical residuals show no evidence of model misspecification.

The vector autoregression (6) does not impose any restrictions implied by REH, but it nests a specification that allows for REH. To see this, first consider the reparameterization of (6) to obtain

$$\Delta X_t = \mu + \gamma\beta' X_{t-1} + B(L)\Delta X_t + \varepsilon_t \tag{7}$$

[in which the number of lags in $B(L)$ is one less than the corresponding number in $A(L)$], and then partition ΔX_t into $(\Delta X_{1t}, \Delta X_{2t})'$ to obtain

$$\begin{aligned} \Delta X_{1t} &= \mu_1 + \gamma_1\beta' X_{t-1} + B_1(L)\Delta X_t + \varepsilon_{1t} \\ \Delta X_{2t} &= \mu_2 + \gamma_2\beta' X_{t-1} + B_2(L)\Delta X_t + \varepsilon_{2t} \end{aligned} \tag{8}$$

in which ΔX_{1t} contains $\Delta R(1,t)$ and ΔX_{2t} contains $\Delta R(k,t)$ and the other variables that might affect ΔX_{1t}. The matrices μ, γ, and coefficients in the matrix polynomial $B(L)$ are partitioned accordingly. The coefficients in γ and β' are not uniquely identified, although the coefficients of their product $\pi = \gamma\beta'$ are identified. The matrix β' defines a basis for linear combinations of X_{t-1} that influence the variables in ΔX_t, while the γ matrices measure the strength of these influences. Like Eqs. (4) and/or (5), Eq. (8) is a vector error-correction model. In the case when the variables in X_t are integrated, the matrix β defines a basis for the cointegration space and the variables in $\beta' X_{t-1}$ define the error-correction terms.[14]

Now consider the following set of restrictions on the framework described by Eq. (8). First restrict β so that β' contains a row that is given $\beta'_{r1} = (-1, 1, 0, \ldots, 0)$ (assume, without loss of generality, that this is the first row), and then impose the further restriction that $\gamma_1 = (k, 0, \ldots, 0)$. These restrictions imply that the lagged yield spread predicts future changes in yields with the coefficient implied by REH and that any other error-correction terms in the system do not influence movements in $\Delta R(1,t)$. Now impose restrictions on the row vector B_1 so that the coefficients on $\Delta R(1, t-i)$ are $(k-1-i)$ for $1 \leq i \leq k-2$; all of the coefficients on $\Delta R(k, t-i)$ are k, for $1 \leq i \leq k-2$; and all other coefficients in this row are zero. These latter restrictions in addition to the spread restrictions imply that future changes in yields are predicted according to (5), which describes yield movements under the REH assumption.

It is now of interest to test all of the above restrictions on Eq. (8). If these restrictions are not rejected, then one can conclude that REH provides an empirically adequate explanation of yield movements with respect to the variables in X_t, but if some of these restrictions are rejected, then it seems appropriate to revise REH in the light of this evidence and to look for other theories that might better explain the data. The test is a system test, rather than a single-equation test, so as to properly account for the cointegration structure. One can compare the log-likelihoods of the system with and without the restrictions to jointly test all of the implications of REH for the data set X_t.[15]

There are several advantages associated with using (8) rather than simple regressions such as

$$\frac{1}{k}\Delta R(1,t) = a + bS(k,1,t-1) + u_t \tag{9}$$

to study REH. The main advantage is that inference based on (8) is empirically justified because (8) is simply a reparameterization of (6) that is constructed in a way that explicitly ensures that the model and the data are consistent. In contrast, the use of (9) involves the imposition of several exclusion and cointegration restrictions, together with assumptions on the distribution of u_t. Since these data restrictions on (9) are not necessarily valid, it follows that inference on $\widehat{b}$ is not necessarily based on a statistically adequate model. Such inference is therefore unreliable. A further advantage of using (8), as opposed to (9), is that framework (8) allows one to test all of the implications of REH (jointly or separately). This is particularly important because specific variables in the information set might help to predict movements in $\Delta R(1,t)$ in (8) and thereby explain an empirical rejection of REH. On the other hand, regression (9) only allows one to test that the spread correctly anticipates movements in $\Delta R(1,t)$.

Vector autoregressive (VAR) frameworks have been used to study REH before, but there are some important differences between this previous work and the setup proposed here. Here, the test of REH explicitly examines the cointegration structure within a broad information set and allows for cointegrating structures other than just $(-1, 1)(R(1,t), R(k,t))'$. Other studies, such as those based on a vector autoregression of $S(k,1,t)$ and $\Delta R(1,t)$, do not allow for any cointegrating relationship other than $(-1, 1)(R(1,t), R(k,t))'$, even if variables other than $R(1,t)$ and $R(k,t)$ are explicitly assumed to be in agent's information sets.

The VAR approach suggested here also examines the validity of the REH decomposition given by

$$R(1, t+j) = E_t\,[R(1, t+j) \mid I_t] + \zeta_{t+j}$$

with $E_t(\zeta_{t+j} \mid I_t) = 0$ in a very direct way, that is, by seeing whether variables other than the lagged spread can predict movements in $\Delta R(1, t)$. In this context, once the researcher has assumed that a particular variable is in agents' information sets, a rejection of the associated orthogonality restriction provides evidence as to why REH has failed. In contrast, other VAR-based methods emphasize the (nonlinear) cross-equation restrictions that REH imposes on companion VAR(1) forms of the model. Since these latter tests do not depend on whether or not agents have information beyond current and lagged $R(1, t)$ and $R(k, t)$, rejections of orthogonality restrictions in this context do not directly suggest which information has not been incorporated into agents' expectations.

There are several different ways of expressing REH that are similar but not logically equivalent to the version presented in this chapter.[16] Alternative formulations of REH, based on present value versions of (1) or on conditions that excess returns be zero lead to single-equation REH regressions of the form

$$\theta[\Delta R(1, t)] = S(k, 1, t-1) - L(k) + \eta_t \tag{10}$$

where η_t, like υ_t in (5), will be orthogonal to the information set, and $E_t[\eta_t \mid I_t] = 0$.[17] One could test the restrictions implied by (10) in the context of (8), instead of testing those implied by (5). However, it is not appropriate to simultaneously test both sets of restrictions in (8) because the two sets of restrictions are derived from different versions of the model. Each set of restrictions is examined separately below.

21.2 EMPIRICAL ANALYSIS

The Treasury bill data used for this study was nominal yield to maturity data derived from the Fama files in the CRSP data set. The yield series used are those relating to bills that have 1 and 2 months to maturity, and these yield series are denoted by $R(1, t)$ and $R(2, t)$, respectively. The primary question to be addressed was whether the spread between these bills could predict future movements in each bill yield, but since a more comprehensive test of REH required an examination of whether other variables could also predict bill movements, a few other potentially relevant variables were also included in the analysis. These other variables included an overnight Federal Funds rate ($FF(t)$), a measure of Government debt ($\ln D(t)$), and the yield on a 5-year Treasury bond ($B(t)$). Together, these five variables make up the observed variables X_t that were used to form the statistical model described by (6)–(8). The analysis is based on monthly observations; data sources and additional information are provided in Appendix 1, and plots are provided in Figs. 21.1 and 21.2.

The tests are based on several assumptions, which are needed to account for the fact that inferences based on observed data do not necessarily translate into inferences about theory. Here, it is assumed that the observed variables $R(1,t)$ and $R(2,t)$ are accurate observations on the theoretical variables $R(k,t)$, that all the observed variables in X_t are also in the theoretical information set I_t, and that X_t contains all variables in I_t that are relevant for forecasting $R(1,t)$ and $R(2,t)$. Given these assumptions on X_t, the statistical findings presented below can then be used to draw inference about the empirical adequacy of REH with respect to the data set X_t.[18]

The variables for X_t were chosen carefully, so that X_t might parsimoniously represent those variables in I_t most relevant for forecasting yields. The Federal Funds rate was used as an indicator of monetary policy, and the use of this variable also allowed for the possibility that substitute instruments at the very short end of the term structure might affect Treasury bill yields. The yield on a 5-year Treasury bond was used to determine how substitute longer-term instruments might affect yield movements, while the Government debt variable

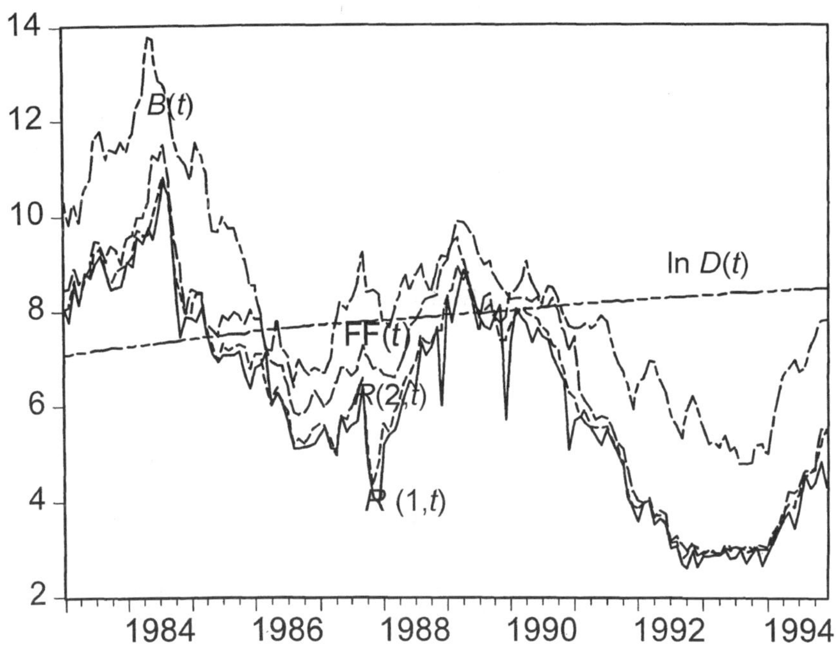

Fig. 21.1 Levels data.

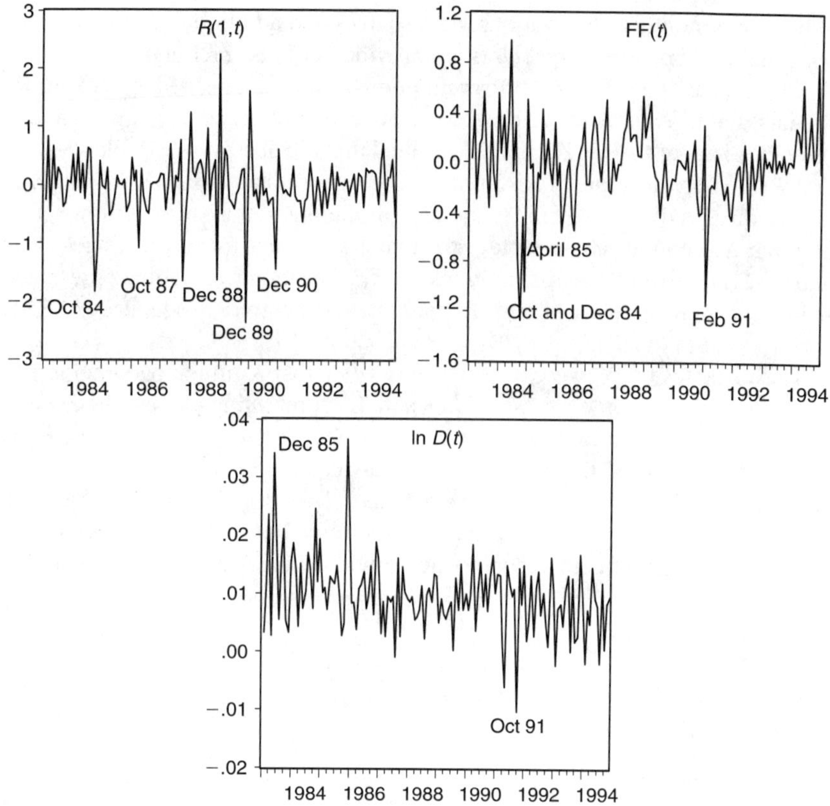

Fig. 21.2 Differenced data (selected series).

was included in X_t as a fiscal policy indicator, which would also reflect factors that potentially influence the supply of Treasury bills.

21.2.1 Standard Tests of REH

It is useful to first study some examples of the regressions that are often run to test REH. Three examples based on the $R(1, t)$ and $R(2, t)$ data are reported in Table 21.1. The top portion of the table shows the regression results that are typically reported, and they are quite similar to those reported elsewhere. The spread coefficient in regression 1 is statistically greater than zero, which is consistent with a hypothesis that the spread incorporates various aspects of agents' forecasts. However, the hypothesis that the spread coefficient is unity is strongly rejected, which suggests that REH does not fully explain yield movements. In regression 2, the spread has limited explanatory ability,

TABLE 21.1
REH Regression Results

Statistic	Regression 1	Regression 2	Regression 3
$\hat{\alpha}$	−0.157	−0.070	−0.315
s.e. $\hat{\alpha}$	0.023	0.039	0.047
Het consistent s.e. $\hat{\alpha}$	0.029	0.040	0.057
$\hat{\beta}$	0.646	0.201	0.292
s.e. $\hat{\beta}$	0.064	0.109	0.129
Het consistent s.e. $\hat{\beta}$	0.079	0.121	0.176
Observed t-stat for test of $H_0 : \beta = 0$	7.342	1.655	1.658
Observed t-stat for test of $H_0 : \beta = 1$	−4.025	See notes	−4.025
R^2	0.439	0.026	0.038
Durbin-Watson	1.583	1.565	1.583
p-Values for selected diagnostic tests			
H_0: No first-order serial correlation	0.001	0.012	0.001
H_0: No first-order ARCH	0.010	0.158	0.010
H_0: Coeff on three lags of $\Delta R(1, t) = 0$	0.200	0.218	0.200
H_0: Coeff on three lags of $\Delta R(2, t) = 0$	0.031	0.093	0.031
H_0: Coeff on $\Delta \ln D(t-3) = 0$	0.049	0.038	0.049
H_0: Coeff on three lags of $\Delta FF(t) = 0$	0.010	0.003	0.010
H_0: Coeff on three lags of $\Delta B(t) = 0$	0.215	0.006	0.215
H_0: Coeff on $\text{Vol}(t) = 0$	0.000	0.000	0.000
Forecast Chow for parameter stability (1995:1–1995:6)	0.996	0.999	0.996
Shapiro-Wilk normality test	0.000	0.001	0.000
McLeod-Li test (six lags)	0.113	0.398	0.113

Notes: Regression 1 is based on Eq. (4), and is given by

$$\tfrac{1}{2}[R(1,t) - R(1,t-1)] = \alpha + \beta[R(2,t-1) - R(1,t-1)] + \varepsilon_{1t}.$$

This regression predicts movements in the yield for the bill of shorter maturity.

Regression 2 is based on Eq. (10), and is given by

$$[R(2,t) - R(2,t-1)] = \alpha + \beta[R(2,t-1) - R(1,t-1)] + \varepsilon_{2t}.$$

This regression predicts movements in the yield for the bill of longer maturity. If this regression is justified by a present value model and the agent's discount factor is assumed to be 0.995, then REH requires that $\beta = 0.005$, and the associated test H_0: $\beta = 1$ of gives rise to a test statistic of 1.62.

Regression 3 is based on Eq. (10) (see note 17), and is given by

$$[R(1,t) - R(2,t-1)] = \alpha + \beta[R(2,t-1) - R(1,t-1)] + \varepsilon_{3t}.$$

This regression predicts movements in returns, and a zero excess returns interpretation of REH requires that $\beta = 1$. Note that regression 3 is just a reparameterized version of regression 1.

Descriptions of the variables are provided in Appendix 1.

and although the data fail to reject the hypothesis that the spread coefficient accords with REH, the coefficient implied by REH is so close to zero that this second result is not at all surprising. The third regression, which is really just a reparameterization of the first, finds no evidence that the spread can predict yield returns, and it rejects the REH implication that the spread coefficient should be unity.

The lower section of Table 21.1 contains statistics that are not usually reported. They provide evidence that the REH test regressions are severely misspecified, and they show that even if one corrects for serial correlation and heteroskedasticity (as is sometimes done), inference based on the estimated coefficients of these regressions is nevertheless problematic. The omitted variables tests point to a potential bias in the coefficient estimates, since they indicate that both monetary and fiscal policy are important explanators of Treasury bill yields, and a volatility variable also seems important, consistent with the ARCH-M literature, which asserts that time-varying risk premia contribute to yield movements. Yields on longer-term instruments also have statistically significant explanatory power.[19]

Without the information in the lower panel, one might simply conclude that the spread has a limited ability to explain yield movements. However, the diagnostics in the lower panel qualify this conclusion. They provide a warning to be wary of making inference on the estimated $\hat{b}$, and they suggest that a better estimate of the information in spreads might be obtained if one were to develop a more comprehensive model of yield movements, which jointly incorporate the effects of risk, debt policies, monetary policies, and substitute instruments.

21.2.2 An Empirical Model of Treasury Bill Yield Movements

This section develops a small model of Treasury bill yield movements along the lines of Eq. (8) in Section 21.1. The choice of variables in X_t explicitly allows long-term yields and monetary and fiscal variables to directly influence yield movements, and the model itself is deliberately consistent with the data so as to allow valid testing of various aspects of REH and other economic theory.

Preliminary analysis described in Appendix 2 leads to an initial error-correction model of the form

$$\begin{aligned} \Delta Y_{1t} &= \mu_1 + \lambda_1 Du_t + \gamma_1 \beta Y_{1t-1} + A_1(L)\Delta Y_t + \varepsilon_{1t} \\ \Delta Y_{2t} &= \mu_2 + \lambda_2 Du_t + \gamma_2 \beta Y_{1t-1} + A_2(L)\Delta Y_t + \varepsilon_{2t} \end{aligned} \tag{11}$$

in which ΔY_{1t} contains the term structure variables (i.e., the bill yields, the Federal Funds rate and the 5-year bond rate), ΔY_{2t} contains the debt variable, and ΔY_t includes both ΔY_{1t} and ΔY_{2t}. The variable Du_t consists of several dummy variables that simultaneously account for a few outlying data points and ensure that the residuals ε_t are well behaved. Details relating to these dummies, and some associated discussion on the interpretation and modeling of outliers

TABLE 21.2
Potentially Cointegrating Regressions (1983:1–1994:12)

$R(2,t) = 0.393 + 0.996\ R(1,t)$ (4.04) (65.65)	$R^2 = 0.97$	$ADF_c = -5.72$	$DW = 1.61$	(1)
$FF(t) = 0.369 + 1.058\ R(1,t)$ (2.51) (46.03)	$R^2 = 0.94$	$ADF_c = -3.82$	$DW = 0.96$	(2)
$B(t) = 2.950 + 0.870\ R(1,t)$ (12.67) (24.06)	$R^2 = 0.80$	$ADF_c = -2.45$	$DW = 0.36$	(3)

Notes: The numbers in brackets are t-statistics, ADF_c are augmented Dickey-Fuller test statistics based on test regressions that contain a constant and two lags of the dependent variables.

are given in Appendix 2. Summary statistics for this general unrestricted model are provided in Tables 21.2 and 21.3. The lower portion of Table 21.3 contains the results of a wide variety of specification tests, which collectively show that this general model provides a statistically adequate characterization of the data. Thus, further inference on this model seems empirically justified.

An important feature of this initial model is that it provides strong evidence that changes in debt Granger cause changes in the term structure variables, and that the converse is also true. This suggests that an empirically valid theory of Treasury bill yield movements should incorporate the interaction between the bill market and the issue of Government debt. However, in this particular case, the residuals of the partial systems for the term structure and debt are uncorrelated, so that efficient estimation can be undertaken by estimating each system separately. The observation that the error-correction terms are not statistically significant in the debt equation is useful because it suggests that debt is "weakly exogenous" in the term structure system and vice-versa. As discussed in Johansen (1992) and Hendry (1995a) this implies that one can validly estimate and make inference about the cointegration parameters in the term structure system without explicitly worrying about the joint probability distribution of each of ΔY_{1t} and ΔY_{2t}. Instead, the cointegration analysis is based on a (partial) model of ΔY_{1t} conditional on ΔY_{2t}, and this does not depend on the marginal model for ΔY_{2t}. See Harbo et al. (1998) for further discussion on the cointegration analysis of partial systems.

The cointegration in Eq. (11) was initially approximated using the first step of an Engle-Granger (1987) two-step procedure, but once appropriate lag lengths for the various explanatory variables had been established, it was then appropriate to analyze the cointegration structure in more detail. Questions of particular interest included whether each of the three error-correction terms were cointegrating, and if so, whether or not the data would fail to reject the restriction that these error-correction terms were the spreads defined by $R(2,t) - R(1,t)$, $FF(t) - R(1,t)$, and $B(t) - R(1,t)$.

TABLE 21.3
Statistics Relating to the General Baseline Model (1984:2–1994:12)

Independent variable	Dependent variable $\Delta R(1,t)$	$\Delta R(2,t)$	$\Delta FF(t)$	$\Delta B(t)$	$\Delta \ln D(t)$
p-Values for groups of explanatory variables					
Three error correction terms	0.0000	0.0000	0.0273	0.3368	0.7302
Four lags of $\Delta R(1,t)$	0.9833	0.1445	0.1760	0.6825	0.0175
Four lags of $\Delta R(2,t)$	0.7709	0.6412	0.0849	0.5204	0.0016
Four lags of $\Delta FF(t)$	0.1285	0.0296	0.6900	0.1266	0.6988
Five lags of $\Delta B(t)$	0.2487	0.0614	0.0021	0.3102	0.0393
$\Delta \ln D(t)$ lagged 3, 6, and 12 months	0.0025	0.0285	0.1766	0.0212	0.0025
Regression R^2	0.8163	0.6969	0.6129	0.2986	0.5244
p-Values for selected diagnostic tests					
H_0: No first-order serial correlation	0.07	0.07	0.11	0.53	0.07
H_0: No third-order serial correlation	0.26	0.29	0.23	0.90	0.16
H_0: No first-order ARCH	0.12	0.73	0.38	0.68	0.56
H_0: No third-order ARCH	0.18	0.59	0.10	0.26	0.12
H_0: Coeff on Vol$(t) = 0$	0.15	0.05	0.49	0.65	0.35
Shapiro-Wilk normality test	0.17	0.09	0.65	0.58	0.32
McLeod-Li test (six lags)	0.43	0.28	0.05	0.41	0.25
Reset test	0.09	0.04	0.08	0.17	0.85
Forecast Chow for parameter stability (1995:1–1995:6)	0.93	0.79	0.48	0.73	0.32

Notes: The error correction terms are lagged residuals from the three potentially cointegrating equations reported in Table 21.2.

All regressions also contain a constant and the dummies reported in Appendix 2.

The *p*-value for a likelihood ratio test that residuals from the term structure equations are uncorrelated with the debt equation is 0.0915. Using Ω to denote the variance/covariance matrix of residuals, the values of $\ln|\Omega|$ for the five variable system, the four variable system, and the debt equation are -23.6394, -12.5836, and -10.9750, respectively.

The *p*-value for a likelihood ratio test that the term structure variables do not Granger cause the debt variable is 0.0214. The *p*-value for a likelihood ratio test that debt does not Granger cause the term structure variable is 0.0138.

Technical details associated with the cointegration analysis are given in Appendix 2, and the statistical results are given in Tables 21.4 and 21.5. Key findings here are that a cointegration rank of three is appropriate, and given this, the data fail to reject the restriction that the three error-correction terms are the spreads defined by $R(2,t) - R(1,t)$, $FF(t) - R(1,t)$, and $B(t) - R(1,t)$. One

TABLE 21.4
Cointegration Analysis of the Term Structure Variables (1984:2–1994:12)

Assumption	ln $\|\Omega\|$	Schwartz criteria	Estimated error correction terms (normalized)
β has rank 3	−12.6038	−11.7479	$-1.001\ R(1,t) + R(2,t)$
			(0.010)
			$-1.103\ R(1,t) + FF(t)$
			(0.043)
			$-0.905\ R(1,t) + B(t)$
			(0.107)
β has rank 2	−12.5016	−11.7201	$-0.992\ R(1,t) - 0.001\ B(t) + R(2,t)$
			(0.029) (0.030)
			$-1.465\ R(1,t) + 0.401\ B(t) + FF(t)$
			(0.105) (0.109)
β has rank 1	−12.3468	−11.6368	$-1.557\ R(1,t) + 0.145\ B(t) + 0.386\ FF(t) + R(2,t)$
			(0.321) (0.081) (0.238)
β has rank 0	−11.9324	−11.2998	

Notes: The analysis was conditioned on all explanatory variables included in the baseline model (excepting the error correction terms). Ω is the variance/covariance matrix of the residuals, and the numbers in brackets are standard errors.

implication of these results is that the spreads contain information that is useful for predicting movements in the term structure, and this is consistent with REH. However, as noted in Section 21.1, the cointegration results by themselves do not verify REH because they do not test any other assumptions or predictions associated with REH.

REH and other theories associated with term structure movements can be studied in a valid fashion by examining the error-correction model that embeds

TABLE 21.5
Tests of Cointegration Restrictions (Conditional on a Cointegration Rank of 3)

Hypothesized cointegration	ln $\|\Omega\|$ (with imposed restriction)	p-Value of likelihood ratio test
(1) $R(2,t) - R(1,t)$	−12.6037	0.950
(2) $FF(t) - R(1,t)$	−12.5748	0.090
(3) $B(t) - R(1,t)$	−12.5986	0.476
All of the Above	−12.5657	0.287

Note: Ω is the variance/covariance matrix of the residuals.

the estimated cointegration structure, but given the large number of parameters in this model, such an analysis is likely to be inefficient. First the restriction that the three error-correction terms be cointegrating vectors was imposed, and then exclusion restrictions consistent with the data were imposed as well so as to develop a parsimonious model of Treasury bill movements. Table 21.6 and Table 21.7 present summary statistics relating to the resulting model. Extensive diagnostic testing on this model finds no specification problems, so that it encompasses the VAR in Eq. (8) and provides a statistically adequate framework for subsequent inference. [See Hendry and Mizon (1993) for discussion on the concept of encompassing.] Forecasts associated with the Table 21.6 regressions are compared in Figs. 21.3 and 21.4 with forecasts that impose the REH restriction. Here, although it appears that the restriction causes forecasts to deteriorate, the forecasts based on the more general information set (from Table 21.6) are not statistically different from those that use just the spread (from Table 21.1). The following section discusses the respects in which inference based on the vector error-correction model is, and is not, consistent with various aspects of REH. Other theory, consistent with this model, is also discussed.

21.3 WHICH THEORIES ARE RELEVANT FOR PREDICTING TREASURY BILL YIELDS?

A cursory glance at the first two equations in Table 21.6 immediately indicates that REH does not explain bill yield movements very well. While the bill spread *does* have predictive power for movements in $R(1, t)$ as REH predicts, the (appropriately normalized) estimated coefficient is only half of the value of 2 predicted by REH. The null hypothesis that this coefficient is 2 is soundly rejected. The contribution of the bill spread toward the R^2 of .8007 is only .0883/.8007, and while this is statistically significant, it constitutes a mere 11 percent of the explained movements in $R(1, t)$. The fact that the second column of Table 21.6 has no entry for $R(2, t-1) - R(1, t-1)$ shows that this variable does not make a significant contribution to the equation for $\Delta R(2, t)$.[20]

Table 21.6 provides very strong evidence against the rational expectations premise embodied in Eqs. (2), (4), and (8). In contrast to the REH prediction that the spread should incorporate all information about future yield movements, we see that the spread has failed to incorporate past information on the Federal Funds, Government debt, and yields on medium-term Government debt instruments. A formal likelihood ratio test of REH, within the context of the $\Delta R(1, t)$ equation in the Table 21.6 model, rejects the null hypothesis with a p-value of 8×10^{-14}. Turning to the $\Delta R(2, t)$ equation, we see that changes in Government debt, the Federal Funds rate, and yields on other Treasury instruments all make significant contributions toward the explanation of yield

TABLE 21.6
Statistics Relating to a Parsimonious Model of the Term Structure Variables (1984:2–1994:12)

Explanatory variable	Endogenous variable $\Delta R(1,t)$		$\Delta R(2,t)$		$\Delta FF(t)$		$\Delta B(t)$	
	Estimated coefficients and standard errors							
$R(2,t-1)-R(1,t-1)$	0.953	(0.103)	—	—	0.203	(0.121)	−0.261	(0.121)
$FF(t-1)-R(1,t-1)$	0.103	(0.050)	0.198	(0.034)	—	—	—	—
$B(t-1)-R(1,t-1)$	0.048	(0.025)	0.102	(0.019)	0.056	(0.021)	—	—
$\Delta R(1,t-1)$	—	—	0.118	(0.052)	0.238	(0.095)	−0.152	(0.069)
$\Delta R(1,t-2)$	—	—	0.060	(0.039)	0.085	(0.059)	—	—
$\Delta R(1,t-3)$	—	—	−0.010	(0.035)	—	—	—	—
$\Delta R(1,t-4)$	—	—	0.086	(0.030)	—	—	—	—
$\Delta R(2,t-1)$	—	—	−0.171	(0.075)	−0.231	(0.121)	—	—
$\Delta R(2,t-2)$	—	—	—	—	−0.117	(0.092)	—	—
$\Delta R(2,t-3)$	—	—	—	—	−0.131	(0.060)	—	—
$\Delta R(2,t-4)$	—	—	—	—	—	—	—	—
$\Delta FF(t-1)$	0.194	(0.081)	0.220	(0.071)	—	—	0.288	(0.110)
$\Delta FF(t-2)$	0.213	(0.078)	0.097	(0.066)	—	—	−0.042	(0.101)
$\Delta FF(t-3)$	−0.023	(0.077)	−0.052	(0.064)	—	—	−0.047	(0.099)
$\Delta FF(t-4)$	−0.130	(0.078)	−0.149	(0.065)	—	—	−0.144	(0.096)
$\Delta B(t-1)$	0.089	(0.064)	0.180	(0.056)	0.268	(0.057)	0.195	(0.087)
$\Delta B(t-2)$	0.027	(0.055)	—	—	0.102	(0.053)	—	—
$\Delta B(t-3)$	−0.098	(0.054)	—	—	0.034	(0.053)	—	—

TABLE 21.6
(Continued)

	Endogenous variable			
Explanatory variable	$\Delta R(1,t)$	$\Delta R(2,t)$	$\Delta FF(t)$	$\Delta B(t)$
	Estimated coefficients and standard errors			
$\Delta B(t-4)$	— —	— —	−0.067 (0.044)	— —
$\Delta B(t-5)$	— —	— —	0.122 (0.047)	— —
$\Delta \ln D(t-3)$	−8.299 (3.666)	−8.804 (2.789)	−6.597 (3.032)	— —
$\Delta \ln D(t-6)$	−7.231 (3.606)	−4.748 (2.782)	— —	−11.051 (4.996)
$\Delta \ln D(t-12)$	−6.089 (3.024)	— —	— —	−12.955 (4.271)
Regression R^2	0.8007	0.6616	0.5651	0.2109
	p-Values for selected diagnostic tests			
H_0: No first-order ARCH	0.1468	0.5836	0.3783	0.4413
H_0: No third-order ARCH	0.4313	0.5259	0.2915	0.0625
Shapiro-Wilk normality test	0.2430	0.2985	0.2903	0.5027
McLeod-Li test (six lags)	0.7853	0.4605	0.2518	0.2830
Reset test	0.4261	0.7551	0.6241	0.1268
Forecast Chow for parameter stability (1995:1–1995:6)	0.9691	0.9255	0.6711	0.4407

Notes: All regressions also contain a constant and the dummies as described in Appendix 2.

Using Ω to denote the variance/covariance matrix of the residuals, $\ln|\Omega| = -12.1787$, and the *p*-value for a likelihood ratio test that this model is a valid restriction of the (four variable) GUM is 0.972.

The *p*-values for portmanteau tests for first-, second-, and third-order serial correlation in the system are 0.256, 0.185, and 0.096.

The *p*-value for including the volatility variable in each equation is 0.390.

TABLE 21.7
Statistics Relating to a Parsimonious Model of the Debt Equation (1984:2–1994:12)

Explanatory variable	Estimated coefficient and standard error	
$\Delta R(1, t-1)$	−0.0028	(0.0014)
$\Delta R(1, t-2)$	−0.0042	(0.0019)
$\Delta R(1, t-3)$	−0.0060	(0.0018)
$\Delta R(1, t-4)$	−0.0046	(0.0014)
$\Delta R(2, t-1)$	0.0008	(0.0022)
$\Delta R(2, t-2)$	0.0052	(0.0025)
$\Delta R(2, t-3)$	0.0034	(0.0026)
$\Delta R(2, t-4)$	0.0084	(0.0084)
$\Delta B(t-1)$	−0.0017	(0.0013)
$\Delta B(t-2)$	−0.0006	(0.0013)
$\Delta B(t-3)$	−0.0015	(0.0013)
$\Delta B(t-4)$	−0.0037	(0.0037)
$\Delta \ln D(t-6)$	0.1422	(0.0736)
$\Delta \ln D(t-12)$	0.2047	(0.0664)
Regression R^2	0.4844	

p-Values for selected diagnostic tests	
H_0: No first-order serial correlation	0.10
H_0: No third-order serial correlation	0.18
H_0: No first-order ARCH	0.81
H_0: No third-order ARCH	0.41
H_0: Coeff on $\text{Vol}(t) = 0$	0.52
Shapiro-Wilk normality test	0.47
McLeod-Li test (six lags)	0.57
Reset test	0.54
Forecast Chow for parameter stability (1995:1–1995:6)	0.38

Notes: The regression also contains a constant and dummies as described in Appendix 2.
Using Ω to denote the variance/covariance matrix of the residuals, $\ln|\Omega| = -10.8942$, and the *p*-value for a likelihood ratio test that this model is a valid restriction of the debt equation in the GUM is .890.

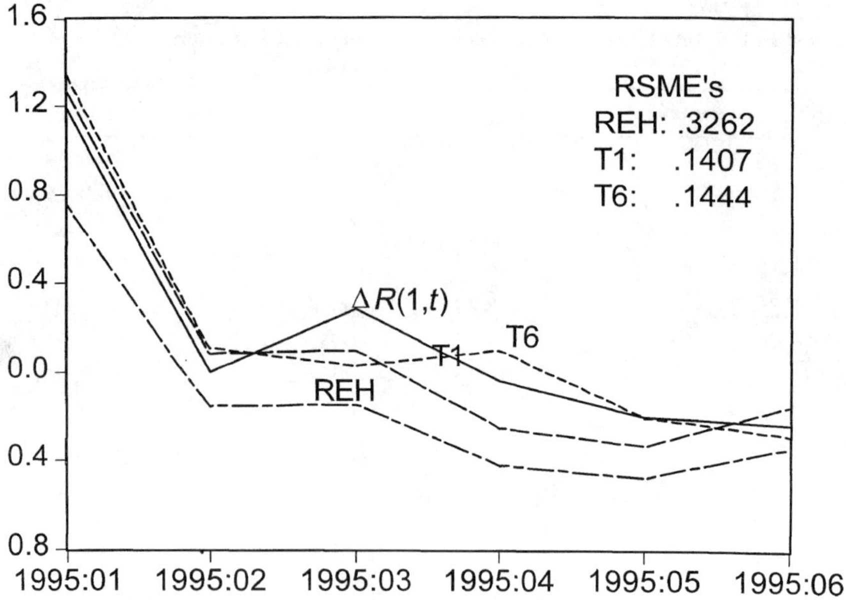

Fig. 21.3 Actual and forecast values of $\Delta R(1, t)$: T1 and T6 are forecasts derived from the models in Tables 21.1 and 21.6, respectively; REH are forecasts derived from a model in which REH has been imposed.

movements, again contradicting the hypothesis that the yield spread incorporates all information relevant for predicting yields.

While the regressions for $\Delta R(1, t)$ in Tables 21.1 and 21.6 lead to the same qualitative conclusion that REH should be rejected, it is important to note that the (normalized) $R(2, t-1) - R(1, t-1)$ coefficients in these equations are quite different. To choose which estimate might be preferred, it should be noted that since the Table 21.6 regression shows that regressors other than the spread are statistically significant, it follows that the estimates in Table 21.1 are likely to be affected by an omitted variables bias. The Table 21.6 regression is also more informative than the Table 21.1 regression because it provides us with directions on *why* REH has failed to explain the data well. This is then useful for determining theory that is likely to provide an improved explanation. Clearly an empirically valid theoretical explanation of these data cannot ignore the direct influence that the Federal Funds, Government debt, and yields on longer-term instruments have on bill movements. Nor can it ignore the evidence that yields respond to changes in these other variables with lags. An empirically relevant theory would incorporate these manifestations of informational inefficiencies rather than simply assume that all available information has been incorporated

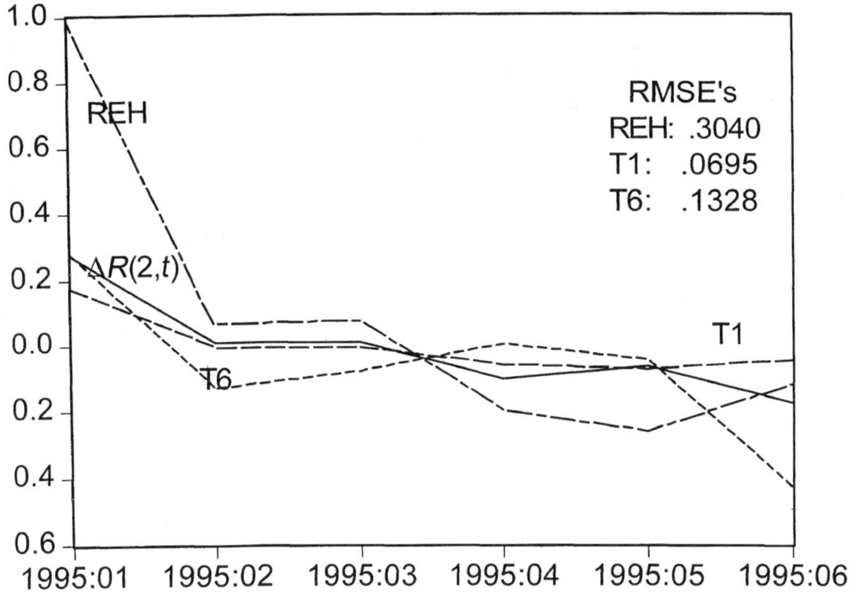

Fig. 21.4 Actual and forecast values of $\Delta R(2, t)$: T1 and T6 are forecasts derived from the models in Tables 21.1 and 21.6, respectively; REH are forecasts derived from a model in which REH has been imposed.

into expectations and hence into the yield spread. It is important to recognize that these "inefficiencies" do not necessarily imply arbitrage opportunities; a relevant theory would ideally differentiate between these two concepts and address the issue of whether or not the inefficiencies observed here do or do not translate into arbitrage opportunities.

There is clear feedback between Treasury bill yield movements, movements in the Federal Funds rate, and movements in the medium-term bond, and therefore an empirically relevant theoretical model would have to appropriately account for this joint endogeneity. Such a model would pay particular attention to the endogeneity of the Federal Funds rate because it appears to affect both long-run relationships within the term structure and short-run movements in individual term structure variables. An empirically relevant theoretical model of the data studied here would probably include a Federal Reserve Bank reaction function, even if movements in the Federal Funds rate were not the focus of the study.[21] The data further indicate that although debt does not appear to affect the long-run relationships *between* different instruments (in the sense that debt does not enter any cointegrating relationships, nor do the error-correction terms influence debt),[22] it does appear to have a strong influence on how the term structure itself moves over time. Thus an empirically relevant model would incorporate theory on how the issue of debt instruments affects equilibrium yield movements.

The presence of three spread terms in the $R(1, t)$ equation deserves comment. First, it suggests that the yield on the 1-month bill changes to prevent arbitrage against (at least) three alternative assets (i.e., 2-month bills, 5-year bonds, and Federal Funds). Thus, it seems that an empirically relevant model might have to abandon the simplification of a two-asset world and allow for at least a few representative assets of different kinds. Alternatively, one might view the presence of the second and third spreads as variables that measure a risk premium associated with holding or off-loading Federal Funds and longer-term instruments, as opposed to just changing holdings of Treasury bills.[23] Under this latter interpretation, REH would have to allow for a time-varying risk premium, rather than the constant premium that is usually assumed.[24]

The long-run relationship between the Federal Funds rate and the yield on the 1-month bill [as reflected by the unrestricted cointegrating combination of $FF(t) - 1.081R(1, t)$ discussed in Appendix 2, rather than in the combination of $FF(t) - R(1, t)$, which was actually imposed in this study] also deserves comment. While this contradicts the usual versions of the expectations hypothesis, since it assumes that the two variables $R(1, t)$ and $FF(t)$ are not separated by a constant premium, one can nevertheless justify a nonconstant premium by specifically considering why Federal Funds are bought and sold. Ho and Saunders (1985) provide a theoretical model that seems relevant in this context. In their model, they assume that the main motive for acquiring Federal Funds has to do with maintaining required reserves, and that the Federal Funds premium relative to other short-term Treasury bills reflects the risk that banks face as they adjust their reserve holdings. If banks do not want to violate reserve requirements, then over the long run, the Federal Funds rate will be proportionately higher than the riskless rate, where the proportion depends on the covariance between the Federal Funds rate and the Treasury bill rate. This is consistent with the estimated relationship of $FF(t) - 1.081R(1, t)$ found here.

21.4 EMPIRICALLY RELEVANT THEORY AND SCIENTIFIC EXPLANATIONS OF DATA

This chapter illustrates the integration of theory and data by examining the ability of REH to explain observed Treasury bill yield movements. The study is based on a multivariate error-correction model of bill yield and related variables, which has been built using data rather than theory to determine both the long-run (cointegrating) relationships among the variables and the short-run dynamics of relevant variables. The analysis shows that although REH can explain why the yield spread seems to contain information that is useful for predicting yields, it has many shortcomings. There are movements in yields that are better predicted by Government debt and the Federal Funds, suggesting that REH provides an incomplete theory of yield movements. Further, the data decisively reject most of the implications of REH, other than those associated with the spread's limited power to predict yield movements. One can conclude from this study that REH cannot explain the data set at hand and hence conclude that a better theory of yield movements is needed.

While this conclusion is not in itself new, the methodology that was used to derive it deserves comment. More often than not, empirical researchers simply translate the theory they are advocating (or trying to discredit) into a structured regression and focus on a single test statistic. As I noted earlier, this in itself is problematic because tests of economic hypotheses do not really provide definitive answers. There are, however, other important shortcomings in this approach. By failing to observe other aspects of the regression, such a procedure ignores information that might have bearing on the validity of the analysis, the theory under consideration, and other theories not explicitly considered. By failing to specify a statistically adequate model in which many possibly relevant theories can be considered on an equal footing, such a procedure also prevents the researcher from seeing which aspects of which theories are borne out by the data and which points associated with these various theories are questionable. The analysis presented here avoids these problems. By taking care to ensure that the specification is consistent with the data, the researcher can have more faith in the validity of his/her analysis. Further, by allowing a general specification in which REH is possible but not enforced, the researcher can see not only which aspects of REH agree or do not agree with the data but also which directions he/she could follow to develop a better theory.

This chapter does not provide a formal theory that explains the analyzed data set, nor does it explore how the empirical implications of the data might change with a different sample or different variables. Further, the empirical results and inferences depend on how well the chosen sample variables represent the true forces that govern Treasury bill movements. As Hausman (1990) cautions, although general analyses might incorporate more information than partial analyses, the former are still based on ceteris paribus assumptions, and may not approximate the truth well if they have omitted important factors.

Clearly, more work is needed to develop an empirically adequate *theoretical* explanation of what has been observed. However, most researchers would agree that scientific investigation assumes an open mind that will consider all the evidence at hand and all possible explanations of this evidence. Further, an empirically adequate explanation of data necessarily accounts for all aspects of those data. A general methodology such as that illustrated in this chapter discourages the researcher from focusing on theory that is not empirically relevant and encourages him/her to think about theories that can explain the data. This seems a sensible first step toward the development of "explanations" of empirical puzzles such as the REH theory-data confrontation discussed here, and ultimately this should be useful for developing theory that is helpful for understanding the phenomena we observe.

APPENDIX 1: THE DATA

The data set consisted of 150 monthly observations, dating from January 1983 through June 1995. Preliminary data analysis and modeling was based on the first 144 of these observations, with the remainder being retained for out-of-sample forecasting analysis. The variables used were:

$R(1, t)$: The (annualized) yield to maturity on Treasury bills with 1 month to maturity. The data (derived from measured prices at the end of each month) were obtained from CRSP. The data measured yields for 30.4 days and were converted to an annual percentage yield by multiplying by 1,200.

$R(2, t)$: The (annualized) yield to maturity on Treasury bills with 2 months to maturity. The data (derived from measured prices at the end of each month) were obtained from CRSP. The data measured yields for 30.4 days and were converted to an annual percentage yield by multiplying by 1,200.

$FF(t)$: The weekly effective (annualized) rate on overnight Federal Funds. Data (from 1984 onward) were obtained from the Federal Reserve, and earlier data were obtained from the *Federal Reserve Bulletin*. Weekly data were converted to monthly data by using the last observation for each month.

$B(t)$: The market bid (annualized) yield to maturity on 5-year Treasury bonds. End-of-the-month data were obtained from the *Treasury Bulletin*.

$\ln D(t)$: Federal debt (total amount outstanding in Bill$). Series FBD from Citibase, converted into natural logarithms.

The volatility variable that is used in some of the test statistics consists of the squared residuals from regression 1 in Table 21.1.

APPENDIX 2: DETAILS RELATING TO THE EMPIRICAL ANALYSIS

Stationarity Properties

Figure 21.1 illustrates the five series of raw data, and preliminary analysis based on these series found that each is integrated [I(1)], with no trend other than some drift in the debt variable. Further analysis on the debt variable rejected the null hypothesis of a second unit root. Preliminary cointegration analysis found cointegration between the first four of these variables, but no cointegration between debt and any subset of these term structure variables.

Modeling Outliers

The presence of several outliers in the differenced data set (see Fig. 21.2) implied that a model consisting of (i) Eq. (8) and (ii) the assumption that ε_t is iid normal would not be consistent with the data. Indeed, tests based on the empirical residuals of this initial model found strong evidence of heteroskedasticity (ARCH), nonlinearity, and nonnormality in each of the five equations.

The "causes" of this model-data conflict are debatable, and "solutions" leading to an amended statistically adequate model of the data are largely a matter of judgment and taste. The researcher's interpretation of ε_t is an important factor in the determination of an appropriate model revision because a change in (ii) is more likely to appeal to those who view ε_t as a spontaneous process, whereas a change in (i) is more likely to appeal to those who view ε_t as a process derived from the specification of (i). The view that ε_t is a derived process is more appropriate in this case, given the procedure used to specify the model in Section 21.1.2, and the choice involved in setting up the data matrix X_t. A detailed study of the standardized residuals of (i) revealed a problem modeling several of the October and December observations, which suggested that a variable such as taxes or firms' profits/returns, which might influence investors at certain times in the year, was missing from (i). However, other possible reasons for the model-versus-data inconsistency, which are more consistent with the interpretation of ε_t as a spontaneous process, include a nonnormal and/or a non-iid data-generating process. A nonlinear relationship between the variables in ΔX_t is a further possibility.

Since the outlying observations were consistent with the view that they resulted from exogenous and possibly seasonal phenomena not incorporated into (i), a crude way of capturing this view was to add some impulse dummy variables to the regressor set.[25] The relevant observations included October 1984, December 1984, April 1985, December 1985, February 1991, October 1991, October/November 1987, and December 1988/1989/1990, and the dummy variables used to account for the first six of these observations were defined in the usual way. For the other outliers, a stock market crash dummy took zero values everywhere, except for October and November 1987 when it took the values two and one, respectively, and an end of the year dummy was defined to be zero everywhere, except for December in 1988, 1989, and 1990, when it took the value of one.

All eight dummies were used in all equations for the general baseline model, and this led to a statistically adequate model [Eq. (11)], which passed standard specification tests. It is possible that the use of these dummies implied a loss of relevant information, but alternative ways of accounting for the data, such as working with nonlinear specifications or incorporating GARCH errors, might have been driven by the fitting of outliers. This latter approach might have placed an incorrect emphasis on a few atypical observations, rather than on the remaining and potentially more representative data points. Some GARCH specifications (which excluded the dummies) were nevertheless estimated, but diagnostic tests based on the standardized residuals of these models found strong evidence of misspecification.

Cointegration Analysis

Study of the cointegration structure was based on the maximum likelihood estimation of a partial system, similar to that discussed in Johansen (1995) and Harbo et al. (1998). All dependent variables other than debt were modeled in the partial system, and the concentrated likelihood was conditioned on all explanatory variables included in the general baseline model equations (excepting the three error- correction terms).

Given that critical values for rank tests in partial systems containing very influential impulse dummies are not readily available (see Doornik et al., 1998, for related discussion), the rank of the cointegrating space was not formally determined via trace tests such as those discussed in Johansen (1995) or Harbo et al. (1998). However, the Schwartz criterion (reported in Table 21.4) and AIC (not reported) support a partial system with three cointegration vectors. Further, an informal examination of estimated systems that uses various combinations of the three normalized error-correction terms in the top portion of Table 21.4, suggests that each makes a large contribution to that likelihood, which appears to be statistically significant. Accordingly, a cointegration rank of three seems to be most appropriate for this data.

Conditional on a cointegration rank of three, the estimated error-correction terms are $R(2,t)-1.001R(1,t)$, $FF(t)-1.103R(1,t)$, and $B(t)-0.905R(1,t)$, and likelihood ratio tests (also conditioned on a cointegration rank of three) indicate that the data accept the restrictions that these error-correction terms are the spreads defined by $R(2,t)-R(1,t)$, $FF(t)-R(1,t)$, and $B(t)-R(1,t)$. The evidence that $FF(t)-R(1,t)$ is error correcting is weak, and if the first and third error-correction hypotheses are imposed, the remaining error-correction term is estimated to be $FF(t)-1.081R(1,t)$.

The similarities between the error-correction terms suggested by the system cointegration analysis and those used in the preliminary model are obvious, which provides some (ex-post) evidence that the latter model was an appropriate baseline model.

The Parsimonious Equations

Once the cointegration analysis had been completed, dummies were included in the individual equations only when they were statistically significant. A list of the dummies used in the various parsimonious equations is given below:

$R(1,t)$: October 1984, April 1985, December 1985, October/November 1987, and December 1988/1989/1990.

$R(2, t)$: October 1984, April 1985, December 1985, October/November 1987, and February 1991.

$FF(t)$: October 1984, December 1984, April 1985, October/November 1987, and February 1991.

$B(t)$: October/November 1987.

$\ln D(t)$: December 1985, December 1988/1989/1990, and October 1991.

NOTES

This chapter is an extended version of work published in the *Journal of Economic Methodology* 6(1), 31–59, 1999. I am grateful to Clive Granger, David Hendry, Dennis Jansen, Bernt Stigum, Farshid Vahid, and two referees for useful comments and suggestions, but I retain the responsibility for any errors and/or omissions.

1. Occasionally these regressions even produce "wrong signed," but statistically significant spread coefficients. Rudebusch (1995) contains a table of relevant regression results, together with appropriate references.

2. The issue is not yet resolved. See Campbell (1995) and Hardouvelis (1994).

3. Integrated and cointegrated are technical time-series terms that describe a special type of long-run behavior. Here, the predicted cointegration implies comovement between yields so that the spread is mean reverting. It also implies a data representation known as an error-correction model in which the spread Granger causes changes in yields. For studies of cointegration in the term structure, see Campbell and Shiller (1988), Hall et al. (1992), Shea (1992), Zhang (1993), and Engsted and Tanggaard (1994).

4. The data need to be suitably normalized to produce this prediction. See Section 21.1.

5. The observation that one cannot "test" REH without simultaneously testing auxiliary assumptions illustrates the Duhem-Quine irrefutability thesis in the context of studying the term structure. Cross (1982) provides an extensive discussion on how this thesis relates to the appraisal of economic theories.

6. See, for instance, Chapters 1 and 3 in Blaug (1980) or Chapter 8 in Hausman (1992) for discussions of this research philosophy.

7. OLS is usually assumed to be consistent in this framework because rational expectations imply that the spread is uncorrelated with expectational errors. However, as pointed out by Tzavalis and Wickens (1997), the consistency of OLS in this framework also relies on the assumption of a constant term premium. If, as they suggest, the term premium is time varying and is correlated with the spread, then instruments will be needed to ensure consistent estimation. Many researchers note that returns are negatively serially correlated and heteroskedastic and adjust their standard errors accordingly.

8. See, for instance, Sargent (1979) or Campbell and Shiller (1988), who assume that I_t contains at least (but possibly more than) current and lagged values of $R(1, t)$ and $R(k, t)$.

9. Strictly speaking, Treasury bill yields cannot be integrated because they never take nonpositive values. However, their behavior closely resembles other aspects of

integrated behavior, so that it is empirically appropriate to treat them as if they are integrated. Stigum (1993) defines a "bridging" relationship between an observed yield $R(k, t)$ (which is not integrated) and a theoretical yield variable $R(k, t)^T$ (which is integrated) so as to both formalize the distinction between theoretical and observed variables and to justify the empirical treatment of observed yields as integrated.

10. If β' is a cointegrating vector for the two integrated variables in X_t, where X_t is a data matrix containing observations on $R(1, t)$ in the first row and $R(k, t)$ in the second, then $\beta' X_t$ is stationary, even though each variable in X_t is nonstationary. In this context, if $\beta' = (-1, 1)$, then $\beta' X_t$ defines the yield spread.

11. Cointegration with $(-1, 1)$ as a cointegrating combination implies that the spread will forecast at least one, but not necessarily both of $\Delta R(1, t)$ and $\Delta R(k, t)$.

12. This lag length is imposed so that subsequent restriction tests will be nested within Eq. (6).

13. This interpretation and use of Eq. (6) follows Hendry (1995b), which views ε_t as a derived process that depends on the model specification, rather than as a spontaneous process generated by nature. Nonlinear relationships between the variables in X_t can be incorporated into the linear framework of (6) by using extra regressors (such as the squares and cross products of X_t) to provide a linear approximation to the relevant nonlinear functional form.

14. See Johansen (1995) for a detailed discussion of multivariate cointegration, cointegration spaces, and multivariate error-correction models.

15. The distribution theory associated with the estimation of the γ and β coefficients is not standard, nor is that for b or d in Eq. (8), if $S(k, 1, t)$ is not cointegrating. However, provided that the cointegration is appropriately accounted for, the likelihood ratio tests that compare the restricted and unrestricted models will have χ^2 distributions. See, for example, Johansen (1995), for discussion.

16. See Cox et al. (1985) for details on why the various versions of the expectations hypothesis are logically incompatible.

17. See, for instance, Campbell and Shiller (1988, 1991). For a present value model in which agents have a discount factor of δ, the parameter θ is given by $\theta = \delta/(1 - \delta)$, whereas if Eq. (10) is based on a zero excess returns argument, then $\theta = k - 1$, and the dependent variable $\Delta R(k, t)$is an approximation for $R(k - 1, t) - R(k, t - 1)$.

18. A more careful theory-data confrontation would use formal theory-data bridging principles to account for measurement error, linear approximation biases, aggregation biases, and other differences between theory and observed data. These principles would then be used to derive and interpret the theoretical implications of the statistical analysis. See Part III of this book for more details.

19. Further tests that looked for whether measures of the monetary base had explanatory power were conducted but not reported. These tests found no evidence that the monetary base was a useful predictor of yield movements. ARCH-M/GARCH-M models (see Engle et al., 1987) were also estimated, but the ARCH/GARCH in mean term in each of these models had no statistically significant explanatory power.

20. If this spread is added to the equation for $\Delta R(2, t)$, its t-statistic is .66.

21. The papers of Abrams et al. (1980), Bradley and Jansen (1986), McNees (1986), and others discuss and estimate such a reaction function.

22. This conclusion might have been different had this study used separate measures of debt classified by maturity rather than the aggregate measure used here.

23. See, for instance, Simon (1990), who adds to his REH regression, the spread between a 3-month Eurodollar time deposit and a 3-month Treasury bill as a "financial market barometer of bank safety."

24. The recent ARCH-M/GARCH-M literature on the term structure (see, for instance, Engle et al., 1987) has emphasized that time-varying risk premia (modeled by volatility in holding returns) can affect yield movements. Although the analysis presented here finds evidence that volatility might be important (see Table 21.1), the GARCH family of models was unable to capture this volatility (see Appendix 2). Such models showed evidence of misspecification (regardless of whether of not the dummy variables were included in the specification). Further, the diagnostics associated with Table 21.6 suggest that the parsimonious model has appropriately incorporated the effects of time-varying volatility on yield movements.

25. Rational expectations may be unsustainable, should some of these exogenous phenomena be unpredictable. See Hendry (2001) for discussion.

REFERENCES

Abrams, R. K., R. Froyen,. and R. N. Waud, 1980, "Monetary Policy Reaction Functions, Consistent Expectations, and the Burns Era," *Journal of Money, Credit and Banking* 12, 30–41.

Blaug, M., 1980, *The Methodology of Economics, or How Economists Explain*, New York: Cambridge University Press.

Bradley, M. D., and D. W. Jansen, 1986, "Federal Reserve Operating Procedure in the Eighties," *Journal of Money, Credit and Banking* 18, 323–335.

Campbell, J. Y., 1995, "Some Lessons from the Yield Curve," *The Journal of Economic Perspectives* 9, 129–152.

Campbell, J. Y., and R. J. Shiller, 1988, "Interpreting Cointegrated Models," *Journal of Economic Dynamics and Control* 12, 505–522.

Campbell, J. Y., and R. J. Shiller, 1991, "Yield Spreads and Interest Rate Movements: A Bird's Eye View," *The Review of Economic Studies* 58, 495–514.

Cox, J. C., J. E. Ingersoll, and S. A. Ross, 1985, "A Theory of the Term Structure of Interest Rates," *Econometrica* 53, 385–407.

Cross, R., 1982, "The Duhem-Quine Thesis, Lakatos and the Appraisal of Theories in Macroeconomics," *The Economic Journal* 92, 320–340.

Doornik, J. A., D. F. Hendry, and B. Nielsen, 1998, "Inference in Cointegrating Models: UK M1 Revisited," *Journal of Economic Surveys* 12, 533–572.

Engle, R. F., and C. W. J. Granger, 1987, "Cointegration and Error Correction Representation, Estimation, and Testing," *Econometrica* 55, 251–276.

Engle, R. F., D. M. Lilien, and R. P. Robins, 1987, "Estimating Time Varying Risk Premia in the Term Structure: The ARCH-M Model," *Econometrica* 55, 391–407.

Engsted, T., and C. Tanggaard, 1994, "Cointegration and the U.S. Term Structure," *Journal of Banking and Finance* 18, 167–181.

Haavelmo, T., 1944, "The Probability Approach in Econometrics," *Econometrica* 12 (Suppl.), 115 pp.

Hall, A. D., H. M. Anderson, and C. W. J. Granger, 1992, "A Cointegration Analysis of Treasury Bill Yields," *The Review of Economics and Statistics* 74, 116–126.

Harbo, I., S. Johansen, B. Nielsen,and A. Rahbek, 1998, "Asymptotic Inference on Cointegrating Rank in Partial Systems," *Journal of Business and Economic Statistics* 16, 388–399.

Hardouvelis, G. A., 1994, "The Term Structure Spread and Future Changes in Long and Short Rates in the G7 Countries: Is There a Puzzle?" *Journal of Monetary Economics* 33, 255–283.

Hausman, D. M., 1990, "Supply and Demand Explanations and Their Ceteris Paribus Clauses," *Review of Political Economy* 2(2), 168–187.

Hausman, D. M., 1992, *The Inexact and Separate Science of Economics*, New York: Cambridge University Press.

Hendry, D. F., 1989, *PC-GIVE: An Interactive Econometric Modelling System*, Oxford: Institute of Economics and Statistics, Oxford University.

Hendry, D. F., 1995a, "On the Interactions of Unit Roots and Exogeneity," *Econometric Reviews* 14(4), 383–419.

Hendry, D. F., 1995b, *Dynamic Econometrics*, New York: Oxford University Press.

Hendry, D. F., 2001, "Forecast Failure, Expectations Formation, and the Lucas Critique," Mimeo, Department of Economics, Oxford University.

Hendry, D. F., and G. Mizon, 1993, "Evaluating Dynamic Econometric Models by Encompassing the VAR," in: *Models, Methods and Applications of Econometrics*, P. C. B. Phillips (ed.), Oxford: Blackwell, pp. 272–300.

Ho, T. Y., and A. Saunders, 1985, "A Micro Model of the Federal Funds Market," *The Journal of Finance* 40(3), 977–988.

Johansen, S., 1992, "Testing Weak Exogeneity and the Order of Cointegration in U.K. Money Demand Data," *Journal of Policy Modeling* 14(3), 313–334.

Johansen, S., 1995, *Likelihood Based Inference in Cointegrated Vector Autoregressive Models*, New York: Oxford University Press.

McNees, S. K., 1986, "Modeling the Fed: A Forward-Looking Monetary Policy Reaction Function," *New England Economic Review* Sept./Oct., 3–8.

Pagan, A. R., 1987, "Three Econometric Methodologies: A Critical Appraisal," *The Journal of Economic Surveys* 1, 3–24.

Popper, K. R., 1968, *The Logic of Scientific Discovery*, 2nd Ed., New York: Harper and Row.

Rudebusch, G. D., 1995, "Federal Reserve Interest Rate Targeting, Rational Expectations and the Term Structure," *Journal of Monetary Economics* 35, 245–276.

Sargent, T. J., 1979, "A Note on the Maximum Likelihood Estimation of the Rational Expectations Model of the Term Structure," *Journal of Monetary Economics* 5, 133–143.

Shea, G. S., 1992, "Benchmarking the Expectations Hypothesis of the Interest Rate Term Structure: An Analysis of Cointegration Vectors," *Journal of Business and Economic Statistics* 10, 347–366.

Simon, D. P., 1990, "Expectations and the Treasury Bill-Federal Funds Rate Spread over Recent Monetary Policy Regimes," *The Journal of Finance* 45(2), 567–577.

Sims, C., 1980, "Macroeconomics and Reality," *Econometrica* 48, 1–48.

Spanos, A., 1995, "On Theory Testing in Econometrics: Modeling with Non-experimental Data," *Journal of Econometrics* 67(1), 189–226.

Stigum, B., 1993, "Hypothesis Testing, Scientific Explanation and Prediction in Economics," *Cahiers d'épistémologie*, Montreal: Université du Québec à Montreal.

Stigum, B., 1998, "Scientific Explanations in Econometrics," in: *Econometrics and Economic Theory in the 20th Century: The Ragnar Frisch Centennial Symposium*, S. Stroem (ed), Cambridge: Cambridge University Press.

Stigum, M., 1990, *The Money Market*, 3rd Ed., Chicago: Dow Jones-Irwin.

Tzavalis E., and M. R. Wickens, 1997, "Explaining the Failures of the Term Spread Models of the Rational Expectations Hypothesis of the Term Structure," *Journal of Money, Credit and Banking* 29, 364–380.

Zhang, H., 1993, "Treasury Yield Curves and Cointegration," *Applied Economics* 25, 361–367.

Chapter Twenty-Two

Scientific Explanation in Economics

This chapter gives a formal account of the meaning of scientific explanations in economics and econometrics.[1] An *explanation* is an answer to a "why" question. It makes clear or intelligible something that is not known or understood by the person asking the question. A *scientific explanation* is one in which the ideas of some scientific theory play an essential role. In economics this is an economic theory and the ideas contained within it are used to provide scientific explanations of regularities that applied economists and econometricians have observed in their data.

There are all sorts of "why" questions and usually many possible answers to the same one. Those of interest here concern the occurrence of certain events: for example, a sudden sharp drop in prices on the N.Y. Stock Exchange; or the characteristics of observed phenomena, for example, prolonged periods of severe unemployment in European economies. An answer to the first kind of question might be a list of the causes of the event(s) in question. An answer to the second might be a list of reasons why the observed phenomena were to be expected.

The form in which the causes of events and the reasons for observed phenomena are listed and used in a scientific explanation differs among scientists even within the same discipline. There is, therefore, a need for formal criteria by which one can distinguish good from bad scientific explanations. These criteria must list the necessary elements of a scientific explanation and explicate the ideas of a logically and an empirically adequate scientific explanation.

In this chapter I give a formal characterization of logically and empirically adequate scientific explanations in economics and econometrics. For motivation and ease of reference I begin by discussing relevant aspects of Carl G. Hempel's fundamental ideas as they appear in Chapters 10 and 12 of his book *Aspects of Scientific Explanation* (Hempel, 1965) and in Wesley C. Salmon's interesting survey article, "Four Decades of Scientific Explanation" (Kitcher and Salmon, 1989, pp. 3–219).

22.1 THE DEDUCTIVE-NOMOLOGICAL SCHEME FOR SCIENTIFIC EXPLANATIONS

Hempel's (1965, pp. 245–251) *deductive-nomological scheme* (DNS) is the most influential existing formal characterization of scientific explanations.

According to the DNS, a scientific explanation of an event or a phenomenon must have four elements: (1) A sentence E that describes the event or the phenomenon in question; (2) a list of sentences $C_1, C_2, \ldots, C_n$ that describes relevant antecedent conditions; (3) a list of general laws $L_1, L_2, \ldots, L_k$; and (4) arguments that demonstrate that E is a logical consequence of the C's and the L's. The following is an example to fix these ideas.

E 22.1 *An explanation is required as to why Per, a human being, cannot live forever. To provide it let* P *denote Per and let* E(x) *insist that* x *is mortal. Then* E *becomes* E(P). *Next, let* C(x) *assert that* x *is a human being and observe that* C(P). *Finally, let* L *denote a law of biology that insists that* $(\forall x)\,[C(x) \supset E(x)]$. *Now, in first-order logic* L *implies that* $[C(P) \supset E(P)]$, *and* C(P) *and* $[C(P) \supset E(P)]$ *imply that* E(P). *Consequently,* E(P) *is a logical consequence of* C(P) *and* L *as required in condition 4 of Hempel's scheme.*

According to the DNS, a scientific explanation is *adequate* only if it is both logically and empirically adequate. An explanation is *logically adequate* only if at least one L plays an essential part in the demonstration that the *explanandum* E is a logical consequence of the *explanans*, the family of C's and L's. Moreover, the explanation is *empirically adequate* only if: (i) it is possible, at least in principle, to establish by experiment or observation whether the C's that are used in condition 4 are satisfied, and (ii) the L's that are used in condition 4 have been subjected to extensive tests and have passed them all.[2] Evidently, the scientific explanation of $E(P)$ in E 22.1 is logically adequate since L plays an essential role in the proof that $E(P)$ is a logical consequence of $C(P)$ and L. The explanation is also empirically adequate since observation alone suffices to determine whether an x satisfies C and history accounts for numerous tests of L, all of which failed to falsify L.

Hempel's DNS has attractive features, and he and others have used it to give interesting scientific explanations of events and phenomena in different sciences (cf., e.g., Hempel, 1965, pp. 335–338; Nagel, 1961, pp. 30–32). Even so, influential philosophers of science have criticized it for many failings and have expressed reservations about applying it in the social sciences. Therefore, a few remarks are called for, and in the course of the ensuing discussion I search for ways to generalize Hempel's scheme so that it can be used in economics and econometrics.[3]

I begin with an example that shows that Hempel's scheme must be used with care. A logically and empirically adequate DNS explanation need not explain a thing.[4]

E 22.2 *Let* E(x) *assert that* x *will have no babies, and let* C(x) *declare that* x *takes* WP, *a wonder pill. Also, let* L *insist that* $(\forall x)\,[C(x) \supset E(x)]$, *and suppose that* L *has been subjected to numerous tests and has passed them all. Finally, let* H *denote Harry, a man, and suppose that Harry takes* WP *regularly. Then* C(H) *and* E(H)*; and* E(H) *is a logical consequence of* C(H) *and* L.

Next the list of C's: In many cases the list of C's is empty. This is always the case when the scientist is asked to give a theoretical explanation of some phenomenon. In other instances the list is incomplete. This is the case when the scientist is ignorant of some of the relevant antecedent conditions. For all practical purposes, it will also be the case whenever the scientist cannot determine by observation or experiment whether all the C's are satisfied.

Example E 22.3 serves to exemplify the import of the preceding observations. Note that the E 22.3 explanation contains no C's, and that it is typical of the kind of scientific explanation that economic theorists provide. It uses essential characteristics of a family of models of a toy economy to explain the phenomenon in question. Note also that if one were to use the ideas of the E 22.3 explanation in a scientific explanation of the severe unemployment that Norwegians experienced during the first half of the 1990s, one would be hard put to specify all the relevant C's.

E 22.3 *In economics one learns that, under reasonable conditions on preferences and production sets, perfectly competitive free-enterprise economies possess full-employment equilibria that have many attractive features, for example, production is efficient and the distribution of goods is Pareto optimal. So why is it that mixed capitalistic economies can and do experience prolonged periods of severe unemployment? There are many answers to this question. Economics professors elaborate on one of them in introductory macroeconomics courses roughly as follows: Let* T *denote an enlarged formal version of Sir J. R. Hicks's (1937, pp. 137–145) model-theoretic account of J. M. Keynes's macroeconomic theory.* T *has models in which* T*'s economy possesses unemployment equilibria that are hard to escape. These models suggest that a downward inflexibility of wages and a possible liquidity trap are major reasons for prolonged periods of unemployment in mixed capitalistic economies.*

Then the list of laws: A *law* is a general lawlike statement that insists that individuals or objects of a given kind *must* have certain properties or that individuals or objects of different given kinds *must* be related in a certain way. Moreover, a general lawlike statement is a law only if it is a logical consequence of an accepted scientific theory and its truth value is independent of place and time. Examples are: "Copper expands when heated" and "When electrons and antielectrons meet head on, they annihilate each other." The former is a theorem in thermodynamics and statistical mechanics and the latter is a theorem in quantum mechanics. Both theorems are believed to be valid irrespective of time and place.

Philosophers of science question the use of Hempel's scheme in the social sciences because they believe that there are no laws in those sciences. Since there are all sorts of theories in economics, the claim that it has no laws amounts to insisting that there are no empirically relevant theorems in economics whose relevance is independent of time and place. This claim cannot be true. To wit:

The first and the last of Nassau Senior's basic postulates of economics, Gresham's law, and Paul Samuelson's fundamental theorem of consumer choice (cf. Stigum, 1990, pp. 4, 554, 186) are theorems that economists believe are empirically relevant irrespective of time and place.

So there are laws in economics, but how prevalent they are is uncertain. Jon Elster believes that economic laws are so rare that economists ought to switch from looking for theorems to looking for what he calls mechanisms. A *mechanism* is a frequently occurring and easily recognizable causal pattern that is triggered under generally unknown conditions. Mechanisms allow us to explain, but not to predict (Elster, 1994, p. 1). Good examples from economics are Daniel Kahnemann and Amos Tversky's (cf. 1972, pp.430–454, 1973, p. 2) availability and representativeness heuristics—heuristics that people supposedly use in uncertain situations to assess likelihoods and make predictions.[5]

E 22.4 *An individual is watching a game of chance, where someone can win or lose a bet with equal probability. There are many players and the game is played many times. He observes that after runs of as much as six wins about half of the players decrease their bets and the other half increase their bets. He can use the representativeness heuristics to explain the behavior of the first half and the availability hypothesis to explain that of the second. Evidently Kahnemann and Tversky's heuristics cannot be used to predict individual behavior in the given context.*[6]

With L's that are valid irrespective of time and place, the requirement that the E of a DNS explanation be a logical consequence of C and L is very strong. It implies that an event whose occurrence can be explained with appropriate C's and L's could have been predicted with the same C's and L's. Thus, with L's that are valid irrespective of time and place the formal analysis that applies to adequate scientific explanations applies to adequate scientific predictions as well. "The difference of the two is of a pragmatic character" (Hempel, 1965, p. 249). In the philosophy of science this observation is referred to as Hempel's symmetry thesis.

There are many situations in which Hempel's symmetry thesis seems to call for a rewording. These are, typically, situations in which one is either unable to ascertain the validity of all the C's or so ignorant about the system under study that all the relevant L's cannot be listed. Good examples from econometrics are a hypothesis that did not test out and a forecast of economic conditions that failed. I discussed such situations at the end of Chapter 20 and showed how Raymond Reiter's logic for diagnostic reasoning can be applied to them. In this chapter I have a different kind of rephrasing in mind. The next example serves to fix the ideas about that.

E 22.5 *An economist is to give a scientific explanation of the occurrence of some event* E. *Suppose that he has been able to show that* $[[[C_1 \wedge C_2] \wedge A] \supset E]$, *where* C_1 *and* C_2 *denote two antecedent conditions and* A *designates a scientific theory. He knows that* C_1 *is valid, but he has his doubts about* C_2. *He also fears that the empirical relevance of* A *is limited. Let* B_1 *and* B_2, *respectively, be sentences that describe conditions under which the validity of* C_2 *and the applicability of* A *are ensured. The economist is certain that* B_1 *and* B_2 *are valid in some world, but does not know whether they are valid in the Real World. Therefore he can claim that* $\sim\Box\sim B_1$ *and* $\sim\Box\sim B_2$, *and assert that* C_1, $[B_1 \supset C_2]$, $[B_2 \supset A]$, *and* $[[[C_1 \wedge C_2] \wedge A] \supset E]$. *These claims and assertions together with arguments of S4 modal logic enable him to show that* $\sim\Box\sim E$, *that is, to establish that there are possible worlds in which* E *is valid. By hypothesis, one of these worlds is the Real World. To the extent that he believes in the possible validity of* B_1 *and* B_2 *in the Real World, he has given an explanation of the occurrence of* E.[7] *However, only if* B_1 *and* B_2 actually *were valid in the Real World would his arguments have sufficed to* predict *the occurrence of* E.

In the idea of a scientific explanation that I develop in this chapter I allow any number of economic theories to play the role of a law in Hempel's scheme. Consequently, the demands for logical and empirical adequacy of a scientific explanation on which I insist appear much weaker than the DNS adequacy requirements. It is, therefore, interesting to observe that Hempel's idea of the adequacy of a DNS explanation has been beset with many problems that cause no difficulties for my account of scientific explanation. Two of these problems are relevant here. First, an explanation is an answer to a "why" question. The same "why" question may call for different answers depending on the context in which it is asked. A valid explanation in one context may be meaningless in another. Just think of pertinent answers to the questions, "Why is Per running?" and "Why is the German interest rate rising?" Second, many scientific explanations display vexing asymmetries. For example, from the laws of mathematical physics one can deduce that the galaxies are receding from Earth if and only if the light Earth receives from them exhibits a shift toward the red end of the spectrum (Van Frassen, 1980, p. 104). Physics and the receding galaxies can explain the red shift. It is hard to see how physics and the red shift can explain why the galaxies are becoming more distant. My account of scientific explanation can handle analogues of the first problem and seems never to have to face analogues of the second problem.

22.2 A FORMAL CHARACTERIZATION OF SCIENTIFIC EXPLANATIONS IN ECONOMICS

I consider a scientific explanation to be a theory-data confrontation in reverse. I have observed interesting aspects of my data and am looking for a theory that

E = Event

I can use to explain them. If my view is correct, I must be able to give an adequate formal characterization of scientific explanations within the framework of theory-data confrontations that I developed in Part III of this book. So here I begin by looking for analogues of Hempel's C's, L's, and E that I can put into the core structures of suitable economic theory-data confrontations.

22.2.1 The Basic Parts of a Scientific Explanation

First the C's: The C's in Hempel's scheme describe relevant antecedent conditions whose validity I can, in principle, determine by experiment or observation. Such C's pertain to objects in the data universe of a theory-data confrontation. Some of them may delineate characteristics of my observations and the data I have constructed. Others may describe properties of the data-generating process. I think of them as building blocks in a formulation of the empirical context in which I am to provide a scientific explanation of an observed event or phenomenon. Hence, in my scheme they appear as members of Γ_p and the axioms that delineate characteristics of the data-generating process.

Then E: In Hempel's scheme E describes an event that has occurred or a phenomenon that has been observed. Such E's pertain to objects in the data universe. They comprise sentences that describe salient characteristics of my data and their probability distribution FP. The sentences in E are taken to be valid in at least one of the models of the pertinent Γ_p and FP. However, they are not logical consequences of Γ_p and the sentences that delineate relevant properties of the FP. Hence, there are models of Γ_p and FP that are not models of E. This characteristic of my E is one that it shares with the E of a logically adequate DNS explanation.

An E that economists observe and want to explain denotes truth in social reality; that is, in the Real World and, for all I know, may denote truth in many other possible worlds as well. However, it is rarely the case that such an E is valid in all possible worlds. Hence, in most situations in economics they stand prepared to assert that $\sim\Box\sim E$ and that the truth value of E is truth in the Real World.

Next the L's: In Hempel's scheme the L's are lawlike statements concerning matters of fact in social reality. They are also logical consequences of an accepted scientific theory and are supposedly valid irrespective of time and place. In the scientific explanations that I envision here the L's are ordinary economic theories that concern characteristics of individuals who roam around in a theory universe. They are members of a particular family of assertions Γ_t, the basic axioms of the theory universe. As such they are not laws in Hempel's sense. Moreover, most of them have rather limited empirical relevance. Since these facts are important, a few remarks concerning the L's in my scheme are called for.

Consider an economic theory of some economic situation, for example, an act or an event or an historical development. *The intended interpretation of the theory delineates the positive analogies that the originator of the theory considered sufficient to describe the kind of situation that he had in mind.* The sentences of the intended interpretation of such a theory are not lawlike statements about matters of fact in the Real World. Instead, they are valid assertions concerning matters of fact in a toy economy. By confronting the theory with data one can discover where and when the positive analogies that the theory identifies are characteristic features of events and phenomena in social reality.

The characteristic features of a toy economy that an interpreted theory describes are not to be identified with Elster's mechanisms. The characteristic features of events and phenomena in social reality that the originator of an economic theory has in mind when he develops his theory are positive analogies of the kind of events and phenomena in question. In contrast, mechanisms are interesting negative analogies of such events and phenomena. To wit Elster's own example: "Perhaps for every child who becomes alcoholic in response to an alcoholic environment, another eschews alcohol in response to the same environment" (Vaillant, 1983, p.65). Here the mechanisms involved are: "doing what your parents do and doing the opposite of what they do" (Elster, 1994, p. 1).

Finally, the bridge that connects theory with data: The theory universe and the data universe are disjoint. So, in order to use an economic theory in a scientific explanation of an event or a phenomenon that resides in the data universe, an economist must find a way of relating variables in the theory universe to variables in the data universe. He does that in the form of a family of bridge principles. The assertions that formulate these principles look like the assertions that formulate axioms in the theory universe as well as in the data universe. Still, they differ in one significant way from the axioms in the two universes. He has no reason to doubt the validity of the pertinent Γ_t in the theory universe since these axioms concern characteristics of toys in a toy economy. Similarly, since he has created the data himself, he has no reason to doubt the validity of Γ_p in the data universe. In an S4 modal-logical framework these axioms are true in all possible worlds. His attitude toward the bridge principles $\Gamma_{t,p}$ is different. Usually, he is sure that there are worlds in which they are valid and stands prepared to assert $\sim\Box\sim\Gamma_{t,p}$. He also *believes* that one of these worlds is the Real World, but cannot be certain of that.

22.2.2 A Characterization of Scientific Explanation in Economics

In this section I present a formal characterization of scientific explanations in economics for situations in which there is no sample population S, no probability measure $P(\cdot)$ on subsets of Ω, and just one model in the intended interpretation of Γ_p. The situations I have in mind are analogues of the kind of situation for which Hempel developed his DNS, that is, a situation in which the explanation can be based on physical or economic theories of deterministic character (cf. Hempel, 1965, p. 351). It is, therefore, interesting that my characterization of scientific explanations, with the proper translation, can be made to fit Hempel's scheme.

22.2.2.1 *The Characterization*

I have observed certain regularities in a set of data and am searching for a scientific explanation of these regularities. Formally, my search can be described as follows:

SE 1 *Let* (Ω_P, Γ_p) *be some given data universe. Assume that the components of the vectors in* Ω_P *denote so many units of objects that have been observed and that* Γ_p *delineates the salient properties of the data. Also, let* H *be a finite family of assertions concerning* Ω_P*, and suppose that there is a model of* (Ω_P, Γ_p)*,* M*, in which all the assertions of* H *are true.* M *is taken to be the intended model of the data universe and it is assumed that* H *delineates the characteristics of the data that are to be explained. Then,* to give a scientific explanation of H means to find a theory universe (Ω_T, Γ_t)*, a sample space,* $\Omega \subset \Omega_T \times \Omega_P$, and a collection of bridge principles $\Gamma_{t,p}$ that in Ω link Ω_T with Ω_P such that H becomes a logical consequence of Γ_t, Γ_p, and $\Gamma_{t,p}$.

Such an explanation is *logically adequate* if *H* is not a logical consequence of Γ_p alone. It is *empirically adequate* if *M* is a model of all the logical consequences of Γ_t, $\Gamma_{t,p}$, and Γ_p that concern components of ω_P.

In SE 1 there are several things to note and to keep in mind for later discussion. First, as in Hempel's DNS, the explanandum is a logical consequence of the explanans, and the explanation is logically adequate if at least one of the components of Γ_t plays an essential role in the proof of *H*. Moreover, as in the case of Hempel's DNS, in my scheme the logical adequacy of a scientific explanation does not entail the symmetry thesis, the reason being that I cannot assert $\Gamma_{t,p}$ and claim that the principles it comprises are valid. At best, I can insist that $\sim\Box\sim\Gamma_{t,p}$ and hope that all the logical consequences of Γ_t, $\Gamma_{t,p}$, and Γ_p are valid in *M*.

Second, the empirical adequacy of an SE 1 scientific explanation hinges on the predictive powers of Γ_t. Specifically, the scientific explanation of *H* is empirically adequate only if Γ_t is relevant in the empirical context that *M* determines. This empirical relevance of Γ_t entails that a logically and empirically adequate scientific explanation of *H* could have been used to predict the happening of *H*. Thus, Hempel's symmetry thesis does apply to logically and empirically adequate SE 1 explanations. More on that in Section 22.3.

Third, both the empirical and the logical adequacy of an SE 1 scientific explanation hinge on the validity of the bridge principles that are adopted. This is an important aspect of SE 1, the meaning of which I explicate in discussing the modal-logical rendition of SE 1 in Section 22.3.

22.2.2.2 An Example

My explication of scientific explanation might sound unfamiliar, so here I offer an example to fix the ideas.[8] Suppose that, for some student, I have constructed the function $W(\cdot) : [0, 1{,}000] \rightarrow [0, 1]$ as I described it in Section 17.3.1 and that this new $W(\cdot)$ satisfies

$$W(x) = 0.5\left\{1 + [(x - 500)/500]^{1/3}\right\}, x \in [0, 1{,}000]. \tag{1}$$

Suppose also that for the same student, I have constructed a function $V(\cdot) : [0, 1{,}000] \rightarrow [0, 1]$ in the following way: I assigned the values 0 and 1, respectively, to $V(0)$ and $V(1{,}000)$, and wherever $V(\cdot)$ had been defined at x and y, I let $V[C(x, y)] = (1/2)V(x) + (1/2)V(y)$, with $C(x, y)$ equal to the student's certainty equivalent of the option x with probability 1/2 and y with probability 1/2. For all $x \in [0, 1{,}000]$ at which I have defined $V(\cdot)$, I have found that it satisfies the relation

$$V(x) = x/1{,}000, x \in [0, 1{,}000]. \tag{2}$$

Now, I am asked to give a scientific explanation of (1) and (2) and the inequalities in

$$V(x) \text{ is } \begin{cases} > W(x) \text{ if } x \in (0, 500) \\ < W(x) \text{ if } x \in (500, 1{,}000). \end{cases} \tag{3}$$

To do that I must describe the data universe (Ω_P, Γ_p), formulate the assertion to be explained H, find the required theory universe (Ω_T, Γ_t) and the sample space Ω, and delineate the bridge principles that in Ω are to connect Ω_T with Ω_P.

The Data Universe and the Explanandum *H*

I begin by letting Ω_P be a set of seven-tuples ω_p that satisfy the following axioms:

EB 1 $\omega_P \in \Omega_P$ *only if* $\omega_P = (q, x, W, y, z, C, V)$, *where* $q \in [0, 1]$, $x, y, z \in [0, 1{,}000]$, $W(\cdot) : [0, 1{,}000] \rightarrow [0, 1]$, $y \leq z$, $V(\cdot) : [0, 1{,}000] \rightarrow [0, 1]$, $V(0) = 0$, $V(1{,}000) = 1$, *and* $C(\cdot) : [0, 1{,}000]^2 \rightarrow [0, 1{,}000]$.

EB 2 *For all* $\omega_P \in \Omega_P$, $W(x) = q$, *and* $V[C(y, z)] = (1/2)V(y) + (1/2)V(z)$.

EB 3 *If* $(q, x, W, y, z, C, V) \in \Omega_P$, *then* $(q, x, W, 0, 1{,}000, C, V) \in \Omega_P$. *Also, there exist two uniquely determined pairs of numbers in* $[0, 1{,}000]$, (v_y, w_y) *and* (v_z, w_z), *that are independent of* q *and* x *and satisfy the relations* $y = C(v_y, w_y)$, $z = C(v_z, w_z)$, $(q, x, W, v_y, w_y, C, V) \in \Omega_P$, *and* $(q, x, W, v_z, w_z, C, V) \in \Omega_P$. *If* $y = 0$, $(v_y, w_y) = (0, 0)$, *and if* $z = 1{,}000$, $(v_z, w_z) = (1{,}000, 1{,}000)$. *Otherwise,* $v_y < w_y$ *and* $v_z < w_z$.

When reading these axioms, observe that the uniqueness of the pairs (v_y, w_y) and (v_z, w_z) on which I insist in EB 3 is a characteristic of the sampling scheme that I used in the construction of $V(\cdot)$. It is not a property of certainty equivalents as such. With that in mind, I can state the explanandum H as follows:

H For all $\omega_P \in \Omega_P$: (i) the value of $W(\cdot)$ at x satisfies Eq. (1) with q instead of p; (ii) the values of $V(\cdot)$ at y, z, and $C(y, z)$ satisfy Eq. (2); and (iii) the value of $W(\cdot)$ at x and the value of $V(\cdot)$ at $C(y, z)$ satisfy the inequalities in Eq. (3) whenever $x = C(y, z)$.

This assertion is true in some model of (Ω_P, Γ_p), but it is not a logical consequence of EB 1 and EB 2.

The Theory Universe

Next I must search for a useful theory universe (Ω_T, Γ_t). One possibility is as follows: Let Ω_T be a set of six-tuples ω_T that satisfy the following axioms:

EB 4 $\omega_T \in \Omega_T$ *only if* $\omega_T = (p, r, U, s, t, \hat{C})$, *where* $p \in [0, 1], r, s, t \in [0, 1{,}000], U(\cdot) : [0, 1{,}000] \rightarrow [0, 1], s \leq t$, *and* $C(\cdot) : [0, 1{,}000]^2 \rightarrow [0, 1{,}000]$.

EB 5 *For all* $\omega_T \in \Omega_T$, $U(r) = p$, *and* $U\left[\hat{C}(s, t)\right] = (1/2)U(s) + (1/2)U(t)$.

EB 6 *For all* $\omega_T \in \Omega_T$, $r = 1{,}000p$, *and* $\hat{C}(s, t) = (1/2)s + (1/2)t$.

In these axioms, the triple (p, r, U) plays the same role as the triple (p, x, U) played in Section 17.3.1 (cf. axioms U 2–U 4). Also, $\hat{C}(s, t)$ is to be interpreted as the certainty equivalent of the random options s and t, both with a perceived probability of 1/2. In its intended interpretation, (Ω_T, EB 4–EB 6) is the universe of a theory in which the decision-maker orders prospects according to their perceived expected value.

The Bridge Principles

Finally, I must describe how the individuals in Ω_T are related to the individuals in Ω_P. I insist on accurate observations on r, s, t, and $\hat{C}$. I also assume that the given student's perceived probabilities, in an appropriate way, overvalue low probabilities and undervalue high probabilities.

EB 7 *The sample space* Ω *is a subset of* $\Omega_T \times \Omega_P$.

EB 8 *If* $(\omega_T, \omega_P) \in \Omega$ *and* $(\omega_T, \omega_P) = (p, r, U, s, t, \hat{C}, q, x, W, y, z, C, V)$, *then* $(p, r, U, 0, 1{,}000, \hat{C}, q, x, W, 0, 1{,}000, C, V) \in \Omega$, , $(p, r, U, v_y, w_y, \hat{C}, q, x, W, v_y, w_y, C, V) \in \Omega$, *and* $(p, r, U, v_z, w_z, \hat{C}, q, x, W, v_z, w_z, C, V) \in \Omega$, *where the pairs* (v_y, w_y) *and* (v_z, w_z) *are as described in EB 3.*

EB 9 *For all* $(\omega_T, \omega_P) \in \Omega$, $r = x$, $s = y$, $t = z$, *and* $\hat{C}(s,t) = C(y,z)$.

EB 10 *For all* $(\omega_T, \omega_P) \in \Omega$, $p = 0.5 + 4(q - 0.5)^3$.

If I pick (Ω_T, Γ_t) and $\Gamma_{t,p}$ as described above, I can show by simple algebra that for all $(\omega_T, \omega_P) \in \Omega$, the value of $W(\cdot)$ at x must satisfy Eq. (1). Moreover, I can show, first by simple algebra, that $C(y, z) = (1/2)y + (1/2)z$, and then, by an obvious inductive argument, that the value of $V(\cdot)$ at y, z, and $C(y, z)$ must satisfy Eq. (2). But if that is so, the value of $W(\cdot)$ at x and the value of $V(\cdot)$ at $C(y, z)$ must satisfy the inequalities in Eq. (3) whenever $x = C(y, z)$. Hence, (Ω_T, Γ_t) and $\Gamma_{t,p}$ provide the required scientific explanation of H.

The explanation of H that I have delineated is obviously logically adequate. Since I have no relevant data, I cannot determine whether the explanation is empirically adequate.

22.2.2.3 Sundry Remarks

There are several striking features of the preceding example of a scientific explanation that I should point out. According to expected utility theory (EUT), the relation $V(x) = W(x)$, $x \in [0, 1{,}000]$, must hold if the student's perception of probabilities are veridical. This is true, moreover, regardless of whether or not $W(\cdot)$ is linear. Furthermore, the relationship between $V(\cdot)$ and $W(\cdot)$ depicted in Eq. (3) seems to be a general feature of experimental results that Maurice Allais and his followers have recorded during the last 50 years (cf., e.g., Allais, 1979, pp. 649–654). Note, therefore, that I use EUT to provide a scientific explanation of Eqs. (1)–(3). In contrast, Allais et al. have used the necessity of the equality of $V(\cdot)$ and $W(\cdot)$ and Eq. (3) to discredit the descriptive power of EUT in risky situations. My analysis shows that they had good reason for their disbelief only if their subjects' perception of probabilities was veridical.

A logically and empirically adequate SE 1 explanation differs in interesting ways from an adequate DNS explanation. Hempel's C's, L's, and E concern individuals in one and the same universe. This universe is in SE 1 my data universe. There the members of Γ_p play the roles of Hempel's C's, the translated versions of the members of Γ_t play the roles of Hempel's L's, and H has taken the place of Hempel's E. Hence, with the proper translation, an SE 1 explanation can be made to look like a DNS explanation. Still, there is a fundamental difference. Hempel's criteria for a DNS explanation to be empirically adequate insist that his L's must have been subjected to extensive tests and have passed them all. I only insist that my L's, the members of Γ_t, be relevant in the given(!) empirical context in which the explanation is formulated.

My criteria cannot differ that much from the criteria on which contemporary philosophers of science insist. The following are two observations in support of my contention: (i) A law of nature is not an assertion that has a truth value.

It is rather a statement that comes with a list of situations in which it has proven possible to apply it (Toulmin, 1953, pp. 86–87). (ii) Theories are applied selectively in scientific explanations. For example, one says that Newton's theory can be used to explain the tides even though it is known that Newton's laws do not satisfy Hempel's criteria for empirical adequacy. Whether a theory explains some fact or other is independent of whether the Real World as a whole fits the theory (Van Frassen, 1980, p. 98).

There is an interesting second way in which an SE 1 explanation differs from a DNS explanation. This difference enables a logically and empirically adequate SE 1 explanation to reason away one of the most serious problems that Hempel's DNS has faced (cf. my remarks at the end of Section 23.1). The problem arises when the same question calls for different answers depending on the circumstances in which it is asked. Then a logically and empirically adequate DNS explanation may be good in one situation and meaningless in another. In logically and empirically adequate SE 1 explanations this problem does not arise because the meaning of H in SE 1 varies with the empirical context M. H may have the same meaning in two different M's, and the same M may be a model of two different Γ_p's. In SE 1, H and M are given in advance. Different M's and/or different Γ_p's might call for different Γ_t's and $\Gamma_{t,p}$'s in the explanation of H.

22.3 A MODAL-LOGICAL FORMULATION OF AN ADEQUATE SCIENTIFIC EXPLANATION

Some of the characteristics that I attribute to my scheme for scientific explanation in economics are easier to demonstrate in modal logic than in my ordinary theory-data confrontation framework, so in this next section I discuss a modal-logical analogue of SE 1, which I denote by SEM 1.

22.3.1 The Modal-Logical Characterization of Scientific Explanations

In the statement of SEM 1 L_{tp} is similar to the multisorted language that I used to discuss Reiter's default logic in Chapter 20. Specifically, $L_{tp} = (L_t, L_p, B_{tp})$, where L_t and L_p are multisorted languages for discussing theory and data and B_{tp} comprises a finite number of predicates that relate individual variables of L_t to individual variables of L_p. The logical symbols of L_{tp} are the standard symbols, $\sim \supset [\ ]\ (\ ,\ )\ \forall =$, a modal operator $\Box$, k nonoverlapping lists of individual variables for L_t, and m nonoverlapping lists of individual variables for L_p. The nonlogical vocabulary of L_{tp} consists of the predicates in B_{tp}; a selection of constants, function symbols, and predicate symbols for L_t; and a selection of constants, function symbols, and predicate symbols for L_p. For ease of exposition, I assume that among the predicate symbols of L_{tp} there is a k-ary predicate symbol Ω_T, an m-ary predicate symbol Ω_P, and a $(k + m)$-ary predicate symbol Ω. The first two belong, respectively, to the vocabulary of L_t and L_p. The third is one of the predicate symbols in B_{tp}.

The other characteristics of the L_{tp} of SEM 1 are also similar to those of the L_{tp} in Chapter 20. Thus, the terms and wffs have been defined the same way, and the logical axiom schemata of the L_{tp} of SEM 1 are the same as the LTPA 1–LTPA 7 of the L_{tp} in Chapter 20. Furthermore, I have described the characteristics of the individual variables in L_p in a finite family of axioms, Γ_p, and have expressed the explanandum H in a finite number of wffs with the vocabulary of L_p. I assume, implicitly, that my search for an explanans has resulted in the choice of a suitable theory and a family of bridge principles. I have expressed the axioms of the theory in a finite family of wffs, Γ_t, with the vocabulary of L_t and the bridge principles in a finite family of wffs, $\Gamma_{t,p}$, with the help of the members of B_{tp}. Finally, I have formulated the nonlogical axioms of L_{tp} as in LTPA 8–LTPA 10, adopted RI 1–RI 3 as the rules of inference, and given the present L_{tp} the interpretation I gave to L_{tp} in Section 20.3.4.

With that much said about the characteristics of L_{tp} I can formulate SEM 1 as follows:

SEM 1 *Let* $\mathrm{L_{tp}}$, Γ_t, Γ_p, $\Gamma_\mathrm{t,p}$, *and* H *be as described above and let* ξ_e *denote the Real World in the intended interpretation of* $\mathrm{L_{tp}}$. *Also, let* σ *be an assignment of values to the variables of* $\mathrm{L_{tp}}$, $\mathrm{a} = (\mathrm{a_t}, \mathrm{a_p})$, *that is admissible in* ξ_e, *that is, an assignment that satisfies* $[[\Omega_\mathrm{T}(\sigma \mathrm{a_t}) \wedge \Omega_\mathrm{P}\sigma\mathrm{a_p})] \wedge \Omega(\sigma\mathrm{a})]$ *in* ξ_e, *and assume that* $\xi_\mathrm{e}[\mathrm{H_{a_p}}(\sigma\mathrm{a_p})] = \mathrm{t}$. *Then the theory and the bridge principles that I have chosen provide a scientific explanation of* H *only if for all such* σ, $\mathrm{H_{a_p}}(\sigma\mathrm{a_p})$ *is a logical consequence of* $[[\Gamma_\mathrm{t}(\sigma\mathrm{a_t}) \wedge \Gamma_\mathrm{p}(\sigma\mathrm{a_p})] \wedge \Gamma_\mathrm{t,p}(\sigma\mathrm{a})]$.

An SEM 1 explanation is *logically adequate* if H is not a logical consequence of Γ_p alone. It is *empirically adequate* if for any assignment σ of values to the variables of $L_{tp}, a = (a_t, a_p)$, that is admissible in ξ_e, all the logical consequences of $\Gamma_t(\sigma a_t)$, $\Gamma_p(\sigma a_p)$, and $\Gamma_{t,p}(\sigma a)$ are valid in ξ_e.

In reading this characterization of logically and empirically adequate scientific explanations in economics there are several things to note. First, the characterization of scientific explanations in SEM 1 only puts restrictions on assignments of values to the variables of L_{tp} that are admissible in ξ_e, that is, that satisfy the predicate $[[\Omega_T \wedge \Omega_p] \wedge \Omega]$ in ξ_e. Thus, what happens outside the sample space is irrelevant,[9] the reason being that the L_{tp} axiom for bridge principles, LTPA 10, concerns only vectors in the sample space.

Second, if σ is an admissible assignment of values to the variables of L_{tp} such that $[[\Omega_T(\sigma a_t) \wedge \Omega_p(\sigma a_p)] \wedge \Omega(\sigma a)]$, and if $C_{a_p}(\sigma a_p)$ is a logical consequence of $\Gamma_t(\sigma a_t)$, $\Gamma_p(\sigma a_p)$, and $\Gamma_{t,p}(\sigma a)$, then (in summary form) $[[[\Gamma_t(\sigma a_t) \wedge \Gamma_p(\sigma a_p)] \wedge \Gamma_{t,p}(\sigma a)] \supset C_{a_p}(\sigma a_p)]$ and $\sim\Box\sim C_{a_p}(\sigma a_p)$ are theorems of L_{tp}. When $C_{a_p}(\sigma a_p)$ is $H_{a_p}(\sigma a_p)$, I know by hypothesis that $H_{a_p}(\sigma a_p)$ is valid in ξ_e. For other $C_{a_p}(\sigma a_p)$ I have no such knowledge unless they are logical consequences of

$\Gamma_p(\sigma a_p)$ alone. I know that there is a possible world ξ such that $\xi[C_{a_p}(\sigma a_p)] = t$ and that if $\xi_e[\Gamma_{t,p}(\sigma a)] = t$, then $\xi_e[C_{a_p}(\sigma a_p)] = t$ as well. Since I just *believe* that $\xi_e[\Gamma_{t,p}(\sigma a)] = t$, I must, for each admissible σ in ξ_e, determine the truth values of all the logical consequences of $\Gamma_t(\sigma a_t)$, $\Gamma_p(\sigma a_p)$, and $\Gamma_{t,p}(\sigma a)$ before I can be sure that the given scientific explanation is empirically adequate.

Third, according to SEM 1, a scientific explanation is empirically adequate only if the theory one has chosen is empirically relevant in the context in which one carries out the explanation. Note, therefore, that the empirical relevance of the theory does entail that Γ_t, Γ_p, and $\Gamma_{t,p}$ could have been used to predict the happening of H. Thus, Hempel's symmetry thesis is valid in the context of SEM 1 for scientific explanations that are both (!) logically and empirically adequate. Logical adequacy alone, however, is not sufficient to ensure the validity of Hempel's symmetry thesis.

22.3.2 An Example

These observations can be illustrated with the help of the example in Section 22.2.2.2, where two experiments were described and bridge principles were used to express the results in vector form:

$$\left(p, r, U(r), s, t, \hat{C}, q, x, W, y, z, C, V\right),$$

where $(p, q) \in [0, 1]^2$, $(r, s, t, x, y, z) \in [0, 1{,}000]^6$, $U(\cdot) : [0, 1{,}000] \to [0, 1]$, $W(\cdot) : [0, 1{,}000] \to [0, 1]$, $\hat{C}(\cdot) : [0, 1{,}000]^2 \to [0, 1{,}000]$, $C(\cdot) : [0, 1{,}000]^2 \to [0, 1{,}000]$, and $V(\cdot) : [0, 1{,}000] \to [0, 1]$. In principle, the vector (q, x, y, z) can assume any value in the set $[0, 1] \times [0, 1{,}000]^3$, but only a finite number of these values are observed. Consequently, no restrictions are placed on the potential values of the given vector in the modal logic of SEM 1, but it is taken for granted that only a finite number of admissible assignments of values to the vector will be relevant.

For all potential values of the vector (q, x, y, z), it is a fact that

$$\begin{aligned}\Big[\big[\big[\big[[W(x) = q] \wedge [r = x]\big] \wedge \big[p = 0.5 + 4(q - 0.5)^3\big]\big] \wedge [r = 1{,}000p]\big] \\ \supset \big[W(x) = 0.5 + 0.5((x - 500)/500)^{1/3}\big]\Big]\end{aligned} \tag{4}$$

Hence, in the S4 modal-logical framework of SEM 1 one can insist that for any admissible assignment σ of values to the components of (p, r, s, t, q, x, y, z),

$$\sim\Box\sim\big[W(\sigma x) = 0.5 + 0.5((\sigma x - 500)/500)^{1/3}\big]. \tag{5}$$

For all potential values of the vector (q, x, y, z), it is also a fact that

$$\begin{aligned}\big[\big[\big[\big[[V(C(y, z)) = (1/2)V(y) + (1/2)V(z)] \wedge [s = y]\big] \wedge [t = z]\big] \\ \wedge \big[\hat{C}(s, t) = C(y, z)\big]\big] \wedge [\hat{C}(s, t) = (1/2)s + (1/2)t]\big] \\ \supset [V((1/2)y + (1/2)z) = (1/2)V(y) + (1/2)V(z)]\big]\end{aligned} \tag{6}$$

Since this is true for all potential values of the vector (q, x, y, z), one finds that

$$V(y) = y/1{,}000, \; y \in [0, 1{,}000]. \tag{7}$$

But if that is so, then in the S4 modal-logical framework of SEM 1 it must also be true that for all admissible assignments σ of values to the vector (p, r, s, t, q, x, y, z),

$$\sim\Box\sim [V(\sigma y) = \sigma y/1{,}000] \tag{(8}$$

In the present case, the wffs in H supposedly express the logical rendition of Eqs. (1)–(3). It can be seen from (5) and (8) that $W(\cdot)$ and $V(\cdot)$ must satisfy (3) for all admissible assignments σ of values to the components of (p, r, s, t, q, x, y, z) that satisfy

$$C(\sigma y, \sigma z) = \sigma x. \tag{9}$$

Hence, the theory axioms and the bridge principles in the modal-logical rendition of the example in 22.2.2.2 give a scientific explanation of H in the sense of SEM 1.

This explanation of H is obviously logically adequate. To ascertain that it is also empirically adequate, one must check to see if the logical consequences of $\Gamma_t(\sigma a_t)$, $\Gamma_p(\sigma a_p)$, and $\Gamma_{t,p}(\sigma a)$ are valid in the Real World for all admissible assignments σ of values to the components of (p, r, s, t, q, x, y, z). For example, for all potential values of the components of (q, x, y, z), it is a fact that

$$\begin{aligned}[][[[[[[V(C(y,z)) = (1/2)V(y) + (1/2)V(z)] \wedge [s = y]] \wedge [t = z]] \\ \wedge \left[\hat{C}(s,t) = C(y,z)\right]\right] \wedge \left[\hat{C}(s,t) = (1/2)s + (1/2)t\right]\right] \\ \supset [C(y,z) = (1/2)y + (1/2)z]\Big]\end{aligned} \tag{10}$$

Hence, it must also be a fact that, for all admissible assignments σ of values to the components of (p, r, s, t, q, x, y, z),

$$\sim\Box\sim [C(\sigma y, \sigma z) = (1/2)\sigma y + (1/2)\sigma z] \tag{11}$$

One must check whether $\xi_e([C(\sigma y, \sigma z) = (1/2)\sigma y + (1/2)\sigma z]) = t$.

22.3.3 A Potential Criticism

Judging from his wonderful book *The Scientific Image*, Bas Van Frassen (1980) would not be satisfied with SE 1 and SEM 1 and their demands for logical and empirical adequacy. He would agree that it is correct to require that the scientific theory on which the explanation is based be empirically relevant in the context in which the explanation is carried out. However, in order that this requirement be meaningful, the description of the "context" must be adequate. Van Frassen would fault my description on two counts: It fails to provide criteria by which one can judge the contextual relevance of the theory and it fails to specify a contrast class for H. These reservations about SE 1 and SEM 1 are interesting, so I take the space here to explain what he has in mind.

First, the contextual relevance of the theory in SE 1 and SEM 1: Van Frassen believes that a person who is asked to explain the occurrence of an event or an observed phenomenon starts by looking for salient features of the cause of the event or salient reasons for the existence of the phenomenon. What appears salient to a given individual depends on his orientation, his interests, and various contextual factors. For example, the cause of a youngster's death might be "multiple hemorrhage" to a physician, "negligence on the part of the driver" to a lawyer, and "a defect in the construction of the brakes" to a car mechanic (Van Frassen, 1980, p. 125). Therefore, the reasons for one theory being chosen instead of another ought to appear in the description of the context in which the given individual carries out his scientific explanation.

Then the required contrast class for H: A *contrast class* for the explanandum is a finite family of assertions $\{H, A, B, \ldots, K\}$ that concern individuals in the data universe and have the property that H and the negations of all the other assertions in the class are logical consequences of the pertinent explanans. Van Frassen believes that the singling out of salient causal factors of an event or salient reasons for a phenomenon depends on the range of contrasting alternatives to the explanandum. For example, it makes a difference in explaining why a given person has paresis whether the contrast class is his brother or the members of his country club, all of whom have a history of untreated syphilis (Van Frassen, 1980, p. 128). By specifying a contrast class, the scientist can communicate to interested parties what question he is out to explain.

There are several interesting aspects of Van Frassen's ideas about contextual relevance and contrast classes that have an important bearing on SE 1 and SEM 1. I note two of them. First, the axioms of the theory in SE 1 and SEM 1 need not constitute more than a small part of the axioms of a complete theory. For example, in Section 22.2.2.2 the axioms of the relevant complete theory are the axioms of von Neumann and Morgenstern's (1953) expected utility theory together with the additional assumption that the utility function is linear. The axioms of the theory universe in that section postulated only the latter assumption. By delineating an appropriate contrast class for H, I can introduce the complete theory, so to say, via the back door. In Section 22.2.2.2, for example, I can insist that the contrast class of H is $\{H, [W(x) = x/1{,}000], [W(x) = V(x)]\}$. Apart from H, this contrast class contains two assertions on which the expected utility theory insists.

Second, in my theory of scientific explanations I have been content with one possible explanation of the explanandum. It is often the case that different scientific theories can be used to provide an explanation of one and the same explanandum. If two different theories can explain a given H, then some of the predictions of one are likely to constitute a contrast class for the other and vice versa. The two contrast classes might provide reasons to prefer one of the explanations over the other. Such uses of contrast classes were met in my discussion of testing one theory against another in Chapter 18.

In concluding this discussion of potential criticisms, I must point out that Van Frassen's (1980, pp. 97–157) pragmatics of scientific explanation is based on an understanding of scientific theories and their empirical relevance that is very different from mine. Hence, chances are good that he might object to aspects of SE 1 and SEM 1 other than the two just noted. The following are paraphrases of two quotes that show how different Van Frassen's idea of a scientific theory and its empirical relevance is from mine. According to Van Frassen (1980, p. 64), a theory is a family of structures, that is, models, that possess empirical substructures to be used for the direct representation of observable phenomena. Science aims to give us theories that are empirically adequate. A theory is empirically adequate if what it says about the observable things and events in this world is true. In different words, a theory is empirically adequate if it has at least one model within which all the actual phenomena fit (Van Frassen, 1980, p. 12).

22.4 CONCLUDING REMARKS

The situation envisaged in SE 1 and SEM 1 is similar to the experimental tests of physical theories that Pierre Duhem described in his book *The Aim and Structure of Physical Theory* (cf. Duhem, 1954, pp.144–147). However, it differs from the situations econometricians usually face when they search for the empirical relevance of economic theories. In SE 1, H is a family of sentences, each one of which has a truth value in every model of (Ω_P, Γ_p) and all of which are true in some model of (Ω_P, Γ_p). In contrast, in econometrics H is often a family of statistical relations. One H might insist that "on the average, families with high incomes save a greater proportion of their incomes than families with low incomes." Another H might claim that "the prices of soybean oil and cottonseed oil vary over time as two cointegrated ARIMA processes." These assertions are about properties of the data-generating process. They need not have a truth value in a model of (Ω_P, Γ_p).

When H is a family of statistical relations, a scientific explanation of H must be based on statistical arguments. Such scientific explanations can be characterized as in SE 2:

statis based Science ?

SE 2 *Let* $(\Omega_{\mathrm{P}}, \Gamma_{\mathrm{p}})$ *be some given data universe; let* $\aleph_{\mathrm{P}}$ *be a* σ*-field of subsets of* Ω_{P}*; let* $\mathrm{P_p}(\cdot) : \aleph_{\mathrm{P}} \rightarrow [0, 1]$ *be a probability measure; and let* FP *denote the joint probability distribution of the components of the vectors in* Ω_{P}*, which, subject to the conditions on which* Γ_{p} *insists, is determined by* $\mathrm{P_p}(\cdot)$*. Also, let* H_1 *and* H_2, *respectively, be a finite family of assertions concerning the characteristics of the vectors in* $\Omega_{\rm P}$ *and the* FP, *and let* $\mathfrak{I}_1$ *and* $\mathfrak{I}_2$, *respectively, be a family of data-admissible models of* $\rm H_1$ *and* $(\Omega_{\rm P}, \Gamma_{\rm p})$ *and of* $\rm H_2$ *and the* FP. *Finally, suppose that* $\mathfrak{I}_1$ *is the intended interpretation of* $\rm H_1$ *and* $(\Omega_{\rm P}, \Gamma_{\rm p})$ *and that* $\mathfrak{I}_2$ *is the intended interpretation of* $\rm H_2$ *and the* FP. *Then, to give a scientific explanation of the pair* $(\rm H_1, H_2)$, *means to find a theory universe* $(\Omega_{\rm T}, \Gamma_{\rm t})$, *a sample space* $\Omega \subset \Omega_{\rm T} \times \Omega_{\rm P}$, *a finite set of bridge principles* $\Gamma_{\rm t,p}$ *that in* Ω *relates members of* $\Omega_{\rm T}$ *to members of* $\Omega_{\rm P}$, *a probability measure* $\rm P(\cdot)$ *on subsets of* Ω, *and an* MPD *that is determined by* $\Gamma_{\rm t}, \Gamma_{\rm p}, \Gamma_{\rm t,p}$, *and the axioms of* $\rm P(\cdot)$ *such that* $\rm H_1$ *becomes a logical consequence of* $\Gamma_{\rm t}, \Gamma_{\rm p}$, *and* $\Gamma_{\rm t,p}$ *and the given* MPD *has the characteristics of* FP *on which* $\rm H_2$ *insists.*

Such an explanation is logically adequate if the pair (H_1, H_2), is not a logical consequence of Γ_p and the axioms of $P_p(\cdot)$. The explanation is empirically adequate if there is a model of $\Gamma_t, \Gamma_{t,p}, \Gamma_p$ and the axioms of $P(\cdot)$ and an associated model of the *MPD* that have the following properties: (1) The logical consequences of $\Gamma_t, \Gamma_{t,p}$, and Γ_p that concern characteristics of the vectors in Ω_P has a model that is a member of $\mathfrak{I}_1$; and (2) there is a member of $\mathfrak{I}_2$ whose associated *FP* shares with the model of *MPD* the characteristics on which the logical consequences of $\Gamma_t, \Gamma_{t,p}, \Gamma_p$, and the axioms of $P(\cdot)$ insist.

It might seem strange that the sample population S plays no role in SE 2. The reason is simple. In SE 2 one imagines that there are data of one of three kinds: (i) Cross-section data, that is, a finite sequence of vectors of observations on different individuals that pertain to some given point in time; (ii) time series of vectors of observations on some individual or some aggregate of individuals; and (iii) panel data, that is, a time series of vectors of observations on more than one individual. For the purposes of the explanation in SE 2 the data are given and so are H_1 and H_2. Hence, in an SE 2 explanation one can work directly with $P(\cdot)$ and $P_p(\cdot)$ without involving $Q(\cdot)$, $\aleph_S$, and S.

I need $Q(\cdot)$, $\aleph_S$, and S when I investigate the empirical adequacy of an SE 2 explanation. The following is one reason why: Since I do not know $\mathfrak{I}_1$ and $\mathfrak{I}_2$, I cannot establish that a given scientific explanation is empirically adequate. The best I can hope for is that I have reason to believe that the likelihood that the explanation is empirically adequate is high. To do that I use data to construct a data-admissible model of the *MPD* and to delineate the contours of a 95 percent confidence band around the parameters of this *MPD*. A large enough family of data-admissible models of the *MPD* whose parameters belong to this confidence band is likely to contain an *MPD* with characteristics shared by some model of the *FP* in $\mathfrak{I}_2$.

It is a difficult task to give logically and empirically adequate SE 2 explanations of regularities in the kind of data I have in mind for SE 2, so a detailed example is called for. Such an example can be found in Chapter 23, where

Heather Anderson, Geir Storvik, and I give an SE 2 explanation of regularities in the behavior over time of Treasury bill yields that A. Hall, H. Anderson, and C. L. M. Granger (HAG) discovered (cf. Hall et al., 1992).

NOTES

1. Most of the material in this chapter is based on ideas that I published in two articles, "Theory-Data Confrontations in Economics" and "Scientific Explanation in Econometrics." The former appeared in a 1995 issue of *Dialogue: The Canadian Philosophical Review* and the latter in the 1998 Ragnar Frisch Centennial Symposium, *Econometrics and Economic Theory in the 20th Century*.

2. Originally, Hempel (1965, p. 248) insisted that the "sentences constituting the explanans must be true."

3. For a different account of the applicability of Hempel's DNS in the social sciences I refer the reader to Merrilee H. Salmon's interesting article, "Explanation in the Social Sciences" (Kitcher and Salmon, 1989, pp. 384–409).

4. I borrowed this example from Van Frassen (1980, p.106).

5. I borrowed the idea of this example from Jon Elster, who cited (Wagenaar, 1988, p. 13) as the original source.

6. According to the *representativeness heuristic*, when the outcome A of an experiment is highly representative of the process B from which it originates, then the conditional probability of A given B is to be judged high. According to the *availability heuristic*, the assessed frequency or probability of an event is to increase with the ease with which instances of similar events can be brought to mind.

7. Sometimes the fact that E is valid in the Real World may supply evidential support for the validity of B_1 and B_2 in the Real World. Hempel calls scientific explanations *self-evidencing* when "the occurrence of the explanandum event provides the only evidence, or an indispensable part of the only evidence, available in support of some of the explanans statements (Hempel, 1965, pp. 372–373). One example in point is the intensely jealous man who killed his wife. The murder demonstrated that the man's jealousy had reached a sufficiently high intensity for him to kill his wife (Scriven, 1959, pp. 468–469, and Hempel, 1965, p. 371).

8. The ideas for this example come from Stigum (1995, pp. 595–597).

9. The sample space consists of all pairs (ω_1, ω_2) that satisfy the predicate $[[\Omega_T \wedge \Omega_p] \wedge \Omega]$.

REFERENCES

Allais, M., 1979, "The So-called Allais Paradox and Rational Decisions under Uncertainty," in: *Expected Utility Hypothesis and the Allais Paradox*, M. Allais and O. Hagen (eds.), Boston: Reidel.

Duhem, P., 1954, *The Aim and Structure of Physical Theory*, P. P. Wiener (trans.), Princeton: Princeton University Press.

Elster, J., 1994, "A Plea for Mechanisms," Unpublished Manuscript, Oslo.

Hall, A. D., H. Anderson, and C. W. J. Granger, 1992, "A Cointegration Analysis of Treasury Bill Yields," *The Review of Economics and Statistics* 74, 116–126.

Hempel, C. G., 1965, *Aspects of Scientific Explanation and Other Essays in the Philosophy of Science,* New York: The Free Press.

Hicks, J. R., 1937, "Mr. Keynes and the 'Classics': A Suggested Interpretation," *Econometrica* 5, 147–159.

Kahnemann, D. and A. Tversky, 1972, "Subjective Probability: A Judgement of Representativeness," *Cognitive Psychology* 3, 430–454.

Kahnemann, D. and A. Tversky, 1973, "Availability: A Heuristic for Judging Frequency and Probability," *Cognitive Psychology* 4, 207–232.

Kitcher, P., and W. C. Salmon (eds.), 1989, *Scientific Explanation*, Minnesota Studies in the Philosophy of Science, Vol. XIII, Minneapolis: University of Minnesota Press.

Nagel, E., 1961, *The Structure of Science*, New York: Harcourt Brace.

Salmon, M. H., 1989, "Explanation in the Social Sciences," in *Scientific Explanation*, P. Kitcher and W. C. Salmon (eds.), Minneapolis: University of Minnesota Press.

Salmon, W. C., 1989, "Four Decades of Scientific Explanation," in *Scientific Explanation*, P. Kitcher and W. C. Salmon (eds.), Minneapolis: University of Minnesota Press.

Scriven, M., 1959, "Truisms as the Grounds for Historical Explanations," in P. Gardiner (ed.), *Theories of History*, New York: The Free Press.

Stigum, B. P., 1990, *Toward a Formal Science of Economics*, Cambridge: MIT Press.

Stigum, B. P., 1995, "Theory-Data Confrontations in Economics," in: *Dialogue: Canadian Philosophical Review* 34, 581–604.

Toulmin, S., 1953, *The Philosophy of Science: An Introduction*, New York: Harper & Row.

Vaillant, G., 1983, *The Natural History of Alcoholism*, Cambridge: Harvard University Press.

Van Frassen, B., 1980, *The Scientific Image*, Oxford: Clarendon Press.

Von Neumann, J., and O. Morgenstern, 1953, *Theory of Games and Economic Behavior*, Princeton: Princeton University Press.

Wagenaar, W. A., 1988, *Paradoxes of Gambling Behaviour*, Hove and London: Erlbaum.

Chapter Twenty-Three

Scientific Explanation in Econometrics: A Case Study

Heather M. Anderson, Bernt P. Stigum, and Geir Olve Storvik

In this chapter we give a scientific explanation of regularities in the behavior over time of U.S. Treasury bill yields that A. Hall, H. Anderson, and C. W. J. Granger (HAG) discovered (cf. Hall et al. 1992). The kind of scientific explanation that we have in mind was described in SE 2 in Chapter 22. For ease of reference we state SE 2 once more here.

SE 2 *Let* (Ω_P, Γ_p) *be some given data universe; let* $\aleph_P$ *be a* σ*-field of subsets of* Ω_P*; let* $P_p(\cdot) : \aleph_P \to [0, 1]$ *be a probability measure; and let* FP *denote the joint probability distribution of the components of the vectors in* Ω_P *which, subject to the conditions on which* Γ_p *insists is determined by* $P_p(\cdot)$*. Also, let* H_1 *and* H_2*, respectively, be a finite family of assertions concerning the characteristics of the vectors in* Ω_P *and the* FP*, and let* $\Im_1$ *and* $\Im_2$*, respectively, be a family of data-admissible models of* H_1 *and* (Ω_P, Γ_p) *and of* H_2 *and the* FP*. Finally, suppose that* $\Im_1$ *is the intended interpretation of* H_1 *and* (Ω_P, Γ_p) *and that* $\Im_2$ *is the intended interpretation of* H_2 *and the* FP*. Then, to give a scientific explanation of the pair* (H_1, H_2) *means to find a theory universe* (Ω_T, Γ_t)*, a sample space,* $\Omega \subset \Omega_T \times \Omega_P$*, a finite set of bridge principles* $\Gamma_{t,p}$*, that in* Ω *relates members of* Ω_T *to members of* Ω_P*, a probability measure* $P(\cdot)$ *on subsets of* Ω*, and an* MPD *that is determined by* Γ_t*,* Γ_p*,* $\Gamma_{t,p}$*, and the axioms of* $P(\cdot)$ *such that* H_1 *becomes a logical consequence of* Γ_t*,* Γ_p*, and* $\Gamma_{t,p}$*, and such that the given* MPD *has the characteristics of* FP *on which* H_2 *insists.*

An SE 2 explanation is logically adequate if the pair (H_1, H_2) is not a logical consequence of Γ_p and the axioms of $P_p(\cdot)$. The explanation is empirically adequate if there is a model of Γ_t, $\Gamma_{t,p}$, Γ_p, and the axioms of $P(\cdot)$ and an associated model of the *MPD* that have the following properties: (1) The logical consequences of Γ_t, $\Gamma_{t,p}$, and Γ_p that concern characteristics of the vectors in Ω_P has a model that is a member of $\Im_1$; and (2) there is a member of $\Im_2$ whose associated *FP* shares with the model of *MPD* the characteristics on which the logical consequences of Γ_t, $\Gamma_{t,p}$, Γ_p, and the axioms of $P(\cdot)$ insist.

23.1 ARIMA PROCESSES AND COINTEGRATED ECONOMIC TIME SERIES

Our explanation of HAG's dictum concerns the behavior of an interesting family of nonstationary random processes known as ARIMA. In this section we describe pertinent characteristics of these processes and explain their relevance for the study of cointegrated economic time series. Our main references are Stigum (1975) for the characteristics of ARIMA processes and Banerjee et al. (1993, ch. 5) and Johansen (1995, chs. 3–5) for cointegrated economic time series.

23.1.1 ARIMA Processes and Their Long-Run Behavior

An *autoregressive integrated moving average process* (an ARIMA process) is a family of real-valued random variables $X = \{x(t, \omega) : t \geq -n + 1\}$ on some probability space $[\Omega, \aleph, P(\cdot)]$ that satisfies the following conditions:

1. There exist constants x_t, $-n + 1 \leq t \leq 0$, such that $x(t, \omega) = x_t$, $t = -n + 1, \ldots, 0$, with probability 1.
2. There exists on $[\Omega, \aleph, P(\cdot)]$ a real-valued purely random process $\eta = \{\eta(t, \omega), t = \ldots, -1, 0, 1, \ldots\}$ with mean zero and finite positive variance σ^2_η and two sequences of constants $\{a_k : k = 0, 1, \ldots, n\}$ and $\{\alpha_s : s = \ldots, -1, 0, 1, \ldots\}$ such that $a_0 = \alpha_0 = 1$, $a_n \neq 0$, $\sum_{-\infty<s<\infty} \alpha_s^2 < \infty$ and $\sum_{0\leq k \leq n} a_k x(t - k, \omega) = \sum_{-\infty<s<\infty} \alpha_s \eta(t + s, \omega)$, $t = 1, 2, \ldots$.
3. There exist a positive integer m_0, nonnegative integers m_j, and complex constants z_j, $j = 1, \ldots, m$, such that $|z_j| < 1$ and $\sum_{0\leq k\leq n} a_k z^{n-k} = (z - 1)^{m_0} \prod_{1\leq j \leq m} (z - z_j)^{m_j}$.

In interpreting the definition, note that when $n = 1$ and $\alpha_s = 0$ for $s \neq 0$, then X is a one-dimensional random walk. Note also that George E. P. Box and Gwilym M. Jenkins (1970) in their seminal treatise always assume that $n = m_0$, $\alpha_s = 0$ for $s > 0$, and $|\alpha_s| \leq K\beta^{|s|}$ for some $\beta \in (0, 1)$ and some suitably large constant K.

The definition of an ARIMA process insists that it satisfy a finite-ordered difference equation. In this chapter we are concerned with the long-run behavior of ARIMA processes. Such behavior can be characterized in different ways. We describe one of them in theorem T 2 and another in theorem T 4. To state these theorems succinctly we need an auxiliary result, T 1.

T 1 *Suppose that* $\{x(t, \omega) : t \geq -n + 1\}$ *is an ARIMA process and that* $\{\eta(t, \omega) : t = \ldots, -1, 01, \ldots\}$ *is the associated* η*-process. Also, let* $y(t, \omega) = \sum_{-\infty<s<\infty} \alpha_s \eta(t + s, \omega)$, $t = 1, 2, \ldots$ *Then there is a function* $\varphi(\cdot)$ *and a sequence of real constants* γ_s *such that:*

1. $\gamma_0 = 1$, $\sum_{0\le k\le v} a_k\gamma_{v-k} = 0$, $v = 1, \ldots, n-1$, and $\sum_{0\le k\le n} a_k\gamma_{v-k} = 0$, $v = n, n+1, \ldots$.
2. $\varphi(t) = x_t$, $t = -n+1, \ldots, 0$, $\sum_{0\le k\le n} a_k\varphi(t-k) = 0$, $t = 1, 2, \ldots$.
3. $x(t,\omega) = \varphi(t) + \sum_{0\le s\le t-1} \gamma_s y(t-s,\omega)$.

From T 1 it follows that there are pairs of constants $(C_{jk}, \hat{C}_{jk})$, $j = 1, \ldots, m$; $k = 0, \ldots, m_j - 1$, and $(D_k, \check{D}_k)$, $k = 0, \ldots, m_0 - 1$, such that

$$D_{m_0-1} \neq 0,$$

$$\gamma_s = \sum_{1\le j\le m} \sum_{0\le k\le m_j-1} C_{jk}\left(s^k z_j^s\right) + \sum_{0\le k\le m_0-1} D_k s^k,\ s = 0, 1, \ldots$$

and

$$\varphi(t) = \sum_{1\le j\le m} \sum_{0\le k\le m_j-1} \hat{C}_{jk}\left(t^k z_j^t\right) + \sum_{0\le k\le m_0-1} \check{D}_k t^k,\ t = 0, 1, \ldots.$$

This characterization of an ARIMA process plays a pivotal role in both the statements and the proofs of T 2 and T 4.

In the statement of T 2, we refer to a constant ϑ and a function $f_y(\cdot)$, which are defined as follows:

$$f_y(\lambda) = \left| \sum_{-\infty<s<\infty} \alpha_s e^{-is\lambda} \right|^2 \sigma_\eta^2,\ \lambda \in [-\pi, \pi) \tag{1}$$

and

$$\vartheta = f_y(0) D_{m_0-1}^2 \big/ (2m_0 - 1). \tag{2}$$

T 2 *Suppose that* $\{x(t,\omega) : t \ge -n+1\}$ *is an ARIMA process and let* $\eta = \{\eta(t,\omega) : -\infty < t < \infty\}$ *be the associated* η*-process. Also let* $\{y(t,\omega) : t \ge 1\}$, $f_y(\cdot)$, *and* ϑ *be as defined in T 1 and Eqs. (1) and (2). Finally, assume that* $0 < \left|\sum_{-\infty<s<\infty} \alpha_s\right|$, *and that* $f_y(\cdot)$ *is piecewise continuous on* $[-\pi, \pi)$ *and continuous in a neighborhood of* $\lambda = 0$. *Then, for all* $z \in R$, $\lim_{t\to\infty} P[x(t)\vartheta^{-1}t^{-(m_0-1/2)} < z] = \lim_{t\to\infty} P[(x(t) - \varphi(t))\vartheta^{-1}t^{-(m_0-1/2)} < z] = (2\pi)^{-1/2} \int_{-\infty<u<z} \exp(-u^2/2)du$.

A formal proof of the theorem can be found in Stigum (1975, p. 327).

The long-run behavior of an ARIMA process can also be characterized by the length of time it tends to spend above its trend line φ. To describe this characteristic precisely, we must first establish the existence of a family of generalized Wiener measures on a space of real-valued functions on the unit interval, and we do that in theorem T 3. In the statement of the theorem, $D([0, 1])$ is the set of functions on $[0, 1]$ to R that are right-continuous and have left-hand limits. Further, $\mathfrak{R}$ is the smallest σ-field of subsets of $D([0, 1])$ that contains all sets that are open in the *Skorohod topology*. An analysis of the

Skorohod topology and a detailed proof of T 3 can be found, respectively, in Parthasarathy (1967, pp. 231–248) and Stigum (1975, pp. 327–330).

T 3 *For each* $q = 0, 1, \ldots$ *there exists a probability measure* $W_q(\cdot)$ *on* $[D([0,1]), \mathfrak{R}]$ *with the following properties:*

1. *For each* $\tau \in (0, 1]$ *and* $\alpha \in (-\infty, \infty)$,

$$W_q(\{x \in D([0,1]) : x(\tau) < \alpha\}) = (2\pi\tau^{2q+1})^{-1/2} \int_{-\infty<u<\alpha} \exp\left[(-1/2)u^2\tau^{-(2q+1)}\right] du,$$

and, for $\tau = 0$,

$$W_q(\{x \in D([0,1]) : x(0) = 0\}) = 1.$$

2. *For each finite* m*-tuple* $(\tau_1, \ldots, \tau_m)$ *such that* $0 \le \tau_1 < \ldots < \tau_m \le 1$, *the vector* $[x(\tau_1), \ldots, x(\tau_m)]$ *is normally distributed with mean zero and covariance matrix* $\Gamma(\tau_1, \ldots, \tau_m) = \{\mu(\tau_i, \tau_j)\}_{1 \le i,j \le m}$, *where, for* $k = \min\{i, j\}$ *and* $p = \max\{i, j\}$,

$$\mu(\tau_i, \tau_j) = (2q+1)\tau_k^{q+1} \sum_{0 \le u \le q} \binom{q}{u} (\tau_p - \tau_k)^u \tau_k^{q-u} (2q+1-u)^{-1}$$

3. *Under* $W_q(\cdot)$, *the random process* $\{x(\tau) : \tau \in [0,1]\}$, *is continuous with pr. 1. Also,* $W_0(\cdot)$ *is an extension of the ordinary Wiener measure to* $[D([0,1], \mathfrak{R}]$.

So much for $W_q(\cdot)$. Next we deal with the second theorem concerning the long-run behavior of an ARIMA process, T 4. In the statement of T 4 we make use of two functions, $\Psi(\cdot)$ and $h(\cdot)$, that we define as follows:

$$\Psi(s) = \begin{cases} 1 \text{ if } s > 0 \\ 0 \text{ otherwise} \end{cases} \tag{3}$$

$$h(x) = \int_{\{\tau \in [0,1] : x(\tau) > 0\}} d\tau, \; x \in D([0,1]). \tag{4}$$

T 4 *Let* $\{x(t, \omega) : t \ge -n+1\}$ *be an ARIMA process that satisfies the conditions of T 2, and suppose that the associated* η*-process has finite fourth-order moments. Moreover let* $\Psi(\cdot)$ *and* $h(\cdot)$ *be as defined in Eqs. (3) and (4), and let* $N_T = \sum_{1 \le t \le T} \Psi[x(t) - \varphi(t)]$, $T = 1, 2, \ldots$.

Then

$$\lim_{T\to\infty} P(\{\omega \in \Omega : N_T/T < \beta\}) = W_{m_0-1}(\{x \in D([0,1]) : h(x) < \beta\}),$$

where β *ranges over the set of continuity points of the distribution of* $h(\cdot)$ *under* $W_{m_0-1}(\cdot)$. *When* $m_0 = 1$,

$$W_{m_0-1}(\{x \in D([0,1]) : h(x) < \beta\}) = (2/\pi) \text{ arc } \sin \beta^{1/2}, \beta \in [0,1].$$

A formal proof of T 4 can be found in Stigum (1975, pp. 336–340). The theorem is interesting in the context of this chapter both because of the way it characterizes the long-run behavior of an ARIMA process and, as we shall see, because of the bearing it has on the way we model the behavior of yields in the money market in our explanation of HAG's dictum. When $m_0 = 1$, T 4 implies that the chances are one in ten that $x(t)$ will be larger than $\varphi(t)$ for more than 97.6 percent of the time and one in five that $x(t)$ will be larger than $\varphi(t)$ for at least 90.5 percent of the time. Similar estimates hold for the likelihood that $x(t)$ will be less than $\varphi(t)$ (Feller, 1957, p. 81). We have not been able to derive the distribution of $h(\cdot)$ under $W_{m_0-1}(\cdot)$ when $m_0 > 1$. However, the results of the simulation experiment in E 33.2 of B. P. Stigum (1990) for a case when $m_0 = 2$ and the fact that the times between crossings tend to be much longer when $m_0 > 1$ than when $m_0 = 1$ suggest that the probabilities of the two given events are higher for $m_0 = 2$ than for $m_0 = 1$.

23.1.2 Cointegrated Economic Time Series

Their characteristics notwithstanding, ARIMA processes and their continuous analogues have been used successfully to study such varied matters as the behavior of prices in the stock market (Cootner, 1964) and the use of feedforward-feedback control systems in chemical engineering (Box and Jenkins, 1970, ch. 12). Until Clive Granger (1981) launched the idea of cointegrated time series, most of these applications concerned the behavior of univariate processes. However, with Granger's ideas and the statistical methods of Søren Johansen (1995), Peter C. B. Phillips (1991), James H. Stock and Mark W. Watson (1993), and many others, the study of multivariate ARIMA processes and their applications to economic time series have experienced a remarkable development. We next discuss those aspects of Granger's ideas that are relevant for our study of cointegrated bond markets.

We need not record here the appropriate multivariate modification of the definition of univariate ARIMA processes. It suffices to describe the most general form of such processes that is relevant for our particular case study. Let $X = \{x(t,\omega) : t \geq -n+1\}$ be a p-dimensional real-vector-valued ARIMA process. There exist constant vectors $x_t, t = -n+1, \ldots, 0$, such that $x(t,\omega) = x_t$ with probability 1 for $t = -n+1, \ldots, 0$. There also exists a sequence of $p \times p$ matrices $A_k, k = 1, \ldots, n$, and a wide-sense stationary p-vector-valued process $\eta = \{\eta(t,\omega) : -\infty < t < \infty\}$ such that, with I_p denoting the p-dimensional identity matrix,

$$A_0 = I_p, A_n \neq 0, \text{ and } \sum_{1 \geq k \leq n} A_k x(t-k,\omega) = \eta(t,\omega), t = 1, 2, \ldots. \quad (5)$$

Finally, let z be a complex-valued variable, let $A(z) = \sum_{1 \leq k \leq n} A_k z^{n-k}$, and let $|A(z)|$ denote the determinant of $A(z)$. Then $|A(z)| = 0$ only if $z = 1$ or $|z| < 1$.

In econometrics the η-process is usually taken to be a purely random one. We have not insisted on that since in our case study η is a moving-average process. The nonrandomness of η required that we rewrite the model in a state-space formulation (Harvey, 1989) and use numerical optimization to estimate the parameters of the ARIMA process. These methods are of interest in themselves.

There is no doubt that Granger's vision of cointegrated time series was a marvelous idea. Time series of observations on univariate ARIMA processes look pretty wild. Therefore, if the behavior of related economic variables can be modeled by a multivariate ARIMA process, there must be some underlying force that keeps them together. Otherwise the corresponding time series would look as though they were flying apart. Now, linear combinations of economic variables often behave as if they were generated by wide-sense stationary processes. Thus there might exist economically relevant multivariate ARIMA processes with variables some linear combinations of which that are wide-sense stationary. Granger discovered such processes and called the time series they generated *cointegrated*. He also found that the error-correction models of J. D. Sargan (1964) generated cointegrated time series. That gave him the idea that cointegrated economic variables move around a common stochastic trend.

The following is an example to indicate the kind of ideas that might have run through Granger's mind.[1]

E 23.1 *Suppose that* $\mathrm{X} = \{\mathrm{x}(\mathrm{t}, \omega) : \mathrm{t} \geq -1\}$ *is a two-dimensional ARIMA process with a purely random* η*-process and matrixes* $\mathrm{A}_0 = \mathrm{I}_2$ *and* $\mathrm{A}_1 = \{\mathrm{a}_{ij}\}_{1 \leq i,j \leq 2}$, *where* $\mathrm{a}_{11} = -0.6$, $\mathrm{a}_{12} = -0.8$, $\mathrm{a}_{21} = -0.1$, *and* $\mathrm{a}_{22} = -0.8$. *Then*

$$x(t, \omega) + A_1 x(t-1, \omega) = \eta(t, \omega),\ t = 1, 2, \ldots \tag{6}$$

and $|\mathrm{A(z)}| = (1 - 0.4\mathrm{z})(1 - \mathrm{z})$. *With* $\alpha' = (-0.4, 0.1)$ *and* $\beta' = (1, -2)$, *we can show that*

$$\Delta x(t, \omega) = (\alpha\beta')x(t-1, \omega) + \eta(t, \omega),\ t = 1, 2, \ldots, \tag{7}$$

$$x_1(t, \omega) - 2x_2(t, \omega) = 0.4\,[x_1(t-1, \omega) - 2x_2(t-1, \omega)] + \left[\eta_1(t, \omega) - 2\eta_2(t, \omega)\right],\ t \geq 1 \tag{8}$$

and

$$\Delta x(t, \omega) = \alpha\,[x_1(t-1, \omega) - 2x_2(t-1, \omega)] + \eta(t, \omega),\ t \geq 2. \tag{9}$$

X *is a solution to the stochastic difference equation in (6) and (7)–(9) describe properties that such a solution might have. Equation (7) suggests that* $\Delta\mathrm{x}(\mathrm{t}, \omega)$ *might be wide-sense stationary if* $\beta'\mathrm{x}(\mathrm{t}, \omega)$ *is wide-sense stationary.*

Equation (8) indicates that $\beta' x(t, \omega)$ *could be a wide-sense stationary solution to a stochastic difference equation. Finally, the error-correction form that* X *satisfies, that is, Eq. (9), suggests that the components of* X *must be in an equilibrium configuration when* $x_1(t, \omega) = 2x_2(t, \omega)$. *If so, the associated common trend (CTR) will satisfy the equation*

$$\mathrm{CTR}(t, \omega) = k(1, 4) \sum_{0 \le s \le t} \eta(s, \omega),\ t = 1, 2, \ldots,$$

where k *is any nonzero number in* R.[2]

We summarize Granger's ideas in the form of a theorem, T 5, that is a paraphrase of theorem 4.2 in Johansen (1995, p. 49). For that purpose we have to introduce several new terms. First, we note that an ARIMA process is integrated of order zero [$I(0)$] or one [$I(1)$] depending on whether $x(t)$ or $\Delta x(t)$ [and not $x(t)$] are wide-sense stationary. We also define Γ_i and π by the equations $\Gamma_i = (A_{i+1} + \ldots + A_k)$, $i = 1, \ldots, k-1$, and $\pi = -I_p - \sum_{1 \le i \le k} A_i$, and rewrite (5), the defining equation of the ARIMA process, as an error-correction model:

$$\Delta x(t, \omega) = \sum_{1 \le i \le k-1} \Gamma_i \Delta x(t-i, \omega) + \pi x(t-1, \omega) + \eta(t, \omega),\ t = 1, 2, \ldots. \quad (10)$$

Finally, for an $I(1)$ process X, we note that X is cointegrated with cointegrating vector $\beta \neq 0$ if $\beta' x(t)$ can be made stationary by a suitable choice for its initial distribution. The cointegrating rank is the number of linearly independent cointegrating vectors, and the space spanned by the cointegrating vectors is the cointegrating space.

T 5 *Consider the* p*-dimensional ARIMA process described earlier, assume that it is integrated of order one, and let* $\Gamma = I_p - \sum_{1 \le i \le k} \Gamma_i$. *Assume also that the* π*-matrix in (10) has rank equal to* r, *where* $r < p$. *Then there exist* $p \times r$ *matrices,* β *and* α, *such that* $\pi = (\alpha\beta')$. *Moreover, a necessary and sufficient condition that* $\Delta x(t)$ *and* $\beta' x(t)$ *can be given initial distributions that will ensure that they become integrated of order zero is that* $\alpha'_\perp \Gamma \beta_\perp$ *has full rank. When* $\alpha'_\perp \Gamma \beta_\perp$ *has full rank, there is a matrix polynomial* $C(\cdot)$ *and an initial vector* $P_{\beta\perp} X_0$ *such that we can represent* x(t) *by (11):*

$$x(t, \omega) = C \sum_{1 \le s \le t} \eta(s, \omega) + C(L)\eta(t, \omega) + P_{\beta\perp} X_0,\ t = 1, 2, \ldots, \quad (11)$$

where $P_\beta = \beta(\beta'\beta)^{-1}\beta'$, $C = \beta_\perp(\alpha'_\perp \Gamma \beta_\perp)^{-1}\alpha'_\perp$, *and* L *is the backward shift operator.*

In the statement of the theorem $\alpha_\perp [\beta_\perp (P_{\beta\perp})]$ is a full-rank matrix such that $(\alpha'\alpha_\perp)\left[(\beta'\beta_\perp), (P'_\beta P_{\beta\perp})\right] = 0(0, 0)$. A proof of the theorem can be found in Johansen (1995, pp. 49–52).

23.2 U.S. TREASURY BILLS AND HAG'S DICTUM

For the purpose of describing what HAG discovered, we consider the relevant part of the U.S. money market to be one in which sellers and buyers meet to determine yields on twenty-one different securities, eleven pure discount bonds that mature in j months, $j = 1, 2, \ldots, 11$, and ten 1-month pure discount bonds that are to be contracted "now" for purchase $j - 1$ months hence, $j = 2, 3, \ldots, 11$. The market opens every day, there are a large number of participants, and no one individual (other than the Treasury) can influence the level of prices in the market by his own actions. The market participants manage through bids and offers to determine the day's equilibrium yields on the various securities.

The equilibrium yields on the twenty-one securities are related. Let $R(j, t)$ be the equilibrium yield at day t of a j-month pure discount bond. Also, let $F(j, t)$ be the equilibrium rate of return from contracting at day t to buy a 1-month pure discount bond $(j - 1)$ months from day t. Then, according to HAG,[3] the $R(j, t)$ and the $F(j, t)$ must satisfy the following equation:

$$R(j, t) = (1/j) \sum_{1 \leq i \leq j} F(i, t),\ j = 1, 2, \ldots, 11. \tag{12}$$

When $j > 1$, the value of $F(j, t)$ need not equal the value of $R(1, \cdot)(j - l)$ months from day t. However, if $\lambda(j, t)$ denotes the expected value of $R(1, \cdot)$ $(j - 1)$ months from day t conditional upon the relevant information at day t, $\Lambda(j, t)$ can be defined by (13) and the $R(j, t)$ must satisfy (14) with $L(j, t) = (1/j) \sum_{1 \leq i \leq j} \Lambda(i, t)$:

$$F(j, t) = \lambda(j, t) + \Lambda(j, t),\ j = 2, \ldots, 11. \tag{13}$$

$$R(j, t) = (1/j) \sum_{1 \leq i \leq j} \lambda(i, t) + L(j, t),\ j = 2, \ldots, 11. \tag{14}$$

Finally, by rearranging the terms in (14), we find that the so-called j-months spreads, $R(j, t) - R(1, t)$, for $j = 2, \ldots, 11$, satisfy

$$R(j, t) - R(1, t) = (1/j) \sum_{1 \leq r \leq (j-1)} \sum_{1 \leq i \leq r} [\lambda(i + 1, t) - \lambda(i, t)] + L(j, t) \tag{15}$$

Equation (15) plays a pivotal role in HAG's analysis of Treasury bill yields. Specifically, HAG assume that the $R(j, t)$ vary with t as if they were realizations of an $I(1)$ process. Moreover, they think it reasonable to assume that the two components on the right-hand side of (15) vary over time as if they were realizations of wide-sense stationary processes. From these assumptions and (15) they deduce that the $R(j, t)$ series for $j = 2, \ldots, 11$ must be cointegrated with the $R(1, t)$ series and that the cointegrating vectors for the vector-valued process $[R(1, t), \ldots, R(11, t)]$ are the ten vectors $(-1, 1, 0, \ldots, 0)$, $(-1, 0,$

$1, 0, \ldots, 0), \ldots$, and $(-1, 0, \ldots, 0, 1)$. In that way they provide an informal scientific explanation of the following two assertions concerning the behavior over time of U.S. Treasury bill yields (Hall et al., 1992, pp. 116–118, 123):

1. Yields to maturity of U.S. Treasury bills are cointegrated $I(1)$ processes.
2. During periods when the Federal Reserve specifically targets short-term interest rates, the spreads between yields of different maturity define the cointegrating vectors.

We use HAG's own arguments to search for a formal scientific explanation of the relationship between U.S. Treasury bill yields that they observed. For that purpose a few preliminary remarks are in order.

The Treasury bill market is part of the money market in the United States. The yields in the money market are interrelated. Consequently, when the relevant positive analogies for the functioning of the Treasury bill market are delineated, one must take into account how the functioning of the remainder of the money market influences the determination of yields in the bill market.

There are many different money market instruments even when they are distinguished just by the name of the issuer and the kind of issue, For example, Treasury versus General Electric, and 3-month bills versus 6-month bills. There are many more when instruments are distinguished by maturity as well. For the purposes of this chapter it is not necessary to take into account this multiplicity of money market instruments. So, to keep the arguments clear and simple, we argue here as if there were just two bills and just one other money market instrument. In due course we show that our arguments' gain in clarity will not come at the expense of loss of insight.

HAG's analysis provided good reasons for believing that yields to maturity of U.S. Treasury bills are cointegrated $I(1)$ processes. However, their theoretical justifications for the claim that the spreads between yields of different maturity define the cointegrating vectors were less convincing. Thus we will impose stronger conditions on the probability distributions of yields in the money market than HAG did.

23.3 COINTEGRATION IN THE U.S. TREASURY BILL MARKET

To provide a formal scientific explanation of HAG's two assertions concerning the behavior over time of U.S. Treasury bill yields, we begin by giving an axiomatic characterization of HAG's data universe.

23.3.1 The Data Universe

The elements in HAG's data universe were series of daily bid and asked quotes on eleven Treasury bills; one series for bills with 1 month to maturity, another for bills with 2 months to maturity, and so on to a series with 11 months to maturity. From these series they obtained eleven nominal yield-to-maturity series, $R(j)$, $j = 1, \ldots, 11$, by taking the average bid and asked quotes of the day as the prices of the respective bills and by insisting that the length of a month be 30.4 days.

HAG's sample consisted of 228 observations on each yield series, dating from January 1970 until December 1988. Our sample consists of 150 observations on the same yields dating from January 1983 until June 1995. Each observed yield pertained to the last trading day of the month and was taken from the Fama Twelve-Month Treasury Bill Term Structure File of the Center for Research in Securities Prices at the University of Chicago.

For the sake of brevity we take the monthly yield series, instead of the bid and asked quotes, to be basic elements in our data universe Ω_P. Further, for the sake of clarity and simplicity, we assume that we have observations only on bills of two different maturities, for example, 3- and 6-month bills or bills that will mature in 1 and 2 months. Since we have monthly observations, we take $\acute{K}(1)$ and $\acute{K}(2)$ to denote series of yields of bills that, respectively, mature in 1 and 2 months. We designate these yields by a $\acute{K}$ instead of an R to avoid confusing them with the R that denotes the set of real numbers.

In addition to our observations on the two Treasury bill yields we have the series of monthly observations on the overnight Federal Funds rate that Anderson used in Chapter 21. Each observation records the weekly effective (annualized) rate on overnight Federal Funds. Data (from 1984 onward) were obtained from the Federal Reserve, and earlier data were obtained from the *Federal Reserve Bulletin*. Further, the weekly data were converted to monthly observations by using the last observation for each month. We denote the series of observations on the Federal Funds rate by *ff*.

With these implicit assumptions, we need only three axioms to characterize the elements in Ω_P. In the intended interpretation of the axioms the $\hat{y}_j$, $j = 1, 2, 3$, are auxiliary series that are needed to delineate the properties of our data, and the numbers in N are taken to denote consecutive "months" beginning at some arbitrary point in time.

D 1 $\omega_P \in \Omega_P$ *only if* $\omega_P = [\acute{K}(1), \acute{K}(2), \mathrm{ff}, \hat{y}_1, \hat{y}_2, \hat{y}_3]$, *where* $\acute{K}(j) \in (R_+)^N, j = 1, 2, \mathrm{ff} \in (R_+)^N, \hat{y}_j \in (R)^N, j = 1, 2, 3,$ *and* $N = \{0, 1, 2, \ldots\}$.

D 2 *For each* $\omega_P \in \Omega_P$ *and all* $t \in N$,

$$\acute{K}(1)_t = \max(\hat{y}_{1t}, 0),\ \acute{K}(2)_t = \max(\hat{y}_{2t}, 0),\ \text{and}\ ff_t = \max(\hat{y}_{3t}, 0), \quad (16)$$

where $\acute{K}(1)_t$, $\hat{y}_{1t}$, $\acute{K}(2)_t$, $\hat{y}_{2t}$, ff_t, $\hat{y}_{3t}$ *denote the* t*th component of* $\acute{K}(1)$, $\hat{y}_1$, $\acute{K}(2)$, $\hat{y}_2$, ff, *and* $\hat{y}_3$.

Instead of thinking of ω_P as a six-tuple of series, we can think of ω_P in Ω_P as a vector-valued function $[\acute{K}(\cdot, \omega_P), ff(\cdot, \omega_p), \hat{y}(\cdot, \omega_P)] : N \to R_+^3 \times R^3$, defined by

$$[\acute{K}(t, \omega_P), \mathit{ff}(t, \omega_P), \hat{y}(t, \omega_P)] = \omega_{Pt}, t \in N, \text{ and } \omega_P \in \Omega_P, \tag{17}$$

where ω_{Pt} is the tth component of ω_P. If we think of the elements of Ω_P in that way, we can state the third axiom concerning the individuals in Ω_P as follows:

D 3 *Let* Ω_P *be as above, and let the vector-valued function* $(\acute{K}, \mathrm{ff}, \hat{y})(\cdot) : N \times \Omega_P \to R^3_+ \times R^3$, *be as described in (17). Also, let* $\aleph_P$ *be the standard Borel field of subsets of* Ω_P. *Then there exists a probability measure* $P_p(\cdot) : \aleph_P \to [0, 1]$ *such that, relative to* $P_p(\cdot)$, *the probability distributions of the family of random vectors* $\{(\acute{K}, \mathrm{ff}, \hat{y})(t, \omega_P); t \in N\}$ *equals the corresponding family of probability distributions of the process that generates the individuals in* Ω_P.

With axioms D 1–D 3 we can formulate the assertion for which we intend to give a scientific explanation:

H *Let* $P_P(\cdot) : \aleph_P \to [0, 1]$ *be the probability measure on whose existence we insisted in D 3. Also, let the vector-valued function* $(\acute{K}, \mathrm{ff}, \hat{y})(\cdot) : N \times \Omega_P \to R^3_+ \times R^3$ *be as described in (17). Then, relative to* $P_p(\cdot)$, *the family of random vectors* $\{(\acute{K}, \mathrm{ff}, \hat{y})(t, \omega_P); t \in N\}$, *satisfies the following conditions:*

1. *For all* $t \in N$, $(\acute{K}, \mathrm{ff})(t, \omega_P) = \max[\hat{y}(t, \omega_P), 0]$ *a.e.*
2. $\{\hat{y}(t, \omega_P); t \in N\}$ *is a vector-valued ARIMA process with one unit root.*
3. *The two first components of* $\{\hat{y}(t, \omega_P); t \in N\}$ *are cointegrated with cointegrating vector* $(-1, 1, 0)$, *that is,* $\{\hat{y}_2(t, \omega_P) - \hat{y}_1(t, \omega_P); t \in N\}$ *is a wide-sense stationary process.*

H does not sound quite like HAG's dictum. However, if we interpret HAG's assertions with their footnote 5 in mind, we must end up with H as stated. In their footnote 5, HAG observe that yields to maturity cannot be integrated processes in the strict sense because nominal yields are bounded below at zero while integrated processes are unbounded.[4]

23.3.2 The Theory Universe

We describe next the theory universe in our scientific explanation of H, and for that six axioms are needed. In the statement of the axioms, with $j = 1, 2$, the $K(j)$, $G(j)$, $\lambda(j)$, and Λ are to be interpreted as the theory universe's series versions of the $R(j, t)$, $F(j, t)$, $\lambda(j, t)$, and $\Lambda(j, t)$ that were dealt with in the earlier discussion of the Treasury bill market, η_j and u_j are series of error terms, and FF is the series of yields to maturity of the one and only non-Treasury bill security in the money market, that is, the "Federal Funds rate" in the theory universe. Finally, $N = \{0, 1, 2, \ldots\}$, and y_1, y_2, and y_3 are auxiliary series whose meanings are determined by the axioms. The members of N are taken to denote consecutive "months" beginning at some arbitrary point in time.

23.3.2.1 The Axioms

B 1 $\omega_T \in \Omega_T$ *only if* $\omega_T \in (R^{16})^N$ *and* $\omega_T = [K(1), K(2), G(1), G(2), FF, \lambda(1), \lambda(2), \Lambda, \eta_1, \eta_2, y_1, y_2, y_3, u_1, u_2, u_3]$.

B 2 *For each* $\omega_T \in \Omega_T$ *and* $t \in N$,

$$K(1)_t = \max(y_{1t}, 0) \text{ and } G(1)_t = K(1)_t, \tag{18}$$

$$y_{2t} = (1/2)\left[y_{1t} + G(2)_t\right], \tag{19}$$

and

$$K(2)_t = \max\left[y_{2t}, G(2)_t, 0\right]. \tag{20}$$

where $K(j)_t$, $G(j)_t$, y_{jt}, *respectively, denote the* t*th component of* $K(j)$, $G(j)$, *and* y_j, $j = 1, 2$.

B 3 *For each* $\omega_T \in \Omega_T$ *and* $t \in N$,

$$G(2)_0 = \lambda(1)_0,\ \Lambda_0 = 0,\ \text{and } G(2)_t = \lambda(1)_t + \Lambda_t,\ \text{for } t \geq 1. \tag{21}$$

where $G(2)_t$, $\lambda(1)_t$, Λ_t, *respectively, denote the* t*th component of* $G(2)$, $\lambda(1)$, *and* Λ.

B 4 *For each* $\omega_T \in \Omega_T$ *and* $t \in N$,

$$y_{1t+1} = \lambda(1)_t + \eta_{1t+1}, \tag{22}$$

and

$$y_{3t+1} = \lambda(2)_t + \eta_{2t+1}. \tag{23}$$

Also, $\eta_{10} = 0, \eta_{20} = 0$*; and there exists a positive pair* $(\acute{y}_1, \acute{y}_3)$ *such that* $y_{10} = \acute{y}_1$, *and* $y_{30} = \acute{y}_3$.

B 5 *For each* $\omega_T \in \Omega_T$ *and all* $t \in N$,

$$FF_t = \max(y_{3t}, 0) \tag{24}$$

B 6 *Let* $\lambda = [\lambda(1), \lambda(2)]$. *There exists a* 2×2 *matrix* $\varphi = (\varphi_{ij})$ *with strictly positive diagonal elements and with largest absolute eigenvalue less than one, such that for each* $\omega_T \in \Omega_T$,

$$\lambda'_0 = \varphi(y_{10}, y_{30})'$$

and

$$\lambda'_t - \lambda'_{t-1} = \varphi\left[(y_{1t}, y_{3t})' - \lambda'_{t-1}\right], t \geq 1. \tag{25}$$

23.3.2.2 The Dynamics of the Market

In our scientific explanation of H the preceding axioms are taken to delineate important positive analogies of the behavior over time of equilibrium yields in the U.S. money market. Some of them, for example, B 2, describe relationships between different yields that must hold because of the possibilities for arbitrage in the market. Others, for example, B 4 and B 6, describe essential features of the dynamics of the money market, as is shown in the following discussion.

The axioms B 2–B 6 have interesting logical consequences. Recall that HAG insisted that the $\lambda(j,t)$ denote the expected value of $R(1,\cdot)(j-1)$ months from day t conditional upon the relevant information at day t. Here, λ_t of B 6 represents the theoretical money market's prediction of the most likely value of $\left[K(1)_{t+1}, FF_{t+1}\right]$ conditional upon the observed values of $[K(1)_s, FF_s]$, $s = 0, 1, \ldots, t$. That such an interpretation of λ_t is a possibility can be inferred from B 2, B 4, B 5, and theorem T 6. The last is a simple logical consequence of B 6.

T 6 *Let* I_2 *be the* 2×2 *identity matrix and* φ *be the* 2×2 *matrix in B 6. Then, for each* $\omega_\mathrm{T} \in \Omega_\mathrm{T}$ *and all* $\mathrm{t} \in \mathrm{N}$,

$$\lambda_t' = \sum_{0 \le s \le t} (I_2 - \varphi)^s \varphi(y_{1t-s}, y_{3t-s})' \tag{26}$$

HAG also claimed that the behavior over time of the yield to maturity on a Treasury bill resembles the behavior of an $I(1)$ process. The possibility of such an interpretation of the pair $[K(1), FF]$ and $K(2)$ can be gathered from B 2, B 5, and the following three theorems.

T 7 *Let* φ *be the* 2×2 *matrix of B 6, and let* $\eta = (\eta_1, \eta_2)'$. *For each* $\omega_\mathrm{T} \in \Omega_\mathrm{T}$, $(\mathrm{y}_{11}, \mathrm{y}_{31})' = \varphi(\mathrm{y}_{10}, \mathrm{y}_{30})' + \eta_1$, *and*

$$(y_{1t+1}, y_{3t+1})' = (y_{1t}, y_{3t})' + \eta_{t+1} - (I - \varphi)\eta_t,\ t \ge 1 \tag{27}$$

T 8 *Let* φ *be the* 2×2 *matrix of B 6, and let* $\xi \in \mathrm{R}$ *be defined by*

$$\xi_0 = 0,\ \xi_1 = (1/2)\left[(1+\varphi_{11})\eta_{11} - (1-\varphi_{11})y_{10} + \varphi_{12}y_{30} + \varphi_{12}\eta_{21} + \Lambda_1\right],$$

and

$$\xi_t = (1/2)\big[(\eta_{1t} - \eta_{1t-1}) + \varphi_{11}(\eta_{1t} + \eta_{1t-1}) + \varphi_{12}(\eta_{2t} + \eta_{2t-1}) + \Lambda_t - \Lambda_{t-1}\big],\ t \ge 2 \tag{28}$$

Then, for each $\omega_\mathrm{T} \in \Omega_\mathrm{T}$,

$$y_{20} = (1/2)\left[(1+\varphi_{11})y_{10} + \varphi_{12}y_{30}\right],$$

and

$$y_{2t} = y_{2t-1} + \xi_t,\ t \ge 1. \tag{29}$$

T 9 *For each* $\omega_\mathrm{T} \in \Omega_\mathrm{T}$ *and all* $\mathrm{t} \in \mathrm{N}$,

$$K(2)_t = \max\left[(1/2)(G(1)_t + G(2)_t, 0\right] \tag{30}$$

Finally HAG insisted that the yields to maturity of Treasury bills are cointegrated and that the spreads between yields of different maturity define the cointegrating vectors. The next theorem establishes the possibility of HAG's dictum being correct in the theory universe, where yields to maturity on Treasury bills might be realizations of cointegrated $I(1)$ processes and the spread between them might determine their cointegrating relationship.

T 10 *Let* φ *be the* 2×2 *matrix of B 6. For each* $\omega_T \in \Omega_T$,

$$y_{20} - y_{10} = (1/2)\left[\Lambda_0 + y_{11} - y_{10} - \eta_{11}\right],$$

and

$$y_{2t} - y_{1t} = (1/2)\left[\Lambda_t - (1 - \varphi_{11})\eta_{1t} + \varphi_{12}\eta_{2t}\right], t \geq 1 \qquad (31)$$

Cointegrated processes have common trends. Looking at the common trend of $y(1)$ and $y(2)$ provides us with new insight into the dynamics of the theory universe's money market. For that purpose, let

$$\mathrm{CTR}_t = (\varphi_{11}, \varphi_{12})\left[(\acute{y}_1, \acute{y}_3)' + \sum_{0 \leq s \leq (t-1)} \eta_{t-1-s}\right]$$

Then it follows from (27), (22), and (21) that

$$y(1)_t = \mathrm{CTR}_t + \eta_{1t},$$

and

$$G(2)_t = \mathrm{CTR}_t + \Lambda_t + (\varphi_{11}, \varphi_{12})\eta_t.$$

But, if that is so, then the equilibrium condition in Eq. (8) implies that

$$y(2)_t = \mathrm{CTR}_t + (1/2)\left[\Lambda_t + \eta_t + (\varphi_{11}, \varphi_{12})\eta_t\right].$$

The equations for y_{1t} and y_{2t} justify referring to CTR_t as the common trend of these variables. In the complete axiom system CTR_t behaves as a generalized random walk.

It is interesting to note here that CTR_t is a function of η_{2t} as well as of η_{1t}. Hence "the other part" of the money market plays an essential role in the construction of the common trend of Treasury bill yields.

It is also interesting to note that the y_1 and y_3 series need not be cointegrated. In the complete axiom system they are cointegrated ARIMA processes if and only if there is a pair of nonzero constants α_1 and α_2 such that $(\alpha_1, \alpha_2)\varphi = 0$. The reason for this is explicated in T 11.

T 11 *Let* φ *be the* 2×2 *matrix of B 6. For each* $\omega_T \in \Omega_T$,

$$(y_{1t+1}, y_{3t+1})' = \varphi(\acute{y}_1, \acute{y}_3)' + \varphi \sum_{0 \leq s \leq (t-1)} \eta_{t-s} + \eta_{t+1},$$

and

$$y_{2t} = (\varphi_{11}, \varphi_{12})\left[(\acute{y}_1, \acute{y}_3)' + \sum_{0 \leq s \leq (t-1)} \eta_{t-1-s}\right] + (1/2)\left[\Lambda_t + \eta_{1t} + (\varphi_{11}, \varphi_{12})\eta_t\right].$$

Since the first component in the equations for y_{2t} is CTR_t, we need only prove the expression for (y_{1t+1}, y_{3t+1}). The proof of that fact goes as follows:

$$\begin{aligned}(y_{1t+1}, y_{3t+1})' &= \lambda_t' + \eta_{t+1}\\ &= \lambda_{t-1}' + \varphi\eta_t + \eta_{t+1}\\ &= \lambda_0' + \varphi \sum_{0\le s\le(t-1)} \eta_{t-s} + \eta_{t+1}\\ &= \varphi(\acute{y}_1, \acute{y}_3)' + \varphi \sum_{0\le s\le(t-1)} \eta_{t-s} + \eta_{t+1}.\end{aligned}$$

If a pair (α_1, α_2) of nonzero constants exists such that $(\alpha_1, \alpha_2)\varphi = 0$, CTR_t or some constant multiple of CTR_t becomes the common trend of y_1 and y_3.

23.3.3 The Bridge Principles

So much for the theory universe. Next we write down the bridge principles of our scientific explanation of H and describe several of the properties of Treasury bill yields in the data universe that can be derived from them and the B axioms. We begin with the bridge principles:

G 1 *The sample space* Ω *is a subset of* $\Omega_T \times \Omega_P$, *that is,* $\Omega \subset \Omega_T \times \Omega_P$.

G 2 *There exists a* 3×3 *matrix,* $\psi = (\psi_{ij})$, *with strictly positive diagonal elements whose largest absolute eigenvalue is less than one, such that for each* $\omega \in \Omega$, $\hat{y}_0 = \acute{y}_0$, $u_0 = 0$, *and*

$$\hat{y}_t - \hat{y}_{t-1} = \psi(y_t - \hat{y}_{t-1}) + u_t,\ t \ge 1, \tag{32}$$

where $\hat{y} = (\hat{y}_1, \hat{y}_2, \hat{y}_3)'$, $y = (y_1, y_2, y_3)'$ *and* $u = (u_1, u_2, u_3)'$.

23.3.4 Characteristic Behavior in the Data Universe

Two interesting theorems from the earlier characterization of the theoretical universe and G 1 and G 2:

T 12 *Let* U *denote the forward shift operator, let* ξ *be as described in Eq. (28), and let* $\zeta = (\zeta_1, \zeta_2, \zeta_3) \in (R^3)^N$ *be defined for arbitrary* t *by*

$$\begin{aligned}\zeta_{1t} = u_{1t} - u_{1t-1} &+ \psi_{11}\left[\eta_{1t} - (1-\varphi_{11})\eta_{1t-1} + \varphi_{12}\eta_{2t-1}\right]\\ &+ \psi_{13}\left[\eta_{2t} - (1-\varphi_{22})\eta_{2t-1} + \varphi_{21}\eta_{1t-1}\right] + \psi_{12}\xi_t\end{aligned} \tag{33}$$

$$\begin{aligned}\zeta_{2t} = u_{2t} - u_{2t-1} &+ \psi_{21}\left[\eta_{1t} - (1-\varphi_{11})\eta_{1t-1} + \varphi_{12}\eta_{2t-1}\right]\\ &+ \psi_{23}\left[\eta_{2t} - (1-\varphi_{22})\eta_{2t-1} + \varphi_{21}\eta_{1t-1}\right] + \psi_{22}\xi_t\end{aligned} \tag{34}$$

$$\zeta_{3t} = u_{3t} - u_{3t-1} + \psi_{31}\left[\eta_{1t} - (1-\varphi_{11})\eta_{1t-1} + \varphi_{12}\eta_{2t-1}\right] + \psi_{33}\left[\eta_{2t} - (1-\varphi_{22})\eta_{2t-1} + \varphi_{21}\eta_{1t-1}\right] + \psi_{32}\xi_t \tag{35}$$

For each $\omega \in \Omega$,

$$\hat{y}_0 = \acute{y}_0,$$

$$\left[I - (I-\Psi)U^{-1}\right]\hat{y}_1 = \Psi\begin{pmatrix}\varphi_{11}y_{10} + \varphi_{12}y_{30} + \eta_{11} \\ y_{20} + \Lambda_1\end{pmatrix} + u_1,$$

and

$$\left[I - (I-\psi)U^{-1}\right](I - IU^{-1})\hat{y}_t = \zeta_t, t \geq 2, \tag{36}$$

T 13 *Let* ε_t *be defined by (37) for all* $t \in N - \{0, 1\}$*:*

$$\varepsilon_t = \left[I - (I-\Psi)U^{-1}\right]^{-1}\zeta_t, \tag{37}$$

where ζ *is as described in (33)–(35). Then, for each* $\omega \in \Omega$ *and all* $t \in N - \{0, 1\}$,

$$\hat{y}_{2t-1} - \hat{y}_{1t-1} = y_{2t} - y_{1t} + (-1, 1, 0)\psi^{-1}(u_t - \varepsilon_t) = (1/2)\left[\Lambda_t - (1-\varphi_{11})\eta_{1t} + \varphi_{12}\eta_{2t}\right] + (-1, 1, 0)\psi^{-1}(u_t - \varepsilon_t) \tag{38}$$

These two theorems and theorems T 7, T 8, and T 10 suggest that the ŷ *and the* y *series might each be realizations of two cointegrated* $I(1)$ *processes with the same cointegrating vector* $(-1, 1, 0)$.

23.3.5 The P Axioms

To establish that the $\hat{y}$ and the y series are in fact realizations of cointegrated $I(1)$ processes we must specify the stochastic properties of the components of ω. These properties can be deduced from the axioms P 1, P 2, and P 3 and from the conditions we delineated in axioms B 2–B 6, D 2, and G 1–G 2.

P 1 *Let the vector-valued function* $(K, G, FF, \lambda, \Lambda, \eta, y, u, \acute{K}, ff, \hat{y})(\cdot) : N \times \Omega \to R^{22}$ *be defined for all* $t \in N$ *by*

$$(K, G, FF, \lambda, \Lambda, \eta, y, u, \acute{K}, ff, \hat{y})(t, \omega) = \omega_t, t \in N, \text{ and } \omega \in \Omega. \tag{39}$$

Let $\aleph$ *be a* σ*-field of subsets of* Ω *and suppose that the functions* $(K, \ldots, \hat{y})(t, \cdot) : \Omega \to R^{22}, t \in N$, *are measurable with respect to* $\aleph$. *There exists a probability measure* $P(\cdot) : \aleph \to [0, 1]$ *relative to which the family of functions* $\{(\Lambda, \eta, u)(t, \omega); t \geq 1\}$ *is a vector-valued wide-sense stationary process.*

P 2 *Let* $P(\cdot) : \aleph \to [0, 1]$ *be as described in P 1. Relative to* $P(\cdot)$, *the families of functions* $\{\eta(t, \omega); t \geq 1\}$ *and* $\{u(t, \omega); t \geq 1\}$ *constitute purely random processes with means zero and covariance matrices* $\sum_\eta$ *and* $\sum_u$.

P 3 *Let* $P(\cdot) : \aleph \rightarrow [0, 1]$ *be as described in P 1, and let the function* $(K, G, FF, \lambda, \Lambda, \eta, y, u, \acute{K}, ff, \hat{y})(\cdot) : N \times \Omega \rightarrow R^{22}$ *be as described in (39). Then, relative to* $P(\cdot)$, *for each* $t \in N - \{0\}$, *the* Λ, η, u, *and* y *components of this family of functions satisfy the following conditions:*

$$E\{\eta(t, \omega) \mid (y_1, y_3)(0), \ldots, (y_1, y_3)(t-1)\} = 0 \text{ a.e.},$$

$$E\{\Lambda(t, \omega) \mid (y_1, y_3)(0), \ldots, (y_1, y_3)(t)\} = \Lambda(t, \omega) \text{ a.e.},$$

and

$$E\{u(t, \omega) \mid (y_1, y_3)(0), \ldots, (y_1, y_3)(t)\} = 0 \text{ a.e.}$$

In reading these axioms there are several things to note: (1) We do not insist that $\sum_\eta$ is diagonal. (2) The family of functions $\{\Lambda(t, \omega); t \geq 0\}$ need not constitute a purely random process. (3) We have only delineated conditions on the Λ, η, u, and y components of $(K, G, FF, \lambda, \Lambda, \eta, y, u, \acute{K}, ff, \hat{y})(\cdot)$. However, from P 1–P 3, the axioms in the theory universe, and the bridge principles, we can derive all the conditions on the components of $(K, G, FF, \lambda, \acute{K}, ff, \hat{y})(\cdot)$ that we need in our scientific explanation of HAG's dictum. (4) The characteristics of the probability distributions of the family of random variables $\{(\acute{K}, ff, \hat{y})(t, \omega); t \geq 0\}$ that we derive from P 1–P 3, B 1–B6, and G 1–G 2 are characteristics of the MPD.

23.3.5.1 The Scientific Explanation

With P 1–P 3 in hand, theorem T 14 below becomes an immediate consequence of B 4, G 2, P 1–P 3, and theorems T 6–T 8 and T 10, T 12, and T 13. Thus there is no need to spell out the details of a proof here. In reading the theorem, note that the random process $\{\hat{y}(t, \omega); t \in N\}$ is defined on $(\Omega, \aleph)$ and not on $(\Omega_P, \aleph_P)$. Hence, H is not an immediate consequence of T 14 and D 2.

T 14 *Let* $P(\cdot) : \aleph \rightarrow [0, 1]$ *be the probability measure in P 1–P 3. Relative to* $P(\cdot)$, *the* λ, y, *and* $\hat{y}$ *components of the family of function* $\{(K, G, FF, \lambda, \Lambda, \eta, y, u, \acute{K}, ff, \hat{y})(t, \omega); t \geq 0\}$ *satisfy the following conditions:*

(i) For all $t \geq 1$, *with* $P(\cdot)$*-probability one,*

$$\lambda(t, \omega) = E\{(y_1, y_3)(t+1) \mid (y_1, y_3)(0), \ldots, (y_1, y_3)(t)\} \tag{40}$$

(ii) For all $t \in N$, $(\acute{K}, ff)(t, \omega) = \max[\hat{y}(t, \omega), 0]$ *a.e.*

(iii) The family of functions $\{y(t, \omega); t \in N\}$ *is an* $I(1)$ *vector-valued ARIMA process, the first two components of which are cointegrated with cointegrating vector* $(-1, 1, 0)$.

(iv) The family of functions $\{\hat{y}(t, \omega); t \in N\}$ *is an* $I(1)$ *vector-valued ARIMA process the first two components of which are cointegrated with cointegrating vector* $(-1, 1, 0)$.

T 14(ii) and T 14(iv) imply that there is an *MPD*, that is, a probability distribution of the family of random vectors on $(\Omega, \aleph)$, $\{(\acute{K}, \mathit{ff}, \hat{y})(t, \omega); t \geq 0\}$, that Γ_t, $\Gamma_{t,p}$, and the axioms of $P(\cdot)$ determine and that satisfies the strictures on which H insists. But if that is so, then standard arguments (cf. Stigum, 1990, pp. 344–347) suffice to establish the existence of a probability measure $\text{þ}(\cdot) : \aleph_P \rightarrow [0, 1]$, relative to which the family of functions $\{(\acute{K}, \mathit{ff}, \hat{y})(t, \omega_P); t \in N\}$, which we defined in Eq. (17), satisfies the conditions of assertion H. To wit: The given *MPD* consists of a family of finite probability distributions of the random vectors in $\{(\acute{K}_t, \mathit{ff}_t, \hat{y}_t); t \in N\}$. These probability distributions determine a probability measure $\text{þ}(\cdot) : \aleph_p \rightarrow [0, 1]$, relative to which the family of functions $\{(\acute{K}, \mathit{ff}, \hat{y})(t, \omega_P); t \in N\}$, satisfies the conditions on which H insists.

The probability measure $\text{þ}(\cdot)$ need not be the same as the probability measure $P_p(\cdot)$ on whose existence we insisted in D 3. However, the probability distributions of the family $\{(\acute{K}, \mathit{ff}, \hat{y})(t, \omega_P) : t \in N\}$ relative to $\text{þ}(\cdot)$ and $P_p(\cdot)$ share the conditions on which H insists. From this and the preceding paragraph it follows that H is true in all models of D 1–D 3, B 1–B 6, G 1–G 2, and P 1–P 3. Since H is true in some, but not all models of D 1–D 3, we conclude that B 1–B 6, G 1–G 2, and P 1–P 3 provide a logically adequate scientific explanation of H.

Taking stock of our formal scientific explanation H so far, calls for several remarks. Note first that we can think of H as a pair (H_1, H_2), where H_1 repeats what is said in D 2 and H_2 comprises the assertions in H. Next, note that the theory universe, the bridge principles, and the axioms of $P(\cdot)$ have many models. The models of the theory universe vary with the values of the pair $(\acute{y}_1, \acute{y}_3)$, in B 4 and the matrix φ in B 6. The models of the bridge principles vary with the values of the vector, $\acute{y}_0$ and the matrix, Ψ, in G 2. And the models of the $P(\cdot)$ axioms vary with the values of the components of the matrices $\sum_\eta$ and $\sum_u$ in P 2. In developing our scientific explanation of H we established its logical adequacy without referring to any of these models. Hence the *MPD* in our explanation comprises a large family of *MPD*s that the models of B 1–B 6, G 1–G2, and the axioms of $P(\cdot)$ determine. When we subsequently set out to establish the empirical adequacy of our explanation, we pick out (estimate), by numerical analysis, one model of the quadruple $(\Gamma_t, \Gamma_p, \Gamma_{t,p}, P(\cdot))$, derive the associated model of the *MPD*, and check whether the explanation of H that the two models provide is empirically adequate. We judge the explanation empirically adequate if there exists a family of models of the *MPD* that with probability 0.95 contains a model whose salient characteristics are shared by some model of the *FP* in $\Im_2$.

23.4 THE EMPIRICAL ADEQUACY

Our scientific explanation of H is logically adequate. Whether it is also empirically adequate remains to be seen. To be reasonably certain of the empirical adequacy of B 1– B 6, G 1–G 2, and P 1–P 3, we must search for a family of data-admissible models of the *MPD*, $\Im$, that with probability 0.95 contains a model whose salient characteristics are shared by FP. Finding an appropriate $\Im$, which we describe next, is a bit of a fishing expedition.

23.4.1 A State-Space Formulation of Eq. (35)

P 1–P 3 do not put stringent conditions on the probability distributions of η, Λ, and u. Thus we begin our search for an appropriate $\Im$ by assuming that η_1, η_2, Λ and the components of u constitute six independently distributed purely random processes. For the sake of argument we also, initially, assume that all these processes are Gaussian.

Next we reformulate the relations in (35) so that they can be expressed by a state-space model. For that purpose we let $v(t) = [u_1(t), u_2(t), u_3(t), \eta_1(t), \eta_2(t), \Lambda(t)]'$ and observe that

$$\zeta(t) = C_0 v(t) - C_1 v(t-1), t = 1, 2, \ldots, \tag{41}$$

with

$$C_0 = \begin{pmatrix} 1 & 0 & 0 & \Psi_{11} + (1/2)\Psi_{12}\left(1+\varphi_{11}\right) & \Psi_{13} + (1/2)\Psi_{12}\varphi_{12} & (1/2)\Psi_{12} \\ 0 & 1 & 0 & \Psi_{21} + (1/2)\Psi_{22}\left(1+\varphi_{11}\right) & \Psi_{23} + (1/2)\Psi_{22}\varphi_{12} & (1/2)\Psi_{22} \\ 0 & 0 & 1 & \Psi_{31} + (1/2)\Psi_{32}\left(1+\varphi_{11}\right) & \Psi_{33} + (1/2)\Psi_{32}\varphi_{12} & (1/2)\Psi_{32} \end{pmatrix},$$

and

$$C_1 = \begin{pmatrix} 1 & 0 & 0 & [\Psi_{11} + (1/2)\Psi_{12}]\left(1-\varphi_{11}\right) - \Psi_{13}\varphi_{21} & -[\Psi_{11} + (1/2)\Psi_{12}]\,\varphi_{12} + \Psi_{13}\left(1-\varphi_{22}\right) & (1/2)\Psi_{12} \\ 0 & 1 & 0 & [\Psi_{21} + (1/2)\Psi_{22}]\left(1-\varphi_{11}\right) - \Psi_{23}\varphi_{21} & -[\Psi_{21} + (1/2)\Psi_{22}]\,\varphi_{12} + \Psi_{23}\left(1-\varphi_{22}\right) & (1/2)\Psi_{22} \\ 0 & 0 & 1 & [\Psi_{31} + (1/2)\Psi_{32}]\left(1-\varphi_{11}\right) - \Psi_{33}\varphi_{21} & -[\Psi_{31} + (1/2)\Psi_{32}]\,\varphi_{12} + \Psi_{33}\left(1-\varphi_{22}\right) & (1/2)\Psi_{32} \end{pmatrix}.$$

Also, we let $A = I_3 - \Psi$, and write (36) as

$$\hat{y}(t) - \hat{y}(t-1) = A\left[\hat{y}(t-1) - \hat{y}(t-2)\right] + C_0 v(t) - C_1 v(t-1) \tag{42}$$

Then with $x(t) = \left[\hat{y}(t)' - \hat{y}(t-1)', v(t)', v(t+1)'\right]'$ the searched for state-space form of (36) becomes:

$$x(t) = \begin{pmatrix} A & -C_1 & C_0 \\ 0 & 0 & I_6 \\ 0 & 0 & 0 \end{pmatrix} x(t-1) + \begin{pmatrix} 0 \\ 0 \\ v(t+1) \end{pmatrix} \tag{43}$$

and

$$\hat{y}(t) = \hat{y}(t-1) + \{I_3 \quad 0 \quad 0\}\, x(t) \tag{44}$$

Equation (43) describes the dynamics of the state vector, while (44) insists that $\hat{y}(t)$ is observed at each time point and that there are no observation errors.

23.4.2 Estimation of Parameters

There are nineteen parameters to be estimated, the nine components of Ψ, the four components of φ, and the six variances of the components of ν. Unfortunately, the likelihoods of the parameter sets

$$\{\sigma_{u1}^2, \sigma_{u2}^2, \sigma_{u3}^2, \sigma_{\wedge}^2\}$$

and

$$\{\sigma_{u1}^2 + (1/4)\Psi_{12}^2\sigma_{\wedge}^2, \sigma_{u2}^2 + (1/4)\Psi_{22}^2\sigma_{\wedge}^2, \sigma_{u3}^2 + (1/4)\Psi_{32}^2\sigma_{\wedge}^2, 0\}$$

are indistinguishable, which shows that we cannot obtain identifiable estimates of all four variances of u and Λ. Since we cannot be certain of the validity of the bridge principles anyway, we decided to assign the value zero to the u-terms in (32) and (36). That left us with sixteen unknown parameters in a new state-space model in which $v(t) = [\eta_1(t), \eta_2(t), \Lambda(t)]'$ and the first three columns of the C_0 and C_1 matrixes are deleted.

To estimate the values of the remaining sixteen parameters we proceeded as follows. We calculated the likelihood of our sample observations with the help of a Kalman filter (Harvey, 1989) and used the resulting likelihood and Powell's method of numerical optimization (Press et al., 1992, p. 412) to search for the parameter values at which the likelihood would attain its maximum height. Powell's method is not fast, but it seemed to give reliable optima.

To obtain uncertainty measures and confidence intervals for our maximum likelihood parameter estimates we used the bootstrapping method (cf. Efron, 1982; Davison and Hinkley, 1997). The main ideas behind the bootstrapping procedure are threefold: (1) Generate a series of artificial data sets by simulation following (almost) the same model as the one that generated the original data set. (2) Estimate the values of the model parameters anew with each one of the simulated data sets. (3) Use the series of parameter estimates obtained from a large number of data sets to determine meaningful measures of the uncertainty that is attached to the original parameter estimates.

In the present case we applied the ideas of bootstrapping in the following way. First, we used the original parameter estimates and the state-space model to obtain estimates of the components of the error term v(t) for all relevant t. Next, we generated new series of error terms by resampling (drawing with replacement) from the estimated time series of $v(t)$. Then we used each new time series of $v(t)$ and the state-space model with the original parameter estimates to construct time series of values of $\hat{y}(t)$, $\hat{y}(t-1)$, and $\hat{y}(t-2)$. Finally, we used each series of the latter variables to estimate the model parameters anew. In that way we obtained a series of parameter values that we could use to construct the uncertainty measures for which we searched. We carried out a total of 1,000 bootstrap simulations.

23.4.3 Table 23.1 and the Empirical Adequacy of the Explanation of HAG's Dictum

Suppose, for now, that our assumptions concerning the probability distributions of η, Λ, and u are correct. This assumption, the estimates of φ, Ψ, $\sum_{\eta}$, and σ^2_Λ that we find in Table 23.1, and arbitrary values of $(\acute{y}_1, \acute{y}_3)$ and $\acute{y}_0$ provide us with a model of the quadruple $(\Gamma_t, \Gamma_p, \Gamma_{t,p}, P(\cdot))$. From this model we can derive a model of the *MPD*.

Here is how: From the estimates in Table 23.1 and Eq. (36) we deduce that

$$\hat{y}(t) - 3.048\hat{y}(t-1) + 3.3614\hat{y}(t-2) - 1.5689\hat{y}(t-3) + 0.2555\hat{y}(t-4) = B(U)\zeta(t),\ t \geq 4 \tag{45}$$

$$\Delta\hat{y}(t) - 2.048\Delta\hat{y}(t-1) + 1.3134\Delta\hat{y}(t-2) - 0.2555\Delta\hat{y}(t-3) = B(U))\zeta(t),\ t \geq 4, \tag{46}$$

and

$$\hat{y}_2(t-1) - \hat{y}_1(t-1) = (1/2)\left[\Lambda_t - 0.213\eta_{1_t} + 0.216\eta_{2_t}\right] - (-1, 1, 0)\Psi^{-1}\epsilon_t, \tag{47}$$

where

$$B(U) = \begin{pmatrix} 1 - 1.652U^{-1} + 0.6675U^{-2} & -0.562U^{-1} + 0.4024U^{-2} & 0.0174U^{-2} \\ -0.012U^{-1} + 0.0133U^{-2} & 1 - 1.112U^{-1} + 0.2835U^{-2} & -0.031U^{-1} + 0.0123U^{-2} \\ -0.15U^{-1} + 0.1415U^{-2} & -0.088U^{-1} + 0.1191U^{-2} & 1 - 1.332U^{-1} + 0.364U^{-2} \end{pmatrix}$$

$$\Psi^{-1} = \begin{pmatrix} 1.527382 & 0.1227996 & -0.8447666 \\ -15.867849 & 17.1085015 & 3.0796806 \\ 1.785835 & -1.8631533 & 3.1552191 \end{pmatrix}$$

and, with $D(U) = \text{Det}(I - AU^{-1}) = 1 - 2.048U^{-1} + 1.3134U^{-2} - 0.2555U^{-3}$,

$$\varepsilon(t) = D(U)^{-1}B(U)\zeta(t).$$

From the estimates in Table 23.1 and Eqs. (36) and (41) we can also deduce that

$$\Delta\hat{y}(t) = A^*\Delta\hat{y}(t-1) + C_0^*(\eta, \Lambda)(t)' - C_1^*(\eta, \Lambda)(t-1)', \tag{48}$$

where

$$A^* = \begin{pmatrix} 0.396 & -0.012 & -0.13 \\ -0.562 & 0.936 & -0.088 \\ 0.01 & -0.031 & 0.716 \end{pmatrix};\ C_0^* = \begin{pmatrix} 0.6147220 & 0.151296 & 0.0060 \\ 0.6191840 & 0.094912 & 0.0320 \\ 0.0176985 & 0.287348 & 0.0155 \end{pmatrix};$$

$$C_1^* = \begin{pmatrix} 0.5032780 & 0.021504 & 0.0320 \\ 0.4668160 & 0.006464 & 0.0320. \\ -0.1998185 & 0.039820 & 0.0155 \end{pmatrix}.$$

TABLE 23.1
Parameter Estimates, Estimates of Bias and Standard Errors, and 95 Percent Confidence Intervals

Parameter	Estimate	Bias	Standard error	95% Confidence Interval	
$\sigma_{\eta,1}$	0.356	−0.179	0.022	0.493	0.577
$\sigma_{\eta,2}$	0.632	−0.446	0.027	1.022	1.128
σ_{Λ}	10.54	−0.779	1.553	8.046	14.119
φ_{11}	0.787	0.003	0.056	0.678	0.899
φ_{12}	0.216	−0.106	0.059	0.208	0.435
φ_{21}	0.68	−0.024	0.076	0.558	0.849
φ_{22}	0.632	−0.049	0.081	0.526	0.837
ψ_{11}	0.604	−0.006	0.016	0.577	0.638
ψ_{12}	0.012	−0.004	0.002	0.012	0.019
ψ_{13}	0.15	0.026	0.01	0.103	0.144
ψ_{21}	0.562	0.005	0.007	0.544	0.57
ψ_{22}	0.064	−0.003	0.002	0.065	0.071
ψ_{23}	0.088	−0.008	0.005	0.087	0.109
ψ_{31}	−0.01	−0.002	0.015	−0.039	0.02
ψ_{32}	0.031	−0.018	0.004	0.042	0.057
ψ_{33}	0.284	−0.016	0.007	0.287	0.313
$\lambda_{1\varphi}$	0.682	−0.085	0.094	0.607	0.976
$\lambda_{2\varphi}$	0.101	−0.03	0.054	0.002	0.199
$\lambda_{1\psi}$	0.825	−0.019	0.02	0.603	0.681
$\lambda_{2\psi}$	0.265	−0.004	0.009	0.253	0.287
$\lambda_{3\psi}$	0.062	−0.001	0.002	0.059	0.068

Note: The confidence intervals were obtained by using the simplest percentile method.

Finally, from Eqs. (28) and (33)–(35) and our assumptions concerning η and Λ, and from the estimates in Table 23.1, we can deduce that the covariance structure of ζ is given by Eqs. (49) and (50).

$$\mathrm{Var}[\zeta(t)] = C_0 \sum C_0' + C_1 \sum C_1' = \begin{pmatrix} 0.154 & 0.154 & 0.026 \\ 0.154 & 0.172 & 0.021 \\ 0.026 & 0.021 & 0.077 \end{pmatrix} \tag{49}$$

and

$$\mathrm{Cov}[\zeta(t), \zeta(t-1)] = -C_0 \sum C_1' = \begin{pmatrix} 0.001 & -0.007 & 0.031 \\ -0.003 & -0.020 & 0.031 \\ 0.0130 & 0.012 & -0.02 \end{pmatrix}, \tag{50}$$

where $\sum = \mathrm{Var}[v(t)] = \mathrm{diag}(0.127, 0.399, 111.092)$.

In looking back at the description of the *MPD* that Eqs. (45)–(50) provide, we note that the characteristic polynomials $P.(z)$ and $P_{\Delta}.(z)$ of Eqs. (45) and (46) are given by (51) and (52), respectively:

$$P_{\hat{y}}(z) = (1 - z)(z - 0.366508)(z - 0.742084)(z - 0.939408) \quad (51)$$

$$P_{\Delta\hat{y}}(z) = (z - 0.366508)(z - 0.742084)(z - 0.939408) \quad (52)$$

Hence, $\Delta\hat{y}(t)$ satisfies the equation of a wide-sense stationary autoregressive moving average process, that is, of an $I(0)$ ARIMA process. Also, $\hat{y}(t)$ satisfies the equation of an $I(1)$ ARIMA process. This and Eq. (47) imply that the $\hat{y}(t)$-process has all the characteristics on which H(ii) and H(iii) insist. Since the components of $\acute{K}(1)$, $\acute{K}(2)$, and ff_t are nonnegative by construction, we see that the *MDP* of the vector $[\acute{K}(t,\cdot), ff(t,\cdot), \hat{y}(t,\cdot)]$ has the characteristics insisted upon by H and, hence, H_2.

Equations (45)–(50) delineate one member of $\Im$, the sought for family of models of the MPD. We obtain other models by varying the values of the components of φ and Ψ and the values of the variances of η and Λ within the relevant confidence bands. There are no restrictions on the values that the variances can assume. However, the φ's and Ψ's must be chosen so that the absolute values of their characteristic roots are less than 1. In describing the contour of $\Im$ we let the limits on the relevant variances equal the estimated 0.95 confidence bands. We use these bands for the φ's and Ψ's and also believe that the associated confidence bands for the characteristic roots that they determine are not too different from the estimated bands. The reason for our belief is that each bootstrap estimate of the characteristic roots is based on the φ and Ψ values of the pertinent sample. Thus the uncertainty measures and the confidence bands for the characteristic roots in Table 23.1 take the relation between the φ and Ψ values and the values of the characteristic roots into account.

23.4.4 The Probability Distributions of η and Λ

If the *MPD* that we have estimated is data admissible, we obtain the sought for family of models of the *MPD* by varying the parameters within their 0.95 percent confidence bands. The *MPD* is data admissible only if the probability distribution of η and Λ satisfy the conditions that we have imposed on them. We next describe the results of various tests of these conditions.

23.4.4.1 Checking for Independence

The Kalman filter provides estimates of the components of $v(t)$ that can be used for model checking. Figure 23.1 shows scatter plots of all combinations of the components of η and Λ. The independence assumption seems to be realistic for these variables.

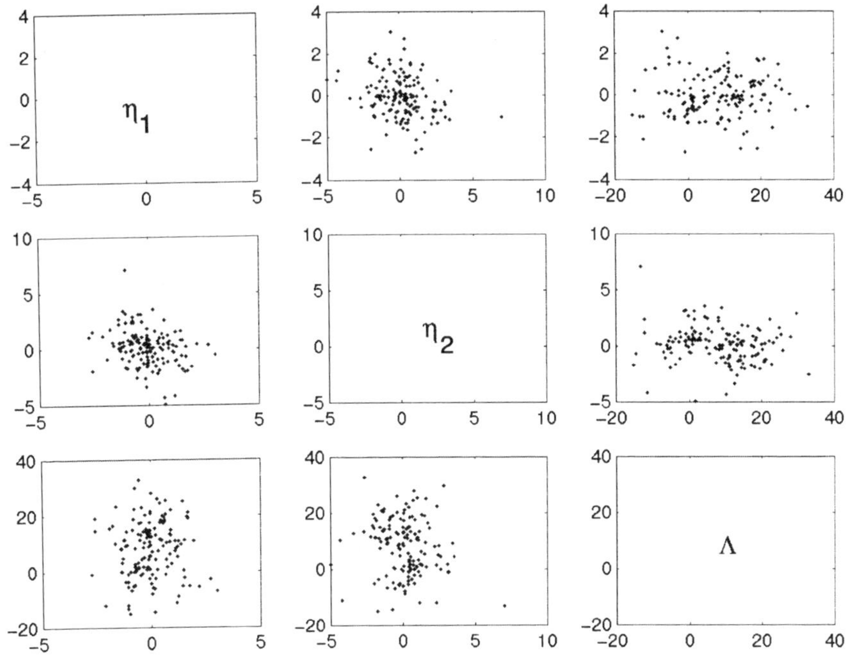

Fig. 23.1 Scatter plots of each pair of random terms calculated from the estimated model by the Kalman filter. The order of random terms on both axes is η_1, η_2, and Λ.

To provide a second check on the independence assumption we also calculated the autocorrelations and the partial autocorrelations of the components of η and Λ. The results are shown in Figs. 23.2 and 23.3. The estimated values of the autocorrelations indicate that independence in time seems reasonable for η_1 and η_2. The small temporal dependence for the latter variable can be blamed on the estimation procedure. Temporal independence for Λ is more suspect. As Fig. 23.3 suggests, an autoregressive model of order two might be a better choice for Λ. This possibility is interesting inasmuch as Λ_t, in contradistinction to the components of η_t, is measurable with respect to the σ-field that the pairs $(y_1, y_3)(0), \ldots, (y_1, y_3)(t)$ generate. However, we do not follow it up with new estimates here.

23.4.4.2 Checking for Normality

Figure 23.4 illustrates *QQ*-plots of the (standardized) values of η and Λ. The plots indicate that a Gaussian distribution is reasonable for η_1 and Λ, whereas there are a couple of outliers in η_2.

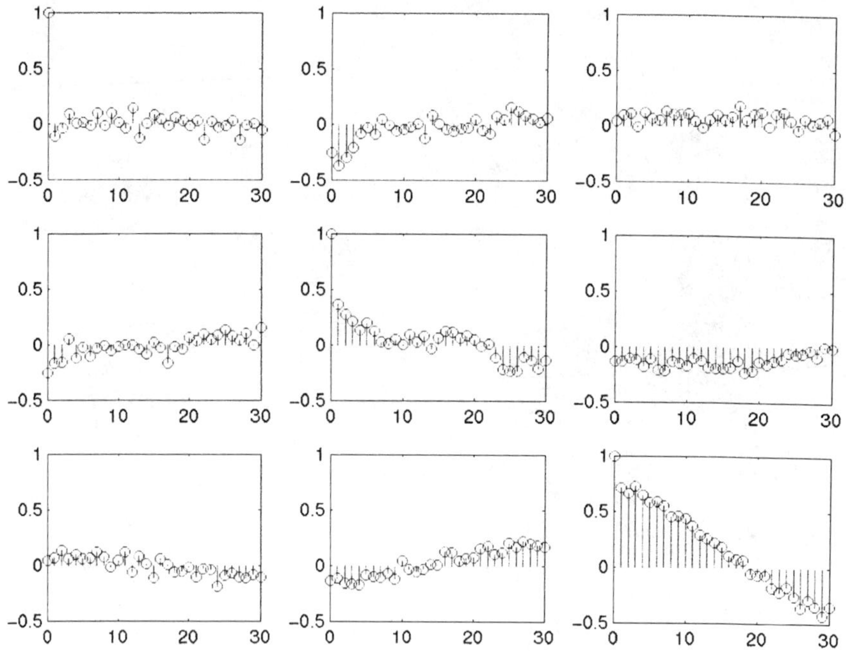

Fig. 23.2 Estimated autocorrelation functions for η_1, η_2, and Λ. The x-axis shows the time lags and the y-axis correlation. The rows pertain to η_1, η_2, and Λ and the columns to η_1, η_2, and Λ in that order.

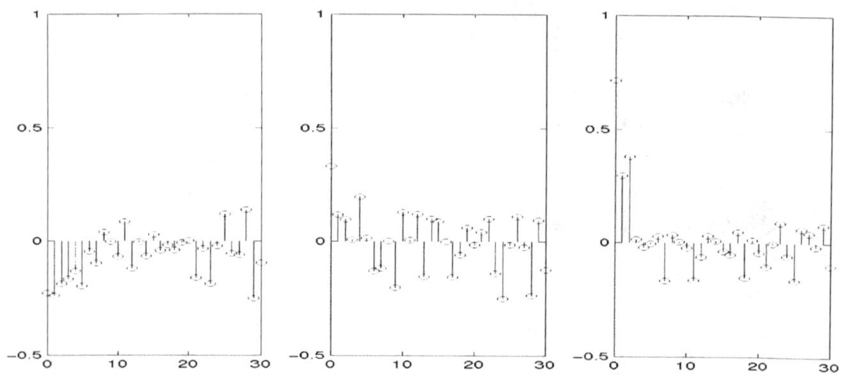

Fig. 23.3 Estimated partial autocorrelation functions for η_1, η_2, and Λ in that order. The x-axis shows the time lags and the y-axis correlation.

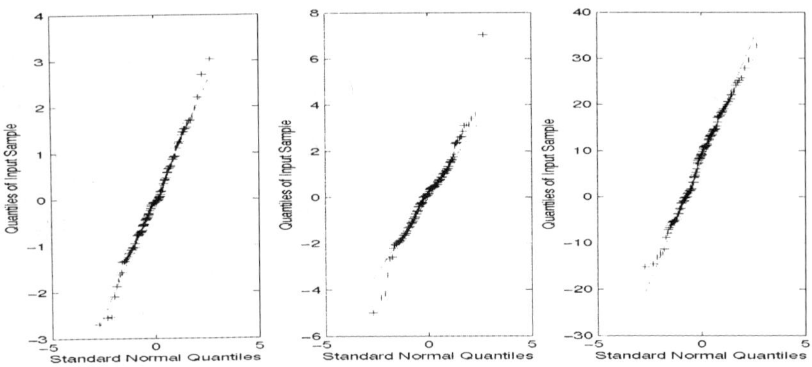

Fig. 23.4 *QQ*-plot of ordered residuals against quantiles in the Gaussian distribution. The order of the variables is η_1, η_2, and Λ.

23.4.5 Summing Up

We noted above that the search for a family of models of the *MPD* and the data universe within which our scientific explanation of HAG's dictum is empirically relevant is like a fishing expedition. In our statistical calculations we assumed that the two η-processes and the Λ-process were independently distributed, purely random Gaussian processes. Our statistical results do not ensure that the Λ-process is purely random and that the η_2-process is Gaussian. Since we did not insist on these characteristics in the $P(\cdot)$ axioms, we ignore this uncertainty and consider this part of our statistical analysis completed.

23.5 THE DATA UNIVERSE AND THE DIMENSION OF THE COINTEGRATION SPACE

Geir's estimates of the components of the φ-matrix and T 11 imply that the y_1 and y_3 processes are not cointegrated in the theory universe. Their aliases seem to be cointegrated in Heather's data universe. Whether they are cointegrated in our data universe is a question that we discuss in this section of the chapter. It is instructive to compare the analysis in Section 23.4 with Heather's analysis in Chapter 21 because the respective results are not entirely consistent. Neither analysis finds evidence against HAG's (1992) dictum [that Treasury bill yields are pairwise cointegrated with a cointegrating vector of $(1, -1)$], but Geir finds no cointegration between his first Treasury bill yield ($\hat{y}_1$) and the yield on Federal Funds ($\hat{y}_3$), whereas Heather cannot reject the null hypothesis that $\hat{y}_1$ and $\hat{y}_3$ are cointegrated with a cointegrating vector of $(-1, 1)$.

Both Geir and Heather use the same data for yields on Treasury bills and Federal Funds [150 monthly observations dating from 1983:1 until 1995:6), but the estimated models relate to different sample periods because different lag structures are employed, and Heather saves several observations for forecast analysis. Geir's model [Eq. (42)] is based on a sample of 148 observations [for 1983:3 until 1995:6). Heather's model is based on a smaller sample of 131 observations (for 1984:2 until 1994:12), but she uses two additional variables, that is, government debt and yields on 5-year Treasury bills in her models, so that her analysis is based on a wider data universe. The different sample periods are unlikely to account for differences between the two authors' conclusions, but it is well known that the dimension of the data set (i.e., the number of variables) and the assumed lag structure can influence cointegration analysis, and these factors may have been relevant here.

Another important difference between the two analyses was that Geir estimates a model that has already been specified, whereas Heather uses the empirical properties of the data to specify her model. In the former case, Geir notes serial correlation and nonnormal residuals in his specified model and then points out that some of the assumptions underlying his analysis are therefore not quite true. In the latter case, Heather uses a sufficiently long lag structure to ensure that her model residuals are serially uncorrelated and impulse dummies to remove the effects of outliers. Outliers (and the use of impulse dummies to reduce their effects) should not affect the asymptotic distribution of cointegration statistics, although they can have profound effects in small samples (see Doornik et al., 1998, for discussion).

Geir checks that his model is consistent with the tenants in HAG'S dictum, but his checks for cointegration are not formal tests, and he does not estimate the cointegration vectors. Heather's analysis (based on Johansen's, 1995, techniques) provides a more direct approach, but given that the effects of dummies and variable dimension on this sort of cointegration analysis are not well known, it is informative to study the robustness of her results with respect to changes in dimension and the use of dummies.

Tables 23.2 and 23.3 provide some analysis that addresses this question of robustness. Two variable systems are studied in Table 23.2, while three are studied in Table 23.3. Each table provides two sets of results, which relate to models that either omit or contain dummies. All models treat the term structure variables as variables with no deterministic trend, and since four lags of (differenced) endogenous variables remove all evidence of serial correlation in the model residuals, all models employ this lag structure. This lag structure leaves an effective sample size of 145 observations for each model (for the period 1983:6–1995:6). When dummies are used, they are chosen so as to remove all evidence of nonnormality in the model residuals.

It is interesting to note that the results of columns 2 and 3 in Table 23.2 (considered together) and the second column of Table 23.3 are very similar.

Monthly

TABLE 23.2
Cointegration Analysis of Two Variable Systems of Term Structure Variables (1983:6–1995:06)

Variables	$\hat{y}_1, \hat{y}_2$	$\hat{y}_1, \hat{y}_3$	$\hat{y}_1, \hat{y}_2$	$\hat{y}_1, \hat{y}_3$
Number of dummies in the VAR	0	0	3	9
Rank of β (tests use 5% critical values)	1	0	1	1
Estimated β (conditional on rank β = 1)	(1, −0.9821)	(1, −0.8764)	(1, −0.9922)	(1, −0.8981)
P-value for test of $H_0: \beta = (1, -1)$	0.1248	0.0649	0.4011	0.0076

In both cases there is clear evidence that $\hat{y}_1$ and $\hat{y}_2$ are cointegrated with cointegrating vector $(1, -1)$, and some (very marginal) support for a claim that $\hat{y}_1$ and $\hat{y}_3$ are as well. The dimension of the system does not seem to change this conclusion. Once we add in the dummies and consider the results of columns 4 and 5 in Table 23.2 (as a unit) and the third column of Table 23.3, it seems clear that there are two cointegrating vectors and that one of them is $(1, -1, 0)\left[\text{for}(\hat{y}_1, \hat{y}_2, \hat{y}_3)'\right]$. Thus HAG's dictum finds further support. However, the second cointegrating vector does not appear to be $(1, 0, -1)$. It seems that the use of dummies weakens the (already weak) support for the claim that the spread between $\hat{y}_1$ and $\hat{y}_3$ is cointegrating.

It is noteworthy that neither the dimension of the system nor the use of dummies has a substantive effect on the cointegration results and that Heather's Table 21.5 (based on a five-variable system with dummies) is consistent with the results for the systems considered here. In Table 21.5 there is no evidence against HAG's dictum and only very weak evidence (at the 9% level of significance) against the claim that the spread between $\hat{y}_1$ and $\hat{y}_3$ is cointegrating. Geir's analysis (based on a three-variable system, without any corrections for nonnormality) does not necessarily disagree with these results. Note that his estimate of φ does not imply any support for the claim that $\hat{y}_1$ and $\hat{y}_3$ are cointegrated, but also note that he does not formally reject the second claim (as one might in a classical hypothesis testing framework). All the models that generated Table 23.2 use four lags of (differenced) endogenous variables and assume no deterministic trend. The residuals in the column 2 and 3 models are not normally distributed (at $< 0.00001\%$ level of significance). The dummies in the column 4 and 5 models ensure that residuals are normally distributed.

All models in Table 23.3 use four lags of (differenced) endogenous variables and assume no deterministic trend. The residuals in the column 2 models are

TABLE 23.3
Cointegration Analysis of ($\hat{y}_1$, $\hat{y}_2$, $\hat{y}_3$) (1983:6–1995:06)

Variables	Model without dummies	Model with dummies
Number of dummies in the VAR	0	8
Rank of β (tests use 5% critical values)	1	2
Estimated β (conditional on rank β = 1)	(1, −1.0889, 0.0960)	(1, −0.8243, 0.1201)
P-value for test of H_0 : β = (1, −1, 0) (conditional on rank β = 1)	0.1529	0.1137
P-value for test of H_0 : β = (1, 0, −1) (conditional on rank β = 1)	0.0002	0.0001
Estimated β (conditional on rank β = 2)	1, −0.9812, 0 1, 0, −0.8743	1, −0.9921, 0 1, 0, −0.8860
P-value for test of H_0 : β_1 = (1, −1, 0 and β_2 = (1, 0, −1) (conditional on rank β = 2)	0.1617	0.0062
P-value for test of H_0 : β_1 = (1, −1, 0) (conditional on rank β = 2)	0.1203	0.4304
P-value for test of H_0 : β = (1, 0, −1) (conditional on rank β = 2)	0.0606	0.0000

not normally distributed (at $< 0.00001\%$ level of significance). The dummies in the column 3 models ensure that residuals are normally distributed.

23.6 CONCLUDING REMARKS

Before our scientific explanation of H can be used in support of HAG's dictum, several remarks concerning the intended interpretation of $P(\cdot)$, the components of ω_P, and the generality and empirical adequacy of our explanation are in order.

First, $P(\cdot)$: In our intended interpretation of the axioms, the initial conditions on y_1 and y_3, axioms B 2–B 6, and the properties of $P(\cdot)$ determine the dynamics of equilibrium yields in the money market of the theory universe. The resulting probability distributions of the components of ω_T can be interpreted as conditional distributions determined by sequences of variables that, for each and every period, specify the supplies of money market instruments and the characteristics of factors that influence the level of demand for such securities. They can also be interpreted as marginal distributions in which the previously mentioned conditioning factors have been expected out.

When considering the positive analogies concerning yields in a money market that our theory identifies, it seems appropriate to interpret the probability distributions of ω_T as marginal distributions. It is difficult to think of the supply of Treasury bills in the U.S. money market, for example, as being entirely exogenously determined. The term structure of interest rates affects the costs of carrying the public debt. Therefore, changes in the term structure will induce the Treasury to make changes in the composition of its outstanding debt and hence in its supply of the various bills. Similarly, it is hard to see how determinants of demand in the U.S. money market, such as the Federal Reserve's monetary policy, can be characterized as entirely exogenous. In endeavoring to carry out the government's monetary policy, the Federal Reserve agents interact with the actors in the money market in interesting ways. Marcia Stigum provides a fascinating description of this interaction in her extraordinary account of the U.S. money market (M. Stigum, 1990, pp. 390–408). Finally, since HAG did not consider variables other than current and lagged values of the components of K, it is in the spirit of HAG's statistical analysis to interpret the probability distributions of the components of ω_T as marginal distributions in which the actions of the Treasury and the agents of the Federal Reserve have been expected out.

In this context it is interesting to take a look at Heather's choice of variables in Chapter 21 and the role they were expected to play in that analysis. The variables are yields on our two Treasury bills, the Federal Funds rate (FF), the yield on a 5-year Treasury bond (B), and a measure of government debt (D). Here FF was used as a monetary policy indicator, D as a fiscal policy indicator, and B to "determine how substitute longer-term instruments might affect yield movements." That statistical analysis suggests that the yields on our Treasury bills, FF, and B are cointegrated and that a cointegration rank of three is appropriate.

Next, *the components of* ω_P: There is a possibility that our formalization of HAG's dictum is incorrect. For example, it might have been better to insist that $K(j)_t = |y_j(t)|$, $\acute{K}(j)_t = |\hat{y}_j(t)|$, $j = 1, 2$; $r = |y_3(t)|$; and $\check{r} = |\hat{y}_3(t)|$. There are many possibilities but no obviously better alternative, so for now we assume that our H is the correct formalization of HAG's dictum.

Then, *the generality of our explanation*: If our H is a correct rendition of HAG's dictum for two Treasury bills, the generality of our scientific explanation of H stands and falls on whether we sacrificed insight into the workings of the U.S. money market by considering just two bills and one other money market instrument. However, as axioms B 2, B 4, and G 2 can be easily generalized to a market with many more securities, it is clear that our gain in clarity has not been at the expense of a loss in generality.

Finally, *the empirical adequacy of our explanation*: We noted above that the search for a family of models of the *MPD* and the data universe within which our scientific explanation of HAG's dictum is empirically relevant is like a fishing expedition. Looking back, we believe that it has been remarkably successful. We have obtained estimates of the values of the relevant parameters in the theory universe as well as in the data universe, and, with the help of sophisticated parametric bootstrapping methods, we have also obtained a 95 percent confidence interval for the various parameter estimates. These estimates and their confidence bands provide the contours of three overlapping families of models—one for the *MPD* and the data universe, one for the theory universe, and one for the bridge principles—with one important property: The members of the family of models of the *MPD* and the data universe satisfy HAG's dictum. In our statistical calculations we assumed that the two η-processes and the Λ-process were independently distributed, purely random Gaussian processes. Our statistical results do not ensure that the Λ-process is purely random and that the η_2-process is Gaussian, but we ignore this uncertainty and consider our statistical analysis complete.

NOTES

Heather Anderson is responsible for Section 23.5, Geir Storvik for Section 23.4, and Bernt Stigum for Sections 23.1–23.3 and 23.6. Section 23.3 builds on ideas that were developed in Stigum (1998).

1. We owe the idea of this example to Banerjee et al. (cf. Banerjee et al. 1993, p. 156).
2. We owe this formulation of the common trend to Heather Anderson.
3. Our account of the Treasury bill market in Section 23.2 accords with the characterization that HAG gave in their paper. Heather Anderson gives a different analysis of the same market in Chapter 21.
4. Section 23.6 contains an analysis of this problem.

REFERENCES

Banerjee, A., J. J. Dolado, J. W. Galbraith, and D. F. Hendry, 1993, *Co-Integration, Error Correction, and Econometric Analysis of Non-stationary Data*, Oxford: Oxford University Press.

Box, G. E. P., and G. M. Jenkins, 1970, *Time Series Analysis, Forecasting and Control*, San Francisco: Holden-Day.

Cootner, P. (ed.), 1964, *The Random Character of Stock Market Prices*, Cambridge: MIT Press

Davison, A. C., and D. V. Hinkley, 1997, *Bootstrap Methods and Their Applications*, Cambridge: Cambridge University Press.

Doornik, J. A., D. F. Hendry, and B. Nielsen, 1998, "Inference in Cointegrating Models: UK M1 Revisited," *Journal of Economic Surveys* 12, 533–572.

Efron, B., 1982, *The Jackknife, The Bootstrap and Other Resampling Plans*, Philadelphia: Siam.

Feller, W., 1957, *An Introduction to Probability Theory and Its Applications, Vol. 1*, 2nd Ed. New York: Wiley.

Granger, C. W. J., 1981, "Some Properties of Time Series Data and their Use in Econometric Model Specification," *Journal of Econometrics* 16, 121–130.

Hall, A. D., H. Anderson, and C. W. J. Granger, 1992, "A Cointegration Analysis of Treasury Bill Yields," *The Review of Economics and Statistics* 74, 116–126.

Harvey, A. C., 1989, *Structural Time Series Models and the Kalman Filter*, Cambridge: Cambridge University Press.

Johansen, S., 1995, *Likelihood-based Inference in Cointegrated Vector Autoregressive Models*, Oxford: Oxford University Press.

Parthasarathy, K. R., 1967, *Probability Measures on Metric Spaces*, New York: Academic.

Phillips, P. C. B., 1991, "Optimal Inference in Cointegrated Systems," *Econometrica* 59, 283–306.

Press, W. H., S. A. Teukolsky, W. T. Vetterling, and B. P. Flannert, 1992, *Numerical Recipes in C*, Cambridge: Cambridge University Press.

Sargan, J. D., 1964, "Wages and Prices in the United Kingdom: A Study in Econometric Methodology," in: *Econometric Analysis for National Economic Planning*, P. E. Hart, G. Mills, and J. K. Whitaker (eds.), London: Butterworth.

Stigum, B. P., 1975, "Asymptotic Properties of Autoregressive Integrated Moving Average Processes," in: *Stochastic Processes and Their Applications, Vol. III.*

Stigum, B. P., 1990, *Toward a Formal Science of Economics*, Cambridge: MIT Press.

Stigum, M., 1990, *The Money Market*, 3rd Ed., Chicago: Dow Jones-Irwin.

Stigum, B. P., 1998, "Scientific Explanation in Econometrics," in: *Econometrics and Economic Theory in the 20th Century: The Ragnar Frisch Centennial Symposium*, S. Stroem (ed.), Cambridge: Cambridge University Press.

Stock, J. H., and M. W. Watson, 1993, "A Simple Estimator of Cointegrating Vectors in Higher Order Integrated Systems," *Econometrica*. 61, 783–820.

PART VII
Contemporary Econometric Analyses

Chapter Twenty-Four

Handling the Measurement Error Problem by Means of Panel Data: Moment Methods Applied on Firm Data

Erik Biørn

Panel data are a valuable source of information for theory-data confrontation in contemporary econometrics. The panel data available are frequently from individuals, firms, or other kinds of microunits. A primary reason for the strongly increasing utilization of panel data during the last three decades seems to be the opportunity that such data offer for "controlling for" unobserved individual and/or time-specific heterogeneity, which may be correlated with the included explanatory variables. As is well known, the effect of individual heterogeneity in a panel data set relative to a linear equation can be removed by measuring all variables from their individual means or by operating on suitably differenced data.

However, microdata, including panel data, and inferences drawn from such data may have deficiencies following from measurement errors. Not only observation errors in the narrow sense, but differences between theoretical variable definitions and their observable counterparts in a wider sense may also be present. A familiar property of the ordinary least squares (OLS) in the presence of random measurement errors (errors-in-variables, EIV) in the regressors is that the slope coefficient estimator is inconsistent. In the one-regressor case (or the multiple-regressor case with uncorrelated regressors), under standard assumptions, the estimator is biased toward zero, often denoted as *attenuation*. More seriously, unless some "extraneous" information is available, for example, the existence of valid parameter restrictions or valid instruments for the error-ridden regressors, slope coefficients cannot generally be identified from standard data (see Fuller, 1987, sec. 1.1.3).[1] This *lack of identification* in EIV models, however, relates to *unidimensional* data, that is, pure (single or repeated) cross sections or pure time series. If the variables are observed as panel data, exhibiting *two-dimensional* variation, it may be possible to handle the heterogeneity and the EIV identification problems jointly and estimate slope coefficients consistently and efficiently without extraneous information, provided that the distribution of the latent regressors and the measurement errors satisfy certain weak conditions.

Briefly, the reason why the existence of variables observed along two dimensions makes the EIV identification problem more manageable is partly (i) the *repeated measurement* property of panel data (each individual and each period is "replicated") so that the effect of measurement errors can be reduced by taking averages, which, in turn, may show sufficient variation to permit consistent estimation; and partly (ii) the larger set of *other linear data transformations* available for estimation. Such transformations may be needed to compensate for unidimensional "nuisance variables" such as unobserved individual or period-specific *heterogeneity* that are potentially correlated with the regressor.

From the panel data literature that disregards the EIV problem, it is known that the effect of, say, additive (fixed or random) individual heterogeneity within a linear model can be eliminated by deducting individual means, taking differences over periods, and so on (see Hsiao, 1986, sec. 1.1; and Baltagi, 2001, ch. 2). Such transformations, however, may magnify the variation in the measurement error component of the observations relative to the variation in the true structural component, that is, they may increase the "noise/signal ratio". Data transformations intended to "solve" the latent heterogeneity problem may then exacerbate the EIV problem. Several familiar estimators for panel data models, including the fixed effects within-group and between-group estimators, and the random effects generalized least squares (GLS) estimators will then be inconsistent, although to a degree depending, inter alia, on the way in which the number of individuals and/or periods tends to infinity and on the heterogeneity of the measurement error process. [See Griliches and Hausman (1986) and Biørn (1992, 1996) for examples for one-regressor models.]

If the distribution of the latent regressor vector is *not* time invariant and the second-order moments of the measurement errors and disturbances are structured to some extent, there are several consistent instrumental variables estimators of the coefficient of the latent regressor vector. Their consistency is robust to correlation between the individual heterogeneity and the latent regressor. Serial correlation or nonstationarity of the latent regressor is favorable from the point of view of identification and estimability of the coefficient vector. Briefly, there should not be "too much structure" on the second-order moments of the latent exogenous regressors across the panel and not "too little structure" on the second-order moments of the errors and disturbances (see Biørn, 2000, sec. 2.b).

24.1 THE BASIC MODEL

The focus of this chapter is on the estimation of linear, static regression equations from balanced panel data with additive, random measurement errors in the regressors by means of methods utilizing instrumental variables (IVs). I consider a data set with N (≥ 2) individuals observed in T (≥ 2) periods and a relationship between y (observable scalar) and a $(1 \times K)$ vector $\boldsymbol{\xi}$ (latent),

$$y_{it} = c + \boldsymbol{\xi}_{it}\boldsymbol{\beta} + \alpha_i + u_{it}, \qquad i = 1, \ldots, N;\ t = 1, \ldots, T, \tag{1}$$

where $(y_{it}, \boldsymbol{\xi}_{it})$ is the value of $(y, \boldsymbol{\xi})$ for individual i in period t, c is a scalar constant, $\boldsymbol{\beta}$ is a $(K \times 1)$ vector, and α_i is a zero (marginal) mean individual effect, which is considered random and potentially correlated with $\boldsymbol{\xi}_{it}$, and u_{it} is a zero mean disturbance that may also contain a measurement error in y_{it}. The regressor vector observed is

$$\boldsymbol{x}_{it} = \boldsymbol{\xi}_{it} + \boldsymbol{v}_{it}, \qquad i = 1, \ldots, N;\ t = 1, \ldots, T, \tag{2}$$

where $\boldsymbol{v}_{it}$ is a zero mean vector of measurement errors. Hence,

$$y_{it} = c + \boldsymbol{x}_{it}\boldsymbol{\beta} + \epsilon_{it}, \qquad \epsilon_{it} = \alpha_i + u_{it} - \boldsymbol{v}_{it}\boldsymbol{\beta}, \tag{3}$$

or in vector form,

$$\boldsymbol{y}_{i\cdot} = \boldsymbol{e}_T c + \boldsymbol{X}_{i\cdot}\boldsymbol{\beta} + \boldsymbol{\epsilon}_{i\cdot}, \qquad \boldsymbol{\epsilon}_{i\cdot} = \boldsymbol{e}_T\alpha_i + \boldsymbol{u}_{i\cdot} - \boldsymbol{V}_{i\cdot}\boldsymbol{\beta}, \qquad i = 1, \ldots, N, \tag{4}$$

where $\boldsymbol{y}_{i\cdot} = (y_{i1}, \ldots, y_{iT})'$, $\boldsymbol{X}_{i\cdot} = (\boldsymbol{x}'_{i1}, \ldots, \boldsymbol{x}'_{iT})'$, and so on; $\boldsymbol{e}_T$ is the $(T \times 1)$ vector of ones and ϵ_{it} is a composite error/disturbance. I assume that $(\boldsymbol{\xi}_{it}, u_{it}, \boldsymbol{v}_{it}, \alpha_i)$ are independent across individuals [which excludes random period specific components in $(\boldsymbol{\xi}_{it}, u_{it}, \boldsymbol{v}_{it})$] and make the following *basic orthogonality assumptions*, corresponding to those in the EIV literature for standard situations[2]:

$$\text{ASSUMPTION (A):} \quad \begin{cases} \mathsf{E}\left(\boldsymbol{v}'_{it}u_{i\theta}\right) = \boldsymbol{0}_{K1}, & \\ \mathsf{E}\left(\boldsymbol{\xi}'_{it}u_{i\theta}\right) = \boldsymbol{0}_{K1}, & i = 1, \ldots, N, \\ \mathsf{E}\left(\boldsymbol{\xi}'_{i\theta} \otimes \boldsymbol{v}_{it}\right) = \boldsymbol{0}_{KK}, & t, \theta = 1, \ldots, T, \\ \mathsf{E}\left(\alpha_i \boldsymbol{v}_{it}\right) = \boldsymbol{0}_{1K}, & \\ \mathsf{E}\left(\alpha_i u_{it}\right) = 0, & \end{cases}$$

where $\boldsymbol{0}_{mn}$ denotes the $(m \times n)$ zero matrix and $\otimes$ is the Kronecker product operator.

One can eliminate α_i from (3) by taking arbitrary backward differences $\Delta y_{it\theta} = y_{it} - y_{i\theta} = \boldsymbol{d}_{t\theta}\boldsymbol{y}_{i\cdot}$, $\Delta\boldsymbol{x}_{it\theta} = \boldsymbol{x}_{it} - \boldsymbol{x}_{i\theta} = \boldsymbol{d}_{t\theta}\boldsymbol{X}_{i\cdot}$, and so on, where $\boldsymbol{d}_{t\theta}$ is the $(1 \times T)$ vector with element t equal to 1, element θ equal to -1, and zero otherwise. Premultiplying (4) by $\boldsymbol{d}_{t\theta}$, yields[3]

$$\Delta y_{it\theta} = \Delta\boldsymbol{x}_{it\theta}\boldsymbol{\beta} + \Delta\epsilon_{it\theta}, \qquad t = 2, \ldots, T;\ \theta = 1, \ldots, t-1. \tag{5}$$

The next section presents an interpretation of this model framework based on production theory and a panel of manufacturing firms, and subsequent sections describe the estimation methods and introduce the additional assumptions needed. The focus is on two kinds of estimation methods: (i) methods operating on period means, illustrating applications of the repeated measurement property of panel data (Section 24.3), and (ii) generalized method of moments (GMM) procedures (Sections 24.4–24.6). The GMM procedures involve *a mixture of level and difference variables* and are of two kinds: (a) The equation is transformed to differences, as in (5), and is estimated by GMM, and as instruments I use level values of the regressors and/or regressands for other periods. (b) The equation is kept in level form, as in (3), and is estimated by GMM, and as instruments I use differenced values of the regressors and/or regressands for other periods. Our (a) procedures extend and modify those proposed in Griliches and Hausman (1986), Wansbeek and Koning (1991), Arellano and Bover (1995), Biørn (1992, 1996), Biørn and Klette (1998, 1999), and Wansbeek (2001).

24.2 APPLICATION: INPUT ELASTICITIES IN MANUFACTURING

I next present an interpretation of (1) with a single regressor ($K = 1$), to be used as basis for the empirical applications. The data are from eight successive annual Norwegian manufacturing censuses for the years 1983–1990 ($T = 8$), collected by Statistics Norway, for four two-digit sectors, comprising 1,647 firms (plants): manufacture of textiles (ISIC 32) ($N = 215$), manufacture of wood and wood products (ISIC 33) ($N = 603$), manufacture of paper and paper products (ISIC 34) ($N = 600$), and manufacture of chemicals (ISIC 35) ($N = 229$). The data base specifies labor, capital, and materials (including energy) inputs, but for illustrative purposes here and in order not to inflate my tables of results, I confine my attention to the last two. This pair of inputs is interesting as capital creates much heavier measurement problems than materials, although both inputs and the output contain potential measurement errors, both in the strict and the wide sense. My measure of capital input is based on deflated fire insurance values, which is a wealth-related measure and hence contains potential errors as indicators of the productive capacity of the capital.

With reference to production theory, I describe two alternative interpretations of the model (1)–(5), but do not go deeply into the problems of theory-data confrontation (see Stigum, 1995, for a thorough discussion).

The first and simplest interpretation is to assume a technology with one output X_{it}^* and one input Y_{it}^*, that is, either capital or materials, both latent. Firm-specific differences in technology are represented by the factor e^{ϕ_i}, indicating firm i's departure from the technology of the average firm (characterized by $\phi_i = 0$). The technology is specified as

$$X_{it}^* = e^{\phi_i} F(Y_{it}^*) = A e^{\phi_i} (Y_{it}^*)^{\mu}, \tag{6}$$

where A is a positive constant, μ is the scale elasticity for this one-factor Cobb-Douglas technology, and $\mathsf{E}(\phi_i) = 0$. One can allow for an unspecified period-specific effect by extending (6) to

$$X_{it}^* = e^{\phi_i} F_t(Y_{it}^*) = Ae^{\phi_i} e^{\psi_t} (Y_{it}^*)^{\mu}, \tag{7}$$

where $\mathsf{E}(\phi_i) = \mathsf{E}(\psi_t) = 0$.

The second interpretation is to assume a (neoclassical) technology with one output and several inputs, of which two are capital and materials, and output constrained *cost minimization*. Let X_{it}^* denote output, $Y_{it}^* = \left(Y_{it}^{*1}, \ldots, Y_{it}^{*G}\right)$ the vector of G inputs, and $w_t^* = \left(w_t^{*1}, \ldots, w_t^{*G}\right)$ the vector of input prices, common to all firms—all treated as latent variables. The technology is described by

$$X_{it}^* = e^{\phi_i} F_t(Y_{it}^*), \tag{8}$$

where F_t is a production function common to all firms, with t reflecting that technological changes are allowed for. I interpret ϕ_i as a constant known to firm i, but unobserved by the econometrician. The dual cost function can then be written as $C_{it}^* = G_t(w_t^*, e^{-\phi_i} X_{it}^*)$ (cf., e.g., Jorgenson, 1986, sec. 5), where $C_{it}^* = \sum_{k=1}^{G} w_t^{*k} Y_{it}^{*k}$. Using Shephard's lemma, one can express firm i's optimal input of factor k in year t as

$$Y_{it}^{*k} = g_t^k \left(w_t^*, e^{-\phi_i} X_{it}^*\right), \tag{9}$$

where $g_t^k(\cdot) = \partial G_t(\cdot)/\partial w_t^{*k}$. Assuming that F_t represents a *homothetic* technology, so that G_t can be separated as $G_t(w_t^*, e^{-\phi_i} X_{it}^*) = H_t(w_t^*) K(e^{-\phi_i} X_{it}^*)$, where the functions H_t and K are monotonically increasing, (9) becomes

$$Y_{it}^{*k} = h_t^k(w_t^*)\, K(e^{-\phi_i} X_{it}^*),$$

with $h_t^k(\cdot) = \partial H_t(\cdot)/\partial w_t^{*k}$. If, in particular, (8) has a *constant scale elasticity* μ for all firms and years, then $K(e^{-\phi_i} X_{it}^*) = e^{-\phi_i/\mu}(X_{it}^*)^{1/\mu}$ for all i, t and, hence,

$$Y_{it}^{*k} = h_t^k(w_t^*) e^{-\phi_i/\mu} (X_{it}^*)^{1/\mu}. \tag{10}$$

Taking logs, one can then write both (7) and (9) in simplified notation as

$$\chi_{it} = c + \alpha_i + \gamma_t + \beta \xi_{it}, \tag{11}$$

where $\chi_{it} = \ln Y_{it}^*$; $\xi_{it} = \ln X_{it}^*$; $\beta = 1/\mu$; $\alpha_i = -(1/\mu)\phi_i$; γ_t is either zero, $-(1/\mu)\psi_t$, or $\ln h_t^k(w_t^*)$; and c is a constant. The observed log-input and log-output are $y_{it} = \chi_{it} + u_{it}$ and $x_{it} = \xi_{it} + v_{it}$, where u_{it} and v_{it} are measurement errors. This gives an equation of the form (3). In the more general case where F_t represents a nonhomothetic technology, separability of G_t does not hold. Then the input elasticity $\boldsymbol{\beta}$ will be different for different inputs and thus cannot be interpreted as an inverse scale elasticity.

Neither of these model interpretations imposes a specific normalization on (11) and (3), as observed input and output are both formally endogenous variables. In the empirical application, two normalizations are considered: (i) y_{it} and x_{it} are, respectively, the log of an observed factor input and the log of observed gross production, both measured as values at constant prices, and β corresponds to $1/\mu$; and (ii) y_{it} and x_{it} have the reverse interpretation and β corresponds to μ.

24.3 ESTIMATORS BASED ON PERIOD MEANS

In this section, I consider various estimators of $\boldsymbol{\beta}$ constructed from differenced period means. From (3), one obtains

$$\Delta_s \bar{y}_{\cdot t} = \Delta_s \bar{\boldsymbol{x}}_{\cdot t}\boldsymbol{\beta} + \Delta_s \bar{\epsilon}_{\cdot t}, \qquad s = 1, \dots, T-1;\ t = s+1, \dots, T, \tag{12}$$

$$(\bar{y}_{\cdot t} - \bar{y}) = (\bar{\boldsymbol{x}}_{\cdot t} - \bar{\boldsymbol{x}})\boldsymbol{\beta} + (\bar{\epsilon}_{\cdot t} - \bar{\epsilon}), \qquad t = 1, \dots, T, \tag{13}$$

where $\bar{y}_{\cdot t} = \sum_i y_{it}/N$, $\bar{y} = \sum_i \sum_t y_{it}/(NT)$, $\bar{\boldsymbol{x}}_{\cdot t} = \sum_i \boldsymbol{x}_{it}/N$, $\bar{\boldsymbol{x}} = \sum_i \sum_t \boldsymbol{x}_{it}/(NT)$, and so on, and Δ_s denotes differencing over s periods.

The (weak) law of the large numbers, when assumption (A) is satisfied, implies under weak conditions (cf. McCabe and Tremayne, 1993, sec. 3.5)[4], that $\text{plim}(\bar{\epsilon}_{\cdot t}) = 0$, $\text{plim}(\bar{\boldsymbol{x}}_{\cdot t} - \bar{\boldsymbol{\xi}}_{\cdot t}) = \boldsymbol{0}_{1K}$, so that $\text{plim}[\bar{\boldsymbol{x}}'_{\cdot t}\bar{\epsilon}_{\cdot t}] = \boldsymbol{0}_{K1}$ even if $\text{plim}[(1/N)\sum_{i=1}^{N} \boldsymbol{x}'_{it}\epsilon_{it}] \neq \boldsymbol{0}_{K1}$. Using (12) and (13) yields

$$\text{plim}[(\Delta_s \bar{\boldsymbol{x}}_{\cdot t})'(\Delta_s \bar{y}_{\cdot t})] = \text{plim}[(\Delta_s \bar{\boldsymbol{x}}_{\cdot t})'(\Delta_s \bar{\boldsymbol{x}}_{\cdot t})]\boldsymbol{\beta}, \tag{14}$$

$$\text{plim}[(\bar{\boldsymbol{x}}_{\cdot t} - \bar{\boldsymbol{x}})'(\bar{y}_{\cdot t} - \bar{y})] = \text{plim}[(\bar{\boldsymbol{x}}_{\cdot t} - \bar{\boldsymbol{x}})'(\bar{\boldsymbol{x}}_{\cdot t} - \bar{\boldsymbol{x}})]\boldsymbol{\beta}. \tag{15}$$

Hence, provided that $\mathsf{E}[(\Delta_s \bar{\boldsymbol{\xi}}_{\cdot t})'(\Delta_s \bar{\boldsymbol{\xi}}_{\cdot t})]$ and $\mathsf{E}[(\bar{\boldsymbol{\xi}}_{\cdot t} - \bar{\boldsymbol{\xi}})'(\bar{\boldsymbol{\xi}}_{\cdot t} - \bar{\boldsymbol{\xi}})]$ have rank K, consistent estimators of $\boldsymbol{\beta}$ can be obtained by applying OLS to (12) or (13), which give, respectively,

$$\widehat{\boldsymbol{\beta}}_{\Delta s} = \left[\sum_{t=s+1}^{T} (\Delta_s \bar{\boldsymbol{x}}_{\cdot t})' (\Delta_s \bar{\boldsymbol{x}}_{\cdot t})\right]^{-1} \left[\sum_{t=s+1}^{T} (\Delta_s \bar{\boldsymbol{x}}_{\cdot t})' (\Delta_s \bar{y}_{\cdot t})\right], \quad s = 1, \dots, T-1, \tag{16}$$

$$\widehat{\boldsymbol{\beta}}_{\text{BP}} = \left[\sum_{t=1}^{T} (\bar{\boldsymbol{x}}_{\cdot t} - \bar{\boldsymbol{x}})'(\bar{\boldsymbol{x}}_{\cdot t} - \bar{\boldsymbol{x}})\right]^{-1} \left[\sum_{t=1}^{T} (\bar{\boldsymbol{x}}_{\cdot t} - \bar{\boldsymbol{x}})'(\bar{y}_{\cdot t} - \bar{y})\right]. \tag{17}$$

The latter is the "between-period" (BP) estimator. The consistency of these estimators relies simply on the fact that, under weak conditions, averages of a large number of repeated measurements of an error-ridden variable give an error-free measure of the true average at the limit, *provided that this average*

TABLE 24.1
Input Elasticities and Inverse Input Elasticities: Standard OLS, Between-Period, and Within-Firm Estimates

y, x	$\widehat{\beta}_{\text{OLS}}$ (1)	$\widehat{\beta}_{\text{BP}}$ (2)	$\widehat{\beta}_{\text{WF}}$ (3)	$\widehat{\beta}_{\text{OLSDC}}$ (4)	$\widehat{\beta}_{\text{BPDC}}$ (5)	$\widehat{\beta}_{\text{WFDC}}$ (6)	$\widehat{\beta}_{\Delta 7}$ (7)	$\widehat{\beta}_{\text{OLSD}}$ (8)
Textiles: $N = 215, T = 8$								
$\ln M, \ln Q$	1.1450	1.0028	1.1033	1.1683	1.0935	1.1750	1.0204	1.1608
$\ln Q, \ln M$	0.7889	0.9859	0.7005	0.5786	0.8742	0.5696	0.9800	0.5894
$\ln K, \ln Q$	0.9899	1.0351	0.6081	0.1621	−0.0170	0.1099	1.5176	0.2313
$\ln Q, \ln K$	0.6751	0.6018	0.3281	0.0852	−0.1584	0.0563	0.6589	0.1203
Wood and wood products: $N = 603, T = 8$								
$\ln M, \ln Q$	1.0940	1.0535	1.0747	1.1062	1.0635	1.1106	1.0779	1.1046
$\ln Q, \ln M$	0.8940	0.9477	0.8127	0.6981	0.9290	0.6869	0.9277	0.7078
$\ln K, \ln Q$	0.9843	1.3865	0.6858	0.2111	0.1081	0.1855	1.7914	0.3004
$\ln Q, \ln K$	0.7816	0.5566	0.3476	0.1272	0.8143	0.1089	0.5582	0.1719
Paper and paper products: $N = 600, T = 8$								
$\ln M, \ln Q$	1.0809	1.0867	1.0759	1.0687	1.0630	1.0664	1.0964	1.0728
$\ln Q, \ln M$	0.8935	0.9194	0.7656	0.5560	0.9088	0.5410	0.9120	0.5907
$\ln K, \ln Q$	0.9711	1.4169	0.9815	0.3001	0.3790	0.2611	1.5207	0.4801
$\ln Q, \ln K$	0.8141	0.6527	0.3757	0.0957	1.0722	0.0812	0.6576	0.1593
Chemicals: $N = 229, T = 8$								
$\ln M, \ln Q$	1.0337	1.0228	1.0275	1.0522	0.9922	1.0573	1.0167	1.0488
$\ln Q, \ln M$	0.9484	0.9764	0.8443	0.6922	0.9644	0.6770	0.9836	0.7121
$\ln K, \ln Q$	1.0499	1.3520	0.8164	0.1929	0.5105	0.1456	1.3626	0.3069
$\ln Q, \ln K$	0.8175	0.7071	0.4447	0.1186	0.8560	0.0883	0.7339	0.1861

Notes: Q = output, M = materials, K = capital; columns 1–3: equation in levels; columns 4–6: equation in differences, with intercept; columns 7–8: equation in differences, without intercept.

shows variation along the remaining dimension, that is, across periods. Basic to these conclusions is the assumption that *the measurement error has no period-specific component*. If such a component is present, it will not vanish when taking plims of period means, that is, $\text{plim}(\bar{\boldsymbol{v}}_{\cdot t})$ will no longer be zero, (14) and (15) will no longer hold, and thus $\widehat{\boldsymbol{\beta}}_{\Delta s}$ and $\widehat{\boldsymbol{\beta}}_{BP}$ will be inconsistent.

Table 24.1 reports between-period estimates of $\boldsymbol{\beta}$ based on levels (column 2) and on differences (column 5)—the latter removing the effect of technical changes represented by a log-linear trend—as well as seven-period difference estimates (column 7) for the four sectors and the two inputs.[5] Since $K = 1$ in this application, the estimators read

$$\widehat{\beta}_{\mathrm{BP}} = \frac{\sum_t (\bar{x}_{\cdot t} - \bar{x})(\bar{y}_{\cdot t} - \bar{y})}{\sum_t (\bar{x}_{\cdot t} - \bar{x})^2},$$

$$\widehat{\beta}_{\mathrm{BPDC}} = \frac{\sum_t (\Delta\bar{x}_{\cdot t} - \Delta\bar{x})(\Delta\bar{y}_{\cdot t} - \Delta\bar{y})}{\sum_t (\Delta\bar{x}_{\cdot t} - \Delta\bar{x})^2},$$

$$\widehat{\beta}_{\Delta 7} = \frac{\bar{y}_{\cdot 8} - \bar{y}_{\cdot 1}}{\bar{x}_{\cdot 8} - \bar{x}_{\cdot 1}}.$$

In each section of the table, rows 1 and 3 can be interpreted as estimates of $1/\mu$ and rows 2 and 4 as estimates of μ. This way of running original and reverse regressions in an EIV context can be related to Frisch's (1934, secs. 5, 10, 11, 14) *confluence analysis*, in which he proposed taking regressions in different directions, for example, in the directions of the x-axis and of the y-axis as a device for handling measurement errors. He did not, however, consider this method in a panel data context.

For *materials*, the BP estimates on levels for the original and the reverse regression imply virtually the same input elasticity, $1/\mu$, in the range 1.00–1.09 for the four sectors considered. They are also very close to the estimates obtained from seven-period differences. The BP estimates based on differences, $\widehat{\beta}_{\mathrm{BPDC}}$, show somewhat larger discrepancies. For *capital*, there are substantial deviations between the level BP, the difference BP, and the seven-period difference estimates. For the BP estimators on levels, the reverse regression gives systematically higher estimates of the input elasticity of capital (lower estimates of μ) than the original regressions. This may indicate that the measurement errors in capital have period-specific, or strongly serially correlated, components, which make both the between-period and all period difference estimators inconsistent. For capital, unlike materials, the results also suggest the presence of period specific heterogeneity in the relationship.

OLS estimates calculated from levels and from one-period differences,

$$\widehat{\beta}_{\mathrm{OLS}} = \frac{\sum_i \sum_t (x_{it} - \bar{x})(y_{it} - \bar{y})}{\sum_i \sum_t (x_{it} - \bar{x})^2},$$

$$\widehat{\beta}_{\mathrm{OLSDC}} = \frac{\sum_i \sum_t (\Delta x_{it} - \Delta\bar{x})(\Delta y_{it} - \Delta\bar{y})}{\sum_i \sum_t (\Delta x_{it} - \Delta\bar{x})^2},$$

$$\widehat{\beta}_{\mathrm{OLSD}} = \frac{\sum_i \sum_t (\Delta x_{it})(\Delta y_{it})}{\sum_i \sum_t (\Delta x_{it})^2},$$

are also reported (columns 1, 4, and 8), $\widehat{\beta}_{\mathrm{OLSDC}}$ removing the possible effect of linear trends. Columns 3 and 6 contain within firm (WF) estimates calculated from levels and differences,

$$\widehat{\beta}_{\mathrm{WF}} = \frac{\sum_i \sum_t (x_{it} - \bar{x}_{i\cdot})(y_{it} - \bar{y}_{i\cdot})}{\sum_i \sum_t (x_{it} - \bar{x}_{i\cdot})^2},$$

$$\widehat{\beta}_{\text{WFDC}} = \frac{\sum_i \sum_t (\Delta x_{it} - \Delta \bar{x}_{i\cdot})(\Delta y_{it} - \Delta \bar{y}_{i\cdot})}{\sum_i \sum_t (\Delta x_{it} - \Delta \bar{x}_{i\cdot})^2},$$

$\widehat{\beta}_{\text{WFDC}}$ removing the possible effect of linear trends. These three OLS and the two WF estimates, all of which are inconsistent in the presence of measurement errors, clearly illustrate the attenuation effect. They have, however, different degrees of robustness. While $\widehat{\beta}_{\text{OLS}}$ is robust neither to firm-specific heterogeneity nor to trend effects, $\widehat{\beta}_{\text{WF}}$ and $\widehat{\beta}_{\text{OLSD}}$ are robust to firm-specific heterogeneity (which is potentially correlated with the regressand or the regressor), but not robust to trend effects, and $\widehat{\beta}_{\text{OLSDC}}$ and $\widehat{\beta}_{\text{WFDC}}$ are robust to both firm-specific heterogeneity and a linear trend. For materials, unlike capital, $\widehat{\beta}_{\text{OLSD}}$, $\widehat{\beta}_{\text{OLSDC}}$, and $\widehat{\beta}_{\text{WFDC}}$ give fairly equal estimates in all sectors.

Although these examples show that it is possible to construct consistent estimators that give estimates of reasonable size (at least for materials) from period means, their efficiency may be low since they do not exploit any interindividual variation in the data, and the latter often tends to dominate. Therefore, there is a potential to improve the estimation by considering methods that utilize this interindividual variation. One such method is the GMM.

24.4 THE PRINCIPLE OF GMM ESTIMATION

Before elaborating the GMM procedures for the panel data situation being discussed, I describe some generalities of this procedure, referring to Davidson and MacKinnon (1993, ch. 17) and Harris and Mátyás (1999) for more detailed expositions. Assume, in general, that one wants to estimate the $(K \times 1)$ coefficient vector $\boldsymbol{\beta}$ in the equation

$$y = \boldsymbol{x}\boldsymbol{\beta} + \epsilon, \tag{18}$$

where y and ϵ are scalars and $\boldsymbol{x}$ is a $(1 \times K)$ regressor vector. There exists an instrument vector z, of dimension $(1 \times G)$, for $\boldsymbol{x}$ $(G \geq K)$ that satisfies the orthogonality conditions

$$\mathsf{E}(z'\epsilon) = \mathsf{E}\left[z'(y - \boldsymbol{x}\boldsymbol{\beta})\right] = \mathbf{0}_{G1}. \tag{19}$$

These conditions are assumed to be derived from the economic theory and the statistical auxiliary hypotheses (e.g., about disturbance/error autocorrelation) underlying the model. There are n observations on $(y, \boldsymbol{x}, z)$, denoted as $(y_j, \boldsymbol{x}_j, z_j)$, $j = 1, \ldots, n$, and I define the vector-valued $(G \times 1)$ function of corresponding means taken over all available observations,

$$\boldsymbol{g}_n(y, \boldsymbol{x}, z; \boldsymbol{\beta}) = (1/n) \textstyle\sum_{j=1}^{n} z_j'(y_j - \boldsymbol{x}_j\boldsymbol{\beta}). \tag{20}$$

It may be considered the empirical counterpart to $\mathsf{E}[z'(y - \boldsymbol{x}\boldsymbol{\beta})]$ based on the sample. The *essence of the GMM* is to choose as an estimator for $\boldsymbol{\beta}$ the value that brings the value of $\boldsymbol{g}_n(y, \boldsymbol{x}, z; \boldsymbol{\beta})$ as close to its theoretical counterpart, the zero vector $\mathbf{0}_{G1}$, as possible. If $G = K$, an exact solution to the equation $\boldsymbol{g}_n(y, \boldsymbol{x}, z; \boldsymbol{\beta}) = \mathbf{0}_{G1}$ exists and is the simple IV estimator

$$\boldsymbol{\beta}^* = \left[\sum_j z_j' \boldsymbol{x}_j\right]^{-1}\left[\sum_j z_j' y_j\right]. \tag{21}$$

If $G > K$, which is the most common situation, the GMM procedure solves the estimation problem by *minimizing a distance measure represented by a quadratic form in* $g_n(y, \boldsymbol{x}, z; \boldsymbol{\beta})$ *for a suitably chosen positive definite* $(G \times G)$ *weighting matrix* $\boldsymbol{W}_n$*, that is,*

$$\boldsymbol{\beta}^*_{\mathrm{GMM}} = \boldsymbol{\beta}^*_{\mathrm{GMM}}(\boldsymbol{W}_n) = \operatorname{argmin}_{\boldsymbol{\beta}}[\boldsymbol{g}_n(y, \boldsymbol{x}, z; \boldsymbol{\beta})' \boldsymbol{W}_n \boldsymbol{g}_n(y, \boldsymbol{x}, z; \boldsymbol{\beta})]. \tag{22}$$

All estimators obtained in this way are consistent. The choice of $\boldsymbol{W}_n$ determines the efficiency of the method. A choice that leads to an asymptotically efficient estimator of $\boldsymbol{\beta}$ is to set this weighting matrix equal (or proportional) to the inverse of (an estimate of) the (asymptotic) covariance matrix of $(1/n)\sum_{j=1}^n z_j' \epsilon_j$ (see, e.g., Davidson and MacKinnon, 1993, theorem 17.3; Harris and Mátyás, 1999, sec. 1.3.3).

If ϵ is serially uncorrelated and homoskedastic, with variance σ_ϵ^2, the appropriate choice is simply $\boldsymbol{W}_n = [n^{-2}\sigma_\epsilon^2 \sum_{j=1}^n z_j' z_j]^{-1}$. The resulting estimator obtained from (22) is

$$\widehat{\boldsymbol{\beta}}_{\mathrm{GMM}} = \left[\left(\sum_j \boldsymbol{x}_j' z_j\right)\left(\sum_j z_j' z_j\right)^{-1}\left(\sum_j z_j' \boldsymbol{x}_j\right)\right]^{-1} \times \left[\left(\sum_j \boldsymbol{x}_j' z_j\right)\left(\sum_j z_j' z_j\right)^{-1}\left(\sum_j z_j' y_j\right)\right], \tag{23}$$

which is the standard two-stage least squares (2SLS) estimator. The method can also be fruitfully applied if ϵ_j has a heteroskedasticity of unspecified (or unknown) form. It can also take account of disturbance/error autocorrelation more or less strictly specified by reformulating the orthogonality conditions in an appropriate way, as will be shown later. This flexibility with respect to the imposition of restrictions on the second-order moments of disturbances/errors is one of the primary virtues of GMM as compared with classical 2SLS. To operationalize the latter method in the presence of unknown heteroskedasticity, one first constructs consistent residuals $\hat{\epsilon}_j$, usually from (23), which is considered a *first-step GMM estimator*, and estimate $\boldsymbol{W}_n$ by $\widehat{\boldsymbol{W}}_n = [n^{-2}\sum_j z_j' \hat{\epsilon}_j^2 z_j]^{-2}$ (see White, 1984, secs. IV.3, VI.2). Inserting this into (22) gives

$$\widetilde{\boldsymbol{\beta}}_{\mathrm{GMM}} = \left[\left(\sum_j \boldsymbol{x}_j' z_j\right)\left(\sum_j z_j' \hat{\epsilon}_j^2 z_j\right)^{-1}\left(\sum_j z_j' \boldsymbol{x}_j\right)\right]^{-1} \times \left[\left(\sum_j \boldsymbol{x}_j' z_j\right)\left(\sum_j z_j' \hat{\epsilon}_j^2 z_j\right)^{-1}\left(\sum_j z_j' y_j\right)\right]. \tag{24}$$

This *second-step GMM estimator*, is in a sense an optimal GMM estimator in the presence of unspecified error/disturbance heteroskedasticity. Both will be considered in the empirical application that follows.

24.5 SIMPLE GMM ESTIMATORS COMBINING DIFFERENCES AND LEVELS

As explained in Section 24.4, the orthogonality conditions (OCs) derived from economic theory (19), their empirical counterparts (20), and other restrictions imposed on second-order moments of observed variables and errors and disturbances all play an essential rôle in GMM procedures. I have already made assumption (A). Before presenting the specific estimators for my panel data measurement error situation, I list the additional assumptions needed.

24.5.1 Additional Assumptions

The additional assumptions with respect to the errors and disturbances are the *nonautocorrelation* assumptions:

Assumption (B1): $\mathsf{E}(\boldsymbol{v}_{it}'\boldsymbol{v}_{i\theta}) = \mathbf{0}_{KK}, \quad t \neq \theta,$

Assumption (C1): $\mathsf{E}(u_{it}u_{i\theta}) = 0, \quad t \neq \theta.$

Sometimes, the following weaker assumptions, allowing for some autocorrelation, are sufficient:

Assumption (B2): $\mathsf{E}(\boldsymbol{v}_{it}'\boldsymbol{v}_{i\theta}) = \mathbf{0}_{KK}, \quad |t-\theta| > \tau,$

Assumption (B3): $\mathsf{E}(\boldsymbol{v}_{it}'\boldsymbol{v}_{i\theta})$ is invariant to $t, \theta, \quad t \neq \theta,$

Assumption (C2): $\mathsf{E}(u_{it}u_{i\theta}) = 0, \quad |t-\theta| > \tau,$

Assumption (C3): $\mathsf{E}(u_{it}u_{i\theta})$ is invariant to $t, \theta, \quad t \neq \theta,$

of which (B2) and (C2) allow for a (vector) moving average (MA) structure up to order τ (≥ 1), and (B3) and (C3) allow for time invariance of the autocorrelation. Assumptions (B3) and (C3) are satisfied if the measurement errors and the disturbances have individual components, say $\boldsymbol{v}_{it} = \boldsymbol{v}_{1i} + \boldsymbol{v}_{2it}$, $u_{it} = u_{1i} + u_{2it}$, where $\boldsymbol{v}_{1i}$, $\boldsymbol{v}_{2it}$, u_{1i}, and u_{2it} are independent iid processes.

The additional assumptions with respect to the *distribution of the latent regressor vector* $\boldsymbol{\xi}_{it}$ are:

Assumption (D1): $\mathsf{E}(\boldsymbol{\xi}_{it})$ is invariant to t,

Assumption (D2): $\mathsf{E}(\alpha_i \boldsymbol{\xi}_{it})$ is invariant to t,

Assumption (E): $\text{rank}\left(\mathsf{E}\left[\boldsymbol{\xi}_{ip}'(\Delta\boldsymbol{\xi}_{it\theta})\right]\right) = K$ for some p, t, θ different.

Assumptions (D1) and (D2) hold when $\boldsymbol{\xi}_{it}$ is mean stationary for all i. Assumption (E) *imposes non-*iid *and some form of autocorrelation or (covariance) nonstationarity on* $\boldsymbol{\xi}_{it}$. It excludes, for example, the case where $\boldsymbol{\xi}_{it}$ has an individual component, so that $\boldsymbol{\xi}_{it} = \boldsymbol{\xi}_{1i} + \boldsymbol{\xi}_{2it}$, where $\boldsymbol{\xi}_{1i}$ and $\boldsymbol{\xi}_{2it}$ are independent (vector) iid processes.

Assumptions (A)–(E) do not go very far in structuring the distributions of the variables of the model, which has both pros and cons. It may be possible to impose more structure on the first- and second-order moments of the u_{it}'s, $\boldsymbol{v}_{it}$'s, $\boldsymbol{\xi}_{it}$'s, and α_i's; confer the "structural approach" to EIV modeling. In this way one might obtain more efficient estimators by operating on the full covariance matrix of the y_{it}'s and the $\boldsymbol{x}_{it}$'s, and possibly higher-order moments, rather than eliminating the α_i's by differencing, as elaborated later. However, such estimators may be less robust to specification errors.

24.5.2 Moment Equations and Orthogonality Conditions

A substantial number of moment conditions involving second-order moments in y_{it}, $\boldsymbol{x}_{it}$, and ϵ_{it} can be derived from assumptions (A)–(E).

From (1)–(3) and assumption (A) one obtains the following moment equations involving observable variables in levels and differences:

$$\mathsf{E}\left[\boldsymbol{x}_{ip}'(\Delta\boldsymbol{x}_{it\theta})\right] = \mathsf{E}\left[\boldsymbol{\xi}_{ip}'(\Delta\boldsymbol{\xi}_{it\theta})\right] + \mathsf{E}\left[\boldsymbol{v}_{ip}'(\Delta\boldsymbol{v}_{it\theta})\right], \tag{25}$$

$$\mathsf{E}\left[\boldsymbol{x}_{ip}'(\Delta y_{it\theta})\right] = \mathsf{E}\left[\boldsymbol{\xi}_{ip}'(\Delta\boldsymbol{\xi}_{it\theta})\right]\boldsymbol{\beta}, \tag{26}$$

$$\mathsf{E}\left[(\Delta\boldsymbol{x}_{ipq})'y_{it}\right] = \mathsf{E}\left[(\Delta\boldsymbol{\xi}_{ipq})'\boldsymbol{\xi}_{it}\right]\boldsymbol{\beta} + \mathsf{E}\left[(\Delta\boldsymbol{\xi}_{ipq})'(\alpha_i + c)\right] \tag{27}$$

and involving observable variables and errors/disturbances:

$$\mathsf{E}\left[\boldsymbol{x}_{ip}'(\Delta\epsilon_{it\theta})\right] = -\,\mathsf{E}\left[\boldsymbol{v}_{ip}'(\Delta\boldsymbol{v}_{it\theta})\right]\boldsymbol{\beta}, \tag{28}$$

$$\mathsf{E}\left[y_{ip}(\Delta\epsilon_{it\theta})\right] = \mathsf{E}\left[u_{ip}(\Delta u_{it\theta})\right], \tag{29}$$

$$\mathsf{E}\left[(\Delta\boldsymbol{x}_{ipq})'\epsilon_{it}\right] = \mathsf{E}\left[(\Delta\boldsymbol{\xi}_{ipq})'\alpha_i\right] - \mathsf{E}\left[(\Delta\boldsymbol{v}_{ipq})'\boldsymbol{v}_{it}\right]\boldsymbol{\beta}, \tag{30}$$

$$\mathsf{E}\left[(\Delta y_{ipq})\epsilon_{it}\right] = \boldsymbol{\beta}'\mathsf{E}\left[(\Delta\boldsymbol{\xi}_{ipq})'\alpha_i\right] + \mathsf{E}\left[(\Delta u_{ipq})u_{it}\right], \tag{31}$$

$$t, \theta, p, q = 1, \ldots, T.$$

The moments on the left-hand side of (25)–(27) are structured by assumptions (D) and (E). The moments on the left-hand side of (28)–(31) are structured by assumptions (B)–(D). Depending on which assumptions are valid, some, or all, of the terms on the right-hand side of (28)–(31) vanish. Provided that $T > 2$, (3), (5), and (28)–(31) imply:

When either (B1) holds and t, θ, p *are different, or (B2) holds and* $|t-p|, |\theta-p| > \tau$, *then*

$$\mathsf{E}\left[\boldsymbol{x}_{ip}'(\Delta\epsilon_{it\theta})\right] = \mathsf{E}\left[\boldsymbol{x}_{ip}'(\Delta y_{it\theta})\right] - \mathsf{E}\left[\boldsymbol{x}_{ip}'(\Delta\boldsymbol{x}_{it\theta})\right]\boldsymbol{\beta} = \boldsymbol{0}_{K1}. \tag{32}$$

When either (C1) holds and t, θ, p *are different, or (C2) holds and* $|t-p|, |\theta-p| > \tau$, *then*

$$\mathsf{E}\left[y_{ip}(\Delta\epsilon_{it\theta})\right] = \mathsf{E}\left[y_{ip}(\Delta y_{it\theta})\right] - \mathsf{E}\left[y_{ip}(\Delta\boldsymbol{x}_{it\theta})\right]\boldsymbol{\beta} = 0. \tag{33}$$

When either (B1), (D1), and (D2) hold and t, p, q *are different, or (B2), (D1), and (D2) hold and* $|\mathrm{t}-\mathrm{p}|, |\mathrm{t}-\mathrm{q}| > \tau$, *then*

$$\mathsf{E}\left[(\Delta \boldsymbol{x}_{ipq})'\epsilon_{it}\right] = \mathsf{E}\left[(\Delta \boldsymbol{x}_{ipq})'y_{it}\right] - \mathsf{E}\left[(\Delta \boldsymbol{x}_{ipq})'\boldsymbol{x}_{it}\right]\boldsymbol{\beta} = \mathbf{0}_{K1}. \tag{34}$$

When either (C1), (D1), and (D2) hold and t, p, q *are different, or (C2), (D1), and (D2) hold and* $|\mathrm{t}-\mathrm{p}|, |\mathrm{t}-\mathrm{q}| > \tau$, *then*

$$\mathsf{E}\left[(\Delta y_{ipq})\epsilon_{it}\right] = \mathsf{E}\left[(\Delta y_{ipq})y_{it}\right] - \mathsf{E}\left[(\Delta y_{ipq})\boldsymbol{x}_{it}\right]\boldsymbol{\beta} = 0. \tag{35}$$

The intercept c needs a comment. When mean stationarity of the latent regressor (D1) holds, then $\mathsf{E}(\Delta \boldsymbol{x}_{ipq}) = \mathbf{0}_{1K}$ and $\mathsf{E}(\Delta y_{ipq}) = 0$. If (D1) is relaxed, which cannot be assumed to hold in many situations owing to nonstationarity, one gets

$$\mathsf{E}\left[(\Delta \boldsymbol{x}_{ipq})'\epsilon_{it}\right] = \mathsf{E}\left[(\Delta \boldsymbol{x}_{ipq})'y_{it}\right] - \mathsf{E}\left[(\Delta \boldsymbol{x}_{ipq})'\right]c - \mathsf{E}\left[(\Delta \boldsymbol{x}_{ipq})'\boldsymbol{x}_{it}\right]\boldsymbol{\beta} = \mathbf{0}_{K1},$$
$$\mathsf{E}\left[(\Delta y_{ipq})\epsilon_{it}\right] = \mathsf{E}\left[(\Delta y_{ipq})y_{it}\right] - \mathsf{E}\left[(\Delta y_{ipq})\right]c - \mathsf{E}\left[(\Delta y_{ipq})\boldsymbol{x}_{it}\right]\boldsymbol{\beta} = 0.$$

Eliminating c by means of $\mathsf{E}(\epsilon_{it}) = \mathsf{E}(y_{it}) - c - E(\boldsymbol{x}_{it})\boldsymbol{\beta} = 0$ leads to the following modifications of (34) and (35):

When either (B1) and (D2) hold and t, p, q *are different, or (B2) and (D2) hold and* $|\mathrm{t}-\mathrm{p}|, |\mathrm{t}-\mathrm{q}| > \tau$, *then*

$$\mathsf{E}\left[(\Delta \boldsymbol{x}_{ipq})'\epsilon_{it}\right] = \mathsf{E}\left[(\Delta \boldsymbol{x}_{ipq})'\{y_{it} - \mathsf{E}(y_{it})\}\right] - \mathsf{E}\left[(\Delta \boldsymbol{x}_{ipq})'\{\boldsymbol{x}_{it} - \mathsf{E}(\boldsymbol{x}_{it})\}\right]\boldsymbol{\beta} = \mathbf{0}_{K1}. \tag{36}$$

When either (C1) and (D2) hold and t, p, q *are different, or (C2) and (D2) hold and* $|\mathrm{t}-\mathrm{p}|, |\mathrm{t}-\mathrm{q}| > \tau$, *then*

$$\mathsf{E}\left[(\Delta y_{ipq})\epsilon_{it}\right] = \mathsf{E}\left[(\Delta y_{ipq})\{y_{it} - \mathsf{E}(y_{it})\}\right] - \mathsf{E}\left[(\Delta y_{ipq})\{\boldsymbol{x}_{it} - \mathsf{E}(\boldsymbol{x}_{it})\}\right]\boldsymbol{\beta} = 0. \tag{37}$$

The OCs (32)–(37), corresponding to (19) in the general exposition of the GMM, are instrumental in constructing the GMM estimators. Of course, not all of these OCs, whose number is substantial even for small T, are independent. In examining the relationships between the OCs in (32) and (33) and between those in (34) and (35), one finds that some of these conditions are redundant, that is, linearly dependent on other conditions. Confining attention to the OCs relating to the $\boldsymbol{x}$'s, one has[6]

1. Assume that (B1) and (C1) are satisfied. Then: (i) All OCs (32) are linearly dependent on all admissible OCs relating to equations differenced over one period and a subset of the OCs relating to two-period differences. (ii) All OCs (34) are linearly dependent on all admissible OCs relating to IVs differenced over one period and a subset of the IVs differenced over two periods.

2. Assume that (B2) and (C2) are satisfied. Then: (i) All OCs (33) are linearly dependent on all admissible OCs relating to equations differenced over one period and a subset of the OCs relating to differences over $2(\tau+1)$ periods. (ii) All OCs (35) are linearly dependent on all admissible OCs relating to IVs differenced over one period and a subset of the IVs differenced over $2(\tau+1)$ periods.

The nonredundant conditions defined by 1 and 2 are denoted as *essential* OCs. The following propositions are shown in Biørn (2000, sec. 2.d):

Proposition 1 *Assume that (B1) and (C1) are satisfied. Then*

(a) $\mathsf{E}[\mathbf{x}'_{ip}(\Delta\epsilon_{it,t-1})] = \mathbf{0}_{K1}$ *for* $p = 1, \ldots, t-2, t+1, \ldots, T;\ t = 2, \ldots, T$ *are* $K(T-1)(T-2)$ *essential OCs for equations differenced over one period.*

(b) $\mathsf{E}\left[\mathbf{x}'_{it}(\Delta\epsilon_{it+1,t-1})\right] = \mathbf{0}_{K1}$ *for* $t = 2, \ldots, T-1$ *are* $K(T-2)$ *essential OCs for equations differenced over two periods.*

(c) The other OCs are redundant: among the $\frac{1}{2}KT(T-1)(T-2)$ *conditions in (32) when* $T > 2$*, only* $KT(T-2)$ *are essential.*

Proposition 2 *Assume that (B1) and (C1) are satisfied. Then*

(a) $\mathsf{E}\left[(\Delta\mathbf{x}_{ip,p-1})'\epsilon_{it}\right] = \mathbf{0}_{K1}$ *for* $t = 1, \ldots, p-2, p+1, \ldots, T;\ p = 2, \ldots, T$ *are* $K(T-1)(T-2)$ *essential OCs for equations in levels, with IVs differenced over one period.*

(b) $\mathsf{E}\left[(\Delta\mathbf{x}_{it+1,t-1})'\epsilon_{it}\right] = \mathbf{0}_{K1}$ *for* $t = 2, \ldots, T-1$ *are* $K(T-2)$ *essential OCs for equations in levels, with IVs differenced over two periods.*

(c) The other OCs are redundant: among the $\frac{1}{2}KT(T-1)(T-2)$ *conditions in (33) when* $T > 2$*, only* $KT(T-2)$ *are essential.*

For generalizations to the case where ϵ_{it} is a *MA(τ) process*, see Biørn (2000, sec. 2.d). These propositions can be (trivially) modified to include the essential and redundant OCs in the y's or the Δy's, given in (33) and (35) as well.

24.5.3 The Estimators

Equations (23) and (24) can now be specialized to define: (i) consistent GMM estimators of $\boldsymbol{\beta}$ in (5) *for one pair of periods* (t, θ), utilizing as IVs for $\Delta\boldsymbol{x}_{it\theta}$ *all admissible* $\boldsymbol{x}_{ip}$*'s*, and (ii) consistent GMM estimators of $\boldsymbol{\beta}$ in (3) *for one period* (t), utilizing as IVs for $\boldsymbol{x}_{it}$ *all admissible* $\Delta\boldsymbol{x}_{ipq}$*'s*. This is a preliminary to Section 24.6, in which I combine, on the one hand, (i) the differenced equations for all pairs of periods, and on the other (ii) the level equations for all periods, respectively, in one equation system.

I let $\boldsymbol{P}_{t\theta}$ denote the $[(T-2) \times T]$ selection matrix obtained by deleting from $\boldsymbol{I}_T$ rows t and θ, and introduce the $[(T-2) \times T]$ matrix

$$
\boldsymbol{D}_t = \begin{bmatrix} \boldsymbol{d}_{21} \\ \vdots \\ \boldsymbol{d}_{t-1,t-2} \\ \boldsymbol{d}_{t+1,t-1} \\ \boldsymbol{d}_{t+2,t+1} \\ \vdots \\ \boldsymbol{d}_{T,T-1} \end{bmatrix}, \qquad t = 1, \ldots, T,
$$

which is a one-period differencing matrix, except that $\boldsymbol{d}_{t,t-1}$ and $\boldsymbol{d}_{t+1,t}$ are replaced by their sum, $\boldsymbol{d}_{t+1,t-1}$, the two-period difference being effective only for $t = 2, \ldots, T-1$, and use the notation

$$
\begin{aligned}
\boldsymbol{y}_{i(t\theta)} &= \boldsymbol{P}_{t\theta}\boldsymbol{y}_{i\cdot}, \quad & \boldsymbol{X}_{i(t\theta)} &= \boldsymbol{P}_{t\theta}\boldsymbol{X}_{i\cdot}, \quad & \boldsymbol{x}_{i(t\theta)} &= \mathrm{vec}(\boldsymbol{X}_{i(t\theta)})', \\
\Delta\boldsymbol{y}_{i(t)} &= \boldsymbol{D}_t\boldsymbol{y}_{i\cdot}, \quad & \Delta\boldsymbol{X}_{i(t)} &= \boldsymbol{D}_t\boldsymbol{X}_{i\cdot}, \quad & \Delta\boldsymbol{x}_{i(t)} &= \mathrm{vec}(\Delta\boldsymbol{X}_{i(t)})',
\end{aligned}
$$

and so on. Here $\boldsymbol{X}_{i(t\theta)}$ denotes the $[(T-2) \times K]$ matrix of $\boldsymbol{x}$ levels obtained by *deleting* rows t and θ from $\boldsymbol{X}_{i\cdot}$, and $\Delta\boldsymbol{X}_{i(t)}$ denotes the $[(T-2) \times K]$ matrix of $\boldsymbol{x}$ differences obtained by stacking all one-period differences between rows of $\boldsymbol{X}_{i\cdot}$ *not including period t* and the single two-period difference between the columns for periods $t+1$ and $t-1$. The vectors $\boldsymbol{y}_{i(t\theta)}$ and $\Delta\boldsymbol{y}_{i(t)}$ are constructed from $\boldsymbol{y}_{i\cdot}$ in a similar way. In general, subscripts $(t\theta)$ and (t) on a matrix or vector denote deletion of $(t\theta)$ differences and t levels, respectively. Stacking $\boldsymbol{y}'_{i(t\theta)}$, $\Delta\boldsymbol{y}'_{i(t)}$, $\boldsymbol{x}_{i(t\theta)}$, and $\Delta\boldsymbol{x}_{i(t)}$ by individuals, gives

$$
\boldsymbol{Y}_{(t\theta)} = \begin{bmatrix} \boldsymbol{y}'_{1(t\theta)} \\ \vdots \\ \boldsymbol{y}'_{N(t\theta)} \end{bmatrix}, \qquad \Delta\boldsymbol{Y}_{(t)} = \begin{bmatrix} \Delta\boldsymbol{y}'_{1(t)} \\ \vdots \\ \Delta\boldsymbol{y}'_{N(t)} \end{bmatrix},
$$

$$
\boldsymbol{X}_{(t\theta)} = \begin{bmatrix} \boldsymbol{x}_{1(t\theta)} \\ \vdots \\ \boldsymbol{x}_{N(t\theta)} \end{bmatrix}, \qquad \Delta\boldsymbol{X}_{(t)} = \begin{bmatrix} \Delta\boldsymbol{x}_{1(t)} \\ \vdots \\ \Delta\boldsymbol{x}_{N(t)} \end{bmatrix},
$$

which have dimensions $[N \times (T-2)]$, $[N \times (T-2)]$, $[N \times (T-2)K]$, and $[N \times (T-2)K]$, respectively. *These four matrices contain the alternative IV sets in the GMM procedures to be considered in what follows.*

Equation in Differences, IVs in Levels: Using $\boldsymbol{X}_{(\mathrm{t}\theta)}$ as IV matrix for $\Delta\boldsymbol{X}_{\mathrm{t}\theta}$, one obtains the following estimator of $\boldsymbol{\beta}$, *specific to period* (t, θ) *differences and utilizing all admissible* **x** *level IVs*,

$$
\begin{aligned}
\widehat{\beta}_{Dx(t\theta)} &= \left[(\Delta X_{t\theta})' X_{(t\theta)} \left(X'_{(t\theta)} X_{(t\theta)}\right)^{-1} X'_{(t\theta)}(\Delta X_{t\theta})\right]^{-1} \\
&\quad \times \left[(\Delta X_{t\theta})' X_{(t\theta)} \left(X'_{(t\theta)} X_{(t\theta)}\right)^{-1} X'_{(t\theta)}(\Delta y_{t\theta})\right] \\
&= \left\{\left[\sum_i (\Delta x_{it\theta})' x_{i(t\theta)}\right]\left[\sum_i x'_{i(t\theta)} x_{i(t\theta)}\right]^{-1}\left[\sum_i x'_{i(t\theta)}(\Delta x_{it\theta})\right]\right\}^{-1} \\
&\quad \times \left\{\left[\sum_i (\Delta x_{it\theta})' x_{i(t\theta)}\right]\left[\sum_i x'_{i(t\theta)} x_{i(t\theta)}\right]^{-1}\left[\sum_i x'_{i(t\theta)}(\Delta y_{it\theta})\right]\right\}. \qquad (38)
\end{aligned}
$$

It exists if $X'_{(t\theta)}X_{(t\theta)}$ has rank $(T-2)K$, which requires $N \geq (T-2)K$. This estimator exemplifies (23), utilizes the OC $\mathsf{E}[x'_{i(t\theta)}(\Delta\epsilon_{it\theta})] = \mathbf{0}_{(T-2)K,1}$—which follows from (32)—and minimizes the quadratic form

$$
\left(N^{-1}X'_{(t\theta)}\Delta\epsilon_{t\theta}\right)'\left(N^{-2}X'_{(t\theta)}X_{(t\theta)}\right)^{-1}\left(N^{-1}X'_{(t\theta)}\Delta\epsilon_{t\theta}\right).
$$

The weight matrix $(N^{-2}X'_{(t\theta)}X_{(t\theta)})^{-1}$ is proportional to the inverse of the (asymptotic) covariance matrix of $N^{-1}X'_{(t\theta)}\Delta\epsilon_{t\theta}$ when $\Delta\epsilon_{it\theta}$ is iid across i. *The consistency of* $\widehat{\beta}_{\mathrm{Dx}(t\theta)}$ *relies on assumptions (A), (B1), and (E).*

Two *modifications* of $\widehat{\beta}_{Dx(t\theta)}$ exist: First, if $\mathrm{var}(\Delta\epsilon_{it\theta})$ varies with i, one can increase the efficiency of (38) by replacing $x'_{i(t\theta)}x_{i(t\theta)}$ by $x'_{i(t\theta)}(\widehat{\Delta\epsilon_{it\theta}})^2 x_{i(t\theta)}$, which gives an asymptotically optimal GMM estimator of the form of (24). Second, instead of using $X_{(t\theta)}$ as IV matrix for $\Delta X_{t\theta}$, one may either, if $K=1$, use $Y_{(t\theta)}$, or, for arbitrary K, use $\left(X_{(t\theta)} : Y_{(t\theta)}\right)$, provided that (C1) is also satisfied.

Equation in Levels, IVs in Differences: Using $\Delta X_{(t)}$ as IV matrix for X_t (for notational simplicity the "dot" subscript on $X_{\cdot t}$ and $y_{\cdot t}$ is omitted) yields the following estimator of β, *specific to period* t *levels, utilizing all admissible* **x** *difference IVs,*

$$
\begin{aligned}
\widehat{\beta}_{Lx(t)} &= \left\{X'_t(\Delta X_{(t)})\left[(\Delta X_{(t)})'(\Delta X_{(t)})\right]^{-1}(\Delta X_{(t)})' X_t\right\}^{-1} \\
&\quad \times \left\{X'_t(\Delta X_{(t)})\left[(\Delta X_{(t)})'(\Delta X_{(t)})\right]^{-1}(\Delta X_{(t)})' y_t\right\} \\
&= \left\{\left[\sum_i x'_{it}(\Delta x_{i(t)})\right]\left[\sum_i (\Delta x_{i(t)})'(\Delta x_{i(t)})\right]^{-1}\left[\sum_i (\Delta x_{i(t)})' x_{it}\right]\right\}^{-1} \\
&\quad \times \left\{\left[\sum_i x'_{it}(\Delta x_{i(t)})\right]\left[\sum_i (\Delta x_{i(t)})'(\Delta x_{i(t)})\right]^{-1}\left[\sum_i (\Delta x_{i(t)})' y_{it}\right]\right\}. \qquad (39)
\end{aligned}
$$

It exists if $(\Delta X_{(t)})'(\Delta X_{(t)})$ has rank $(T-2)K$, which requires $N \geq (T-2)K$. This estimator exemplifies (23), utilizes the OC $\mathsf{E}[(\Delta x_{i(t)})'\epsilon_{it}] = \mathbf{0}_{(T-2)K,1}$—which follows from (34)—and minimizes the quadratic form

$$
\left[N^{-1}(\Delta X_{(t)})'\epsilon_t\right]'\left[N^{-2}(\Delta X_{(t)})'(\Delta X_{(t)})\right]^{-1}\left[N^{-1}(\Delta X_{(t)})'\epsilon_t\right].
$$

The weight matrix $[N^{-2}(\Delta X_{(t)})'(\Delta X_{(t)})]^{-1}$ is proportional to the inverse of the (asymptotic) covariance matrix of $N^{-1}(\Delta X_{(t)})'\epsilon_t$ when ϵ_{it} is iid across i. *The consistency of* $\widehat{\beta}_{\mathrm{Lx}(t)}$ *relies on assumptions (A), (B1), (D1), (D2), and (E).*

Three *modifications* of $\widehat{\beta}_{Lx(t)}$ exist: First, if var(ϵ_{it}) varies with i, one can increase the efficiency of (39) by replacing $(\Delta \boldsymbol{x}_{i(t)})'(\Delta \boldsymbol{x}_{i(t)})$ by $(\Delta \boldsymbol{x}_{i(t)})'(\hat{\epsilon}_{it})^2$ $(\Delta \boldsymbol{x}_{i(t)})$, which gives an asymptotically optimal GMM estimator of the form of (24). Second, instead of using $\Delta \boldsymbol{X}_{(t)}$ as an IV matrix for $\boldsymbol{X}_t$, one may either, if $K = 1$, use $\Delta \boldsymbol{Y}_{(t)}$, or, for arbitrary K, use $(\Delta \boldsymbol{X}_{(t)} : \Delta \boldsymbol{Y}_{(t)})$, provided that (C1) is also satisfied. Third, one can deduct period means from $\boldsymbol{x}_{it}$ and y_{it} and relax the stationarity in mean assumption of the latent regressor, (D1) [cf. (36) and (37)].

If assumptions (B1) or (C1) are relaxed and replaced by (B2) or (C2), the OCs underlying (38) and (39) must be reconstructed to ensure that the variables in the IV matrix have a lead or lag of at least $\tau + 1$ periods to the regressor to "get clear of" the τ period memory of the MA(τ) process. The IV sets will then be reduced.

24.6 COMPOSITE GMM ESTIMATORS COMBINING DIFFERENCES AND LEVELS

I now take the single-equation GMM estimators (38) and (39) and their heteroskedasticity robust modifications one step further and construct GMM estimators of the common coefficient vector $\boldsymbol{\beta}$ when I combine the essential OCs for all periods, that is, for all differences or for all levels. This gives *multiequation, or overall, GMM estimators* for panel data with measurement errors that still belong to the general framework described in Section 24.4. The procedures to be described in this section, like the single-equation procedures in Section 24.5.3, may be modified to be applicable to situations with disturbance/error autocorrelation.

Equation in Differences, IVs in Levels: Consider the differenced equation (5) for *all* $\theta = t - 1$ and $\theta = t - 2$. These $(T - 1) + (T - 2)$ equations stacked for individual i read

$$\begin{bmatrix} \Delta y_{i21} \\ \vdots \\ \Delta y_{i,T,T-1} \\ \Delta y_{i31} \\ \vdots \\ \Delta y_{i,T,T-2} \end{bmatrix} = \begin{bmatrix} \Delta \boldsymbol{x}_{i21} \\ \vdots \\ \Delta \boldsymbol{x}_{i,T,T-1} \\ \Delta \boldsymbol{x}_{i31} \\ \vdots \\ \Delta \boldsymbol{x}_{i,T,T-2} \end{bmatrix} \boldsymbol{\beta} + \begin{bmatrix} \Delta \epsilon_{i21} \\ \vdots \\ \Delta \epsilon_{i,T,T-1} \\ \Delta \epsilon_{i31} \\ \vdots \\ \Delta \epsilon_{i,T,T-2} \end{bmatrix}, \tag{40}$$

or, compactly,

$$\Delta \boldsymbol{y}_i = (\Delta \boldsymbol{X}_i)\boldsymbol{\beta} + \Delta \boldsymbol{\epsilon}_i.$$

The IV matrix (cf. proposition 1) is the $[(2T-3)\times KT(T-2)]$ matrix

$$\boldsymbol{Z}_i = \begin{bmatrix} \boldsymbol{x}_{i(21)} & \cdots & \mathbf{0} & \mathbf{0} & \cdots & \mathbf{0} \\ \vdots & \ddots & \vdots & \vdots & \vdots & \vdots \\ \mathbf{0} & \cdots & \boldsymbol{x}_{i(T,T-1)} & \mathbf{0} & \cdots & \mathbf{0} \\ \mathbf{0} & \cdots & \mathbf{0} & \boldsymbol{x}_{i2} & \cdots & \mathbf{0} \\ \vdots & \vdots & \vdots & \vdots & \ddots & \vdots \\ \mathbf{0} & \cdots & \mathbf{0} & \mathbf{0} & \cdots & \boldsymbol{x}_{i,T-1} \end{bmatrix}. \quad (41)$$

Here different IVs are used for the $(T-1)+(T-2)$ equations in (40), with $\boldsymbol{\beta}$ as a common slope coefficient. Let

$$\Delta\boldsymbol{y} = \big[(\Delta\boldsymbol{y}_1)',\ldots,(\Delta\boldsymbol{y}_N)'\big]', \quad \Delta\boldsymbol{\epsilon} = \big[(\Delta\boldsymbol{\epsilon}_1)',\ldots,(\Delta\boldsymbol{\epsilon}_N)'\big]',$$
$$\Delta\boldsymbol{X} = \big[(\Delta\boldsymbol{X}_1)',\ldots,(\Delta\boldsymbol{X}_N)'\big]', \quad \boldsymbol{Z} = \big[\boldsymbol{Z}_1',\ldots,\boldsymbol{Z}_N'\big]'.$$

The overall GMM estimator corresponding to (32), which I now write as $\mathsf{E}\big[\boldsymbol{Z}_i'(\Delta\boldsymbol{\epsilon}_i)\big] = \mathbf{0}_{T(T-2)K,1}$, minimizing $\big[N^{-1}(\Delta\boldsymbol{\epsilon})'\boldsymbol{Z}\big](N^{-2}\boldsymbol{V})^{-1}\big[N^{-1}\boldsymbol{Z}'(\Delta\boldsymbol{\epsilon})\big]$ for $\boldsymbol{V} = \boldsymbol{Z}'\boldsymbol{Z}$, can be written as

$$\begin{aligned}\widehat{\boldsymbol{\beta}}_{Dx} &= \big[(\Delta\boldsymbol{X})'\boldsymbol{Z}(\boldsymbol{Z}'\boldsymbol{Z})^{-1}\boldsymbol{Z}'(\Delta\boldsymbol{X})\big]^{-1}\big[(\Delta\boldsymbol{X})'\boldsymbol{Z}(\boldsymbol{Z}'\boldsymbol{Z})^{-1}\boldsymbol{Z}'(\Delta\boldsymbol{y})\big] \\ &= \Big\{\big[\textstyle\sum_i(\Delta\boldsymbol{X}_i)'\boldsymbol{Z}_i\big]\big[\sum_i \boldsymbol{Z}_i'\boldsymbol{Z}_i\big]^{-1}\big[\sum_i \boldsymbol{Z}_i'(\Delta\boldsymbol{X}_i)\big]\Big\}^{-1} \\ &\quad\times\Big\{\big[\textstyle\sum_i(\Delta\boldsymbol{X}_i)'\boldsymbol{Z}_i\big]\big[\sum_i \boldsymbol{Z}_i'\boldsymbol{Z}_i\big]^{-1}\big[\sum_i \boldsymbol{Z}_i'(\Delta\boldsymbol{y}_i)\big]\Big\}. \end{aligned} \quad (42)$$

This estimator exemplifies (23). *The consistency of* $\boldsymbol{\beta}_{\mathrm{Dx}}$ *relies on assumptions (A), (B1), and (E).* If $\Delta\boldsymbol{\epsilon}$ has a nonscalar covariance matrix, a more efficient estimator is obtained for $\boldsymbol{V} = \boldsymbol{V}_{Z(\Delta\epsilon)} = \mathsf{E}[\boldsymbol{Z}'(\Delta\boldsymbol{\epsilon})(\Delta\boldsymbol{\epsilon})'\boldsymbol{Z}]$, which gives

$$\widetilde{\boldsymbol{\beta}}_{Dx} = \Big[(\Delta\boldsymbol{X})'\boldsymbol{Z}\boldsymbol{V}_{Z(\Delta\epsilon)}^{-1}\boldsymbol{Z}'(\Delta\boldsymbol{X})\Big]^{-1}\Big[(\Delta\boldsymbol{X})'\boldsymbol{Z}\boldsymbol{V}_{Z(\Delta\epsilon)}^{-1}\boldsymbol{Z}'(\Delta\boldsymbol{y})\Big].$$

We can estimate $\boldsymbol{V}_{Z(\Delta\epsilon)}/N$ consistently from the residuals obtained from (42), $\widehat{\Delta\boldsymbol{\epsilon}}_i = \Delta\boldsymbol{y}_i - (\Delta\boldsymbol{X}_i)\widehat{\boldsymbol{\beta}}_{Dx}$, by

$$\widehat{\boldsymbol{V}}_{Z(\Delta\epsilon)}/N = (1/N)\textstyle\sum_i \boldsymbol{Z}_i'\big(\widehat{\Delta\boldsymbol{\epsilon}}_i\big)\big(\widehat{\Delta\boldsymbol{\epsilon}}_i\big)'\boldsymbol{Z}_i.$$

The resulting asymptotically optimal GMM estimator, which exemplifies (24), is

$$\begin{aligned}\widetilde{\boldsymbol{\beta}}_{Dx} &= \Big\{\big[\textstyle\sum_i(\Delta\boldsymbol{X}_i)'\boldsymbol{Z}_i\big]\big[\sum_i \boldsymbol{Z}_i'\widehat{\Delta\boldsymbol{\epsilon}}_i\widehat{\Delta\boldsymbol{\epsilon}}_i'\boldsymbol{Z}_i\big]^{-1}\big[\sum_i \boldsymbol{Z}_i'(\Delta\boldsymbol{X}_i)\big]\Big\}^{-1} \\ &\quad\times\Big\{\big[\textstyle\sum_i(\Delta\boldsymbol{X}_i)'\boldsymbol{Z}_i\big]\big[\sum_i \boldsymbol{Z}_i'\widehat{\Delta\boldsymbol{\epsilon}}_i\widehat{\Delta\boldsymbol{\epsilon}}_i'\boldsymbol{Z}_i\big]^{-1}\big[\sum_i \boldsymbol{Z}_i'(\Delta\boldsymbol{y}_i)\big]\Big\}. \end{aligned} \quad (43)$$

The estimators $\widehat{\boldsymbol{\beta}}_{Dx}$ and $\widetilde{\boldsymbol{\beta}}_{Dx}$ can be modified by extending $\boldsymbol{x}_{i(t,t-1)}$ to $(\boldsymbol{x}_{i(t,t-1)} : \boldsymbol{y}_{i(t,t-1)}')$ and $\boldsymbol{x}_{it}$ to $(\boldsymbol{x}_{it} : \boldsymbol{y}_{it})$ in (41), also exploiting assumption (C1) and the OCs in the y's. This is indicated by replacing subscript Dx by Dy or Dxy on the estimator symbols.

Table 24.2 contains the overall GMM estimates obtained from the complete set of *differenced equations* for the four manufacturing sectors and the two inputs. The standard error estimates are computed as described in the appendix.[7] The estimated input-output elasticities (column 1, rows 1 and 3) are always lower than the inverse output-input elasticities (column 2, rows 2 and 4). This attenuation effect, also found for the OLS estimates (cf. Table 24.1), is consonant with the fact that $\widehat{\beta}_{Dx}$ and $\widehat{\beta}_{Dy}$ can be interpreted as having been obtained by running standard 2SLS on the "original" and on the "reverse regression" version of (40), respectively. Under both normalizations, the estimates utilizing the y instruments (column 2) tend to exceed those based on the x instruments (column 1). Using the optimal weighting (columns 4 and 5), one finds that the estimates are more precise, according to the standard error estimates, than those in columns 1 and 2, as they should be. The standard error estimates for capital are substantially higher than for materials.

Sargan-Hansen orthogonality test statistics, which are asymptotically distributed as χ^2 with the number of degrees of freedom equal to the number of OCs imposed less the number of coefficients estimated (one in this case) under the null hypothesis of orthogonality (cf. Hansen, 1982; Newey, 1985; Arellano and Bond, 1991), corresponding to the asymptotically efficient estimates in columns 4 and 5, are reported in columns 6 and 7. For materials, these statistics indicate nonrejection of the full set of OCs when using the x's as IVs for the original regression (row 1 in each section) and the y's as IVs for the reverse regression (row 2 in each section)—that is, the output variable in both cases—with p-values exceeding 5 percent. However, the OCs when using the y's as IVs for the original regression and the x's as IVs for the reverse regression—that is, the material input variable in both cases—are rejected. For capital the tests come out with very low p-values in all cases, indicating rejection of the OCs. This may be due to lagged response, autocorrelated measurement errors, or disturbances and/or (deterministic or stochastic) trends in the capital-input relationship. The last, for example, would violate the stationarity assumption for capital. However, owing to the short time span of my data, I have not performed a cointegration analysis.

All the results in Table 24.2 uniformly indicate *a marginal input elasticity of materials,* $1/\mu$, *larger than one*; $\widehat{\beta}_{Dx}$ and $\widetilde{\beta}_{Dx}$ are, however, lower than the (inconsistent) estimate obtained by running an OLS regression on differences (cf. $\widehat{\beta}_{\text{OLSD}}$ for the materials-output regression in Table 24.1), and $\widehat{\beta}_{Dy}$ and $\widetilde{\beta}_{Dy}$ are higher than the (inconsistent) estimate obtained by running reverse an OLS regression on differences (cf. $\widehat{\beta}_{\text{OLSD}}$ for the output-materials regression in Table 24.1).

Equation in Levels, IVs in Differences: I next consider the procedures for estimating all the level equations (3) with the IVs in differences. The T stacked level equations for individual i are

TABLE 24.2
Input Elasticities and Inverse Input Elasticities: GMM Estimates of Differenced Equations, with All IVs in Levels

y, x	$\widehat{\beta}_{Dx}$ (1)	$\widehat{\beta}_{Dy}$ (2)	$\widehat{\beta}_{Dxy}$ (3)	$\widetilde{\beta}_{Dx}$ (4)	$\widetilde{\beta}_{Dy}$ (5)	$\chi^2(\widetilde{\beta}_{Dx})$ (6)	$\chi^2(\widetilde{\beta}_{Dy})$ (7)
Textiles: $N = 215$, $T = 8$							
ln M, ln Q	1.0821	1.1275	1.0900	1.0546	1.0825	51.71	70.39
	(0.0331)	(0.0346)	(0.0350)	(0.0173)	(0.0169)	(0.2950)	(0.0152)
ln Q, ln M	0.8404	0.8931	0.8064	0.8917	0.9244	86.55	59.08
	(0.0283)	(0.0283)	(0.0363)	(0.0143)	(0.0148)	(0.0004)	(0.1112)
ln K, ln Q	0.5095	0.6425	0.5004	0.5239	0.6092	115.68	121.29
	(0.0735)	(0.0700)	(0.0745)	(0.0407)	(0.0314)	(0.0000)	(0.0000)
ln Q, ln K	0.4170	0.6391	0.4021	0.4499	0.6495	130.50	133.94
	(0.0409)	(0.0561)	(0.0382)	(0.0248)	(0.0330)	(0.0000)	(0.0000)
Wood and wood products: $N = 603$, $T = 8$							
ln M, ln Q	1.0604	1.0784	1.0632	1.0615	1.0772	63.97	90.28
	(0.0123)	(0.0124)	(0.0128)	(0.0089)	(0.0098)	(0.0502)	(0.0002)
ln Q, ln M	0.9171	0.9362	0.9117	0.9195	0.9370	91.40	64.13
	(0.0106)	(0.0108)	(0.0115)	(0.0083)	(0.0078)	(0.0001)	(0.0489)
ln K, ln Q	0.7454	0.8906	0.7494	0.8094	0.9398	290.60	281.57
	(0.0409)	(0.0439)	(0.0425)	(0.0305)	(0.0310)	(0.0000)	(0.0000)
ln Q, ln K	0.4862	0.6003	0.4806	0.5261	0.6377	283.25	280.65
	(0.0229)	(0.0258)	(0.0223)	(0.0189)	(0.0212)	(0.0000)	(0.0000)
Paper and paper products: $N = 600$, $T = 8$							
ln M, ln Q	1.0766	1.1102	1.0726	1.0680	1.0820	43.12	81.97
	(0.0150)	(0.0162)	(0.0155)	(0.0119)	(0.0123)	(0.6340)	(0.0012)
ln Q, ln M	0.8847	0.9204	0.8853	0.9119	0.9301	90.18	44.50
	(0.0140)	(0.0131)	(0.0145)	(0.0101)	(0.0102)	(0.0002)	(0.5769)
ln K, ln Q	1.0713	1.2134	1.0818	1.0854	1.2543	193.21	220.93
	(0.0430)	(0.0477)	(0.0435)	(0.0324)	(0.0398)	(0.0000)	(0.0000)
ln Q, ln K	0.5591	0.7048	0.5559	0.5377	0.7075	225.95	193.33
	(0.0198)	(0.0243)	(0.0198)	(0.0170)	(0.0198)	(0.0000)	(0.0000)
Chemicals: $N = 229$, $T = 8$							
ln M, ln Q	1.0166	1.0540	1.0263	1.0009	1.0394	54.29	81.64
	(0.0245)	(0.0241)	(0.0251)	(0.0135)	(0.0138)	(0.2166)	(0.0013)
ln Q, ln M	0.9205	0.9609	0.8972	0.9323	0.9815	87.10	57.90
	(0.0230)	(0.0239)	(0.0231)	(0.0122)	(0.0130)	(0.0003)	(0.1324)
ln K, ln Q	0.9706	1.2497	0.9579	1.0051	1.2672	90.42	85.36
	(0.0583)	(0.0633)	(0.0582)	(0.0336)	(0.0489)	(0.0001)	(0.0005)
ln Q, ln K	0.5550	0.7459	0.5637	0.5700	0.7762	96.70	89.57
	(0.0317)	(0.0374)	(0.0314)	(0.0236)	(0.0273)	(0.0000)	(0.0002)

Notes: Q = output, M = materials, K = capital; in parentheses: columns 1–5: standard error estimates; columns 6–7: p values.

$$\begin{bmatrix} y_{i1} \\ \vdots \\ y_{iT} \end{bmatrix} = \begin{bmatrix} c \\ \vdots \\ c \end{bmatrix} + \begin{bmatrix} \boldsymbol{x}_{i1} \\ \vdots \\ \boldsymbol{x}_{iT} \end{bmatrix} \boldsymbol{\beta} + \begin{bmatrix} \epsilon_{i1} \\ \vdots \\ \epsilon_{iT} \end{bmatrix}, \tag{44}$$

or compactly, omitting the "dot" subscript [cf. (4)],

$$\boldsymbol{y}_i = \boldsymbol{e}_T c + \boldsymbol{X}_i \boldsymbol{\beta} + \boldsymbol{\epsilon}_i.$$

The IV matrix (cf. proposition 2) is the $[T \times T(T-2)K]$ matrix

$$\Delta \boldsymbol{Z}_i = \begin{bmatrix} \Delta \boldsymbol{x}_{i(1)} & \cdots & \boldsymbol{0} \\ \vdots & \ddots & \vdots \\ \boldsymbol{0} & \cdots & \Delta \boldsymbol{x}_{i(T)} \end{bmatrix}. \tag{45}$$

Again, one uses different IVs for different equations, considering (44) as T equations with $\boldsymbol{\beta}$ as a common slope coefficient. Let

$$\boldsymbol{y} = \left[\boldsymbol{y}_1', \ldots, \boldsymbol{y}_N'\right]', \qquad \boldsymbol{\epsilon} = \left[\boldsymbol{\epsilon}_1', \ldots, \boldsymbol{\epsilon}_N'\right]',$$
$$\boldsymbol{X} = \left[\boldsymbol{X}_1', \ldots, \boldsymbol{X}_N'\right]', \qquad \Delta \boldsymbol{Z} = \left[(\Delta \boldsymbol{Z}_1)', \ldots, (\Delta \boldsymbol{Z}_N)'\right]'.$$

The overall GMM estimator corresponding to (34), which I now write as $\mathsf{E}[(\Delta \boldsymbol{Z}_i)'\boldsymbol{\epsilon}_i] = \boldsymbol{0}_{T(T-2)K,1}$, minimizing $[N^{-1}\boldsymbol{\epsilon}'(\Delta \boldsymbol{Z})](N^{-2}\boldsymbol{V}_\Delta)^{-1}[N^{-1}(\Delta \boldsymbol{Z})'\boldsymbol{\epsilon}]$ for $\boldsymbol{V}_\Delta = (\Delta \boldsymbol{Z})'(\Delta \boldsymbol{Z})$, can be written as

$$\begin{aligned}
\widehat{\boldsymbol{\beta}}_{Lx} &= \left\{\boldsymbol{X}'(\Delta \boldsymbol{Z})\left[(\Delta \boldsymbol{Z})'(\Delta \boldsymbol{Z})\right]^{-1}(\Delta \boldsymbol{Z})'\boldsymbol{X}\right\}^{-1}\left\{\boldsymbol{X}'(\Delta \boldsymbol{Z})\left[(\Delta \boldsymbol{Z})'(\Delta \boldsymbol{Z})\right]^{-1}(\Delta \boldsymbol{Z})'\boldsymbol{y}\right\} \\
&= \left\{\left[\sum_i \boldsymbol{X}_i'(\Delta \boldsymbol{Z}_i)\right]\left[\sum_i (\Delta \boldsymbol{Z}_i)'(\Delta \boldsymbol{Z}_i)\right]^{-1}\left[\sum_i (\Delta \boldsymbol{Z}_i)'\boldsymbol{X}_i\right]\right\}^{-1} \\
&\quad \times \left\{\left[\sum_i \boldsymbol{X}_i'(\Delta \boldsymbol{Z}_i)\right]\left[\sum_i (\Delta \boldsymbol{Z}_i)'(\Delta \boldsymbol{Z}_i)\right]^{-1}\left[\sum_i (\Delta \boldsymbol{Z}_i)'\boldsymbol{y}_i\right]\right\}.
\end{aligned} \tag{46}$$

This estimator exemplifies (23). *The consistency of* $\boldsymbol{\beta}_{\mathrm{Lx}}$ *relies on assumptions (A), (B1), (D1), (D2), and (E).* If $\boldsymbol{\epsilon}$ has a nonscalar covariance matrix, a more efficient estimator is obtained for $\boldsymbol{V}_\Delta = \boldsymbol{V}_{(\Delta Z)\epsilon} = \mathsf{E}[(\Delta \boldsymbol{Z})'\boldsymbol{\epsilon}\boldsymbol{\epsilon}'(\Delta \boldsymbol{Z})]$, which gives

$$\widetilde{\boldsymbol{\beta}}_{Lx} = \left[\boldsymbol{X}'(\Delta \boldsymbol{Z})\boldsymbol{V}_{(\Delta Z)\epsilon}^{-1}(\Delta \boldsymbol{Z})'\boldsymbol{X}\right]^{-1}\left[\boldsymbol{X}'(\Delta \boldsymbol{Z})\boldsymbol{V}_{(\Delta Z)\epsilon}^{-1}(\Delta \boldsymbol{Z})'\boldsymbol{y}\right].$$

One can estimate $\boldsymbol{V}_{(\Delta Z)\epsilon}/N$ consistently from the residuals obtained from (46), $\widehat{\boldsymbol{\epsilon}}_i = \boldsymbol{y}_i - \boldsymbol{X}_i \widehat{\boldsymbol{\beta}}_{Lx}$, by

$$\widehat{\boldsymbol{V}}_{(\Delta Z)\epsilon}/N = (1/N)\sum_i (\Delta \boldsymbol{Z}_i)'\hat{\boldsymbol{\epsilon}}_i\hat{\boldsymbol{\epsilon}}_i'(\Delta \boldsymbol{Z}_i).$$

The intercept c can be omitted here; (see Section 24.5.2). The resulting asymptotically optimal GMM estimator, which exemplifies (24), is

$$\widetilde{\boldsymbol{\beta}}_{Lx} = \left\{\left[\sum_i \boldsymbol{X}_i'(\Delta \boldsymbol{Z}_i)\right]\left[\sum_i (\Delta \boldsymbol{Z}_i)'\hat{\boldsymbol{\epsilon}}_i\hat{\boldsymbol{\epsilon}}_i'(\Delta \boldsymbol{Z}_i)\right]^{-1}\left[\sum_i (\Delta \boldsymbol{Z}_i)'\boldsymbol{X}_i\right]\right\}^{-1}$$
$$\times \left\{\left[\sum_i \boldsymbol{X}_i'(\Delta \boldsymbol{Z}_i)\right]\left[\sum_i (\Delta \boldsymbol{Z}_i)'\hat{\boldsymbol{\epsilon}}_i\hat{\boldsymbol{\epsilon}}_i'(\Delta \boldsymbol{Z}_i)\right]^{-1}\left[\sum_i (\Delta \boldsymbol{Z}_i)'\boldsymbol{y}_i\right]\right\}. \quad (47)$$

The estimators $\widehat{\boldsymbol{\beta}}_{Lx}$ and $\widetilde{\boldsymbol{\beta}}_{Lx}$ can be modified by extending $\Delta \boldsymbol{x}_{i(t)}$ to $(\Delta \boldsymbol{x}_{i(t)} : \Delta \boldsymbol{y}_{i(t)}')$ in (45), also exploiting assumption (C1) and the OCs in the Δy's. This is indicated be replacing subscript Lx by Ly or Lxy on the estimator symbols. One can also deduct period means from the level variables in (44) to take account of possible nonstationarity of these variables and relax assumption (D1) [cf. (36) and (37)].

Tables 24.3 and 24.4 contain the overall GMM estimates obtained from the complete set of *level equations*, the first using the untransformed observations and the second based on observations measured from their year means. The orthogonality test statistics (columns 6 and 7) for materials lead to conclusions similar to those for the differenced equation in Table 24.2 for textiles and chemicals (for which there are fewer observations): nonrejection of the OCs when using the x's as IVs [cf. $\chi^2(\widetilde{\boldsymbol{\beta}}_{Lx})$ in row 1] and the y's as IVs [cf. $\chi^2(\widetilde{\boldsymbol{\beta}}_{Ly})$ in row 2]—that is, the output variable in both cases—and rejection when using the y's as IVs in the materials-output regression and the x's as IVs in the output-materials regression—that is, the material input variable in both cases. For capital, the orthogonality test statistics once again come out with very low p-values in all cases, which again may reflect misspecified dynamics or trend effects. There is, however, a striking difference between Tables 24.3 and 24.4. In Table 24.3—in which no adjustment is made for nonstationarity in means and (D1) is imposed—one finds uniform rejection of the OCs for capital in all sectors and for wood and paper products for materials. In Table 24.4—in which adjustment is made for nonstationarity in means by deducting period means from the level variables and (D1) is relaxed—we find nonrejection when using output as an instrument for all sectors for materials (p-values exceeding 5 percent), and for capital in all sectors except textiles and wood and wood products (p-values exceeding 1 percent). Note that the set of orthogonality conditions under test in Tables 24.3 and 24.4 is larger than in Table 24.2, since it also includes assumption (D2), time invariance of the covariance between the firm-specific effect α_i and the latent regressor $\boldsymbol{\xi}_{it}$.

However, these estimates for the level equation, unlike those for the differenced equation in Table 24.2 do not give uniformly marginal input elasticity estimates greater than one for materials. Using level observations measured from year means (Table 24.4) and relaxing mean stationarity of the latent regressor yield estimates exceeding one, whereas using untransformed observations and imposing mean stationarity lead to estimates less than one. There are also substantial differences for capital.

A tentative conclusion that can be drawn from the examples in Tables 24.2–24.4 is that overall GMM estimates of the input elasticity of materials with

TABLE 24.3
Input Elasticities and Inverse Input Elasticities: GMM Estimates of Level Equations, with All IVs in Differences (No Mean Deduction)

y, x	$\widehat{\beta}_{Lx}$ (1)	$\widehat{\beta}_{Ly}$ (2)	$\widehat{\beta}_{Lxy}$ (3)	$\widetilde{\beta}_{Lx}$ (4)	$\widetilde{\beta}_{Ly}$ (5)	$\chi^2(\widetilde{\beta}_{Lx})$ (6)	$\chi^2(\widetilde{\beta}_{Ly})$ (7)
Textiles: $N = 215, T = 8$							
$\ln M, \ln Q$	0.9308	0.9325	0.9274	0.9351	0.9404	56.76	81.49
	(0.0031)	(0.0052)	(0.0036)	(0.0024)	(0.0022)	(0.1557)	(0.0013)
$\ln Q, \ln M$	1.0718	1.0743	1.0772	1.0628	1.0690	80.64	56.69
	(0.0060)	(0.0035)	(0.0039)	(0.0025)	(0.0028)	(0.0016)	(0.1572)
$\ln K, \ln Q$	0.7408	0.7355	0.7381	0.7505	0.7502	107.05	116.19
	(0.0079)	(0.0079)	(0.0072)	(0.0059)	(0.0055)	(0.0000)	(0.0000)
$\ln Q, \ln K$	1.3533	1.3483	1.3490	1.3211	1.3231	115.18	106.84
	(0.0145)	(0.0144)	(0.0129)	(0.0097)	(0.0105)	(0.0000)	(0.0000)
Wood and wood products: $N = 603, T = 8$							
$\ln M, \ln Q$	0.9473	0.9469	0.9471	0.9484	0.9496	141.10	159.95
	(0.0011)	(0.0011)	(0.0011)	(0.0010)	(0.0010)	(0.0000)	(0.0000)
$\ln Q, \ln M$	1.0561	1.0557	1.0558	1.0529	1.0543	159.80	141.07
	(0.0013)	(0.0012)	(0.0012)	(0.0011)	(0.0011)	(0.0000)	(0.0000)
$\ln K, \ln Q$	0.7545	0.7560	0.7546	0.7598	0.7699	207.64	272.33
	(0.0030)	(0.0033)	(0.0029)	(0.0027)	(0.0029)	(0.0000)	(0.0000)
$\ln Q, \ln K$	1.3197	1.3244	1.3221	1.2927	1.3124	270.29	207.00
	(0.0056)	(0.0053)	(0.0050)	(0.0049)	(0.0046)	(0.0000)	(0.0000)
Paper and paper products: $N = 600, T = 8$							
$\ln M, \ln Q$	0.9301	0.9300	0.9301	0.9304	0.9347	140.14	150.10
	(0.0015)	(0.0016)	(0.0015)	(0.0013)	(0.0013)	(0.0000)	(0.0000)
$\ln Q, \ln M$	1.0751	1.0751	1.0749	1.0695	1.0744	149.82	140.18
	(0.0019)	(0.0017)	(0.0017)	(0.0015)	(0.0015)	(0.0000)	(0.0000)
$\ln K, \ln Q$	0.7703	0.7658	0.7692	0.7761	0.7745	196.22	254.48
	(0.0033)	(0.0034)	(0.0031)	(0.0028)	(0.0029)	(0.0000)	(0.0000)
$\ln Q, \ln K$	1.3025	1.2974	1.2970	1.2848	1.2850	252.95	195.79
	(0.0057)	(0.0055)	(0.0051)	(0.0048)	(0.0046)	(0.0000)	(0.0000)
Chemicals: $N = 229, T = 8$							
$\ln M, \ln Q$	0.9521	0.9518	0.9520	0.9532	0.9535	53.01	87.76
	(0.0015)	(0.0015)	(0.0015)	(0.0012)	(0.0013)	(0.2537)	(0.0003)
$\ln Q, \ln M$	1.0506	1.0503	1.0503	1.0486	1.0490	87.69	52.98
	(0.0017)	(0.0017)	(0.0016)	(0.0014)	(0.0014)	(0.0003)	(0.2544)
$\ln K, \ln Q$	0.7877	0.7886	0.7884	0.7881	0.7994	96.57	117.54
	(0.0046)	(0.0048)	(0.0045)	(0.0040)	(0.0037)	(0.0000)	(0.0000)
$\ln Q, \ln K$	1.2662	1.2686	1.2659	1.2470	1.2652	117.00	96.55
	(0.0077)	(0.0074)	(0.0072)	(0.0058)	(0.0064)	(0.0000)	(0.0000)

Notes: Q = output, M = materials, K = capital; in parentheses: columns 1–5: standard error estimates; columns 6–7: p-values.

TABLE 24.4
Input Elasticities and Inverse Input Elasticities: GMM Estimates of Level Equations, with All IVs in Differences (with Mean Deduction)

y, x	$\widehat{\beta}_{Lx}$ (1)	$\widehat{\beta}_{Ly}$ (2)	$\widehat{\beta}_{Lxy}$ (3)	$\widetilde{\beta}_{Lx}$ (4)	$\widetilde{\beta}_{Ly}$ (5)	$\chi^2(\widetilde{\beta}_{Lx})$ (6)	$\chi^2(\widetilde{\beta}_{Ly})$ (7)
Textiles: $N = 215$, $T = 8$							
$\ln M, \ln Q$	1.0219	1.2148	1.1881	1.0739	1.1749	54.66	73.56
	(0.0644)	(0.1202)	(0.0786)	(0.0289)	(0.0316)	(0.2065)	(0.0079)
$\ln Q, \ln M$	0.7345	0.9392	0.7048	0.7428	0.8834	64.48	52.42
	(0.0730)	(0.0559)	(0.0621)	(0.0225)	(0.0242)	(0.0460)	(0.2720)
$\ln K, \ln Q$	1.0348	1.2201	1.0776	0.7504	1.3279	84.43	76.36
	(0.1471)	(0.1514)	(0.1153)	(0.0703)	(0.0808)	(0.0007)	(0.0043)
$\ln Q, \ln K$	0.5967	0.7045	0.5902	0.4599	0.6675	69.04	94.75
	(0.0755)	(0.1190)	(0.0682)	(0.0322)	(0.0546)	(0.0198)	(0.0000)
Wood and wood products: $N = 603$, $T = 8$							
$\ln M, \ln Q$	1.0501	1.1174	1.0813	1.0646	1.1328	63.26	65.06
	(0.0219)	(0.0245)	(0.0235)	(0.0140)	(0.0188)	(0.0567)	(0.0415)
$\ln Q, \ln M$	0.8740	0.9425	0.8888	0.8644	0.9277	62.69	62.27
	(0.0192)	(0.0189)	(0.0194)	(0.0145)	(0.0123)	(0.0625)	(0.0671)
$\ln K, \ln Q$	0.6696	1.4487	0.8460	0.4414	1.4470	100.40	126.86
	(0.0927)	(0.1615)	(0.0794)	(0.0489)	(0.1093)	(0.0000)	(0.0000)
$\ln Q, \ln K$	0.5188	0.7927	0.5363	0.3165	0.9208	102.10	149.90
	(0.0655)	(0.0905)	(0.0546)	(0.0339)	(0.0617)	(0.0000)	(0.0000)
Paper and paper products: $N = 600$, $T = 8$							
$\ln M, \ln Q$	1.0797	1.0883	1.0766	1.0799	1.1376	42.95	83.36
	(0.0242)	(0.0410)	(0.0216)	(0.0185)	(0.0310)	(0.6408)	(0.0009)
$\ln Q, \ln M$	0.8911	0.9172	0.8911	0.8271	0.9124	79.18	43.00
	(0.0334)	(0.0209)	(0.0185)	(0.0233)	(0.0158)	(0.0023)	(0.6388)
$\ln K, \ln Q$	0.9242	1.2121	0.9624	0.8171	1.2018	59.67	158.86
	(0.0641)	(0.1117)	(0.0540)	(0.0427)	(0.0791)	(0.1017)	(0.0000)
$\ln Q, \ln K$	0.5953	1.0319	0.7451	0.3715	1.0560	141.11	62.95
	(0.0635)	(0.0711)	(0.0444)	(0.0321)	(0.0506)	(0.0000)	(0.0598)
Chemicals: $N = 229$, $T = 8$							
$\ln M, \ln Q$	0.9721	1.0217	0.9950	0.9805	1.0253	55.85	83.10
	(0.0269)	(0.0278)	(0.0225)	(0.0179)	(0.0179)	(0.1765)	(0.0009)
$\ln Q, \ln M$	0.9619	1.0196	0.9760	0.9429	0.9992	81.75	55.71
	(0.0262)	(0.0279)	(0.0214)	(0.0159)	(0.0179)	(0.0013)	(0.1798)
$\ln K, \ln Q$	1.1013	1.4280	1.1151	0.9795	1.4408	68.96	69.82
	(0.0692)	(0.1429)	(0.0623)	(0.0465)	(0.0838)	(0.0201)	(0.0170)
$\ln Q, \ln K$	0.6348	0.8281	0.7261	0.5150	0.8536	67.88	71.83
	(0.0680)	(0.0550)	(0.0428)	(0.0355)	(0.0390)	(0.0247)	(0.0113)

Notes: Q = output, M = materials, K = capital; in parentheses: columns 1–5: standard error estimates; columns 6–7: p-values.

respect to output tend to be larger than one if one uses either the equation in differences with IVs in levels or the equation in levels, measuring the observations from their year means, with IVs in differences. If the nonadjusted equation in levels with IVs in differences is used, the GMM estimates tend to be less than one. For capital, the picture is less clear. Overall, there is a considerable difference between the elasticity estimates of materials and those of capital. An interpretation one may give of this difference is that the underlying production technology is nonhomothetic (cf. Section 24.2).

24.7 CONCLUDING REMARKS

In this chapter, I have constructed and illustrated several estimators that may handle in conjunction the heterogeneity and the measurement error problems in panel data. These problems may be untractable when only pure (single or repeated) cross-section data or pure time-series data are available. The estimators considered are estimators operating on period specific means, inter alia, the between-period (BP) estimator and generalized method of moments (GMM) estimators. The GMM estimators use either equations in differences with level values as instruments or equations in levels with differenced values as instruments. In both cases, the differences may be taken over one period or more.

In GMM estimation, not only instruments constructed from the observed regressors (x's), but also instruments constructed from the observed regressands (y's) may be useful, even if both are, formally, endogenous variables. My empirical examples—using materials and capital input data and output data for firms in a single-regressor case—indicate that for both normalizations of the equation, GMM estimates using y instruments tend to exceed those using x instruments. Even if the GMM estimates, unlike the OLS estimates, are consistent, they seem to some extent to be affected by the attenuation known for the OLS in errors-in-variables situations. However, using levels as instruments for differences or vice versa as a general estimation strategy within a GMM framework may raise problems related to "weak instruments" (cf. Nelson and Startz, 1990; Staiger and Stock, 1997). It is left for future research to explore these problems, for example, by means of Monte Carlo experiments.

The BP estimates on levels for the original and the reverse regression give virtually the same input elasticity for materials. For capital, I find substantial deviations between the two sets of BP estimators, which may indicate that measurement errors or disturbances have period-specific, or strongly serially correlated, components.

Finally, I find that GMM estimates based on the equation in levels have lower standard errors than those based on the equation in differences. Deducting period means from levels to compensate for nonstationarity of the latent regressor gives estimates for the level equation that are less precise and more sensitive to the choice of instrument set than those operating on untransformed levels. On the other hand, this kind of transformation of level variables may be needed to compensate for period effects, misspecified dynamics, or nonstationarity of the variables, in particular for the capital input variable. It should come as no surprise that the adjustment of material input is far easier to model within the framework considered than is capital.

APPENDIX

In this appendix, I elaborate the procedures for estimating asymptotic covariance matrices of the GMM estimators. All models in the main text, with suitable interpretations of $\boldsymbol{y}$, $\boldsymbol{X}$, $\boldsymbol{Z}$, $\boldsymbol{\epsilon}$, and $\boldsymbol{\Omega}$, have the form:

$$\boldsymbol{y} = \boldsymbol{X\beta} + \boldsymbol{\epsilon}, \quad \mathsf{E}(\boldsymbol{\epsilon}) = \boldsymbol{0}, \quad \mathsf{E}(\boldsymbol{Z}'\boldsymbol{\epsilon}) = \boldsymbol{0}, \quad \mathsf{E}(\boldsymbol{\epsilon\epsilon}') = \boldsymbol{\Omega}, \tag{48}$$

where $\boldsymbol{y} = (\boldsymbol{y}_1', \ldots, \boldsymbol{y}_N')'$, $\boldsymbol{X} = (\boldsymbol{X}_1', \ldots, \boldsymbol{X}_N')'$, $\boldsymbol{Z} = (\boldsymbol{Z}_1', \ldots, \boldsymbol{Z}_N')'$, and $\boldsymbol{\epsilon} = (\boldsymbol{\epsilon}_1', \ldots, \boldsymbol{\epsilon}_N')'$, $\boldsymbol{Z}_i$ being the IV matrix of $\boldsymbol{X}_i$. The two generic GMM estimators considered are

$$\widehat{\boldsymbol{\beta}} = [\boldsymbol{X}'\boldsymbol{P}_Z\boldsymbol{X}]^{-1}[\boldsymbol{X}'\boldsymbol{P}_Z\boldsymbol{y}], \qquad \boldsymbol{P}_Z = \boldsymbol{Z}(\boldsymbol{Z}'\boldsymbol{Z})^{-1}\boldsymbol{Z}', \tag{49}$$

$$\widetilde{\boldsymbol{\beta}} = [\boldsymbol{X}'\boldsymbol{P}_Z(\boldsymbol{\Omega})\boldsymbol{X}]^{-1}[\boldsymbol{X}'\boldsymbol{P}_Z(\boldsymbol{\Omega})\boldsymbol{y}], \qquad \boldsymbol{P}_Z(\boldsymbol{\Omega}) = \boldsymbol{Z}(\boldsymbol{Z}'\boldsymbol{\Omega}\boldsymbol{Z})^{-1}\boldsymbol{Z}'. \tag{50}$$

Let the residual vector calculated from $\widehat{\boldsymbol{\beta}}$ be $\widehat{\boldsymbol{\epsilon}} = \boldsymbol{y} - \boldsymbol{X}\widehat{\boldsymbol{\beta}}$, and use the notation

$$\boldsymbol{S}_{XZ} = \boldsymbol{X}'\boldsymbol{Z}/N, \quad \boldsymbol{S}_{ZX} = \boldsymbol{Z}'\boldsymbol{X}/N, \quad \boldsymbol{S}_{ZZ} = \boldsymbol{Z}'\boldsymbol{Z}/N,$$
$$\boldsymbol{S}_{\epsilon Z} = \boldsymbol{\epsilon}'\boldsymbol{Z}/N, \quad \boldsymbol{S}_{Z\epsilon} = \boldsymbol{Z}'\boldsymbol{\epsilon}/N, \quad \boldsymbol{S}_{Z\Omega Z} = \boldsymbol{Z}'\Omega\boldsymbol{Z}/N,$$
$$\boldsymbol{S}_{Z\epsilon\epsilon Z} = \boldsymbol{Z}'\boldsymbol{\epsilon\epsilon}'\boldsymbol{Z}/N, \quad \boldsymbol{S}_{Z\hat{\epsilon}\hat{\epsilon}Z} = \boldsymbol{Z}'\hat{\boldsymbol{\epsilon}}\hat{\boldsymbol{\epsilon}}'\boldsymbol{Z}/N.$$

Inserting for $\boldsymbol{y}$ from (48) in (49) and (50), yields

$$\begin{aligned}\sqrt{N}(\widehat{\boldsymbol{\beta}} - \boldsymbol{\beta}) &= \sqrt{N}[\boldsymbol{X}'\boldsymbol{P}_Z\boldsymbol{X}]^{-1}[\boldsymbol{X}'\boldsymbol{P}_Z\boldsymbol{\epsilon}] \\ &= \left[\boldsymbol{S}_{XZ}\boldsymbol{S}_{ZZ}^{-1}\boldsymbol{S}_{ZX}\right]^{-1}\left[\boldsymbol{S}_{XZ}\boldsymbol{S}_{ZZ}^{-1}(\boldsymbol{Z}'\boldsymbol{\epsilon}/\sqrt{N})\right], \\ \sqrt{N}(\widetilde{\boldsymbol{\beta}} - \boldsymbol{\beta}) &= \sqrt{N}\left[\boldsymbol{X}'\boldsymbol{P}_Z(\boldsymbol{\Omega})\boldsymbol{X}\right]^{-1}\left[\boldsymbol{X}'\boldsymbol{P}_Z(\boldsymbol{\Omega})\boldsymbol{\epsilon}\right] \\ &= \left[\boldsymbol{S}_{XZ}\boldsymbol{S}_{Z\Omega Z}^{-1}\boldsymbol{S}_{ZX}\right]^{-1}\left[\boldsymbol{S}_{XZ}\boldsymbol{S}_{Z\Omega Z}^{-1}(\boldsymbol{Z}'\boldsymbol{\epsilon}/\sqrt{N})\right],\end{aligned}$$

and hence,

$$\begin{aligned}N(\widehat{\boldsymbol{\beta}} - \boldsymbol{\beta})(\widehat{\boldsymbol{\beta}} - \boldsymbol{\beta})' &= \left[\boldsymbol{S}_{XZ}\boldsymbol{S}_{ZZ}^{-1}\boldsymbol{S}_{ZX}\right]^{-1}\left[\boldsymbol{S}_{XZ}\boldsymbol{S}_{ZZ}^{-1}\boldsymbol{S}_{Z\epsilon\epsilon Z}\boldsymbol{S}_{ZZ}^{-1}\boldsymbol{S}_{ZX}\right] \\ &\quad \times \left[\boldsymbol{S}_{XZ}\boldsymbol{S}_{ZZ}^{-1}\boldsymbol{S}_{ZX}\right]^{-1}, \\ N(\widetilde{\boldsymbol{\beta}} - \boldsymbol{\beta})(\widetilde{\boldsymbol{\beta}} - \boldsymbol{\beta})' &= \left[\boldsymbol{S}_{XZ}\boldsymbol{S}_{Z\Omega Z}^{-1}\boldsymbol{S}_{ZX}\right]^{-1}\left[\boldsymbol{S}_{XZ}\boldsymbol{S}_{Z\Omega Z}^{-1}\boldsymbol{S}_{Z\epsilon\epsilon Z}\boldsymbol{S}_{Z\Omega Z}^{-1}\boldsymbol{S}_{ZX}\right] \\ &\quad \times \left[\boldsymbol{S}_{XZ}\boldsymbol{S}_{Z\Omega Z}^{-1}\boldsymbol{S}_{ZX}\right]^{-1}.\end{aligned}$$

The asymptotic covariance matrices of $\sqrt{N}\widehat{\boldsymbol\beta}$ and $\sqrt{N}\widetilde{\boldsymbol\beta}$ can then, under suitable regularity conditions, be written as (see Bowden and Turkington, 1984, pp. 26, 69)

$$a\mathsf{V}(\sqrt{N}\widehat{\boldsymbol\beta}) = \lim \mathsf{E}\left[N(\widehat{\boldsymbol\beta}-\boldsymbol\beta)(\widehat{\boldsymbol\beta}-\boldsymbol\beta)'\right] = \operatorname{plim}\left[N(\widehat{\boldsymbol\beta}-\boldsymbol\beta)(\widehat{\boldsymbol\beta}-\boldsymbol\beta)'\right],$$

$$a\mathsf{V}(\sqrt{N}\widetilde{\boldsymbol\beta}) = \lim \mathsf{E}\left[N(\widetilde{\boldsymbol\beta}-\boldsymbol\beta)(\widetilde{\boldsymbol\beta}-\boldsymbol\beta)'\right] = \operatorname{plim}\left[N(\widetilde{\boldsymbol\beta}-\boldsymbol\beta)(\widetilde{\boldsymbol\beta}-\boldsymbol\beta)'\right].$$

Since $\boldsymbol{S}_{Z\epsilon\epsilon Z}$ and $\boldsymbol{S}_{Z\Omega Z}$ coincide asymptotically, using bars to denote plims, one gets,

$$a\mathsf{V}(\sqrt{N}\widehat{\boldsymbol\beta}) = \left[\bar{\boldsymbol S}_{XZ}\bar{\boldsymbol S}_{ZZ}^{-1}\bar{\boldsymbol S}_{ZX}\right]^{-1}\left[\bar{\boldsymbol S}_{XZ}\bar{\boldsymbol S}_{ZZ}^{-1}\bar{\boldsymbol S}_{Z\Omega Z}\bar{\boldsymbol S}_{ZZ}^{-1}\bar{\boldsymbol S}_{ZX}\right]\left[\bar{\boldsymbol S}_{XZ}\bar{\boldsymbol S}_{ZZ}^{-1}\bar{\boldsymbol S}_{ZX}\right]^{-1}, \quad (51)$$

$$a\mathsf{V}(\sqrt{N}\widetilde{\boldsymbol\beta}) = \left[\bar{\boldsymbol S}_{XZ}\bar{\boldsymbol S}_{Z\Omega Z}^{-1}c\bar{\boldsymbol S}_{ZX}\right]^{-1}. \quad (52)$$

Replacing the plims $\bar{\boldsymbol S}_{XZ}$, $\bar{\boldsymbol S}_{ZX}$, $\bar{\boldsymbol S}_{ZZ}$, and $\bar{\boldsymbol S}_{Z\Omega Z}$ by their sample counterparts, $\boldsymbol S_{XZ}$, $\boldsymbol S_{ZX}$, $\boldsymbol S_{ZZ}$, and $\boldsymbol S_{Z\hat\epsilon\hat\epsilon Z}$ and dividing by N, one gets from (51) and (52) the following estimators of the asymptotic covariance matrices of $\widehat{\boldsymbol\beta}$ and $\widetilde{\boldsymbol\beta}$:

$$\widehat{\mathsf{V}(\widehat{\boldsymbol\beta})} = (1/N)\left[\boldsymbol S_{XZ}\boldsymbol S_{ZZ}^{-1}\boldsymbol S_{ZX}\right]^{-1}\left[\boldsymbol S_{XZ}\boldsymbol S_{ZZ}^{-1}\boldsymbol S_{Z\hat\epsilon\hat\epsilon Z}\boldsymbol S_{ZZ}^{-1}\boldsymbol S_{ZX}\right]\left[\boldsymbol S_{XZ}\boldsymbol S_{ZZ}^{-1}\boldsymbol S_{ZX}\right]^{-1}$$
$$= \left[\boldsymbol X'\boldsymbol P_Z\boldsymbol X\right]^{-1}\left[\boldsymbol X'\boldsymbol P_Z\hat{\boldsymbol\epsilon}\hat{\boldsymbol\epsilon}'\boldsymbol P_Z\boldsymbol X\right]\left[\boldsymbol X'\boldsymbol P_Z\boldsymbol X\right]^{-1}, \quad (53)$$

$$\widehat{\mathsf{V}(\widetilde{\boldsymbol\beta})} = (1/N)\left[\boldsymbol S_{XZ}\boldsymbol S_{Z\hat\epsilon\hat\epsilon Z}^{-1}\boldsymbol S_{ZX}\right]^{-1}$$
$$= \left[\boldsymbol X'\boldsymbol Z(\boldsymbol Z'\hat{\boldsymbol\epsilon}\hat{\boldsymbol\epsilon}'\boldsymbol Z)^{-1}\boldsymbol Z'\boldsymbol X\right]^{-1} = \left[\boldsymbol X'\boldsymbol P_Z(\hat{\boldsymbol\epsilon}\hat{\boldsymbol\epsilon}')\boldsymbol X\right]^{-1}. \quad (54)$$

These are the generic expressions that are used for estimating variances and covariances of the GMM estimators considered.

When calculating $\widetilde{\boldsymbol\beta}$ from (50) in practice, $\boldsymbol P_Z(\boldsymbol\Omega)$ is replaced by $\boldsymbol P_Z(\hat{\boldsymbol\epsilon}\hat{\boldsymbol\epsilon}') = \boldsymbol Z(\boldsymbol Z'\hat{\boldsymbol\epsilon}\hat{\boldsymbol\epsilon}'\boldsymbol Z)^{-1}\boldsymbol Z'$ (see White, 1982, 1984).

NOTES

I thank Harald Goldstein and Bernt P. Stigum for helpful comments, which led to improvement in the organization of the chapter. The usual disclaimer applies.

1. However, identification under nonnormality of the true regressor is possible by utilizing moments of the distribution of the observable variables of order higher than the second (see Reiersøl, 1950). Even under nonidentification, bounds on the parameters can be established from the distribution of the observable variables (see Fuller, 1987, p. 11). These bounds may be wide or narrow, depending on the covariance structure of the variables; see, e.g., Klepper and Leamer (1984); Bekker et al. (1987).

2. The last two assumptions are stronger than strictly needed; time invariance of $\mathsf{E}(\alpha_i \boldsymbol v_{it})$ and $\mathsf{E}(\alpha_i u_{it})$ is sufficient. A modification to this effect will be of minor practical importance, however.

3. Premultiplication of (4) by $\boldsymbol{d}_{t\theta}$ is not the only way of eliminating α_i. Any $(1 \times T)$ vector $\boldsymbol{c}_{t\theta}$ such that $\boldsymbol{c}_{t\theta}\boldsymbol{e}_T = 0$, for example, the rows of the within individual transformation matrix $\boldsymbol{I}_T - \boldsymbol{e}_T\boldsymbol{e}_T'/T$, where $\boldsymbol{I}_T$ is the T-dimensional identity matrix, has this property.

4. Here and in the following plim always denotes probability limits when N goes to infinity and T is finite.

5. I report no standard error estimates in Table 24.1, since some of the methods are inconsistent.

6. The OCs involving y's can be treated similarly. Essential and redundant moment conditions in the context of AR models for panel data are discussed in, inter alia, Ahn and Schmidt (1995), Arellano and Bover (1995), and Blundell and Bond (1998). This problem resembles, in some respects, the problem for static measurement error models discussed here.

7. All numerical calculations are performed by means of procedures I have constructed in the GAUSS software code.

REFERENCES

Ahn, S. C., and P. Schmidt, 1995, "Efficient Estimation of Models for Dynamic Panel Data," *Journal of Econometrics* 68, 5–27.

Arellano, M., and S. Bond, 1991, "Some Tests of Specification for Panel Data: Monte Carlo Evidence and an Application to Employment Equations," *Review of Economic Studies* 58, 277–297.

Arellano, M., and O. Bover, 1995, "Another Look at the Instrumental Variable Estimation of Error-Components Models," *Journal of Econometrics* 68, 29–51.

Baltagi, B. H., 2001, *Econometric Analysis of Panel Data*, 2nd ed., Chichester: Wiley.

Bekker, P., A. Kapteyn, and T. Wansbeek, 1987, "Consistent Sets of Estimates for Regressions with Correlated or Uncorrelated Measurement Errors in Arbitrary Subsets of All Variables," *Econometrica* 55, 1223–1230.

Biørn, E., 1992, "The Bias of Some Estimators for Panel Data Models with Measurement Errors," *Empirical Economics* 17, 51–66.

Biørn, E., 1996, "Panel Data with Measurement Errors," in: *The Econometrics of Panel Data: Handbook of the Theory with Applications*, L. Mátyás and P. Sevestre (eds.), Dordrecht: Kluwer, ch. 10.

Biørn, E., 2000, "Panel Data with Measurement Errors: Instrumental Variables and GMM Estimators Combining Levels and Differences," *Econometric Reviews* 19, 391–424.

Biørn, E., and T. J. Klette, 1998, "Panel Data with Errors-in-Variables: Essential and Redundant Orthogonality Conditions in GMM-Estimation," *Economics Letters* 59, 275–282.

Biørn, E., and T. J. Klette, 1999, "The Labour Input Response to Permanent Changes in Output: An Errors in Variables Analysis Based on Panel Data," *Scandinavian Journal of Economics* 101, 379–404.

Blundell, R., and S. Bond, 1998, "Initial Conditions and Moment Restrictions in Dynamic Panel Data Models," *Journal of Econometrics* 87, 115–143.

Bowden, R. J., and D. A. Turkington, 1984, *Instrumental Variables*, Cambridge: Cambridge University Press.

Davidson, R., and J. G. MacKinnon, 1993, *Estimation and Inference in Econometrics*, Oxford: Oxford University Press.

Frisch, R., 1934, *Statistical Confluence Analysis by Means of Complete Regression Systems*, Oslo: Universitetets Økonomiske Institutt.

Fuller, W. A., 1987, *Measurement Error Models*, New York: Wiley.

Griliches, Z., and J. A. Hausman, 1986, "Errors in Variables in Panel Data," *Journal of Econometrics* 31, 93–118.

Hansen, L. P., 1982, "Large Sample Properties of Generalized Method of Moments Estimators," *Econometrica* 50, 1029–1054.

Harris, D., and L. Mátyás, 1999, "Introduction to the Generalized Method of Moments Estimation," in: *Generalized Method of Moments Estimation*, L. Mátyás (ed.), Cambridge: Cambridge University Press, ch. 1.

Hsiao, C., 1986, *Analysis of Panel Data*, Cambridge: Cambridge University Press.

Jorgenson, D. W., 1986, "Econometric Methods for Modeling Producer Behavior," in: *Handbook of Econometrics*, Vol. III, Z. Griliches and M. D. Intriligator (eds.), Amsterdam, North-Holland, ch. 31.

Klepper, S., and E. Leamer, 1984, "Consistent Sets of Estimates for Regressions with Errors in All Variables," *Econometrica* 52, 163–183.

McCabe, B., and A. Tremayne, 1993, *Elements of Modern Asymptotic Theory with Statistical Applications*, Manchester: Manchester University Press.

Nelson, C. R., and R. Startz, 1990, "Some Further Results on the Exact Small Sample Properties of the Instrumental Variable Estimator," *Econometrica* 58, 967–976.

Newey, W. K., 1985, "Generalized Method of Moments Specification Testing," *Journal of Econometrics* 29, 229–256.

Reiersøl, O., 1950, "Identifiability of a Linear Relation Between Variables which are Subject to Error," *Econometrica* 18, 375–389.

Staiger, D., and J. H. Stock, 1997, "Instrumental Variables Regression with Weak Instruments," *Econometrica* 65, 557–586.

Stigum, B., 1995, "Theory-Data Confrontations in Economics," *Dialogue* 34, 581–604.

Wansbeek, T. J., 2001, "GMM Estimation in Panel Data Models with Measurement Error," *Journal of Econometrics* 104, 259–268.

Wansbeek, T. J., and R. H. Koning, 1991, "Measurement Error and Panel Data," *Statistica Neerlandica* 45, 85–92.

White, H., 1982, "Instrumental Variables Regression with Independent Observations," *Econometrica* 50, 483–499.

White, H., 1984, *Asymptotic Theory for Econometricians*, Orlando: Academic Press.

Chapter Twenty-Five

On Bayesian Structural Inference in a Simultaneous Equation Model

Herman K. van Dijk

A fundamental feature of economic systems based on the market mechanism is that prices are jointly determined by the laws of demand and supply. Another feature of a dynamic market system is the joint expansion and contraction of such economic variables as consumption, investment, and gross national output during the business cycle. The econometric analysis of market price behavior and the nature of business cycles was greatly advanced in the twentieth century by the specification of the *simultaneous equation model* (SEM). Important statistical implications of a linear SEM have been indicated by Haavelmo (1943), and seminal studies on the identification and the estimation of SEM parameters are contained in two Cowles Commission monographs (Koopmans, 1950; Hood and Koopmans, 1953). In most cases use is made of the classical method of maximum likelihood, where an unknown "true" model structure is assumed. The classical econometrician is "condemned" to find this true structure. However, Drèze (1962) argues that such classical inference is not adequate since, on the one hand, available information on parameters is ignored (e.g., the marginal propensity to consume is in the unit interval) while, on the other hand, too many exact zero restrictions are imposed (e.g., zero restrictions due to the omission of certain variables in each equation). Drèze's paper has been a major stimulus for Bayesian structural inference of the SEM.

In this chapter I discuss some issues that have dominated the development of Bayesian inference of the SEM in the second half of the twentieth century. The first issue is the specification of prior information. As I mentioned earlier, Drèze started this discussion in 1962 with the common sense arguments that many structural parameters are restricted to a priori plausible regions. This does not hold only for these parameters but also for dynamic characteristics of the SEM such as correct signs of multipliers and plausible restrictions on the period of oscillation. It is, however, not trivial to incorporate these inequality restrictions in a class of analytically tractable priors such as the natural conjugate class. Further, Rothenberg (1963) pointed out that this natural conjugate class is by itself highly restrictive for systems of equations. This result is known as Rothenberg's problem. The difficulty in incorporating flexible prior information such as inequality conditions or nonlinear restrictions and the restrictiveness of the natural conjugate class of priors by itself were the starting points of new research that began in the late 1960s and the early 1970s.

Two developments took place. First, in order to simplify the analysis, single-equation inference was pursued by Drèze (1976) and Zellner (1971). In this approach a connection can be made with instrumental variable estimation. I discuss some motivating examples in Section 25.1 and analyze the limited information approach in detail in Section 25.2.

A second development was tackling the problem of finding numerical integration procedures that are computationally efficient and that allow for the use of flexible prior information that is of interest to economists. The use of Monte Carlo integration methods turned out to be revolutionary. The method of importance sampling was introduced in Bayesian inference by Kloek and van Dijk (1978) [see also Geweke (1989)]. This was followed by Markov chain Monte Carlo methods as Metropolis Hastings and Gibbs sampling. An excellent survey is provided by Geweke (1999). I refer to that paper and the references cited there, in particular, Hastings (1970) and Tierney (1994). I do not focus on the description of Monte Carlo integration in this chapter.

The application of numerical procedures to the case of the SEM has not been trivial. Here we come to an important econometric issue in Bayesian inference of the SEM. The shape of the likelihood of a SEM is nonstandard. This holds not only for the case of a model with no restrictions on the parameters but also for a standard model of a market that is identified according to classical identification conditions. This is different from the case of the linear regression model, where the marginal likelihood of parameters of interest belongs to the class of Student-t densities. The problem of a nonstandard shape of the likelihood has been analyzed by van Dijk (1985), Bauwens and van Dijk (1989), and Kleibergen and van Dijk (1992, 1994a, 1998). The basic reason is the presence of singularities in the parameter space owing to reduced rank restrictions. I illustrate Bayesian structural inference in simultaneous equation analysis through simple examples in Section 25.2. Section 25.3 contains a condition that is sufficient for the existence of posterior moments in the full information case.

The flexibility of Monte Carlo integration procedures using simulation methods has greatly advanced Bayesian inference of dynamic features of a SEM. The elicitation of informative priors by investigation of the implications for short- and long-term prediction is rather trivial using simulation methods. The potential use of Bayesian structural inference using a simple predictive approach combined with Monte Carlo as a computational tool is illustrated in Section 25.4 through an analysis of the U.S. business cycle in the period of the Great Depression.

The SEM itself came under attack by Liu (1960) and, in particular, Sims (1980) because of its "incredible" restrictions. The class of vector autoregressive (VAR) models advocated by Sims is considered to be more "data driven" whereas the SEM is more "theory driven." In Section 25.5 I discuss Bayesian inference in structural VAR models. Section 25.6 contains my conclusions.

25.1 MOTIVATION AND TWO EXAMPLES

Consider the stylized wage regression popular in empirical labor studies:

$$y_1 = \beta y_2 + x_1\gamma + u_1 \tag{1}$$

where y_1 is the log of hourly wage, y_2 denotes education, which is measured as the number of years of schooling, and x_1 equal to age − years of schooling − 6. This last variable captures work experience. Note that all variables are given in deviations from their mean values. The structural parameter of interest, β ideally measures the rate of return to schooling. The variable y_2 (years of schooling) is potentially endogenous, however, and correlated with u_1 owing to the omission of a variable measuring (unobservable) ability. The degree of endogeneity is potentially very high owing to a high expected correlation between education and ability. Classical inference makes use of instrumental variable estimation methods but potential instruments for y_2 are hard to find as these variables must be correlated with education but uncorrelated with unobserved ability. Angrist and Krueger (1991) suggest using quarter of birth as a dummy variable. They argue that quarter of birth is randomly distributed across the population and so is uncorrelated with ability and affects years of schooling weakly, through a combination of the age at which a person begins school and the compulsory education laws in a person's state. Staiger and Stock (1997) provide evidence that inference on the rate of return to schooling can be greatly affected by the weak quarter of birth instruments.

As a second example, consider the problem of determining the fraction of temporary income consumers spend in a permanent-income–consumption model. Campbell and Mankiw (1989) use the simple regression equation

$$\Delta c = \beta \Delta y + u_1 \tag{2}$$

where c is log consumption and y is log income. In this simple model, β measures the fraction of temporary income consumed. Consumption and income are simultaneously determined and so Δy is potentially highly correlated with u_1. In the permanent-income model c and y are cointegrated with cointegrating vector $(1, -1)$ and the error-correction model for Δy suggests using lagged values of Δy and Δc and the lagged error correction term, $c - y$, as instruments. However, the growth rate of income is not predicted very well from this error-correction model so that the suggested instruments are expected to be fairly weak. Note that in this example the quality of the instruments is determined by the short-run dynamics in the growth rate of income.

More formally, consider the following two-equation SEM

$$y_1 = \beta y_2 + X_1\gamma + u_1 \tag{3}$$

$$y_2 = X_1\pi_{21} + X_2\pi_{22} + v_2 \tag{4}$$

where y_1 is a $(T \times 1)$ vector of observations on the structural equation of interest, y_2 is a $(T \times 1)$ vector of observations on the included endogenous variable, β is the scalar structural parameter of interest, X_1 is a $(T \times k_1)$ matrix of included weakly exogenous variables, γ is a $(k_1 \times 1)$ vector of structural parameters (not of direct interest), X_2 is a $(T \times k_2)$ matrix of excluded weakly exogenous variables or instruments and π_{21} and π_{22} are $(k_1 \times 1)$ and $(k_2 \times 1)$ vectors of reduced form parameters, respectively. It is assumed that $k_2 \geq 1$ so that the necessary condition for identification of β is satisfied and we call $k_2 - 1$ the degree of overidentification. The variables in $X = [X_1 \vdots X_2]$, which may contain lagged predetermined variables, are assumed to be weakly exogenous for the structural parameters β and γ (see Engle et al., 1983). I assume that the rows of the error terms u_1 and v_2 are independently normally distributed with covariance matrix Σ, which has elements σ_{ij} $(i, j = 1, 2)$. Note that (3) and (4) together are known as the incomplete simultaneous equation model (INSEM).[1]

The interpretation of the parameters is crucial in this context. The parameter $\rho = \sigma_{12}/(\sigma_{11}\sigma_{22})^{1/2}$ measures the degree of endogeneity of y_2 in (1), and π_{22} captures the quality of the instruments. The weak instrument problem occurs in (1) and (2) when $\mid \rho \mid \approx 1$ and $\pi_{22} \approx 0$ so that β is nearly nonidentified.[2] The weak instrument problem in the INSEM has been examined from a Bayesian point of view by Kleibergen and Zivot (1998) and Gao and Lahiri (1999). In the next section I discuss the connection between weak instruments and Bayesian limited information.

25.2 LIMITED INFORMATION OR INCOMPLETE SIMULTANEOUS EQUATION ANALYSIS

25.2.1 Parameterizations

There are several equivalent ways to parameterize the INSEM, and Bayesian analysis is influenced by the adopted parameterization. The *structural form* of the INSEM is given in (3) and (4) and was the parameterization originally analyzed by Zellner (1971) (see also Zellner et al., 1988). The multivariate regression representation of the structural form is

$$YB = X\Gamma + U, \tag{5}$$

where $Y = [y_1, y_2]$, $X = [X_1, X_2]$ and $U = [u_1, v_2]$ with

$$B = \begin{bmatrix} 1 & 0 \\ -\beta & 1 \end{bmatrix}, \qquad \Gamma = \begin{bmatrix} \gamma & \pi_{21} \\ 0 & \pi_{22} \end{bmatrix}.$$

Since $|B| = 1$ the likelihood function for the INSEM is of the same form as a seemingly unrelated regressions (SUR) model.

The *unrestricted reduced form* of the model is

$$y_1 = X_1\pi_{11} + X_2\pi_{12} + v_1, \tag{6}$$

$$y_2 = X_1\pi_{21} + X_2\pi_{22} + v_2. \tag{7}$$

In systems form the unrestricted reduced form is

$$Y = X\Pi + V,$$

where the rows of V are independently normally distributed with mean zero and covariance matrix Ω. Since (6) and (7) represent simply a multivariate linear model, all of the reduced-form parameters are identified.

The identifying restrictions that tie the structural form to the reduced form are $\gamma = \pi_{11} - \pi_{21}\beta$, $\pi_{21} - \pi_{22}\beta = 0$, $\sigma_{11} = \omega_{11} - 2\beta\omega_{12} + \beta^2\omega_{22}$, $\sigma_{12} = \omega_{12} - \beta\omega_{22}$, and $\sigma_{22} = \omega_{22}$.

The *restricted reduced form* of the INSEM is obtained by imposing the identifying restrictions on the unrestricted reduced form and is given by

$$y_1 = X_1(\pi_{21}\beta + \gamma) + X_2\pi_{22}\beta + v_1 \tag{8}$$

$$y_2 = X_1\pi_{21} + X_2\pi_{22} + v_2, \tag{9}$$

where $v_1 = u_1 - v_2\beta$. In system form we have

$$Y = -X\Gamma B^{-1} + UB^{-1},$$

where $\Omega = B^{-1'}\Sigma B^{-1}$. The restricted reduced form is a multivariate regression model with nonlinear restrictions on the parameters. In the absence of restrictions on the covariance structure of Σ, β is identified if and only if $\pi_{22} \neq 0$ and $k_2 \geq 1$. If $\rho = 0$, however, then β is identified even if $\pi_{22} = 0$.

The *orthogonal structural form* (Zellner et al., 1988) reads

$$y_1 = y_2\beta + X_1\gamma_1 + v_2\phi + \eta_1, \tag{10}$$

$$y_2 = X_1\pi_{21} + X_2\pi_{22} + v_2, \tag{11}$$

where

$$\begin{pmatrix} \eta_1 \\ v_2 \end{pmatrix} \sim N\left[\begin{pmatrix} 0 \\ 0 \end{pmatrix}, \begin{pmatrix} \sigma_{11.2} & 0 \\ 0 & \sigma_{22} \end{pmatrix}\right],$$

$$\sigma_{11.2} = \sigma_{11} - \sigma_{12}\sigma_{22}^{-1}\sigma_{21}, \qquad \phi = \sigma_{22}^{-1}\sigma_{12}.$$

The parameter ϕ measures the degree of endogeneity. Note that $\phi = \rho(\sigma_{11}/\sigma_{22})^{\frac{1}{2}}$.

The interest here is in cases where there are different degrees of identifiability. It is well known that the likelihood is flat when there are nonidentified parameters. It is of interest to note that different degrees of identification correspond to different degrees of the quality of instrumental variables in classical IV estimation.

For convenience I consider the case of a *just identified model*, where $k_2 = 1$. The structural representation is now

$$y_1 = y_2\beta + u_1, \tag{12}$$

$$y_2 = x\pi_{22} + v_2; \tag{13}$$

the unrestricted reduced form is

$$y_1 = x\pi_{12} + v_1, \tag{14}$$

$$y_2 = x\pi_{22} + v_2; \tag{15}$$

and the restricted reduced form is

$$y_1 = x\pi_{22}\beta + \beta v_2 + u_1, \tag{16}$$

$$y_2 = x\pi_{22} + v_2. \tag{17}$$

If $\rho \neq 0$, the structural parameter β is identified provided $\pi_{22} \neq 0$ and can be uniquely recovered from the reduced form via the transformation $\beta = \pi_{12}/\pi_{22}$. In addition, if β is identified then the structural correlation coefficient ρ can be recovered via the transformation $\rho = (\omega_{12} - \beta\omega_{22})/[(\omega_{11} - 2\beta\omega_{12} + \beta^2\omega_{22})\omega_{22}]^{1/2}$. Similarly, if ρ is identified then β can be recovered from the elements of Ω.

The orthogonal structural form is

$$y_1 = y_2\beta + v_2\phi + \eta_1, \tag{18}$$

$$y_2 = x\pi_{22} + v_2. \tag{19}$$

The case of nearly nonidentified parameters or weak instruments occurs when $\pi_{22} \approx 0$ and there is strong endogeneity when $\mid \rho = \phi \mid \approx 1$.

25.2.2 Marginal Likelihood or Posterior Analysis with a Uniform Prior of the Structural Model

In this subsection I present a Bayesian analysis of the INSEM for the simple bivariate just identified model with no exogenous variables in the structural equation. I use flat priors for the parameters of interest and avoid getting into the complicated algebra that accompanies the general analysis. The discussion draws on Zellner (1971), Drèze (1976), Bauwens and van Dijk (1989), Zellner et al., (1988), Kleibergen and van Dijk (1992, 1994a, 1998), and Chao and Phillips (1998). A flat or diffuse prior for the structural parameters β, π_{22}, and Σ is of the form

$$p(\beta, \pi_{22}, \Sigma) \propto |\, \Sigma \,|^{-\frac{1}{2}h}, \; h > 0. \tag{20}$$

The likelihood function of the structural model for a sample of size T is

$$L(\beta, \pi_{22}, \Sigma \mid y_1, y_2, x) \propto |\, \Sigma \,|^{-\frac{1}{2}T} \exp\left\{-\tfrac{1}{2}\mathrm{tr}\left[\Sigma^{-1}U'U\right]\right\}. \tag{21}$$

Thus the joint posterior based on the flat prior is

$$p(\beta, \pi_{22}, \Sigma \mid y_1, y_2, x) \propto |\, \Sigma \,|^{-\frac{1}{2}(T+h)} \exp\left\{-\tfrac{1}{2}\mathrm{tr}\left[\Sigma^{-1}U'U\right]\right\}. \tag{22}$$

With the use of properties of the inverted Wishart distribution (see Zellner, 1971 and Bauwens and van Dijk, 1989), Σ^{-1} may be analytically integrated out of the joint posterior to give the following joint posterior for (β, π_{22}):

$$p(\beta, \pi_{22} \mid y_1, y_2, x) \propto |\, U'U \,|^{-\frac{1}{2}(T+h-3)} = |\, (u_1 v_2)'(u_1 v_2) \,|^{-\frac{1}{2}(T+h-3)}. \tag{23}$$

Note that $p(\beta, \pi_{22} \mid y_1, y_2, x)$ is of the same form as the concentrated likelihood function for (β, π_{22}) from the maximum likelihood analysis of the INSEM, apart from the degrees-of-freedom parameter h.

The marginal posteriors for β and π_{22} can be determined from (23) using properties of the Student-t distribution and the decomposition

$$|\, (u_1 v_2)'(u_1 v_2) \,| = |\, u_1' u_1 \,||\, v_2' M_{u1} v_2 \,| = |\, v_2' v_2 \,||\, u_1' M_{v2} u_1 \,|, \tag{24}$$

where $M_A = I - P_A$, $P_A = A(A'A)^{-1}A'$ for any full rank matrix A. Straightforward calculations yield the following result.[3]

Theorem 1 *Weak Structural Inference (Drèze, 1976). The marginal posterior for β is a ratio of Student-t densities and is similar in form to the concentrated likelihood function.*

For the exactly identified model one obtains

$$p(\beta \mid y_1, y_2, x) \propto \frac{|\, (y_1 - y_2\beta)' M_x (y_1 - y_2\beta) \,|^{\frac{1}{2}(T+h-5)}}{|\, (y_1 - y_2\beta)'(y_1 - y_2\beta) \,|^{\frac{1}{2}(T+h-4)}}. \tag{25}$$

The concentrated likelihood is given as

$$l(\beta \mid y_1, y_2, x) \propto \left[\frac{(y_1 - y_2\beta)' M_x (y_1 - y_2\beta)}{(y_1 - y_2\beta)'(y_1 - y_2\beta)}\right]^{\frac{1}{2}T}.$$

The difference between the concentrated likelihood function and the marginal posterior reflects the difference between concentration and marginalization of the likelihood function (21). The concentrated likelihood function may be interpreted as the posterior density for β resulting from a flat prior *conditional* on the modal values of Σ and π_{22}, whereas the marginal posterior for β is obtained after integrating out these parameters for the joint posterior.

For the just identified model we proceed as follows. Choose $h = G + 1 = 3$ and rewrite (23) as

$$p(\beta \mid y_1, y_2, x) \propto c(\beta) \mid (y_1 - y_2\beta)' M_x (y_1 - y_2\beta) \mid^{-\frac{1}{2}(1+0)} \quad (26)$$

where $1+0$ refers to the dimension of β and the degrees-of-freedom parameter, respectively and $c(\beta)$ is given as

$$c(\beta) = \left[\frac{\mid (y_1 - y_2\beta)' M_x (y_1 - y_2\beta) \mid}{\mid (y_1 - y_2\beta)'(y_1 - y_2\beta) \mid} \right]^{\frac{1}{2}(T+h-4)}.$$

It is easily seen that $c(\beta)$ is bounded from above and below by extreme eigenvalues of data matrices of moments of (y_1, y_2) and $M_x(y_1, y_2)$. Thus (23) is bounded by a Student-t density $t(\beta \mid \hat{\beta}_{2SLS}, s^2 y_2' M_x y_2, 0)$, which is not proper (integrable) for $-\infty \leq \beta \leq \infty$. The nonintegrability or "fat-tails" of the posterior is the result of integrating the joint posterior for (β, π_{22}) across the infinite ridge in the β direction that occurs at $\pi_{22} = 0$. Consequently, unless the range of β is truncated a priori, posterior inference regarding β is not possible.

For overidentified models, it can be shown that the moments of the marginal posterior for β exist up to the order of overidentification. Note that the difference in the exponents of (25) then becomes larger (for details see Kleibergen and van Dijk, 1998). Hence, the marginal posterior of β is proper if there are at least two instruments. One consequence of this result is that the existence of posterior moments of β depends on the order condition for identification and not the rank condition. *Hence, it is possible to sharpen inference about* β *by simply adding more instruments to the model.* This result was first pointed out by Maddala (1976) and was explained analytically by Kleibergen and van Dijk (1998).

Finally, for large values of T, the marginal posterior for β may be approximated by

$$p(\beta \mid y_1, y_2, x) \propto \exp\left[-\tfrac{1}{2}(y_1 - y_2\beta)' P_x (y_1 - y_2\beta)\right],$$

which is a normal density centered at the 2SLS estimate of β. Thus, for large T the Bayesian results based on flat priors for the structural model coincide with classical results.

A second result is obtained by marginalizing (23) with respect to β.

Theorem 2 *Local Nonidentification and Impossible Reduced Form Inference (Kleibergen and van Dijk, 1998). The marginal posterior of* π_{22} *is equal to the kernel of a univariate Student-t centered at* $\hat{\pi}_{22}^{\mathrm{OLS}}$ *multiplied by the factor* $\mid \pi_{22} \mid^{-1}$ *and is given as*

$$p(\pi_{22} \mid y_1, y_2, x) \propto \mid \pi_{22} \mid^{-1} \mid (y_2 - x\pi_{22})'(y_2 - x\pi_{22}) \mid^{-\frac{1}{2}(T+h-4)}. \quad (27)$$

The factor $\mid \pi_{22} \mid^{-1}$ creates a nonintegrable asymptote since the posterior density is infinite at $\pi_{22} = 0$ and, therefore, the posterior is not a proper density. As a consequence, forecasting and decision analysis are not feasible. The intuition behind this result stems from the nonidentifiability of β when $\pi_{22} = 0$. When $\pi_{22} = 0$, β is not identified and the joint posterior of (β, π_{22})

is flat in the β direction along the axis where $\pi_{22} = 0$ (see Figs. 25.7–25.9 in Section 25.2.3). As a result, the integral of the joint posterior over β is infinite, which produces the asymptote at zero in the marginal posterior of π_{22}.

Kleibergen and van Dijk (1994a) and Chao and Phillips (1998) point out that the nonintegrability of (27) can be interpreted as a pathology that has been imposed on the model by a peculiar prior induced on the reduced-form parameters (π_{12}, π_{22}) of (14) and (15). Since $\pi_{12} = \beta\pi_{22}$ there is a 1-1 relationship between (β, π_{22}) and (π_{12}, π_{22}) and a flat prior over (β, π_{22}) implies, by the change-of-variables formula, the nonflat prior for (π_{12}, π_{22}):

$$p(\pi_{12}, \pi_{22}) \propto p_F^S(\beta, \pi_{22} \left| \frac{\partial(\beta, \pi_{22})}{\partial(\pi_{21}, \pi_{22})} \right| = |\pi_{22}|^{-1}.$$

The induced prior for (π_{12}, π_{22}) gives infinite density to the point $\pi_{22} = 0$ in the reduced form and thus the flat prior (20) is far from noninformative for π_{22} since it infinitely favors the point π_{22} in the posterior. Another way of explaining the result is that correlation between β and π_{22} that is present in the likelihood is not reflected in the flat prior. Kleibergen and van Dijk (1994a) point out the similarity between the discontinuity in the Bayesian results and the breakdown of standard classical asymptotic results when $\pi_{22} = 0$. They note that a classical solution is to not allow π_{22} to equal zero, as in the local-to-zero asymptotics of Staiger and Stock (1997), and they argue that a sensible Bayesian procedure should also have this type of restriction. A procedure for dealing with this problem is given by Kleibergen and van Dijk (1998) and discussed in the next subsection.

25.2.3 A Simple Example with Artificially Generated Data

For illustrative purposes, posteriors are calculated from simulated data from (12) and (13) with $T = 100$, $\beta = 0$, $\sigma_{11} = \sigma_{22} = 1$, $x \sim N(0, 1)$ for three cases representing: (1) strong identification/good instruments ($\pi_{22} = 1$); (2) weak identification/weak instruments ($\pi_{22} = 0.1$), and (3) nonidentification/irrelevant instruments ($\pi_{22} = 0$). These cases are combined with cases of: strong ($\rho = 0.99$), medium ($\rho = 0.5$), and no ($\rho = 0$) degree of endogeneity. The joint posterior (23) from the simulated data is plotted in Figs. 25.1–25.9 for the three cases.[4] The bivariate and contour plots are highly informative and give three typical shapes of the marginal likelihood: *bell shaped, multimodality, and elongated ridges* (Table 25.1).

1. *Strong identification/good instruments give regular bell shaped posterior curves*: Consider Figs. 25.1–25.3. When $\rho = 0$, the bivariate posterior has the familiar bell-like shape of a bivariate normal distribution and is centered near the 2SLS estimate of β [which is also the limited information maximum likelihood (LIML) estimator since the model is just identified]

and the OLS estimate of π_{22}. When $\rho = 0.99$, the bivariate posterior reduces to a thin single-peaked bell-like shape. It must be emphasized that the plots of $p_F^S(\pi_{22} \mid Y, x)$ do not always display the spike at $\pi_{22} = 0$, owing to the fact that they are drawn for a finite grid of points that excludes $\pi_{22} = 0$.

2. *Weak identification/weak instruments give multimodal posterior curves*: Consider Figs. 25.4–25.6. For the case with $\rho = 0.99$, the bivariate posterior for (β, π_{22}) is multimodal and actually separates into two L-shaped regions about the point $\pi_{22} = 0$ and $\beta = 0$. In addition, the bivariate posterior develops a long series of bell curves in the β direction at $\pi_{22} = 0$, suggesting that β is undetermined at that value of π_{22}. This "shelf" is the result of the lack of identification of β at $\pi_{22} = 0$.
3. *Nonidentification/irrelevant instruments give elongated ridges in posterior surface*: Consider Figs. 25.7–25.9. In the irrelevant instrument (unidentified) case, the bivariate posterior is again multimodal but now the "shelf" in the β direction at $\pi_{22} = 0$, is very prominent. The posterior does not separate this time and the contour plot indicates a wide range of possible values for β. This is what we expect with data generated from an unidentified model.

Given the generated data one can easily compute OLS and IV/2SLS estimates for β and π_{22}. For the good instrument case the OLS estimate of β has a strong bias and a small standard error. The IV/2SLS estimate of β is closer to the true value of zero. The 95 percent confidence interval easily covers zero. The OLS results for the reduced form give a 95 percent confidence interval that does not cover zero, confirming the good quality of the instrument. The marginal posterior for β is very similar to the shape of a normal curve centered on the IV estimate with a standard deviation equal to the standard error of the IV estimate, so the classical and Bayesian analyses give very similar information. Note, however, the spike in the posterior of π_{22}.

For the weak-instrument case, the OLS estimate of β is even more biased and the estimated standard error is smaller than in the good instrument case. The marginal posterior for β is multimodal and has extremely fat tails with secondary modes. The wide distribution of mass reflects a great deal of uncertainty about the true value of β and its convoluted shape reflects the width and prominence of the "shelf" in the bivariate posterior. Interestingly, the posterior degenerates near the OLS estimate which, in turn, is close to the point of concentration of the finite sample distribution of the IV estimate in the case of poor instruments.

In the irrelevant instrument case, the IV estimate of β has a Cauchy distribution centered at the point of concentration (see Phillips, 1989). The marginal posterior for β is unimodal and tightly peaked about the point of concentration, but with long fat tails. The posterior is remarkably similar to the finite sample

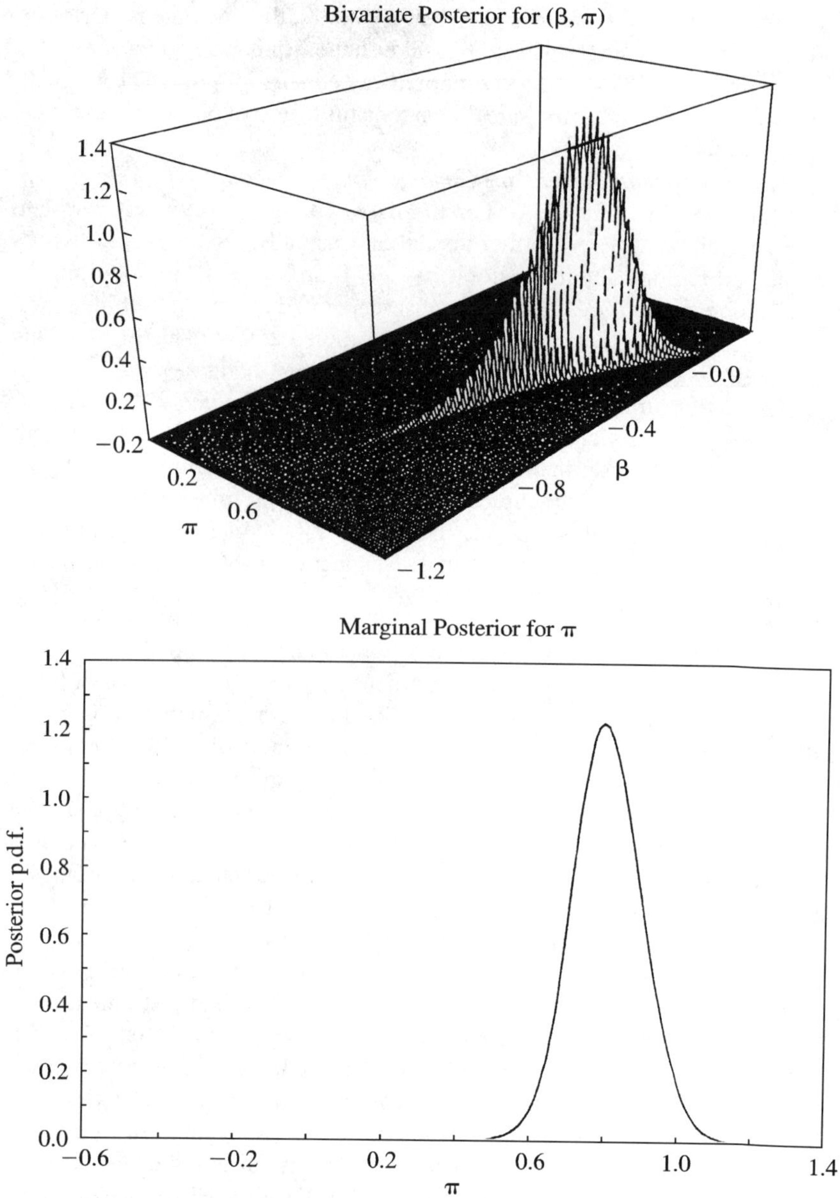

Fig. 25.1 Shape of marginal likelihood with strong identification/good instruments and strong endogeneity.

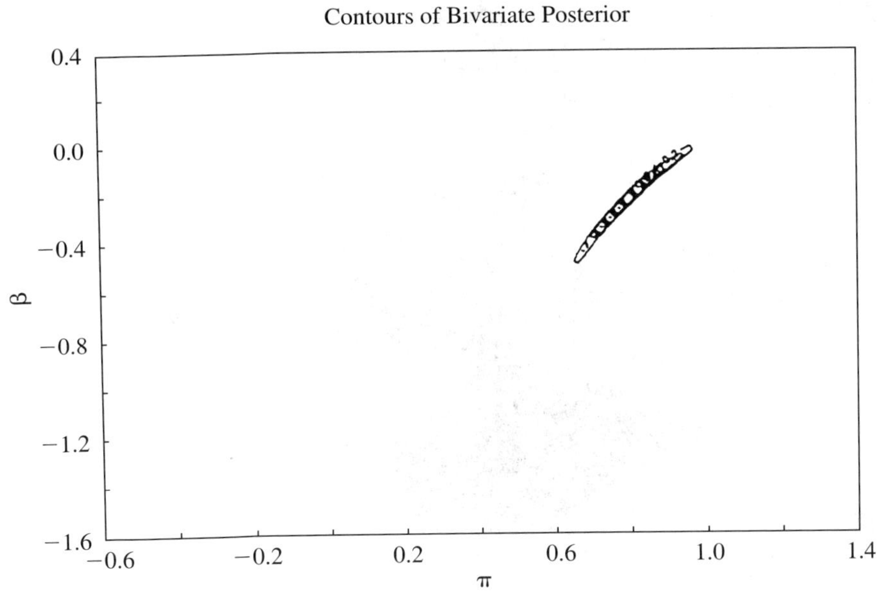

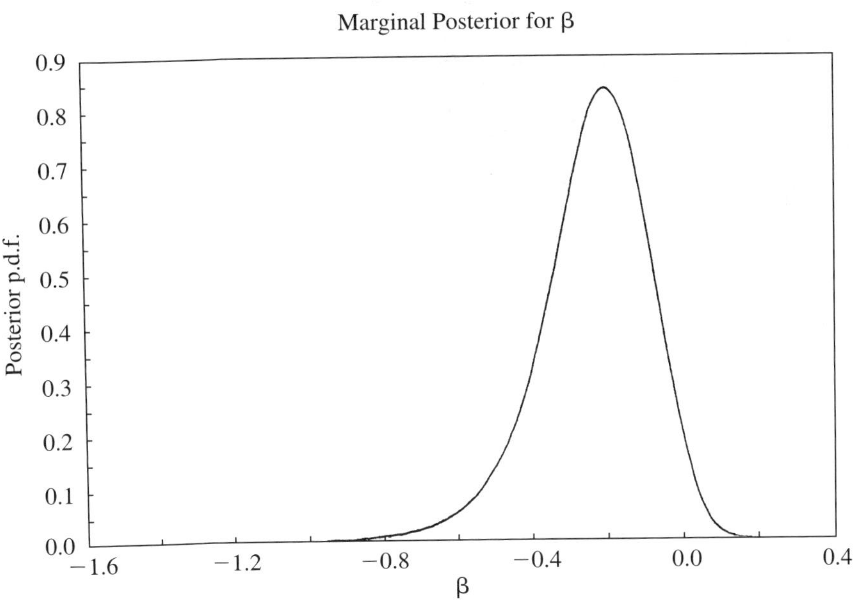

Fig. 25.1 *(Continued)*

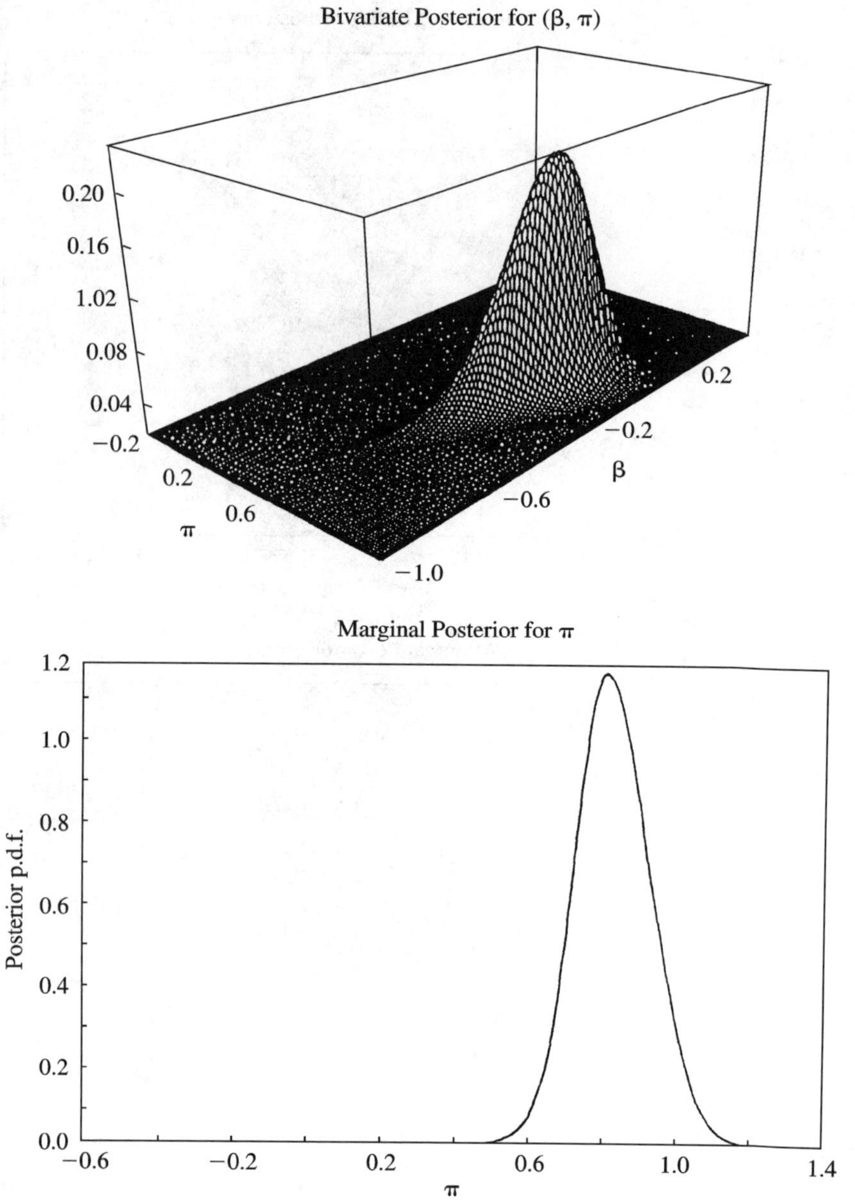

Fig. 25.2 Shape of marginal likelihood with strong identification/good instruments and medium endogeneity.

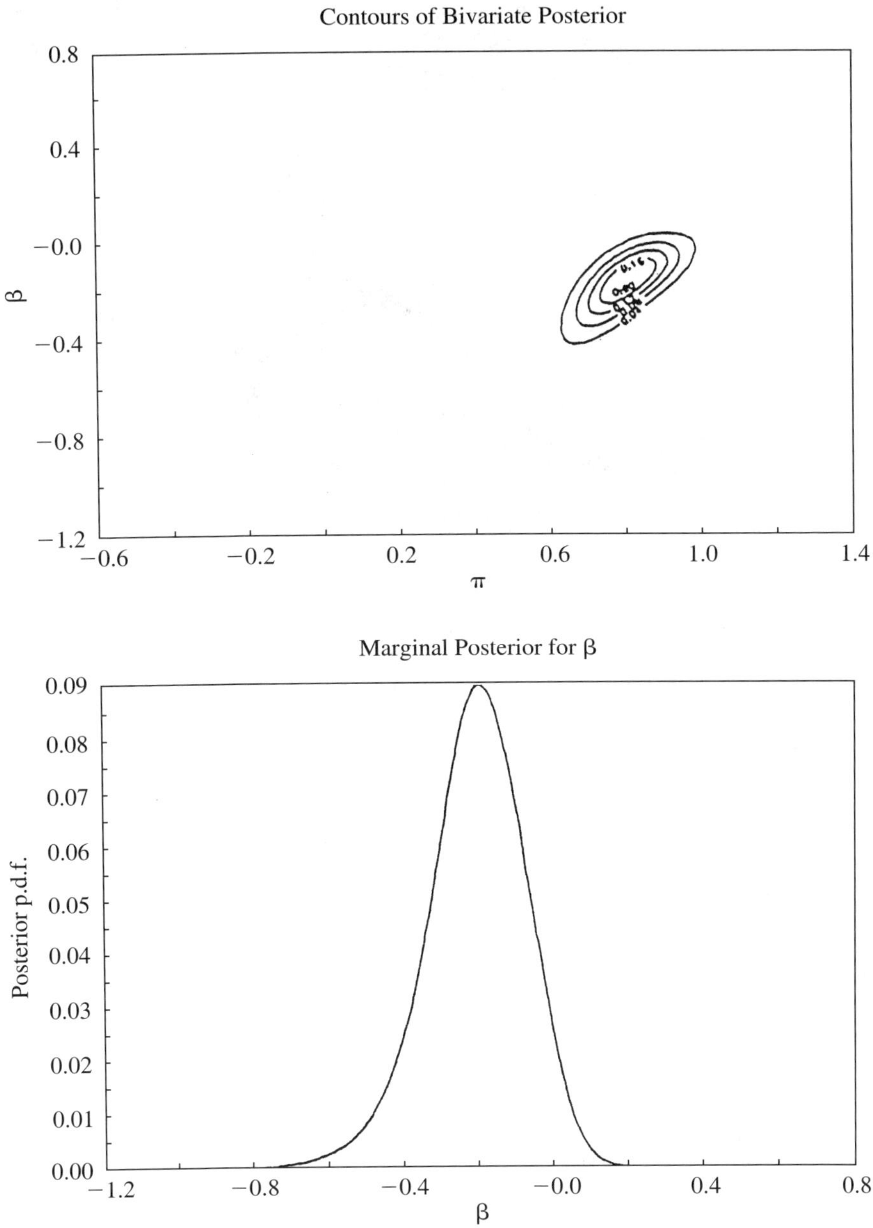

Fig. 25.2 (*Continued*)

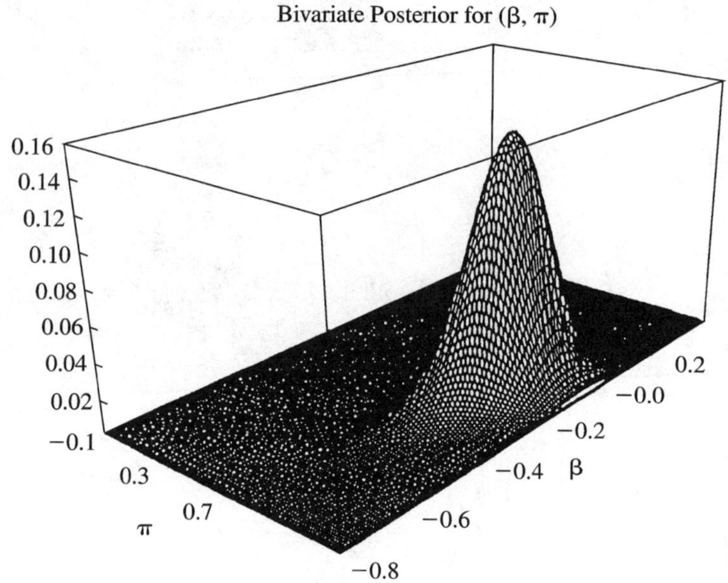

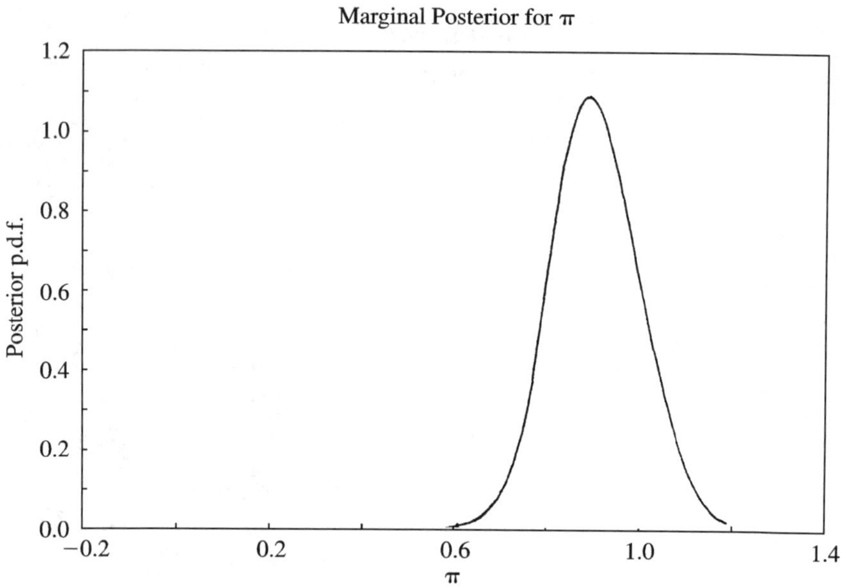

Fig. 25.3 Shape of marginal likelihood with strong identification/good instruments and no endogeneity.

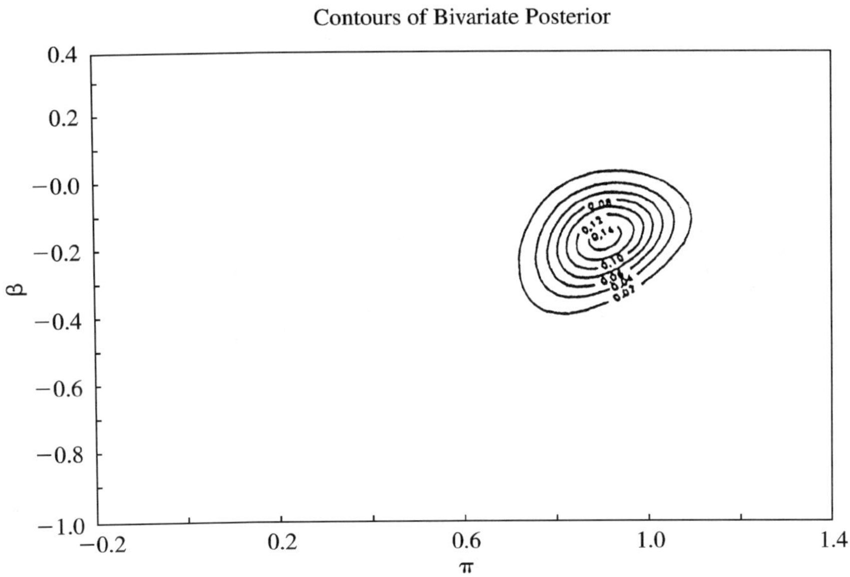

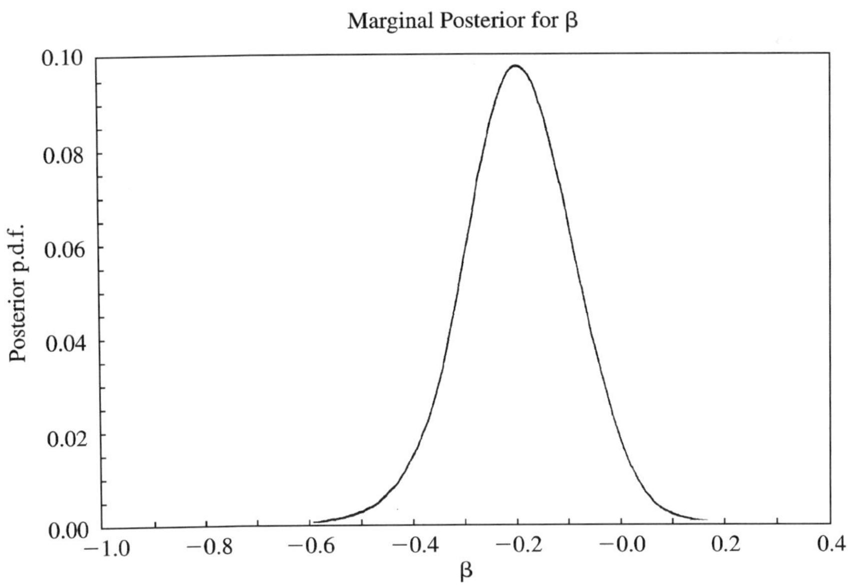

Fig. 25.3 (*Continued*)

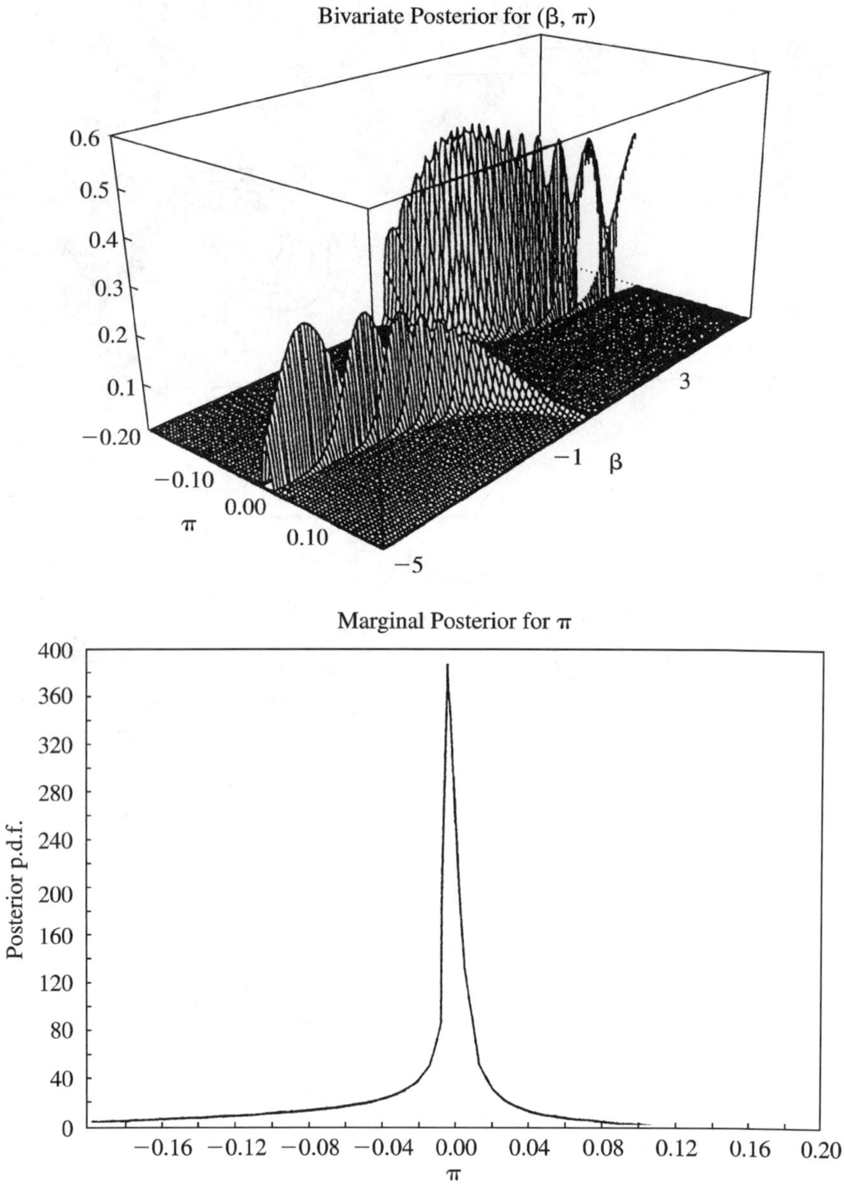

Fig. 25.4 Shape of marginal likelihood with weak identification/weak instruments and strong endogeneity.

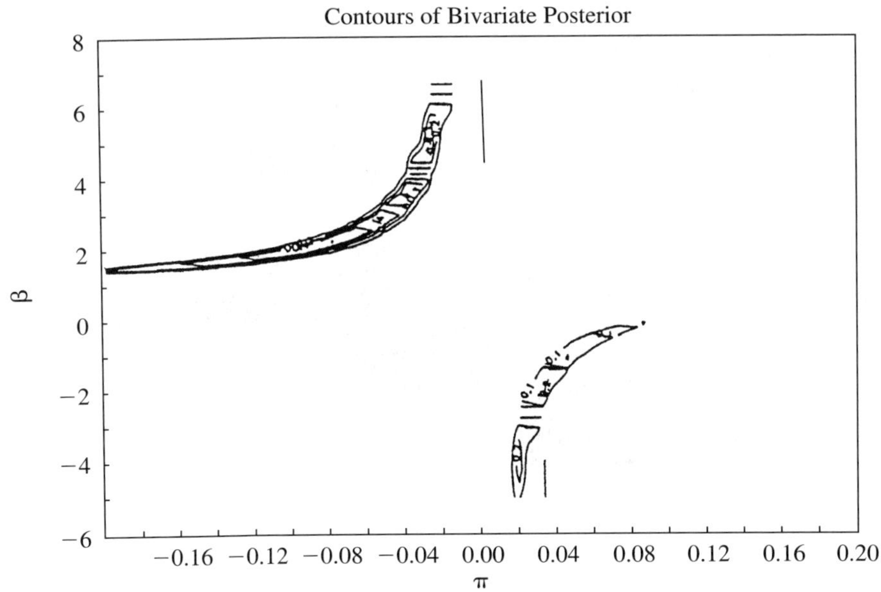

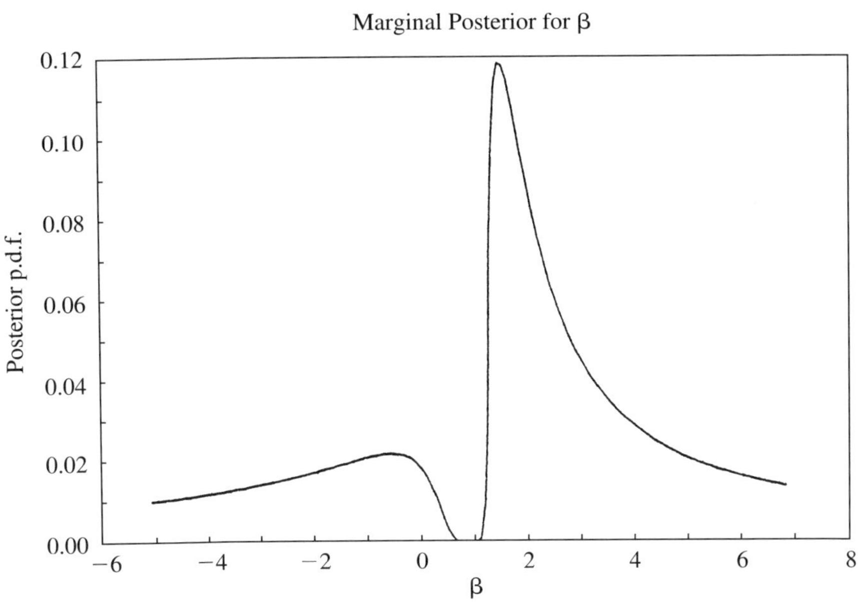

Fig. 25.4 (*Continued*)

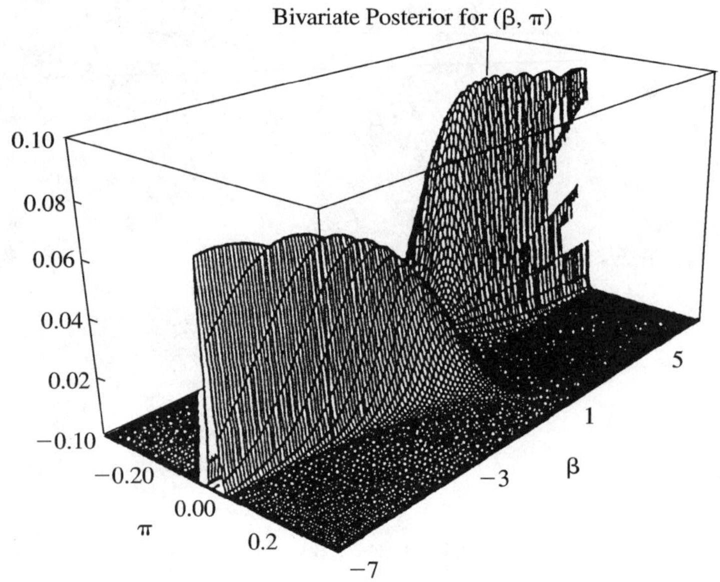

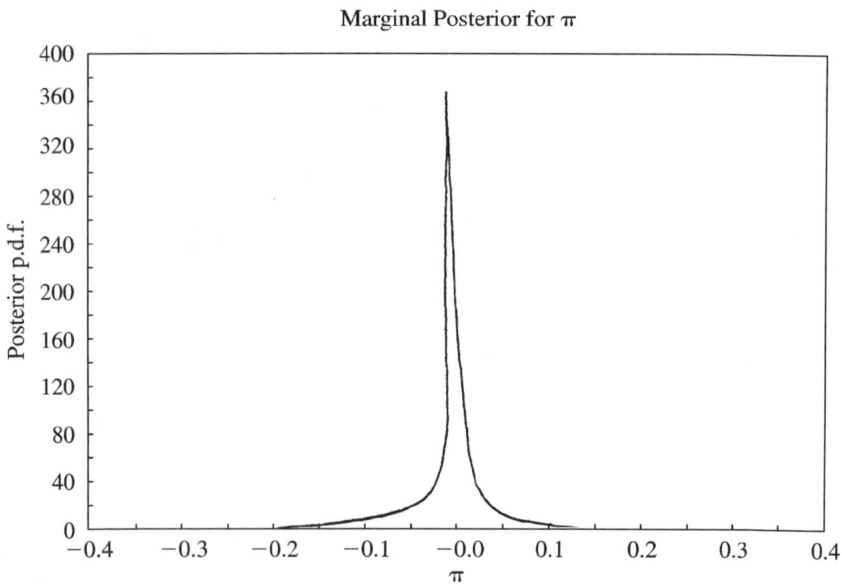

Fig. 25.5 Shape of marginal likelihood with weak identification/weak instruments and medium endogeneity.

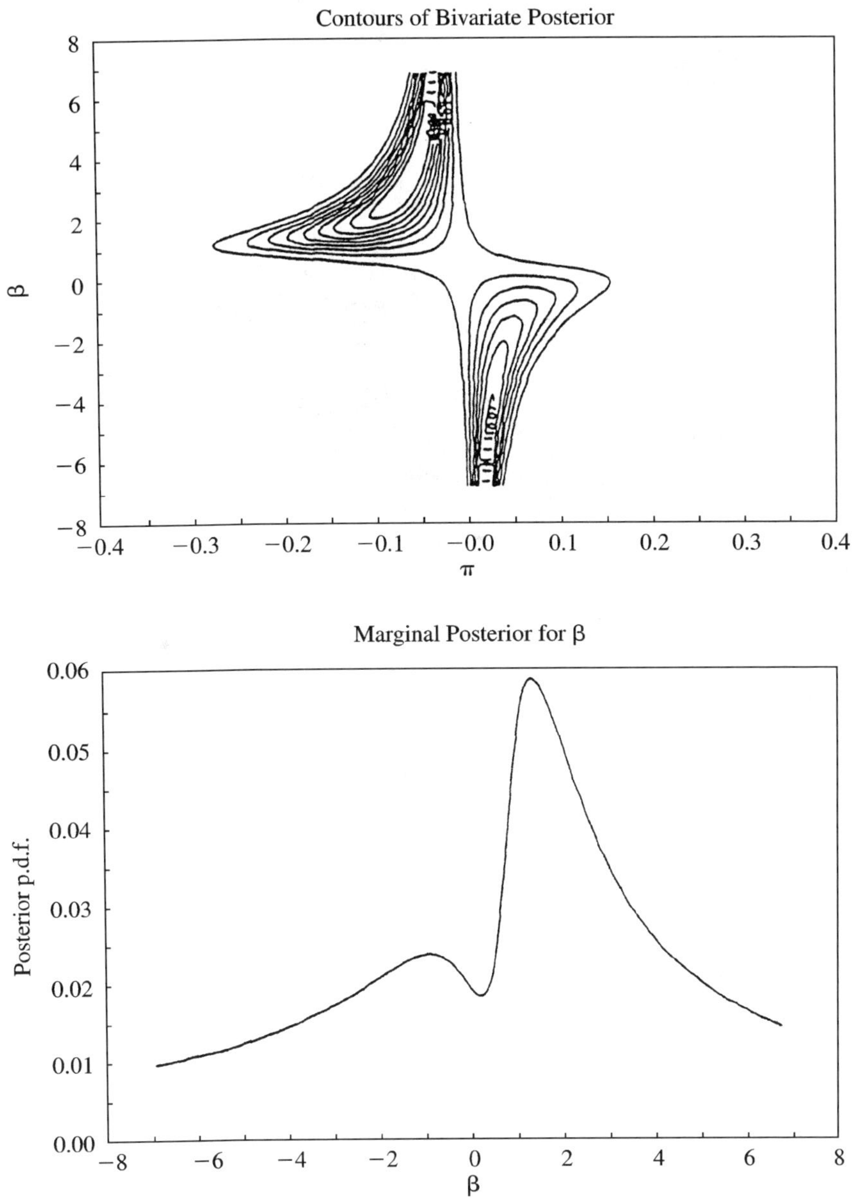

Fig. 25.5 *(Continued)*

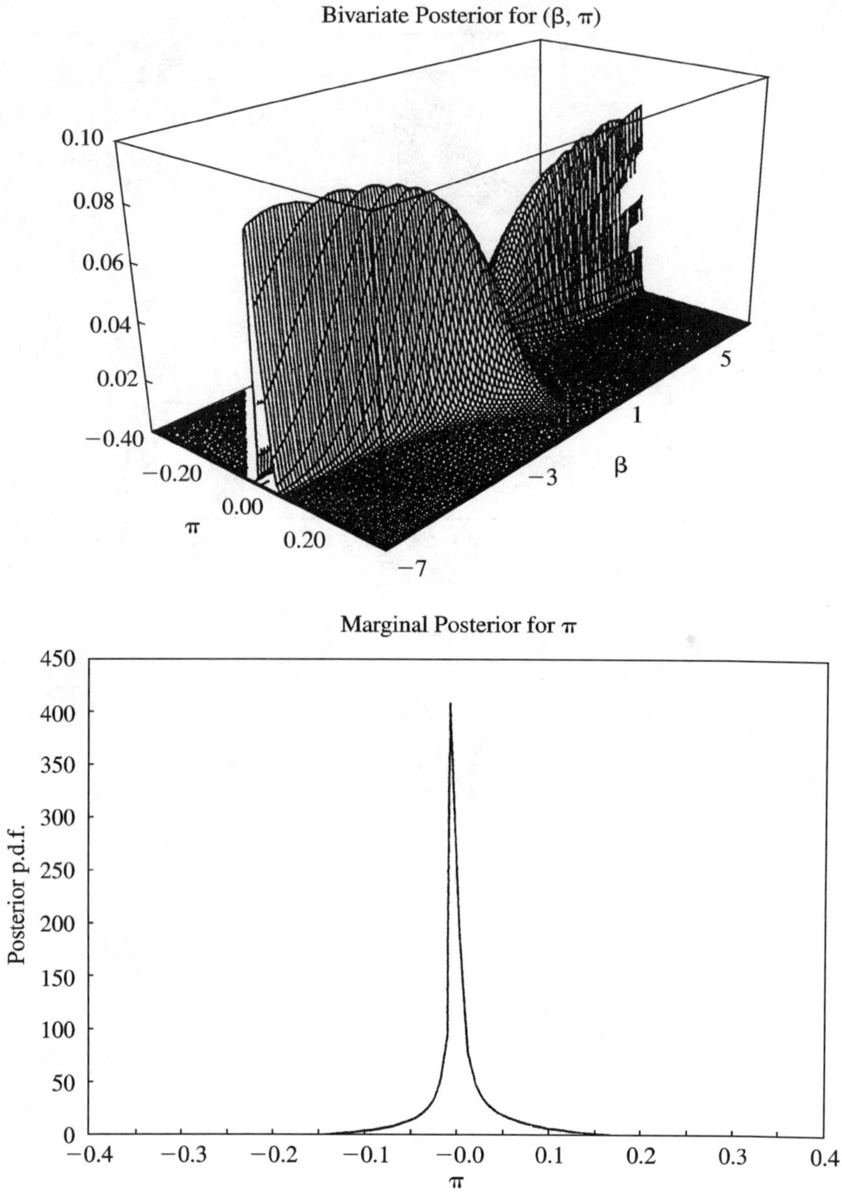

Fig. 25.6 Shape of marginal likelihood with weak identification/weak instruments and no endogeneity.

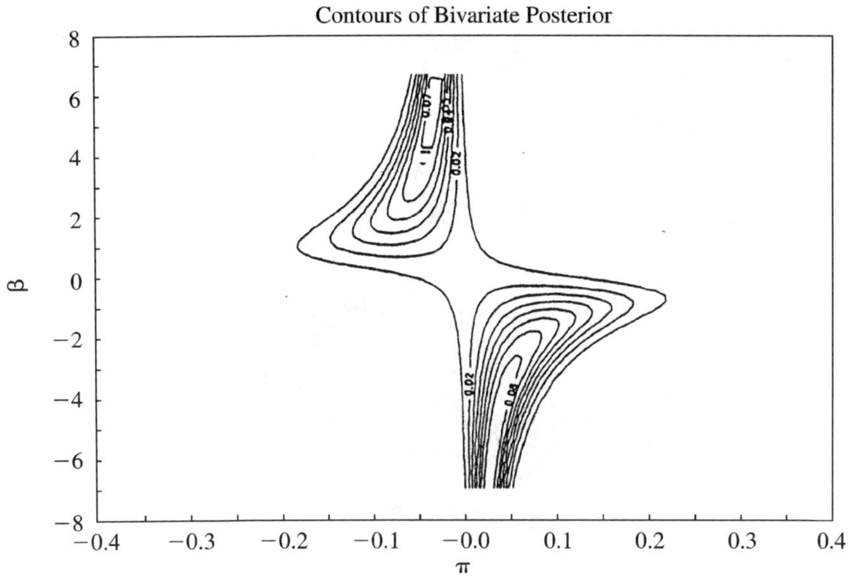

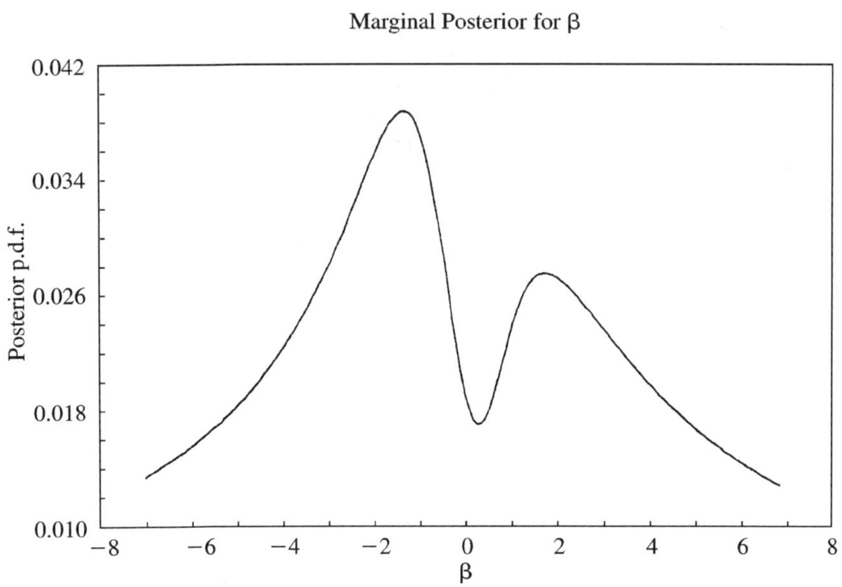

Fig. 25.6 (*Continued*)

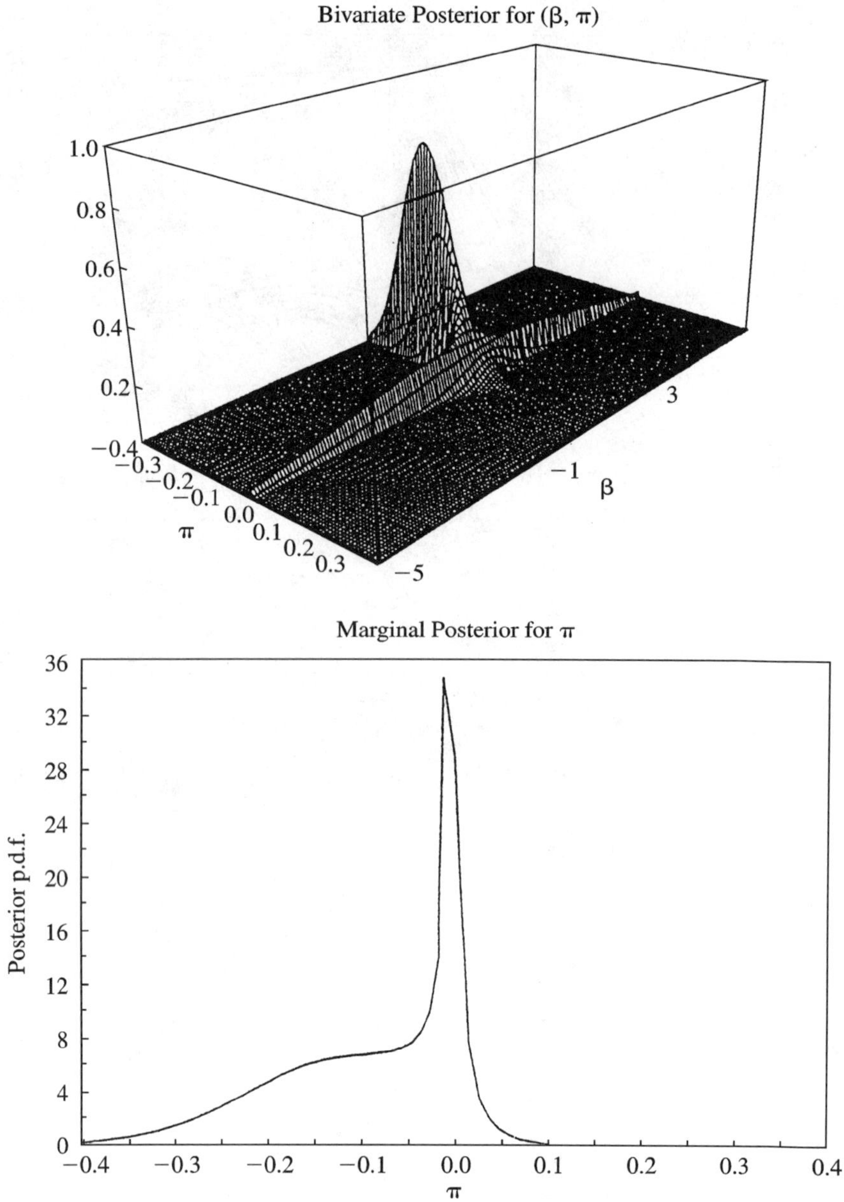

Fig. 25.7 Shape of marginal likelihood with unidentification/irrelevant instruments and strong endogeneity.

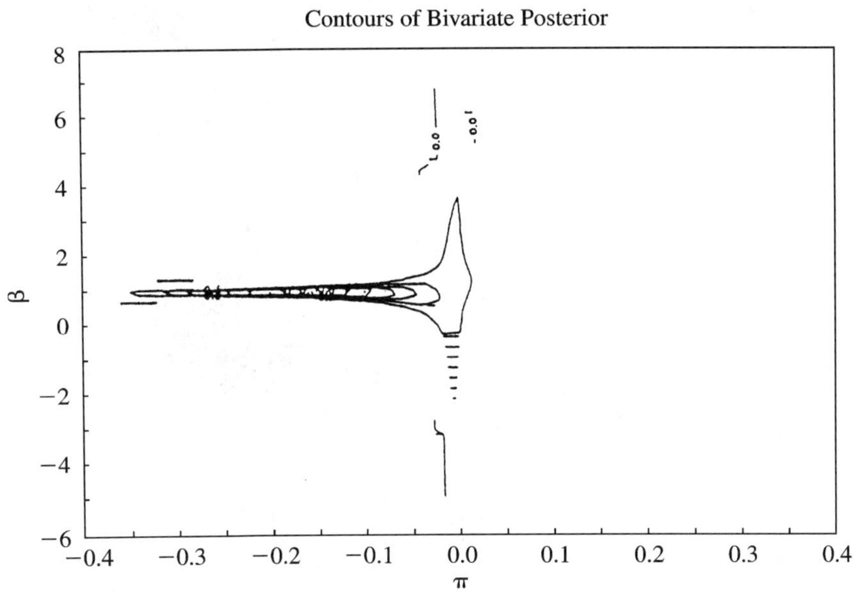

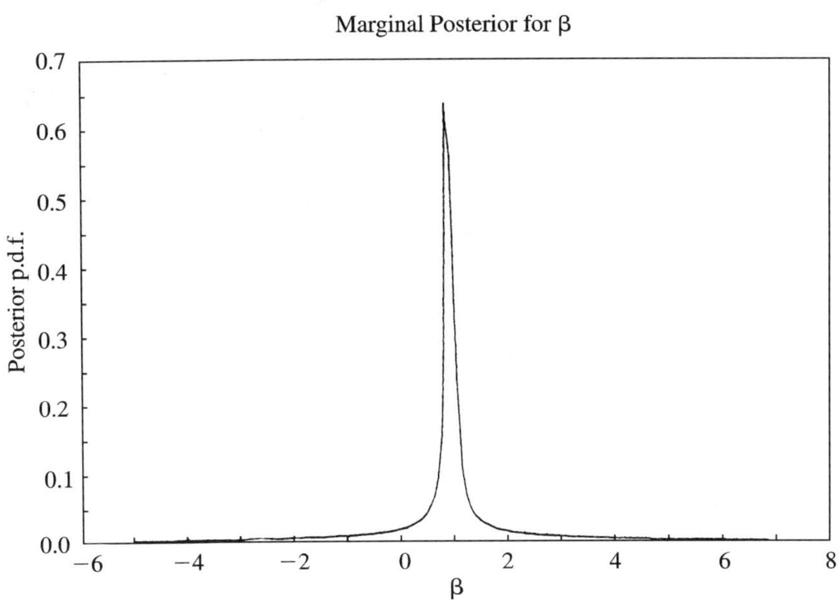

Fig. 25.7 (*Continued*)

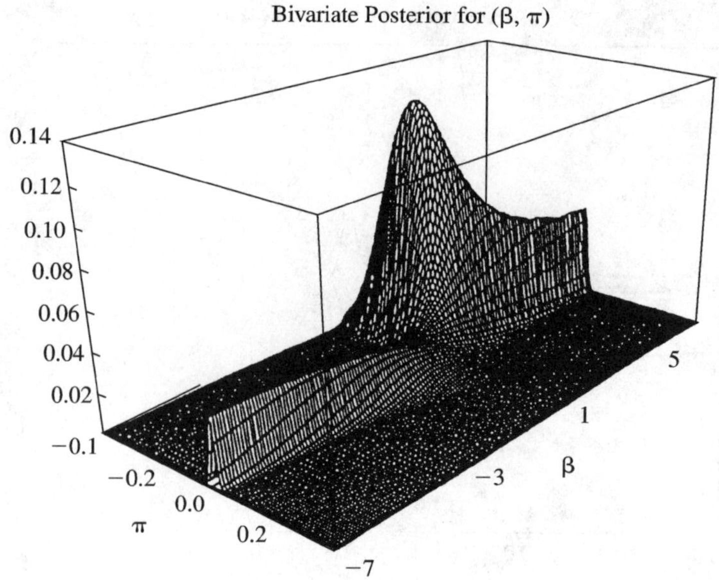

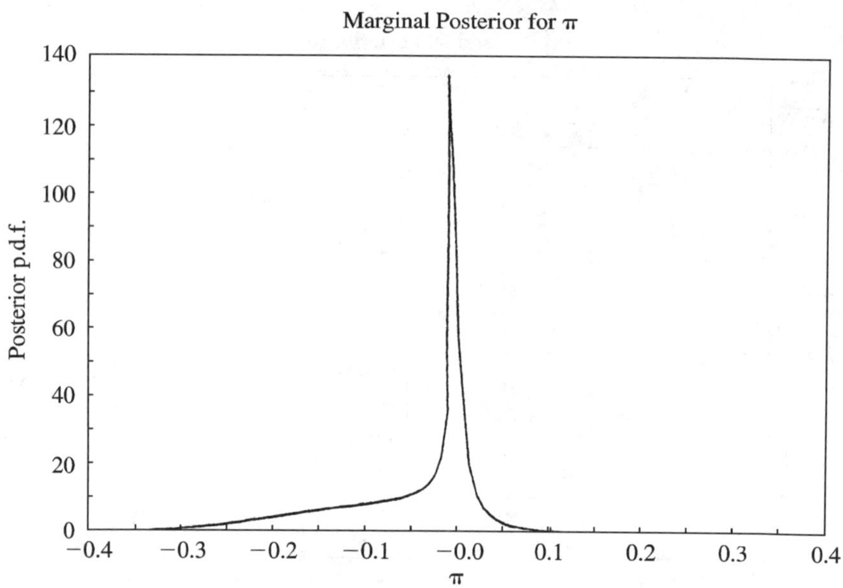

Fig. 25.8 Shape of marginal likelihood with unidentification/irrelevant instruments and medium endogeneity.

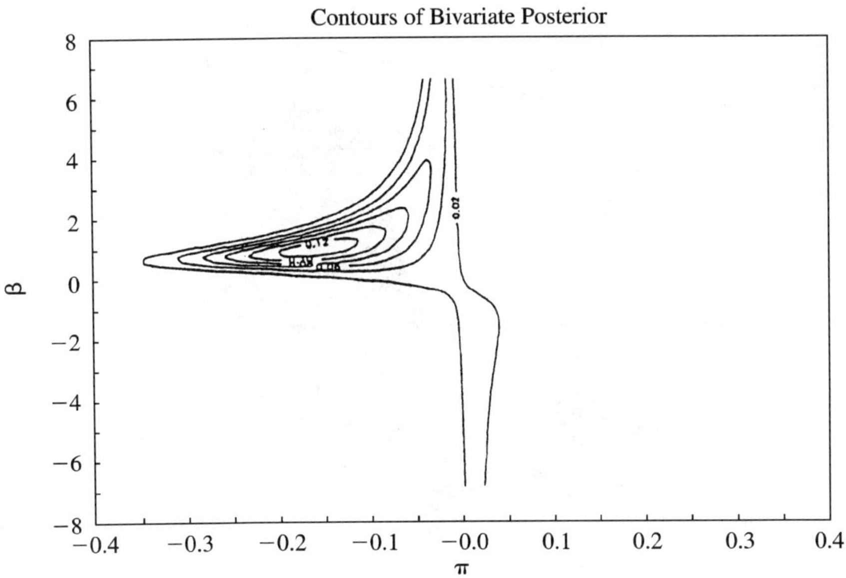

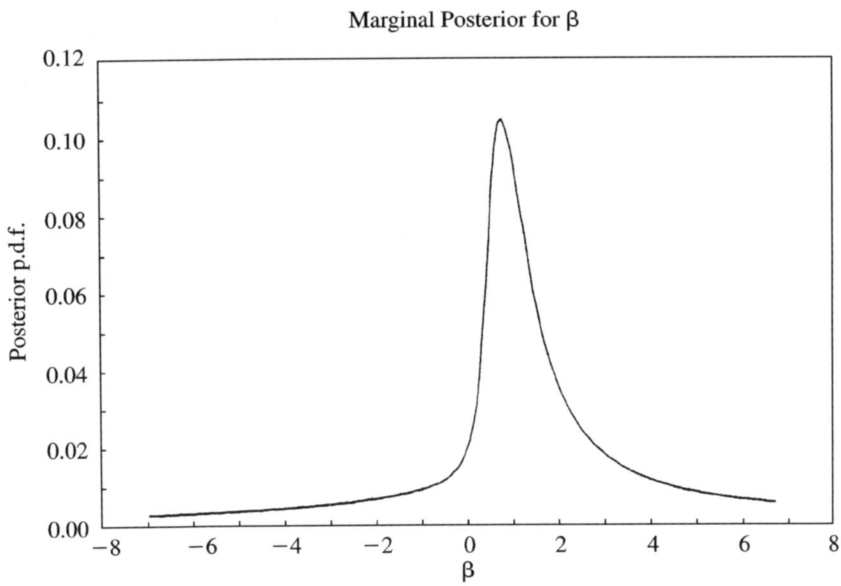

Fig. 25.8 (*Continued*)

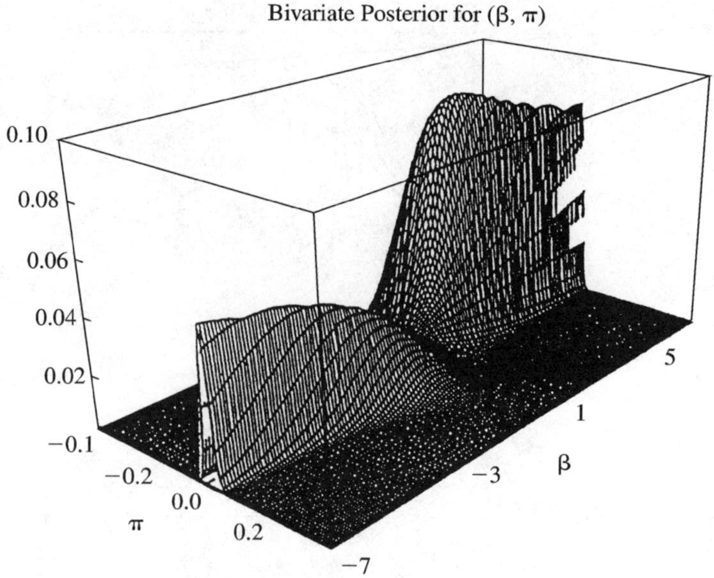

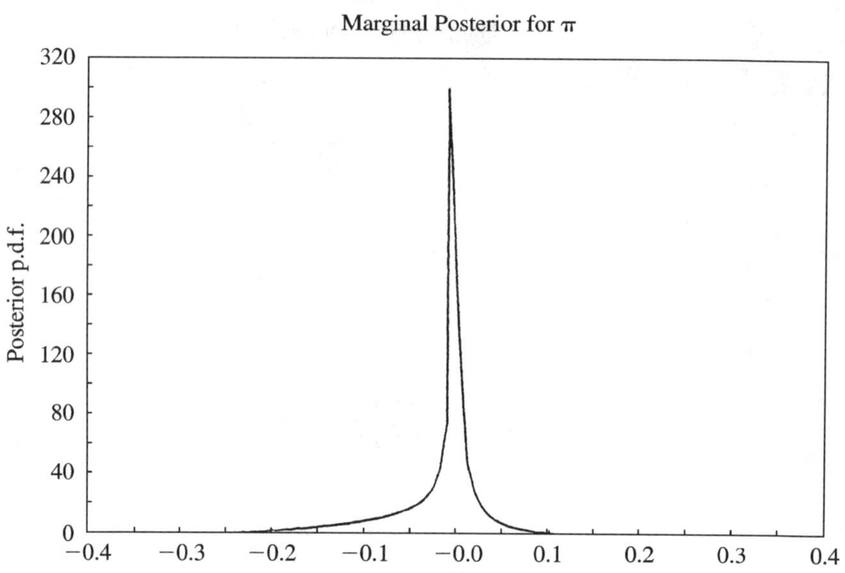

Fig. 25.9 Shape of marginal likelihood with unidentification/irrelevant instruments and no endogeneity.

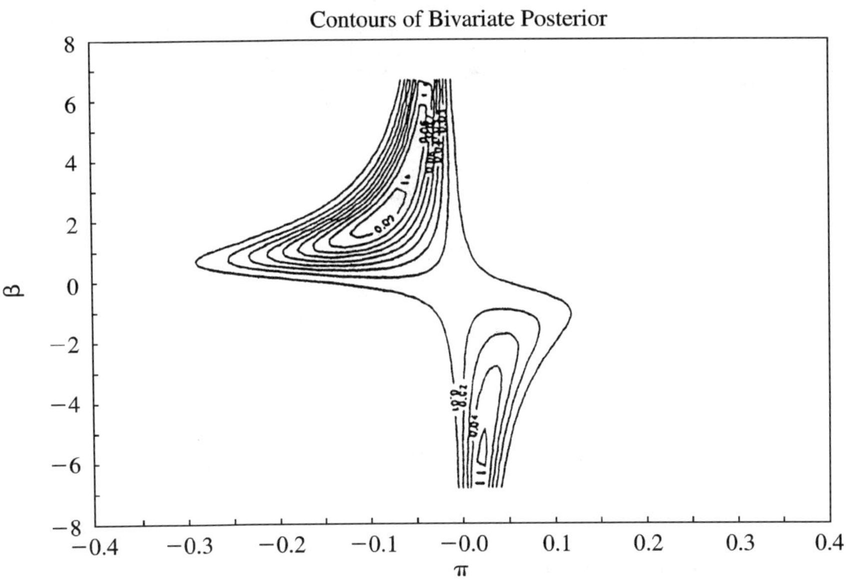

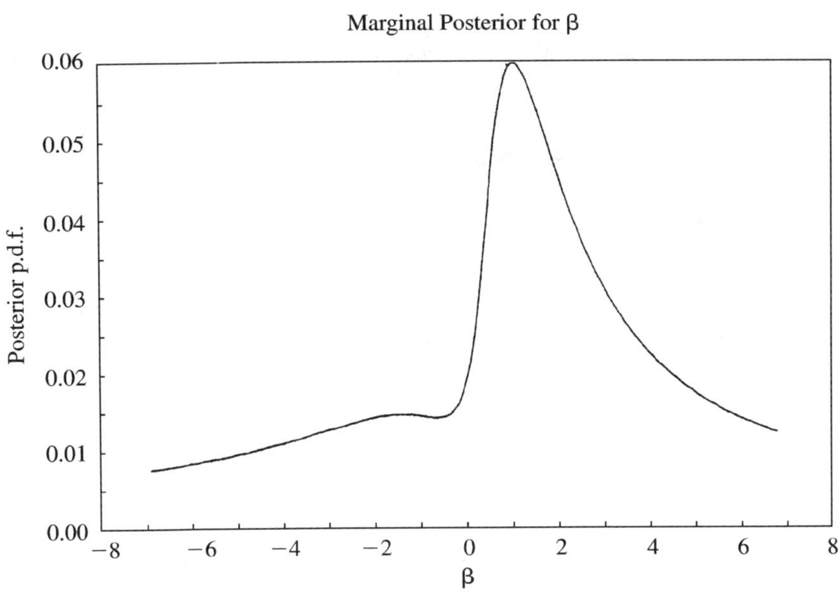

Fig. 25.9 (*Continued*)

TABLE 25.1
The Shape of the Marginal Likelihood/Posterior with Uniform Prior

		Degree of endogeneity: ρ		
		Strong endogeneity ($\rho = 0.99$)	Medium endogeneity ($\rho = 0.5$)	No endogeneity ($\rho = 0$)
Level of identification or quality of instruments	None $\pi = 0$	Elongated ridges (1,1)	(1,2)	(1,3)
	Weak $\pi = 0.1$	(2,1)	Multimodality (2,2)	(2,3)
	Strong $\pi = 1$	(3,1)	(3,2)	Bell shaped (3,3)

distribution of the IV estimate in the totally unidentified case determined by Phillips (1989). The tightness of the posterior about the point of concentration reflects the inability of the instrument to remove any of the bias due to simultaneity, while the fat tails of the distribution reflect the lack of information in the data about the true value of β.

25.2.4 Weakly Informative Priors

25.2.4.1 The Embedding Approach

The incomplete SEM can be considered as a multivariate regression model with nonlinear restrictions on the parameters. In the embedding approach one starts from an unrestricted reduced-form model and considers the transformation to the restricted reduced form. For the exact identified case Kleibergen and van Dijk (1998) start with a flat prior for the unrestricted reduced-form parameters $(\pi_{12}, \pi_{22}, \Omega)$,

$$p(\pi_{12}, \pi_{22}, \Omega) \propto |\, \Omega \,|^{-\frac{1}{2}h}, \quad h > 0, \tag{28}$$

and use this prior to deduce a prior for the restricted reduced-form parameters β, π_{22}, and Ω via the change-of-variable formula. The absolute value of the Jacobian of the transformation from (π_{21}, π_{22}) to (β, π_{22}) is

$$|\, J \,| = \left| \frac{\partial(\pi_{12}, \pi_{22})}{\partial(\beta, \pi_{22})} \right| = |\, \pi_{22} \,|,$$

so the implied prior for the restricted reduced-form parameters is

$$p(\beta, \pi_{22}, \Omega) \propto |\, \pi_{22} \,||\, \Omega \,|^{-\frac{1}{2}h}, \quad h > 0. \tag{29}$$

Note that the implied prior for the restricted reduced-form parameters degenerates at $\pi_{22} = 0$ and so gives zero prior weight to a model for which β is not identified. Intuitively, one can think of the joint prior (29) as the product of three priors

$$p(\beta, \pi_{22}, \Omega) = p(\beta \mid \pi_{22}) p(\pi_{22}) p(\Omega),$$

where

$$\begin{aligned} p(\beta \mid \pi_{22}) &\propto \mid \pi_{22} \mid, \\ p(\pi_{22}) &\propto \text{ constant}, \\ p(\Omega) &\propto \mid \Omega \mid^{-\frac{1}{2}h}, \ h > 0. \end{aligned}$$

The conditional prior, $p(\beta \mid \pi_{22})$, can be thought of as a limiting form of a normal prior with mean β_0 and variance σ_0^2/π_{22}^2. Such a normal prior has a variance that increases as π_{22} approaches zero.

For the overidentified case the transformation is nontrivial. Here one can make use of a singular value decomposition [see Kleibergen and van Dijk (1998) and Kleibergen (2001) for details].

25.2.4.2 The Information Matrix Approach

The implied prior (29) is very similar to the Jeffreys prior derived from the structural model (12) and (13). The Jeffreys prior is invariant to smooth 1-1 transformations of the parameter space and is proportional to the square root of the determinant of the information matrix of the model. Kleibergen and van Dijk (1994a) derive the Jeffreys prior for the general structural model (4) and (5) and in the just identified case this prior reduces to

$$p(\beta, \pi_{22}, \Sigma) \propto \mid \pi_{22} \mid\mid \Sigma \mid^{-2}.$$

Combining the likelihood function (21) with the prior (29) gives the joint posterior

$$p(\beta, \pi_{22}, \Omega \mid y_1, y_2, x) \propto \mid \pi_{22} \mid\mid \Omega \mid^{-\frac{1}{2}(T+h)} \exp\left\{-\tfrac{1}{2}\text{tr}\left[\Omega^{-1}V'V\right]\right\}. \quad (30)$$

and integrating out Ω^{-1} leaves

$$p(\beta, \pi_{22} \mid y_1, y_2, x) \propto \mid\mid V'V \mid^{-\frac{1}{2}(T+h-3)} = \mid \pi_{22} \mid\mid U'U \mid^{-\frac{1}{2}(T+h-3)} \quad (31)$$

The result of the embedding and information matrix approach is that inference on the reduced form parameters is possible but structural inference with weakly or exactly identified models is not feasible for a finite sample. One solution in this respect is to use a penalty function as discussed in Kleibergen and Paap (2002) and Paap and van Dijk (2002). Another approach is to limit the range of the structural parameters, which is presented in the next section

25.3 FULL INFORMATION ANALYSIS AND RESTRICTIONS ON THE RANGE OF STRUCTURAL PARAMETERS

Consider the linear SEM shown in (5). The prior information with respect to the structural parameters (B, Γ, Σ) is given as follows. The diagonal elements of B are restricted to unity owing to normalization, and a certain number of zero elements of B and Γ follow from zero identifying restrictions. The unrestricted elements of B and Γ are denoted by the s-vector θ. The stochastic prior information on θ and Σ can be described by the prior density

$$p(\theta, \Sigma) \propto | \Sigma |^{-1/2h}, \tag{32}$$

where h is interpreted as a prior degrees-of-freedom parameter. So, we have a uniform prior on θ defined on the region of integration S, where S is equal to the s-dimensional real space.

The likelihood function of the parameters (θ, Σ) can be derived using the assumptions on the model. Combining the prior density (2) with the likelihood gives the joint posterior density of (θ, Σ). Marginalization with respect to Σ can be performed by making use of properties of the inverted-Wishart density. Then one obtains the kernel of the marginal posterior density of θ as

$$p(\theta \mid Y, X) \propto \| B \|^T | Q |^{-1/2(T+h-G-1)}, \tag{33}$$

with

$$\begin{aligned} Q &= U'U \\ &= (YB + X\Gamma)'(YB + X\Gamma). \end{aligned} \tag{34}$$

[For details, see Drèze and Richard (1984), Zellner (1971, ch. 9), or Bauwens and van Dijk (1989).] The right-hand side of (33) is similar to a concentrated likelihood function of θ as defined by Koopmans and Hood (1953, p. 191). The difference is the exponent of $| Q |$, which is $-(1/2T)$ for the concentrated likelihood function and in this case depends on the particular value of h. For $h = G + 1$ the expressions are proportional.

One can derive an upper bound function to this marginal posterior. This result is given in the following theorem.

Theorem 3 *An Existence Condition for Posterior Moments. Given* $\mathrm{R(Z)} = \mathrm{G + K}$*, it follows that*

$$\| B \|^T | Q |^{-1/2(T+h-G-1)} \leq c \, | Q |^{-1/2(h-G-1)} \qquad (c > 0) \tag{35}$$

if and only if $\mathrm{R}\begin{pmatrix} \mathrm{B} \\ \Gamma \end{pmatrix} = \mathrm{G}.$

A proof for theorem 3 is given in van Dijk (1985).

I analyze both the condition $R(B' \ \Gamma')' = G$ as well as a bound on the range of the degrees-of-freedom parameter h. For convenience, define $ZA = YB + X\Gamma$, where $Z = (Y, X)$ and $A' = (B', \Gamma')$. Next, let p be a vector of constants, $p \neq 0$, then $p'A'Z'ZAp \geq \varepsilon p'p$, with $\varepsilon > 0$. It follows that

$$p'A'Z'ZAp \geq (1/2)p'(A'Z'ZA + \varepsilon I)p > 0. \tag{36}$$

Given that $\mid A'Z'ZA \mid = \prod_{i=1}^{G} \lambda_i$, where λ_i is the ith characteristic root ($\lambda_1 \geq \lambda_2 \geq \cdots \geq \lambda_G > 0$), and that $\mid A'Z'ZA + \varepsilon I \mid = \prod_{i=1}^{G}(\lambda_i + \varepsilon)$, one obtains

$$\mid A'Z'ZA \mid \geq (1/2)^G \mid A'Z'ZA + \varepsilon I \mid > 0, \tag{37}$$

with $\lambda_G \geq \varepsilon > 0$. The determinant given at the right-hand side of the inequality (35) has the same functional form as the determinant of the inverse of a *matricvariate* Student-t density (see, e.g., Dickey, 1967; Zellner, 1971, app. B5); Drèze and Richard, 1984, p. 589). The difference is, however, the presence of exact restrictions in the matrix A.

It is important to distinguish between the interpretation of the rank conditions on A in a classical and a Bayesian framework. The classical rank condition for identification is derived for a set of unknown *constant* structural parameters. Given this rank condition, the event of underidentification of the structural parameters is a set of measure zero in the classical approach. In our Bayesian case the rank condition on A (or on U) has another interpretation. That is, since the unrestricted elements of A, given in the vector θ, are random variables, $R(A)$ is a random variable. The assumption $R(A) = G$ is interpreted as follows. The event that a nontrivial linear combination of vectors of parameters of the G equations is zero has prior probability zero and the event $R(A) = G$ has prior probability one. Given $R(A) = G$ with probability one, it follows that $\mid A'Z'ZA \mid > 0$ with probability one. But it is important to distinguish between three cases of SEMs.

The first case is one where $\mid A'Z'ZA \mid$ tends to zero in the prior parameter region of θ, which we denote by S. It follows that the right-hand side of (35) tends to infinity if $h > G + 1$. The assumption $P[R(A) = G] = 1$ implies, therefore, that the probability function of $R(A)$ has to be truncated at the value $R(A) = G$. In order to obtain a finite upper bound for the right-hand side of (35) one can make use of the following solution. Truncate the uniform prior density $p(\theta)$ in such a way that it is zero on an open subset of the region S, where $\mid A'Z'ZA \mid < \varepsilon$, $\varepsilon > 0$ and $p(\theta)$ is equal to a positive constant elsewhere on S. This implies that $\mid Q \mid = \mid A'Z'ZA \mid \geq \varepsilon$ on a subset of S. One can investigate the sensitivity of the upper bound by varying ε.

This approach implies that in the evaluation of posterior moments one replaces an infinite integral by a (truncated) finite value of the integral, and it may be an unattractive one. Consider, for instance, the following simple two-equation model, which is interpreted as a market model for a particular commodity,

$$q + \beta_1 p + \gamma_1 I = u_1, \qquad (38)$$
$$q + \beta_2 p + \gamma_2 W = u_2,$$

where q represents the quantity traded of a certain commodity and p its price. Values of the endogenous variables p and q are jointly determined given a value of the exogenous variables I and W (e.g., I represents income and W represents weather conditions). If $h > G + 1$, and if γ_1 and γ_2 tend toward zero and β_1 tends toward β_2, then the upper bound function given at the right-hand side of (35) and the kernel $p(\theta \mid Y, Z)$, eq. (34), both tend to infinity. The rate at which $p(\theta \mid Y, Z)$ tends to infinity depends on the particular value of h. Note that if $\gamma_1 = \gamma_2 = 0$ and $\beta_1 = \beta_2$, then $\mid A'Z'ZA \mid = 0$ **and** $\| B \| = \mid \beta_2 - \beta_1 \mid = 0$. So, in this case the upper bound function, mentioned above, is infinitely large, but $p(\theta \mid Y, Z)$ is zero [see Bauwens and van Dijk (1989) for illustrative examples].

The second case is one where the exact restrictions on the structural parameters are such that $\mid A'Z'ZA \mid \neq \eta$, $\eta > 0$, for all values of θ in the original region of S. In this case the discrete random variable $R(A)$ has degenerated to the constant G. A simple example is

$$C = \gamma + \beta Y + u, \qquad (39)$$
$$Y = C + Z,$$

where C, Y, and Z represent T-vectors of observations on consumption expenditure (C), total expenditure (Y), and autonomous expenditure (Z). After substitution of the second equation into the first, one can verify in a straightforward way that $\mid Q \mid = \mid u'u \mid \neq \eta$, $\eta > 0$, for all values of γ and β. Note that (39) is a SEM with identities.

A third case is to use different normalization restrictions; in particular, a natural restriction is $A'A = I$. In recent work Strachan (2000), Villani (2000), and Strachan and van Dijk (2001) use these types of restrictions on the parameters such that the condition of this section is fulfilled. As a consequence structural moments do exist.

25.4 PRIOR AND POSTERIOR ANALYSIS OF THE U.S. BUSINESS CYCLE DURING THE GREAT DEPRESSION

In this Section[5] we use an informal predictive approach to construct priors and illustrate Bayesian structural inference within the context of a well-known econometric model: Klein's model I (see Klein, 1950). The prior information on B, Γ, and Σ is specified as follows. The prior specification with respect to the nuisance parameters is taken from a noninformative approach. The exactly known parameter values of B and Γ are implied by the specification of Klein's model I. Then there remain nine unrestricted structural parameters collected in the vector θ.

We specify a number of prior densities of θ and demonstrate how Monte Carlo can be used to investigate the implied prior information with respect to the reduced form parameters, the stability characteristics of the model, and the final form parameters (if these exist).

Our first and simplest prior for the vector θ is uniform on the nine-dimensional unit region minus the region where $\| B \| < 0.01$. We investigate the implications of our prior information for the multipliers and dynamic characteristics of the model. We obtained the implied prior means and standard deviations of these functions of θ by drawing θ vectors from the nine-dimensional standard uniform distribution. Each θ vector was checked with respect to the condition $\| B \| > 0.01$. In case this condition was not satisfied and the vector was rejected and replaced by a new vector.

As a next step the first prior was modified in several ways by adding sets of extra constraints, given as follows:

1. The system is assumed to be stable. For that reason only vectors θ satisfying $| DRT | < 1$, where DRT is the dominant root of the characteristic polynomial, were accepted.
2. The long-run effects in the structural equations are all assumed to be in the unit interval.
3. The short-run multipliers are assumed to be less than five in absolute value and to have the correct sign.
4. The same set of constraints as noted under 3 was applied to the long-run multipliers.
5. The period of oscillation is assumed to be between 3 and 10 years, which is in accordance with the observed length of business cycles in the period 1890–1920 (see *Historical Statistics of the United States* 1975).

Eight different priors were obtained by combining the sets of extra constraints, 1 to 5, in several ways. Note that, owing to space limitations, I present only results based on prior 2 (prior 1 with extra constraint 1) and prior 8 (prior 1 with extra constraints 1–5). Prior and posterior means and standard deviations of the period of oscillation and the dominant root are given, as are prior and posterior probabilities of the four states of the system (Table 25.2).

We observe that the prior constraints on the period of oscillation have rather large effects. The question arises whether this information is acceptable. The posterior mean and standard deviation of the period of oscillation under prior 2 suggest that the hypothesis of a 10-year period is acceptable. Inspection of the prior and posterior densities of the period of oscillation in Fig. 25.10 reveals that for the case of prior 2 the information from the likelihood function has

TABLE 25.2
Means and Standard Deviations of Period of Oscillation and Dominant Root: Probability of States

	Period of oscillation (years)	| DRT |	Damped		Explosive	
			Oscillatory	Monotone	Oscillatory	Monotone
FIML (no prior)	34.83	0.76	NA	NA	NA	NA
Prior 2	5.22 (4.74)	0.78 (.17)	0.96	0.04	0	0
Posterior 2′	15.06 (2.90)	0.84 (.08)	0.9999	0.0001	0	0
Prior 8	5.42 (1.57)	0.72 (.18)	0.98	0.02	0	0
Posterior 8′	9.61 (0.37)	0.77 (.08)	0.9927	0.0073	0	0

Note: NA = not available.

modified the prior information substantially. The posterior probability that the period of oscillation is less than or equal to 10 years is less than .02. Further, the effect of constraint 5 is clearly reflected in the posterior density 8′. These results suggest rejection of constraint 5. When considering these results we investigated specification errors. Bayesian diagnostic results indicate that there are errors in the dynamic specification of the consumption function. So, instead of reducing the parameter space by making use of the sets of prior constraints 1–5, one has to enlarge the parameter space by including, for example, lagged consumption in the consumption equation. Preliminary results obtained with an enlarged version of Klein's model I confirm this.

25.5 REMARKS ON STRUCTURAL INFERENCE IN VECTOR AUTOREGRESSIVE MODELS

The empirical validity of the large number of structurally identifying restrictions in large-scale macroeconometric models was questioned by several researchers in the 1960s and 1970s. These restrictions were considered to be "incredible." Further, owing to the oil price shock in the 1970s and to the deregulation in several Western economic systems in the 1980s, many economic time series, in particular financial series, appear to be nonstationary. As a consequence, research in the field of dynamic econometric modeling was redirected toward the analysis of systems of equations that have very few restrictions and allow for nonstationarity.

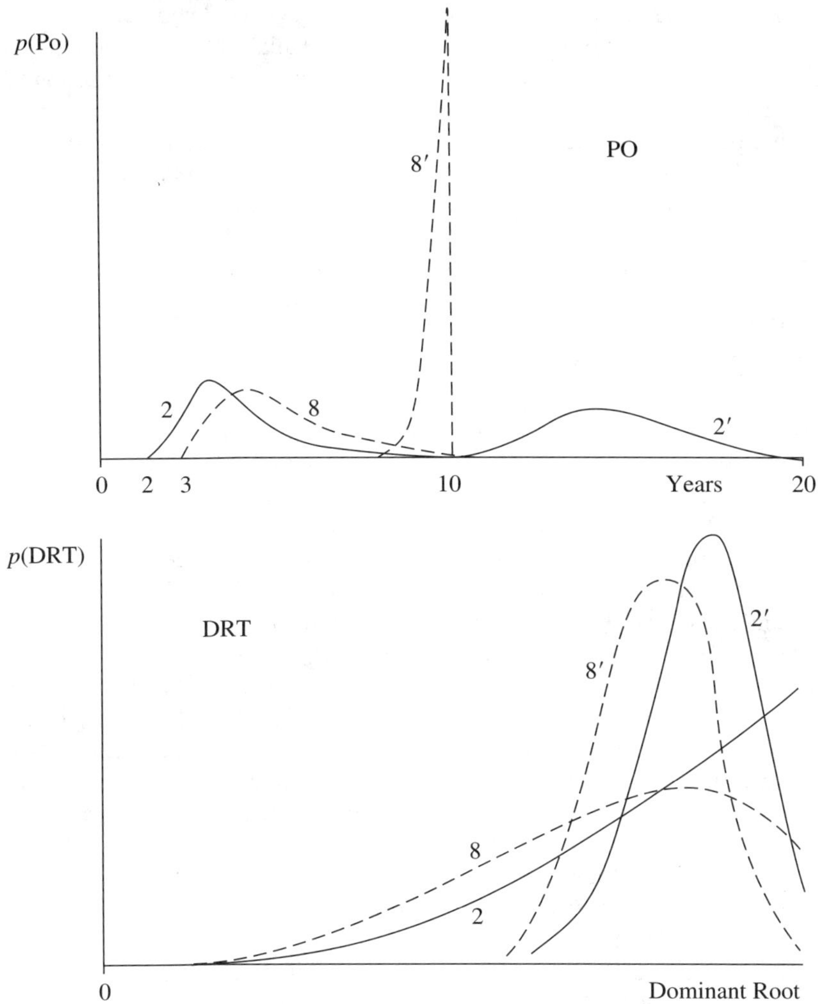

Fig. 25.10 Prior and posterior densities of the period of oscillation and the dominant root.

As an alternative to the class of SEMs the class of vector autoregressive (VAR) models was proposed (see Sims, 1980). Within this class of models one may investigate the issue of stationary versus nonstationary behavior of linear combinations of economic variables, otherwise known as cointegration restrictions and the existence of error-correction models (see, Engle and Granger, 1987; Johansen, 1991). Well-known examples of cointegration models are permanent-income hypotheses and other present-value models such as prices and dividends of stocks, and short- and long-term interest rates. It is of interest to observe that the mathematical structure of a cointegration model and a SEM are the same (see Hoogerheide and van Dijk, 2001). As a consequence the same *local nonidentification* problem occurs as discussed in Section 25.2 (see Kleibergen and van Dijk, 1994b).

In order to obtain meaningful inference in such models, research should be directed toward the construction of flexible VAR models with some structural restrictions referring to the long run. Interesting results have been obtained in the field of macroeconometric modeling by Garratt et al., (2001), Strachan and van Dijk (2001), Sims and Zha (1999), and Paap and van Dijk (2002).

25.6 CONCLUSIONS

Given the advances in computing methods and the analytical insight into the shape of the likelihood and the marginal posterior of a SEM, the Bayesian approach to a SEM can provide useful insight into the structural effect of certain variables. However, using only vague prior information and relatively short data periods implies that structural inference is very often fragile. The conclusion on fragile finite sample inference is also reached in classical instrumental variable inference (see Dufour, 1997; Staiger and Stock, 1997; Zivot et al., 1998). These authors show that traditional classical asymptotic inference, for example, Wald tests on the structural parameters based on 2SLS, breaks down when instruments are weak owing to the near nonidentification of β. As a result, nonstandard methods are required for inference on structural parameters. Using the results of Kleibergen (2001) and Kleibergen and van Dijk (1998), I have shown that similar results hold for Bayesian inference methods. Using information from a predictive approach strengthens inference considerably. Data based priors may also be useful in this respect (see Chapter 13 in this volume). Flexible VAR models with some structural restrictions are an interesting topic for research, forecasting, and policy analysis.

It may be concluded that Bayesian structural inference is like a phoenix. It was almost a dead topic in the late 1980s and early 1990s but has become of renewed importance in the following classes of models in which reduced rank analysis occurs: structural VARs; APT, and CAPM models in finance; factor models and dynamic panel models; state-space models; consumer demand and factor demand systems in production theory; and error in variables models.

NOTES

I am indebted to Eric Zivot, Rodney Strachan, and, in particular, to Frank Kleibergen for stimulating discussions on the topic of this paper. They are, of course, not responsible for any errors.

1. There is a slight difference between this model and a complete SEM, which is analyzed under limited information, as is done by Drèze (1976). For details see Bauwens and van Dijk (1989). In this chapter I make use of the INSEM.

2. Empirically, the weak instrument problem is often characterized by a low first-stage R^2 or a low first-stage F-statistic for testing $\pi_{22} = 0$.

The effects of weak instruments on IV-based inference is discussed in Nelson and Startz (1990a,b), Bound et al., (1995), Hall et al., (1996), Staiger and Stock (1997), Wang and Zivot (1998) and Zivot, et al., (1998). In these papers it is shown that the 2SLS/IV estimator of β is biased in the same direction as the OLS estimator and the 2SLS/IV estimated standard errors are often spuriously too small, which leads to seriously size-distorted confidence intervals for β. Wang and Zivot (1998) and Zivot et al. (1998) show that inferences based on likelihood ratio and Lagrange multiplier statistics are more robust than inferences based on Wald statistics.

3. See Bauwens and van Dijk (1989) and Kleibergen and van Dijk (1992, 1994a, 1998) for details.

4. The author is heavily indebted to Eric Zivot for helpful discussion on the topic of these experiments and for providing the figures. The posteriors are normalized over the displayed range. All plots are computed using GAUSS 3.2.

5. The material in this subsection is taken from van Dijk (1987) and van Dijk and Kloek (1978).

REFERENCES

Angrist, J. D., and A. B. Krueger, 1991, "Does Compulsory School Attendance Affect Schooling and Earnings?" *Quarterly Journal of Economics* 106, 979–1014.

Bauwens, L., and H. K. van Dijk, 1989, "Bayesian Limited Information Analysis Revisited," in: *Economic Decision-Making: Games, Econometrics and Optimisation*, J. J. Gabszewicz et al. (eds.), Amsterdam: North-Holland.

Bound, J., D. A. Jaeger, and R. M. Baker, 1995, "Problems with Instrumental Variables Estimation when the Correlation Between the Instruments and the Endogenous Explanatory Variable is Weak," *Journal of the American Statistical Association* 90, 443–450.

Campbell, J. Y., and G. N. Mankiw, 1989, "Consumption, Income, and Interest Rates: Reinterpreting the Time Series Evidence," *NBER Macroeconomics Annual 1989*, Cambridge: MIT Press, pp. 185–216.

Chao, J. C., and P. C. B. Phillips, 1998, "Bayesian Posterior Distributions in Limited Information Analysis of the Simultaneous Equation Model using Jeffreys' Prior," *Journal of Econometrics* 87, 49–86.

Dickey, J. M., 1967, "Matricvariate Generalizations of the Multivariate *t* Distribution and the Inverted Multivariate *t* Distribution," *The Annals of Mathematical Statistics* 38, 511–518.

Drèze, J. H., 1962, "The Bayesian Approach to Simultaneous Equations Estimation," ONR Research Memorandum 67, The Technological Institute, Northwestern University.

Drèze, J. H., 1976, "Bayesian Limited Information Analysis of the Simultaneous Equations Model," *Econometrica* 44, 1045–1075.

Drèze, J. H., and J. F. Richard, 1984, "Bayesian Analysis of Simultaneous Equations Systems," in: *Handbook of Econometrics*, Vol. 1, Z. Griliches and M. D. Intrilligator (eds.), Amsterdam: North-Holland.

Dufour, J-M, 1997, "Some Impossibility Theorems in Econometrics with Applications to Structural and Dynamic Models," *Econometrica* 65, 1365–1388.

Engle, R. F., and C. W. J. Granger, 1987, "Co-integration and Error Correction: Representation, Estimation and Testing," *Econometrica* 55: 251–276.

Engle, R. F., D. F. Hendry, and J. F. Richard, 1983, "Exogeneity," *Econometrica* 51, 277–304.

Gao C., and K. Lahiri, 1999, "A Comparison of Some Recent Bayesian and Classical Procedures for Simultaneous Equations Models with Weak Instruments," Manuscript.

Garratt, A., K. Lee, M. H. Pesaran, and Y. Shin, 2001, "A Long Run Structural Macroeconometric Model of the UK," Manuscript (to appear in *Economic Journal*).

Geweke, J., 1989, "Bayesian Inference in Econometric Models Using Monte-Carlo Integration," *Econometrica* 57, 1317–1339.

Geweke, J., 1999, "Using Simulation Methods for Bayesian Econometric Models: Inference, Development, and Communication," *Econometric Reviews* 18(1), 1–74.

Haavelmo, T., 1943, "The Statistical Implications of a System of Simultaneous Equations," *Econometrica* 11, 1–12.

Hall, A. R., G. D. Rudebusch, and D. W. Wilcox, 1996, "Judging Instrument Relevance in Instrumental Variables Estimation," *International Economic Review* 37, 283–289.

Hastings, W. K., 1970, "Monte Carlo Sampling Using Markov Chains and Their Applications," *Biometrika* 57, 97–109.

Hood, W. C., and T. C. Koopmans (eds.), 1953, *Studies in Econometric Method*, New Haven: Yale University Press.

Hoogerheide, L. F., and H. K. van Dijk, 2001, "Comparison of the Anderson-Rubin Test for Overidentification and the Johansen Test for Cointegration," Econometric Institute Report 2001-04, 14 pp.

Johansen, S., 1991, "Estimation and Hypothesis Testing of Cointegration Vectors in Gaussian Vector Autoregressive Models," *Econometrica* 59: 1551–1580.

Kleibergen, F. R., 2001, "How to Overcome the Jeffreys-Lindleys Paradox for Invariant Bayesian Inference in Regression Models," Manuscript, 22 pp.

Kleibergen, F. R., and R. Paap, 2002, "Priors, Posteriors and Bayes Factors for a Bayesian Analysis of Cointegration," *Journal of Econometrics* 111, 223–249.

Kleibergen, F. R., and H. K. van Dijk, 1992, "Bayesian Simultaneous Equation Models Analysis: On the Existence of Structural Posterior Moments," Econometric Institute Report 9269/A, Erasmus University Rotterdam.

Kleibergen, F. R., and H. K. van Dijk, 1994a, "Bayesian Analysis of Simultaneous Equation Models Using Noninformative Priors," Discussion Paper TI 94-134, Tinbergen Institute.

Kleibergen, F. R., and H. K. van Dijk, 1994b, "On the Shape of the Likelihood/Posterior in Cointegration Models," *Econometric Theory* 10, 514–552.

Kleibergen, F. R., and H. K. van Dijk, 1998, "Bayesian Simultaneous Equations Analysis Using Reduced Rank Structures," *Econometric Theory* 14, 701–743.

Kleibergen, F. R., and E. Zivot, 1998, "Bayesian and Classical Approaches to Instrumental Variable Regression," Manuscript (to appear in *Journal of Econometrics*).

Klein, L. R., 1950, *Economic Fluctuations in the United States, 1921–1941*, New York: Wiley.

Kloek, T., and H. K. van Dijk, 1978, "Bayesian Estimates of Equation System Parameters: An Application of Integration by Monte Carlo," *Econometrica* 46, 1–19.

Koopmans, T. C. (ed.), 1950, *Statistical Inference in Dynamic Economic Models*, New York: Wiley.

Koopmans, T. C., and W. C. Hood, 1953, "The Estimation of Simultaneous Linear Economic Relations," in: *The Studies in Econometric Method*, W. C. Hood and T. C. Koopmans (eds.), New Haven: Yale University Press.

Liu, T. C., 1960, "Underidentification, Structural Estimation, and Forecasting," *Econometrica* 28, 855–865.

Maddala, G. S., 1976, "Weak Priors and Sharp Posteriors in Simultaneous Equation Models," *Econometrica* 44, 345–351.

Nelson, C. R., and R. Startz, 1990a, "Some Further Results on the Exact Small Sample Properties of the Instrumental Variables Estimator," *Econometrica* 58, 967–976.

Nelson, C. R., and R. Startz, 1990b, "The Distribution of the Instrumental Variables Estimator and Its *t*-ratio when the Instrument is a Poor One," *Journal of Business* 63, S125–S140.

Paap, R., and H. K. van Dijk, 2002, "Bayes Estimates of Markov Trends in Possibly Cointegrated Series: An Application to US Consumption and Income," Report 2002–42, Econometric Institute, 47 pp.

Phillips, P. C. B., 1989, "Partially Identified Econometric Models," *Econometric Theory* 5, 181–240.

Rothenberg, T., 1963, "A Bayesian Analysis of Simultaneous Equation Systems," Report 6315, Econometric Institute, Erasmus University, Rotterdam.

Sims, C., 1980, "Macroeconomics and Reality," *Econometrica* 48, 1–48.

Sims, C. A., and T. Zha, 1999, "Error Bands for Impulse Responses," *Econometrica* 67(5), 1113–1155.

Staiger, D., and J. H. Stock, 1997, "Instrumental Variables Regression with Weak Instruments," *Econometrica* 65, 557–586.

Strachan, R. W., 2000, "Valid Bayesian Estimation of the Cointegrating Error Correction Model," Report 6/2000, Department of Econometrics and Business Statistics, Monash University.

Strachan, R. W., and H. K. van Dijk, 2001, "The Value of Structural Information in Vector Autoregressive Models," Manuscript.

Tierney, L., 1994, "Markov Chains for Exploring Posterior Distributions," *Annals of Statistics* 22, 1701–1762.

van Dijk, H. K., 1985, "Existence Conditions for Posterior Moments of Simultaneous Equation Model Parameters," Report 8551, Econometric Institute, Erasmus University, Rotterdam, 31 pp.

van Dijk, H. K., 1987, "Some Advances in Bayesian Estimation Methods Using Monte Carlo Integration," in: *Advances in Econometrics* 6, T. B. Fomby and G. F. Rhodes (eds.), Greenwich, Conn.: JAI Press.

van Dijk, H. K., and T. Kloek, 1978, "Posterior Analysis of Klein's Model I," *Szigma, Hungarian Journal of Mathematical Economics*, 121–143.

Villani, M., 2000, *Aspects of Bayesian Cointegration*, Thesis, Department of Statistics, Stockholm University.

Wang, J., and E. Zivot, 1998, "Inference on Structural Parameters in Instrumental Variables Regression with Weak Instruments," *Econometrica* 66, 1389–1404.

Zellner, A., 1971, *An Introduction to Bayesian Inference in Econometrics*, New York: Wiley.

Zellner, A., L. Bauwens, and H. K. van Dijk, 1988, "Bayesian Specification Analysis and Estimation of Simultaneous Equation Models Using Monte-Carlo Integration," *Journal of Econometrics* 38, 39–72.

Zivot, E., R. Startz, and C. R. Nelson, 1998, "Valid Confidence Intervals and Inference in the Presence of Weak Instruments," *International Economic Review* 39, 1119–1246.

Chapter Twenty-Six

An Econometric Analysis of Residential Electric Appliance Holdings and Consumption

Jeffrey A. Dubin and Daniel L. McFadden

Econometric specification and estimation of the demand for electricity have posed a rich set of problems for the econometrician. Early studies recognized that the demand for electricity was derived through the use of energy-using durables. Somewhat later it was recognized that the long- and short-run responses to price changes might differ greatly as households adjusted their appliance portfolios.[1] Recently, microsimulation studies have attempted to model jointly the demand for appliances and the demand for electricity by appliance, termed unit electricity consumption (UEC).[2] Within this latter context it becomes important to test the statistical exogeneity of appliance dummy variables typically included in demand for electricity equations. If, as the theory suggests, the demand for durables and their use are related decisions by the consumer, specifications that ignore this lead to biased and inconsistent estimates of price and income elasticities. As these long-run simulations are both very costly and important for future energy policy, it would appear useful to test commonly used demand equations for specification error. This problem has been noted and discussed in McFadden et al. (1978).

The present chapter attempts to test this bias using a subsample of the 1975 survey of 3,249 households carried out by the Washington Center for Metropolitan Studies (WCMS) for the Federal Energy Administration. Matched with these observations were the actual rate schedules faced by each household. The use of disaggregated data in this form is desirable as we can avoid the confounding effects of misspecification owing either to aggregation bias or to approximation of rate data.

The demand systems derived in what follows are simultaneous equations with dummy endogenous variables. Functional forms have been chosen that offer relatively easy implementation while maintaining economic consistency between discrete decisions on durable purchase and continuous decisions on usage. We use econometric methods adapted from Heckman (1978). Related studies are the papers by Lee and Trost (1978) on housing demand and by Hay (1979) on wage earnings.

In Section 26.1 we discuss and derive a unified model of the demand for consumer durables and the derived demand for electricity. In Section 26.2 we introduce and estimate a joint water-heat–space-heat choice model. In Section 26.3 we conclude with the estimations and specification tests of demand for electricity equations under alternative assumptions. Variable definitions and constructions are discussed in an appendix.

26.1 UTILITY MAXIMIZING MODELS FOR DISCRETE/CONTINUOUS CHOICE

In this section we specify a unified model of the demand for electricity consistent with discrete appliance choice. Within this model we illustrate several technical points relating to the economic theory of the demand for electricity. Particular functional forms are chosen with a view toward attempting to remain within the spirit of previous work in this area. Finally, we indicate the source of the simultaneous equation bias mentioned above.

Economic analysis of the demand for consumer durables suggests that such demand arises from the flow of services provided by durables ownership. The utility associated with a consumer durable is then best characterized as indirect. Durables may vary in capacity, efficiency, versatility, and of course vary correspondingly in price. Although durables differ, the consumer ultimately utilizes the durable at an intensity level that provides the "necessary" service. Corresponding to this usage is the cost of the derived demand for the fuel that the durable consumes. The optimization problem posed is thus quite complex. The consumer unit in the spirit of the theory must weigh the alternatives of each appliance against expectations of future use, future energy prices, and current financing decisions.

We first outline several econometric models consistent with utility maximization that can be used to describe appliance choice and electricity consumption. In the present analysis, block rate structure is ignored, and electricity is treated as a commodity available in any quantity at a fixed marginal (= average) price.[3] Moreover, appliance-holding decisions are analyzed as if they are contemporaneous with usage decisions, and do not involve intertemporal considerations—a realistic assumption only if there are perfect competitive rental markets for consumer durables.[4] The approach we use combines the method of development of discrete choice models from conditional indirect utility functions employed in McFadden (1981) and the method developed by Hausman (1979a) for recovery of indirect utility functions from econometric partial demand systems.

The consumer faces a choice of m mutually exclusive, exhaustive appliance portfolios, which can be indexed $i = 1, \ldots, m$. Portfolio i has a rental price (annualized cost) r_i. Given portfolio i, the consumer has a conditional indirect utility function

$$u = V(i, y - r_i, p_1, p_2, s_i, \epsilon_i, \eta), \tag{1}$$

where p_1 is price of electricity, p_2 is price of alternative energy sources, y is income, s_i denotes observed attributes of portfolio i, ϵ_i denotes unobserved attributes of portfolio i, r_i is price of portfolio i, η denotes unobserved characteristics of the consumer, and all prices and income are deflated by an index of nonenergy commodity prices. Electricity and alternative energy consumption levels, given portfolio i, are (by Roy's identity)

$$x_1 = \frac{-\partial V(i, y - r_i, p_1, p_2, s_i, \epsilon_i, \eta)/\partial p_1}{\partial V(i, y - r_i, p_1, p_2, s_i, \epsilon_i, \eta)/\partial y}, \tag{2}$$

$$x_2 = \frac{-\partial V(i, y - r_i, p_1, p_2, s_i, \epsilon_i, \eta)/\partial p_2}{\partial V(i, y - r_i, p_1, p_2, s_i, \epsilon_i, \eta)/\partial y}. \tag{3}$$

The probability that portfolio i is chosen is

$$\begin{aligned} P_i = \text{Prob}\big\{(\epsilon_1, \ldots, \epsilon_m, \eta) : V(i, y - r_i, p_1, p_2, s_i, \epsilon_i, \eta) \\ > V(j, y - r_j, p_1, p_2, s_j, \epsilon_j, \eta), \quad \text{for} \quad j \neq i\big\}. \end{aligned} \tag{4}$$

Any function V with the necessary and sufficient properties of an indirect utility function can be used to construct econometric forms for joint discrete/continuous choice.[5]

A second method of obtaining a discrete/continuous demand system is to start from a parametric specification of the UEC equation, treat Roy's identity as a partial differential equation whose solution defines a conditional indirect utility function, and then define the discrete choice probabilities from the indirect utility function. This procedure can be carried through for functions in which UEC levels exhibit some income elasticity.

First consider systems in which the UEC equation is linear in income:

$$x_1 = \beta_i(y - r_i) + m^i(p_1, p_2) + \nu_{1i}, \tag{5}$$

with m^i linear in parameters and the distribution of ν_{1i} depending in general on discrete choice i. A general solution for an indirect utility function yielding this demand equation is

$$u = \Psi\left(\left[M^i(p_1, p_2) + y - r_i + \nu_{1i}/\beta_i\right]e^{-\beta_i p_1}, p_2, \nu_{2i}\right), \tag{6}$$

where

$$M^i(p_1, p_2) = \int_{p_1}^{0} m^i(t, p_2)e^{\beta_i(p_1 - t)}dt \tag{7}$$

and Ψ is a function that is increasing in its first argument.[6] The demand for substitute energy satisfies

$$x_2 = -M_2^i(p_1, p_2) - e^{-\beta_i p_1}\Psi_2/\Psi_1, \tag{8}$$

where $M_2^i = \partial M^i/\partial p_2$ and $\Psi_2/\Psi_1 = (\partial\Psi/\partial p_2)/(\partial\Psi/\partial p_1)$ is evaluated at the arguments in (6).

Consider a special case of (6) in which $\nu_{2i} = \nu_{21}$ is the same for all i. The discrete choice probabilities satisfy

$$P_i = \text{Prob}\Big\{\big[M^i(p_1, p_2) + y - r_i + \nu_{1i}/\beta_i\big]e^{-\beta p_1} \geq \big[M^j(p_1, p_2) + y - r_j + \nu_{ij}/\beta_j\big]e^{-\beta_j p_1} \quad \text{for } j \neq i\Big\}. \tag{9}$$

A special case of this system that yields a simple functional form is

$$u = \ln\Big\{\big[\alpha_0^i + \alpha_1^i/\beta + \alpha_1^i p_1 + \alpha_2^i p_2 + \beta(y - r_i) + \nu_{li}\big]e^{-\beta p_1}\Big\} - \alpha_5 \ln p_2 \tag{10}$$

with $\beta_i = \beta$ common across alternatives, and

$$x_1 = \alpha_0^i + \alpha_1^i p_1 + \alpha_2^i p_2 + \beta(y - r_i) + \nu_{1i} \tag{11}$$

$$x_2 = \frac{\alpha_2^i}{\beta}(\alpha_5 - 1) + \frac{\alpha_5}{\beta}\left(\alpha_0^i + \frac{\alpha_1^i}{\beta}\right)\frac{1}{p_2} + \frac{\alpha_5\alpha_1^i}{\beta}\frac{p_1}{p_2} + \alpha_5\frac{y - r_i}{p_2} + \frac{\alpha_5\nu_{1i}}{\beta p_2}. \tag{12}$$

Alternatively, consider the special case of (6) in which $\nu_{1i} = \eta$ and

$$u = \big[M^i(p_1, p_2) + y - r_i + \eta/\beta_i\big]e^{-\beta_i p_1} + \nu_{2i}. \tag{13}$$

Analogously to (10), define

$$u = \big[\alpha_0^i + \alpha_1^i/\beta + \alpha_1^i p_1 + \alpha_2^i p_2 + \beta(y - r_i) + \eta\big]e^{-\beta p_1} - \alpha_5 \ln p_2 + \nu_{2i}. \tag{14}$$

The UEC equation is then

$$x_1 = \alpha_0^i + \alpha_1^i p_1 + \alpha_2^i p_2 + \beta(y - r_i) + \eta \tag{15}$$

and the choice probabilities satisfy

$$P_i = \text{Prob}(\nu_{2j} - \nu_{2i} < W_i - W_j \qquad \text{for } j \neq i), \tag{16}$$

with

$$W_i = V_i e^{-\beta p_1} = \left(\alpha_0^i + \alpha_1^i/\beta + \alpha_1^i p_1 + \alpha_2^i p_2 - \beta r_i\right)e^{-\beta p_1}. \tag{17}$$

Econometric studies of UEC have in most cases assumed, implicitly or explicitly, statistical independence of appliance portfolio choice and the additive error in the UEC equation and have proceeded to estimate the UEC equation by ordinary least squares. Examples are Houthakker (1951), McFadden et al. (1978), Cambridge Systematics/West (1979), California State Energy Conservation Commission (1979), and Parti and Parti (1980). In practice some correlation of unobserved variables is likely. For an appliance such as an air conditioner, an unobserved effect that increases the utility of the service supplied by the appliance (e.g., poor natural ventilation in a housing unit) is likely to increase both its probability of selection and its intensity of use. For an appliance such as a water heater, unobserved factors which increase intensity of use (e.g., tastes for washing clothes in hot water) are likely to decrease the probability of choosing the electric alternative, which has a higher operating-to-capital cost ratio than the alternative fuel. In either case, ordinary least squares estimation of the UEC equation induces a classical bias owing to correlation of an explanatory variable and the equation error.[7]

In our empirical work, we adopt the specifications (15)–(17) with modifications to accommodate varying climate and household characteristics and employ statistical procedures that are consistent in the presence of the suspect correlation.

26.2 A SPACE AND WATER HEAT CHOICE MODEL

Household demand for electricity is determined by choice of fuel type for space and water heating, ownership of electrical appliances such as an air conditioner, range, dishwasher, clothes dryer, and color television, and the intensity of use of these devices. Table 26.1 summarizes typical saturations and UEC's.

Our analysis isolates the space- and water-heating choice, treating the portfolio of other appliances owned by the household as statistically exogenous. The space- and water-heating choice is usually associated with selection of a housing unit, and is often made at a different point in time than purchase or retrofit decisions on portable appliances, so that a hypothesis of behavioral independence is plausible.

We make the following assumptions on housing market behavior: First, the supply of housing units with each heating type is assumed to be perfectly elastic at price differentials that accurately reflect the contemporary capital costs of these systems. Second, real capital costs of heating systems evolve sufficiently slowly so that real prices in 1975 reflect costs at date of housing unit acquisition. Third, consumer evaluation of heating system life-cycle operating costs at the time of housing choice anticipates future real energy prices equal to 1975 levels.

These assumptions permit us to model space and water heating type holdings and electricity consumption in 1975 as contemporaneous decisions, with choices of other durables treated as exogenous. In reality these assumptions are at best only approximately true and should be tested against a more complete dynamic model of expectations, durable purchase, and intensity of use, using panel data on consumer behavior.

Our model of space and water heat choice and electricity consumption employs a version of the indirect utility function (14):

$$u = \left[\alpha_0^i + \alpha_1/\beta + \alpha_1 p_1 + \alpha_2 p_2 + w'\gamma + \beta(y - r_i) + \eta\right] e^{-\beta p_1} + \epsilon_i, \quad (18)$$

TABLE 26.1
Typical Appliance Saturation and UEC

Appliance	Saturation[a]	UEC[b]
Electric space heater	0.23	6,440[c]
Electric water heater	0.23	3,431[d]
Dishwasher	0.49	1,453[e]
Central air conditioner	0.39	2,856[f]
Room air conditioner	0.37[g]	413
Freezer	0.56	1,340
Electric range	0.67	780
Color television	0.81	480
Electric dryer	0.56	1,030

[a] From WCMS survey (1975) subsample of 313 households.

[b] Annual consumption in KWH, from BLS survey (1972) fitted by regression of consumption on household appliance dummies. (These estimates are subject to the potential bias discussed in the text.)

[c] The average number of heating degree days per year is 4,318.

[d] Excludes hot water consumption by a dishwasher.

[e] UEC determined by hot water consumption if electric water heater.

[f] The average number of cooling degree days per year is 1,229.

[g] Average number of room air conditioners/number of households.

where p_1 is electricity price, p_2 is the price of alternative energy (in KWH equivalents), i indexes the water- and space-heating alternatives, r_i is the annualized total life-cycle cost of alternative i, and w is a vector of household characteristics including number of persons, climate, and the portfolio of portable appliances.

Annualized total life-cycle cost is assumed to have the form

$$r_i = \sum_{j=1}^{m} p_j q_{ji} + \rho r_{ki}, \tag{19}$$

where

$$\rho = \rho_0 + \rho_1 y, \tag{20}$$

$$q_{ji} = \tilde{q}_j + \tilde{q}_{ji}, \tag{21}$$

with r_{ki} the capital cost of portfolio alternative i, ρ the discount rate, and q_{ji} the typical total annual consumption by the household of fuel type j given portfolio i. Equation (21) shows q_{ji} as the sum of two terms, $\tilde{q}_j$, the typical annual consumption of fuel j, which is independent of portfolio choice, and $\tilde{q}_{ji}$, the annual consumption of fuel j by portfolio i. In our analysis q_{ji} is calculated using typical UEC, as detailed in the appendix, and hence is exogenous. All q_{ji} are calculated in KWH equivalents. The discount rate ρ is assumed to be a linear function of income, to reflect credit availability; ρ_0 and ρ_1 are unknown parameters.

The unobserved factors ϵ_i in (18) are assumed to have independent extreme value distributions:

$$\text{Prob}(\epsilon_i \leq \epsilon) = \exp\left(-e^{-\epsilon\pi/\lambda\sqrt{3}-\gamma}\right), \tag{22}$$

where $\gamma = .577\ldots$ is Euler's constant. The distribution of η conditional on $(\epsilon_1, \epsilon_2, \ldots, \epsilon_m)$ is assumed to have mean $(\sqrt{2}\sigma/\lambda)\sum_{i=1}^m R_i\epsilon_i$ and variance $\sigma^2(1-\sum_{i=1}^m R_i^2)$, where $\sum_{i=1}^m R_i = 0$ and $\sum_{i=1}^m R_i^2 < 1$. Then R_i is the correlation of η and ϵ_i, ϵ_i has unconditional mean zero and unconditional variance $\lambda^2/2$, and η has unconditional mean zero and unconditional variance σ^2.

The expected value of ϵ_i given that portfolio j is chosen satisfies

$$E\left[\epsilon_i \mid \delta_j(\epsilon) = 1\right] = \begin{cases} -\ln P_j \cdot \lambda\sqrt{3}/\pi, & \text{if } i = j \\ \dfrac{P_i}{1-P_i}\ln P_i \cdot \lambda\sqrt{3}/\pi, & \text{if } i \neq j, \end{cases} \tag{23}$$

where $\delta_j(\epsilon)$ is an indicator random variable that is equal to one if and only if j is the chosen alternative.

It then follows that

$$E\left(\eta \mid \delta_j(\epsilon) = 1\right) = \frac{\sqrt{6}\sigma}{\pi} \cdot \left(\sum_{i=1}^m R_i \frac{P_i}{1-P_i}\ln P_i - R_j \frac{\ln P_j}{1-P_j}\right). \tag{24}$$

The portfolio choice probabilities have a nonlinear multinomial logit form,

$$\begin{aligned} P_i &= \text{Prob}\left[u_i > u_j, \quad \text{for} \quad j \neq i\right] \\ &= \text{Prob}\Big[\epsilon_j - \epsilon_i < \big\{\alpha_0^i - \alpha_0^j - \beta\left[p_1(q_{1i} - q_{1j}) + p_2(q_{2i} - q_{2j})\right] \\ &\qquad - \beta\rho(r_{ki} - r_{kj})\big\}e^{-\beta p_1}, \quad \text{for} \quad j \neq i\Big] \\ &= \frac{\exp\left\{\left[\alpha_0^i - \beta(p_1q_{1i} + p_2q_{2i}) - \beta\rho r_{ki}\right]\left(e^{-\beta p_1}\right)/\theta\right\}}{\sum_{j=1}^m \exp\left[\left(\alpha_0^i - \beta(p_1q_{1j} + p_2q_{2j}) - \beta\rho r_{kj}\right)\left(e^{-\beta p_1}\right)/\theta\right]}, \end{aligned} \tag{25}$$

where $\rho = \rho_0 + \rho_1 y$ and $\theta = \sqrt{3}\lambda/\pi$ is a positive scale factor.

We have estimated the model (25) using a subsample of 313 households from the 1975 WCMS survey for which water and space heat were either both electric or both gas. Mixed systems were excluded because of the difficulty of measuring their capital cost. If the logit specification for portfolio choice is correct, then no bias is introduced by restricting analysis to a subset of alternatives (see McFadden, 1981). The subsample also eliminated households with missing data (details are given in the appendix).

Table 26.2 gives the variables used in the choice model and their sample means. The maximum likelihood parameter estimates are given in Table 26.3.

TABLE 26.2
Variables in the Water-Space–Heat-Choice Model

		Means by alternative	
Variable	Mnemonic	Electric space and water	Gas space and water
Choice dummy	Choice	0.2332	0.7668
Annual operating cost ($)	*PIOP*[a]	392.8	208.0
Capital cost ($)	*PICP*[b]	996.1	1,136.0
Capital cost · income ($ · $10^3$$)	*PICPY*	17,160	20,100
Gas availability index in alternative one	*GASAV*751	0.7294	0
Marginal price of electricity in alternative one	*WMPE*751	0.02194	0
Electricity price ($/KWH)	p_e, p_1, *WMPE*75	0.02194	0.02194
Gas price ($/KWH equivalent)	p_g, p_2, *MPG*75	0.006449	0.006449
Annual typical electric demand (KWH)	q_{1i}	17570	6432
Annual typical gas demand (KWH equivalent)	q_{2i}	0	11,138.0
Income (10^3)	y	14.97	17.55

[a] $PIOP_i \equiv \sum_{j=1}^{m} p_j q_{ji}$.
[b] $PICP_i \equiv r_{ki}$.

Note that the coefficients of *PIOP*, *PICP*, and *PICPY* are $-\beta/\theta$, $\beta\rho_0/\theta$, and $-\beta\rho_1/\theta$, respectively. From the estimates of these parameters and their asymptotic covariances, one obtains the linear-in-income predicted discount factor

$$\hat{\rho} = \underset{(0.0780)}{0.3793} - \underset{(0.00289)}{0.01028} \cdot \text{(annual income)},$$

with annual income in thousands of 1975 dollars and standard errors in parentheses. The negative estimate of ρ_1 implies that the discount rate declines with income. This result is consistent with a similar finding of Hausman (1979b). The formula yields a predicted discount factor of 0.205 at the sample mean income of $16,948. Classical economic consumers who are not credit constrained can be expected to have discount factors equal to the real interest rate plus depreciation rate, roughly 0.10 to 0.15. This range is attained for households with incomes over $22,300. Households below this income level appear to be credit constrained. However, it should be noted that: (1) failure of consumers to correctly anticipate energy price increases between the time of housing choice and 1975, or (2) an imperfectly elastic housing market in which the capital

TABLE 26.3
Estimated Water-Space–Heat-Choice Model

Alternative	Frequency	Proportion	
Electric water and space	73	23.32	
Gas water and space	240	76.68	
	313	100.00	
Explanatory variable	**Estimated coefficient**	**Standard error**	**Asymptotic t-statistic**
Capital cost ($PICP$)	−0.0029	0.0084	−2.73
Capital cost · income (10^3) ($PICPY$)	0.621	0.244	2.55
Annual operating cost ($PIOP$)	−0.0604	0.026	−2.29
Gas availability in alternative one ($GASAV751$)	−7.16	3.49	−2.05
Alternative-one dummy ($C1$)	−1.32	2.32	−0.57
Marginal price of electricity in alternative one ($WMPE751$)	496.77	228.20	2.18
Utility scale factor $\exp((-\beta)^* WMPE75)$	−39.09	14.30	−2.73
log likelihood: at convergence	−102.4		
with alternative dummy only	−217.0		

cost variable *PICP* overestimates the implicit capital cost component in the price of houses with systems that have higher expected operating costs in 1975 than at the time of construction both introduce specification errors that bias the estimate of ρ upward.

Observe from Table 26.3 that we have defined $\alpha_0^i \equiv (\gamma_0 \cdot GASAV75 + \gamma_1 p_e + \gamma_2) \cdot C1_i$. It then follows that the elasticity of demand for alternative i with respect to the price of electricity satisfies

$$\frac{\partial \ln P_i}{\partial \ln p_e} = p_e \Bigg[\left(\frac{\gamma_1}{\theta}\right) e^{-\beta p_e} (C1_i - P_1) + (\beta) \sum_{j=1}^{2} P_j \ln\left(\frac{P_j}{P_i}\right) - \left(\frac{\beta}{\theta}\right)\left(\tilde{q}_{ei} - \sum_{j=1}^{2} P_j \tilde{q}_{ej}\right) e^{-\beta p_e} \Bigg]. \qquad (27)$$

Noting that (γ_1/θ) and $(-\beta/\theta)$ are, respectively, the coefficients of *WMPE*751 and *PIOP* in Table 26.3 and that β is estimated in the utility scale factor term $e^{-\beta p_e}$, the elasticities calculated at the means of right-hand-side variables are −0.473 for electric water and space heat and +0.144 for gas. For the price of gas, the elasticity is given by the analogue of (27) with $\tilde{q}_{ei}$ replaced by gas consumption (in KWH equivalents); the elasticity of P_i with respect to the price of gas is

$$\frac{\partial \ln P_i}{\partial \ln p_g} = \left(\frac{-\beta}{\theta}\right)(p_g)\left(e^{-\beta p_e}\right)\left(\tilde{q}_{gi} - \sum_{j=1}^{2} P_j \tilde{q}_{gj}\right). \tag{28}$$

For the electric and gas portfolios these are +1.41 and −0.43, respectively.

26.2.1 The Demand for Electricity

Application of Roy's identity to (18), taking into account the dependence of life-cycle cost r_i on the price of electricity in (19), but treating the discount rate ρ as exogenous to the household, yields annual electricity demand conditioned on space and water heating choice i,

$$x = q_{1i} + \alpha_0^i + \alpha_1 p_1 + \alpha_2 p_2 + w'\gamma + \beta(y - r_i) + \eta. \tag{29}$$

A more convenient form for estimation is

$$\begin{aligned} x - q_{1i} = \sum_{j=1}^{m} \alpha_0^j \delta_{ji} + \alpha_1 p_1 + \alpha_2 p_2 + w'\gamma + \beta\left(y - \sum_{j=1}^{m} PIOP_j \cdot \delta_{ji}\right) \\ - \beta\rho \sum_{j=1}^{m} PICP_j \cdot \delta_{ji} + \eta, \end{aligned} \tag{30}$$

where δ_{ji} is a dummy variable that is equal to one when $i = j$. The postulated distribution of η and ϵ_i implies $E\eta = 0$ and

$$\begin{aligned} E(\eta \mid i) &= \frac{\sigma\sqrt{6}}{\pi}\left(\sum_{j=1}^{m} \frac{R_j P_j}{1 - P_j} \ln P_j - \frac{R_i}{1 - P_i} \ln P_i\right) \\ &= \sum_{j=1}^{m} \left(\frac{\sigma\sqrt{6} R_j}{\pi}\right)\left(\frac{\ln P_j}{1 - P_j}\right) \cdot (P_j - \delta_{ji}) \\ &= \sum_{j \neq 1}^{m} \left(\frac{\sigma\sqrt{6} R_j}{\pi}\right)\left(\frac{P_j \ln P_j}{1 - P_j} + \ln P_i\right). \end{aligned} \tag{31}$$

One can estimate (29) using ordinary least squares and by three alternative methods that are consistent in the presence of correlation of the residual and the choice dummies δ_{ji}:

1. *Instrumental Variable Method:* The estimated probability, $\hat{P}_j$, from the discrete choice model is used as an instrument for δ_{ji}: the list of instruments is $p_1, p_2, w, y - \sum_{j=1}^{m} PIOP_j \cdot \hat{P}_j, \sum_{j=1}^{m} PICP_j \cdot \hat{P}_j$, and $\hat{P}_j, \ldots, \hat{P}_m$.

2. *Reduced Form Method:* Ordinary least squares is applied to the equation

$$x - q_{1i} = \sum_{j=1}^{m} \alpha_0^j \hat{P}_j + \alpha_1 p_1 + \alpha_2 p_2 + w'\gamma + \beta\left(y - \sum_{j=1}^{m} PIOP_j \cdot \hat{P}_j\right) - \beta\rho \sum_{j=1}^{m} PICP_j \cdot \hat{P}_j + \xi_1. \tag{32}$$

3. *Conditional Expectation Correction Method:* Ordinary least squares is applied to the equation

$$x - q_{1i} = \sum_{j=1}^{m} \alpha_0^j \delta_{ji} + \alpha_1 p_1 + \alpha_2 p_2 + w'\gamma + \beta\left(y - \sum_{j=1}^{m} PIOP_j \cdot \delta_{ji}\right) - \beta\rho \sum_{j=1}^{m} PICP_j \delta_{ji} + \sum_{j \neq 1}^{m} \gamma_j \left(\frac{\hat{P}_j \ln \hat{P}_j}{1 - \hat{P}_j} + \ln \hat{P}_i\right) + \xi_2, \tag{33}$$

where the terms involving estimated probabilities permit a consistent estimate of $E(\eta \mid i)$.

Table 26.4 lists the variables included in the estimation of (30) and gives their sample means. Table 26.5 gives the ordinary least squares estimates of

TABLE 26.4
Variables Entering the Electricity Demand Equation

Variable	Mnemonic	Mean
Income less energy cost (chosen alternative)($)	*NETINC*	16,710
Capital cost (chosen alternative)($)	*PICPI*	1,044
Gas availability index if alternative one chosen	*GASAV*751	0.1509
Marginal price of electricity if alternative one chosen	*WMPE*751	0.004526
If alternative one chosen	*A*1	0.2332
If homeowner	*OWN*	0.9457
Gas availability index	*GASAV*75	0.7294
Number of persons in household	*PERSONS*	3.78
Number of rooms	*ROOMS*	6.265
Marginal price of electricity ($/KWH)	*WMPE*75	0.02194
Marginal price of gas ($/KWH equivalent)	*MPG*75[a]	0.00645
Annual electricity consumption (KWH)		
Households choosing alternative 1	—	24,240
Households choosing alternative 2	—	8,645

[a] Conversion factor equals 4.6597×10^{-2} so that marginal price of gas in $/KWH equivalent is $(4.6597 \times 10^{-2}) \times$ (marginal price of gas in dollars per therm). Details are given in the appendix.

TABLE 26.5
Estimated Electricity Demand Model

Explanatory[a] variable	Method 1[b] OLS estimates coefficient (standard error)	Method 1[b] IV estimates coefficient (standard error)	Method 2[c] coefficient (standard error)[e]	Method 3[d] coefficient (standard error)[e]
NETINC	0.04020 (.03579)	0.01102 (.03823)	0.03254 (.04093)	0.01416 (.03947)
PICPI	4.653 (.9748)	6.260 (1.149)	5.844 (1.418)	6.073 (1.2820)
*GASAV*751	−4,779 (3,211)	−2,477 (5,674)	−3,453 (6,669)	−5,316 (3,514.5)
*WMPE*751	$-.2262E+6$ ($.7956E+5$)	$-.3594E+6$ ($.1366E+6$)	$-.3492E+6$ ($.1599E+6$)	$-.2789E+6$ ($.9387E+5$)
*A*1	$0.1275E+5$ (2,866)	$0.1206E+5$ (5,468)	$0.1327E+5$ (6,449)	$0.1245E+5$ (3,284.2)
OWN	−260.0 (1,078)	134.2 (1,122)	345.7 (1,167)	−254.4 (1,113.8)
*GASAV*75	−1,320 (1,796)	−3,465 (2,314)	−2,676 (2,597)	−2,347 (2,009.6)
PERSONS	918.2 (151.4)	929.5 (156.7)	930.4 (165.9)	871.8 (160.9)
ROOMS	−193.0 (213.3)	−345.1 (225.0)	−445.3 (242.4)	−288.2 (232.8)
*WMPE*75	8,728 ($.3790E+5$)	$.1662E+5$ ($.4351E+5$)	$.3012E+5$ ($.4899E+5$)	−1323 ($.4087E+5$)
*MPG*75	$-.1243E+6$ ($.1319E+6$)	$-.4898E+5$ ($.1402E+6$)	$-.1334E+6$ ($.1549E+6$)	$-.3985E+5$ ($.1477E+6$)
ONE	−3,602 (2,047)	−2,934 (2,434)	−2,954 (2,522)	−3,060 (2,189.4)
H_1	— —	— —	— —	987.1 (603.93)[f]
Standard error of regression	4,139	4,270	4,205.6[e]	4,239.1[e]

[a] Estimated on a subsample of 313 observations from the 1975 WCMS survey. The dependent variable is electricity consumption. For variable definitions, see Table 26.4 and the appendix.

[b] The instruments are the listed explanatory variables, except for *NETINC*, *PICPI*, *WMPE751*, *GASAV*751, and *A*1. Instruments for these variables are formed by replacing the dummy variable indicating actual choice of alternative one by the estimated probability from the logit model.

[c] Explanatory variables are those listed except *NETINC*, *PICPI*, *GASAV*751, *WMPE751*, and *A*1. These variables are replaced by their instruments as defined in note *b*.

[d] Included variables are those listed and the variable $H_1 = [(ESTPB1 - A1) \cdot \log(ESTPB1)/ESTPB2 - (ESTPB2 - A2) \cdot \log(ESTPB2)/ESTPB1]$. *ESTPB*1 is the probability of choosing alternative one, estimated in the discrete choice model.

[e] Corrected standard errors.

[f] Standard error uncorrected is 409.11.

(30) as well as the estimates from the three procedures outlined earlier. These procedures utilized a corrected covariance matrix whose form was derived using the methods of Amemiya (1978).[8]

Note that the dependent variable in (33) is net consumption, defined earlier as the difference between annual electricity consumption and "typical electric usage" of appliances that are not included in the modeled portfolio decision. As a consequence, explanatory dummy variables indicating ownership of, for instance, an electric clothes dryer, electric range, air conditioning system, or color television, are excluded from the demand specification.

Using net consumption as the dependent variable follows our definition of the annualized total cost r_i. Recall that r_i is defined as the operating plus discounted capital cost for alternative i plus the charge for typical fuel usage by appliances that are not choice specific. The inclusion of this latter cost, which is constant across alternatives for each individual, cannot have an effect on the coefficient estimates within the logit model. This follows as only the differences in the explanatory variables between alternatives enter the probability calculation. However, the inclusion of this term does imply a specification with net consumption as the dependent variable.

The price and income elasticities implied by the fitted equation are given in Table 26.6. The formula used for the calculation of price elasticity is modified to include the effects of a change in price on the variable net income. Net income is defined simply as the difference between income and annual operating cost in the chosen alternative. The first two sets of elasticities in Table 26.6 are calculated to correspond to short-run responses conditional on a particular choice of water-heat–space-heat portfolio. In principle, the conditional expectation of the error term in the usage equation is a function of the portfolio choice probabilities, which in turn respond to changes in price. In making our conditional elasticity calculations we are holding this effect constant by assuming that the representative individual cannot switch his appliance portfolio in the short run.

The last set of elasticities includes the effect of portfolio shift. We make these calculations by writing expected consumption as a probability weighted sum of the conditional expectations: $Ex = E(x \mid 1) \cdot P_1 + E(x \mid 2) \cdot P_2$, where $E(x \mid 1)$ is the expected consumption of electricity given that portfolio one is chosen and P_1 is the probability of choosing portfolio one. Then if $\epsilon\,[x, p]$ denotes the elasticity of x with respect to p we have

$$\epsilon\,[Ex, p] = \epsilon\,[E(x \mid 1), p]\, P_1 E(x \mid 1)/Ex + \epsilon\,[E(x \mid 2), p]\, P_2 E(x \mid 2)/ \\ Ex + P_1\,[E(x \mid 1) - E(x \mid 2)]\,/EX \cdot \epsilon\,[P_1, p]\,. \qquad (34)$$

Each of the consistent procedures produced quantitatively similar elasticities. Portfolio shifts are the primary contributor to the price sensitivity of average demand calculated from (34).

TABLE 26.6
Price and Income Elasticities

	Least squares	Method 1, instrumental variable	Method 2, reduced form	Method 3, conditional expectation correction
Elasticities of electricity demand with electric space and water heaters				
With respect to income	0.028	0.008	0.023	0.010
With respect to price of electricity	−0.197	−0.310	−0.289	−0.254
With respect to price of gas	−0.033	−0.013	−0.035	−0.011
Elasticities of electricity demand with gas space and water heater				
With respect to income	0.079	0.022	0.064	0.028
With respect to price of electricity	0.021	0.042	0.076	−0.004
With respect to price of gas	−0.093	−0.037	−0.100	−0.030
Elasticities of expected electricity demand, including portfolio shift				
With respect to income	0.06	0.02	0.05	0.02
With respect to price of electricity	−0.22	−0.26	−0.23	−0.26
With respect to price of gas	0.35	0.39	0.35	0.40

[a] Calculated at sample means.

Comparing the final group of elasticities, we see that the elasticity of income is both smaller than the ordinary least squares estimates and considerably smaller than previous studies have indicated. Own price elasticity is larger in magnitude for methods one and three than that given by ordinary least squares. Finally, we note that the cross-elasticity of the demand for electricity with respect to the price of gas (in KWH equivalents) is larger when estimated by consistent procedures one and three compared to the least squares estimates. Again the price sensitivity comes almost entirely from portfolio shift. Based on a qualitative comparison, reasonable point estimates for average demand under the consistent methods would be +0.02 for income elasticity, −0.26 for own price elasticity, and +0.39 for cross-price elasticity.

We have performed two tests of the independence of the choice variables and the error in (29). Results with method one, the instrumental variable method, were compared to the least squares estimates using the Wu-Hausman statistic.[9] The statistic $\Upsilon = (\hat{\gamma}_{IV} - \hat{\gamma}_{LS})'(\hat{V}_{IV} - \hat{V}_{LS})^{-1}(\hat{\gamma}_{IV} - \hat{\gamma}_{LS})$ computed for the estimates in Table 26.5 on the suspected endogenous variables *PICPI*, *GASAV*751, *WMPE*751, and *A*1 is 15.07 (*NETINC* is excluded because to the limits of numerical accuracy it is perfectly correlated with its instrument.)

Under the null hypothesis, this statistic is asymptotically χ^2 with four degrees of freedom, and thus exceeds the 95 percent critical level of 9.49.

The second specification test compares the results of the least squares and Heckman methods of estimation and is identical to the Wald test of the significance of the "Heckman type" correction term.[10] Recall that the variable H_1 entered as the conditional expectation correction factor in procedure three has the coefficient $\left(-\sigma\sqrt{6}R_2/\pi\right)$. This implies that the consistently estimated value of R_2 is -0.299 with a standard error (corrected) of 0.179. The unadjusted standard error (given in Table 26.5, footnote f) is correct for the null hypothesis of no correlation between η and ϵ. Under the null hypothesis of no correlation, the coefficient of H_1 would be zero. The asymptotic t-statistic for the Wald test of this hypothesis is 2.41, which exceeds the 95 percent critical level.[11]

One might thus infer that an unobserved effect that increases the attractiveness of all gas heat alternative tends at the same time to decrease use of electricity. This pattern could be produced, for example, by an unobserved marginal cost of the electricity component.

We therefore reject the null hypothesis that the unobserved factors influencing portfolio choice are independent of the unobserved factors influencing intensity of use. If these results are confirmed in further analyses, one must conclude that estimation of UEC by least squares decomposition of total demand has the potential for severe bias and that appropriate statistical methods, such as the instrumental variables procedure, are feasible and have satisfactory statistical properties.

APPENDIX

Here we present an account of variable construction and definition for the two-alternative all-electric versus all-gas water-heat–space-heat choice model. The WCMS data survey with matched rate structure and temperature information consisted of 1,502 observations. To have comparable information for both the water-heat–space-heat model and the demand for electricity equation we selected a sample of 313 observations from which there were no missing observations and for which: (1) Income, rate, and cost data were strictly positive (this included the marginal prices of electricity and gas in 1975 as well as space-heating capital costs as calculated by Hittman Associates for CSI/ WEST). (2) Annual consumption of electricity in 1975 was positive. (3) Housing units used either gas or electric water-heat fuel and either gas or electric space-heat fuel but were selected so that the same fuel choice was made for both appliances in the portfolio. (4) Housing construction date from 1950.

Water-Heat and Space-Heat Operating Costs

The definition of operating costs for water heaters and space heaters by fuel type is as follows:

Gas :

$$\begin{aligned}\$/\text{year} = {} & (\$/\text{therm-in})(\text{therm-in/Btu-in}) \\ & \cdot (\text{Btu-in/Btu-out})(\text{Btu-out/KWH-out}) \\ & \cdot (\text{KWH-out/KWH-in})(\text{KWH-in/day})(\text{days/year}).\end{aligned}$$

Electric :

$$\$/\text{year} = (\$/\text{KWH-in})(\text{KWH-in/day})(\text{days/year}),$$

where \$/therm-in is marginal price of gas in 1975, \$/KWH-in is marginal price of electricity in 1975, therm/Btu = 1/100,000, Btu/KWH = 3,413, Btu-in/Btu-out = 1/.72, KWH-out/ KWH-in = 983, KWH-in/day is average consumption. Average consumption for electric water heating depends on the number of residents. (See pp. 5–13 of EPRI report EA-682, "Patterns of Energy Use by Electrical Appliances.")

Average consumption for electric space heat per day is related to the number of rooms in the residence as well as the number of heating degree days. Heating degree days are the number of degrees the daily average temperature is below 65°F. Normally heating is not required when the outdoor temperature averages above 65°F. Using BLS data we constructed the following relationship:

$$\begin{aligned}\frac{\text{KWH} - \text{in}}{\text{day}}[\text{for electric space heat}] = {} & 5.9 - (0.00217)(\text{ANNUAL HDD}) \\ & + (0.000833)(\text{ROOMS} \cdot \text{ANNUAL HDD}).\end{aligned}$$

Note: Sample means and definitions for all variables are found in Table 26.2.

The operating cost used in our econometric analysis differed in one minor respect. As discussed in the text it proved useful to add the annual operating cost for base consumption of all other electric appliances to the space heat operating cost. As this cost is constant across alternatives, its inclusion allows one to think of the household as choosing a certain space-heat–water-heat portfolio as well as the portfolio of all other electric utilizing durables. This latter portfolio of durables is predetermined across the choices we are modeling.

Using the MRI survey we constructed an electric utilization base rate that depends on the presence of appliance durables measured at their average or base usage rates. Thus, we have defined:

$$\begin{aligned}QEBASE = {} & 2496 + (82.8 + 0.93 \cdot CDD + 0.51 \cdot ROOMS \cdot CDD) \\ & \cdot (\text{Central Air Conditioning}) + (-144.6 + 0.447 \cdot CDD) \\ & \cdot (\text{Number of Room Air Conditioners}) + 1{,}340 \cdot FOODFRZ + 780 \\ & \cdot ELECRNGE + 480 \cdot CLRTV + 1030 \cdot ECLTHDR\end{aligned}$$

Water-Heat and Space-Heat Capital Costs

Capital costs for water heaters were not available with the WCMS data set. Estimates were obtained from the National Construction Estimator (Craftsman

Book Co., Solano Beach, California, 1978). These constructions again follow the specifications of Cambridge Systematics/West (1979). They are then related to 1975 prices with a consumer price index adjustment.

Space-heating capital costs for each fuel type were available within the WCMS matched data set. These numbers were calculated using a residential thermal load model developed by Hittman Associates.

NOTES

This research has been supported by NSF Grant No. 79-20052. We are indebted to Cambridge Systematics, Inc., for provision of data and unpublished research reports. We have benefited from discussions with D. Brownstone, A. Goett, J. Hausman, R. Parks, and S. Sen. This chapter revises and extends a paper presented by McFadden to an EPRI Workshop on the Choice and Utilization of Energy-Using Durables in November 1979.

1. Classical studies of aggregate electricity consumption given appliance stock are Houthakker (1951), Houthakker and Taylor (1970), and Fisher and Kaysen (1962). A number of other studies postulate an adaptive adjustment of consumption to long-run equilibrium, which can be attributed to long-run adjustments in holdings of appliances (see Taylor, 1975).

2. Cross-section studies with this structure are McFadden et al. (1978), the residential forecasting model of the California Energy Conservation and Development Commission (1979), and the microsimulation model developed by Cambridge Systematics/West for the Electric Power Research Institute.

3. For a discussion of the treatment of rate structure in demand for electricity, see Dubin (1980).

4. A neoclassical consumer will base appliance purchase, replacement, and retirement decisions on the life-cycle capital and operating costs of alternative appliance portfolios. The first econometric problem in analyzing appliance choice is that the components of life-cycle appliance costs are usually not all observable. A second difficulty is that contemporary energy prices may be a poor indicator of the operating cost expectations of a household. A third, and more fundamental, difficulty in analyzing appliance choice decisions lies in the question of the interaction of supply and demand. These issues are discussed in Dubin (1982).

5. A function $V(y, p_1, p_2)$ of normalized income and prices is the indirect utility function of some locally nonsatiated utility function if and only if it is lower semicontinuous, quasi-convex, increasing in y, nonincreasing in (p_1, p_2), and has $V(\lambda y, \lambda p_1, \lambda p_2)$ nondecreasing in λ.

6. Additional restrictions on ψ and M^i will be imposed by the lower semicontinuity, monotonicity, and quasi-convexity of the indirect utility function.

7. Alternatively, an ordinary least squares regression of individually metered consumption by appliance for a sample of households that have chosen portfolios containing this appliance induces a sample selection bias, with positive UEC residuals and low electricity prices more common in appliance-holding households.

8. Dubin (1981) presents the form of the corrected covariance matrix for each consistent procedure. Details are available on request.

9. For details regarding this test see Hausman (1978) and Hausman and Taylor (1981).

10. We wish to thank an anonymous referee for directing our attention to this identity derived in Holly (1982). We should emphasize that the Heckman estimation method embodies specific assumptions regarding the joint distribution of η and ϵ, whereas the instrumental variable and reduced form methods are more robust in this sense. Four is the appropriate figure for degrees of freedom from Wu-Hausman tests using these latter estimation methods and is the number of dummies and their interactions whose exogeneity is under test. The single degree of freedom in the Wu-Hausman test utilizing the Heckman estimation method reflects the imposition of the implicit distributional assumptions.

11. An alternative method of obtaining consistent estimates of the correlation coefficient R_2 is to run an auxilary regression of the squared fitted residuals from procedures one, two, or three against an expression from conditional expectation given portfolio choice, evaluated at the estimated choice probabilities. The point estimates of R_2 are -0.369, -0.337, and -0.332, respectively. These estimates are close to the estimate of -0.299 obtained earlier from the coefficient of H_1. Details of the calculation are available from the authors on request.

REFERENCES

Amemiya, T., 1973, "Regression Analysis when the Dependent Variable is Truncated Normal," *Econometrica* 41, 997–1016.

Amemiya, T., 1978, "The Estimation of a Simultaneous Equation Generalized Probit Model," *Econometrica* 46, 1193–1206.

Amemiya, T., and G. Sen, 1977, "The Consistency of the Maximum Likelihood Estimator in a Disequilibrium Model," Technical Report 238, Institute for Mathematical Studies in Social Sciences, Stanford University.

Anderson, K., 1973, "Residential Energy Use: An Econometric Analysis," RAND Corporation.

California State Energy Conservation Commission, "California Energy Demand 1978–2000," Working Paper.

Cambridge Systematics/West, 1979, "An Analysis of Household Survey Data in Household Time-of-Day and Annual Electricity Consumption," Working Paper, Cambridge Systematics/West.

Dubin, J., 1980, "Rate Structure and Price Specification in the Demand for Electricity," Mimeo, Massachusetts Institute of Technology.

Dubin, J., 1981, "Two-Stage Single Equation Estimation Methods: An Efficiency Comparison," Mimeo, Massachusetts Institute of Technology.

Dubin, J., 1982, "Economic Theory and Estimation of the Demand for Consumer Durable Goods and Their Utilization: Appliance Choice and the Demand for Electricity," Discussion Paper No. 23, Massachusetts Institute of Technology Energy Laboratory.

Duncan, G., 1980, "Formulation and Statistical Analysis of the Mixed Continuous/Discrete Variable Model in Classical Production Theory," *Econometrica* 48, 839–852.

Fisher, F., and C. Kaysen, 1962, *A Study in Econometrics: The Demand for Electricity in the U. S.*, Amsterdam: North-Holland.

Goett, A., 1979, "A Structured Logit Model of Appliance Investment and Fuel Choice," Working Paper, Cambridge Systematics/West.

Goldfeld, S., and R. Quandt, 1973, "The Estimation of Structural Shifts by Switching Regressions," *Annals of Economic and Social Measurement* 2, 475–485.

Goldfeld, S., and R. Quandt, 1976, "Techniques for Estimating Switching Regression," in: *Studies in Non-Linear Estimation,* S. Goldfeld and R. Quandt (eds.), Cambridge: Ballinger.

Hausman, J., 1978, "Specification Tests in Econometrics," *Econometrica* 46, 1251–1271.

Hausman, J., 1979a, "Exact Consumer's Surplus and Deadweight Loss," *American Economic Review* 71, 663–676.

Hausman, J., 1979b, "Individual Discount Rates and the Purchase and Utilization of Energy-Using Durables," *Bell Journal of Economics* 10, 33–54.

Hausman, J., and W. Taylor, 1981, "A Generalized Specification Test," *Economic Letters* 8, 239–245.

Hay, J., 1979, "An Analysis of Occupational Choice and Income," Ph. D. Dissertation, Yale University.

Heckman, J., 1978, "Dummy Endogenous Variables in a Simultaneous Equation System," *Econometrica* 46, 931–960.

Heckman, J., 1979, "Sample Selection Bias as a Specification Error," *Econometrica* 47, 153–162.

Holly, A., 1982, "A Remark on Hausman's Specification Test," *Econometrica* 50, 749–759.

Houthakker, H., 1951, "Some Calculations of Electricity Consumption in Great Britain," *Journal of the Royal Statistical Society A,* 114, 351–371.

Houthakker, H., and L. Taylor, 1970. *Consumer Demand in the U.S.*, 2nd Ed., Cambridge: Harvard University Press.

Lee, L. F., 1981, "Simultaneous Equations Models with Discrete and Continuous Variables," in: *Structural Analysis of Discrete Date,* C. Manski and D. McFadden (eds.), Cambridge: MIT Press.

Lee, L. F., and R. Trost, 1978, "Estimation of Some Limited Dependent Variable Models with Application to Housing Demand," *Journal of Econometrics* 8, 357–382.

Maddala, G., and F. Nelson, 1974, "Maximum Likelihood Methods for Markets in Disequilibrium," *Econometrica* 42, 1013–1030.

McFadden, D., 1973, "Conditional Logit Analysis of Qualitative Choice Behavior," in: *Frontiers in Econometrics,* P. Zarembka (ed.), New York: Academic Press.

McFadden, D., 1981, "Econometric Models of Probabilistic Choice," in: *Structural Analysis of Discrete Data,* C. Manski and D. McFadden (eds.), Cambridge: MIT Press.

McFadden, D., D. Kirschner, and C. Puig, 1978, "Determinants of the Long-run Demand for Electricity," in: *Proceedings of the American Statistical Association.*

Parti, M., and C. Parti, 1980, "The Total and Appliance-Specific Conditional Demand for Electricity in the Household Sector," *Bell Journal of Economics* 11, 309–321.

Taylor, L., 1975, "The Demand for Electricity: A Survey," *Bell Journal of Economics* 6, 74–110.

Chapter Twenty-Seven

Econometric Methods for Applied General Equilibrium Analysis

Dale W. Jorgenson

The development of computational methods for solving nonlinear general equilibrium models along the lines pioneered by Scarf and Hansen (1973, ch. 1) has been the focus of much recent research. By comparison, the development of econometric methods for estimating the unknown parameters describing technology and preferences in such models has been neglected. The purpose of this chapter is to summarize the results of recent research on econometric methods for estimating the parameters of nonlinear general equilibrium models. For this purpose, I present econometric models of producer and consumer behavior suitable for incorporation into a general equilibrium model of the U.S. economy. The most important feature of these models is that they encompass all of the restrictions implied by economic theories of producer and consumer behavior.

It is essential to recognize at the outset that the predominant tradition in applied general equilibrium modeling, which originated with the seminal work of Leontief (1951, 1953) and his implementations of the static input-output model more than half a century ago, does not employ econometric methods. Leontief gave a further impetus to the development of general equilibrium modeling by introducing a dynamic input-output model. Empirical work associated with input-output analysis is based on estimating the unknown parameters of a general equilibrium model from a single interindustry transactions table.

The usefulness of the "fixed-coefficients" assumption that underlies input-output analysis is hardly subject to disput. By linearizing technology and preferences, it is possible to solve at one stroke the two fundamental problems that arise in the practical implementation of general equilibrium models. First, the resulting model can be solved as a system of linear equations with constant coefficients. Second, the unknown parameters describing technology and preferences can be estimated from a single data point.

Johansen (1960) was the first researcher to successfully implement an applied general equilibrium model without the fixed-coefficients assumption of input-output analysis. He retained the fixed-coefficients assumption in modeling demands for intermediate goods, but employed linear-logarithmic or Cobb-Douglas production functions in modeling the substitution between capital and labor services and technical change. He replaced the fixed-coefficients assumption for household behavior by a system of demand functions originated by Frisch (1959).

Linear-logarithmic production functions imply that relative shares of inputs in the value of output are fixed, so that the unknown parameters characterizing substitution between capital and labor inputs can be estimated from a single data point. In describing producer behavior, Johansen employed econometric methods only in estimating constant rates of technical change. Similarly, the unknown parameters of the demand system proposed by Frisch can be determined from a single data point, except for one parameter that must be estimated econometrically.

The essential features of Johansen's approach have been preserved in the applied general equilibrium models surveyed by Fullerton et al. (1984) and by Mansur and Whalley (1984). The unknown parameters describing technology and preferences in these models are determined by "calibration" to a single data point. Data from a single interindustry transactions table are supplemented by a small number of parameters estimated econometrically. The obvious disadvantage of this approach is that highly restrictive assumptions on technology and preferences are required in order to make calibration feasible.

As an example of the restrictive assumptions on technology employed in the calibration approach, note that almost all applied general equilibrium models retain the fixed-coefficients assumption of Leontief and Johansen for modeling demand for intermediate goods. This assumption is directly contradicted by recent evidence of changes in energy utilization in response to the higher energy prices that have prevailed since 1973. As an example of a restrictive assumption on preferences employed in the calibration approach, note that preferences are commonly assumed to be homothetic, which is contradicted by empirical evidence on consumer behavior going back more than a century.

To implement models of producer and consumer behavior that are less restrictive than those of Johansen, it is essential to employ econometric methods. A possible econometric extension of Johansen's approach would be to estimate elasticities of substitution between capital and labor inputs along the lines suggested by Arrow et al. (1961). Unfortunately, constant elasticity of substitution (CES) production functions cannot easily be extended to encompass substitution among capital, labor, and intermediate inputs or among intermediate inputs. As Uzawa (1962) and McFadden (1963) have shown, constant elasticities of substitution among more than two inputs imply, essentially, that they must be the same among all inputs.

An alternative approach to the implementation of econometric models of producer behavior is to generate complete systems of demand functions for inputs in each industrial sector. Each system gives quantities of inputs demanded as functions of prices and output. This approach to modeling producer behavior was first implemented by Berndt and Jorgenson (1973). As in the descriptions of technology by Leontief and Johansen, production is characterized by constant returns to scale in each sector. As a consequence, commodity prices can be expressed as function-of-factor prices, using the nonsubstitution theorem of Samuelson (1951). This greatly facilitates the solution of the econometric general equilibrium model constructed by Hudson and Jorgenson (1974) by permitting a substantial reduction in dimensionality of the space of prices to be determined by the model.

The implementation of econometric models of producer behavior is very demanding in terms of data requirements. These models require the construction of a consistent time series of inter-industry transactions tables. By comparison, the noneconometric approaches of Leontief and Johansen require only a single interindustry transactions table. The implementation of systems of input demand functions requires methods for the estimation of parameters in systems of nonlinear simultaneous equations. Finally, the restrictions implied by the economic theory of producer behavior require estimation under both equality and inequality constraints.

Similarly, econometric models of consumer behavior can be employed in applied general equilibrium models. Econometric models stemming from the pathbreaking contributions of Schultz (1938), Wold (1953), and Stone (1954) consist of complete systems of demand functions giving quantities demanded as functions of prices and total expenditure. A possible approach to incorporating the restrictions implied by the theory of consumer behavior is to treat aggregate demand functions (ADFs) as if they can be generated by a single representative consumer. Demanded per capita quantities can be expressed as functions of prices and per capita expenditure.

The obvious difficulty with the representative consumer approach is that ADFs can be expressed as the sum of individual demand functions (IDFs). The former depend on prices and total expenditures, as in the theory of individual consumer behavior, but the dependence is on individual total expenditures rather than on aggregate expenditure. If individual expenditures are allowed to vary independently, models of aggregate consumer behavior based on a single representative consumer imply restrictions that severely limit the dependence of the latter on individual expenditure.

An alternative approach to the construction of econometric models of aggregate consumer behavior is provided by Lau's (1977b, 1982) theory of exact aggregation. In this approach, systems of ADFs depend on statistics of the joint distribution of individual total expenditures and attributes of individuals associated with differences in preferences. One of the most remarkable features of models based on exact aggregation is that systems of demand functions for individuals can be recovered uniquely from the system of ADFs. This feature makes it possible to exploit all the implications of the economic theory of the individual consumer in constructing an econometric model of aggregate consumer behavior.

Jorgenson et al. (1980, 1981, 1982) have implemented an econometric model of aggregate consumer behavior based on the theory of exact aggregation. Their approach requires time-series data on prices and aggregate quantities consumed, as well as cross-section data on individual quantities consumed, individual total expenditures, and attributes of individual households, such as demographic characteristics. By comparison, the noneconometric approaches of Leontief and Johansen require only a single data point for prices and aggregate quantities consumed. The implementation of a system of aggregate demand functions requires methods for combining time-series and cross-section data for the estimation of parameters in systems of nonlinear simultaneous equations.

Section 27.1 presents an econometric model of producer behavior, originally implemented for thirty-five industrial sectors of the U.S. economy by Jorgenson and Fraumeni (1981). This model is based on a production function for each sector, giving output as a function of inputs of intermediate goods produced by other sectors and inputs of the primary factors of production, capital, and labor services. Output also depends on time as an index of the level of technology. Producer equilibrium under constant returns to scale implies the existence of a sectoral price function (SPF), giving the price of output as a function of input prices and time. In order to incorporate the restrictions implied by the economic theory of producer behavior, I generate my econometric model from a price function for each sector.

Section 27.2 presents an econometric model of aggregate consumer behavior that has been implemented for the U.S. economy by Jorgenson et al. (1980, 1981, 1982), which is based on a utility function for each consumer, giving utility as a function of quantities of individual commodities. Consumer equilibrium implies the existence of an indirect utility function (IUF) for each consumer, which gives the level of utility as a function of the prices of individual commodities, total expenditure, and attributes of the consumer associated with differences in preferences among consumers. In order to incorporate the restrictions implied by the economic theory of consumer behavior this econometric model is generated from an IUF for each consumer.

Section 27.3 presents the empirical results of implementing these econometric models for the U.S. economy. The presentation of results for the model of producer behavior described in Section 27.1 is limited to the first stage of the two-stage process for the allocation of the value of sectoral output, and that of the model of consumer behavior described in Section 27.2 is similarly limited to the first stage of the two-stage process for the allocation of total expenditure. Family size, age of head, region of residence, race, and urban versus rural residence constitute the attributes of individual households associated with differences in preferences.

27.1 PRODUCER BEHAVIOR

The objective here is to analyze technical change and the distribution of the value of output for thirty-five industrial sectors of the U.S. economy. My most important conceptual innovation is the determination of the rate of technical change and the distributive shares of productive inputs simultaneously as functions of relative prices. I show that the effects of technical change on the distributive shares are precisely the same as the effects of relative prices on the rate of technical change.

My methodology is based on a model of production treating substitution among inputs and changes in technology symmetrically. The model is based on a production function for each industrial sector, giving output as a function of time and of four inputs: capital, labor, energy, and materials. Necessary conditions for producer equilibrium in each sector are given by equalities between the distributive shares of the four productive inputs and the corresponding elasticities of output with respect to each of these inputs.

Producer equilibrium under constant returns to scale implies that the value of output is equal to the sum of the value of the four inputs into each sector. Given this identity and the equalities between the distributive shares and the elasticities of output with respect to each of the inputs, the price of output or the SPF can be expressed as a function of the prices of the four inputs and time.

Given SPFs for all thirty-five industrial sectors, I can generate econometric models that determine the rate of technical change and the distributive shares of the four productivity inputs endogenously for each sector. The distributive shares and the rate of technical change, like the price of sectoral output, are functions of relative prices and time. I assume that the prices of sectoral outputs are transcendental-logarithmic or, more simply, translog functions of the prices of the four inputs and time.

Although technical change is endogenous in these models of production, they must be carefully distinguished from models of induced technical change, such as those analyzed by Hicks (1932), von Weizsäcker (1962), Kennedy (1964), Samuelson (1965), and many others.[1] In those models, the biases of technical change are endogenous and depend on relative prices. In my models, the biases of technical change are fixed, whereas the rate of technical change is endogenous and depends on relative prices.

As Samuelson (1965) pointed out, models of induced technical change require intertemporal optimization, since technical change at any point of time affects future production possibilities. In my models myopic decision rules are appropriate, even though the rate of technical change is endogenous, provided that the price of capital input is treated as a rental price for capital services.[2] The rate of technical change at any point of time is a function of relative prices, but does not affect future production possibilities. This vastly simplifies the modeling of producer behavior and greatly facilitates the implementation of the present models.

27.1.1 Translog Model of Producer Behavior

Given myopic decision rules for producers in each industrial sector, all of the implications of the theory of production can be described in terms of the SPFs.[3] These functions must be homogeneous of degree one, nondecreasing, and concave in the prices of the four inputs. A novel feature of this econometric methodology is fitting econometric models of sectoral production and technical change that incorporate all of these implications of the theory of production.

Representing these models of producer behavior requires some notation. There are I industrial sectors, indexed by $i = 1, 2, \ldots, I$. I denote the quantities of sectoral outputs by $\{Z_i\}$ and the quantities of the four sectoral inputs by $\{K_i, L_i, E_i, M_i\}$. Similarly, the prices of the sectoral outputs are given by $\{q_i\}$ and the prices of the four sectoral inputs by $\{p_K^i, p_L^i, p_E^i, p_M^i\}$. The shares of inputs in the value of output for each of the sectors can be defined by

$$\nu_K^i = \frac{p_K^i K_i}{q_i Z_i}, \qquad \nu_L^i = \frac{p_L^i L_i}{q_i Z_i}, \qquad \nu_E^i = \frac{p_E^i E_i}{q_i Z_i}, \qquad V_M^i = \frac{p_M^i M_i}{q_i Z_i} \qquad (i = 1, 2, \ldots, I).$$

Outputs are valued in producers' prices, whereas inputs are valued in purchasers' prices. The following notation is also required: $\nu_i = (\nu_K^i, \nu_L^i, \nu_E^i, \nu_M^i)$ is the vector of value shares of the ith industry and $\ln p_i = (\ln p_K^i, \ln p_L^i, \ln p_E^i, \ln p_M^i)$ is the vector of logarithms of prices of sectoral inputs both of the ith industry $(i = 1, 2, \ldots, I)$; and t is time as an index of technology.

I assume that the ith industry allocates the value of its output among the four inputs in accordance with the price function

$$\ln q_i = \alpha_0^i + \ln p_i' \alpha_p^i + \alpha_t^i \cdot t + \tfrac{1}{2} \ln p_i' \beta_{pp}^i \ln p_i + \ln p_i' \beta_{pt}^i \cdot t + \tfrac{1}{2} \beta_{tt} \cdot t^2 \qquad (i = 1, 2, \ldots, I). \tag{1}$$

For these price functions, the prices of outputs are transcendental or, more specifically, exponential functions of the logarithms of the prices of inputs, referred to as *transcendental-logarithmic* price functions or, more simply, as translog price functions,[4] indicating the role of the variables that enter the price functions. In this reorientation, the scalars $\{\alpha_0^i, \alpha_t^i, \beta_{tt}^i\}$, the vectors $\{\alpha_p^i, \beta_{pt}^i\}$, and the matrices $\{\beta_{pp}^i\}$ are constant parameters that differ among industries, reflecting differences among sectoral technologies. Differences in technology among time periods within an industry are represented by time as an index of technology.

The value shares of the ith industry can be expressed in terms of the logarithmic derivatives of the SPF with respect to the logarithms of the prices of the corresponding inputs:

$$\nu_i = \frac{\partial \ln q_i}{\partial \ln p_i} \qquad (i = 1, 2, \ldots, I). \tag{2}$$

Applying this relationship to the translog price function yields the system of sectoral value shares:

$$\nu_i = \alpha^i_p + \beta^i_{pp} \ln p_i + \beta^i_{pt} \cdot t \qquad (i = 1, 2, \ldots, I). \tag{3}$$

The *rate of technical change* for each of the sectors, say $\{\nu^i_t\}$, can be defined as the negative of the rate of growth of the price of sectoral output with respect to time, holding the prices of the four sectoral inputs constant:

$$\nu^i_t = -\frac{\partial \ln q_i}{\partial t} \qquad (i = 1, 2, \ldots, I). \tag{4}$$

For the translog price function this relationship takes the form

$$-\nu^i_t = \alpha^i_t + \beta^{i\prime}_{pt} \ln p_i + \beta^i_{tt} \cdot t \qquad (i = 1, 2, \ldots, I). \tag{5}$$

Given the SPFs, the *share elasticities with respect to price* can be defined as the derivatives of the value shares with respect to the logarithms of the prices of the four inputs.[5] For the translog price functions, the matrices of share elasticities with respect to price $\{\beta^i_{pp}\}$ are constant. One can also characterize these functions as *constant share elasticity* or CSE price functions, indicating the role of fixed parameters that enter the SPFs.[6] Similarly, the *biases of technical change with respect to price* can be defined as derivatives of the value shares with respect to time.[7] Alternatively, the biases of technical change with respect to price can be defined as derivatives of the rate of technical change with respect to the logarithms of the prices of the four inputs.[8] These two definitions are equivalent. For the translog price functions, the vectors of biases of technical change with respect to price $\{\beta^i_{pt}\}$ are constant. Finally, the *rate of change of the negative of the rate of technical change* can be defined as the derivative of the rate of technical change with respect to time.[9] For the translog price functions, these rates of change $\{\beta^i_{tt}\}$ are constant.

The negative of the average rates of technical change at any two points of time, say t and $t-1$, can be expressed as the difference between successive logarithms of the price of output less a weighted average of the differences between successive logarithms of the prices given by the average value shares:

$$\begin{aligned} -\bar{\nu}^i_t =& \ln q_i(t) - \ln q_i(t-1) - \bar{\nu}^i_K \left[\ln p^i_K(t) - \ln p^i_K(t-1)\right] \\ & - \bar{\nu}^i_L \left[\ln p^i_L(t) - \ln p^i_L(t-1)\right] - \bar{\nu}^i_E \left[\ln p^i_E(t) - \ln p^i_E(t-1)\right] \\ & - \bar{\nu}^i_M \left[\ln p^i_M(t) - \ln p^i_M(t-1)\right] \qquad (i = 1, 2, \ldots, I), \end{aligned} \tag{6}$$

where

$$\bar{\nu}^i_t = \tfrac{1}{2}\left[\nu^i_t(t) + \nu^i_t(t-1)\right] \qquad (i = 1, 2, \ldots, I)$$

and the average value shares in the two periods are given by

$$\begin{aligned} \bar{\nu}^i_K &= \tfrac{1}{2}\left[\nu^i_K(t) + \nu^i_K(t-1)\right], \\ \bar{\nu}^i_L &= \tfrac{1}{2}\left[\nu^i_L(t) + \nu^i_L(t-1)\right], \\ \bar{\nu}^i_E &= \tfrac{1}{2}\left[\nu^i_E(t) + \nu^i_E(t-1)\right], \\ \bar{\nu}^i_M &= \tfrac{1}{2}\left[\nu^i_M(t) + \nu^i_M(t-1)\right] \qquad (i = 1, 2, \ldots, I). \end{aligned}$$

The expressions for the average rates of technical change $\{\bar{v}_t^i\}$ are known as the *translog price indexes of the sectoral rates of technical change*.

The present model of producer behavior is based on a two-stage allocation. In the first stage, the value of sectoral output is allocated among the four sectoral inputs. In the second stage, the value of each of these inputs is allocated among individual types of that input. The behavior of the ith industry ($i = 1, 2, \ldots, I$) is characterized in terms of the price function that underlies the two-stage process. In addition to homogeneity, monotonicity, and concavity, this price function has the property of homothetic separability in prices of individual types of the four inputs.

Each of the input prices $\{p_K^i, p_L^i, p_E^i, p_M^i\}$ can be regarded as a function of its components. These functions must be homogeneous of degree one, nondecreasing, and concave in the prices of the individual inputs. Specific forms for price indexes of each of the four inputs can be considered as functions of the individual types of that input. If each of these prices is a translog function of its components, the differences between successive logarithms of the prices can be expressed as a weighted average of differences between successive logarithms of process of individual types of that input with weights given by the average value shares. The resulting expressions are known as *translog indexes of the prices of capital, labor, energy and materials inputs.*[10]

27.1.2 Integrability

The next step in representing the present models is to employ the implications of the theory of production in specifying econometric models of technical change and the distribution of the value of output. If a system of equations consisting of sectoral value shares and the rate of technical change can be generated from a SPF, then the system is *integrable*. A complete set of conditions for integrability expressed in terms of the system of equations is as follows:

1. *Homogeneity*. The sectoral value shares and the rate of technical change are homogeneous of degree zero in the input prices, and can be written in the form:

$$\begin{aligned} v_i &= \alpha_p^i + \beta_{pp}^i \ln p_i + \beta_{pt}^i \cdot t, \\ -v_t &= \alpha_t^i + \beta_{pt}^i \ln p_i + \beta_{tt}^i \cdot t \qquad (i = 1, 2, \ldots, I), \end{aligned} \tag{7}$$

where the parameters $\{\alpha_p^i, \alpha_t^i, \beta_{pp}^i, \beta_{pt}^i, \beta_{tt}^i\}$ are constant. Homogeneity implies that these parameters must satisfy

$$\beta_{pp}^i \iota = 0, \qquad \beta_{pt}^{i'} \iota = 0\, I \qquad (i = 1, 2, \ldots, I). \tag{8}$$

For four sectoral inputs there are five restrictions implied by homogeneity.

2. *Product Exhaustion*. The sum of the sectoral value shares is equal to unity:

$$v_i' \iota = 1 \qquad (i = 1, 2, \ldots, I).$$

Product exhaustion implies that the value of the four sectoral inputs exhausts the value of the product and that the parameters must satisfy the restrictions

$$\alpha_p^{i'}\iota = 1, \qquad \beta_{pp}^{i'}\iota = 0, \qquad \beta_{pt}^{i'}\iota = 0 \qquad (i = 1, 2, \ldots, I). \tag{9}$$

For four sectoral inputs there are six restrictions implied by product exhaustion.

3. *Symmetry*. The matrix of share elasticities and biases and rate of change of technical change must be symmetric. Imposing homogeneity and product exhaustion restrictions, one can write the system of sectoral value shares and the rate of technical change without imposing symmetry in the form:

$$\nu_i = \alpha_p^i + \beta_{pp}^i \ \ln\ p_i + \beta_{pt}^i \cdot t, \qquad -\nu_t^i = \alpha_t^i + \beta_{tp}^{i'} \ \ln\ p_i + \beta_{tt}^i \cdot t$$
$$(i = 1, 2, \ldots, I). \tag{10}$$

A necessary and sufficient condition for symmetry is that the matrix of parameters satisfy the restrictions

$$\begin{bmatrix} \beta_{pp}^i & \beta_{pt}^i \\ \beta_{tp}^{i'} & \beta_{tt}^i \end{bmatrix} = \begin{bmatrix} \beta_{pp}^i & \beta_{pt}^i \\ \beta_{pt}^{i'} & \beta_{tt}^i \end{bmatrix} \tag{11}$$

For four sectoral inputs there are a total of ten symmetry restrictions.

4. *Nonnegativity*. The sectoral value shares must be nonnegative:

$$\nu_i \geqq 0 \qquad (i = 1, 2, \ldots, I).$$

By product exhaustion the sectoral value shares sum to unity, so that one can write

$$\nu_i \geq 0 \qquad (i = 1, 2, \ldots, I),$$

where $\nu_i \geq 0$ implies $\nu_i \geq 0$ and $\nu_i \neq 0$. Nonnegativity of the sectoral value shares is implied by monotonicity of the SPFs:

$$\frac{\partial \ln q_t}{\partial \ln p_i} \geqq 0 \qquad (i = 1, 2, \ldots, I).$$

For the translog price function the conditions for monotonicity take the form

$$\frac{\partial \ln q_i}{\partial \ln p_i} = \alpha_p^i + \beta_{pp}^i \ln p_i + \beta_{pt}^i \cdot t \geqq 0 \qquad (i = 1, 2, \ldots, I). \tag{12}$$

Since the translog price functions are quadratic in the logarithms of sectoral input prices $\ln p_i$ $(i = 1, 2, \ldots, I)$, one can always choose prices so that the monotonicity of the SPFs is violated. Accordingly, one cannot impose restrictions on the parameters of the translog price functions that would imply nonnegativity of the sectoral value shares for all prices and times. Instead one considers restrictions on the parameters that imply concavity of the SPFs or monotonicity of the sectoral value shares for all nonnegative value shares.

5. *Monotonicity*. The matrix of share elasticities must be nonpositive-definite. Concavity of the SPFs implies that the matrices of second-order partial derivatives, say $\{H_i\}$, are nonpositive-definite,[11] so that the matrices $\{\beta^i_{pp} + \nu_i \nu_i' - V_i\}$ are nonpositive-definite[12]:

$$(1/q_i) \cdot N_i \cdot H_i \cdot N_i = \beta^i_{pp} + \nu_i \nu_i' - V_i \qquad (i = 1, 2, \ldots, I), \qquad (13)$$

where the SPFs are positive and

$$N_i = \begin{bmatrix} p^i_K & 0 & 0 & 0 \\ 0 & p^i_L & 0 & 0 \\ 0 & 0 & p^i_E & 0 \\ 0 & 0 & 0 & p^i_M \end{bmatrix}, \quad V_i = \begin{bmatrix} \nu^i_K & 0 & 0 & 0 \\ 0 & \nu^i_L & 0 & 0 \\ 0 & 0 & \nu^i_E & 0 \\ 0 & 0 & 0 & \nu^i_M \end{bmatrix} \quad (i = 1, 2, \ldots, I)$$

and $\{\beta^i_{pp}\}$ are CSE matrices as defined above.

Without violating the product exhaustion and nonnegativity restrictions on the sectoral value shares, the matrices $\{\nu_i \nu_i' - V_i\}$ can be set equal to zero, for example, by choosing one of the value shares to be equal to unity and the other equal to zero. Necessary conditions for the matrices $\{\beta^i_{pp} + \nu_i \nu_i' - V_i\}$ to be nonpositive-definite are that the CSE matrices $\{\beta^i_{pp}\}$ must be nonpositive-definite. These conditions are also sufficient, since the matrices $\{\nu_i \nu_i' - V_i\}$ are nonpositive-definite for all nonnegative value shares summing to unity and the sum of two nonpositive-definite matrices is nonpositive-definite.

To impose concavity in the translog price functions, the CSE matrices $\{\beta^i_{pp}\}$ can be represented in terms of their Cholesky factorizations:

$$\beta^i_{pp} = T_i D_i T_i' \qquad (i = 1, 2, \ldots, I),$$

where $\{T_i\}$ are unit lower triangular matrices and $\{D_i\}$ are diagonal matrices. For four inputs one can write the matrices $\{\beta^i_{pp}\}$ in terms of their Cholesky factorizations as follows:

$$\beta^i_{pp} = \begin{bmatrix} \delta^i_1 & \lambda^i_{21}\delta^i_1 & \lambda^i_{31}\delta^i_1 & \lambda^i_{41}\delta^i_1 \\ \lambda^i_{21}\delta^i_1 & \lambda^i_{21}\lambda^i_{21}\delta^i_1 + \delta^i_2 & \lambda^i_{21}\lambda^i_{31}\delta^i_1 + \lambda^i_{32}\delta^i_2 & \lambda^i_{41}\lambda^i_{21}\delta^i_1 + \lambda^i_{42}\delta^i_2 \\ \lambda^i_{31}\delta^i_1 & \lambda^i_{31}\lambda^i_{21}\delta^i_1 + \lambda^i_{32}\delta^i_2 & \lambda^i_{31}\lambda^i_{31}\delta^i_1 + \lambda^i_{32}\lambda^i_{32}\delta^i_2 + \delta^i_3 & \lambda^i_{41}\lambda^i_{31}\delta^i_1 + \lambda^i_{42}\lambda^i_{32}\delta^i_2 + \lambda^i_{43}\delta^i_3 \\ \lambda^i_{41}\delta^i_1 & \lambda^i_{41}\lambda^i_{21}\delta^i_1 + \lambda^i_{42}\delta^i_2 & \lambda^i_{41}\lambda^i_{31}\delta^i_1 + \lambda^i_{42}\lambda^i_{32}\delta^i_2 + \lambda^i_{43}\delta^i_3 & \lambda^i_{41}\lambda^i_{41}\delta^i_1 + \lambda^i_{42}\lambda^i_{42}\delta^i_2 + \lambda^i_{43}\lambda^i_{43}\delta^i_3 + \delta^i_4 \end{bmatrix} \quad (i = 1, 2, \ldots, I),$$

where

$$T_i = \begin{bmatrix} 1 & 0 & 0 & 0 \\ \lambda_{21}^i & 1 & 0 & 0 \\ \lambda_{31}^i & \lambda_{32}^i & 1 & 0 \\ \lambda_{41}^i & \lambda_{42}^i & \lambda_{43}^i & 1 \end{bmatrix}, \qquad D_i = \begin{bmatrix} \delta_1^i & 0 & 0 & 0 \\ 0 & \delta_2^i & 0 & 0 \\ 0 & 0 & \delta_3^i & 0 \\ 0 & 0 & 0 & \delta_4^i \end{bmatrix} (i = 1, 2, \dots, I).$$

The CSE matrices $\{\beta_{pp}^i\}$ must satisfy both the symmetry restrictions and those implied by product exhaustion. The parameters of the Cholesky factorizations must then satisfy the following conditions:

$$\begin{aligned} 1 + \lambda_{21}^i + \lambda_{31}^i + \lambda_{41}^i &= 0, \\ 1 + \lambda_{32}^i + \lambda_{42}^i &= 0, \\ 1 + \lambda_{43}^i &= 0, \\ \delta_4^i &= 0 \qquad (i = 1, 2, \dots, I). \end{aligned}$$

Under these conditions, there is a one-to-one transformation between the CSE matrices $\{\beta_{pp}^i\}$ and the parameters of the Cholesky factorizations $\{T_i, D_i\}$. The CSE matrices are nonpositive-definite, if and only if the diagonal elements of the matrices $\{D_i\}$, the so-called Cholesky values, are nonpositive.

Similarly, one can provide a complete set of conditions for integrability of the systems of sectoral value shares for individual inputs for the second stage of the two-stage allocation process. For example, the sectoral value shares for individual capital inputs are homogeneous of degree zero in the prices of these inputs, the sum of these shares is equal to unity, and the matrix of share elasticities with respect to prices of individual capital inputs must be symmetric. These conditions can be used to generate restrictions on the parameters of the translog price indexes for capital input. The restrictions are analogous to those for the first stage of the two-stage allocation process, except that restrictions on the equation for the rate of technical change are omitted.

The sectoral value shares for individual capital inputs must be nonnegative; as before, one cannot impose conditions on the parameters of the translog price indexes for capital input that would imply nonnegativity of these shares for all prices and times. Instead, one can consider restrictions on the parameters that imply concavity of the SPFs for capital input for all nonnegative value shares. These restrictions are precisely analogous to those for concavity of the SPFs, and can be imposed by representing the CSE matrices in terms of their factorizations, requiring that the corresponding Cholesky values be nonpositive. Similar restrictions can be imposed on the parameters of translog price functions for labor, energy, and materials inputs.

27.1.3 Stochastic Specifications

The present models of producer behavior are generated from translog price functions for each industrial sector. To formulate an econometric model of production and technical change, I add a stochastic component to the equations for the value shares and the rate of technical change and associate it with unobservable random disturbances at the level of the individual industry. The industry maximizes profits for given prices of inputs, but the value shares of inputs are chosen with a random disturbance. This disturbance may result from errors in implementation of production plans, random elements in sectoral technologies not reflected in the models of producer behavior, or errors of measurements in the value shares. I assume that each of these equations have two additive components[13]: a nonrandom function of the prices of the four inputs and time, and an unobservable random disturbance that is functionally independent of these variables.

Representing an econometric model of production and technical change requires some additional notation. Consider observations on expenditure patterns by I industries, indexed by $i = 1, 2, \ldots, I$, for T time periods, indexed by $t = 1, 2, \ldots, T$. For the ith industry in the tth time period the vector of value shares is ν_{it}, the rate of technical change is ν_{it}^{t}, the vector of price indexes for the four inputs is p_{it}, and the vector of logarithms of input price indexes is $\ln p_{it}$. As before, time as an index of technology is denoted by t.

Econometric models of production and technical change corresponding to translog price functions are obtained by adding random disturbances to the equations for the value shares and the rate of technical change in each industry:

$$\nu_{it} = \alpha_p^i + \beta_{pp}^i \ \ln p_{it} + \beta_{pt}^i \cdot t + \varepsilon_{it},$$

$$-\nu_{it}^t = \alpha_t^i + \beta_{pt}^{i'} \ \ln p_{it} + \beta_{it}^i \cdot t + \varepsilon_{it}^t$$

$$(i = 1, 2, \ldots, I; \ t = 1, 2, \ldots, T), \tag{14}$$

where $\{\varepsilon_{it}\}$ is the vector of unobservable random disturbances for the value shares of the ith industry and the tth time period and $\{\varepsilon_{it}^t\}$ is the corresponding disturbance for the rate of technical change. Since the value shares for all inputs sum to unity for each industry in each time period, the random disturbances corresponding to the four value shares sum to zero in each time period:

$$\imath' \varepsilon_{it} = 0 \qquad (i = 1, 2, \ldots, I; \ t = 1, 2, \ldots, T), \tag{15}$$

so that these disturbances are not distributed independently.

It is assumed that the unobservable random disturbances for all five equations have expected value equal to zero for all observations,

$$E \begin{pmatrix} \varepsilon_{it} \\ \varepsilon_{it}^t \end{pmatrix} = 0 \qquad (i = 1, 2, \ldots, I; \ t = 1, 2, \ldots, T). \tag{16}$$

and that these disturbances have a covariance matrix that is the same for all observations. Since the random disturbances corresponding to the four value shares sum to zero, this matrix is nonnegative-definite with rank equal at most to four. The covariance matrix of the random disturbances, say $\left\{ \sum^i \right\}$, for instance, is assumed to be rank four, where

$$V\begin{pmatrix}\varepsilon_{it}\\ \varepsilon^{t}_{it}\end{pmatrix}=\sum{}^{i} \qquad (i=1,2,\ldots,I;\ t=1,2,\ldots,T).$$

Finally, as the random disturbances corresponding to distinct observations in the same or different equations are assumed to be uncorrelated,[14] the covariance matrix of random disturbances for all observations has the Kronecker product form:

$$V\begin{pmatrix}\varepsilon^{i}_{K1}\\ \varepsilon^{i}_{K2}\\ \vdots\\ \varepsilon^{i}_{KT}\\ \varepsilon^{i}_{L1}\\ \vdots\\ \varepsilon^{t}_{tT}\end{pmatrix}=\sum{}^{i}\otimes i=1,2,\ldots,I;\ t=1,2,\ldots,T). \qquad (17)$$

The sectoral rates of technical change $\{v^{t}_{it}\}$ are not directly observable; however, the equation for the translog price indexes of the sectoral rates of technical change can be written as

$$-\bar{v}^{t}_{it}=\alpha^{i}_{t}+\beta^{i'}_{pt}\,\overline{\ln p_{it}}+\beta^{i}_{tt}\cdot\bar{t}+\bar{\varepsilon}^{t}_{it} \qquad (i=1,2,\ldots,I;\ t=2,3,\ldots,T), \qquad (18)$$

where $\bar{\varepsilon}^{t}_{it}$ is the average disturbance in the two periods:

$$\bar{\varepsilon}^{t}_{it}=\tfrac{1}{2}\left(\varepsilon^{t}_{it}+\varepsilon^{t}_{i,t-1}\right) \qquad (i=1,2,\ldots,I;\ t=2,3,\ldots,T).$$

Similarly, $\overline{\ln p_{it}}$ is a vector of averages of the logarithms of the prices of the four inputs and $\bar{t}$ is the average of time as an index of technology in the two periods.

With this new notation, the equations for the value shares of these inputs can be written as

$$\bar{v}_{it}=\alpha^{i}_{p}+\beta^{i}_{pp}\,\overline{\ln p_{it}}+\beta^{i}_{pt}\cdot\bar{t}+\bar{\varepsilon}_{it} \qquad (i=1,2,\ldots,I;\ t=2,3,\ldots,T), \qquad (19)$$

where $\bar{\varepsilon}_{it}$ is a vector of averages of the disturbances in the two periods. As before, the average value shares sum to unity, so that the average disturbances for the equations corresponding to value shares sum to zero:

$$\imath'\bar{\varepsilon}_{it}=0 \qquad (i=1,2,\ldots,I;\ t=2,3,\ldots,T). \qquad (20)$$

The covariance matrix of the average disturbances corresponding to the equation for the rate of technical change for all observations, say Ω, is proportional to a Laurent matrix:

$$V\begin{pmatrix}\bar{\varepsilon}^{i}_{t2}\\ \bar{\varepsilon}^{i}_{t3}\\ \vdots\\ \bar{\varepsilon}^{i}_{tT}\end{pmatrix}\sim\Omega \qquad (i=1,2,\ldots,I), \qquad (21)$$

where

$$\Omega = \begin{bmatrix} \frac{1}{2} & \frac{1}{4} & 0 & \cdots & 0 \\ \frac{1}{4} & \frac{1}{2} & \frac{1}{4} & \cdots & 0 \\ 0 & \frac{1}{4} & \frac{1}{2} & \cdots & 0 \\ \vdots & \vdots & \vdots & & \vdots \\ 0 & 0 & 0 & \cdots & \frac{1}{2} \end{bmatrix}.$$

The covariance matrices of the average disturbance corresponding to the equations for the four value shares are all the same, so that the covariance matrix of the average disturbances for all observations has the Kronecker product form:

$$V \begin{pmatrix} \bar{\varepsilon}^i_{K2} \\ \bar{\varepsilon}^i_{K3} \\ \vdots \\ \bar{\varepsilon}^i_{KT} \\ \bar{\varepsilon}^i_{L2} \\ \vdots \\ \bar{\varepsilon}^t_{tT} \end{pmatrix} = \sum\nolimits^i \otimes \Omega \qquad (i = 1, 2, \ldots, I). \tag{22}$$

Although disturbances in equations for the average rate of technical change and the average value shares are autocorrelated, the data can be transformed to eliminate the autocorrelation. The matrix Ω is positive-definite, so that there is a matrix P such that

$$P\Omega P' = I, \qquad P'P = \Omega^{-1}.$$

To construct the matrix P one first inverts the matrix Ω to obtain the inverse matrix Ω^{-1}, which is positive-definite. The Cholesky factorization of the inverse matrix Ω^{-1} is then calculated:

$$\Omega^{-1} = TDT',$$

where T is a unit lower triangular matrix and D is a diagonal matrix with positive elements along the main diagonal. Finally, one can write the matrix P in the form

$$P = D^{\frac{1}{2}}T',$$

where $D^{\frac{1}{2}}$ is a diagonal matrix with elements along the main diagonal equal to the square roots of the corresponding elements of D.

Equations for the average rates of technical change can be transformed by the matrix $P = D^{\frac{1}{2}}T'$ to obtain equations with uncorrelated random disturbances.

$$D^{\frac{1}{2}}T' \begin{pmatrix} \bar{v}^i_{t2} \\ \bar{v}^i_{t3} \\ \vdots \\ \bar{v}^i_{tT} \end{pmatrix} = D^{\frac{1}{2}}T' \begin{pmatrix} 1 \ \overline{\ln p^i_{K2}} & \cdots & 2 - \frac{1}{2} \\ 1 \ \overline{\ln p^i_{K3}} & \cdots & 3 - \frac{1}{2} \\ \vdots & & \vdots \\ 1 \ \overline{\ln p^i_{KT}} & \cdots & T - \frac{1}{2} \end{pmatrix} \begin{pmatrix} \alpha^i_t \\ \beta^i_{Kt} \\ \vdots \\ \beta^i_{tt} \end{pmatrix}$$

$$+ D^{\frac{1}{2}}T' \begin{pmatrix} \bar{\varepsilon}^i_{t2} \\ \bar{\varepsilon}^i_{t3} \\ \vdots \\ \bar{\varepsilon}^i_{tT} \end{pmatrix} \qquad (i = 1, 2, \ldots, I), \qquad (23)$$

since

$$P\Omega P' = \left(D^{\frac{1}{2}}T'\right)\Omega\left(D^{\frac{1}{2}T'}\right)' = I.$$

The transformation $P = D^{\frac{1}{2}}T'$ is applied to data on the average rates of technical change $\{\bar{v}^i_t\}$ and on the average values of the variables that appear on the right-hand side of the corresponding equation.

The transformation $P = D^{\frac{1}{2}}T'$ can be applied to the equations for average value shares to obtain equations with uncorrelated disturbances. As before, the transformation is applied to data on the average value shares and the average values of variables that appear in the corresponding equations. The covariance matrix of the transformed disturbances from the equations for these shares and for the average rate of technical change has the Kronecker product form:

$$\left(I \otimes D^{\frac{1}{2}}T'\right)\left(\sum\nolimits^i \otimes \Omega\right)\left(I \otimes D^{\frac{1}{2}}T'\right)' = \sum\nolimits^i \otimes I \qquad (i = 1, 2, \ldots, I). \qquad (24)$$

To estimate the unknown parameters of the translog price function, the first three equations for the average value shares are combined with the equation for the average rate of technical change to obtain a complete econometric model of production and technical change. The parameters of the equations for the remaining average value share are estimated using the restrictions on these parameters given earlier. The complete model involves fourteen unknown parameters. A total of sixteen additional parameters can be estimated as functions of these fourteen, given the restrictions. My estimate of the unknown parameters of this model is based on the nonlinear three-stage least squares estimator introduced by Jorgenson and Laffont (1974).

27.2 CONSUMER BEHAVIOR

I now turn to models of aggregate consumer behavior. First, some notation: There are J consumers, indexed by $j = 1, 2, \ldots, J$ and N commodity groups in the economy, indexed by $n = 1, 2, \ldots, N$; p_n is the price of the nth commodity group, assumed to be the same for all consumers. The vector of prices of all commodity groups are denoted by $p = (p_1, p_2, \ldots, p_N)$. The quantity of the nth commodity group demanded by the jth consumer is x_{nj} and total expenditure of the jth consumer is $Y_j = \sum_{n=1}^{N} p_n x_{nj}$. Finally, A_j is a vector of individual attributes of the jth consumer.[15]

I assume that the demand for the nth commodity group by the jth consumer x_{nj} can be expressed as a function f_{nj} of the price vector p, total expenditure Y_j, and the vector of attributes A_j:

$$x_{nj} = f_{nj}(p, Y_j, A_j). \tag{25}$$

Aggregate demand for the nth commodity group is given by

$$\sum_{j=1}^{J} x_{nj} = \sum_{j=1}^{J} f_{nj}(p, Y_j, A_j).$$

In models of consumer behavior based on aggregate quantities consumed, the ADF depends on the price vector p, aggregate expenditure $\sum_{j=1}^{J} Y_j$, and possibly some index of aggregate attributes, say $\sum_{j=1}^{J} A_j$. Thus, one may write

$$\sum_{j=1}^{J} f_j(p, Y_j, A_j) = F\left(p, \sum_{j=1}^{J} Y_j, \sum_{j=1}^{J} A_j\right), \tag{26}$$

where f_j is a vector-valued IDF,

$$f_j = \begin{bmatrix} f_{1j} \\ f_{2j} \\ \vdots \\ f_{Nj} \end{bmatrix} \qquad (j = 1, 2, \ldots, J),$$

giving the vector of demands for all N commodities by the jth consumer, and F is a vector-valued ADF, giving the vector of demands for all N commodities by all J consumers.

The conditions under which equation (26) holds for all expenditures $\{Y_j\}$, all prices, and all possible attributes were derived by Gorman (1953) under the assumption of utility maximization by individual consumers. Gorman's conditions imply

1. $f_j(p, Y_j, A_j) = h_1(p)Y_j + h_2(p)A_j + C_j(p) \quad (j = 1, 2, \ldots, J)$,
2. $F\left(p, \sum_{j=1}^{j} Y_j, \sum_{j=1}^{J} A_j\right) = h_1(p) \sum_{j=1}^{J} Y_j + h_2(p) \sum_{j=1}^{J} A_j + \sum_{j=1}^{J} C_j(p)$,

where the vector-valued function $h_1(p)$ is homogeneous of degree minus one and the vector-valued functions $\{h_2(p), C_j(p)\}$ are homogeneous of degree zero. In other words, the IDFs are linear in expenditure and attributes and identical up to the addition of a function that is independent of expenditure and attributes. Furthermore, if aggregate demands are equal to zero when aggregate expenditure is equal to zero, individuals must have identical homothetic preferences.[16]

Homothetic preferences are inconsistent with well-established empirical regularities in the behavior of individual consumers, such as Engel's law, which states that the proportion of expenditure devoted to food is a decreasing function of total expenditure.[17] Identical preferences for individual households are inconsistent with empirical findings that expenditure patterns depend on the demographic characteristics of individual households.[18] Even the weaker form of Gorman's results—that quantities consumed are linear functions of expenditure with identical slopes for all individuals—is inconsistent with empirical evidence from budget studies.[19]

Despite this lack of agreement, Gorman's characterization provided an important stimulus to empirical research based on aggregate time-series data. The linear expenditure system, proposed by Klein and Rubin (1947) and implemented by Stone (1954), has the property that IDFs are linear in total expenditure. The resulting system of ADFs has been widely used as the basis for econometric models of aggregate consumer behavior. Generalizations of the linear expenditure system that retain the critical property of linearity of IDFs in total expenditure have also been employed in empirical research.[20]

Muellbauer (1975, 1976a,b) substantially generalized Gorman's characterization of the representative consumer model. Aggregate expenditure shares, interpreted as the expenditure shares of a representative consumer, may depend on prices and on a function of individual expenditure not restricted to aggregate or per capita expenditure. In Muellbauer's model of the representative consumer, individual preferences are identical but not necessarily homothetic. Furthermore, quantities consumed may be nonlinear functions of expenditure, rather than linear functions as in Gorman's characterization. An important consequence of this nonlinearity is that ADFs depend on the distribution of expenditure among individuals. Berndt et al. (1977), and Deaton and Muellbauer (1980a,b), have implemented aggregate models of consumer behavior that conform to Muellbauer's characterization of the representative consumer model, retaining the assumption that preferences are identical among individuals.

Lau (1977b, 1982) has developed a theory of exact aggregation that makes it possible to incorporate differences in individual preferences. One first generalizes the concept of an ADF to that of a function that depends on general symmetric functions of individual expenditures and attributes:

$$\sum_{j=1}^{J} f_j(p, Y_j, A_j) = F\big[(p, g_1(Y_1, Y_2, \ldots, Y_J, A_1, A_2, \ldots, A_j), \\ g_2(Y_1, Y_2, \ldots, Y_J, A_1, A_2, \ldots, A_J), \ldots, \\ g_1(Y_1, Y_2, \ldots, Y_J, A_1, A_2, \ldots, A_j)\big], \qquad (27)$$

where each g_i $(i = 1, 2, \ldots, I)$ is such a function, so that the value of (27) is independent of the ordering of the individuals. The $\{g_i\}$ are known as index functions and can be interpreted as statistics describing the population. To avoid triviality it is assumed that the function $\{g_i\}$ is functionally independent.

The fundamental theorem of exact aggregation establishes conditions for (27) to hold for all prices and all individual expenditures and attributes. These conditions are as follows:

1. All the IDFs for the same commodity are identical up to the addition of a function independent of individual attributes and expenditure.
2. All the IDFs must be sums of products of separate functions of the prices and of the individual attributes and expenditure.
3. The ADFs depend on certain index functions of individual attributes and expenditures, the only admissible index functions are additive in these functions.
4. The ADFs can be written as linear functions of the index functions.[21]

Specialization of the fundamental theorem of exact aggregation has already appeared in the literature. For example, if there is only one index function and one takes $g_1 = \sum_{j=1}^{J} Y_j$, aggregate expenditure for the economy, then this theorem implies that for given prices, all consumers must have parallel linear Engel curves. Restricting demands to be nonnegative for all prices and expenditures implies that for given prices, these curves are identical for all consumers. These are Gorman's (1953) results. Muellbauer's condition for the existence of a representative consumer,

$$\sum_{j=1}^{j} f_{nj}(p, Y_j) - F_n(g_2(Y_{1,2}, \ldots, Y_j), p)\left(\sum_{j=1}^{J} y_j\right) \qquad (n = 1, 2, \ldots, N),$$

can be viewed as a special case of (27) with the number of indexes I equal to two and the first index function $g_1(Y_1,\ Y_2, \ldots, Y_j) = \sum_{j=1}^{J} Y_j$ equal to aggregate expenditure. The representative consumer interpretation fails for the case of more than two index functions.

27.2.1 Translog Model of Consumer Behavior

I next present individual and aggregate models of consumer behavior based on the theory of exact aggregation, which requires that the IDFs be linear in a number of functions of individual attributes and expenditure. Representing ADFs as the sum of IDFs, one finds that the former depend on the distribution of expenditure among individuals, on the level of per capita expenditure and prices, and also on the joint distribution of expenditures and demographic characteristics among individuals.

In the present model of consumer behavior, the individual consuming units are households. I assume that household expenditures on commodity groups are allocated so as to maximize a household welfare function. As a consequence, the household behaves in the same way as an individual maximizing a utility function.[22] The IDFs must be integrable, so that they can be generated by Roy's (1943) identity from an IUF for each consuming unit.[23] These IUFs are assumed to be homogeneous of degree zero in prices and expenditure, nonincreasing in prices and nondecreasing in expenditure, and quasi-convex in prices and expenditure.

To allow for differences in preferences among consuming units, the IUFs for the jth unit are allowed to depend on the vector of attributes A_j; each attribute is represented by a dummy variable equal to unity when the consuming unit has the corresponding characteristic and zero otherwise. There are several groups of attributes in this model of consumer behavior, and each consuming unit is assigned one of the attributes in each of the groups.

Some additional notation is required here. For the jth consuming unit ($j = 1, 2, \ldots, J$): $w_{nj} = p_n x_{nj}/Y_j$ is the expenditure shares of the nth commodity group in the budget; $w_j = (w_{1j}, w_{2j}, \ldots, 2_{Nj})$ is the vector of expenditure shares; $\ln(p/Y_j) = (\ln(p_{1/Y_j}), \ln(p_{2/Y_j}), \ldots, ln(p_{N/Y_j}))$ is the vector of logarithms of ratios of prices to expenditure; and $\ln p = (\ln p_1, \ln p_2, \ldots, \ln p_N)$ is the vector of logarithms of prices.

It is assumed that the jth consuming unit allocates its expenditures in accordance with the transcendental logarithmic or translog IUF,[24] say U_j, where

$$\ln U_j = G(A_j) + \ln\left(p/Y_j\right)' \alpha_p + \tfrac{1}{2} \ln\left(p/Y_j\right)' \beta_{pp} \ln p/Y_j$$
$$+ \ln\left(p/Y_j\right)' \beta_{pA} A_j \qquad (j = 1, 2, \ldots, J). \tag{28}$$

In this representation the function G depends on the attribute vector A_j but is independent of the prices p and expenditure Y_j. The vector α_p and the matrices β_{pp} and β_{pA} are constant parameters that are the same for all consuming units.

The expenditure shares of the jth consuming unit can be derived by the logarithmic form of Roy's identity:

$$w_{nj} = \frac{\partial \ln U_j}{\partial \ln(p_n/Y_j)} + \sum \frac{\partial \ln U_j}{\partial \ln(p_n/Y_j)} \qquad (n = 1, 2, \ldots, N;\; j = 1, 2, \ldots, J). \tag{29}$$

Applying this identity to the translog IUF yields the system of individual expenditure shares:

$$w_j = (1/B_j)\left(\alpha_p + \beta_{pp} \ln(p/Y_j) + \beta_{pA}\, A_j\right) \qquad (j = 1, 2, \ldots, J), \tag{30}$$

where the denominators $\{B_j\}$ take the form

$$B_j = \iota'\alpha_p + \iota'\beta_{pp} \ln(p/Y_j) + \iota'\beta_{pA}\, A_j \qquad (j = 1, 2, \ldots, J) \tag{31}$$

and ι is a vector of ones.

The function G that appears in the translog IUF does not enter into the determination of the individual expenditure shares and is not identifiable from observed patterns of individual expenditure allocation. Since these shares can be expressed as ratios of functions that are homogeneous and linear in the unknown parameters $(\alpha_p, \beta_{pp}, \beta_{pA})$, they are homogeneous of degree zero in the parameters. Multiplying a given set of the unknown parameters by a constant gives another set of parameters that generates the same system of individual budget shares. Accordingly, a normalization for the parameters can be chosen without affecting observed patterns of individual expenditure allocation. It is convenient here to employ the normalization

$$\iota'\alpha_p = -1.$$

Under this restriction any change in the set of unknown parameters is reflected in changes in individual expenditure patterns.

The conditions for exact aggregation are that the individual expenditure shares are linear in functions of the attributes $\{A_j\}$ and total expenditures $\{Y_j\}$ for all consuming units.[25] These conditions are satisfied if and only if the terms involving the attributes and expenditures do not appear in the denominators of the expressions given earlier for the individual expenditure shares, so that

$$\iota'\beta_{pp}\iota = 0, \qquad \iota'\beta_{pA} = 0.$$

These restrictions imply that the denominators $\{B_j\}$ reduce to

$$B = -1 + \iota'\beta_{pp} \ \ln\ p,$$

where the subscript j is no longer required, since the denominator is the same for all consuming units. Under these restrictions the individual expenditure shares can be written as

$$w_j = (1/B)\left(\alpha_p + \beta_{pp} \ \ln\ p - \beta_{pp}\iota \cdot \ln\ Y_j + \beta_{pA}\ A_j\right) \qquad (j = 1, 2, \ldots, J). \tag{32}$$

The shares are linear in the logarithms of expenditures $\{\ln\ Y_j\}$ and the attributes $\{A_j\}$, as required by exact aggregation.

Aggregate expenditure shares, say w, were obtained by multiplying individual expenditure shares by expenditure for each consuming unit, adding over all consuming units, and dividing by aggregate expenditure,

$$W = \frac{\sum Y_j w_j}{\sum Y_j}. \tag{33}$$

and they can be written as

$$w = \frac{1}{B}\left(\alpha_p + \beta_{pp} \ \ln\ p - \beta_{pp}\iota\frac{\sum Y_j \ln Y_j}{\sum Y_j} + \beta_{pA}\frac{\sum Y_j A_j}{\sum Y_j}\right). \tag{34}$$

These shares depend on prices p as well as on the distribution of expenditures over all consuming units through the function $\sum Y_j \ \ln Y_j / \sum Y_j$, which may be regarded as a statistic of the distribution. This single statistic summarizes the impact of changes in the distribution of expenditures among individual consuming units on aggregate expenditure allocation. Finally, they depend on the distribution of expenditures among demographic groups through the functions $\{\sum Y_j A_j / \sum Y_j\}$, which may be regarded as statistics of the joint distribution of expenditures and attributes. As the attributes are represented as dummy variables, equal to one for a consuming unit with that characteristic and zero otherwise, these functions are equal to the shares of the corresponding demographic groups in aggregate expenditure. One can conclude that aggregate expenditure patterns depend on the distribution of expenditure over all consuming units through the statistic $\sum Y_j \ln Y_j / \sum Y_j$ and the distribution among demographic groups through the statistics $\{\sum Y_j A_j / \sum Y_j\}$.

The present model of individual consumer behavior is based on a two-stage allocation. In the first stage, total expenditure is allocated among N commodity groups, and in the second, total expenditure on each commodity group is allocated among the individual commodities within each group.[26] I have characterized the behavior of the individual consumer in terms of properties of the IUF. In addition to the properties of homogeneity, monotonicity, and quasi-convexity, the IUF that underlies the two-stage process is homothetically separable in prices of the individual commodities.

Each of the prices of commodity groups $\{p_n\}$ can be regarded as a function of the prices of individual commodities within the group. These functions must be homogeneous of degree one, nondecreasing, and concave in the prices of the individual commodities. Specific forms for price indexes can be considered for each commodity group. If each of these prices is a translog function of its components, the difference between successive logarithms of the price of each group can be expressed as a weighted average of the differences between successive logarithms of prices of individual commodities within it, with weights given by the average value shares. These expressions for the prices of the N commodity groups $\{p_n\}$ are known as *translog price indexes*.[27]

27.2.2 Integrability

Systems of individual expenditure shares for consuming units with identical demographic characteristics can be recovered in one and only one way from the system of aggregate expenditure shares under exact aggregation. This makes it possible to employ all the implications of the theory of individual consumer behavior in specifying an econometric model of aggregate expenditure allocation. If a system of individual expenditure shares can be generated from an IUF by means of the logarithmic form of Roy's identity, the system is said to be integrable. A complete set of conditions for integrability, expressed in terms of the system of individual expenditure shares, is as follows:

1. *Homogeneity*. The individual expenditure shares are homogeneous of degree zero in prices and expenditure, and can take the form

$$w_j = (1/B)\left(\alpha_p + \beta_{pp}\ \ln\ p - \beta_{pY} \ln\ Y_j + \beta_{pA}\ A_j\right) \qquad (j = 1, 2, \ldots, J),$$

where the parameters $\{B_{pY}\}$ are constant and the same for all consuming units. Homogeneity implies that this vector must satisfy the restrictions

$$\beta_{pY} = \beta_{pp}\iota. \tag{35}$$

Given the exact aggregation restriction, $N - 1$ restrictions are implied by homogeneity.

2. *Summability*. The sum of the individual expenditure shares over all commodity groups is equal to unity:

$$\sum w_{nj} = 1 \qquad (j = 1, 2, \ldots, J).$$

The denominator B can be written as

$$B = -1 + \beta_{Yp}\ \ln\ p,$$

where the parameters $\{B_{Yp}\}$ are constant and the same for all commodity groups and all consuming units. Summability implies that these parameters must satisfy the restrictions

$$\beta_{Yp} = \iota'\beta_{pp}. \tag{36}$$

Given the exact aggregation restrictions, $N - 1$ restrictions are implied by summability.

3. *Symmetry*. The matrix of compensated own- and cross-price effects must be symmetric. With the homogeneity and summability restrictions, the individual expenditure shares take the form

$$w_j = (1/B)\left(\alpha_p + \beta_{pp}\ \ln(p/Y_j) + \beta_{pA}\ A_j\right) \qquad (j = 1, 2, \ldots, J),$$

where the denominator B can be written as

$$B = -1 + \iota'\beta_{pp}\ \ln\ p.$$

The typical element of the matrix of uncompensated own- and cross-price effects is then

$$\frac{\partial x_{nj}}{\partial(p_m/Y_j)} = \frac{1}{(p_n/Y_j)(p_m/Y_j)}\left[\frac{1}{B}\,(\beta_{nm} - w_{nj}\beta_{Ym}) - \delta_{nm}w_{nj}\right]$$
$$(n, m = 1, 2, \ldots, N;\ j = 1, 2, \ldots, J),$$

where

$$\beta_{Ym} = \sum \beta_{nm} \qquad (m = 1, 2, \ldots, N),$$

$$\delta_{nm}\begin{cases} = 0 & \text{if } n \neq m \\ = 1 & \text{if } n = m \end{cases} \qquad (n, m = 1, 2, \ldots, N).$$

The corresponding element of the matrix of compensated own- and cross-price effects takes the form

$$\frac{\partial x_{nj}}{\partial(p_m/Y_j)} - x_{mj}\sum \frac{\partial x_{nj}}{\partial(p_1/Y_j)} \cdot \frac{p_1}{Y_j}$$

$$= \frac{1}{(p_n/Y_j)(p_m/Y_j)}\left[\frac{1}{B}\left(\beta_{nm} - w_{nj}\beta_{Ym}\right) - \delta_{nm}w_{nj}\right]$$

$$- x_{mj}\sum \frac{1}{(p_n/Y_j)(p_l/Y_j)}\left[\frac{1}{B}\left(\beta_{nl} - w_{nj}\beta_{Yl}\right) - \delta_{nl}w_{nj}\right]\frac{p_l}{Y_j}$$

$$(n, m = 1, 2, \ldots, N;\ j = 1, 2, \ldots, J).$$

The full matrix of compensated own- and cross-price effects, say S_j, becomes

$$S_j = P_j^{-1}\left[(1/B)\left(\beta_{pp} - w_j\iota'\beta_{pp} - \beta_{pp}\iota w_j' + w_j\iota'\beta_{pp}\iota w_j'\right) + w_j w_j' - W_j\right]P_j^{-1}, \qquad (j = 1, 2, \ldots, J) \qquad (37)$$

where

$$P_j^{-1} = \begin{bmatrix} \frac{1}{p_1/Y_j} & 0 & \cdots & 0 \\ 0 & \frac{1}{p_2/Y_j} & \cdots & 0 \\ \vdots & \vdots & & \vdots \\ 0 & 0 & \cdots & \frac{1}{p_N/Y_j} \end{bmatrix},$$

$$W_j = \begin{bmatrix} w_{1j} & 0 & \cdots & 0 \\ 0 & w_{2j} & \cdots & 0 \\ \vdots & \vdots & & \vdots \\ 0 & 0 & \cdots & w_{Nj} \end{bmatrix}$$

$$(j = 1, 2, \ldots, J).$$

The matrices $\{S_j\}$ must be symmetric for all consuming units.

If the system of individual expenditure shares is to be generated from a translog IUF, a necessary and sufficient condition for symmetry is that the matrix β_{pp} be symmetric. Without imposing this condition one can write the individual expenditure shares in the form

$$w_j = (1/B)\left(\alpha_p + \beta_{pp}\ \ln(p/Y_j) + \beta_{pA}\ A_j\right) \qquad (j = 1, 2, \ldots, J).$$

Symmetry implies that the matrix of parameters β_{pp} must satisfy the restrictions

$$\beta_{pp} = \beta_{pp}'. \qquad (38)$$

The total number of symmetry restrictions is $\frac{1}{2}\ N(N-1)$.

4. *Nonnegativity*. The individual expenditure shares must be nonnegative:

$$w_{nj} \geqq 0 \qquad (n = 1, 2, \ldots, N;\ j = 1, 2, \ldots, J).$$

By summability they sum to unity, so that one can write

$$w_j \geq 0 \qquad (J = 1, 2, \ldots, J),$$

where $w_j \geqq 0$ implies $w_{nj} \geq 0,\ (n = 1, 2, \ldots, N)$ and $w_j \neq 0$. Nonnegativity of these shares is implied by monotonicity of the IUF,

$$\frac{\partial \ln U_j}{\partial \ln (p/Y_j)} \leqq 0 \qquad (j = 1, 2, \ldots, J).$$

For the translog IUF the conditions for monotonicity take the form

$$\frac{\partial \ln U_j}{\partial \ln (p/Y_j)} = \alpha_p + \beta_{pp} \ln (p/Y_j) + \beta_{pA}\, A_j \leqq 0 \qquad (j = 1, 2, \ldots, J). \quad (39)$$

Summability implies that not all the expenditure shares are zero, so that

$$B = -1 + \iota' \beta_{pp} \ln\ p < 0. \quad (40)$$

Since the translog IUF is quadratic in the logarithms of prices in $\ln p$, the prices can always be chosen so that the individual expenditure shares violate the nonnegativity conditions. In other words, it is possible to choose the prices so that the monotonicity of that function is violated. Accordingly, one cannot impose restrictions on the parameters of the translog IUF that would imply nonnegativity of the individual expenditure shares or monotonicity of that function for all prices and expenditures. Instead, one considers restrictions on the parameters that imply quasi-convexity of the IUF or monotonicity of the system of individual demand functions for all nonnegative expenditure shares.

5. *Monotonicity*. The matrix of compensated own- and cross-price effects must be nonpositive-definite. First homogeneity, summability, and symmetry restrictions are imposed on the expenditure shares. Consideration is restricted to values of the prices p, expenditures $\{Y_j\}$, and attributes $\{A_j\}$ for which the individual expenditure shares satisfy the nonnegativity restrictions, so that $w_j \geqq 0 (j = 1, 2, \ldots, J)$. The summability restrictions imply that $\iota' w_j = 1$ $(j = 1, 2, \ldots, J)$. The matrix of price effects can be written in the form

$$S_j = P_j^{-1} \big[(1/B)(I - \iota w_j')' \beta_{pp} (I - \iota w_j') + w_j w_j' - W_j \big] P_j^{-1} \quad (j = 1, 2, \ldots, J).$$

A necessary and sufficient condition for monotonicity of the systems of individual expenditure shares is that the matrices

$$\big\{ (1/B)(I - \iota w_j') \beta_{pp} (I - \iota w_j') + w_j w_j' - W_j \big\}$$

are nonpositive-definite for all expenditure shares satisfying the nonnegativity and summability conditions.

Next I consider restrictions on the parameters of the translog IUF implied by monotonicity of the individual expenditure shares. If $\iota' \beta_{pp} = 0$, the denominator B is independent of prices and the translog IUF is homothetic; otherwise, for a given value of the individual expenditure shares the denominator B can be made as large or as small as one wishes by a suitable choice of prices p. A necessary and sufficient condition for monotonicity of these systems is that the matrices

$$\{(1/B)(I - \iota w')\beta_{pp}(I - \iota w_j')\} \qquad \text{and} \qquad \{w_j w_j' - W_j\}$$

are both nonpositive-definite.

The matrices $\{w_j w_j' - W_j\}$ are nonpositive-definite for all expenditure shares satisfying the nonnegativity and summability restrictions. A sufficient condition for nonpositive definiteness of the matrices

$$\{(1/B)(I - \iota w_j')'\beta_{pp}(I - \iota w_j')\}$$

is that the matrix β_{pp} is nonnegative-definite. However, if the quadratic form $z'\beta_{pp}z$ achieves the value zero, which must be a minimum, for any vector z not equal to zero, then z is a characteristic vector of β_{pp} corresponding to a zero characteristic value if β_{pp} is nonnegative-definite. Hence, $\beta_{pp}\iota = 0$ and the translog IUF is homothetic.

Martos (1969) defined a *merely positive-subdefinite matrix*, say P, which is a real symmetric matrix such that

$$x'Px < 0$$

implies $Px \geq 0$ or $Px \leq 0$ and P is not nonnegative-definite. Similarly, a *strictly merely positive-subdefinite* matrix is a real symmetric matrix such that

$$x'Px < 0$$

implies $Px > 0$ or $Px < 0$. Cottle and Ferland (1972) provided a complete characterization of merely positive-subdefinite matrices and showed that such matrices must satisfy the conditions:

1. P consists of only nonpositive elements.
2. P has exactly one negative characteristic value.

Martos (1969) did the same for a strictly merely positive-subdefinite matrix and showed that such a matrix must satisfy the additional condition:

3. P does not contain a row (or column) of zeros.

Note that this final condition does not in itself imply that a strictly merely positive-subdefinite matrix is nonsingular.

A necessary and sufficient condition for monotonicity is either that the translog IUF is homothetic or that β_{pp}^{-1} exists and is strictly merely positive-subdefinite. To impose restrictions on the matrix β_{pp} implied by monotonicity of the systems of individual expenditure shares, one first provides a Cholesky factorization of this matrix:

$$\beta_{pp} = TDT',$$

where T is a unit lower triangular matrix and D is a diagonal matrix.

Since the matrix β_{pp}^{-1} is strictly merely positive-subdefinite, all its elements are nonpositive. The nonpositivity constraints on these elements can be expressed in terms of the elements of the Cholesky factorization of the matrix β_{pp}, where $\beta_{pp} = TDT'$. Finally, one includes restrictions on the Cholesky values; the matrix β_{pp} has exactly one negative Cholesky value, the last in order, and $N-1$ positive Cholesky values. Combining these restrictions with nonpositivity restrictions on the elements of β_{pp}^{-1} yields a complete set of restrictions implied by the monotonicity of the system of individual expenditure shares.

Similarly, a complete set of conditions can be described for integrability of the system of individual expenditure shares for the second stage of the two-stage allocation process. For example, the shares for commodities within each group are homogeneous of degree zero in commodity prices, their sum is equal to unity, and the matrix of compensated own- and cross-price effects must be symmetric for each group. The restrictions are analogous to those for price indexes I used in my models of producer behavior.

The individual expenditure shares must be nonnegative for each commodity group; as before, one can always choose prices so that the monotonicity of the IUF for each commodity group is violated. One can consider restrictions on the parameters that imply quasi-convexity of the homothetic translog IUF or monotonicity of the system of individual demand functions for all nonnegative expenditure shares for each commodity group. Again, the conditions for monotonicity for expenditure shares that satisfy the nonnegativity restrictions are precisely analogous to those I used earlier.

27.2.3 Stochastic Specifications

The model of consumer behavior presented in Section 27.2.2 is generated from a translog IUF for each consuming unit. To formulate an econometric model of consumer behavior, I add a stochastic component to the equations for the individual expenditure shares and associate it with unobservable random disturbances at the level of the individual consuming unit. The consuming unit maximizes utility, but the expenditure shares are chosen with a random disturbance. This disturbance may result from errors in implementation of consumption plans, random elements in the determination of consumer preferences not reflected in the list of attributes of consuming units, or errors of measurement of the shares. I assume that each of the equations for the individual shares has two additive components: a nonrandom function of prices, expenditure, and demographic characteristics and an unobservable random disturbance that is functionally independent of these variables.

My econometric model of consumer behavior requires some additional notation. I consider observations on expenditure patterns by J consuming units, indexed by $j = 1, 2, \ldots, J$, for T time periods, indexes by $t = 1, 2, \ldots, T$. In the tth time period, the vector of expenditure shares for the jth consuming unit is w_{jt}; the expenditure for the jth unit on all commodity groups is Y_{jt}; the vector of prices faced by all consuming units is p_t; the vector of logarithms of prices in $\ln p_t$; and the vector of logarithms of ratios of prices to expenditure for the jth consuming unit is $\ln(p_t/Y_{jt})$.

With this notation, the individual expenditure shares can be written as

$$w_{jt} = (1/B_t)\left(\alpha_p + \beta_{pp}\ \ln\left(p_t/Y_{jt}\right) + \beta_{pA}\ A_j\right) + \varepsilon_{jt}$$
$$(j = 1, 2, \ldots, J;\ t = 1, 2, \ldots, T), \qquad (41)$$

where $B_t = -1 + \iota'\beta_{pp} \ln\ p_t \quad (t = 1, 2, \ldots, T)$ and $\{\varepsilon_{jt}\}$ are the vectors of unobservable random disturbances for all J consuming units and all T time periods. Since these shares for all commodities sum to unity for each consuming unit in each time period, the unobservable random disturbances for all commodities sum to zero for each unit in each time period:

$$\iota'\varepsilon_{jt} = 0 \quad (j = 1, 2, \ldots, J;\ t = 1, 2, \ldots, T). \qquad (42)$$

These disturbances are not distributed independently.

I assume that for all observations the unobservable random disturbances for all commodities have expected value equal to zero:

$$E(\varepsilon_{jt}) = 0 \quad (j = 1, 2, \ldots, J;\ t = 1, 2, \ldots, T). \qquad (43)$$

and that these disturbances have the same covariance matrix:

$$V(\varepsilon_{jt}) = \Omega^{\varepsilon} \quad (j = 1, 2, \ldots, J;\ t = 1, 2, \ldots, T).$$

Since the disturbances sum to zero for each observation, this matrix is nonnegative-definite with rank equal at most to $N - 1$, where N is the number of commodities and the covariance matrix has rank equal to $N - 1$.

Under the assumption that disturbances corresponding to distinct observations are uncorrelated, the covariance matrix of the disturbances for all consuming units at a given point of time has the Kronecker product form:

$$V\begin{pmatrix} \varepsilon_{1t} \\ \varepsilon_{2t} \\ \vdots \\ \varepsilon_{jt} \end{pmatrix} = \Omega_t \otimes I. \qquad (44)$$

The covariance matrix of the disturbances for all time periods for a given individual has an analogous form. The unknown parameters of the system of equations determining the individual expenditure shares can be estimated from time-series data on these shares and on prices, total expenditure, and demographic characteristics.

At any point of time, the aggregate expenditure shares are equal to the individual expenditure shares multiplied by the ratio of individual to aggregate expenditure. Although the data for individual consuming units and for the aggregate of all consuming units are based on the same definitions, the aggregate data are not obtained by summing over the data for individuals. Observations on individual consuming units are based on a random sample from the population of all consuming units. Observations for the aggregate of all consuming units are constructed from data on production of commodities and on consumption of these commodities by households and other consuming units such as businesses, governments, and the rest of the world. Accordingly, one must introduce an additional source of random error into the equations for the aggregate expenditure shares, corresponding to unobservable errors of measurement in the observations that underlie these shares.

Each of the equations for the aggregate expenditure shares is assumed to have three additive components. The first is a weighted average of the nonrandom functions of prices, expenditure, and demographic characteristics that determine the individual expenditure shares; the second is a weighted average of the unobservable random disturbances in the relevant equations; and the third is a weighted average of the unobservable random errors of measurement in the observations on the aggregate expenditure shares.

Denoting the vector of aggregate expenditure shares at time t by w_t $(t = 1, 2, \ldots, T)$, these shares can be expressed in the form:

$$w_t = \frac{1}{B_t}\left(\alpha_p + \beta_{pp} \ln p_t\right) - \frac{1}{B_t}\beta_{pp}\iota \frac{\sum_{j=1}^{J} Y_{jt} \ln Y_{jt}}{\sum_{j=1}^{J} Y_{jt}} + \frac{1}{B_t}\beta_{pA}\frac{\sum_{j=1}^{J} Y_{jt} A_j}{\sum_{j=1}^{J} Y_{jt}} + \varepsilon_t \quad (t = 1, 2, \ldots, T), \tag{45}$$

where $B_1 = -1 + \iota'\beta_{pp} \ln p_t \quad (t = 1, 2, \ldots, T)$ as before, and $\{\varepsilon_t\}$ are the vectors of unobservable random disturbances for the tth time period.

The aggregate disturbances ε_t can be written as:

$$\varepsilon_t = \frac{\sum_{j=1}^{J} Y_{jt}\varepsilon_{jt}}{\sum_{j=1}^{J} Y_{jt}} + \frac{\sum_{j=1}^{J} Y_{jt}\nu_{jt}}{\sum_{j=1}^{J} Y_{jt}} \qquad (t = 1, 2, \ldots, T), \tag{46}$$

where $\{\nu_{jt}\}$ are the vectors of errors of measurement that underlie the data on the aggregate expenditure shares. Since the random disturbances for all commodities sum to zero in each time period,

$$\iota'\varepsilon_t = 0 \qquad (j = 1, 2, \ldots, J;\ t = 1, 2, \ldots, T). \tag{47}$$

These disturbances are not distributed independently.

I assume that for all observations the errors of measurement that underlie the data on the aggregate expenditure shares have expected value equal to zero:

$$E(\nu_{jt}) = 0 \qquad (j = 1, 2, \ldots, J;\ t = 1, 2, \ldots, T),$$

that these errors have the same covariance matrix:

$$V(\nu_{jt}) = \Omega_\nu \qquad (j = 1, 2, \ldots, J;\ t = 1, 2, \ldots, T),$$

and that the rank of this matrix is equal to $N - 1$.

If the errors of measurement are distributed independently of expenditure and of the disturbances in the equations for the individual expenditure shares, the aggregate disturbances have expected value equal to zero for all time periods,

$$E(\varepsilon_t) = 0 \qquad (t = 1, 2, \ldots, T), \tag{48}$$

and a covariance matrix given by

$$V(\varepsilon_t) = \frac{\sum_{j=1}^{J} Y_{jt}^2}{\left(\sum_{j=1}^{J} Y_{jt}\right)^2} \Omega_\varepsilon + \frac{\sum_{j=1}^{J} Y_{jt}^2}{\left(\sum_{j=1}^{J} Y_{jt}\right)^2} \Omega_\nu \qquad (t = 1, 2, \ldots, T),$$

so that the aggregate disturbances for different time periods are heteroskedastic.

One can correct for heteroskedasticity of the aggregate disturbances by transforming the observations on the aggregate expenditure shares as follows:

$$\rho_t w_t = \frac{\rho_t}{B_t}(\alpha_p + \beta_{pp} \ln p_t) - \frac{\rho_t}{B_t} \beta_{pp} \iota \frac{\sum_{j=1}^{J} Y_{jt} \ln Y_{jt}}{\sum_{j=1}^{J} Y_{jt}}$$

$$+ \frac{\rho_t}{B_t} \beta_{pA} \frac{\sum_{j=1}^{J} Y_{jt} A_j}{\sum_{j=1}^{J} Y_{jt}} + \rho_t \varepsilon_t \qquad (t = 1, 2, \ldots, T),$$

where

$$\rho_t^2 = \frac{\left(\sum_{j=1}^{J} Y_{jt}\right)^2}{\sum_{j=1}^{J} Y_{jt}^2} \qquad (t = 1, 2, \ldots, T).$$

The covariance matrix of the transformed disturbances, say Ω, becomes

$$V(\rho_t \varepsilon_t) = \Omega_\varepsilon + \Omega_\nu = \Omega.$$

This matrix is nonnegative-definite with rank equal to $N - 1$. Finally, under the assumption that the errors of measurement corresponding to distinct observations are uncorrelated, the covariance matrix of the transformed disturbances at all points of time has the Kronecker product form:

$$V \begin{pmatrix} \rho_1 \varepsilon_1 \\ \rho_2 \varepsilon_2 \\ \vdots \\ \rho_T \varepsilon_T \end{pmatrix} = \Omega \otimes I. \tag{49}$$

I discuss next the estimation of the translog model of aggregate consumer behavior, combining a single cross section of observations on individual expenditure patterns with several time-series observations on aggregate expenditure patterns. Take first a random sample of observations on individual expenditure patterns at a given point of time. Prices for all consumers are the same. The translog model (41) takes the form

$$w_j = \gamma_1 + \gamma_2 \ln Y_j + \Gamma_3 A_j + \varepsilon_j \qquad (j = 1, 2, \dots, J), \tag{50}$$

where the time subscript is dropped. In this model γ_1 and γ_2 are vectors and Γ_3 is a matrix, all of unknown parameters. Random sampling implies that disturbances for different individuals are uncorrelated, and the data matrix with $(1, \ln Y_j, A_j)$ as its jth row is assumed to be of full rank.

The parameters of γ_1, γ_2, and Γ_3 are identified in the cross section. Moreover, (50) is a multivariate regression model, except that the vector of disturbances ε_j has a singular distribution. A model in which one equation has been dropped is a multivariate regression model so that the unique, minimum-variance, unbiased estimator of the unknown parameters γ_1, γ_2, and Γ_3 is obtained by applying ordinary least squares to each equation separately.

To link the parameters γ_1, γ_2, and Γ_3 to the parameters of the translog model of aggregate consumer behavior, first note that the parameters of the translog model can be identified only up to a normalization since multiplying all of the parameters by the same nonzero constant leaves the expenditure shares unchanged. The usual normalization is $\iota'\alpha_p = -1$, giving the unknown parameters the same sign as those in the translog IUF. Second, without loss of generality the prices of all goods can be taken as equal to unity for a particular time period. In the application to a single cross section, all prices on the date of the survey are taken as equal to unity. The prices for all other time periods are expressed relative to prices of this base period.

Given the normalization of the parameters and the choice of base period for measurement of the prices, one obtains the following correspondence between the unknown parameters of the cross-section model and the parameters of the translog model of aggregate consumer behavior:

$$\gamma_1 = -\alpha_p \qquad \gamma_2 = \beta_{pp}\iota \qquad \Gamma_3 = -\beta_{pA} \tag{51}$$

The constants α_p and the parameters associated with demographic characteristics of individual households β_{pA} as well as the parameters associated with total expenditure $\beta_{pp}\iota$ can be estimated from a single cross section. The remaining parameters, those associated with prices, can be estimated from time-series data on aggregate expenditure patterns. Since the model is linear in parameters for a cross section, ordinary least squares regression can be used to estimate the impact of the demographic structure on aggregate expenditure patterns.

After correction for heteroskedasticity the translog model of aggregate consumer behavior is given by

$$\rho_t w_t = \frac{\rho_t}{B_t}\left(\alpha_p + \beta_{pp} \ln p_t\right) - \frac{\rho_t}{B_t}\beta_{pp}\iota \frac{\sum_{j=1}^{J} Y_{jt} \ln Y_{jt}}{\sum_{j=1}^{J} Y_{jt}}$$

$$+\frac{\rho_t}{B_t}\beta_{pA}\frac{\sum_{j=1}^{J} Y_{jt}A_j}{\sum_{j=1}^{J} Y_{jt}} + \rho_1\varepsilon_t \qquad (t = 1, 2, \ldots, T), \tag{52}$$

where $B_t = -1 + \iota'\beta_{pp} \ln p_t \quad (t = 1, 2, \ldots, T)$ and ε_t is a vector of unobservable random disturbances. One also has time-series observations on prices p_t, the expenditure statistic $\sum Y_{jt} \ln Y_{jt}/\sum Y_{jt}$, the vector of attribute-expenditure statistics $\{\sum Y_{jt} A_j/\sum Y_{jt}\}$, and the heteroskedasticity correction $\rho_t (t = 1, 2, \ldots, T)$.

The translog model in (51) might appear to be a nonlinear regression model with additive errors, indicates that nonlinear regression techniques might be employed.[28] However, the existence of supply functions for all commodities makes it more appropriate to treat some of the right-hand side variables as endogenous. For example, shifts in prices owing to demand-supply interactions may cause significant shifts in the distribution of expenditure. To obtain a consistent estimator for this model, one can specify supply functions for all commodities and estimate the complete model by full-information maximum likelihood.

Alternatively, to estimate the model in (52) one can consider limited information techniques utilizing instrumental variables. In particular, a sufficient number of instrumental variables can be introduced to identify all parameters. The model is estimated by nonlinear three-stage least squares (NL3SLS).[29] Using NL3SLS here would be straightforward except for the fact that the covariance matrix of the disturbances is singular, so NL3SLS estimators of the complete system are obtained by dropping one equation and estimating the resulting system of $N-1$ equations by NL3SLS. An estimator for parameters of the remaining equation is derived from the conditions for summability. The parameter estimates are invariant to the choice of the equation omitted in the model for aggregate time-series data and the model for individual cross-section data.

In the analysis of the model to be applied to cross-section data on individual expenditure patterns, I have assumed that individual disturbances and individual total expenditure are uncorrelated. If aggregate demand-supply interactions induce shifts in the distribution of expenditure, the zero correlation assumption cannot be strictly valid for all consumers at the individual level. However, the cross section is a random sample that includes a minute percentage of the total population, so that it is reasonable to assume that the correlations between total expenditure and disturbances at the individual level are negligible.

The NL3SLS estimator can be employed to estimate all parameters of the model of aggregate expenditures, provided that these parameters are identified. Since I wish to obtain a detailed characterization of the impact of changes in the demographic structure of the population, (52) contains a large number of parameters and requires a large number of time-series observations for identification. The technical conditions for identification are quite complicated: A sufficient condition for underidentification is that the number of instruments is less than the number of parameters. For the translog model of aggregate consumer behavior, this occurs if

$$(N-1)(1+S)=[(N+1)N]/2-1>(N-1)-(V,T), \qquad (53)$$

where N is the number of commodities, S is the number of components of A_{jt}, and V is the number of instruments. The left-hand side of (53) is the number of free parameters of the translog model under symmetry of the matrix β_{pp} and the right-hand side is the number of instruments, assuming that no collinearity exists among them.

Condition (53) is met in the present application, so that not all parameters are identified in the model for aggregate time-series data. I next consider methods utilizing individual cross-section data together with aggregate time-series data to obtain identification. Again, cross-section data can be used to identify the constant α_p, the coefficients of total expenditure $-\beta_{pp}\iota$, and the demographic coefficients β_{pA}. Only the price coefficients β_{pp} must be identified from aggregate time-series data. A necessary condition for identification of these parameters is

$$[(N-1)N]/2<(N-1)-(V,T) \qquad (54)$$

or

$$N/2<-(V,T). \qquad (55)$$

This condition is met in the present application. Sufficient conditions amount to the nonlinear analogue of the absence of multicollinearity. These conditions are quite weak and hold in this application.

In order to pool cross-section and time-series data, I combine the model for individual expenditures with that for aggregate expenditure and apply NL3SLS to the whole system. The instruments for the cross-section model are the microdata themselves; for the aggregate model, the instruments are variables that can be taken to be distributed independently of the aggregate disturbances. The data sets are pooled statistically, where estimates of the covariance matrix of the aggregate disturbances from time-series data and the covariance matrix of the individual disturbances from cross-section data are used to weight aggregate and cross-section data, respectively. The resulting estimator is consistent and asymptotically efficient in the class of instrumental variable estimators utilizing the instruments chosen.

27.3 EMPIRICAL RESULTS

Sections 27.1 and 27.2 described econometric models of producer and consumer behavior suitable for incorporation into general equilibrium models of the U.S. economy. The most important innovation in these econometric models is that they encompass all the restrictions on the parameters implied by the economic theories of producer and consumer behavior, which take the form of equalities required for monotonicity subject to nonnegativity restriction.

My model of producer behavior is based on industries as producing units. Each industry behaves as an individual producer, maximizing profit subject to a production function characterized by constant returns to scale. The allocation of the value of output among inputs can be generated from a translog price function for each industry. This model also determines the rate of technical change endogenously for each industry. Time is included in the price function for each sector as an index of technology.

My model of consumer behavior is based on households as consuming units. Expenditures within the household are allocated so as to maximize a household welfare function. Each household behaves in the same way as an individual maximizing a utility function subject to a budget constraint. All consuming units are classified by demographic characteristics associated with differences in preferences among households. For each of these characteristics, households are divided among mutually exclusive and exhaustive groups. Each demographic characteristic is represented by a qualitative or dummy variable, equal to unity when the household is in the group and zero otherwise.

27.3.1 Producer Behavior

The first objective here is to present the empirical results of implementing the model of producer behavior described in Section 27.1 for thirty-five U.S. industrial sectors. This model is based on a two-stage process for the allocation of the value of output in each sector among capital, labor, energy, and materials inputs. The value of inputs from these four commodity groups exhausts the value of the output for each of the thirty-five sectors. This presentation of empirical results deals only with the first stage.

To implement my econometric models of production and technical change I assembled a time-series data base for the thirty-five sectors. For capital and labor inputs, I first compiled data by sector on the basis of the U.S. Census Bureau's National Income and Product Accounts classification of economic activities. I then transformed these data into a format appropriate for the U.S. Census Bureau's Interindustry Transactions Accounts. For energy and materials inputs, I compiled data by sector on interindustry transactions on the basis of the latter's classification of activities.[30]

The endogenous variables in my model of producer behavior are value shares of sectoral inputs for four commodity groups and the sectoral rate of technical change. I can estimate four equations for each industry, corresponding to three of the value shares and the rate of technical change. Three elements of the vector $\{\alpha_p^i\}$, the scalar $\{\alpha_t^i\}$, six share elasticities in the matrix $\{\beta_{pp}^i\}$, which is constrained to be symmetric, three biases of technical change in the vector $\{\beta^i_{pt}\}$, and the scalar $\{\beta^i_{tt}\}$, make up a total of fourteen unknown parameters for each industry. These are estimated from time-series data for the period 1958–1974, subject to the inequality restrictions implied by monotonicity of the sectoral input value shares. The results are given in Table 27.1.

My interpretation of the empirical results reported in Table 27.1 begins with an analysis of the estimates of the parameters $\{\alpha^i_p, \alpha^i_t\}$. If all other parameters were set equal to zero, the SPFs would be linear-logarithmic in prices and linear in time. The parameters $\{\alpha^i_p\}$ would correspond to constant-value shares of inputs and the negative of the parameters $\{\alpha^i_t\}$ to constant rates of technical change. The parameters $\{\alpha^i_p\}$ are nonnegative for all thirty-five sectors included in the study and are estimated very precisely. The parameters $\{\alpha^i_t\}$, which are estimated less precisely, are negative in fifteen sectors and positive in twenty.

The estimated share elasticities with respect to price $\{\beta^i_{pp}\}$ describe the implications of patterns of substitution for the distribution of the value of output among the four inputs. Positive, negative, and zero share elasticities imply, respectively, that the corresponding value shares increase with an increase in price, decrease with price, and are independent of price. The concavity constraints on the SPFs contribute substantially to the precision of the estimates, but require that the share of each input be nonincreasing in the price of the input itself.

Imposing monotonicity on the sectoral input value shares or concavity of the SPFs reduced the number of share elasticities to be fitted from 350, or ten for each industrial sector, to 132, or an average of fewer than five per sector. All share elasticities are constrained to be zero for eleven of the thirty-five industries, so that the representation of technology reduces to a price function that is linear-logarithmic in the input prices at any given time for these industries. For fifteen of the thirty-five industries the share elasticities with respect to the price of labor input are set to equal zero. Finally, for all thirty-five the share elasticities with respect to the price of capital input are set to equal zero.

The interpretation of the parameter estimates given in Table 27.1 is continued with estimated biases of technical change with respect to price $\{\beta^i_{pt}\}$. These parameters can be interpreted as the change in the share of each input with respect to time, holding price constant, or alternatively, as the change in the negative of the rate of technical change with respect to the price of the corresponding input. For example, if the bias of technical change with respect to the price of capital input is positive, technical change is described as capital-using; if the bias is negative, it is capital-saving.

A classification of industries by patterns of the biases of technical change is given in Table 27.2: the patterns that occur with greatest frequency are capital-saving, labor-saving, energy-using, and materials-saving. Each of these patterns occurs for eight of the thirty-five industries for which there are fitted

TABLE 27.1
Parameter Estimates: Sectoral Models of Production and Technical Change

Parameter	Agriculture, forestry, and fisheries	Metal mining	Coal mining	Crude petroleum and natural gas	Nonmetallic mining	Construction
AK	.170 (.00445)	.216 (.0108)	.237 (.00643)	.449 (.00559)	.270 (.00346)	.0686 (.000640)
AL	.254 (.00475)	.313 (.0226)	.469 (.0121)	.103 (.00272)	.310 (.00963)	.439 (.00310)
AE	.0243 (.000580)	.0393 (.00251)	.121 (.00279)	.0565 (.000676)	.0746 (.000921)	.0254 (.000393)
AM	.551 (.00430)	.432 (.0242)	.173 (.0102)	.391 (.00736)	.345 (.00882)	
AT	–.0329 (.0546)	.0151 (.0602)	.00643 (.0757)	.0246 (.0759)	.0767 (.0271)	.0471 (.00565)
BKK						
BKL						
BKE						
BKM						
BKT	–.00247 (.000603)	.000775 (.00147)	.00868 (.000873)	–.0795 (.000759)	.00187 (.0470)	.000295 (.00008680)
BLL	–.220 (.0356a)	–.405 (.265)	–.433 (.0420)			
BLE	–.00158 (.00427)	.0255 (.0224)	–.0526 (.00385)			
BLM	.222 (.0342)	.379 (.244)	.485 (.0459)			
BLT	.00530 (.00147)	.0154 (.00671)	.00472 (.00165)	–.000914 (.000369)	–.00189 (.00131)	–.00923 (.00158)
BEE	–.0000114 (.0000620)	–.00161 (.00181)	–.00639 (.00113)			
BEM	.00159 (.00433)	–.0239 (.0206)	.0590 (.00689)			
BET	.000210 (.000175)	–.000104 (.000607)	–.00731 (.000378)	.000814 (.0000916)	.00172 (.000125)	–.00159 (.000222)
BMM	–.223 (.0333)	–.356 (.224)	–.544 (.0507)			
BMT	–.00798 (.00139)	–.0160 (.00639)	–.00609 (.00138)	.000895 (.000998)	–.00170 (.00120)	.0105 (.00174)
BTT	–.00966 (.00741)	–.000849 (.00815)	–.00180 (.0103)	.00291 (.0103)	.00781 (.00364)	.00343 (.000771)

Parameter	Food and kindred products	Tobacco manufacturers	Textile mill products	Apparel and other fabrics; textile production	Lumber and wood products	Furniture and fixtures
AK	.0548 (.000404)	.162 (.00238)	.0698 (.00158)	.0405 (.000285)	.151 (.00192)	.0635 (.000857)
AL	.146 (.00267)	.136 (.00345)	.200 (.00476)	.306 (.00225)	.267 (.00583)	.360 (.00516)
AE	.0114 (.000457)	.00347 (.000345)	.0150 (.000216)	.00628 (.0000910)	.0178 (.000828)	.00912 (.000217)
AM	.788 (.00290)	.699 (.00495)	.715 (.00634)	.647 (.00634)	.647 (.00229)	.564 (.00530)
AT	.0188 (.0115)	.0850 (.119)	−.0183 (.0126)	−.0126 (.0299)	−.00477 (.0357)	−.00306 (.0203)
BKK						
BKL						
BKE						
BKM						
BKT	−.00130 (.0000548)	.000955 (.000322)	−.000395 (.000214)	.000240 (.0000386)	.00456 (.000260)	−.000677 (.000116)
BLL	−.132 (.0205)	−.0269 (.0158)	−1.022 (.0830)			
BLE	.00631 (.00352)	.00126 (.00154)	−.0687 (.00393)			
BLM	.126 (.0214)	.0256 (.0157)	1.090 (.0814)			
BLT	.00104 (.000569)	.00456 (.000953)	−.000195 (.000646)	−.00232 (.0006)	−.00120 (.000791)	.0189 (.00170)
BEE	−.000301 (.000348)	−.0000588 (.00143)	−.00185 (.000651)	−.00462 (.000768)		
BEM	−.00601 (.00318)	−.00120 (.00140)	.00185 (.000651)	.0733 (.00463)		
BET	−.0000788 (.0000977)	.0000296 (.0000914)	.000291 (.0000293)	.000267 (.00005)	.000625 (.000112)	.00144 (.0000744)
BMM	−.120 (.0226)	−.0244 (.0157)	−.00185 (.000651)	−1.164 (.0794)		
BMT	.000332 (.000603)	−.00555 (.000107)	.000299 (.000860)	.00181 (.0000)	−.00399 (.000719)	−.01 (.00169)
BTT	.00230 (.00156)	.0157 (.0161)	−.000871 (.00168)	−.00203 (.00405)	.000383 (.00483)	.00110 (.00276)

TABLE 27.1
(Continued)

Parameter	Paper and allied products	Printing, publishing, and allied industries	Chemicals and allied products	Petroleum refining	Rubber and miscellaneous plastic products	Leather and leather products
AK	.111 (.000562)	.103 (.00741)	.128 (.00135)	.105 (.00582)	.0982 (.00151)	.0467 (.00143)
AL	.242 (.00292)	.362 (.00450)	.201 (.00311)	.0670 (.00199)	.271 (.00334)	.342 (.00469)
AE	.0322 (.000333)	.00822 (.000218)	.0885 (.00165)	.599 (.00373)	.0261 (.000279)	.00795 (.000188)
AM	.615 (.00290)	.526 (.00494)	.582 (.00412)	.229 (.00268)	.605 (.00431)	.604 (.00469)
AT	.0372 (.0301)	−.0129 (.0233)	.0130 (.0206)	.00582 (.0375)	.0318 (.0291)	−.00105 (.0239)
BKK						
BKL						
BKE						
BKM						
BKT	−.00208 (.0000762)	.000400 (.000101)	−.00545 (.000183)	.0001333 (.00789)	−.00356 (.000204)	−.000401 (.000193)
BLL	−.316 (.0393)	−.327 (.0704)	−.0237 (.0449)	−.280 (.0208)		
BLE	.0196 (.00578)	−.00875 (.00384)	−.000362 (.0164)	.0346 (.00870)		
BLM	.336 (.0382)	.335 (.0726)	.0240 (.0520)	.246 (.0272)		
BLT	.00708 (.00107)	.00948 (.00234)	−.00241 (.00160)	−.00130 (.000291)	−.00238 (.000453)	−.00141 (.000636)
BEE	−.00122 (.000772)	−.00339 (.00100)	−.00000555 (.000499)	−.00428 (.00237)		
BEM	.0208 (.00654)	.0121 (.00436)	.000368 (.0169)	−.0304 (.00635)		
BET	.00109 (.000156)	.000493 (.000129)	.00177 (.000610)	.000948 (.000508)	.00059 (.0000378)	.000225 (.0000255)
BMM	−.357 (.0378)	−.347 (.0751)	−.0244 (.0631)	−.215 (.0325)		
BMT	−.00610 (.00104)	−.0104 (.00242)	.00608 (.00186)	.000217 (.000407)	.00535 (.000584)	.00159 (.000637)
BTT	.00916 (.00409)	−.00181 (.00316)	.00440 (.00281)	.00135 (.00509)	.00651 (.00395)	−.000777 (.00326)

Parameter	Stone, clay, and glass products	Primary metal industries	Fabricated metal	Machinery (except electrical)	Electrical machinery	Motor vehicles and motor vehicle equipment
AK	.119 (.00139)	.0893 (.00110)	.0874 (.000893)	.0966 (.00211)	.0923 (.00187)	.108 (.00185)
AL	.371 (.00189)	.277 (.00302)	.337 (.00253)	.311 (.00193)	.343 (.00342)	.188 (.00029)
AE	.0432 (.00100)	.0407 (.000492)	.0115 (.000194)	.0115 (.000158)	.0104 (.000215)	.00737 (.0000757)
AM	.467 (.00281)	.593 (.00361)	.564 (.00293)	.581 (.00343)	.554 (.00278)	.697 (.00429)
AT	.0132 (.0180)	−.00898 (.0257)	.0312 (.0199)	.00187 (.0133)	−.00690 (.0178)	.0208 (.0327)
BKK						
BKL						
BKE						
BKM						
BKT	−.00405 (.000189)	−.00226 (.000149)	.000220 (.000121)	−.00156 (.000286)	−.000289 (.000254)	−.000485 (.000251)
BLL	−.738 (.0696)		−.174 (.0229)	.455 (.0488)		−.174 (.0510)
BLE	−.114 (.0119)		−.0302 (.00276)	−.0280 (.00596)		−.174 (.0510)
BLM	.852 (.0778)		.204 (.0221)	.483 (.0524)		.174 (.0509)
BLT	.0209 (.00169)	.00176 (.000409)	.00505 (.000554)	.00746 (.00104)	−.00252 (.000464)	.00959 (.00186)
BEE	−.0176 (.00288)		−.00526 (.00137)	−.00173 (.000646)		−.00000126 (.0000977)
BEM	.132 (.0145)		.0355 (.00402)	.0298 (.00659)		.000470 (.00182)
BET	.00262 (.000317)	−.000389 (.0000667)	.000634 (.0000489)	.000854 (.000125)	.000195 (.0000292)	.000150 (.0000652)
BMM	−.983 (.0883)		−.239 (.0208)	−.513 (.0567)		−.175 (.0509)
BMT	−.0194 (.00191)	.000893 (.000490)	−.00590 (.000582)	−.00675 (.00118)	.00262 (.000378)	−.00926 (.00190)
BTT	.00273 (.00243)	−.00121 (.00348)	.00537 (.00271)	.00119 (.00181)	.00226 (.00241)	.00428 (.00444)

TABLE 27.1
(Continued)

Parameter	Transportation equipment and ordinance	Instruments	Miscellaneous manufacturing industries	Transportation	Communications	Electric utilities
AK	.0371 (.00160)	.123 (.00276)	.0905 (.00242)	.169 (.00126)	.364 (.00275)	.324 (.00249)
AL	.371 (.00497)	.325 (.00391)	.329 (.00295)	.425 (.00174)	.388 (.00252)	.229 (.00187)
AE	.00933 (.000148)	.00676 (.000162)	.0112 (.000198)	.0550 (.0009)	.0125 (.000821)	.247 (.00513)
AM	.583 (.00482)	.545 (.00627)	.569 (.00253)	.351 (.00226)	.236 (.00329)	.201 (.00480)
AT	−.0259 (.0235)	.0348 (.0382)	.0273 (.0182)	−.0367 (.0112)	−.00449 (.0299)	.0303 (.0203)
BKK						
BKL						
BKE						
BKM						
BKT	−.00173 (.000217)	−.00145 (.000375)	.000132 (.000328)	−.000768 (.00017)	−.00280 (.000373)	−.00604 (.000338)
BLL	−.327 (.0771)	−.645 (.0298)				
BLE	.00982 (.00247)	−.00159 (.00194)				
BLM	.317 (.0778)	.646 (.0298)				
BLT	.00389 (.00164)	.00974 (.000661)	−.000581 (.000400)	−.00131 (.000236)	.0000186 (.000342)	−.00681 (.000254)
BEE	−.000295 (.000181)	−.00000392 (.00000956)		−.00481 (.00258)	−.0905 (.0183)	
BEM	−.00953 (.00230)	.00159 (.00195)		.00481 (.00258)	.0905 (.0183)	
BET	−.0000433 (.0000533)	.0000853 (.0000338)	.000316 (.0000269)	.000712 (.000119)	−.000272 (.000115)	.0079 (.000679)
BMM	−.308 (.0785)	−.648 (.0299)		−.00481 (.00258)	−.0905 (.0183)	
BMT	−.00212 (.00165)	−.00837 (.000937)	.000134 (.000344)	.00136 (.000307)	.00306 (.00044)	.00488 (.000631)
BTT	−.00263 (.00319)	.00569 (.00518)	.00264 (.00247)	−.00257 (.00151)	.00188 (.00406)	.00754 (.00275)

Parameter	Gas utilities	Trade	Finance, insurance, and real estate	Services	Government enterprises
AK	.219 (.00410)	.148 (.00144)	.244 (.00784)	.0984 (.000536)	.0954 (.00669)
AL	.180 (.00188)	.560 (.00460)	.238 (.00196)	.509 (.00356)	.567 (.0112)
AE	.548 (.00485)	.0230 (.00128)	.0175 (.000357)	.0204 (.000435)	.0336 (.00166)
AM	.0527 (.00137)	.270 (.00466)	.501 (.00852)	.372 (.00346)	.304 (.00723)
AT	.0153 (.0201)	.00327 (.0148)	−.0429 (.0567)	−.0136 (.00797)	−.0166 (.0519)
BKK					
BKL					
BKE					
BKM					
BKT	−.00609 (.000556)	.000106 (.000195)	−.00429 (.00106)	.00066 (.0000727)	.00437 (.000908)
BLL		−1.023 (.0905)	−.0414 (.0491)	−.335 (.102)	−.194 (.184)
BLE		.0303 (.0106)	−.00109 (.00797)	.00444 (.0108)	.0306 (.0308)
BLM		.992 (.0929)	.0425 (.0492)	.330 (.0978)	.164 (.156)
BLT	.00779 (.000255)	.0320 (.00261)	.00140 (.00102)	.0121 (.00256)	.0215 (.00972)
BEE	−.0767 (.00705)	−.000900 (.000646)	−.0000289 (.000425)	−.0000590 (.000279)	−.00481 (.00572)
BEM	.0767 (.00705)	−.0294 (.00993)	.00112 (.00839)	−.00439 (.0105)	−.0258 (.0254)
BET	.00155 (.000659)	−.00150 (.000353)	.0000309 (.000160)	.00000105 (.000270)	−.00222 (.00163)
BMM	−.0767 (.00705)	−.963 (.0961)	−.0436 (.0506)	−.326 (.0949)	−.138 (.133)
BMT	−.00325 (.000190)	−.0306 (.00266)	.00286 (.00151)	−.0128 (.00245)	−.0237 (.00818)
BTT	.00213 (.00272)	.240 (.00200)	.000351 (.00764)	−.00142 (.00108)	−.00157 (.00706)

Notation:

Text	Table 27.1	Text	Table 27.1				Text	Table 27.1
	AK		BKK	BKL	BKE	BKM	$\beta^i_{pt} =$	BET
	AL		.	BLL	BLE	BLM		BMT
$\alpha^i_p =$	AE	$\beta^i_{pp} =$	.	.	BEE	BEM	$\beta^i_{tt} =$	BTT
	AM		.	.	.	BMM		
$\alpha^i_t =$	AT		BKT					
			BLT					

TABLE 27.2
Classification of Industries by Biases of Technical Change

Pattern of biases	Industries
Capital-using Labor-using Energy-using Materials-saving	Tobacco; printing and publishing; fabricated metal; services
Capital-using Labor-using Energy-saving Materials-saving	Metal mining; coal mining; trade; government enterprises
Capital-using Labor-saving Energy-using Materials-using	Apparel; petroleum refining; miscellaneous manufacturing
Capital-using Labor-saving Energy-using Materials-saving	Nonmetallic mining; lumber and wood
Capital-using Labor-saving Energy-saving Materials-using	Construction
Capital-saving Labor-using Energy-using Materials-using	Finance, insurance, and real estate
Capital-saving Labor-using Energy-using Materials-saving	Agriculture; furniture; paper; stone, clay, and glass; nonelectrical machinery; motor vehicles; instruments; gas utilities
Capital-saving Labor-using Energy-saving Materials-using	Food; primary metal; communications
Capital-saving Labor-saving Energy-using Materials-using	Crude petroleum and natural gas; textiles; chemicals; rubber and plastic; leather; electric machinery; transportation; electric utilities
Capital-saving Labor-using Energy-saving Materials-saving	Transportation equipment

biases. Technical change is found to be capital-saving for twenty-one of the thirty-five industries, labor-using for twenty-one, energy-using for twenty-six, and materials-saving for twenty-four.

The final parameter in this model of producer behavior is the rate of change of the negative of the rate of technical change $\{\beta^i_{tt}\}$. The rate of technical change is found to be decreasing with time for twenty-four of the thirty-five industries and increasing for the remaining ten. Whereas the biases of technical change with respect to the prices of the four inputs are estimated very precisely, the rate of change is estimated with much less precision. Overall, the empirical results suggest a considerable degree of similarity across the industries, especially in the qualitative character of the distribution of the value of output among inputs and of changes in technology.

27.3.2 Consumer Behavior

I present next the empirical results of implementing the model of consumer behavior described in Section 27.2, which is based on a two-stage process for the allocation of consumer expenditures among commodities. The presentation of empirical results is again limited to the first stage of the two-stage allocation process. Consumer expenditures are divided among five commodity groups:

1. *Energy*: Expenditure on electricity, gas, heating oil, and gasoline.
2. *Food and Clothing*: Expenditures on food, beverages, and tobacco; clothing expenditures; and other related expenditures.
3. *Other Nondurable Expenditure*: The remainder of the budget, which includes some transportation and trade margins from other expenditures.
4. *Capital Services*: The service flow from consumer durables as well as a service flow from housing.
5. *Consumer Services*: Expenditures on services such as entertainment, maintenance and repairs of automobiles and housing, tailoring, cleaning, and insurance.

The following demographic characteristics are employed as attributes of individual households:

1. *Family Size*: 1, 2, 3, 4, 5, 6, and 7 or more persons.
2. *Age of Head*: 15–24, 25–34, 35–44, 45–54, 55–65, 65 and over.
3. *Region of Residence*: Northeast, North-Central, South, and West.
4. *Race*: White, nonwhite.
5. *Type of Residence*: Urban, rural.

Cross-section observations on individual expenditures for each commodity group and the demographic characteristics are for the year 1972 from the 1972–1973 Survey of Consumer Expenditures.[31] Time-series observations of prices and aggregate expenditures for each group come from data on personal consumption expenditures from the U.S. Interindustry Transaction Accounts for the period 1958–1974.[32] Time-series data on the distribution of expenditures over all households and among demographic groups are based on *Current Population Reports*, as is the time-series data set that was compiled to complete the data for our heteroskedasticity adjustment.[33]

The application has expenditure shares for five commodity groups as endogenous variables at the first stage, so that there are four estimated equations. Four elements of the vector α_p, four expenditure coefficients of the vector $\beta_{pp}\iota$, sixteen attribute coefficients for each of the four equations in the matrix β_{pA}, and ten price coefficients in the matrix β_{pp}, which is constrained to be symmetric, constitute the unknown parameters. The expenditure coefficients are sums of price coefficients in the corresponding equation, giving a total of eighty-two unknown parameters. The complete model, subject to inequality restrictions implied by monotonicity of the individual expenditure shares, is estimated by pooling time-series and cross-section data. The results are given in Table 27.3.

The impacts of changes in total expenditures and demographic characteristics of individual households are estimated very precisely, which reflects the fact that these estimates incorporate a relatively large number of cross-section observations. The impacts of prices enter through the denominator of the equations for expenditure shares, and these price coefficients are estimated very precisely as they also incorporate cross-section data. Finally, the price impacts also enter through the numerators of equations for the expenditure shares, but these are estimated less precisely, since they are based on a much smaller number of time-series observations on prices.

Individual expenditure shares for capital services increase with total expenditure, whereas all other shares decrease. As family size increases, the shares of energy, food, clothing, and other nondurable expenditures increase, whereas the shares of capital and consumer services decrease. The energy share increases with age of head of household, whereas the share of consumer services decreases. The shares of food and clothing and other nondurables increase with age of head, whereas the share of capital services decreases.

The effects of region of residence on patterns of individual expenditures is small for energy and other nondurables. Households in the North-Central and South regions use relatively more capital services, slightly more energy, and fewer consumer services. The only difference between whites and nonwhites is a smaller share of capital services and a larger share of consumer services for nonwhites. Finally, shares of food and clothing, consumer services, and other nondurables are smaller for rural families, whereas the shares of capital services and energy are much larger. The overall conclusion is that differences in preferences among consuming units are very significant empirically and must be incorporated into models of aggregate consumer behavior.

TABLE 27.3
Pooled Estimation Results

Variable	Numerator coefficient	Standard error
For Equation W_{EN}		
Constant	−0.17874	0.005363
ln p_{EN}	0.01805	0.003505
ln p_{FC}	−0.08745	0.014618
ln p_{O}	0.02325	0.011342
ln p_{CAP}	−0.02996	0.009905
ln p_{SERV}	0.05898	0.015862
ln *M*	0.01712	0.000614
*F*2	−0.01784	0.000971
*F*3	−0.02281	0.001140
*F*4	−0.02675	0.001243
*F*5	−0.02677	0.001424
*F*6	−0.02861	0.001723
*F*7	−0.02669	0.001908
*A*30	−0.00269	0.001349
*A*40	−0.00981	0.001440
*A*50	−0.00844	0.001378
*A*60	−0.01103	0.001374
*A*70	−0.00971	0.001336
RNC	−0.00727	0.000909
RS	−0.00481	0.000906
RW	0.00621	0.000974
RLK	0.00602	0.001157
RUR	−0.01463	0.000890
For Equation W_{FC}		
Constant	−0.56700	0.011760
ln p_{EN}	−0.08745	0.014618
ln p_{FC}	0.58972	0.094926
ln p_{O}	−0.11121	0.064126
ln p_{CAP}	0.00158	0.057450
ln p_{SERV}	−0.44384	0.101201
ln *M*	0.05120	0.001357
*F*2	−0.03502	0.002030
*F*3	−0.05350	0.002390
*F*4	−0.07016	0.002605
*F*5	−0.08486	0.002987
*F*6	−0.08947	0.003613
*F*7	−0.11520	0.003799
*A*30	−0.02189	0.002813
*A*40	−0.04961	0.003015
*A*50	−0.05067	0.002878
*A*60	−0.05142	0.002870
*A*70	−0.03929	0.002791
RNC	0.01993	0.001897
RS	0.01511	0.001893
RW	0.01854	0.002039
RLK	−0.01026	0.002419
RUR	0.01547	0.001878
For Equation W_o		
Constant	−0.32664	0.010446
ln p_{EN}	0.02325	0.011342
ln p_{FC}	−0.11121	0.064126
ln p_{O}	0.19236	0.083095
ln p_{CAP}	−0.16232	0.023397
ln p_{SERV}	0.03887	0.028097
ln *M*	0.01903	0.001203
*F*2	−0.01616	0.001921
*F*3	−0.02748	0.002143
*F*4	−0.03584	0.002336
*F*5	−0.03882	0.002678
*F*6	−0.04298	0.003239
*F*7	−0.05581	0.003406
*A*30	−0.01293	0.002524
*A*40	−0.02584	0.002703
*A*50	−0.02220	0.002582
*A*60	−0.02199	0.002574
*A*70	−0.00826	0.002503
RNC	0.01160	0.001702
RS	0.00278	0.001698
RW	0.01375	0.001827
RLK	−0.00320	0.002169
RUR	0.00783	0.001680
For Equation W_{CAP}		
Constant	0.85630	0.026022
ln p_{EN}	−0.02996	0.009905
ln p_{FC}	0.00158	0.057450
ln p_{O}	−0.16232	0.023397
ln p_{CAP}	0.51464	0.053931
ln p_{SERV}	−0.20176	0.079587
ln *M*	−0.12217	0.002995
*F*2	0.00161	0.004557
*F*3	0.01074	0.005361
*F*4	0.01928	0.005843

continued

TABLE 27.3
(Continued)

Variable	Numerator coefficient	Standard error	Variable	Numerator coefficient	Standard error
For Equation W_{CAP} *(continued)*			$\ln p_{\mathrm{CAP}}$	−0.20176	0.079587
$F5$	0.02094	0.006700	$\ln p_{\mathrm{SERV}}$	0.51293	0.143707
$F6$	0.02976	0.008106	$\ln M$	0.03481	0.002772
$F7$	0.05885	0.008522	$F2$	0.06742	0.004242
$A30$	0.03385	0.006320	$F3$	0.09306	0.004989
$A40$	0.05225	0.006761	$F4$	0.11348	0.005437
$A50$	0.04761	0.006463	$F5$	0.12952	0.006234
$A60$	0.03685	0.006444	$F6$	0.13130	0.007543
$A70$	0.00492	0.006267	$F7$	0.13886	0.007928
RNC	−0.04438	0.004261	$A30$	0.00367	0.005885
RS	−0.03193	0.004250	$A40$	0.03301	0.006292
RW	−0.02574	0.004574	$A50$	0.03371	0.006018
RLK	0.02338	0.005431	$A60$	0.04758	0.006001
RUR	−0.05752	0.004198	$A70$	0.05233	0.005836
			RNC	0.02011	0.003968
For Equation W_{SERV}			RS	0.01884	0.003957
Constant	−0.78391	0.024099	RW	−0.01277	0.004258
$\ln p_{\mathrm{EN}}$	0.05898	0.015862	RLK	−0.01592	0.005055
$\ln p_{\mathrm{FC}}$	−0.44384	0.101201	RUR	0.04885	0.003907
$\ln p_{\mathrm{O}}$	0.03887	0.028097			

Notes: Notation: W = budget share; $\ln p$ = log price. In order to designate the proper good to which W or $\ln p$ refers, the following subscripts and appended where appropriate:

EN: energy, FC: food and clothing, O: other nondurable goods, CAP: capital services, SERV: consumer services.

Further notation is given as

$\ln M$ = log total expenditure
$F2$ = dummy for family size 2
$F3$ = dummy for family size 3
$F4$ = dummy for family size 4
$F5$ = dummy for family size 5
$F6$ = dummy for family size 6
$F7$ = dummy for family size 7 or more
$A30$ = dummy for age class 25–34
$A40$ = dummy for age class 35–44
$A50$ = dummy for age class 45–54
$A60$ = dummy for age class 55–64
$A70$ = dummy for age class 65 and older
RNC = dummy for region North-Central
RS = dummy for region South
RW = dummy for region West
BLK = dummy for nonwhite head
RUR = dummy for rural residence

27.4 CONCLUSION

My empirical results for sector patterns of production and technical change are very striking and suggest a considerable degree of similarity across industries. However, it is important to emphasize that these results were obtained under strong simplifying assumptions. First, for all industries, I used conditions for producer equilibrium under perfect competition, assumed constant returns to scale at the industry level, and employed a description of technology that led to myopic decision rules. These assumptions may be justified primarily by their usefulness in implementing production models that are uniform for all thirty-five industrial sectors of the U.S. economy.

Although it might be worthwhile to weaken each of the assumptions enumerated above, a more promising direction for further research appears to lie within the framework they provided. First, one can develop a more detailed model for allocation among productive inputs. Energy and materials have been disaggregated into thirty-five groups—five types of energy and thirty types of materials—by constructing a hierarchy of models for allocation within the energy and materials aggregates. The second research objective suggested by these results is to incorporate the production models for all thirty-five industrial sectors into a general equilibrium model of production in the U.S. economy. Such a model has been constructed by Jorgenson and Wilcoxen (1993).

In this chapter, I have presented an econometric model of aggregate consumer behavior and implemented it for households in the United States. The model incorporates aggregate time series data on quantities consumed, prices, the level and distribution of total expenditures, and demographic characteristics of the population. It also incorporates individual cross-section data on the allocation of consumer expenditures among commodities for households with different demographic characteristics. I have obtained evidence of very significant differences in preferences among U.S. households based on differing demographic characteristics.

My next research objective is to provide a more detailed model for allocation of consumer expenditures among commodity groups. For this purpose, I have disaggregated the five commodity groups into thirty-six individual commodities by constructing a hierarchy of models for allocation within each of the five groups—energy, food and clothing, other nondurable goods, capital services, and consumer services. My final research objective is to incorporate this model of aggregate consumer behavior into the thirty-five-sector general equilibrium model of the U.S. economy developed by Jorgenson and Wilcoxen (1993). The resulting model can be employed in assessing the impacts of alternative economic policies on the welfare of individuals with different levels of income and different demographic characteristics, including family size, age of head, region, type of residence, and race (see Jorgenson, 1998).

NOTES

1. A review of the literature on induced technical change is given by Binswanger (1978a), who distinguishes between models, like mine and those of Schmookler (1966), Lucas (1967), and Ben-Zion and Ruttan (1978), with an endogenous range of technical change, and models, such as those of Hicks (1932), von Weizsäcker (1962), Kennedy (1964), Samuelson (1965), and others, with an endogenous bias of technical change. Additional references are given in Binswanger (1978a).

2. For further discussion of myopic decision rules, see Jorgenson (1973).

3. The price function was introduced by Samuelson (1953).

4. The translog price function was introduced by Christensen et al. (1971, 1973). The translog price function was first applied at the sectoral level by Berndt and Jorgenson (1973) and Berndt and Wood (1975). References to sectoral production studies incorporating energy and materials inputs are given by Berndt and Wood (1979).

5. The share elasticity with respect to price was introduced by Christensen et al. (1971, 1973) as a fixed parameter of the translog price function. An analogous concept was employed by Samuelson (1973). The terminology is due to Jorgenson and Lau (1983).

6. The terminology *constant share elasticity price function* is due to Jorgenson and Lau (1983), who have shown that constancy of share elasticities with respect to price, biases of technical change with respect to price, and the rate of change of the negative of the rate of technical change are necessary and sufficient for representation of the price function in translog form.

7. The bias of technical change was introduced by Hicks (1932). An alternative definition of the bias of technical change is analyzed by Burmeister and Dobell (1969). Binswanger (1974) has introduced a translog cost function with fixed biases of technical change. Alternative definitions of biases of technical change are compared by Binswanger (1978b).

8. This definition of the bias of technical change with respect to price is due to Jorgenson and Lau (1983).

9. The rate of change of the negative of the rate of technical change was introduced by Jorgenson and Lau (1983).

10. The price indexes were introduced by Fisher (1922) and have been discussed by Tornqvist (1936), Theil (1965), and Kloek (1966). These indexes were first derived from the translog price function by Diewert (1976). The corresponding index of technical change was introduced by Christensen and Jorgenson (1973). The translog index of technical change was first derived from the translog price function by Diewert (1980) and by Jorgenson and Lau (1983). Earlier, Diewert (1976) had interpreted the ratio of translog indexes of the prices of input and output as an index of productivity under the assumption of Hicks neutrality.

11. The following discussion of share elasticities with respect to price and concavity follows that of Jorgenson and Lau (1983). Representation of conditions for concavity in terms of the Cholesky factorization is due to Lau (1978).

12. The following discussion of concavity for the translog price function is based on that of Jorgenson and Lau (1983).

13. The following formulation of an econometric model of production and technical change is based on that of Jorgenson and Lau (1983).

14. The Cholesky factorization is used to obtain an equation with uncorrelated random disturbances by Jorgenson and Lau (1983).

15. Note that when one considers only a single commodity or a single consumer, one can suppress the corresponding commodity or individual subscript. This is done to keep the notation as simple as possible; any omission of subscripts will be clear from the context.

16. If aggregate demands are zero when aggregate expenditure is equal to zero, $C_j(p) = 0$.

17. See, e.g., Houthakker (1957) and the references given therein.

18. Alternative approaches to the representation of the effects of household characteristics on expenditure allocation are presented by Prais and Houthakker (1955), Barten (1964), and Gorman (1976). Empirical evidence on the impact of variations in demographic characteristics on expenditure allocation is given by Parks and Barten (1973), Muellbauer (1977), Lau et al. (1978), and Pollak and Wales (1980). A review of the literature is presented by Deaton and Muellbauer (1980b, pp. 191–213).

19. Alternative approaches to the representation of the effects of total expenditure on expenditure allocation are reviewed by Deaton and Muellbauer (1980b, pp. 148–60). Gorman (1981) shows that Engel curves for an individual consumer that are linear in certain functions of total expenditure, as required in the theory of exact aggregation considered below, involve at most three linearly independent functions of total expenditure. Evidence from budget studies on the nonlinearity of Engel curves is presented by Prais and Houthakker (1955), Leser (1963), Muellbauer (1976b), and Pollak and Wales (1978).

20. See, e.g., Blackorby et al. (1978a), and the references given therein.

21. I omit the proof of this theorem, referring the interested reader to Lau (1977b, 1982).

22. See Samuelson (1956) for details.

23. The specification of a system of individual demand functions by means of Roy's identity was first implemented empirically in a path-breaking study by Houthakker (1960). A detailed review of econometric models of consumer behavior based on Roy's identity is given by Lau (1977a).

24. Alternative approaches to the representation of the effects of prices on expenditure allocation are reviewed by Barten (1977), Lau (1977a), and Deaton and Muellbauer (1980b, pp. 60–85). The indirect translog utility function was introduced by Christensen et al. (1975) and was extended to encompass changes in preferences over time by Jorgenson and Lau (1975).

25. These conditions are implied by the fundamental theorem of exact aggregation presented in Section 27.1.

26. Two-stage allocation is discussed by Blackorby et al. (1978b, especially pp. 103–216); they give detailed references to the literature.

27. See Diewert (1976) for a detailed justification of this approach to price index numbers.

28. See Malinvaud (1980, ch. 9) for a discussion of these techniques.

29. Nonlinear two-stage least squares estimators were introduced by Amemiya (1974). Subsequently, nonlinear three-stage least squares estimators were introduced by Jorgenson and Laffont (1974). For detailed discussion of nonlinear three-stage least squares estimators, see Amemiya (1977), Gallant (1977), Gallant and Jorgenson (1979), and Malinvaud (1980, ch. 20).

30. Data on energy and materials are based on annual interindustry transactions tables for the United States, 1958–1974, compiled by Jack Faucett and Associates (1977) for the Federal Preparedness Agency. Data on labor and capital are based on estimates by Fraumeni and Jorgenson (1980).

31. The cross-section data are described by Carlson (1974).

32. The preparation of these data is described in detail in Jack Faucett and Associates (1977).

33. This series is published annually by the U.S. Bureau of the Census. For this study, numbers 33, 35, 37, 39, 41, 43, 47, 51, 53, 59, 60, 62, 66, 72, 75, 79, 80, 84, 85, 90, 96, 97, and 101 were employed together with technical report numbers 8 and 17.

REFERENCES

Amemiya, T., 1974, "The Nonlinear Two-Stage Least-Squares Estimator," *Journal of Econometrics* 2(2), 105–110.

Amemiya, T., 1977, "The Maximum Likelihood Estimator and the Nonlinear Three-Stage Least-Squares Estimator in the General Nonlinear Simultaneous Equation Model," *Econometrica* 45(4), 955–968.

Arrow, K. J., H. B. Chenery, B. S. Minhas, and R. M. Solow, 1961, "Capital-Labor Substitution and Economic Efficiency," *Review of Economics and Statistics* 43(3), 225–250.

Barten, A. P., 1964, "Family Composition, Prices and Expenditure Patterns," in: *Econometric Analysis for National Economic Planning: The 16th Symposium of the Colston Society*, P. Hart, G. Mills, and J. K. Whitaker (eds.), London: Butterworth, pp. 277–292.

Barten, A. P., 1977, "The Systems of Consumer Demand Functions Approach: A Review," in: *Frontiers of Quantitative Economics, Vol. 3*, M. D. Intriligator (ed.), Amsterdam: North-Holland, pp. 23–58.

Ben-Zion, U., and V. W. Ruttan, 1978, "Aggregate Demand and the Rate of Technical Change," in: *Induced Innovation*, H. P. Binswanger and V. W. Ruttan (eds.), Baltimore: Johns Hopkins University Press, pp. 261–275.

Berndt, E. R., and D. W. Jorgenson, 1973, "Production Structure," in: *U.S. Energy Resources and Economic Growth*, D. W. Jorgenson and H. S. Houthakker (eds.), Washington, D.C.: Energy Policy Project, ch. 3.

Berndt, E. R., and D. O. Wood, 1975, "Technology Prices and the Derived Demand for Energy," *Review of Economics and Statistics* 56(3), 259–268.

Berndt, E. R., and D. O. Wood, 1979, "Engineering and Econometric Interpretations of Energy-Capital Complementarity," *American Economic Review* 69(3), 342–354.

Berndt, E. R., M. N. Darrough, and W. E. Diewert, 1977, "Flexible Functional Forms and Expenditure Distributions: An Application to Canadian Consumer Demand Functions," *International Economic Review* 18(3), 651–676.

Binswanger, H. P., 1974, "The Measurement of Technical Change Biases with Many Factors of Production," *American Economic Review* 64(5), 964–974.

Binswanger, H. P., 1978a, "Induced Technical Change: Evolution of Thought," in: *Induced Innovation*, H. P. Binswanger and V. W. Ruttan (eds.), Baltimore: Johns Hopkins University Press, pp. 13–43.

Binswanger, H. P., 1978b, "Issues in Modeling Induced Technical Change," in: *In Induced Innovation*, H. P. Binswanger and V. W. Ruttan (eds.), Baltimore: Johns Hopkins University Press, pp. 128–163.

Blackorby, C., R. Boyce, and R. R. Russell, 1978a, "Estimation of Demand Systems Generated by the Gorman Polar Form: A Generalization of the S-Branch Utility Tree," *Econometrica* 46(2), 345–364.

Blackorby, C., D. Primont, and R. R. Russell, 1978b, *Duality, Separability, and Functional Structure*, Amsterdam: North-Holland.

Burmeister, E., and A. R. Dobell, 1969, "Disembodied Technological Change with Several Factors," *Journal of Economic Theory* 1(1), 1–18.

Carlson, M. D., 1974, "The 1972–1973 Consumer Expenditure Survey," *Monthly Labor Review* 97(12), 16–23.

Christensen, L. R., and D. W. Jorgenson, 1973, "Measuring Economic Performance in the Private Sector," in: *The Measurement of Economic and Social Performance*, M. Moss (ed.), NBER Studies in Income and Wealth, Vol. 37, New York: Columbia University Press, pp. 233–351.

Christensen, L. R., D. W. Jorgenson, and L. J. Lau, 1971, "Conjugate Duality and the Transcendental Logarithmic Production Function," *Econometrica* 39(4), 255–256.

Christensen, L. R., D. W. Jorgenson, and L. J. Lau, 1973, "Transcendental Logarithmic Production Frontiers" *Review of Economics and Statistics* 55(1), 28–45.

Christensen, L. R., D. W. Jorgenson, and L. J. Lau, 1975, "Transcendental Logarithmic Utility Functions," *American Economic Review* 65(3), 367–383.

Cottle, R. W., and J. A. Ferland, 1972, "Matrix-Theoretic Criteria for the Quasi-Convexity and Pseudo-Convexity of Quadratic Functions," *Linear Algebra and Its Applications* 5, 123–136.

Deaton, A. S., and J. S. Muellbauer, 1980a, "An Almost Ideal Demand System," *American Economic Review* 70(3), 312–326.

Deaton, A. S., and J. S. Muellbauer, 1980b, *Economics and Consumer Behavior*, Cambridge: Cambridge University Press.

Diewert, W. E., 1976, "Exact and Superlative Index Numbers," *Journal of Econometrics* 4(2), 115–146.

Diewert, W. E., 1980, "Aggregation Problems in the Measurement of Capital," in: *The Measurement of Capital*, D. Usher (ed.), Chicago: University of Chicago Press, pp. 433–528.

Faucett, J., and Associates, 1977, "Development of 35 Order Input-Output Tables, 1958–1974," Final Report, October, Washington, D.C.: Federal Emergency Management Agency.

Fisher, I., 1922, *The Making of Index Numbers*, Boston: Houghton Mifflin.

Fraumeni, B. M., and D. W. Jorgenson, 1980, "The Role of Capital in U.S. Economic Growth, 1948–1976," in: *Capital, Efficiency and Growth*, G. M. von Furstenberg (ed.), Cambridge, Mass.: Ballinger, pp. 9–250.

Frisch, R., 1959, "A Complete Scheme for Computing All Direct and Cross Demand Elasticities in a Model with Many Sectors," *Econometrica* 27(2), 177–196.

Fullerton, D., Y. K. Henderson, and J. B. Shoven, 1984, "A Comparison of Methodologies in Empirical General Equilibrium Models of Taxation," in: *Applied General Equilibrium Analysis*, H. E. Scarf and J. B. Shoven (eds.), Cambridge: Cambridge University Press, pp. 367–409.

Gallant, A. R., (1977), "Three-Stage Least-Squares Estimation for a System of Simultaneous, Nonlinear, Implicit Equations," *Journal of Econometrics* 5(1), 71–88.

Gallant, A. R., and D. W. Jorgenson, 1979, "Statistical Inference for a System of Simultaneous, Nonlinear, Implicit Equations in the Context of Instrumental Variable Estimation," *Journal of Econometrics* 11(2/3), 275–302.

Gorman, W. M., 1953, "Community Preference Fields," *Econometrica* 21(1), 63–80.

Gorman, W. M., 1976, "Tricks with Utility Functions," in: *Essays in Economic Analysis: Proceedings of the 1975 AUTE Conference, Sheffield*, M. J. Artis and A. R. Nobay (eds.), Cambridge: Cambridge University Press, pp. 211–243.

Gorman, W. M., 1981, "Some Engel Curves," in: *Essays in the Theory and Measurement of Consumer Behavior*, New York: Cambridge University Press, pp. 7–29.

Hicks, J. R., 1932, *The Theory of Wages*, 2nd Ed., London: Macmillan.

Houthakker, H. S., 1957, "An International Comparison of Household Expenditure Patterns Commemorating the Centenary of Engel's Law," *Econometrica* 25(4), 532–551.

Houthakker, H. S., 1960, "Additive Preferences," *Econometrica* 28(21), 244–257.

Hudson, E. A., and D. W. Jorgenson, 1974, "U.S. Energy Policy and Economic Growth, 1975–2000," *Bell Journal of Economics and Management Science* 5(2): 461–514.

Johansen, L., 1960, *A Multi-Sectoral Study of Economic Growth*, Amsterdam: North-Holland.

Jorgenson, D. W., 1973, "Technology and Decision Rules in the Theory of Investment Behavior," *Quarterly Journal of Economics* 87(4), 523–543.

Jorgenson, D. W., 1998, *Energy, the Environment, and Economic Growth*, Cambridge: MIT Press.

Jorgenson, D. W., and B. M. Fraumeni, 1981, "Relative Prices and Technical Change," in: *Modeling and Measuring Natural Resource Substitution*, E. R. Berndt and B. C. Field (eds.), Cambridge: MIT Press, pp. 17–47.

Jorgenson, D. W., and J.-J. Laffont, 1974, "Efficient Estimation of Nonlinear Simultaneous Equations with Additive Disturbances," *Annals of Social and Economic Measurement* 3(4), 615–640.

Jorgenson, D. W., and L. J. Lau, 1975, "The Structure of Consumer Preferences," *Annals of Economic and Social Measurement* 4(1), 49–101.

Jorgenson, D. W., and L. J. Lau, 1983, *Transcendental Logarithmic Production Functions*, Amsterdam: North-Holland.

Jorgenson, D. W., and P. J. Wilcoxen, 1993, "Energy, the Environment, and Economic Growth," in: *Handbook of Energy and Natural Resource Economics, Vol. 3*, A. V. Kneese and J. L. Sweeney (eds.), pp. 1267–1349.

Jorgenson, D. W., L. J. Lau, and T. M. Stoker, 1980, "Welfare Comparison under Exact Aggregation," *American Economic Review* 70(2), 268–272 .

Jorgenson, D. W., L. J. Lau, and T. M. Stoker, 1981, "Aggregate Consumer Behavior and Individual Welfare," *Macroeconomic Analysis*, D. Currie, R. Nobay, and D. Peel (eds.), London: Croom-Helm, pp. 35–61.

Jorgenson, D. W., L. J. Lau, and T. M. Stoker, 1982, "The Transcendental Logarithmic Model of Aggregate Consumer Behavior," in: *Advances in Econometrics, Vol. 1*, R. L. Basmann and G. Rhodes (eds.), Greenwich, Conn.: JAI, pp. 97–238.

Kennedy, C., 1964, "Induced Bias in Innovation and the Theory of Distribution," *Economic Journal* 74(295), 541–547.

Klein, L. R., and H. Rubin, 1947, "A Constant-Utility Index of the Cost of Living," *Econometrica* 15(2), 84–87.

Kloek, T., 1966, *Indexciffers: Enige methodologisch aspecten*, The Hague: Pasmans.

Lau, L. J., 1977a, "Complete Systems of Consumer Demand Functions through Duality," in: *Frontiers of Quantitative Economics, Vol. 3*, M. D. Intriligator and D. A. Kendrick (eds.), Amsterdam: North-Holland, pp. 59–86.

Lau, L. J., 1977b. "Existence Conditions for Aggregate Demand Functions: The Case of Multiple Indexes," Technical Report 248 (October), Institute for Mathematical Studies in Social Sciences, Stanford University (revised 1980 and 1982).

Lau, L. J., 1978, "Testing and Imposing Monotonicity, Convexity, and Quasi Convexity," in: *Production Economics: A Dual Approach to Theory and Applications, Vol. 1*, M. Fuss and D. L. McFadden (eds.), Amsterdam: North-Holland, pp. 409–453.

Lau, L. J., 1982, "A Note on the Fundamental Theorem of Exact Aggregation," *Economics Letters* 9(2), 119–126.

Lau, L. J., W.-L. Lin, and P. A. Yotopoulos, 1978, "The Linear Logarithmic Expenditure System: An Application to Consumption-Leisure Choice," *Econometrica* 46(4), 843–868.

Leontief, W., 1951, *The Structure of the American Economy, 1919–1939*, 2nd Ed. (1st Ed. 1941), New York: Oxford University Press.

Leontief, W. (ed.), 1953, *Studies in the Structure of the American Economy*, New York: Oxford University Press.

Leser, C. E. V., 1963, "Forms of Engel Functions," *Econometrica* 31(4), 694–703.

Lucas, R. E., Jr., 1967, "Tests of a Capital-Theoretic Model of Technological Change," *Review of Economic Studies* 34(9), 175–180.

Malinvaud, E., 1980, *Statistical Methods of Econometrics*, 3rd Ed, Amsterdam: North-Holland.

Mansur, A., and J. Whalley, 1984, "Numerical Specification of Applied General Equilibrium Models: Estimation, Calibration, and Data," in: *Applied General Equilibrium Analysis*, H. E. Scarf and J. B. Shoven (eds.), Cambridge: Cambridge University Press, pp. 69–127.

Martos, B., 1969, "Subdefinite Matrices and Quadratic Forms," *SIAM Journal of Applied Mathematics* 17, 1215–1223.

McFadden, D. L., 1963, "Further Results on CES Production Functions," *Review of Economic Studies* 30 (83), 73–83.

Muellbauer, J. S., 1975, "Aggregation, Income Distribution, and Consumer Demand," *Review of Economic Studies* 42(132), 525–543.

Muellbauer, J. S., 1976a, "Community Preferences and the Representative Consumer," *Econometrica* 44(5), 979–999.

Muellbauer, J. S., 1976b, "Economics and the Representative Consumer," in: *Private and Enlarged Consumption*, L. Solari and J. N. Du Pasquier (eds.), Amsterdam: North-Holland, pp. 29–54.

Muellbauer, J. S., 1977, "Testing the Barten Model of Household Composition Effects and the Cost of Children," *Economic Journal* 87(347), 460–487.

Parks, R. W., and A. P. Barten, 1973, "A Cross-Country Comparison of the Effects of Prices, Income, and Population Compensation on Consumption Patterns," *Economic Journal* 83(331), 834–852.

Pollak, R. A., and T. J. Wales, 1978, "Estimation of Complete Demand Systems from Household Budget Data: The Linear and Quadratic Expenditure Systems," *American Economic Review* 68(3), 348–359.

Pollak, R. A., and T. J. Wales, 1980, "Comparison of the Quadratic Expenditure System and Translog Demand Systems with Alternative Specifications of Demographic Effects," *Econometrica* 48(3), 595–612.

Prais, S. J., and H. S. Houthakker, 1955,. *The Analysis of Family Budgets*, 2nd Ed., Cambridge: Cambridge University Press.

Roy, R., 1943, *De l'utilite: Contribution a la theorie des choix*. Paris: Herman and Cie.

Samuelson, P. A., 1951, "Abstract of a Theorem Concerning Substitutability in Open Leontief Models," in: *Activity Analysis of Production and Allocation*, T. C. Koopmans (ed.), New York: Wiley, pp. 142–146.

Samuelson, P. A., 1953, "Prices of Factors and Goods in General Equilibrium," *Review of Economic Studies* 21(54), 1–20.

Samuelson, P. A., 1956, "Social Indifference Curves," *Quarterly Journal of Economics* 70(1), 1–22.

Samuelson, P. A., 1965, "A Theory of Induced Innovation along Kennedy-Weizsäcker Lines," *Review of Economics and Statistics* 47(3), 343–356.

Samuelson, P. A., 1973, "Relative Shares and Elasticities Simplified: Comment," *American Economic Review* 63(4), 770–771.

Scarf, H. E., and T. Hansen, 1973, *Computation of Economic Equilibria*, New Haven: Yale University Press.

Schmookler, J., 1966, *Invention and Economic Growth*, Cambridge: Harvard University Press.

Schultz, H., 1938, *The Theory and Measurement of Demand*, Chicago: University of Chicago Press.

Stone, R., 1954. *Measurement of Consumers' Expenditures and Behavior in the United Kingdom, Vol. 1*, Cambridge: Cambridge University Press.

Theil, H., 1965, "The Information Approach to Demand Analysis," *Econometrica* 33(1), 67–87.

Tornqvist, L., 1936, The Bank of Finland's Consumption Price Index, *Bank of Finland Monthly Bulletin* 10, 1–8

Uzawa, H., 1962, "Production Functions with Constant Elasticities of Substitution," *Review of Economic Studies* 29(81), 291–299.

von Weizsäcker, C. C., 1962, "A New Technical Progress Function," Department of Economics, MIT, Unpublished.

Wold, H., 1953, *Demand Analysis: A Study in Econometrics*, New York: Wiley.

Index